OFFICIAL TOURIST BOARD GUIDE

# B&B

# Contents



## Further information



## Useful indexes

Guernsey and Jersey are not drawn to scale

### VisitBritain

VisitBritain is the organisation created to market Britain to the rest of the world, and England to the British.

Formed by the merger of the British Tourist Authority and the English Tourism Council, its mission is to build the value of tourism by creating world-class destination brands and marketing campaigns.

It will also build partnerships with – and provide insights to – other organisations which have a stake in British and English tourism.

Botany Bay, Kent

# How to use this guide

**This official VisitBritain guide is packed with information from where to stay, to how to get there and what to see. In fact, everything you need to know to enjoy England and the Channel Islands.**

**Choose from a wide range of quality-assessed accommodation** to suit all budgets and tastes. This guide contains a comprehensive listing of all bed and breakfast establishments participating in VisitBritain's Enjoy England Quality Rose assessment scheme, including guesthouses, farmhouses, inns, restaurants with rooms, hostels and campus accommodation.

Each property has been visited annually by professional assessors who apply nationally agreed standards so that you can book with confidence knowing your accommodation has been checked and rated for quality.

**Check out the places to visit** in each region, from towns and cities to spectacular coast and countryside, plus historic homes, castles and great family attractions! Regional maps show selected destinations as well as National Trails and sections of the National Cycle Network. For even more ideas go online at enjoyengland.com, jersey.com and visitguernsey.com.

**Regional tourism contacts and tourist information centres** are listed – contact them for further information. You'll also find **events, travel information, maps** and useful **indexes**.

# Finding accommodation is easy...

## 1. REGIONAL SECTIONS

The guide is divided into regions (see page 3) and accommodation is listed alphabetically by place name within each region.

Start your search for accommodation in these sections. For an even wider choice in England, turn to the listings starting on page 438 where you will find ALL Enjoy England assessed bed and breakfast establishments, including those that have not taken a paid entry.

## 2. COLOUR MAPS

Use the colour maps, starting on page 32, to pinpoint the location of all accommodation featured in the regional sections.

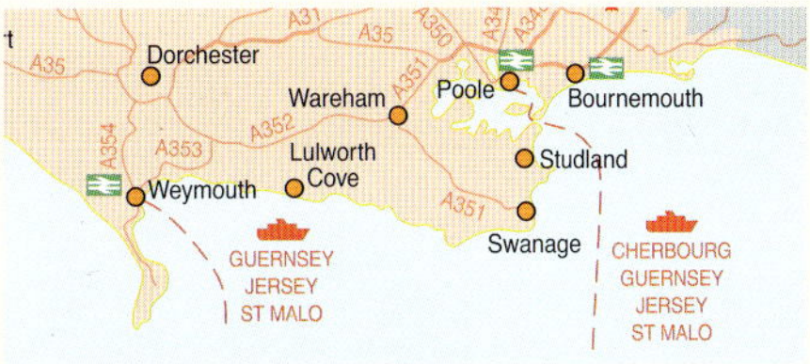


Then refer to the place index at the back of the guide to find the page number. The index also includes tourism areas such as the New Forest and the Cotswolds.

## 3. INDEXES

The indexes, listed on page 659, make it easy to find accommodation that matches specific requirements; for example, establishments suitable for guests with disabilities or those that offer an evening meal by arrangement. And if you know the name of the establishment, use the property index.

# Accommodation entries explained

Each accommodation entry contains detailed information to help you decide if it is right for you. This has been provided by proprietors and our aim is to ensure that it is as objective and factual as possible.

1 2 3 4 5 6 7 8
HUNSTANTON, Norfolk Map ref 3B1
★★★★
INN
SILVER AWARD
B&B PER ROOM PER NIGHT
S £50.00–£60.00
D £75.00–£90.00
EVENING MEAL PER PERSON
£8.00–£25.00
3rd night half price with double occupancy.
The King William IV Country Inn & Restaurant
Heacham Road, Sedgeford, Hunstanton PE36 5LU t (01485) 571765
e info@thekingwilliamsedgeford.co.uk
thekingwilliamsedgeford.co.uk SPECIAL OFFERS • REAL-TIME BOOKING
open All year
bedrooms 4 double
bathrooms All en suite
payment Credit/debit cards, cash, cheques
Popular and busy traditional country inn, amid Norfolk countryside. Close to North Norfolk's beautiful coastline, Peddars Way, RSPB bird reserves and golf. High-standard, comfortable en suite accommodation with king-size beds. Extensive menu and daily specials served in two non-smoking restaurants, bar and garden. A delightful escape – whatever the season.
SAT NAV PE36 5LU ONLINE MAP
WALKERS WELCOME
CYCLISTS WELCOME
Room TV
General P
Leisure
Sample enhanced entry
9 10 11 12 13


1 Listing under town or village with map reference

2 Quality rating plus Gold or Silver Award where applicable

3 Classification

4 Prices per room for bed and breakfast (B&B) and per person for evening meal

5 Establishment name, address, telephone and email

6 Indicates when the establishment is open

7 Website information (web addresses are shown without the prefix www.)

8 Accommodation details and payment accepted

9 Accessible rating where applicable

10 Walkers, cyclists, pets and families welcome where applicable

11 Special promotions and themed breaks

12 At-a-glance facility symbols

13 Travel directions

# Key to symbols

Information about many of the accommodation services and facilities is given in the form of symbols.

## General

- Children welcome (a number following gives minimum age)
- Cots
- Highchairs
- Parking on site
- Wi-Fi
- Internet access
- Bar
- Evening meals served
- Special diets by arrangement
- Games console available
- Laundry facilities
- Garden/patio
- Pets welcome by arrangement

### National Accessible Scheme

The National Accessible Scheme includes standards for hearing and visual impairment as well as mobility impairment – see pages 16-17 for further information.

### Welcome schemes

Walkers, cyclists, families and pet owners are warmly welcomed where you see these signs – see page 12 for further information.

## Rooms

- Bedroom(s) on ground floor
- Four-poster bed(s)
- Telephone in all bedrooms
- TV in all bedrooms
- Satellite/cable channels in all bedrooms
- Tea/coffee facilities in all bedrooms
- Hairdryer in all bedrooms
- Smoking rooms available

## Leisure

- Swimming pool – indoor
- Swimming pool – outdoor
- Tennis court(s)
- Riding/pony-trekking nearby
- Fishing nearby
- Access to golf
- Cycle hire nearby

## Campus/Hostels

- Cooking facilities available
- Lounge
- Games room

# Ratings and awards at a glance

**Reliable, rigorous, easy to use – look out for the following ratings and awards to help you choose with confidence.**

## Star ratings

Bed and breakfast establishments are awarded a rating of one to five stars based on a combination of quality of facilities and services provided. Put simply, **the more stars, the higher the quality and the greater the range of facilities and level of service.**

The process to arrive at a star rating is very thorough. National tourist board professional assessors visit establishments annually and work to strict criteria to check the available facilities and service. A quality score is awarded for every aspect of the experience including the comfort of the bed, the standard of the breakfast (and dinner if offered) and, most importantly, the cleanliness. They also score the warmth of welcome and the level of care that each offers its guests.

From January 2006, all the national assessing bodies (VisitBritain, VisitScotland, Visit Wales, Jersey Tourism, VisitGuernsey and the AA) have operated to a common set of standards, giving holidaymakers and travellers a clear guide on exactly what to expect at each level (see page 660).

For information on awards see overleaf

## Ratings made easy

★
Simple, practical, no frills

★★
Well presented and well run

★★★
Good level of quality and comfort

★★★★
Excellent standard throughout

★★★★★
Exceptional with a degree of luxury

For full details of the quality assessment schemes, go online at **enjoyengland.com/quality**

## Gold and Silver Awards

If you want a superior level of quality guaranteed seek out accommodation with a Gold or Silver Award. They are only given to bed and breakfast establishments offering the highest levels of quality within their star rating (see page 14).

## Enjoy England Awards for Excellence

The prestigious and coveted Enjoy England Awards for Excellence showcase the very best in English tourism. Run by VisitBritain in association with England's regions, they include a Bed & Breakfast of the Year category (see page 18).

## National Accessible Scheme

Hotels with a National Accessible Scheme rating have been thoroughly assessed to set criteria and provide access to facilities and services for guests with visual, hearing or mobility impairment (see page 16).

## Welcome schemes

Enjoy England runs four special Welcome schemes: Cyclists Welcome, Walkers Welcome, Welcome Pets! and Families Welcome. Scheme participants actively encourage these types of visitors and make special provision to ensure a welcoming, comfortable stay (see page 12).

## Visitor Attraction Quality Assurance

Attractions participating in this scheme are visited every year by a professional assessor and must achieve high standards in all aspects of the visitor experience to receive this Enjoy England award. The assessment focuses on the nature of the welcome, hospitality, services and presentation as well as the standards of toilets, shop and café where provided.

**Accommodation with a lower star rating may be more suited to your needs:** sometimes a bed and breakfast establishment has exceptional bedrooms and bathrooms and offers guests a very special welcome, but cannot achieve a higher star rating because, for example, there are no en suite bedrooms, or it is difficult to put washbasins in the bedrooms (three star). This is sometimes the case with period properties. Look out for accommodation with Gold or Silver Awards which recognise quality rather than specific facilities.

# What to expect

All bed and breakfast accommodation that is awarded a star rating will meet the minimum standards – so you can be confident that you will find the basic services that you would expect, such as:

- A clear explanation of booking charges, services offered and cancellation terms
- A full cooked breakfast or substantial continental breakfast
- At least one bathroom or shower room for every six guests
- For a stay of more than one night, rooms cleaned and beds made daily
- Printed advice on how to summon emergency assistance at night
- All statutory obligations will be met.

Proprietors of bed and breakfast accommodation have to provide certain additional facilities and services at the higher star levels, some of which may be important to you:

**THREE-STARs must provide** ★★★

- Private bathroom/shower room (cannot be shared with the owners)
- Bedrooms must have a washbasin if not en suite.

**FOUR-STARs must provide** ★★★★

- 50% of bedrooms en suite or with private bathroom.

**FIVE-STARs must provide** ★★★★★

- All bedrooms with en suite or private bathroom.

Increasingly you will find accommodation at all star levels where all bedrooms have an en suite or private bathroom, but at five stars you can be guaranteed these facilities.

# A special welcome

To help make your selection of accommodation easier VisitBritain has four special Welcome schemes which accommodation in England can be assessed to. Owners participating in these schemes go the extra mile to welcome walkers, cyclists, families or pet owners and provide additional facilities and services to make your stay even more comfortable.

## Families Welcome

If you are searching for a great family break look out for the Families Welcome sign. The sign indicates that the proprietor offers additional facilities and services catering for a range of ages and family units. For families with young children, the accommodation will have special facilities such as cots and highchairs, storage for push-chairs and somewhere to heat baby food or milk. Where meals are provided, children's choices will be clearly indicated, with healthy options available.They'll also have information on local walks, attractions, activities or events suitable for children, as well as local child-friendly pubs and restaurants. Not all accommodation is able to cater for all ages or combinations of family units, so do check when you book.

## Welcome Pets!

Want to travel with your faithful companion? Look out for accommodation displaying the Welcome Pets! sign. Participants in this scheme go out of their way to meet the needs of guests bringing dogs, cats and/or small birds. In addition to providing water and food bowls, torches or nightlights, spare leads and pet washing facilities, they'll buy in food on request, and offer toys, treats and bedding. They'll also have information on pet-friendly attractions, pubs, restaurants and recreation. Of course, not everyone is able to offer suitable facilities for every pet, so do check if there are any restrictions on the type, size and number of animals when you book.

## Walkers Welcome

If walking is your passion seek out accommodation participating in the Walkers Welcome scheme. Facilities include a place for drying clothes and boots, maps and books for reference and a first-aid kit. Packed breakfasts and lunch are available on request in hotels and guesthouses, and you have the option to pre-order basic groceries in self-catering accommodation. A wide range of information is provided including public transport, weather, local restaurants and attractions, details of the nearest bank and all night chemists.

## Cyclists Welcome

If you like to explore by bike seek out accommodation displaying the Cyclists Welcome symbol. Facilities include a lockable undercover area and a place to dry outdoor clothing and footwear, an evening meal if there are no eating facilities available within one mile, and a packed breakfast or lunch on request. Information is also provided on cycle hire and cycle repair shops, maps and books for reference, weather and details of the nearest bank and all night chemists and more.

**For further information go online at enjoyengland.com/quality**

# Classifications explained

Bed and breakfast accommodation varies greatly in style and facilities. The following will help you decide which type of establishment is right for you, whether you are seeking a seaside escape for two or family fun on the farm.

## Guest Accommodation

Encompassing a wide range of establishments from one-room bed and breakfasts to larger properties, which may offer dinner and hold an alcohol licence.

## Bed and Breakfast

Accommodating generally no more than six people, the owners of these establishments welcome you into their home as a special guest.

## Guest House

Generally comprising more than three rooms. Dinner is unlikely to be available (if it is, it will need to be booked in advance). May possibly be licensed.

## Farmhouse

Bed and breakfast, and sometimes dinner, but always on a farm.

## Restaurant with Rooms

A licensed restaurant is the main business but there will be a small number of bedrooms, with all the facilities you would expect, and breakfast the following morning.

## Inn

Pubs with rooms, and many with restaurants as well.

## Hostel

Safe, budget-priced, short-term accommodation for individuals and groups. The Hostel classification includes Group Hostel, Backpacker and Activity Accommodation (all of which are awarded star ratings), and Bunkhouses and Camping Barns.

## Campus

Accommodation provided by educational establishments, including university halls of residence and student village complexes. May be offered on a bed and breakfast or sometimes a self catering basis.

# Gold and Silver Awards

## Enjoy England's unique Gold and Silver Awards are given in recognition of exceptional quality in bed and breakfast accommodation.

Enjoy England professional assessors make recommendations for Gold and Silver Awards during assessments. They will look at the quality provided in all areas, in particular housekeeping, hospitality, bedrooms, bathrooms and food, to see if it meets the highest quality for the star level achieved.

While star ratings are based on a combination of quality, range of facilities and level of service offered, Gold and Silver Awards are based solely on quality.

Here we feature bed and breakfast establishments with a Gold Award for which detailed entries are included in the regional pages. Use the property index starting on page 710 to find their page numbers.

An index of all Gold and Silver Award-winning accommodation can be found at the back of this guide.

## Gold Award Bed and Breakfast Accommodation 2009

**17 Burgate**
Pickering, *North Yorkshire*

**Anchorage House**
St Austell, *Cornwall*

**Arundel House Restaurant & Rooms**
Arundel, *West Sussex*

**Athole Guest House**
Bath, *Somerset*

**The Ayrlington**
Bath, *Somerset*

**Bays Farm**
Stowmarket, *Suffolk*

**Brayscroft House**
Eastbourne, *East Sussex*

**Brookfield House**
Bovey Tracey, *Devon*

**Cold Cotes**
Harrogate, *North Yorkshire*

**Cotteswold House**
Bibury, *Gloucestershire*

**Crake Trees Manor**
Crosby Ravensworth, *Cumbria*

**The Dairy Barns**
Hickling, *Norfolk*

**Farnham Farm House**
Blandford Forum, *Dorset*

**Folly Farm Cottage**
Stratford-upon-Avon, *Warwickshire*

**Giffard House**
Winchester, *Hampshire*

**Grassington Lodge**
Grassington, *North Yorkshire*

**Grendon Guest House**
Buxton, *Derbyshire*

**Hazel Bank Country House**
Borrowdale, *Cumbria*

**Highland Court Lodge**
St Austell, *Cornwall*

**Hill Farm B&B For Country Lovers**
Cartmel, *Cumbria*

**Holmans**
Burley, *Hampshire*

**Holme House**
Hebden Bridge, *West Yorkshire*

**Incleborough House Luxury Bed and Breakfast**
Cromer, *Norfolk*

**The Inn at Whitewell**
Whitewell, *Lancashire*

**Iwood Bed & Breakfast**
Heathfield, *East Sussex*

**Jeake's House**
Rye, *East Sussex*

**Magnolia House**
Canterbury, *Kent*

**Moresby Hall**
Whitehaven, *Cumbria*

**Old Bakery**
Pulham Market, *Norfolk*

**Old Pump House**
Aylsham, *Norfolk*

**The Old Vicarage**
Pickering, *North Yorkshire*

**The Residence**
Bath, *Somerset*

**Rookhurst Country House**
Hawes, *North Yorkshire*

**The Salty Monk**
Sidmouth, *Devon*

**Shave Cross Inn**
Shave Cross, *Dorset*

**Sheepscombe House**
Broadway, *Worcestershire*

**Spanhoe Lodge**
Uppingham, *Rutland*

**The Summer House**
Penzance, *Cornwall*

**Sunnybank Guesthouse**
Holmfirth, *West Yorkshire*

**Tor Cottage**
Tavistock, *Devon*

**Underleigh House**
Hope, *Derbyshire*

**West Acre House**
Alnwick, *Northumberland*

**White Hart Inn**
Nayland, *Suffolk*

**Yew Tree House**
Vowchurch, *Herefordshire*

# National Accessible Scheme

**Finding suitable accommodation is not always easy, especially if you have to seek out rooms with level entry or large print menus. Use the National Accessible Scheme to help you make your choice.**

Proprietors of accommodation taking part in the National Accessible Scheme have gone out of their way to ensure a comfortable stay for guests with special hearing, visual or mobility needs. These exceptional places are full of extra touches to make everyone's visit trouble-free, from handrails, ramps and step-free entrances (ideal for buggies too) to level-access showers and colour contrast in the bathrooms. Owners may have attended a disability awareness course and will know what assistance will really be appreciated.

Appropriate National Accessible Scheme symbols are included in the guide entries (shown opposite). If you have additional needs or special requirements we strongly recommend that you make sure these can be met by your chosen establishment before you confirm your reservation. The index at the back of the guide gives a list of hotels that have received a National Accessible rating.

For a wider selection of accessible accommodation, order a copy of the *Easy Access Britain* guide featuring almost 500 places to stay. It is available from Tourism for All for £9.99 (plus P&P). Alternatively, visit tourismforall.org.uk for a directory of National Accessible Scheme and Tourism for All members.

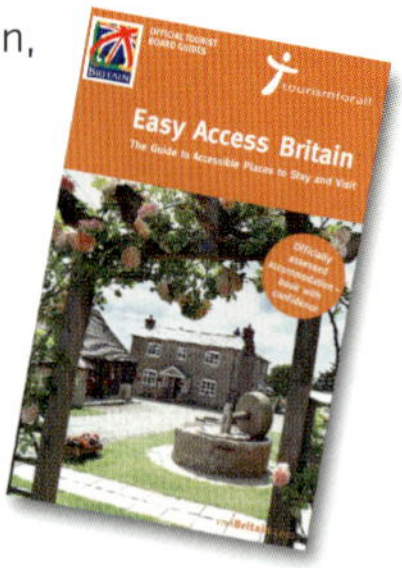

The criteria VisitBritain and national/regional tourism organisations have adopted do not necessarily conform to British Standards or to Building Regulations. They reflect what the organisations understand to be acceptable to meet the practical needs of guests with mobility or sensory impairments and encourage the industry to increase access to all.

tourismforall

The National Accessible Scheme forms part of the Tourism for All campaign that is being promoted by VisitBritain and national/regional tourism organisations. Additional help and guidance on finding suitable holiday accommodation can be obtained from:

**Tourism for All**
**c/o Vitalise, Shap Road Industrial Estate, Kendal LA9 6NZ**

**information helpline** 0845 124 9971
**reservations** 0845 124 9973
(lines open 9-5 Mon-Fri)

**f** (01539) 735567

**e** info@tourismforall.org.uk

**w** tourismforall.org.uk

# England

## Mobility Impairment Symbols

Typically suitable for a person with sufficient mobility to climb a flight of steps but who would benefit from fixtures and fittings to aid balance.

Typically suitable for a person with restricted walking ability and for those who may need to use a wheelchair some of the time and can negotiate a maximum of three steps.

Typically suitable for a person who depends on the use of a wheelchair and transfers unaided to and from the wheelchair in a seated position. This person may be an independent traveller.

Typically suitable for a person who depends on the use of a wheelchair and needs assistance when transferring to and from the wheelchair in a seated position.

EXCEPTIONAL

EXCEPTIONAL

Access Exceptional is awarded to establishments that meet the requirements of independent wheelchair users or assisted wheelchair users shown above and also fulfil more demanding requirements with reference to the British Standards BS8300:2001.

## Visual Impairment Symbols

1 Typically provides key additional services and facilities to meet the needs of visually impaired guests.

2 Typically provides a higher level of additional services and facilities to meet the needs of visually impaired guests.

## Hearing Impairment Symbols

1 Typically provides key additional services and facilities to meet the needs of guests with hearing impairment.

2 Typically provides a higher level of additional services and facilities to meet the needs of guests with hearing impairment.

# Enjoy England Awards for Excellence

**Enjoy England Awards for Excellence are all about telling the world what a fantastic place England is to visit, whether it's for a day trip, a weekend break or a fortnight's holiday.**

Organised by VisitBritain and sponsored by The Caravan Club, The Enjoy England Awards for Excellence are the annual accolades for English tourism, recognising the best places to stay and visit. Now in their 20th year, the Awards are known throughout the industry, promoting healthy competition and high standards. Competition is fierce, and entries are submitted to regional tourism organisations across England before being short-listed for the national finals, culminating in an Awards ceremony held in April each year.

"The Enjoy England Awards for Excellence highlight the rising quality and diversity of holiday experiences on offer in England. From foodie gems and unique attractions to magnificent hotels and sustainable B&Bs, England is an exciting world-class tourism destination in which to discover something new. We are proud to honour the people behind those outstanding tourism businesses who play a vital role in encouraging visitors to holiday in England," said Hugh Taylor, VisitEngland chairman.

There are fifteen categories, from visitor attractions and hotels to self-catering accommodation and caravan parks. This year's winners include a country house hotel in the Yorkshire Dales, Europe's largest free airshow in Sunderland, an environmentally sustainable villa and restaurant in Norfolk and a children's attraction and story centre in Buckinghamshire. Seek them out and experience them for yourself – you won't be disappointed.

**The complete list of winners can be found online at enjoyengland.com.**

Clockwise: Clow Beck House; Boltongate Old Rectory; The Old Manse;

The Salty Monk Restaurant with Rooms

## Bed & Breakfast of the Year 2008

GOLD WINNER

**The Salty Monk Restaurant with Rooms**, Sidmouth, Devon

★★★★★ **GOLD** *Restaurant with Rooms*

SILVER WINNERS

**Boltongate Old Rectory**, Boltongate, Cumbria ★★★★★ **GOLD** *Guest Accommodation*

**Clow Beck House**, Darlington, Tees Valley ★★★★★ **GOLD** *Guest Accommodation*

**The Old Manse**, Chatton, near Wooller, Northumberland ★★★★★ **GOLD** *Guest Accommodation*

## The Salty Monk

**"The Salty Monk represents a new breed of English B&B offering all-round excellent cuisine and very high quality accommodation".** *Judges comment*

The Salty Monk in Sidmouth is a 16th-century restaurant with rooms. What is a restaurant with rooms? It's a licensed restaurant with a small number of quality-assessed bedrooms. Great if you really enjoy your food. And what's more, you're guaranteed a delicious breakfast in the morning, too!

The place gets its name from its interesting history, as a salt house used by Benedictine Monks who traded salt at Exeter Cathedral. Set in the beautiful Devonshire countryside, it's just two miles from the seaside Regency town of Sidmouth, so you can enjoy the best of both coast and country. Explore magnificent Heritage Coastline, Dartmoor or Exeter. There's also a wealth of golf courses, National Trust properties and gardens within easy driving distance.

The Salty Monk offers five individually furnished rooms with equally individual water therapy: choose from a sauna shower, a hydro massage power shower, a hydro spa bath or a king-size water bed.

One of the highlights is, of course, the dining experience. The menu offers contemporary English cuisine and uses the freshest ingredients sourced from the West Country where possible, and there's an extensive wine list. A wide selection of seafood is delivered daily from Brixham and select cuts of meat or game come from their butcher's own herd.

Freshly baked rolls, brioche, scones, cakes and biscuits all add to the gastronomic experience. Round off with mouth-watering desserts including home made ice creams or a selection of West Country Cheese from the huge cheese board. House parties can also be arranged in The Abbott's Den private dining room, so it's a great place to get together with family and friends.

**t** (01395) 513174
**w** saltymonk.co.uk

**great ideas**

# Family fun

## Kids and weather. They change mood from one moment to the next. Fortunately, that's also one of the most striking things about England's great outdoors and attractions: you just step across the threshold and its landscapes and entertainment venues offer all the varied play potential you need to fill holidays, sunny afternoons or rainy weekends.

So, there you are on the beach building sandcastles, paddling, eating ice cream and basking in the warm memory that you'll take home. You watch the teenagers hanging out with their surfboards, part of the family outing but doing their own thing. There's something for all ages and that's priceless in every sense of the word. Next time, maybe picnicking in woods, leaping through treetops on an aerial adventure, or getting your hands on heritage – whatever makes everyone happy.

Then it rains and you want to stay indoors. London's Science Museum is free, like a good number of England's top attractions, and that pleases Money Bags. Everyone immediately vanishes into one of the galleries: in Who Am I? you're morphing your face older and younger, in another you're discovering how to forecast weather, which could be useful for planning your next trip!

Anticipate the family's next mood. Animal magic at Chester Zoo, following Harry Potter to Alnwick Castle, or screaming your heads off at Drayton Manor Theme Park in Staffordshire? There's always another boredom-buster just around the corner.

**For lots more great ideas visit enjoyEngland.com/ideas**

Clockwise: Botany Bay, Kent; Blackpool Pleasure Beach, Lancashire; Wookey Hole Caves and Papermill, near Wells; Woburn Safari Park, Bedfordshire

Clockwise: At Bristol, Bristol; the British Museum, London; NewcastleGateshead; Spinnaker Tower, Portsmouth

greatideas

# City breaks

## Cities today exude confidence. It's a self-belief that comes from bold investment. And as you gaze up at yet another remarkable new building that demands your attention and sparks your imagination, you realize that nowhere is this confidence more visible than in the architecture of the now.

Architects have done us proud in this country. Many of our cities are studded with gleaming out-of-this-world structures that find the fulcrum between form and function. And today you've taken time out to see the Lowry Museum in Manchester's Salford Quays. Just glimpsing the metal hull of the building from a distance makes you speed your step. Somehow, the thrilling combination of stainless steel and glass makes this inspirational waterside building a fitting home for the world's greatest collection of Lowry works inspirational waterside building a fitting home for the world's greatest collection of Lowry works.

It's just the kind of landmark building that you can seek out in many English cities these days. Portsmouth Harbour's 170-metre Spinnaker Tower, in the design of a billowing sail, conjures thoughts of sea breezes. So you take the lift to its Crow's Nest view deck, open to the elements, and see for miles, wind in your hair. Wembley Stadium, Gateshead Millennium Bridge, each one is a vigorous marriage of art and purpose.

Why not set a day aside, fish out your A to Z, and go on a safari of spectacular structures in a city near to (or far from) you.

**For lots more great ideas visit enjoyEngland.com/ideas**

Clockwise: Whinstone Lee Tor, Peak District, Derbyshire; Waterhead, Cumbria; Porlock Bay, Somerset; North York Moors

greatideas

# Rural escapes

Take one of hundreds of footpaths along the eastern end of Hope Valley in the Peak District and you'll find yourself at Stanage Edge. The wind whips around the gritstone outcrop, but all you can think about are the exhilarating panoramic views. Just a five-minute walk from the roadside car park, what a reward!

Ramble, cycle, relax over a picnic – in Britain's national parks you're quickly a world away from the day-to-day routine. Sea views across Porlock Bay, Exmoor, or purple waves of heather on the North York Moors work the yin and yang magic of nature. Wander with ponies on Dartmoor, enjoy the people-free hillsides of the Cheviots in Northumberland. What a sense of complete escape!

For a different experience follow the footpaths and cycleways to East Lancashire's Panopticons: gateway landmarks to magnificent countryside. Discover Burnley's huge Singing Ringing Tree crooning its low, mysterious song at Crown Point, or the striking steel Halo at Top o' Slate in Rossendale. They're fun, imaginative and easy to reach.

England boasts an astonishing diversity of natural wonders on the doorstep. From the flat waterscapes of the Norfolk Broads to the jutting peaks of the Lake District, from the ancient woodlands of the New Forest to Dorset's fossil-jewelled Jurassic Coast – there's scenery and breathing spaces to suit every activity and mood.

This is our natural heritage, shaped by primeval forces and just waiting to be explored. Step out and do so: you'll return with happily weary legs, a ravenous appetite and that wonderful tingling sensation on your face from a day in the fresh air.

**For lots more great ideas visit enjoyEngland.com/ideas**

Make your break memorable with fresh local flavours and chefs with passion

greatideas

# Food & drink

**A quiet revolution has been simmering away in England's eateries. Fresh, local and organic ingredients have become the order of the day. As you tuck into a light lunch of crisp salad and garlic mayo (made with free range eggs) you really begin to wonder if Chicken in a Basket wasn't just a bad dream.**

Yes, the wake-up call has been heard. Inventiveness, quality and choice are top of menus and eating out is about more than munching in candlelit corners – so give your tastebuds a holiday too! Try a waffle house for a change (with waffles made from organic flour, of course). How about a topping of chickpea curry and mango chutney? Ethnic cuisines serve up a spicy sense of adventure. Restaurants create works of art on a plate – imaginatively conjured from seasonal ingredients and local produce bursting with regional flavour. Some now have beer menus alongside wine menus, bringing new connoisseurship to our national drink.

Then, let's not forget the gastro pub phenomenon, it's still going strong. Stylish cooked-from-scratch bistro meals at bar room prices appeal to tummy and wallet in equal measure. Traditional inns, too, have raised their game. When the chef appears, he'll happily tell you where he sources his artisan cheeses (just down the road), herbs (grown in his kitchen garden), and orchard fruit and cream (from the nearby farm) for the scrumptious pie you just devoured.

And this is the true legacy of the contemporary food revolution in England today: wherever you dine, you'll more than likely be presented with fresh, wholesome food that has been beautifully cooked with passion, pride and care. Enjoy!

**For lots more great ideas visit enjoyEngland.com/ideas**

# enjoyEngland™

## official tourist board guides

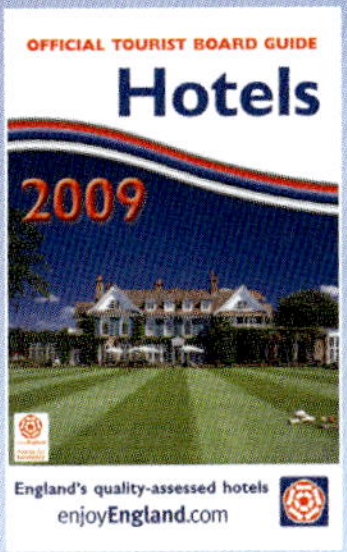


Hotels, including country house and town house hotels, metro and budget hotels and serviced apartments in England 2009

**£10.99**

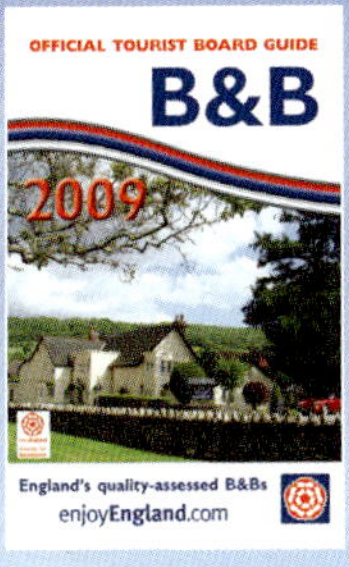


Guest accommodation, B&Bs, guest houses, farmhouses, inns, restaurants with rooms, campus and hostel accommodation in England 2009

**£11.99**

Self-catering holiday homes, including serviced apartments and approved caravan holiday homes, boat accommodation and holiday cottage agencies in England 2009

**£11.99**

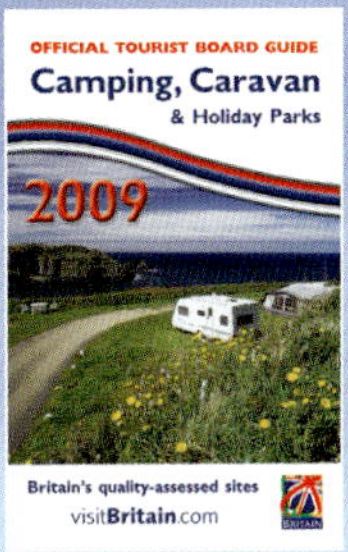


Touring parks, camping holidays and holiday parks and villages in Britain 2009

**£8.99**

## informative, easy to use and great value for money

Pet-friendly hotels, B&Bs and self-catering accommodation in England 2009

**£9.99**

Great Places to Stay Four and five star accommodation in Britain

**£17.99**

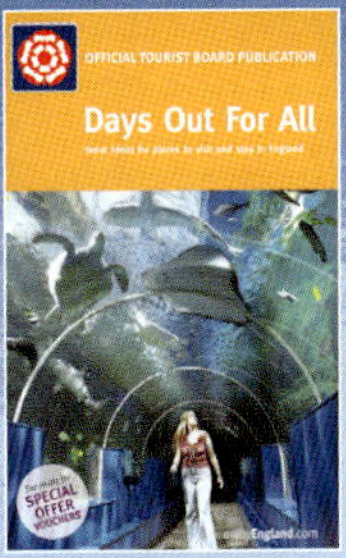


Great ideas for places to visit, eat and stay in England

**£10.99**

Accessible places to stay in Britain

**£9.99**

Now available in good bookshops.
For special offers on VisitBritain publications, please visit **enjoyenglanddirect.com**

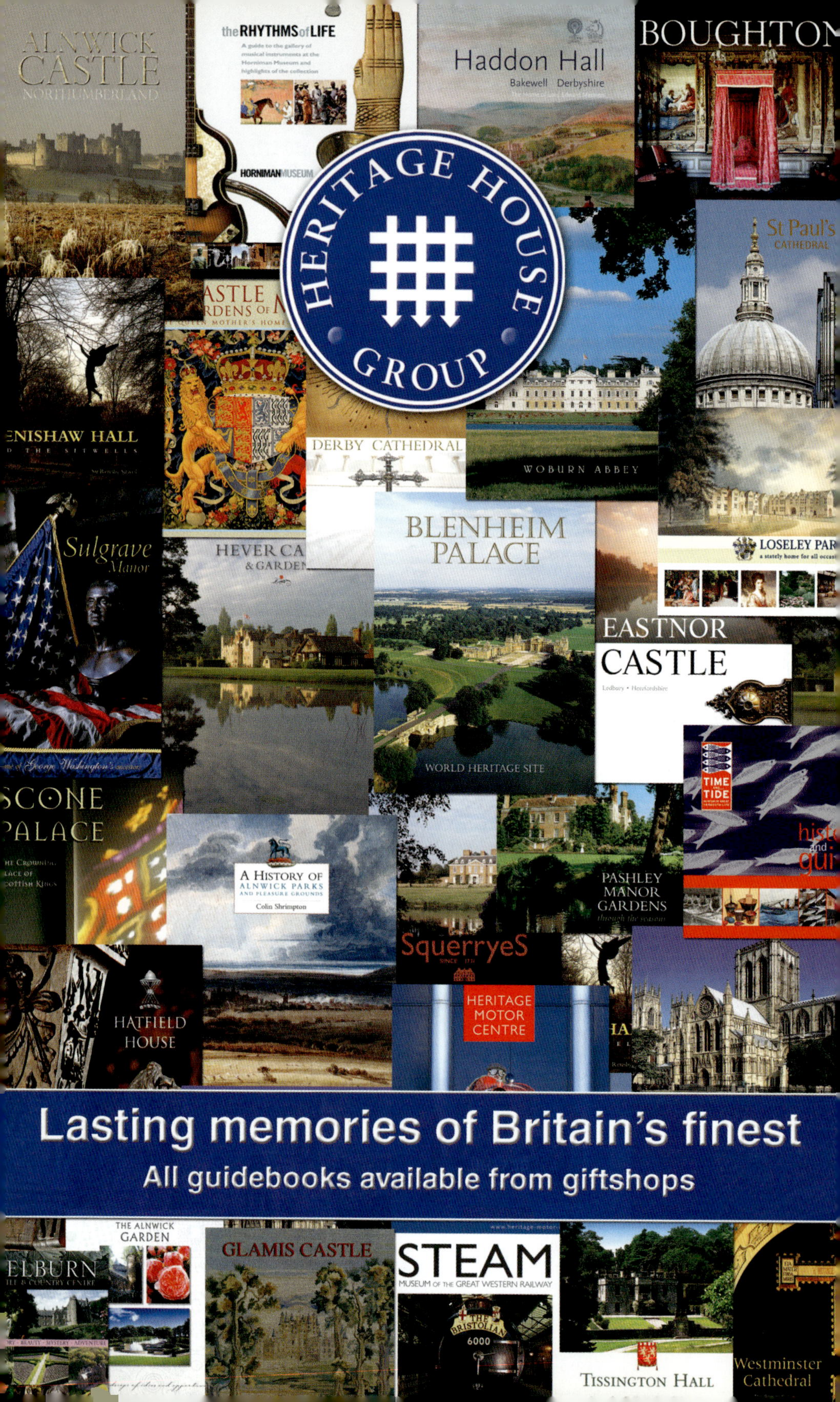
ALNWICK CASTLE
NORTHUMBERLAND
the RHYTHMS of LIFE
HORNIMAN MUSEUM
Haddon Hall
Bakewell Derbyshire
HERITAGE HOUSE GROUP
St Paul's
CATHEDRAL
DERBY CATHEDRAL
WOBURN ABBEY
Sulgrave
Manor
BLENHEIM
PALACE
WORLD HERITAGE SITE
EASTNOR
CASTLE
Ledbury • Herefordshire
TIME AND TIDE
A HISTORY OF
ALNWICK PARKS
AND PLEASURE GROUNDS
Colin Shrimpton
PASHLEY
MANOR
GARDENS
through the seasons
SquerryeS
HERITAGE
MOTOR
CENTRE
HATFIELD
HOUSE
Lasting memories of Britain's finest
All guidebooks available from giftshops
THE ALNWICK
GARDEN
GLAMIS CASTLE
STEAM
MUSEUM OF THE GREAT WESTERN RAILWAY
THE BRISTOLIAN
6000
TISSINGTON HALL
Westminster
Cathedral

# Location Maps

Every place name featured in the regional accommodation sections of this Enjoy England guide has a map reference to help you locate it on the maps which follow. For example, to find Colchester, Essex, which has 'Map ref 3B2', turn to Map 3 and refer to grid square B2.

All place names appearing in the regional sections are shown with orange circles on the maps. This enables you to find other places in your chosen area which may have suitable accommodation – the place index (at the back of this guide) gives page numbers.

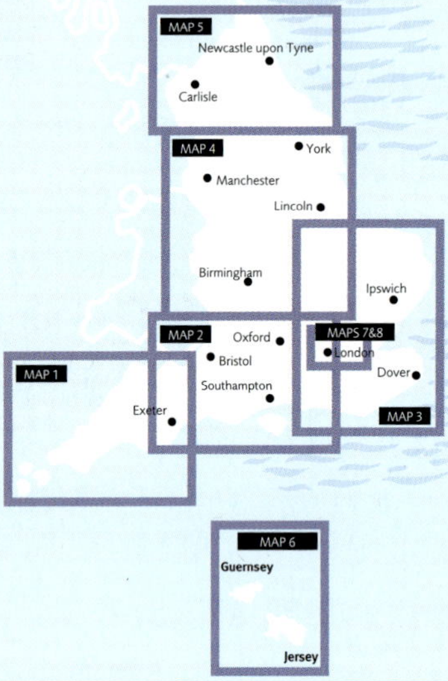


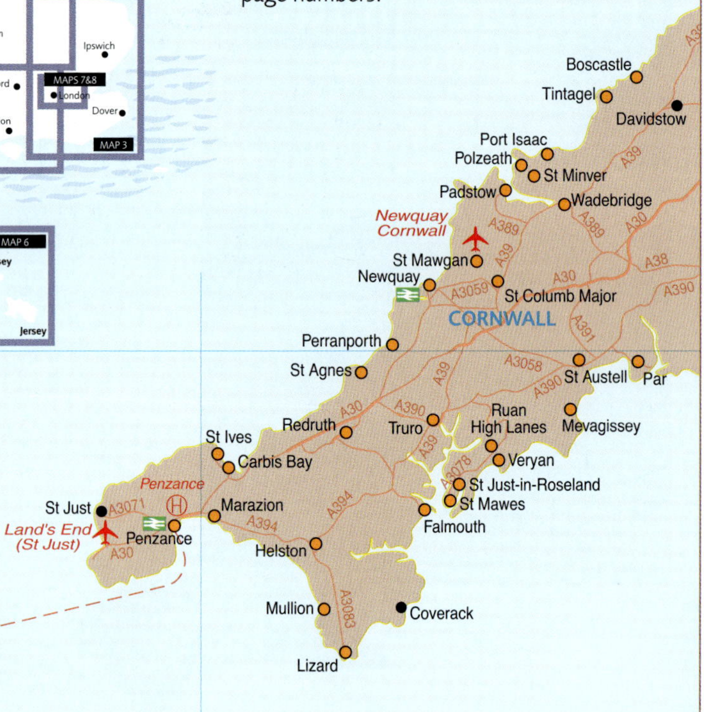

Key to regions: South West England

Orange circles indicate accommodation within the regional sections of this guide

# Map 2

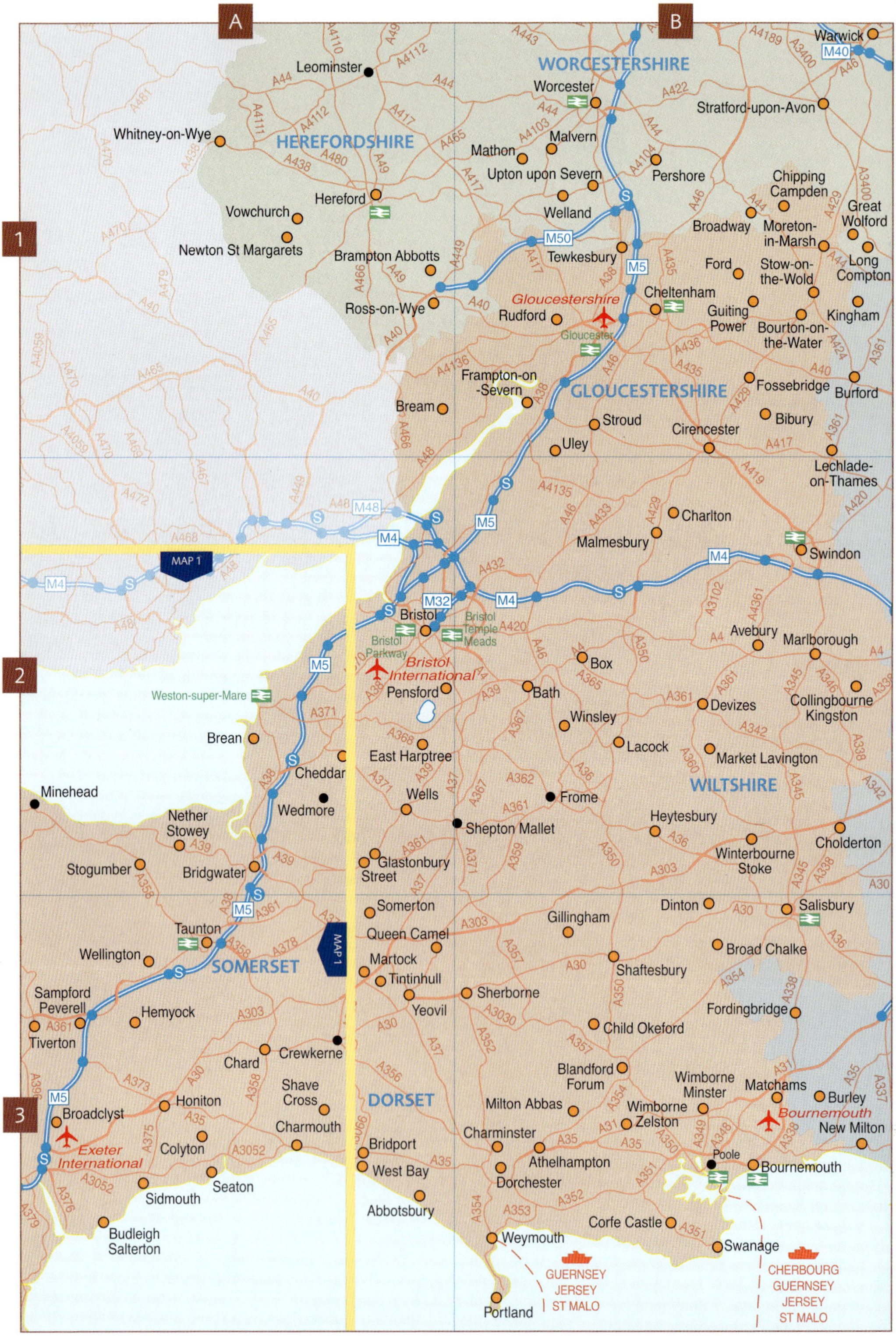


Key to regions: South West England | Central England | South East England

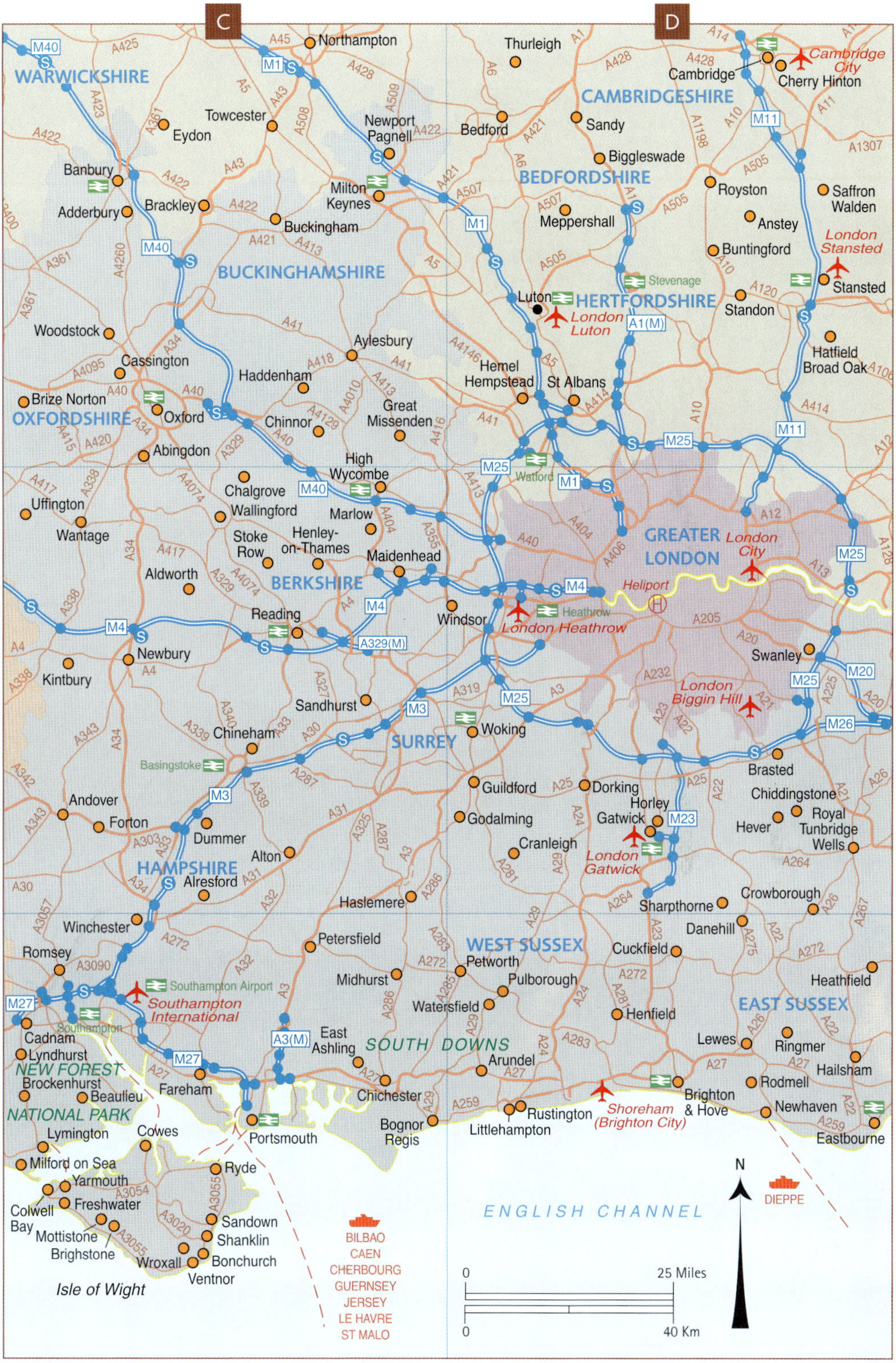


London

Orange circles indicate accommodation within the regional sections of this guide

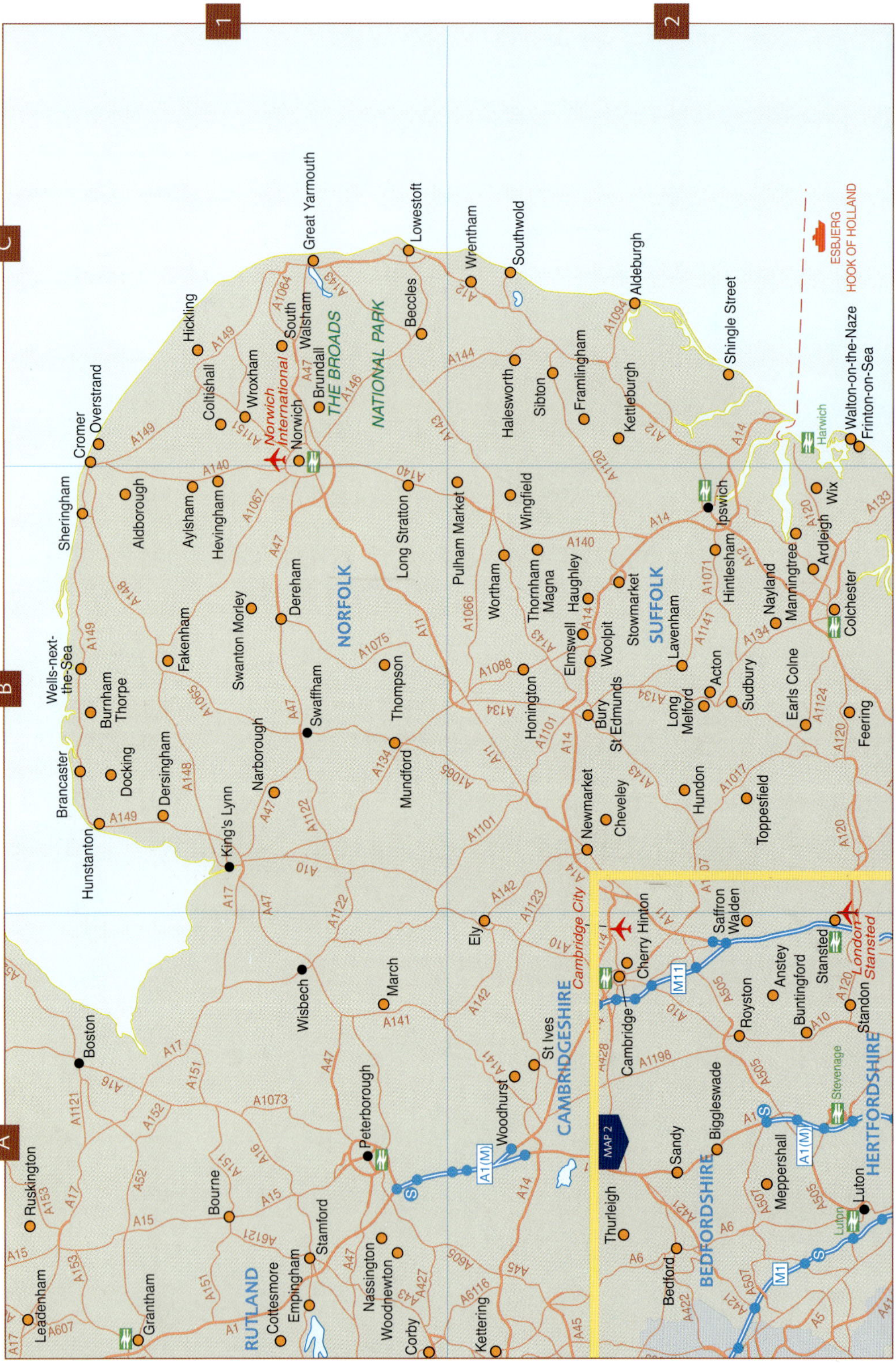


Key to regions: Central England South East England London

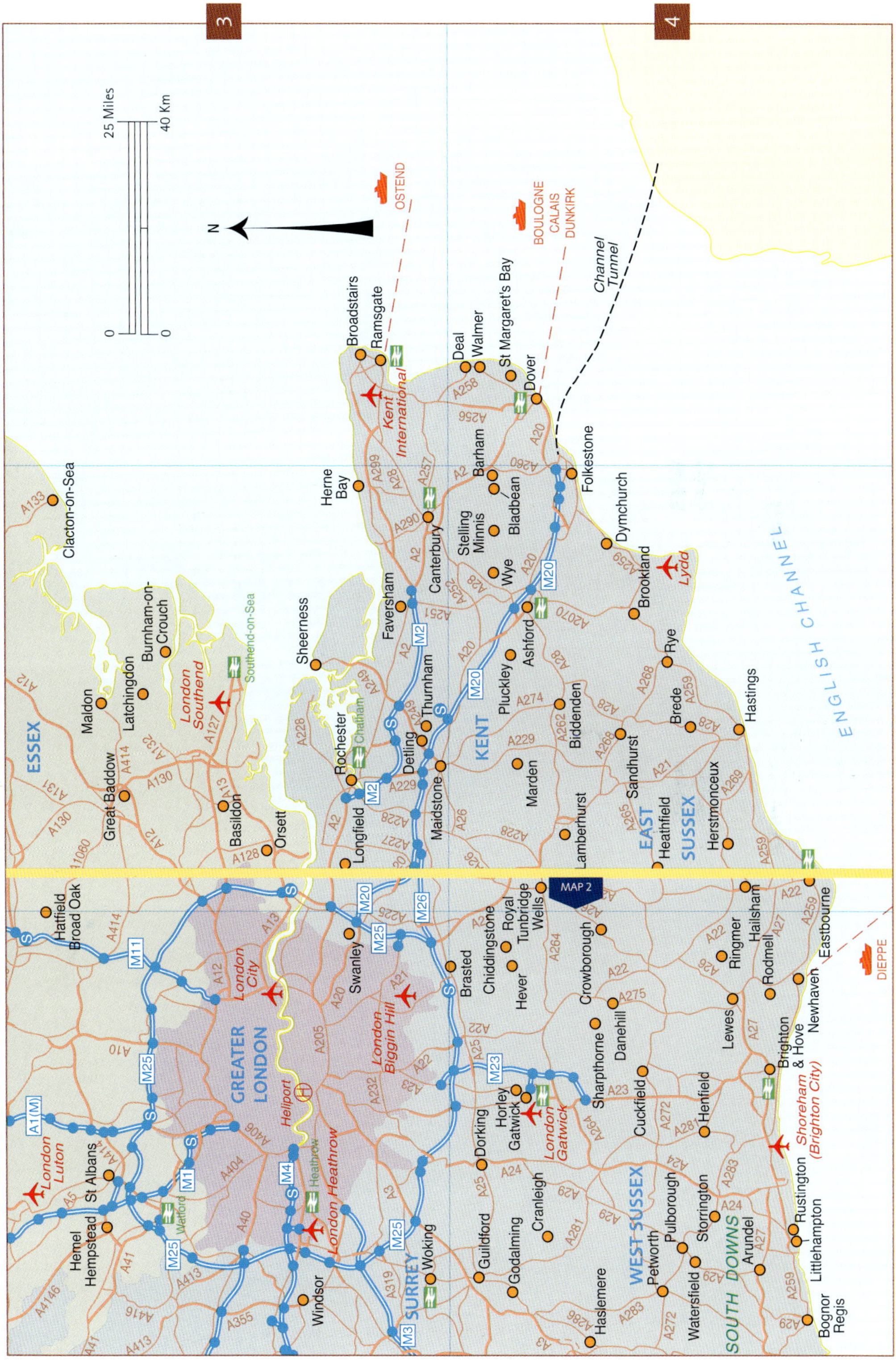
3
4
25 Miles
40 Km
0
0
N
OSTEND
BOULOGNE
CALAIS
DUNKIRK
Channel Tunnel
ENGLISH CHANNEL
DIEPPE
MAP 2
ESSEX
KENT
EAST SUSSEX
WEST SUSSEX
SURREY
SOUTH DOWNS
GREATER LONDON
Clacton-on-Sea
Maldon
Latchingdon
Burnham-on-Crouch
Great Baddow
Basildon
Orsett
London Southend
Southend-on-Sea
Sheerness
Herne Bay
Broadstairs
Ramsgate
Kent International
Deal
Walmer
St Margaret's Bay
Dover
Barham
Bladbean
Stelling Minnis
Canterbury
Faversham
Wye
Folkestone
Dymchurch
Brookland
Lydd
Rye
Ashford
Pluckley
Biddenden
Thurnham
Detling
Rochester
Chatham
Maidstone
Longfield
Marden
Lamberhurst
Sandhurst
Brede
Hastings
Heathfield
Herstmonceux
Hailsham
Eastbourne
Hatfield Broad Oak
London City
Swanley
Brasted
London Biggin Hill
Chiddingstone
Royal Tunbridge Wells
Hever
Crowborough
Danehill
Sharpthorne
Ringmer
Rodmell
Lewes
Newhaven
Brighton & Hove
Shoreham (Brighton City)
Cuckfield
Henfield
Horley
Gatwick
London Gatwick
Dorking
Heliport
London Heathrow
Heathrow
London Luton
St Albans
Hemel Hempstead
Watford
Windsor
Woking
Guildford
Godalming
Cranleigh
Haslemere
Petworth
Pulborough
Storrington
Waterfield
Arundel
Rustington
Littlehampton
Bognor Regis
M2
M20
M25
M26
M23
M11
M1
M4
M3
A1(M)

## Map 4

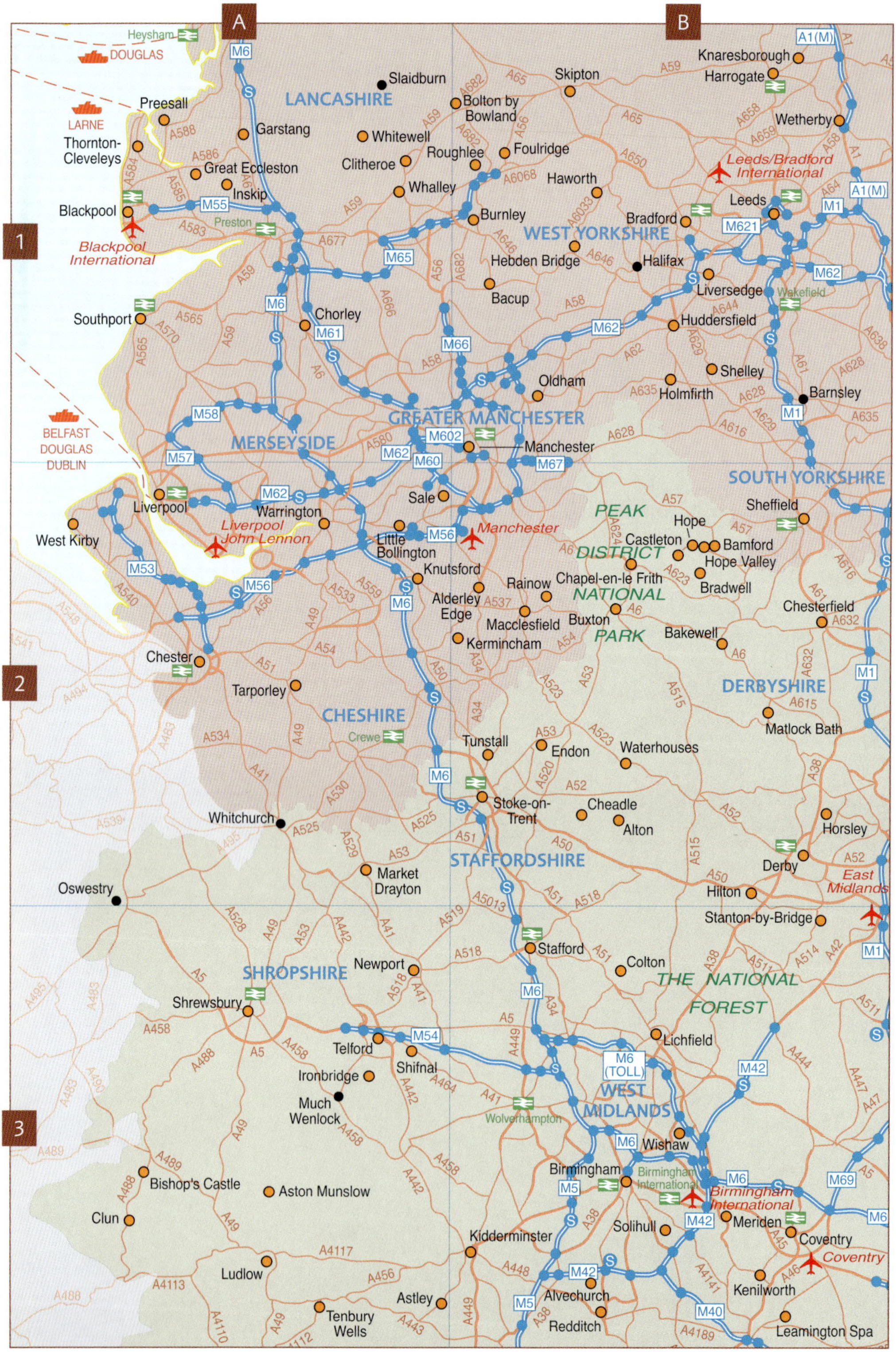


Key to regions: Northern England Central England

Orange circles indicate accommodation within the regional sections of this guide

## Map 5

Key to regions: Northern England

Orange circles indicate accommodation within the regional sections of this guide

## Map 6

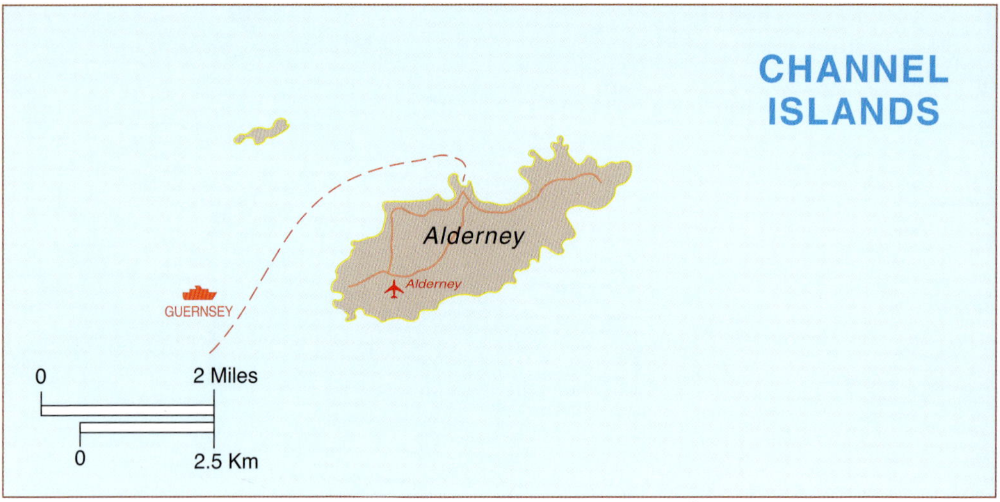


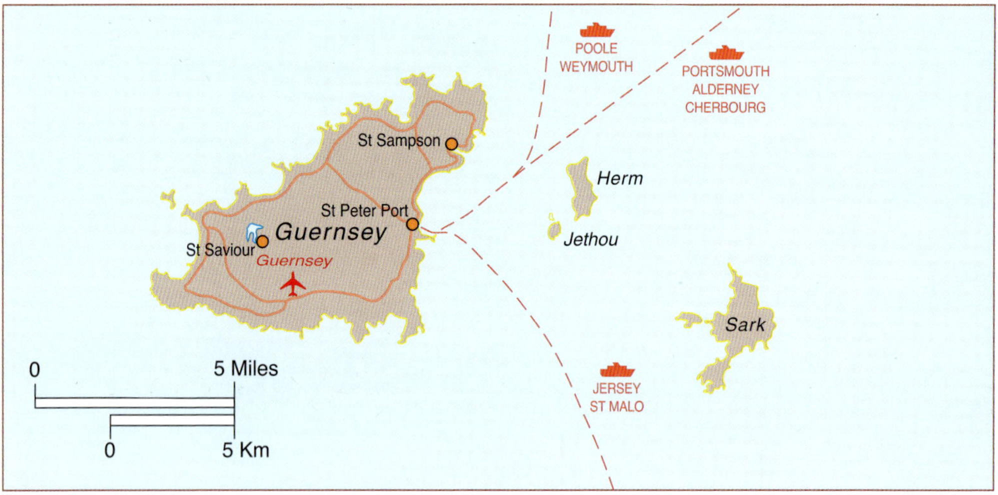

Key to regions: Channel Islands

Orange circles indicate accommodation within the regional sections of this guide

Central London
© Arka Cartographics Ltd. 1999
HOXTON
FINSBURY
EC1
EC2
EC3
EC4
CLERKENWELL
PENTONVILLE
N1
BLOOMSBURY
WC1
WC2
ST. PANCRAS
SOMERS TOWN
HOLBORN
CITY
SOHO
W1
MAYFAIR
MARYLEBONE
NW1
NW8
ST. JOHN'S WOOD
MAIDA VALE
MAIDA HILL
KILBURN
WEST KILBURN
KENSAL TOWN
W9
W2
BAYSWATER
PADDINGTON
WESTBOURNE GREEN
NOTTING HILL
W11
W8
KENSINGTON
WEST KENSINGTON
W14
SW7
SOUTH KENSINGTON
BROMPTON
SW3
CHELSEA
SW10
SW5
EARLS COURT
WEST BROMPTON
SW6
BELGRAVIA
SW1
WESTMINSTER
PIMLICO
VAUXHALL
SW8
LAMBETH
SE11
SE1
SOUTHWARK
THE BOROUGH
NEWINGTON
KENNINGTON
SE17
WALWORTH
CAMBERWELL
SE5
SE15
BERMONDSEY
Regent's Park
Primrose Hill
Hyde Park
Kensington Gardens
Holland Park
Green Park
St James's Park
RIVER THAMES
King's Cross
St. Pancras
Euston
King's Cross Thameslink
Farringdon
Barbican
Moorgate
Old Street
Liverpool Street
Fenchurch Street
Cannon Street
London Bridge
City Thameslink
Blackfriars
Waterloo
Waterloo East
Charing Cross
Victoria
Vauxhall
Elephant and Castle
Marylebone
Paddington
Kilburn High Road
Queen's Park
Kensington (Olympia)
West Brompton
A40(M)
WESTWAY
TOWER BRIDGE
LONDON BRIDGE
SOUTHWARK BRIDGE
BLACKFRIARS BRIDGE
WATERLOO BRIDGE
WESTMINSTER BRIDGE
LAMBETH BRIDGE
VAUXHALL BRIDGE
CHELSEA BRIDGE
ALBERT BRIDGE
BATTERSEA BRIDGE
EUSTON ROAD
MARYLEBONE ROAD
OXFORD STREET
REGENT STREET
PICCADILLY
WHITEHALL
STRAND
VICTORIA EMBANKMENT
ALBERT EMBANKMENT
CHELSEA EMBANKMENT
KINGSWAY
PARK LANE
KNIGHTSBRIDGE
KENSINGTON ROAD
BAYSWATER ROAD
EDGWARE ROAD
CROMWELL ROAD
KING'S ROAD
FULHAM ROAD
HOLLAND PARK AVE
LADBROKE GROVE
HARROW ROAD
CITY ROAD
OLD STREET
MOORGATE
CHEAPSIDE
BISHOPSGATE
KENNINGTON ROAD
WALWORTH ROAD
CAMBERWELL RD
NEW KENT RD
OLD KENT RD
BOROUGH HIGH STREET
LONG LANE
TOOLEY ST

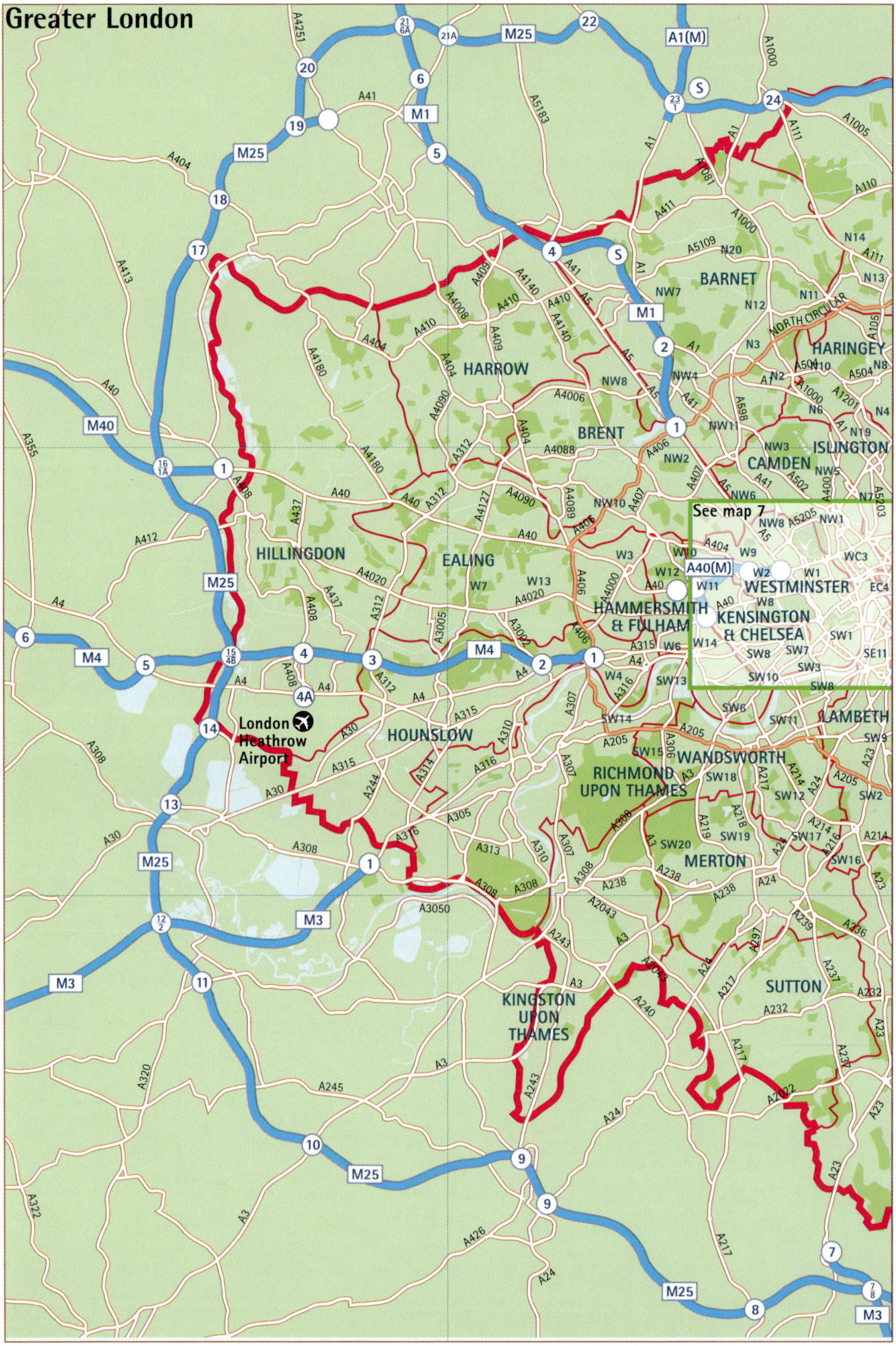
Greater London
M25
A1(M)
A1000
A4251
A41
M1
A5183
A1005
A111
A110
A404
A1081
A411
A1000
A5109
N20
N14
N13
BARNET
NW7
N12
N11
NORTH CIRCULAR
HARINGEY
N8
N3
N2
N10
N6
N4
A413
A4180
A410
A4008
A409
A4140
HARROW
NW8
A4006
NW4
NW11
A598
A1201
N19
A40
M40
A4090
A312
A404
BRENT
A4088
NW3
CAMDEN
ISLINGTON
A355
A408
A437
A4127
NW2
NW5
NW6
N7
A5203
A4090
A4089
NW10
A407
See map 7
NW8
A5205
NW1
A412
HILLINGDON
EALING
W7
W13
A4020
A4000
W3
W10
W9
W12
A40(M)
W2
W1
WC3
WESTMINSTER
EC4
W11
W8
HAMMERSMITH
& FULHAM
KENSINGTON
& CHELSEA
A3005
A3002
A315
W6
W14
SW1
SW8
SW7
SW3
SE11
SW10
SW5
M4
A4
A4A
W4
A316
SW13
London
Heathrow
Airport
A30
A315
HOUNSLOW
A310
A307
SW14
SW6
SW11
LAMBETH
SW9
A205
SW15
A306
WANDSWORTH
A3
SW18
A217
A214
A24
SW12
SW2
A308
A244
A314
A316
RICHMOND
UPON THAMES
A305
A313
A308
SW20
A218
A219
SW19
SW17
A216
SW16
MERTON
A23
A238
A3050
A2043
A239
A236
A297
A243
A237
SUTTON
A232
A240
KINGSTON
UPON
THAMES
A320
A245
A2022
M3
A24
A322
A426
A217

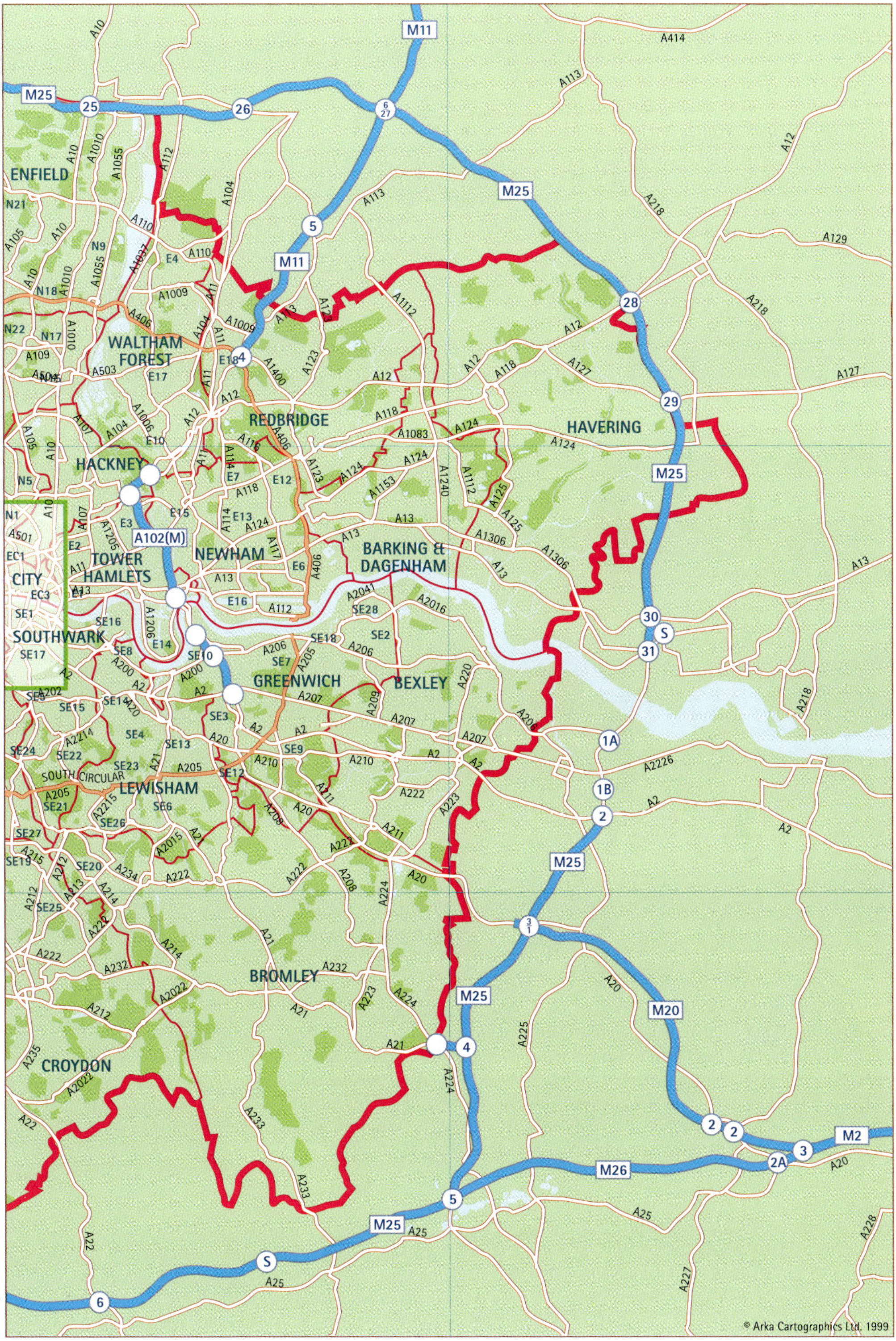
ENFIELD
WALTHAM FOREST
REDBRIDGE
HAVERING
HACKNEY
NEWHAM
TOWER HAMLETS
CITY
SOUTHWARK
BARKING & DAGENHAM
GREENWICH
BEXLEY
LEWISHAM
BROMLEY
CROYDON
M25
M11
M20
M26
M2
A102(M)
SOUTH CIRCULAR
© Arka Cartographics Ltd. 1999

# Northern England

Cheshire, Cumbria, Durham, Greater Manchester, Lancashire, Merseyside, Northumberland, Tees Valley, Tyne and Wear, Yorkshire

Clockwise: Bamburgh Castle, Northumberland; Liverpool; North Yorkshire Moors Railway

# Great days out

## Explore windswept moors and breathtaking coastlines. Admire mirrored-glass lakes and magnificent cathedrals. Discover pioneering industrial heritage and cutting-edge cities. Northern England is a proud fusion of history, dramatic landscapes and modern culture – not forgetting fun-filled seaside resorts!

### Relive the revolution

Where did the Industrial Revolution gather pace? In Northern England, of course! Experience its legacy in so many ways. At **Beamish Museum**, a town, colliery village and farm have been recreated using authentic early 19th and 20thC buildings – get around by tramcar and chat to costumed interpreters. Children love living history this way. Hear vivid tales at the **National Coal Mining Museum for England** at Wakefield, put on hat, belt and battery and tour underground with an experienced miner. Clamber onto historic craft at **The National Waterways Museum**, Ellesmere Port. Or maybe trains are more your style? Go spotting at **Locomotion, The National Railway Museum** in Shildon, one of the oldest railway towns in the world. Steaming Days get dads as excited as the kids.

### Natural highs

Wide-open spaces abound in the National Parks – Yorkshire alone has over 1,000 square miles to explore. Escape and hear your laughter in the breeze as you fly a kite from high on the **North York Moors**. You can always pick up tips from the professionals at Sunderland International Kite Festival. **The Lake District and Cumbria** have inspired poets, painters and climbers, and Wastwater was recently voted 'Britain's favourite view'. Enjoy it at ground level or hike up Scafell Pike, England's highest peak, for a stunning aerial picture. You'll also feel on top of the world cycling or walking to **East Lancashire's Panopticons**, a series of innovative structures pointing the way to panoramic countryside: Halo, illuminating the Rossendale night sky, is simply breathtaking.

For more firsts and highs, ramble the **North Pennines Area of Outstanding Natural Beauty**, Britain's first geopark. Weardale and Teesdale are renowned for dazzling waterfalls – aptly named **High Force** is England's highest. Build castles along rippled-sand beaches, such as Spittal and St Aidans, in the North East. Board a boat to **Holy Island** to learn the secrets of the Lindisfarne Gospels. And remember the binoculars on the **Farne Islands** – home to hundreds of thousands of puffins and dewy-eyed grey seals.

Wastwater, Cumbria

### Join the Romans

Pace along **Hadrian's Wall** in the footsteps of soldiers nearly two millennia ago. Built in just six years, it runs for an amazing 73 miles. **Chesters** is Britain's best-preserved Roman cavalry fort  and you can find out more about Romans in the region at **Tullie House**

Left to right: Alnwick Castle, Northumberland; York Minster

**why not...** cycle the shoreline of Coniston Water, perfect for easygoing family rides?

**Museum and Art Gallery**, Carlisle. In the walled city of Chester, Britain's best-preserved Roman town, visit the partially excavated amphitheatre or the **Dewa Roman Experience** where you can step aboard a Roman galley, stroll a reconstructed street and handle 'dig' discoveries.

## Grand designs

Northern England has more than its fair share of remarkable buildings. Please the children with a visit to **Alnwick Castle**, aka Hogwarts in the first Harry Potter films. They'll be enthralled by one of the world's largest treehouses, too. **Tatton Park** in Cheshire is among the most complete historic estates, featuring a mansion, gardens, farm, Tudor Old Hall, deer park and speciality shops. And **Castle Howard**, near York, sets an impressive standard in home décor with its Canalettos, Holbeins and Gainsboroughs. Seek green-fingered inspiration at **Sheffield's Winter Garden**, which grows more than 2,500 plants from around the world in a huge temperate glasshouse the size of 5,000 domestic greenhouses!

Tiptoe beneath the towering vaulted ceilings of **York Minster**, the largest medieval Gothic cathedral in Northern Europe and home to glittering stained glass collections. Durham City's medieval cobbled streets are crowned by the magnificent towers of **Durham Castle and Cathedral** – 'the best cathedral on planet earth', according to travel writer Bill Bryson. And now's the time to discover the twin **Anglo-Saxon monasteries at Wearmouth and Jarrow**, the UK's nomination for World Heritage Status in 2009.

## Young hearts and minds

Candyfloss and sticky rock, thrills and spills – **Blackpool** is your dream ticket for family fun. Book ringside seats at the **Tower Circus**, and gasp in amazement as international artists

Blackpool

perform superhuman feats. Hop onto sock-popping rides at **Camelot Theme Park** near Chorley or **Go Ape!** in Grizedale Forest on rope bridges and Tarzan swings. Then stimulate the brain cells at **Rotherham's Magna** on an elemental interactive adventure through fire, earth, air and water. Or take the plunge at **The Deep** in Hull and come nose to nose with sharks in the submarium.

## Modern city culture

There's also plenty to keep pulses racing in Northern England's dynamic cities where regeneration is the name of the game. Enjoy the renaissance of **NewcastleGateshead**, highlighted by the stunning architecture of the **Gateshead Millennium Bridge**. New artists at the **Baltic Centre for Contemporary Art** keep pushing the boundaries. Explore **Liverpool** and **Manchester**, both vibrant club scenes – of the soccer and night-time variety. Liverpool, revered birthplace of The Beatles, is still sparking from its European Capital of Culture 2008 status. Tour the revitalised **Albert Dock** along the World Heritage waterfront and sample the contemporary art of **Tate Liverpool**.

**why not...** join a ghost walk around York, claimed as Europe's most haunted city?

In **Manchester** head for **Salford Quays** and **The Lowry**, the inspirational waterfront centre for the visual arts and entertainment. The daring aluminium **Imperial War Museum North** designed by Daniel Libeskind is a showstopper, one of Manchester's many free museums. Next up: **Leeds** has a new must-see **City Museum** featuring an astounding Treasures Gallery. Middlesbrough, though not a city, also beckons with the recently opened **Middlesbrough Institute of Modern Art** housing works by Tracey Emin and other headline names.

Clockwise: NewcastleGateshead; The Deep, Hull; The Lowry, Manchester

# Destinations

## Berwick-upon-Tweed

England's northernmost town guards the mouth of the River Tweed. Marvel at some of the finest 16thC city walls in Europe, built by Elizabeth I to protect the town. Visit Bamburgh Castle and the beautiful gardens at Alnwick. Roam magnificent Heritage coastline and see Holy Island and the fairytale Lindisfarne Castle.

Bamburgh near Berwick-upon-Tweed

## Blackpool

Britain's favourite holiday resort. Experience thrills and excitement at the Pleasure Beach, take tea in the magnificent Tower Ballroom, or stroll the seven miles of sandy beaches. Blackpool offers you world-class shows, cosmopolitan restaurants, vibrant nightlife, an active sports scene and breathtakingly beautiful scenery on the doorstep.

## Chester

Experience one of Europe's top heritage cities. Walk the unique city walls, then visit the famous Rows, unique two-tiered galleries, to shop for everything from antiques to high fashion. Stroll along the banks of the beautiful River Dee, explore the Roman amphitheatre, and spend a day at Chester's famous Roodee Racecourse.

## Cumbria – The Lake District

With breathtaking mountains and sparkling lakes, the unsurpassed scenery of Cumbria – The Lake District has inspired writers and poets across the ages. Explore the best walking and climbing routes that England has to offer, and see for yourself 'Britain's favourite view'. Take a lake cruise, visit wonderful homes and gardens or simply enjoy the views.

## Durham

Described by Bill Bryson as 'a perfect little city.' Explore majestic Durham Cathedral, a World Heritage Site, and thought by many to be the finest Norman church architecture in England. Visit the tombs of St Cuthbert and the Venerable Bede. Take a coffee in the cobbled Market Place and enjoy the stunning floral displays, or walk down to the riverbank for magnificent views.

## Hull

Enjoy the invigorating yet relaxing atmosphere that only a waterfront city can offer. Visit the Museum Quarter linking four of Hull's eight free museums. Don't miss 'The Deep', home to 40 sharks and one of the most spectacular sea-life attractions in the world. Marvel at the engineering of the Humber Bridge and, after dark, experience Hull's very own café bar culture.

## Leeds

Rich local history, world-class sport, outstanding museums and galleries, and diverse year-round entertainment, that's Leeds. It's a shopaholic's dream, from the elegant Corn Exchange to the exquisite Victoria Quarter, not to mention the only Harvey Nichols outside London. See opera and dance at the Opera North and Northern Ballet and explore the Yorkshire Dales right on the doorstep.

National Park
Area of Outstanding Natural Beauty
Heritage Coast
National Trails
nationaltrail.co.uk
3
Sections of the
National Cycle Network
nationalcyclenetwork.org.uk
Berwick-upon-Tweed
Holy Island/
Lindisfarne
Bamburgh
Northumberland
Coast
Wooler
1
68
PENNINE
WAY
Alnwick
Kielder Water
and Forest Park
NORTHUMBERLAND
Druridge
Druridge
Bay
Bellingham
HADRIAN'S
WALL PATH
7
72
Tynemouth
South Shields
Solway
Coast
Carlisle
PENNINE
WAY
72
Newcastle
Gateshead
Sunderland
Silloth
7
7
Derwent
Reservoir
Durham
North
Pennines
Stanhope
14
14
Maryport
Penrith
Middleton-
in-Teesdale
1
Hartlepool
Workington
71
Keswick
71
Stockton-
on-Tees
Middlesbrough
Whitehaven
Kirkby
Stephen
Barnard
Castle
Darlington
Saltburn-by-the-Sea
LAKE DISTRICT
Whitby
Ambleside
Dalegarth
Windermere
NORTH YORK
MOORS
Ravenglass
68
PENNINE
WAY
71
CLEVELAND
WAY
Scarborough
Grange-
over-Sands
6
Kirkby
Lonsdale
YORKSHIRE
DALES
Helmsley
Filey
Ulverston
Arnside &
Silverdale
DALES WAY
Ripon
65
Howardian
Hills
Barrow-
in-Furness
Nidderdale
Bridlington
Lancaster
Forest of
Bowland
Harrogate
York
Skipton
YORKSHIRE
WOLDS WAY
1
Ilkley
Haworth
Leeds
65
Blackpool
Hull
Bradford
Preston
Blackburn
Wakefield
67
62
Withernsea
Southport
Halifax
Huddersfield
Chorley
PENNINE
BRIDLEWAY
Barnsley
62
PEAK
DISTRICT
Doncaster
Manchester
Liverpool
Rotherham
Sheffield
Neston
Knutsford
Ellesmere Port
Chester
Macclesfield
Nantwich
0
50 miles
0
75 kms

Durham

## Liverpool

Experience the unique atmosphere of Liverpool. The birthplace of the Beatles and European Capital of Culture 2008 offers you more theatres, museums and galleries than any UK city outside London. Its history as one of the world's great ports has left a remarkable legacy of art and architecture to explore, not forgetting, the city's famous sporting pedigree. So if it's Strawberry Fields, Premiership football or Europe's finest culture you're looking for, it has to be Liverpool.

## Manchester

Explore a city that has reinvented itself as a truly contemporary metropolis. You'll find modern landmark buildings, a wealth of art and culture, great bars and world-class hospitality. There's every experience imaginable, from fine dining and top-class theatre, to major sporting events and year-round festivals. It's a shopping destination in its own right, rivalling that of the capital, with top stores and chic boutiques.

Clockwise: Chester; Leeds; Martindale, Cumbria

## NewcastleGateshead

Must-see attractions including the award-winning Gateshead Millennium Bridge, the Baltic Centre for Contemporary Art and the magnificent new Sage Gateshead, a stunning Sir Norman Foster building, with billowing curves of glass and steel catering for every genre of music. Rich in culture, architecture and history and with a great reputation for style, shopping and nightlife, the variety of life in NewcastleGateshead surprises even the most well travelled visitor.

## Whitby

With its quaint cobbled streets and picturesque houses standing on the steep slopes of the River Esk, Whitby is dominated by its cliff top Abbey. Explore one of Britain's finest stretches of coastline. Climb the steps to the parish church of St Mary, whose churchyard inspired Bram Stocker's 'Dracula'. Then down to the historic quayside of this 1,000-year-old port and celebrate the town's seafaring tradition at the Captain Cook Festival, named in honour of Whitby's most famous son.

## York

Visit award-winning attractions including the magnificent York Minster, and the world's biggest and best railway museum. Let 21stC technology transport you back to the Viking age at Jorvik, and wander through the terrifying York Dungeon. Pedestrianised streets make York an ideal city to explore on foot. Follow the city's specialist shopping trails '5 Routes to Shopping Heaven', or browse the specialist antique and book dealers.

**For lots more great ideas visit enjoyEngland.com/destinations**

# Visitor attractions

## Family and Fun

**Aquarium of the Lakes**
*Lakeside, Cumbria*
(015395) 30153
aquariumofthelakes.co.uk
*Freshwater aquarium complete with underwater viewing tunnel.*

**Beamish, The North of England Open Air Museum**
*Beamish, Durham*
(0191) 370 4000
beamish.org.uk
*Award-winning open-air museum of working life.*

**Blackpool Tower & Circus**
*Blackpool, Lancashire*
(01253) 622242
blackpooltower.co.uk
*Entertainment for all ages, night and day.*

**Blue Planet Aquarium**
*Ellesmere Port, Cheshire*
(0151) 357 8804
blueplanetaquarium.com
*Underwater adventure in the UK's largest aquarium.*

**Chester Zoo**
*Chester, Cheshire*
(01244) 380280
chesterzoo.org
*Meet over 7,000 animals and 500 species.*

**Darlington Railway Centre and Museum**
*Darlington, Durham*
(01325) 460532
drcm.org.uk
*See, touch and feel living railway heritage.*

**The Deep**
*Hull, East Yorkshire*
(01482) 381000
thedeep.co.uk
*One of the world's most spectacular aquariums.*

**Hartlepool's Maritime Experience**
*Hartlepool, Durham*
(01429) 860077
hartlepoolsmaritimeexperience.com
*Authentic reconstruction of an 18thC seaport.*

**JORVIK Viking Centre**
*York, North Yorkshire*
(01904) 543400
jorvik-viking-centre.co.uk
*Meet the Vikings, face-to-face.*

**Killhope, The North of England Lead Mining Museum**
*Cowshill, Durham*
(01388) 537505
durham.gov.uk/killhope
*Award-winning underground experience.*

**Liverpool Football Club Museum and Stadium Tour**
*Liverpool*
(0151) 260 6677
liverpoolfc.tv
*Touch the famous 'This is Anfield' sign!*

**Locomotion: The National Railway Museum at Shildon**
*Shildon, Durham*
(01388) 777999
locomotion.uk.com
*Historic buildings and vehicles celebrate railway heritage.*

**Magna Science Adventure Centre**
*Rotherham, South Yorkshire*
(01709) 720002
visitmagna.co.uk
*An unforgettable, interactive science adventure.*

**Manchester United Museum & Tour**
*Manchester*
0870 442 1994
manutd.com
*Official tour of the 'Theatre of Dreams'.*

**Merseyside Maritime Museum**
*Liverpool*
(0151) 478 4499
merseysidemaritimemuseum.org.uk
*Liverpool's seafaring heritage brought to life.*

**MOSI (Museum of Science and Industry)**
*Manchester*
(0161) 832 2244
mosi.org.uk
*Five historic buildings packed with fascinating displays.*

**The National Waterways Museum**
*Ellesmere Port, Cheshire*
(0151) 355 5017
nwm.org.uk
*Britain's largest collection of inland waterway craft.*

**Nature's World**
*Middlesbrough*
(01642) 594895
naturesworld.org.uk
*Pioneering eco-garden of the future.*

**Saltburn Smugglers Heritage Centre**
*Saltburn-by-the-Sea, Tees Valley*
(01287) 625252
redcar-cleveland.gov.uk/leisure
*Meet costumed characters in ancient fishermens' cottages.*

**Seven Stories, The Centre for Children's Books**
*Newcastle upon Tyne, Tyne and Wear*
0845 271 0777
sevenstories.org.uk
*Britain's first centre dedicated to children's literature.*

**Yorkshire Waterways Museum**
*Goole, East Yorkshire*
(01405) 768730
waterwaysmuseum.org.uk
*Museum, adventure centre and nature trail.*

## Heritage

**Alnwick Castle**
*Alnwick, Northumberland*
(01665) 510777
alnwickcastle.com
*Dazzling medieval castle with glorious state rooms.*

**Arley Hall & Gardens**
*Northwich, Cheshire*
(01565) 777353
arleyhallandgardens.com
*Charming stately home and award-winning gardens.*

**Bamburgh Castle**
*Bamburgh, Northumberland*
(01668) 214515
bamburghcastle.com
*Imposing castle in dramatic coastal setting.*

**Beeston Castle**
*Beeston, Cheshire*
(01829) 260464
english-heritage.org.uk
*13thC castle with views over eight counties.*

**Belsay Hall, Castle and Gardens**
*Newcastle upon Tyne, Tyne and Wear*
(01661) 881636
english-heritage.org.uk
*Medieval castle, 17thC manor and gardens.*

**Brodsworth Hall and Gardens**
*Doncaster, South Yorkshire*
(01302) 724969
english-heritage.org.uk
*Italianate house with marvellous labyrinthine gardens.*

**Castle Howard**
*York, North Yorkshire*
(01653) 648444
castlehoward.co.uk
*Magnificent 18thC house in stunning parkland.*

**Chester Cathedral**
*Chester, Cheshire*
(01244) 324756
chestercathedral.com
*Medieval cathedral with spectacular carved choir stalls.*

**Durham Castle**
*Durham*
(0191) 334 3800
durhamcastle.com
*Superb Norman castle in World Heritage Site.*

**Fountains Abbey and Studley Royal Water Garden**
*Ripon, North Yorkshire*
(01765) 608888
fountainsabbey.org.uk
*12thC monastic ruin with captivating landscaped gardens.*

**Harewood House**
*Harewood, West Yorkshire*
(0113) 218 1010
harewood.org
*Stunning architecture and exquisite Adam interiors.*

**Holker Hall and Gardens**
*Cark in Cartmel, Cumbria*
(015395) 58328
holker-hall.co.uk
*Magnificent Neo-Elizabethan mansion and award-winning gardens.*

**Levens Hall & Gardens**
*Levens, Cumbria*
(015395) 60321
levenshall.co.uk
*Elizabethan mansion and world-famous topiary gardens.*

**Lyme Park**
*Disley, Cheshire*
(01663) 766492
nationaltrust.org.uk
*Tudor house transformed into an Italianate palace.*

**National Coal Mining Museum for England**
*Wakefield, West Yorkshire*
(01924) 848806
ncm.org.uk
*Award-winning museum of the English coalfields.*

**Newby Hall & Gardens**
*Ripon, North Yorkshire*
0845 450 4068
newbyhall.com
*One of England's renowned Adam houses.*

**North Yorkshire Moors Railway**
*Pickering, North Yorkshire*
(01751) 472508
nymr.co.uk
*Nostalgic steam excursions through spectacular landscapes.*

**Ripley Castle**
*Ripley, North Yorkshire*
(01423) 770152
ripleycastle.co.uk
*Medieval castle set in a delightful estate.*

**Sewerby Hall and Gardens**
*Sewerby, East Yorkshire*
(01262) 673769
sewerby-hall.co.uk
*Country house and gardens in cliff-top location.*

**Speke Hall, Garden and Estate**
*Speke, Merseyside*
(0151) 427 7231
nationaltrust.org.uk
*Wonderful, rambling Tudor mansion with Victorian interiors.*

## Indoors

**1853 Gallery**
*Shipley, West Yorkshire*
(01274) 531163
saltsmill.org.uk
*Works by Hockney in historic mill buildings.*

**BALTIC Centre for Contemporary Art**
*Gateshead, Tyne and Wear*
(0191) 478 1810
balticmill.com
*Dynamic international art.*

**The Bowes Museum**
*Barnard Castle, Durham*
(01833) 690606
thebowesmuseum.org.uk
*Outstanding European fine and decorative arts.*

**Captain Cook Birthplace Museum**
*Middlesbrough*
(01642) 311211
captcook-ne.co.uk
*Learn about Cook's life.*

**Discovery Museum**
*Newcastle upon Tyne, Tyne and Wear*
(0191) 232 6789
twmuseums.org.uk/discovery
*The history of Tyneside brought to life.*

**Imperial War Museum North**
*Manchester*
(0161) 836 4000
iwm.org.uk
*Dynamic displays reflecting the impact of war.*

**Jodrell Bank Visitor Centre**
*Holmes Chapel, Cheshire*
(01477) 571339
jb.man.ac.uk/scicen
*Home of the world-famous Lovell Telescope.*

**Leeds City Art Gallery**
*Leeds, West Yorkshire*
(0113) 247 8256
leeds.gov.uk/artgallery
*Remarkable collection of 20thC British art.*

**The Lowry**
*Salford, Manchester*
(0161) 876 2000
thelowry.com
*World-renowned art gallery, exhibitions and theatre.*

**Millennium Galleries**
*Sheffield, South Yorkshire*
(0114) 278 2600
sheffieldgalleries.org.uk
*Vibrant galleries of arts, craft and design.*

**mima, Middlesbrough Institute of Modern Art**
*Middlesbrough*
(01642) 726720
visitmima.com
*Inspiring modern and contemporary art.*

**National Glass Centre**
*Sunderland, Tyne and Wear*
(0191) 515 5555
nationalglasscentre.com
*Stunning displays and live glass-blowing.*

**National Media Museum**
*Bradford, West Yorkshire*
0870 701 0200
nationalmediamuseum.org.uk
*Seven-floor gallery featuring giant IMAX screen.*

**Royal Armouries Museum**
*Leeds, West Yorkshire*
(0113) 220 1916
royalarmouries.org
*Thrilling entertainment and world-famous arms collection.*

**Tullie House Museum and Art Gallery**
**Large Visitor Attraction of the Year - Silver**
*Carlisle, Cumbria*
(01228) 618718
tulliehouse.co.uk
*Jacobean house, Pre-Raphaelite art and interactive fun.*

**South Shields Museum and Art Gallery**
*South Shields, Tyne and Wear*
(0191) 456 8740
twmuseums.org.uk/southshields
*Explore the history of South Tyneside.*

**Sunderland Museum and Winter Gardens**
*Sunderland, Tyne and Wear*
(0191) 553 2323
twmuseums.org.uk/sunderland
*Stunning winter gardens and imaginative galleries.*

**Tate Liverpool**
*Liverpool*
(0151) 702 7400
tate.org.uk/liverpool
*Housing the National Collection of Modern Art.*

**Thackray Museum**
*Leeds, West Yorkshire*
(0113) 244 4343
thackraymuseum.org
*Experience Victorian slums, explore the human body.*

**The Whitworth Art Gallery**
*Manchester*
(0161) 275 7450
whitworth.man.ac.uk
*Internationally famous collection of British watercolours.*

**World Museum Liverpool**
*Liverpool*
(0151) 478 4393
liverpoolmuseums.org.uk
*Featuring the award-winning Natural History Centre.*

**The World of Glass**
*St Helens, Merseyside*
(01744) 22766
worldofglass.com
*Live glass-blowing and multi-media shows.*

## Outdoors

**Chesters Roman Fort (Hadrian's Wall)**
*Chollerford, Northumberland*
(01434) 681379
english-heritage.org.uk
*The best-preserved Roman cavalry fort in Britain.*

**Go Ape! High Wire Forest Adventure – Grizedale**
*Grizedale, Cumbria*
0845 643 9215
goape.co.uk
*High-adrenaline adventure in the trees.*

**Go Ape! High Wire Forest Adventure – Dalby**
*Low Dalby, North Yorkshire*
0845 643 9215
goape.co.uk
*Exhilarating course of bridges, swings and slides.*

**Hadrian's Wall Path National Trail**
*Hexham, Northumberland*
(01434) 322002
nationaltrail.co.uk/hadrianswall
*84-mile trail stretching from coast to coast.*

**Kielder Castle Forest Park Centre**
*Kielder, Northumberland*
(01434) 250209
forestry.gov.uk
*Visitor centre for England's largest forest.*

**National Wildflower Centre**
*Liverpool*
(0151) 738 1913
nwc.org.uk
*A peaceful haven with seasonal wildflower displays.*

**RHS Garden Harlow Carr**
*Harrogate, North Yorkshire*
(01423) 565418
rhs.org.uk/harlowcarr
*Spectacular 58-acre garden with year-round interest.*

**RSPB Blacktoft Sands Nature Reserve**
*Whitgift, East Yorkshire*
(01405) 704665
rspb.org.uk
*Spot avocets, bitterns and marsh harriers.*

**Windermere Lake Cruises**
*Lakeside, Cumbria*
(015394) 43360
windermere-lakecruises.co.uk
*Sail the Lakes on launches and steamers.*

**WWT Washington Wetland Centre**
*Washington, Tyne and Wear*
(0191) 416 5454
wwt.org.uk
*100-acre conservation site with diverse wildlife.*

**Yorkshire Sculpture Park**
*Wakefield, West Yorkshire*
(01924) 832631
ysp.co.uk
*Browse art alfresco on beautiful 18thC parkland.*

**ASSURANCE OF A GREAT DAY OUT**
Attractions with this sign participate in the Visitor Attraction Quality Assurance Scheme which recognises high standards in all aspects of the visitor experience.

## Events 2009

**Bradford International Film Festival**
Bradford
bradfordfilmfestival.org.uk
**Feb - Mar**

**Jorvik Viking Festival**
York
jorvik-viking-centre.co.uk
**18 - 22 Feb**

**John Smith's Grand National**
Liverpool
aintree.co.uk
**2 - 4 Apr**

**Chester Food and Drink Festival 2009**
Chester
chesterfoodanddrink.com
**10 - 13 Apr**

**Arley Horse Trials and Country Fair 2009**
Northwich
arleyhallandgardens.com
**16 - 17 May**

**Great Yorkshire Show**
Harrogate
greatyorkshireshow.co.uk
**Jul**

**Sunderland International Air Show**
Sunderland
sunderland-airshow.com
**25 - 26 Jul**

**Stockton International Riverside Festival**
Stockton
sirf.co.uk
**29 Jul - 2 Aug**

**St Leger Festival**
Doncaster
doncaster-racecourse.co.uk
**Sep**

# Regional contacts and information

For more information on accommodation, attractions, activities, events and holidays in Northern England, contact one of the following regional or local tourism organisations. Their websites have a wealth of information and many produce free publications to help you get the most out of your visit.

## England's Northwest

There are various publications and guides about England's Northwest available from the following Tourist Boards or by logging on to **visitenglandsnorthwest.com** or calling **0845 600 6040**:

**Visit Chester and Cheshire**
Chester Railway Station, 1st Floor, West Wing Offices, Station Road, Chester CH1 3NT
**t** (01244) 405600
**t** 0845 073 1324 (accommodation booking)
**e** info@visitchesterandcheshire.co.uk
**w** visitchester.com or visitcheshire.com

**Cumbria Tourism**
Windermere Road, Staveley, Kendal LA8 9PL
**t** (015398) 22222
**e** info@cumbriatourism.org
**w** golakes.co.uk

**The Lancashire and Blackpool Tourist Board**
St George's House, St George's Street
Chorley PR7 2AA
**t** (01257) 226600 (Brochure request)
**e** info@visitlancashire.com
**w** visitlancashire.com

**Visit Manchester – The Tourist Board For Greater Manchester**
Carver's Warehouse, 77 Dale Street
Manchester M2 2HG
**t** 0161 237 1010
**t** 0871 222 8223 (information and brochure request)
**e** touristinformation@visitmanchester.com
**w** visitmanchester.com

**The Mersey Partnership – The Tourist Board for the Liverpool City Region**
12 Princes Parade, Liverpool L3 1BG
**t** (0151) 233 2008 (information enquiries)
**t** 0844 870 0123 (accommodation booking)
**e** info@visitliverpool.com (accommodation enquiries)
**e** 08place@liverpool.gov.uk (information enquiries)
**w** visitliverpool.com

Clockwise: Arley Hall and Gardens, Cheshire; Ilkley Moor, Yorkshire; Beamish, Durham

## Yorkshire

The following publications are available from the Yorkshire Tourist Board by logging on to **yorkshire.com** or calling **0844 888 5123**:

- **Yorkshire Accommodation Guide 2009**
  Information on Yorkshire, including hotels, self catering, camping and caravan parks.

- **Make Yorkshire Yours Magazine**
  This entertaining magazine is full of articles and features about what's happening in Yorkshire, including where to go and what to do.

## North East

Log on to the North East England website at **visitnortheastengland.com** for further information on accommodation, attractions, events and special offers throughout the region. A range of free guides are available for you to order online or by calling **0870 160 1781**:

- **Holiday and Short Breaks Guide**
  Information on North East England, including hotels, bed and breakfast, self-catering, caravan and camping parks and accessible accommodation as well as events and attractions throughout the region.

- **Cycling Guide**
  A guide to day rides, traffic-free trails and challenging cycling routes.

- **Gardens Guide**
  A guide to the region's most inspirational gardens.

- **Walking Guide**
  Circular trails and long distance routes through breathtaking countryside.

# Tourist Information Centres

When you arrive at your destination, visit an Official Partner Tourist Information Centre for quality assured help with accommodation and information about local attractions and events, or email your request before you go. To search for attractions and Tourist Information Centres on the move just text INFO to 62233, and a web link will be sent to your mobile phone. To find a Tourist Information Centre by region visit enjoyEngland.com/find-tic.

| | | | |
|---|---|---|---|
| **Accrington** | Town Hall, Blackburn Rd | (01254) 872595 | tourism@hyndburnbc.gov.uk |
| **Alnwick** | 2 The Shambles | (01665) 511333 | alnwicktic@alnwick.gov.uk |
| **Altrincham** | 20 Stamford New Road | (0161) 912 5931 | tourist.information@trafford.gov.uk |
| **Ashton-under-Lyne** | Wellington Road | (0161) 343 4343 | tourist.information@tameside.gov.uk |
| **Aysgarth Falls** | Aysgarth Falls National Park Centre | (01969) 662910 | aysgarth@ytbtic.co.uk |
| **Barnard Castle** | Flatts Road | (01833) 690909 | tourism@teesdale.gov.uk |
| **Barnoldswick** | Fernlea Avenue | (01282) 666704 | tourist.info@pendle.gov.uk |
| **Barrow-in-Furness** | Duke Street | (01229) 876505 | touristinfo@barrowbc.gov.uk |
| **Batley** | Bradford Road | (01924) 426670 | batley@ytbtic.co.uk |
| **Beverley** | 34 Butcher Row | (01482) 391672 | beverley.tic@eastriding .gov.uk |
| **Blackburn** | 50-54 Church Street | (01254) 53277 | visit@blackburn.gov.uk |
| **Blackpool** | 1 Clifton Street | (01253) 478222 | tic@blackpool.gov.uk |
| **Bolton** | Le Mans Crescent | (01204) 334321 | tourist.info@bolton.gov.uk |
| **Bowness** | Glebe Road | (015394) 42895 | bownesstic@lake-district.gov.uk |
| **Bradford** | Centenary Square | (01274) 433678 | tourist.information@bradford.gov.uk |
| **Bridlington** | 25 Prince Street | (01262) 673474 | bridlington.tic@eastriding.gov.uk |
| **Brigg** | Market Place | (01652) 657053 | brigg.tic@northlincs.gov.uk |
| **Burnley** | Croft Street | (01282) 664421 | tic@burnley.gov.uk |
| **Bury** | Market Street | (0161) 253 5111 | touristinformation@bury.gov.uk |
| **Carlisle** | Greenmarket | (01228) 625600 | tourism@carlisle-city.gov.uk |
| **Chester (Town Hall)** | Northgate Street | (01244) 402111 | tis@chester.gov.uk |
| **Cleethorpes** | 42-43 Alexandra Road | (01472) 323111 | cleetic@nelincs.gov.uk |
| **Cleveleys** | Victoria Square | (01253) 853378 | cleveleystic@wyrebc.gov.uk |
| **Clitheroe** | 12-14 Market Place | (01200) 425566 | tourism@ribblevalley.gov.uk |
| **Congleton** | High Street | (01260) 271095 | tourism@congleton.gov.uk |
| **Coniston** | Ruskin Avenue | (015394) 41533 | mail@conistontic.org |
| **Danby** | Lodge Lane | (01439) 772737 | moorscentre@northyorkmoors-npa.gov.uk |
| **Darlington** | 13 Horsemarket | (01325) 388666 | tic@darlington.gov.uk |
| **Doncaster** | 38-40 High Street | (01302) 734309 | tourist.information@doncaster.gov.uk |

| | | | |
|---|---|---|---|
| **Durham** | 2 Millennium Place | (0191) 384 3720 | touristinfo@durhamcity.gov.uk |
| **Ellesmere Port** | Kinsey Road | (0151) 356 7879 | cheshireoaks.cc@visitor-centre.net |
| **Filey*** | The Evron Centre, John Street | (01723) 383637 | fileytic@scarborough.gov.uk |
| **Fleetwood** | The Esplanade | (01253) 773953 | fleetwoodtic@wyrebc.gov.uk |
| **Garstang** | High Street | (01995) 602125 | garstangtic@wyrebc.gov.uk |
| **Grassington** | Colvend, Hebden Road | (01756) 751690 | grassington@ytbtic.co.uk |
| **Guisborough** | Church Street | (01287) 633801 | guisborough_tic@redcar-cleveland.gov.uk |
| **Halifax** | Piece Hall | (01422) 368725 | halifax@ytbtic.co.uk |
| **Harrogate** | Crescent Road | (01423) 537300 | tic@harrogate.gov.uk |
| **Hartlepool** | Church Square | (01429) 869706 | hpooltic@hartlepool.gov.uk |
| **Hawes** | Station Yard | (01969) 666210 | hawes@ytbtic.co.uk |
| **Haworth** | 2/4 West Lane | (01535) 642329 | haworth@ytbtic.co.uk |
| **Hebden Bridge** | New Road | (01422) 843831 | hebdenbridge@ytbtic.co.uk |
| **Helmsley** | Helmsley Castle | (01439) 770173 | helmsley@ytbtic.co.uk |
| **Hexham** | Wentworth Car Park | (01434) 652220 | hexham.tic@tynedale.gov.uk |
| **Holmfirth** | 49-51 Huddersfield Road | (01484) 222444 | holmfirth.tic@kirklees.gov.uk |
| **Hornsea*** | 120 Newbegin | (01964) 536404 | hornsea.tic@eastriding.gov.uk |
| **Huddersfield** | 3 Albion Street | (01484) 223200 | huddersfield.tic@kirklees.gov.uk |
| **Hull** | 1 Paragon Street | (01482) 223559 | tourist.information@hullcc.gov.uk |
| **Humber Bridge** | Ferriby Road | (01482) 640852 | humberbridge.tic@eastriding.gov.uk |
| **Ilkley** | Station Rd | (01943) 602319 | ilkley@ytbtic.co.uk |
| **Kendal** | Highgate | (01539 725758 | kendaltic@southlakeland.gov.uk |
| **Keswick** | Market Square | (017687) 72645 | keswicktic@lake-district.gov.uk |
| **Knaresborough** | 9 Castle Courtyard | 0845 389 0177 | kntic@harrogate.gov.uk |
| **Knutsford** | Toft Road | (01565) 632611 | ktic@macclesfield.gov.uk |
| **Lancaster** | 29 Castle Hill | (01524) 32878 | lancastertic@lancaster.gov.uk |
| **Leeds** | The Arcade, City Station | (0113) 242 5242 | tourinfo@leeds.gov.uk |
| **Leeming Bar** | The Yorkshire Maid, The Great North Road | (01677 424262 | leeming@ytbtic.co.uk |

Left to right: Holker Hall and Gardens, Cumbria;
Locomotion: The National Railway Museum, Durham

| | | | |
|---|---|---|---|
| **Leyburn** | Railway Street | (01969) 623069 | leyburn@ytbtic.co.uk |
| **Liverpool 08 Place** | Whitechapel | (0151) 233 2459 | contact@liverpool.08.com |
| **Liverpool John Lennon Airport** | Speke Hall Avenue | 0906 680 6886** | info@visitliverpool.com |
| **Lytham St Annes** | 67 St Annes Road West | (01253) 725610 | touristinformation@fylde.gov.uk |
| **Macclesfield** | Town Hall | (01625) 504114 | informationcentre@macclesfield.gov.uk |
| **Malham** | National Park Centre | (01969) 652380 | malham@ytbtic.co.uk |
| **Malton** | 58 Market Place | (01653) 600048 | maltontic@btconnect.com |
| **Manchester Visitor Information Centre** | Lloyd St | 0871 222 8223 | touristinformation@marketing-manchester.co.uk |
| **Morecambe** | Marine Road Central | (01524) 582808 | morecambetic@lancaster.gov.uk |
| **Morpeth** | Bridge Street | (01670) 500700 | tourism@castlemorpeth.gov.uk |
| **Nantwich** | Market Street | (01270) 537359 | touristi@crewe-nantwich.gov.uk |
| **Newcastle-upon-Tyne** | 8-9 Central Arcade | (0191) 277 8000 | tourist.info@newcastle.gov.uk |
| **Northwich** | 1 The Arcade | (01606) 353534 | tourism@valeroyal.gov.uk |
| **Oldham** | 12 Albion Street | (0161) 627 1024 | ecs.tourist@oldham.gov.uk |
| **Otley** | Nelson Street | (01943) 462485 | otleytic@leedslearning.net |
| **Pateley Bridge*** | 18 High Street | 0845 389 0177 | pbtic@harrogate.gov.uk |
| **Pendle Heritage Centre** | Park Hill | (01282) 661701 | heritage.centre@pendle.gov.uk |
| **Penrith** | Middlegate | (01768) 867466 | pen.tic@eden.gov.uk |
| **Pickering** | The Ropery | (01751) 473791 | pickering@ytbtic.co.uk |
| **Preston** | Lancaster Road | (01772) 253731 | tourism@preston.gov.uk |
| **Redcar** | Esplanade | (01642) 471921 | redcar_tic@redcar-cleveland.gov.uk |
| **Reeth** | Hudson House, The Green | (01748) 884059 | reeth@ytbtic.co.uk |
| **Richmond** | Victoria Road | (01748) 828742 | richmond@ytbtic.co.uk |
| **Ripon** | Minster Road | (01765) 604625 | ripontic@harrogate.gov.uk |
| **Rochdale** | The Esplanade | (01706) 924928 | tic@link4life.org |
| **Rotherham** | 40 Bridgegate | (01709) 835904 | tic@rotherham.gov.uk |
| **St Helens** | The World of Glass | (01744) 755150 | info@sthelenstic.com |
| **Salford** | The Lowry, Pier 8 | (0161) 848 8601 | tic@salford.gov.uk |
| **Saltburn-by-the-Sea** | 3 Station Buildings | (01287) 622422 | saltburn_tic@redcar-cleveland.gov.uk |
| **Scarborough** | Brunswick Shopping Centre | (01723) 383636 | tourismbureau@scarborough.gov.uk |
| **Scarborough (Harbourside)** | Sandside | (01723) 383636 | harboursidetic@scarborough.gov.uk |
| **Settle** | Cheapside | (01729) 825192 | settle@ytbtic.co.uk |
| **Sheffield** | 14 Norfolk Row | (0114) 2211900 | visitor@sheffield.gov.uk |
| **Skipton** | 35 Coach Street | (01756) 792809 | skipton@ytbtic.co.uk |
| **Stockport** | 30 Market Place | (0161) 474 4444 | tourist.information@stockport.gov.uk |
| **Sunderland** | 50 Fawcett Street | (0191) 553 2000 | tourist.info@sunderland.gov.uk |
| **Sutton Bank** | Sutton Bank Visitor Centre | (01845) 597426 | suttonbank@ytbtic.co.uk |

| | | | |
|---|---|---|---|
| **Thirsk** | 49 Market Place | (01845) 522755 | thirsktic@hambleton.gov.uk |
| **Todmorden** | 15 Burnley Road | (01706) 818181 | todmorden@ytbtic.co.uk |
| **Wakefield** | 9 The Bull Ring | 0845 601 8353 | tic@wakefield.gov.uk |
| **Warrington** | Academy Way | (01925) 428585 | informationcentre@warrington.gov.uk |
| **Wetherby** | 17 Westgate | (01937) 582151 | wetherbytic@leedslearning.net |
| **Whitby** | Langborne Road | (01723) 383637 | whitbytic@scarborough.gov.uk |
| **Whitehaven** | Market Place | (01946) 598914 | tic@copelandbc.gov.uk |
| **Wigan** | 62 Wallgate | (01942) 825677 | tic@wlct.org |
| **Wilmslow** | Rectory Fields | (01625) 522275 | i.hillaby@macclesfield.gov.uk |
| **Windermere** | Victoria Street | (015394) 46499 | windermeretic@southlakeland.gov.uk |
| **Withernsea*** | 131 Queen Street | (01964) 615683 | withernsea.tic@eastriding.gov.uk |
| **York (De Grey Rooms)** | Exhibition Square | (01904) 550099 | info@visityork.org |
| **York (Railway Station)** | Station Road | (01904) 550099 | info@visityork.org |

*seasonal opening

**calls to this number are charged at premium rate

Clockwise: High Force, Durham; Royal Armouries Museum, Yorkshire; Manchester United Museum and Tour

where to stay in

# Northern England

All place names in the blue bands are shown on the maps at the front of this guide.

A complete listing of all Enjoy England assessed accommodation covered by this guide appears at the back.

## Accommodation symbols

Symbols give useful information about services and facilities. On page 7 you can find a key to these symbols.

## ALDERLEY EDGE, Cheshire Map ref 4B2

★★★
BED & BREAKFAST

B&B PER ROOM PER NIGHT
S £26.50–£28.50
D £53.00–£57.00

EVENING MEAL PER PERSON
£15.00–£25.00

### Mayfield Bed & Breakfast @ Sheila's

Wilmslow Road, Alderley Edge SK9 7QW **t** (01625) 583991 & 07703 289663

Bed and breakfast with optional dinner (notice required). If flying from Manchester Airport, car may be left (at owner's risk) with Sheila taking and picking up from the airport. No pets.

**open** All year
**bedrooms** 2 twin, 2 single
**payment** Cash, cheques

Room General P

## ALLENDALE, Northumberland Map ref 5B2

★★★★
FARMHOUSE

B&B PER ROOM PER NIGHT
S £35.00–£40.00
D £60.00–£70.00

EVENING MEAL PER PERSON
£15.00–£25.00

### High Keenley Fell Farm

Allendale NE47 9NU **t** (01434) 618344 **e** camaclean@btinternet.com

**highkeenleyfarm.co.uk**

Traditional, recently refurbished Northumbrian farmhouse built round a courtyard with stunning views around Allendale and up to the Cheviots and Scottish Borders.

**open** All year
**bedrooms** 2 double, 1 twin
**bathrooms** All en suite
**payment** Cash, cheques

Room General P Leisure

## ALNMOUTH, Northumberland Map ref 5C1

★★★
GUEST ACCOMMODATION

B&B PER ROOM PER NIGHT
S £35.00
D £70.00

### Alnmouth Golf Club

Foxton Hall, Alnwick NE66 3BE **t** (01665) 830231 **e** secretary@alnmouthgolfclub.com

**alnmouthgolfclub.com**

Situated on the magnificent Northumberland coast, Foxton Hall provides the perfect base to tour the delights of Northumberland.

**open** All year except Christmas and New Year
**bedrooms** 8 twin, 2 single
**bathrooms** All en suite
**payment** Credit/debit cards, cash, cheques

Room General P

### B&B prices

Rates for bed and breakfast are shown per room per night.
Double room prices are usually based on two people sharing the room.

## ALNMOUTH, Northumberland Map ref 5C1

★★★★
BED & BREAKFAST
SILVER AWARD

B&B PER ROOM PER NIGHT
D £68.00–£72.00

### Beech Lodge

8 Alnwood, Alnwick NE66 3NN **t** (01665) 830709 **e** beechlodge@hotmail.com

**welcomenorthumberland.co.uk**

**open** February to November
**bedrooms** 2 double
**bathrooms** 1 en suite, 1 private
**payment** Cash, cheques

A warm and friendly welcome awaits guests at our spacious, detached, modern bungalow in a quiet woodland setting, close to village shops, pubs and restaurants. Our en suite rooms are decorated and furnished to a high and modern standard. An ideal base for exploring all the wonderful coast and countryside.

**SAT NAV** *NE66 3NN*

Room General P

## ALNWICK, Northumberland Map ref 5C1

★★★
GUEST ACCOMMODATION

B&B PER ROOM PER NIGHT
S £45.00
D £70.00–£120.00

EVENING MEAL PER PERSON
£15.00–£20.00

### Alnwick Lodge

West Cawledge Park, Alnwick NE66 2HJ **t** (01665) 604363 & (01665) 603377
**e** bookings@alnwicklodge.com

**alnwicklodge.com** REAL-TIME BOOKING

**open** All year
**bedrooms** 3 double, 2 twin, 2 single, 2 family, 1 suite
**bathrooms** All en suite
**payment** Credit/debit cards, cash, cheques

A unique creation AD1650-2007. Alnwick Lodge at West Cawledge Park is a combination of history and rural charm with an air of sophistication, whilst linked to technology. Fascinating and incomparable accommodation set in beautiful Northumberland, one mile south of Alnwick, off the A1. For business or pleasure, conferences, functions, parties. Antique galleries and log fires.

**SAT NAV** *NE66 2HJ* **ONLINE MAP**

Room General P Leisure

## ALNWICK, Northumberland Map ref 5C1

★★★★
INN

B&B PER ROOM PER NIGHT
S £45.00
D £38.00–£47.50

### The Masons Arms Country Inn

Stamford Cott NE66 3RX **t** (01665) 577275 **e** bookings@masonsarms.net

**masonsarms.net**

Country inn with real ale, a good selection of wine and malt whiskies and good, fresh food. Comfortable en suite accommodation. Well positioned for Alnwick and the coast.

**open** All year
**bedrooms** 11 double, 2 twin, 1 single, 1 family, 2 suites
**bathrooms** All en suite
**payment** Credit/debit cards, cash, cheques

Room General P Leisure

## Gold and Silver Awards

Gold and Silver Awards are given to establishments achieving the highest levels of quality and service. You can find more information at the front of the guide, and an index to all accommodation achieving these awards at the back.

## ALNWICK, Northumberland Map ref 5C1

★★★★
INN

B&B PER ROOM PER NIGHT
S £55.00–£65.00
D £90.00

EVENING MEAL PER PERSON
£5.95–£18.00

# The Queens Head Hotel

25 Market Street, Alnwick NE66 1SS **t** (01665) 604691 **e** stay@alnwickqueensheadhotel.co.uk

**alnwickqueensheadhotel.co.uk**

**open** All year
**bedrooms** 2 double, 1 twin
**bathrooms** All en suite
**payment** Credit/debit cards, cash, cheques

This 16thC coaching inn – 'the oldest pub in Alnwick' – has kept many of its original features and offers quality, en suite accommodation, recently refurbished to a high standard. Luxurious king-size, double and twin bedrooms. Within easy walking distance of Alnwick Castle and Gardens.

**SAT NAV** *NE66 1SS* **ONLINE MAP**

Room General P Leisure

## ALNWICK, Northumberland Map ref 5C1

★★★★★
GUEST ACCOMMODATION
GOLD AWARD

B&B PER ROOM PER NIGHT
D £80.00–£90.00

# West Acre House

West Acres, Alnwick NE66 2QA **t** (01665) 510374 & 07746 038180 **e** info@westacrehouse.co.uk

**westacrehouse.co.uk** GUEST REVIEWS

**open** All year
**bedrooms** 3 double, 1 twin
**bathrooms** All en suite
**payment** Credit/debit cards, cash, cheques, euros

Elegant detached Edwardian villa influenced by the Arts and Crafts movement. Set in its own one-acre garden in a leafy suburb on the edge of Alnwick. Beautifully appointed with much attention to detail and guest comfort. Lovely en suite bathrooms. Close to Alnwick Castle and central for all Northumberland's attractions.

**SAT NAV** *NE66 2QA* **ONLINE MAP**

Room General P

## AMBLESIDE, Cumbria Map ref 5A3

★★★★
BED & BREAKFAST

B&B PER ROOM PER NIGHT
S £33.00
D £65.00

EVENING MEAL PER PERSON
£17.50

# Dower House

Wray Castle, Low Wray, Ambleside LA22 0JA **t** (015394) 33211

The house overlooks Lake Windermere, three miles from Ambleside. Situated through the main gates of Wray Castle and up the drive. A bird-watcher's paradise.

**open** All year
**bedrooms** 2 double, 1 twin
**bathrooms** All en suite
**payment** Cash, cheques

Room General 5 P Leisure

## AMBLESIDE, Cumbria Map ref 5A3

★★★
GUEST HOUSE

B&B PER ROOM PER NIGHT
S £25.00–£30.00
D £50.00–£60.00

# Ferndale Lodge

Lake Road, Ambleside LA22 0DB **t** (015394) 32207 **e** stay@ferndalelodge.co.uk

**ferndalelodge.co.uk**

Small, family-run guesthouse close to the centre of Ambleside offering excellent accommodation at realistic prices. Superb breakfasts and a friendly welcome assured. Private car park. An ideal walking base.

**open** All year except Christmas
**bedrooms** 7 double, 2 twin, 1 single
**bathrooms** All en suite
**payment** Credit/debit cards, cash, cheques

Room General P Leisure

## AMBLESIDE, Cumbria Map ref 5A3

★★★★
GUEST ACCOMMODATION

B&B PER ROOM PER NIGHT
S £35.00–£50.00
D £66.00–£100.00

# The Gables

Church Walk, Ambleside LA22 9DJ **t** (015394) 33272 **e** info@thegables-ambleside.co.uk

**thegables-ambleside.co.uk**

**open** All year except Christmas
**bedrooms** 6 double, 3 twin, 3 single, 2 family
**bathrooms** All en suite
**payment** Credit/debit cards, cash, cheques

Sharyn and Mark welcome you to The Gables overlooking the bowling green and surrounding fells. Ideally situated in the heart of Ambleside, our guesthouse makes an excellent base for exploring the Lake District. Stylish rooms, all en suite. Hearty breakfasts. Car parking. Drying room. Bike storage. Non-smoking.

**SAT NAV** *LA22 9DJ*

Room General P Leisure

## AMBLESIDE, Cumbria Map ref 5A3

★★★
GUEST ACCOMMODATION

B&B PER ROOM PER NIGHT
S £28.00–£35.00
D £55.00–£70.00

# Lyndale Guest House

Low Fold, Lake Road, Ambleside LA22 0DN **t** (015394) 34244 **e** alison@lyndale-guesthouse.co.uk

**lyndale-guesthouse.co.uk**

Victorian guesthouse providing spacious, comfortable accommodation. Hearty breakfasts and excellent services. Located midway between Lake Windermere and Ambleside. Great for touring and walking. Great value for money.

**open** All year
**bedrooms** 2 double, 2 single, 2 family
**bathrooms** 4 en suite, 2 private
**payment** Credit/debit cards, cash, cheques

Room General

## AMBLESIDE, Cumbria Map ref 5A3

★★★
GUEST ACCOMMODATION

B&B PER ROOM PER NIGHT
S £29.00–£35.00
D £58.00–£70.00

# Meadowbank

Rydal Road, Ambleside LA22 9BA **t** (015394) 32710 **e** enquiries@meadowbank.org.uk

Country house in private garden with ample parking in grounds. Overlooking meadowland and fells, yet a level, easy walk to Ambleside. Good walking base.

**open** All year except Christmas
**bedrooms** 3 double, 2 twin, 1 single, 1 family
**bathrooms** 6 en suite, 1 private
**payment** Credit/debit cards, cash, cheques

Room General P Leisure

## AMBLESIDE, Cumbria Map ref 5A3

★★★★
GUEST ACCOMMODATION

B&B PER ROOM PER NIGHT
S Min £100.00
D £100.00–£150.00

# The Old Vicarage

Vicarage Road, Ambleside LA22 9DH **t** (015394) 33364 **e** info@oldvicarageambleside.co.uk

**oldvicarageambleside.co.uk**

**open** All year except Christmas
**bedrooms** 4 double, 4 twin, 2 family, 4 suites
**bathrooms** All en suite
**payment** Credit/debit cards, cash, cheques, euros

Quiet central situation. Car park. Pets welcome. Heated indoor swimming pool, sauna and hot tub. Quality accommodation with TV/DVD/VCR, hairdryer, fridge, en suite. Some four-posters, spa baths and some ground-floor rooms.

**SAT NAV** *LA22 9DH*

Room General P
Leisure

PETS! WELCOME

## AMBLESIDE, Cumbria Map ref 5A3

★★★★★
BED & BREAKFAST SILVER AWARD

B&B PER ROOM PER NIGHT
D £70.00–£90.00

# Red Bank

Wansfell Road, Ambleside LA22 0EG **t** (015394) 34637 **e** info@red-bank.co.uk

**red-bank.co.uk** SPECIAL OFFERS

**open** All year
**bedrooms** 2 double, 1 twin
**bathrooms** All en suite
**payment** Cash, cheques, euros

Elegant, traditionally built Lakeland house in residential fringes of Ambleside. Three tastefully furnished en suite rooms offering spacious, deluxe accommodation. Village centre five minutes. An ideal base for discovering the grandeur of the Lake District National Park. We will do our very best to make your stay as relaxing and comfortable as possible. Private parking.

**SAT NAV** *LA22 0EG* **ONLINE MAP**

Room General 9 P Leisure

## AMBLESIDE, Cumbria Map ref 5A3

★★★★
INN

B&B PER ROOM PER NIGHT
S £40.00–£70.00
D £80.00–£160.00

EVENING MEAL PER PERSON
£15.85–£29.95

*3-night midweek breaks from £96pp.*

# Wateredge Inn

Waterhead Bay, Ambleside LA22 0EP **t** (015394) 32332 **e** stay@wateredgeinn.co.uk

**wateredgeinn.co.uk**

**open** All year except Christmas
**bedrooms** 9 double, 6 twin, 3 single, 3 family, 1 suite
**bathrooms** All en suite
**payment** Credit/debit cards, cash, cheques

Delightfully situated family-run inn on the shores of Windermere at Waterhead Bay. Enjoy country-inn-style dining, freshly prepared gourmet bar food, real ales and fine wines, all served overlooking the lake. Pretty bedrooms, many with lake views, offer the best of Lakeland comfort.

**SAT NAV** *LA22 0EP* **ONLINE MAP**

Room General P Leisure

## AMBLESIDE, Cumbria Map ref 5A3

★★★★
GUEST ACCOMMODATION

B&B PER ROOM PER NIGHT
S £30.00–£45.00
D £30.00–£45.00

*Free passes to Langdale Country Club: swimming pool, steam room, Turkish sauna, gymnasium, beautiful restaurant. Winter/spring breaks, fabulous offers!*

# Wordsworths Guest House

Lake Road, Ambleside LA22 0DB **t** (015394) 32095 **e** anna@wordsworthsguesthouse.co.uk

**wordsworthsguesthouse.co.uk** SPECIAL OFFERS

**open** All year
**bedrooms** 2 double, 1 twin, 1 single, 1 family
**bathrooms** All en suite
**payment** Credit/debit cards, cash, cheques

An elegant Victorian house with quality en suite accommodation. Level walk to village and Lake Windermere. Wonderful Lakeland fell walks from the front door. Hearty Cumbrian breakfasts. Relax in our beautiful award-winning garden, surrounded by stunning views. Free Wi-Fi access. Private car park. Home from home!

**SAT NAV** *LA22 0DB* **ONLINE MAP**

Room General 4 P Leisure

## AUSTWICK, North Yorkshire Map ref 5B3

★★★★
GUEST HOUSE

B&B PER ROOM PER NIGHT
S £40.00–£59.00
D £54.00–£76.00

### Wood View

The Green, Austwick LA2 8BB **t** (015242) 51190 **e** woodview@austwick.org

**woodviewbandb.com**

**open** All year except Christmas
**bedrooms** 4 double, 2 twin
**bathrooms** All en suite
**payment** Credit/debit cards, cash, cheques

Enjoy the warm, friendly atmosphere of log fires and beamed ceilings in one of Austwick's oldest farmhouses. Wood View is situated in the centre of this typical Dales village and is the ideal base for exploring stunning limestone scenery in the Three Peaks area of the Yorkshire Dales National Park.

**SAT NAV** *LA2 8BB*

Room General 12 P Leisure

## AYSGARTH, North Yorkshire Map ref 5B3

★★★★★
GUEST ACCOMMODATION
SILVER AWARD

B&B PER ROOM PER NIGHT
D £80.00–£120.00

EVENING MEAL PER PERSON
£15.00–£20.00

### Thornton Lodge

Thornton Rust, Leyburn DL8 3AP **t** (01969) 663375 **e** enquiries@thorntonlodgenorthyorkshire.co.uk

**thorntonlodgenorthyorkshire.co.uk** REAL-TIME BOOKING

**open** Easter to mid-October
**bedrooms** 2 double, 2 twin, 2 single, 2 family, 1 suite
**bathrooms** All en suite
**payment** Credit/debit cards, cash, cheques, euros

Thornton Lodge is a beautiful Edwardian country house with something for everyone. Its setting, within acres of landscaped grounds, woodlands and pasture, offers peace and tranquillity, which visitors find difficult to draw away from. Located in the National Park, there are walks and cycle routes from the doorstep. Available for house parties in winter.

**SAT NAV** *DL8 3AP*

Room General P Leisure

## AYSGARTH, North Yorkshire Map ref 5B3

★★★
INN

B&B PER ROOM PER NIGHT
S £35.00
D £68.00–£85.00

EVENING MEAL PER PERSON
£6.25–£16.95

### Wheatsheaf Inn

Main Street, Carperby, Nr Aygarth DL8 4DF **t** (01969) 663216 **e** wheatsheaf@paulmit.globalnet.uk

**wheatsheafinwensleydale.co.uk** SPECIAL OFFERS • REAL-TIME BOOKING

Delightful Dales country hotel made famous when the real-life James Herriot spent his honeymoon here. Log fires in winter. Cosy panelled dining room. Some four-poster beds. New luxury rooms added.

**open** All year except Christmas
**bedrooms** 9 double, 2 twin, 1 single, 1 family
**bathrooms** All en suite
**payment** Credit/debit cards, cash, cheques

Room General P Leisure

## BACUP, Lancashire Map ref 4B1

★★★★
GUEST ACCOMMODATION

B&B PER ROOM PER NIGHT
S £30.00–£40.00
D £50.00–£65.00

### Rossbrook House

New Line, Bacup OL13 0BY **t** (01706) 878187 **e** rossbkhouse@aol.com

**a1touristguide.com/rossbrookhouse**

Spacious former vicarage set in own grounds with ample parking. Refurbished to retain the charm of its Victorian past and providing excellent facilities for guests.

**open** All year except Christmas
**bedrooms** 3 double, 1 twin
**bathrooms** All en suite
**payment** Cash, cheques

Room General P Leisure

## BAMBURGH, Northumberland Map ref 5C1

★★★★
BED & BREAKFAST
SILVER AWARD

B&B PER ROOM PER NIGHT
S £40.00–£65.00
D £65.00–£75.00

### Glenander Bed & Breakfast

27 Lucker Road, Bamburgh NE69 7BS **t** (01668) 214336 **e** enquiries@glenander.com

**glenander.com**

Long-established, quality bed and breakfast. All rooms are individually and tastefully furnished with hospitality tray, hairdryer, colour TV. Selected in the top 20 Good Bed and Breakfast Guide 2004, published by Which? Books.

**open** All year
**bedrooms** 2 double, 1 twin
**bathrooms** All en suite
**payment** Cash, cheques

Room General

## BARDON MILL, Northumberland Map ref 5B2

★★★
INN

B&B PER ROOM PER NIGHT
S £30.00–£35.00
D £50.00–£80.00

EVENING MEAL PER PERSON
£8.00–£15.50

*Bridge weekends held first weekend in Mar and first weekend in Nov. 1 Nov – end Feb: 3 nights for 2 B&B (excl Christmas period).*

### Twice Brewed Inn

Bardon Mill, Hexham NE47 7AN **t** (01434) 344534 **e** info@twicebrewedinn.co.uk

**twicebrewedinn.co.uk** SPECIAL OFFERS

**open** All year except Christmas
**bedrooms** 6 double, 6 twin, 2 single
**bathrooms** 6 en suite
**payment** Credit/debit cards, cash, cheques

Family-run inn situated 0.5 miles from Hadrian's Wall offering accommodation, a warm welcome, good food, real ales, breathtaking views and wide-open spaces. Centrally placed for visits to Scotland, Cumbria and the North East (all within one hour's drive).

**SAT NAV** *NE47 7AN* **ONLINE MAP**

Room General Leisure

## BARNARD CASTLE, Durham Map ref 5B3

★★★★
GUEST ACCOMMODATION
SILVER AWARD

B&B PER ROOM PER NIGHT
S £42.00–£46.00
D £65.00–£70.00

### Crich House Bed & Breakfast

94 Galgate, Barnard Castle DL12 8BJ **t** (01833) 630357 **e** info@crich-house.co.uk

**crich-house.co.uk**

Beautiful Victorian family house close to centre of town, offering luxurious bedrooms with attention to detail. Wonderful breakfasts using local produce, all making for a warm and friendly stay.

**open** All year except Christmas and New Year
**bedrooms** 1 double, 1 twin
**bathrooms** All en suite
**payment** Cash, cheques

Room General 6

## BARROW-IN-FURNESS, Cumbria Map ref 5A3

★★★★
BED & BREAKFAST
SILVER AWARD

B&B PER ROOM PER NIGHT
D £50.00–£55.00

EVENING MEAL PER PERSON
£15.00–£25.00

### November House B&B

Hawcoat Lane, Barrow-in-Furness LA14 4HE **t** (01229) 827247 **e** november-house@tiscali.co.uk

**novemberhouse.co.uk**

We offer guests quality B&B accommodation and aim to provide genuine hospitality, making your stay enjoyable and memorable.

**open** All year except Christmas
**bedrooms** 2 double, 1 family
**bathrooms** All en suite
**payment** Cash, cheques

Room General

## What shall we do today?

For ideas on places to visit, see the beginning of this regional section or go online at enjoyengland.com.

## BASSENTHWAITE, Cumbria Map ref 5A2

★★★★
GUEST HOUSE

B&B PER ROOM PER NIGHT
S £32.00–£36.00
D £65.00–£90.00

EVENING MEAL PER PERSON
£18.50

*3 nights DB&B £149-£175pp. Also offer special anniversary/ honeymoon package in deluxe room with lake views, champagne and flowers.*

### Ouse Bridge House

Dubwath, Bassenthwaite Lake, Bassenthwaite CA13 9YD **t** (017687) 76322
**e** enquiries@ousebridge.com

**ousebridge.com** GUEST REVIEWS • SPECIAL OFFERS • REAL-TIME BOOKING

**open** All year except Christmas
**bedrooms** 6 double, 1 twin, 2 single, 2 family
**bathrooms** 9 en suite, 2 private
**payment** Credit/debit cards, cash, cheques

Friendly, family-run guesthouse with amazing views over Bassenthwaite Lake and Skiddaw. Excellent menu, using local produce, available in our restaurant. Overall, we offer a relaxed atmosphere, excellent service and delicious food in a stunning and peaceful location.

**SAT NAV** *CA13 9YD* **ONLINE MAP**

Room General Leisure

## BEAL, Northumberland Map ref 5B1

★★★
GUEST ACCOMMODATION

B&B PER ROOM PER NIGHT
S Min £35.00
D Min £57.00

*Midweek deals. Christmas and New Year packages on self-catering basis. Discount for 3 or more nights.*

### Brock Mill Farmhouse

Brock Mill, Beal, Berwick-upon-Tweed TD15 2PB **t** (01289) 381283 & 07889 099517
**e** brockmillfarmhouse@btinternet.com

**lindisfarne.org.uk/brock-mill-farmhouse**

**open** All year except Christmas
**bedrooms** 1 double, 1 twin, 1 single, 1 family
**bathrooms** 1 private
**payment** Credit/debit cards, cash, cheques

A 220-acre mixed farm. Peaceful, idyllic surroundings, ideal as a base for touring north Northumberland and Scottish Borders. Quality accommodation with spacious, well-furnished rooms. Residents' lounge. Enjoy our superb English breakfasts or our tasty vegetarian alternatives. Golf and fishing nearby. A warm, friendly welcome awaits.

**SAT NAV** *TD15 2PB*

WALKERS WELCOME CYCLISTS WELCOME

Room General Leisure

## BEDALE, North Yorkshire Map ref 5C3

★★★★
INN

B&B PER ROOM PER NIGHT
S £55.00–£65.00
D £75.00–£85.00

*Special seasonal rates available Oct-Mar.*

### The Castle Arms Inn

Bedale DL8 2TB **t** (01677) 470270 **e** castlearms@aol.com

**thecastlearms.co.uk**

**open** All year
**bedrooms** 6 double, 3 twin
**bathrooms** All en suite
**payment** Credit/debit cards, cash, cheques

A family-run, 14thC inn which has been completely refurbished. All twin and double bedrooms are en suite, and have been furnished to an exceptional standard, and include TV and tea-/coffee-making facilities. A warm welcome awaits you, with open fires, traditional ales and real home cooking.

**SAT NAV** *DL8 2TB*

Room General 5 Leisure

## BEDALE, North Yorkshire Map ref 5C3

★★★★
GUEST HOUSE
SILVER AWARD

B&B PER ROOM PER NIGHT
S £52.00–£58.00
D £70.00–£82.00

EVENING MEAL PER PERSON
£14.50–£20.50

*Seasonal offers and discounts on stays of 7 or more nights – see website. Packages for group bookings – please enquire.*

### Elmfield House

Bedale DL8 1NE **t** (01677) 450558 **e** stay@elmfieldhouse.co.uk

**elmfieldhouse.co.uk**

**open** All year
**bedrooms** 4 double, 2 twin, 1 family
**bathrooms** All en suite
**payment** Credit/debit cards, cash, cheques

A warm welcome, hearty Yorkshire breakfast using local produce and spacious en suite rooms await you at this friendly family-run guest house. Guests are welcome to walk in 24 acres of fields and woods with lake to say hello to the livestock and spot wildlife. Evening meals by arrangement. Residential licence.

**SAT NAV** *DL8 1NE*

Room General P Leisure

## BERWICK-UPON-TWEED, Northumberland Map ref 5B1

★★★★
BED & BREAKFAST
SILVER AWARD

B&B PER ROOM PER NIGHT
S £35.00–£45.00
D £60.00–£65.00

WALKERS WELCOME CYCLISTS WELCOME

### Alannah House

84 Church Street, Berwick-upon-Tweed TD15 1DU **t** (01289) 307252
**e** steven@berwick1234.freeserve.co.uk

**alannahhouse.com**

Georgian town house, originally married quarters of historic barracks. Situated in town centre with walled garden and residential parking. Close to all amenities.

**open** All year
**bedrooms** 1 double, 1 twin, 1 family
**bathrooms** All en suite
**payment** Cash, cheques

Room General

## BERWICK-UPON-TWEED, Northumberland Map ref 5B1

★★★★
BACKPACKER

PER PERSON PER NIGHT
B&B £16.95-£29.95

WALKERS WELCOME CYCLISTS WELCOME

### Berwick Backpackers

56 Bridge Street, Berwick-upon-Tweed TD15 1AQ **t** (01289) 331481
**e** bkbackpacker@aol.com

**berwickbackpackers.co.uk**

This excellent hostel has a series of rooms around a central courtyard in the outbuildings of a Grade II Listed Georgian town house. Free internet access. Highly recommended.

**open** All year
**bedrooms** 1 single, 1 double, 1 twin, 1 triple, 1 quad, 1 dormitory. Total no of beds 20
**bathrooms** 2 en suite, 3 public
**meals** Breakfast available
**payment** Cash/cheques

Room General Leisure

## BERWICK-UPON-TWEED, Northumberland Map ref 5B1

★★★
INN

B&B PER ROOM PER NIGHT
S £32.00
D £54.00

### The Cat Inn

Great North Road, Cheswick, Berwick-upon-Tweed TD15 2RL **t** (01289) 387251

Seven-bedroom inn situated five miles south of Berwick, providing accommodation, good food and range of ales and lagers.

**open** All year except Christmas and New Year
**bedrooms** 1 double, 4 twin, 2 family
**bathrooms** All en suite
**payment** Credit/debit cards, cash, cheques

Room General 5 P Leisure

## What do the star ratings mean?

Detailed information about star ratings can be found at the back of this guide.

## BERWICK-UPON-TWEED, Northumberland Map ref 5B1

★★★★
GUEST HOUSE

B&B PER ROOM PER NIGHT
s £28.00–£45.00
d £56.00–£70.00

### Ladythorne Guest House

Cheswick, Berwick-upon-Tweed TD15 2RW **t** (01289) 387382
**e** valparker@ladythorne.wanadoo.co.uk

**ladythorne.wanadoo.co.uk SPECIAL OFFERS**

Grade II Listed Georgian house dated 1721. Magnificent views of the countryside, close to unspoilt beaches. Large garden, families welcome. Meals available within five minutes' drive.

**open** All year
**bedrooms** 2 double, 1 twin, 2 family
**bathrooms** 2 en suite, 1 private
**payment** Cash, cheques

Room General Leisure

## BEVERLEY, East Riding of Yorkshire Map ref 4C1

★★★★
GUEST ACCOMMODATION

B&B PER ROOM PER NIGHT
s £25.00–£50.00
d £45.00–£80.00

### Eastgate Guest House

7 Eastgate, Beverley HU17 0DR **t** (01482) 868464 **e** dodd@dodd.karoo.co.uk

Family-run Victorian guesthouse, established and run by the same proprietor for 38 years. Close to town centre, Beverley Minster and railway station. Fifteen minutes to Hull city centre and The Deep. Excellent central location for exploring the surrounding wolds

**open** All year
**bedrooms** 7 double, 2 twin, 4 single, 2 family
**bathrooms** 7 en suite
**payment** Credit/debit cards

Room General

## BISHOP WILTON, East Riding of Yorkshire Map ref 4C1

★★★
FARMHOUSE

B&B PER ROOM PER NIGHT
s £30.00
d £25.00

EVENING MEAL PER PERSON
£15.00

### High Belthorpe

Thorny Lane, Bishop Wilton, Driffield YO42 1SB **t** (01759) 368238 **e** meg@holidaysfordogs.plus.com

**holidayswithdogs.com**

**open** All year except Christmas
**bedrooms** 1 double, 2 family
**bathrooms** 2 en suite, 1 private
**payment** Cash, cheques

Set on an ancient site in the Yorkshire Wolds, this Victorian farmhouse has large, comfortable bedrooms with uninterrupted panoramic views. The centre of a working livery yard, the house has its own private fishing lake and access to fabulous country walks. Dogs very welcome. York 12 miles, coast 20 miles.

**SAT NAV** *YO42 1SB* **ONLINE MAP**

Room General Leisure

## BLACKPOOL, Lancashire Map ref 4A1

★★★
GUEST HOUSE

B&B PER ROOM PER NIGHT
s £25.00–£27.00
d £50.00–£68.00

### Ash Lodge

131 Hornby Road, Blackpool FY1 4JG **t** (01253) 627637 **e** admin@ashlodgehotel.co.uk

**ashlodgehotel.co.uk REAL-TIME BOOKING**

**open** All year except Christmas
**bedrooms** 1 double, 2 twin, 3 single, 2 family
**bathrooms** 7 en suite, 1 private
**payment** Credit/debit cards, cash, cheques

The Ash Lodge is located in central Blackpool but in a quiet residential area. The hotel is a late Victorian house with many of its original features. However, it has all the modern facilities needed for a comfortable stay. The Ash Lodge has a residential licence.

**SAT NAV** *FY1 4JG* **ONLINE MAP**

Room General

## BLACKPOOL, Lancashire Map ref 4A1

★★★★
GUEST ACCOMMODATION

B&B PER ROOM PER NIGHT
S £23.00–£35.00
D £46.00–£60.00

EVENING MEAL PER PERSON
Min £9.00

*Weekend breaks from £20pppn (excl Bank Holidays). Special rates for over 55s (excl Bank Holidays).*

### The Berwick

23 King Edward Avenue, Blackpool FY2 9TA **t** (01253) 351496 **e** theberwickhotel@btconnect.com

**theberwickhotel.co.uk**

**open** All year
**bedrooms** 5 double, 3 twin
**bathrooms** All en suite
**payment** Credit/debit cards, cash, cheques

Adjacent to Queen's Promenade and close to Gynn Gardens. Conveniently placed for all Blackpool's attractions. Close to local transport. A friendly home-from-home welcome awaits visitors to our attractively decorated, fully non-smoking hotel. All meals are home cooked and served in our pleasant dining room. Car park at rear.

**SAT NAV** *FY2 9TA*

Room General 5 P Leisure

## BLACKPOOL, Lancashire Map ref 4A1

★★★
GUEST HOUSE

B&B PER ROOM PER NIGHT
S £25.00–£30.00
D £20.00–£28.00

EVENING MEAL PER PERSON
£9.00

### Cardoh Lodge

21 Hull Road, Blackpool FY1 4QB **t** (01253) 627755

Friendly, centrally located hotel catering for families and couples, offering a high standard of accommodation and choice of menu.

**open** All year except Christmas and New Year
**bedrooms** 4 double, 2 twin, 2 single, 2 family
**bathrooms** All en suite
**payment** Cash, cheques, euros

Room General

## BLACKPOOL, Lancashire Map ref 4A1

★★★★
GUEST HOUSE

B&B PER ROOM PER NIGHT
S £22.50–£30.00
D £45.00–£60.00

EVENING MEAL PER PERSON
£7.50–£10.00

### Edenfield Guest House

17 Cocker Street, Blackpool FY1 2BY **t** (01253) 624009 **e** info@edenfieldguesthouse.com

**edenfieldguesthouse.com** GUEST REVIEWS

A warm welcome awaits you at an award-winning, true home away from home. Situated in a quieter area of Blackpool, close to all attractions. Adults only.

**open** All year except Christmas
**bedrooms** 6 double, 1 single
**payment** Credit/debit cards, cash, cheques

Room SC General

## BLACKPOOL, Lancashire Map ref 4A1

★★★
GUEST ACCOMMODATION

B&B PER ROOM PER NIGHT
S £23.00–£30.00
D £46.00–£60.00

EVENING MEAL PER PERSON
£10.00

### Hadley

225 Promenade, Blackpool FY1 5DL **t** (01253) 621197 **e** admin@hadley-hotel.com

**hadley-hotel.com** REAL-TIME BOOKING

Friendly, family-run hotel, recently refurbished. Twenty en suite bedrooms. Situated on Central Promenade overlooking the Irish Sea.

**open** All year
**bedrooms** 11 double, 6 twin, 1 single, 2 family
**bathrooms** All en suite
**payment** Credit/debit cards

Room General

## Using map references

Map references refer to the colour maps at the front of this guide.

**BLACKPOOL, Lancashire Map ref 4A1**

★★
GUEST HOUSE

B&B PER ROOM PER NIGHT
D £44.00–£56.00

## The Manor Grove

24 Leopold Grove, Blackpool FY1 4LD **t** (01253) 625577 **e** themanorgrove@blueyonder.co.uk

**themanorgrove.co.uk**

Lovely, bright, clean, modern rooms. Family-run guesthouse, central location behind the Winter Gardens. All rooms en suite, TV, hairdryers, tea/coffee.

**open** All year
**bedrooms** 2 double, 4 single, 3 family
**bathrooms** All en suite
**payment** Credit/debit cards, cash, cheques

Room General

**BLACKPOOL, Lancashire Map ref 4A1**

★★★
GUEST ACCOMMODATION

B&B PER ROOM PER NIGHT
S £25.00–£30.00
D £50.00–£60.00

EVENING MEAL PER PERSON
£10.00

## Norville House

44 Warbreck Hill Road, Blackpool FY2 9SU **t** (01253) 352714 **e** norvillehouse@btconnect.com

**norvillehousehotel.co.uk** SPECIAL OFFERS

Norville House is a small, family-run bed and breakfast, recently refurbished with the highest standards of cleanliness assured. Evening meal is available Monday to Friday. Special diets catered for with prior notice.

**open** All year
**bedrooms** 3 double, 3 twin, 2 single, 1 family
**bathrooms** All en suite
**payment** Cash, cheques

Room General Leisure

**BLACKPOOL, Lancashire Map ref 4A1**

★★★★
GUEST ACCOMMODATION

B&B PER ROOM PER NIGHT
S £31.00–£36.00
D £62.00–£72.00

EVENING MEAL PER PERSON
£8.95–£10.50

*3 nights for the price of 2, Mon-Fri (excl Bank Holidays), Jan-Aug.*

## The Raffles Guest Accommodation

73-77 Hornby Road, Blackpool FY1 4QJ **t** (01253) 294713
**e** enquiries@raffleshotelblackpool.fsworld.co.uk

**raffleshotelblackpool.co.uk**

**open** All year
**bedrooms** 12 double, 3 twin, 1 single, 1 family, 3 suites
**bathrooms** All en suite
**payment** Credit/debit cards, cash, cheques

Excellent central location for promenade, shopping centre, Winter Gardens, theatres. All rooms en suite. Licensed bar, English tea rooms, parking and daily housekeeping. Imaginative choice of menus. Listed in the Good Hotel Guide and the Which? Guide to Good Hotels. Three new family apartments each sleeping up to four people.

**SAT NAV** *FY1 4QJ*

Room General

**BLACKPOOL, Lancashire Map ref 4A1**

★★★
GUEST ACCOMMODATION

B&B PER ROOM PER NIGHT
S £25.00–£50.00
D £40.00–£80.00

## The South Beach

367 Promenade, Blackpool FY1 6BJ **t** (01253) 342250 **e** info@southbeachhotel.co.uk

**southbeachhotel.co.uk** GUEST REVIEWS · SPECIAL OFFERS · REAL-TIME BOOKING

Above-average, friendly family-run licensed bed and breakfast situated in the main holiday area on Blackpool's South Promenade. Great for families and couples.

**open** All year
**bedrooms** 10 double, 4 twin, 2 single, 12 family
**bathrooms** All en suite
**payment** Credit/debit cards, cash

Room General

### Has every property been assessed?

All accommodation in this guide has been rated for quality, or is awaiting assessment, by a professional national tourist board assessor.

## BLACKPOOL, Lancashire Map ref 4A1

★★★
GUEST ACCOMMODATION

B&B PER ROOM PER NIGHT
s £22.00–£30.00
d £45.00–£60.00

EVENING MEAL PER PERSON
£6.00–£8.00

### The Valentine

35 Dickson Road, Blackpool FY1 2AT **t** (01253) 622775
**e** anthony@anthonypalmer.orangehome.co.uk

**valentinehotelblackpool.co.uk** SPECIAL OFFERS

A very high standard in presentation and cleanliness. Licensed to residents only. Couples and families welcome. Five minutes to Winter Gardens, Tower, North Pier, shopping centre and rail station.

**open** All year
**bedrooms** 8 double, 1 twin, 4 family
**bathrooms** All en suite
**payment** Credit/debit cards, cash

Room General

## BOLTON-BY-BOWLAND, Lancashire Map ref 4B1

★★★★
GUEST HOUSE

B&B PER ROOM PER NIGHT
s £40.00–£50.00
d £60.00–£75.00

EVENING MEAL PER PERSON
£25.00–£35.00

### Middle Flass Lodge

Forest Becks Brow, Clitheroe BB7 4NY **t** (01200) 447259 **e** middleflasslodge@btconnect.com

**middleflasslodge.co.uk**

**open** All year
**bedrooms** 4 double, 2 twin, 1 family
**bathrooms** All en suite
**payment** Credit/debit cards, cash, cheques

Tastefully converted barn/cow byre, set in idyllic countryside location of Forest of Bowland. Ideal touring base on Lancashire/Yorkshire border. Always personal and professional attention with neat and cosy bedrooms. Lounge with stove, dining room with chef-prepared cuisine. Licensed. Gardens and ample parking.

**SAT NAV** *BB7 4NY*

Room General P Leisure

## BORROWDALE, Cumbria Map ref 5A3

★★★★★
GUEST HOUSE
GOLD AWARD

B&B PER ROOM PER NIGHT
s £33.50–£62.50
d £67.00–£125.00

EVENING MEAL PER PERSON
Min £32.50

*Discounts available when bookings are made more than 3 months in advance of arrival.*

### Hazel Bank Country House

Rosthwaite, Borrowdale, Keswick CA12 5XB **t** (017687) 77248 **e** enquiries@hazelbankhotel.co.uk

**hazelbankhotel.co.uk**

**open** All year except Christmas
**bedrooms** 7 double, 1 twin
**bathrooms** All en suite
**payment** Credit/debit cards, cash, cheques

Award-winning, Victorian country house set in four-acre grounds. Peaceful location, superb views of central Lakeland fells. Bedrooms all en suite. Rosette-standard cuisine using local produce. Ideal base for walking. No smokers. No pets. Self-catering cottage for two. Best in Cumbria 2001, 2002 and 2004. Finalist Best in England 2003.

**SAT NAV** *CA12 5XB*

Room General 12 P Leisure

## BRADFORD, West Yorkshire Map ref 4B1

★★
GUEST HOUSE

B&B PER ROOM PER NIGHT
s £25.00
d £38.00

### Ivy Guest House

3 Melbourne Place, Bradford BD5 0HZ **t** (01274) 727060 **e** enquiries@ivyguesthousebradford.com

**ivyguesthousebradford.com**

Large, detached, listed, Yorkshire-stone house. Close to city centre, National Media Museum, Alhambra Theatre and the University of Bradford.

**open** All year
**bedrooms** 4 double, 4 twin, 2 single
**payment** Credit/debit cards, cash, cheques, euros

Room General

## BRAITHWAITE, Cumbria Map ref 5A3

★★★
INN

B&B PER ROOM PER NIGHT
S £32.00–£38.00
D £64.00–£76.00

EVENING MEAL PER PERSON
£8.95–£12.50

### Coledale Inn

Braithwaite, Keswick CA12 5TN **t** (017687) 78272 **e** info@coledale-inn.com

**coledale-inn.co.uk** GUEST REVIEWS • SPECIAL OFFERS • REAL-TIME BOOKING

Victorian country-house hotel and Georgian inn. Peaceful hillside position away from traffic, with superb mountain views. Families and pets welcome. Fine selection of real ales. Special midweek winter breaks available.

**open** All year
**bedrooms** 11 double, 3 twin, 1 single, 5 family
**bathrooms** All en suite
**payment** Credit/debit cards, cash, cheques

Room General Leisure

## BRAMPTON, Cumbria Map ref 5B2

★★★★
INN

B&B PER ROOM PER NIGHT
S £40.00–£50.00
D £55.00–£70.00

EVENING MEAL PER PERSON
£5.25–£25.00

### Blacksmiths Arms

Talkin, Brampton CA8 1LE **t** (01697) 73452 **e** blacksmithsarmstalkin@yahoo.co.uk

**blacksmithstalkin.co.uk**

**open** All year except Christmas
**bedrooms** 6 double, 2 twin
**bathrooms** All en suite
**payment** Credit/debit cards, cash, cheques, euros

Village inn in scenic countryside, three miles south of Brampton and eight miles east of junction 43 on the M6 motorway. Close to Talkin Tarn and within easy reach of Hadrian's Wall, the Lake District, the Borders and Carlisle. Restaurant and bar meals served every day, cask ales, open fire. Closed Christmas day.

**SAT NAV** *CA8 1LE* **ONLINE MAP**

Room General Leisure

## BRAMPTON, Cumbria Map ref 5B2

★★★★
BED & BREAKFAST

B&B PER ROOM PER NIGHT
S £40.00–£50.00
D £64.00–£80.00

EVENING MEAL PER PERSON
£20.00–£25.00

### Scarrowhill House

Scarrow Hill House, Denton Mill, Brampton CA8 2QU **t** (01697) 746759 & 07789 950322
**e** ianmac2949@aol.com

**scarrowhillhouse.co.uk** GUEST REVIEWS

**open** All year except Christmas and New Year
**bedrooms** 1 double, 1 twin
**bathrooms** All en suite
**payment** Credit/debit cards, cash, cheques, euros

Scarrow Hill House is a Victorian gamekeeper's dwelling set in secluded grounds on the Naworth Castle estate. It offers first-class accommodation and food, fine hospitality and relaxation in its own extensive gardens. It is close to Hadrian's Wall, the Scottish Borders and the Lake District.

**SAT NAV** *CA8 2QU* **ONLINE MAP**

Room General Leisure

## Do you have access needs?

Look for the National Accessible Scheme symbols if you have special hearing, visual or mobility needs. An index of accommodation participating in the scheme can be found at the back of this guide.

## BRIDLINGTON, East Riding of Yorkshire Map ref 5D3

★★★★
BED & BREAKFAST

B&B PER ROOM PER NIGHT
S £45.00–£50.00
D £50.00–£60.00

*7 nights for the price of 6.*

# Lincoln House

43 Wellington Road, Bridlington YO15 2AX **t** (01262) 679595 **e** lincolnhousebrid@fsmail.net

**lincolnhousebridlington.co.uk** GUEST REVIEWS

**open** All year except Christmas and New Year
**bedrooms** 3 double
**bathrooms** All en suite
**payment** Cash, cheques

Lincoln House, built c1892, is recently renovated and offers three tastefully decorated and spacious bedrooms with en suite facilities and is ideally situated to take advantage of all that Bridlington has to offer. Just a ten-minute stroll to the town centre, promenade, theatres, historic harbour, bus and rail stations.

**SAT NAV** *YO15 2AX* **ONLINE MAP**

Room General

## BRIDLINGTON, East Riding of Yorkshire Map ref 5D3

★★★★
GUEST HOUSE

B&B PER ROOM PER NIGHT
S Min £25.00
D Min £56.00

EVENING MEAL PER PERSON
Min £8.00

# Providence Place

11 North View Terrace, Bridlington YO15 2QP **t** (01262) 603840 **e** enquiries@providenceplace.info

**providenceplace.info**

Fully accessible, family-run establishment, home-from-home atmosphere. Ground-floor rooms. Quiet location close to sea and all amenities. Licensed guest lounge, attractive garden. Ample on-site parking.

**open** All year
**bedrooms** 1 double, 3 twin, 1 single, 1 family
**bathrooms** 5 en suite, 1 private
**payment** Credit/debit cards, cash, cheques

Room General P Leisure

## BRIDLINGTON, East Riding of Yorkshire Map ref 5D3

★★★
GUEST HOUSE

B&B PER ROOM PER NIGHT
S £24.00–£25.00
D £48.00–£50.00

# The Waverley

105 Cardigan Road, Bridlington YO15 3LP **t** (01262) 671040 **e** info@waverley-bridlington.co.uk

**waverley-bridlington.co.uk**

Small, friendly, family-run bed and breakfast in a quiet residential area close to the South Beach, Spa Theatre and golf course. Parking.

**open** All year except Christmas and New Year
**bedrooms** 2 double, 1 twin, 2 family
**bathrooms** All en suite
**payment** Credit/debit cards, cash, cheques

Room General P

## BROUGHTON IN FURNESS, Cumbria Map ref 5A3

★★★★
FARMHOUSE

B&B PER ROOM PER NIGHT
S Min £33.00
D Min £58.00

# Low Hall Farm

Kirkby-in-Furness, Broughton in Furness LA17 7TR **t** (01229) 889220 **e** enquiries@low-hall.co.uk

**low-hall.co.uk**

**open** All year
**bedrooms** 1 double, 1 twin, 1 family
**bathrooms** All en suite
**payment** Credit/debit cards, cash, cheques

Low Hall is a working farm with stunning views across the Duddon estuary and Lakeland fells. A warm, friendly welcome awaits you. High quality en suite accommodation and a traditional farmhouse breakfast our speciality. Ideal for exploring the South Lakes, beautiful walks with many places of interest on our doorstep.

**SAT NAV** *LA17 7TR*

Room General 10 P Leisure

## BUCKDEN, North Yorkshire Map ref 5B3

★★★
INN

B&B PER ROOM PER NIGHT
S £35.00–£55.00
D £35.00–£85.00

EVENING MEAL PER PERSON
£8.50–£13.50

### The White Lion Inn

Cray, Skipton BD23 5JB **t** (01756) 760262 **e** admin@whitelioncray.com

**whitelioncray.com**

Traditional 17thC Dales inn. Idyllic location, stone-flagged floors, roaring log fire, quality home-cooked food, Camra Pub of the Season. Special offers available midweek and weekends.

**open** All year
**bedrooms** 6 double, 3 twin
**bathrooms** All en suite
**payment** Credit/debit cards, cash, cheques

Room General P Leisure

## BURNLEY, Lancashire Map ref 4B1

★★★
GUEST ACCOMMODATION

B&B PER ROOM PER NIGHT
S £29.00–£32.00
D £45.00–£47.00

### Ormerod

123 Ormerod Road, Burnley BB11 3QW **t** (01282) 423255

**open** All year
**bedrooms** 2 double, 2 twin, 4 single, 2 family
**bathrooms** All en suite
**payment** Cash, cheques

Small bed and breakfast guesthouse in quiet, pleasant surroundings facing local parks. Recently refurbished, all en suite facilities. Five minutes from town centre.

**SAT NAV** *BB11 3QW*

Room TV General

## CALDBECK, Cumbria Map ref 5A2

★★★★
GUEST HOUSE
SILVER AWARD

B&B PER ROOM PER NIGHT
S £31.00
D £56.00

*Honeymoon extras. Special nature walks. Badger-watching evenings.*

### Swaledale Watch

Whelpo, Caldbeck CA7 8HQ **t** (01697) 478409 **e** nan.savage@talk21.com

**swaledale-watch.co.uk**

**open** All year except Christmas
**bedrooms** 2 double, 1 twin, 2 family
**bathrooms** 4 en suite, 1 private
**payment** Cash, cheques

A working farm outside picturesque Caldbeck. Enjoy great comfort, excellent food and a warm welcome amidst peaceful, unspoilt countryside. Central for touring, walking or discovering the northern fells. A memorable walk is through 'The Howk', a limestone gorge. Relax 'at home' with open fires.

**SAT NAV** *CA7 8HQ*

Room TV General P

## CARTMEL, Cumbria Map ref 5A3

★★★★★
BED & BREAKFAST
GOLD AWARD

B&B PER ROOM PER NIGHT
S £40.00–£45.00
D £80.00–£90.00

### Hill Farm B&B For Country Lovers

Cartmel, Grange-over-Sands LA11 7SS **t** (015395) 36477 **e** hillfarmbb@btinternet.com

**hillfarmbb.co.uk**

Hill Farm is an historic farmhouse with peaceful grounds, small tarns and beautiful views. It is not suitable for very young children. Arrival times are always kept open to assist guests.

**open** 1 February to 31 October
**bedrooms** 2 double, 1 single
**bathrooms** All en suite
**payment** Cash, cheques

Room TV General 7 P Leisure

## CASTLE HOWARD, North Yorkshire Map ref 5C3

★★★
FARMHOUSE

B&B PER ROOM PER NIGHT
S £35.00–£40.00
D £70.00–£80.00

EVENING MEAL PER PERSON
£15.00–£20.00

### Ganthorpe Gate Farm

Ganthorpe, Terrington, York YO60 6QD **t** (01653) 648269 **e** millgate001@msn.com

**ganthorpegatefarm.co.uk** REAL-TIME BOOKING

Working dairy farm in quiet hamlet near to Castle Howard, offering friendly, traditional, Yorkshire hospitality. Convenient for the Moors, east coast and York.

**open** All year
**bedrooms** 1 double, 1 twin, 1 family
**bathrooms** 1 en suite
**payment** Cash, cheques, euros

Room General Leisure

## CASTLESIDE, Durham Map ref 5B2

★★★★
GUEST HOUSE

B&B PER ROOM PER NIGHT
S £45.00–£48.00
D £70.00–£76.00

EVENING MEAL PER PERSON
£20.00

*Special prices for 3-day breaks and winter breaks. DB&B. See website.*

### Bee Cottage Guesthouse

Castleside, Nr Consett DH8 9HW **t** (01207) 508224 **e** beecottage68@aol.com

**beecottage.co.uk** SPECIAL OFFERS

**open** All year
**bedrooms** 2 double, 2 twin, 3 family, 1 suite
**bathrooms** All en suite
**payment** Credit/debit cards, cash, cheques, euros

Situated on the edge of the Durham Dales with stunning views. A wonderful place to relax. Peaceful walking and cycling (next to C2C). Ideal base for Beamish, Durham, Newcastle, Hadrian's Wall, Hexham and Corbridge. Some ground-floor rooms, all en suite. Home-cooked evening meals. Licensed. You will be most welcome.

**SAT NAV** *DH8 9HW* **ONLINE MAP**

WALKERS WELCOME CYCLISTS WELCOME

Room General Leisure

## CHATTON, Northumberland Map ref 5B1

★★★★
FARMHOUSE
SILVER AWARD

B&B PER ROOM PER NIGHT
S £35.00–£40.00
D £60.00–£70.00

### South Hazelrigg Farmhouse

Chatton, Alnwick NE66 5RZ **t** (01668) 215216 & 07710 346076 **e** sed@hazelrigg.fsnet.co.uk

**farmhousebandb.co.uk**

**open** All year except Christmas and New Year
**bedrooms** 2 double, 1 twin
**bathrooms** All en suite
**payment** Cash, cheques

Spacious farmhouse with magnificent views over lovely countryside. Elegant dining room and large drawing room with access to extensive grounds. Full central heating, tea-/coffee-making facilities, TV, private parking.

**SAT NAV** *NE66 5RZ* **ONLINE MAP**

Room General Leisure

## CHESTER, Cheshire Map ref 4A2

★★★★
BED & BREAKFAST

B&B PER ROOM PER NIGHT
S £35.00–£45.00
D £60.00–£75.00

### Golborne Manor

Platts Lane, Hatton Heath, Chester CH3 9AN **t** (01829) 770310 & 07774 695268
**e** info@golbornemanor.co.uk

**golbornemanor.co.uk**

A 19thC manor house renovated to a high standard, set in 3.5 acres. Five miles south of Chester, off A41 Whitchurch road, turning right just after Cheshire Van Sales. Ample parking.

**open** All year
**bedrooms** 1 double, 1 twin, 1 family
**bathrooms** All en suite
**payment** Cash, cheques

Room General Leisure

## CHORLEY, Lancashire Map ref 4A1

★★★★
GUEST ACCOMMODATION

B&B PER ROOM PER NIGHT
S £40.00–£50.00
D £70.00–£80.00

### Parr Hall Farm

Parr Lane, Eccleston, Chorley PR7 5SL **t** (01257) 451917 **e** enquiries@parrhallfarm.com

**parrhallfarm.com**

**open** All year
**bedrooms** 7 double, 2 twin
**bathrooms** All en suite
**payment** Credit/debit cards, cash, cheques

Georgian farmhouse built in 1721 and tastefully restored. Quiet, rural location within easy walking distance of good public houses, restaurants and village amenities. Conveniently situated for Lancashire coast and countryside, Lake District and Yorkshire Dales. Manchester Airport 45 minutes, Liverpool Airport 45 minutes.

**SAT NAV** *PR7 5SL*

Room General Leisure

## CLITHEROE, Lancashire Map ref 4A1

★★★★
INN

B&B PER ROOM PER NIGHT
S £40.00–£55.00
D £70.00–£75.00

EVENING MEAL PER PERSON
£8.50–£20.00

### Bayley Arms

Avenue Road, Hurst Green, Clitheroe, Nr Blackburn BB7 9QB **t** (01254) 826478
**e** sales@bayleyarms.co.uk

**bayleyarms.co.uk** GUEST REVIEWS • SPECIAL OFFERS • REAL-TIME BOOKING

16thC country inn, sensational home-cooked food, sensible prices, stylish bedrooms. Close to motorway network, rural village location, ideal for walking, sightseeing, in fact any occasion. A warm welcome is assured.

**open** All year
**bedrooms** 5 double, 2 twin, 1 family
**bathrooms** All en suite
**payment** Credit/debit cards, cash, cheques

Room General Leisure

## COCKERMOUTH, Cumbria Map ref 5A2

★★★★
GUEST HOUSE

B&B PER ROOM PER NIGHT
S £45.00–£70.00
D £60.00–£85.00

EVENING MEAL PER PERSON
£20.00–£25.00

*Midweek or weekend breaks available all year (min 2 nights). Family group packages also available all year (min 12 people).*

PETS! WELCOME

### Rose Cottage

Lorton Road, Cockermouth CA13 9DX **t** (01900) 822189 **e** bookings@rosecottageguest.co.uk

**rosecottageguest.co.uk** REAL-TIME BOOKING

**open** All year except Christmas and New Year
**bedrooms** 3 double, 2 twin, 1 single, 2 family
**bathrooms** All en suite
**payment** Credit/debit cards, cash, cheques

In a pleasant position and only a ten-minute walk from the town, this family-run guesthouse is within easy reach of the Lakes and coast. Home cooking. Large, private car park. An ideal base for walking or touring.

**SAT NAV** *CA13 9DX* **ONLINE MAP**

Room General

## Check the maps for accommodation locations

Colour maps at the front pinpoint all the places where accommodation is featured within the regional sections of this guide. Pick your location and then refer to the place index at the back to find the page number.

## CONISTON, Cumbria Map ref 5A3

★★★★
GUEST HOUSE

B&B PER ROOM PER NIGHT
S £32.50
D £60.00–£65.00

### Oaklands

Yewdale Road, Coniston LA21 8DX **t** (015394) 41245 **e** judithzeke@oaklandsguesthouse.fsnet.co.uk

**oaklandsconiston.co.uk**

Spacious 100-year-old Lakeland house, village location, mountain views. Quality breakfast, special diets, owners' personal attention. Parking. Non-smoking.

**open** All year
**bedrooms** 2 double, 1 twin, 1 single
**bathrooms** 2 en suite, 1 private
**payment** Cash, cheques, euros

Room General 10 P Leisure

## CONISTON, Cumbria Map ref 5A3

★★★★★
FARMHOUSE
SILVER AWARD

B&B PER ROOM PER NIGHT
S £70.00–£80.00
D £110.00–£130.00

EVENING MEAL PER PERSON
£15.00–£35.00

### Yew Tree Farm

Coniston LA21 8DP **t** (015394) 41433 **e** info@yewtree-farm.com

**yewtree-farm.com**

**open** All year
**bedrooms** 3 double
**bathrooms** 2 en suite, 1 private
**payment** Credit/debit cards

In the beautiful Yew Dale Valley this picturesque farmhouse once owned by Beatrix Potter featured in the film 'Miss Potter'. Luxurious accommodation recently refurbished in period style, extra touches come as standard. Enjoy open fires, oak-panelled walls and private gardens with hot tub. A warm welcome awaits.

**SAT NAV** *LA21 8DP* **ONLINE MAP**

Room General P Leisure

## CONISTON, Cumbria Map ref 5A3

★★★
INN

B&B PER ROOM PER NIGHT
S £32.50–£50.00
D £60.00–£90.00

EVENING MEAL PER PERSON
£7.50–£15.00

### Yewdale Inn

Yewdale Road, Coniston LA21 8DU **t** (015394) 41280 **e** mail@yewdalehotel.com

**yewdalehotel.com**

Small, family-run inn situated in the centre of Coniston, within walking distance of the lake. Ideally positioned for walkers and cyclists. Children and pets welcome.

**open** All year
**bedrooms** 3 double, 4 family
**bathrooms** All en suite
**payment** Credit/debit cards, cash, cheques

Room General P Leisure

## CORBRIDGE, Northumberland Map ref 5B2

★★★★
BED & BREAKFAST

B&B PER ROOM PER NIGHT
S £25.00–£30.00
D £50.00–£60.00

### Broxdale

Station Road, Corbridge NE45 5AY **t** (01434) 632492 **e** mike@broxdale.co.uk

Bed and breakfast accommodation within the historic and picturesque village of Corbridge. Close to Hadrian's Wall, Housesteads and other noted Roman sites. The property is tastefully decorated, retaining many original fixtures and fittings.

**open** All year
**bedrooms** 2 double
**bathrooms** All en suite
**payment** Cash, cheques

Room General P Leisure

## CORBRIDGE, Northumberland Map ref 5B2

★★★★
BED & BREAKFAST

B&B PER ROOM PER NIGHT
S £35.00
D £55.00

EVENING MEAL PER PERSON
Min £12.00

### Fellcroft

Station Road, Corbridge NE45 5AY **t** (01434) 632384 **e** tove.brown@ukonline.co.uk

Well-appointed, stone-built Edwardian house with full, private facilities. Quiet road in country setting, 0.5 miles south of market square. Non-smokers only please. Family room (three-four sharing) £65.00.

**open** All year except Christmas and New Year
**bedrooms** 1 twin, 1 family
**bathrooms** 1 en suite, 1 private
**payment** Cash, cheques

Room General P

## CORBRIDGE, Northumberland Map ref 5B2

★★★
GUEST ACCOMMODATION

B&B PER ROOM PER NIGHT
S £29.50–£39.50
D £59.00–£65.00

### The Hayes

Newcastle Road, Corbridge NE45 5LP **t** (01434) 632010 **e** camon@surfree.co.uk

**hayes-corbridge.co.uk**

Large, late-19thC country house with splendid views southwards. Set in spacious grounds, in historic village with easy access to Hadrian's Wall, A69 and A68. Family-run.

**open** All year except Christmas and New Year
**bedrooms** 1 twin, 1 single, 2 family
**bathrooms** 2 en suite, 2 private
**payment** Credit/debit cards, cash, cheques

Room General P Leisure

## CRASTER, Northumberland Map ref 5C1

★★★
FARMHOUSE

B&B PER ROOM PER NIGHT
D £50.00–£56.00

### Howick Scar Farmhouse

Craster, Alnwick NE66 3SU **t** (01665) 576665 **e** stay@howickscar.co.uk

**howickscar.co.uk**

Comfortable farmhouse with television lounge. Sea view from bedrooms. Shared bathroom. Seven miles from Alnwick between Craster and Howick on the coast. Lovely scenery and walks.

**open** April to October
**bedrooms** 2 double
**payment** Cash, cheques

Room General 12 P Leisure

## CRAYKE, North Yorkshire Map ref 5C3

★★★
BED & BREAKFAST

B&B PER ROOM PER NIGHT
S Min £32.00
D Min £64.00

### The Hermitage

Mill Lane, Crayke YO61 4TD **t** (01347) 821635

Peaceful location with panoramic views. Overlooking our own farm and the Howardian Hills. Offering a warm and friendly welcome at our comfortable modern farmhouse. Hot tub on patio.

**open** All year except Christmas
**bedrooms** 1 double, 2 twin
**bathrooms** 1 en suite
**payment** Cash, cheques

Room General P

## CROSBY RAVENSWORTH, Cumbria Map ref 5B3

★★★★★
GUEST ACCOMMODATION
GOLD AWARD

B&B PER ROOM PER NIGHT
S £60.00
D £90.00–£110.00

EVENING MEAL PER PERSON
Min £25.00

### Crake Trees Manor

Crosby Ravensworth, Penrith CA10 3JG **t** (01931) 715205 **e** ruth@craketreesmanor.co.uk

**craketreesmanor.co.uk** GUEST REVIEWS • REAL-TIME BOOKING

At Crake Trees, traditional skills and local materials of green oak, slate, ash and limestone create a stylish home from a 19thC barn at the centre of our family farm. Two courtyard apartments and two bedroom suites furnished with easy mix of modern and antique furnishings.

**open** All year
**bedrooms** 2 double, 2 suites
**bathrooms** All en suite
**payment** Credit/debit cards, cash

Room General P Leisure

For **key to symbols** see page 7

## DALBY, North Yorkshire Map ref 5C3

★★★★
FARMHOUSE

B&B PER ROOM PER NIGHT
D £54.00–£65.00

EVENING MEAL PER PERSON
£10.00–£20.00

*Reduced rates for children under 14 years. Discounts on stays of 5 nights or more.*

### South Moor Farm

Dalby Forest Drive, Scarborough YO13 0LW **t** (01751) 460285 **e** tbg@southmoorfarm.co.uk

**southmoorfarm.co.uk** REAL-TIME BOOKING

**open** All year
**bedrooms** 1 double, 1 twin, 1 single, 1 family
**bathrooms** 3 en suite, 1 private
**payment** Credit/debit cards, cash, cheques

Quiet rural location on Dalby Forest Drive between Pickering and Scarborough. An excellent base to explore Dalby Forest on foot, bike or horse after a full English breakfast. Packed lunches and evening meals by arrangement. Children's play area, orienteering courses, quad bikes, 4x4 driving and astronomy in Dalby Forest.

**SAT NAV** *YO13 0LW*

Room General Leisure

## DANBY, North Yorkshire Map ref 5C3

★★★★
INN

B&B PER ROOM PER NIGHT
S £45.00–£60.00
D £75.00–£90.00

### The Fox & Hounds Inn

45 Brook Lane, Ainthorpe, Whitby YO21 2LD **t** (01287) 660218 **e** info@foxandhounds-ainthorpe.com

**foxandhounds-ainthorpe.com**

**open** All year except Christmas
**bedrooms** 3 double, 3 twin, 1 family
**bathrooms** All en suite
**payment** Credit/debit cards, cash, cheques

16thC former coaching inn, now a high-quality residential country inn and restaurant. Set amidst the beautiful North York Moors National Park. Enjoy freshly prepared dishes, cask ales or selected quality wines in our restaurant or oak-beamed bar.

**SAT NAV** *YO21 2LD*

Room General Leisure

## DARLINGTON, Tees Valley Map ref 5C3

★★★
INN

B&B PER ROOM PER NIGHT
S £30.00–£35.00
D £50.00

### Boot & Shoe

Church Row, Darlington DL1 5QD **t** (01325) 287501 **e** enquiries@bootandshoe.com

**bootandshoe.com**

A Grade II Listed building situated on Darlington's busy marketplace, fully refurbished in 2000. Only minutes from train and bus station, and A1.

**open** All year
**bedrooms** 5 double, 2 twin, 2 family
**bathrooms** 7 en suite
**payment** Cash, cheques

Room General

## DENT, Cumbria Map ref 5B3

★★★
BED & BREAKFAST

B&B PER ROOM PER NIGHT
S £35.00–£40.00
D £50.00–£70.00

### Stone Close Tea Room & Guest House

Main Street, Dent, Sedbergh LA10 5QL **t** (015396) 25231 **e** stoneclose@btinternet.com

**dentdale.com**

Lovely 17thC listed building. Use of quiet room with stunning view across the dale. Ground-floor twin room has walk-in wetroom. Fresh organic breakfast served in Tea Room, fire lit in cast-iron range in cold weather.

**open** All year
**bedrooms** 1 double, 2 twin
**bathrooms** 1 en suite
**payment** Cash, cheques

Room General Leisure

## DONCASTER, South Yorkshire Map ref 4C1

★★★
GUEST ACCOMMODATION

B&B PER ROOM PER NIGHT
S £25.00–£40.00
D £40.00–£55.00

EVENING MEAL PER PERSON
Min £8.50

### The Balmoral

129 Thorne Road, Doncaster DN2 5BH **t** (01302) 364385 **e** thebalmoralhotel@blueyonder.co.uk

The Balmoral Hotel is located in Doncaster. This family-run hotel offers clean and comfortable accommodation with a choice of facilities. Prime location, and a warm Yorkshire welcome.

**open** All year
**bedrooms** 4 double, 1 twin, 3 single
**bathrooms** 3 en suite
**payment** Credit/debit cards, cash, cheques, euros

Room General Leisure

## DONCASTER, South Yorkshire Map ref 4C1

★★★
INN

B&B PER ROOM PER NIGHT
S £35.00
D £40.00–£58.00

EVENING MEAL PER PERSON
£4.95–£10.95

### Park Inn

232 Carrhouse Road, Doncaster DN4 5DS **t** (01302) 364008

The recently refurbished Park Inn is situated in a popular area of Doncaster, close to the racecourse. It has a large lounge/restaurant area and a separate games room and function room with a licensed bar.

**open** All year
**bedrooms** 4 double, 5 twin, 1 single, 2 family
**bathrooms** All en suite
**payment** Cash, cheques

Room General Leisure

## DONCASTER, South Yorkshire Map ref 4C1

★★★
FARMHOUSE

B&B PER ROOM PER NIGHT
S £28.00–£36.00
D £50.00–£60.00

### Rock Farm

Hooton Pagnell, Doncaster DN5 7BT **t** (01977) 642200 & 07785 916186 **e** info@rockfarm.info

**rockfarm.info**

**open** All year
**bedrooms** 1 double, 1 twin, 1 family
**bathrooms** 1 en suite
**payment** Cash, cheques, euros

A warm welcome and hearty breakfast await you at our Grade II Listed stone farmhouse on a 200-acre mixed farm. Situated in the picturesque stone-built village of Hooton Pagnell, six miles north-west of Doncaster. Five minutes A1 and Brodsworth Hall, ten minutes M62, M1 and M18.

**SAT NAV** *DN5 7BT*

Room General Leisure

## DUFTON, Cumbria Map ref 5B3

★★★★
FARMHOUSE
SILVER AWARD

B&B PER ROOM PER NIGHT
S £28.00–£30.00
D £56.00–£60.00

### Brow Farm Bed & Breakfast

Dufton, Appleby-in-Westmorland CA16 6DF **t** (017683) 52865 **e** stay@browfarm.com

**browfarm.com**

**open** All year except Christmas
**bedrooms** 2 double, 1 twin
**bathrooms** All en suite
**payment** Credit/debit cards, cash, cheques

Situated on the edge of the Pennines, with superb views from every room. Tasteful barn conversion offers rest and relaxation.

**SAT NAV** *CA16 6DF*

Room General

## DUNSWELL, East Riding of Yorkshire Map ref 4C1

★★★
INN

B&B PER ROOM PER NIGHT
S £50.00
D £55.00

### The Ship's Quarters

Beverley High Road, Dunswell, Hull HU6 0AJ **t** (01482) 859160

**theshipsquarters.co.uk**

**open** All year
**bedrooms** 7 double, 2 twin
**bathrooms** All en suite
**payment** Credit/debit cards, cash

Ideally situated between Hull and Beverley, this all-en suite accommodation nestles in the grounds of a 19thC ale house, with hand-pulled beers, open fires and wholesome food.

**SAT NAV** *HU6 0AJ*

Room General Leisure

## DURHAM Map ref 5C2

★★
INN

B&B PER ROOM PER NIGHT
S £23.00–£35.00
D £45.00–£65.00

### The Avenue Inn

Avenue Street, High Shincliffe DH1 2PT **t** (0191) 386 5954 **e** info@theavenue.biz

**theavenue.biz** REAL-TIME BOOKING

Cosy village inn with eight bedrooms, mainly en suite. Real ales and a friendly atmosphere.

**open** All year
**bedrooms** 2 double, 2 twin, 3 single, 1 family
**bathrooms** 4 en suite
**payment** Credit/debit cards, cash, cheques

Room General Leisure

## DURHAM Map ref 5C2

★★★★
GUEST ACCOMMODATION

B&B PER ROOM PER NIGHT
S £50.00–£60.00
D £75.00–£80.00

### Castle View Guest House

4 Crossgate, Durham DH1 4PS **t** (0191) 386 8852 **e** castle_view@hotmail.com

**castle-view.co.uk**

Two-hundred-and-fifty-year-old listed building in the heart of the old city, with woodland and riverside walks and a magnificent view of the cathedral and castle.

**open** All year except Christmas and New Year
**bedrooms** 3 double, 2 twin, 1 single
**bathrooms** All en suite
**payment** Credit/debit cards, cash, cheques

Room General 2

## DURHAM Map ref 5C2

★★★★
GUEST ACCOMMODATION
SILVER AWARD

B&B PER ROOM PER NIGHT
S £60.00–£80.00
D £80.00–£90.00

### Cathedral View Town House

212 Gilesgate, Durham DH1 1QN **t** (0191) 386 9566 **e** cathedralview@hotmail.com

**cathedralview.com**

**open** All year except Christmas and New Year
**bedrooms** 4 double, 2 twin
**bathrooms** All en suite
**payment** Credit/debit cards, cash, cheques

Georgian town house in conservation area of the city centre. Close to restaurants, shops and theatre. Ten minutes' walk to cathedral and castle. Elevated position with panoramic views of the cathedral and surrounding countryside. Comfortable, well equipped accommodation with extensive breakfast menu using only top quality ingredients. Complimentary parking provided.

**SAT NAV** *DH1 1QN*

Room General

## DURHAM Map ref 5C2

★★★
INN

B&B PER ROOM PER NIGHT
S £45.00
D £65.00

EVENING MEAL PER PERSON
£2.50–£15.00

### Garden House

North Road, Durham DH1 4NQ **t** (0191) 384 3460

**open** All year
**bedrooms** 2 double, 3 family
**bathrooms** All en suite
**payment** Credit/debit cards, cash, cheques

Family-run business within walking distance of Durham city centre. Traditional bar menu and top quality Four Seasons Conservatory menu. A very warm welcome to all visitors.

**SAT NAV** *DH1 4NQ*

Room General Leisure

## DURHAM Map ref 5C2

★★★
GUEST ACCOMMODATION

B&B PER ROOM PER NIGHT
S £35.00
D £60.00–£70.00

### Hillrise Guest House

13 Durham Road West, Bowburn, Durham DH6 5AU **t** (0191) 377 0302 **e** enquiries@hill-rise.com

**hill-rise.com**

Conveniently placed 200yds from junction 61 A1(M). Family, twin and double rooms with en suite facilities. Friendly atmosphere and a high standard of cleanliness.

**open** All year
**bedrooms** 2 double, 2 twin, 1 family
**bathrooms** All en suite
**payment** Credit/debit cards, cash, euros

Room General 12

## DURHAM Map ref 5C2

★★
GUEST ACCOMMODATION

B&B PER ROOM PER NIGHT
S £25.00–£32.00
D £40.00–£50.00

### St Chad's College

18 North Bailey, Durham DH1 3RH **t** (0191) 334 3358 **e** St-Chads.www@durham.ac.uk

**dur.ac.uk/StChads**

**open** All year except Christmas
**bedrooms** 3 double, 40 twin, 66 single
**bathrooms** 23 en suite
**payment** Credit/debit cards, cash, cheques

In the heart of historic Durham, adjacent to the castle and cathedral, designated a World Heritage Site. Comfortable and convenient accommodation, friendly service.

**SAT NAV** *DH1 3RH*

Room General Leisure

## DURHAM Map ref 5C2

★★
GUEST ACCOMMODATION

B&B PER ROOM PER NIGHT
S £24.00–£27.00
D £24.00–£27.00

### St Johns College

3 South Bailey, Durham DH1 3RJ **t** (0191) 334 3877 **e** s.l.hobson@durham.ac.uk

**durham.ac.uk/st-johns.college**

Located in the heart of Durham City alongside the cathedral, St John's offers accommodation in distinctive, historic buildings with riverside gardens.

**open** All year except Christmas and New Year
**bedrooms** 9 twin, 36 single
**payment** Credit/debit cards, cash, cheques

Room General

## DURHAM Map ref 5C2

★★★★
GUEST ACCOMMODATION
SILVER AWARD

B&B PER ROOM PER NIGHT
D £60.00–£75.00

### The Victorian Town House

2 Victoria Terrace, Durham DH1 4RW **t** 05601 459168
**e** thevictoriantownhouse-durham@yahoo.co.uk

**durhambedandbreakfast.co.uk**

Victorian terraced family home. Three en suite rooms. City centre, train, bus all five minutes' walk. Private and nearby parking.

**open** All year
**bedrooms** 1 double, 1 twin, 1 family
**bathrooms** All en suite
**payment** Credit/debit cards, cash, cheques

Room General 5 P

## EGTON BRIDGE, North Yorkshire Map ref 5D3

★★★★
GUEST HOUSE
SILVER AWARD

B&B PER ROOM PER NIGHT
D £73.00–£118.00

### Broom House

Egton Bridge, Whitby YO21 1XD **t** (01947) 895279 **e** mw@broom-house.co.uk

**egton-bridge.co.uk** GUEST REVIEWS • SPECIAL OFFERS • REAL-TIME BOOKING

**open** All year except Christmas
**bedrooms** 3 double, 1 twin, 2 suites
**bathrooms** All en suite
**payment** Credit/debit cards, cash, cheques

Broom House is an excellent place to stay. We provide comfortable en suite rooms, with two new guest suites for 2009 and a guest lounge. An idyllic setting with views over the Esk Valley. Visit website for more details.

**SAT NAV** *YO21 1XD* **ONLINE MAP**

WALKERS WELCOME CYCLISTS WELCOME

Room General P Leisure

## ELLINGHAM, Northumberland Map ref 5C1

★★★
INN

B&B PER ROOM PER NIGHT
S £35.00–£45.00
D £60.00–£80.00

EVENING MEAL PER PERSON
£10.00–£25.00

*For stays of more than 3 nights special rates can be negotiated – please call.*

### The Pack Horse Inn

Ellingham, Chathill NE67 5HA **t** (01665) 589292 **e** graham_c_simpson@hotmail.co.uk

**packhorseinn-ellingham.co.uk** GUEST REVIEWS • SPECIAL OFFERS • REAL-TIME BOOKING

**open** All year
**bedrooms** 3 double, 2 twin
**bathrooms** All en suite
**payment** Credit/debit cards, cash, cheques

The Pack Horse Inn is a 200-year-old traditional Northumbrian inn situated at one end of the village main street. It provides comfortable guest accommodation for bed and breakfast and has a self-catering cottage which sleeps two. The restaurant serves only the best local ingredients, all freshly prepared.

**SAT NAV** *NE67 5HA* **ONLINE MAP**

Room General P Leisure

## Don't forget www.

Web addresses throughout this guide are shown without the prefix www. Please include www. in the address line of your browser. If a web address does not follow this style it is shown in full.

## FIR TREE, Durham Map ref 5C2

★★★★
GUEST ACCOMMODATION

B&B PER ROOM PER NIGHT
S £60.00
D £75.00

### Greenhead Country House

Green Head, Fir Tree DL15 8BL **t** (01388) 763143 **e** info@thegreenheadhotel.co.uk

**thegreenheadhotel.co.uk** GUEST REVIEWS · SPECIAL OFFERS

**open** All year
**bedrooms** 4 double, 2 twin, 2 single
**bathrooms** All en suite
**payment** Credit/debit cards, cash, cheques

Converted from 1704 Dales longhouse and situated at the foot of rural Weardale, surrounded by fields and woodland, the multiple award-winning Greenhead Country House is only twenty minutes from the historic city of Durham. High standards of hospitality, service, food and comfort with attention to detail. Restricted to resident guests.

**SAT NAV** *DL15 8BL* **ONLINE MAP**

Room General P

## FOULRIDGE, Lancashire Map ref 4B1

★★★
INN

B&B PER ROOM PER NIGHT
S £40.00–£50.00
D £50.00–£60.00

EVENING MEAL PER PERSON
£5.00–£15.00

### Hare & Hounds Foulridge

Skipton Old Road, Foulridge, Colne BB8 7PD **t** (01282) 864235 **e** cherylcrabtree@btconnect.com

**hare&houndsfoulridge.co.uk**

Personalised country hotel, family-owned, serving breakfast, lunch and dinner seven days per week. Licensed bar and restaurant, five spacious en suite bedrooms.

**open** All year
**bedrooms** 1 double, 3 twin, 1 family
**bathrooms** All en suite
**payment** Credit/debit cards, cash, cheques

Room General P Leisure

## GARSTANG, Lancashire Map ref 4A1

★★★
GUEST ACCOMMODATION

B&B PER ROOM PER NIGHT
S £30.00–£32.00
D £42.00–£44.00

### Ashdene

Parkside Lane, Nateby, Garstang PR3 0JA **t** (01995) 602676 **e** ashdene@supanet.com

**ashdenebedandbreakfast.gbr.cc**

Small, family-run bed and breakfast. All rooms have en suite facilities. Shops, laundry, public house nearby. On the edge of Garstang, Six miles from M6 junctions 31 and 32.

**open** All year
**bedrooms** 2 double, 1 twin
**bathrooms** All en suite
**payment** Cash, cheques

Room General P

## GARSTANG, Lancashire Map ref 4A1

★★★★
GUEST ACCOMMODATION

B&B PER ROOM PER NIGHT
S £51.56–£74.00
D £56.12–£80.00

EVENING MEAL PER PERSON
£5.00–£30.00

*Champagne weekend from £165. Sunday saver only £65 for 2 people, DB&B.*

### Guys Thatched Hamlet

Canalside, St Michael's Road, Bilsborrow, Preston PR3 0RS **t** (01995) 640010
**e** info@guysthatchedhamlet.com

**guysthatchedhamlet.com** SPECIAL OFFERS • REAL-TIME BOOKING

**open** All year except Christmas
**bedrooms** 48 double, 10 twin, 7 family
**bathrooms** All en suite
**payment** Credit/debit cards, cash, cheques

A canalside haven of thatched-roof buildings, just off the A6 at Bilsborrow near Garstang. Featuring Guy's Lodge, Owd Nell's Tavern, Guy's Restaurant and Pizzeria, craft shops, bowling green and cricket ground. Guy's Lodge offers rooms from only £52.00. Executive spa rooms and deluxe rooms available. All have Sky TV, tea/coffee etc.

**SAT NAV** *PR3 0RS* **ONLINE MAP**

Room General
Leisure

## GIGGLESWICK, North Yorkshire Map ref 5B3

★★★★
INN

B&B PER ROOM PER NIGHT
S £42.50–£50.00
D £55.00–£85.00

EVENING MEAL PER PERSON
£8.00–£20.00

WALKERS WELCOME · CYCLISTS WELCOME

### The Harts Head Inn

Belle Hill, Giggleswick, Settle BD24 0BA **t** (01729) 822086 **e** info@hartsheadinn.co.uk

**hartsheadinn.co.uk** GUEST REVIEWS • SPECIAL OFFERS • REAL-TIME BOOKING

Family-run inn offering quality food and accommodation. Beer garden, log fires, pool and other facilities. Cask ales and superb food.

**open** All year except Christmas
**bedrooms** 5 double, 2 twin, 2 single, 1 family
**bathrooms** All en suite
**payment** Credit/debit cards, cash, cheques

Room General Leisure

## GILSLAND, Cumbria Map ref 5B2

★★★★
GUEST ACCOMMODATION

B&B PER ROOM PER NIGHT
S £37.50
D £75.00

### Gilsland Spa

Gilsland, Brampton CA8 7AR **t** (01697) 747203

**gilslandspa.co.uk**

**open** All year
**bedrooms** 28 double, 49 twin, 13 single, 4 family
**bathrooms** All en suite
**payment** Credit/debit cards, cash, cheques

Situated in the heart of Roman Wall country, commanding spectacular views over the Cumbrian countryside. Many scenic walks to be found in the hotel's 140 acres of park and woodland. No age limit for children. Half-board rates available.

**SAT NAV** *CA8 7AR*

Room General Leisure

## Where can I get help and advice?

Tourist Information Centres offer friendly help with accommodation and holiday ideas as well as suggestions of places to visit and things to do. You'll find contact details at the beginning of each regional section.

## GOATHLAND, North Yorkshire Map ref 5D3

★★★★

**GUEST HOUSE**

**B&B PER ROOM PER NIGHT**
S £38.50–£50.00
D £77.00–£100.00

### Fairhaven Country Guest House

The Common, Goathland, Whitby YO22 5AN **t** (01947) 896361
**e** enquiries@fairhavencountryguesthouse.co.uk

**fairhavencountryguesthouse.co.uk** SPECIAL OFFERS

**open** All year except Christmas
**bedrooms** 4 double, 1 twin, 2 single, 1 family
**bathrooms** 7 en suite, 1 private
**payment** Credit/debit cards, cash, cheques

Edwardian country guesthouse set in the heart of the North York Moors National Park, in the picturesque village of Goathland. A warm welcome awaits you in comfortable and relaxed surroundings. Excellent breakfasts are served in our dining room with panoramic views of the surrounding countryside.

**SAT NAV** *YO22 5AN*

Room General

## GRANGE-OVER-SANDS, Cumbria Map ref 5A3

★★★★

**GUEST HOUSE**

**B&B PER ROOM PER NIGHT**
S £38.00–£48.00
D £68.00–£74.00

**EVENING MEAL PER PERSON**
£20.00–£25.00

### Greenacres Country Guesthouse

Lindale, Grange-over-Sands LA11 6LP **t** (015395) 34578 **e** greenacres.lindale@googlemail.com

**greenacres-lindale.co.uk**

**open** All year
**bedrooms** 2 double, 1 twin, 1 single, 1 family
**payment** Credit/debit cards, cash, cheques, euros

Friendly hospitality and quality service our pride. Tea and cakes on arrival. Excellent Cumbrian breakfasts await you in our attractive guesthouse. All bedrooms en suite. Comfortable conservatory and lounges with log fire. Ideal base for Lakeland attractions, ten miles from junction 36 of M6, Lake Windermere six miles, convenient for Morecambe Bay and the Dales.

**SAT NAV** *LA11 6LP*

Room General Leisure

## GRANGE-OVER-SANDS, Cumbria Map ref 5A3

★★★★

**GUEST ACCOMMODATION**

**B&B PER ROOM PER NIGHT**
S £36.00–£39.00
D £39.00–£45.00

**EVENING MEAL PER PERSON**
£10.50–£19.95

*Competitive rates available for 4 nights or more.*

### The Lymehurst

Kents Bank Road, Grange-over-Sands LA11 7EY **t** (015395) 33076 **e** enquiries@lymehurst.co.uk

**lymehurst.co.uk** GUEST REVIEWS · SPECIAL OFFERS · REAL-TIME BOOKING

**open** All year
**bedrooms** 5 double, 2 twin, 3 single
**bathrooms** All en suite
**payment** Credit/debit cards, cash

A beautiful Victorian building with a welcoming and peaceful atmosphere retaining many original features, in the centre of Grange-over-Sands, a charming town with many individual shops and cafes. Lymestone restaurant on the lower ground floor open for lunch every day with seasonal menus prepared by Master Chef of Great Britain Kevin Wyper.

**SAT NAV** *LA11 7EY* **ONLINE MAP**

Room General Leisure

### Where are the maps?

Colour maps can be found at the front of the guide. They pinpoint the location of all accommodation found in the regional sections.

## GRANTLEY, North Yorkshire Map ref 5C3

★★★★
FARMHOUSE

B&B PER ROOM PER NIGHT
S £50.00–£65.00
D £70.00–£80.00

### St Georges Court

Old Home Farm, Ripon HG4 3PJ **t** (01765) 620618 **e** stgeorgescourt@bronco.co.uk

**stgeorges-court.co.uk**

**open** All year
**bedrooms** 3 double, 1 twin, 1 family
**bathrooms** All en suite
**payment** Credit/debit cards, cash, cheques

Farmhouse B&B with five en suite rooms, all on ground level, situated around a pretty courtyard.

**SAT NAV** *HG4 3PJ*

Room General Leisure

## GRASSINGTON, North Yorkshire Map ref 5B3

★★★★★
GUEST ACCOMMODATION
GOLD AWARD

B&B PER ROOM PER NIGHT
D £85.00–£100.00

### Grassington Lodge

8 Wood Lane, Grassington, Skipton BD23 5LU **t** (01756) 752518 **e** relax@grassingtonlodge.co.uk

**grassingtonlodge.co.uk**

**open** All year
**bedrooms** 6 double, 5 twin, 1 suite
**bathrooms** 11 en suite, 1 private
**payment** Credit/debit cards, cash, cheques, euros

Grassington Lodge is a contemporary-styled, comfortable Victorian guesthouse in a quiet setting less than 100yds from the centre of Grassington, the capital village of Upper Wharfedale.

**SAT NAV** *BD23 5LU*

Room General 12 Leisure

## GRASSINGTON, North Yorkshire Map ref 5B3

★★★★
GUEST ACCOMMODATION

B&B PER ROOM PER NIGHT
D £62.00–£78.00

### New Laithe House

Wood Lane, Grassington, Skipton BD23 5LU **t** (01756) 752764 **e** enquiries@newlaithehouse.co.uk

**newlaithehouse.co.uk** GUEST REVIEWS

**bedrooms** 4 double, 1 twin, 1 family
**bathrooms** 4 en suite, 1 private
**payment** Cash, cheques, euros

Family-run guesthouse with spacious rooms. Situated in a quiet location in Grassington with lovely views over open countryside. Ideal base for walking, fishing and visiting the many historic towns in North and West Yorkshire. Large garden with private parking. Closed January to February.

**SAT NAV** *BD23 5LU* **ONLINE MAP**

Room General Leisure

## What if I need to cancel?

It's advisable to check the proprietor's cancellation policy at the time of booking in case you have to change your plans.

## GREAT AYTON, North Yorkshire Map ref 5C3

★★★★
GUEST ACCOMMODATION
SILVER AWARD

B&B PER ROOM PER NIGHT
S £59.50–£85.00
D £75.00–£99.50

EVENING MEAL PER PERSON
£10.00–£40.00

*Business rates available. Winter offers available, from 1 Oct – 31 Mar inclusive.*

### The Kings Head at Newton under Roseberry

The Green, Newton under Roseberry, Middlesbrough TS9 6QR **t** (01642) 722318
**e** info@kingsheadhotel.co.uk

**kingsheadhotel.co.uk** REAL-TIME BOOKING

**open** All year except Christmas and New Year
**bedrooms** 5 double, 1 twin, 1 single, 1 family
**bathrooms** All en suite
**payment** Credit/debit cards, cash, cheques

Tourism North East Bed and Breakfast of the Year 2005. Delightful family-owned hotel and restaurant, situated at the foot of Roseberry Topping. Individually designed, luxurious en suite bedrooms developed from two adjoining 18thC cottages oozing character and charm. Guest bedrooms are fitted with the latest facilities, and our restaurant serves a selection of freshly cooked dishes.

**SAT NAV** *TS9 6QR* **ONLINE MAP**

Room General Leisure

## GREAT ECCLESTON, Lancashire Map ref 4A1

★★★★
INN

B&B PER ROOM PER NIGHT
S £50.00–£85.00
D £70.00–£120.00

EVENING MEAL PER PERSON
£10.00–£25.00

*For details of our special promotions, please visit our website which will be updated on a regular basis.*

### The Cartford Inn

Cartford Lane, Little Eccleston, Nr Great Eccleston PR3 0YP **t** (01995) 670166
**e** info@thecartfordinn.co.uk

**thecartfordinn.co.uk** REAL-TIME BOOKING

**open** All year except Christmas Day
**bedrooms** 7 double
**bathrooms** All en suite
**payment** Credit/debit cards, cash, cheques, euros

An 17thC coaching inn, nestling on the banks of the river Wyre. Newly refurbished, it combines traditional charm with modern chic. Famous for its real ales, its delightful beer garden overlooks the river and surrounding countryside. Quality food is available in the bar and upstairs in 'Mushrooms' restaurant.

**SAT NAV** *PR3 0YP* **ONLINE MAP**

Room General Leisure

## GRINTON, North Yorkshire Map ref 5B3

★★★
INN

B&B PER ROOM PER NIGHT
S £46.00–£48.00
D £72.00–£76.00

EVENING MEAL PER PERSON
£7.95–£28.00

PETS! WELCOME!

### The Bridge Inn

Grinton, Reeth DL11 6HH **t** (01748) 884224 **e** atkinbridge@btinternet.com

**bridgeinngrinton.co.uk**

The Bridge Inn is situated on the banks of the beautiful River Swale in the heart of the Yorkshire Dales National Park. A former coaching inn dating back to the 13th century, it sits in the picturesque village of Grinton.

**open** All year
**bedrooms** 1 double/single, 2 double, 1 twin, 1 family
**bathrooms** All en suite
**payment** Credit/debit cards, cash, cheques

Room General Leisure

## It's all quality-assessed accommodation

Our commitment to quality involves wide-ranging accommodation assessment. Ratings and awards were correct at the time of going to press but may change following a new assessment. Please check at time of booking.

## GUISBOROUGH, Tees Valley Map ref 5C3

★★★
INN

B&B PER ROOM PER NIGHT
S Min £35.00
D Min £50.00

EVENING MEAL PER PERSON
Min £5.00

### Fox Inn

Bow Street, Guisborough TS14 6BP **t** (01287) 632958 **e** val.baines@btconnect.com

Situated in the ancient town of Guisborough, the Fox Inn is centrally located just off the main High Street. With newly and beautifully refurbished rooms, the Fox Inn is an excellent base from which to explore the local area.

**open** All year
**bedrooms** 4 double, 1 twin, 1 single, 2 family
**bathrooms** 6 en suite, 2 private
**payment** Credit/debit cards, cash, cheques

Room General P

## GUISBOROUGH, Tees Valley Map ref 5C3

★★
INN

B&B PER ROOM PER NIGHT
S Min £25.00
D Min £42.00

### Three Fiddles

34 Westgate, Guisborough TS14 6BA **t** (01287) 632417 **e** jill@hendersoncampbell.co.uk

Inn set in the market town of Guisborough, recently refurbished to a high standard with excellent quality of service.

**open** All year
**bedrooms** 1 double, 3 twin, 1 family
**payment** Credit/debit cards, cash, cheques

Room General

## HALTWHISTLE, Northumberland Map ref 5B2

★★★★
BED & BREAKFAST

B&B PER ROOM PER NIGHT
S £27.50–£45.00
D £56.00–£60.00

### Hall Meadows

Main Street, Haltwhistle NE49 0AZ **t** (01434) 321021 **e** richardhumes@tiscali.co.uk

**hallmeadows.co.uk**

Built in 1888, a large family house with pleasant garden in the centre of town. Ideally placed for Hadrian's Wall and close to bus and rail connections.

**open** All year except Christmas and New Year
**bedrooms** 2 double, 1 twin
**bathrooms** 2 en suite
**payment** Cash, cheques

Room General P

## HAMSTERLEY FOREST

*See under Barnard Castle*

## HARBOTTLE, Northumberland Map ref 5B1

★★★★
BED & BREAKFAST

B&B PER ROOM PER NIGHT
S £23.00–£25.00
D £46.00–£50.00

### Parsonside Bed & Breakfast

Newton Farm, Harbottle, Morpeth NE65 7DP **t** (01669) 650275 **e** carolyn.graham@harbottle.net

Parsonside is situated in the Upper Coquet Valley, close to Alwinton village. A peaceful setting with a large garden.

**open** All year except Christmas and New Year
**bedrooms** 1 double, 1 twin
**bathrooms** All en suite
**payment** Cash, cheques

Room General

## HARROGATE, North Yorkshire Map ref 4B1

★★★★
GUEST HOUSE

B&B PER ROOM PER NIGHT
S £38.00–£45.00
D £65.00–£70.00

### Alamah Guest House

88 Kings Road, Harrogate HG1 5JX **t** (01423) 502187 & (01423) 502187
**e** alamahguesthouse@btconnect.com

An ideal base from which to explore North Yorkshire. A short walk to Harrogate's stylish shops, restaurants, theatre, gardens and Harrogate International Conference Centre. Yorkshire's breathtaking countryside within a short drive.

**open** All year
**bedrooms** 2 double, 2 twin, 2 single, 1 family
**bathrooms** 6 en suite, 1 private
**payment** Credit/debit cards, cash, cheques

Room General 5 P

Where can I get live travel information?
For the latest travel update – call the RAC on 1740 from your mobile phone.

## HARROGATE, North Yorkshire Map ref 4B1

★★★★★ GUEST ACCOMMODATION GOLD AWARD

B&B PER ROOM PER NIGHT
D Min £80.00

EVENING MEAL PER PERSON
Min £15.00

### Cold Cotes

Cold Cotes Road, Felliscliffe, Harrogate HG3 2LW **t** (01423) 770937 **e** info@coldcotes.com

**coldcotes.com** GUEST REVIEWS

Situated in a tranquil, relaxing and beautiful setting on the edge of Nidderdale in the picturesque Yorkshire Dales. Cold Cotes is conveniently located for Harrogate, York and Leeds. Extensive gardens.

**open** All year
**bedrooms** 3 double, 1 twin, 1 suite
**bathrooms** All en suite
**payment** Credit/debit cards, cash, cheques

Room General 12 P

## HARROGATE, North Yorkshire Map ref 4B1

★★ GUEST HOUSE

B&B PER ROOM PER NIGHT
S £35.00–£40.00
D £65.00–£75.00

### Scotia Guest House

66 Kings Road, Harrogate HG1 5JR **t** (01423) 504361 **e** enquiries@scotiahotel.co.uk

**scotiahotel.co.uk**

Warm and friendly guesthouse opposite the conference centre within minutes of town and amenities. En suite bedrooms offering colour TV, telephone, tea/coffee and Wi-Fi internet. Free car parking.

**open** All year
**bedrooms** 2 double, 2 twin, 3 single
**bathrooms** 6 en suite, 1 private
**payment** Credit/debit cards, cash, cheques, euros

Room General P Leisure

## HAWES, North Yorkshire Map ref 5B3

★★★★★ GUEST HOUSE GOLD AWARD

B&B PER ROOM PER NIGHT
S £55.00–£100.00
D £90.00–£130.00

EVENING MEAL PER PERSON
£15.00–£25.00

*3 nights' B&B for the price of 2, Sun-Thu, Nov-Mar inclusive.*

### Rookhurst Country House

West End, Gayle, Hawes DL8 3RT **t** (01969) 667454 **e** enquiries@rookhurst.co.uk

**rookhurst.co.uk** SPECIAL OFFERS · REAL-TIME BOOKING

**open** All year except Christmas and New Year
**bedrooms** 4 double, 1 twin
**bathrooms** All en suite
**payment** Credit/debit cards, cash, cheques, euros

Relax, wind down and let us pamper you in our 'no smoking, no children' ambience. Enjoy a glass or two with dinner (food award). The house is part Victorian-Gothic and part 17th/18thC Dales farmhouse with many original features – oak and pine beams, tiled floor, open fire, carved stone and ironwork.

**SAT NAV** *DL8 3RT*

Room General 12 P Leisure

## HAWKSHEAD, Cumbria Map ref 5A3

★★★★ FARMHOUSE

B&B PER ROOM PER NIGHT
S £32.00–£38.00
D £27.00–£32.00

EVENING MEAL PER PERSON
£14.00

### Crosslands Farm

Rusland, Hawkshead LA22 8JU **t** (01229) 860242 **e** enquiries@crosslandsfarm.co.uk

**crosslandsfarm.co.uk**

**open** All year except Christmas
**bedrooms** 2 double, 1 twin
**bathrooms** 2 en suite, 1 private
**payment** Cash, cheques

Crosslands is a 17thC farmhouse with original features in the unspoilt valley of Rusland between the lakes of Windermere and Coniston. Perfect base for walking and cycling. Lots of lovely walks from the farm. Near Hawkshead, Grizedale Forest and all the lakeland hills. Plenty of parking. Great breakfast. Lovely views.

**SAT NAV** *LA22 8JU*

Room General P Leisure

## HAWKSHEAD, Cumbria Map ref 5A3

★★★★
GUEST HOUSE

B&B PER ROOM PER NIGHT
S £55.00–£60.00
D £110.00–£120.00

EVENING MEAL PER PERSON
£20.00–£35.00

### Ivy House & Restaurant

Main Street, Hawkshead LA22 0NS **t** (015394) 36204 **e** ivyhousehotel@btinternet.com

**ivyhousehotel.com**

**open** All year except Christmas
**bedrooms** 3 double, 1 twin, 2 family
**bathrooms** All en suite
**payment** Credit/debit cards, cash, cheques

Ivy House is an attractive Georgian house and a Grade II Listed building located in the centre of this attractive village. The Ivy House restaurant provides a beautiful setting to enjoy superbly cooked local produce.

**SAT NAV** *LA22 0NS*

Room General

## HAWORTH, West Yorkshire Map ref 4B1

★★
GUEST HOUSE

B&B PER ROOM PER NIGHT
S £25.00–£30.00
D £45.00–£55.00

### The Apothecary Guest House

86 Main Street, Haworth, Keighley BD22 8DP **t** (01535) 643642 **e** Nicholasapt@aol.com

**theapothecaryguesthouse.co.uk**

**open** All year
**bedrooms** 3 double, 2 twin, 1 single, 1 family
**bathrooms** All en suite
**payment** Credit/debit cards, cash, cheques

Friendly, family-run guesthouse at the top of Haworth Main Street, opposite the famous Brontë church. We are one minutes' walk from the Brontë Parsonage, and ten minutes' walk from the KWV Railway. All rooms are en suite, have colour TVs and tea-making facilities. Enjoy your stay!

**SAT NAV** *BD22 8DP*

Room General Leisure

## HAWORTH, West Yorkshire Map ref 4B1

★★★
GUEST ACCOMMODATION

B&B PER ROOM PER NIGHT
S £30.00–£40.00
D £50.00–£70.00

### The Bronte

Lees Lane, Haworth, Keighley BD22 8RA **t** (01535) 644112 **e** bookings@bronte-hotel.co.uk

**bronte-hotel.co.uk**

On the edge of the Moors, five minutes' walk from the station and 15 minutes' walk to the Parsonage, the former home of the Brontës.

**open** All year except Christmas
**bedrooms** 3 double, 1 twin, 4 single, 3 family
**bathrooms** 8 en suite
**payment** Credit/debit cards, cash, cheques

Room General

## HAWORTH, West Yorkshire Map ref 4B1

★★★★
GUEST ACCOMMODATION

B&B PER ROOM PER NIGHT
S £35.00–£45.00
D £70.00–£80.00

EVENING MEAL PER PERSON
£17.00

WALKERS WELCOME CYCLISTS WELCOME

### Rosebud Cottage

1 Belle Isle Road, Haworth BD22 8QQ **t** (01535) 640321 **e** info@rosebudcottage.co.uk

**rosebudcottage.co.uk** GUEST REVIEWS • SPECIAL OFFERS • REAL-TIME BOOKING

A traditional Yorkshire-stone cottage, deceptively spacious. All rooms are en suite, and all double rooms have a four-poster bed.

**open** All year except Christmas
**bedrooms** 3 double, 1 twin, 1 single
**bathrooms** All en suite
**payment** Credit/debit cards, cash, cheques

Room General

## HAYDON BRIDGE, Northumberland Map ref 5B2

★★★★
BED & BREAKFAST

B&B PER ROOM PER NIGHT
S £40.00–£45.00
D £70.00–£80.00

EVENING MEAL PER PERSON
£18.00–£20.00

### Grindon Cartshed

Haydon Bridge, Hexham NE47 6NQ **t** (01434) 684273 **e** cartshed@grindon.force9.co.uk

**grindon-cartshed.co.uk** REAL-TIME BOOKING

**open** All year
**bedrooms** 1 double, 2 twin
**bathrooms** All en suite
**payment** Credit/debit cards, cash, cheques

A warm welcome awaits at the beautifully converted cartshed, within walking distance of Hadrian's Wall. Ideal location for touring. Licensed and offering delicious meals prepared from local produce.

**SAT NAV** *NE47 6NQ* **ONLINE MAP**

WALKERS WELCOME CYCLISTS WELCOME

Room General Leisure

## HEBDEN, North Yorkshire Map ref 5B3

★★★
BED & BREAKFAST

B&B PER ROOM PER NIGHT
D £50.00–£70.00

### Court Croft

Church Lane, Hebden, Skipton BD23 5DX **t** (01756) 753406

Five-hundred-acre livestock farm. Farmhouse in village location close to the Dales Way. Ideal for touring the Dales, Nidderdale and Ribblesdale.

**open** All year
**bedrooms** 3 twin
**bathrooms** 2 en suite, 1 private
**payment** Cash, cheques

Room General Leisure

## HEBDEN BRIDGE, West Yorkshire Map ref 4B1

★★★★★
BED & BREAKFAST
GOLD AWARD

B&B PER ROOM PER NIGHT
S £55.00
D £70.00–£85.00

### Holme House

New Road, Hebden Bridge HX7 8AD **t** (01422) 847588 **e** mail@holmehousehebdenbridge.co.uk

**holmehousehebdenbridge.co.uk** GUEST REVIEWS

Magnificent Georgian house situated in the centre of Hebden Bridge. All bedrooms en suite. Close to shops and restaurants. Efficient, friendly service. Extensive breakfast menu. Private car park.

**open** All year
**bedrooms** 2 double, 1 twin
**bathrooms** All en suite
**payment** Credit/debit cards, cash, cheques

Room General Leisure

## HEDDON-ON-THE-WALL, Northumberland Map ref 5B2

★★★★
HOSTEL

B&B PER PERSON PER NIGHT
D £24.00-£40.00

### Houghton North Farm

Heddon-on-the-Wall NE15 0EZ **t** (01661) 854364 & 07708 419911
**e** wjlaws@btconnect.com

**houghtonnorthfarm.co.uk**

Comfortable, attractive, luxurious and spacious accommodation in converted barn setting. Bunk-style rooms, some en suite. Self-catering kitchen, luxurious lounge, courtyard. Internet, laundry, parking. Ideally situated on Hadrian's Wall.

**open** All year except Christmas
**bedrooms** 1 double, 1 twin, 1 triple, 4 quad
4 dormitories. Total no of beds 22
**bathrooms** 2 en suite, 2 public
**meals** Breakfast available
**payment** Credit/debit cards, cash/cheques

WALKERS WELCOME CYCLISTS WELCOME

Room General 8 Leisure

**Looking for a wide range of facilities?**
More stars means higher quality accommodation plus a greater range of facilities and services.

## HEXHAM, Northumberland Map ref 5B2

★★★★
FARMHOUSE

B&B PER ROOM PER NIGHT
S £30.00–£40.00
D £60.00–£90.00

EVENING MEAL PER PERSON
£12.00–£15.00

*Discounts on 4-day stays or more, excl Sat.*

### HallBarns B&B

Simonburn, Hexham NE48 3AQ **t** (01434) 681419 & 07788 998959
**e** enquiries@hallbarns-simonburn.co.uk

**hallbarns-simonburn.co.uk** SPECIAL OFFERS · REAL-TIME BOOKING

**open** All year
**bedrooms** 2 twin, 1 family
**bathrooms** 2 en suite, 1 private
**payment** Cash, cheques

A welcoming and friendly stay awaits you in a tranquil and peaceful setting with scenic views near Hadrian's Wall, the National Park and historic Corbridge. Garden in which to relax and enjoy the sunsets or have a barbecue. Comfortable lounge with log fire, quality en suite rooms. Hearty breakfast.

**SAT NAV** *NE48 3AQ* **ONLINE MAP**

Room General Leisure

## HEXHAM, Northumberland Map ref 5B2

★★★★
GUEST ACCOMMODATION

B&B PER ROOM PER NIGHT
S £35.00–£40.00
D £70.00–£80.00

### Loughbrow House

Dipton Mill Road, Hexham NE46 1RS **t** (01434) 603351 **e** patricia@loughbrow.fsnet.co.uk

**loughbrow.fsnet.co.uk**

**open** All year except Christmas and New Year
**bedrooms** 2 double, 2 twin, 2 single
**bathrooms** 3 en suite, 2 private
**payment** Cash, cheques

Standing 600ft above the River Tyne and set in nine acres of garden. The house, built in 1780, is comfortably furnished with antique furniture, where all are given a friendly welcome and are well fed, using mostly local produce from the estate. Within easy distance of the Lake District, Durham and National Trust properties.

**SAT NAV** *NE46 1RS*

Room General 5 Leisure

## HOLMFIRTH, West Yorkshire Map ref 4B1

★★★
GUEST ACCOMMODATION

B&B PER ROOM PER NIGHT
S £34.00
D £56.00

### Elephant and Castle

Hollowgate, Huddersfield HD9 2DG **t** (01484) 683178

Situated in the heart of the Pennines, a traditional local with a friendly welcoming atmosphere. The rooms are all centrally heated and en suite.

**open** All year
**bedrooms** 2 double, 1 twin, 1 family
**bathrooms** All en suite
**payment** Credit/debit cards, cash, cheques

Room General

## HOLMFIRTH, West Yorkshire Map ref 4B1

★★★★★
GUEST ACCOMMODATION
GOLD AWARD

B&B PER ROOM PER NIGHT
D £65.00–£100.00

### Sunnybank Guesthouse

78 Upperthong Lane, Holmfirth HD9 3BQ **t** (01484) 684857 **e** info@sunnybankguesthouse.co.uk

**sunnybankguesthouse.co.uk** GUEST REVIEWS · SPECIAL OFFERS · REAL-TIME BOOKING

An elegant Victorian house in large wooded gardens near the centre of Holmfirth yet overlooking the countryside, as seen on the BBC's 'Last of the Summer Wine'. Attractive, stylish, with a welcoming atmosphere.

**open** All year except Christmas and New Year
**bedrooms** 2 double, 1 family
**bathrooms** All en suite
**payment** Credit/debit cards, cash, cheques, euros

Room General 8 Leisure

## HUDDERSFIELD, West Yorkshire Map ref 4B1

★★★
GUEST ACCOMMODATION

B&B PER ROOM PER NIGHT
S £40.00
D £50.00

### Cambridge Lodge

4 Clare Hill, Huddersfield HD1 5BS **t** (01484) 519892 **e** cambridge.lodge.hudd@btconnect.com

**cambridgelodge.co.uk**

Thirty-four en suite rooms with tea-/coffee-making facilities, telephones, colour TV. Free parking. Less than 0.5 miles from train and bus station. Easy to find on Clare Hill off St Johns Road.

**open** All year
**bedrooms** 11 double, 7 twin, 12 single, 4 family
**bathrooms** All en suite
**payment** Credit/debit cards, cash, cheques, euros

Room General

## HUDDERSFIELD, West Yorkshire Map ref 4B1

★★★★
GUEST ACCOMMODATION
SILVER AWARD

B&B PER ROOM PER NIGHT
S £47.00–£55.00
D £65.00

*Discounts available for long-stay or group bookings. Company accounts can be arranged. Self-catering rooms with kitchenettes available.*

### Huddersfield Central Lodge

11-15 Beast Market, Huddersfield HD1 1QF **t** (01484) 515551 **e** enquiries@centrallodge.com

**centrallodge.com** GUEST REVIEWS

**open** All year
**bedrooms** 7 double, 7 twin, 4 single, 4 family
**bathrooms** All en suite
**payment** Credit/debit cards, cash, cheques

The Huddersfield Central Lodge is family owned and managed. All rooms are fully en suite. Free Sky channels, free, secure, on-site, overnight parking. Fully licensed bar in refurbished lounge area. Large, newly constructed conservatory. Within five minutes' walk are the Kingsgate Shopping Centre, theatre, bus and train stations.

**SAT NAV** *HD1 1QF* **ONLINE MAP**

Room General

## HUDDERSFIELD, West Yorkshire Map ref 4B1

★★★
CAMPUS

PER PERSON PER NIGHT
BED ONLY £25.00
B&B £30.00

PER PERSON PER WEEK
HB £190.00-£230.00
FB £220.00-£250.00

*Perfect for holidays, training and team-building courses, away days, and residential conferences. Special discounted rates for large group bookings.*

### Storthes Hall Park

Storthes Hall Lane, Kirkburton, Huddersfield HD8 0WA **t** (01484) 488820

**campusdigs.com**

**open** July to September
**bedrooms** 1365 single, 52 double/twin
Total no of beds 1417
**bathrooms** 1417 en suite
**meals** Breakfast, lunch and evening meals available
**payment** Credit/debit cards, cash/cheques

With prices starting from just £25.00 per night, we offer quality accommodation at amazing prices. Purpose-built adult/student accommodation. Lounge, shop, bar, gym, sports and conferencing facilities all on site. A wide variety of packages available from self-catering to full board for any size of group.

**SAT NAV** *HD8 0WA*

Room General Leisure

## Remember to check when booking

Please remember that all information in this guide has been supplied by the proprietors well in advance of publication. Since changes do sometimes occur it's a good idea to check details at the time of booking.

## INGLETON, North Yorkshire Map ref 5B3

★★★★
GUEST ACCOMMODATION

B&B PER ROOM PER NIGHT
s £33.00–£35.00
d £50.00–£54.00

*Special terms for 2 or more days: single £33, double £54. B&B £171pp weekly. Weekly single supplement £56.*

### Springfield Country Guest House

26 Main Street, Ingleton, Carnforth LA6 3HJ **t** (015242) 41280

**destination-england.co.uk/springfield.html**

**open** All year except Christmas and New Year
**bedrooms** 2 double, 1 twin, 1 single, 1 family
**bathrooms** All en suite
**payment** Credit/debit cards, cash, cheques

Detached Victorian villa, large garden with patio down to River Greta. Home-grown vegetables in season, home cooking. Private fishing. Pets welcome. All credit cards are accepted.

**SAT NAV** *LA6 3HJ*

Room General P Leisure

## INSKIP, Lancashire Map ref 4A1

★★★
FARMHOUSE

B&B PER ROOM PER NIGHT
s Min £35.00
d Min £60.00

### Chesham Hill B&B

Pinfold Lane, Inskip, Preston PR4 0UA **t** (01995) 679424

**cheshamhillfarm.co.uk**

We are a working farm in lovely countryside offering two comfortable en suite double rooms, close to main traffic routes. We also have a delightful tearoom using local produce and home baking.

**open** All year
**bedrooms** 2 double
**bathrooms** All en suite
**payment** Cash, cheques

Room General P Leisure

## IRTHINGTON, Cumbria Map ref 5B2

★★★
FARMHOUSE

B&B PER ROOM PER NIGHT
s £35.00
d Min £56.00

EVENING MEAL PER PERSON
£8.00–£12.00

### Newtown Farm

Newtown, Irthington, Carlisle CA6 4NX **t** (01697) 72768 **e** susangrice@tiscali.co.uk

**newtownfarmbedandbreakfast.co.uk**

Susan and Malcolm welcome you to Newtown Farm bed and breakfast, a family-run working farm located on Hadrian's Wall Path. An ideal resting place for your visit to the Highlands.

**open** All year except Christmas and New Year
**bedrooms** 1 double, 1 family
**bathrooms** All en suite
**payment** Cash, cheques

Room General P Leisure

## KENDAL, Cumbria Map ref 5B3

★★★★
BED & BREAKFAST

B&B PER ROOM PER NIGHT
s £40.00–£45.00
d £70.00–£80.00

### Burrow Hall

Plantation Bridge, Kendal LA8 9JR **t** (01539) 821711 **e** burrow.hall@virgin.net

**burrowhall.co.uk** REAL-TIME BOOKING

**open** All year except Christmas
**bedrooms** 2 double, 1 twin, 1 family
**bathrooms** All en suite
**payment** Credit/debit cards, cash, cheques

Tastefully furnished, 17thC Lakeland house enjoying modern-day comforts. Sits peacefully in idyllic South Lakeland countryside between Kendal and Windermere, on A591. Ideal stopover for Scotland. Ample, safe parking.

**SAT NAV** *LA8 9JR* **ONLINE MAP**

Room General 12 P Leisure

## KENDAL, Cumbria Map ref 5B3

★★★★ GUEST HOUSE

B&B PER ROOM PER NIGHT
D £60.00–£80.00

# The Glen

Oxenholme, Kendal LA9 7RF **t** (01539) 726386 & 07743 604599 **e** greenintheglen@btinternet.com

**glen-kendal.co.uk**

The Glen is in a quiet location under the Helm (local walk and view point), but within walking distance of inn and restaurant. Relax in the hot tub after a day's touring!

**open** All year
**bedrooms** 2 double, 1 twin, 2 family, 1 suite
**bathrooms** All en suite
**payment** Credit/debit cards, cash, cheques

PETS! WELCOME

Room General P Leisure

## KERMINCHAM, Cheshire Map ref 4B2

★★★★ FARMHOUSE

B&B PER ROOM PER NIGHT
S £35.00–£40.00
D £70.00–£80.00

EVENING MEAL PER PERSON
£12.00–£25.00

# The Fields Farm

Forty Acre Lane, Crewe CW4 8DY **t** (01477) 571224

**theenglishdiningroom.co.uk** GUEST REVIEWS

Quality accommodation in English country house. Ideal for business people, families and small groups. Cordon bleu evening meal available. Ideally located for opera, market towns and attractions.

**open** All year
**bedrooms** 2 double, 1 twin, 1 single
**bathrooms** 2 en suite, 2 private
**payment** Cash, cheques, euros

Room General P Leisure

## KESWICK, Cumbria Map ref 5A3

★★★★ GUEST HOUSE SILVER AWARD

B&B PER ROOM PER NIGHT
S £55.00–£60.00
D £66.00–£80.00

# Acorn House

Ambleside Road, Keswick CA12 4DL **t** (017687) 72553 **e** info@acornhousehotel.co.uk

**acornhousehotel.co.uk**

**open** All year except Christmas
**bedrooms** 7 double, 2 family
**bathrooms** All en suite
**payment** Credit/debit cards, cash, cheques

Detached Georgian house quietly situated close to town centre with private car park and well-maintained gardens. Friendly and relaxed atmosphere with traditional furniture and individually styled bedrooms with four-poster rooms available. Acorn House prides itself on providing its guests with a hearty Lakeland breakfast and a warm welcome.

**SAT NAV** *CA12 4DL*

Room General 6 P

## KESWICK, Cumbria Map ref 5A3

★★★★ GUEST HOUSE

B&B PER ROOM PER NIGHT
S £35.00–£40.00
D £60.00–£75.00

# Appletrees

The Heads, Keswick CA12 5ER **t** (017687) 80400 **e** john@armstrong2001.fsnet.co.uk

**appletreeskeswick.com**

**open** All year except Christmas
**bedrooms** 5 double, 1 twin, 1 single
**bathrooms** All en suite
**payment** Credit/debit cards, cash, cheques

Strictly non-smoking. Appletrees is a spacious Victorian house with spectacular views over Crow Park, Borrowdale Valley and Derwentwater to the south and Skiddaw and Latrigg to the north. Friendly hosts, full English and vegetarian breakfasts, limited parking. Ideal location close to town centre, lake, park and theatre.

**SAT NAV** *CA12 5ER*

WALKERS WELCOME

Room General 3 P Leisure

## KESWICK, Cumbria Map ref 5A3

★★★★
GUEST ACCOMMODATION

B&B PER ROOM PER NIGHT
S £32.00–£36.00
D £64.00–£72.00

*Weekly B&B rate from £210.*

# Avondale Guest House

20 Southey Street, Keswick CA12 4EF **t** (017687) 72735 **e** enquiries@avondaleguesthouse.com

**avondaleguesthouse.com** SPECIAL OFFERS

**open** All year
**bedrooms** 4 double, 1 twin, 1 single
**bathrooms** All en suite
**payment** Credit/debit cards, cash, cheques

Comfortable Victorian guesthouse with well-appointed, en suite rooms. Close to town centre, theatre, lake and parks. Excellent English and vegetarian breakfasts. In our guest lounge you can just relax and chat to fellow guests or read from the choice of books and magazines. Non-smokers only please.

**SAT NAV** *CA12 4EF* **ONLINE MAP**

Room General 12 Leisure

## KESWICK, Cumbria Map ref 5A3

★★★★
GUEST HOUSE
SILVER AWARD

B&B PER ROOM PER NIGHT
S Min £31.00
D Min £60.00

# Badgers Wood

30 Stanger Street, Keswick CA12 5JU **t** (017687) 72621 **e** ctb@badgers-wood.co.uk

**badgers-wood.co.uk**

**bedrooms** 3 double, 1 twin, 2 single
**bathrooms** All en suite
**payment** Cash, cheques

Award-winning and charmingly restored Victorian guesthouse situated in a quiet cul-de-sac just a two-minute walk from the heart of the town and the bus station. Totally refurbished bedrooms and new en suite facilities, all with colour TVs, tea/coffee facilities and views towards the surrounding fells. Special diets catered for. Maps/guidebooks available. Closed Christmas. Open New Year.

**SAT NAV** *CA12 5JU*

Room General 10 Leisure

## KESWICK, Cumbria Map ref 5A3

★★★★
GUEST HOUSE

B&B PER ROOM PER NIGHT
D £60.00–£90.00

# Burleigh Mead

The Heads, Keswick CA12 5ER **t** (017687) 75935 **e** info@burleighmead.co.uk

**burleighmead.co.uk**

Conveniently situated between town centre and Derwentwater, our charming Victorian house offers excellent accommodation with outstanding views of surrounding fells.

**open** All year except Christmas and New Year
**bedrooms** 2 double, 2 twin, 2 family
**bathrooms** All en suite
**payment** Cash, cheques

Room General P Leisure

## KESWICK, Cumbria Map ref 5A3

CAMPING BARN

B&B PER PERSON PER NIGHT
s £10.00-£11.00

### Fisher-Gill Camping Barn

Stybeck Farm Experience, Thirlmere, Keswick CA12 4TN **t** (017687) 73232
**e** stybeckfarm@farming.co.uk

**members.farmline.com/stybeckfarm**

Situated in central Lake District. Walks from the barn, easy access and ample parking. Lovely scenery. Camping barn with kitchen/dinner room. Bunk room sleeping ten (curtains for semi-privacy), shower room, wc/washbasin.

**open** All year
**bedrooms** 1 dormitory. Total no of beds 10
**bathrooms** 1 public
**payment** Cash/cheques

Room General P Leisure

## KESWICK, Cumbria Map ref 5A3

★★★★★
GUEST HOUSE
SILVER AWARD

B&B PER ROOM PER NIGHT
s £72.00–£86.00
D £90.00–£106.00

*Special rates are normally available for a stay of three or more nights, please contact us to find out more.*

### The Grange Country House

Manor Brow, Ambleside Road, Keswick CA12 4BA **t** (017687) 72500 **e** info@grangekeswick.com

**grangekeswick.com** GUEST REVIEWS • SPECIAL OFFERS • REAL-TIME BOOKING

**open** All year except mid-December to early February
**bedrooms** 6 double, 3 twin, 1 single
**bathrooms** All en suite
**payment** Credit/debit cards, cash, cheques

Spacious rooms, beautifully decorated, furnished with quality bedding, flat-screen televisions, Fairtrade beverage trays, mineral water and super toiletries. Superb freshly prepared Cumbrian breakfast, free 24-hour Wi-Fi access, lounge and scenic outdoor terrace. Ample off-street parking.

**SAT NAV** *CA12 4BA* **ONLINE MAP**

Room TV SC General 10 P Leisure

## KESWICK, Cumbria Map ref 5A3

★★★★
GUEST HOUSE

B&B PER ROOM PER NIGHT
s £30.00–£31.00
D £62.00–£64.00

EVENING MEAL PER PERSON
£16.00–£16.50

### Lindisfarne House

21 Church Street, Keswick CA12 4DX **t** (017687) 73218 **e** alison230@btinternet.com

**lindisfarnehouse.com**

Close to town centre, lake and parks. We cater for vegetarians, vegans and people with special diets. Our minimum age for children is two years.

**open** All year
**bedrooms** 3 single, 3 double, 1 double/twin/family
**bathrooms** 4 en suite, 2 private
**payment** Credit/debit cards, cash, cheques

Room TV General 2

## KESWICK, Cumbria Map ref 5A3

★★★
FARMHOUSE

B&B PER ROOM PER NIGHT
S £34.00–£40.00
D £68.00–£80.00

### Littletown Farm

Newlands, Keswick CA12 5TU **t** (017687) 78353 **e** info@littletownfarm.co.uk

**littletownfarm.co.uk**

**bedrooms** 4 double, 2 twin, 2 family
**bathrooms** 6 en suite, 2 private
**payment** Credit/debit cards, cash, cheques

A 150-acre mixed farm in the beautiful, unspoilt Newlands Valley. The perfect place for hard or leisurely walking, relaxing round lakes Derwent and Buttermere, or strolling around the market towns of Keswick and Cockermouth. Breakfast comprises a selection of fruits and cereals followed by our famous farmhouse grill, to keep you going all day.

**SAT NAV** *CA12 5TU*

Room General P Leisure

## KESWICK, Cumbria Map ref 5A3

★★★
GUEST HOUSE

B&B PER ROOM PER NIGHT
D £58.00–£80.00

EVENING MEAL PER PERSON
£4.50–£8.00

*Weekend breaks from £52.00-£70.00 pppn B&B (full rates apply Bank Holidays). Minimum 2 nights, children half price.*

### Newlands Fell Guesthouse

Newlands Valley, Keswick CA12 5TS **t** (017687) 78477 **e** kelly.wood8@btinternet.com

**lakedistrict-bandb.co.uk** GUEST REVIEWS • SPECIAL OFFERS • REAL-TIME BOOKING

**open** All year
**bedrooms** 4 double, 1 twin, 1 family
**bathrooms** All en suite
**payment** Credit/debit cards, cash, cheques

Newlands Fell Guest House on the Newlands Valley is a traditional Lakeland property full of charm and character. Situated in a quiet location ten minutes from Keswick and ten minutes from Buttermere village with stunning views right outside your window as far as the eye can see. We look forward to hearing from you soon.

**SAT NAV** *CA12 5TS* **ONLINE MAP**

Room TV General P Leisure

## KESWICK, Cumbria Map ref 5A3

★★★★
GUEST HOUSE

B&B PER ROOM PER NIGHT
S £25.00–£35.00
D £50.00–£70.00

### Sandon Guesthouse

13 Southey Street, Keswick CA12 4EG **t** (017687) 73648 **e** enquiries@sandonguesthouse.com

**sandonguesthouse.com**

Charming Lakeland-stone Victorian guesthouse, conveniently situated for town, theatre or lake. Friendly, comfortable accommodation. Ideal base for walking or cycling holidays. Superb English breakfast.

**open** All year except Christmas
**bedrooms** 3 double, 1 twin, 2 single
**bathrooms** 5 en suite, 1 private
**payment** Credit/debit cards, cash, cheques

Room TV General 4 Leisure

## KIELDER, Northumberland Map ref 5B1

★★
BED & BREAKFAST

B&B PER ROOM PER NIGHT
S £30.00–£35.00
D £64.00–£70.00

EVENING MEAL PER PERSON
£6.50–£15.00

### Twenty Seven

27 Castle Drive, Kielder, Hexham NE48 1EQ **t** (01434) 250462 & (01434) 250366
**e** twentyseven@staykielder.co.uk

**staykielder.co.uk** SPECIAL OFFERS

Twenty Seven offers three rooms, bed and breakfast, evening meals on request, TV, tea-/coffee-making facilities. Dining room/lounge, with wood-burning stove. Cyclists, walkers and dogs welcome. Laundry facilities and secure bike storage.

**open** All year
**bedrooms** 1 twin, 1 single, 1 family
**bathrooms** 1 en suite
**payment** Cash, cheques

Room General Leisure

## KIELDER FOREST

*See under Kielder, Kielder Water, Wark, West Woodburn*

## KIELDER WATER, Northumberland Map ref 5B2

★★★★
INN
SILVER AWARD

B&B PER ROOM PER NIGHT
S £50.00–£55.00
D £85.00–£90.00

EVENING MEAL PER PERSON
£8.25–£14.50

*Reduced rates 1 Nov-30 Apr, DB&B £65pppn.*

### The Pheasant Inn (by Kielder Water)

Stannersburn, Hexham NE48 1DD **t** (01434) 240382 **e** enquiries@thepheasantinn.com

**thepheasantinn.com**

**open** All year except Christmas
**bedrooms** 4 double, 3 twin, 1 family
**bathrooms** All en suite
**payment** Credit/debit cards, cash, cheques

Charming 16thC inn, retaining its character while providing comfortable, modern, en suite accommodation. Stone walls and low-beamed ceilings in the bars, antique artefacts and open fires. Traditional home cooking, using fresh vegetables, served in bar or dining room. Renowned Sunday roasts. Closed Monday and Tuesday between November and March.

**SAT NAV** *NE48 1DD*

Room General Leisure

## KIRKBY LONSDALE, Cumbria Map ref 5B3

★★
GUEST ACCOMMODATION

B&B PER ROOM PER NIGHT
S £28.00
D £41.00–£48.00

EVENING MEAL PER PERSON
£5.50–£9.00

*Seven nights B&B for the price of six.*

### Copper Kettle Restaurant & Guest House

3-5 Market Street, Kirkby Lonsdale, Carnforth LA6 2AU **t** (015242) 71714

**open** All year
**bedrooms** 3 double, 1 twin, 1 family
**bathrooms** 3 en suite, 2 private
**payment** Credit/debit cards, cash, cheques, euros

Part of an old manor house, built in 1610, on the border between the Yorkshire Dales and the Lakes. Very handy for shops, enjoying yourself and walking days out at Lakes, or travel to Yorkshire Dales or seaside.

**SAT NAV** *LA6 2AU*

Room General

WALKERS WELCOME

## Do you like walking?

Walkers feel at home in accommodation participating in our Walkers Welcome scheme. Look out for the symbol. Consider walking all or part of a long-distance route – go online at nationaltrail.co.uk.

## KIRKBY LONSDALE, Cumbria Map ref 5B3

★★★★
GUEST ACCOMMODATION

B&B PER ROOM PER NIGHT
S £28.00–£35.00
D £50.00–£56.00

*Stay 3 nights or more and receive a 10% discount (excl Bank Holidays).*

### Ullathorns Farm

Middleton, Kirkby Lonsdale, Carnforth LA6 2LZ **t** (015242) 76214 & 07800 990689
**e** pauline@ullathorns.co.uk

**ullathorns.co.uk** SPECIAL OFFERS

**open** All year except Christmas and New Year
**bedrooms** 1 double, 1 family
**bathrooms** All en suite
**payment** Cash, cheques

A warm welcome awaits you at Ullathorns, a working farm situated in the unspoilt Lune Valley midway between Sedbergh and Kirkby Lonsdale. An ideal touring base for lakes and dales. Good overnight stopping-off point, situated between junctions of the M6. Refreshments served upon arrival. Individual breakfast tables.

**SAT NAV** *LA6 2LZ* **ONLINE MAP**

Room General Leisure

## KIRKBYMOORSIDE, North Yorkshire Map ref 5C3

★★★★
GUEST HOUSE
SILVER AWARD

B&B PER ROOM PER NIGHT
D £75.00–£110.00

EVENING MEAL PER PERSON
Min £30.00

### The Cornmill

Kirby Mills, Kirkbymoorside, York YO62 6NP **t** (01751) 432000 **e** cornmill@kirbymills.demon.co.uk

**kirbymills.demon.co.uk**

**open** All year
**bedrooms** 4 double, 1 twin
**bathrooms** All en suite
**payment** Credit/debit cards, cash, cheques

Converted 18thC watermill and Victorian farmhouse providing well-appointed bed and breakfast accommodation on the River Dove. Bedrooms (two with four-posters), lounge, wood-burning stove and bootroom are in the farmhouse. Sumptuous breakfasts and pre-booked group dinners are served in the mill, with viewing panel in the floor.

**SAT NAV** *YO62 6NP*

Room General Leisure

## KNARESBOROUGH, North Yorkshire Map ref 4B1

★★★★★
GUEST HOUSE

B&B PER ROOM PER NIGHT
S Min £75.00
D Min £110.00

EVENING MEAL PER PERSON
Min £27.00

*Discounts are available for stays of 3 or more nights. Special midweek DB&B rates.*

### Gallon House

47 Kirkgate, Knaresborough HG5 8BZ **t** (01423) 862102 **e** gallon-house@ntlworld.com

**gallon-house.co.uk**

**open** All year except Christmas and New Year
**bedrooms** 2 double, 1 twin
**bathrooms** All en suite
**payment** Cash, cheques

Overlooking the beautiful Nidd Gorge, Gallon House offers award-winning accommodation and mouthwatering, locally sourced fresh food. Recognised as a unique, special hotel, Gallon House offers individual service in a breathtaking setting. A recent guest said: 'thank you for making your special place our special place too.'

**SAT NAV** *HG5 8BZ*

Room General Leisure

### What shall we do today?

For ideas on places to visit, see the beginning of this regional section or go online at enjoyengland.com.

## KNUTSFORD, Cheshire Map ref 4A2

★★★
GUEST ACCOMMODATION

B&B PER ROOM PER NIGHT
S £30.00–£45.00
D £40.00–£60.00

### Moat Hall Motel

Chelford Road, Marthall, Knutsford WA16 8SU **t** (01625) 860367 **e** val@moathall.fsnet.co.uk

**moat-hall-motel.co.uk**

**open** All year
**bedrooms** 2 double, 2 twin, 1 single, 1 family
**bathrooms** All en suite
**payment** Credit/debit cards, cash, cheques

Attractive accommodation on Cheshire farm, six miles from Manchester Airport. Knutsford three miles (M6 junction 19). All rooms en suite with TV, microwave and fridge. Suitable for business and touring guests.

**SAT NAV** *WA16 8SU*

Room General

## LEEDS, West Yorkshire Map ref 4B1

★★★★
GUEST HOUSE

B&B PER ROOM PER NIGHT
S £30.00–£40.00
D £45.00–£50.00

### Avalon Guest House

132 Woodsley Road, Leeds LS2 9LZ **t** (0113) 243 2545 **e** info@woodsleyroad.com

**avalonguesthouseleeds.co.uk**

Superbly decorated Victorian establishment close to the university and Leeds General Infirmary. Less than one mile from the city centre. Most of the rooms have en suite facilities.

**open** All year
**bedrooms** 5 double, 2 twin, 6 single, 2 family
**bathrooms** 10 en suite
**payment** Credit/debit cards, cash, cheques, euros

Room General

## LEEDS, West Yorkshire Map ref 4B1

★★
GUEST HOUSE

B&B PER ROOM PER NIGHT
S £30.00–£45.00
D £55.00–£59.00

### City Centre Guest House

51a New Briggate, Leeds LS2 8JD **t** (0113) 242 9019 **e** info@leedscitycentrehotel.com

**citycentrehotelleeds.co.uk**

Family-run hotel in the heart of the city opposite Grand Theatre and close to all major shops, restaurants and nightlife.

**open** All year
**bedrooms** 3 double, 2 twin, 4 single, 3 family
**bathrooms** 9 en suite
**payment** Credit/debit cards, cash, cheques

Room General

## LEEDS, West Yorkshire Map ref 4B1

★★★
GUEST HOUSE

B&B PER ROOM PER NIGHT
S £30.00–£40.00
D £45.00–£50.00

### The Glengarth

162 Woodsley Road, Leeds LS2 9LZ **t** (0113) 245 7940 **e** info@woodsleyroad.com

**glengarthhotel.co.uk**

Attractive, clean, family-run hotel close to city centre, university and city hospital. Twenty minutes from Leeds City Airport. Easy access to M1 and M62. Most of the rooms have en suite facilities and colour TV.

**open** All year
**bedrooms** 6 double, 3 twin, 2 single, 3 family
**bathrooms** 8 en suite
**payment** Credit/debit cards, cash, cheques, euros

Room General

PETS! WELCOME WELCOME PETS!

## Where is my pet welcome?

Want to take your cherished companion with you on holiday? Proprietors participating in our Welcome Pets! scheme go out of their way to make special provision for you and your pet. Look out for the symbol.

## LEEDS, West Yorkshire Map ref 4B1

★★
GUEST ACCOMMODATION

B&B PER ROOM PER NIGHT
S £34.00–£44.00
D £48.00–£60.00

EVENING MEAL PER PERSON
£6.00–£10.00

*Special three-night weekend stay. Double en suite £54pn incl breakfast.*

### The Moorlea

146 Woodsley Road, Leeds LS2 9LZ **t** (0113) 243 2653 **e** themoorleahotel@aol.com

**open** All year
**bedrooms** 3 double, 1 twin, 5 single, 2 family
**bathrooms** 6 en suite
**payment** Credit/debit cards, cash, cheques

Five minutes from the university and 15 minutes from the city centre. Friendly atmosphere and fully licensed bar. Quality cooked English breakfasts. Two miles from Test Match cricket ground in Headingley.

**SAT NAV** *LS2 9LZ*

Room General

## LEEDS, West Yorkshire Map ref 4B1

★★★
GUEST HOUSE

B&B PER ROOM PER NIGHT
S £27.00–£37.00
D £40.00–£50.00

### St Michael's Guest House

5 St Michael's Villas, Cardigan Road, Leeds LS6 3AF **t** (0113) 275 5557
**e** stmichaels-guesthouse@hotmail.co.uk

**stmichaels-guesthouse.co.uk**

Well-presented B&B, 1.5 miles from city centre and close to Headingley Cricket Ground and university. Easy access to Headingley and the city centre. Warm welcome from friendly staff.

**open** All year except Christmas and New Year
**bedrooms** 8 double, 6 twin, 8 single, 2 family
**bathrooms** 13 en suite
**payment** Credit/debit cards, cash, cheques

Room General P

## LEEDS BRADFORD INTERNATIONAL AIRPORT

*See under Bradford, Leeds*

## LEYBURN, North Yorkshire Map ref 5B3

★★★★
GUEST ACCOMMODATION
SILVER AWARD

B&B PER ROOM PER NIGHT
S £35.00–£45.00
D £60.00–£75.00

### Clyde House

5 Railway Street, Leyburn DL8 5AY **t** (01969) 623941 **e** lucia.fisher1@btinternet.com

**clydehouseleyburn.co.uk** SPECIAL OFFERS

Clyde House is a stylish, furnished, period house with a lovely garden and beautiful views. Its position off the main market square offers easy access to many excellent eateries.

**open** All year
**bedrooms** 3 double, 2 twin, 1 single
**bathrooms** All en suite
**payment** Credit/debit cards, cash, cheques

Room General 12 Leisure

## LITTLE BOLLINGTON, Greater Manchester Map ref 4A2

★★
BED & BREAKFAST

B&B PER ROOM PER NIGHT
S £25.00–£30.00
D £45.00–£50.00

### Bollington Hall Farm

Park Lane, Little Bollington, Altrincham WA14 4TJ **t** (0161) 928 1760

18thC Georgian farmhouse, family-run, comfortable rooms with exceptional views overlooking Dunham Hall, superb, quiet location, outstanding hospitality and good food. Pub within five minutes' walk for evening meals.

**open** All year except Christmas and New Year
**bedrooms** 1 single, 2 family
**payment** Cash, cheques, euros

Room General P Leisure

### B&B prices

Rates for bed and breakfast are shown per room per night.
Double room prices are usually based on two people sharing the room.

## LIVERPOOL, Merseyside Map ref 4A2

★★★
GUEST ACCOMMODATION

B&B PER ROOM PER NIGHT
S £35.00–£45.00
D £54.00–£65.00

### Aachen

89-91 Mount Pleasant, Liverpool L3 5TB **t** (0151) 709 3477 **e** enquiries@aachenhotel.co.uk

**aachenhotel.co.uk**

**open** All year except Christmas
**bedrooms** 5 double, 5 twin, 2 single, 4 family
**bathrooms** 9 en suite
**payment** Credit/debit cards, cash, cheques

Award-winning hotel situated in the heart of the city convenient for all road, rail and air links. Within walking distance of all attractions, and famous for the 'Eat as much as you like' breakfast. Late bar.

**SAT NAV** *L3 5TB*

Room General

## LIVERPOOL, Merseyside Map ref 4A2

★★★
GUEST ACCOMMODATION

B&B PER ROOM PER NIGHT
S £21.00–£28.00
D £48.00–£59.00

### Holme-Leigh Guest House

93 Woodcroft Road, Wavertree, Liverpool L15 2HG **t** (0151) 734 2216 **e** info@holmeleigh.com

**holmeleigh.com** GUEST REVIEWS • SPECIAL OFFERS • REAL-TIME BOOKING

Victorian, red-brick, three-storey corner guesthouse, just 2.5 miles from city centre, two miles from M62 and close to Sefton Park.

**open** All year
**bedrooms** 2 double, 9 twin, 2 single, 2 family
**bathrooms** All en suite
**payment** Credit/debit cards, cash, cheques

Room General

## LIVERPOOL, Merseyside Map ref 4A2

★★★★
HOSTEL

PER PERSON PER NIGHT
B&B £16.95–£24.95

### YHA Liverpool

25 Tabley Street, off Wapping, Liverpool L1 8EE **t** 0870 770 5924
**e** liverpool@yha.org.uk

**yha.org.uk**

YHA Liverpool, situated adjacent to the historic Albert Dock, has excellent facilities. With the city centre a ten-minute stroll away, 2008's Capital of Culture is truly on your doorstep.

**open** All year except Christmas
**bedrooms** 1 double, 5 triple, 10 quad, 11 dormitories. Total no of beds 125
**bathrooms** 25 en suite, 2 public
**meals** Breakfast, lunch and evening meals available
**payment** Cash/cheques/credit card

WALKERS WELCOME WALKERS CYCLISTS WELCOME CYCLISTS

Room General Leisure

## LIVERSEDGE, West Yorkshire Map ref 4B1

★★
BED & BREAKFAST

B&B PER ROOM PER NIGHT
S £35.00
D £45.00–£90.00

EVENING MEAL PER PERSON
Min £13.50

### Heirloom Carriage Driving B&B

9 Windsor Drive, Norristhorpe WF15 7RA **t** (01924) 235120

**open** All year except Christmas
**bedrooms** 1 double, 1 twin
**payment** Cash, cheques

B&B specialising in local carriage-driving courses (pony/horse) and horse-drawn guided tours. Full English breakfast. No single-occupancy supplement. Quiet location with easy access to M62/M1 for touring West Yorkshire.

**SAT NAV** *WF15 7RA*

Room General 10 P Leisure

## MACCLESFIELD, Cheshire Map ref 4B2

★★
FARMHOUSE

B&B PER ROOM PER NIGHT
S £25.00–£35.00
D £45.00–£60.00

### Astle Farm East

Chelford, Macclesfield SK10 4TA **t** (01625) 861270 **e** gill.farmhouse@virgin.net

**open** All year
**bedrooms** 1 double, 1 twin, 1 family
**bathrooms** 2 en suite
**payment** Credit/debit cards, cash, cheques

A warm and friendly welcome awaits you and your family on our picturesque arable farm. Astle Farm East is surrounded by a large garden, down a small rural lane, where we can offer you a quiet stay in an idyllic setting. Farm tours and nature walks available by appointment.

**SAT NAV** *SK10 4TA*

FAMILIES WELCOME PETS! WELCOME

Room General P

## MACCLESFIELD, Cheshire Map ref 4B2

★★★
GUEST ACCOMMODATION

B&B PER ROOM PER NIGHT
S £35.00–£40.00
D £60.00–£65.00

### Moorhayes House

27 Manchester Road, Tytherington, Macclesfield SK10 2JJ **t** (01625) 433228
**e** helen@moorhayes.co.uk

**moorhayes.co.uk**

Warm welcome. Comfortable home in mature gardens. About 0.5 miles north of town centre. Hearty full English breakfast. Car park. Non-smoking. Rooms with small en suite shower rooms, TV, tea/coffee, telephone. Wi-Fi available.

**open** All year except Christmas and New Year
**bedrooms** 4 double, 1 twin, 1 single, 2 family
**bathrooms** All en suite
**payment** Credit/debit cards, cash, cheques

WALKERS WELCOME CYCLISTS WELCOME

Room General 5 P

## MANCHESTER, Greater Manchester Map ref 4B1

★★★
GUEST ACCOMMODATION

B&B PER ROOM PER NIGHT
S Min £42.50
D Min £49.50

### Luther King House

Brighton Grove, Wilmslow Road, Manchester M14 5JP **t** (0161) 224 6404 **e** reception@lkh.co.uk

**lkh.co.uk** REAL-TIME BOOKING

**open** All year except Christmas and New Year
**bedrooms** 11 double, 6 twin, 25 single, 3 family
**bathrooms** All en suite
**payment** Credit/debit cards, cash, cheques

Located in a tree-lined suburb just a short way from the city centre in a private two-acre site, Luther King House provides a full range of bed and breakfast and conference/meeting facilities. Noted for its peaceful location and very friendly atmosphere, it is the perfect choice for quality, inexpensive accommodation.

**SAT NAV** *M14 5JP*

Room General

## MANCHESTER, Greater Manchester Map ref 4B1

★★★
GUEST ACCOMMODATION

B&B PER ROOM PER NIGHT
S £55.00–£60.00
D £58.00–£65.00

EVENING MEAL PER PERSON
£5.00–£14.00

### Stay Inn – Manchester

55 Blackfriars Road, Salford, Manchester M3 7DB **t** (0161) 907 2277 **e** info@stayinn.co.uk

**stayinn.co.uk** GUEST REVIEWS • REAL-TIME BOOKING

**open** All year
**bedrooms** 41 double, 12 twin, 12 family
**bathrooms** All en suite
**payment** Credit/debit cards, cash, euros

Modern, purpose-built hotel offering excellent value for money. Free car parking, city-centre location, close to railway station. Five minutes' walk from the MEN Arena, and further five minutes from GMEX and MICC. Residents' bar open until 0100. Breakfast from £5.95 to £7.25 for a full English.

**SAT NAV** *M3 7DB* **ONLINE MAP**

Room General

## MANCHESTER AIRPORT

*See under Alderley Edge, Knutsford, Manchester, Sale*

## MASHAM, North Yorkshire Map ref 5C3

★★★★
GUEST ACCOMMODATION

B&B PER ROOM PER NIGHT
S £40.00–£45.00
D £65.00–£70.00

### Garden House

1 Park Street, Masham, Ripon HG4 4HN **t** (01765) 689989 **e** suefurbymasham@gmail.com

Three-hundred-year-old listed building just off large market square. Private parking. Excellent breakfast and tea on the lawn. TV, tea/coffee, toiletries, hairdryer in beautiful bedrooms. A home from home.

**open** All year except Christmas
**bedrooms** 2 double, 1 single
**bathrooms** All en suite
**payment** Cash, cheques

Room General Leisure

FAMILIES WELCOME

## Looking for an ideal family break?

For accommodation offering additional facilities and services for a range of ages and family units, look out for the Families Welcome symbol. Owners of these properties will go out of their way to welcome families.

## MORECAMBE, Lancashire Map ref 5A3

★★★
GUEST ACCOMMODATION

B&B PER ROOM PER NIGHT
S Min £30.00
D £58.00–£60.00

EVENING MEAL PER PERSON
Min £9.00

### The Clifton

Marine Road West, Morecambe LA3 1BZ **t** (01524) 411573 **e** clifton.hotel@btinternet.com

**hotel-clifton.co.uk**

Family-run seafront guesthouse with 45 en suite rooms, bar and dance floor. Comfortable, with great service. Groups welcome.

**open** All year except January and February
**bedrooms** 18 double, 11 twin, 9 single, 7 family
**bathrooms** All en suite
**payment** Credit/debit cards, cash, cheques

Room General P

## MORECAMBE, Lancashire Map ref 5A3

★★★
GUEST HOUSE

B&B PER ROOM PER NIGHT
S £21.00–£25.00
D £40.00–£50.00

EVENING MEAL PER PERSON
£6.00–£12.00

### Silverwell

20 West End Road, Morecambe LA4 4DL **t** (01524) 410532 **e** svlerwll@aol.com

**silverwellguesthouse.co.uk**

Victorian terraced guesthouse 100yds from promenade. Within easy reach of shops and amenities. Ideal as base for the Lakes and dales.

**open** All year
**bedrooms** 4 double, 2 twin, 7 single, 1 family
**bathrooms** 6 en suite
**payment** Credit/debit cards

Room General 8

## MORPETH, Northumberland Map ref 5C2

★★
GUEST HOUSE

B&B PER ROOM PER NIGHT
S £35.00–£40.00
D £55.00–£60.00

*Child discounts available.*

### Cottage View Guesthouse

6 Staithes Lane, Morpeth NE61 1TD **t** (01670) 518550 **e** bookings@cottageview.co.uk

**cottageview.co.uk** REAL-TIME BOOKING

**open** All year
**bedrooms** 10 double, 6 twin, 6 single, 3 family
**bathrooms** 19 en suite, 6 private
**payment** Credit/debit cards, cash, cheques

Centrally situated, family-run guesthouse. Private car parking, reception bar, two lounges (one private), email and fax facilities (small charge made). Night porter available for late arrivals/early departures. We can accommodate over 50 people – ideal for wedding guests. So don't delay, book today!

**SAT NAV** *NE61 1TD* **ONLINE MAP**

Room General P

## MORPETH, Northumberland Map ref 5C2

★★★
BED & BREAKFAST

B&B PER ROOM PER NIGHT
S £27.50–£30.00
D £55.00–£60.00

### Kington

East Linden, Longhorsley, Morpeth NE65 8TH **t** (01670) 788554 **e** clivetaylor.services@tiscali.co.uk

**kington-longhorsley.com**

Attractive converted farm building. Rural location six miles north of Morpeth and close to Alnwick Castle and Gardens. Friendly atmosphere, wonderful breakfasts. Suite consists of one double and one twin room, both en suite.

**open** All year
**bedrooms** 1 suite
**bathrooms** 1 private
**payment** Cash, cheques

Room General P Leisure

## MUNCASTER, Cumbria Map ref 5A3

★★★★
GUEST ACCOMMODATION

B&B PER ROOM PER NIGHT
S Max £45.00
D £75.00–£100.00

### Muncaster Coachman's Quarters

Muncaster Castle, Muncaster, Ravenglass CA18 1RQ **t** (01229) 717614 **e** info@muncaster.co.uk

**muncaster.co.uk**

**open** All year
**bedrooms** 4 double, 4 twin, 2 family
**bathrooms** 9 en suite
**payment** Credit/debit cards, cash, cheques

The Coachman's Quarters are within the stable yard of the magnificent Muncaster Gardens. One room has facilities for people with disabilities. The Granary is a large bedroom with lounge area and kitchenette. Tariff includes admission to the Gardens, World Owl Centre, MeadowVole Maze, Darkest Muncaster when operational, and reduced entry to the Castle.

**SAT NAV** *CA18 1RQ*

Room General Leisure

## NEWBIGGIN-ON-LUNE, Cumbria Map ref 5B3

★★★★
GUEST ACCOMMODATION

B&B PER ROOM PER NIGHT
S £30.00–£35.00
D £52.00–£56.00

EVENING MEAL PER PERSON
£13.00

### Tranna Hill

Newbiggin-on-Lune, Kirkby Stephen CA17 4NY **t** (015396) 23227 & 07989 892368
**e** enquiries@trannahill.co.uk

**trannahill.co.uk** REAL-TIME BOOKING

A warm welcome guaranteed. Large, en suite bathrooms and fantastic views of Howgill Fells yet only five minutes from M6 (jct 38). Great for breaking journey, walking or exploring area.

**open** All year except Christmas
**bedrooms** 1 double, 1 twin, 1 family
**bathrooms** All en suite
**payment** Cash, cheques

Room General Leisure

## NEWCASTLE UPON TYNE, Tyne and Wear Map ref 5C2

★★★
GUEST ACCOMMODATION

B&B PER ROOM PER NIGHT
S £29.00–£40.00
D £69.00–£72.00

EVENING MEAL PER PERSON
£12.50–£20.00

### Clifton House

46 Clifton Road, Off Grainger Park Road, Newcastle upon Tyne NE4 6XH **t** (0191) 273 0407
**e** cliftonhousehotel@hotmail.com

**cliftonhousehotel.com**

Comfortable, elegant country-style house with private grounds and car park. Close to the city, central for travel, sightseeing and shopping. Evening meals by arrangement.

**open** All year except Christmas
**bedrooms** 2 double, 2 twin, 4 single, 3 family
**bathrooms** 9 en suite
**payment** Credit/debit cards, cash, cheques

Room General

## NEWCASTLE UPON TYNE, Tyne and Wear Map ref 5C2

★★★★
GUEST ACCOMMODATION

B&B PER ROOM PER NIGHT
S £47.00
D £67.00

EVENING MEAL PER PERSON
£5.00–£15.00

### The Keelman's Lodge

Grange Road, Newcastle upon Tyne NE15 8NL **t** (0191) 267 1689 & (0191) 414 0156
**e** admin@biglampbrewers.co.uk

**keelmanslodge.co.uk**

The Keelman's Lodge is a purpose-built accommodation lodge which stands in its own grounds on the edge of the Tyne Riverside Country Park. Sharing its grounds are the Big Lamp Brewery (listed building) and the very popular Keelman pub, selling good food and real ale on tap.

**open** All year
**bedrooms** 8 double, 5 twin, 1 family
**bathrooms** All en suite
**payment** Credit/debit cards, cash, cheques

Room General Leisure

For **key to symbols** see page 7

## NEWCASTLE UPON TYNE, Tyne and Wear Map ref 5C2

★★★
GUEST HOUSE

B&B PER ROOM PER NIGHT
S £25.00–£30.00
D £50.00–£60.00

### Stonehaven Lodge

Prestwick Road Ends, Ponteland, Newcastle upon Tyne NE20 9BX **t** (01661) 872363
**e** stonehavenlodge@hotmail.co.uk

Stone semi-detached property facing the Cheviots on the Prestwick roundabout, on the A696 to Jedburgh, 200yds past Newcastle Airport.

**open** All year except Christmas and New Year
**bedrooms** 1 double, 2 twin, 1 single
**bathrooms** 2 en suite, 2 private
**payment** Cash, cheques, euros

Room General P Leisure

## OLDHAM, Greater Manchester Map ref 4B1

★★★
GUEST ACCOMMODATION

B&B PER ROOM PER NIGHT
S £28.00–£37.50
D £53.00–£65.00

EVENING MEAL PER PERSON
£5.00–£8.00

### Grains Bar Farm

Ripponden Road, Oldham OL1 4SX **t** (0161) 624 0303 **e** info@grainsbarhotel.co.uk

Set in nine acres of land where horses graze. Fabulous views of Saddleworth and the Pennines. Warm, relaxed atmosphere with two comfortable lounges and licensed bar with Sky TV. Ideal for motorway links.

**open** All year
**bedrooms** 8 double, 8 twin, 6 single, 2 family
**bathrooms** 16 en suite
**payment** Credit/debit cards, cash, cheques

Room General P Leisure

## OTTERBURN, Northumberland Map ref 5B1

★★★★
GUEST HOUSE

B&B PER ROOM PER NIGHT
S £33.00–£38.00
D £60.00–£70.00

### Butterchurn Guest House

Main Street, Otterburn NE19 1NP **t** (01830) 520585 **e** keith@butterchurn.freeserve.co.uk

**butterchurnguesthouse.co.uk**

**open** All year
**bedrooms** 4 double, 2 twin, 1 family
**bathrooms** All en suite
**payment** Credit/debit cards, cash, cheques

Excellent family-run guesthouse, quiet village location, renowned for its welcome, very high quality of service and ambience. Situated in Northumberland National Park, close to Hadrian's Wall, Kielder Water, Northumbria's coast and castles and the historic Scottish Borders.

**SAT NAV** *NE19 1NP*

Room General P Leisure

## OVINGTON, Durham Map ref 5B3

★★★
INN

B&B PER ROOM PER NIGHT
S £32.50
D £60.00

EVENING MEAL PER PERSON
£7.50–£15.00

*2 nights' B&B £110 – based on 2 people sharing double or twin room. Subject to availability.*

### The Four Alls

Ovington, Richmond DL11 7BP **t** (01833) 627302 **e** john.stroud@virgin.net

**thefouralls-teesdale.co.uk** SPECIAL OFFERS · REAL-TIME BOOKING

**open** All year
**bedrooms** 1 double, 2 twin, 2 single
**bathrooms** 3 en suite, 2 private
**payment** Credit/debit cards

Privately run establishment offering quality accommodation and food in a quiet and beautiful village setting. Centrally located for exploring local area and places of interest.

**SAT NAV** *DL11 7BP* **ONLINE MAP**

Room General 8 P

## PICKERING, North Yorkshire Map ref 5D3

★★★★★
**GUEST HOUSE GOLD AWARD**

**B&B PER ROOM PER NIGHT**
S £65.00–£75.00
D £85.00–£105.00

**EVENING MEAL PER PERSON**
Min £7.50

*Midweek Madness deals available in selected periods – see our website for details.*

# 17 Burgate

Pickering YO18 7AU **t** (01751) 473463 **e** info@17burgate.co.uk

**17burgate.co.uk** GUEST REVIEWS · SPECIAL OFFERS

**open** All year except Christmas
**bedrooms** 2 double, 1 twin, 2 suites
**bathrooms** All en suite
**payment** Credit/debit cards, cash, cheques, euros

Superb, award-winning, renovated town house between town centre and castle. Luxury for the stressed and weary. 17 Burgate is different, 17 Burgate is special – indulge yourselves, and make it part of your North Yorkshire experience. 'The boutique B&B has arrived in North Yorkshire' – The Times.

**SAT NAV** *YO18 7AU* **ONLINE MAP**

Room TV General 12 P Leisure

## PICKERING, North Yorkshire Map ref 5D3

★★★★
**GUEST HOUSE SILVER AWARD**

**B&B PER ROOM PER NIGHT**
S £40.00–£45.00
D £70.00–£75.00

# Cawthorne House

42 Eastgate, Pickering YO18 7DU **t** (01751) 477364 **e** info@cawthornehouse.co.uk

**cawthornehouse.co.uk**

An imposing Victorian house offering first-class accommodation. Luxury bedrooms all with shower en suite. Non-smoking. Private parking available.

**open** All year except Christmas and New Year
**bedrooms** 4 double, 1 twin
**payment** Cash, cheques

Room TV General P Leisure

## PICKERING, North Yorkshire Map ref 5D3

★★★★
**BED & BREAKFAST SILVER AWARD**

**B&B PER ROOM PER NIGHT**
S £35.00–£55.00
D £55.00–£70.00

*Mountain-biking holidays (Dalby Forest and North York Moors) including guiding and instruction from £50pppn. Instructor and mechanic on site.*

# Eleven Westgate

Eden House, Pickering YO18 8BA **t** (01751) 475111 **e** info@elevenwestgate.co.uk

**elevenwestgate.co.uk** GUEST REVIEWS · SPECIAL OFFERS

**open** All year except Christmas and New Year
**bedrooms** 3 double/twin
**bathrooms** All en suite
**payment** Credit/debit cards, cash, cheques

Elegant Victorian town house offering luxury accommodation and hospitality, three minutes' walk from Pickering town centre. Spacious en suite rooms. Home comforts include log fire, Wi-Fi, Sky+, DVD, iPod dock. Lovely garden. Aga-cooked breakfast using fresh local produce. Ideal for North Yorkshire and renowned steam railway. Secure bike storage, bikewash and workshop.

**SAT NAV** *YO18 8BA* **ONLINE MAP**

Room TV SC General Leisure

## Using map references

The map references refer to the colour maps at the front of this guide. The first figure is the map number, the letter and figure that follow indicate the grid reference on the map.

## PICKERING, North Yorkshire Map ref 5D3

★★★★
BED & BREAKFAST

B&B PER ROOM PER NIGHT
S £35.00–£40.00
D £64.00–£70.00

EVENING MEAL PER PERSON
£15.00–£20.00

### The Hawthornes

High Back Side, Middleton, Pickering YO18 8PB **t** (01751) 474755 **e** paulaappleby@btinternet.com

**the-hawthornes.com**

The Hawthornes offers comfortable accommodation in three generous-sized rooms, two on ground floor. Aga-cooked breakfast, home-baked bread. Tea and fresh baked scones on arrival. Ample parking.

**open** All year except Christmas and New Year
**bedrooms** 2 double, 1 twin
**bathrooms** All en suite
**payment** Cash, cheques

Room General P Leisure

## PICKERING, North Yorkshire Map ref 5D3

★★★★★
GUEST ACCOMMODATION
GOLD AWARD

B&B PER ROOM PER NIGHT
S £60.00–£80.00
D £75.00–£95.00

WALKERS WELCOME CYCLISTS WELCOME

### The Old Vicarage

Toftly View, Pickering YO18 8QD **t** (01751) 476126 **e** oldvic@toftlyview.co.uk

**toftlyview.co.uk**

The Old Vicarage at Toftly View offers stylish accommodation in a stunning location with wonderful south-facing views towards the Wolds. You will find a warm welcome and a high standard of comfort.

**open** February to October
**bedrooms** 4 double
**bathrooms** All en suite
**payment** Credit/debit cards, cash, cheques

Room General 10 P

## PORT CARLISLE, Cumbria Map ref 5A2

★★★★★
BED & BREAKFAST
SILVER AWARD

B&B PER ROOM PER NIGHT
S Max £60.00
D Max £85.00

EVENING MEAL PER PERSON
Max £17.50

### Brockelrigg

Port Carlisle, Wigton CA7 5BU **t** (01697) 351953 **e** mu.atkinson@btopenworld.com

**brockelrigg.co.uk**

Luxury guest suite with private lounge. Tranquil setting in beautiful area close to North Lakes. Good local food.

**open** All year except Christmas and New Year
**bedrooms** 1 suite
**payment** Cash, cheques

Room General P

## POWBURN, Northumberland Map ref 5B1

★★★★★
FARMHOUSE
SILVER AWARD

B&B PER ROOM PER NIGHT
S Min £45.00
D £70.00

### Low Hedgeley Farm

Powburn, Alnwick NE66 4JD **t** (01665) 578815

**open** All year except Christmas and New Year
**bedrooms** 1 double, 1 twin
**bathrooms** 1 en suite, 1 private
**payment** Cash, cheques

Grade II Listed farmhouse with extensive grounds. Situated in the Breamish Valley at the foot of the Cheviot Hills. Ideal base for visiting Cragside, and Alnwick Castle and Garden.

**SAT NAV** *NE66 4JD*

Room General P Leisure

## PREESALL, Lancashire Map ref 4A1

★★★
BED & BREAKFAST

B&B PER ROOM PER NIGHT
S £20.00–£30.00
D £40.00–£60.00

### Grassendale

Green Lane, Preesall, Poulton-le-Fylde FY6 0NS t (01253) 812331 e rondeyo@aol.com

Family home in a quiet location offering bed and breakfast. Three rooms available, ample parking and pets welcome. Only one hour from Southern Lakes and 30 minutes from Blackpool.

**open** All year
**bedrooms** 1 double, 1 twin, 1 family
**bathrooms** 2 en suite, 1 private
**payment** Cash, cheques

Room General P

## RAINOW, Cheshire Map ref 4B2

★★★★
BED & BREAKFAST

B&B PER ROOM PER NIGHT
S £40.00
D £60.00

### Common Barn Farm B&B

Smith Lane, Rainow, Macclesfield SK10 5XJ t (01625) 574878 e g_greengrass@hotmail.com

**commonbarnfarm.co.uk** GUEST REVIEWS

**open** All year
**bedrooms** 1 double, 3 twin, 1 family
**bathrooms** All en suite
**payment** Credit/debit cards, cash, cheques, euros

Our bed and breakfast accommodation, on a working sheep farm, is ideal for groups, families, couples and individuals. The perfect base for exploring the Peak District, Lyme Park, and Cheshire. All rooms have wireless broadband, en suite bathrooms and underfloor heating. One room with an en suite wet room is particularly suitable for disabled guests.

SAT NAV *SK10 5XJ* ONLINE MAP

Room General P Leisure

## REDCAR, Tees Valley Map ref 5C3

★★★
GUEST HOUSE

B&B PER ROOM PER NIGHT
S £20.00–£25.00
D £40.00–£45.00

### Armada Guest House

28-30 Henry Street, Redcar TS10 1BJ t (01642) 471710 e info@armadaguesthouse.co.uk

**armadaguesthouse.co.uk**

**open** All year
**bedrooms** 2 double, 5 twin, 5 single, 3 family
**bathrooms** 6 en suite
**payment** Cash, cheques

Small, friendly, family-run B&B close to all local amenities. Only seconds from seafront, also very close to the town centre.

SAT NAV *TS10 1BJ* ONLINE MAP

Room General Leisure

## RIBBLE VALLEY

*See under Clitheroe, Whalley, Whitewell*

### What if I need to cancel?

It is advisable to check the proprietor's cancellation policy in case you have to change your plans at a later date.

## RICHMOND, North Yorkshire Map ref 5C3

★★★★
GUEST ACCOMMODATION

B&B PER ROOM PER NIGHT
S £55.00–£74.00
D Min £65.00

### Frenchgate Guest House

66 Frenchgate, Richmond DL10 7AG **t** (01748) 823421 & 07889 768696 **e** info@66frenchgate.co.uk

**open** All year
**bedrooms** 3 double, 2 twin, 2 family
**bathrooms** All en suite
**payment** Credit/debit cards, cash, cheques, euros

Panoramic views overlooking the Swale Valley, Richmond Castle, Easby Abbey and rolling countryside over the Dales. The historic marketplace and castle are nearby.

**SAT NAV** *DL10 7AG*

Room General 8 Leisure

## RICHMOND, North Yorkshire Map ref 5C3

★★★★★
BED & BREAKFAST
SILVER AWARD

B&B PER ROOM PER NIGHT
S £40.00
D £60.00

*3rd night half price.*

### New Skeeby Grange

Sedbury Lane, Skeeby, Richmond DL10 5ED **t** (01748) 822276 **e** gandmf@tiscali.co.uk

**newskeebygrange.co.uk** GUEST REVIEWS

**open** All year except Christmas and New Year
**bedrooms** 1 double, 1 family
**bathrooms** All en suite
**payment** Cash, cheques

We welcome you to our lovely, luxury accommodation, peaceful and quiet, surrounded by farmland. Both attractive en suite bedrooms overlook our garden, full of birds; watch our woodpecker family feeding whilst you enjoy a hearty English breakfast of locally produced bacon, sausage and free range eggs to set you up for a day's sightseeing!

**SAT NAV** *DL10 5ED* **ONLINE MAP**

Room General 5 P Leisure

## RICHMOND, North Yorkshire Map ref 5C3

★★★★
GUEST ACCOMMODATION

B&B PER ROOM PER NIGHT
S £60.00–£70.00
D £70.00–£80.00

### Nuns Cottage

5 Hurgill Road, Richmond DL10 4AR **t** (01748) 822809 **e** the.flints@ukgateway.net

**nunscottage.co.uk**

Nuns Cottage is an 18thC house set in secluded gardens. Comfortable bedrooms. Five minutes from the centre of Richmond. Easy access to the A1 and the beautiful Yorkshire Dales.

**open** All year except Christmas and New Year
**bedrooms** 1 double, 1 twin
**bathrooms** 2 private
**payment** Cash, cheques, euros

Room General 12 Leisure

## What do the star ratings mean?

For a detailed explanation of the quality and facilities represented by the stars, please refer to the information pages at the back of this guide.

## RIPON, North Yorkshire Map ref 5C3

★★★★
GUEST HOUSE

B&B PER ROOM PER NIGHT
S £45.00–£70.00
D £60.00–£80.00

# Box Tree Cottages

Coltsgate Hill, Ripon HG4 2AB **t** (01765) 698006 **e** boxtreecottages@gmail.com

**boxtreecottages.com**

**open** All year except Christmas and New Year
**bedrooms** 3 double, 2 twin, 1 family
**bathrooms** All en suite
**payment** Credit/debit cards, cash, cheques

A pretty row of listed cottages now combined into one property. Very quietly situated but only minutes from the marketplace. Completely refurbished, furnished with antiques. Homely atmosphere, spacious rooms, best-quality food. Ample parking, large gardens.

**SAT NAV** *HG4 2AB*

Room General

## RIPON, North Yorkshire Map ref 5C3

★★★★★
GUEST ACCOMMODATION

B&B PER ROOM PER NIGHT
S £35.00–£45.00
D £69.00–£89.00

*Check out our website for offers/ promotions.*

# The Old Coach House

2 Stable Cottages, North Stainley, Ripon HG4 3HT **t** (01765) 634900
**e** enquiries@oldcoachhouse.info

**oldcoachhouse.info**

**open** All year
**bedrooms** 5 double, 1 twin, 2 single
**bathrooms** All en suite
**payment** Credit/debit cards, cash, cheques

The Old Coach House is an accommodation jewel and one of Yorkshire's best kept secrets. The 18thC coaching house stands proud in the grounds of North Stainley Hall in the picturesque village of North Stainley just north of Ripon. All eight rooms are en suite and designed with modern living in mind.

**SAT NAV** *HG4 3HT* **ONLINE MAP**

Room General Leisure

## RIPON, North Yorkshire Map ref 5C3

★★★★
INN

B&B PER ROOM PER NIGHT
S £40.00–£50.00
D £70.00–£80.00

EVENING MEAL PER PERSON
£8.00–£15.00

*Call for details of off-peak special rates.*

# The Royal Oak

36 Kirkgate, Ripon HG4 1PB **t** (01765) 602284 **e** info@royaloakripon.co.uk

**royaloakripon.co.uk**

**open** All year
**bedrooms** 4 double, 1 twin, 1 family
**bathrooms** All en suite
**payment** Credit/debit cards, cash

The recently refurbished Royal Oak is one of Ripon's historic inns and is conveniently located close to the bustling market place and the city's shops and tourist attractions. Time-honoured Yorkshire hospitality with busy, lively bars serving Timothy Taylor's award-winning cask ales and excellent food every day using fresh local produce.

**SAT NAV** *HG4 1PB* **ONLINE MAP**

Room General Leisure

## Using map references

Map references refer to the colour maps at the front of this guide.

## RIPON, North Yorkshire Map ref 5C3

★★★
INN

B&B PER ROOM PER NIGHT
S £30.00
D £50.00

### The White Horse

61 North Street, Ripon HG4 1EN **t** (01765) 603622 **e** david.bate13@btopenworld.com

**white-horse-ripon.co.uk**

A friendly, family-run pub close to Ripon market square. Entertainment at weekends and various midweek activities.

**open** All year
**bedrooms** 3 twin, 4 single, 5 family
**bathrooms** All en suite
**payment** Credit/debit cards, cash, cheques

Room General Leisure

## ROUGHLEE, Lancashire Map ref 4B1

★★★★
GUEST ACCOMMODATION

B&B PER ROOM PER NIGHT
S £40.00–£50.00
D £60.00–£80.00

### Dam Head Barn

Dam Head Farm, Nelson BB9 6MX **t** (01282) 617190 **e** sagarbarn@btinternet.com

Dam Head Barn is a 400-year-old, Grade II Listed barn found in the small village of Roughlee, at the foot of the majestic Pendle Hill, within the Forest of Bowland Area of Outstanding Natural Beauty.

**open** All year
**bedrooms** 1 double, 1 twin
**bathrooms** All en suite
**payment** Cash, cheques

Room General Leisure

## RUNSWICK BAY, North Yorkshire Map ref 5D3

★★★★
GUEST HOUSE

B&B PER ROOM PER NIGHT
S £48.00
D £75.00

EVENING MEAL PER PERSON
£19.50

### The Firs

26 Hinderwell Lane, Runswick Bay, Nr Whitby TS13 5HR **t** (01947) 840433
**e** mandy.shackleton@talk21.com

**the-firs.co.uk**

In a coastal village, eight miles north of Whitby. All rooms en suite with colour TV, tea/coffee facilities. Private parking. Children and dogs welcome.

**open** April to October
**bedrooms** 3 double, 2 twin, 1 single, 5 family
**bathrooms** All en suite
**payment** Cash, cheques, euros

Room General Leisure

## RYTON, Tyne and Wear Map ref 5C2

★★★
GUEST ACCOMMODATION

B&B PER ROOM PER NIGHT
S £25.00–£50.00
D £60.00–£90.00

### A1 Hedgefield House

Stella Road, Blaydon-on-Tyne NE21 4LR **t** (0191) 413 7373 **e** david@hedgefieldhouse.co.uk

**hedgefieldhouse.co.uk** GUEST REVIEWS • SPECIAL OFFERS • REAL-TIME BOOKING

**open** All year
**bedrooms** 4 double, 3 twin, 3 single, 2 family, 2 suites
**bathrooms** 5 en suite
**payment** Credit/debit cards, cash, cheques

Georgian residence in three acres of wooded gardens. Sauna and gym facilities. Peaceful, yet only minutes from Newcastle city centre, Gateshead MetroCentre and A1(M). A warm welcome guaranteed.

**SAT NAV** *NE21 4LR* **ONLINE MAP**

Room General Leisure

## Place index

If you know where you want to stay, the index by place name at the back of the guide will give you the page number listing accommodation in your chosen town, city or village. Check out the other useful indexes too.

## ST BEES, Cumbria Map ref 5A3

★★★★★
GUEST ACCOMMODATION

B&B PER ROOM PER NIGHT
S £50.00–£59.95
D £80.00–£85.00

### Fleatham House

High House Road, St Bees CA27 0BX **t** (01946) 822341 **e** fleathamhouse@aol.com

**fleathamhouse.com**

Victorian country house set in several acres of garden overlooking St Bees Head. Fleatham House offers a personal service in a peaceful setting. All rooms are spacious and en suite.

**open** All year except Christmas and New Year
**bedrooms** 3 double, 3 single
**bathrooms** All en suite
**payment** Credit/debit cards, cash, cheques

Room General P Leisure

## ST BEES, Cumbria Map ref 5A3

★★★★
FARMHOUSE

B&B PER ROOM PER NIGHT
S £30.00–£35.00
D £60.00–£65.00

### Stonehouse Farm

133 Main Street, St Bees CA27 0DE **t** (01946) 822224 **e** csmith.stonehouse@btopenworld.com

**stonehousefarm.net**

150-acre livestock farm. Modernised, Georgian, listed farmhouse, conveniently and attractively situated next to station, shops and hotels. Start of coast-to-coast walk. Golf course, long-stay car park.

**open** All year except Christmas
**bedrooms** 2 double, 1 twin, 1 single, 2 family, 1 suite
**bathrooms** All en suite
**payment** Credit/debit cards, cash, cheques, euros

Room General P Leisure

## SALE, Greater Manchester Map ref 4A2

★★★
GUEST ACCOMMODATION

B&B PER ROOM PER NIGHT
S £32.00–£42.50
D £45.00–£50.00

EVENING MEAL PER PERSON
£4.95–£12.95

### The Belforte House

7-9 Broad Road, Sale M33 2AE **t** (0161) 973 8779 **e** belfortehotel@aol.com

**belfortehousehotel.co.uk**

Privately owned hotel with a personal, friendly approach. Ideally located for Manchester Airport, the Metrolink and the city centre. Situated directly opposite Sale Leisure Centre.

**open** All year except Christmas
**bedrooms** 2 double, 3 twin, 14 single, 2 family
**bathrooms** 17 en suite
**payment** Credit/debit cards, cash, cheques

Room General P

## SALTBURN-BY-THE-SEA, Tees Valley Map ref 5C3

★★★★
GUEST HOUSE

B&B PER ROOM PER NIGHT
S £35.00–£40.00
D £60.00–£80.00

### The Arches

Low Farm, Ings Lane, Brotton, Saltburn-by-the-Sea TS12 2QX **t** (01287) 677512
**e** hotel@gorallyschool.co.uk

**thearcheshotel.co.uk**

**open** All year
**bedrooms** 4 double, 3 twin, 1 family
**bathrooms** All en suite
**payment** Credit/debit cards, cash, cheques

The Arches offers a relaxing environment and overlooks spectacular views of cliffs and golf course. All the rooms are individually furnished with en suite bathrooms.

**SAT NAV** *TS12 2QX*

Room General P Leisure

## Has every property been assessed?

All accommodation in this guide has been rated for quality, or is awaiting assessment, by a professional national tourist board assessor.

## SAWREY, Cumbria Map ref 5A3

★★★★
GUEST HOUSE

B&B PER ROOM PER NIGHT
s £37.50–£40.00
d £75.00–£80.00

### Buckle Yeat Guest House

Nr Sawrey, Ambleside LA22 0LF **t** (015394) 36446 **e** info@buckle-yeat.co.uk

**buckle-yeat.co.uk**

17thC oak-beamed cottage, famous for its connections with Beatrix Potter, provides a warm, friendly and centrally located base, and excellent value for money.

**open** All year except Christmas
**bedrooms** 4 double, 2 twin, 1 single
**bathrooms** 6 en suite, 1 private
**payment** Credit/debit cards, cash, cheques

Room General P Leisure

## SCARBOROUGH, North Yorkshire Map ref 5D3

★★★
GUEST HOUSE

B&B PER ROOM PER NIGHT
s £16.00–£20.00
d £18.00–£26.00

*Special offers Nov – Mar. Please ring for details.*

### Brontes Guest House

135 Columbus Ravine, Scarborough YO12 7QZ **t** (01723) 362934 **e** ericwatson@talktalk.net

**brontesguesthouse.co.uk** SPECIAL OFFERS • REAL-TIME BOOKING

**open** All year
**bedrooms** 4 double, 1 twin, 1 single, 1 family
**bathrooms** All en suite
**payment** Credit/debit cards, cash, cheques, euros

Family-run guesthouse in excellent location near Peasholm Park and North Bay. Highly recommended by guests. All rooms en suite, TV, drinks, centrally heated, licensed bar, wireless internet. Refurbished 2007. We specialise in comfort, cleanliness and genuine quality accommodation. Free parking permits provided.

**SAT NAV** *YO12 7QZ* **ONLINE MAP**

Room General Leisure

## SCARBOROUGH, North Yorkshire Map ref 5D3

★★★
GUEST HOUSE

B&B PER ROOM PER NIGHT
s £25.00–£35.00
d £40.00–£50.00

### Dolphin Guest House

151 Columbus Ravine, Scarborough YO12 7QZ **t** (01723) 341914
**e** dolphinguesthouse@btinternet.com

**thedolphin.info**

**open** All year
**bedrooms** 2 double, 2 twin, 2 family
**bathrooms** 5 en suite, 1 private
**payment** Credit/debit cards, cash, cheques

The Dolphin Guest House offers a comfortable and friendly stay. All rooms are double glazed and centrally heated with tea-/coffee-making facilities, colour TV, clock/radio, hairdryer. Modern decor in all rooms. We welcome families, walking groups and motorcyclists. Two-minute walk to Peasholm Park.

**SAT NAV** *YO12 7QZ*

Room General

## SCARBOROUGH, North Yorkshire Map ref 5D3

★★★★
GUEST HOUSE

B&B PER ROOM PER NIGHT
S £23.00–£26.00
D £52.00–£64.00

*Mini-breaks (3 nights min) Mar-early Jul, Sep and Oct, from £24pppn.*

### Howdale

121 Queen's Parade, Scarborough YO12 7HU **t** (01723) 372696 **e** mail@howdalehotel.co.uk

**howdalehotel.co.uk**

**open** All year except Christmas and New Year
**bedrooms** 10 double, 2 twin, 1 single, 2 family
**bathrooms** 13 en suite
**payment** Credit/debit cards, cash

Beautifully situated overlooking North Bay and Scarborough Castle, yet close to town. We are renowned for cleanliness and the friendly, efficient service provided in a comfortable atmosphere. Our substantial breakfasts are deservedly famous. Thirteen of our excellent bedrooms are en suite, many have sea views. All have TV, tea/coffee facilities, hairdryer etc.

**SAT NAV** *YO12 7HU*

Room General P

## SCARBOROUGH, North Yorkshire Map ref 5D3

★★★★
BED & BREAKFAST
SILVER AWARD

B&B PER ROOM PER NIGHT
S £40.00–£50.00
D £60.00–£80.00

EVENING MEAL PER PERSON
Min £15.00

### Killerby Cottage Farm

Killerby Lane, Cayton, Scarborough YO11 3TP **t** (01723) 581236 **e** val@stainedglasscentre.co.uk

**smoothhound.co.uk/hotels/killerby** REAL-TIME BOOKING

Situated between Scarborough and Filey, 1.5 miles from Cayton Bay. Farmhouse of character adjacent to Stained-Glass Centre. Good food, lovely garden, warm welcome.

**open** All year except Christmas
**bedrooms** 2 double, 1 twin
**bathrooms** All en suite
**payment** Credit/debit cards, cash, cheques

Room General P Leisure

## SCARBOROUGH, North Yorkshire Map ref 5D3

★★★
GUEST HOUSE

B&B PER ROOM PER NIGHT
S £30.00–£35.00
D £52.00–£56.00

EVENING MEAL PER PERSON
£12.00–£14.00

### Robyn's Guest House

139 Columbus Ravine, Scarborough YO12 7QZ **t** (01723) 374217 **e** info@robynsguesthouse.co.uk

**robynsguesthouse.co.uk** GUEST REVIEWS

Robyn's Guest House offers you the very best in comfortable, luxury accommodation at affordable rates in the heart of Yorkshire's premier seaside resort.

**open** All year
**bedrooms** 3 double, 3 family
**bathrooms** All en suite
**payment** Credit/debit cards, cash, cheques

Room General Leisure

## SCARBOROUGH, North Yorkshire Map ref 5D3

★★★★
FARMHOUSE
SILVER AWARD

B&B PER ROOM PER NIGHT
S £35.00–£40.00
D £60.00–£70.00

### Sawdon Heights

Scarborough YO13 9EB **t** (01723) 859321 **e** info@sawdonheights.com

**sawdonheights.com**

A warm welcome awaits on our family farm adjacent to forest. Quiet location, stunning views. Cycle hire and storage, walks and pack-ups available. Ideal location for exploring east coast and moors. Extra bed available.

**open** All year except Christmas
**bedrooms** 2 double, 1 twin
**bathrooms** All en suite
**payment** Cash, cheques

Room General 10 P Leisure

### Where are the maps?

Colour maps can be found at the front of the guide. They pinpoint the location of all accommodation found in the regional sections.

**SCARBOROUGH, North Yorkshire Map ref 5D3**

★★★★
GUEST ACCOMMODATION

B&B PER ROOM PER NIGHT
s £37.00–£39.00
d £32.00–£34.00

## Smugglers Rock Country House

Staintondale Road, Ravenscar, Scarborough YO13 0ER **t** (01723) 870044
**e** info@smugglersrock.co.uk

**smugglersrock.co.uk** REAL-TIME BOOKING

**open** Easter to mid-October
**bedrooms** 3 double, 1 twin, 1 single, 3 family
**bathrooms** All en suite
**payment** Credit/debit cards, cash, cheques

Georgian country house in Ravenscar with panoramic views over surrounding National Park and sea. Ideal country holiday area, with wonderful walks in all directions, located at southern end of Robin Hood's Bay. Whitby, Scarborough and 'Heartbeat' Country within easy reach. Friendly farm animals. Self-catering cottages also available.

**SAT NAV** *YO13 0ER* **ONLINE MAP**

Room General 5 P Leisure

**SCARBOROUGH, North Yorkshire Map ref 5D3**

★★★
GUEST HOUSE

B&B PER ROOM PER NIGHT
s £21.00–£22.50
d £42.00–£45.00

EVENING MEAL PER PERSON
£6.00–£9.00

## The Thoresby

53 North Marine Road, Scarborough YO12 7EY **t** (01723) 365715

Friendly, family-run guesthouse. Near to town centre, sea views, car parking at rear. Full English or continental breakfast.

**open** All year
**bedrooms** 2 double, 2 twin, 2 single, 3 family
**bathrooms** 8 en suite
**payment** Cash, cheques

Room General P

**SCARBOROUGH, North Yorkshire Map ref 5D3**

★★★★
GUEST ACCOMMODATION

B&B PER ROOM PER NIGHT
s £30.50–£32.00
d £24.50–£30.00

*Oct-May inclusive (excl Bank Holidays): reduction of £1.50pppn when staying 2 nights or more.*

## The Whiteley

99-101 Queens Parade, Scarborough YO12 7HY **t** (01723) 373514 **e** whiteleyhotel@bigfoot.com

**yorkshire-coast.co.uk/whiteley**

**open** February to November
**bedrooms** 7 double, 3 family
**bathrooms** All en suite
**payment** Credit/debit cards, cash, cheques

Small, family-run, non-smoking, licensed guest accommodation located in an elevated position overlooking the North Bay, close to the town centre and ideally situated for all amenities. The bedrooms are well co-ordinated and equipped with useful extras, many with sea views. Good home cooking is served in the traditional dining room.

**SAT NAV** *YO12 7HY*

Room General 3 P

## Gold and Silver Awards

Gold and Silver Awards are given to establishments achieving the highest levels of quality and service. You can find more information at the front of the guide, and an index to all accommodation achieving these awards at the back.

## SETTLE, North Yorkshire Map ref 5B3

★★★
INN

B&B PER ROOM PER NIGHT
S £34.00–£39.00
D £60.00–£65.00

EVENING MEAL PER PERSON
£7.95–£13.95

*Midweek and winter breaks available – please telephone for details.*

### Maypole Inn

Maypole Green, Long Preston, Skipton BD23 4PH **t** (01729) 840219 **e** robert@maypole.co.uk

**maypole.co.uk** GUEST REVIEWS • SPECIAL OFFERS • REAL-TIME BOOKING

**open** All year
**bedrooms** 2 double, 1 twin, 1 single, 2 family
**bathrooms** All en suite
**payment** Credit/debit cards, cash, cheques, euros

Traditional 17thC village inn on the Maypole Green, situated within the Yorkshire Dales and close to the Trough of Bowland and the Lake District. Restaurant serving home-made food with a good local reputation. Traditional beers – we are four-times winner of the CAMRA Pub of the Season.

**SAT NAV** *BD23 4PH* **ONLINE MAP**

Room General Leisure

## SHEFFIELD, South Yorkshire Map ref 4B2

★★★
GUEST ACCOMMODATION

B&B PER ROOM PER NIGHT
S £45.00
D £45.00

EVENING MEAL PER PERSON
£5.00–£15.00

### Parson House Farm

Longshaw, Sheffield S11 7TZ **t** (01433) 631017 **e** deb_bel@hotmail.co.uk

**parsonhouse.co.uk**

Quality comfortable rooms with private bathroom. Set in Peak District, great for families/couples, breakfast, half or full board available. Pets welcome. Outdoor activities available.

**open** All year
**bedrooms** 2 family
**bathrooms** 2 private
**payment** Cash, cheques

Room General Leisure

## SHELLEY, West Yorkshire Map ref 4B1

★★★★
RESTAURANT WITH ROOMS

B&B PER ROOM PER NIGHT
S £65.00–£70.00
D £90.00–£100.00

EVENING MEAL PER PERSON
£15.00–£35.00

### Three Acres Inn and Restaurant

Roydhouse, Shelley HD8 8LR **t** (01484) 602606 **e** 3acres@globalnet.co.uk

**3acres.com**

An attractive country inn conveniently situated for all of Yorkshire's major conurbations and motorway networks. Restaurant. Traditional beers.

**open** All year except Christmas and New Year
**bedrooms** 10 double, 1 twin, 8 single, 1 suite
**bathrooms** All en suite
**payment** Credit/debit cards, cash, cheques

Room General Leisure

## SKIPTON, North Yorkshire Map ref 4B1

★★★★★
BED & BREAKFAST
SILVER AWARD

B&B PER ROOM PER NIGHT
S £45.00–£50.00
D £70.00–£80.00

*Stays of 3 nights or more only £35pp (based on 2 people sharing). Children aged 3 and under – free.*

### Cononley Hall Bed & Breakfast

Main Street, Cononley, Skipton BD20 8LJ **t** (01535) 633923 **e** cononleyhall@madasafish.com

**cononleyhall.co.uk**

**open** All year except Christmas and New Year
**bedrooms** 2 double, 1 twin
**bathrooms** All en suite
**payment** Credit/debit cards, cash, cheques

Grade II Listed Georgian house in unspoilt village, near to Skipton. Cononley Hall is ideally located for those wishing to explore the picturesque Yorkshire Dales or the Brontë countryside and attractions. All rooms are en suite and offer excellent facilities. Breakfast consists of local produce, including our own free-range eggs.

**SAT NAV** *BD20 8LJ*

Room General Leisure

For **key to symbols** see page 7

**SKIPTON, North Yorkshire Map ref 4B1**

★★★★
RESTAURANT WITH ROOMS

B&B PER ROOM PER NIGHT
S Max £69.50
D Max £79.50

EVENING MEAL PER PERSON
£10.00–£30.00

*Book 3 nights and receive 10% discount on accommodation.*

## Napier's Restaurant & Accommodation

Chapel Hill, Skipton BD23 1NL **t** (01756) 799688 **e** info@accommodation-skipton.co.uk

**restaurant-skipton.co.uk**

**open** 14 January to 31 December
**bedrooms** 4 double, 2 twin
**bathrooms** All en suite
**payment** Credit/debit cards, cash, cheques, euros

Originally a large farmhouse dating back to the 13th century, offering relaxed and friendly accommodation. Come away and stay with us in the most picturesque corner of Skipton.

**SAT NAV** *BD23 1NL* **ONLINE MAP**

Room General Leisure

**SKIPTON, North Yorkshire Map ref 4B1**

★★★★
BED & BREAKFAST

B&B PER ROOM PER NIGHT
S £37.00–£47.00
D £74.00

## Newton Grange

Bank Newton, Gargrave, Skipton BD23 3NT **t** (01756) 748140 & (01756) 796016
**e** bookings@banknewton.fsnet.co.uk

**cravencountryconnections.co.uk**

A Grade II Listed Georgian farmhouse in rolling countryside, suitable for walking, cycling, horse-riding or touring. Rooms en suite or with private bathroom. Eating places nearby.

**open** All year
**bedrooms** 2 double, 1 twin
**bathrooms** 2 en suite, 1 private
**payment** Cash, cheques

Room General Leisure

**SKIPTON, North Yorkshire Map ref 4B1**

★★★
INN

B&B PER ROOM PER NIGHT
S £40.00
D £65.00–£75.00

EVENING MEAL PER PERSON
£5.95–£9.95

## The Woolly Sheep

38 Sheep Street, Skipton BD23 1HY **t** (01756) 700966

**timothytaylor.co.uk/woollysheep**

A traditional English inn in the centre of Skipton. Busy bar and dining area serving home-cooked food. Luxuriously fitted en suite rooms with TV and tea-/coffee-making facilities. Parking available.

**open** All year
**bedrooms** 3 double, 2 twin, 1 single, 3 family
**bathrooms** All en suite
**payment** Credit/debit cards, cash, cheques

Room General

**SOUTHPORT, Merseyside Map ref 4A1**

★★★
FARMHOUSE

B&B PER ROOM PER NIGHT
S Min £30.00
D Max £50.00

## Sandy Brook Farm

52 Wyke Cop Road, Scarisbrick, Southport PR8 5LR **t** (01704) 880337 & 07719 468712
**e** sandybrookfarm@lycos.co.uk

**sandybrookfarm.co.uk**

Twenty-seven-acre arable farm. Comfortable accommodation in converted farm buildings in rural area of Scarisbrick, 3.5 miles from Southport. Special facilities for disabled guests.

**open** All year except Christmas
**bedrooms** 1 double, 2 twin, 1 single, 2 family
**bathrooms** All en suite
**payment** Cash, cheques

Room General Leisure

### What if I need to cancel?

It's advisable to check the proprietor's cancellation policy at the time of booking in case you have to change your plans.

## SPENNYMOOR, Durham Map ref 5C2

★★★★
GUEST HOUSE

B&B PER ROOM PER NIGHT
S £35.00–£40.00
D £55.00–£60.00

### Highview Country House

Kirk Merrington, Spennymoor DL16 7JT **t** (01388) 811006 **e** jayne@highviewcountryhouse.co.uk

**highviewcountryhouse.com** REAL-TIME BOOKING

Country house in one acre of gardens surrounded by countryside. Peace and tranquillity await. Safe parking. Situated on the edge of delightful village. Good pubs, Saxon church. Ten minutes from motorway/Durham.

**open** All year
**bedrooms** 5 double, 1 twin, 1 single, 1 family
**bathrooms** All en suite
**payment** Credit/debit cards, cash, cheques

Room General P Leisure

## STAITHES, North Yorkshire Map ref 5C3

★★★
BED & BREAKFAST

B&B PER ROOM PER NIGHT
S Min £30.00
D Min £55.00

### Brooklyn

Browns Terrace, Staithes TS13 5BG **t** (01947) 841396 **e** m.heald@tesco.net

**brooklynuk.com**

**open** All year except Christmas
**bedrooms** 2 double, 1 twin
**payment** Cash, cheques

Sea-captain's house in picturesque, historic fishing village. Comfortable, individually decorated rooms with view of Cowbar cliffs. Pets and children welcome. Generous breakfasts. Vegetarians welcome.

**SAT NAV** *TS13 5BG*

Room General

## STANLEY, Durham Map ref 5C2

★★
INN

B&B PER ROOM PER NIGHT
D £54.00–£60.00

### Oak Tree Inn

Front Street, Tantobie, Stanley DH9 9RF **t** (01207) 235445

A beautiful old coach house inn, dating back to the 1700s. Warm and friendly atmosphere and inviting decor. Close to Tanfield Railway and Beamish Museum.

**open** All year
**bedrooms** 2 double, 2 twin, 1 family
**bathrooms** All en suite
**payment** Credit/debit cards, cash, cheques

Room General P Leisure

## STAPE, North Yorkshire Map ref 5D3

★★★★
BED & BREAKFAST
SILVER AWARD

B&B PER ROOM PER NIGHT
S £38.00–£42.00
D £66.00–£72.00

### High Muffles

Pickering YO18 8HP **t** (01751) 417966 **e** candrew840@aol.com

**highmuffles.co.uk**

Beautifully renovated farmhouse accommodation with en suite bathrooms. Situated within Cropton Forest, North Yorkshire National Park. Perfect for walking and cycling.

**open** All year except Christmas and New Year
**bedrooms** 2 double
**bathrooms** All en suite
**payment** Cash, cheques

Room General 14 P Leisure

## Do you have access needs?

Look for the National Accessible Scheme symbols if you have special hearing, visual or mobility needs. An index of accommodation participating in the scheme can be found at the back of this guide.

## STOCKSFIELD, Northumberland Map ref 5B2

★★★
GUEST ACCOMMODATION

B&B PER ROOM PER NIGHT
S £30.00–£35.00
D £60.00–£70.00

### Old Ridley Hall

Stocksfield NE43 7RU **t** (01661) 842816 **e** josephinealdridge@oldridleyhall.force9.co.uk

**oldridley.co.uk**

**open** All year except Christmas
**bedrooms** 2 twin, 1 single, 1 family
**bathrooms** 1 private
**payment** Cash, cheques

Country house with rambling garden, dovecote. Listed buildings. Easy reach of MetroCentre, places to eat, Prudhoe, Corbridge Roman Wall, Newcastle, railway.

**SAT NAV** *NE43 7RU*

Room General

## STOCKTON-ON-TEES, Tees Valley Map ref 5C3

★★★
INN

B&B PER ROOM PER NIGHT
S £45.00
D £59.00

EVENING MEAL PER PERSON
£7.95–£13.95

### The Parkwood

64-66 Darlington Road, Stockton-on-Tees TS18 5ER **t** (01642) 587933
**e** theparkwoodhotel@aol.co.uk

**theparkwoodhotel.com**

**open** All year
**bedrooms** 4 double, 1 twin
**bathrooms** 5 en suite
**payment** Cash, cheques

A very friendly welcome awaits you at this family-run inn. The well-equipped, comfortable rooms boast en suite facilities, along with practical and homely extras. A range of meals are professionally prepared and served in the cosy, non-smoking restaurant and conservatory.

**SAT NAV** *TS18 5ER*

Room General

## SUNDERLAND, Tyne and Wear Map ref 5C2

★★★
BED & BREAKFAST

B&B PER ROOM PER NIGHT
S £25.00–£42.50
D £50.00–£60.00

### Felicitations

94 Ewesley Road, High Barnes, Sunderland SR4 7RJ **t** (0191) 522 0960 **e** felicitations_uk@talk21.com

**felicitations.biz** REAL-TIME BOOKING

Adjacent shower rooms and own use wc. Double with private bathroom facility, power shower and bidet. Heating on all year, good quality food, near to bus routes, university, Royal Hospital.

**open** All year
**bedrooms** 2 double, 1 twin, 1 single, 1 suite
**bathrooms** 1 en suite, 3 private
**payment** Credit/debit cards, cash, cheques, euros

Room General

## Check the maps for accommodation locations

Colour maps at the front pinpoint all the places where accommodation is featured within the regional sections of this guide. Pick your location and then refer to the place index at the back to find the page number.

## TARPORLEY, Cheshire Map ref 4A2

★★★
INN

B&B PER ROOM PER NIGHT
S £40.00
D £55.00

EVENING MEAL PER PERSON
£3.50–£9.25

### Foresters Arms

92 High Street, Tarporley CW6 0AX **t** (01829) 733151 **e** foresters-arms@btconnect.com

**theforesters.co.uk**

A country public house on the edge of Tarporley offering a homely and friendly service. Weekly rates negotiable.

**open** All year
**bedrooms** 2 double, 2 twin, 2 single
**bathrooms** All en suite
**payment** Credit/debit cards, cash, cheques

Room General 10 Leisure

## THIRSK, North Yorkshire Map ref 5C3

★★★★
GUEST ACCOMMODATION
SILVER AWARD

B&B PER ROOM PER NIGHT
S £47.50–£49.50
D £70.00–£75.00

EVENING MEAL PER PERSON
£21.50–£22.50

*In spring and autumn we run courses in all types of embroidery. Please ask for our brochure.*

### Borrowby Mill, Bed and Breakfast

Borrowby, Nr Thirsk YO7 4AW **t** (01845) 537717 **e** markandvickipadfield@btinternet.com

**borrowbymill.co.uk**

**open** All year except Christmas and New Year
**bedrooms** 1 double, 2 twin
**bathrooms** All en suite
**payment** Credit/debit cards, cash, cheques

Tastefully converted 18thC flour mill in a secluded location between Thirsk and Northallerton. Convenient for touring North Yorkshire Moors and Dales. Cosy en suite rooms, excellent breakfasts and dinners prepared by chef/proprietor. Relax in our drawing room with library or explore our woodland gardens.

**SAT NAV** *YO7 4AW*

Room General Leisure

## THIRSK, North Yorkshire Map ref 5C3

★★★★
GUEST ACCOMMODATION

B&B PER ROOM PER NIGHT
S £40.00–£55.00
D £50.00–£65.00

EVENING MEAL PER PERSON
£12.95–£15.95

### Manor House Cottage

Hag Lane, South Kilvington, Thirsk YO7 2NY **t** (01845) 527712 **e** info@manor-house-cottage.co.uk

**manor-house-cottage.co.uk** REAL-TIME BOOKING

**open** All year
**bedrooms** 2 double, 1 twin
**bathrooms** 2 en suite, 1 private
**payment** Cash, cheques

Superior accommodation in quiet rural location, three minutes from town centre, close to the dales and the North York Moors.

**SAT NAV** *YO7 2NY*

Room General Leisure

## THIRSK, North Yorkshire Map ref 5C3

★★★★
FARMHOUSE

B&B PER ROOM PER NIGHT
S £35.00–£40.00
D £50.00–£65.00

### Town Pasture Farm

Thirsk YO7 2DY **t** (01845) 537298

Comfortable farmhouse in picturesque Boltby village within the North York Moors National Park. Views of the Hambleton Hills. Excellent walks. Horse-riding available in village. Central for east coast, York and the Dales. Colour TV in lounge.

**open** All year except Christmas
**bedrooms** 1 twin, 1 family
**bathrooms** All en suite
**payment** Cash, cheques

Room General Leisure

For **key to symbols** see page 7

## THIXENDALE, North Yorkshire Map ref 4C1

★★★
INN

B&B PER ROOM PER NIGHT
S Max £27.50
D Max £55.00

# The Cross Keys

Thixendale, Malton YO17 9TG **t** (01377) 288272

Family-run, award-winning, small village pub nestling in the valleys of the Yorkshire Wolds. Well situated on four major and several short, circular walks. Single occupancy available.

**open** All year except Christmas and New Year
**bedrooms** 1 double, 2 twin
**bathrooms** All en suite
**payment** Credit/debit cards, cash, cheques

Room General 14

## THORNTON-CLEVELEYS, Lancashire Map ref 4A1

★★
GUEST ACCOMMODATION

B&B PER ROOM PER NIGHT
S £20.00–£22.50
D £40.00–£45.00

# Four Seasons Guest House

9 Cambridge Road, Thornton-Cleveleys FY5 1EP **t** (01253) 853537
**e** fourseasonsguesthouse@talktalk.net

**open** All year
**bedrooms** 3 double, 2 twin, 1 single
**bathrooms** 1 en suite
**payment** Cash, cheques, euros

The Four Seasons, where you are assured of a warm welcome, friendly atmosphere, comfortable rooms and an excellent full English breakfast. Situated yards from the bus station, excellent shopping centre, lively pubs and clubs and the newly modernised promenade. Blackpool and Fleetwood are just a tram ride away.

**SAT NAV** *FY5 1EP*

Room TV SC General 2 P

## THORNTON DALE, North Yorkshire Map ref 5D3

★★★★
GUEST HOUSE

B&B PER ROOM PER NIGHT
S Min £28.00
D £60.00–£70.00

EVENING MEAL PER PERSON
£10.00–£30.00

# Bridgefoot Guest House

Pickering YO18 7RR **t** (01751) 474749 **e** enquire@bridgefoot-house.co.uk

**bridgefoot-house.co.uk**

Seventeenth-century house of character providing a warm welcome with emphasis on food and comfort. By a trout beck in a beautiful village.

**open** All year
**bedrooms** 5 double, 1 twin, 1 single, 1 family
**bathrooms** All en suite
**payment** Cash, cheques

Room TV General P

## THORNTON DALE, North Yorkshire Map ref 5D3

★★★★
BED & BREAKFAST
SILVER AWARD

B&B PER ROOM PER NIGHT
S £65.00
D £80.00

# Cherry Garth

Church Hill, Pickering YO18 7QH **t** (01751) 473404 **e** claire@cherrygarthholidays.com

**cherrygarthholidays.com** SPECIAL OFFERS

Central to Thornton-le-Dale and the famous thatched cottage. Charming separate studio apartments with fully equipped kitchens, giving the choice of serviced or self-catering accommodation. Based on Scandinavian comforts.

**bedrooms** 2 double
**bathrooms** All en suite
**payment** Cash, cheques

WALKERS WELCOME · CYCLISTS WELCOME

Room TV General P Leisure

## THRELKELD, Cumbria Map ref 5A3

★★★★
INN

B&B PER ROOM PER NIGHT
S £35.00–£50.00
D £70.00–£100.00

EVENING MEAL PER PERSON
£7.50–£16.50

### Horse and Farrier Inn

Threlkeld, Keswick CA12 4SQ **t** (017687) 79688 **e** info@horseandfarrier.com

**horseandfarrier.com** GUEST REVIEWS • SPECIAL OFFERS

**open** All year
**bedrooms** 4 double, 1 twin, 6 double/twin
**bathrooms** 9 en suite, 2 private
**payment** Credit/debit cards, cash, cheques

This award-winning inn is situated beneath Blencathra and is ideally located for walking or touring the Lake District. All nine bedrooms are en suite with TV, tea-/coffee-making facilities and hairdryer. Our Head Chef won the Cumbria Tourist Board's Most Inspiring Chef of the Year 2005/2006. Numerous guide book recommendations.

**SAT NAV** *CA12 4SQ* **ONLINE MAP**

Room General Leisure

## ULLSWATER, Cumbria Map ref 5A3

★★★
GUEST HOUSE

B&B PER ROOM PER NIGHT
S £38.00–£50.00
D £66.00–£72.00

*Rheged discount vouchers.*

### Knotts Mill Country Lodge

Watermillock, Penrith CA11 0JN **t** (017684) 86699 **e** relax@knottsmill.com

**knottsmill.com**

**open** All year
**bedrooms** 4 double, 2 twin, 3 family
**bathrooms** All en suite
**payment** Credit/debit cards, cash, cheques, euros

A country lodge offering quality, serviced accommodation and big breakfasts. In private grounds, set in magnificent scenery around Ullswater with stunning views of the surrounding hills. Ideal for walking, touring, bird-watching and sailing. Relaxed, welcoming atmosphere in a peaceful setting, yet only ten minutes from the M6. Pets by arrangement.

**SAT NAV** *CA11 0JN* **ONLINE MAP**

Room General Leisure

## WALL, Northumberland Map ref 5B2

★★★
INN

B&B PER ROOM PER NIGHT
S £45.00–£50.00
D £58.00–£68.00

EVENING MEAL PER PERSON
£6.25–£14.25

### The Hadrian Wall Inn

Wall, Hexham NE46 4EE **t** (01434) 681232 **e** david.lindsay13@btinternet.com

**hadrianhotel.com**

Attractive 18thC former coaching inn. Excellent bar meals, real ales, open fires and tranquil gardens. Situated close to Hadrian's Wall and near Hexham.

**open** All year
**bedrooms** 2 double, 4 twin
**bathrooms** 4 en suite
**payment** Credit/debit cards, cash, cheques

Room General

## Where can I get help and advice?

Tourist Information Centres offer friendly help with accommodation and holiday ideas as well as suggestions of places to visit and things to do. You'll find contact details at the beginning of each regional section.

## WARK, Northumberland Map ref 5B2

★★★★
INN
SILVER AWARD

B&B PER ROOM PER NIGHT
S £55.00–£60.00
D £90.00–£110.00

EVENING MEAL PER PERSON
£8.50–£18.50

*Changing offers throughout the year. Please see website.*

### Battlesteads Country Inn & Restaurant

Wark, Hexham NE48 3LS **t** (01434) 230209 **e** info@battlesteads.com

**battlesteads.com**

**open** All year
**bedrooms** 7 double, 7 twin, 1 single, 2 family
**bathrooms** All en suite
**payment** Credit/debit cards, cash, cheques

18thC inn, formerly a farmhouse, in the heart of rural Northumberland, close to the Roman Wall and Kielder Water. An ideal centre for exploring Border country and for relaxing, walking or cycling. Ground-floor bedrooms available. Excellent restaurant using fresh, local produce. Five cask ales.

**SAT NAV** *NE48 3LS*

Room General Leisure

## WARRINGTON, Cheshire Map ref 4A2

★★
BED & BREAKFAST

B&B PER ROOM PER NIGHT
S Min £37.00
D Min £52.00

EVENING MEAL PER PERSON
Min £7.00

### New House Farm Cottages

Hatton Lane, Hatton, Warrington WA4 4BZ **t** (01925) 730567 **e** newhousefarmcottages@goggle.com

**newhousefarmcottages.co.uk**

Fully modernised farm-workers' cottages which still retain their original features. Fields surround the cottages. Organic fruit sold from garden. Close to motorways. Evening meals available. Pick-ups arranged.

**open** All year
**bedrooms** 1 double, 1 twin, 1 single, 1 family
**bathrooms** 2 en suite, 2 private
**payment** Cash, cheques, euros

Room General Leisure

## WARRINGTON, Cheshire Map ref 4A2

★★★
GUEST ACCOMMODATION

B&B PER ROOM PER NIGHT
S £46.00–£53.00
D £46.00–£53.00

### Tall Trees Lodge

Tarporley Road, Lower Whitley, Warrington WA4 4EZ **t** (01928) 790824 & (01928) 715117
**e** booking@talltreeslodge.co.uk

**talltreeslodge.co.uk**

Set in the beautiful Cheshire countryside, a warm welcome awaits you at Tall Trees. The rooms are large, bright and have TV, hairdryer, telephone and coffee-making facilities. All en suite.

**open** All year except Christmas and New Year
**bedrooms** 14 double, 1 twin, 5 family
**bathrooms** All en suite
**payment** Cash, cheques

Room General

## WATERMILLOCK-ON-ULLSWATER, Cumbria Map ref 5A3

★★★★
FARMHOUSE

B&B PER ROOM PER NIGHT
D Min £60.00

### Mellfell House Farm B&B

Watermillock-on-Ullswater, Penrith CA11 0LS **t** (017684) 86295 **e** ben@mellfell.co.uk

**mellfell.co.uk**

Lovely old farmhouse high above Ullswater in Lake District National Park. Log fires. Central heating. En suite. Hearty breakfasts. Guest lounge. Use of kitchen facilities. Delightful walks from door. Excellent base.

**open** February to October
**bedrooms** 2 double, 1 twin
**bathrooms** All en suite
**payment** Cash, cheques

Room General Leisure

**Where can I get live travel information?**
For the latest travel update – call the RAC on 1740 from your mobile phone.

## WELBURN, North Yorkshire Map ref 5C3

★★★

BED & BREAKFAST

B&B PER ROOM PER NIGHT
D £60.00–£80.00

### The Barley Basket

Main Road, York YO60 7DX **t** (01653) 618352 **e** marianlacey@btinternet.com

A warm welcome awaits you. Situated on the fringe of Castle Howard, York, Scarborough and the Howardian Hills.

**open** All year
**bedrooms** 2 family
**bathrooms** 1 en suite, 1 private
**payment** Cash, cheques

Room General 10 P

## WEST KIRBY, Merseyside Map ref 4A2

★★★★

GUEST HOUSE
SILVER AWARD

B&B PER ROOM PER NIGHT
S Min £65.00
D Min £85.00

*Winter breaks available.*

### At Peel Hey

Frankby Road, Frankby, Wirral CH48 1PP **t** (0151) 677 9077 **e** enquiries@peelhey.co.uk

**peelhey.co.uk** SPECIAL OFFERS • REAL-TIME BOOKING

**open** All year
**bedrooms** 4 double, 2 twin, 1 single, 2 family
**bathrooms** All en suite
**payment** Credit/debit cards, cash, cheques

Award-winning country house offering luxury, en suite accommodation, a warm welcome and excellent breakfasts and cream teas. Located in picturesque village, yet minutes from Hoylake, British Open Championship venue 2006 and West Kirby for restaurants and bars. Close to M53 for Chester and 15 minutes from Liverpool – European Capital of Culture 2008. Wi-Fi.

**SAT NAV** *CH48 1PP*

Room General P Leisure

## WEST KIRBY, Merseyside Map ref 4A2

★★★★★

BED & BREAKFAST

B&B PER ROOM PER NIGHT
S Min £65.00
D Min £85.00

*Oct-Mar: 3 nights for the price of 2 (excl Christmas and New Year). Special weekly rates.*

### Caldy Warren Cottage

42 Caldy Road, West Kirby, Wirral CH48 2HQ **t** (0151) 625 8740 **e** office@warrencott.demon.co.uk

**warrencott.demon.co.uk**

**open** All year except Christmas and New Year
**bedrooms** 2 double, 1 twin
**bathrooms** All en suite
**payment** Credit/debit cards, cash, cheques

Beautiful, privately owned guesthouse offering luxury accommodation. Spectacular views across Dee Estuary towards Wales. Close to all local amenities, marine lake, restaurants and bars, and conveniently located for Hoylake – Open Championship venue 2006, Liverpool – European Capital of Culture 2008, and Chester, making us an excellent touring base. Non-smoking.

**SAT NAV** *CH48 2HQ*

Room General P

## Country Code always follow the Country Code

- Be safe – plan ahead and follow any signs
- Leave gates and property as you find them
- Protect plants and animals, and take your litter home
- Keep dogs under close control
- Consider other people

## WEST WITTON, North Yorkshire Map ref 5B3

★★★
GUEST ACCOMMODATION

B&B PER ROOM PER NIGHT
S £26.00–£38.00
D £48.00–£54.00

*We offer a price reduction for stays of 3 or more nights and a further reduction for a week or more.*

### The Old Star

Main Street, West Witton, Leyburn DL8 4LU **t** (01969) 622949 **e** enquiries@theoldstar.com

**theoldstar.com**

**open** All year except Christmas
**bedrooms** 4 double, 1 twin, 2 family
**bathrooms** 5 en suite
**payment** Cash, cheques

Seventeenth-century, stone-built former coaching inn set in the Yorkshire Dales National Park with uninterrupted views of Wensleydale from the rear of the property. Oak beams, log fire and a friendly atmosphere, The Old Star is an excellent centre for exploring the Dales. West Witton has two excellent pubs for food.

**SAT NAV** *DL8 4LU*

Room General P Leisure

## WEST WOODBURN, Northumberland Map ref 5B2

★★★
INN

B&B PER ROOM PER NIGHT
S £40.00–£50.00
D £60.00–£84.00

EVENING MEAL PER PERSON
£7.95–£20.00

### Bay Horse Inn

West Woodburn NE48 2RX **t** (01434) 270218 **e** enquiry@bayhorseinn.org

**bayhorseinn.org** SPECIAL OFFERS · REAL-TIME BOOKING

An 18thC coaching inn nestling on the banks of the River Rede. Personally run, friendly locals. Super food using mostly local produce. Central for Hadrian's Wall, Kielder Water, border towns.

**open** All year except Christmas Day
**bedrooms** 3 double, 2 twin
**bathrooms** All en suite
**payment** Credit/debit cards, cash, cheques

Room General P Leisure

## WETHERBY, West Yorkshire Map ref 4B1

★★
GUEST HOUSE

B&B PER ROOM PER NIGHT
S £28.00–£30.00
D £56.00–£60.00

### Prospect House

8 Caxton Street, Wetherby LS22 6RU **t** (01937) 582428

Established 45 years. En suite rooms available. Near York, Harrogate, Dales, Herriot Country. Midway London/Edinburgh. Restaurants nearby. Pets welcome.

**open** All year
**bedrooms** 2 double, 2 twin, 2 single
**bathrooms** 4 en suite
**payment** Cash, cheques

Room General

## WHALLEY, Lancashire Map ref 4A1

★★★★
GUEST ACCOMMODATION

B&B PER ROOM PER NIGHT
S £35.00
D £70.00

### Whalley Abbey

The Sands, Whalley, Clitheroe BB7 9SS **t** (01254) 828400 **e** office@whalleyabbey.org

**whalleyabbey.co.uk** SPECIAL OFFERS

Whalley Abbey Conference House offers en suite accommodation with TV, phone and free internet connection. The 14thC Cistercian Abbey ruins, gardens and coffee shop are open daily.

**open** All year except Christmas and New Year
**bedrooms** 1 double, 9 twin, 6 single, 1 family
**bathrooms** 16 en suite, 1 private
**payment** Credit/debit cards, cash, cheques

Room General P Leisure

## It's all quality-assessed accommodation

Our commitment to quality involves wide-ranging accommodation assessment. Ratings and awards were correct at the time of going to press but may change following a new assessment. Please check at time of booking.

## WHITBY, North Yorkshire Map ref 5D3

★★★★
BED & BREAKFAST
SILVER AWARD

B&B PER ROOM PER NIGHT
D £60.00–£85.00

### Gramarye Suites B&B

15 Coach Road, Sleights, Whitby YO22 5AA **t** (01947) 811656 **e** gramaryesuites@btinternet.com

**gramaryesuites.co.uk**

**open** All year
**bedrooms** 2 double, 1 family
**bathrooms** All en suite
**payment** Cash, cheques

Three-bedroom, luxury bed and breakfast in a former village shop in Sleights, Whitby. Ideally suited for the North York Moors and the Yorkshire coast. The rooms have king-size four-poster/high-post beds, satellite LCD TVs, free Wi-Fi, irons, hairdryers, fridges, room safes, very generous beverage trays and high-quality en suites.

**SAT NAV** *YO22 5AA* **ONLINE MAP**

Room General Leisure

## WHITBY, North Yorkshire Map ref 5D3

★★★
HOSTEL

PER PERSON PER NIGHT
B&B £24.00-£34.00

PER PERSON PER WEEK
HB £224.00-£294.00
FB £273.00-£343.00

### Sneaton Castle Centre

Castle Road, Whitby YO21 3QN **t** (01947) 600051
**e** sneaton@globalnet.co.uk

**sneatoncastle.co.uk**

Excellent facilities in beautiful location for bed and breakfast, holidays, conferences, meetings and many other events. Excellent home cooking, ample free and safe parking. Ideal base for touring the North York Moors area.

**open** All year except Christmas and New Year
**bedrooms** 34 single, 16 twin, 7 quad, 1 dormitory. Total no of beds 120
**bathrooms** 12 en suite, 24 public
**meals** Breakfast, lunch and evening meals available
**payment** Credit/debit cards, cash/cheques

Room General P Leisure

## WHITBY, North Yorkshire Map ref 5D3

★★★★
GUEST ACCOMMODATION

B&B PER ROOM PER NIGHT
S Min £33.50
D Min £67.00

EVENING MEAL PER PERSON
Min £8.50

### Sneaton Castle Centre

Sneaton Castle, Whitby YO21 3QN **t** (01947) 600051 **e** sneaton@globalnet.co.uk

**sneatoncastle.co.uk**

St Francis House, set in stunning grounds of Sneaton Castle, on outskirts of Whitby and edge of the North York Moors. High quality en suite accommodation. Excellent breakfast. Ample parking.

**open** All year except Christmas and New Year
**bedrooms** 9 twin, 3 family
**bathrooms** All en suite
**payment** Credit/debit cards, cash, cheques

Room General P Leisure

## WHITBY, North Yorkshire Map ref 5D3

★★★
GUEST HOUSE

B&B PER ROOM PER NIGHT
S £25.00–£29.00
D £48.00–£56.00

EVENING MEAL PER PERSON
£15.00

### Wentworth House

27 Hudson Street, Whitby YO21 3EP **t** (01947) 602433 **e** info@whitbywentworth.co.uk

**whitbywentworth.co.uk** GUEST REVIEWS · REAL-TIME BOOKING

Small, friendly family-run guesthouse. Pets welcome. Central location for beach, town pubs, restaurant and all the facilities of the North York coast and moors.

**open** All year
**bedrooms** 2 double, 1 twin, 1 single, 3 family
**bathrooms** 6 en suite, 1 private
**payment** Cash, cheques

Room General Leisure

For **key to symbols** see page 7

## WHITEHAVEN, Cumbria Map ref 5A3

★★★★★
GUEST HOUSE
GOLD AWARD

B&B PER ROOM PER NIGHT
S £80.00–£100.00
D £100.00–£140.00

EVENING MEAL PER PERSON
£25.00–£30.00

*Sep-Mar: book dinner on 2 consecutive nights and receive a free bottle of house wine each night (2 or more diners).*

### Moresby Hall

Moresby, Whitehaven CA28 6PJ **t** (01946) 696317 **e** info@moresbyhall.co.uk

**moresbyhall.co.uk** REAL-TIME BOOKING

**open** All year
**bedrooms** 1 double, 1 twin, 2 suites
**bathrooms** All en suite
**payment** Credit/debit cards, cash, cheques, euros

A Grade I Listed building (circa 1620) – one of the oldest residences in Cumbria. Delightful four-poster rooms with hydromassage power shower, sauna or jacuzzi bath and TileVision colour TV. Delicious breakfasts and imaginative dinners. Semi-rural location, walled gardens, good parking. Near Whitehaven, a Georgian harbour town.

**SAT NAV** *CA28 6PJ*

Room General 10 P Leisure

## WHITEWELL, Lancashire Map ref 4A1

★★★★★
INN
GOLD AWARD

B&B PER ROOM PER NIGHT
S £70.00–£160.00
D £96.00–£197.00

### The Inn at Whitewell

Dunsop Road, Whitewell BB7 3AT **t** (01200) 448222 **e** reception@innatwhitewell.com

**innatwhitewell.com**

Award-winning inn with superb restaurant, own wine merchant and very individual bedrooms. Residential fishing.

**open** All year
**bedrooms** 18 double, 4 twin, 1 suite
**bathrooms** All en suite
**payment** Credit/debit cards, cash, cheques

Room General P Leisure

## WHITLEY BAY, Tyne and Wear Map ref 5C2

★★★★
GUEST HOUSE

B&B PER ROOM PER NIGHT
S £39.00–£45.00
D £65.00–£70.00

### Lindsay Guest House

50 Victoria Avenue, Whitley Bay NE26 2BA **t** (0191) 252 7341 **e** info@lindsayguesthouse.co.uk

**lindsayguesthouse.co.uk**

Small, family-run guesthouse offering quality en suite accommodation, close to the sea, town, transport system and all amenities.

**open** All year
**bedrooms** 2 double, 1 twin, 1 family
**bathrooms** All en suite
**payment** Credit/debit cards, cash, cheques, euros

Room General P Leisure

## WILTON, North Yorkshire Map ref 5D3

★★★★
GUEST ACCOMMODATION

B&B PER ROOM PER NIGHT
S Min £39.50
D Min £65.00

*Bargain breaks available.*

### The Old Forge

Wilton, Pickering YO18 7JY **t** (01751) 477399

**open** All year
**bedrooms** 2 double, 1 twin
**bathrooms** All en suite
**payment** Cash, cheques

Blacksmith's cottage and forge, dating from 1701, converted to create comfortable, quality bed and breakfast with all rooms en suite. Many local attractions including steam railway, Dalby Forest, Yorkshire Moors, Eden Camp. Close to Thornton-le-Dale, a beautiful 'chocolate-box' village (one mile), and Pickering (four miles).

**SAT NAV** *YO18 7JY*

Room General 12 P Leisure

**WINDERMERE, Cumbria Map ref 5A3**

★★★★★
GUEST HOUSE

B&B PER ROOM PER NIGHT
D £80.00–£150.00

## Beaumont House

Holly Road, Windermere LA23 2AF **t** (015394) 47075 **e** thebeaumonthotel@btinternet.com

**lakesbeaumont.co.uk** SPECIAL OFFERS • REAL-TIME BOOKING

Beaumont House, an elegant Victorian property occupying an enviable position close to all amenities of Windermere/Bowness, providing superb quality bed and breakfast. Ideal base from which to tour Lakeland.

**open** All year except Christmas
**bedrooms** 8 double, 2 twin
**bathrooms** All en suite
**payment** Credit/debit cards, cash, cheques, euros

Room General 12 P Leisure

**WINDERMERE, Cumbria Map ref 5A3**

★★★
BED & BREAKFAST

B&B PER ROOM PER NIGHT
S Min £30.00
D £48.00–£56.00

EVENING MEAL PER PERSON
Min £13.50

## Bowfell Cottage

Middle Entrance Drive, Bowness-on-Windermere, Windermere LA23 3JY **t** (015394) 44835

**open** All year
**bedrooms** 1 double, 1 twin, 1 family
**bathrooms** 1 en suite
**payment** Cash, cheques

Cottage in a delightful setting, about one mile south of Bowness just off the A5074, offering traditional Lakeland hospitality with comfortable accommodation and good home-cooking. Secluded parking in own grounds surrounding the property.

**SAT NAV** *LA23 3JY*

Room General P Leisure

**WINDERMERE, Cumbria Map ref 5A3**

★★★★
GUEST HOUSE

B&B PER ROOM PER NIGHT
D £48.00–£72.00

## College House

15 College Road, Windermere LA23 1BU **t** (015394) 45767 **e** clghse@aol.com

**college-house.com** REAL-TIME BOOKING

**open** All year
**bedrooms** 2 double, 1 twin
**bathrooms** All en suite
**payment** Cash, cheques

Quiet, comfortable, Victorian family house offering a warm and friendly welcome. Close to village centre and bus/railway station. Front rooms have superb mountain views, all are en suite and have colour TV, tea/coffee-making facilities and full central heating. Delicious breakfast choice. Colourful, sunny garden. Non-smoking. Private parking.

**SAT NAV** *LA23 1BU*

Room General 12 P Leisure

## WINDERMERE, Cumbria Map ref 5A3

★★★
GUEST HOUSE

B&B PER ROOM PER NIGHT
S £75.00–£180.00
D £65.00–£180.00

*Offer – 1 Jan–30 Jun 2009: 3 nights' B&B midweek from £125, standard room per person. Subject to availability.*

### The Cranleigh

Kendal Road, Bowness-on-Windermere, Windermere LA23 3EW **t** (015394) 43293
**e** enquiries@thecranleigh.com

**thecranleigh.com** GUEST REVIEWS • SPECIAL OFFERS • REAL-TIME BOOKING

**open** All year
**bedrooms** 11 double, 2 twin, 2 family
**bathrooms** 14 en suite, 1 private
**payment** Credit/debit cards, cash, cheques

The Cranleigh is situated only one minute's walk from Lake Windermere and the central village. Stunning new luxury and superior rooms with fantastic in-room facilities that rival the best hotels around. Air-spa baths, large TVs, DVD recorders, iPod docking stations, mood lighting, luxury bedding, towels, robes and much, much more.

**SAT NAV** *LA23 3EW* **ONLINE MAP**

Room SC General P Leisure

## WINDERMERE, Cumbria Map ref 5A3

★★★
GUEST HOUSE

B&B PER ROOM PER NIGHT
S £20.00–£30.00
D £22.00–£40.00

*Discounts for stays of 3 or more nights (excl school holidays). Phone for last-minute deals.*

### Elim Lodge

Biskey Howe Road, Bowness-on-Windermere LA23 2JP **t** (015394) 47299
**e** enquiries@elimlodge.co.uk

**elimlodge.co.uk** SPECIAL OFFERS • REAL-TIME BOOKING

**open** All year except Christmas
**bedrooms** 2 double, 1 twin, 1 single, 2 family
**bathrooms** 3 en suite, 1 private
**payment** Credit/debit cards, cash, cheques

An attractive, family-run B&B only five minutes' walk from Lake Windermere. Clean, smart, value-for-money accommodation with private parking and garden in a quiet and pretty part of Bowness village. Superb breakfasts with local ingredients and Fairtrade tea/coffee. Gay-friendly. Pets welcome by arrangement.

**SAT NAV** *LA23 2JP*

Room TV General P Leisure

## WINDERMERE, Cumbria Map ref 5A3

★★★★
GUEST HOUSE
SILVER AWARD

B&B PER ROOM PER NIGHT
S £40.00–£88.00
D £64.00–£88.00

### Fair Rigg

Ferry View, Bowness-on-Windermere, Windermere LA23 3JB **t** (015394) 43941 **e** stay@fairrigg.co.uk

**fairrigg.co.uk**

Fine Victorian house with superb views, in rural setting on edge of Bowness. Lovely rooms, plenty of space to relax and unwind. High standards assured.

**open** All year except Christmas and New Year
**bedrooms** 5 double, 1 twin
**bathrooms** All en suite
**payment** Credit/debit cards, cash, cheques

Room TV General 14 P Leisure

## Remember to check when booking

Please remember that all information in this guide has been supplied by the proprietors well in advance of publication. Since changes do sometimes occur it's a good idea to check details at the time of booking.

## WINDERMERE, Cumbria Map ref 5A3

★★★★
GUEST HOUSE
SILVER AWARD

B&B PER ROOM PER NIGHT
s £45.00–£60.00
d £66.00–£140.00

EVENING MEAL PER PERSON
Min £27.50

*Reduced prices for 3 nights during weekdays, or extended weekends in low season. DB&B available Nov-Mar.*

### Fairfield House and Gardens

Brantfell Road, Bowness Bay LA23 3AE **t** (015394) 46565 **e** relax@the-fairfield.co.uk

**the-fairfield.co.uk** GUEST REVIEWS · SPECIAL OFFERS · REAL-TIME BOOKING

**open** All year except Christmas
**bedrooms** 4 double, 2 twin, 1 family, 3 suites
**bathrooms** All en suite
**payment** Credit/debit cards, cash, cheques, euros

Secluded Georgian house set in own grounds with beautiful garden and private car park. Informally run B&B with exceptional breakfasts. King-size four-poster and spa-bath bedrooms available. All rooms en suite, some with state-of-the-art, deluxe bathrooms. Guest lounge with internet access. Located central Bowness – close to Lake Windermere, restaurants, shops and pubs.

**SAT NAV** *LA23 3AE* **ONLINE MAP**

Room General 10 P Leisure

## WINDERMERE, Cumbria Map ref 5A3

★★★★
GUEST ACCOMMODATION

B&B PER ROOM PER NIGHT
s £27.00–£35.00
d £52.00–£70.00

### Holly Lodge

6 College Road, Windermere LA23 1BX **t** (015394) 43873 **e** enquiries@hollylodge20.co.uk

**hollylodge20.co.uk** SPECIAL OFFERS

Traditional Lakeland, family-run guesthouse in a quiet location close to shops, restaurants, buses and trains. Friendly atmosphere. Hearty English breakfast. Each bedroom individually furnished.

**open** All year except Christmas
**bedrooms** 4 double, 1 single, 4 family
**bathrooms** All en suite
**payment** Credit/debit cards, cash, cheques

Room General P Leisure

## WINDERMERE, Cumbria Map ref 5A3

★★★★
GUEST HOUSE

B&B PER ROOM PER NIGHT
s £35.00–£50.00
d £70.00–£85.00

*See website for details of all special offers.*

### Holly-Wood Guest House

Holly Road, Windermere LA23 2AF **t** (015394) 42219 **e** info@hollywoodguesthouse.co.uk

**hollywoodguesthouse.co.uk** REAL-TIME BOOKING

**open** All year
**bedrooms** 3 double, 1 twin, 1 single, 1 family
**bathrooms** All en suite
**payment** Credit/debit cards, cash, cheques

Minutes from Windermere village centre and a short stroll from Lake Windermere, Holly-Wood is a family-run guesthouse where you are assured of a warm welcome. Our comfortable bedrooms are equipped with thoughtful extras. Private parking available. Excellent, hearty English breakfast. A perfect base to explore the Lake District.

**SAT NAV** *LA23 2AF* **ONLINE MAP**

Room General 10 P Leisure

## Check the maps for accommodation locations

Colour maps at the front pinpoint all the cities, towns and villages where you will find accommodation entries in the regional sections. Pick your location and then refer to the place index at the back to find the page number.

## WINDERMERE, Cumbria Map ref 5A3

★★★★
GUEST HOUSE

B&B PER ROOM PER NIGHT
D £48.00–£90.00

### Lindisfarne Guest House

Sunny Bank Road, Windermere LA23 2EN **t** (015394) 46295 **e** enquiries@lindisfarne-house.co.uk

**lindisfarne-house.co.uk**

**open** All year except Christmas
**bedrooms** 2 double, 1 twin, 1 family
**bathrooms** 3 en suite, 1 private
**payment** Cash, cheques

A traditional, detached Lakeland-stone house built in 1881. Situated in a quiet area within easy walking distance of Windermere village centre, shops, restaurants, pubs and scenic walks, Bowness and Lake Windermere. Healthy, home-cooked English breakfasts. Non-smoking. Garage storage for bicycles/motorbikes.

**SAT NAV** *LA23 2EN*

Room General 5 P Leisure

## WINDERMERE, Cumbria Map ref 5A3

★★★★
GUEST HOUSE

B&B PER ROOM PER NIGHT
D £65.00–£90.00

*Seasonal specials – please see our website for details. Discounts on stays of 3 nights or longer.*

### New Hall Bank

Fallbarrow Road, Windermere LA23 3DJ **t** (015394) 43558 **e** info@newhallbank.co.uk

**newhallbank.com** SPECIAL OFFERS

**open** All year
**bedrooms** 12 double, 3 twin, 3 family
**bathrooms** 10 en suite, 2 private
**payment** Credit/debit cards, cash, cheques

Wonderful Victorian guesthouse standing in one of the most envied positions in Bowness overlooking the lake! Comfortable en suite rooms, many with lake views, contain all you require for a relaxing stay in the heart of the Lake District. English or vegetarian breakfasts provided, on-site car parking, personal attention.

**SAT NAV** *LA23 3DJ*

Room General 5 P Leisure

## WINDERMERE, Cumbria Map ref 5A3

★★★
GUEST ACCOMMODATION

B&B PER ROOM PER NIGHT
S £35.00–£50.00
D £55.00–£110.00

*3-day breaks (price per person): low season from £60, mid-season from £75, high season from £84.*

### St John's Lodge

Lake Road, Windermere LA23 2EQ **t** (015394) 43078 **e** mail@st-johns-lodge.co.uk

**st-johns-lodge.co.uk** GUEST REVIEWS · SPECIAL OFFERS · REAL-TIME BOOKING

**open** All year except Christmas
**bedrooms** 9 double, 1 twin, 1 single, 1 family
**bathrooms** All en suite
**payment** Credit/debit cards, cash, euros

Pretty guesthouse between Windermere and lake, and close to all amenities including Beatrix Potter attraction. Exclusively for adult non-smokers. Large breakfast menu including traditional English, veggie/vegan, gluten-free, fresh fish and some house speciality dishes. Free internet access via communal PC and 24-hour Wi-Fi. Free use of nearby luxury leisure club.

**SAT NAV** *LA23 2EQ* **ONLINE MAP**

Room General 12 P Leisure

## Looking for a wide range of facilities?

More stars means higher quality accommodation plus a greater range of facilities and services.

## WINDERMERE, Cumbria Map ref 5A3

★★★★
GUEST HOUSE
SILVER AWARD

B&B PER ROOM PER NIGHT
S £35.00–£100.00
D £50.00–£120.00

*Stay any 3 nights Sun-Thu and get a short-break discount. Weekend breaks from £100.00.*

### Southview House & Indoor Pool

Cross Street, Windermere LA23 1AE **t** (015394) 42951 **e** stay@southviewwindermere.co.uk

**southviewwindermere.co.uk**

**open** All year except Christmas
**bedrooms** 9 double, 1 twin
**bathrooms** All en suite
**payment** Credit/debit cards, cash, cheques

The Southview is a licensed B&B with its own heated indoor swimming pool. A bed and breakfast guesthouse with a 'splash of luxury'. Southview consists of ten en suite bedrooms: five superior with en suite spa baths or body-jet showers, one contemporary king-size four-poster room and four classic rooms.

**SAT NAV** *LA23 1AE*

Room General 6 P Leisure

## WINDERMERE, Cumbria Map ref 5A3

★★★★
GUEST HOUSE

B&B PER ROOM PER NIGHT
S £45.00–£60.00
D £55.00–£90.00

*Special off-peak offer: 3 nights for £165 per en suite double. Discount from high-season prices available all year for 3-night stays.*

### Tarn Rigg Guest House

Thornbarrow Road, Windermere LA23 2DG **t** (015394) 88777 **e** info@tarnrigg-guesthouse.co.uk

**tarnrigg-guesthouse.co.uk** GUEST REVIEWS • SPECIAL OFFERS

**open** All year except Christmas
**bedrooms** 3 double, 2 family
**bathrooms** All en suite
**payment** Credit/debit cards, cash, cheques, euros

Welcome to the Lake District. Built in 1903, Tarn Rigg is situated in an ideal position midway between Windermere and Bowness. Panoramic Langdale Pike views. Quiet, convenient location, ample parking, beautiful 0.75-acre grounds. Spacious, en suite rooms with excellent modern facilities. Rooms with lake views available.

**SAT NAV** *LA23 2DG*

Room General P Leisure

## WIRRAL

*See under West Kirby*

## WORKINGTON, Cumbria Map ref 5A2

★★★★
INN

B&B PER ROOM PER NIGHT
S £55.00–£65.00
D £70.00–£110.00

### Old Ginn House

Moor Road, Great Clifton, Workington CA14 1TS **t** (01900) 64616 **e** enquiries@oldginnhouse.co.uk

**oldginnhouse.co.uk**

The Old Ginn House has been successfully converted from a 17thC farm into a charming village inn offering quality accommodation, great food and a warm welcome. Ideal for exploring the Western Lake District.

**open** All year except Christmas
**bedrooms** 11 double, 3 twin, 4 family, 1 suite
**bathrooms** All en suite
**payment** Credit/debit cards, cash, cheques

Room General P Leisure

CYCLISTS WELCOME

## Fancy a cycling holiday?

For a fabulous freewheeling break, seek out accommodation participating in our Cyclists Welcome scheme. Look out for the symbol and plan your route online at nationalcyclenetwork.org.

## YORK, North Yorkshire Map ref 4C1

★★★★
GUEST HOUSE
SILVER AWARD

B&B PER ROOM PER NIGHT
s £45.00–£55.00
D £70.00–£90.00

*3rd night at 50% reduction (excl peak periods).*

# 23 St Marys

Bootham, York YO30 7DD **t** (01904) 622738 **e** stmarys23@hotmail.com

**23stmarys.co.uk** GUEST REVIEWS • SPECIAL OFFERS • REAL-TIME BOOKING

**open** All year except Christmas
**bedrooms** 6 double, 1 twin, 1 single, 1 family
**bathrooms** All en suite
**payment** Credit/debit cards, cash, cheques, euros

Large Victorian terraced house peacefully set within five minutes' stroll of city centre. Spacious rooms, antique furnishings, en suite bedrooms of different sizes and character. Extensive breakfast menu in elegant surroundings. Julie and Chris will offer you a warm welcome to their home.

**SAT NAV** *YO30 7DD* **ONLINE MAP**

Room General Leisure

## YORK, North Yorkshire Map ref 4C1

★★★★
GUEST HOUSE

B&B PER ROOM PER NIGHT
s £50.00–£55.00
D £70.00–£80.00

# Abbey Guest House

13-14 Earlsborough Terrace, Marygate YO30 7BQ **t** (01904) 627782 **e** info@abbeyghyork.co.uk

**abbeyghyork.co.uk** GUEST REVIEWS • REAL-TIME BOOKING

Small, family-run guesthouse on banks of river. Private car park, well-appointed rooms all en suite, no-smoking. Five minutes' walk to city centre. Lovely garden and terrace.

**open** All year except Christmas
**bedrooms** 3 double, 1 twin, 1 family
**bathrooms** All en suite
**payment** Credit/debit cards, cash, cheques

Room General

## YORK, North Yorkshire Map ref 4C1

★★★★
GUEST HOUSE

B&B PER ROOM PER NIGHT
s £40.00–£68.00
D £56.00–£75.00

# Alcuin Lodge Guest House

15 Sycamore Place, Bootham, York YO30 7DW **t** (01904) 632222 **e** info@alcuinlodge.com

**alcuinlodge.com** GUEST REVIEWS • REAL-TIME BOOKING

Edwardian house in a quiet cul-de-sac. Bowling green opposite. Five minutes' walk to York Minster and all other attractions. Non-smoking property. Children welcome.

**open** All year
**bedrooms** 3 double, 1 twin, 1 family
**bathrooms** 4 en suite, 1 private
**payment** Credit/debit cards, cash, cheques

Room General 1

## YORK, North Yorkshire Map ref 4C1

★★★
GUEST HOUSE

B&B PER ROOM PER NIGHT
D £64.00–£80.00

# Ambleside Guest House

62 Bootham Crescent, Bootham YO30 7AH **t** (01904) 637165 **e** ambles@globalnet.co.uk

**ambleside-gh.co.uk**

Tastefully furnished Victorian townhouse, a few minutes' walk to the city centre. Cleanliness and hospitality guaranteed at all times. Non-smoking establishment.

**open** All year except Christmas and New Year
**bedrooms** 6 double, 1 twin, 1 family
**bathrooms** 6 en suite
**payment** Credit/debit cards, cash, cheques

Room General 10

WALKERS WELCOME

## Do you like walking?

Walkers feel at home in accommodation participating in our Walkers Welcome scheme. Look out for the symbol. Consider walking all or part of a long-distance route – go online at nationaltrail.co.uk.

## YORK, North Yorkshire Map ref 4C1

★★★★ GUEST ACCOMMODATION SILVER AWARD

B&B PER ROOM PER NIGHT
S £55.00–£70.00
D £70.00–£80.00

# Ascot House

80 East Parade, York YO31 7YH **t** (01904) 426826 **e** admin@ascothouseyork.com

**ascothouseyork.com**

**open** All year except Christmas
**bedrooms** 8 double, 2 twin, 3 family
**bathrooms** 12 en suite, 1 private
**payment** Credit/debit cards, cash, cheques

A family-run Victorian villa, built in 1869, with en suite rooms of character and many four-poster or canopy beds. Delicious English, continental and vegetarian breakfasts served. Fifteen minutes' walk to historic walled city centre, castle museum or York Minster. Residential licence and residents' lounge, sauna and private, enclosed car park.

**SAT NAV** *YO31 7YH*

Room General

## YORK, North Yorkshire Map ref 4C1

★★★★ GUEST ACCOMMODATION

B&B PER ROOM PER NIGHT
S £30.00–£35.00
D £60.00–£70.00

*Single-night price reduction for 2 or more nights' stay.*

# Ascot Lodge

112 Acomb Road, York YO24 4EY **t** (01904) 798234 **e** info@ascotlodge.com

**ascotlodge.com**

**open** All year
**bedrooms** 1 twin, 4 single, 5 family
**bathrooms** 7 en suite
**payment** Cash, cheques

Receive a warm welcome at this beautiful mid-Victorian guesthouse on the west side of York. Peaceful, yet near to the city centre – 25 minutes' walk or 5-10 minutes by regular bus service. Luxurious, en suite double, family and single rooms. Non-smoking throughout. Secure, private car park. Vegetarians catered for.

**SAT NAV** *YO24 4EY*

Room General Leisure

## YORK, North Yorkshire Map ref 4C1

★★★★ GUEST ACCOMMODATION

B&B PER ROOM PER NIGHT
S £35.00–£40.00
D £60.00–£80.00

# The Ashberry

103 The Mount, York YO24 1AX **t** (01904) 647339 **e** kevlyon@ashberryhotel.co.uk

**ashberryhotel.co.uk**

The Ashberry is a double-fronted Victorian town house, only five minutes from the town centre, Minster, railway station and racecourse. Enjoy an award-winning breakfast.

**open** All year except Christmas
**bedrooms** 3 double, 2 twin, 1 family
**bathrooms** All en suite
**payment** Credit/debit cards, cash, cheques, euros

Room General

## Where is my pet welcome?

Some proprietors welcome well-behaved pets. Look for the symbol in the accommodation listings. You can also buy a copy of our popular guide – Pets Come Too! – available from good bookshops and online at visitbritaindirect.com.

## YORK, North Yorkshire Map ref 4C1

★★★★
GUEST ACCOMMODATION
SILVER AWARD

B&B PER ROOM PER NIGHT
S £68.00–£84.00
D £78.00–£92.00

*Discount on stays of 3 or more days (excl Fri and Sat). See website for details.*

# Barbican House

20 Barbican Road, York YO10 5AA **t** (01904) 627617 **e** info@barbicanhouse.com

**barbicanhouse.com** GUEST REVIEWS • SPECIAL OFFERS • REAL-TIME BOOKING

**open** All year except Christmas and New Year
**bedrooms** 6 double, 1 twin, 1 family
**bathrooms** All en suite
**payment** Credit/debit cards, cash, cheques

Welcome to our wonderful restored Victorian villa overlooking the medieval city walls. Delightful bedrooms, each individually decorated to complement the charm and character of the period. All rooms are en suite and non-smoking. Full English breakfast using local, free-range produce. Free private parking available.

**SAT NAV** *YO10 5AA* **ONLINE MAP**

Room General 10 P Leisure

## YORK, North Yorkshire Map ref 4C1

★★★★
GUEST ACCOMMODATION

B&B PER ROOM PER NIGHT
S £38.00–£45.00
D £70.00–£82.00

*Why not book our celebrations package too? Please call or visit the website for details.*

# The Bentley Guest House

25 Grosvenor Terrace, Bootham, York YO30 7AG **t** (01904) 644313 **e** enquiries@bentleyofyork.com

**bentleyofyork.com**

**open** All year except Christmas
**bedrooms** 3 double, 1 twin, 1 single
**bathrooms** All en suite
**payment** Credit/debit cards, cash, cheques

Steve and Margaret Bradley look forward to welcoming you to The Bentley, an elegant Victorian town house situated close to York's historic centre. All our rooms are en suite and prettily decorated with colourful linen and interesting pictures. A highlight of a stay here is a superb breakfast.

**SAT NAV** *YO30 7AG* **ONLINE MAP**

Room General 10 Leisure

## YORK, North Yorkshire Map ref 4C1

★★★★★
GUEST ACCOMMODATION
SILVER AWARD

B&B PER ROOM PER NIGHT
S £40.00–£50.00
D £70.00–£120.00

*Celebration Package of flowers, chocolates and champagne. Business-traveller and off-peak, midweek, short-break rates available Sun-Thu.*

# Bishops

135 Holgate Road, York YO24 4DF **t** (01904) 628000 **e** enquiries@bishopshotel.co.uk

**bishopshotel.co.uk**

**open** All year except Christmas
**bedrooms** 2 double, 1 twin, 1 single, 3 family, 6 suites
**bathrooms** 11 en suite
**payment** Credit/debit cards, cash, cheques

Elegant Victorian villa, peaceful yet near to the city centre. Spacious, comfortable interior with individually styled suites and bedrooms all en suite. Hearty breakfast using fresh, local produce. Fully licensed establishment with a friendly family atmosphere and off-road parking. Ideal base for exploring our beautiful Roman city and the Yorkshire countryside. 5% surcharge on credit cards.

**SAT NAV** *YO24 4DF*

Room General P Leisure

## What shall we do today?

For ideas on places to visit, see the beginning of this regional section or go online at enjoyengland.com.

## YORK, North Yorkshire Map ref 4C1

★★★★
GUEST ACCOMMODATION

B&B PER ROOM PER NIGHT
S £40.00–£65.00
D £60.00–£80.00

### Carlton House

134 The Mount, York YO24 1AS **t** (01904) 622265 **e** etb@carltonhouse.co.uk

**carltonhouse.co.uk**

**open** All year except Christmas and New Year
**bedrooms** 9 double, 4 family
**bathrooms** All en suite
**payment** Credit/debit cards, cash, cheques

Charming Georgian townhouse situated on The Mount, gateway to the City of York. Five minutes' walk to city walls, ten minutes to city centre, railway station, racecourse and all major tourist attractions.

**SAT NAV** *YO24 1AS*

Room General P

## YORK, North Yorkshire Map ref 4C1

★★★
GUEST HOUSE

B&B PER ROOM PER NIGHT
S £28.00–£30.00
D £54.00–£60.00

### Cumbria House

2 Vyner Street, York YO31 8HS **t** (01904) 636817 **e** candj@cumbriahouse.freeserve.co.uk

**cumbriahouse.com** SPECIAL OFFERS

Family-run guesthouse, warm welcome assured, 12 minutes' walk from York Minster. En suites available. Easily located from ring road. Private car park. Special winter offers.

**open** All year except Christmas
**bedrooms** 3 double, 1 single, 2 family
**bathrooms** 2 en suite
**payment** Credit/debit cards, cash, cheques, euros

Room General P

## YORK, North Yorkshire Map ref 4C1

★★★★
GUEST HOUSE

B&B PER ROOM PER NIGHT
S £49.50–£58.00
D £65.00–£85.00

*Midweek and 3-night-stay deals off-peak – please enquire.*

### Curzon Lodge and Stable Cottages

23 Tadcaster Road, York YO24 1QG **t** (01904) 703157 **e** admin@curzonlodge.com

**smoothhound.co.uk/hotels/curzon.html**

**open** All year except Christmas and New Year
**bedrooms** 6 double, 2 twin, 1 single, 1 family
**bathrooms** All en suite
**payment** Credit/debit cards, cash, cheques

Charming 17thC listed house and former stables in a conservation area overlooking York racecourse. Comfortable, en suite rooms, some with four-poster or brass beds. Country antiques, books, prints, fresh flowers and complimentary sherry lend traditional ambience. Delicious breakfasts. Warm, relaxed atmosphere with restaurants a minute's walk. Entirely non-smoking. Parking in grounds.

**SAT NAV** *YO24 1QG*

Room General 10 P Leisure

## YORK, North Yorkshire Map ref 4C1

★★★★
GUEST HOUSE

B&B PER ROOM PER NIGHT
S £50.00–£65.00
D £60.00–£85.00

### Dairy Guest House

3 Scarcroft Road, York YO23 1ND **t** (01904) 639367 **e** stay@dairyguesthouse.co.uk

**dairyguesthouse.co.uk** REAL-TIME BOOKING

A lovingly restored and upgraded Victorian town house with original features, situated just 300yds from the medieval city walls and within an easy stroll of York's many attractions and museums.

**open** All year
**bedrooms** 4 double, 1 twin, 1 family
**bathrooms** All en suite
**payment** Credit/debit cards, cash, cheques

Room General

For **key to symbols** see page 7

## YORK, North Yorkshire Map ref 4C1

★★★
GUEST HOUSE

B&B PER ROOM PER NIGHT
S £28.00–£70.00
D £45.00–£95.00

*Reduction for 3 nights or more, all year round.*

### Fourposter Lodge

68-70 Heslington Road, York YO10 5AU **t** (01904) 651170 **e** fourposter.lodge@virgin.net

**fourposterlodge.co.uk** SPECIAL OFFERS • REAL-TIME BOOKING

**open** All year except New Year
**bedrooms** 7 double, 1 twin, 1 single, 1 family
**bathrooms** 8 en suite, 2 private
**payment** Credit/debit cards, cash, cheques

Your hosts Shirley and Gary welcome you to their Victorian villa. Enjoy the comfort and luxury of our four-poster beds. Start the day with the house speciality – 'a hearty English breakfast'. Ten minutes' walk to the city centre, close to Fulford Golf Course and York University. Licensed. Car park.

**SAT NAV** *YO10 5AU* **ONLINE MAP**

Room General P Leisure

## YORK, North Yorkshire Map ref 4C1

★★★
GUEST HOUSE

B&B PER ROOM PER NIGHT
S Min £28.00
D Min £46.00

### Greenside

124 Clifton, York YO30 6BQ **t** (01904) 623631 **e** greenside@surfree.co.uk

**greensideguesthouse.co.uk**

**open** All year except Christmas and New Year
**bedrooms** 2 double, 2 twin, 1 single, 3 family
**bathrooms** 3 en suite
**payment** Cash, cheques, euros

Charming, detached, conservation area, owner-run guesthouse fronting onto Clifton Green. Ideally situated, ten minutes' walk from the city walls and all York's attractions. Offers many facilities, including an enclosed, locked car park. All types of ground-/first-floor bedrooms are available in a warm, homely atmosphere.

**SAT NAV** *YO30 6BQ*

Room General P

## YORK, North Yorkshire Map ref 4C1

★★★★
GUEST ACCOMMODATION
SILVER AWARD

B&B PER ROOM PER NIGHT
S £50.00–£95.00
D £80.00–£125.00

*3 nights for the price of 2, Sun-Thu, 1 Nov-Easter (excl school holidays).*

### The Hazelwood

24-25 Portland Street, York YO31 7EH **t** (01904) 626548 **e** reservations@thehazelwoodyork.com

**thehazelwoodyork.com**

**open** All year
**bedrooms** 7 double, 3 twin, 1 single, 2 family
**bathrooms** All en suite
**payment** Credit/debit cards, cash, cheques

Situated in the very heart of York only 400yds from York Minster in an extremely quiet residential area. An elegant Victorian town house with private car park providing high-quality accommodation in individually designed en suite bedrooms. Extensive breakfast menu catering for all tastes including vegetarian. Completely non-smoking. Licensed.

**SAT NAV** *YO31 7EH*

Room General 8 P Leisure

## B&B prices

Rates for bed and breakfast are shown per room per night.
Double room prices are usually based on two people sharing the room.

**YORK, North Yorkshire Map ref 4C1**

★★★★
GUEST ACCOMMODATION

B&B PER ROOM PER NIGHT
S £58.00–£118.00
D £69.00–£129.00

*10% discount to guests booking online. See also 'Sunday Saver', stay 5 nights arriving Sunday, get Sunday at half price.*

## Heworth Court

Heworth Green, York YO31 7TQ **t** (01904) 425156 **e** hotel@heworth.co.uk

**heworth.co.uk** GUEST REVIEWS · SPECIAL OFFERS · REAL-TIME BOOKING

**open** All year except Christmas and New Year
**bedrooms** 22 double, 2 twin, 2 single, 2 family
**bathrooms** All en suite
**payment** Credit/debit cards, cash

Heworth Court offers guests bed and full English breakfast. Twelve minutes from York Minster and York's numerous restaurants. Free parking. Our 'Minster Bells' bar features over 30 malt whiskies as well as draught beers and soft drinks. Superking-size, king-size with rolltop bath, four-poster, executive, VIP chandelier and standard rooms.

**SAT NAV** *YO31 7TQ* **ONLINE MAP**

Room General P Leisure

**YORK, North Yorkshire Map ref 4C1**

★★★★
GUEST ACCOMMODATION

B&B PER ROOM PER NIGHT
S £58.00–£88.00
D £68.00–£98.00

## Holly Lodge

206 Fulford Road, York YO10 4DD **t** (01904) 646005 **e** geoff@thehollylodge.co.uk

**thehollylodge.co.uk**

**open** All year except Christmas
**bedrooms** 3 double, 1 twin, 1 family
**bathrooms** All en suite
**payment** Credit/debit cards, cash

Award-winning, beautifully appointed, Georgian Grade II Listed building where you are assured of a warm welcome. Ten minutes' riverside stroll to centre, conveniently located for all York's attractions including the university. All rooms individually furnished, each overlooking garden or terrace. On-site parking, easy to find. Booking recommended.

**SAT NAV** *YO10 4DD*

Room General 7

**YORK, North Yorkshire Map ref 4C1**

★★★★
INN

B&B PER ROOM PER NIGHT
S £25.00–£45.00
D £50.00–£70.00

## The Lighthorseman

124 Fulford Road, Fishergate YO10 4BE **t** (01904) 624818 **e** janinerobinson03@aol.com

**lighthorseman.co.uk** GUEST REVIEWS · SPECIAL OFFERS

**open** All year
**bedrooms** 5 double, 2 twin, 1 single
**bathrooms** All en suite
**payment** Credit/debit cards, cash, cheques

Local inn with eight letting bedrooms all en suite. Full breakfast, car parking. Short walk along river to town centre and racecourse. For more information visit our website.

**SAT NAV** *YO10 4BE* **ONLINE MAP**

Room General P Leisure

### Do you have access needs?

Look for the National Accessible Scheme symbols if you have special hearing, visual or mobility needs.

## YORK, North Yorkshire Map ref 4C1

★★★★
GUEST ACCOMMODATION

B&B PER ROOM PER NIGHT
S £45.00–£55.00
D £65.00–£80.00

EVENING MEAL PER PERSON
£12.50–£25.00

*Book full week and pay for 6 nights. Various seasonal and midweek offers. Excellent dinners available on request from £12.50.*

### Manor Guest House

Main Street, Linton-on-Ouse YO30 2AY **t** (01347) 848391 **e** manorguesthouse@tiscali.co.uk

**manorguesthouse.co.uk**

**open** All year
**bedrooms** 2 double, 2 twin, 1 single, 2 family, 1 suite
**bathrooms** All en suite
**payment** Credit/debit cards, cash, cheques, euros

Award-winning en suite accommodation in a listed Georgian manor house. Period oak-beamed rooms and ground-floor family suite. Ideal for Yorkshire Dales and Moors and picturesque towns, yet only 10 minutes York 'park and ride'. Lovely village location, river walks, pubs/restaurants. Spacious grounds with ample private parking. Dogs welcome.

**SAT NAV** *YO30 2AY*

Room General Leisure

## YORK, North Yorkshire Map ref 4C1

★★★
GUEST HOUSE

B&B PER ROOM PER NIGHT
S £40.00–£50.00
D £60.00–£90.00

*Winter breaks 10% discount for 3 midweek nights or more (Sun-Thu) Nov 1st 2008 – March 31st 2009.*

### Mont-Clare Guest House

32 Claremont Terrace, Gillygate, York YO31 7EJ **t** (01904) 651011 **e** info@mont-clare.co.uk

**mont-clare.co.uk**

**open** All year except Christmas
**bedrooms** 4 double, 2 twin, 1 single
**bathrooms** All en suite
**payment** Credit/debit cards, cash, cheques

Enjoy city-centre accommodation with free parking. Located in a quiet cul-de-sac close to York Minster, within easy walking distance of the city centre and all the historic attractions. The railway station is a fifteen-minute walk. All rooms are en suite and we offer a traditional English breakfast including vegetarian option.

**SAT NAV** *YO31 7EJ*

Room General 8 Leisure

## YORK, North Yorkshire Map ref 4C1

★★★★
GUEST ACCOMMODATION

B&B PER ROOM PER NIGHT
D £61.00–£64.00

### Palm Court

17 Huntington Road, York YO31 8RB **t** (01904) 639387 **e** helencoll_2000@hotmail.com

**thepalmcourt.org.uk**

A very warm welcome awaits you at our elegant Victorian family-run guest accommodation, offering excellent value. Overlooking River Foss and five-minute walk to city. En suite rooms, free private parking.

**open** All year except Christmas and New Year
**bedrooms** 2 double, 2 twin, 4 family
**bathrooms** All en suite
**payment** Cash, cheques

Room General

FAMILIES WELCOME WELCOME FAMILIES

## Looking for an ideal family break?

For accommodation offering additional facilities and services for a range of ages and family units, look out for the Families Welcome symbol. Owners of these properties will go out of their way to welcome families.

## YORK, North Yorkshire Map ref 4C1

★★★★
INN

B&B PER ROOM PER NIGHT
s Min £55.00
D Min £80.00

EVENING MEAL PER PERSON
£6.95–£15.75

### The Windmill

Hull Road, Dunnington, York YO19 5LP **t** (01904) 481898 **e** j.saggers@btopenworld.com

**thewindmilldunnington.co.uk** REAL-TIME BOOKING

**open** All year
**bedrooms** 5 double, 5 twin
**bathrooms** All en suite
**payment** Credit/debit cards, cash, cheques

Eat – drink – relax – sleep. Home-made food is available daily; traditional Sunday lunches; a selection of ales and lagers. A function/meeting room is also available. Large car park.

**SAT NAV** *YO19 5LP*

Room General

## YORK, North Yorkshire Map ref 4C1

★★★★
GUEST ACCOMMODATION

B&B PER ROOM PER NIGHT
s £28.00–£33.00
D £58.00–£68.00

*Four-poster rooms £34.00-£39.00 pppn.*

### York House

62 Heworth Green, York YO31 7TQ **t** (01904) 427070 **e** yorkhouse.bandb@tiscali.co.uk

**yorkhouseyork.co.uk**

**open** All year except Christmas and New Year
**bedrooms** 5 double, 1 twin, 1 single, 1 family
**bathrooms** 7 en suite, 1 private
**payment** Credit/debit cards, cash, cheques

Located a short stroll from the heart of one of Europe's most historic cities. York House is the perfect base for a visit to beautiful York or the surrounding area. A Georgian house with later additions, rooms feature all the modern conveniences you could possibly need for a relaxing, enjoyable stay.

**SAT NAV** *YO31 7TQ*

Room General

enjoyEngland.com
Gold AWARD
enjoyEngland.com
Silver AWARD
Gold and Silver Awards
Enjoy England's unique Gold and Silver Awards recognise exceptional quality in serviced accommodation.
Our assessors make recommendations for Gold and Silver Awards during assessments in recognition of levels of quality over and above that expected of a particular rating.
Look for the Gold and Silver Awards in the regional sections, or you can find an index to accommodation with a Gold or Silver Award at the back of this guide.

# Central England

Bedfordshire, Cambridgeshire, Derbyshire, Essex, Herefordshire, Hertfordshire, Leicestershire, Lincolnshire, Norfolk, Northamptonshire, Nottinghamshire, Rutland, Shropshire, Staffordshire, Suffolk, Warwickshire, West Midlands, Worcestershire

Clockwise: Holkham Hall, Norfolk; Royal Worcester, Worcestershire; Lincoln Cathedral, Lincolnshire

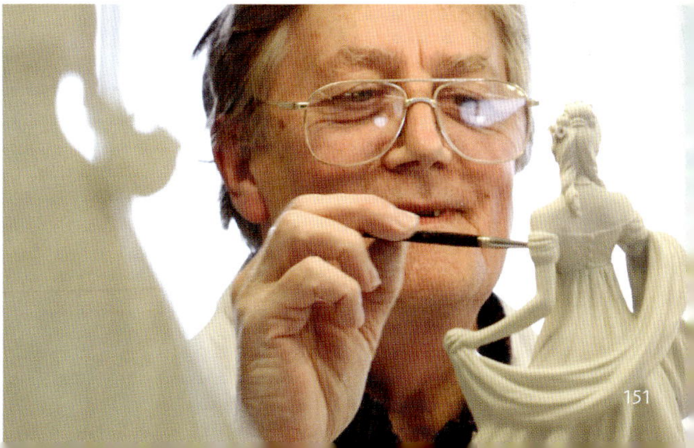

# Great days out

Active pursuits, lazy days and family fun – find them all in Central England. Pull on your walking boots and challenge the Pennines, drift along the canals that criss-cross the region, follow the trail to the Major Oak in Sherwood Forest. And do come for the world-class – sometimes uniquely quirky – culture.

## It's child's play

Game for anything? Then plunge in – there's such a wide choice of fun family days out. Start with a Thrill Hopper ticket giving great value access to four hair-raising theme park attractions: **Alton Towers** (try the exciting new Battle Galleons interactive water ride), **Drayton Manor Theme Park** (now with Europe's first Thomas Land for engine fiends), Tamworth **SnowDome** and **Waterworld**.

Bewilderwood, Norfolk

Next up, how about the **National Space Centre**, Leicester, where you can see if you cut it as an astronaut. Check your pulse and hit the assault course at **Conkers**, Swadlincote, in the heart of the National Forest, or tackle the zip wires and crocklebogs of **Bewilderwood**, Wroxham. Encounter lions, tigers and elephants at **Woburn Safari Park**, and get to **Dudley Zoological Gardens** for feeding time.

## Good sport!

Discover natural sporting arenas to suit every pace and purpose. Walking, cycling, climbing, potholing: it's all here. Saunter along **Offa's Dyke Path**, stride part of the **Heart of England Way**, or dip into stretches of the **Pennine Way**. In the west of the region, the vistas that embrace the **Malverns** are superb. Cyclists of all ages love the flat terrain in the East of England, and you can hire bikes to explore the woodland trails at **Clumber Park**, Worksop. Mountain bikers (especially keen youngsters) can enjoy a challenge on traffic-free circular rides in **Bacton Woods**, Norfolk.

Then up the ante because action and adventure are bywords for the **Peak District and Derbyshire**. Climbers of all abilities come to grapple with limestone and gritstone crags. Potholers relish some of the most challenging caves in Britain. And if you're really more of a spectator, book your place trackside for sensational, high-octane Formula 1 racing at **Silverstone**, or have a flutter at **Newmarket**, the historical home of British horseracing.

## Take the waters

Pack buckets, spades and binoculars then head for mile upon mile of sandy and shingle beaches from Essex to Lincolnshire. Hunker down in a hide along the coast at **RSPB Minsmere** to spy wading birds and waterfowl. Share the bustling delights of seaside resorts like Felixstowe, Southend-on-Sea and Great Yarmouth. For something quieter, seek out the havens of Frinton-on-Sea, Covehithe and Anderby Creek plus numerous quaint fishing villages.

Left to right: The Roaches, Staffordshire; RSPB Minsmere Nature Reserve, Suffolk

**did you know...** Derbyshire's Dovedale was formed from ancient coral reefs? Enjoy the ultimate ramble!

Inland, explore rivers and dykes in the **Fens**, a magical water world extending over Cambridgeshire, Lincolnshire, Norfolk and Rutland. At **Fenscape** interactive discovery centre in Spalding, learn all about the unique landscape and heritage. For lazy days with friends and family, what could be more calming than the reed-fringed waterways of the **Norfolk Broads**? When energy levels rise again, cast off for some sailing at **Rutland Water & Nature Reserve** and exhilarating watersports at **Carsington Water**.

## Creative culture

With such a rich mix of history and raw natural beauty it's not surprising Central England inspires creativity. Visit the haunts of famous local lads: the **Stour Valley** of John Constable immortalised in *The Hay Wain* and **Stratford-upon-Avon** where young William Shakespeare lived – look around his birthplace then catch a performance by the **Royal Shakespeare Company**, there's nothing like Shakespeare enacted in his home town. Tour Gothic **Newstead Abbey**, full of Lord Byron's possessions and manuscripts, and gain insights into the life and music of Sir Edward Elgar at **The Elgar Birthplace Museum**, Lower Broadheath.

Today the region thrives with festivals and events ranging from classical to contemporary culture. On a musical note, Benjamin Britten's **Aldeburgh Festival** at Snape Maltings, Suffolk, is the place for classical concerts in a rural setting.

Royal Shakespeare Company, Warwickshire

The annual **DH Lawrence Festival** helps to attract thousands to the author's home town of Eastwood. Unique and quirky happenings are also to the fore, at **Whittlesea Straw Bear Festival** and **Shrewsbury's Cartoon Festival**.

## Historic highlights

Linger in **Shrewsbury** to savour the historic atmosphere, or browse the streets of **Worcester** – places noted for their charming Tudor half-timbered architecture. Reach for your camera as you pass through **Much Wenlock**, one of the beautiful black and white villages of Shropshire. Castles and grand homes dot the landscape – **Warwick Castle, Hatfield House** and **Chatsworth** are favourites. For Elizabethan architecture at its most impressive, **Hardwick Hall** is hard to beat. Gothic **Lincoln Cathedral** on its lofty hill and **Lincoln Castle**, where one of only four surviving copies of Magna Carta is held, are must-visit heritage showpieces.

**did you know...** Lincoln Cathedral doubled as Westminster Abbey in The Da Vinci Code film?

Also step back into the area's proud industrial past, at the **Ironbridge Gorge Museums** – kids soon switch on their imaginations to design and technology at **Enginuity**. Have a chat with working craftsmen at **The Black Country Living Museum**. Trace the history of fighter planes at the **Imperial War Museum Duxford**, Europe's premier aviation museum. At the **Wedgwood Visitor Centre**, Stoke-on-Trent, you can tour the factory and throw a pot or two under the helpful eye of an expert.

## Plumbread, pies and shopping

Central England serves up a mouthwatering range of distinctive foods: succulent Melton Mowbray pork pies, Red Leicester and Stilton, Lincolnshire plumbread and Bakewell pudding – often imitated, never matched. Head for Britain's food capital, pretty **Ludlow** on the Welsh borders, to discover what lures so many top chefs to the **Ludlow Marches Food and Drink Festival**. And then there's retail therapy at its most irresistible. Remember the **Bullring** in **Birmingham**? A space the size of more than 26 football pitches – all dedicated to shopping and entertainment. Soak up the colourful atmosphere of multicultural **Leicester** and try on a sari or two.

Clockwise: Imperial War Museum Duxford, Cambridgeshire; Wedgwood Visitor Centre, Staffordshire; Henry Moore Foundation, Hertfordshire

# Destinations

## Birmingham

A dynamic city combining a fascinating history with a world-class cultural scene. Lose yourself in shopping heaven in the stunningly remodelled Bullring, wander through the historic Jewellery Quarter then sit back and enjoy the Symphony Orchestra in the magnificent Symphony Hall. Indulge your sweet tooth at Cadbury World, or take in a major event at the NEC or NIA. You'll also find yourself at the heart of a region full of history and heritage, beautiful quaint villages and access to lush rolling countryside – Birmingham really is a gateway to the heart of England!

Cambridge

## Cambridge

The name Cambridge instantly summons breathtaking images – the Backs carpeted with spring flowers, King's College Chapel, punting on the river Cam and, of course, the calm of the historic college buildings. Cambridge still has the atmosphere of a bustling market town, notwithstanding its international reputation. Explore its winding streets and splendid architecture, and choose from a range of attractions, museums, hotels, restaurants and pubs. Situated in the heart of East Anglia but less than an hour from London by high-speed rail link.

## Colchester

Find internationally important treasures located in award-winning museums or visit cutting-edge contemporary galleries. It's a shopper's heaven with specialist shops and big name stores, and the range of cuisine makes Colchester a magnet for food lovers – don't miss the annual Colchester Oyster Feast.

## Great Yarmouth

One of the UK's most popular seaside resorts, with an enviable mix of sandy beaches, attractions, entertainment and heritage. Beyond the seaside fun is a charming town that is steeped in history. Visit the medieval town walls, stroll the historic South Quay and discover Nelson's 'other' column. When the sun goes down colourful illuminations light up the night sky.

## Hereford

In this ancient city on the banks of the River Wye, you'll find historic buildings housing modern shops and modern buildings holding historic treasures. Don't miss Hereford Cathedral with its priceless Mappa Mundi and Chained Library. Wander through the spacious High Town and the new Left Bank Village. Visit the Cider Museum to learn about Hereford's claim to be 'The Apple of England's Eye'.

## Lincoln

Possessing magnificent architectural heritage, centred on its world famous Cathedral and Castle, Lincoln is a vivacious City – mixing 2,000 years of heritage with excellent shopping and lively arts and events. The Brayford Waterfront quarter is home to some of the newest places to eat and drink. Events include the famous Christmas Market and the Brayford Waterfront Festival.

Left to right: Chatsworth, Derbyshire; Alton Towers, Staffordshire

Ludlow

## Ludlow

Discover the place Betjemen described as 'the loveliest town in England.' Britain's first 'slow' town is also a gastronomic capital and host to the renowned Ludlow Marches Food & Drink Festival. You'll find a host of speciality food shops, and more restaurants and inns than you can shake a cocktail stick at. To walk off lunch, stroll in the enchanting Angel Gardens, or take in a performance at the open-air theatre in the stunning medieval ruin of Ludlow Castle.

## Norwich

Norwich, county town of Norfolk, is an enchanting cathedral city and a thriving modern metropolis. See some of the finest medieval architecture in Britain in the cathedral and castle, and wander an intricate network of winding streets. The city's newest centrepiece, The Forum, represents contemporary architecture at its best. You'll find excellent shopping as well as a vibrant mix of theatres, cinemas, arts festivals, exhibitions, museums, and a vast array of restaurants.

Clockwise: Brayford Waterfront, Lincoln; Colchester Castle; Birmingham

## Nottingham

Nottingham is the undisputed capital of the East Midlands, boasting a sophisticated urban environment with an enviable reputation for clubs, theatres, cinemas and galleries, not to mention a deserved reputation as one of the top retail centres in the country. History is never far away, though, with reminders of Nottingham's legendary hero Robin Hood and his adversary the Sheriff of Nottingham. Explore the Castle Museum and Art Gallery, and Wollaton Hall, one of the most ornate Tudor buildings in Britain, complete with 500-acre deer park.

## Peak District

The Peak District is Britain's first and most popular National Park. Roam on open moorland to the north and take in the magnificent views over the Derwent Dams. Further south, stroll alongside sparkling rivers in wildlife-rich valleys far from the hustle and bustle of town. The Peak Park Rangers lead regular guided walks – choose from long hikes to village tours. Take in the grandeur of Chatsworth House or Haddon Hall, and sample the local oatcakes with Hartington Stilton, followed by a delicious Bakewell pudding.

## Stratford-upon-Avon

Unearth a magical blend of heritage and drama in and around Shakespeare's home town. Explore five houses with Shakespeare connections including Anne Hathaway's Cottage and Shakespeare's Birthplace. Visit one of England's most beautiful parish churches at Holy Trinity to see Shakespeare's grave and enjoy some of his great works performed by the world's largest classical theatre company, the RSC. Take a boat out on the River Avon, wander the boutiques, specialist stores and gift shops, and discover some of Britain's finest historic houses and gardens.

**For lots more great ideas visit enjoyEngland.com/destinations**

# Visitor attractions

## Family and Fun

**Adventure Island Southend**
*Southend-on-Sea, Essex*
(01702) 443400
adventureisland.co.uk
*Great rides and attractions for all ages.*

**Alton Towers Theme Park**
*Alton, Staffordshire*
0870 520 4060
altontowers.com
*High-adrenalin adventure and family fun.*

**Banham Zoo**
*Banham, Norfolk*
(01953) 887771
banhamzoo.co.uk
*Wildlife spectacular featuring rare and endangered animals.*

**Bewilderwood**
*Wroxham, Norfolk*
(01603) 783900
bewilderwood.co.uk
*Treehouses, zip wires and jungle bridges.*

**Black Country Living Museum**
*Dudley, West Midlands*
(0121) 557 9643
bclm.co.uk
*Twenty-six acres of fascinating living history.*

**Cadbury World**
*Birmingham*
0845 450 3599
cadburyworld.co.uk
*Chocolate-making demonstrations and free samples.*

**Colchester Zoo**
*Stanway, Essex*
(01206) 331292
colchester-zoo.com
*Featuring superb cat and primate collections.*

**Conkers**
*Swadlincote, Leicestershire*
(01283) 216633
visitconkers.com
*Interactive adventure in the National Forest.*

**Coventry Transport Museum**
*Coventry, West Midlands*
(024) 7623 4270
transport-museum.com
*World-renowned exhibition of British road transport.*

**Drayton Manor Theme Park**
*Tamworth, Staffordshire*
0844 472 1950
draytonmanor.co.uk
*The biggest, wettest and scariest rides around.*

**Dudley Zoological Gardens**
*Dudley, West Midlands*
(01384) 215313
dudleyzoo.org.uk
*Lions and tigers, snakes and spiders!*

**Imperial War Museum Duxford**
**Large Visitor Attraction of the Year – Gold**
*near Cambridge*
(01223) 835000
duxford.iwm.org.uk
*The sights, sounds and power of aircraft.*

**Ironbridge Gorge Museums**
*Ironbridge, Shropshire*
(01952) 884391
ironbridge.org.uk
*World Heritage Site featuring ten superb museums.*

**National Sea Life Centre**
*Birmingham*
(0121) 643 6777
sealifeeurope.com
*Marvel at over 3,000 sea creatures.*

**National Space Centre**
*Leicester*
0870 607 7223
spacecentre.co.uk
*Test your abilities as an astronaut.*

**Nene Valley Railway**
*Peterborough, Cambridgeshire*
(01780) 784444
nvr.org.uk
*The golden age of steam comes alive.*

**The Poppy Line – North Norfolk Railway**
*Sheringham, Norfolk*
(01263) 820800
nnr.co.uk
*5.5 mile heritage railway through delightful countryside.*

**Pleasurewood Hills Leisure Park**
*Lowestoft, Suffolk*
(01502) 586000
pleasurewoodhills.co.uk
*Adrenaline-fuelled thrills and spills.*

**Severn Valley Railway**
*Bewdley, Worcestershire*
(01299) 403816
svr.co.uk
*Journey through 16 miles of beautiful countryside.*

**Twycross Zoo**
*Twycross, Leicestershire*
(01827) 880250
twycrosszoo.com
*Meet the famous gorillas, orang-utans and chimpanzees.*

**Warwick Castle**
*Warwick, Warwickshire*
(01926) 406611
warwick-castle.co.uk
*Enthralling medieval castle in 60-acre grounds.*

**Woburn Safari Park**
*Woburn, Bedfordshire*
(01525) 290407
woburnsafari.co.uk
*Wild animals just a windscreen's width away.*

## Heritage

**Alford Manor House**
*Alford, Lincolnshire*
(01507) 463073
alfordmanorhouse.co.uk
*Britain's largest thatched manor house.*

**Althorp**
*Althorp, Northamptonshire*
(01604) 770107
althorp.com
*Historic Spencer family seat containing Diana exhibition.*

**Belton House, Park and Gardens**
*Belton, Lincolnshire*
(01476) 566116
nationaltrust.org.uk
*Fine example of Restoration country-house architecture.*

**Belvoir Castle**
*Belvoir, Leicestershire*
(01476) 871002
belvoircastle.com
*Fine stately home in stunning setting.*

**Burghley House**
*Stamford, Lincolnshire*
(01780) 752451
burghley.co.uk
*The grandest house of the Elizabethan age.*

**Canons Ashby House**
*Canons Ashby, Northamptonshire*
(01327) 861900
nationaltrust.org.uk
*Tranquil Elizabethan home of the Dryden family.*

**Chatsworth House**
*Bakewell, Derbyshire*
(01246) 565300
chatsworth.org
*One of Britain's truly great historic houses.*

**Doddington Hall & Gardens**
*Lincoln*
(01522) 694308
doddingtonhall.com
*Superb Elizabethan mansion set in romantic gardens.*

**Ely Cathedral**
*Ely, Cambridgeshire*
(01353) 667735
cathedral.ely.anglican.org
*Tour one of England's finest cathedrals.*

**Gainsborough Old Hall**
*Gainsborough, Lincolnshire*
(01427) 612669
lincolnshire.gov.uk
*Medieval manor house with original interiors.*

**Haddon Hall**
*Bakewell, Derbyshire*
(01629) 812855
haddonhall.co.uk
*Medieval and Tudor manor house with gardens.*

**Hardwick Hall**
*Chesterfield, Derbyshire*
(01246) 850430
nationaltrust.org.uk
*Elizabethan country house, gardens and parkland.*

**Hatfield House**
*Hatfield, Hertfordshire*
(01707) 287010
hatfield-house.co.uk
*Magnificent childhood home of Elizabeth I.*

**Hedingham Castle**
*Castle Hedingham, Essex*
(01787) 460261
hedinghamcastle.co.uk
*The finest Norman keep in England.*

**Hereford Cathedral**
*Hereford, Herefordshire*
(01432) 374200
herefordcathedral.org
*Magnificent cathedral housing the precious Mappa Mundi.*

**Holkham Hall**
*Wells-next-the-Sea, Norfolk*
(01328) 713103
holkham.co.uk
*Classic 18thC Palladian-style mansion.*

**Kirby Hall**
*Corby, Northamptonshire*
(01536) 203230
*Elizabethan house with superb carved decoration.*

**Knebworth House**
*Knebworth, Hertfordshire*
(01438) 812661
knebworthhouse.com
*Re-fashioned Tudor house in 250-acre grounds.*

**Lincoln Cathedral**
*Lincoln*
(01522) 561600
lincolncathedral.com
*One of Europe's finest gothic buildings.*

**Newstead Abbey**
*near Nottingham*
(01623) 455900
newsteadabbey.org.uk
*The ancestral home of Lord Byron.*

**Norwich Cathedral**
*Norwich, Norfolk*
(01603) 218300
cathedral.org.uk
*Majestic Norman cathedral with 14thC roof bosses.*

**Nottingham Castle**
*Nottingham*
(0115) 915 3700
nottinghamcity.gov.uk/museums
*17thC mansion on a medieval-castle site.*

**Rockingham Castle**
**Small Visitor Attraction of the Year – Silver**
*Rockingham, Northamptonshire*
(01536) 770240
rockinghamcastle.com
*Elizabethan house with splendid artworks and gardens.*

**Sandringham**
*Sandringham, Norfolk*
(01553) 612908
sandringham-estate.co.uk
*The country retreat of HM The Queen.*

**Shugborough – The Complete Working Historic Estate**
*Shugborough, Staffordshire*
(01889) 881388
shugborough.org.uk
*Fine mansion set in rare, surviving estate.*

**Sulgrave Manor**
*Sulgrave, Northamptonshire*
(01295) 760205
sulgravemanor.org.uk
*The home of George Washington's ancestors.*

**Weston Park**
*near Shifnal, Shropshire*
(01952) 852100
weston-park.com
*Charming stately home with beautiful gardens.*

**Woburn Abbey**
*Woburn, Bedfordshire*
(01525) 290333
woburnabbey.co.uk
*Palladian mansion set in 3,000-acre deer park.*

## Indoors

**78 Derngate**
*Northampton*
(01604) 603407
78derngate.org.uk
*Terraced house transformed by Charles Rennie Mackintosh.*

**Birmingham Museum & Art Gallery**
*Birmingham*
(0121) 303 2834
bmag.org.uk
*Fine and applied arts featuring Pre-Raphaelites.*

**Compton Verney**
*Compton Verney, Warwickshire*
(01926) 645500
comptonverney.org.uk
*Art gallery housed in Robert Adam mansion.*

**The Elgar Birthplace Museum**
*Lower Broadheath, Worcestershire*
(01905) 333224
elgarmuseum.org
*Fascinating insight into the great composer's life.*

**Fitzwilliam Museum**
*Cambridge*
(01223) 332900
fitzmuseum.cam.ac.uk
*Internationally renowned collection of antiques and art.*

**Newark Castle**
*Newark, Nottinghamshire*
(01636) 655765
newark-sherwooddc.gov.uk
*Discover an exciting Civil War history.*

**Red House Glass Cone**
*Stourbridge, West Midlands*
(01384) 812750
dudley.gov.uk/redhousecone
*Live glassmaking, craft studios, tunnels and furnaces.*

**Royal Air Force Museum, Cosford**
*Cosford, Shropshire*
(01902) 376200
rafmuseum.org
*Warplanes, missiles, aero-engines and flight simulator.*

**Royal Shakespeare Company**
*Stratford-upon-Avon, Warwickshire*
(01789) 403444
rsc.org.uk
*Year-round performances of the great works.*

**Shakespeare's Birthplace**
*Stratford-upon-Avon, Warwickshire*
(01789) 204016
shakespeare.org.uk
*Acclaimed exhibition housed in Shakespeare's childhood home.*

**Shuttleworth Collection**
*Biggleswade, Bedfordshire*
(01767) 627927
shuttleworth.org
*Unique collection of historic aircraft.*

**Time and Tide – Museum of Great Yarmouth Life**
*Great Yarmouth, Norfolk*
(01493) 743930
museums.norfolk.gov.uk
*Discover a rich maritime and fishing heritage.*

**The Wedgwood Visitor Centre**
*Stoke-on-Trent, Staffordshire*
(01782) 282986
thewedgwoodvisitorcentre.com
*Famous pottery set in glorious Staffordshire countryside.*

## Outdoors

**Castle Ashby Gardens**
*Castle Ashby, Northamptonshire*
(01604) 696187
castleashby.co.uk
*Capability Brown landscaped gardens and parkland.*

**Foxton Locks**
*Foxton, Leicestershire*
(01908) 302500
foxtonlocks.com
*Fascinating ten-lock 'staircase' climbing a 75ft hill.*

**Go Ape! High Wire Forest Adventure – Sherwood**
*Mansfield, Nottinghamshire*
0845 643 9215
goape.co.uk
*Rope bridges, swings and zip slides.*

**Peveril Castle**
*Castleton, Derbyshire*
(01433) 620613
english-heritage.org.uk
*Ruined Norman castle with impressive curtain wall.*

**RHS Garden Hyde Hall**
*Chelmsford, Essex*
(01245) 400256
rhs.org.uk
*28-acre hill-top garden with year-round interest.*

**RSPB Minsmere Nature Reserve**
*Saxmundham, Suffolk*
(01728) 648281
rspb.org.uk
*One of the RSPB's finest reserves.*

**Rutland Water & Nature Reserve**
*Oakham, Rutland*
(01572) 770651
rutlandwater.org.uk
*Important wildfowl sanctuary with leisure centre.*

**Sherwood Forest Country Park**
*Edwinstowe, Nottinghamshire*
(01623) 823202
sherwoodforest.org.uk
*Native woodland packed with adventure.*

**Silverstone Circuit**
*Silverstone, Northamptonshire*
0870 4588 200
silverstone.co.uk
*The home of British motor racing.*

**Sutton Hoo Burial Site**
*Woodbridge, Suffolk*
(01394) 389700
nationaltrust.org.uk
*Anglo-Saxon royal burial site.*

**The Trentham Estate**
*Stoke-on-Trent, Staffordshire*
(01782) 646646
trentham.co.uk
*One of Britain's most important historic gardens.*

**Welney Wetland Centre**
*Welney, Norfolk*
(01353) 860711
wwt.org.uk
*1,000-acre wetland reserve attracting wild swans.*

**Wrest Park**
*Silsoe, Bedfordshire*
(01525) 860152
english-heritage.org.uk
*Magnificent 18thC formal gardens with orangery.*

**ASSURANCE OF A GREAT DAY OUT**
Attractions with this sign participate in the Visitor Attraction Quality Assurance Scheme which recognises high standards in all aspects of the visitor experience.

## Events 2009

**Crufts**
Birmingham
the-kennel-club.org.uk
**5 - 8 Mar**

**St George's Day Festival, Wrest Park Gardens**
Silsoe
english-heritage.org.uk
**Apr**

**Luton Carnival**
Luton
luton.gov.uk
**May**

**Southend Airshow**
Southend-on-Sea
southendairshow.com
**May**

**University of the Great Outdoors - Activity event**
Ledbury
visitherefordshire.co.uk
**3 - 4 May**

**Aldeburgh Festival of Music and the Arts**
Snape
aldeburgh.co.uk
**Jun**

**Althorp Literary Festival**
Northampton
althorp.com
**Jun**

**Stamford Shakespeare Festival**
Rutland
stamfordshakespeare.co.uk
**Jun - Aug**

**Robin Hood Festival**
Nottingham
nottinghamshire.gov.uk/robinhoodfestival
**Jul - Aug**

**Flavours of Herefordshire Food Festival**
Holmer
visitherefordshire.co.uk
**24 - 25 Oct**

**Lincoln Christmas Market**
Lincoln
**Dec**

# Regional contacts and information

For more information on accommodation, attractions, activities, events and holidays in Central England, contact one of the following regional or local tourism organisations. Their websites have a wealth of information and many produce free publications to help you get the most out of your visit.

## Heart of England

Further information is available from the following organisations:

**Marketing Birmingham**
t (0121) 202 5115
w visitbirmingham.com

**Black Country Tourism**
w blackcountrytourism.co.uk

**Visit Coventry & Warwickshire**
t (024) 7622 7264
w visitcoventryandwarwickshire.co.uk

**Visit Herefordshire**
t (01432) 260621
w visitherefordshire.co.uk

**Shakespeare Country**
t 0870 160 7930
w shakespeare-country.co.uk

**Shropshire Tourism**
t (01743) 462462
w shropshiretourism.info

**Destination Staffordshire**
t 0870 500 4444
w enjoystaffordshire.com

**Stoke-on-Trent**
t (01782) 236000
w visitstoke.co.uk

**Destination Worcestershire**
t (01905) 728787
w visitworcestershire.org

### Help before you go

To search for attractions and Tourist Information Centres on the move just text INFO to 62233, and a web link will be sent to your mobile phone.

Clockwise: Warwick Castle, Warwickshire; Rutland Water, Rutland; The Broads, Norfolk

## East of England

**East of England Tourism**
t (01284) 727470
e info@eet.org.uk
w visiteastofengland.com

The comprehensive website is updated daily. Online brochures and information sheets can be downloaded including What's New; Major Events; Lights, Camera, Action! (film and television locations); Stars and Stripes (connections with the USA) and a range of Discovery Tours around the region.

## East Midlands

The publications listed are available from the following organisations:

**East Midlands Tourism**
w discovereastmidlands.com
- **Discover East Midlands**

**Experience Nottinghamshire**
t 0844 477 5678
w visitnotts.com
- **Nottinghamshire Essential Guide, Where to Stay Guide, Stay Somewhere Different, City Breaks, Family Days Out**
- **Robin Hood Breaks**
- **Pilgrim Fathers**

**Peak District and Derbyshire**
t 0870 444 7275
w visitpeakdistrict.com
- **Peak District and Derbyshire Visitor Guide**
- **Peak District and Derbyshire Short Break Ideas**
- **Camping and Caravanning Guide**
- **Bess of Hardwick 400th Anniversary**

**Lincolnshire**
t (01522) 873800
w visitlincolnshire.com
- **Visit Lincolnshire – Destination Guide, Great days out, Gardens & Nurseries, Aviation Heritage, Good Taste**
- **Keep up with the flow**

**Explore Northamptonshire**
t (01604) 838800
w explorenorthamptonshire.co.uk
- **Explore Northamptonshire Visitor Guide, County Map**

**Leicestershire**
t 0844 888 5181
w goleicestershire.com
- **Inspiring short breaks and holidays in Leicestershire**
- **Stay, Play, Explore**
- **Great Days Out in Leicestershire**

**Discover Rutland**
t (01572) 653026
w discover-rutland.co.uk
- **Discover Rutland**

# Tourist Information Centres

When you arrive at your destination, visit an Official Partner Tourist Information Centre for quality assured help with accommodation and information about local attractions and events, or email your request before you go. To search for attractions and Tourist Information Centres on the move just text INFO to 62233, and a web link will be sent to your mobile phone. To find a Tourist Information Centre by region visit enjoyEngland.com/find-tic.

| | | | |
|---|---|---|---|
| **Aldeburgh** | 152 High Street | (01728) 453637 | atic@suffolkcoastal.gov.uk |
| **Ashbourne** | 13 Market Place | (01335) 343666 | ashbourneinfo@derbyshiredales.gov.uk |
| **Ashby-de-la-Zouch** | North Street | (01530) 411767 | ashby.tic@nwleices.gov.uk |
| **Bakewell** | Bridge Street | (01629) 813227 | bakewell@peakdistrict-npa.gov.uk |
| **Bewdley** | Load Street | (01299) 404740 | bewdleytic@wyreforestdc.gov.uk |
| **Birmingham Rotunda** | 150 New Street | 0844 888 3883 | callcentre@marketingbirmingham.com |
| **Bishop's Stortford** | The Old Monastery | (01279) 655831 | tic@bishopsstortford.org |
| **Brackley** | 2 Bridge Street | (01280) 700111 | tic@southnorthants.gov.uk |
| **Braintree** | Market Square | (01376) 550066 | tic@braintree.gov.uk |
| **Bridgnorth** | Listley Street | (01746) 763257 | bridgnorth.tourism@shropshire.gov.uk |
| **Burton upon Trent** | Horninglow Street | (01283) 508111 | tic@eaststaffsbc.gov.uk |
| **Bury St Edmunds** | 6 Angel Hill | (01284) 764667 | tic@stedsbc.gov.uk |
| **Buxton** | The Crescent | (01298) 25106 | tourism@highpeak.gov.uk |
| **Castleton** | Buxton Road | (01433) 620679 | castleton@peakdistrict-npa.gov.uk |
| **Chesterfield** | Rykneld Square | (01246) 345777 | tourism@chesterfield.gov.uk |
| **Church Stretton** | Church Street | (01694) 723133 | churchstretton.scf@shropshire.gov.uk |
| **Colchester** | Trinity Street | (01206) 282920 | vic@colchester.gov.uk |
| **Coventry Cathedral** | Cathedral Ruins, 1 Hill Top | (024) 7623 4297 | tic@cvone.co.uk |
| **Coventry Ricoh** | Phoenix Way | 0844 873 6397 | richoh@cvone.co.uk |
| **Coventry Transport Museum** | Hales Street | (024) 7622 7264 | tic@cvone.co.uk |
| **Derby** | Market Place | (01332) 255802 | tourism@derby.gov.uk |
| **Felixstowe** | 91 Undercliff Road West | (01394) 276770 | ftic@suffolkcoastal.gov.uk |
| **Flatford** | Flatford Lane | (01206) 299460 | flatfordvic@babergh.gov.uk |
| **Harwich** | Iconfield Park | (01255) 506139 | harwichtic@btconnect.com |
| **Hereford** | 1 King Street | (01432) 268430 | tic-hereford@herefordshire.gov.uk |
| **Hunstanton** | The Green | (01485) 532610 | hunstanton.tic@west-norfolk.gov.uk |
| **Ipswich** | St Stephens Lane | (01473) 258070 | tourist@ipswich.gov.uk |
| **Ironbridge** | Coalbrookdale | (01952) 884391 | tic@ironbridge.org.uk |

| | | | |
|---|---|---|---|
| **King's Lynn** | Purfleet Quay | (01553) 763044 | kings-lynn.tic@west-norfolk.gov.uk |
| **Lavenham** | Lady Street | (01787) 248207 | lavenhamtic@babergh.gov.uk |
| **Leamington Spa** | The Parade | (01926) 742762 | leamington@shakespeare-country.co.uk |
| **Leek** | Stockwell Street | (01538) 483741 | tourism.services@staffsmoorlands.gov.uk |
| **Leicester** | 7/9 Every Street | 0906 294 1113** | info@goleicestershire.com |
| **Lichfield** | Castle Dyke | (01543) 412112 | info@visitlichfield.com |
| **Lincoln** | 9 Castle Hill | (01522) 873213 | tourism@lincoln.gov.uk |
| **Lowestoft** | Royal Plain | (01502) 533600 | touristinfo@waveney.gov.uk |
| **Ludlow** | Castle Street | (01584) 875053 | ludlow.tourism@shropshire.gov.uk |
| **Maldon** | Coach Lane | (01621) 856503 | tic@maldon.gov.uk |
| **Malvern** | 21 Church Street | (01684) 892289 | malvern.tic@malvernhills.gov.uk |
| **Matlock** | Crown Square | (01629) 583388 | matlockinfo@derbyshiredales.gov.uk |
| **Matlock Bath** | The Pavillion | (01629) 55082 | matlockbathinfo@derbyshiredales.gov.uk |
| **Newmarket** | Palace Street | (01638) 667200 | tic.newmarket@forest-heath.gov.uk |
| **Northampton** | The Royal & Dernage Theatre | (01604) 838800 | northampton.tic@northamptonshire enterprise.ltd.uk |
| **Oswestry** | Mile End | (01691) 662488 | tic@oswestry-bc.gov.uk |
| **Oundle** | 14 West Street | (01832) 274333 | oundletic@east-northamptonshire.gov.uk |
| **Peterborough** | 3-5 Minster Precincts | (01733) 452336 | tic@peterborough.gov.uk |
| **Ripley** | Market Place | (01773) 841488 | touristinformation@ambervalley.gov.uk |
| **Ross-on-Wye** | Edde Cross Street | (01989) 562768 | tic-ross@herefordshire.gov.uk |
| **Rugby** | Rugby Art Gallery Museum & Library | (01788) 533217 | visitor.centre@rugby.gov.uk |
| **Saffron Walden** | Market Square | (01799) 510444 | tourism@uttleford.gov.uk |
| **Shrewsbury** | The Square | (01743) 281200 | visitorinfo@shrewsbury.gov.uk |
| **Sleaford** | Carre Street | (01529) 414294 | tic@n-kesteven.gov.uk |
| **Solihull** | Homer Road | (0121) 704 6130 | artscomplex@solihull.gov.uk |
| **Southwold** | 69 High Street | (01502) 724729 | southwold.tic@waveney.gov.uk |
| **Stafford** | Market Street | (01785) 619619 | tic@staffordbc.gov.uk |
| **Stoke-on-Trent** | Victoria Hall, Bagnall Street | (01782) 236000 | stoke.tic@stoke.gov.uk |
| **Stowmarket** | The Museum of East Anglian Life | (01449) 676800 | tic@midsuffolk.gov.uk |
| **Stratford-upon-Avon** | Bridgefoot | 0870 160 7930 | stratfordtic@shakespeare-country.co.uk |
| **Sudbury** | Market Hill | (01787) 881320 | sudburytic@babergh.gov.uk |
| **Swadlincote** | West Street | (01283) 222848 | Jo@sharpespotterymuseum.org.uk |
| **Tamworth** | 29 Market Street | (01827) 709581 | tic@tamworth.gov.uk |
| **Warwick** | Jury Street | (01926) 492212 | touristinfo@warwick-uk.co.uk |
| **Witham** | 61 Newland Street | (01376) 502674 | ticwitham@braintree.gov.uk |
| **Woodbridge** | Station Buildings | (01394) 382240 | wtic@suffolkcoastal.gov.uk |
| **Worcester** | High Street | (01905) 728787 | touristinfo@cityofworcester.gov.uk |

*seasonal opening

**calls to this number are charged at premium rate

where to stay in

# Central England

All place names in the blue bands are shown on the maps at the front of this guide.

A complete listing of all Enjoy England assessed accommodation covered by this guide appears at the back.

## Accommodation symbols

Symbols give useful information about services and facilities. On page 7 you can find a key to these symbols.

## ACTON, Suffolk Map ref 3B2

★★
GUEST ACCOMMODATION

B&B PER ROOM PER NIGHT
s £22.50
d £38.50–£45.50

### Barbies

25 Clay Hall Place, Sudbury CO10 0BT **t** (01787) 373702

**tiscover.co.uk**

Barbies Guesthouse is in Acton, a small village surrounded by farmland, and is within an easy drive of beautiful Long Melford, Lavenham and, of course, the market town of Sudbury.

**open** All year except Christmas and New Year
**bedrooms** 1 double, 2 twin, 1 single
**bathrooms** 1 en suite
**payment** Cash, cheques

Room General 5

## ALDBOROUGH, Norfolk Map ref 3B1

★★★★
GUEST HOUSE

B&B PER ROOM PER NIGHT
s £30.00–£35.00
d £60.00–£70.00

EVENING MEAL PER PERSON
£13.00–£15.00

### Butterfly Cottage

The Green, Aldborough, Norwich NR11 7AA **t** (01263) 768198 & (01263) 761689
**e** butterflycottage@btopenworld.com

**butterflycottage.com**

On the Weavers Way. Comfortable, cottage-style, well equipped, friendly atmosphere. Rooms overlook large garden or village green. Each has DVD player, fridge and own entrance. Car parking.

**open** All year
**bedrooms** 1 double, 1 twin, 1 single, 1 family, 1 suite
**bathrooms** 4 en suite, 1 private
**payment** Cash, cheques

Room General Leisure

## ALDEBURGH, Suffolk Map ref 3C2

★★★★
GUEST HOUSE

B&B PER ROOM PER NIGHT
s Max £60.00
d Max £80.00

### Toll House

50 Victoria Road, Aldeburgh IP15 5EJ **t** (01728) 453239 **e** tollhouse@fsmail.net

**tollhouse.travelbugged.com**

**open** All year
**bedrooms** 5 double, 2 twin
**bathrooms** All en suite
**payment** Credit/debit cards, cash, cheques, euros

The Toll House is a delightful Victorian guesthouse which offers en suite rooms with TV and tea-/coffee-making facilities. Freshly prepared, full English breakfast using local produce is served daily, with vegetarian/continental option provided. Parking available.

**SAT NAV** *IP15 5EJ*

Room General 1 Leisure

## ALTON, Staffordshire Map ref 4B2

★★★
INN

B&B PER ROOM PER NIGHT
s £35.00–£45.00
d £55.00–£65.00

EVENING MEAL PER PERSON
£5.95–£13.95

*Group bookings welcome if over 18 years of age. Birthday celebrations and hen parties accommodated. Small-conference facilities available.*

### Bulls Head Inn

High Street, Alton, Stoke-on-Trent ST10 4AQ **t** (01538) 702307 **e** janet@thebullsheadalton.co.uk

**altontowers-bedandbreakfast.co.uk**

**open** All year
**bedrooms** 5 double, 1 twin, 1 family
**bathrooms** All en suite
**payment** Credit/debit cards, cash, cheques

This family-owned business is in the village of Alton, close to Alton Towers. An 18thC inn offering traditional cask ales and home cooking, with a real log fire and a friendly atmosphere. All rooms en suite, separate restaurant.

**SAT NAV** *ST10 4AQ*

Room General Leisure

## ALTON, Staffordshire Map ref 4B2

★★★★
BED & BREAKFAST

B&B PER ROOM PER NIGHT
s £28.00–£35.00
d £42.00–£48.00

EVENING MEAL PER PERSON
£8.00–£15.00

### Fields Farm

Chapel Lane, Threapwood Alton, Stoke-on-Trent ST10 4QZ **t** (01538) 752721 & 07850 310381
**e** pat.massey@fieldsfarmbb.co.uk

**fieldsfarmbb.co.uk**

Traditional farmhouse hospitality and comfort in picturesque Churnet Valley, ten minutes from Alton Towers near Peak District National Park, Potteries, stately homes. Stabling available. Ideal walking, cycling, riding, fishing. Family rooms.

**open** All year
**bedrooms** 1 double, 1 twin, 1 family
**bathrooms** 2 en suite, 1 private
**payment** Cash, cheques

Room General Leisure

FAMILIES WELCOME WELCOME FAMILIES

## Looking for an ideal family break?

For accommodation offering additional facilities and services for a range of ages and family units, look out for the Families Welcome symbol. Owners of these properties will go out of their way to welcome families.

## ALTON, Staffordshire Map ref 4B2

★★★
BED & BREAKFAST

B&B PER ROOM PER NIGHT
S £25.00–£30.00
D £40.00–£60.00

### Hillside Farm

Alton Road, Uttoxeter ST14 5HG **t** (01889) 590760

**smoothhound.co.uk/hotels/hillside.html**

**open** All year
**bedrooms** 1 double, 3 family
**bathrooms** 1 en suite, 1 private
**payment** Cash, cheques

Victorian farmhouse with extensive views to the Weaver Hills and Churnet Valley. Situated two miles south of Alton Towers on B5032.

**SAT NAV** *ST14 5HG*

Room General

## ALTON, Staffordshire Map ref 4B2

★★★★
GUEST HOUSE

B&B PER ROOM PER NIGHT
S £30.00
D £50.00

*Family rooms: £60 (4 sharing), £80 (5 sharing), £100 (8 sharing). 4 nights for 3; 7 nights for 5.*

### Windy Arbour

Hollis Lane, Denstone, Uttoxeter ST14 5HP **t** (01889) 591013 **e** stay@windyarbour.co.uk

**windyarbour.co.uk** GUEST REVIEWS · SPECIAL OFFERS · REAL-TIME BOOKING

**open** All year
**bedrooms** 1 double, 1 twin, 2 family, 2 suites
**bathrooms** 5 en suite, 1 private
**payment** Credit/debit cards, cash, cheques

Windy Arbour is a peaceful haven graced with superb views and big skies. A warm country welcome is guaranteed. The farmhouse and converted outbuildings can accommodate up to 24. Alton Towers, Peak District and Derbyshire Dales all within easy reach.

**SAT NAV** *ST14 5HP* **ONLINE MAP**

Room General

## ALVECHURCH, Worcestershire Map ref 4B3

★★★
FARMHOUSE

B&B PER ROOM PER NIGHT
S £40.00
D £60.00

### Alcott Farm

Icknield Street, Weatheroak, Alvechurch B48 7EH **t** (01564) 824051 **e** alcottfarm@btinternet.com

**alcottfarm.co.uk**

**open** All year
**bedrooms** 2 double, 2 twin
**bathrooms** All en suite
**payment** Cash, cheques

Country residence close to M42 junction 3. Twenty minutes from Birmingham International Airport and NEC. Solihull, Stratford and Redditch are close by. This interesting country home has spacious en suite bedrooms with one double room located on the ground floor. Good pubs and restaurants close by.

**SAT NAV** *B48 7EH*

Room General 10 Leisure

## What do the star ratings mean?

Detailed information about star ratings can be found at the back of this guide.

## ALVECHURCH, Worcestershire Map ref 4B3

★★★★
BED & BREAKFAST

B&B PER ROOM PER NIGHT
S £45.00
D £75.00–£85.00

EVENING MEAL PER PERSON
£8.50–£10.00

### Woodlands Bed and Breakfast

Coopers Hill, Alvechurch, Nr Bromsgrove B48 7BX **t** (0121) 445 6772 **e** john.impey@gmail.com

**woodlandsbedandbreakfast.com**

**open** All year except Christmas and New Year
**bedrooms** 4 double
**bathrooms** All en suite
**payment** Credit/debit cards, cash, cheques, euros

Set in delightful countryside with extensive gardens and heated swimming pool. A warm welcome is offered by John and Amanda. Bedrooms are en suite, spacious and comfortable. A substantial breakfast is served in the elegant dining room. Close to Birmingham and the NEC and a short drive from Stratford and Warwick.

**SAT NAV** *B48 7BX* **ONLINE MAP**

Room General Leisure

## ANSTEY, Hertfordshire Map ref 2D1

★★★★
FARMHOUSE

B&B PER ROOM PER NIGHT
S £50.00–£60.00
D £80.00–£100.00

### Anstey Grove Barn

The Grove, Buntingford SG9 0BJ **t** (01763) 848828 **e** enquiries@ansteygrovebarn.co.uk

**ansteygrovebarn.co.uk** GUEST REVIEWS

**open** All year
**bedrooms** 3 double, 2 twin, 1 suite
**bathrooms** All en suite
**payment** Credit/debit cards, cash, cheques, euros

Beautiful timber barn set in walled garden, recently converted to offer high quality bed and breakfast accommodation. Set in the heart of the tranquil Hertfordshire countryside, there are a wealth of country walks to enjoy with many village pubs nearby. Within easy reach of Cambridge and London.

**SAT NAV** *SG9 0BJ* **ONLINE MAP**

Room General 12 Leisure

## ARDLEIGH, Essex Map ref 3B2

★★★★
BED & BREAKFAST

B&B PER ROOM PER NIGHT
S £35.00–£40.00
D £65.00–£70.00

### Old Shields Farm

Waterhouse Lane, Ardleigh, Colchester CO7 7NE **t** (01206) 230251 & 07831 278036
**e** ruthemarshall@btinternet.com

**oldshieldsbedandbreakfast.co.uk**

Family-run fruit farm. Peaceful location. Ground-floor accommodation with en suite facilities. Charming single/twin room. Close to Constable Country, Harwich and Beth Chatto's garden.

**open** All year except Christmas and New Year
**bedrooms** 1 twin/double
**bathrooms** En suite
**payment** Cash, cheques, euros

Room General

## ASTLEY, Worcestershire Map ref 4A3

★★★★
BED & BREAKFAST

B&B PER ROOM PER NIGHT
S £35.00–£40.00
D £60.00

### Woodhampton House

Weather Lane, Astley, Stourport-on-Severn DY13 0SF **t** (01299) 826510
**e** pete-a@sally-a.freeserve.co.uk

**woodhamptonhouse.co.uk**

Delightful coach house set in rural location, yet close to Stourport and other places of interest. Always a warm and friendly welcome. Excellent breakfast. Family room £70.00-£80.00.

**open** All year except Christmas
**bedrooms** 1 twin, 1 family
**bathrooms** All en suite
**payment** Cash, cheques

Room General

## ASTON MUNSLOW, Shropshire Map ref 4A3

★★★★★
BED & BREAKFAST
SILVER AWARD

B&B PER ROOM PER NIGHT
S £30.00–£38.00
D £60.00–£74.00

EVENING MEAL PER PERSON
£20.00

### Chadstone

Aston Munslow, Craven Arms SY7 9ER **t** (01584) 841675 **e** chadstone.lee@btinternet.com

**chadstonebandb.co.uk**

**open** All year
**bedrooms** 1 double, 2 twin
**bathrooms** All en suite
**payment** Cash, cheques, euros

Chadstone offers friendly, personal service and luxurious en suite accommodation in the renowned Corvedale. Enjoy panoramic views and the peace and quiet of the South Shropshire countryside. Quoting our guests: 'Superb accommodation, delicious food served by wonderful hosts'. 'Highly recommended. Will come again soon'. 'Every detail made it all so perfect'.

**SAT NAV** *SY7 9ER*

Room General 12 P Leisure

## AYLSHAM, Norfolk Map ref 3B1

★★★★★
GUEST ACCOMMODATION
GOLD AWARD

B&B PER ROOM PER NIGHT
S £60.00–£85.00
D £75.00–£95.00

### Old Pump House

Holman Road, Aylsham NR11 6BY **t** (01263) 733789 **e** theoldpumphouse@btconnect.com

**theoldpumphouse.com**

**open** All year except Christmas and New Year
**bedrooms** 1 double, 2 twin, 2 family
**bathrooms** All en suite
**payment** Credit/debit cards, cash, cheques

Creature comforts, home cooking. Rambling 1750s house beside the thatched pump, a minute from church and market place. Non-smoking.

**SAT NAV** *NR11 6BY* **ONLINE MAP**

Room General P Leisure

## BAKEWELL, Derbyshire Map ref 4B2

★★★★
BED & BREAKFAST

B&B PER ROOM PER NIGHT
S £34.00–£38.00
D £50.00–£56.00

*Family room (sleeps 4): children half price. 10% reduction when booking 3 or more nights. See website for latest offers.*

### Housley Cottage

Housley, Nr Foolow, Hope Valley S32 5QB **t** (01433) 631505 **e** kevin@housleycottages.co.uk

**housleycottages.co.uk**

**open** All year except Christmas and New Year
**bedrooms** 2 double, 1 twin, 1 family
**bathrooms** All en suite
**payment** Credit/debit cards, cash, cheques, euros

A 16thC farm cottage set in open countryside but within ten minutes' walk of the Bulls Head pub in Foolow village. Public footpaths pass our garden gate to Millers Dale, Chatsworth House, Eyam and Castleton. All rooms en suite with views over open countryside. Full English breakfast or vegetarian.

**SAT NAV** *S32 5QB*

Room General P

## B&B prices

Rates for bed and breakfast are shown per room per night.
Double room prices are usually based on two people sharing the room.

## BAMFORD, Derbyshire Map ref 4B2

★★★★
BED & BREAKFAST
SILVER AWARD

B&B PER ROOM PER NIGHT
S £40.00
D £55.00–£58.00

### Pioneer House

Station Road, Bamford, Hope Valley S33 0BN **t** (01433) 650638 **e** pioneerhouse@yahoo.co.uk

**pioneerhouse.co.uk** GUEST REVIEWS · SPECIAL OFFERS

Pioneer House is set in the stunning Hope Valley between Hathersage, Hope and Castleton and is an ideal base for exploring this beautiful and interesting area, whether walking, climbing or just sightseeing.

**open** All year
**bedrooms** 2 double, 1 twin
**bathrooms** 2 en suite, 1 private
**payment** Credit/debit cards, cash, cheques

Room General 1 P Leisure

## BAMFORD, Derbyshire Map ref 4B2

★★★★
INN
SILVER AWARD

B&B PER ROOM PER NIGHT
S Min £55.00
D £76.00–£110.00

*Special breaks available – 3 nights or more; Bank Holiday special breaks; Christmas and New Year breaks.*

### Yorkshire Bridge Inn

Ashopton Road, Bamford, Hope Valley S33 0AZ **t** (01433) 651361 **e** info@yorkshire-bridge.co.uk

**yorkshire-bridge.co.uk**

**open** All year
**bedrooms** 10 double, 2 twin, 2 family
**bathrooms** All en suite
**payment** Credit/debit cards, cash, cheques

This famous inn enjoys an idyllic setting by the beautiful reservoirs of Ladybower, Derwent and Howden in the Peak District, and was voted one of the top six freehouses of the year for all-year-round excellence. Superb, en suite rooms, lovely bar and dining areas offering excellent cuisine with a friendly welcome all year. Brochure available.

**SAT NAV** *S33 0AZ*

Room General P Leisure

## BARROW UPON SOAR, Leicestershire Map ref 4C3

★★★★
INN

B&B PER ROOM PER NIGHT
S £90.00–£120.00
D £90.00–£120.00

EVENING MEAL PER PERSON
£8.00–£20.00

*Register with us online to receive all the latest offers and promotions.*

### Hunting Lodge

38 South Street, Barrow upon Soar, Loughborough LE12 8LZ **t** (01509) 412337

**probablythebestpubsintheworld.com** REAL-TIME BOOKING

**open** All year
**bedrooms** 3 double, 3 twin
**bathrooms** All en suite
**payment** Credit/debit cards, cash, cheques

This beautiful, spectacular, three-storey granite building boasts open fires, leather sofas, private dining and restaurant areas, all suited perfectly to any type of occasion. The rooms, each individually designed, range from the traditional and ornate 'Fagin' room, the luxurious 'Louis' suite to the quirky 'Dali' room.

**SAT NAV** *LE12 8LZ* **ONLINE MAP**

Room General P Leisure

## Don't forget www.

Web addresses throughout this guide are shown without the prefix www. Please include www. in the address line of your browser. If a web address does not follow this style it is shown in full.

For **key to symbols** see page 7

## BASILDON, Essex Map ref 3B3

★★★★
GUEST ACCOMMODATION

B&B PER ROOM PER NIGHT
S £58.00
D £68.00

### Frasers

5 Maltings Road, Wickford SS11 7RF **t** (01268) 561700 & 07876 717353 **e** frasers@battlesbridge.com

**battlesbridge.com/guesthouse.php** SPECIAL OFFERS • REAL-TIME BOOKING

**open** All year
**bedrooms** 4 double, 1 twin, 1 family
**bathrooms** 7 en suite
**payment** Credit/debit cards, cash, cheques, euros

Quality accommodation serving the picturesque village of Battlesbridge, on the River Crouch. Centrally situated between Basildon, Chelmsford and Southend close to the A130. Two excellent food pubs within walking distance and home to the largest antiques centre in the South East.

**SAT NAV** *SS11 7RF* **ONLINE MAP**

Room General

## BECCLES, Suffolk Map ref 3C1

★★★★
GUEST ACCOMMODATION

B&B PER ROOM PER NIGHT
S £37.00–£45.00
D £54.00–£56.00

### Catherine House

2 Ringsfield Road, Beccles NR34 9PQ **t** (01502) 716428

**catherinehouse.net** GUEST REVIEWS

Family home, tastefully decorated to high standard, in quiet position overlooking Waveney Valley. Five minutes' walk to town centre. Private parking. Good breakfast with local produce.

**open** All year except Christmas
**bedrooms** 2 double, 1 family
**bathrooms** 2 en suite, 1 private
**payment** Cash, cheques

Room General

## BECCLES, Suffolk Map ref 3C1

★★★★
GUEST ACCOMMODATION

B&B PER ROOM PER NIGHT
S £40.00–£42.00
D £50.00–£52.00

### Pinetrees

Park Drive, Beccles NR34 7DQ **t** (01502) 470796 **e** info@pinetrees.net

**pinetrees.net** GUEST REVIEWS

Attractive timber-constructed, contemporary-style, eco-friendly B&B set in 6.25 acres of the peaceful Waveney Valley in Beccles, North Suffolk. Organic food served, plus our free-range hens' eggs.

**open** All year except Christmas
**bedrooms** 3 double
**bathrooms** All en suite
**payment** Cash, cheques

Room General Leisure

## BEDFORD, Bedfordshire Map ref 2D1

★★★★
RESTAURANT WITH ROOMS
SILVER AWARD

B&B PER ROOM PER NIGHT
S £80.00–£90.00
D £120.00–£150.00

EVENING MEAL PER PERSON
£12.00–£25.00

### Cornfields

Wilden Road, Roothams Green, Bedford MK44 2NJ **t** (01234) 378990
**e** reservations@cornfieldsrestaurant.co.uk

**cornfieldsrestaurant.co.uk** GUEST REVIEWS • SPECIAL OFFERS • REAL-TIME BOOKING

**open** All year
**bedrooms** 3 double, 2 twin, 5 single
**bathrooms** 5 en suite
**payment** Credit/debit cards, cash, cheques

A fresh-food restaurant with individually furnished rooms in the heart of the Bedfordshire countryside at Colmworth near Bedford.

**SAT NAV** *MK44 2NJ* **ONLINE MAP**

Room General Leisure

## BEESTON, Nottinghamshire Map ref 4C2

★★★
GUEST HOUSE

B&B PER ROOM PER NIGHT
S £27.50–£50.00
D £60.00

EVENING MEAL PER PERSON
£7.95–£15.00

*Discounts available for groups and stays of 4 nights or longer. Extra discounts during winter. Please contact for details.*

### Hylands

Queens Road, Beeston, Nottingham NG9 1JB **t** (0115) 925 5472 **e** hyland.hotel@btconnect.com

**accommodation.uk.net/hylands.htm** REAL-TIME BOOKING

**open** All year except Christmas
**bedrooms** 6 double, 7 twin, 17 single, 8 family
**bathrooms** 23 en suite
**payment** Credit/debit cards, cash

A family-run hotel offering comfortable, clean accommodation within a warm and friendly atmosphere. Situated close to Nottingham University, the city indoor tennis centre and Attenborough nature reserve. Within easy walking distance of an award-winning pub and several excellent restaurants, and with frequent transport links to the city centre.

**SAT NAV** *NG9 1JB* **ONLINE MAP**

Room General Leisure

## BIGGLESWADE, Bedfordshire Map ref 2D1

★★★
BED & BREAKFAST

B&B PER ROOM PER NIGHT
S Min £35.00
D Min £55.00

### Old Warden Guesthouse

Shop & Post Office, Old Warden SG18 9HQ **t** (01767) 627201 **e** owgh@idnet.co.uk

Listed 19thC building, adjacent to shop and post office. Between Biggleswade and Bedford. One mile from Shuttleworth Collection. All rooms en suite. In the heart of the Bedfordshire countryside.

**open** All year except Christmas and New Year
**bedrooms** 2 double, 1 twin
**bathrooms** All en suite
**payment** Credit/debit cards, cash, cheques

Room General

## BIRMINGHAM, West Midlands Map ref 4B3

★★★
GUEST ACCOMMODATION

B&B PER ROOM PER NIGHT
S £36.00–£45.00
D £45.00–£58.00

### Elmdon Guest House

2369 Coventry Road, Sheldon, Birmingham B26 3PN **t** (0121) 688 1720 & (0121) 742 1626
**e** elmdonhouse@blueyonder.co.uk

**elmdonguesthouse.co.uk** SPECIAL OFFERS

Family-run guesthouse with en suite facilities. TV in all rooms, including Sky. On main A45 close to the NEC, airport, railway and city centre. We now have Wi-Fi internet connection.

**open** All year except Christmas and New Year
**bedrooms** 1 double, 2 twin, 2 single, 1 family, 1 suite
**bathrooms** All en suite
**payment** Credit/debit cards, cash, cheques

Room General Leisure

## BIRMINGHAM, West Midlands Map ref 4B3

★★
GUEST ACCOMMODATION

B&B PER ROOM PER NIGHT
S £22.00–£40.00
D £38.50–£49.95

EVENING MEAL PER PERSON
£5.00–£8.50

### Rollason Wood

130 Wood End Road, Erdington, Birmingham B24 8BJ **t** (0121) 373 1230 **e** rollwood@globalnet.co.uk

**rollasonwoodhotel.co.uk**

Friendly, family-run hotel, one mile from M6, exit 6. Convenient for city centre, NEC and Convention Centre. A la carte restaurant and bar.

**open** All year except Christmas and New Year
**bedrooms** 3 double, 5 twin, 19 single, 8 family
**bathrooms** 10 en suite, 1 private
**payment** Credit/debit cards, cash, cheques

Room General

## BIRMINGHAM INTERNATIONAL AIRPORT

*See under Birmingham, Coventry, Meriden, Solihull*

## BISHOP'S CASTLE, Shropshire Map ref 4A3

★★★★
INN

B&B PER ROOM PER NIGHT
S Min £50.00
D Min £70.00

EVENING MEAL PER PERSON
£6.00–£20.00

*Discounts for longer stays – 3 nights or more. Please ask.*

### Inn on the Green

Wentnor, Bishop's Castle SY9 5EF **t** (01588) 650105 **e** sempleaj@aol.com

**theinnonthegreen.net**

**open** All year
**bedrooms** 3 double, 1 twin, 1 family
**bathrooms** All en suite
**payment** Credit/debit cards, cash, cheques, euros

Family-run country inn situated in the heart of the Shropshire Hills walking country. Local real ales, bar snacks, restaurant meals using local produce. Dishes of the day including vegetarian. Snacks start at £4.00, main dishes start at £10.00. Wheelchair access to all public rooms and disabled toilet.

**SAT NAV** *SY9 5EF* **ONLINE MAP**

Room General Leisure

## BOURNE, Lincolnshire Map ref 3A1

★★★★
GUEST ACCOMMODATION
SILVER AWARD

B&B PER ROOM PER NIGHT
S £24.00–£32.00
D £46.00–£54.00

### Maycroft Cottage Bed and Breakfast

6 Edenham Road, Hanthorpe, Bourne PE10 0RB **t** (01778) 571689
**e** enquiries@maycroftcottage.co.uk

**maycroftcottage.co.uk** GUEST REVIEWS

Maycroft Cottage is a modern residence with a cottage atmosphere, accommodating the tourist or the business person wishing to relax in this idyllic setting. Walkers and cyclists welcome.

**open** All year except Christmas and New Year
**bedrooms** 1 double, 1 twin
**bathrooms** 2 private
**payment** Cash, cheques

Room General 8 P Leisure

## BRACKLEY, Northamptonshire Map ref 2C1

★★★★
FARMHOUSE

B&B PER ROOM PER NIGHT
S Min £30.00
D Min £50.00

### Astwell Mill

Helmdon, Brackley NN13 5QU **t** (01295) 760507 **e** astwell01@aol.com

**astwellmill.co.uk**

Converted water mill and sheep farm overlooking large lake. Great welcome. Excellent breakfasts using local produce. Picturesque surroundings. Stowe, Canons Ashby, Silverstone nearby. Warwick, Blenheim, Oxford, Stratford, one hour.

**open** All year except Christmas
**bedrooms** 2 double
**bathrooms** 1 en suite, 1 private
**payment** Cash, cheques

Room General P

## BRACKLEY, Northamptonshire Map ref 2C1

★★★★
FARMHOUSE

B&B PER ROOM PER NIGHT
S £45.00–£55.00
D £55.00–£70.00

### Hill Farm

Halse, Brackley NN13 6DY **t** (01280) 703300 & 07860 865146 **e** j.g.robinson@btconnect.com

A charming Georgian farmhouse set in beautiful countryside. Antique four-poster bed. Close to Silverstone, Stowe, Oxford, Blenheim and the Cotswolds. Peaceful location, warm welcome, delicious breakfasts.

**open** All year except Christmas and New Year
**bedrooms** 2 double, 1 twin, 2 suites
**bathrooms** 2 en suite, 3 private
**payment** Cash, cheques, euros

Room General P

## Using map references

The map references refer to the colour maps at the front of this guide. The first figure is the map number, the letter and figure that follow indicate the grid reference on the map.

## BRADWELL, Derbyshire Map ref 4B2

★★★
INN

B&B PER ROOM PER NIGHT
s £30.00–£45.00
D £55.00–£80.00

EVENING MEAL PER PERSON
£6.95–£12.95

### Travellers Rest

Brough Lane End, Brough, Hope Valley S33 9HG **t** (01433) 620363 **e** elliottstephen@btconnect.com

**travellers-rest.net**

Country inn set in the picturesque Hope Valley in the Peak District. Friendly, with great food and beer.

**open** All year except Christmas
**bedrooms** 3 double, 2 twin
**bathrooms** All en suite
**payment** Credit/debit cards, cash, cheques

Room General Leisure

## BRAMPTON ABBOTTS, Herefordshire Map ref 2A1

★★★
BED & BREAKFAST

B&B PER ROOM PER NIGHT
s £25.00–£30.00
D £50.00–£60.00

EVENING MEAL PER PERSON
£12.50–£15.00

### Brampton Cottage

Brampton Abbotts, Ross-on-Wye HR9 7JD **t** (01989) 562459 **e** caroline-keen@btconnect.co.uk

Comfortable 18thC cottage in rural location with the River Wye within walking distance and only three miles from Ross-on-Wye. One double and one twin/family room. Brand new bathroom. Well established, sunny garden.

**open** All year except Christmas and New Year
**bedrooms** 1 double, 1 twin
**bathrooms** 2 private
**payment** Cash, cheques

Room General Leisure

## BRANCASTER, Norfolk Map ref 3B1

★★★
INN

B&B PER ROOM PER NIGHT
s £50.00–£60.00
D £60.00–£80.00

EVENING MEAL PER PERSON
£8.00–£15.00

### Ship Inn

Main Road, Brancaster PE31 8AP **t** (01485) 210333 **e** mike.ali.ship@btinternet.com

**shipinnbrancaster.co.uk**

The Ship Inn at Brancaster is warm and welcoming. Serving home-cooked food in the bars, dining room or beer garden. A traditional, old-fashioned 18thC English pub.

**open** All year
**bedrooms** 3 double, 1 twin
**bathrooms** 3 en suite, 1 private
**payment** Credit/debit cards, cash, cheques

Room General Leisure

## BRIGG, Lincolnshire Map ref 4C1

★★★★
GUEST HOUSE

B&B PER ROOM PER NIGHT
s £20.00–£27.50
D £30.00–£45.00

EVENING MEAL PER PERSON
£6.00–£10.00

### Holcombe Guest House

34 Victoria Road, Barnetby DN38 6JR **t** 07850 764002 **e** holcombe.house@virgin.net

**holcombeguesthouse.co.uk**

Pleasant, homely accommodation near the railway station and airport. Only 15 minutes from Scunthorpe, Grimsby and Hull. Bedroom for disabled guests.

**open** All year
**bedrooms** 3 twin, 8 single, 2 family
**bathrooms** 7 en suite
**payment** Credit/debit cards, cash, cheques

Room General

**BROADWAY, Worcestershire Map ref 2B1**

★★★★
GUEST ACCOMMODATION

B&B PER ROOM PER NIGHT
S £65.00–£70.00
D £80.00–£85.00

EVENING MEAL PER PERSON
£10.25–£14.95

## The Bell at Willersey

The Bell Inn, Willersey, Broadway WR12 7PJ **t** (01386) 858405 **e** enq@bellatwillersey.fsnet.co.uk

**the-bell-willersey.com**

**open** All year
**bedrooms** 2 double, 1 twin, 2 suites
**bathrooms** All en suite
**payment** Credit/debit cards, cash, cheques

17thC inn overlooking the village green and duck pond. One mile from Broadway, a perfect location for touring. Enjoys a high reputation for home-produced food. Restaurant open lunchtime and evenings. Relax in our superb bedrooms situated in our courtyard.

**SAT NAV** *WR12 7PJ*

Room General P Leisure

**BROADWAY, Worcestershire Map ref 2B1**

★★★★
GUEST ACCOMMODATION

B&B PER ROOM PER NIGHT
S £51.50
D £93.00

EVENING MEAL PER PERSON
£15.65

*Weekend leisure-course breaks and 3-night deals throughout the year. Last-minute discounts available.*

## Farncombe Estate Centre

Broadway WR12 7LJ **t** (01386) 854100 **e** visit@farncombeestate.co.uk

**farncombeestate.co.uk** SPECIAL OFFERS

**open** All year except Christmas and New Year
**bedrooms** 9 double, 5 twin, 39 single
**bathrooms** All en suite
**payment** Credit/debit cards, cash, cheques

Comfortable B&B accommodation set in 300 acres of beautiful grounds in the North Cotswolds near the picturesque village of Broadway. 53 en suite bedrooms and fully equipped meeting rooms are available for hire. Group travel or exclusive-use bookings welcome by arrangement. Weekend leisure course and event programme available.

**SAT NAV** *WR12 7LJ*

Room General P Leisure

**BROADWAY, Worcestershire Map ref 2B1**

★★★★
FARMHOUSE

B&B PER ROOM PER NIGHT
S £52.00–£65.00
D £62.00–£80.00

EVENING MEAL PER PERSON
£20.00

*Off-season discounts. Please see website.*

WALKERS WELCOME · CYCLISTS WELCOME

## Lowerfield Farm

Willersey Fields, Broadway WR11 7HF **t** (01386) 858273 **e** info@lowerfieldfarm.com

**lowerfieldfarm.com** GUEST REVIEWS · SPECIAL OFFERS · REAL-TIME BOOKING

**open** All year
**bedrooms** 3 double, 2 twin, 1 single, 2 family
**bathrooms** All en suite
**payment** Credit/debit cards, cash, cheques

A largely 17thC farmhouse just outside Broadway, with wonderful views of the Cotswold escarpment. All rooms en suite, beautifully furnished and with digital TV and DVD players. Doubles have king-size beds. We offer a varied and high quality breakfast menu, and farmhouse dinner by request. Licensed premises; Wi-Fi internet available.

**SAT NAV** *WR11 7HF* **ONLINE MAP**

Room General P Leisure

### Has every property been assessed?

All accommodation in this guide has been rated for quality, or is awaiting assessment, by a professional national tourist board assessor.

## BROADWAY, Worcestershire Map ref 2B1

★★★★
BED & BREAKFAST
GOLD AWARD

B&B PER ROOM PER NIGHT
S Min £60.00
D £80.00–£100.00

### Sheepscombe House

Snowshill, Broadway WR12 7JU **t** (01386) 853769 **e** reservations@snowshill-broadway.co.uk

**broadway-cotswolds.co.uk/sheepscombe.html**

In the heart of the Cotswolds, Sheepscombe House is surrounded by beautiful countryside with spectacular views. Very comfortable. Try the Cotswold breakfast. Ample parking. Ideal walking.

**open** 1 March to Christmas
**bedrooms** 1 double, 1 twin, 1 family
**bathrooms** 2 en suite, 1 private
**payment** Credit/debit cards, cash, cheques

Room TV SC General P Leisure

## BRUNDALL, Norfolk Map ref 3C1

★★★★
BED & BREAKFAST

B&B PER ROOM PER NIGHT
S £40.00
D £60.00

### Breckland B&B

12 Strumpshaw Road, Brundall NR13 5PA **t** (01603) 712122 **e** brecklandbandb@hotmail.co.uk

**breckland-bandb.co.uk**

At Breckland B&B in Brundall, David and Tina Ward have two superior, self-contained bedrooms both with en suite facilities. Convenient for Strumpshaw RSPB, the Broads and Norwich. Recommended.

**open** All year except Christmas and New Year
**bedrooms** 1 double, 1 twin
**bathrooms** All en suite
**payment** Cash, cheques, euros

Room TV General P Leisure

## BUNTINGFORD, Hertfordshire Map ref 2D1

★★
GUEST ACCOMMODATION

B&B PER ROOM PER NIGHT
S £30.00–£40.00
D £55.00–£65.00

### Buckland Bury Farm

Buckland Bury, Buckland, Buntingford SG9 0PY **t** 07760 227366
**e** bucklandbury@shrubbsfarm.demon.co.uk

**tiscover.co.uk**

17thC creeper-clad farmhouse offering homely accommodation, within easy reach of Duxford, Audley End, Wimpole Hall and Cambridge.

**open** All year
**bedrooms** 1 double, 2 twin
**bathrooms** 1 en suite
**payment** Credit/debit cards, cash, cheques

Room TV General P

## BURNHAM-ON-CROUCH, Essex Map ref 3B3

★★★★
INN
SILVER AWARD

B&B PER ROOM PER NIGHT
S Min £51.00
D Min £67.00

### The Railway Hotel

Station Road, Burnham-on-Crouch CM0 8BQ **t** (01621) 786868

**therailwayhotelburnham.co.uk**

Originally built in the late 1800s, and lovingly restored by Jenny and Colin Newcombe to incorporate 21st-century luxuries with Victorian charm.

**open** All year
**bedrooms** 6 double, 1 twin, 1 single
**bathrooms** All en suite
**payment** Credit/debit cards, cash, cheques

Room TV General P

## BURNHAM THORPE, Norfolk Map ref 3B1

★★★★
FARMHOUSE
SILVER AWARD

B&B PER ROOM PER NIGHT
S £45.00–£80.00
D £72.00

### Whitehall Farm

Burnham Thorpe PE31 8HN **t** (01328) 738416 **e** barrysoutherland@aol.com

**tiscover.co.uk**

Barry and Valerie welcome you for a quiet, relaxed stay in North Norfolk, two miles from the coast. Family rooms with full facilities in 16thC farmhouse.

**open** All year except Christmas
**bedrooms** 1 double, 1 twin, 1 family
**bathrooms** 2 en suite, 1 private
**payment** Credit/debit cards, cash, cheques, euros

Room TV General P Leisure

For **key to symbols** see page 7

## BURY ST EDMUNDS, Suffolk Map ref 3B2

★★★★
BED & BREAKFAST
SILVER AWARD

B&B PER ROOM PER NIGHT
S £35.00–£45.00
D £55.00–£65.00

### Brambles Lodge

Welham Lane, Risby, Bury St Edmunds IP28 6QS **t** (01284) 810701

**open** All year except Christmas
**bedrooms** 1 double, 1 twin, 1 single, 1 family
**bathrooms** 3 en suite
**payment** Cash, cheques

The lodge stands amid attractive landscape gardens in the delightful and peaceful village of Risby, three miles from Bury St Edmunds. The individual rooms, which are beautifully furnished, are equipped with many thoughtful touches. Breakfast is served in a smart conservatory overlooking a large pond and garden which attract wildlife. Two village pubs serve food.

**SAT NAV** *IP28 6QS*

Room TV General 6 P Leisure

## BURY ST EDMUNDS, Suffolk Map ref 3B2

★★★
GUEST HOUSE

B&B PER ROOM PER NIGHT
S £30.00–£45.00
D £65.00–£75.00

### Dunston Guesthouse

8 Springfield Road, Bury St Edmunds IP33 3AN **t** (01284) 767981

**dunstonguesthouse.co.uk**

Victorian hotel in quiet, tree-lined road five to ten minutes' walk from town centre and close to all amenities. Comfortable lounge and peaceful sun lounge. Garden, car park. Groups up to 12 welcome. All rooms may be let as single occupancy.

**open** All year except Christmas and New Year
**bedrooms** 10 single, 5 double/family, 2 twin
**bathrooms** 9 en suite, 4 private
**payment** Cash, cheques

Room TV General P

## BUXTON, Derbyshire Map ref 4B2

★★★
INN

B&B PER ROOM PER NIGHT
S Min £45.00
D Min £55.00

EVENING MEAL PER PERSON
£7.50–£12.50

### Devonshire Arms

Peak Forest, Buxton SK17 8EJ **t** (01298) 23875 **e** fiona.clough@virgin.net

**devarms.com** SPECIAL OFFERS • REAL-TIME BOOKING

**open** All year except Christmas
**bedrooms** 4 double, 2 family
**bathrooms** All en suite
**payment** Credit/debit cards, cash, cheques

Traditional Peak District inn. High-standard, en suite rooms with TV and coffee facilities. Excellent food, traditional ales, coal fire. Dogs and children free. Guaranteed warm welcome.

**SAT NAV** *SK17 8EJ* **ONLINE MAP**

Room TV General P Leisure

WALKERS WELCOME WELCOME WALKERS

## Do you like walking?

Walkers feel at home in accommodation participating in our Walkers Welcome scheme. Look out for the symbol. Consider walking all or part of a long-distance route – go online at nationaltrail.co.uk.

## BUXTON, Derbyshire Map ref 4B2

★★★★
FARMHOUSE
SILVER AWARD

B&B PER ROOM PER NIGHT
S £39.00–£45.00
D £60.00–£78.00

*Discounts on stays of 4 or more nights (excl Bank Holidays).*

### Fernydale Farm

Earl Sterndale, Nr Buxton SK17 0BS **t** (01298) 83236 **e** wjnadin@btconnect.com

**fernydalefarmbandb.co.uk**

**open** All year
**bedrooms** 1 double, 1 twin, 1 family
**bathrooms** All en suite
**payment** Cash, cheques

A friendly, warm welcome awaits you at Fernydale. A working farm nestling in the Peaks with stunning views. Attractive bedrooms with modern bathrooms. Spacious conservatory and garden to relax in. Excellent breakfast to set you up for the day. Buxton, Bakewell, Ashbourne and numerous attractions/walks within easy access. Occasional evening meals.

**SAT NAV** *SK17 0BS*

WALKERS WELCOME · CYCLISTS WELCOME

Room General P Leisure

## BUXTON, Derbyshire Map ref 4B2

★★★★★
GUEST HOUSE
GOLD AWARD

B&B PER ROOM PER NIGHT
S £33.00–£50.00
D £65.00–£90.00

EVENING MEAL PER PERSON
£15.00

### Grendon Guest House

Bishops Lane, Buxton SK17 6UN **t** (01298) 78831 **e** grendonguesthouse@hotmail.com

**grendonguesthouse.co.uk** GUEST REVIEWS • REAL-TIME BOOKING

Grendon is spacious and elegant, with exquisite bedrooms, scrumptious food and the friendliest hospitality. Set in lovely one-acre gardens. Easy driveway parking. Beautiful location, fifteen minutes' walk to town centre.

**open** All year
**bedrooms** 3 double, 1 twin, 1 single
**bathrooms** All en suite
**payment** Credit/debit cards, cash, cheques

Room General 9 P

## BUXTON, Derbyshire Map ref 4B2

★★★★
GUEST HOUSE
SILVER AWARD

B&B PER ROOM PER NIGHT
S Min £45.00
D £65.00–£80.00

### Grosvenor House

Broad Walk, Buxton SK17 6JE **t** (01298) 72439 **e** grosvenor.buxton@btopenworld.com

**grosvenorbuxton.co.uk**

**open** All year except Christmas
**bedrooms** 6 double, 1 twin, 1 family
**bathrooms** All en suite
**payment** Credit/debit cards, cash, cheques

Quiet, privately run, Grade II Listed Victorian residence situated in the heart of this historic spa town. All en suite rooms have many interesting features. Imaginative, freshly cooked breakfast menu. Non-smoking throughout. Stairlift to first floor.

**SAT NAV** *SK17 6JE*

Room General P Leisure

## Place index

If you know where you want to stay, the index by place name at the back of the guide will give you the page number listing accommodation in your chosen town, city or village. Check out the other useful indexes too.

**BUXTON, Derbyshire Map ref 4B2**

★★★★
GUEST HOUSE
SILVER AWARD

B&B PER ROOM PER NIGHT
S £35.00–£45.00
D £60.00–£80.00

*10% discount on stays of 4 nights or more.*

## Kingscroft Guest House

10 Green Lane, Buxton SK17 9DP **t** (01298) 22757

**open** All year
**bedrooms** 6 double, 1 twin, 1 single
**bathrooms** All en suite
**payment** Cash, cheques

Late-Victorian luxury guesthouse, in a central yet quiet position in the heart of the Peak District. Comfortable surroundings with period decor. Enjoy our hearty, delicious, home-cooked full English or continental breakfasts.

**SAT NAV** *SK17 9DP*

Room General P Leisure

**BUXTON, Derbyshire Map ref 4B2**

★★★★
GUEST HOUSE

B&B PER ROOM PER NIGHT
D £70.00–£80.00

## Lakenham Guest House

11 Burlington Road, Buxton SK17 9AL **t** (01298) 79209 **e** enquiries@lakenhambuxton.co.uk

**lakenhambuxton.co.uk** GUEST REVIEWS

**open** All year
**bedrooms** 4 double, 3 twin
**bathrooms** 5 en suite, 2 private
**payment** Credit/debit cards, cash, cheques

Sample Victorian elegance in one of Buxton's finest guesthouses. Lakenham offers all modern facilities yet retains its Victorian character. Period furniture and antiques. Superb, central location overlooking picturesque Pavilion Gardens. Spacious, tastefully furnished bedrooms with TV, hospitality tray. First-class, personal service in a friendly, relaxed atmosphere.

**SAT NAV** *SK17 9AL* **ONLINE MAP**

Room TV SC General P

**CAENBY CORNER, Lincolnshire Map ref 4C2**

★★★★
BED & BREAKFAST
SILVER AWARD

B&B PER ROOM PER NIGHT
S £40.00
D £55.00–£75.00

## Ermine Lodge Bed and Breakfast

Ermine Lodge, Caenby Corner LN8 2AR **t** (01673) 878152 & 07771 740722
**e** info@erminelodgebandb.com

**erminelodgebandb.com** SPECIAL OFFERS

A friendly and comfortable home with four lovely en suite bedrooms, set in two acres of gardens and with our own free-range eggs for breakfast. Single-occupancy discount for midweek guests. Free Wi-Fi.

**open** All year except Christmas
**bedrooms** 2 double, 1 twin, 1 family
**bathrooms** All en suite
**payment** Credit/debit cards, cash, cheques, euros

Room TV General P Leisure

**CAMBRIDGE, Cambridgeshire Map ref 2D1**

★★★★
BED & BREAKFAST

B&B PER ROOM PER NIGHT
S £40.00–£50.00
D £60.00–£75.00

## Allenbell

517a Coldham Lane, Cambridge CB1 3JS **t** (01223) 210353 **e** sandragailturner@hotmail.com

**allenbell.co.uk**

Warm, friendly bed and breakfast providing newly-furnished, en suite, comfortable accommodation. Quality breakfast served in light, spacious dining room. Easy access from A14/M11, close to city centre.

**open** All year except Christmas
**bedrooms** 3 double, 1 twin
**bathrooms** 3 en suite, 1 private
**payment** Credit/debit cards, cash, cheques

Room TV General 5 P Leisure

## CAMBRIDGE, Cambridgeshire Map ref 2D1

★★★★
GUEST HOUSE

B&B PER ROOM PER NIGHT
S £30.00–£65.00
D £55.00–£75.00

### Arbury Lodge Guesthouse

82 Arbury Road, Cambridge CB4 2JE **t** (01223) 364319 **e** arbury-lodge@btconnect.com

**arburylodgeguesthouse.co.uk**

Comfortable, family-run guesthouse offering excellent service, good home cooking, cleanliness and friendly atmosphere. 1.5 miles north of city centre and colleges. Easy access from A14/M11. Large car park, garden.

**open** All year except Christmas and New Year
**bedrooms** 2 double, 2 twin, 1 single, 1 family
**bathrooms** 3 en suite
**payment** Credit/debit cards, cash, cheques

Room General P

## CAMBRIDGE, Cambridgeshire Map ref 2D1

★★★
BED & BREAKFAST

B&B PER ROOM PER NIGHT
S £35.00–£40.00
D £50.00–£60.00

### Avondale

35 Highfields Road, Caldecote CB3 7NX **t** (01954) 210746 **e** avondalecambs@amserve.com

**tiscover.co.uk**

Small exclusive bungalow offering friendly accommodation. Situated in peaceful village location. Long country walkways.

**open** All year except Christmas
**bedrooms** 1 twin, 1 family
**bathrooms** All en suite
**payment** Cash, cheques

Room General P Leisure

## CAMBRIDGE, Cambridgeshire Map ref 2D1

★★★
GUEST HOUSE

B&B PER ROOM PER NIGHT
S £45.00–£60.00
D £65.00–£75.00

### Bridge Guest House

151 Hills Road, Cambridge CB2 2RJ **t** (01223) 247942 **e** bghouse@gmail.com

**bridgeguesthouse.co.uk**

Family-run business. Close to Addenbrooks Hospital, Cambridge Leisure Park, Botanic Gardens and city centre. M11 (Stansted) two miles. Easy access to buses and railway.

**open** All year except Christmas and New Year
**bedrooms** 2 double, 2 twin, 2 single, 1 family
**bathrooms** All en suite
**payment** Credit/debit cards, cash, cheques, euros

Room General P

## CAMBRIDGE, Cambridgeshire Map ref 2D1

★★★★
BED & BREAKFAST

B&B PER ROOM PER NIGHT
S Min £35.00
D Min £70.00

### City Centre North Bed And Breakfast

328a Histon Road, Cambridge CB4 3HT **t** (01223) 312843 **e** gscambs@tiscali.co.uk

**citycentrenorth.co.uk**

Light and airy contemporary house. Off A14/M11 with parking. Ten-minute bus journey to town centre with market, shops, restaurant and colleges.

**open** April to December
**bedrooms** 1 twin, 1 single
**bathrooms** 1 private
**payment** Cash, cheques

Room General 3 P

## CAMBRIDGE, Cambridgeshire Map ref 2D1

★★★
BED & BREAKFAST

B&B PER ROOM PER NIGHT
S £40.00–£45.00
D £60.00

### Granta House

53 Eltisley Avenue, Newnham CB3 9JQ **t** (01223) 560466 **e** tj.dathan@ntlworld.com

**tiscover.co.uk**

Edwardian family home in quiet location, within walking distance of city centre, the Backs and library. Delightful walk across meadows to village of Grantchester. Easy access to M11 junction 12.

**open** All year
**bedrooms** 1 double, 1 single
**payment** Cash, cheques

Room General Leisure

### Where are the maps?

Colour maps can be found at the front of the guide. They pinpoint the location of all accommodation found in the regional sections.

## CAMBRIDGE, Cambridgeshire Map ref 2D1

★★★★
GUEST HOUSE

B&B PER ROOM PER NIGHT
S £55.00–£65.00
D £65.00–£75.00

### Harry's Bed and Breakfast

39 Milton Road, Cambridge CB4 1XA **t** (01223) 503866 **e** cjmadden@ntlworld.com

**welcometoharrys.co.uk**

**open** All year
**bedrooms** 3 double, 1 twin, 1 family
**bathrooms** All en suite
**payment** Credit/debit cards, cash, cheques, euros

Edwardian semi-detached house only ten minutes from centre. Close to science park and all major routes. All rooms with full en suite and flat-screen LCD TV with Freeview. Excellent local amenities.

**SAT NAV** *CB4 1XA*

Room General Leisure

## CAMBRIDGE, Cambridgeshire Map ref 2D1

★★★★
BED & BREAKFAST

B&B PER ROOM PER NIGHT
S £30.00–£40.00
D £50.00–£60.00

### The Poplars

12 East Drive, Highfields Caldecote, Cambridge CB23 7NZ **t** (01954) 210396
**e** thepoplars@onetel.com

**tiscover.co.uk**

Peaceful village bungalow. Close to M11/A14, Cambridge, Duxford, Papworth hospital, Bourn Hall. Near 'park and ride'. Pets/children warmly welcomed. This is a non-smoking establishment.

**open** All year except Christmas and New Year
**bedrooms** 1 double, 1 twin, 1 family
**bathrooms** 2 en suite, 1 private
**payment** Cash, cheques

Room General

## CAMBRIDGE, Cambridgeshire Map ref 2D1

★★★
GUEST HOUSE

B&B PER ROOM PER NIGHT
S £35.00–£45.00
D £48.00–£58.00

### Southampton Guest House

7 Elizabeth Way, Cambridge CB4 1DE **t** (01223) 357780 **e** southamptonhouse@btinternet.com

**southamptonguesthouse.com**

Victorian property with friendly atmosphere, only 15 minutes' walk along riverside to city centre, colleges and shopping mall.

**open** All year
**bedrooms** 1 double, 1 single, 3 family
**bathrooms** All en suite
**payment** Cash, cheques, euros

Room General

## CAMBRIDGE, Cambridgeshire Map ref 2D1

★★★★
BED & BREAKFAST

B&B PER ROOM PER NIGHT
S £25.00–£45.00
D £45.00–£60.00

### Tudor Cottage

292 Histon Road, Cambridge CB4 3HS **t** (01223) 565212 **e** email@tudor-cottage.net

**tudorcottageguesthouse.co.uk** REAL-TIME BOOKING

**open** All year
**bedrooms** 2 double, 1 twin, 1 single
**bathrooms** 2 en suite
**payment** Cash, cheques

Comfortable, friendly, Tudor-style cottage situated within 30 minutes' walking distance of city centre. En suite or shared facilities, central heating, colour TV, tea-/coffee-making facilities. Excellent food and friendly, personal service. Off-street parking. Easy access to A14/M11.

**SAT NAV** *CB4 3HS* **ONLINE MAP**

Room General

## CAMBRIDGE, Cambridgeshire Map ref 2D1

★★★★
GUEST HOUSE
SILVER AWARD

B&B PER ROOM PER NIGHT
S £40.00–£65.00
D £60.00–£85.00

### Worth House

152 Chesterton Road, Cambridge CB4 1DA **t** (01223) 316074 **e** enquiry@worth-house.co.uk

**worth-house.co.uk** GUEST REVIEWS • SPECIAL OFFERS

Worth House offers quiet, comfortable and spacious accommodation in this Victorian home. Within easy reach of the city centre. 'Which?' recommended.

**open** All year
**bedrooms** 4 suites
**bathrooms** All en suite
**payment** Credit/debit cards, cash, cheques, euros

Room General Leisure

## CASTLETON, Derbyshire Map ref 4B2

★★★
INN

B&B PER ROOM PER NIGHT
S £35.00–£40.00
D £65.00–£80.00

### Ye Olde Cheshire Cheese Inn

How Lane, Castleton, Hope Valley S33 8WJ **t** (01433) 620330 **e** info@cheshirecheeseinn.co.uk

**cheshirecheeseinn.co.uk**

**open** All year except Christmas Day
**bedrooms** 8 double, 1 twin, 1 single
**bathrooms** All en suite
**payment** Credit/debit cards, cash, cheques

Situated in the heart of the picturesque Peak District. A delightful family-run, 17thC free house. Cosy bar areas and restaurant. The inn offers a wide selection of draught beers and has an excellent reputation for award-winning cask ales and good quality, freshly cooked food. Large car park adjacent to the premises.

**SAT NAV** *S33 8WJ*

Room General Leisure

## CHAPEL-EN-LE-FRITH, Derbyshire Map ref 4B2

★★★★★
GUEST HOUSE
SILVER AWARD

B&B PER ROOM PER NIGHT
S £55.00–£70.00
D £65.00–£90.00

*Discounts on stays of 4 or more days (excl Sat).*

### High Croft

Manchester Road, Chapel-en-le-Frith, High Peak SK23 9UH **t** (01298) 814843
**e** elaine@highcroft-guesthouse.co.uk

**highcroft-guesthouse.co.uk** GUEST REVIEWS • SPECIAL OFFERS

**open** All year
**bedrooms** 2 double, 2 family
**bathrooms** All en suite
**payment** Cash, cheques

A luxurious Edwardian country house set in 1.5 acres of peaceful, mature gardens adjoining Chapel-en-le-Frith golf course and Combs Reservoir with magnificent views and superb walks from the door. Beautifully furnished, en suite bedrooms, spacious, comfortable sitting room, log fires, elegant dining room, and an extensive and appetizing breakfast menu.

**SAT NAV** *SK23 9UH* **ONLINE MAP**

Room General Leisure

## Gold and Silver Awards

Gold and Silver Awards are given to establishments achieving the highest levels of quality and service. You can find more information at the front of the guide, and an index to all accommodation achieving these awards at the back.

## CHEADLE, Staffordshire Map ref 4B2

★★★★
FARMHOUSE

B&B PER ROOM PER NIGHT
S £25.00
D £50.00

EVENING MEAL PER PERSON
£7.50–£10.00

### Rakeway House Farm B&B

Rakeway Road, Cheadle, Alton Towers Area ST10 1RA **t** (01538) 755295
**e** enquiries@rakewayhousefarm.co.uk

**rakewayhousefarm.co.uk**

Charming farmhouse, beautiful gardens. Fantastic views over Cheadle and surrounding countryside. Alton Towers 15 minutes' drive. Good base for Peak District and Potteries. First-class accommodation, excellent menu, superb hospitality.

**open** All year
**bedrooms** 1 double, 1 twin, 1 family
**bathrooms** All en suite
**payment** Cash, cheques

Room General 2 P

## CHERRY HINTON, Cambridgeshire Map ref 2D1

★★
BED & BREAKFAST

B&B PER ROOM PER NIGHT
S £30.00–£40.00
D £45.00–£55.00

### Old Rosemary Branch

Church End, Cherry Hinton, Cambridge CB1 3LF **t** (01223) 247161 **e** saa30@cam.ac.uk

**theoldrosemarybranch.co.uk**

Friendly comfortable family house dating back to mid-eighteenth century.

**open** All year except Christmas and New Year
**bedrooms** 1 double, 1 twin
**payment** Cash, cheques

Room General

## CHESTERFIELD, Derbyshire Map ref 4B2

★★★
GUEST HOUSE

B&B PER ROOM PER NIGHT
S Min £36.00
D Min £48.00

### Abigails Guest House

62 Brockwell Lane, Chesterfield S40 4EE **t** (01246) 279391 **e** gail@abigails.fsnet.co.uk

**abigailsguesthouse.co.uk**

Relax taking breakfast in the conservatory overlooking Chesterfield and surrounding moorlands. Garden with pond and waterfall, private car park. Best B&B winners 2000.

**open** All year
**bedrooms** 3 double, 2 twin, 2 single
**bathrooms** All en suite
**payment** Cash, cheques

Room General P

## CHESTERFIELD, Derbyshire Map ref 4B2

★★★
GUEST ACCOMMODATION

B&B PER ROOM PER NIGHT
S £23.00–£29.00
D £45.00

EVENING MEAL PER PERSON
£7.50–£10.00

### Clarendon Guest House

32 Clarence Road, Chesterfield S40 1LN **t** (01246) 235004

Victorian residence near town centre, leisure facilities, theatres and Peak National Park. Special diets catered for. Overnight laundry service always available.

**open** All year
**bedrooms** 1 double, 2 twin, 2 single
**bathrooms** 4 en suite
**payment** Cash, cheques

Room General Leisure

## CHEVELEY, Cambridgeshire Map ref 3B2

★★★★
BED & BREAKFAST

B&B PER ROOM PER NIGHT
S £35.00–£40.00
D £60.00–£70.00

EVENING MEAL PER PERSON
£18.00–£25.00

### Old Farmhouse

165 High Street, Cheveley, Newmarket CB8 9DG **t** (01638) 730771 & 07909 970047
**e** amrobinson@clara.co.uk

**cheveleybandb.co.uk** REAL-TIME BOOKING

Grade II Listed farmhouse offering a warm welcome and good dining. Perfect base to explore East Anglia, and for horse-racing and Icknield Way for walkers. Private parking. French, Spanish and some German spoken. Pre-booked evening meals. Closed Christmas and Easter.

**bedrooms** 1 double, 1 twin
**bathrooms** 1 en suite, 1 private
**payment** Credit/debit cards, cash, cheques

Room General P

## CLACTON-ON-SEA, Essex Map ref 3B3

★★★★
GUEST ACCOMMODATION

B&B PER ROOM PER NIGHT
S £45.00–£47.00
D £70.00–£72.00

*Reduced terms by negotiation Oct-Mar (excl Christmas and Bank Holidays).*

### The Chudleigh

13 Agate Road, Marine Parade West, Clacton-on-Sea CO15 1RA **t** (01255) 425407
**e** reception@chudleighhotel.com

**tiscover.co.uk/chudleigh-hotel**

**open** All year
**bedrooms** 4 double, 2 twin, 2 single, 2 family
**bathrooms** All en suite
**payment** Credit/debit cards, cash, cheques, euros

An oasis in a town centre location, 200m from seafront gardens, near pier and main shops. Ideal for the business visitor, the tourist and for overnight stays. Free parking. The Chudleigh, owned by the same family since 1963, welcomes you and assures you of every comfort, with friendly atmosphere and attention to detail.

**SAT NAV** *CO15 1RA*

Room General 1 P Leisure

## CLUN, Shropshire Map ref 4A3

★★★
INN

B&B PER ROOM PER NIGHT
S Min £32.50
D Min £55.00

EVENING MEAL PER PERSON
£5.25–£12.00

WALKERS WELCOME CYCLISTS WELCOME

### The White Horse Inn

The Square, Clun SY7 8JA **t** (01588) 640305 **e** jack@whi-clun.co.uk

**whi-clun.co.uk**

Small, friendly, Good Beer Guide-listed public house with well-appointed, en suite family bedrooms in traditional style. Wide-ranging menu available in dining room. Shrewsbury and SW Shropshire Pub of the Year 2007.

**open** All year except Christmas
**bedrooms** 1 double, 3 family
**bathrooms** All en suite
**payment** Credit/debit cards, cash, cheques

Room General Leisure

## COLCHESTER, Essex Map ref 3B2

★★
GUEST HOUSE

B&B PER ROOM PER NIGHT
S £31.00–£40.00
D £47.00–£55.00

### Scheregate Guesthouse

36 Osborne Street, Via St John's Street, Colchester CO2 7DB **t** (01206) 573034

Interesting 15thC building, centrally situated, providing accommodation at moderate prices.

**open** All year except Christmas
**bedrooms** 6 double, 8 twin, 12 single, 2 family
**bathrooms** 10 en suite
**payment** Credit/debit cards, cash, cheques

Room General P

## COLTISHALL, Norfolk Map ref 3C1

★★★★
GUEST ACCOMMODATION

B&B PER ROOM PER NIGHT
S £30.00–£44.00
D £53.00–£58.00

*3 nights for the price of 2 Nov-Apr. Quote 342 when booking.*

### Hedges Guesthouse

Tunstead Road, Coltishall NR12 7AL **t** (01603) 738361 **e** info@hedgesbandb.co.uk

**hedgesbandb.co.uk**

**open** All year except Christmas
**bedrooms** 1 double, 2 twin, 2 family
**bathrooms** All en suite
**payment** Credit/debit cards, cash, cheques

Hear evening owlsong and the dawn chorus at this friendly, family-run guesthouse. Set in large, peaceful gardens surrounded by open countryside, yet convenient for local amenities. Ideal base for exploring the Norfolk Broads, Norwich and Norfolk coast. Families welcome, lounge, plenty of parking.

**SAT NAV** *NR12 7AL*

Room General P Leisure

## COLTISHALL, Norfolk Map ref 3C1

★★★★★ BED & BREAKFAST SILVER AWARD

B&B PER ROOM PER NIGHT
S £55.00
D £68.00–£78.00

*10% reduction for 3 or more nights' stay.*

### Seven Acres House

Great Hautbois, Coltishall NR12 7JZ **t** (01603) 736737 **e** william@hautbois.plus.com

**norfolkbroadsbandb.com**

**open** All year except Christmas and New Year
**bedrooms** 1 double, 1 twin
**bathrooms** All en suite
**payment** Credit/debit cards, cash, cheques, euros

Edwardian Seven Acres House is surrounded by extensive grounds in a peaceful rural location, yet close to village amenities. Easy access to the Broads, Norwich, National Trust properties and coast. Two spacious well-equipped, beautifully furnished south-facing bedrooms. A delicious cooked breakfast is served in the bright morning room leading onto the terrace.

**SAT NAV** *NR12 7JZ*

Room General P Leisure

## COLTON, Staffordshire Map ref 4B3

★★★★★ GUEST HOUSE SILVER AWARD

B&B PER ROOM PER NIGHT
S £50.00–£75.00
D £66.00–£96.00

EVENING MEAL PER PERSON
£8.00–£11.00

*Occasional special offers.*

### Colton House

Bellamour Way, Colton, Rugeley WS15 3LL **t** (01889) 578580 **e** mail@coltonhouse.com

**coltonhouse.com**

**open** All year
**bedrooms** 4 double
**bathrooms** All en suite
**payment** Credit/debit cards, cash, cheques

In a pretty, peaceful village with two pubs and church, this Georgian home has views across the 1.5-acre garden to Cannock Chase. All rooms individually designed; choice of bedrooms: a four-poster, or a 6ft x 7ft bed and round 5ft jacuzzi, to those with beamed ceilings and superb views.

**SAT NAV** *WS15 3LL*

Room General P

## CORBY, Northamptonshire Map ref 3A1

★★★ BED & BREAKFAST

B&B PER ROOM PER NIGHT
S Min £35.00
D £60.00

*Discount for full occupancy.*

### Home Farm

Main Street, Sudborough, Kettering NN14 3BX **t** (01832) 730488 **e** bandbhomefarmsud@aol.com

**homefarmsudborough.co.uk**

**open** All year
**bedrooms** 1 double, 1 twin
**bathrooms** 2 private
**payment** Cash, cheques, euros

Just three miles from the A14, a restored barn to yourself in the picturesque village of Sudborough. The barn has a breakfast room, double bedroom, shower room, lounge with sofa bed and single bed, lockable storage room, private parking, and seating area in the garden, and includes a self-service continental breakfast.

**SAT NAV** *NN14 3BX*

Room General P Leisure

## What if I need to cancel?

It's advisable to check the proprietor's cancellation policy at the time of booking in case you have to change your plans.

## CORBY, Northamptonshire Map ref 3A1

★★★★
GUEST ACCOMMODATION

B&B PER ROOM PER NIGHT
S Min £35.00
D Min £70.00

### Manor Farm Guest House

Station Road, Rushton, Kettering NN14 1RL **t** (01536) 710305

**rushtonmanorfarm.co.uk**

16thC manor house, family home in small village of Rushton, situated between Kettering, Corby and Desborough. 15 minutes to Rockingham Speedway.

**open** All year
**bedrooms** 6 double
**bathrooms** 5 en suite, 1 private
**payment** Credit/debit cards, cash, cheques

Room General P

## COTSWOLDS

*See under Broadway, Long Compton*
*See also Cotswolds in the South East and South West England sections*

## COTTESMORE, Rutland Map ref 3A1

★★★★
GUEST ACCOMMODATION

B&B PER ROOM PER NIGHT
S £35.00–£40.00
D £55.00–£70.00

*Discounts on stays of 5 or more days.*

### Tithe Barn

Clatterpot Lane, Cottesmore, Oakham LE15 7DW **t** (01572) 813591 **e** jp@thetithebarn.co.uk

**tithebarn-rutland.co.uk**

**open** All year
**bedrooms** 3 double, 2 twin, 2 family
**bathrooms** 5 en suite, 2 private
**payment** Credit/debit cards, cash, cheques

An attractive 17thC converted tithe barn. Spacious, comfortable, en suite rooms. Two superior rooms have power showers and king-size beds. Five minutes from Rutland Water, Barnsdale Gardens and A1. A warm and friendly home with a panelled dining room, striking hall and a wealth of original features. All rooms have tea/coffee facilities.

**SAT NAV** *LE15 7DW*

Room General P Leisure

## COVENTRY, West Midlands Map ref 4B3

★★★
GUEST HOUSE

B&B PER ROOM PER NIGHT
S £30.00–£45.00
D £50.00–£60.00

### Ashdowns Guest House

12 Regent Street, Earlsdon, Coventry CV1 3EP **t** (024) 7622 9280

**open** All year except Christmas and New Year
**bedrooms** 3 double, 2 twin, 2 single, 1 family
**bathrooms** 7 en suite
**payment** Cash, cheques

Family-run guesthouse offering quality accommodation convenient for city centre, rail and bus services, NEC, NAC, university and Coventry and Birmingham airports. A warm welcome awaits you in this relaxed, non-smoking family home. Own private car park.

**SAT NAV** *CV1 3EP*

Room General 12 P

## Do you have access needs?

Look for the National Accessible Scheme symbols if you have special hearing, visual or mobility needs. An index of accommodation participating in the scheme can be found at the back of this guide.

## COVENTRY, West Midlands Map ref 4B3

★★★
GUEST HOUSE

B&B PER ROOM PER NIGHT
S £29.50–£37.50
D £45.00–£52.00

EVENING MEAL PER PERSON
£6.00–£8.00

### Ashleigh House

17 Park Road, Coventry CV1 2LH **t** (024) 7622 3804

Experience a warm welcome from friendly, helpful staff. Well maintained and equipped, en suite accommodation. All city amenities and railway station five minutes' walk. Licensed. Evening meals (varied menu available).

**open** All year except Christmas and New Year
**bedrooms** 2 twin, 5 single, 3 family
**bathrooms** All en suite
**payment** Cash, cheques

Room General

## COVENTRY, West Midlands Map ref 4B3

★★★
BED & BREAKFAST

B&B PER ROOM PER NIGHT
S £20.00–£30.00
D £35.00–£55.00

### Bede Guest House

250 Radford Road, Radford, Coventry CV6 3BU **t** (024) 7659 7837 **e** bedehouse@aol.com

**bedeguesthouse.co.uk** SPECIAL OFFERS

We are based near the city centre. Most rooms are en suite and all have TVs, tea/coffee facilities. All rooms changed daily and guests have the added peace of mind of secure parking.

**open** All year
**bedrooms** 1 double, 1 twin, 1 single
**bathrooms** 2 private
**payment** Credit/debit cards, cash, cheques

Room General

## COVENTRY, West Midlands Map ref 4B3

★★★
GUEST HOUSE

B&B PER ROOM PER NIGHT
S £22.00–£35.00
D £36.00–£46.00

EVENING MEAL PER PERSON
£3.00–£5.00

### Highcroft Guest House

65 Barras Lane, Coundon, Coventry CV1 4AQ **t** (024) 7622 8157 **e** deepakcov@hotmail.com

**open** All year
**bedrooms** 1 double, 2 single, 2 family
**bathrooms** 2 en suite, 3 private
**payment** Cash, cheques

Large, detached guesthouse close to city centre. A family-run business that endeavours to make guests feel at home. Discounts available. Good transport to airports, train stations and motorways.

**SAT NAV** *CV1 4AQ*

Room General

## CREATON, Northamptonshire Map ref 4C3

★★★★
GUEST ACCOMMODATION

B&B PER ROOM PER NIGHT
S £55.00–£130.00
D £75.00–£155.00

EVENING MEAL PER PERSON
£20.00–£35.00

### Highgate House – A Sundial Group Venue

Grooms Lane, Creaton, Northampton NN6 8NN **t** (01604) 731999 **e** highgate@sundialgroup.com

**sundialgroup.com** SPECIAL OFFERS · REAL-TIME BOOKING

**open** All year except Christmas
**bedrooms** 50 double, 18 twin, 30 single
**bathrooms** All en suite
**payment** Credit/debit cards, cash, cheques

Highgate House is a striking property in the picturesque Northamptonshire village of Creaton. Originally a coaching inn, it has evolved over the years into a superb destination. Its continued development has carefully maintained the beauty of the original building, successfully combining 17thC charm with 21stC comfort. Under one hour from M25. 20 minutes from M1.

**SAT NAV** *NN6 8NN* **ONLINE MAP**

Room General
Leisure

## CROMER, Norfolk Map ref 3C1

★★★★★
BED & BREAKFAST
GOLD AWARD

B&B PER ROOM PER NIGHT
D £160.00–£185.00

EVENING MEAL PER PERSON
£20.00–£25.00

*Special offers for midweek breaks, see our website or ring for details. Honeymoon, birthday and anniversary stays.*

### Incleborough House Luxury Bed and Breakfast

Lower Common, East Runton, Cromer NR27 9PG **t** (01263) 515939
**e** enquiries@incleboroughhouse.co.uk

**incleboroughhouse.co.uk** GUEST REVIEWS • SPECIAL OFFERS

**open** All year
**bedrooms** 3 double
**bathrooms** All en suite
**payment** Credit/debit cards, cash, cheques

Incleborough House, built in 1687, (King James II was on the throne) is a stunning Grade II Listed country house overlooking the Lower Common in the heart of a small unspoilt fishing village just 300 metres from the beach, on the coast at East Runton, near Cromer in Norfolk.

**SAT NAV** *NR27 9PG* **ONLINE MAP**

Room General 14 P Leisure

## DERBY, Derbyshire Map ref 4B2

★★★
BED & BREAKFAST

B&B PER ROOM PER NIGHT
S £25.00–£30.00
D Min £52.00

### Bonehill Farm

Etwall Road, Mickleover, Derby DE3 0DN **t** (01332) 513553 **e** bonehillfarm@hotmail.com

**bonehillfarm.co.uk**

**open** All year except Christmas
**bedrooms** 1 double, 1 twin, 1 family
**bathrooms** 2 en suite
**payment** Cash, cheques

A 120-acre mixed farm. Comfortable Georgian farmhouse in rural setting, three miles from Derby. Alton Towers, Peak District, historic houses and the Potteries within easy reach. Peaceful location.

**SAT NAV** *DE3 0DN*

Room General P

## DEREHAM, Norfolk Map ref 3B1

★★★★
FARMHOUSE

B&B PER ROOM PER NIGHT
S £40.00–£60.00
D £60.00–£80.00

### Hunters Hall

Park Farm, Swanton Morley, Dereham NR20 4JU **t** (01362) 637457 **e** office@huntershall.com

**huntershall.com**

A traditional working farm offering accommodation, function and conference facilities in a conservation area.

**open** All year
**bedrooms** 5 double, 5 twin, 2 family
**bathrooms** 8 en suite
**payment** Credit/debit cards, cash, cheques, euros

Room General P Leisure

## Check the maps for accommodation locations

Colour maps at the front pinpoint all the places where accommodation is featured within the regional sections of this guide. Pick your location and then refer to the place index at the back to find the page number.

## DERSINGHAM, Norfolk Map ref 3B1

★★★★
GUEST ACCOMMODATION

B&B PER ROOM PER NIGHT
S £35.00–£50.00
D £55.00–£70.00

### Barn House Bed And Breakfast

14 Station Road, Dersingham, King's Lynn PE31 6PP **t** (01485) 543086
**e** tom@d14mxs.wanadoo.co.uk

**smoothhound.co.uk/hotels/barnho** GUEST REVIEWS

**open** All year
**bedrooms** 1 double, 1 twin
**bathrooms** All en suite
**payment** Cash, cheques

Barn conversion offering comfortable, relaxed, character accommodation. Lovely, spacious en suite rooms provide a warm welcome and home comforts for holidaymakers, walkers, birdwatchers and cyclists. Sandringham Estate and Country Park one mile. RSPB reserve 2.5 miles. Peddars Way four miles. Drying room. Cycle facilities. Extensive beach, woodland and countryside walks.

**SAT NAV** *PE31 6PP*

Room TV General 10 P Leisure

## DOCKING, Norfolk Map ref 3B1

★★★★
GUEST ACCOMMODATION

B&B PER ROOM PER NIGHT
S £30.00
D £50.00

### Jubilee Lodge

Station Road, Docking PE31 8LS **t** (01485) 518473 **e** eghoward62@hotmail.com

**jubilee-lodge.com**

Bed and breakfast in a Tudor-style, centrally heated, double-glazed house, in a pleasant village setting, only four miles from the beach.

**open** All year
**bedrooms** 2 double, 1 twin
**bathrooms** All en suite
**payment** Cash, cheques

Room TV General P Leisure

## EARLS COLNE, Essex Map ref 3B2

★★★
GUEST ACCOMMODATION

B&B PER ROOM PER NIGHT
S £50.00–£52.00
D £58.00–£62.00

### Riverside Lodge

40 Lower Holt Street, Earls Colne, Colchester CO6 2PH **t** (01787) 223487
**e** bandb@riversidelodge-uk.com

**riversidelodge-uk.com**

Single, en suite chalets on banks of River Colne. Restaurants, pubs and village amenities within walking distance. Fine country walks from lodge. All rooms on ground level.

**open** All year
**bedrooms** 2 double, 3 twin
**bathrooms** All en suite
**payment** Credit/debit cards, cash, cheques

Room TV General P

## ELMSWELL, Suffolk Map ref 3B2

★★★★
GUEST HOUSE

B&B PER ROOM PER NIGHT
S £40.00–£50.00
D £80.00–£100.00

EVENING MEAL PER PERSON
£12.50

### Kiln Farm

Kiln Lane, Elmswell, Bury St Edmunds IP30 9QR **t** (01359) 240442 **e** davejankilnfarm@btinternet.com

**open** All year
**bedrooms** 4 double, 2 twin, 2 family
**bathrooms** All en suite
**payment** Credit/debit cards, cash, cheques, euros

Welcoming Victorian farmhouse with a courtyard of converted barns set in two acres enjoying a secluded location among country roads just off the A14. Licensed bar with conservatory for breakfasts and pre-booked evening meals. Ideally placed for exploring Suffolk's finest towns and villages. The kettle's always on.

**SAT NAV** *IP30 9QR*

Room TV General P

## ELY, Cambridgeshire Map ref 3A2

★★★★
RESTAURANT WITH ROOMS

B&B PER ROOM PER NIGHT
S £59.50–£89.50
D £79.50–£155.00

EVENING MEAL PER PERSON
£13.00–£30.00

### Anchor Inn

Sutton Gault, Sutton CB6 2BD **t** (01353) 778537 **e** anchorinn@popmail.bta.com

**anchorsuttongault.co.uk** REAL-TIME BOOKING

Tranquil and peaceful, friendly 17thC riverside inn. Spotless, quality well-equipped rooms, most with stunning fen views. Close to Ely, Cambridge, Welney and Newmarket. Good Food Guide, Michelin, Sawdays, Good Pub Guide, AA Rosette.

**open** All year
**bedrooms** 1 double, 1 twin, 2 suites
**bathrooms** All en suite
**payment** Credit/debit cards, cash, cheques

Room General Leisure

## ELY, Cambridgeshire Map ref 3A2

★★★★
BED & BREAKFAST

B&B PER ROOM PER NIGHT
S £35.00
D £56.00

### The Old School B & B

The Old School, School Lane, Coveney, Ely CB6 2DB **t** (01353) 777087
**e** info@theoldschoolbandb.co.uk

**theoldschoolbandb.co.uk**

Quality accommodation in former village school, quiet location three miles from Ely. Set in gardens with views onto Ely Cathedral. Ground-floor bedrooms. Dogs welcome. Euros accepted. Wir sprechen Deutsch.

**open** All year except Christmas and New Year
**bedrooms** 1 double, 2 twin
**bathrooms** 1 en suite, 2 private
**payment** Cash, cheques, euros

PETS! WELCOME

Room General P Leisure

## ELY, Cambridgeshire Map ref 3A2

★★★★
FARMHOUSE

B&B PER ROOM PER NIGHT
D £65.00

### Spinney Abbey

Stretham Road, Wicken CB7 5XQ **t** (01353) 720971 **e** spinney.abbey@tesco.net

**spinneyabbey.co.uk**

**open** All year except Christmas
**bedrooms** 1 double, 1 twin, 1 family
**bathrooms** 2 en suite, 1 private
**payment** Cash, cheques, euros

This attractive Georgian Grade II Listed farmhouse, surrounded by pasture fields, stands next to our livestock farm which borders the National Trust Nature Reserve, 'Wicken Fen', on the southern edge of the Fens. Guests are welcome to make full use of the spacious garden and all-weather tennis court. All rooms have en suite or private facilities.

**SAT NAV** *CB7 5XQ*

Room General 5 P Leisure

## EMPINGHAM, Rutland Map ref 3A1

★★★★
BED & BREAKFAST

B&B PER ROOM PER NIGHT
S £40.00–£45.00
D £55.00

EVENING MEAL PER PERSON
£15.00

### Shacklewell Lodge

Stamford Road, Empingham, Oakham LE15 8QQ **t** (01780) 460646 **e** shacklewell@hotmail.com

Ancaster stone farmhouse set in large gardens close to Rutland Water. Family rooms available £65 – £85.

**open** All year except Christmas and New Year
**bedrooms** 1 double, 1 twin, 1 family
**bathrooms** 2 en suite, 1 private
**payment** Cash, cheques

Room General P Leisure

## ENDON, Staffordshire Map ref 4B2

★★★
FARMHOUSE

B&B PER ROOM PER NIGHT
S £20.00–£25.00
D £44.00–£50.00

### Hollinhurst Farm

Park Lane, Endon, Stoke-on-Trent ST9 9JB **t** (01782) 502633 **e** joan.hollinhurst@btconnect.com

A 17thC farmhouse on our working stock farm above the tranquil Caldon Canal. Within easy reach of the Potteries attractions, Peak District, Alton Towers and Trentham. Panoramic views, walking and touring.

**open** All year
**bedrooms** 1 double, 1 twin, 1 family
**bathrooms** 2 en suite, 1 private
**payment** Cash, cheques

Room General Leisure

## EYDON, Northamptonshire Map ref 2C1

★★★★
FARMHOUSE

B&B PER ROOM PER NIGHT
S £44.00–£49.00
D £78.00–£88.00

### Crockwell Farm

Eydon, Daventry NN11 3QA **t** (01327) 361358 **e** info@crockwellfarm.co.uk

**crockwellfarm.co.uk** GUEST REVIEWS

**open** All year
**bedrooms** 3 twin, 4 family
**bathrooms** All en suite
**payment** Credit/debit cards, cash, cheques

Beautiful 18thC ironstone farmhouse and cottages in an idyllic rural setting. Delicious breakfasts, featuring local and home-made specialities, served in the farmhouse. The cottages are self-contained. Evening meals and lunches are available in a good local pub approximately one mile away. Ideal location for walking and visiting local attractions.

**SAT NAV** *NN11 3QA* **ONLINE MAP**

Room General Leisure

## EYE KETTLEBY, Leicestershire Map ref 4C3

★★★★
FARMHOUSE

B&B PER ROOM PER NIGHT
S £30.00–£35.00
D £50.00–£80.00

### Old Guadaloupe B&B

Old Guadaloupe, Kirby Lane, Melton Mowbray LE14 2TS **t** 07989 960588
**e** sue@suelomas.orengehome.co.uk

**oldguadaloupeb&b.co.uk**

**open** All year
**bedrooms** 1 double, 1 twin, 1 family
**bathrooms** All en suite
**payment** Credit/debit cards, cash, cheques

A 500-year-old farmhouse. Well-equipped rooms with Freeview TV and DVD, tea/coffee, hairdryer. One family, one double, one twin. Doubles have 5ft bed, all en suite. Bathrooms fitted to a high standard. Own lounge. Plenty of parking. Near Melton Mowbray and Eye Kettleby Lakes.

**SAT NAV** *LE14 2TS*

Room General Leisure

## FAKENHAM, Norfolk Map ref 3B1

★★★
FARMHOUSE

B&B PER ROOM PER NIGHT
S £26.00–£30.00
D £52.00–£60.00

### Abbott Farm

Walsingham Road, Binham NR21 0AW **t** (01328) 830519 **e** abbot.farm@btinternet.com

**abbottfarm.co.uk**

A 190-acre arable farm. Rural views of North Norfolk including the historic Binham Priory. Liz and Alan offer a warm welcome to their guesthouse.

**open** All year except Christmas
**bedrooms** 1 double, 2 twin
**bathrooms** All en suite
**payment** Cash, cheques, euros

Room General Leisure

## FEERING, Essex Map ref 3B2

★★★★
FARMHOUSE
SILVER AWARD

B&B PER ROOM PER NIGHT
S £40.00
D £60.00–£90.00

### Old Wills Farm

Little Tey Road, Feering, Colchester CO5 9RP **t** (01376) 570259 **e** janecrayston@btconnect.com

**open** All year except Christmas
**bedrooms** 1 double, 1 twin, 1 family
**bathrooms** All en suite
**payment** Cash, cheques

Attractive and comfortable Essex farmhouse on a working arable farm with large garden offering homely surroundings and atmosphere. Ample, safe parking. We are within reach of the historic town of Colchester and its zoo, Dedham Vale, Constable Country and Colne Valley Railway.

**SAT NAV** *CO5 9RP*

Room General Leisure

## FRAMLINGHAM, Suffolk Map ref 3C2

★★★
FARMHOUSE

B&B PER ROOM PER NIGHT
S £36.00–£46.00
D £50.00–£60.00

### High House Farm

Cransford, Woodbridge IP13 9PD **t** (01728) 663461 **e** info@highhousefarm.co.uk

**highhousefarm.co.uk** SPECIAL OFFERS

A warm welcome awaits you in our beautifully restored 15thC farmhouse, featuring exposed beams, inglenook fireplaces and attractive gardens. Situated midway between Framlingham and Saxmundham.

**open** All year
**bedrooms** 1 double, 1 family
**bathrooms** 1 en suite, 1 private
**payment** Cash, cheques

Room General Leisure

## FRINTON-ON-SEA, Essex Map ref 3C2

★★★
BED & BREAKFAST

B&B PER ROOM PER NIGHT
S £25.00
D £50.00

### Russell Lodge

47 Hadleigh Road, Frinton-on-Sea CO13 9HQ **t** (01255) 675935 & 07891 899824
**e** stay@russell-lodge.fsnet.co.uk

**russell-lodge.fsnet.co.uk**

A friendly, homely bed and breakfast in a quiet seaside town. Situated close to beaches, shops and train station. Approximately 300yds to the Greensward, town centre and Crescent Gardens.

**open** All year
**bedrooms** 1 double, 1 single, 1 family
**bathrooms** 2 en suite
**payment** Cash, cheques

Room General Leisure

## GAINSBOROUGH, Lincolnshire Map ref 4C2

★★★
BED & BREAKFAST

B&B PER ROOM PER NIGHT
D £60.00–£65.00

EVENING MEAL PER PERSON
Min £7.50

### Blyton (Sunnyside) Ponds

Sunnyside Farm, Station Road, Blyton, Gainsborough DN21 3LE **t** (01427) 628240
**e** blytonponds@msn.com

**blytonponds.co.uk** REAL-TIME BOOKING

Detached log cabins offering B&B and evening meals in rural setting with complimentary fishing facilities. Each cabin has en suite bathroom and private patio. Self-catering facilities also available.

**open** All year except Christmas and New Year
**bedrooms** 1 double, 1 twin
**bathrooms** All en suite
**payment** Credit/debit cards, cash, cheques

Room General Leisure

## Need some ideas?

Big city buzz or peaceful panoramas? Take a fresh look at England and you may be surprised at what's right on your doorstep. Explore the diversity online at enjoyengland.com

## GRANTHAM, Lincolnshire Map ref 3A1

★★★★
BED & BREAKFAST

B&B PER ROOM PER NIGHT
S £27.00–£35.00
D £54.00–£65.00

EVENING MEAL PER PERSON
£10.00–£15.00

### The Cedars

Low Road, Barrowby, Grantham NG32 1DL **t** (01476) 563400 **e** pbcbennett@mac.com

**open** All year
**bedrooms** 1 double, 1 twin
**bathrooms** 2 private
**payment** Cash, cheques, euros

Enjoy the relaxed atmosphere of this Grade II Listed farmhouse and its gardens. Delicious breakfasts, and evening meals if required, using our own, and local fresh produce. Italian cuisine a speciality. A five-minute drive from A1 motorway, and two miles from Grantham mainline station. French and Italian spoken. Horse and pony stabling available.

**SAT NAV** *NG32 1DL*

Room General P

## GREAT BADDOW, Essex Map ref 3B3

★★★
GUEST ACCOMMODATION

B&B PER ROOM PER NIGHT
S £25.00–£30.00
D £45.00–£50.00

### Homecroft

Southend Road, Great Baddow, Chelmsford CM2 7AD **t** (01245) 475070
**e** jesse@pryke.fsbusiness.co.uk

**tiscover.co.uk**

Detached Victorian family home. Offering home cooking, friendly atmosphere, off-road parking.

**open** All year except Christmas
**bedrooms** 2 double, 1 twin
**payment** Cash, cheques

Room General 3 P Leisure

## GREAT WOLFORD, Warwickshire Map ref 2B1

★★★★★
BED & BREAKFAST
SILVER AWARD

B&B PER ROOM PER NIGHT
S £40.00–£50.00
D £60.00–£80.00

### The Old Coach House

Great Wolford, Shipston-on-Stour CV36 5NQ **t** (01608) 674152
**e** theoldcoachhouse@thewolfords.net

**theoldcoachhouseatthewolfords.co.uk**

**open** All year
**bedrooms** 2 double
**bathrooms** All en suite
**payment** Cash, cheques

This delightful old coach house, formerly part of the pub next door, with many original features, is set in a lovely garden, perfect for afternoon tea. A night in our pretty, en suite rooms and a delicious breakfast with local produce will prepare you for a day exploring the Cotswolds.

**SAT NAV** *CV36 5NQ*

Room General 10 P

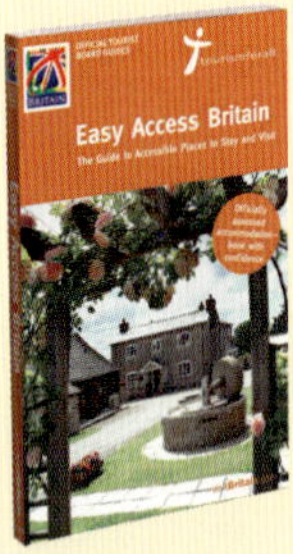


## Where can I find accessible accommodation?

If you have special hearing, visual or mobility needs, there's an index of National Accessible Scheme participants featured in this guide. For more accessible accommodation buy a copy of Easy Access Britain available online at visitbritaindirect.com, and from Tourism for All on 0845 124 997 or visit tourismforall.org.uk.

## GREAT YARMOUTH, Norfolk Map ref 3C1

★★★
GUEST ACCOMMODATION

B&B PER ROOM PER NIGHT
S £18.00–£25.00
D £35.00–£50.00

EVENING MEAL PER PERSON
£9.00–£25.00

### Cavendish House

19-20 Princes Road, Great Yarmouth NR30 2DG **t** (01493) 843148
**e** cavendishhousehotel@yahoo.co.uk

**cavendishhousehotel.com** SPECIAL OFFERS · REAL-TIME BOOKING

**open** All year
**bedrooms** 7 double, 4 twin, 3 single, 4 family, 1 suite
**bathrooms** 18 en suite, 1 private
**payment** Cash, cheques, euros

In a prominent position, close to all holiday amenities, shopping centre, theatres and beaches. En suite rooms with colour TV available. Special rate for group bookings.

**SAT NAV** *NR30 2DG*

Room General Leisure

## HALESWORTH, Suffolk Map ref 3C2

★★★★
BED & BREAKFAST

B&B PER ROOM PER NIGHT
S £24.99–£30.00
D £40.00–£50.00

### Fen-Way Guest House

Fen-Way, School Lane, Halesworth IP19 8BW **t** (01986) 873574

Spacious bungalow in seven acres of peaceful meadowland. Pets include sheep and lambs. Five minutes' walk from town centre. Convenient for many places including Southwold (nine miles).

**open** All year
**bedrooms** 2 double, 1 twin
**bathrooms** 1 en suite
**payment** Cash, cheques

Room General 5 P Leisure

## HATFIELD BROAD OAK, Essex Map ref 2D1

★★★
BED & BREAKFAST

B&B PER ROOM PER NIGHT
S £30.00–£35.00
D £50.00

### Bury House

High Street, Bishop's Stortford CM22 7HQ **t** (01279) 718259 **e** bswan@buryhouse.wanadoo.co.uk

**tiscover.co.uk**

A comfortable house with a beautiful garden in the middle of this attractive village, and only five miles from Stansted Airport. Off-street parking.

**open** All year except Christmas and New Year
**bedrooms** 2 double, 1 single
**payment** Cash, cheques

Room General 10 P

## HAUGHLEY, Suffolk Map ref 3B2

★★★★
FARMHOUSE

B&B PER ROOM PER NIGHT
S £40.00–£45.00
D £65.00–£70.00

### Red House Farm

Haughley, Stowmarket IP14 3QP **t** (01449) 673323 **e** mary@redhousefarmhaughley.co.uk

**farmstayanglia.co.uk**

Attractive farmhouse in rural location on small grassland farm. First-class breakfast. Central heating and large garden.

**open** All year except Christmas and New Year
**bedrooms** 1 double, 1 twin, 2 single
**bathrooms** All en suite
**payment** Credit/debit cards, cash, cheques

Room General 8 P

## Where can I get help and advice?

Tourist Information Centres offer friendly help with accommodation and holiday ideas as well as suggestions of places to visit and things to do. You'll find contact details at the beginning of each regional section.

## HEMEL HEMPSTEAD, Hertfordshire Map ref 2D1

★★★★
BED & BREAKFAST

B&B PER ROOM PER NIGHT
S Min £55.00
D Min £65.00

### Marsh Farm

Ledgemore Lane, Great Gaddesden HP2 6HA **t** (01442) 252517 **e** nicky@bennett-baggs.com

**marshfarm.org.uk**

**open** All year except Christmas and New Year
**bedrooms** 1 twin
**bathrooms** En suite
**payment** Cash, cheques

Situated on the private Gaddesden Estate, Marsh Farm is a beautiful 18thC farmhouse in a stunning rural location with excellent local pubs, restaurants and wonderful country walks from our front door. You can be assured of a comfortable, well-appointed room with good breakfasts using local produce.

**SAT NAV** *HP2 6HA*

Room General P Leisure

## HEREFORD, Herefordshire Map ref 2A1

Dinner Bed & Breakfast breaks available all year

## HEREFORD, Herefordshire Map ref 2A1

★★★★
GUEST ACCOMMODATION

B&B PER ROOM PER NIGHT
S £45.00–£55.00
D £65.00–£75.00

EVENING MEAL PER PERSON
£7.00–£15.00

### Hedley Lodge

Belmont Abbey, Abergavenny Road, Hereford HR2 9RZ **t** (01432) 374747
**e** hedley@belmontabbey.org.uk

**hedleylodge.com**

Set in lovely grounds of Belmont Abbey, this friendly, modern guesthouse offers comfortably appointed rooms with en suite facilities. Licensed restaurant. 2.5 miles from Hereford. Ideal for visiting the Wye Valley.

**open** All year
**bedrooms** 6 double, 10 twin, 1 family
**bathrooms** All en suite
**payment** Credit/debit cards, cash, cheques

Room General P Leisure

## HEVINGHAM, Norfolk Map ref 3B1

★★★★
INN

B&B PER ROOM PER NIGHT
S £54.50–£65.00
D £95.00–£110.00

EVENING MEAL PER PERSON
£17.50–£30.00

*See website for our special room deals. Enjoy our monthly jazz evenings or attend our informal wine tastings.*

### Marsham Arms Inn

Holt Road, Hevingham NR10 5NP **t** (01603) 754268 **e** info@marshamarms.co.uk

**marshamarms.co.uk** SPECIAL OFFERS

**open** All year
**bedrooms** 3 double, 8 family
**bathrooms** All en suite
**payment** Credit/debit cards, cash, cheques

Country inn on B1149 north of Horsford. Extensive menu using fresh local produce. Real ales, comprehensive wine list. Restaurant and function room for weddings, private parties and training courses. Heated patio area, breeze house and large garden to enjoy an alfresco meal. Spacious ground-floor en suite bedrooms.

**SAT NAV** *NR10 5NP* **ONLINE MAP**

Room General Leisure

## HICKLING, Norfolk Map ref 3C1

★★★★
FARMHOUSE
GOLD AWARD

B&B PER ROOM PER NIGHT
S £46.00
D £60.00–£66.00

### The Dairy Barns

Lound Farm, Hickling, Norwich NR12 0BE **t** (01692) 598243 **e** enquiries@dairybarns.co.uk

**dairybarns.co.uk**

The accommodation is in self-contained, converted barns. Breakfast is the best farmhouse cooking using local produce. Spacious en suite rooms. One mile from beaches and Norfolk Broads. Disabled facilities. Children welcome.

**open** All year
**bedrooms** 3 double, 3 twin
**bathrooms** All en suite
**payment** Credit/debit cards, cash

Room General Leisure

## HILTON, Derbyshire Map ref 4B2

★★★★
GUEST ACCOMMODATION

B&B PER ROOM PER NIGHT
S £40.00–£43.99
D £60.00–£63.99

EVENING MEAL PER PERSON
£5.99–£9.99

### Tudor Rose

Main Street, Derby DE65 5FF **t** (01283) 734564 **e** hilton-tudor-rose@tiscali.co.uk

**hilton-tudor-rose.co.uk**

Small friendly family-run B&B. Home from home in heart of Derbyshire village. Use of garden and patio. On edge of National Forest, close to Derby, Burton, A50 and A38.

**open** All year except Christmas and New Year
**bedrooms** 1 double, 1 twin, 2 single
**bathrooms** All en suite
**payment** Credit/debit cards, cash, cheques

Room General

## HINTLESHAM, Suffolk Map ref 3B2

★★★★
FARMHOUSE
SILVER AWARD

B&B PER ROOM PER NIGHT
S £38.00–£44.00
D £60.00–£68.00

### College Farm

Hintlesham, Ipswich IP8 3NT **t** (01473) 652253 **e** bandb@collegefarm.plus.com

**collegefarm.net**

Peaceful 500-year-old house on 600-acre arable farm near Ipswich (six miles). Convenient for Constable Country, Sutton Hoo (National Trust) and the coast. Well-appointed, comfortable rooms. Good food locally.

**open** All year except Christmas and New Year
**bedrooms** 2 double, 1 twin
**bathrooms** 2 en suite, 1 private
**payment** Cash, cheques

Room General 10 P Leisure

## Looking for a wide range of facilities?

More stars means higher quality accommodation plus a greater range of facilities and services.

## HONINGTON, Suffolk Map ref 3B2

★★★
GUEST ACCOMMODATION

B&B PER ROOM PER NIGHT
s £20.00–£25.00
d £40.00–£50.00

### North View Guesthouse

North View, Malting Row, Honington IP31 1RE **t** (01359) 269423

North View Guesthouse is situated in the village of Honington opposite the church. Close to Thetford and Bury St Edmunds stations.

**open** All year
**bedrooms** 1 double, 1 single, 1 family
**payment** Cash, cheques

Room General 8 P Leisure

## HOPE, Derbyshire Map ref 4B2

★★★★★
GUEST ACCOMMODATION
GOLD AWARD

B&B PER ROOM PER NIGHT
s £60.00
d £80.00–£95.00

### Underleigh House

Off Edale Road, Hope, Hope Valley S33 6RF **t** (01433) 621372 **e** info@underleighhouse.co.uk

**underleighhouse.co.uk** REAL-TIME BOOKING

**bedrooms** 4 double, 1 twin, 1 suite
**bathrooms** All en suite
**payment** Credit/debit cards, cash, cheques

Secluded cottage and barn conversion near the village of Hope with magnificent countryside views. Ideal for walking and exploring the Peak District. Delicious breakfasts, featuring local and home-made specialities, served in flagstoned dining hall. Welcoming and relaxing atmosphere with a log fire on chilly evenings in the charming, beamed lounge. Closed Christmas, New Year and January.

**SAT NAV** *S33 6RF*

Room General 12 P Leisure

## HOPE VALLEY, Derbyshire Map ref 4B2

★★★★
INN
SILVER AWARD

B&B PER ROOM PER NIGHT
s £75.00–£100.00
d £75.00–£100.00

### The Chequers Inn

Froggatt Edge, Hope Valley S32 3ZJ **t** (01433) 630231 **e** info@chequers-froggatt.com

**chequers-froggatt.com**

A traditional coaching inn offering first-class accommodation and exquisite food. Further seating available in our woodland garden. Five beautifully appointed en suite rooms.

**open** All year except Christmas
**bedrooms** 4 double, 1 twin
**bathrooms** All en suite
**payment** Credit/debit cards, cash, cheques

Room General P

## HORNCASTLE, Lincolnshire Map ref 4D2

★★★★
GUEST HOUSE

B&B PER ROOM PER NIGHT
s Max £40.00
d Max £60.00

### Bank Cottage Guest House

16 Bank Street, Horncastle LN9 5BW **t** (01507) 526666 **e** horncastleinfo@e-lindsey.gov.uk

**bankcottage-guesthouse.com**

Our friendly family-run guesthouse, Bank Cottage, is situated in the centre of Horncastle close to the town's most popular shops, restaurants and public houses.

**open** All year except Christmas
**bedrooms** 2 suites
**bathrooms** All en suite
**payment** Credit/debit cards, cash, cheques

Room General P

## It's all quality-assessed accommodation

Our commitment to quality involves wide-ranging accommodation assessment. Ratings and awards were correct at the time of going to press but may change following a new assessment. Please check at time of booking.

## HORSLEY, Derbyshire Map ref 4B2

★★★★
GUEST ACCOMMODATION
SILVER AWARD

**B&B PER ROOM PER NIGHT**
S £69.00–£79.00
D £90.00–£106.00

**EVENING MEAL PER PERSON**
£10.00–£15.00

*'Learn to golf' breaks. Discounts available Sun nights.*

### Horsley Lodge

Smalley Mill Road, Horsley, Derby DE21 5BL **t** (01332) 780838 **e** enquiries@horsleylodge.co.uk

**horsleylodge.co.uk** GUEST REVIEWS · SPECIAL OFFERS

**open** All year
**bedrooms** 6 double, 4 twin
**bathrooms** All en suite
**payment** Credit/debit cards, cash, cheques, euros

Magnificent stone country-house hotel. This hidden gem specialises in exclusive breaks. Great restaurant, lovely views, championship golf course. All rooms individually themed.

**SAT NAV** *DE21 5BL* **ONLINE MAP**

Room General 1
Leisure

## HUNDON, Suffolk Map ref 3B2

Rating Applied For
INN

**B&B PER ROOM PER NIGHT**
S £60.00
D £85.00

**EVENING MEAL PER PERSON**
£7.95–£25.00

### The Plough Inn

Brockley Green, Sudbury CO10 8DT **t** (01440) 786789 **e** info@theploughhundon.co.uk

**theploughhundon.co.uk**

**open** All year
**bedrooms** 5 double, 2 twin
**bathrooms** All en suite
**payment** Credit/debit cards, cash, cheques

Delightfully situated in an Area of Outstanding Natural Beauty, the Plough Inn is a gem. It blends the finest features of a country pub and dining experience with the more contemporary feel of the seven en suite bedrooms.

**SAT NAV** *CO10 8DT* **ONLINE MAP**

Room General

## HUNSTANTON, Norfolk Map ref 3B1

★★★★
INN
SILVER AWARD

**B&B PER ROOM PER NIGHT**
S £50.00–£60.00
D £75.00–£90.00

**EVENING MEAL PER PERSON**
£8.00–£25.00

*3rd night half price with double occupancy.*

### The King William IV Country Inn & Restaurant

Heacham Road, Sedgeford, Hunstanton PE36 5LU **t** (01485) 571765
**e** info@thekingwilliamsedgeford.co.uk

**thekingwilliamsedgeford.co.uk** SPECIAL OFFERS · REAL-TIME BOOKING

**open** All year
**bedrooms** 4 double
**bathrooms** All en suite
**payment** Credit/debit cards, cash, cheques

Popular and busy traditional country inn, amid Norfolk countryside. Close to North Norfolk's beautiful coastline, Peddars Way, RSPB bird reserves and golf. High-standard, comfortable en suite accommodation with king-size beds. Extensive menu and daily specials served in two non-smoking restaurants, bar and garden. A delightful escape – whatever the season.

**SAT NAV** *PE36 5LU* **ONLINE MAP**

Room General Leisure

For **key to symbols** see page 7

## HUNSTANTON, Norfolk Map ref 3B1

★★★★
INN

B&B PER ROOM PER NIGHT
S £45.00–£70.00
D £70.00–£120.00

EVENING MEAL PER PERSON
£10.00–£35.00

# The Lodge

Old Hunstanton, Hunstanton PE36 6HX **t** (01485) 532896 **e** thelodge@norfolk-hotels.co.uk

**norfolk-hotels.co.uk**

**open** All year
**bedrooms** 8 double, 6 twin, 1 family
**bathrooms** All en suite
**payment** Credit/debit cards, cash, euros

A pub with rooms 500yds from a quiet sandy beach and Hunstanton Golf Course. A former dower house, it is a listed building. Real ales, wooden floors and food sourced from local producers contribute to a relaxed atmosphere. Open all year.

**SAT NAV** *PE36 6HX*

Room General Leisure

## IRONBRIDGE, Shropshire Map ref 4A3

★★★★★
GUEST ACCOMMODATION
SILVER AWARD

B&B PER ROOM PER NIGHT
S £52.00–£55.00
D £70.00–£75.00

# Bridge House

Buildwas Road, Ironbridge, Telford TF8 7BN **t** (01952) 432105 **e** the-bridgehouse@bt.com

**smoothhound.co.uk**

**open** All year except Christmas and New Year
**bedrooms** 2 double, 1 twin, 1 family
**bathrooms** All en suite
**payment** Credit/debit cards, cash, cheques

Charming 17thC country house situated by the River Severn and close to the famous Ironbridge. A house full of character and charm. Beautiful rooms all individually decorated and en suite, with a breakfast to be remembered. In all, the place to stay when visiting the famous Ironbridge Gorge. Family room rates also available.

**SAT NAV** *TF8 7BN*

Room General Leisure

## IRONBRIDGE, Shropshire Map ref 4A3

★★★★★
GUEST HOUSE
SILVER AWARD

B&B PER ROOM PER NIGHT
S £39.95–£89.95
D £69.95–£139.95

*Please go to our website where our current and future promotions can be seen.*

# The Old Rectory at Broseley

46 Ironbridge Road, Broseley TF12 5AF **t** (01952) 883399 **e** info@theoldrectoryatbroseley.co.uk

**theoldrectoryatbroseley.co.uk** GUEST REVIEWS · SPECIAL OFFERS

**open** All year except Christmas and New Year
**bedrooms** 8 double, 1 twin, 1 single, 2 family
**bathrooms** 10 en suite, 5 private
**payment** Credit/debit cards, cash

The Old Rectory at Broseley is located within a mile of the Iron Bridge and the other gorge attractions, enjoys a tranquil setting in two acres of established gardens, and has recently been tastefully restored to very high standards. It offers comfort, quality, charm and character second to none.

**SAT NAV** *TF12 5AF* **ONLINE MAP**

Room General 1 Leisure

## What shall we do today?

For ideas on places to visit, see the beginning of this regional section or go online at enjoyengland.com.

## KENILWORTH, Warwickshire Map ref 4B3

★★★★
GUEST HOUSE

B&B PER ROOM PER NIGHT
S £35.00–£37.00
D £55.00–£59.00

### Abbey Guest House

41 Station Road, Kenilworth CV8 1JD **t** (01926) 512707 **e** the.abbey@btinternet.com

**abbeyguesthouse.com**

A quiet location, yet only a minute's walk to the town centre. With Egyptian cotton linen, TV, refreshments, hairdryers and free wireless internet access, your comfort is our priority.

**open** All year
**bedrooms** 3 double, 2 twin, 2 single
**bathrooms** 6 en suite, 1 private
**payment** Credit/debit cards, cash, cheques

Room General P Leisure

## KENILWORTH, Warwickshire Map ref 4B3

★★★★
GUEST HOUSE

B&B PER ROOM PER NIGHT
S £45.00–£55.00
D £75.00–£85.00

### Castle Laurels Guest House

22 Castle Road, Kenilworth CV8 1NG **t** (01926) 856179 **e** reception@castlelaurels.co.uk

**castlelaurels.co.uk** GUEST REVIEWS · SPECIAL OFFERS · REAL-TIME BOOKING

Victorian house in conservation area beside Kenilworth Castle and Abbey fields, convenient for Warwick, Coventry, Leamington Spa, National Exhibition and Agriculture centres. Non-smoking hotel.

**open** All year except Christmas and New Year
**bedrooms** 6 double, 3 twin, 3 single
**bathrooms** All en suite
**payment** Credit/debit cards, cash, cheques

Room General 3 P Leisure

## KENILWORTH, Warwickshire Map ref 4B3

★★★★
GUEST ACCOMMODATION
SILVER AWARD

B&B PER ROOM PER NIGHT
S £49.00–£62.00
D £72.00–£80.00

### Victoria Lodge

180 Warwick Road, Kenilworth CV8 1HU **t** (01926) 512020 **e** info@victorialodgehotel.co.uk

**victorialodgehotel.co.uk** GUEST REVIEWS · SPECIAL OFFERS · REAL-TIME BOOKING

**open** All year except Christmas
**bedrooms** 7 double, 2 twin, 1 single
**bathrooms** All en suite
**payment** Credit/debit cards, cash, cheques

Small, friendly hotel with individually styled en suite bedrooms, guest lounge, licensed bar, garden and off-street parking. Non-smoking establishment. Ideal for NEC, NAC, university, M40, airports.

**SAT NAV** *CV8 1HU* **ONLINE MAP**

Room General P Leisure

## KETTERING, Northamptonshire Map ref 3A2

★★★
FARMHOUSE

B&B PER ROOM PER NIGHT
S £25.00–£38.00
D £50.00–£76.00

EVENING MEAL PER PERSON
Max £18.00

### Dairy Farm

Cranford St Andrew, Kettering NN14 4AQ **t** (01536) 330273

17thC thatched farmhouse in a lovely Northamptonshire village just off the A14. Large garden containing ancient dovecote and summerhouse. Good food and friendly welcome. Safe off-road parking. Many places of interest nearby.

**open** All year except Christmas and New Year
**bedrooms** 2 double, 1 twin
**bathrooms** 2 en suite, 1 private
**payment** Cash, cheques

Room General P Leisure

## Remember to check when booking

Please remember that all information in this guide has been supplied by the proprietors well in advance of publication. Since changes do sometimes occur it's a good idea to check details at the time of booking.

## KETTLEBURGH, Suffolk Map ref 3C2

★★★
FARMHOUSE

B&B PER ROOM PER NIGHT
S £30.00–£32.00
D £60.00–£64.00

EVENING MEAL PER PERSON
£16.00

### Church Farm

Kettleburgh, Woodbridge IP13 7LF **t** (01728) 723532 **e** jbater@suffolkonline.net

**churchfarmkettleburgh.co.uk** REAL-TIME BOOKING

**open** All year
**bedrooms** 1 double, 1 twin
**bathrooms** 1 en suite, 1 private
**payment** Cash, cheques

Oak-beamed, 400-year-old farmhouse on a working farm. Bedrooms with lovely views and every comfort. Excellent food from home-grown produce.

**SAT NAV** *IP13 7LF*

Room General P Leisure

## KEXBY, Lincolnshire Map ref 4C2

★★★
FARMHOUSE

B&B PER ROOM PER NIGHT
S Min £26.00
D Min £46.00

### The Grange

Kexby, Gainsborough DN21 5PJ **t** (01427) 788265

650-acre mixed farm. Victorian farmhouse offering warm welcome. Four miles from Gainsborough. Convenient for Lincoln, Hemswell Antique Centre and Wolds. Double room has private bathroom.

**open** All year except Christmas and New Year
**bedrooms** 1 double, 1 twin
**bathrooms** 1 private
**payment** Cash, cheques

Room TV General P Leisure

## KIDDERMINSTER, Worcestershire Map ref 4B3

★★★★
GUEST HOUSE

B&B PER ROOM PER NIGHT
S £35.00
D £55.00

### Bewdley Hill House

8 Bewdley Hill, Kidderminster DY11 6BS **t** (01562) 60473 **e** info@bewdleyhillhouse.co.uk

**bewdleyhillhouse.co.uk** GUEST REVIEWS

Attractive, en suite accommodation, colour TVs, tea/coffee facilities. Noted for full English breakfasts. Cosy surroundings, warm welcome and off-road parking. Wi-Fi internet.

**open** All year except Christmas
**bedrooms** 2 double, 2 twin, 2 family
**bathrooms** All en suite
**payment** Credit/debit cards, cash, cheques

Room TV General 3 P Leisure

## KNIPTON, Leicestershire Map ref 4C2

★★★★
RESTAURANT WITH ROOMS

B&B PER ROOM PER NIGHT
S £56.00–£70.00
D £90.00–£130.00

EVENING MEAL PER PERSON
£10.00–£27.95

PETS! WELCOME PETS! WELCOME

### Manners Arms

Croxton Road, Knipton, Grantham NG32 1RH **t** (01476) 879222 **e** info@mannersarms.com

**mannersarms.com** SPECIAL OFFERS

**open** All year
**bedrooms** 6 double, 2 twin, 2 single
**bathrooms** All en suite
**payment** Credit/debit cards, cash, cheques

Nestled in the charming village of Knipton, close to Belvoir Castle, this delightful country inn has ten bedrooms, a bar and restaurant, serving fresh, local seasonal food seven days a week.

**SAT NAV** *NG32 1RH*

Room TV General P Leisure

## LATCHINGDON, Essex Map ref 3B3

★★★
GUEST ACCOMMODATION

B&B PER ROOM PER NIGHT
S £50.00–£80.00
D £65.00–£90.00

EVENING MEAL PER PERSON
£16.00–£40.00

*Special weekend deals available throughout the year, i.e. 3 nights for the price of 2.*

### Crouch Valley Lodge

Burnham Road, Latchingdon CM3 6EX **t** (01621) 740770 **e** reservations@crouchvalley.com

**crouchvalley.com**

**open** All year
**bedrooms** 9 double, 1 twin
**bathrooms** All en suite
**payment** Credit/debit cards, cash, cheques, euros

Expect a warm welcome at this purpose-built lodge (all en suite) with ample parking. The adjoining fully licensed restaurant is open 365 days of the year. With Sky Sports, adult channel and Wi-Fi all included in this quality packaged-accommodation pricing.

**SAT NAV** *CM3 6EX* **ONLINE MAP**

Room General Leisure

## LAVENHAM, Suffolk Map ref 3B2

★★★★
BED & BREAKFAST

B&B PER ROOM PER NIGHT
S £40.00–£65.00
D £65.00–£70.00

### Brett Farm

The Common, Sudbury, Lavenham CO10 9PG **t** (01787) 248533 **e** brettfarmbandb@aol.com

**brettfarm.com**

Riverside bungalow set in rural surroundings within walking distance of Lavenham High Street. Comfortable bedrooms, with either en suite or private bathroom. Stabling available.

**open** All year
**bedrooms** 2 double, 1 twin
**bathrooms** 2 en suite, 1 private
**payment** Cash, cheques

Room General Leisure

## LAVENHAM, Suffolk Map ref 3B2

★★★★
BED & BREAKFAST
SILVER AWARD

B&B PER ROOM PER NIGHT
D £75.00–£90.00

### Guinea House Bed & Breakfast

16 Bolton Street, Lavenham, Sudbury CO10 9RG **t** (01787) 249046 **e** gdelucy@aol.com

**guineahouse.co.uk**

Very comfortable, heavily beamed medieval house, tucked away yet close to market square and Guildhall. Excellent Suffolk breakfasts with local or home-grown produce. Excellent base for exploring Suffolk.

**open** All year
**bedrooms** 1 double, 1 twin/double
**bathrooms** All en suite
**payment** Cash, cheques, euros

Room General Leisure

## LEADENHAM, Lincolnshire Map ref 3A1

★★★
INN

B&B PER ROOM PER NIGHT
S £22.00–£35.00
D £40.00–£48.00

EVENING MEAL PER PERSON
£8.00–£18.00

### George Hotel

20 High Street, Leadenham LN5 0PN **t** (01400) 272251 **e** thegeorge.hotel@btconnect.com

**thegeorgeatleadenham.co.uk**

Old-world coaching inn famous for Lincoln Red Beef, local produce and hosting over 600 whiskies. Situated just off the A17, ten miles from Lincoln, Grantham, Sleaford and Newark.

**open** All year
**bedrooms** 3 double, 1 twin, 1 single, 1 family
**bathrooms** 4 en suite
**payment** Cash, cheques

Room General Leisure

### B&B prices

Rates for bed and breakfast are shown per room per night.
Double room prices are usually based on two people sharing the room.

**LEAMINGTON SPA, Warwickshire Map ref 4B3**

★★★★
BED & BREAKFAST

B&B PER ROOM PER NIGHT
D £50.00–£60.00

## Braeside Bed & Breakfast

26 Temple End, Harbury, Nr Royal Leamington Spa CV33 9NE **t** (01926) 613402
**e** rosemary@braesidebb.co.uk

**braesidebb.co.uk**

Comfortable accommodation in Warwickshire village, close to historic Warwick. Within reach of Stratford-upon-Avon, the Cotswolds, Kenilworth, Coventry, Oxford, NEC, Stoneleigh Park, Gaydon Heritage Centre and the M40.

**open** All year except Christmas
**bedrooms** 1 double, 1 twin
**bathrooms** 1 en suite, 1 private
**payment** Cash, cheques

Room General

**LEAMINGTON SPA, Warwickshire Map ref 4B3**

★★★
GUEST HOUSE

B&B PER ROOM PER NIGHT
S £30.00–£35.00
D £45.00–£55.00

## Charnwood Guest House

47 Avenue Road, Leamington Spa CV31 3PF **t** (01926) 831074 **e** ray@charnwoodguesthouse.com

**charnwoodguesthouse.com**

Semi-detached Victorian guesthouse, established for over 25 years, situated within walking distance of Leamington Spa town centre, railway station and leisure facilities. Parking.

**open** All year
**bedrooms** 2 double, 2 twin, 1 single, 1 family
**bathrooms** 4 en suite, 1 private
**payment** Cash, cheques

Room General 3 P Leisure

**LEAMINGTON SPA, Warwickshire Map ref 4B3**

★★★★
FARMHOUSE
SILVER AWARD

B&B PER ROOM PER NIGHT
S £40.00–£42.00
D £50.00–£52.00

## The Coach House

Snowford Hall Farm, Hunningham, Royal Leamington Spa CV33 9ES **t** (01926) 632297
**e** the_coach_house@lineone.net

**http://website.lineone.net/~the_coach_house**

A 200-acre arable farm. Converted barn farmhouse off the Fosse Way, on the edge of Hunningham village. On elevated ground overlooking quiet surrounding countryside.

**open** All year except Christmas
**bedrooms** 1 double, 2 twin
**bathrooms** 2 en suite, 1 private
**payment** Cash, cheques

Room General P

**LEAMINGTON SPA, Warwickshire Map ref 4B3**

★★★★
GUEST HOUSE

B&B PER ROOM PER NIGHT
S £52.00
D £70.00–£75.00

## Victoria Park Lodge

12 Adelaide Road, Leamington Spa CV31 3PW **t** (01926) 424195
**e** info@victoriaparkhotelleamingtonspa.co.uk

**victoriaparkhotelleamingtonspa.co.uk** REAL-TIME BOOKING

**open** All year except Christmas and New Year
**bedrooms** 10 double, 2 twin, 8 single, 9 family
**bathrooms** All en suite
**payment** Credit/debit cards, cash, cheques

Twenty-nine well-appointed bedrooms, all with en suite facilities and Wi-Fi. We pride ourselves on cleanliness and comfort, offering a home away from home in an excellent location. Four minutes' walk from the town centre and five minutes' drive from Warwick Castle. We also provide free off-street parking.

**SAT NAV** *CV31 3PW*

Room General P Leisure

## Where are the maps?

Colour maps can be found at the front of the guide. They pinpoint the location of all accommodation found in the regional sections.

## LEICESTER, Leicestershire Map ref 4C3

★★★
GUEST HOUSE

B&B PER ROOM PER NIGHT
S £33.00–£39.00
D £45.00–£52.00

### Abinger Guest House

175 Hinckley Road, Leicester LE3 0TF **t** (0116) 255 4674 **e** abinger@btinternet.com

**leicesterguest.co.uk** REAL-TIME BOOKING

Extensively modernised guesthouse situated 0.8 miles from Leicester city centre. Friendly staff, great breakfasts and extremely comfortable beds. Freeview TV in every room, and free Wi-Fi internet throughout.

**open** All year except Christmas and New Year
**bedrooms** 2 double, 3 twin, 1 single, 2 family
**payment** Credit/debit cards, cash, cheques, euros

Room General

## LEICESTER, Leicestershire Map ref 4C3

★★★
BED & BREAKFAST

B&B PER ROOM PER NIGHT
S £35.00
D £50.00

*Weekend breaks £45 per room based on 2 people sharing, 2 nights minimum, off-peak.*

### Wondai B&B

47-49 Main Street, Newtown Linford, Leicester LE6 0AE **t** (01530) 242728

**open** All year except Christmas
**bedrooms** 1 twin, 1 family
**bathrooms** All en suite
**payment** Credit/debit cards, cash, cheques

Our bed and breakfast is located in the village just a short walk from Bradgate Deer Park which was home to Lady Jane Grey, Queen of England for nine days in 1553. Great Central Railway, the only twin-track mainline steam train in England, is a short drive away.

**SAT NAV** *LE6 0AE*

WALKERS WELCOME CYCLISTS WELCOME

Room General Leisure

## LICHFIELD, Staffordshire Map ref 4B3

★★★★
GUEST HOUSE

B&B PER ROOM PER NIGHT
S £35.00–£43.00
D £52.00–£64.00

### Coppers End Guest House

Walsall Road, Muckley Corner, Lichfield WS14 0BG **t** (01543) 372910
**e** info@coppersendguesthouse.co.uk

**coppersendguesthouse.co.uk** REAL-TIME BOOKING

**open** All year except Christmas and New Year
**bedrooms** 3 double, 3 twin
**bathrooms** 4 en suite
**payment** Credit/debit cards, cash, cheques

Detached guesthouse of character and charm in its own grounds. Conservatory dining room, large walled garden with patio, guests' lounge. All bedrooms non-smoking. Vegetarians catered for. Off-road parking, safes in rooms, luggage racks. Easy access M6, M42 and M1, Lichfield, Walsall and Birmingham. Sixteen miles to NEC, six miles Whittington Barracks. Motorcyclist, cyclist and walker friendly.

**SAT NAV** *WS14 0BG* **ONLINE MAP**

Room General Leisure

## LINCOLN, Lincolnshire Map ref 4C2

★★★★★
GUEST HOUSE
SILVER AWARD

B&B PER ROOM PER NIGHT
S £40.00–£45.00
D £55.00

### Creston Villa Guest House

27 St Catherines, Lincoln LN5 8LW **t** (01522) 872511 **e** info@crestonvilla.co.uk

**crestonvilla.co.uk** GUEST REVIEWS · REAL-TIME BOOKING

Victorian guesthouse located one mile from city centre, providing old-fashioned elegance with your comfort in mind. Superior accommodation, delicious breakfast, helpful hosts. A better than home-from-home experience.

**open** All year except Christmas
**bedrooms** 3 double, 2 twin
**bathrooms** 3 en suite, 2 private
**payment** Credit/debit cards, cash, cheques

Room General Leisure

## LINCOLN, Lincolnshire Map ref 4C2

★★★★
GUEST ACCOMMODATION

B&B PER ROOM PER NIGHT
S £76.90
D £76.90

### Damon's Motel

997 Doddington Road, Lincoln LN6 3SE **t** (01522) 887733 **e** motel@damons.co.uk

**damons.co.uk**

Four miles from the historic city of Lincoln, a superior-grade motel. Relax in our indoor pool, gym and solarium or dine in the adjacent, world-famous Damon's Restaurant.

**open** All year except Christmas
**bedrooms** 37 double, 10 single
**bathrooms** All en suite
**payment** Credit/debit cards, cash, cheques

Room General Leisure

## LINCOLN, Lincolnshire Map ref 4C2

★★★
INN

B&B PER ROOM PER NIGHT
S £65.00–£80.00
D £75.00–£105.00

EVENING MEAL PER PERSON
Min £15.00

### Duke William Inn

44 Bailgate, Lincoln LN1 3AP **t** (01522) 533351 **e** enquiries@dukewilliam.com

**dukewilliam.com**

**open** All year
**bedrooms** 7 double, 1 twin, 1 single, 3 family
**bathrooms** 11 en suite, 1 private
**payment** Credit/debit cards, cash, cheques

First registered as an inn in 1791, this establishment combines modern facilities with an old-world atmosphere. Near to historic Newport Arch, Lincoln Cathedral and Lincoln Castle. Boasting 12 newly refurbished en suite bedrooms.

**SAT NAV** *LN1 3AP*

Room General

## LINCOLN, Lincolnshire Map ref 4C2

★★★
BED & BREAKFAST

B&B PER ROOM PER NIGHT
S £26.00
D £52.00

*Free internet access. No charge for children under the age of ten. Lock-up for bikes. Discounts available.*

### Goodlane B&B

31 Good Lane, Lincoln LN1 3EH **t** (01522) 542994 & 07778 061494 **e** sue@goodlane.co.uk

**goodlane.co.uk** GUEST REVIEWS · SPECIAL OFFERS

**open** All year
**bedrooms** 2 double, 1 twin, 1 single
**payment** Cash, cheques

Home from home. Georgian house situated in a quiet street within a few minutes' walk of the old town, cathedral, shops and over 20 restaurants. All rooms are newly decorated and furnished to suit the original features. Luxury Victorian-style bathroom. Overlooks a beautiful secluded garden.

**SAT NAV** *LN1 3EH* **ONLINE MAP**

Room General Leisure

## LINCOLN, Lincolnshire Map ref 4C2

★★★★
RESTAURANT WITH ROOMS
SILVER AWARD

B&B PER ROOM PER NIGHT
S £50.00
D £53.00–£65.00

EVENING MEAL PER PERSON
£25.00–£30.00

# The Old Bakery Restaurant with Rooms

26/28 Burton Road, Lincoln LN1 3LB **t** (01522) 576057 **e** enquiries@theold-bakery.co.uk

**theold-bakery.co.uk** GUEST REVIEWS · REAL-TIME BOOKING

**open** All year
**bedrooms** 2 double, 1 twin, 1 family
**bathrooms** 2 en suite, 2 private
**payment** Credit/debit cards, cash, cheques

Converted Victorian bakery full of rustic charm, minutes from Lincoln Cathedral and castle. International restaurant serving full a la carte evening, lunchtime meals and Sunday lunch. Superb climate-controlled garden room. All rooms have colour TV with Freeview, wireless broadband internet access and central heating with either en suite or private bathrooms. Strictly non-smoking throughout.

**SAT NAV** *LN1 3LB* **ONLINE MAP**

Room General

## LINCOLN, Lincolnshire Map ref 4C2

★★★★
GUEST ACCOMMODATION
SILVER AWARD

B&B PER ROOM PER NIGHT
S Max £45.00
D Max £60.00

# The Old Vicarage

East Street, Nettleham, Lincoln LN2 2SL **t** (01522) 750819 **e** susan@oldvic.net

**oldvic.net**

**open** All year
**bedrooms** 1 double, 1 twin
**bathrooms** 1 en suite, 1 private
**payment** Credit/debit cards, cash, cheques

Welcome to our listed Georgian farmhouse near the centre of an attractive village with traditional village green and beck. A warm welcome, tastefully furnished rooms and excellent location make us an ideal base when visiting historic Lincoln and surrounding counties.

**SAT NAV** *LN2 2SL*

Room General 15 P

## LINCOLN, Lincolnshire Map ref 4C2

★★★★
GUEST ACCOMMODATION

B&B PER ROOM PER NIGHT
S £35.00–£45.00
D £50.00–£60.00

# Savill Guest House

203 Yarborough Road, Lincoln LN1 3NQ **t** (01522) 523261 **e** info@savillguesthouse.co.uk

**savillguesthouse.co.uk**

The unrivalled position of the Savill Guest House offers outstanding views over the Trent Valley, yet is within walking distance of Lincoln's famous cathedral and castle, and the shopping centre.

**open** All year except Christmas
**bedrooms** 3 double, 3 twin
**bathrooms** All en suite
**payment** Credit/debit cards, cash, cheques

Room General 14 P

WALKERS WELCOME

## Do you like walking?

Walkers feel at home in accommodation participating in our Walkers Welcome scheme. Look out for the symbol. Consider walking all or part of a long-distance route – go online at nationaltrail.co.uk.

For **key to symbols** see page 7

## LINCOLN, Lincolnshire Map ref 4C2

★★★★
BED & BREAKFAST

B&B PER ROOM PER NIGHT
S £30.00
D £50.00

EVENING MEAL PER PERSON
Min £10.00

### Welbeck Cottage B&B

19 Meadow Lane, South Hykeham, Lincoln LN6 9PF **t** (01522) 692669 **e** maggied@hotmail.co.uk

**open** All year except Christmas and New Year
**bedrooms** 2 double, 1 twin
**bathrooms** All en suite
**payment** Cash, cheques

A friendly welcome to our home, set in a quiet village location on the outskirts of the city of Lincoln. Use as a base to explore many local attractions. Close to Whisby Nature Park and Doddington Hall. Only a short drive to Lincoln's beautiful and historic cathedral area and shopping centre.

**SAT NAV** *LN6 9PF*

Room General Leisure

## LITTLE CAWTHORPE, Lincolnshire Map ref 4D2

★★★★
INN

B&B PER ROOM PER NIGHT
S £45.00–£55.00
D £70.00–£85.00

EVENING MEAL PER PERSON
£10.00–£25.00

### The Royal Oak Inn – The Splash

Watery Lane, Little Cawthorpe, Louth LN11 8LZ **t** (01507) 600750 **e** info@royaloaksplash.co.uk

**royaloaksplash.co.uk** REAL-TIME BOOKING

**open** All year
**bedrooms** 3 double, 2 twin, 1 single, 1 family
**bathrooms** All en suite
**payment** Credit/debit cards, cash, cheques

Royal Oak Inn is an historic country public house situated in its own large lawned gardens next to a picturesque ford in a peaceful Wolds village. With our period bars, open fire, restaurant, conservatory and seven en suite bedrooms, you're always sure of a warm welcome.

**SAT NAV** *LN11 8LZ* **ONLINE MAP**

Room General Leisure

## LONG COMPTON, Warwickshire Map ref 2B1

★★★
FARMHOUSE

B&B PER ROOM PER NIGHT
S £35.00
D £50.00

### Butlers Road Farm

Long Compton, Shipston-on-Stour CV36 5JZ **t** (01608) 684262 **e** eileen@butlersroad.com

**butlersroadfarm.co.uk**

120-acre stock farm. Listed Cotswold-stone farmhouse adjacent to A3400 between Oxford and Stratford-upon-Avon. Home comforts. Local pub nearby. Rooms also function as family rooms.

**open** All year
**bedrooms** 1 double, 1 twin
**payment** Cash, cheques

Room General Leisure

## LONG MELFORD, Suffolk Map ref 3B2

★★★★
BED & BREAKFAST
SILVER AWARD

B&B PER ROOM PER NIGHT
S £30.00–£60.00
D £50.00–£70.00

### High Street Farmhouse

High Street, Long Melford, Sudbury CO10 9BD **t** (01787) 375765 **e** mail@gallopingchef.co.uk

**highstreetfarmhouse.co.uk**

**open** All year
**bedrooms** 2 double, 1 twin
**bathrooms** All en suite
**payment** Cash, cheques

Add to the perfect picture postcard of a traditional Suffolk farmhouse, the friendliest of welcomes, the cosiest of rooms, the tastiest of breakfasts, the charm of an English village, the gem of a location and that little touch of magic that is the countryside on your doorstep.

**SAT NAV** *CO10 9BD*

Room General Leisure

## LONG STRATTON, Norfolk Map ref 3B1

★★★★
BED & BREAKFAST

B&B PER ROOM PER NIGHT
S £38.00–£45.00
D £55.00–£70.00

*Reduced rates for two or more nights.*

### Greenacres Farm

Wood Green, Long Stratton NR15 2RR **t** (01508) 530261 **e** greenacresfarm@tinyworld.co.uk

**abreakwithtradition.co.uk**

**open** All year
**bedrooms** 2 double, 1 twin
**bathrooms** 2 en suite, 1 private
**payment** Cash, cheques

17thC farmhouse on a 30-acre common with ponds and natural wildlife (ten miles south of Norwich). Bedrooms are tastefully furnished. Tea/coffee facilities, TV. Beams and inglenooks create a relaxing atmosphere. Jo is able to offer therapeutic massage/reflexology to guests. Come and enjoy the peace and tranquillity of our home.

**SAT NAV** *NR15 2RR*

Room General Leisure

## LOUGHBOROUGH, Leicestershire Map ref 4C3

★★★★
GUEST HOUSE

B&B PER ROOM PER NIGHT
S £38.00–£55.00
D £50.00–£80.00

EVENING MEAL PER PERSON
£8.95–£17.50

### Charnwood Lodge

136 Leicester Road, Loughborough LE11 2AQ **t** (01509) 211120
**e** reservations@charnwoodlodge.com

**charnwoodlodge.com**

Elegant, Victorian, licensed hotel in pretty gardens with private parking. Spacious, comfortable interior with very attractive en suite rooms, including a four-poster suite. Guests' lounge, bar. Warm, friendly service assured.

**open** All year
**bedrooms** 5 double, 4 twin, 1 single, 3 family, 1 suite
**bathrooms** All en suite
**payment** Credit/debit cards, cash, cheques

Room General Leisure

WELCOME PETS!

## Where is my pet welcome?

Want to take your cherished companion with you on holiday? Proprietors participating in our Welcome Pets! scheme go out of their way to make special provision for you and your pet. Look out for the symbol.

## LOUGHBOROUGH, Leicestershire Map ref 4C3

★★★★
GUEST HOUSE

B&B PER ROOM PER NIGHT
S Min £35.00
D Min £50.00

### Highbury Guest House

146 Leicester Road, Loughborough LE11 2AQ **t** (01509) 230545
**e** cosmo@thehighburyguesthouse.co.uk

**thehighburyguesthouse.co.uk**

Well-run family guesthouse surrounded by well-kept gardens. Conservatory/dining room, large car park for off-road parking.

**open** All year except Christmas and New Year
**bedrooms** 4 double, 3 twin, 3 single, 6 family
**bathrooms** 14 en suite
**payment** Credit/debit cards, cash, cheques

Room General

## LOUGHBOROUGH, Leicestershire Map ref 4C3

★★
GUEST ACCOMMODATION

B&B PER ROOM PER NIGHT
S £15.00–£35.00
D £40.00–£45.00

### Peachnook Guest House

154 Ashby Road, Loughborough LE11 3AG **t** (01509) 264390

Friendly Victorian villa, family-run. Good English breakfasts, vegans and vegetarians catered for.

**open** All year
**bedrooms** 2 double, 1 twin, 1 single
**bathrooms** 2 en suite
**payment** Cash, cheques

Room General 1

## LOWESTOFT, Suffolk Map ref 3C1

★★★★
BED & BREAKFAST

B&B PER ROOM PER NIGHT
S £45.00–£60.00
D £65.00–£85.00

### Fairways Bed and Breakfast

288 Normanston Drive, Oulton Broad, Lowestoft NR32 2PS **t** (01502) 582756
**e** info@fairwaysbb.co.uk

**fairwaysbb.co.uk**

A warm and friendly welcome awaits you at Fairways, where we offer a very comfortable and relaxing break. Family rates from £95.00.

**open** All year
**bedrooms** 1 double, 1 twin, 1 family
**bathrooms** 2 en suite
**payment** Credit/debit cards, cash, cheques

Room General Leisure

## LOWESTOFT, Suffolk Map ref 3C1

★★★
BED & BREAKFAST

B&B PER ROOM PER NIGHT
S Max £24.00
D Max £48.00

### Saint Catherines House

186 Denmark Road, Lowestoft NR32 2EN **t** (01502) 500951

**tiscover.co.uk**

Victorian-built terraced house close to railway station.

**open** All year except Christmas and New Year
**bedrooms** 1 double, 2 single
**payment** Cash, cheques

Room General

## LUDLOW, Shropshire Map ref 4A3

★★★★
BED & BREAKFAST

B&B PER ROOM PER NIGHT
S £75.00–£110.00
D £110.00–£115.00

### Bromley Court

18-20 Lower Broad Street, Ludlow SY8 1PQ **t** (01584) 876996 & 07809 699665
**e** phil@ludlowhotels.com

**ludlowhotels.com** SPECIAL OFFERS

Tudor cottages of great charm, in Ludlow town. Each cottage forms a delightful, individually furnished suite – for total privacy and relaxation. Within walking distance of everything in Ludlow.

**open** All year
**bedrooms** 3 suites
**bathrooms** All en suite
**payment** Credit/debit cards, cash, cheques

Room General Leisure

### What do the star ratings mean?

Detailed information about star ratings can be found at the back of this guide.

## LUDLOW, Shropshire Map ref 4A3

★★★
GUEST HOUSE

B&B PER ROOM PER NIGHT
S £24.00–£43.00
D £60.00–£66.00

EVENING MEAL PER PERSON
£18.00

### Cecil Guest House

Sheet Road, Ludlow SY8 1LR **t** (01584) 872442

Attractive guesthouse 15 minutes' walk from town centre and station. Freshly cooked food from local produce. Residents' bar and lounge. Off-street parking.

**open** All year
**bedrooms** 2 double, 4 twin, 2 single, 1 family
**bathrooms** 7 en suite
**payment** Cash, cheques

Room General P Leisure

## LUDLOW, Shropshire Map ref 4A3

★★★★★
RESTAURANT WITH ROOMS
SILVER AWARD

B&B PER ROOM PER NIGHT
S £60.00–£85.00
D £85.00–£110.00

EVENING MEAL PER PERSON
£25.00–£30.00

*3 nights for the price of 2, Sun-Thu nights (excl Christmas, New Year and Bank Holiday weekends). Oct-May only.*

### The Clive Bar and Restaurant With Rooms

Bromfield, Ludlow SY8 2JR **t** (01584) 856565 & (01584) 856665 **e** info@theclive.co.uk

**theclive.co.uk**

**open** All year except Christmas
**bedrooms** 8 double, 5 twin, 2 family
**bathrooms** All en suite
**payment** Credit/debit cards, cash, cheques

Set in the heart of South Shropshire's beautiful countryside, The Clive offers en suite bedrooms in period outbuildings that have been tastefully converted to provide contemporary accommodation and complimented by the 2 AA rosette Clive Restaurant, open every day. Located on main A49 road in the village of Bromfield, just two miles north of Ludlow with ample parking.

**SAT NAV** *SY8 2JR* **ONLINE MAP**

Room General P Leisure

## LUDLOW, Shropshire Map ref 4A3

★★★★★
GUEST ACCOMMODATION
SILVER AWARD

B&B PER ROOM PER NIGHT
S £65.00–£130.00
D £85.00–£190.00

*For last-minute offers please check our website.*

### DeGreys

5-6 Broad Street, Ludlow SY8 1NG **t** (01584) 872764 **e** degreys@btopenworld.com

**degreys.co.uk**

**open** All year except Christmas and New Year
**bedrooms** 5 double, 3 twin, 1 suite
**bathrooms** All en suite
**payment** Credit/debit cards, cash, cheques

An irresistible fusion of the past and present is how one would describe our nine new bedrooms and suites. Each with its own individual charm, they ensure a feeling of luxury and comfort. All the rooms have en suite facilities and some feature stunning bathrooms with roll-top baths and large, powerful showers.

**SAT NAV** *SY8 1NG*

Room General

## LUDLOW, Shropshire Map ref 4A3

★★★★
BED & BREAKFAST

B&B PER ROOM PER NIGHT
S Min £50.00
D Min £60.00

WALKERS WELCOME CYCLISTS WELCOME

### Elm Lodge B&B

Elm Lodge, Fishmore, Ludlow SY8 3DP **t** (01584) 872308 **e** info@elm-lodge.org.uk

**elm-lodge.org.uk**

Converted Georgian coach house on outskirts of town. Overlooks own golf course. Views to Ludlow and Welsh Borders. Short breaks available. Self-catering apartments also available.

**open** All year
**bedrooms** 4 double/twin
**bathrooms** All en suite
**payment** Credit/debit cards, cash, cheques

Room General 1 Leisure

## MABLETHORPE, Lincolnshire Map ref 4D2

★★★
GUEST HOUSE

B&B PER ROOM PER NIGHT
S Min £20.00
D £50.00–£55.00

EVENING MEAL PER PERSON
£5.00–£7.00

### The Cannon Guest House

7 Waterloo Road, Mablethorpe LN12 1JR **t** (01507) 473148 **e** info@cannon-guesthouse.co.uk

**cannon-guesthouse.co.uk**

Open all year round for a warm and friendly welcome and good food. This delightful, small guesthouse comprises four comfortable letting bedrooms. You can even choose from a four-poster bed with en suite or a 7ft 7in bed with en suite.

**open** All year except Christmas and New Year
**bedrooms** 2 double, 1 twin, 1 family
**bathrooms** All en suite
**payment** Cash, cheques, euros

Room General Leisure

## MALDON, Essex Map ref 3B3

★★★★
BED & BREAKFAST

B&B PER ROOM PER NIGHT
D Max £55.00

### Tatoi Bed & Breakfast

31 Acacia Drive, Maldon CM9 6AW **t** (01621) 853841 & 07860 162328
**e** diana.rogers2@btinternet.com

Detached family house standing on a large plot in a quiet residential area. It is within easy walking distance of the town and historic maritime quay.

**open** All year except Christmas
**bedrooms** 2 double
**payment** Cash, cheques

Room General Leisure

## MALVERN, Worcestershire Map ref 2B1

★★★★
GUEST HOUSE
SILVER AWARD

B&B PER ROOM PER NIGHT
S £35.00–£50.00
D £60.00–£80.00

### Cannara Guest House

147 Barnards Green Road, Malvern WR14 3LT **t** (01684) 564418 **e** info@cannara.co.uk

**cannara.co.uk**

Feel at home at Cannara, where style, ambience, attention to detail and guest comfort is of paramount importance to us. Family rates from £90.00.

**open** All year
**bedrooms** 2 double, 2 twin, 1 family
**bathrooms** All en suite
**payment** Credit/debit cards, cash, cheques

Room General

## MALVERN, Worcestershire Map ref 2B1

★★★
BED & BREAKFAST

B&B PER ROOM PER NIGHT
S £32.50–£40.00
D £55.00–£65.00

### Harmony House Malvern

184 West Malvern Road, Malvern WR14 4AZ **t** (01684) 891650 **e** catherine@harmonymalvern.com

**harmonyhousemalvern.com**

A warm and spacious home set on the western slopes of the Malvern Hills. Close to footpaths and bus route. Wonderful views. Double/twin bed option. Organic/local food.

**open** All year
**bedrooms** 1 double, 1 twin, 1 family
**bathrooms** All en suite
**payment** Cash, cheques

Room General

## MANNINGTREE, Essex Map ref 3B2

★★★★
BED & BREAKFAST
SILVER AWARD

B&B PER ROOM PER NIGHT
S £50.00–£60.00
D £60.00–£75.00

*The perfect place to stay for walkers and birdwatchers. Single-let discounts on twin rooms.*

### Curlews

Station Road, Bradfield, Manningtree CO11 2UP **t** (01255) 870890
**e** margherita@curlewsaccommodation.co.uk

**curlewsacccommodation.co.uk**

**open** All year
**bedrooms** 3 double, 5 twin, 1 family, 1 suite
**bathrooms** All en suite
**payment** Credit/debit cards, cash, cheques

Curlews is a superb property situated on the outskirts of Bradfield village offering luxury bed and breakfast and self-catering accommodation including facilities for the disabled. Located approximately 30m above sea level, all bedrooms provide stunning elevated panoramic views over farmland and the Stour Estuary.

**SAT NAV** *CO11 2UP* **ONLINE MAP**

Room General 8 P Leisure

## MANNINGTREE, Essex Map ref 3B2

★★★★
BED & BREAKFAST

B&B PER ROOM PER NIGHT
S £40.00–£55.00
D £55.00–£65.00

### Emsworth House

Station Road, Ship Hill, Bradfield, Manningtree CO11 2UP **t** (01255) 870860
**e** emsworthhouse@hotmail.com

**emsworthhouse.co.uk**

**open** All year
**bedrooms** 1 double, 1 twin, 1 single, 1 family
**bathrooms** 2 en suite
**payment** Cash, cheques

Formerly the vicarage. Spacious rooms with stunning views of the countryside and River Stour. Near Colchester and Harwich. On holiday, business or en route to the continent, it's perfect!

**SAT NAV** *CO11 2UP* **ONLINE MAP**

Room General P Leisure

## MARCH, Cambridgeshire Map ref 3A1

★★★
GUEST HOUSE

B&B PER ROOM PER NIGHT
S Max £30.00
D Max £50.00

### Causeway Guest House

6 The Causeway, March PE15 9NT **t** (01354) 650823

**causewayguesthouse.co.uk**

This 19thC house offers en suite accommodation, colour TV and tea/coffee facilities in all rooms. Private car park. Situated five minutes' walk from town centre.

**open** All year
**bedrooms** 13 double, 5 twin, 6 single, 1 family
**bathrooms** All en suite
**payment** Credit/debit cards, cash, cheques

Room General P

FAMILIES WELCOME

## Looking for an ideal family break?

For accommodation offering additional facilities and services for a range of ages and family units, look out for the Families Welcome symbol. Owners of these properties will go out of their way to welcome families.

## MARKET DRAYTON, Shropshire Map ref 4A2

★★★
GUEST HOUSE

B&B PER ROOM PER NIGHT
S £30.00–£35.00
D £50.00–£60.00

EVENING MEAL PER PERSON
£7.50–£25.00

### The Hermitage

44 Stafford Street, Market Drayton TF9 1JB **t** (01630) 658508 **e** info@thehermitagebb.co.uk

**thehermitagebb.co.uk**

A large Victorian house offering a quality environment for holidays or business, set in the pretty market town of Market Drayton.

**open** All year
**bedrooms** 5 double, 1 twin, 1 family
**bathrooms** 4 en suite
**payment** Cash, cheques

Room General

## MARKET HARBOROUGH, Leicestershire Map ref 4C3

★★★★
FARMHOUSE

B&B PER ROOM PER NIGHT
S £35.00
D £55.00

### Langton Brook Farm

Langton Road, Great Bowden, Market Harborough LE16 7EZ **t** (01858) 545730
**e** mervyn@langtonbrookfarm.freeserve.co.uk

**langtonbrookfarm.com**

**open** All year
**bedrooms** 1 double, 1 family
**bathrooms** All en suite
**payment** Credit/debit cards, cash, cheques, euros

Private, en suite accommodation in annexe adjoining modern farmhouse in peaceful, open countryside. Foxton Locks and Market Harborough nearby. Historic towns of Stamford and Uppingham within easy reach. Rutland Water and Grafham Water 40 minutes' drive. Corby raceway ten minutes. Coventry, Birmingham, Nottinghamshire Airports 40 minutes.

**SAT NAV** *LE16 7EZ*

Room General Leisure

## MATHON, Herefordshire Map ref 2B1

★★★★
BED & BREAKFAST
SILVER AWARD

B&B PER ROOM PER NIGHT
S Min £55.00
D £70.00–£80.00

### Weobley Cross Cottage

South End Lane, Mathon, Malvern WR13 5PB **t** (01684) 541488 **e** anne@hanleyinteriors.co.uk

**bedandbreakfastmalvernhills.co.uk**

Quality accommodation set in picturesque and peaceful surroundings within easy reach of many local attractions. Excellent walking, lovely garden. Be assured of a warm welcome and helpful hosts.

**open** All year except Christmas
**bedrooms** 1 double, 1 twin
**bathrooms** All en suite
**payment** Cash, cheques

Room General Leisure

## MATLOCK BATH, Derbyshire Map ref 4B2

★★★
GUEST ACCOMMODATION

B&B PER ROOM PER NIGHT
S £35.00–£40.00
D £60.00–£65.00

### Ashdale Guest House

92 North Parade, Matlock Bath, Matlock DE4 3NS **t** (01629) 57826
**e** ashdale@matlockbath.fsnet.co.uk

**ashdaleguesthouse.co.uk** SPECIAL OFFERS

A Grade II Listed Victorian villa situated in the centre of Matlock Bath. Large, comfortable rooms, level walking to restaurants, pubs, museums and station. Home-made bread and marmalade.

**open** All year
**bedrooms** 1 double, 1 twin, 2 family
**bathrooms** All en suite
**payment** Credit/debit cards, cash, cheques, euros

Room General Leisure

## Do you have access needs?

Look for the National Accessible Scheme symbols if you have special hearing, visual or mobility needs.

## MEPPERSHALL, Bedfordshire Map ref 2D1

★★
BED & BREAKFAST

B&B PER ROOM PER NIGHT
S £30.00
D £45.00

### Old Joe's

90 Fildyke Road, Meppershall, Shefford SG17 5LU **t** (01462) 815585 & 07831 111062
**e** cih@freenet.co.uk

Double-fronted, modernised and extended detached cottage. Spacious rooms, central heating, parking. Village location. One mile A507/A600. One mile to pubs and restaurants. Home-made marmalade.

**open** All year
**bedrooms** 2 double, 1 single
**payment** Cash, cheques

Room General 5 P Leisure

## MERIDEN, West Midlands Map ref 4B3

★★★
GUEST HOUSE

B&B PER ROOM PER NIGHT
S Min £25.00
D Min £45.00

### Bonnifinglas Guest House

3 Berkswell Road, Meriden, Coventry CV7 7LB **t** (01676) 523193 **e** bookings@bonnifinglas.co.uk

**bonnifinglas.co.uk**

Country house, all rooms en suite with TV. Several pubs and restaurants within walking distance. Fire certificate. Large, off-road car park. Five minutes NEC. Wi-Fi internet.

**open** All year except Christmas and New Year
**bedrooms** 2 double, 3 twin, 2 single, 1 family
**bathrooms** All en suite
**payment** Credit/debit cards, cash, cheques, euros

Room General P Leisure

## MUMBY, Lincolnshire Map ref 4D2

★★★★
GUEST ACCOMMODATION

B&B PER ROOM PER NIGHT
S £25.00–£30.00
D £50.00–£70.00

EVENING MEAL PER PERSON
£5.00–£15.00

### Brambles

Occupation Lane, Alford LN13 9JU **t** (01507) 490174 **e** suescrimshaw@btinternet.com

Newly built rural bungalow, quiet scenic setting, close to the costal resorts. Two en suite double rooms for bed and breakfast.

**open** All year
**bedrooms** 1 double, 1 family
**bathrooms** All en suite
**payment** Cash, cheques

Room General P Leisure

## MUNDFORD, Norfolk Map ref 3B1

★★★★
FARMHOUSE

B&B PER ROOM PER NIGHT
S £35.00–£40.00
D £30.00–£40.00

EVENING MEAL PER PERSON
£20.00

### Colveston Manor

Mundford, Thetford IP26 5HU **t** (01842) 878218 **e** mail@colveston-manor.co.uk

**colveston-manor.co.uk**

Colveston Manor is set in the heart of the Breckland countryside. A birdwatcher's paradise, so quiet and peaceful. Delicious Norfolk breakfasts. National Trust properties, cathedrals, gardens and coast within easy reach.

**open** All year except Christmas and New Year
**bedrooms** 2 double, 1 twin, 1 single
**bathrooms** 1 en suite, 1 private
**payment** Cash, cheques

Room General 8 P Leisure

## NARBOROUGH, Norfolk Map ref 3B1

★★★★
BED & BREAKFAST

B&B PER ROOM PER NIGHT
S £30.75–£35.00
D £55.00–£60.00

### Mill View Rooms

Main Road, King's Lynn PE32 1TE **t** (01760) 338005 **e** narfish@supanet.com

**millviewbandb.co.uk** SPECIAL OFFERS

In the beautiful Nar Valley, our quality accommodation has the added convenience of a kitchenette and is 25yds from one of our five lakes.

**open** All year
**bedrooms** 3 twin
**bathrooms** All en suite
**payment** Credit/debit cards, cash, cheques

Room General P Leisure

For **key to symbols** see page 7

## NASSINGTON, Northamptonshire Map ref 3A1

★★★★
BED & BREAKFAST

B&B PER ROOM PER NIGHT
S £40.00–£50.00
D £60.00–£70.00

# Fairlands

35 Church Street, Nassington, Peterborough PE8 6QG **t** (01780) 783603
**e** enquiries@fairlandsbandb.co.uk

**fairlandsbandb.co.uk**

**open** All year except Christmas
**bedrooms** 2 double, 1 twin
**bathrooms** 1 en suite
**payment** Cash, cheques

Ann and John welcome you to their Grade II Listed building with a wealth of character, oak beams and inglenook fireplace. Situated in the heart of a thriving village in a conservation area, the beautiful south-facing garden overlooks open countryside. Two excellent pub/restaurants within easy walking distance, ample parking to rear.

**SAT NAV** *PE8 6QG* **ONLINE MAP**

Room General P Leisure

## NAYLAND, Suffolk Map ref 3B2

★★★★
FARMHOUSE

B&B PER ROOM PER NIGHT
S £45.00–£55.00
D £65.00–£75.00

# Gladwins Farm

Harpers Hill, Nayland CO6 4NU **t** (01206) 262261 **e** gladwinsfarm@aol.com

**gladwinsfarm.co.uk**

**open** All year except Christmas and New Year
**bedrooms** 2 double
**bathrooms** All en suite
**payment** Credit/debit cards, cash, cheques, euros

Homely farmhouse B&B set in 22 acres of Suffolk's beautiful, rolling Constable Country. Marvellous views, charming heritage villages, birdwatching and NT gardens. Only 25 minutes from the sea. Heated indoor pool, sauna, hot tub, tennis court, fishing, farm animals. Plus nine charming award-winning self-catering cottages sleeping from two to eight.

**SAT NAV** *CO6 4NU* **ONLINE MAP**

Room General Leisure

## NAYLAND, Suffolk Map ref 3B2

★★★★★
RESTAURANT WITH ROOMS
GOLD AWARD

B&B PER ROOM PER NIGHT
S £76.00–£109.00
D £96.00–£129.00

EVENING MEAL PER PERSON
£23.00–£42.00

# White Hart Inn

High Street, Nayland CO6 4JF **t** (01206) 263382 **e** nayhart@aol.com

**whitehart-nayland.co.uk** GUEST REVIEWS

**open** All year
**bedrooms** 5 double, 1 twin
**bathrooms** All en suite
**payment** Credit/debit cards, cash, cheques

The White Hart, a 15thC coaching inn, is a restaurant with rooms located in the sleepy but pretty Suffolk village of Nayland, on the border with Essex, close to the coast.

**SAT NAV** *CO6 4JF* **ONLINE MAP**

Room General P Leisure

## Has every property been assessed?

All accommodation in this guide has been rated for quality, or is awaiting assessment, by a professional national tourist board assessor.

## NEWARK, Nottinghamshire Map ref 4C2

★★★
FARMHOUSE

B&B PER ROOM PER NIGHT
S Min £35.00
D Min £48.00

### Ivy Farm B&B

Newark Road, Barnby in the Willows, Newark NG24 2SL **t** (01636) 672568
**e** clare@ivyfarnewark.co.uk

**ivyfarmnewark.co.uk**

Comfortable, working family farm, three miles east of Newark, easy access from A17 and A1. Close to Newark Showground. Separate annexe to farmhouse. Free Wi-Fi internet, Freeview in rooms.

**open** All year
**bedrooms** 1 double, 2 twin, 1 family
**bathrooms** 3 en suite, 1 private
**payment** Credit/debit cards, cash

Room General

## NEWMARKET, Suffolk Map ref 3B2

★★★★
GUEST ACCOMMODATION

B&B PER ROOM PER NIGHT
S £30.00–£35.00
D £60.00

### Meadow House

2a High Street, Burwell, Cambridge CB25 0HB **t** (01638) 741926 **e** hilary@themeadowhouse.co.uk

**themeadowhouse.co.uk**

**open** All year
**bedrooms** 1 double, 1 twin, 3 family, 1 suite
**bathrooms** 4 en suite
**payment** Cash, cheques, euros

Large, well-equipped, modern house set in grounds of two acres, close to Newmarket Racecourse, Cambridge and Ely. King-size beds. Family suites available, also coach house available in grounds. Large car park. Generous breakfasts. Two rooms suitable for moderately disabled people. More colour pictures available on our website.

**SAT NAV** *CB25 0HB*

Room General

## NEWPORT, Shropshire Map ref 4A3

★★★★
BED & BREAKFAST
SILVER AWARD

B&B PER ROOM PER NIGHT
D £60.00–£70.00

WALKERS WELCOME · CYCLISTS WELCOME

### Red Gables Country B&B

Longford, Newport TF10 8LN **t** (01952) 811118 **e** sandracorbett@red-gables.com

**red-gables.com**

Red Cables Country B&B is a beautiful country house offering newly converted three bedroomed, en suite accommodation in coach house set in five acres of private grounds.

**open** All year
**bedrooms** 2 double, 1 twin
**bathrooms** All en suite
**payment** Cash, cheques

Room General

## NEWTON ST MARGARETS, Herefordshire Map ref 2A1

★★★★
GUEST ACCOMMODATION

B&B PER ROOM PER NIGHT
S £30.00–£40.00
D £60.00–£80.00

EVENING MEAL PER PERSON
£14.50–£20.00

### Marises Barn

Newton St Margarets, Hereford HR2 0QG **t** (01981) 510101 **e** marisesbandb@aol.com

**marisesbarn.co.uk** GUEST REVIEWS · SPECIAL OFFERS

Marises Barn offers a very warm welcome and quality bed and breakfast accommodation in Herefordshire's beautiful Golden Valley.

**open** All year
**bedrooms** 2 double, 1 twin, 1 single
**bathrooms** 2 en suite, 2 private
**payment** Cash, cheques

Room General 12 Leisure

## NORFOLK BROADS

*See under Aylsham, Beccles, Brundall, Coltishall, Great Yarmouth, Hevingham, Hickling, Lowestoft, Norwich, South Walsham, Wroxham*

## NORTHAMPTON, Northamptonshire Map ref 2C1

★★★★
BED & BREAKFAST

B&B PER ROOM PER NIGHT
S £55.00–£65.00
D £65.00–£80.00

*Grand Prix Silverstone – Jul 3-night special weekend B&B. Champagne, transport to circuit and return. POA. Advance booking essential.*

### Lake House Bed and Breakfast

Brixworth Hall Park, Brixworth, Northampton NN6 9DE **t** (01604) 880280
**e** rosemarytuckley@talktalk.net

**brixworthlakehouse.com** SPECIAL OFFERS • REAL-TIME BOOKING

**open** All year except Christmas and New Year
**bedrooms** 1 double, 1 family
**bathrooms** All en suite
**payment** Cash, cheques, euros

A deluxe 18thC converted coach house and stables set in 4.5 acres of tranquil gardens and koi lake. The bedrooms, having lake view, are beautifully appointed and are supplied with large fluffy towels and dressing gowns. Breakfast served in grand dining room or conservatory. We use locally grown products where possible.

**SAT NAV** *NN6 9DE* **ONLINE MAP**

Room General Leisure

## NORTHAMPTON, Northamptonshire Map ref 2C1

★★★★
GUEST ACCOMMODATION
SILVER AWARD

B&B PER ROOM PER NIGHT
S Min £34.00
D Min £62.50

EVENING MEAL PER PERSON
Min £12.00

### The Poplars

Cross Street, Moulton NN3 7RZ **t** (01604) 643983 **e** info@thepoplarshotel.com

**thepoplarshotel.com**

**open** All year except Christmas and New Year
**bedrooms** 6 double, 1 twin, 6 single, 4 family
**bathrooms** 13 en suite
**payment** Credit/debit cards, cash, cheques

A small, comfortable, family-run country hotel of character, situated in picturesque village of Moulton. Perfect location for visiting family, friends and local attractions. Special weekend rates. Quality food provided, sourced locally whenever possible. Licensed.

**SAT NAV** *NN3 7RZ* **ONLINE MAP**

Room General Leisure

## NORTON DISNEY, Lincolnshire Map ref 4C2

★★★★
BED & BREAKFAST

B&B PER ROOM PER NIGHT
S £45.00
D £57.00–£60.00

### River Farm House B&B

Clay Lane, Norton Disney LN6 9JS **t** (01522) 788600 **e** amandajane500@aol.com

**pyrah.com/riverfarmhouse**

A warm welcome awaits you at this traditional Lincolnshire farmhouse. Well placed for access to the historic town of Newark and the cathedral city of Lincoln.

**open** All year
**bedrooms** 2 double, 1 twin
**payment** Cash, cheques

Room General P

## NORWICH, Norfolk Map ref 3C1

★★★★
GUEST ACCOMMODATION

B&B PER ROOM PER NIGHT
S £35.00–£40.00
D £55.00–£60.00

### Becklands

105 Holt Road, Norwich NR10 3AB **t** (01603) 898582 **e** becklands@aol.com

**becklandsguesthouse.com**

Quietly located modern house overlooking open countryside five miles north of Norwich. Central for the Broads and coastal areas.

**open** All year
**bedrooms** 3 double, 2 twin, 2 single, 1 family
**bathrooms** All en suite
**payment** Credit/debit cards, cash, cheques

Room General P

## NORWICH, Norfolk Map ref 3C1

★★★★
CAMPUS

PER PERSON PER NIGHT
BED ONLY £43.00-£49.00
B&B £48.00-£54.00

*Discounts available at weekends on single rooms.*

# Broadview Lodge

University of East Anglia, Earlham Road, Norwich NR4 7TJ **t** (01603) 591918
**e** guestsuite@uea.ac.uk

**uea.ac.uk/conferences** SPECIAL OFFERS

**open** All Year except Christmas and New Year
**bedrooms** 29 single, 31 double/twin, 2 triple
Total no of beds 74
**bathrooms** 60 en suite
**payment** Credit/debit cards, cash/cheques

At the heart of the UEA campus, hotel-standard bedrooms at value-for-money prices. On campus, visit the Sportspark with Olympic-size pool or the iconic Sainsbury Centre for visual arts. The city centre is a few minutes by car and there is a frequent direct bus service.

**SAT NAV** *NR4 7TJ*

Room General Leisure

## NORWICH, Norfolk Map ref 3C1

★★★★
BED & BREAKFAST

B&B PER ROOM PER NIGHT
S Max £29.50
D Max £55.00

# Cavell House

The Common, Swardeston, Norwich NR14 8DZ **t** (01508) 578195 **e** joljean.harris@virgin.net

Birthplace of nurse Edith Cavell. Georgian farmhouse on edge of Swardeston village. Off B1113 five miles south of Norwich centre. Near university, new hospital and showground.

**open** All year except Christmas
**bedrooms** 1 double, 1 twin/single
**payment** Cash, cheques

WALKERS WELCOME CYCLISTS WELCOME

Room General Leisure

## NORWICH, Norfolk Map ref 3C1

★★★
GUEST ACCOMMODATION

B&B PER ROOM PER NIGHT
S £38.00–£43.00
D £43.00–£48.00

# Edmar Lodge

64 Earlham Road, Norwich NR2 3DF **t** (01603) 615599 **e** mail@edmarlodge.co.uk

**edmarlodge.co.uk** GUEST REVIEWS

**open** All year
**bedrooms** 3 double, 1 twin, 1 family
**bathrooms** All en suite
**payment** Credit/debit cards, cash, cheques, euros

Edmar Lodge is a family-run guesthouse where you will receive a warm welcome from Ray and Sue. We are situated only ten minutes' walk from the city centre. All rooms have en suite facilities and digital TV. We are well known for our excellent breakfasts that set you up for the day.

**SAT NAV** *NR2 3DF* **ONLINE MAP**

Room General

## Using map references

The map references refer to the colour maps at the front of this guide. The first figure is the map number, the letter and figure that follow indicate the grid reference on the map.

## NORWICH, Norfolk Map ref 3C1

★★★★
GUEST ACCOMMODATION

B&B PER ROOM PER NIGHT
S £30.00–£35.00
D £58.00–£62.00

### Manor Barn House

Back Lane, Rackheath, Norwich NR13 6NN **t** (01603) 783543 **e** jane.roger@manorbarnhouse.co.uk

**manorbarnhouse.co.uk** SPECIAL OFFERS

**open** All year
**bedrooms** 3 double, 2 twin
**bathrooms** 4 en suite, 1 private
**payment** Cash, cheques

A warm welcome awaits you at our 17thC Norfolk barn conversion set in pleasant gardens. Excellent selection of locally produced and home-cooked foods. Good pub food within walking distance. Situated five miles north of Norwich down a quiet lane just off A1151. Very convenient for Broads and coast. Ample parking.

**SAT NAV** *NR13 6NN* **ONLINE MAP**

Room General 5 P Leisure

## NORWICH, Norfolk Map ref 3C1

★★★
GUEST HOUSE

B&B PER ROOM PER NIGHT
S £30.00–£40.00
D £54.00–£58.00

### Marlborough House

22 Stracey Road, Norwich NR1 1EZ **t** (01603) 628005

Long-established family hotel close to city centre, new Riverside development, Castle Mall, museum and cathedral. All double, twin and family rooms are en suite. Licensed bar, car park.

**open** All year except Christmas
**bedrooms** 3 double, 1 twin, 5 single, 2 family
**bathrooms** 6 en suite
**payment** Cash, cheques, euros

Room General P

## OAKHAM, Rutland Map ref 4C3

★★★★
BED & BREAKFAST

B&B PER ROOM PER NIGHT
S £45.00–£55.00
D £75.00–£85.00

*Discounts are available for stays of 3 or more nights.*

### 17 Northgate

Oakham LE15 6QR **t** (01572) 759271 **e** dane@danegould.wanadoo.co.uk

**17northgate.co.uk**

**open** All year except Christmas and New Year
**bedrooms** 1 double, 1 twin
**bathrooms** All en suite
**payment** Credit/debit cards, cash, cheques, euros

A recently renovated, 300-year-old thatched farmhouse in the centre of Oakham close to Rutland Water, the church, railway station and the excellent pubs and restaurants. The two en suite rooms are newly built, with their own patios and private entrance from the drive, where off-road parking is available.

**SAT NAV** *LE15 6QR*

Room General P Leisure

## ORSETT, Essex Map ref 3B3

★★★★
GUEST ACCOMMODATION

B&B PER ROOM PER NIGHT
S £30.00–£35.00
D Min £45.00

### Jays Lodge

Chapel Farm, Baker Street, Grays RM16 3LJ **t** (01375) 891663 **e** info@jayslodge.co.uk

**jayslodge.co.uk**

Barn conversion to provide twelve rooms all with en suite, mini kitchen and colour television. Ample, free and secure parking available.

**open** All year
**bedrooms** 2 double, 8 twin, 2 single
**bathrooms** All en suite
**payment** Credit/debit cards, cash, cheques, euros

Room General P

## OVERSTRAND, Norfolk Map ref 3C1

★★★
BED & BREAKFAST

B&B PER ROOM PER NIGHT
S £30.00–£32.00
D £50.00–£54.00

### Cliff Cottage Bed and Breakfast

18 High Street, Overstrand NR27 0AB **t** (01263) 578179 **e** roymin@btinternet.com

**cliffcottagebandb.com** GUEST REVIEWS

18thC cottage offering one double and one twin room, both en suite. Tea/coffee facilities, colour TV, central heating, private parking, use of garden. Good food.

**open** All year
**bedrooms** 1 double, 1 twin
**bathrooms** All en suite
**payment** Cash, cheques, euros

Room TV General 5 P

## PEAK DISTRICT

*See under Bakewell, Bamford, Buxton, Castleton, Chapel-en-le-Frith, Hope*

## PERSHORE, Worcestershire Map ref 2B1

★★★
INN

B&B PER ROOM PER NIGHT
S £30.00–£45.00
D £50.00–£75.00

EVENING MEAL PER PERSON
£8.50–£15.00

### Anchor Inn & Restaurant

Cotheridge Lane, Eckington, Nr Pershore WR10 3BA **t** (01386) 750356 **e** anchoreck@aol.com

**anchoreckington.co.uk**

**open** All year
**bedrooms** 2 double, 3 twin
**bathrooms** All en suite
**payment** Credit/debit cards, cash, cheques

Owner operated free house, real ales, log fires and comfortable en suite rooms, in a village location.

**SAT NAV** *WR10 3BA* **ONLINE MAP**

Room TV General P Leisure

## PERSHORE, Worcestershire Map ref 2B1

★★★★
BED & BREAKFAST
SILVER AWARD

B&B PER ROOM PER NIGHT
S £40.00–£45.00
D £65.00–£70.00

*Special 3- and 4-night breaks available – see website for details.*

### Arbour House

Main Road, Wyre Piddle, Pershore WR10 2HU **t** (01386) 555833 **e** liz@arbour-house.com

**arbour-house.com** SPECIAL OFFERS

**open** All year
**bedrooms** 2 double, 2 twin
**bathrooms** 3 en suite, 1 private
**payment** Cash, cheques, euros

A fine Grade II Listed character home with oak beams, overlooking Bredon Hill and close to the River Avon. Comfortable accommodation and generous breakfasts in a relaxed, friendly atmosphere. Riverside pub in village. No smoking. Private car park. An ideal base for visiting the Cotswolds, Stratford, Worcester and Malvern.

**SAT NAV** *WR10 2HU* **ONLINE MAP**

WALKERS WELCOME CYCLISTS WELCOME

Room TV General P Leisure

## What if I need to cancel?

It is advisable to check the proprietor's cancellation policy in case you have to change your plans at a later date.

## PULHAM MARKET, Norfolk Map ref 3B2

★★★★★
GUEST ACCOMMODATION
GOLD AWARD

B&B PER ROOM PER NIGHT
S £45.00–£65.00
D £65.00–£80.00

### Old Bakery

The Old Bakery, Church Walk, Pulham Market IP21 4SL **t** (01379) 676492 **e** info@theoldbakery.net

**theoldbakery.net** GUEST REVIEWS • SPECIAL OFFERS

Oak-beamed former bakery in Waveney Valley conservation village with two inns. Beautifully appointed spacious en suite bedrooms, garden and delicious locally produced breakfasts. Ideally located for Broads, coast and countryside.

**open** All year
**bedrooms** 1 double, 1 twin, 1 family
**bathrooms** All en suite
**payment** Credit/debit cards, cash, cheques

Room General 10 P Leisure

## REDDITCH, Worcestershire Map ref 4B3

★★★
INN

B&B PER ROOM PER NIGHT
S £50.00–£55.00
D £50.00–£55.00

### White Hart Inn

157 Evesham Road, Redditch B97 5EJ **t** (01527) 545442 **e** enquiries@whitehartredditch.co.uk

Ten bedrooms. Newly completed free large car park. Specially adapted disabled room. No smoking. Free internet access.

**open** All year
**bedrooms** 3 double, 6 twin, 1 family
**bathrooms** All en suite
**payment** Credit/debit cards, cash, cheques

Room General P

## ROSS-ON-WYE, Herefordshire Map ref 2A1

★★★★
BED & BREAKFAST

B&B PER ROOM PER NIGHT
S £25.00–£45.00
D £40.00–£60.00

EVENING MEAL PER PERSON
Max £18.50

*Pay a maximum of £18.50 for an a la carte dinner, regardless of the menu price, if you are a resident.*

### Broome Farm

Peterstow, Ross-on-Wye HR9 6QG **t** (01989) 562824 **e** broomefarm@tesco.net

**broomefarmhouse.co.uk**

**open** All year
**bedrooms** 2 double, 1 family
**bathrooms** All en suite
**payment** Credit/debit cards, cash, cheques

Working cider farm, providing en suite accommodation. Licensed dining room with a la carte menu featuring local produce. Set in tranquil countryside, looking over rural Herefordshire. Only two miles from the town of Ross-on-Wye. Orchard walks, cream teas and cider tasting available.

**SAT NAV** *HR9 6QG* **ONLINE MAP**

Room General 10 P Leisure

## ROYSTON, Hertfordshire Map ref 2D1

★★★★
GUEST ACCOMMODATION

B&B PER ROOM PER NIGHT
S £50.00–£55.00
D £70.00–£75.00

### Hall Farm

Hall Lane, Great Chishill Nr Royston SG8 8SH **t** (01763) 838263 **e** wisehall@tiscali.co.uk

**hallfarmbb.co.uk**

**open** All year
**bedrooms** 1 double, 1 twin, 1 family
**bathrooms** All en suite
**payment** Credit/debit cards, cash, cheques, euros

Georgian manor house in secluded garden. Ground-floor room with wheelchair access and flat-floor shower available. Quiet accommodation only 30 minutes Cambridge/Stansted. London one hour by train. On B1039 at Saffron Walden end of village.

**SAT NAV** *SG8 8SH* **ONLINE MAP**

Room General P Leisure

## RUSKINGTON, Lincolnshire Map ref 3A1

★★★
FARMHOUSE

B&B PER ROOM PER NIGHT
S Min £25.00
D Min £50.00

### Sunnyside Farm

Leasingham Lane, Ruskington, Sleaford NG34 9AH **t** (01526) 833010
**e** sunnyside_farm@btinternet.com

**sunnysidefarm.co.uk**

A family-run farmhouse with en suite guest bedrooms. Warm, friendly welcome. Local golf courses. Coast 40 miles. Boston, Grantham, Lincoln, Newark all within easy reach.

**open** All year
**bedrooms** 1 double, 1 twin
**bathrooms** All en suite
**payment** Cash, cheques

Room General Leisure

## RUTLAND WATER

*See under Empingham, Oakham*

## SAFFRON WALDEN, Essex Map ref 2D1

★★★★
FARMHOUSE

B&B PER ROOM PER NIGHT
S £28.00–£35.00
D £56.00–£70.00

### Rockells Farm

Duddenhoe End, Saffron Walden CB11 4UY **t** (01763) 838053 **e** evert.westerhuis@tiscali.co.uk

**rockellsfarm.co.uk**

Georgian house in rolling countryside with plenty of opportunities for walking and sightseeing. The three-acre lake provides excellent fishing. Stansted Airport is 30 minutes away. London one hour.

**open** All year except Christmas
**bedrooms** 1 twin, 1 single, 1 family
**bathrooms** All en suite
**payment** Cash, cheques, euros

Room General Leisure

## ST ALBANS, Hertfordshire Map ref 2D1

★★★
BED & BREAKFAST

B&B PER ROOM PER NIGHT
S £30.00–£36.00
D £50.00–£58.00

### Tresco

76 Clarence Road, St Albans AL1 4NG **t** (01727) 864880 **e** pat_leggatt@hotmail.com

**geocities.com/patleggatt/index.htm**

Spacious Edwardian house with quiet, comfortable rooms and pleasant conservatory. Park nearby. Easy walk to station for fast trains to London (20 minutes).

**open** All year
**bedrooms** 1 twin, 1 single
**payment** Cash, cheques

Room General

## ST IVES, Cambridgeshire Map ref 3A2

★★★★★
GUEST ACCOMMODATION
SILVER AWARD

B&B PER ROOM PER NIGHT
S £65.00–£72.00
D £75.00–£85.00

*Close to Huntingdon and Newmarket races. Ask too about our walking, cycling and birdwatching breaks including maps and packed lunches.*

### Cheriton House

Mill Street, Houghton PE28 2AZ **t** (01480) 464004 **e** sales@cheritonhousecambs.co.uk

**cheritonhousecambs.co.uk**

**open** All year
**bedrooms** 4 double, 1 twin
**bathrooms** All en suite
**payment** Credit/debit cards, cash, cheques

Award-winning B&B 150yds from the river and the mill in picturesque village of Houghton. Two miles from Huntingdon, just 20-25 minutes from Cambridge and Ely. Great breakfasts, home-made breads, jams, marmalade, cakes. Large garden, riverside walks to several good pubs with attractive gardens in summer and roaring log fires in winter.

**SAT NAV** *PE28 2AZ* **ONLINE MAP**

Room General Leisure

## Where are the maps?

Colour maps can be found at the front of the guide. They pinpoint the location of all accommodation found in the regional sections.

## SANDY, Bedfordshire Map ref 2D1

★★★★
BED & BREAKFAST

B&B PER ROOM PER NIGHT
S £40.00
D £65.00

### Pantiles

6 Swaden, Sandy SG19 2DA **t** (01767) 680668 **e** pantilesbandb@live.com

**thepantilesbandb.co.uk**

**open** All year except Christmas and New Year
**bedrooms** 2 double, 1 twin
**bathrooms** All en suite
**payment** Credit/debit cards, cash, cheques

The Pantiles is a converted onion loft in a lovely wooded valley, overlooking large gardens with potager and fruit trees. A warm welcome is assured and we offer home-made jam and cakes. Easy access to A1, mainline railway and local services and attractions. French and some Spanish spoken.

**SAT NAV** *SG19 2DA*

Room General P Leisure

## SANDY, Bedfordshire Map ref 2D1

★★★★
BED & BREAKFAST

B&B PER ROOM PER NIGHT
S £30.00
D £50.00–£60.00

### The Tythe Barn

Drove Road, Gamlingay, Sandy SG19 2HT **t** (01767) 650156 **e** thetythebarn@supanet.com

**tythebb.co.uk**

A sympathetically converted listed barn, surrounded by our own paddocks. Rooms are en suite and comfortably furnished. Situated on Bedfordshire/Cambridgeshire border.

**open** All year except Christmas and New Year
**bedrooms** 1 double, 1 twin, 1 single
**bathrooms** All en suite
**payment** Credit/debit cards, cash, cheques

Room General P Leisure

## SHERINGHAM, Norfolk Map ref 3B1

★★★★
GUEST HOUSE

B&B PER ROOM PER NIGHT
S £26.00–£28.00
D £52.00–£56.00

### Sheringham Lodge

Cromer Road, Sheringham NR26 8RS **t** (01263) 821954 **e** mikewalker19@hotmail.com

**sheringhamlodge.co.uk**

Edwardian detached house. Centrally located. Convenient for beach and town. Off-road parking. Non-smoking. No pets. No children under five years.

**open** All year except Christmas and New Year
**bedrooms** 3 double, 1 twin, 1 single
**bathrooms** 4 en suite, 1 private
**payment** Cash, cheques

Room General 5 P Leisure

## SHERINGHAM, Norfolk Map ref 3B1

★★★★
GUEST ACCOMMODATION
SILVER AWARD

B&B PER ROOM PER NIGHT
S £45.00–£50.00
D £70.00–£76.00

EVENING MEAL PER PERSON
£15.00–£20.00

*Anniversary stays, alone or with friends and family. Packages include celebratory meal (2-8 covers dinner, 6-20 covers buffet). Price on application.*

### Viburnham House B&B

Augusta Street, Sheringham NR26 8LB **t** (01263) 822528 **e** viburnhamhouse@aol.com

**viburnhamhouse.co.uk**

**open** All year
**bedrooms** 2 double, 1 twin
**bathrooms** All en suite
**payment** Credit/debit cards, cash, cheques

Relax, unwind, and refresh in real comfort at Viburnham House. Great hospitality, personal friendly service in period surroundings. An easy stroll to the sea and the town centre. All rooms en suite. Visit us by car or train. Children over six and well-behaved dogs welcome too.

**SAT NAV** *NR26 8LB*

Room General 6 Leisure

## SHERWOOD FOREST

*See under Newark*

## SHIFNAL, Shropshire Map ref 4A3

★★★
INN

B&B PER ROOM PER NIGHT
S Min £42.50
D £52.50–£57.50

EVENING MEAL PER PERSON
£10.00–£25.00

### Odfellows – The Wine Bar

Market Place, Shifnal TF11 9AU **t** (01952) 461517 **e** odfellows@odley.co.uk

**open** All year
**bedrooms** 5 double, 1 twin, 1 family
**bathrooms** All en suite
**payment** Credit/debit cards, cash, cheques

Comfortable, well-appointed bedrooms upstairs, with a lively, friendly bar/restaurant downstairs. Modern British food delights, complemented by an intelligently assembled wine list and draught-beer range. Served caddishly late, the cooked breakfast is well worth the wait, whilst the early birds are amply served the continental.

**SAT NAV** *TF11 9AU*

Room General P

## SHINGLE STREET, Suffolk Map ref 3C2

★★★★
BED & BREAKFAST

B&B PER ROOM PER NIGHT
D Min £60.00

EVENING MEAL PER PERSON
£12.50–£15.00

### Lark Cottage

Shingle Street, Nr Woodbridge IP12 3BE **t** (01394) 411292

Beachside bungalow, very quiet location. Interesting sea/land birds, plants of special interest. Sutton Hoo four miles, Snape Maltings 14 miles. One double with private shower/wc and lounge with TV.

**open** All year except Christmas and New Year
**bedrooms** 1 double
**bathrooms** 1 private
**payment** Cash, cheques

Room General P Leisure

## SHREWSBURY, Shropshire Map ref 4A3

★★★★
GUEST HOUSE

B&B PER ROOM PER NIGHT
S £40.00–£45.00
D £60.00–£70.00

*Discounted rates available for longer stays.*

### Abbey Court House

134 Abbey Foregate, Shrewsbury SY2 6AU **t** (01743) 364416 **e** info@abbeycourt.biz

**abbeycourt.biz**

**open** All year
**bedrooms** 3 double, 4 twin, 2 single, 1 family
**bathrooms** All en suite
**payment** Credit/debit cards, cash, cheques, euros

Abbey Court offers quality accommodation in a Grade II Listed building. Refurbished to a high standard. Comfortable en suite guest rooms each with hospitality tray, TV and telephone. Convenient for the town centre. Off-road parking and some ground-floor rooms. Superb breakfasts include vegetarian options. A warm welcome is guaranteed.

**SAT NAV** *SY2 6AU* **ONLINE MAP**

Room General P

## Place index

If you know where you want to stay, the index by place name at the back of the guide will give you the page number listing accommodation in your chosen town, city or village. Check out the other useful indexes too.

## SIBTON, Suffolk Map ref 3C2

★★★★
INN

B&B PER ROOM PER NIGHT
S £50.00–£60.00
D £75.00–£85.00

EVENING MEAL PER PERSON
£20.00–£30.00

*Discounts on 4 or more nights. Special winter deals often available. Telephone or see website for further details.*

### Sibton White Horse Inn

Halesworth Road, Sibton, Saxmundham IP17 2JJ **t** (01728) 660337 **e** info@sibtonwhitehorseinn.co.uk

**sibtonwhitehorseinn.co.uk** GUEST REVIEWS • SPECIAL OFFERS

**open** All year
**bedrooms** 3 double, 1 twin, 2 single, 1 family
**bathrooms** All en suite
**payment** Credit/debit cards, cash, cheques

You probably couldn't find a more quintessential country inn. Grade II Listed, wonderful features and timber frame dating back to 1580. Quiet village 15 minutes from coast. Peaceful attractive en suite bedrooms in separate building within spacious gardens. Good food, all freshly prepared, enchanting dining areas. Special in both summer and winter.

**SAT NAV** *IP17 2JJ* **ONLINE MAP**

Room General Leisure

## SKEGNESS, Lincolnshire Map ref 4D2

★★★
GUEST ACCOMMODATION

B&B PER ROOM PER NIGHT
S £30.00–£47.00
D £60.00–£90.00

EVENING MEAL PER PERSON
£11.50–£15.00

### Chatsworth

15-16 North Parade, Skegness PE25 2UB **t** (01754) 764177 **e** info@chatsworthhotel.co.uk

**chatsworthskegness.co.uk**

The Chatsworth is centrally situated close to many of the main attractions. Delicious home-made food, friendly staff, passenger lift, comfortable beds and an outstanding position overlooking the seafront.

**open** March to December
**bedrooms** 14 double, 15 twin, 10 single, 1 family
**bathrooms** All en suite
**payment** Credit/debit cards, cash, cheques, euros

Room General

## SKEGNESS, Lincolnshire Map ref 4D2

★★★
GUEST ACCOMMODATION

B&B PER ROOM PER NIGHT
S £20.00–£23.00
D £40.00 £46.00

### The Grafton Guest House

15 Seaview Road, Skegness PE25 1BW **t** (01574) 766158 **e** thegraftonhotelskegness@fsmail.net

**grafton-skegness.co.uk** SPECIAL OFFERS

The Grafton is a coastal bed & breakfast guesthouse, offering quality accommodation. Situated just off the seafront and close to the bowling green, gardens, theatre, town centre and all other amenities.

**open** All year except Christmas
**bedrooms** 5 double, 2 twin, 1 single, 5 family
**bathrooms** All en suite
**payment** Cash, cheques

Room General Leisure

## SKEGNESS, Lincolnshire Map ref 4D2

★★★
GUEST ACCOMMODATION

B&B PER ROOM PER NIGHT
D £42.00–£52.00

EVENING MEAL PER PERSON
£8.50–£10.50

### Roosevelt Lodge

59 Drummond Road, Skegness PE25 3EQ **t** (01754) 766548 **e** skegnessinfo@e-lindsey.gov.uk

A warm and friendly welcome awaits you at Roosevelt Lodge, a popular family-run hotel, which offers an excellent menu and comfortable accommodation. Situated near the seafront, town centre, bowling green, theatre and all other amenities.

**open** All year
**bedrooms** 3 double, 3 twin, 1 family
**bathrooms** 6 en suite, 1 private
**payment** Credit/debit cards, cash, cheques

Room General Leisure

### What if I need to cancel?

It's advisable to check the proprietor's cancellation policy at the time of booking in case you have to change your plans.

## SOLIHULL, West Midlands Map ref 4B3

★★★
GUEST HOUSE
SILVER AWARD

B&B PER ROOM PER NIGHT
S Min £25.00
D Min £50.00

### Acorn Guest House

29 Links Drive, Solihull B91 2DJ **t** (0121) 705 5241 **e** acorn.wood@btinternet.com

**acorn-guest-house.com**

**open** All year except Christmas and New Year
**bedrooms** 1 double, 2 twin, 2 single
**bathrooms** 1 en suite
**payment** Cash, cheques

Homely service in a comfortable, quiet, superb family home overlooking golf course. All rooms have wash basin, fridge, microwave, hairdryer, hospitality tray. Walk to Solihull centre and Touchwood Shopping Centre. Plentiful choice of local restaurants. Three miles to NEC, Birmingham International Rail and Airport. Car parking.

**SAT NAV** *B91 2DJ*

Room TV General P

## SOUTH COCKERINGTON, Lincolnshire Map ref 4D2

★★★★
BED & BREAKFAST
SILVER AWARD

B&B PER ROOM PER NIGHT
S £37.50–£42.50
D £55.00–£65.00

### West View Bed & Breakfast

South View Lane, South Cockerington, Louth LN11 7ED **t** (01507) 327209 & 07855 291185
**e** enquiries@west-view.co.uk

**west-view.co.uk** GUEST REVIEWS • SPECIAL OFFERS • REAL-TIME BOOKING

Single-storey barn conversion with old-world charm. All bedrooms en suite. beamed ceilings, disabled facilities, newly painted and furnished, broadband internet access.

**open** All year except Christmas
**bedrooms** 2 double, 1 twin
**bathrooms** All en suite
**payment** Cash, cheques

Room TV General P Leisure

## SOUTH WALSHAM, Norfolk Map ref 3C1

★★★★
GUEST ACCOMMODATION

B&B PER ROOM PER NIGHT
S Min £35.00
D £50.00–£55.00

### Old Hall Farm

Newport Road, South Walsham, Norwich NR13 6DS **t** (01603) 270271 **e** veronica@oldhallfarm.co.uk

**oldhallfarm.co.uk**

**open** April to October
**bedrooms** 2 double, 1 twin
**bathrooms** All en suite
**payment** Cash, cheques

17thC thatched farmhouse with large garden on the edge of Broadland village. Within walking distance of Fairhaven Gardens, Ranworth and St Lawrence Arts Centre, South Walsham. Wide range of cooked breakfasts using our own free-range eggs. Business guests welcome. Wireless broadband available. Non-smoking.

**SAT NAV** *NR13 6DS*

Room TV General P Leisure

## What do the star ratings mean?

For a detailed explanation of the quality and facilities represented by the stars, please refer to the information pages at the back of this guide.

## SOUTHWOLD, Suffolk Map ref 3C2

★★★★
**BED & BREAKFAST**

**B&B PER ROOM PER NIGHT**
S Min £45.00
D £75.00–£85.00

*7 nights for the price of 6 (weekly).*

### Poplar Hall

Frostenden Corner, Frostenden, Southwold NR34 7JA **t** (01502) 578549 **e** poplarhall@tiscali.co.uk

**southwold.ws/poplar-hall**

**open** All year except Christmas and New Year
**bedrooms** 1 double, 1 single, 1 suite
**bathrooms** 1 en suite, 2 private
**payment** Cash, cheques

Peaceful and quiet, yet only minutes from the lovely seaside town of Southwold, Poplar Hall is a 16thC thatched house in a 1.5-acre garden. Luxury accommodation with TV, tea/coffee facilities and vanity units in all rooms. Enjoy our famed breakfasts of fresh fruit, local fish, sausage, bacon and home-made preserves.

**SAT NAV** *NR34 7JA*

Room General 9 P Leisure

## SPILSBY, Lincolnshire Map ref 4D2

★★★★
**BED & BREAKFAST SILVER AWARD**

**B&B PER ROOM PER NIGHT**
S £30.00
D £60.00

### Spye House

Main Road, West Keal, Spilsby PE23 4BE **t** (01790) 752102 **e** spye.house@btinternet.com

**open** All year
**bedrooms** 2 double
**bathrooms** 1 en suite, 1 private
**payment** Cash, cheques

Spye House is a large, detached, comfortable family home with quality en suite accommodation, standing in large attractive grounds. Home baking and local produce are specialities. Parking is on the house drive.

**SAT NAV** *PE23 4BE*

Room General P

## STAFFORD, Staffordshire Map ref 4B3

★★★
**FARMHOUSE**

**B&B PER ROOM PER NIGHT**
S Max £35.00
D Max £55.00

### Rooks Nest Farm

Weston Bank, Weston, Stafford ST18 0BA **t** (01889) 270624 **e** info@rooksnest.co.uk

**rooksnest.co.uk**

Modern farmhouse on working farm, with far-reaching views over the Trent valley. Close to Weston Hall and County Showground, easy access to all Staffordshire attractions.

**open** All year
**bedrooms** 1 double, 1 twin
**bathrooms** All en suite
**payment** Cash, cheques

Room General P

## STAFFORD, Staffordshire Map ref 4B3

★★★
GUEST HOUSE

B&B PER ROOM PER NIGHT
S £30.00–£40.00
D £54.00–£60.00

EVENING MEAL PER PERSON
£6.00–£14.00

### Wyndale Guest House

199 Corporation Street, Stafford ST16 3LQ **t** (01785) 223069 **e** wyndale@aol.com

**wyndaleguesthouse.co.uk**

**open** All year except Christmas
**bedrooms** 2 double, 2 twin, 2 single, 2 family
**bathrooms** 5 en suite
**payment** Credit/debit cards, cash, cheques

The Wyndale is a comfortable Victorian house conveniently situated 0.25 miles from the town centre and en route to the county showground, hospital, university and technology park.

**SAT NAV** *ST16 3LQ* **ONLINE MAP**

Room General

## STAMFORD, Lincolnshire Map ref 3A1

★★★
RESTAURANT WITH ROOMS

B&B PER ROOM PER NIGHT
S £50.00–£75.00
D £65.00–£75.00

EVENING MEAL PER PERSON
£15.00–£20.00

### Candlesticks

1 Church Lane, Stamford PE9 2JU **t** (01780) 764033 **e** pinto@breathemail.com

**candlestickshotel.co.uk**

**open** All year
**bedrooms** 3 double, 3 twin, 2 single
**bathrooms** All en suite
**payment** Credit/debit cards

Family-run since 1975. Located in a quiet lane in the oldest part of Stamford town centre. Easy access to rail, bus and road travel. The award-winning restaurant has an extensive menu with Portuguese and French influences, with a superb list of wines and ports to complement your food.

**SAT NAV** *PE9 2JU*

Room General

## STANDON, Hertfordshire Map ref 2D1

★★★★
GUEST ACCOMMODATION

B&B PER ROOM PER NIGHT
S £45.00–£50.00
D £60.00–£70.00

### The Granary – Mill End Farm

Mill End Farm, Standon, Ware SG11 1LR **t** (01920) 823955 **e** tricia@thegranaryatmillendfarm.co.uk

**thegranaryatmillendfarm.co.uk**

The Granary, a recently converted barn, is located at the end of Mill End Lane, in the historic Hertfordshire village of Standon, a short distance from the A120/A10 junction.

**open** All year except Christmas and New Year
**bedrooms** 1 double, 1 twin
**bathrooms** All en suite
**payment** Cash, cheques

Room

## Country Code always follow the Country Code

- Be safe – plan ahead and follow any signs
- Leave gates and property as you find them
- Protect plants and animals, and take your litter home
- Keep dogs under close control
- Consider other people

**STANSTED, Essex Map ref 2D1**

★★★★
GUEST ACCOMMODATION
SILVER AWARD

B&B PER ROOM PER NIGHT
S £50.00–£60.00
D £75.00–£90.00

## The Cottage

71 Birchanger Lane, Birchanger, Bishop's Stortford CM23 5QA **t** (01279) 812349
**e** bookings@thecottagebirchanger.co.uk

**thecottagebirchanger.co.uk**

**open** All year except Christmas and New Year
**bedrooms** 7 double, 5 twin, 2 single
**bathrooms** 13 en suite, 1 private
**payment** Credit/debit cards, cash, cheques

17thC Listed house with panelled rooms and woodburning stove. Conservatory-style breakfast room overlooks mature garden. Quiet, peaceful village setting yet near M11 junction 8, Stansted Airport and Bishop's Stortford. Ample off-road parking. Guest rooms furnished in traditional cottage style, with colour TV, tea/coffee facilities and free Wi-Fi Internet. Award-winning pub in village.

**SAT NAV** *CM23 5QA* **ONLINE MAP**

Room General Leisure

**STANSTED, Essex Map ref 2D1**

★★★★
GUEST ACCOMMODATION

B&B PER ROOM PER NIGHT
S £60.00
D £65.00

EVENING MEAL PER PERSON
£7.50–£20.00

## The White House

Smiths Green, Takeley CM22 6NR **t** (01279) 870257 **e** enquiries@whitehousestansted.co.uk

**whitehousestansted.co.uk** GUEST REVIEWS • SPECIAL OFFERS • REAL-TIME BOOKING

**open** All year except Christmas and New Year
**bedrooms** 1 double, 1 twin, 1 single
**bathrooms** 2 en suite, 1 private
**payment** Credit/debit cards, cash, cheques, euros

A 15thC manor house set in one acre with ample parking. Two miles from Stansted Airport (but not on flight path). Recently renovated. Modern, en suite facilities in a traditional family environment. Evening meal available at nearby Lion and Lamb pub/restaurant, which is also owned by Mike and Linda.

**SAT NAV** *CM22 6NR* **ONLINE MAP**

Room General Leisure

**STANTON-BY-BRIDGE, Derbyshire Map ref 4B3**

★★★★
GUEST ACCOMMODATION
SILVER AWARD

B&B PER ROOM PER NIGHT
S £35.00
D £55.00–£65.00

## Ivy House Farm

Ingleby Road, Stanton-by-Bridge, Derby DE73 7HT **t** (01332) 863152 **e** info@ivy-house-farm.com

**ivy-house-farm.com**

The bed and breakfast has been converted from farm buildings and completed in February 2000. We offer peace, comfort and relaxation. Three rooms are on the ground floor, one with disabled facilities.

**open** All year
**bedrooms** 4 double, 2 twin
**bathrooms** All en suite
**payment** Credit/debit cards, cash, cheques

Room General Leisure

**STOKE-ON-TRENT, Staffordshire Map ref 4B2**

★★★★
BED & BREAKFAST
SILVER AWARD

B&B PER ROOM PER NIGHT
S £35.00–£40.00
D £55.00–£65.00

## Cedar Tree Cottage

41 Longton Road, Trentham, Stoke-on-Trent ST4 8ND **t** (01782) 644751 **e** n.portas@btinternet.com

A warm welcome is assured with comfortable bedrooms, beamed lounge with seasonal log fire, and hearty Staffordshire breakfasts. 300yds from Trentham Gardens. Wedgewood factory shop one mile.

**open** All year except Christmas and New Year
**bedrooms** 1 double, 1 twin
**bathrooms** 1 en suite, 1 private
**payment** Cash, cheques

Room General Leisure

## STOKE-ON-TRENT, Staffordshire Map ref 4B2

★★★★
GUEST ACCOMMODATION

B&B PER ROOM PER NIGHT
S £25.00
D £44.00–£46.00

EVENING MEAL PER PERSON
£12.00–£15.00

### Reynolds Hey

Park Lane, Endon, Stoke-on-Trent ST9 9JB **t** (01782) 502717 **e** reynoldshey@hotmail.com

**reynoldshey.co.uk** REAL-TIME BOOKING

Set in the rolling countryside, this modernised farmhouse offers comfortable accommodation in a friendly atmosphere. Situated close to The Potteries, Alton Towers, and beautiful Peak District and Caldon Canal.

**open** All year except Christmas
**bedrooms** 2 double, 1 twin, 1 family
**bathrooms** All en suite
**payment** Cash, cheques

Room General P Leisure

## STOKE-ON-TRENT, Staffordshire Map ref 4B2

★★
GUEST HOUSE

B&B PER ROOM PER NIGHT
S Min £24.00
D £40.00–£44.00

### Verdon Guest House

44 Charles Street, Stoke-on-Trent ST1 3JY **t** (01782) 264244

**verdonguesthouse.co.uk**

Newly renovated, large, friendly guesthouse in Hanley town centre. Alton Towers 20 minutes. All rooms have large flat-screen televisions with HD Freeview channels and DVD. Exceptionally comfortable beds. Excellent value.

**open** All year
**bedrooms** 4 double, 3 twin, 1 single, 5 family
**bathrooms** 5 en suite
**payment** Credit/debit cards, cash, cheques

PETS! WELCOME

Room General P

## STOWMARKET, Suffolk Map ref 3B2

★★★★★
GUEST ACCOMMODATION
GOLD AWARD

B&B PER ROOM PER NIGHT
S Min £60.00
D Min £70.00

### Bays Farm

Forward Green, Stowmarket IP14 5HU **t** (01449) 711286 **e** info@baysfarmsuffolk.co.uk

**baysfarmsuffolk.co.uk**

**open** All year
**bedrooms** 3 double
**bathrooms** All en suite
**payment** Credit/debit cards, cash, cheques, euros

A 17thC beamed farmhouse in the heart of the Suffolk countryside stands ready to welcome you. Four acres of formal garden and grassland with a wealth of wildlife, including bats, owls and bird life.

**SAT NAV** *IP14 5HU*

Room General P

## STRATFORD-UPON-AVON, Warwickshire Map ref 2B1

★★★★
GUEST HOUSE

B&B PER ROOM PER NIGHT
S £28.00–£35.00
D £58.00–£80.00

### Ambleside Guest House

41 Grove Road, Stratford-upon-Avon CV37 6PB **t** (01789) 297239 **e** ruth@amblesideguesthouse.com

**amblesideguesthouse.com** GUEST REVIEWS

Completely refurbished guesthouse in town centre with on-site car park and free Wi-Fi. Five minutes' walk to station and restaurants. Ten minutes to the Courtyard Theatre.

**open** All year
**bedrooms** 1 double, 2 single, 4 family
**bathrooms** 5 en suite
**payment** Credit/debit cards, cash, cheques

Room General 5 P Leisure

Where can I get live travel information?
For the latest travel update – call the RAC on 1740 from your mobile phone.

## STRATFORD-UPON-AVON, Warwickshire Map ref 2B1

★★★★
BED & BREAKFAST
GOLD AWARD

B&B PER ROOM PER NIGHT
s £55.00
d £68.00–£84.00

EVENING MEAL PER PERSON
£15.00–£18.50

*Discounts on stays of 3 nights or more. Call for further details.*

### Folly Farm Cottage

Back Street, Ilmington, Chipping Campden CV36 4LJ **t** (01608) 682425
**e** bruceandpam@follyfarm.co.uk

**follyfarm.co.uk** SPECIAL OFFERS

**open** All year
**bedrooms** 3 double
**bathrooms** All en suite
**payment** Credit/debit cards, cash, cheques

Old-world country cottage accommodation. Double or king-size four-poster rooms, en suite bathroom with bath and shower or whirlpool, hospitality tray, clock/radio, TV, video, free video library. Home cooking is our speciality. Ideal for exploring the Cotswolds and nearby Stratford. A warm welcome guaranteed.

**SAT NAV** *CV36 4LJ*

Room General P Leisure

## STRATFORD-UPON-AVON, Warwickshire Map ref 2B1

★★★★★
INN
SILVER AWARD

B&B PER ROOM PER NIGHT
s £87.50–£95.00
d £120.00–£150.00

EVENING MEAL PER PERSON
£15.00–£25.00

### The Howard Arms

Lower Green, Ilmington, Shipston-on-Stour CV36 4LT **t** (01608) 682226 **e** info@howardarms.com

**howardarms.com**

Idyllic award-winning country inn, recognised nationally for good food, superb accommodation and warm, friendly hospitality.

**open** All year
**bedrooms** 6 double, 2 twin
**bathrooms** All en suite
**payment** Credit/debit cards, cash, cheques

Room General 8 P Leisure

## STRATFORD-UPON-AVON, Warwickshire Map ref 2B1

★★★
BED & BREAKFAST

B&B PER ROOM PER NIGHT
s £30.00
d £52.00

### Larkrise Cottage

Upper Billesley, Stratford-upon-Avon CV37 9RA **t** (01789) 268618 **e** alanbailey17@hotmail.com

**larkrisecottage.co.uk**

Larkrise Cottage provides quality fare in a tranquil rural location. It is within easy reach of the theatres of Stratford and the charm of the Cotswolds.

**open** All year except Christmas and New Year
**bedrooms** 1 double, 1 twin
**bathrooms** 2 private
**payment** Cash, cheques, euros

Room General P

## STRATFORD-UPON-AVON, Warwickshire Map ref 2B1

★★★★
GUEST ACCOMMODATION

B&B PER ROOM PER NIGHT
s £45.00–£59.00
d £69.00–£89.00

*Discounts available Oct-May (excl Sat and locally important dates).*

### Melita

37 Shipston Road, Stratford-upon-Avon CV37 7LN **t** (01789) 292432 **e** info@melitaguesthouse.co.uk

**melitaguesthouse.co.uk** SPECIAL OFFERS

**open** All year except Christmas and New Year
**bedrooms** 5 double, 2 twin, 3 single, 2 family
**bathrooms** 10 en suite, 2 private
**payment** Credit/debit cards, cash, cheques

Once a Victorian home, the Melita is now a warm, friendly establishment managed by caring proprietors. Accommodation and service are of a high standard. Breakfasts are individually prepared to suit guests' requirements. The Melita is only 400m from the theatres and town centre and has free, private, on-site car parking.

**SAT NAV** *CV37 7LN*

Room General P Leisure

## SUDBURY, Suffolk Map ref 3B2

★★★

BED & BREAKFAST

B&B PER ROOM PER NIGHT
S Min £37.50
D Min £50.00

### Hillview Studio

58 Clarence Road, Sudbury CO10 1NJ **t** (01787) 374221 & 07779 854199 **e** sooteapot@hotmail.com

Friendly, modern, self-contained, en suite room with own access. Five minutes' walk to town centre and water meadows.

**open** All year
**bedrooms** 1 twin
**bathrooms** En suite
**payment** Cash, cheques

Room General P Leisure

## SWANTON MORLEY, Norfolk Map ref 3B1

★★★★★
GUEST ACCOMMODATION
SILVER AWARD

B&B PER ROOM PER NIGHT
S Min £55.00
D Min £85.00

### Carricks at Castle Farm

Castle Farm, Elsing Road, Dereham NR20 4JT **t** (01362) 638302 **e** jean@castlefarm-swanton.co.uk

**carricksatcastlefarm.co.uk** GUEST REVIEWS

**open** All year
**bedrooms** 2 double, 1 twin
**bathrooms** 2 en suite, 1 private
**payment** Credit/debit cards, cash, cheques

Carricks at Castle Farm is the family home of the Carrick family and is a large Victorian farmhouse surrounded by beautiful gardens on the banks of the River Wensum where the peace and quiet is only interrupted by the bird song.

**SAT NAV** *NR20 4JT* **ONLINE MAP**

Room General P Leisure

## TELFORD, Shropshire Map ref 4A3

★★★★

BED & BREAKFAST

B&B PER ROOM PER NIGHT
S £35.00–£40.00
D £48.00–£55.00

### The Mill House

Shrewsbury Road, High Ercall, Telford TF6 6BE **t** (01952) 770394 **e** cjpy@lineone.net

**ercallmill.co.uk**

**open** All year
**bedrooms** 1 double, 1 twin, 1 family
**bathrooms** All en suite
**payment** Cash, cheques

Beautiful, Grade II Listed, converted water mill (no machinery) beside River Roden. Peaceful, rural setting. All rooms en suite with colour TV, Freeview and DVD. Large, timbered guest lounge with colour TV. Working smallholding. Ideal for visiting Ironbridge, Telford, Shrewsbury and mid-Wales.

**SAT NAV** *TF6 6BE* **ONLINE MAP**

Room General P Leisure

## TELFORD, Shropshire Map ref 4A3

★★★★★ INN SILVER AWARD

B&B PER ROOM PER NIGHT
S £65.00–£98.00
D £75.00–£128.00

EVENING MEAL PER PERSON
£12.00–£35.00

*Stay & Eat offer (DBB for £125 per couple) or the Wrekin Weekend (3 nights DBB plus extras £299). These prices may vary.*

### The Old Orleton

Holyhead Road, Wellington TF1 2HA **t** (01952) 255011 **e** info@theoldorleton.com

**theoldorleton.com** GUEST REVIEWS • SPECIAL OFFERS • REAL-TIME BOOKING

**open** Closed for two weeks in January
**bedrooms** 6 double, 2 twin, 2 single
**bathrooms** All en suite
**payment** Credit/debit cards, cash, cheques

Contemporary-styled 17thC coaching inn facing the famous Wrekin Hill. The Old Orleton Inn, Wellington, Shropshire is a charming retreat for both work and pleasure. With ten boutique-style bedrooms, each one unique in design and character. A comprehensive selection of carefully prepared vegetarian, fish and meat dishes are served using fresh, quality, local produce.

**SAT NAV** *TF1 2HA* **ONLINE MAP**

Room General P Leisure

## TELFORD, Shropshire Map ref 4A3

★★★★ GUEST ACCOMMODATION

B&B PER ROOM PER NIGHT
S £36.00–£39.00
D £51.00–£54.00

### Stone House

Shifnal Road, Priorslee, Telford TF2 9NN **t** (01952) 290119 **e** stonehousegh@aol.com

**stonehouseguesthouse.co.uk**

Comfortable, friendly guesthouse well situated for exploring the World Heritage Site of Ironbridge. Close to town centre, M54, station and university. Personal attention assured. Excellent food and Platinum Healthy Eating Award holders.

**open** All year
**bedrooms** 2 double, 3 twin
**bathrooms** All en suite
**payment** Cash, cheques

Room General P Leisure

## TENBURY WELLS, Worcestershire Map ref 4A3

★★★★ BED & BREAKFAST

B&B PER ROOM PER NIGHT
S £43.00–£48.00
D £76.00–£80.00

WALKERS WELCOME

### Millbrook

Eastham, Tenbury Wells WR15 8NP **t** (01584) 781720 **e** keithoddy@millbrook01584.co.uk

**millbrook01584.co.uk** SPECIAL OFFERS

Set in the beautiful Teme Valley, a centre for retreat and renewal. Ideally situated as a base for exploring. Organic local produce where possible.

**open** All year
**bedrooms** 2 double
**bathrooms** 1 en suite, 1 private
**payment** Credit/debit cards, cash, cheques

Room General P Leisure

## THOMPSON, Norfolk Map ref 3B1

★★★★ INN

B&B PER ROOM PER NIGHT
S £40.00
D £60.00

EVENING MEAL PER PERSON
£6.00–£25.00

### Chequers Inn

Griston Road, Thompson IP24 1PX **t** (01953) 483360 **e** richard@chequers-inn.wanadoo.co.uk

**thompson-chequers.co.uk**

**open** All year
**bedrooms** 2 double, 1 twin
**bathrooms** All en suite
**payment** Credit/debit cards, cash, cheques

The Chequers is a 16thC village inn with a thatched roof, still retaining all of its original character. A true country retreat, in the heart of Breckland. Local produce and fresh fish a speciality. Local real ales include Breckland Gold, Wolf, Wherry, Adnams and Greene King IPA to name a few.

**SAT NAV** *IP24 1PX*

Room General P Leisure

## THORNHAM MAGNA, Suffolk Map ref 3B2

★★★★★
GUEST ACCOMMODATION
SILVER AWARD

B&B PER ROOM PER NIGHT
S £55.00–£100.00
D £100.00

EVENING MEAL PER PERSON
£18.00–£25.00

### Thornham Hall

Thornham Magna, Eye IP23 8HA **t** (01379) 783314 **e** thornhamhall@aol.com

**thornhamhall.com**

**open** All year
**bedrooms** 2 double, 1 suite
**bathrooms** All en suite
**payment** Credit/debit cards, cash, cheques

Thornham Hall offers exclusive accommodation and function facilities, and is an idyllic wedding reception venue. The Hall is situated in its own private park at the centre of the Thornham estate, the baronial home of the Henniker family since 1750.

**SAT NAV** *IP23 8HA* **ONLINE MAP**

Room General P Leisure

## THORNTON CURTIS, Lincolnshire Map ref 4C1

★★★★
INN

B&B PER ROOM PER NIGHT
S £39.70–£41.70
D £65.45–£67.45

EVENING MEAL PER PERSON
£7.39–£14.95

### Thornton Hunt Inn

17 Main Street, Thornton Curtis, Nr Ulceby DN39 6XW **t** (01469) 531252
**e** peter@thornton-inn.co.uk

**thornton-inn.co.uk**

Family-run, Grade II Listed building. Traditional home-made bar meals and desserts available lunch and dinner. Extensive garden with children's fun trail and slide. Convenient for airport, Humber Bridge and M180.

**open** All year except Christmas and New Year
**bedrooms** 5 double, 1 single
**bathrooms** All en suite
**payment** Credit/debit cards, cash, cheques

Room TV General P Leisure

## THURLEIGH, Bedfordshire Map ref 2D1

★★★★
BED & BREAKFAST

B&B PER ROOM PER NIGHT
S £40.00–£45.00
D £60.00–£80.00

### The Windmill

Milton Road, Thurleigh, Bedford MK44 2DF **t** (01234) 771016 **e** wendy.armitage1@talk21.com

**thewindmill.uk.com**

A recently converted windmill which offers unique views over the surrounding countryside. Comfortable, spacious accommodation. Large gardens and ample parking space.

**open** All year except Christmas and New Year
**bedrooms** 1 double, 1 family, 1 suite
**bathrooms** 1 en suite, 1 private
**payment** Cash, cheques, euros

Room TV General 8 P Leisure

## TOPPESFIELD, Essex Map ref 3B2

★★★
BED & BREAKFAST

B&B PER ROOM PER NIGHT
D £44.00–£50.00

EVENING MEAL PER PERSON
Max £12.00

### Harrow Hill Cottage

Harrow Hill, Toppesfield CO9 4LX **t** (01787) 237425

**tiscover.co.uk**

A 17thC cottage in a quiet location, set in one-acre gardens with outdoor swimming pool, surrounded by pleasant views and farmland.

**open** All year except Christmas
**bedrooms** 1 double, 1 family
**bathrooms** 1 en suite
**payment** Cash, cheques

Room TV General 10 P Leisure

### Looking for a wide range of facilities?

More stars means higher quality accommodation plus a greater range of facilities and services.

## TOWCESTER, Northamptonshire Map ref 2C1

★★★★
FARMHOUSE
SILVER AWARD

B&B PER ROOM PER NIGHT
S £30.00–£45.00
D £50.00–£65.00

### Slapton Manor Accommodation

Slapton Manor, Slapton NN12 8PF **t** (01327) 860344 **e** accommodation@slaptonmanor.co.uk

En suite rooms within stable/hay loft conversion and self-catering studios adjoining village 12thC manor house on working farm.

**open** All year
**bedrooms** 1 double, 1 twin, 1 family
**bathrooms** All en suite
**payment** Cash, cheques, euros

Room General P Leisure

## TUNSTALL, Staffordshire Map ref 4B2

★★★
GUEST ACCOMMODATION

B&B PER ROOM PER NIGHT
S £23.00–£30.00
D £48.00

### The Victoria

4 Roundwell Street, Tunstall, Stoke-on-Trent ST6 5JJ **t** (01782) 835964
**e** victoriahoteltunstall@hotmail.com

Once a Victorian public house, now a comfortable, family-run guesthouse in a quiet, residential area. City centre is 2.5 miles away, Royal Doulton 1 mile. Convenient for all potteries and for Alton Towers (17 miles).

**open** All year
**bedrooms** 2 double, 1 twin, 4 single, 2 family
**bathrooms** 5 en suite
**payment** Credit/debit cards, cash, cheques, euros

Room General P

## UPPINGHAM, Rutland Map ref 4C3

★★★★★
GUEST ACCOMMODATION
GOLD AWARD

B&B PER ROOM PER NIGHT
S £60.00–£80.00
D £75.00–£90.00

EVENING MEAL PER PERSON
£12.00–£18.00

### Spanhoe Lodge

Harringworth Road, Laxton, Corby NN17 3AT **t** (01780) 450328 **e** jennie.spanhoe@virgin.net

**spanhoelodge.co.uk** GUEST REVIEWS · REAL-TIME BOOKING

**open** All year
**bedrooms** 6 double, 2 twin, 2 family
**bathrooms** 8 en suite
**payment** Credit/debit cards, cash, cheques

A warm, friendly welcome awaits you at this gold-awarded establishment in the heart of Rockingham Forest. Luxuriously appointed, en suite accommodation, wide choice of gourmet breakfasts, fine dining, licensed bar, conferencing. Ideally situated for Stamford, Corby, Uppingham, Oundle, Oakham, Rutland Water and Rockingham Motor Speedway. You will not be disappointed!

**SAT NAV** *NN17 3AT* **ONLINE MAP**

Room General P
Leisure

## UPTON UPON SEVERN, Worcestershire Map ref 2B1

★★★★
BED & BREAKFAST

B&B PER ROOM PER NIGHT
S £40.00–£60.00
D £65.00–£80.00

### Sunnyside Bed & Breakfast

Station Road, Ripple GL20 6EY **t** (01684) 592461 **e** sunnysideripple@btinternet.com

**sunnysidebandb.co.uk**

Charming cottage set in the shadow of the Malverns offering a relaxed friendly atmosphere, real fires. High standard of accommodation. Home-made and locally-sourced produce. Excellent motorway links.

**open** All year except Christmas and New Year
**bedrooms** 2 double
**bathrooms** 1 en suite, 1 private
**payment** Cash, cheques

Room General P Leisure

## What shall we do today?

For ideas on places to visit, see the beginning of this regional section or go online at enjoyengland.com.

## VOWCHURCH, Herefordshire Map ref 2A1

★★★★
BED & BREAKFAST
GOLD AWARD

B&B PER ROOM PER NIGHT
S £35.00–£50.00
D £60.00–£75.00

EVENING MEAL PER PERSON
£15.00–£25.00

### Yew Tree House

Vowchurch, Hereford HR2 9PF **t** (01981) 251195 **e** enquiries@yewtreehouse-hereford.co.uk

**yewtreehouse-hereford.co.uk**

Two-hundred-year-old house with magnificent views of the Golden Valley, offering luxurious accommodation in an extremely comfortable family home.

**open** All year
**bedrooms** 1 double, 1 twin, 1 family
**bathrooms** All en suite
**payment** Cash, cheques, euros

Room General Leisure

## WAINFLEET, Lincolnshire Map ref 4D2

★★★
FARMHOUSE

B&B PER ROOM PER NIGHT
S £25.00
D £50.00

EVENING MEAL PER PERSON
£5.00–£10.00

### Willow Farm

Thorpe Fendykes, Skegness PE24 4QH **t** (01754) 830316 **e** willowfarmhols@aol.com

**willowfarmholidays.co.uk**

Working family farm with ponies, goats, ducks and hens in peaceful countryside yet only ten to fifteen minutes from Skegness. Disabled-accessible, comfortable en suite rooms. Please ring for brochure.

**open** All year
**bedrooms** 1 double, 1 twin, 1 family
**bathrooms** All en suite
**payment** Cash, cheques

Room General Leisure

## WALTON-ON-THE-NAZE, Essex Map ref 3C2

★★★★
GUEST ACCOMMODATION

B&B PER ROOM PER NIGHT
S £24.50–£27.00
D £49.00–£54.00

### Bufo Villae Guest House

31 Beatrice Road, Walton-on-the-Naze CO14 8HJ **t** (01255) 672644 **e** bufovillae@btinternet.com

**bufovillae.co.uk**

Close to the seafront in a quiet area of Walton. Two rooms have sea views, all rooms are en suite with tea-/coffee-making facilities. Colour television, parking available, downstairs room available for those with mobility difficulties.

**open** All year
**bedrooms** 1 double, 1 twin, 1 single
**bathrooms** All en suite
**payment** Cash, cheques

Room General Leisure

## WARWICK, Warwickshire Map ref 2B1

★★★★
GUEST HOUSE

B&B PER ROOM PER NIGHT
S Min £40.00
D £60.00–£70.00

### Croft Guesthouse

Haseley Knob, Warwick CV35 7NL **t** (01926) 484447 **e** david@croftguesthouse.co.uk

**croftguesthouse.co.uk**

A friendly, non-smoking family guesthouse providing clean, high-quality, en suite accommodation at reasonable prices. Centrally located for exploring Warwick, Stratford, Coventry and Kenilworth, or for visiting the NEC (15 minutes).

**open** All year except Christmas and New Year
**bedrooms** 3 double, 2 twin, 1 single, 3 family
**bathrooms** 6 en suite, 3 private
**payment** Credit/debit cards, cash, cheques, euros

Room General Leisure

## WARWICK, Warwickshire Map ref 2B1

★★★
BED & BREAKFAST

B&B PER ROOM PER NIGHT
S £42.50–£47.50
D £65.00–£67.50

### Peacock Lodge

97 West Street, Warwick CV34 6AH **t** (01926) 419480

Three-storey, early-Victorian terraced house. One of the guest rooms is a converted stable.

**open** All year except Christmas and New Year
**bedrooms** 3 double
**bathrooms** All en suite
**payment** Credit/debit cards, cash, cheques

Room General Leisure

For **key to symbols** see page 7

## WATERHOUSES, Staffordshire Map ref 4B2

★★★★
BED & BREAKFAST
SILVER AWARD

B&B PER ROOM PER NIGHT
S £30.00–£35.00
D £50.00–£60.00

### Leehouse Farm

Leek Road, Waterhouses, Leek ST10 3HW **t** (01538) 308439

Charming 18thC house in centre of a Staffordshire Moorlands village in Peak District National Park. Ideal for Derbyshire Dales, the Potteries and Alton Towers.

**open** All year except Christmas
**bedrooms** 2 double, 1 twin
**bathrooms** All en suite
**payment** Cash, cheques

Room General 8 P Leisure

## WELLAND, Worcestershire Map ref 2B1

★★★
GUEST ACCOMMODATION

B&B PER ROOM PER NIGHT
S £30.00–£35.00
D £60.00–£65.00

### North Farm

Hancocks Lane, Welland, Malvern WR13 6LG **t** (01684) 574365

North Farm is a welcoming B&B with comfortable en suite rooms. Set in a beautiful rural location close to Three Counties Showground, Upton upon Severn, and the Malvern Hills.

**open** All year
**bedrooms** 1 double, 1 twin
**bathrooms** All en suite
**payment** Cash, cheques

Room General P

## WELLS-NEXT-THE-SEA, Norfolk Map ref 3B1

★★★★
GUEST HOUSE

B&B PER ROOM PER NIGHT
S Min £40.00
D Min £80.00

### The Cobblers

Standard Road, Wells-next-the-Sea NR23 1JU **t** (01328) 710155 **e** info@cobblers.co.uk

**cobblers.co.uk**

The Cobblers is situated in the centre of town, close to the harbour and restaurants, in Wells-next-the-Sea. An ideal base for exploring north Norfolk. Pets by arrangement. Midwinter midweek specials. Off-street parking.

**open** All year except Christmas and New Year
**bedrooms** 4 double, 1 twin, 3 single
**bathrooms** 7 en suite, 1 private
**payment** Credit/debit cards, cash, cheques

Room General P Leisure

## WEST BRIDGFORD, Nottinghamshire Map ref 4C2

★★★
GUEST HOUSE

B&B PER ROOM PER NIGHT
S £25.00–£29.00
D £35.00–£45.00

### Firs Guesthouse

96 Radcliffe Road, West Bridgford, Nottingham NG2 5HH **t** (0115) 981 0199
**e** firs.hotel@btinternet.com

High-quality Victorian establishment, well maintained with reasonable rates. Guest lounge with pool table and Sky TV. Close to Trent Bridge, Nottingham Forest FC, watersports and all amenities. Good city accessibility.

**open** All year except Christmas
**bedrooms** 3 twin, 6 family
**bathrooms** 2 en suite
**payment** Credit/debit cards, cash, cheques

Room General P Leisure

## WHITNEY-ON-WYE, Herefordshire Map ref 2A1

★★★★
INN

B&B PER ROOM PER NIGHT
S Min £42.50
D Min £85.00

EVENING MEAL PER PERSON
£20.00–£35.00

### Rhydspence Inn

Whitney-on-Wye, Hay-on-Wye HR3 6EU **t** (01497) 831262 **e** info@rhydspence-inn.co.uk

**rhydspence-inn.co.uk**

14thC drovers' inn, in superb Wye Valley, serving top-quality local produce in comfortable surroundings. Beautiful en suite bedrooms and oak-beamed bars.

**open** All year except Christmas
**bedrooms** 4 double, 2 twin, 1 single
**bathrooms** All en suite
**payment** Credit/debit cards, cash, cheques

Room General P Leisure

## B&B prices

Rates for bed and breakfast are shown per room per night.
Double room prices are usually based on two people sharing the room.

## WINGFIELD, Suffolk Map ref 3B2

★★★★
BED & BREAKFAST
SILVER AWARD

B&B PER ROOM PER NIGHT
S £40.00–£50.00
D £62.00–£65.00

### Gables Farm

Earsham Street, Wingfield, Diss IP21 5RH **t** (01379) 586355 & 07824 445464
**e** enquiries@gablesfarm.co.uk

**gablesfarm.co.uk** GUEST REVIEWS

**open** All year except Christmas and New Year
**bedrooms** 2 double, 1 twin
**bathrooms** All en suite
**payment** Cash, cheques

A 16thC timbered farmhouse in moated gardens. Wingfield is a quiet village in the centre of East Anglia, central to everywhere and in the middle of nowhere!

**SAT NAV** *IP21 5RH* **ONLINE MAP**

Room General P Leisure

## WISHAW, Warwickshire Map ref 4B3

★★★★
BED & BREAKFAST

B&B PER ROOM PER NIGHT
S £38.00–£45.00
D £50.00–£60.00

### Ash House

The Gravel, Wishaw, Sutton Coldfield B76 9QB **t** (01675) 475782 **e** kate@rectory80.freeserve.co.uk

Former rectory with lovely views. Few minutes' walk from Belfry Golf and Leisure Hotel. Half a mile M42, ten minutes' drive from Birmingham Airport/NEC. Drayton Manor Park and zoo five miles.

**open** All year except Christmas and New Year
**bedrooms** 1 double, 1 twin, 1 family
**bathrooms** All en suite
**payment** Cash, cheques

Room General P Leisure

## WIX, Essex Map ref 3B2

★★★★
BED & BREAKFAST
SILVER AWARD

B&B PER ROOM PER NIGHT
S £38.00
D £59.50

### Periwinkle Cottage

Colchester Road, Wix, Nr Harwich CO11 2PD **t** (01255) 870167

**tiscover.co.uk** REAL-TIME BOOKING

**open** All year except Christmas and New Year
**bedrooms** 1 double, 1 twin, 1 family
**bathrooms** All en suite
**payment** Cash, cheques, euros

Periwinkle Cottage is set in a semi-rural position, close to the busy passenger port of Harwich, Constable Country and Clacton-on-Sea. Direct access to UK trunk road network, approximately one hour from London. All rooms well furnished, TV/DVD, teasmade, ironing facility, toiletries. Family rate £80.00.

**SAT NAV** *CO11 2PD* **ONLINE MAP**

Room General 5 P Leisure

## Check the maps for accommodation locations

Colour maps at the front pinpoint all the cities, towns and villages where you will find accommodation entries in the regional sections. Pick your location and then refer to the place index at the back to find the page number.

## WOODHALL SPA, Lincolnshire Map ref 4D2

★★★★
GUEST ACCOMMODATION SILVER AWARD

B&B PER ROOM PER NIGHT
S £45.00–£60.00
D £60.00

EVENING MEAL PER PERSON
£20.00

*Indulge in midweek 3-night break (two people sharing a double/twin room) Mon-Thu for £165 (£15 discount).*

### Chaplin House

92 High Street, Martin LN4 3QT **t** (01526) 378795 **e** info@chaplin-house.co.uk

**chaplin-house.co.uk** GUEST REVIEWS • SPECIAL OFFERS • REAL-TIME BOOKING

**open** All year except Christmas and New Year
**bedrooms** 2 double, 1 twin, 1 family
**bathrooms** All en suite
**payment** Cash, cheques

Award-winning accommodation at Chaplin House, in the heart of the Lincolnshire countryside. In our barn conversion, we have three spacious en suite rooms, together with a guests' lounge; there is one guest room in the house. Most of our produce is locally sourced, free-range and organic.

**SAT NAV** *LN4 3QT* **ONLINE MAP**

Room General P Leisure

## WOODHALL SPA, Lincolnshire Map ref 4D2

★★★★
GUEST ACCOMMODATION SILVER AWARD

B&B PER ROOM PER NIGHT
S £30.00–£60.00
D £60.00–£80.00

### Kirkstead Old Mill Cottage

Tattershall Road, Woodhall Spa LN10 6UQ **t** (01526) 353637 **e** barbara@woodhallspa.com

**woodhallspa.com** GUEST REVIEWS • SPECIAL OFFERS

**open** All year except Christmas
**bedrooms** 1 double, 2 twin
**bathrooms** All en suite
**payment** Cash, cheques, euros

Barbara and Tony Hodgkinson would like to offer you a warm welcome to their detached home near the river Witham. They hope you will treasure the peace and tranquillity if you choose to sleep in one of their three en suite guest bedrooms, before enjoying a Gold Award breakfast. Pets only welcome in one bedroom.

**SAT NAV** *LN10 6UQ* **ONLINE MAP**

Room General P Leisure

## WOODHALL SPA, Lincolnshire Map ref 4D2

★★★
BED & BREAKFAST

B&B PER ROOM PER NIGHT
S Max £50.00
D Max £50.00

### The Limes

Tattershall Road, Woodhall Spa LN10 6TW **t** (01526) 352219

A warm welcome assured in this elegant Edwardian house, set in the leafy village of Woodhall Spa. Convenient for the golf course and all the amenities in Woodhall Spa.

**open** All year except Christmas and New Year
**bedrooms** 2 double
**payment** Cash, cheques

General P

## Where is my pet welcome?

Some proprietors welcome well-behaved pets. Look for the symbol in the accommodation listings. You can also buy a copy of our popular guide – Pets Come Too! – available from good bookshops and online at visitbritaindirect.com.

## WOODHALL SPA, Lincolnshire Map ref 4D2

★★★★
GUEST ACCOMMODATION

B&B PER ROOM PER NIGHT
S £42.00–£50.00
D £65.00–£75.00

*10% discount for 4 nights or more.*

### Village Limits Motel

Stixwould Road, Woodhall Spa LN10 6UJ **t** (01526) 353312 **e** info@villagelimits.co.uk

**villagelimits.co.uk**

**open** All year
**bedrooms** 8 twin
**bathrooms** All en suite
**payment** Credit/debit cards, cash, cheques

Award-winning Tastes of Lincolnshire Best Accommodation 2007. Village Limits Country Pub and Restaurant has a friendly, relaxing welcome. The comfortable ground-floor bedrooms all have en suite bathrooms, one with full facilities for the disabled. Food daily 1200-1400 and 1900-2100. Closed Sunday evening and Mondays. B&B seven days.

**SAT NAV** *LN10 6UJ* **ONLINE MAP**

Room General

## WOODHURST, Cambridgeshire Map ref 3A2

★★★
GUEST ACCOMMODATION

B&B PER ROOM PER NIGHT
S £40.00
D £40.00–£60.00

### The Raptor Foundation

The Heath, St Ives Road, Huntingdon PE28 3BT **t** (01487) 741140 **e** heleowl@aol.com

**raptorfoundation.org.uk** REAL-TIME BOOKING

Stay with us at the Falcon's Nest and take a relaxing stroll around the birds. Have breakfast in the conservatory overlooking the park.

**open** All year
**bedrooms** 6 double, 1 twin, 1 family
**bathrooms** 6 en suite, 1 private
**payment** Credit/debit cards, cash, cheques

Room General

## WOODNEWTON, Northamptonshire Map ref 3A1

★★★★
BED & BREAKFAST

B&B PER ROOM PER NIGHT
S £38.00–£50.00
D £70.00–£85.00

### Bridge Cottage

Oundle Road, Woodnewton PE8 5EG **t** (01780) 470779 & 07979 644864
**e** enquiries@bridgecottage.net

**bridgecottage.net**

Newly renovated family-run bed and breakfast in lovely countryside. Ideal for businessmen or weekend relaxing, walking and birdwatching. Eight miles from Peterborough, ten from Stamford, four from Oundle.

**open** All year except Christmas
**bedrooms** 2 double, 1 twin
**payment** Cash, cheques

Room General

## WOOLPIT, Suffolk Map ref 3B2

★★★
INN

B&B PER ROOM PER NIGHT
S £40.00–£45.00
D £75.00–£80.00

EVENING MEAL PER PERSON
£4.75–£20.00

### Bull Inn and Restaurant

The Street, Woolpit, Bury St Edmunds IP30 9SA **t** (01359) 240393 **e** info@bullinnwoolpit.co.uk

**bullinnwoolpit.co.uk**

Public house and restaurant offering good accommodation in centre of pretty village. Large garden, ample parking. Ideal base for touring Suffolk.

**open** All year
**bedrooms** 4 double, 1 twin, 2 single, 1 family
**bathrooms** All en suite
**payment** Credit/debit cards, cash, cheques

Room General 2 Leisure

## Do you have access needs?

Look for the National Accessible Scheme symbols if you have special hearing, visual or mobility needs.

## WORCESTER, Worcestershire Map ref 2B1

★★★
FARMHOUSE

B&B PER ROOM PER NIGHT
S £35.00–£40.00
D £55.00–£60.00

### The Barn House

Broadwas in Teme, Worcester WR6 5NS **t** (01886) 888733 & 07778 274328
**e** info@barnhouseonline.co.uk

**barnhouseonline.co.uk**

Period property set in over two acres of mature garden, surrounded by open countryside, 15 minutes from Worcester city centre.

**open** All year
**bedrooms** 1 double, 1 twin
**bathrooms** All en suite
**payment** Cash, cheques

Room General 3 P Leisure

## WORCESTER, Worcestershire Map ref 2B1

★★★★
BED & BREAKFAST
SILVER AWARD

B&B PER ROOM PER NIGHT
S £45.00
D £45.00–£75.00

### Hill Farm House

Dormston Lane, Dormston, Worcester WR7 4JS **t** (01386) 793159 **e** jim@hillfarmhouse.co.uk

**hillfarmhouse.co.uk**

A traditional former farmhouse and converted buildings in quiet rural location. King-size, en suite rooms with pastoral views. Ideal for Stratford, Cotswolds, Worcester and the Malverns.

**open** All year except Christmas
**bedrooms** 1 double, 1 twin, 2 suites
**bathrooms** All en suite
**payment** Cash, cheques

Room General P Leisure

## WORCESTER, Worcestershire Map ref 2B1

★★★
BED & BREAKFAST

B&B PER ROOM PER NIGHT
S £42.00–£52.50
D £52.50–£56.00

EVENING MEAL PER PERSON
£7.00–£10.00

### Holland House

210 London Road, Worcester WR5 2JT **t** (01905) 353939 **e** beds@holland-house.me.uk

**holland-house.me.uk** REAL-TIME BOOKING

A warm welcome awaits you at this Victorian mid-terrace house, situated within easy walk of the cathedral and shops. It retains many original features and offers fully en suite rooms throughout.

**open** All year
**bedrooms** 2 double, 1 twin
**bathrooms** All en suite
**payment** Credit/debit cards, cash, cheques

Room General P

## WORTHAM, Suffolk Map ref 3B2

★★★★
FARMHOUSE
SILVER AWARD

B&B PER ROOM PER NIGHT
S Max £35.00
D £50.00–£70.00

### Rookery Farm

Old Bury Road, Wortham, Diss IP22 1RB **t** (01379) 783236 **e** russell.ling@ukgateway.net

**tiscover.co.uk**

**open** All year except Christmas and New Year
**bedrooms** 2 double, 1 twin
**bathrooms** All en suite
**payment** Cash, cheques

A warm welcome awaits at this comfortable Georgian farmhouse with its spacious, tastefully decorated, fully en suite rooms. Enjoy a traditional farmhouse breakfast made, wherever possible, from fresh local produce.

**SAT NAV** *IP22 1RB* **ONLINE MAP**

Room General P

## What do the star ratings mean?

Detailed information about star ratings can be found at the back of this guide.

## WRENTHAM, Suffolk Map ref 3C2

★★★
INN

B&B PER ROOM PER NIGHT
S £60.00–£70.00
D £80.00–£90.00

### Five Bells

Southwold Road, Wrentham NR34 7JF **t** (01502) 675249 **e** victoriapub@aol.com

**five-bells.com**

Traditional country inn set in a rural location. Close to Southwold.

**open** All year except Christmas
**bedrooms** 1 double, 3 twin, 1 family
**bathrooms** All en suite
**payment** Credit/debit cards, cash, cheques

Room General P Leisure

## WROXHAM, Norfolk Map ref 3C1

★★★★
BED & BREAKFAST

B&B PER ROOM PER NIGHT
S £36.00–£42.00
D £56.00–£60.00

### Wroxham Park Lodge

142 Norwich Road, Wroxham, Norwich NR12 8SA **t** (01603) 782991
**e** parklodge@computer-assist.net

**wroxhamparklodge.com**

Warm welcome in comfortable Victorian house. Tastefully furnished en suite rooms all with TV and tea/coffee tray. Hearty breakfast menu, large garden, patio and car park. Situated in Norfolk Broads.

**open** All year
**bedrooms** 2 double, 1 twin
**bathrooms** All en suite
**payment** Cash, cheques

Room TV General P Leisure

## WYE VALLEY

*See under Hereford, Ross-on-Wye*

# South East England

Berkshire, Buckinghamshire, East Sussex, Hampshire, Isle of Wight, Kent, Oxfordshire, Surrey, West Sussex

Clockwise: Portsmouth Historic Dockyard, Hampshire; Deal, Kent; Oxford

# Great days out

The South East is your quintessential slice of England. Explore iconic chalk cliffs and 400 miles of glorious coastline, fairytale castles, colourful gardens and historic cities. Whilst singles and couples will find plenty to enjoy, this region is bursting with great family days out that the kids will treasure forever.

## Enjoy the ride!

Get set, **Go Ape!** on a high-wire forest adventure course, now at Bedgebury Pinetum and Wendover Woods as well as other exciting locations across the South East. White-knuckle rides like **Thorpe Park's** Inferno and Slammer keep the thrills coming and there's always something new to try: take a dizzying spin on **Legoland Windsor's** Longboat Invader, twirl and tilt on the amazing

Paultons Park, Hampshire

Sky Swinger at **Paultons Park**, or hop aboard the spooky ghost train Horror Hotel at **Brighton Pier**. At Winchester's **Intech Science Centre and Planetarium** you can even fly through the solar system and visit a black hole. Enjoy the rides of your life!

## Who killed Harold?

Explore a region that has witnessed some of the most momentous events in British history, from the Battle of Hastings in 1066 to the air raids of the Second World War. At **Battle Abbey** stand on the exact spot where tradition says King Harold fell and take the interactive audio tour of the battlefield to find out what really happened on that fateful day. Clamber aboard the world-famous HMS Victory at **Portsmouth Historic Dockyard**, then experience the challenges of the modern Navy in Action Stations.

Formidable **Dover Castle** on the Kent coast puts you right on the frontline of history: tour the **Secret Wartime Tunnels** deep beneath the gleaming White Cliffs, where the evacuation of Dunkirk was masterminded. Another of the country's dazzling landmarks, **Canterbury Cathedral**, opens the door on the infamous murder of Thomas Becket. And just for fun, why not follow in the footsteps of Morse and Lewis beneath the dreaming spires of **Oxford** to solve a fictional mystery or two?

## Shore pleasures

South coast beaches keep alive all the best traditions of the seaside, with a zesty twist of watersport action. **Eastbourne**, **Bournemouth**, **Brighton** and **Margate** were popular playgrounds for the Victorians – Queen Victoria loved to escape to her Isle of Wight home, **Osborne House**. Save your small change for the slot machines on the pier where it's hot doughnuts or fish and chips all round. If you're looking for something a bit more peaceful, there are still many gems to uncover. Scamper about the sand dunes at **West Wittering**, just down the Sussex coast from **Bognor Regis**, and watch the zigzagging kitesurfers at **Pevensey Bay**. Get your own adrenalin fix at the **Calshot Activities Centre** where you can try all sorts of watersports, including sailing on the Solent.

Left to right: Hever Castle, Kent; Royal Pavilion, Brighton, East Sussex

**did you know...** you're walking on 80 million years of geological history along the White Cliffs of Dover?

## Castles, castles everywhere

Become king, queen, lord or lady for a day visiting the South East's magnificent castles. **Bodiam** is a picture-perfect medieval moated fortress and **Arundel** is full of priceless collections. Dreamy **Leeds** in Kent was restored by Henry VIII for his first queen, Catherine of Aragon. It might have been the ultimate romantic gesture, except that he abandoned her for his second wife, Anne Boleyn – visit Anne's beautiful childhood home, **Hever Castle**, too. **Windsor Castle** has been a royal residence for nine centuries and reflects changing royal tastes through the ages. But nothing quite prepares you for the **Royal Pavilion** at Brighton, George IV's eccentric Indian-style palace!

## Follow nature's way

Kent is rightly famed as the Garden of England, so sample some real horticultural treats like **Sissinghurst Castle Garden**, lovingly created by Vita Sackville-West. Discover Kew's country garden and the Millennium Seed Bank at **Wakehurst Place**, near Haywards Heath. Follow the ancient tracks of the **South Downs Way** for an exhilarating breath of fresh air, or hop over to the **Isle of Wight** where you can cycle Round the Island in eight hours. Phew! Play hide and seek along the paths and bridleways of the **New Forest** and watch out for wild ponies as they gently graze. You'll encounter elephants and other exotic creatures at **Howletts Wild Animal Park**.

New Forest ponies

## Have a Dickens of a time

Catch the buzz of a festival or event, whatever the time of year. From rock 'n' pop to hops, from rowing to sailing, from Dickens to dancing round a maypole – the rich tapestry of life. **The Brighton Festival** comes to the funky seaside town every May and is an exuberant celebration of world-class art and entertainment. If you're looking for the epitome of elegance, dress up for **Glyndebourne's** season of opera, **Royal Ascot**, **Henley Royal Regatta** or **Cowes Week** – four internationally famous spectacles.

Or join Mr Pickwick and other jolly characters in Victorian costume on the streets of Broadstairs during the **Dickens Festival**. The town was the author's favourite 'English watering place'. There's rock, pop and hip hop mixed with liberal helpings of mud at August's **Reading Festival**. And kids can always find something fantabulous to fill the school holidays at **The Roald Dahl Museum and Story Centre**, Great Missenden: from whizzpopping, hands-on science workshops to delumptious cookery classes.

## Time to indulge

Had your fill of sightseeing? Then it's time to indulge! Shopaholics: head for the charming world of The Lanes, **Brighton**, to hunt out stylish gifts and antiques. Browse for hours in the country's largest second-hand bookshop, Baggins at **Rochester**. Pop into **Oxford Castle** where boutique stalls, outdoor music performances, wining and dining are set against an unusual prison backdrop. If you need to boost your energy levels, you're in just the right region, too: embark on an epicurean journey through lots of orchards, breweries and vineyards, including England's largest vineyard at **Denbies Wine Estate**. Then savour more of the genuine flavours of South East England in the oyster houses and fine restaurants.

**why not...** visit the world's oldest and largest occupied castle – Windsor Castle?

Clockwise: The Roald Dahl Museum and Story Centre, Buckinghamshire; Cowes, Isle of Wight; Denbies Wine Estate, Surrey

# Destinations

## Brighton

England's favourite seaside city, Brighton is historic, elegant and offbeat. Wander a beachfront packed with cafés and bars, then step into town for fine antiques and designer boutiques. Don't miss the Royal Pavilion, surely the most extravagant royal palace in Europe, and come in springtime for an arts festival second to none. Find the world's cuisine in over 400 restaurants, and then relax with dance, comedy or music in the thriving pub and club culture. Brighton has it all – and just 50 minutes by train from central London.

Brighton

## Canterbury

Marvel with fellow 'pilgrims' from the four corners of the world as Canterbury Cathedral dominates your approach to this World Heritage Site. Let Canterbury Tales 'Medieval Misadventures' take you on a journey back to Chaucer's England. Wander traffic-free daytime streets to enjoy historic buildings and modern attractions, and then head further afield to explore the valleys, woods and coastline of this beautiful region of Kent.

## Dover

Discover the rich history of Dover – 'the lock and key of England'. Tour Dover Castle and relive the epic sieges of 1216-17. Delve into the secrets contained in the Wartime Tunnels, nerve centre for the evacuation of Dunkirk. Enjoy the pier and stroll the stylish marina before heading out of town to tour the scenic beaches of White Cliffs Country.

## Isle of Wight

Sixty miles of spectacular coastline, picturesque coves and safe bathing in bays of golden sand. Explore the maritime history of Cowes, the beautiful and historic town of Newport and take the family to the welcoming resorts of Shanklin and Ventnor. Follow the trail of dinosaurs, ancient tribes, Romans and monarchs.

## New Forest

Roam a landscape little changed since William the Conqueror gave it his special protection over 900 years ago. Discover wild heath and dappled woodland, roaming ponies, thatched hamlets, bustling market towns, and tiny streams meandering to the sparkling expanse of the Solent. Explore great attractions too, from Buckler's Hard to the National Motor Museum Beaulieu.

## Oxford

This ancient university city is both timeless and modern. Wander among its 'dreaming spires' and tranquil college quadrangles. Find national and international treasures displayed in a family of museums. Hire a punt and spend the afternoon drifting along the River Cherwell or seek out bustling shops and fashionable restaurants. Experience candlelit evensong in college chapels or Shakespeare in the park, and after dark enjoy the cosmopolitan buzz.

Left to right: Great Dixter, East Sussex; Thorpe Park, Surrey

Royal Tunbridge Wells

## Portsmouth

At the heart of the city is Portsmouth Historic Dockyard where there is so much naval heritage to explore. Climb the new striking Spinnaker Tower or take a harbour tour to see naval ships. If you're after retail therapy, head for Gunwharf Quays. Portsmouth also has its own resort area, Southsea, with four miles of beach and promenade.

## Royal Tunbridge Wells

Ever since the discovery of the Chalybeate Spring 400 years ago, visitors have been coming here. The health-giving waters still flow and the Pantiles, the famous colonnaded walkway, is now home to a wonderful selection of boutiques, antiques shops, bars and cafés. The village atmosphere of the old high street and Chapel Place, adds to the town's reputation as one of the most desirable destinations in the South East. Surrounded by beautiful countryside, and a wealth of castles, stately homes and gardens, there's so much to explore.

Clockwise: Portsmouth; Windsor Castle; Dover Castle

## Winchester

Winchester is best known for its 11thC cathedral and the Great Hall, which for over 600 years has housed the mysterious Arthurian round table. Wander through the city's popular shopping streets, admire the architecture and enjoy quirky open air events. Home of good food, birthplace of cricket, resting place of author Jane Austen and inspiration to the many craft-makers and artists who live here, Winchester is a destination for all seasons.

Winchester Cathedral

## Windsor

Explore Windsor and the Royal Borough to the west of London. Gaze at the priceless treasures in the Royal Collection at Windsor Castle, royal home and fortress for over 900 years. Henry VI founded Eton College in 1440. Lose yourself in the history of the cloisters and the chapel. Sail the rapids at Legoland's incredible Vikings' River Splash, and find peace and quiet in the rural landscape of Royal Berkshire, traversed by the timeless flow of the Thames.

**For lots more great ideas visit enjoyEngland.com/destinations**

# Visitor attractions

## Family and Fun

**Blue Reef Aquarium**
*Hastings, East Sussex*
(01424) 718776
discoverhastings.co.uk
*Meet tropical sharks and giant crabs.*

**The Canterbury Tales**
*Canterbury, Kent*
(01227) 479227
canterburytales.org.uk
*Audiovisual recreation of life in medieval England.*

**Didcot Railway Centre**
*Didcot, Oxfordshire*
(01235) 817200
didcotrailwaycentre.org.uk
*Living museum of the Great Western Railway.*

**Dinosaur Isle**
*Sandown, Isle of Wight*
(01983) 404344
dinosaurisle.com
*Britain's first purpose-built dinosaur attraction.*

**Farming World**
*Boughton, Kent*
(01227) 751144
farming-world.com
*Working farm packed with family fun.*

**Guildford Spectrum**
*Guildford, Surrey*
(01483) 443322
guildfordspectrum.co.uk
*Olympic-sized ice rink and tenpin bowling.*

**Gulliver's Land**
*Milton Keynes, Buckinghamshire*
(01925) 444888
gulliversfun.co.uk
*Family magic for children aged 2-13 years.*

**Harbour Park**
*Littlehampton, West Sussex*
(01903) 721200
harbourpark.com
*All-weather theme park with dodgems.*

**The Historic Dockyard Chatham**
*Chatham, Kent*
(01634) 823800
chdt.org.uk
*Maritime heritage site with stunning architecture.*

**The Hop Farm Country Park**
*Paddock Wood, Kent*
(01622) 872068
thehopfarm.co.uk
*Once-working hop farm in 400 unspoilt acres.*

**Howletts Wild Animal Park**
*Canterbury, Kent*
(01227) 721286
totallywild.net
*Gorillas and tigers in 90-acre parkland.*

**Isle of Wight Zoo**
*Sandown, Isle of Wight*
(01983) 403883
isleofwightzoo.com
*Zoo specialising in big cats and primates.*

**LEGOLAND Windsor**
*Windsor, Berkshire*
0870 504 0404
legoland.co.uk
*More Lego bricks than you dreamed possible.*

**The Look Out Discovery Centre**
*Bracknell, Berkshire*
(01344) 354400
bracknell-forest.gov.uk/lookout
*Interactive science park with over 70 exhibits.*

**Marwell Zoological Park**
*Winchester, Hampshire*
(01962) 777407
marwell.org.uk
*Relaxing and fascinating zoological park.*

**Mid-Hants Railway Watercress Line**
*Alresford, Hampshire*
(01962) 733810
watercressline.co.uk
*Ten-mile steam railway through beautiful countryside.*

**National Motor Museum Beaulieu**
*Beaulieu, Hampshire*
(01590) 612345
beaulieu.co.uk
*Vintage cars in glorious New Forest setting.*

**Paultons Park**
*Romsey, Hampshire*
(023) 8081 4442
paultonspark.co.uk
*Over 50 rides for all the family.*

**Port Lympne Wild Animal Park, Mansion and Gardens**
*Lympne, Kent*
(01303) 264647
totallywild.net
*Rare and endangered species in 600-acre park.*

**Portsmouth Historic Dockyard**
*Portsmouth, Hampshire*
(023) 9283 9766
historicdockyard.co.uk
*Home to the Mary Rose and HMS Victory.*

**River & Rowing Museum**
*Henley-on-Thames, Oxfordshire*
(01491) 415600
rrm.co.uk
*Award-wining museum with year-round exhibitions.*

**The Roald Dahl Museum and Story Centre**
**Small Visitor Attraction of the Year - Gold**
*Great Missenden, Buckinghamshire*
(01494) 892192
roalddahlmuseum.org
*The life behind so many well-loved books.*

**Romney, Hythe and Dymchurch Railway**
*Littlestone-on-Sea, Kent*
(01797) 362353
rhdr.org.uk
*The world's only main line in miniature.*

**Thorpe Park**
*Chertsey, Surrey*
0870 444 4466
thorpepark.com
*Thrills and spills for all the family.*

**Weald & Downland Open Air Museum**
*Chichester, West Sussex*
(01243) 811348
wealddown.co.uk
*Rescued historic buildings in beautiful 50-acre setting.*

## Heritage

**1066 Battle Abbey and Battlefield**
*Battle, East Sussex*
(01424) 775705
english-heritage.org.uk
*William the Conqueror's abbey commemorates the fallen.*

**Arundel Castle**
*Arundel, West Sussex*
(01903) 883136
arundelcastle.org
*Castle and stately home with priceless collections.*

**Bateman's**
*Burwash, East Sussex*
(01435) 882302
nationaltrust.org.uk
*Jacobean house, the home of Rudyard Kipling.*

**Blenheim Palace**
*Woodstock, Oxfordshire*
(01993) 811091
blenheimpalace.com
*Baroque palace and beautiful Capability Brown parkland.*

**Bodiam Castle**
*Bodiam, East Sussex*
(01580) 830196
nationaltrust.org.uk
*Magical late-medieval moated castle.*

**Canterbury Cathedral**
*Canterbury, Kent*
(01227) 762862
canterbury-cathedral.org
*Seat of the Archbishop of Canterbury.*

**Chichester Cathedral**
*Chichester, West Sussex*
(01243) 782595
chichestercathedral.org.uk
*Splendid medieval cathedral with art treasures.*

**Dapdune Wharf**
*Guildford, Surrey*
(01483) 561389
nationaltrust.org.uk
*Interactive exhibitions and a restored Wey barge.*

**Dover Castle and Secret Wartime Tunnels**
*Dover, Kent*
(01304) 211067
english-heritage.org.uk
*Historic nerve centre for Battle of Britain.*

**Farnham Castle**
*Farnham, Surrey*
(01252) 721194
farnhamcastle.com
*Historic home of the Bishops of Winchester.*

**Fishbourne Roman Palace**
*Chichester, West Sussex*
(01243) 785859
sussexpast.co.uk/fishbourne
*Remains of Roman residence with beautiful mosaics.*

**Goodwood House**
*Chichester, West Sussex*
(01243) 755048
goodwood.co.uk
*Stately home with superb art and furniture.*

**Guildford Castle**
*Guildford, Surrey*
(01483) 444750
guildford.gov.uk
*Imposing ruins and restored 12thC stone keep.*

**Hever Castle and Gardens**
*near Edenbridge, Kent*
(01732) 865224
hevercastle.co.uk
*Moated castle, the childhood home of Anne Boleyn.*

**Leeds Castle and Gardens**
*near Maidstone, Kent*
(01622) 765400
leeds-castle.com
*Medieval castle set on two islands.*

**Mottisfont Abbey Garden, House and Estate**
*Mottisfont, Hampshire*
(01794) 340757
nationaltrust.org.uk
*Glorious grounds of 13thC former priory.*

**Osborne House**
*East Cowes, Isle of Wight*
(01983) 200022
english-heritage.org.uk
*Queen Victoria's opulent seaside retreat.*

**Penshurst Place and Gardens**
*Penshurst, Kent*
(01892) 870307
penshurstplace.com
*Medieval manor house with Tudor gardens.*

**Petworth House & Park**
*Petworth, West Sussex*
(01798) 342207
nationaltrust.org.uk
*Magnificent house and internationally important art collection.*

**Polesden Lacey**
*near Dorking, Surrey*
(01372) 452048
nationaltrust.org.uk
*Opulent Edwardian interiors in downland setting.*

**Royal Pavilion**
*Brighton, East Sussex*
(01273) 290900
royalpavilion.org.uk
*King George IV's extravagant seaside palace.*

**Waverley Abbey**
*Farnham, Surrey*
(01483) 252000
english-heritage.org.uk
*Ruins of England's first Cistercian abbey.*

**Winchester Cathedral**
*Winchester, Hampshire*
(01962) 857200
winchester-cathedral.org.uk
*Magnificent medieval cathedral with soaring Gothic nave.*

**Windsor Castle**
*Windsor, Berkshire*
(020) 7766 7304
royalcollection.org.uk
*Official residence of HM The Queen.*

## Indoors

**Ashford Designer Outlet**
*Ashford, Kent*
(01233) 895900
ashforddesigneroutlet.com
*One of Europe's most spectacular shopping destinations.*

**Bletchley Park**
*Bletchley, Buckinghamshire*
(01908) 640404
bletchleypark.org.uk
*Wartime code-breaking with the famous Enigma machines.*

**De La Warr Pavilion**
*Bexhill-on-Sea, East Sussex*
(01424) 229111
dlwp.com
*Superb Modernist pavilion housing theatre and gallery.*

**Denbies Wine Estate**
*Dorking, Surrey*
(01306) 876616
denbiesvineyard.co.uk
*Englands largest vineyard, set in 265 acres.*

**Dickens World**
*Chatham, Kent*
(01634) 890421
dickensworld.co.uk
*Fascinating journey through Dickens' life and times.*

**Gunwharf Quays**
*Portsmouth, Hampshire*
(023) 9283 6700
gunwharf-quays.com
*Innovative retail, restaurant and leisure destination.*

**Mercedes-Benz World**
*Weybridge, Surrey*
0870 400 4000
mercedes-benzworld.co.uk
*Thrilling driving experiences and fascinating attractions.*

**Pallant House Gallery**
*Chichester, West Sussex*
(01243) 774557
pallant.org.uk
*Queen Anne house holding renowned art collection.*

## Outdoors

**Ascot Racecourse**
*Ascot, Berkshire*
0870 727 1234
ascot.co.uk
*Flat and jump racing throughout the year.*

**Bedgebury National Pinetum**
*Goudhurst, Kent*
(01580) 879820
forestry.gov.uk/bedgebury
*The world's finest collection of conifers.*

**Borde Hill Garden**
*Haywards Heath, West Sussex*
(01444) 450326
bordehill.co.uk
*Beautiful and botanically rich heritage garden.*

**Claremont Landscape Garden**
*Esher, Surrey*
(01372) 467806
nationaltrust.org.uk
*One of the finest English landscape gardens.*

**Exbury Gardens and Steam Railway**
*Exbury, Hampshire*
(023) 8089 1203
exbury.co.uk
*Vast woodland garden with circular railway.*

**Gardens and Grounds of Herstmonceux Castle**
*Herstmonceux, East Sussex*
(01323) 833816
herstmonceux-castle.com
*Magnificent moated castle with Elizabethan gardens.*

**Go Ape!**
*Choose from three South East locations*

*Bracknell, Berkshire*

*Leeds Castle, near Maidstone, Kent*

*Wendover Woods, Buckinghamshire*

0845 643 9215
goape.co.uk
*Rope bridges, swings and zip slides.*

**High Beeches Gardens**
*Handcross, West Sussex*
(01444) 400589
highbeeches.com
*Peaceful, landscaped woodland and water gardens.*

**Leonardslee Lakes and Gardens**
*Lower Beeding, West Sussex*
(01403) 891212
leonardslee.com
*Glorious rhododendrons and azaleas in 240-acre valley.*

**Loseley Park**
*Guildford, Surrey*
(01483) 304440
loseley-park.com
*Beautiful Elizabethan mansion and gardens.*

**Nymans Garden**
*Handcross, West Sussex*
(01444) 405250
nationaltrust.org.uk
*Romantic garden with outstanding rare tree collection.*

**Painshill Park**
*Cobham, Surrey*
(01932) 868113
painshill.co.uk
*Beatifully restored and renovated park with follies.*

**RHS Garden Wisley**
*Woking, Surrey*
(01483) 224234
rhs.org.uk
*A working encyclopedia of British gardening.*

**Sissinghurst Castle Garden**
*Sissinghurst, Kent*
(01580) 710700
nationaltrust.org.uk
*Celebrated gardens of enclosed compartments around mansion.*

**Spinnaker Tower**
*Portsmouth, Hampshire*
(023) 9285 7520
spinnakertower.co.uk
*Breathtaking views from 170m landmark.*

**Wakehurst Place Gardens**
*near Haywards Heath, West Sussex*
(01444) 894066
kew.org
*Kew's beautiful country garden.*

**ASSURANCE OF A GREAT DAY OUT**
Attractions with this sign participate in the Visitor Attraction Quality Assurance Scheme which recognises high standards in all aspects of the visitor experience.

## Events 2009

**Sea your history**
Portsmouth
seayourhistory.org.uk
**Until Apr 2009**

**A Study in Sherlock**
Portsmouth
portsmouthmuseums.co.uk
**All year**

**New Year Steam Day**
Didcot
didcotrailwaycentre.org.uk
**1 Jan**

**Sandown Park's Golden Cup Final**
Esher
sandown.co.uk
**Apr**

**Brighton Festival**
Brighton
brightonfestival.org
**2 - 24 May**

**Derby Day at Epsom Downs Racecourse**
Epsom
epsomderby.co.uk
**Jun**

**Royal Ascot**
Ascot
royalascot.co.uk
**16 - 20 Jun**

**Henley Royal Regatta**
Henley-on-Thames
hrr.co.uk
**1 Jul - 5 Jul**

**Skandia Cowes Week**
Cowes
skandiacowesweek.co.uk
**1 - 8 Aug**

**Ringwood Carnival at Market Place and The Bickerley**
Ringwood
ringwoodcarnival.org
**19 Sep***

** provisional date at time of going to press*

# Regional contacts and information

For more information on accommodation, attractions, activities, events and holidays in South East England, contact the regional tourism organisation below. The website has a wealth of information and you can order or download publications.

## South East England

The following publications are available from Tourism South East by logging on to **visitsoutheastengland.com** or calling **(023) 8062 5400**:

### Publications

- **Escape into the Countryside**
- **Distinctive Country Inns**
- **We Know Just the Place**

### E-Brochures

- **Family Fun**
- **Timeless Treasures**
- **Just the Two of Us**

Clockwise: Freshwater Bay, Isle of Wight; Savill Garden, Surrey; Bewl Water, Kent; Canterbury Cathedral, Kent

# Tourist Information Centres

When you arrive at your destination, visit an Official Partner Tourist Information Centre for quality assured help with accommodation and information about local attractions and events, or email your request before you go. To search for attractions and Tourist Information Centres on the move just text INFO to 62233, and a web link will be sent to your mobile phone. To find a Tourist Information Centre by region visit enjoyEngland.com/find-tic.

| | | | |
|---|---|---|---|
| **Bicester** | Unit 86a, Bicester Village | (01869) 369055 | bicester.vc@cherwell-dc.gov.uk |
| **Brighton** | Pavilion Buildings | 0906 711 2255** | brighton-tourism@brighton-hove.gov.uk |
| **Canterbury** | 12/13 Sun Street | (01227) 378100 | canterburyinformation@canterbury.gov.uk |
| **Chichester** | 29a South Street | (01243) 775888 | chitic@chichester.gov.uk |
| **Cowes** | 9 The Arcade | (01983) 813818 | info@islandbreaks.co.uk |
| **Dover** | The Old Town Gaol | (01304) 205108 | tic@doveruk.com |
| **Hastings** | Queens Square | (01424) 781111 | hic@hastings.gov.uk |
| **Newport** | High Street | (01983) 813818 | info@islandbreaks.co.uk |
| **Oxford** | 15/16 Broad Street | (01865) 726871 | tic@oxford.gov.uk |
| **Portsmouth** | Clarence Esplanade | (023) 9282 6722 | vis@portsmouthcc.gov.uk |
| **Portsmouth** | The Hard | (023) 9282 6722 | vis@portsmouthcc.gov.uk |
| **Rochester** | 95 High Street | (01634) 843666 | visitor.centre@medway.gov.uk |
| **Royal Tunbridge Wells** | The Pantiles | (01892) 515675 | touristinformationcentre @tunbridgewells.gov.uk |
| **Ryde** | 81-83 Union Street | (01983) 813818 | info@islandbreaks.co.uk |
| **Sandown** | 8 High Street | (01983) 813818 | info@islandbreaks.co.uk |
| **Shanklin** | 67 High Street | (01983) 813818 | info@islandbreaks.co.uk |
| **Southampton** | 9 Civic Centre Road | (023) 8083 3333 | tourist.information@southampton.gov.uk |
| **Winchester** | High Street | (01962 840500 | tourism@winchester.gov.uk |
| **Windsor** | Royal Windsor Central Station | (01753) 743900 | windsor.tic@rbwm.gov.uk |
| **Yarmouth** | The Quay | (01983) 813818 | info@islandbreaks.co.uk |

**calls to this number are charged at premium rate

# Ratings you can trust

enjoyEngland.com
★★★
GUEST HOUSE

When you're looking for a place to stay, you need a rating system you can trust. Star ratings are your clear guide to what to expect and are easy to understand. Properties are visited annually by our professional assessors, so you can be confident that your accommodation has been thoroughly checked and rated for quality before you make a booking.

Based on the internationally recognised rating scheme of one to five stars operated by all national assessing bodies, the system puts great emphasis on quality and is based on research which shows exactly what consumers are looking for when choosing accommodation.

Progressively higher levels of quality and customer care must be provided for each of the one to five star ratings. The rating reflects the unique character of bed and breakfast accommodation, and covers areas such as cleanliness, hospitality, bedrooms, bathrooms and food quality.

Look out, too, for Enjoy England's Gold and Silver Awards, that are awarded to those establishments which not only achieve the overall quality required for their star rating, but also reach the highest levels of quality in those specific areas which guests identify as being really important for them.

where to stay in

# South East England

All place names in the blue bands are shown on the maps at the front of this guide.

A complete listing of all Enjoy England assessed accommodation covered by this guide appears at the back.

## Accommodation symbols

Symbols give useful information about services and facilities. On page 7 you can find a key to these symbols.

## ABINGDON, Oxfordshire Map ref 2C1

★★★★
GUEST ACCOMMODATION

B&B PER ROOM PER NIGHT
S £64.00–£67.00
D £81.00–£84.00

*Sign up on our website for special offers and last-minute bookings. Discounts available for block bookings. Everyone is welcome!*

### Kingfisher Barn

Rye Farm, Abingdon OX14 3NN **t** (01235) 537538 **e** info@kingfisherbarn.com

**kingfisherbarn.com** SPECIAL OFFERS • REAL-TIME BOOKING

**open** All year
**bedrooms** 2 double, 8 twin
**bathrooms** All en suite
**payment** Credit/debit cards, cash, cheques

Situated around a pretty courtyard garden, our attractive rooms are very comfortable, homely and fresh. A continental-style breakfast is delivered to your room in the morning at a time you request. Located in the Oxfordshire countryside, close to the River Thames, with easy access to A34, M4 and M40.

**SAT NAV** *OX14 3NN*

Room General Leisure

## ADDERBURY, Oxfordshire Map ref 2C1

★★★
INN

B&B PER ROOM PER NIGHT
S £45.00–£65.00
D £55.00–£85.00

EVENING MEAL PER PERSON
£6.00–£15.00

### The Bell Inn

High Street, Adderbury, Banbury OX17 3LS **t** (01295) 810338 **e** info@the-bell.com

**the-bell.com**

**open** All year
**bedrooms** 1 double, 1 twin
**bathrooms** 1 en suite, 1 private
**payment** Credit/debit cards, cash, cheques

Traditional English inn serving award-winning ales and home-cooked food. With its striking inglenook fireplace, the Bell offers a warm and friendly welcome to customers old and new. Quiet location, pretty village on the edge of the Cotswolds. Regular folk and quiz nights. Traditional pub games including 'Aunt Sally'!

**SAT NAV** *OX17 3LS*

Room General Leisure

For **key to symbols** see page 7

## ALDWORTH, Berkshire Map ref 2C2

★★★★
BED & BREAKFAST

B&B PER ROOM PER NIGHT
S £30.00–£35.00
D £60.00–£70.00

### Fieldview Cottage

Bell Lane, Aldworth, Reading RG8 9SB **t** (01635) 578964 **e** hunt@fieldvu.freeserve.co.uk

**bedrooms** 1 double, 1 twin, 1 single
**bathrooms** 2 private
**payment** Cash, cheques

Fieldview is a pretty cottage in the centre of Aldworth, situated high on the Downs and adjoining the Ridgeway, an ideal base for walking, cycling and horse-riding. M4/A34 junction 12/13, Oxford, Bath, Windsor and Heathrow within easy reach. Only 2.5 miles from main railway line – Paddington 45 minutes.

**SAT NAV** *RG8 9SB*

Room TV General P

## ALRESFORD, Hampshire Map ref 2C2

★★★
BED & BREAKFAST

B&B PER ROOM PER NIGHT
S £30.00
D £60.00

### Haygarth

Val Ramshaw, 82 Jacklyns Lane, Alresford SO24 9LJ **t** (01962) 732715 & 07986 372895

**open** All year
**bedrooms** 3 double
**bathrooms** 2 en suite, 1 private
**payment** Cash, cheques

A pleasant welcome awaits visitors to Haygarth. Located close to town centre and golf course. Convenient for Winchester, Salisbury, New Forest, Watercress Line and Wayfarers Walk. Relax and unwind in the heart of Hampshire. Guest annexe includes separate entrance, lounge, kitchen, en suite bedrooms. Sky TV.

**SAT NAV** *SO24 9LJ*

Room TV General P Leisure

## ALTON, Hampshire Map ref 2C2

★★★★
BED & BREAKFAST

B&B PER ROOM PER NIGHT
S £53.00–£59.00
D £70.00–£78.00

### Neatham Barn

Holybourne, Neatham, Alton GU34 4NP **t** (01420) 544215 **e** neathambarn@f2s.com

**neathambarn.com**

**open** All year
**bedrooms** 1 double/twin
**bathrooms** En suite
**payment** Cash, cheques

Situated in a tiny hamlet, up a quiet country lane, this detached oak-barn annexe occupies a lovely setting in the grounds of Neatham Cottage. Self-catering an option. Please enquire for prices.

**SAT NAV** *GU34 4NP*

Room TV General P Leisure

enjoyEngland.com Gold AWARD

## Gold and Silver Awards

Gold and Silver Awards are given to establishments achieving the highest levels of quality and service. You can find more information at the front of the guide, and an index to all accommodation achieving these awards at the back.

enjoyEngland.com Silver AWARD

## ALTON, Hampshire Map ref 2C2

★★★★
BED & BREAKFAST

B&B PER ROOM PER NIGHT
S £40.00–£45.00
D £60.00–£70.00

*The lower rates are for long-term, uninterrupted stays.*

### St Mary's Hall

18 Albert Road, Alton GU34 1LP **t** (01420) 88269 **e** joanmossop@stmaryshall.com

**stmaryshall.com**

**open** All year
**bedrooms** 2 twin, 1 single
**bathrooms** 1 en suite, 1 private
**payment** Cash, cheques

Beautifully converted church in a quiet town location with Jane Austen's house, restaurants, pubs and good transport links all within easy walking distance. All rooms have recently been refurbished to a very high standard, with a spacious, relaxing guest lounge overlooking the garden with satellite TV, DVD player and fridge.

**SAT NAV** *GU34 1LP*

Room General P

## ANDOVER, Hampshire Map ref 2C2

★★★★
BED & BREAKFAST
SILVER AWARD

B&B PER ROOM PER NIGHT
S £40.00–£55.00
D £65.00–£90.00

### May Cottage

Thruxton, Andover SP11 8LZ **t** (01264) 771241 **e** info@maycottage-thruxton.co.uk

**maycottage-thruxton.co.uk**

**open** All year
**bedrooms** 2 double, 1 twin
**bathrooms** 2 en suite, 1 private
**payment** Cash, cheques

May Cottage dates back to 1740 and is situated in the heart of this picturesque, tranquil village with two old inns serving food. All rooms have en suite/private bathroom, TV, radio, beverage tray. Guests' own sitting/dining room. Pretty, secluded garden with stream. Many National Trust properties and stately homes/gardens within easy reach. Private parking. Non-smoking establishment.

**SAT NAV** *SP11 8LZ*

Room TV General P Leisure

## ARUNDEL, West Sussex Map ref 2D3

★★★★★
RESTAURANT WITH ROOMS
GOLD AWARD

B&B PER ROOM PER NIGHT
D £100.00–£180.00

EVENING MEAL PER PERSON
£16.00–£30.00

*Enjoy a three-course dinner with coffee for £20 per person from Mon-Thu, saving £10 per person.*

### Arundel House Restaurant & Rooms

11 High Street, Arundel BN18 9AD **t** (01903) 882136 & (01903) 882136
**e** mail@arundelhouseonline.co.uk

**arundelhouseonline.co.uk** SPECIAL OFFERS

**open** All year except Christmas
**bedrooms** 5 double
**bathrooms** All en suite
**payment** Credit/debit cards, cash

Relax in one of our five contemporary yet cosseting bedrooms. Revive yourself under the deluge of hot water delivered from eight-inch shower roses, and revitalise in our intimate and welcoming restaurant serving modern British-led cuisine, with an occasional French or Mediterranean twist. Reward yourself with a stay at Arundel House.

**SAT NAV** *BN18 9AD* **ONLINE MAP**

Room TV SC General 16 Leisure

## Using map references

Map references refer to the colour maps at the front of this guide.

## ASHFORD, Kent Map ref 3B4

★★★
GUEST ACCOMMODATION

B&B PER ROOM PER NIGHT
S Min £35.00
D Min £60.00

EVENING MEAL PER PERSON
£12.00–£15.00

### Dean Court Farm

Challock Lane, Westwell, Ashford TN25 4NH **t** (01233) 712924

**open** All year except Christmas
**bedrooms** 1 double, 1 twin, 1 family
**bathrooms** 1 en suite
**payment** Cash, cheques

Period farmhouse on working farm with modern amenities. Magnificent views in quiet valley. Comfortable accommodation with separate sitting room for guests.

**SAT NAV** *TN25 4NH*

Room General P

## AYLESBURY, Buckinghamshire Map ref 2C1

★★★★
BED & BREAKFAST
SILVER AWARD

B&B PER ROOM PER NIGHT
S £40.00
D £70.00

### Tanamera

37 Bishopstone Village, Bishopstone, Aylesbury HP17 8SH **t** (01296) 748551 **e** tanamera@tesco.net

**open** All year except Christmas and New Year
**bedrooms** 1 double
**bathrooms** En suite
**payment** Cash, cheques, euros

A warm welcome with owner's personal attention. Quality English breakfast, excellent accommodation, large, attractive, en suite, twin or king-size double, TV/video, tea/coffee, central heating. Central location, good train service, interesting area, historic houses (Waddesdon Manor, Chequers), Quainton working-steam museum. Country pub in village, private parking, non-smoking.

**SAT NAV** *HP17 8SH*

Room TV General P

## BANBURY, Oxfordshire Map ref 2C1

★★★★
BED & BREAKFAST

B&B PER ROOM PER NIGHT
S £30.00–£32.50
D £60.00–£65.00

EVENING MEAL PER PERSON
Min £18.00

### St Martins House

Warkworth, Banbury OX17 2AG **t** (01295) 712684

**open** All year
**bedrooms** 2 double
**bathrooms** 1 en suite, 1 private
**payment** Cash, cheques

600-year-old listed converted barn with galleried dining room. Comfortable en suite rooms with TV. Safe parking, evening meals by arrangement, French and English country cooking.

**SAT NAV** *OX17 2AG*

Room TV General 2

## Do you have access needs?

Look for the National Accessible Scheme symbols if you have special hearing, visual or mobility needs. An index of accommodation participating in the scheme can be found at the back of this guide.

## BARHAM, Kent Map ref 3B4

★★★★
INN

B&B PER ROOM PER NIGHT
S £40.00–£50.00
D £55.00–£75.00

EVENING MEAL PER PERSON
£6.25–£19.95

*Discounts available when staying 3 or more nights.*

### The Duke of Cumberland

The Street, Canterbury CT4 6NY **t** (01227) 831396 **e** info@dukeofcumberland.co.uk

**dukeofcumberland.co.uk** GUEST REVIEWS

**open** All year
**bedrooms** 2 double, 1 family
**bathrooms** All en suite
**payment** Credit/debit cards, cash, cheques

This 18thC inn is located in the beautiful village of Barham nestled in the scenic Elham valley. First and foremost a traditional English country pub, we offer comfortable and attractive bedrooms and home-cooked food. Ideally situated for exploring Canterbury and the surrounding 'Garden of England', a warm welcome awaits.

**SAT NAV** *CT4 6NY* **ONLINE MAP**

Room General Leisure

## BEAULIEU, Hampshire Map ref 2C3

★★★★
GUEST ACCOMMODATION

B&B PER ROOM PER NIGHT
S £30.00–£45.00
D £56.00–£80.00

*15% discount for Christmas breaks on a room-only basis. 3-for-2 weekend breaks Oct-Mar (excl Bank Holidays).*

### Dale Farm House

Manor Road, Applemore Hill, Dibden, Southampton SO45 5TJ **t** (023) 8084 9632

**dalefarmhouse.co.uk** GUEST REVIEWS • SPECIAL OFFERS • REAL-TIME BOOKING

**open** All year
**bedrooms** 3 double, 2 family
**bathrooms** 4 en suite
**payment** Cash, cheques

Beautiful 18thC farmhouse in secluded wooded setting with direct access for walks or cycling. Peaceful garden in which to unwind and a bird-watcher's paradise. Excellent food to satisfy your appetite. Barbecues on request. Near beaches and ferry link to Southampton. Spoil yourself at this BBC-holiday-programme-featured bed and breakfast.

**SAT NAV** *SO45 5TJ* **ONLINE MAP**

Room General Leisure

## BIDDENDEN, Kent Map ref 3B4

★★★★
GUEST ACCOMMODATION

B&B PER ROOM PER NIGHT
S £45.00–£55.00
D £55.00–£70.00

EVENING MEAL PER PERSON
£17.50

### Heron Cottage

Biddenden, Ashford TN27 8HH **t** (01580) 291358

**heroncottage.info**

**open** February to December.
**bedrooms** 3 double, 2 twin, 2 family
**bathrooms** 6 en suite
**payment** Cash, cheques

Situated between historic Biddenden and Sissinghurst Castle, and set in five acres surrounded completely by farmland. The bedrooms are thoughtfully equipped and have co-ordinated soft furnishings. Breakfast is served in the smart dining room and there is a cosy lounge with an open fire. One room with wheelchair access.

**SAT NAV** *TN27 8HH*

Room General Leisure

## Has every property been assessed?

All accommodation in this guide has been rated for quality, or is awaiting assessment, by a professional national tourist board assessor.

## BLADBEAN, Kent Map ref 3B4

★★★★
GUEST ACCOMMODATION

B&B PER ROOM PER NIGHT
S £35.00–£40.00
D £50.00–£60.00

EVENING MEAL PER PERSON
£8.00–£12.00

### Molehills

Bladbean, Canterbury CT4 6LU **t** (01303) 840051 **e** molehills84@hotmail.com

**molehillsbedbreakfast.co.uk**

**open** All year except Christmas
**bedrooms** 1 double, 1 twin
**bathrooms** All en suite
**payment** Cash, cheques, euros

The house, in large gardens, is in a peaceful hamlet within the beautiful Elham Valley. We are within easy reach of Canterbury and the Channel terminals. We produce home-grown vegetables and excellent home cooking. Our comfortable accommodation includes ground floor bedrooms, sitting room with woodburning stove and conservatory.

**SAT NAV** *CT4 6LU*

Room TV General P

## BOGNOR REGIS, West Sussex Map ref 2C3

★★★
GUEST ACCOMMODATION

B&B PER ROOM PER NIGHT
S £25.00–£40.00
D £50.00–£80.00

### Jubilee Guest House

5 Gloucester Road, Bognor Regis PO21 1NU **t** (01243) 863016 **e** jubileeguesthouse@tiscali.co.uk

**jubileeguesthouse.com**

Family-run business, 75yds from seafront and beach. Ideal for visiting Butlins family entertainment resort, Chichester, Goodwood, Fontwell, Arundel, Portsmouth and the Isle of Wight.

**open** All year except Christmas and New Year
**bedrooms** 1 double, 2 single, 3 family
**bathrooms** 2 en suite, 1 private
**payment** Credit/debit cards, cash, cheques, euros

Room TV General P

## BOGNOR REGIS, West Sussex Map ref 2C3

★★★★
BED & BREAKFAST

B&B PER ROOM PER NIGHT
S £40.00–£45.00
D £70.00–£90.00

### White Horses Felpham

Clyde Road, Felpham, Bognor Regis PO22 7AH **t** (01243) 824320 **e** info@whitehorsesfelpham.co.uk

**whitehorsesfelpham.co.uk**

**open** All year
**bedrooms** 2 double, 1 twin, 1 family
**bathrooms** 3 en suite, 1 private
**payment** Cash, cheques

White Horses is located in a quiet cul-de-sac 20yds from Felpham beach. It has recently been refurbished and offers high-quality accommodation in a friendly environment. A three-mile promenade close to the entrance provides easy seaside walking with a variety of amenities for all ages.

**SAT NAV** *PO22 7AH* **ONLINE MAP**

WALKERS WELCOME CYCLISTS WELCOME

Room TV General P

## Don't forget www.

Web addresses throughout this guide are shown without the prefix www. Please include www. in the address line of your browser. If a web address does not follow this style it is shown in full.

## BONCHURCH, Isle of Wight Map ref 2C3

★★★★
GUEST ACCOMMODATION

B&B PER ROOM PER NIGHT
S £35.00–£43.00
D £70.00–£88.00

EVENING MEAL PER PERSON
£12.00

*4-night special break including breakfast, dinner and car ferry from any port from £160.00.*

### The Lake

Shore Road, Bonchurch, Ventnor PO38 1RF **t** (01983) 852613 **e** enquiries@lakehotel.co.uk

**lakehotel.co.uk**

**open** February to November
**bedrooms** 10 double, 5 twin, 1 single, 4 family
**bathrooms** All en suite
**payment** Credit/debit cards, cash, cheques, euros

Charming country-house hotel in two acres of beautiful gardens. Located on the seaward side of Bonchurch Pond in the 'olde worlde' village of Bonchurch. Run by the same family for over 40 years, we are confident of offering you the best-value accommodation and food on our beautiful island.

**SAT NAV** *PO38 1RF*

Room General 3 P Leisure

## BONCHURCH, Isle of Wight Map ref 2C3

★★★★★
GUEST HOUSE
SILVER AWARD

B&B PER ROOM PER NIGHT
S £65.00–£150.00
D £110.00–£190.00

### Winterbourne Country House

Bonchurch Village Road, Ventnor PO38 1RQ **t** (01983) 852535 **e** info@winterbournehouse.co.uk

**winterbournehouse.co.uk**

**open** All year except Christmas and New Year
**bedrooms** 3 double, 1 twin, 1 single, 2 suites
**bathrooms** 6 en suite, 1 private
**payment** Credit/debit cards, cash, cheques

Winterbourne is a country house of great charm and character, located in one of the most beautiful and tranquil settings on the island. Enchanting gardens ablaze with colour in season. You will receive a welcome of genuine warmth in the house where Charles Dickens made his home whilst writing 'David Copperfield'.

**SAT NAV** *PO38 1RQ*

Room General 11 P Leisure

## BRASTED, Kent Map ref 2D2

★★★★
BED & BREAKFAST

B&B PER ROOM PER NIGHT
S £30.00–£35.00
D £60.00–£70.00

### The Mount House

Brasted, Westerham TN16 1JB **t** (01959) 563617 **e** diana@themounthouse.com

**themounthouse.com**

Large, early-Georgian family residence in centre of village. Listed Grade II. Convenient for Knole, Hever, Penshurst and fast trains to London from Sevenoaks.

**open** All year except Christmas and New Year
**bedrooms** 1 double, 1 twin, 1 single
**bathrooms** 1 en suite, 1 private
**payment** Cash, cheques

Room General 1 P Leisure

## BREDE, East Sussex Map ref 3B4

★★
BED & BREAKFAST

B&B PER ROOM PER NIGHT
S £25.00–£30.00
D £50.00–£55.00

EVENING MEAL PER PERSON
£12.00–£18.00

### 2 Stonelink Cottages

Stubb Lane, Brede, Rye TN31 6BL **t** (01424) 882943 & 07802 573612 **e** stonelinkC@aol.com

**visit-rye.co.uk**

Traditional clapboard house overlooking Brede Valley, surrounded on all sides by 134 acres of farming land. Quiet, relaxing. Close to Rye, Hastings and Tunbridge Wells. Evening meals by prior arrangement.

**open** All year except Christmas and New Year
**bedrooms** 1 double, 1 single
**payment** Cash, cheques

Room General P

For **key to symbols** see page 7

## BRIGHSTONE, Isle of Wight Map ref 2C3

★★★★
FARMHOUSE

B&B PER ROOM PER NIGHT
S £35.00–£45.00
D £60.00–£70.00

### Chilton Farm B&B

Chilton Farm, Chilton Lane, Newport PO30 4DS **t** (01983) 740338 **e** info@chiltonfarm.co.uk

**chiltonfarm.co.uk**

A warm welcome assured on our 800-acre working farm. All rooms en suite in separate accommodation behind main farmhouse. Breakfast in farmhouse. Two tennis courts, large garden, close to sea.

**open** All year except Christmas and New Year
**bedrooms** 2 double, 1 twin, 1 suite
**bathrooms** All en suite
**payment** Credit/debit cards, cash, cheques

Room General P Leisure

## BRIGHTON & HOVE, East Sussex Map ref 2D3

★★★★
GUEST ACCOMMODATION

B&B PER ROOM PER NIGHT
S £45.00–£55.00
D £70.00–£140.00

### Adelaide House

51 Regency Square, Brighton BN1 2FF **t** (01273) 205286 **e** info@adelaidehotel.co.uk

**adelaidehotel.co.uk**

Elegant Regency town-house hotel, centrally situated in Brighton's premier seafront square convenient for all amenities, NCP parking and conference venues. No lift.

**open** All year
**bedrooms** 7 double, 1 twin, 3 single, 1 family
**bathrooms** 9 en suite, 3 private
**payment** Credit/debit cards, cash

Room General

## BRIGHTON & HOVE, East Sussex Map ref 2D3

★★★
GUEST ACCOMMODATION

B&B PER ROOM PER NIGHT
S £25.00–£40.00
D £60.00–£80.00

### Andorra Guest Accommodation

15-16 Oriental Place, Brighton BN1 2LJ **t** (01273) 321787

**andorrahotelbrighton.co.uk**

Try our established, comfortable guesthouse with well-appointed bedrooms. Whether your stay is for a holiday, attending a conference or visiting town overnight, it will be an enjoyable one.

**open** All year
**bedrooms** 7 double, 2 twin, 6 single, 4 family
**bathrooms** 17 en suite, 2 private
**payment** Credit/debit cards

Room General 16 Leisure

## BRIGHTON & HOVE, East Sussex Map ref 2D3

★★★
GUEST ACCOMMODATION

B&B PER ROOM PER NIGHT
S £25.00–£40.00
D £50.00–£90.00

### Atlantic Seafront

16 Marine Parade, Brighton BN2 1TL **t** (01273) 695944 **e** majanatlantic@hotmail.com

**atlantichotelbrighton.co.uk**

Attractive, newly refurbished, centrally located sea-facing hotel right opposite Brighton Pier and Sea Life Centre. The historic Royal Pavilion and famous Lanes are across the road. Brighton Centre nearby.

**open** All year except Christmas
**bedrooms** 6 double, 2 single, 2 family
**bathrooms** All en suite
**payment** Credit/debit cards, cash, cheques

Room General

## BRIGHTON & HOVE, East Sussex Map ref 2D3

★★★★
GUEST ACCOMMODATION

B&B PER ROOM PER NIGHT
S £55.00–£70.00
D £110.00–£170.00

# The Neo

19 Oriental Place, Brighton BN1 2LL **t** (01273) 711104 **e** info@neohotel.com

**neohotel.com** SPECIAL OFFERS

**open** All year except Christmas
**bedrooms** 8 double, 1 single
**bathrooms** All en suite
**payment** Credit/debit cards, cash, cheques

The Neo is a chic, stylish hotel with nine uniquely designed rooms, a cool cocktail bar, elegant dining room and massage/treatment room. Neo's friendly, professional staff place great emphasis on attention to detail and really care about your experience. Perfect for weddings/small conferences. This hotel is an absolute gem. Free Wi-Fi and ten minutes from The Brighton Centre, shopping and nightlife.

**SAT NAV** *BN1 2LL*

Room General Leisure

## BRIGHTON & HOVE, East Sussex Map ref 2D3

★★★
GUEST ACCOMMODATION

B&B PER ROOM PER NIGHT
D £58.00–£80.00

# Russell Guest House

19 Russell Square, Brighton BN1 2EE **t** (01273) 327969 **e** info@therussell.co.uk

**therussell.co.uk**

Five-storey town-centre guesthouse in pleasant garden square. Close to the Brighton Centre, seafront and main shopping area. Unrestricted access. Theatres, cinemas and nightclubs all nearby. No lift.

**open** All year except Christmas
**bedrooms** 3 double, 2 twin, 3 family
**bathrooms** All en suite
**payment** Credit/debit cards, cash

Room General Leisure

## BRIGHTON & HOVE, East Sussex Map ref 2D3

★★★★
GUEST ACCOMMODATION

B&B PER ROOM PER NIGHT
D £75.00–£135.00

# The Townhouse Brighton

19 New Steine, Brighton BN2 1PD **t** (01273) 607456 **e** info@thetownhousebrighton.com

**thetownhousebrighton.com** GUEST REVIEWS · REAL-TIME BOOKING

**open** All year
**bedrooms** 7 double, 1 twin
**bathrooms** All en suite
**payment** Credit/debit cards, cash, cheques

Stunning themed rooms await you in this unique boutique hotel based in the heart of Brighton with views of the sea and the pier. Eight highly individual rooms help you to travel the world without ever leaving Brighton. Boutique, bespoke and bijou.

**SAT NAV** *BN2 1PD* **ONLINE MAP**

Room General Leisure

## Check the maps for accommodation locations

Colour maps at the front pinpoint all the places where accommodation is featured within the regional sections of this guide. Pick your location and then refer to the place index at the back to find the page number.

## BRIZE NORTON, Oxfordshire Map ref 2C1

★★★
GUEST ACCOMMODATION

B&B PER ROOM PER NIGHT
S £30.00–£45.00
D £55.00–£80.00

### The Priory

Manor Farm, Manor Road, Brize Norton OX18 3NA **t** (01993) 843062
**e** mail@priorymanor.wanadoo.co.uk

**priorymanor.co.uk**

Situated in Brize Norton village, a beautiful character house in natural stone, set in 0.75 acres of beautiful gardens. Ample parking, comfortable rooms with tea-/coffee-making facilities and colour TV.

**open** All year
**bedrooms** 2 double, 1 twin, 1 family, 2 suites
**bathrooms** 5 en suite, 1 private
**payment** Cash, cheques, euros

Room General P Leisure

## BROADSTAIRS, Kent Map ref 3C3

★★★★
GUEST ACCOMMODATION

B&B PER ROOM PER NIGHT
S £40.00–£60.00
D £80.00–£90.00

EVENING MEAL PER PERSON
£25.00

### Bay Tree Broadstairs

12 Eastern Esplanade, Broadstairs CT10 1DR **t** (01843) 862502

**open** All year except Christmas and New Year
**bedrooms** 9 double, 1 twin, 1 single
**bathrooms** All en suite
**payment** Credit/debit cards, cash, cheques

Situated on the lovely Eastern Esplanade overlooking Stone Bay, the hotel enjoys panoramic sea views across the English Channel. Minutes from the town centre and sandy beaches. A warm welcome awaits you at this family-run hotel.

**SAT NAV** *CT10 1DR*

Room General 10 P

## BROCKENHURST, Hampshire Map ref 2C3

★★
BED & BREAKFAST

B&B PER ROOM PER NIGHT
S £20.00–£25.00
D £40.00–£50.00

### Goldenhayes

9 Chestnut Road, Brockenhurst SO42 7RF **t** (01590) 623743

Single-storey, owner-occupied home, in central but quiet situation. Close to village, station and open forest. Large garden.

**open** All year
**bedrooms** 1 twin, 1 family
**payment** Cash, cheques, euros

Room General P Leisure

## BROOKLAND, Kent Map ref 3B4

★★★★
INN

B&B PER ROOM PER NIGHT
S £50.00–£70.00
D £50.00–£70.00

EVENING MEAL PER PERSON
£8.00–£25.00

### The Royal Oak

High Street, Brookland, Romney Marsh TN29 9QR **t** (01797) 344215 **e** dzrj@btinternet.com

**royaloakbrookland.co.uk**

**open** All year
**bedrooms** 1 double, 1 twin
**bathrooms** 1 en suite, 1 private
**payment** Credit/debit cards, cash, cheques

An historic country inn offering top quality food with menus to suit all pockets and superbly appointed B&B accommodation. Short-listed as a finalist in the 'Newcomer of the Year' Publican Awards 2008.

**SAT NAV** *TN29 9QR* **ONLINE MAP**

Room General P

## BUCKINGHAM, Buckinghamshire Map ref 2C1

★★★★
**BED & BREAKFAST**

**B&B PER ROOM PER NIGHT**
S £40.00
D £60.00

*Rate reduced for stays of more than one night.*

### Huntsmill Farm B&B

Shalstone, Nr Buckingham MK18 5ND **t** (01280) 704852 & 07970 871104 **e** fiona@huntsmill.com

**huntsmill.com**

**open** All year except Christmas
**bedrooms** 2 double, 1 twin
**bathrooms** All en suite
**payment** Credit/debit cards, cash, cheques, euros

Home-made bread and preserves welcome you at Huntsmill Farm. Accommodation is in comfortable, en suite rooms adjacent to farmhouse, set in stone courtyard. Set in quiet location with views over open countryside. Close to many National Trust properties and Silverstone.

**SAT NAV** *MK18 5ND*

Room General 5 Leisure

## BURFORD, Oxfordshire Map ref 2B1

★★★★
**GUEST ACCOMMODATION**

**B&B PER ROOM PER NIGHT**
S £35.00–£45.00
D £60.00–£80.00

*Midweek special offers available on two nights or more. Discount given on Sunday night when staying the weekend.*

### Cotland House B&B

Fulbrook Hill, Burford OX18 4BH **t** (01993) 822382 **e** info@cotlandhouse.com

**otlandhouse.com** GUEST REVIEWS • SPECIAL OFFERS

**open** All year except Christmas and New Year
**bedrooms** 1 double, 1 twin, 1 single, 1 family
**bathrooms** All en suite
**payment** Cash, cheques

Cotland House B&B is a charming Cotswold-stone home restored to an exceptional standard with stylish, luxurious en suite rooms. A fabulous breakfast, made from organic/local produce, is served in front of a wood-burning stove or on the sunny terrace depending on the season. A perfect Cotswold base.

**SAT NAV** *OX18 4BH* **ONLINE MAP**

Room General Leisure

## BURLEY, Hampshire Map ref 2B3

★★★★
**BED & BREAKFAST GOLD AWARD**

**B&B PER ROOM PER NIGHT**
S £45.00–£50.00
D £75.00–£80.00

### Holmans

Bisterne Close, Burley, Ringwood BH24 4AZ **t** (01425) 402307 **e** holmans@talktalk.net

Charming country house set in four acres overlooking New Forest. All bedrooms en suite and tastefully furnished. Superb walking. Pub within walking distance. Own horses welcome, stabling available.

**open** All year except Christmas
**bedrooms** 2 double, 1 twin
**bathrooms** All en suite
**payment** Cash, cheques

Room General Leisure

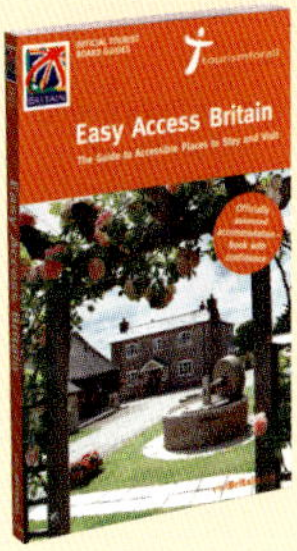


## Where can I find accessible accommodation?

If you have special hearing, visual or mobility needs, there's an index of National Accessible Scheme participants featured in this guide. For more accessible accommodation buy a copy of Easy Access Britain available online at visitbritaindirect.com, and from Tourism for All on 0845 124 997 or visit tourismforall.org.uk.

For **key to symbols** see page 7

## BURLEY, Hampshire Map ref 2B3

★★★★
BED & BREAKFAST

B&B PER ROOM PER NIGHT
S £35.00–£75.00
D £60.00–£75.00

EVENING MEAL PER PERSON
£18.00–£25.00

### Wayside Cottage

27 Garden Road, Burley, Ringwood BH24 4EA **t** (01425) 403414 **e** jwest@wayside-cottage.co.uk

**wayside-cottage.co.uk**

**open** All year
**bedrooms** 3 double, 2 twin, 1 family
**bathrooms** 5 en suite, 1 private
**payment** Cash, cheques

Enchanting wisteria-covered Edwardian cottage in peaceful location in the heart of the New Forest. A haven of tranquillity, full of antique furniture and china, ideal for walking, cycling or exploring the forest and coast, or just relax in our delightful cottage gardens. Local produce cooked by ex-professional chef. Dinners by arrangement.

**SAT NAV** *BH24 4EA*

Room General Leisure

## CADNAM, Hampshire Map ref 2C3

★★★★
GUEST HOUSE
SILVER AWARD

B&B PER ROOM PER NIGHT
S £35.00–£50.00
D £75.00–£80.00

### Twin Oaks Guest House

Southampton Road, Cadnam, New Forest SO40 2NQ **t** (023) 8081 2305
**e** enquiries@twinoaks-guesthouse.co.uk

Victorian guesthouse in beautiful village location. All en suite, off-road parking, close to restaurants, open forest and much more.

**open** All year except Christmas and New Year
**bedrooms** 3 double, 1 twin, 2 single
**bathrooms** All en suite
**payment** Cash, cheques, euros

Room General P

## CANTERBURY, Kent Map ref 3B3

★★★★
GUEST ACCOMMODATION

B&B PER ROOM PER NIGHT
S £35.00
D £55.00–£65.00

### Alexandra House

1 Roper Road, Canterbury CT2 7EH **t** (01227) 786617 **e** alexandrahouse2@aol.com

**alexandrahouse.net**

Family-run guesthouse close to city centre, cathedral, university, Canterbury West station and Marlowe Theatre. Private car parking. Full English breakfast with vegetarian options. All rooms are en suite.

**open** All year
**bedrooms** 2 double, 2 twin, 1 single, 2 family
**bathrooms** All en suite
**payment** Credit/debit cards, cash, cheques

Room General P Leisure

## CANTERBURY, Kent Map ref 3B3

★★★★
BED & BREAKFAST
SILVER AWARD

B&B PER ROOM PER NIGHT
S £42.00
D £60.00

### Bower Farm House

Bossingham Road, Stelling Minnis, Canterbury CT4 6BB **t** (01227) 709430
**e** anne@bowerbb.freeserve.co.uk

**bowerfarmhouse.co.uk**

**open** All year except Christmas
**bedrooms** 1 double, 1 twin
**bathrooms** All en suite
**payment** Cash, cheques, euros

Delightful, heavily beamed, 17thC farmhouse between the villages of Stelling Minnis and Bossingham. Canterbury and Hythe are approximately seven miles away. Home-laid eggs, home-made bread ... a peaceful countryside experience.

**SAT NAV** *CT4 6BB*

Room General P Leisure

## CANTERBURY, Kent Map ref 3B3

★★★★
GUEST HOUSE

B&B PER ROOM PER NIGHT
S £32.00–£34.00
D £56.00–£68.00

*Discounts for 2-/3-night stay Nov-Mar (excl Christmas and New Year).*

### Clare Ellen Guest House

9 Victoria Road, Canterbury CT1 3SG **t** (01227) 760205 **e** enquiry@clareellenguesthouse.co.uk

**clareellenguesthouse.co.uk** SPECIAL OFFERS

**open** All year
**bedrooms** 3 double, 2 twin, 1 single, 1 family
**bathrooms** 6 en suite, 1 private
**payment** Credit/debit cards, cash, cheques, euros

A family-run Victorian guesthouse, situated in quiet area minutes from town centre, benefits from private parking, garden, swimming pool and free internet access. Large, elegant en suite bedrooms feature TV, hairdryer, clock radio, mini-fridge and tea-/coffee-making facilities. Full English breakfast, vegetarian and special diets catered for on request.

**SAT NAV** *CT1 3SG* **ONLINE MAP**

WALKERS WELCOME CYCLISTS WELCOME FAMILIES WELCOME

Room General P Leisure

## CANTERBURY, Kent Map ref 3B3

★★★★
FARMHOUSE

B&B PER ROOM PER NIGHT
S £35.00–£45.00
D £70.00–£80.00

EVENING MEAL PER PERSON
£15.00–£20.00

### Hornbeams

Jesses Hill, Kingston, Canterbury CT4 6JD **t** (01227) 830119 **e** bandb@hornbeams.co.uk

**hornbeams.co.uk**

**open** All year except Christmas
**bedrooms** 1 double, 1 twin, 1 single
**bathrooms** 1 en suite, 1 private
**payment** Cash, cheques

Rolling hills and woodland, long views over luscious Kent, and a lovely garden. Full English breakfast on patio (weather permitting). Hornbeams is an idyllic place to stay, the ultimate escapism, yet near to local town and historical landmarks. Canterbury seven miles, Dover ten miles, Channel Tunnel 20 minutes. Good private parking.

**SAT NAV** *CT4 6JD*

Room General P Leisure

## CANTERBURY, Kent Map ref 3B3

★★★★★
GUEST ACCOMMODATION
GOLD AWARD

B&B PER ROOM PER NIGHT
S £55.00–£65.00
D £95.00–£125.00

EVENING MEAL PER PERSON
£30.00–£35.00

### Magnolia House

36 St Dunstans Terrace, Canterbury CT2 8AX **t** (01227) 765121
**e** info@magnoliahousecanterbury.co.uk

**magnoliahousecanterbury.co.uk** REAL-TIME BOOKING

Charming, late-Georgian house in quiet residential street, a ten-minute stroll from the city centre. Bedrooms have every facility for an enjoyable stay. Varied breakfasts are served overlooking the attractive walled garden.

**open** All year except Christmas
**bedrooms** 5 double, 1 twin, 1 single
**bathrooms** All en suite
**payment** Credit/debit cards, cash, cheques

Room General 12 P

## Need some ideas?

Big city buzz or peaceful panoramas? Take a fresh look at England and you may be surprised at what's right on your doorstep. Explore the diversity online at enjoyengland.com

## CANTERBURY, Kent Map ref 3B3

★★★★
GUEST ACCOMMODATION
SILVER AWARD

B&B PER ROOM PER NIGHT
S £35.00–£40.00
D £60.00–£70.00

### Oak Cottage

Elmsted, Ashford TN25 5JT **t** (01233) 750272 **e** oakcottage@invictanet.co.uk

**oakcottage-elmsted.co.uk**

An attractive 17thC cottage with independent guest wing with own TV, conservatory and beautiful garden set in unspoilt, wooded countryside. Ideally placed for Canterbury, castles, gardens, golf, steam trains, restaurants.

**open** All year except Christmas
**bedrooms** 1 double, 2 single
**bathrooms** 1 en suite
**payment** Cash, cheques, euros

Room General Leisure

## CANTERBURY, Kent Map ref 3B3

★★★★★
GUEST ACCOMMODATION

B&B PER ROOM PER NIGHT
S £50.00–£60.00
D £90.00–£115.00

*Special low season deals. See website or ring for details.*

### Yorke Lodge

50 London Road, Canterbury CT2 8LF **t** (01227) 451243 **e** info@yorkelodge.com

**yorkelodge.com**

**open** All year
**bedrooms** 5 double, 1 twin, 1 single, 1 family
**bathrooms** All en suite
**payment** Credit/debit cards, cash, cheques

Yorke Lodge is the ideal retreat after a long day sightseeing or a busy day at the office. Built in 1887 and fully refurbished over the last two years, this quintessential Victorian town house offers a warm home-from-home atmosphere, with all the modern conveniences now expected by the discerning traveller.

**SAT NAV** *CT2 8LF*

Room General Leisure

## CASSINGTON, Oxfordshire Map ref 2C1

★★★★
FARMHOUSE

B&B PER ROOM PER NIGHT
D £70.00

### Burleigh Farm

Bladon Road, Nr Cassington, Oxford OX29 4EA **t** (01865) 881352 **e** cook_jane@btconnect.com

**oxfordcity.co.uk/accom/burleighfarm**

Warm and comfortable stone farmhouse in a quiet location near Woodstock, six miles from Oxford, on Blenheim Palace Estate. On the edge of the Cotswolds, yet only an hour's drive from London.

**open** All year
**bedrooms** 1 double, 1 family
**bathrooms** All en suite
**payment** Cash, cheques

Room General

## CHALGROVE, Oxfordshire Map ref 2C2

★★
BED & BREAKFAST

B&B PER ROOM PER NIGHT
S Min £30.00
D Min £50.00

### Cornerstones

1 Cromwell Close, Chalgrove, Oxford OX44 7SE **t** (01865) 890298 **e** corner.stones@virgin.net

**http://freespace.virgin.net/corner.stones**

Bungalow in pretty village with thatched cottages. The Red Lion (0.5 miles away) serves good and reasonably priced food.

**open** All year except Christmas and New Year
**bedrooms** 2 twin
**payment** Cash, cheques

Room General 5

### Where can I get help and advice?

Tourist Information Centres offer friendly help with accommodation and holiday ideas as well as suggestions of places to visit and things to do. You'll find contact details at the beginning of each regional section.

## CHICHESTER, West Sussex Map ref 2C3

★★★
BED & BREAKFAST

B&B PER ROOM PER NIGHT
S £30.00
D £60.00

### Kia-ora

Main Road, Nutbourne, Chichester PO18 8RT **t** (01243) 572858 **e** ruthiefp@tiscali.co.uk

Views to Chichester Harbour. Warm welcome in comfortable family house. Large garden. Restaurants and country pubs within walking distance. Closed Christmas.

**open** All year except Christmas
**bedrooms** 1 double
**bathrooms** En suite
**payment** Cash, cheques, euros

Room General P

## CHICHESTER, West Sussex Map ref 2C3

★★★
BED & BREAKFAST

B&B PER ROOM PER NIGHT
S £30.00–£45.00
D £60.00–£80.00

### Pen Cottage

The Drive, Summersdale, Chichester PO19 5QA **t** (01243) 783667
**e** monicaandcolinkaye@talktalk.net

**visitsussex.org/pencottage**

Conveniently situated for the city, theatre and university, and a few minutes' drive to Goodwood. Open countryside a short walk away. A warm welcome guaranteed.

**open** All year except Christmas and New Year
**bedrooms** 1 double, 1 twin, 1 single
**bathrooms** 2 private
**payment** Cash, cheques, euros

Room General 10 P

## CHICHESTER, West Sussex Map ref 2C3

★★★★
GUEST HOUSE
SILVER AWARD

B&B PER ROOM PER NIGHT
S £64.00–£67.00
D £75.00–£118.00

### Woodstock House

Charlton, Chichester PO18 0HU **t** (01243) 811666 **e** info@woodstockhousehotel.co.uk

**woodstockhousehotel.co.uk** SPECIAL OFFERS • REAL-TIME BOOKING

Situated in the heart of the South Downs, our comfortable, friendly B&B hotel is an ideal base for the Downs, Goodwood and many local attractions. Many excellent country inns for dining.

**open** All year
**bedrooms** 7 double, 4 twin, 1 single
**bathrooms** All en suite
**payment** Credit/debit cards, cash, cheques

Room General P Leisure

## CHIDDINGSTONE, Kent Map ref 2D2

★★★
GUEST ACCOMMODATION

B&B PER ROOM PER NIGHT
S £35.00–£40.00
D £65.00–£70.00

### Hoath House

Chiddingstone, Edenbridge TN8 7DB **t** (01342) 850362
**e** janestreatfeild@hoath-house.freeserve.co.uk

**hoathhouse.co.uk**

Medieval and Tudor family house in extensive grounds near Penshurst, Hever and Chartwell. Off-street parking. Single bookings accepted. Price on application. French spoken.

**open** All year except Christmas
**bedrooms** 1 double, 1 twin, 1 family
**bathrooms** 1 private
**payment** Cash, cheques

Room General P Leisure

## CHINEHAM, Hampshire Map ref 2C2

★★★
GUEST ACCOMMODATION

B&B PER ROOM PER NIGHT
S Max £33.00
D Max £48.00

### Ashfields, 51A Reading Road

Chineham, Basingstoke RG24 8LT **t** (01256) 324629

Friendly family-run bungalow within walking distance of Chineham and business park. Pubs and restaurants close by. Outskirts of Basingstoke. Suitable bus/train services for area.

**open** All year except Christmas and New Year
**bedrooms** 2 double, 1 twin
**bathrooms** 2 en suite, 1 private
**payment** Cash, cheques

Room General 10 P

### Where are the maps?

Colour maps can be found at the front of the guide. They pinpoint the location of all accommodation found in the regional sections.

## CHINNOR, Oxfordshire Map ref 2C1

★★★★
BED & BREAKFAST

B&B PER ROOM PER NIGHT
S £40.00–£42.00
D £52.00–£57.00

### The Croft

Chinnor Hill, Chinnor OX39 4BS **t** (01844) 353654 **e** beth@acornhomesltd.co.uk

**bethatthecroft.co.uk**

Comfortable country house set high in the Chilterns. Close to M40, surrounded by fields and lovely views.

**open** All year except Christmas and New Year
**bedrooms** 2 double
**bathrooms** 1 en suite, 1 private
**payment** Cash, cheques

Room General

## COLWELL BAY, Isle of Wight Map ref 2C3

★★★★
GUEST HOUSE

B&B PER ROOM PER NIGHT
S £39.00–£43.00
D £58.00–£66.00

*Please ask about our out-of-season special offers.*

### Rockstone Cottage

Colwell Chine Road, Colwell Bay, Freshwater PO40 9NR **t** (01983) 753723
**e** enquiries@rockstonecottage.co.uk

**rockstonecottage.co.uk** SPECIAL OFFERS

**open** All year
**bedrooms** 2 double, 2 twin, 1 family
**bathrooms** All en suite
**payment** Cash, cheques

Charming cottage built in 1790, 300m from the coastal path and sandy beach at Colwell Bay and surrounded by lovely walks in rural West Wight. Our breakfast menu includes quality local produce. We offer a warm welcome, plenty of parking, en suite rooms and will collect foot passengers from Yarmouth.

**SAT NAV** *PO40 9NR* **ONLINE MAP**

Room General Leisure

## COTSWOLDS

*See under Brize Norton, Burford, Cassington, Kingham, Woodstock*
*See also Cotswolds in the Central and South West England sections*

## COWES, Isle of Wight Map ref 2C3

★★★★
GUEST ACCOMMODATION

B&B PER ROOM PER NIGHT
S Min £35.00
D £60.00–£80.00

### Anchorage Guest House

23 Mill Hill Road, Cowes PO31 7EE **t** (01983) 247975 **e** peterandjenni@anchoragecowes.co.uk

**anchoragecowes.co.uk**

Detached guesthouse with parking, recently refurbished to a high standard, all rooms en suite, either double, twin or family. Located close to water, marinas, shops and restaurants.

**open** All year
**bedrooms** 2 double, 1 twin, 1 family
**bathrooms** All en suite
**payment** Credit/debit cards, cash, cheques

Room General Leisure

## CRANLEIGH, Surrey Map ref 2D2

★★★
GUEST ACCOMMODATION

B&B PER ROOM PER NIGHT
s Max £40.00
d Max £65.00

### Long Copse

Pitch Hill, Ewhurst GU6 7NN **t** (01483) 277458 **e** shhandley@btinternet.com

**open** All year
**bedrooms** 2 double, 2 twin
**payment** Cash, cheques, euros

A warm welcome awaits you at Long Copse, a beautiful Arts and Crafts house set high in the Surrey Hills with magnificent views and 80 miles of footpaths at the gate. Within easy reach are National Trust properties, pubs, picturesque villages and historic towns. Walkers, cyclists and children are welcome.

**SAT NAV** *GU6 7NN*

Room General P Leisure

## CROWBOROUGH, East Sussex Map ref 2D2

★★★★
GUEST ACCOMMODATION
SILVER AWARD

B&B PER ROOM PER NIGHT
s £37.40–£40.00
d £67.40–£80.00

EVENING MEAL PER PERSON
£15.00–£20.00

### Yew House Bed & Breakfast

Crowborough Hill, Crowborough TN6 2EA **t** (01892) 610522 **e** yewhouse@yewhouse.com

**yewhouse.com** GUEST REVIEWS • SPECIAL OFFERS

Two en suite rooms, one four-poster bed, double shower. Double room use of bathroom. Single/twin room use of shower room. Close to shops, station and buses. Off-road parking. Quiet location.

**open** All year except Christmas Day
**bedrooms** 1 single/twin/triple, 3 double
**bathrooms** 2 en suite, 2 private
**payment** Credit/debit cards, cash, cheques

Room TV SC General P Leisure

## CUCKFIELD, West Sussex Map ref 2D3

★★★★
BED & BREAKFAST
SILVER AWARD

B&B PER ROOM PER NIGHT
s Min £50.00
d Min £80.00

EVENING MEAL PER PERSON
£40.00

### Highbridge Mill

Cuckfield Road, Haywards Heath RH17 5AE **t** (01444) 450881

**highbridgemill.com**

**open** 1 April to 1 December
**bedrooms** 1 double, 1 twin
**bathrooms** 1 en suite, 1 private
**payment** Cash, cheques

A slightly eccentric welcome awaits you at this converted water mill. Highbridge Mill was built in 1810 and was converted into a family home 20 years ago. Nestling in its own hidden valley of some five acres, the garden offers peace and tranquillity with the River Adur flowing through it. Minimum stay 2 nights.

**SAT NAV** *RH17 5AE*

Room General P

## It's all quality-assessed accommodation

Our commitment to quality involves wide-ranging accommodation assessment. Ratings and awards were correct at the time of going to press but may change following a new assessment. Please check at time of booking.

For **key to symbols** see page 7

## DANEHILL, East Sussex Map ref 2D3

★★★★
GUEST ACCOMMODATION

B&B PER ROOM PER NIGHT
D £50.00–£70.00

### New Glenmore

Sliders Lane, Furners Green, Uckfield TN22 3RU **t** (01825) 790783 **e** alan.robinson@bigfoot.com

**open** All year except Christmas and New Year
**bedrooms** 1 twin, 1 family
**bathrooms** 1 en suite, 1 private
**payment** Cash, cheques

Spacious bungalow set in six acres of grounds. Rural location close to Bluebell Steam Railway and Sheffield Park. Breakfast includes our own eggs, honey and home-baked bread.

**SAT NAV** *TN22 3RU*

Room TV General P

## DEAL, Kent Map ref 3C4

★★★★
GUEST ACCOMMODATION

B&B PER ROOM PER NIGHT
S £45.00–£50.00
D £60.00–£70.00

### Ilex Cottage

Temple Way, Worth, Deal CT14 0DA **t** (01304) 617026 **e** info@ilexcottage.com

**ilexcottage.com**

Renovated 1736 house with lovely conservatory and country views. Secluded yet convenient village location north of Deal. Sandwich five minutes, Canterbury, Dover and Ramsgate 25 minutes.

**open** All year
**bedrooms** 1 double, 2 twin
**bathrooms** All en suite
**payment** Credit/debit cards, cash, cheques

Room TV General P Leisure

## DETLING, Kent Map ref 3B3

★★★★
BED & BREAKFAST

B&B PER ROOM PER NIGHT
S £45.00–£55.00
D £55.00–£65.00

*Discounts available for longer stays. Check our website for special offers.*

### Wealden Hall

Pilgrims Way, Detling, Maidstone ME14 3JY **t** (01622) 739622 & 07934 489041
**e** johnwatson@wealdenhall.net

**wealdenhall.net** SPECIAL OFFERS

**open** All year except Christmas and New Year
**bedrooms** 1 double, 1 twin
**bathrooms** 1 en suite, 1 private
**payment** Credit/debit cards, cash, cheques, euros

Spacious family-owned establishment offering comfortable fully equipped en suite rooms in rural setting, with stunning views. Conveniently situated close to Maidstone; good motorway access and secure parking. Large gardens and heated swimming pool (April-September). Quality breakfasts using our own produce including home-reared bacon and sausages.

**SAT NAV** *ME14 3JY* **ONLINE MAP**

Room TV SC General P Leisure

## Remember to check when booking

Please remember that all information in this guide has been supplied by the proprietors well in advance of publication. Since changes do sometimes occur it's a good idea to check details at the time of booking.

## DORKING, Surrey Map ref 2D2

★★★
BED & BREAKFAST

B&B PER ROOM PER NIGHT
S £40.00–£45.00
D £60.00–£65.00

### Broomhill

15 Broomfield Park, Dorking RH4 3QQ **t** (01306) 885565 **e** suzanne.willis@virgin.net

**open** All year except Christmas and New Year
**bedrooms** 1 double, 1 family
**payment** Cash, cheques

Spacious house, walking distance of Westcott village. Dorking 1.5 miles. Two double/family rooms, shared bathroom, TV/DVD, coffee/tea. Magnificent views and safe parking. Gatwick 30 mins, M25 15 mins (junctions 8/9), London 40 mins by train. Fabulous walking countryside (North Downs and Greensand Way). Children welcome.

**SAT NAV** *RH4 3QQ*

Room General P Leisure

## DORKING, Surrey Map ref 2D2

★★★★
FARMHOUSE
SILVER AWARD

B&B PER ROOM PER NIGHT
S £65.00–£95.00
D £95.00

### Denbies Farmhouse

Denbies Wine Estate, London Road, Dorking RH5 6AA **t** (01306) 876777
**e** bandb@denbiesvineyard.co.uk

**denbiesvineyard.co.uk** REAL-TIME BOOKING

**open** All year
**bedrooms** 5 double, 2 family
**bathrooms** All en suite
**payment** Credit/debit cards, cash, cheques

Denbies Farmhouse, a favourite for overnight business trips and romantic short stays, is located on England's largest vineyard. Denbies Vineyard visitor centre nearby, offers wine tours and tasting, restaurants, shops and conference facilities. Within walking distance of the historic market town of Dorking with direct train links to London.

**SAT NAV** *RH5 6AA*

Room General 6 P Leisure

## DOVER, Kent Map ref 3C4

★★★★
BED & BREAKFAST
SILVER AWARD

B&B PER ROOM PER NIGHT
S £35.00–£40.00
D £60.00–£65.00

### Colret House

The Green, Coldred, Dover CT15 5AP **t** (01304) 830388 **e** jackiecolret@aol.com

**colrethouse.co.uk**

**open** All year
**bedrooms** 1 double, 1 twin
**bathrooms** All en suite
**payment** Cash, cheques, euros

An early-Edwardian property with modern, purpose-built, en suite garden rooms, standing in extensive, well-maintained grounds. Situated beside the village green in a conservation area on downs above Dover. Ideally situated for overnight stays when travelling by ferries or shuttle. Close to Canterbury and Sandwich. Ample, secure parking.

**SAT NAV** *CT15 5AP* **ONLINE MAP**

Room General P Leisure

### What if I need to cancel?

It's advisable to check the proprietor's cancellation policy at the time of booking in case you have to change your plans.

## DUMMER, Hampshire Map ref 2C2

★★★
FARMHOUSE

B&B PER ROOM PER NIGHT
S £30.00–£35.00
D £40.00–£50.00

### Oakdown Farm Bungalow

Oakdown Farm, Dummer, Basingstoke RG23 7LR **t** (01256) 397218

Mixed, 600-acre farm. Comfortable bungalow in a secluded cul-de-sac next to M3, junction 7, overlooking farmland.

**open** All year
**bedrooms** 1 double, 2 twin
**payment** Cash, cheques, euros

Room General 10 P Leisure

## DYMCHURCH, Kent Map ref 3B4

★★★★
GUEST ACCOMMODATION

B&B PER ROOM PER NIGHT
S £37.50–£67.50
D £60.00–£67.50

EVENING MEAL PER PERSON
Min £12.50

### Waterside Guest House

15 Hythe Road, Dymchurch, Romney Marsh TN29 0LN **t** (01303) 872253
**e** info@watersideguesthouse.co.uk

**watersideguesthouse.co.uk**

Cottage-style house offering comfortable rooms and attractive gardens, ideally situated for Channel crossings and historic Romney Marsh. Experience the RH&D railway, visit Port Lympne Wild Animal Park or stroll nearby sandy beaches.

**open** All year
**bedrooms** 2 double, 2 twin, 1 family
**bathrooms** All en suite
**payment** Credit/debit cards, cash, cheques, euros

Room General P Leisure

## EAST ASHLING, West Sussex Map ref 2C3

★★★★
INN

B&B PER ROOM PER NIGHT
S Min £45.00
D Min £70.00

EVENING MEAL PER PERSON
£6.50–£15.95

### Horse & Groom

East Ashling, Chichester PO18 9AX **t** (01243) 575339 **e** info@thehorseandgroomchichester.co.uk

**thehorseandgroomchichester.co.uk**

**open** All year
**bedrooms** 6 double, 5 twin
**bathrooms** All en suite
**payment** Credit/debit cards, cash, cheques

A traditional 17thC inn with en suite accommodation. Friendly, country-style inn with fine cuisine, real ales and cast-iron range. Plenty of parking. Close to Goodwood. All rooms can function as single/double.

**SAT NAV** *PO18 9AX*

Room General P Leisure

## EASTBOURNE, East Sussex Map ref 3B4

★★★
GUEST ACCOMMODATION

B&B PER ROOM PER NIGHT
S £35.00–£65.00
D £60.00–£80.00

EVENING MEAL PER PERSON
£8.00–£19.00

*3 nights for the price of 2, Oct-Mar (excl Bank Holidays, Christmas and New Year). Pre-booked only.*

### The Birling Gap

Birling Gap, Seven Sisters Cliffs, Eastbourne BN20 0AB **t** (01323) 423197
**e** reception@birlinggaphotel.co.uk

**birlinggaphotel.co.uk**

**open** All year
**bedrooms** 5 double, 2 twin, 1 single, 1 family
**bathrooms** All en suite
**payment** Credit/debit cards, cash, cheques, euros

Magnificent cliff-top position on Seven Sisters cliffs with views of country, sea and beach. Superb downland and beach walks. Old-world Thatched Bar and Oak Room Restaurant. Coffee shop and games room, function and conference suite. Off A259 coast road at East Dean, 1.5 miles west of Beachy Head.

**SAT NAV** *BN20 0AB*

Room General P Leisure

## EASTBOURNE, East Sussex Map ref 3B4

★★★★
GUEST HOUSE
GOLD AWARD

B&B PER ROOM PER NIGHT
S £36.00–£40.00
D £72.00–£80.00

EVENING MEAL PER PERSON
Min £15.00

### Brayscroft House

13 South Cliff Avenue, Eastbourne BN20 7AH **t** (01323) 647005 **e** brayscroft@hotmail.com

**brayscrofthotel.co.uk** GUEST REVIEWS • REAL-TIME BOOKING

**open** All year except Christmas
**bedrooms** 3 double, 2 twin, 1 single
**bathrooms** All en suite
**payment** Credit/debit cards, cash, cheques

Elegant, award-winning, small hotel, one of only a handful in Eastbourne with coveted rating and award for 'outstanding accommodation and hospitality'. Superb position. Selected by the Which? Hotel Guide. Near to the sea, theatres and tennis.

**SAT NAV** *BN20 7AH*

Room General 12

## EASTBOURNE, East Sussex Map ref 3B4

★★★★
GUEST HOUSE

B&B PER ROOM PER NIGHT
S £40.00–£45.00
D £70.00–£80.00

### The Gladwyn

16 Blackwater Road, Eastbourne BN21 4JD **t** (01323) 733142 **e** contact@thegladwyn.com

**thegladwyn.com** SPECIAL OFFERS • REAL-TIME BOOKING

**open** All year except Christmas and New Year
**bedrooms** 4 double, 3 twin, 2 single, 1 family
**bathrooms** All en suite
**payment** Credit/debit cards, cash, cheques, euros

You can be assured of a warm and friendly welcome at the Gladwyn in Eastbourne. We are conveniently located for theatres, shops and seafront. Our comfortable en suite rooms have been refurbished using unique themes and imaginative colours. There is a welcoming residents' lounge, a licensed bar and a large garden.

**SAT NAV** *BN21 4JD* **ONLINE MAP**

PETS! WELCOME

Room General

## FAREHAM, Hampshire Map ref 2C3

★★★
BED & BREAKFAST

B&B PER ROOM PER NIGHT
S £40.00–£45.00
D £60.00–£65.00

### Bridge House

1 Waterside Gardens, Wallington, Fareham PO16 8SD **t** (01329) 287775 **e** maryhb8@aol.com

Comfortable Georgian family home, all facilities, Japanese garden. Full English or continental breakfast. Ample parking. Immediate access to M27 junction 11 and town centre.

**open** All year except Christmas
**bedrooms** 2 twin
**bathrooms** 1 en suite, 1 private
**payment** Cash, cheques

Room General P

## FAREHAM, Hampshire Map ref 2C3

★★★
GUEST ACCOMMODATION

B&B PER ROOM PER NIGHT
S £55.00–£75.00
D £65.00–£90.00

### Travelrest Solent Gateway

22 The Avenue, Fareham PO14 1NS **t** (01329) 232175 **e** solentreservations@travelrest.co.uk

**travelrest.co.uk/fareham**

Recently refurbished, comfortable accommodation, in landscaped gardens. Free car park and within walking distance of town-centre bars, restaurants and railway station. Ideal location on A27 between Southampton and Portsmouth.

**open** All year
**bedrooms** 11 double, 5 twin, 1 single, 2 family
**bathrooms** All en suite
**payment** Credit/debit cards, cash, euros

Room General P

For **key to symbols** see page 7

## FAVERSHAM, Kent Map ref 3B3

★★★
GUEST ACCOMMODATION

B&B PER ROOM PER NIGHT
S £28.00–£48.00
D £42.00–£72.00

### Barnsfield

Fostall, Hernhill, Faversham ME13 9JG **t** (01227) 750973 **e** barnsfield@yahoo.com

**barnsfield.co.uk**

Grade II Listed country cottage accommodation, just off A299, set in three acres of orchards, six miles from Canterbury. Convenient for ports and touring.

**open** All year
**bedrooms** 1 double, 1 twin, 1 family
**bathrooms** 1 private
**payment** Cash, cheques

Room General Leisure

## FAVERSHAM, Kent Map ref 3B3

★★★
GUEST ACCOMMODATION

B&B PER ROOM PER NIGHT
S £39.00–£50.00
D £50.00–£65.00

### Tenterden House

209 The Street, Boughton ME13 9BL **t** (01227) 751593 **e** platham@tesco.net

**faversham.org/tenterdenhouse**

Gardener's cottage containing two en suite bedrooms. Breakfast served in main 16thC house. Pubs and restaurants within walking distance. Off-road parking.

**open** All year except Christmas and New Year
**bedrooms** 1 double, 1 twin
**bathrooms** All en suite
**payment** Cash, cheques, euros

Room General P Leisure

## FOLKESTONE, Kent Map ref 3B4

★★★
GUEST HOUSE

B&B PER ROOM PER NIGHT
S £29.00–£39.00
D £43.00–£57.00

*Weekend and midweek breaks from £84-£122pp, min 2 nights. Also free child off-peak offers.*

### The Rob Roy Guest House

227 Dover Road, Folkestone CT19 6NH **t** (01303) 253341 **e** robroy.folkestone@ntlworld.com

**therobroyguesthouse.co.uk** GUEST REVIEWS • SPECIAL OFFERS • REAL-TIME BOOKING

**open** All year except Christmas
**bedrooms** 3 double, 3 twin, 1 family
**bathrooms** 3 en suite
**payment** Credit/debit cards, cash, cheques, euros

The Rob Roy: friendly service, comfortable accommodation and tasty breakfasts. Ideally situated ten minutes from M20 and Channel Tunnel and 20 minutes from Dover ferries and Eurostar Ashford. Only minutes from Folkestone's famous Leas, cliffs, beaches and promenade and the lovely Folkestone Downs and North Downs Way.

**SAT NAV** *CT19 6NH* **ONLINE MAP**

Room General P Leisure

## FORDINGBRIDGE, Hampshire Map ref 2B3

★★★★
RESTAURANT WITH ROOMS

B&B PER ROOM PER NIGHT
S £69.00–£79.00
D £80.00–£125.00

EVENING MEAL PER PERSON
£29.00–£38.00

### The Three Lions

Stuckton, Fordingbridge SP6 2HF **t** (01425) 652489 **e** the3lions@btinternet.com

**thethreelionsrestaurant.co.uk**

**open** All year
**bedrooms** 2 double, 1 twin, 1 family, 3 suites
**bathrooms** All en suite
**payment** Credit/debit cards, cash, cheques

Welcome to the Three Lions, a restaurant with rooms in the New Forest National Park set in two acres of beautiful gardens. Enjoy Mike's rustic though refined cooking in front of our open log fire. Wheelchair access, whirlpool jacuzzi and sauna. Hampshire Restaurant of the Year 2006, Good Food Guide.

**SAT NAV** *SP6 2HF*

Room General P Leisure

## FORTON, Hampshire  Map ref 2C2

★★★★★
**BED & BREAKFAST**
**SILVER AWARD**

B&B PER ROOM PER NIGHT
S £60.00–£75.00
D £80.00–£105.00

Discounts on stays of 4 or more days (excl Sat). See website for details.

### The Barn House B&B
Andover SP11 6NU  t (01264) 720544  e hello@thebarnhousebandb.co.uk

**thebarnhousebandb.co.uk**

**open** All year except Christmas and New Year
**bedrooms** 1 double, 1 twin
**bathrooms** All en suite
**payment** Credit/debit cards, cash, cheques

A luxury B&B in a quiet, pretty village situated in Hampshire's picturesque Test Valley. There are many places of interest nearby, as well as local pubs and a variety of interesting walks. We provide the highest standards of accommodation, food and hospitality. For more information please visit our website.

**SAT NAV** SP11 6NU **ONLINE MAP**

Room 📺 ♨ 🍵   General P 🍴

## FRESHWATER, Isle of Wight  Map ref 2C3

★★★★
**BED & BREAKFAST**

B&B PER ROOM PER NIGHT
S £25.00–£40.00
D £50.00–£60.00

EVENING MEAL PER PERSON
£12.00–£15.00

### The Orchards
Princes Road, Freshwater PO40 9ED  t (01983) 753795  e paulagerrish@vodafoneemail.co.uk

**theorchardsbandb.co.uk**

Located in Freshwater village. Central to Yarmouth ferry, local walks, beaches and amenities. All rooms are en suite. Locally sourced food when available.

**open** All year
**bedrooms** 1 double, 2 single
**bathrooms** 2 en suite, 1 private
**payment** Cash, cheques

Room ♿ 📺 ♨   General 🍽 ⚡ P ✗   Leisure 🎣 U ♪ 🚴

## FRESHWATER, Isle of Wight  Map ref 2C3

★★★★
**GUEST ACCOMMODATION**

B&B PER ROOM PER NIGHT
S £29.00–£33.00
D £58.00–£66.00

### Seahorses
Victoria Road, Freshwater PO40 9PP  t (01983) 752574  e seahorses-iow@tiscali.co.uk

**seahorsesisleofwight.com** REAL-TIME BOOKING

A charming early-19thC rectory, standing in 2.5 acres of lovely gardens with direct footpath access to Yarmouth and Freshwater Bay. Art courses available in our studio. Pets welcome.

**open** All year
**bedrooms** 1 double, 1 twin, 2 family
**bathrooms** All en suite
**payment** Cash, cheques

Room 📺 ♨ 🍵   General 🐴 P 🍴 🔔 ❋ 🐕   Leisure U ♪ 🚴

## GATWICK, West Sussex  Map ref 2D2

★★★★
**GUEST HOUSE**
**SILVER AWARD**

B&B PER ROOM PER NIGHT
S £45.00–£50.00
D £60.00–£65.00

### The Lawn Guest House
30 Massetts Road, Horley RH6 7DF  t (01293) 775751  e info@lawnguesthouse.co.uk

**lawnguesthouse.co.uk** GUEST REVIEWS

**open** All year
**bedrooms** 3 double, 3 twin, 6 family
**bathrooms** All en suite
**payment** Credit/debit cards, cash, cheques, euros

Imposing Victorian house in pretty gardens. Five minutes Gatwick. Two minutes' walk Horley. Station 300yds. London 40 minutes. Bedrooms all en suite. Full English breakfast and continental for early departures. Guests' ice machine. On-line residents' computer for emails. Overnight/long-term parking. Airport transfers by arrangement.

**SAT NAV** RH6 7DF **ONLINE MAP**

Room ☎ 📺 ♨ 🍵   General 🐴 🍽 ⚡ P 💡 ✻ ❋ 🐕   Leisure ▶

For **key to symbols** see page 7

## GATWICK, West Sussex Map ref 2D2

★★★★
GUEST HOUSE

B&B PER ROOM PER NIGHT
S £47.00–£53.00
D £63.00–£68.00

### Southbourne Guest House Gatwick

34 Massetts Road, Horley RH6 7DS **t** (01293) 771991 **e** reservations@southbournegatwick.com

**southbournegatwick.com**

**open** All year
**bedrooms** 3 double, 3 twin, 2 single, 4 family
**bathrooms** All en suite
**payment** Credit/debit cards, cash, cheques

A warm welcome awaits you in our family-run guesthouse. Ideally located for Gatwick Airport, and exploring Surrey, Sussex and London. Five minutes' walk from Horley train station, restaurants, shops and pubs and 30 minutes by train from London. Five minutes' drive from Gatwick with free courtesy transport from 0930-2130.

**SAT NAV** *RH6 7DS*

Room General P

## GATWICK AIRPORT

*See under Horley*

## GODALMING, Surrey Map ref 2D2

★★★
BED & BREAKFAST

B&B PER ROOM PER NIGHT
S £35.00–£40.00
D £70.00–£80.00

### Combe Ridge

Pook Hill, Chiddingfold, Godalming GU8 4XR **t** (01428) 682607 **e** brendaessex@btinternet.com

**open** All year except Christmas and New Year
**bedrooms** 2 double, 1 single
**bathrooms** 1 en suite, 1 private
**payment** Cash, cheques

Combe Ridge is in an Area Of Outstanding Natural Beauty with grazing sheep and views of gently wooded hills. London is an hour away by train, and both Heathrow and Gatwick are less than an hour by car. Combe Ridge is a family-run B&B where there's always a warm welcome.

**SAT NAV** *GU8 4XR*

Room General

## GODALMING, Surrey Map ref 2D2

★★★
FARMHOUSE

B&B PER ROOM PER NIGHT
S £32.00–£37.00
D £62.00–£67.00

### Heath Hall Farm

Bowlhead Green, Godalming GU8 6NW **t** (01428) 682808 **e** heathhallfarm@btinternet.com

**heathhallfarm.co.uk**

**open** All year
**bedrooms** 1 double, 1 twin, 1 single, 1 family
**bathrooms** 3 en suite, 1 private
**payment** Credit/debit cards, cash, cheques, euros

Secluded farmhouse, converted stable courtyard, surrounded by own land. Free-range fowl. Tennis court. Relaxed atmosphere. Ground-floor accommodation. Ample parking. Single pet welcome by arrangement. Wonderful walking. Green Sand Way and National Nature Reserve. Easy access to A3.

**SAT NAV** *GU8 6NW*

Room General P Leisure

## GREAT MISSENDEN, Buckinghamshire  Map ref 2C1

★★★★
**BED & BREAKFAST**

B&B PER ROOM PER NIGHT
S £29.50
D £55.00

### Forge House
10 Church Street, Great Missenden HP16 0AX  t (01494) 867347

**open** All year
**bedrooms** 2 double, 1 twin, 1 single
**bathrooms** 3 en suite
**payment** Cash, cheques

Set in the wooded Chiltern Hills, quiet village location – a charming 18thC beamed house traditionally refurbished with three en suite double bedrooms. English/continental breakfast included. Chiltern Line to Marylebone 35 minutes. Car access to Waddesdon Manor, Hughendon Manor, West Wycombe Park and caves, Milton's Cottage, Bekonscot Model Village. Walking/cycling The Ridgeway, Chiltern Way.

**SAT NAV** HP16 0AX

Room [TV] 🍵 🍽  General ✻ Leisure 🍃

## GUILDFORD, Surrey  Map ref 2D2

★★★
**BED & BREAKFAST**

B&B PER ROOM PER NIGHT
S £38.00–£43.00

### East Woodhay
86a Epsom Road, Guildford GU1 2DH  t (01483) 575986  e eastwoodhaybandb@hotmail.co.uk

Large single room with en suite shower and wc. Quiet area, within easy reach town of centre. Television, tea/coffee facilities in room. French/Italian spoken. Non-smoking. Off-street parking.

**open** All year
**bedrooms** 1 single
**bathrooms** En suite
**payment** Cash, cheques

Room [TV] 🍵 🍽  General P ✻

## GUILDFORD, Surrey  Map ref 2D2

★★★
**FARMHOUSE**

B&B PER ROOM PER NIGHT
S Max £50.00
D Max £70.00

### Littlefield Manor
Littlefield Common, Guildford GU3 3HJ  t (01483) 233068  e john@littlefieldmanor.co.uk

**littlefieldmanor.co.uk**

A 17thC listed manor house with Tudor origins set in large walled garden surrounded by farmland.

**open** All year except Christmas
**bedrooms** 2 double, 1 twin
**bathrooms** 1 en suite, 2 private
**payment** Credit/debit cards, cash, cheques

Room [TV] 🍵 🍽  General 🍼1 P 🐾 ✗ ✻  Leisure ▶

## GUILDFORD, Surrey  Map ref 2D2

★★
**GUEST ACCOMMODATION**

B&B PER ROOM PER NIGHT
S Min £28.00
D Min £56.00

### Matchams
35 Boxgrove Avenue, Guildford GU1 1XQ  t (01483) 567643

**open** All year
**bedrooms** 1 twin, 2 single
**payment** Cash, cheques

Detached private residence in quiet road. Close to bus routes and only five minutes' walk from Spectrum Leisure Complex. Equidistant from Heathrow and Gatwick airports. Within easy reach of south coast, London and Windsor.

**SAT NAV** GU1 1XQ

Room [TV] 🍵  General 🍼 ✻

### Looking for a wide range of facilities?
More stars means higher quality accommodation plus a greater range of facilities and services.

For **key to symbols** see page 7

## GUILDFORD, Surrey Map ref 2D2

★★★★
BED & BREAKFAST
SILVER AWARD

B&B PER ROOM PER NIGHT
s £45.00
d £60.00

### Plaegan House

96 Wodeland Avenue, Guildford GU2 4LD **t** (01483) 822181 & 07961 919430
**e** froxanephillips@yahoo.co.uk

**plaeganhouse.co.uk**

Large room in friendly, accommodating house with three cats in central Guildford. Lovely views and garden. Tastefully refurbished. Walking distance of town centre and university. French and Spanish spoken. Discount for non-breakfast customers.

**open** All year
**bedrooms** 1 twin
**bathrooms** En suite
**payment** Cash, cheques, euros

Room General P

## HADDENHAM, Buckinghamshire Map ref 2C1

★★★
BED & BREAKFAST

B&B PER ROOM PER NIGHT
s £30.00–£50.00

### New Hadden

3a High Street, Haddenham, Aylesbury HP17 8ES **t** (01844) 291347

Modern architect-designed house. One double room with en suite, one double room with shower room. Breakfast in conservatory overlooking large garden. Bus route to Oxford and fast train to London.

**open** All year
**bedrooms** 2 double, 2 single
**bathrooms** All en suite
**payment** Cash, cheques

Room General P Leisure

## HAILSHAM, East Sussex Map ref 2D3

★★★★★
GUEST ACCOMMODATION
SILVER AWARD

B&B PER ROOM PER NIGHT
s £60.00–£75.00
d £95.00–£120.00

### Hailsham Grange

Vicarage Road, Hailsham BN27 1BL **t** (01323) 844248 **e** noel-hgrange@amserve.com

**hailshamgrange.co.uk**

**open** All year except Christmas and New Year
**bedrooms** 3 double, 1 twin
**bathrooms** All en suite
**payment** Cash, cheques

Hailsham is conveniently located for the numerous historic houses and gardens in East Sussex/West Kent. Also ideal for those wishing to explore the south coast and the South Downs, while Glyndebourne is close by. The accommodation epitomises the comfort and elegance of classic English style and the garden is a haven of peace and tranquillity.

**SAT NAV** *BN27 1BL*

Room General P

## HASLEMERE, Surrey Map ref 2C2

★★★★
BED & BREAKFAST

B&B PER ROOM PER NIGHT
s Min £38.00
d £56.00–£60.00

### Deerfell

Blackdown, Haslemere GU27 3BU **t** (01428) 653409 **e** deerfell@tesco.net

**deerfell.co.uk**

**open** All year except Christmas and New Year
**bedrooms** 1 double, 1 twin, 1 single
**bathrooms** 2 en suite, 1 private
**payment** Cash, cheques

Delightful country house only four miles from Haslemere. Spacious, comfortable, en suite rooms with TV and tea-/coffee-making facilities. Good local pubs/restaurants.

**SAT NAV** *GU27 3BU*

Room General

**HASLEMERE, Surrey Map ref 2C2**

★★★
BED & BREAKFAST

B&B PER ROOM PER NIGHT
S £50.00–£60.00
D £70.00–£80.00

EVENING MEAL PER PERSON
£10.00–£25.00

## Sheps Hollow

Henley Common, Henley, Haslemere GU27 3HB **t** (01428) 653120 **e** bizzielizziebee@msn.com

**tuckedup.com/accommodation/840/sheps-hollow.php**

Charming, rural 16thC cottage featuring honeymoon suite. This totally private little barn also available for holiday lets. Sky and video channels in all rooms. Oak-framed dining room available, seats 20.

**open** All year
**bedrooms** 1 double, 1 twin, 1 family
**bathrooms** All en suite
**payment** Cash, cheques

Room General Leisure

**HASLEMERE, Surrey Map ref 2C2**

★★★
INN

B&B PER ROOM PER NIGHT
S Min £55.00
D Min £75.00

## The Wheatsheaf Inn

Grayswood Road, Haslemere GU27 2DE **t** (01428) 644440 **e** ken@thewheatsheafgrayswood.co.uk

A delightful building in wooded area. Award-winning menu. Comfortable en suite rooms. Also has a bright and airy non-smoking conservatory.

**open** All year
**bedrooms** 4 double, 1 twin, 2 single
**bathrooms** All en suite
**payment** Credit/debit cards, cash, cheques

Room General

**HASTINGS, East Sussex Map ref 3B4**

Rating Applied For
GUEST ACCOMMODATION

B&B PER ROOM PER NIGHT
S £25.00–£40.00
D £50.00–£65.00

## The Old Town Guest House

1a George Street, Hastings TN34 3EG **t** (01424) 423342 & 07870 163818 **e** sophiew84@hotmail.com

A guesthouse of character situated in the heart of Hastings Old Town. Relax in our simple, yet comfortable rooms and wake up to a full English breakfast.

**open** All year
**bedrooms** 1 double, 1 twin, 1 single
**bathrooms** 1 en suite
**payment** Cash, cheques

Room General Leisure

**HASTINGS, East Sussex Map ref 3B4**

★★★★
GUEST ACCOMMODATION
SILVER AWARD

B&B PER ROOM PER NIGHT
S £30.00–£35.00
D £60.00–£75.00

*Discounts for 3 or more nights booked. Complimentary wine and gift with all honeymoon and anniversary stays.*

## Seaspray

54 Eversfield Place, St Leonards-on-Sea, Hastings TN37 6DB **t** (01424) 436583
**e** jo@seaspraybb.co.uk

**seaspraybb.co.uk** GUEST REVIEWS • SPECIAL OFFERS • REAL-TIME BOOKING

**open** All year
**bedrooms** 3 double, 3 twin, 3 single, 1 family
**bathrooms** 8 en suite
**payment** Cash, cheques

Victorian seafront B&B on Hastings promenade. Your home from home with a bit extra. Refurbished to very high standard. Quiet location five minutes to town and all amenities. Rooms are modern and clean: superking beds, Wi-Fi, plasma TV, Freeview, fridge. Parking permits. Extensive breakfast menu, all diets catered for.

**SAT NAV** *TN37 6DB* **ONLINE MAP**

Room General Leisure

CYCLISTS WELCOME

## Fancy a cycling holiday?

For a fabulous freewheeling break, seek out accommodation participating in our Cyclists Welcome scheme. Look out for the symbol and plan your route online at nationalcyclenetwork.org.

## HASTINGS, East Sussex Map ref 3B4

★★★★★
GUEST ACCOMMODATION
SILVER AWARD

B&B PER ROOM PER NIGHT
S £70.00–£95.00
D £100.00–£135.00

EVENING MEAL PER PERSON
£9.00–£24.00

### Swan House

1 Hill Street, Old Town, Hastings TN34 3HU **t** (01424) 430014 **e** res@swanhousehastings.co.uk

**swanhousehastings.co.uk** REAL-TIME BOOKING

**open** All year except Christmas
**bedrooms** 2 double, 1 twin, 1 suite
**bathrooms** All en suite
**payment** Credit/debit cards, cash, cheques, euros

Swan House continues to receive widespread press recognition for its service and style. More than just a guesthouse, we offer luxury and relaxation unprecedented in Hastings Old Town. Guests enjoy a gourmet, locally-sourced breakfast menu, spacious guest lounge, computer room, wireless broadband internet access and a landscaped patio garden.

**SAT NAV** *TN34 3HU*

Room General 5 Leisure

## HEATHFIELD, East Sussex Map ref 3B4

★★★★
GUEST ACCOMMODATION
GOLD AWARD

B&B PER ROOM PER NIGHT
S £30.00–£50.00
D £55.00–£75.00

*Concessionary rates for stays 7+ nights.*

### Iwood Bed & Breakfast

Mutton Hall Lane, Heathfield TN21 8NR **t** (01435) 863918 **e** iwoodbb@aol.com

**iwoodbb.com**

**open** All year except Christmas and New Year
**bedrooms** 1 single, 2 double, 1 twin/suite
**bathrooms** 3 en suite, 1 private
**payment** Credit/debit cards, cash, cheques

Secluded house in lovely gardens with distant views of South Downs and sea. Situated within easy reach of coastal towns, including 1066 attractions around Hastings, and historic towns of Battle, Rye, Lewes and Tunbridge Wells. Excellent standards maintained to ensure a comfortable stay. Be prepared for an excellent breakfast! Suitable for partially disabled guests.

**SAT NAV** *TN21 8NR* **ONLINE MAP**

Room General 7 P Leisure

## HENFIELD, West Sussex Map ref 2D3

★★★★
BED & BREAKFAST

B&B PER ROOM PER NIGHT
S £25.00–£35.00
D Min £60.00

### 1 The Laurels

Martyn Close, Henfield BN5 9RQ **t** (01273) 493518 **e** malc.harrington@lineone.net

**no1thelaurels.co.uk**

A detached house faced with traditional knapped Sussex flint stones. Comfortable rooms, a warm welcome, easy access to Brighton. Many places of interest nearby.

**open** All year
**bedrooms** 2 double, 1 twin, 1 single
**bathrooms** 3 en suite
**payment** Cash, cheques

Room General P

## HENLEY-ON-THAMES, Oxfordshire Map ref 2C2

★★★
BED & BREAKFAST

B&B PER ROOM PER NIGHT
S £32.00–£45.00
D £55.00–£65.00

### Avalon

36 Queen Street, Henley-on-Thames RG9 1AP **t** (01491) 577829 **e** avalon@henleybb.co.uk

**henleybb.co.uk**

Spacious Victorian terraced house in a quiet, central location two minutes' walk from river, station and town centre.

**open** All year
**bedrooms** 1 double, 1 twin, 1 single
**bathrooms** All en suite
**payment** Cash, cheques

Room General 10

## HENLEY-ON-THAMES, Oxfordshire Map ref 2C2

★★
FARMHOUSE

B&B PER ROOM PER NIGHT
S £28.00–£56.00
D £56.00

### Bank Farm

The Old Road, Pishill RG9 6HS **t** (01491) 638601 **e** e.f.lakey@btinternet.com

**stayatbankfarm.co.uk**

Peaceful listed farmhouse in an Area of Outstanding Natural Beauty. Good for walking, birdwatching, reading. Ideal for visiting London and Thameside towns from Oxford to Windsor.

**open** All year except Christmas
**bedrooms** 2 double, 1 twin
**payment** Cash, cheques

Room General

## HENLEY-ON-THAMES, Oxfordshire Map ref 2C2

★★★★
INN
SILVER AWARD

B&B PER ROOM PER NIGHT
S £75.00
D £85.00

### The Baskerville

Station Road, Lower Shiplake RG9 3NY **t** (0118) 940 3332 **e** enquiries@thebaskerville.com

**thebaskerville.com**

**open** All year
**bedrooms** 2 double, 1 twin, 1 family
**bathrooms** All en suite
**payment** Credit/debit cards, cash, cheques

A small village pub close to the River Thames and just minutes from Henley-on-Thames. Good Pub Guide County Dining Pub of the Year 2007, excellent wine list, cosy, comfortable bar with a good choice of cask-conditioned ales.

**SAT NAV** *RG9 3NY* **ONLINE MAP**

Room General

## HENLEY-ON-THAMES, Oxfordshire Map ref 2C2

★★★★★
BED & BREAKFAST
SILVER AWARD

B&B PER ROOM PER NIGHT
S £50.00–£60.00
D £70.00–£75.00

### Lenwade

3 Western Road, Henley-on-Thames RG9 1JL **t** (01491) 573468 **e** jacquie@lenwade.com

**lenwade.com**

**open** All year except Christmas
**bedrooms** 2 double, 1 twin
**bathrooms** 2 en suite, 1 private
**payment** Cash, cheques, euros

A premier B&B in a quiet residential road within walking distance of Henley town centre, river, restaurants etc. Superb buffet and individually cooked breakfasts. All rooms have en suite or private facilities with many electrical extras. Free Wi-Fi. Ample parking. Wonderful walking in Chiltern Hills and Thames Path. Convenient Heathrow, Windsor.

**SAT NAV** *RG9 1JL*

Room General Leisure

## HENLEY-ON-THAMES, Oxfordshire Map ref 2C2

★★★★
BED & BREAKFAST

B&B PER ROOM PER NIGHT
S £30.00–£35.00
D £50.00–£70.00

### Orchard Dene Cottage

Lower Assendon, Henley-on-Thames RG9 6AG **t** (01491) 575490 **e** info@orcharddenecottage.co.uk

**orcharddenecottage.co.uk**

**open** All year
**bedrooms** 1 double, 1 single
**payment** Cash, cheques, euros

Two miles from Henley in beautiful Chilterns countryside, with all the comfort and friendly relaxation you'd expect in an old family home. Enjoy an interesting garden in summer, log fires in winter and full English breakfast all year. Excellent evening meals in nearby village pub. Ideal for London Heathrow access.

**SAT NAV** *RG9 6AG*

Room General Leisure

## HERNE BAY, Kent Map ref 3B3

★★★★
BED & BREAKFAST

B&B PER ROOM PER NIGHT
S £40.00–£45.00
D £55.00–£65.00

### Bayview

Central Parade, Herne Bay CT6 5JJ **t** (01227) 741458 **e** info@the-bayview-guesthouse.co.uk

**the-bayview-guesthouse.co.uk** GUEST REVIEWS

Centrally located in this popular seaside resort, Bayview offers eleven individually designed double bedrooms, each enjoying views of the beautiful Herne Bay coastline.

**open** All year
**bedrooms** 7 double, 2 twin, 1 family, 1 suite
**bathrooms** 5 en suite, 2 private
**payment** Credit/debit cards

Room General Leisure

## HERSTMONCEUX, East Sussex Map ref 3B4

★★★★
GUEST ACCOMMODATION

B&B PER ROOM PER NIGHT
S £40.00–£60.00
D £60.00–£80.00

### Sandhurst

Church Road, Herstmonceux, Hailsham BN27 1RG **t** (01323) 833088 **e** junealanruss@aol.com

Large bungalow with plenty of off-road parking. Within walking distance of Herstmonceux village and close to Herstmonceux Castle. Twenty minutes' drive to sea. No smoking.

**open** All year except Christmas
**bedrooms** 2 double, 2 family
**bathrooms** 3 en suite, 1 private
**payment** Cash, cheques

Room General P

## HEVER, Kent Map ref 2D2

★★★★
BED & BREAKFAST
SILVER AWARD

B&B PER ROOM PER NIGHT
S £48.00–£65.00
D £70.00–£85.00

*Discount for stays of 4 days or more.*

### Becketts

Pylegate Farm, Hartfield Road, Cowden, Edenbridge TN8 7HE **t** (01342) 850514
**e** jacqui@becketts-bandb.co.uk

**becketts-bandb.co.uk** SPECIAL OFFERS · REAL-TIME BOOKING

**open** All year except Christmas
**bedrooms** 1 double, 2 twin
**bathrooms** All en suite
**payment** Credit/debit cards, cash, cheques, euros

Beautiful, character 300-year-old barn with vaulted dining room and beams throughout, set in glorious countryside. Antique four-poster bed. All rooms en suite. Hever Castle, Penshurst and Chartwell all within four miles. Many other NT properties. Great walking and cycling. Cosy pubs with good food nearby. Wireless broadband. Online booking.

**SAT NAV** *TN8 7HE* **ONLINE MAP**

Room General P Leisure

## HIGH WYCOMBE, Buckinghamshire Map ref 2C2

★★★★
BED & BREAKFAST
SILVER AWARD

B&B PER ROOM PER NIGHT
S £40.00–£50.00
D £55.00–£65.00

### 9 Green Road

High Wycombe HP13 5BD **t** (01494) 437022

**lovetostayat9.co.uk**

Quiet family home with ample off-street parking. Rooms furnished to a high standard with power showers in all bathrooms. Full English breakfast. Easy access to M40 and M25. Family occupancy from £75.00 per night.

**open** All year except Christmas and New Year
**bedrooms** 2 double
**bathrooms** 1 en suite, 1 private
**payment** Credit/debit cards, cash, cheques

Room General

## HIGH WYCOMBE, Buckinghamshire Map ref 2C2

★★★
BED & BREAKFAST

B&B PER ROOM PER NIGHT
S Min £35.00
D Min £55.00

### 9 Sandford Gardens

Daws Hill, High Wycombe HP11 1QT **t** (01494) 441723 & 07980 439560

Georgian-style house in quiet residential area with off-street parking. Self-contained annexe. Easy access to motorways and Heathrow.

**open** All year
**bedrooms** 1 twin, 1 single
**payment** Cash, cheques

Room General

## HIGH WYCOMBE, Buckinghamshire Map ref 2C2

★★★
GUEST HOUSE

B&B PER ROOM PER NIGHT
S £35.00–£45.00
D £58.00–£68.00

### Amersham Hill Guest House

52 Amersham Hill, High Wycombe HP13 6PQ **t** (01494) 520635

Conveniently located five minutes' walk from High Wycombe station. Easy access to M40 and M4. All rooms have colour TV, radio alarm, tea-/coffee-making facilities. Full English breakfast included. Ample parking.

**open** All year
**bedrooms** 2 double, 1 twin, 4 single
**bathrooms** 2 en suite
**payment** Cash, cheques

Room General 5 P

## HORLEY, Surrey Map ref 2D2

★★★
GUEST ACCOMMODATION

B&B PER ROOM PER NIGHT
S £39.00–£45.00
D £54.00–£57.00

*Special offers on accommodation plus 8 days parking from £55.*

### The Turret Guest House

48 Massetts Road, Horley RH6 7DS **t** (01293) 782490 & 07970 066471 **e** info@theturret.com

**theturret.com**

**open** All year
**bedrooms** 3 double, 2 twin, 2 single, 3 family
**bathrooms** All en suite
**payment** Credit/debit cards, cash, cheques

Very comfortable, non-smoking Victorian house. All rooms en suite. Five minutes' walk to pubs, restaurants and station. Gatwick Airport 1.5 miles. Broadband internet access.

**SAT NAV** *RH6 7DS*

Room General Leisure

## HOVE

*See under Brighton & Hove*

## ISLE OF WIGHT

*See under Bonchurch, Brighstone, Colwell Bay, Cowes, Freshwater, Mottistone, Ryde, Sandown, Shanklin, Ventnor, Wroxall, Yarmouth*

### What shall we do today?

For ideas on places to visit, see the beginning of this regional section or go online at enjoyengland.com.

## KINGHAM, Oxfordshire Map ref 2B1

★★★★
INN

B&B PER ROOM PER NIGHT
S £65.00
D £90.00–£100.00

EVENING MEAL PER PERSON
£20.00–£30.00

### Tollgate Inn & Restaurant

Church Street, Kingham OX7 6YA **t** (01608) 658389 **e** info@thetollgate.com

**thetollgate.com** GUEST REVIEWS

The Tollgate Inn and Restaurant is a renovated 17thC farmhouse nestling in Kingham. Recommended in Egon Ronay's Best Restaurants and Gastropubs and Michelin Eating Out in Pubs 2008. Ideally situated for touring the Cotswolds.

**open** All year
**bedrooms** 7 double, 1 twin, 1 family
**bathrooms** All en suite
**payment** Credit/debit cards, cash, cheques

Room General Leisure

## KINTBURY, Berkshire Map ref 2C2

★★★
INN

B&B PER ROOM PER NIGHT
S £80.00–£90.00

EVENING MEAL PER PERSON
£8.00–£18.00

### The Dundas Arms

Station Road, Kintbury, Hungerford RG17 9UT **t** (01488) 658263 **e** info@dundasarms.co.uk

**dundasarms.co.uk**

Canal and riverside pub selling good food, beer and wine in both bar and restaurant, with hotel rooms overlooking the river.

**open** All year except Christmas and New Year
**bedrooms** 3 double, 2 twin
**bathrooms** All en suite
**payment** Credit/debit cards, cash, cheques

Room General Leisure

## LAMBERHURST, Kent Map ref 3B4

★★★★★
BED & BREAKFAST
SILVER AWARD

B&B PER ROOM PER NIGHT
S £40.00–£45.00
D £70.00–£75.00

EVENING MEAL PER PERSON
£13.00–£23.00

### Woodpecker Barn

Wickhurst Farm, Tunbridge Wells TN3 8BH **t** (01892) 891958 **e** martinloveday@btinternet.com

**woodpeckerbarn.co.uk** SPECIAL OFFERS

Elegantly converted 17thC barn, combining traditional and contemporary styles, set in a tranquil spot on Kent/East Sussex borders.

**open** All year
**bedrooms** 2 suites
**bathrooms** 2 private
**payment** Cash, cheques, euros

Room General Leisure

## LEWES, East Sussex Map ref 2D3

★★★★
INN
SILVER AWARD

B&B PER ROOM PER NIGHT
S £50.00–£70.00
D £65.00–£80.00

EVENING MEAL PER PERSON
£9.00–£18.00

### The Blacksmiths Arms

London Road, Offham, Lewes BN7 3QD **t** (01273) 472971 **e** blacksmithsarms@tiscali.co.uk

**theblacksmithsarms-offham.co.uk**

18thC village inn close to South Downs Way on main A275. Close to historic town of Lewes. Convenient for Sussex University and Glyndebourne. Mentioned in Good Pub Guide.

**open** All year
**bedrooms** 4 double
**bathrooms** All en suite
**payment** Credit/debit cards, cash, cheques

Room General 3 P Leisure

## LITTLEHAMPTON, West Sussex Map ref 2D3

★★
INN

B&B PER ROOM PER NIGHT
S £27.50–£35.00
D £42.50–£50.00

EVENING MEAL PER PERSON
£6.95–£25.00

### Arun View Inn

Wharf Road, Littlehampton BN17 5DD **t** (01903) 722335

**thearunview.co.uk**

A pleasant riverside pub, offering a good range of home-cooked food and a wide selection of drinks in a friendly atmosphere.

**open** All year except Christmas and New Year
**bedrooms** 1 double, 4 twin
**payment** Credit/debit cards, cash, cheques, euros

Room General Leisure

## LONGFIELD, Kent Map ref 3B3

★★★
INN

B&B PER ROOM PER NIGHT
S £50.00–£55.00
D £65.00–£75.00

EVENING MEAL PER PERSON
£7.00–£20.00

### The Rising Sun Inn

Fawkham Green, Fawkham, Longfield DA3 8NL **t** (01474) 872291

**open** All year
**bedrooms** 2 double, 3 twin
**bathrooms** All en suite
**payment** Credit/debit cards, cash, cheques

The Rising Sun Inn is a 16thC public house situated close to Brands Hatch. A popular inn with en suite rooms, two with superb four-poster beds. Other facilities include a busy restaurant, main bar with inglenook fireplace and large patio for al fresco dining in warmer weather.

**SAT NAV** *DA3 8NL*

Room General 2 P

## LYMINGTON, Hampshire Map ref 2C3

★★★★★
GUEST ACCOMMODATION
SILVER AWARD

B&B PER ROOM PER NIGHT
S £60.00–£85.00
D £75.00–£90.00

*Private yacht hire, horse-riding and many more outside activities can be arranged. Picnic hampers can be organised.*

### Britannia House

Mill Lane, Lymington SO41 9AY **t** (01590) 672091 **e** enquiries@britannia-house.com

**britannia-house.com** GUEST REVIEWS · SPECIAL OFFERS

**open** All year
**bedrooms** 5 double, 1 twin
**bathrooms** All en suite
**payment** Credit/debit cards, cash, cheques, euros

Luxurious guesthouse, non-smoking establishment, very comfortable rooms, all en suite. Traditional four-course breakfast in farmhouse kitchen, large guest lounge with spectacular views over harbour and Isle of Wight. Beautiful courtyard garden, on-site parking. Only two minutes' walking distance to quay, high street, shops, pubs and restaurants.

**SAT NAV** *SO41 9AY* **ONLINE MAP**

Room General 12 P Leisure

## LYMINGTON, Hampshire Map ref 2C3

★★★
GUEST HOUSE

B&B PER ROOM PER NIGHT
S £45.00–£55.00
D £90.00–£120.00

EVENING MEAL PER PERSON
£30.00

### Gorse Meadow Guest House

Sway Road, Pennington, Lymington SO41 8LR **t** (01590) 673354 **e** gorsemeadow@btconnect.com

**gorsemeadowguesthouse.co.uk**

**open** All year
**bedrooms** 3 double, 1 twin, 2 family
**bathrooms** All en suite
**payment** Credit/debit cards, cash, cheques

Beautiful Edwardian residence in 16 acres, close to New Forest. Period furniture, modern utilities. Splendid galleried hall, impressive dining room (evening dinners) seating 12. Licensed. Residents'/visitors' lounge. Landscaped grounds with fish pond. Cookery courses, bike and boat hire, beaches, riding, golf and good pubs nearby.

**SAT NAV** *SO41 8LR* **ONLINE MAP**

Room General P Leisure

### B&B prices

Rates for bed and breakfast are shown per room per night.
Double room prices are usually based on two people sharing the room.

## LYNDHURST, Hampshire Map ref 2C3

★★★
BED & BREAKFAST

B&B PER ROOM PER NIGHT
S £30.00–£35.00
D £60.00–£70.00

EVENING MEAL PER PERSON
Max £13.00

### Rosedale Bed & Breakfast

24 Shaggs Meadow, Lyndhurst SO43 7BN **t** (023) 8028 3793 & (023) 8013 4253
**e** rosedalebandb@btinternet.com

**rosedalebedandbreakfast.co.uk**

Family-run bed and breakfast in the centre of Lyndhurst. We cater for all. Colour TV, tea/coffee facilities. New Forest breakfast served up to 0900. Evening meals by arrangement.

**open** All year
**bedrooms** 1 family
**bathrooms** 2 en suite
**payment** Cash, cheques

Room General P Leisure

## MAIDENHEAD, Berkshire Map ref 2C2

★★★★
RESTAURANT WITH ROOMS
SILVER AWARD

B&B PER ROOM PER NIGHT
D £85.00–£95.00

EVENING MEAL PER PERSON
£7.95–£30.00

### The Black Boys Inn

Henley Road, Hurley, Maidenhead SL6 5NQ **t** (01628) 824212

**open** All year except Christmas and New Year
**bedrooms** 7 double, 1 twin
**bathrooms** All en suite
**payment** Credit/debit cards, cash, cheques

This 16thC inn has en suite bedrooms of style and character and looks onto sweeping views of the Chilterns. Water is supplied by the inn's very own well. The restaurant retains original beams and polished oak floors and has gained many awards over the years.

**SAT NAV** *SL6 5NQ*

Room General 12 P Leisure

## MAIDENHEAD, Berkshire Map ref 2C2

★★
BED & BREAKFAST

B&B PER ROOM PER NIGHT
S £35.00–£47.50
D £55.00–£70.00

### Cartlands Cottage

Kings Lane, Cookham Dean, Maidenhead SL6 9AY **t** (01628) 482196

Family room in self-contained garden studio. Meals in delightful, timbered character cottage with exposed beams. Traditional cottage garden opposite National Trust common land. Very quiet.

**open** All year
**bedrooms** 1 family
**bathrooms** En suite
**payment** Cash, cheques

Room General P

## MAIDSTONE, Kent Map ref 3B3

★★★★
BED & BREAKFAST
SILVER AWARD

B&B PER ROOM PER NIGHT
S £35.00–£40.00
D £60.00–£65.00

### Grove House

Grove Green Road, Maidstone ME14 5JT **t** (01622) 738441

**open** All year except Christmas and New Year
**bedrooms** 1 double, 1 twin
**bathrooms** 1 en suite, 1 private
**payment** Credit/debit cards, cash, cheques

Attractive comfortable detached house in quiet road. Off-street parking. Close to Leeds Castle, pubs, restaurants, M20 and M2 motorways.

**SAT NAV** *ME14 5JT*

Room General P Leisure

## MARDEN, Kent Map ref 3B4

★★★★
FARMHOUSE

B&B PER ROOM PER NIGHT
S Min £45.00
D £55.00–£60.00

### Tanner House

Tanner Farm, Goudhurst Road, Tonbridge TN12 9ND **t** (01622) 831214
**e** enquiries@tannerfarmpark.co.uk

**tannerfarmpark.co.uk**

Tudor farmhouse in centre of family farm. Good access in secluded, rural position. Shire horses kept on farm. Also, award-winning caravan and camping park.

**open** All year except Christmas
**bedrooms** 1 double, 2 twin
**bathrooms** All en suite
**payment** Credit/debit cards, cash, cheques, euros

Room General 12 P Leisure

## MARLOW, Buckinghamshire Map ref 2C2

★★★★★
INN

B&B PER ROOM PER NIGHT
D £140.00–£190.00

EVENING MEAL PER PERSON
£27.50–£35.50

### The Hand and Flowers

West Street, Marlow SL7 2BP **t** (01628) 482277

**thehandandflowers.co.uk**

**open** All year except Christmas
**bedrooms** 4 double
**bathrooms** All en suite
**payment** Credit/debit cards, cash, cheques

Cottages are described as quirky and luxurious, perfect for a romantic weekend or as an escape from the city. Enjoy a short walk to the river or relax in the spa. Have breakfast in bed or full English in our pub.

**SAT NAV** *SL7 2BP* **ONLINE MAP**

Room General P

## MIDHURST, West Sussex Map ref 2C3

★★
BED & BREAKFAST

B&B PER ROOM PER NIGHT
S £40.00–£50.00
D £35.00–£50.00

### Oakhurst Cottage

Carron Lane, Midhurst GU29 9LF **t** (01730) 813523

Beautifully converted early Victorian coach house next to Midhurst Common, yet within walking distance of Midhurst town centre. Great breakfasts. Access to lovely walking and cycling countryside.

**open** All year except Christmas and New Year
**bedrooms** 1 double
**payment** Cash, cheques

Room General

## MIDHURST, West Sussex Map ref 2C3

★★★
BED & BREAKFAST

B&B PER ROOM PER NIGHT
D £70.00–£90.00

### Sunnyside

Cocking Causeway, Midhurst GU29 9QH **t** (01730) 814370

Sunnyside is close to the South Downs Way, Goodwood for golf, motor-racing and horse-racing, and Cowdray Park for polo. Easy reach of Arundel and the south coast. Always a friendly welcome.

**open** All year except Christmas and New Year
**bedrooms** 2 double, 1 twin
**bathrooms** 2 en suite, 1 private
**payment** Cash, cheques, euros

Room General P Leisure

WALKERS WELCOME

### Do you like walking?

Walkers feel at home in accommodation participating in our Walkers Welcome scheme. Look out for the symbol. Consider walking all or part of a long-distance route – go online at nationaltrail.co.uk.

## MILFORD ON SEA, Hampshire Map ref 2C3

★★★★
BED & BREAKFAST

B&B PER ROOM PER NIGHT
D £60.00–£70.00

### Alma Mater

4 Knowland Drive, Milford on Sea, Lymington SO41 0RH **t** (01590) 642811
**e** bandbalmamater@aol.com

**almamater.org.uk**

**open** All year
**bedrooms** 2 double, 1 twin
**bathrooms** 2 en suite, 1 private
**payment** Cash, cheques, euros

Detached, quiet, spacious, non-smoking chalet bungalow with en suite bedrooms overlooking lovely garden. In quiet residential area close to village, beaches, New Forest and IOW. Secure, off-road parking.

**SAT NAV** *SO41 0RH*

Room General 15 P Leisure

## MILTON KEYNES, Buckinghamshire Map ref 2C1

★★★
FARMHOUSE

B&B PER ROOM PER NIGHT
S £30.00–£40.00
D £60.00–£70.00

### Chantry Farm

Pindon End, Hanslope, Milton Keynes MK19 7HL **t** (01908) 510269 **e** chuff.wake@tiscali.co.uk

**chantryfarmbandb.com** GUEST REVIEWS

A 600-acre friendly working farm. Old stone farmhouse (1650) with inglenook fireplace, in beautiful countryside overlooking lake. Near Milton Keynes, London train 40 minutes. Convenient for Northampton, Silverstone, Woburn Abbey.

**open** All year except Christmas and New Year
**bedrooms** 1 double, 2 twin
**bathrooms** 1 en suite
**payment** Cash, cheques, euros

Room General P Leisure

## MILTON KEYNES, Buckinghamshire Map ref 2C1

★
GUEST HOUSE

B&B PER ROOM PER NIGHT
S £25.00–£30.00
D £30.00–£35.00

### Kingfishers

9 Rylstone Close, Heelands, Milton Keynes MK13 7QT **t** 07866 424417
**e** enquiry@kingfishersmk.co.uk

**kingfishersmk.co.uk**

Large, private home in 0.25 acres of grounds, convenient for city centre, shopping, theatre and railway station. Very comfortable; a warm welcome assured.

**open** All year
**bedrooms** 1 double, 1 twin, 2 single, 1 family
**bathrooms** 4 en suite, 1 private
**payment** Cash, cheques

Room General 2 P

## MOTTISTONE, Isle of Wight Map ref 2C3

★★★★
GUEST ACCOMMODATION

B&B PER ROOM PER NIGHT
S £36.00–£45.00
D £64.00–£70.00

### Mottistone Manor Farmhouse

Mottistone PO30 4ED **t** (01983) 740207 **e** bookings@bolthols.co.uk

**bolthols.co.uk**

Tranquil 17th/18thC farmhouse B&B nestling in an Area of Outstanding Natural Beauty. Rural views to the sea; ideal for walking, cycling, beaches, sightseeing. Within easy reach of buses, pubs, village shops etc.

**open** All year except Christmas
**bedrooms** 3 double, 1 twin
**bathrooms** 3 en suite, 1 private
**payment** Credit/debit cards, cash, cheques

Room General P Leisure

## NEW FOREST

*See under Beaulieu, Brockenhurst, Burley, Cadnam, Fordingbridge, Lymington, Lyndhurst, Milford on Sea, New Milton*

## NEW MILTON, Hampshire Map ref 2B3

★★★★
BED & BREAKFAST
SILVER AWARD

B&B PER ROOM PER NIGHT
S £34.00–£45.00
D £58.00–£66.00

*Winter discounts (excl Bank Holidays). Discount for more than 7 days.*

### Taverners Cottage

Bashley Cross Road, Bashley, New Milton BH25 5SZ **t** (01425) 615403
**e** judith@tavernerscottage.co.uk

**tavernerscottage.co.uk**

**open** All year except Christmas and New Year
**bedrooms** 1 double, 1 family
**bathrooms** All en suite
**payment** Cash, cheques, euros

Attractive 300-year-old cob cottage overlooking open farmland. Warm welcome guaranteed. Great breakfasts. Care and attention to detail a priority. Ideal for touring, golf, cycling, walking and riding.

**SAT NAV** *BH25 5SZ* **ONLINE MAP**

Room General P Leisure

## NEW MILTON, Hampshire Map ref 2B3

★★★★
BED & BREAKFAST

B&B PER ROOM PER NIGHT
S £45.00–£50.00
D £65.00–£75.00

*Midweek reduced breaks: 4 nights for the price of 3.*

### Willy's Well

Bashley Common Road, Bashley, New Milton BH25 5SF **t** (01425) 616834
**e** moyramac2@hotmail.com

**open** All year
**bedrooms** 1 double, 1 twin
**bathrooms** All en suite
**payment** Cash, cheques, euros

A warm welcome awaits you at our mid-17thC listed thatched cottage standing in one acre of mature gardens, also available for your enjoyment. We have direct forest access through six acres of pasture and are three miles from the sea. Ideal for walking, cycling, horse-riding.

**SAT NAV** *BH25 5SF*

Room General 12 P Leisure

## NEWBURY, Berkshire Map ref 2C2

★★★
INN

B&B PER ROOM PER NIGHT
S £50.00–£75.00
D £60.00–£85.00

*Please see website for current offers.*

### The Bell at Boxford

Boxford, Newbury RG20 8DD **t** (01488) 608721 **e** paul@bellatboxford.com

**bellatboxford.com** SPECIAL OFFERS

**open** All year
**bedrooms** 6 double, 2 twin, 2 single
**bathrooms** All en suite
**payment** Credit/debit cards, cash, cheques, euros

Situated in the beautiful Lambourn valley, only four miles from both Newbury and Lambourn. Newbury racecourse is only ten minutes away. Golf, fishing and riding are all local pursuits.

**SAT NAV** *RG20 8DD* **ONLINE MAP**

Room General P Leisure

### What do the star ratings mean?

Detailed information about star ratings can be found at the back of this guide.

## NEWBURY, Berkshire Map ref 2C2

★★★★
INN

B&B PER ROOM PER NIGHT
S £69.95–£79.95
D £79.95–£89.95

*2-night weekend break DB&B based on two people sharing a room £220.00.*

# The Carnarvon Arms

Winchester Road, Whitway, Burghclere, Newbury RG20 9LE **t** (01635) 278222
**e** info@carnarvonarms.com

**carnarvonarms.com** SPECIAL OFFERS · REAL-TIME BOOKING

**open** All year
**bedrooms** 13 double, 5 twin, 5 family
**bathrooms** All en suite
**payment** Credit/debit cards, cash, cheques

The Carnarvon Arms is a truly modern-day country inn with 23 beautifully appointed en suite bedrooms. We offer sensational, sensibly priced food in stylish yet informal surroundings. You will find a warm, welcoming and positive atmosphere making the Carnarvon Arms a place where you can unwind in homely but modern comfort.

**SAT NAV** *RG20 9LE* **ONLINE MAP**

Room General Leisure

## NEWBURY, Berkshire Map ref 2C2

★★★★
GUEST ACCOMMODATION

B&B PER ROOM PER NIGHT
S £40.00–£45.00
D £68.00–£80.00

*Packages available for riders, walkers and cyclists, including stabling/grazing, meals and luggage drop-off service.*

# East End Farm

East End, Newbury RG20 0AB **t** (01635) 254895 **e** mp@eastendfarm.co.uk

**eastendfarm.co.uk**

**open** All year
**bedrooms** 1 double, 1 twin
**bathrooms** All en suite
**payment** Cash, cheques, euros

Five miles south of Newbury, in an Area of Outstanding Natural Beauty, this small working farm will give you a warm welcome. Accommodation is in a beautifully converted barn. Choice of breakfasts with home-made and local produce. Ideal base for country lovers or stopover for business or travel.

**SAT NAV** *RG20 0AB*

Room General Leisure

## NEWBURY, Berkshire Map ref 2C2

★★★★
FARMHOUSE
SILVER AWARD

B&B PER ROOM PER NIGHT
S £44.00–£47.00
D £73.00–£76.00

# Manor Farm House

Church Street, Hampstead Norreys, Newbury RG18 0TD **t** (01635) 201276
**e** bettsbedandbreakfast@hotmail.com

**bettsbedandbreakfast.co.uk**

**open** All year
**bedrooms** 1 double, 1 twin, 1 suite
**bathrooms** All en suite
**payment** Cash, cheques

Welcoming and superbly comfortable accommodation on our working farm in centre of peaceful village. A 17thC farmhouse with 21stC comfort, including whirlpool bath, and self-contained ground-floor apartment. Wi-Fi in all rooms. Pub two minutes' stroll. Labrador dogs available for longer walks on farm or in neighbouring woods.

**SAT NAV** *RG18 0TD*

Room General 10

## Using map references

Map references refer to the colour maps at the front of this guide.

## NEWBURY, Berkshire Map ref 2C2

★★★★
BED & BREAKFAST

B&B PER ROOM PER NIGHT
S £45.00–£55.00
D £75.00–£85.00

### The Old Farmhouse

Downend Lane, Chieveley, Newbury RG20 8TN **t** (01635) 248361 **e** palletts@aol.com

**smoothhound.co.uk/hotels/oldfarmhouse**

**open** All year
**bedrooms** 1 suite
**bathrooms** En suite
**payment** Cash, cheques

Period farmhouse on edge of village within two miles of M4/A34 (jct13), five miles north of Newbury. Accommodation in ground-floor annexe comprising hall, kitchenette, sitting room (with bed-settee), double bedroom, bathroom. Large gardens overlooking countryside. Oxford, Bath, Windsor and Heathrow Airport within easy reach. London approximately one hour. Family room rates from £85.00.

**SAT NAV** *RG20 8TN*

Room General

## NEWHAVEN, East Sussex Map ref 2D3

★★★
GUEST HOUSE

B&B PER ROOM PER NIGHT
S £29.00–£35.00
D £54.00–£64.00

### Newhaven Lodge Guest House

12 Brighton Road, Newhaven BN9 9NB **t** (01273) 513736 **e** newhavenlodge@aol.com

**newhavenlodge.co.uk** GUEST REVIEWS

A comfortable, bright, family-run establishment located close to the Newhaven/Dieppe ferry terminal. Brighton, Lewes and South Downs nearby. The establishment motto is 'Arrive as a guest and leave as a friend'.

**open** All year
**bedrooms** 1 double, 2 single, 3 family
**bathrooms** 4 en suite
**payment** Credit/debit cards, cash, cheques, euros

Room General Leisure

## NEWPORT PAGNELL, Buckinghamshire Map ref 2C1

★★★
GUEST ACCOMMODATION
SILVER AWARD

B&B PER ROOM PER NIGHT
S £33.00–£39.00
D £55.00–£65.00

EVENING MEAL PER PERSON
£6.99–£12.99

### Rosemary House

7 Hill View, Newport Pagnell MK16 8BE **t** (01908) 612198 **e** rosemaryhouse@btinternet.com

All rooms have TV and video, tea and coffee facilities and hot and cold water vanity units. Full English breakfast included. Ample parking. Wi-Fi internet.

**open** All year
**bedrooms** 2 twin, 1 suite
**bathrooms** 1 en suite, 2 private
**payment** Cash, cheques

Room General Leisure

## OXFORD, Oxfordshire Map ref 2C1

★★
GUEST ACCOMMODATION

B&B PER ROOM PER NIGHT
S £40.00–£60.00
D £50.00–£70.00

### Becket House

5 Becket Street, Oxford OX1 1PP **t** (01865) 724675 **e** becketguesthouse@yahoo.co.uk

Friendly guesthouse convenient for rail and bus station, within walking distance of city centre and colleges. Good, clean accommodation, en suite rooms.

**open** All year
**bedrooms** 4 double, 2 twin, 2 single, 2 family
**bathrooms** 5 en suite
**payment** Credit/debit cards

Room General

## Has every property been assessed?

All accommodation in this guide has been rated for quality, or is awaiting assessment, by a professional national tourist board assessor.

## OXFORD, Oxfordshire Map ref 2C1

★★★★
BED & BREAKFAST

B&B PER ROOM PER NIGHT
s £40.00–£50.00
d £60.00–£80.00

### Broomhill

Lincombe Lane, Boars Hill, Oxford OX1 5DZ **t** (01865) 735339 **e** sara@broomhill-oxford.co.uk

**broomhill-oxford.co.uk**

**open** All year
**bedrooms** 2 double, 1 twin, 2 single
**bathrooms** 4 en suite
**payment** Cash, cheques, euros

Broomhill is situated five minutes from Oxford. Heathrow 45 minutes. Large house in family environment in extensive grounds. Large double and single rooms, all en suite. Excellent pub five minutes' walk, serving good, all-day food. See website or email for more information.

**SAT NAV** *OX1 5DZ*

Room General P Leisure

## OXFORD, Oxfordshire Map ref 2C1

★★★★
GUEST HOUSE

B&B PER ROOM PER NIGHT
s £65.00–£85.00
d £95.00–£130.00

### The Buttery

11-12 Broad Street, Oxford OX1 3AP **t** (01865) 811950 **e** enquiries@thebutteryhotel.co.uk

**thebutteryhotel.co.uk**

Set on Broad Street, surrounded by historic Oxford colleges and museums, The Buttery welcomes you to explore the wonders of Oxford from its central location. Spacious well-furnished en suite rooms.

**open** All year
**bedrooms** 10 double, 2 twin, 1 single, 3 family
**bathrooms** All en suite
**payment** Credit/debit cards, cash, cheques, euros

Room General Leisure

## OXFORD, Oxfordshire Map ref 2C1

★★★★
GUEST ACCOMMODATION

B&B PER ROOM PER NIGHT
s £52.00–£62.00
d £80.00–£90.00

### Cotswold House

363 Banbury Road, Oxford OX2 7PL **t** (01865) 310558 **e** d.r.walker@talk21.com

**cotswoldhouse.co.uk** REAL-TIME BOOKING

A well-situated and elegant property, offering good accommodation and service. Cotswold House is in a most desirable part of Oxford.

**open** All year
**bedrooms** 2 double, 1 twin, 2 single, 2 family
**bathrooms** All en suite
**payment** Credit/debit cards, cash, cheques

Room General 5 P

## OXFORD, Oxfordshire Map ref 2C1

★★★
BED & BREAKFAST

B&B PER ROOM PER NIGHT
s £35.00–£40.00
d £60.00

### Park House

7 St Bernard's Road, Oxford OX2 6EH **t** (01865) 310824 **e** krynpark@hotmail.com

Traditional Victorian terraced house in north Oxford, five minutes' walk from city centre and within easy reach of all amenities.

**open** All year except Christmas
**bedrooms** 1 double, 1 single
**bathrooms** 1 private
**payment** Cash, cheques

Room General P

PETS! WELCOME WELCOME PETS!

## Where is my pet welcome?

Want to take your cherished companion with you on holiday? Proprietors participating in our Welcome Pets! scheme go out of their way to make special provision for you and your pet. Look out for the symbol.

## OXFORD, Oxfordshire Map ref 2C1

★★★★
GUEST HOUSE

B&B PER ROOM PER NIGHT
S £30.00–£55.00
D £70.00–£90.00

### Pickwick's Guest House

15-17 London Road, Headington, Oxford OX3 7SP **t** (01865) 750487 **e** pickwicks@tiscali.co.uk

**pickwicksguesthouse.co.uk**

**open** All year except Christmas and New Year
**bedrooms** 4 double, 3 twin, 4 single, 4 family
**bathrooms** 13 en suite
**payment** Credit/debit cards, cash, cheques

Comfortable guesthouse within easy reach of Oxford's universities and hospitals. Nearby coach stop for 24-hour service to central London, Heathrow, Gatwick and Stansted Airports. Free car parking and Wi-Fi internet. Please contact us for family room rates.

**SAT NAV** *OX3 7SP* **ONLINE MAP**

Room General P

## OXFORD, Oxfordshire Map ref 2C1

★★
GUEST HOUSE

B&B PER ROOM PER NIGHT
S £30.00–£35.00
D £50.00–£55.00

### Whitehouse View Guest House

9 Whitehouse Road, Grandpont, Oxford OX1 4PA **t** (01865) 721626 & 07831 201259
**e** sramdoo@aol.com

Whitehouse View is situated in peaceful surroundings in the heart of Oxford. Ten minutes' walking distance to city centre, its historic universities and amenities. Well-appointed rooms including ground floor. A warm welcome awaits.

**open** All year except Christmas and New Year
**bedrooms** 2 double, 2 twin, 2 single, 2 family
**bathrooms** 2 en suite
**payment** Cash, cheques, euros

Room General Leisure

## PETERSFIELD, Hampshire Map ref 2C3

★★★★
BED & BREAKFAST

B&B PER ROOM PER NIGHT
S £40.00–£45.00
D £60.00–£64.00

### 1 The Spain

Sheep Street, Petersfield GU32 3JZ **t** (01730) 263261 **e** allantarver@ntlworld.com

**1thespain.com**

18thC house with charming walled garden, in conservation area of Petersfield. Good eating places nearby, lovely walks, plenty to see and do.

**open** All year
**bedrooms** 2 double, 1 twin
**bathrooms** 2 en suite, 1 private
**payment** Cash, cheques

Room General Leisure

## PETERSFIELD, Hampshire Map ref 2C3

★★★★
BED & BREAKFAST

B&B PER ROOM PER NIGHT
S £35.00–£45.00
D £65.00–£75.00

### Quinhay Farmhouse

Alton Road, Froxfield, Petersfield GU32 1BZ **t** (01730) 827183 **e** janerothery@quinhaybandb.co.uk

**quinhaybandb.co.uk** GUEST REVIEWS

**open** All year except Christmas and New Year
**bedrooms** 1 double, 1 twin, 1 single
**bathrooms** 1 en suite, 2 private
**payment** Credit/debit cards, cash, cheques

We offer three rooms, a double en suite and a single and a twin room, both with private bathrooms. There is a large guest lounge with garden access. Close to Winchester, Chichester and Portsmouth. Access to glorious countryside. Non-smoking.

**SAT NAV** *GU32 1BZ* **ONLINE MAP**

Room General 10 P Leisure

For **key to symbols** see page 7

## PETWORTH, West Sussex Map ref 2D3

★★★★
BED & BREAKFAST

B&B PER ROOM PER NIGHT
S £40.00
D £65.00–£70.00

### Eedes Cottage

Bignor Park Road, Bury Gate, Pulborough RH20 1EZ **t** (01798) 831438
**e** eedes.bandb@btinternet.com

**visitsussex.org/eedescottage**

Quiet country house surrounded by farmland. Convenient for main roads to Arundel, Chichester and Brighton. Dogs and children welcome. All bedrooms large and comfortable.

**open** All year
**bedrooms** 2 double, 2 twin
**bathrooms** 2 en suite
**payment** Cash, cheques, euros

Room General Leisure

## PLUCKLEY, Kent Map ref 3B4

★★★★
GUEST ACCOMMODATION

B&B PER ROOM PER NIGHT
S £64.00–£84.00
D £80.00–£140.00

EVENING MEAL PER PERSON
£19.95–£23.95

### Elvey Farm

Elvey Lane, Ashford TN27 0SU **t** (01233) 840442 **e** bookings@elveyfarm.co.uk

**elveyfarm.co.uk** GUEST REVIEWS • SPECIAL OFFERS • REAL-TIME BOOKING

**open** All year
**bedrooms** 1 double, 2 family, 4 suites
**bathrooms** All en suite
**payment** Credit/debit cards, cash, cheques

Medieval farmstead set in 75 acres in the heart of Darling Buds of May country. Suites in stable block and 16thC barn, packed with period features and stylish, contemporary en suites. Private entrances and living rooms. Stunning Kentish restaurant.

**SAT NAV** *TN27 0SU* **ONLINE MAP**

WALKERS WELCOME CYCLISTS WELCOME PETS! WELCOME

Room General Leisure

## PORTSMOUTH, Hampshire Map ref 2C3

★★★★
GUEST ACCOMMODATION

B&B PER ROOM PER NIGHT
S £45.00–£60.00
D £60.00–£70.00

### Hamilton House Bed & Breakfast

95 Victoria Road North, Portsmouth PO5 1PS **t** (023) 9282 3502 **e** sandra@hamiltonhouse.co.uk

**hamiltonhouse.co.uk**

Delightful Victorian town house, many original features. Five minutes continental/Isle of Wight ferry ports, stations, University of Portsmouth, The Historic Dockyard, museums, Gunwharf Quays, tourist attractions. Ideal touring base. Breakfast served from 0600.

**open** All year
**bedrooms** 5 double, 2 twin, 2 family
**bathrooms** 5 en suite
**payment** Credit/debit cards, cash, cheques, euros

Room General

## PULBOROUGH, West Sussex Map ref 2D3

★★★★
INN

B&B PER ROOM PER NIGHT
S £50.00–£60.00
D £90.00–£120.00

EVENING MEAL PER PERSON
£6.95–£16.95

### The Labouring Man

Old London Road, Pulborough RH20 1LF **t** (01798) 872215 **e** philip.beckett@btconnect.com

**thelabouringman.co.uk** GUEST REVIEWS · SPECIAL OFFERS

**open** All year
**bedrooms** 4 double, 1 twin
**bathrooms** All en suite
**payment** Credit/debit cards, cash, cheques

Pub/restaurant with five luxury bed and breakfast rooms. Walkers, car park, home-cooked food, real ales, log fire.

**SAT NAV** *RH20 1LF* **ONLINE MAP**

Room General Leisure

## RAMSGATE, Kent Map ref 3C3

★★★★
GUEST HOUSE

B&B PER ROOM PER NIGHT
S £35.00–£40.00
D £55.00–£60.00

### Glendevon Guest House

8 Truro Road, Ramsgate CT11 8DB **t** (01843) 570909 **e** rebekah.smith1@btinternet.com

**glendevonguesthouse.co.uk**

Delightful Victorian house near beach, harbour and town. Very comfortable rooms, all en suite, and each containing attractive feature of modern kitchen/dining area. TV/VCR, Fairtrade tea and coffee.

**open** All year
**bedrooms** 3 double, 1 twin, 2 family
**bathrooms** All en suite
**payment** Credit/debit cards, cash, cheques

Room General Leisure

## READING, Berkshire Map ref 2C2

★★★★
GUEST ACCOMMODATION

B&B PER ROOM PER NIGHT
S £30.00–£65.00
D £65.00–£80.00

### Belle Vue House

2 Tilehurst Road, Reading RG1 7TN **t** (0118) 959 4445 **e** bellevuehotel@btconnect.com

**bellevuehousehotel.co.uk**

Central location, newly refurbished, ample parking, wireless broadband, walking distance to shops, bars, restaurants. Five minutes to mainline railway station.

**open** All year except Christmas
**bedrooms** 4 double, 1 twin, 10 single, 1 family
**bathrooms** 9 en suite
**payment** Credit/debit cards

Room General

## READING, Berkshire Map ref 2C2

★★★
GUEST ACCOMMODATION

B&B PER ROOM PER NIGHT
S £29.00–£37.50
D £37.50–£60.00

### Dittisham Guest House

63 Tilehurst Road, Reading RG30 2JL **t** (0118) 956 9483 **e** dittishamgh@aol.com

**open** All year
**bedrooms** 1 double, 1 twin, 3 single
**bathrooms** 3 en suite
**payment** Credit/debit cards, cash, cheques, euros

Renovated Edwardian property with garden, in a quiet but central location. Good value and quality. On bus routes for centre of town. Car park.

**SAT NAV** *RG30 2JL*

Room General

## RINGMER, East Sussex Map ref 2D3

★★★★
GUEST ACCOMMODATION

B&B PER ROOM PER NIGHT
s £40.00–£60.00
d £60.00–£70.00

### Bryn-Clai

Uckfield Road, Ringmer, Lewes BN8 5RU **t** (01273) 814042

**brynclai.co.uk** REAL-TIME BOOKING

**open** All year
**bedrooms** 1 double, 1 twin, 1 family
**bathrooms** 1 en suite, 1 private
**payment** Credit/debit cards, cash, cheques

Large, modern house set in seven acres with beautiful garden and good parking. Spacious, comfortable interior. Large, airy bedrooms (including ground-floor rooms) with views over farmland. Within walking distance of 16thC country pub with excellent food. Nearby attractions include Glyndebourne, East Sussex Golf Course, South Downs and Brighton.

**SAT NAV** *BN8 5RU*

Room General Leisure

## ROCHESTER, Kent Map ref 3B3

★★
BED & BREAKFAST
SILVER AWARD

B&B PER ROOM PER NIGHT
s £26.00–£28.00
d £52.00–£55.00

### Churchfields B&B

6 Churchfields Terrace, St Margarets Street, Rochester ME1 1TQ **t** (01634) 400 679
**e** info@churchfieldsbandb.co.uk

**churchfieldsbandb.co.uk**

A modern townhouse with river views, which provides a warm welcome and high standard comfortable accommodation. Five-minute walk from centre of Rochester, 15 minutes from station.

**open** All year except Christmas and New Year
**bedrooms** 1 double, 1 single
**bathrooms** 2 private
**payment** Cash, cheques

Room General 12

## RODMELL, East Sussex Map ref 2D3

★★★★
GUEST ACCOMMODATION

B&B PER ROOM PER NIGHT
s £35.00
d £60.00

### Garden Studio

Robin Hill, Mill Lane, Rodmell, Lewes BN7 3HS **t** (01273) 476715 & 07775 624235

Self-contained studio flat on South Downs Way. Twin beds, bed-settee, own kitchen, breakfast supplied. Close to Glyndebourne, Brighton, port of Newhaven. Use of garden. Popular village inn.

**open** All year
**bedrooms** 1 family
**bathrooms** En suite
**payment** Cash, cheques

Room General Leisure

## ROMSEY, Hampshire Map ref 2C3

★★★★★
BED & BREAKFAST

B&B PER ROOM PER NIGHT
s £35.00–£45.00
d £55.00–£70.00

### Ranvilles Farm House

Pauncefoot Hill, Romsey SO51 6AA **t** (023) 8081 4481 **e** info@ranvilles.com

**ranvilles.com**

A historic farmhouse near Winchester, Salisbury and the New Forest, and one mile from Romsey. Peaceful situation, set in five acres of gardens and paddocks. Extra-large beds.

**open** All year
**bedrooms** 1 double, 1 twin, 1 single, 1 family
**bathrooms** All en suite
**payment** Cash, cheques

Room General Leisure

FAMILIES WELCOME

## Looking for an ideal family break?

For accommodation offering additional facilities and services for a range of ages and family units, look out for the Families Welcome symbol. Owners of these properties will go out of their way to welcome families.

## ROYAL TUNBRIDGE WELLS, Kent Map ref 2D2

★★★★
GUEST ACCOMMODATION

B&B PER ROOM PER NIGHT
S Max £68.50
D Max £97.00

EVENING MEAL PER PERSON
£10.00–£28.00

### The Beacon

Tea Garden Lane, Tunbridge Wells TN3 9JH **t** (01892) 524252 **e** beaconhotel@btopenworld.com

**the-beacon.co.uk**

**open** All year
**bedrooms** 2 double, 1 single
**bathrooms** All en suite
**payment** Credit/debit cards, cash, cheques

Situated 1.5 miles from Tunbridge Wells, The Beacon, with its magnificent views and reputation for excellent cuisine and friendly, welcoming atmosphere, offers delightfully unique bedrooms – the Colonial (double), the Georgian (double) and the Contemporary (single) – each one attractively designed to make your stay a memorable one.

**SAT NAV** *TN3 9JH*

Room General P Leisure

## ROYAL TUNBRIDGE WELLS, Kent Map ref 2D2

★★
BED & BREAKFAST

B&B PER ROOM PER NIGHT
S Min £40.00
D Min £60.00

### Great Oaks

163 St Johns Road, Tunbridge Wells TN4 9UP **t** (01892) 529992 **e** greatoaks163@tiscali.co.uk

Detached family home, off road-parking, five to seven cars, large back garden, easy to find. Bedrooms – one double plus one extra bed, two bathrooms and two separate toilets.

**open** All year except Christmas
**bedrooms** 1 double
**payment** Cash, cheques

Room General 8 P

## ROYAL TUNBRIDGE WELLS, Kent Map ref 2D2

★★★★
BED & BREAKFAST

B&B PER ROOM PER NIGHT
D £50.00–£60.00

### Hawkenbury Farm

Hawkenbury Road, Royal Tunbridge Wells TN3 9AD **t** (01892) 536977 **e** rhwright1@aol.com

Accommodation on small working farm, set in quiet location 1.5 miles south east of Tunbridge Wells. Unlimited parking, views and walks.

**open** All year except Christmas and New Year
**bedrooms** 2 double, 1 twin
**bathrooms** All en suite
**payment** Credit/debit cards, cash, cheques, euros

Room General P Leisure

## ROYAL TUNBRIDGE WELLS, Kent Map ref 2D2

★★★
FARMHOUSE

B&B PER ROOM PER NIGHT
S £28.00–£42.00
D £56.00–£66.00

*Reductions for longer stays. Reductions for children.*

### Manor Court Farm

Ashurst Road, Ashurst, Tunbridge Wells TN3 9TB **t** (01892) 740279 **e** jsoyke@jsoyke.freeserve.co.uk

**manorcourtfarm.co.uk**

**open** All year
**bedrooms** 1 double, 2 twin
**payment** Cash, cheques, euros

Georgian farmhouse with friendly atmosphere, spacious rooms and lovely views of Medway Valley. Mixed 350-acre farm, many animals. Good base for walking. Penshurst Place, Hever Castle, Chartwell, Sissinghurst etc all within easy reach by car. Excellent camping facilities. Good train service to London from Ashurst station (two minutes away).

**SAT NAV** *TN3 9TB*

Room General P Leisure

For **key to symbols** see page 7

## RUSTINGTON, West Sussex Map ref 2D3

★★★★
GUEST ACCOMMODATION
SILVER AWARD

B&B PER ROOM PER NIGHT
S £35.00–£45.00
D £60.00–£65.00

### Kenmore

Claigmar Road, Rustington, Littlehampton BN16 2NL **t** (01903) 784634 **e** thekenmore@hotmail.co.uk

**kenmoreguesthouse.co.uk**

Secluded Edwardian house in a garden setting in the heart of the village and close to the sea. Attractive en suite rooms, individually decorated and comfortably furnished. Private parking. Family rates £75.00–£80.00.

**open** All year except Christmas and New Year
**bedrooms** 2 double, 2 twin, 2 single, 1 family
**bathrooms** All en suite
**payment** Credit/debit cards, cash, cheques, euros

Room General P

## RYDE, Isle of Wight Map ref 2C3

★★★★
BED & BREAKFAST

B&B PER ROOM PER NIGHT
D £50.00–£70.00

### Claverton House Bed and Breakfast

Claverton House, 12 The Strand, Ryde PO33 1JE **t** (01983) 613015 **e** clavertonhouse@aol.com

**clavertonhouse.co.uk** REAL-TIME BOOKING

Family-run bed and breakfast in a Victorian house providing panoramic views across the Solent. Landscaped garden with pond. Convenient for the town centre and beaches.

**open** All year
**bedrooms** 1 double, 1 family
**payment** Cash, cheques, euros

Room General P

## RYDE, Isle of Wight Map ref 2C3

★★★★
BED & BREAKFAST

B&B PER ROOM PER NIGHT
D £45.00–£50.00

### Fern Cottage

8 West Street, Ryde PO33 2NW **t** (01983) 565856 **e** sandra@psdferguson.freeserve.co.uk

Fern Cottage is a family-run, non-smoking guest house, close to the beach, shops, ferries and golf course. There is always a warm welcome on arrival with a tray of tea and biscuits.

**open** All year except Christmas
**bedrooms** 3 double
**bathrooms** 1 en suite
**payment** Cash, cheques

Room General 10 Leisure

## RYDE, Isle of Wight Map ref 2C3

★
GUEST HOUSE

B&B PER ROOM PER NIGHT
S £23.00–£30.00
D £38.00–£54.00

### Seaward Guest House

14-16 George Street, Ryde PO33 2EW **t** (01983) 563168 **e** bookings@seawardguesthouse.co.uk

Guesthouse, conveniently located for beach, pier and all amenities. English, continental or vegetarian breakfast served.

**open** All year
**bedrooms** 3 double, 1 twin, 1 single, 2 family
**bathrooms** 2 en suite
**payment** Credit/debit cards, cash, cheques

Room General

## RYE, East Sussex Map ref 3B4

★★★
GUEST HOUSE

B&B PER ROOM PER NIGHT
S £35.00–£40.00
D £60.00–£65.00

### Aviemore Guest House

28-30 Fishmarket Road, Rye TN31 7LP **t** (01797) 223052 **e** info@aviemorerye.co.uk

**aviemorerye.co.uk**

Owner-operated, imposing Victorian guesthouse overlooking green expanse of the Salts. Five minutes' walk town centre. En suite and standard rooms, breakfast room, guests' lounge and bar.

**open** All year except Christmas
**bedrooms** 5 double, 3 twin
**bathrooms** 4 en suite, 4 private
**payment** Credit/debit cards, cash, cheques

Room General Leisure

## Using map references

The map references refer to the colour maps at the front of this guide. The first figure is the map number, the letter and figure that follow indicate the grid reference on the map.

## RYE, East Sussex Map ref 3B4

★★★★★
BED & BREAKFAST

B&B PER ROOM PER NIGHT
S £55.00–£65.00
D £80.00–£100.00

EVENING MEAL PER PERSON
£20.00–£30.00

*Discounts on stays of 3 days or more (excluding Saturdays).*

### Hayden's

108 High Street, Rye TN31 7JE **t** (01797) 224501 **e** richard.hayden@mac.com

**cheynehouse.co.uk**

**open** All year except Christmas
**bedrooms** 2 double
**bathrooms** All en suite
**payment** Credit/debit cards, cash, cheques

Hayden's is a small, family-run, eco-friendly B&B and restaurant in the heart of the ancient town of Rye, set in a beautiful 18thC town house. Visitors can enjoy home cooking using organic local produce while gazing out at panoramic views across the Romney Marsh.

**SAT NAV** *TN31 7JE*

Room General Leisure

## RYE, East Sussex Map ref 3B4

★★★★★
GUEST ACCOMMODATION
GOLD AWARD

B&B PER ROOM PER NIGHT
S £70.00–£79.00
D £90.00–£124.00

*Reductions for a stay of 7 or more nights. Midweek winter breaks.*

### Jeake's House

Mermaid Street, Rye TN31 7ET **t** (01797) 222828 **e** stay@jeakeshouse.com

**jeakeshouse.com**

**open** All year
**bedrooms** 6 double, 2 twin, 3 suites
**bathrooms** 10 en suite, 1 private
**payment** Credit/debit cards, cash, cheques

Ideally located historic house on winding, cobbled street in the heart of ancient medieval town. Individually restored rooms provide traditional luxury combined with all modern facilities. Book-lined bar, cosy parlours, extensive breakfast menu to suit all tastes. Easy walking distance to restaurants and shops. Private car park.

**SAT NAV** *TN31 7ET*

Room General 8 Leisure

## RYE, East Sussex Map ref 3B4

★★★★
GUEST ACCOMMODATION
SILVER AWARD

B&B PER ROOM PER NIGHT
D £65.00–£120.00

EVENING MEAL PER PERSON
Min £27.50

*Christmas and New Year house party. Dinner, bed and breakfast special offers. Licensed for weddings and civil partnerships.*

### Strand House

Strand House, Tanyards Lane, The Strand, Winchelsea TN36 4JT **t** (01797) 226276
**e** info@thestrandhouse.co.uk

**thestrandhouse.co.uk** GUEST REVIEWS • SPECIAL OFFERS • REAL-TIME BOOKING

**open** All year
**bedrooms** 7 double, 1 twin, 2 family
**bathrooms** 9 en suite, 1 private
**payment** Credit/debit cards, cash, cheques, euros

A Tudor house with rooms full of character with an inglenook fireplace in the lounge. Food is the heart of the house with Sussex breakfast, tea on the lawn and evening dinner. Explore the many houses and gardens in the area. A house of calm to while away the hours.

**SAT NAV** *TN36 4JT* **ONLINE MAP**

Room General 5 P Leisure

**Where can I get live travel information?**
For the latest travel update – call the RAC on 1740 from your mobile phone.

## ST MARGARET'S BAY, Kent Map ref 3C4

★★★★
GUEST ACCOMMODATION
SILVER AWARD

B&B PER ROOM PER NIGHT
S £40.00–£70.00
D £50.00–£85.00

### Small Acre

Sea View Road, St Margarets Bay, Dover CT15 6EE **t** (01304) 851840 **e** marion@smallacre.co.uk

**smallacre.co.uk** REAL-TIME BOOKING

**open** All year except Christmas
**bedrooms** 1 double, 1 twin, 1 suite
**bathrooms** 1 en suite, 1 private
**payment** Cash, cheques, euros

Luxury home-from-home accommodation, a short walk from the White Cliffs of Dover. Quiet and peaceful location with fantastic views over the channel to Calais yet only 15 minutes' drive from the ferry terminal and 30 minutes from the Channel Tunnel. Great walking country. Many historic places of interest nearby.

**SAT NAV** *CT15 6EE* **ONLINE MAP**

Room General 10 P Leisure

## SANDHURST, Berkshire Map ref 2C2

★★★
INN

B&B PER ROOM PER NIGHT
S £55.00–£62.95
D £55.00–£70.90

EVENING MEAL PER PERSON
£4.95–£14.95

### The Wellington Arms

203 Yorktown Road, Sandhurst GU47 9BN **t** (01252) 872408

**thewellingtonarms.co.uk**

En suite rooms in converted stable block next to friendly local pub serving great food and drinks. View our rooms and our menu on our website.

**open** All year except Christmas and New Year
**bedrooms** 3 double, 2 twin, 1 single
**bathrooms** All en suite
**payment** Credit/debit cards, cash, cheques

Room General P

## SANDHURST, Kent Map ref 3B4

★★★★
BED & BREAKFAST

B&B PER ROOM PER NIGHT
S £35.00–£45.00
D £55.00–£65.00

EVENING MEAL PER PERSON
£18.00–£22.00

### Lamberden Cottage

Rye Road, Cranbrook TN18 5PH **t** (01580) 850743 **e** thewalledgarden@hotmail.co.uk

**lamberdencottage.co.uk**

**open** All year except Christmas
**bedrooms** 1 double, 1 twin
**bathrooms** All en suite
**payment** Cash, cheques

An 18thC detached cottage with sympathetic additions in approximately 1.75 acres. Friendly and peaceful atmosphere. Many historic places and gardens of interest to visit. Great Dixter, Sissinghurst, Pashley Manor, Bodiam Castle, the Kent and East Sussex Steam Train Railway are a few of the many attractions. Family room from £70 per night.

**SAT NAV** *TN18 5PH* **ONLINE MAP**

Room General P Leisure

## SANDOWN, Isle of Wight Map ref 2C3

★★★
GUEST ACCOMMODATION

B&B PER ROOM PER NIGHT
S £23.00–£29.00
D £46.00–£58.00

### The Montpelier

Pier Street, Sandown PO36 8JR **t** (01983) 403964 **e** enquiries@themontpelier.co.uk

**themontpelier.co.uk**

The Montpelier is situated opposite the pier and beaches with the high street just around the corner. We offer B&B, room-only and ferry-inclusive packages. Sea views available.

**open** All year
**bedrooms** 3 double, 2 twin, 1 single, 2 family
**bathrooms** All en suite
**payment** Credit/debit cards, cash, cheques

Room General

## SANDOWN, Isle of Wight  Map ref 2C3

★★★
GUEST HOUSE

B&B PER ROOM PER NIGHT
S £22.00–£29.00
D £44.00–£58.00

### Mount Brocas Guest House

15 Beachfield Road, Sandown PO36 8LT **t** (01983) 406276 **e** mountbrocas1@btconnect.com

**wightstay.co.uk/brocas.html**

Our home is a family-run guesthouse, which has a warm, friendly and relaxed feeling. We are conveniently located on the main road in Sandown, a minute's walk away from the shops, pier and beach.

**open** All year except Christmas
**bedrooms** 4 double, 1 twin, 1 single, 2 family
**bathrooms** 6 en suite, 2 private
**payment** Cash, cheques

Room General

## SHANKLIN, Isle of Wight  Map ref 2C3

★★★★
GUEST HOUSE
SILVER AWARD

B&B PER ROOM PER NIGHT
S £45.00–£55.00
D £56.00–£64.00

### The Heatherleigh

17 Queens Road, Shanklin PO37 6AW **t** (01983) 862503 **e** enquiries@heatherleigh.co.uk

**heatherleigh.co.uk** GUEST REVIEWS • REAL-TIME BOOKING

Heatherleigh Guest House is family-run and ideally situated minutes from beach, shops, restaurants, Old Village and Chine, with a friendly family atmosphere. Extensive breakfast menu. Doggies welcome. No grumpy people!

**open** All year
**bedrooms** 2 double/twin, 2 family, 2 suites
**bathrooms** All en suite
**payment** Credit/debit cards, cash

Room General 1 P

## SHANKLIN, Isle of Wight  Map ref 2C3

★★★
GUEST ACCOMMODATION

B&B PER ROOM PER NIGHT
S £24.00–£30.00
D £24.00–£30.00

### Ingress Bed & Breakfast

St Pauls Crescent, Shanklin PO37 7AN **t** (01983) 862623 **e** info@ingressbandb.co.uk

**ingressbandb.co.uk**

A warm and friendly welcome awaits you at Ingress B&B. Our Victorian home is ideally situated within a short walk of beaches and picturesque Shanklin Old Village, bus and train routes.

**open** All year except Christmas
**bedrooms** 2 double, 1 twin, 1 family
**bathrooms** All en suite
**payment** Cash, cheques

Room General 13 Leisure

## SHANKLIN, Isle of Wight  Map ref 2C3

★★★
GUEST ACCOMMODATION

B&B PER ROOM PER NIGHT
S £25.00–£35.00
D £50.00–£70.00

### The Palmerston

16 Palmerston Road, Shanklin PO37 6AS **t** (01983) 865547 **e** info@palmerston-hotel.co.uk

**palmerston-hotel.co.uk**

Located in an ideal position in Shanklin just a few minutes' walk to the beach, town centre and Old Village. A family-run hotel offering a friendly and attentive service.

**open** All year
**bedrooms** 3 double, 1 twin, 1 single, 2 family, 1 suite
**bathrooms** All en suite
**payment** Credit/debit cards, cash, cheques

Room General P Leisure

## SHARPTHORNE, West Sussex  Map ref 2D2

★★★★
BED & BREAKFAST

B&B PER ROOM PER NIGHT
S £30.00–£40.00
D £60.00–£70.00

### Courtlands Nurseries

Chilling Street, Sharpthorne, East Grinstead RH19 4JF **t** (01342) 810780 **e** lindsay.shurvell@virgin.net

**courtlandsnurseries.co.uk**

Courtlands Nurseries is a two-acre walled kitchen garden and nursery in a quiet, peaceful old Sussex country estate, ideally placed for visiting many local attractions. Spacious ground-floor rooms.

**open** All year
**bedrooms** 2 twin, 1 family
**bathrooms** 2 en suite
**payment** Cash, cheques

Room General P Leisure

For **key to symbols** see page 7

## SHEERNESS, Kent Map ref 3B3

★★★★
GUEST ACCOMMODATION
SILVER AWARD

B&B PER ROOM PER NIGHT
S £50.00
D £85.00–£95.00

EVENING MEAL PER PERSON
£8.50–£20.00

*Stay 3 nights, get 3rd night half price (excl Bank Holidays). Murder Mystery evenings.*

### The Ferry House Inn

Harty Ferry Road, Leysdown-on-Sea, Sheerness ME12 4BQ **t** (01795) 510214
**e** info@theferryhouseinn.co.uk

**theferryhouseinn.co.uk** GUEST REVIEWS • SPECIAL OFFERS • REAL-TIME BOOKING

**open** All year except Christmas and New Year
**bedrooms** 3 double, 1 twin
**bathrooms** All en suite
**payment** Credit/debit cards, cash, cheques

Traditional 16thC inn. Set in a peaceful location overlooking the Swale estuary. Great for walking, birdwatching or just relaxing. Luxury en suite accommodation complemented by our barn restaurant. The inn prides itself on home cooking from locally sourced produce, specialising in game, steak and fresh fish.

**SAT NAV** *ME12 4BQ* **ONLINE MAP**

Room General P Leisure

## SOUTHSEA

*See under Portsmouth*

## STELLING MINNIS, Kent Map ref 3B4

★★★★
FARMHOUSE
SILVER AWARD

B&B PER ROOM PER NIGHT
S £35.00–£65.00
D £50.00–£80.00

### Great Field Farm

Misling Lane, Stelling Minnis, Canterbury CT4 6DE **t** (01227) 709223 **e** Greatfieldfarm@aol.com

**great-field-farm.co.uk** GUEST REVIEWS

Delightful farmhouse set amidst lovely gardens and countryside. Spacious, private suites; B&B or self-catering. Hearty breakfasts with home-grown fruits and eggs. Ten minutes to Canterbury/ Channel Tunnel.

**open** All year
**bedrooms** 2 double, 1 twin
**bathrooms** All en suite
**payment** Credit/debit cards, cash, cheques, euros

Room General P Leisure

## STOKE ROW, Oxfordshire Map ref 2C2

★★★★
INN

B&B PER ROOM PER NIGHT
D £95.00

EVENING MEAL PER PERSON
£9.95–£22.50

### The Cherry Tree Inn

Stoke Row, Henley-on-Thames RG9 5QA **t** (01491) 680430 **e** info@thecherrytreeinn.com

**thecherrytreeinn.com**

**open** All year except Christmas
**bedrooms** 4 double
**bathrooms** All en suite
**payment** Credit/debit cards, cash, cheques

The Cherry Tree is situated in an Area of Outstanding Natural Beauty within the Chilterns, and is a perfect blend of classic and contemporary: modern, but with classic original features such as beamed ceilings and flagstone floors. Both the bar and restaurant are non-smoking. Rosette awarded for food. Brakspears Ale, ten wines by the glass.

**SAT NAV** *RG9 5QA*

Room General P Leisure

## What if I need to cancel?

It is advisable to check the proprietor's cancellation policy in case you have to change your plans at a later date.

## SWANLEY, Kent Map ref 2D2

★★★★
BED & BREAKFAST

B&B PER ROOM PER NIGHT
S Max £40.00
D Max £80.00

### Greenacres

15 Greenacre Close, Swanley BR8 8HT **t** (01322) 613656 **e** pauline.snow1@btinternet.com

**greenacrebandb.co.uk**

**open** All year except Christmas and New Year
**bedrooms** 1 double, 1 twin
**bathrooms** 2 private
**payment** Cash, cheques

Quality ground-floor annexe, double and twin rooms with private bathroom and private garden, kitchen with fridge and microwave, private conservatory. Four miles Brands Hatch, close Bluewater shopping centre.

**SAT NAV** *BR8 8HT*

Room General P

## THURNHAM, Kent Map ref 3B3

★★★★
INN

B&B PER ROOM PER NIGHT
S £60.00–£70.00
D £80.00–£100.00

EVENING MEAL PER PERSON
£7.50–£18.00

### Black Horse Inn

Pilgrims Way, Thurnham, Maidstone ME14 3LD **t** (01622) 737185 **e** info@wellieboot.net

**wellieboot.net** GUEST REVIEWS • SPECIAL OFFERS • REAL-TIME BOOKING

Kentish country pub with award-winning restaurant in the heart of the North Downs. Beautiful gardens with fountains and ponds. Alfresco terrace dining. Fantastic walking area.

**open** All year
**bedrooms** 8 double, 4 twin, 4 family
**bathrooms** All en suite
**payment** Credit/debit cards, cash, cheques

Room General P Leisure

## TUNBRIDGE WELLS

*See under Royal Tunbridge Wells*

## UFFINGTON, Oxfordshire Map ref 2C2

★★★★
GUEST ACCOMMODATION
SILVER AWARD

B&B PER ROOM PER NIGHT
S £35.00–£40.00
D £55.00–£60.00

### Norton House

Broad Street, Uffington, Faringdon SN7 7RA **t** (01367) 820230 **e** carloberman@aol.com

Comfortable 18thC home with secluded garden in heart of attractive village. Free-range produce, home-made bread and preserves a speciality. Friendly local pub for food.

**open** All year except Christmas
**bedrooms** 1 double, 1 single, 1 family
**bathrooms** 2 private
**payment** Cash, cheques

Room General P

## VENTNOR, Isle of Wight Map ref 2C3

★★★★
GUEST HOUSE

B&B PER ROOM PER NIGHT
S £36.00–£41.00
D £72.00

*Family suite £150.00. Rates are discounted for people staying 3 nights or more. All special promotions can be seen via our website.*

### Brunswick House

Victoria Street, Ventnor PO38 1ET **t** (01983) 852656 **e** brunswick@unicombox.co.uk

**brunswickhouse-web.co.uk** SPECIAL OFFERS

**open** All year
**bedrooms** 2 double, 2 twin, 2 single, 1 family
**bathrooms** All en suite
**payment** Credit/debit cards, cash, cheques, euros

A family-run guesthouse, over 150 years old, but retaining its spacious Victorian character and, with its recent refurbishment, offering warm, comfortable and welcoming accommodation. Located in the heart of Ventnor, ideally situated for walking, cycling and the many places of interest locally and around the island. Additional en suite family room available.

**SAT NAV** *PO38 1ET* **ONLINE MAP**

Room General

## WALLINGFORD, Oxfordshire Map ref 2C2

★★★
BED & BREAKFAST

B&B PER ROOM PER NIGHT
S Min £35.00
D Min £55.00

### Huntington House

18 Wood Street, Wallingford OX10 0AX **t** (01491) 839201 **e** hunting311@aol.com

18thC, Grade II Listed building. Quiet town-centre location, easy parking. Traditional decor and delightful walled garden.

**open** All year except Christmas
**bedrooms** 1 double, 1 twin
**payment** Cash, cheques, euros

Room General Leisure

## WALLINGFORD, Oxfordshire Map ref 2C2

★★★★
BED & BREAKFAST

B&B PER ROOM PER NIGHT
S £50.00–£65.00
D £65.00–£85.00

### Little Gables

166 Crowmarsh Hill, Crowmarsh Gifford, Wallingford OX10 8BG **t** (01491) 837834 & 07860 148882
**e** marketing@littlegables.co.uk

**stayingaway.com** GUEST REVIEWS • REAL-TIME BOOKING

Welcoming B&B in detached 1930s house with flexible accommodation and well-furnished, well-equipped rooms (one on ground floor). Garden seating, off-road parking, bike storage. Many attractions close by. Easy access M4/M40.

**open** All year
**bedrooms** 3 double/twin/family/single
**bathrooms** All en suite
**payment** Credit/debit cards, cash, cheques, euros

Room General P Leisure

## WALMER, Kent Map ref 3C4

★★★★
BED & BREAKFAST

B&B PER ROOM PER NIGHT
S Min £30.00
D £56.00–£65.00

*7 nights for the price of 6.*

### Hardicot Guest House

Kingsdown Road, Walmer, Deal CT14 8AW **t** (01304) 373867 **e** guestboss@btopenworld.com

**hardicot-guest-house.co.uk** GUEST REVIEWS • REAL-TIME BOOKING

**open** All year except Christmas
**bedrooms** 1 double, 2 twin
**bathrooms** 2 en suite, 1 private
**payment** Cash, cheques, euros

Large, quiet, detached Victorian house with Channel views and secluded garden, situated 100yds from the beach. Guests have unrestricted access to rooms. Close to three championship golf courses, ferries and the Channel Tunnel. Ideal centre for cliff walks and exploring Canterbury and the castles and gardens of East Kent.

**SAT NAV** *CT14 8AW* **ONLINE MAP**

Room General P Leisure

## WANTAGE, Oxfordshire Map ref 2C2

★★★★
BED & BREAKFAST

B&B PER ROOM PER NIGHT
S £26.00–£30.00
D £40.00–£48.00

### B&B in Wantage

50 Foliat Drive, Wantage OX12 7AL **t** (01235) 760495 **e** eleanor@eaturner.freeserve.co.uk

**geocities.com/bandbinwantage**

B&B in Wantage is a clean, comfortable and quiet establishment within easy walking distance of the town centre and buses.

**open** All year
**bedrooms** 1 double, 2 twin
**bathrooms** 2 en suite, 1 private
**payment** Credit/debit cards

Room General P

## Place index

If you know where you want to stay, the index by place name at the back of the guide will give you the page number listing accommodation in your chosen town, city or village. Check out the other useful indexes too.

## WATERSFIELD, West Sussex  Map ref 2D3

★★★★
**BED & BREAKFAST**

**B&B PER ROOM PER NIGHT**
S  Min £35.00
D  Min £60.00

### The Willows
London Road, Watersfield, Pulborough RH20 1NB  t (01798) 831576  e mount@ukonline.co.uk

**mountbandb.co.uk**

**open** All year except Christmas
**bedrooms** 2 double
**bathrooms** 1 en suite, 1 private
**payment** Cash, cheques

Comfortable family house on A29, close to South Downs, Parham House, Petworth, Arundel, Goodwood, RSPB Reserve Pulborough. Ample off-road parking, clock radio, colour TV, tea-/coffee-making facilities, friendly atmosphere.

**SAT NAV** RH20 1NB **ONLINE MAP**

Room 📺 ♨ 🍴  General 🛏8 P 📶 ♿ ▪ ❄ 🐕  Leisure ▶

## WINCHESTER, Hampshire  Map ref 2C3

★★★
**BED & BREAKFAST**

**B&B PER ROOM PER NIGHT**
S  £35.00–£40.00
D  £45.00–£50.00

### 12 Christchurch Road
Winchester SO23 9SR  t (01962) 854272  e pjspatton@yahoo.co.uk

Elegant Victorian house furnished with style. Easy, pleasant walk to city centre, cathedral and water meadows. Breakfast in conservatory, overlooking beautiful gardens, features home-made bread, preserves and local produce.

**open** All year except Christmas and New Year
**bedrooms** 1 double, 1 twin
**payment** Cash, cheques

Room ♨ 🍴  General 🛏 🍽 🔑 📺 🐕

## WINCHESTER, Hampshire  Map ref 2C3

★★★★★
**GUEST ACCOMMODATION**
**GOLD AWARD**

**B&B PER ROOM PER NIGHT**
S  £69.00–£109.00
D  £87.00–£115.00

### Giffard House
50 Christchurch Road, Winchester SO23 9SU  t (01962) 852628  e giffardhotel@aol.com

**giffardhotel.co.uk**

**open** All year
**bedrooms** 6 double, 2 twin, 4 single, 1 suite
**bathrooms** All en suite
**payment** Credit/debit cards, cash, cheques, euros

A warm welcome awaits those who visit this stunning Victorian house, recently refurbished to the highest standard. Relax in crisp, white bed linen and in luxurious, en suite bathrooms. Start the day with a traditional breakfast in our elegant dining room. Ten minutes' walk to town centre.

**SAT NAV** SO23 9SU **ONLINE MAP**

Room 🛗 📞 📺 ♨ 🍴  General 🛏 🍽 🔑 P 📶 ♿ 🍷 🔑 ▪ ❄  Leisure ∪ ♦ ▶ 🚲

# enjoyEngland.com

Get in the know – log on for a wealth of information and inspiration. All the latest news on places to visit, events and quality-assessed accommodation is literally at your fingertips. Explore all that England has to offer.

## WINCHESTER, Hampshire Map ref 2C3

★★★
CAMPUS

PER PERSON PER NIGHT
BED ONLY £19.60-£26.90
B&B £23.70-£30.80

### The University of Winchester

West Hill, Winchester SO22 4NR **t** (01962) 827332 **e** conferences@winchester.ac.uk

Located on the outskirts of the ancient city of Winchester, the university offers high quality and value for money for groups and tours. Self-catering and full board available.

**open** Mid-June to mid-September
**bedrooms** 903 single, 10 double/twin
Total no of beds 913
**Groups only** 923
**bathrooms** 267 en suite
**meals** Breakfast, lunch and evening meal available
**payment** Credit/debit cards, cash/cheques

Room General P Leisure

## WINCHESTER, Hampshire Map ref 2C3

★★★
INN

B&B PER ROOM PER NIGHT
S £62.00–£100.00
D £99.00–£150.00

EVENING MEAL PER PERSON
£16.00–£25.00

### The Wykeham Arms

75 Kingsgate Street, Winchester SO23 9PE **t** (01962) 853834 **e** wykeham.arms@fullers.co.uk

**fullersinns.co.uk**

**open** All year except Christmas and New Year
**bedrooms** 8 double, 3 twin, 2 single, 1 suite
**bathrooms** All en suite
**payment** Credit/debit cards, cash

Award-winning public house with first-class accommodation, excellent cuisine, fine wines and real ales. Close to the cathedral and Winchester College.

**SAT NAV** *SO23 9PE*

Room General

## WINDSOR, Berkshire Map ref 2D2

★★★
BED & BREAKFAST

B&B PER ROOM PER NIGHT
S £45.00–£50.00
D Min £60.00

### Barbara's Bed & Breakfast

16 Maidenhead Road, Windsor SL4 5EQ **t** (01753) 840273 **e** bbandb@btinternet.com

Welcoming, friendly, Victorian family home, many original features. Situated close to the River Thames and leisure centre. Ten minutes' walk from Windsor Castle and town centre. Heathrow 20 minutes.

**open** All year except Christmas
**bedrooms** 2 double, 1 twin
**bathrooms** 1 en suite, 2 private
**payment** Cash, cheques, euros

Room General 12 P

## WINDSOR, Berkshire Map ref 2D2

★★★★
GUEST ACCOMMODATION

B&B PER ROOM PER NIGHT
S £59.00–£79.00
D £69.00–£89.00

*We offer special weekend winter-break prices.*

### Bluebell House

Lovel Lane, Woodside, Winkfield, Windsor SL4 2DG **t** (01344) 886828
**e** registrations@bluebellhousehotel.co.uk

**bluebellhousehotel.co.uk** GUEST REVIEWS · SPECIAL OFFERS · REAL-TIME BOOKING

**open** All year except Christmas
**bedrooms** 3 double, 2 twin
**bathrooms** 3 en suite, 2 private
**payment** Credit/debit cards, cash, cheques

This charming ex-coaching inn situated between Windsor and Ascott offers classic accommodation but with all modern conveniences. We have private parking and all our rooms have TV, fridge, hairdryer and kettle. We are an ideal base for visiting Windsor, Legoland, Ascot races, and polo. Close to several good pubs.

**SAT NAV** *SL4 2DG* **ONLINE MAP**

Room General P Leisure

## WINDSOR, Berkshire Map ref 2D2

★★★
GUEST HOUSE

B&B PER ROOM PER NIGHT
S £45.00–£71.00
D £55.00–£82.00

### The Clarence

9 Clarence Road, Windsor SL4 5AE **t** (01753) 864436 **e** clarence.hotel@btconnect.com

**clarence-hotel.co.uk**

**open** All year except Christmas
**bedrooms** 4 double, 6 twin, 4 single, 6 family
**bathrooms** All en suite
**payment** Credit/debit cards, cash, cheques

Comfortable hotel with licensed bar and steam-sauna. Located near town centre and short walk from Windsor Castle, Eton College and River Thames. All rooms with en suite bathroom, TV, tea-/coffee-making facilities, hairdryer and radio-alarm. Free Wi-Fi Internet. Convenient for Legoland and Heathrow Airport.

**SAT NAV** *SL4 5AE*

Room TV General P

## WOKING, Surrey Map ref 2D2

★★
GUEST ACCOMMODATION

B&B PER ROOM PER NIGHT
S Max £47.00
D Max £69.00

EVENING MEAL PER PERSON
Max £25.00

*Enquire about our exclusive-use rates.*

### St Columba's House

Maybury Hill, Woking GU22 8AB **t** (01483) 766498 **e** retreats@stcolumbas.org.uk

**stcolumbashouse.org.uk** SPECIAL OFFERS

**open** All year except Easter, Christmas and New Year
**bedrooms** 4 twin, 23 single
**bathrooms** All en suite
**payment** Cash, cheques

A quiet retreat house and conference centre with 21stC facilities for business, leisure, and spiritual renewal. We welcome individuals and groups from all over the world and provide a range of meeting and catering facilities for groups of up to 50, whether for business or leisure.

**SAT NAV** *GU22 8AB* **ONLINE MAP**

Room TV General P

## What if I need to cancel?

It's advisable to check the proprietor's cancellation policy at the time of booking in case you have to change your plans.

For **key to symbols** see page 7

## WOODSTOCK, Oxfordshire Map ref 2C1

★★★★ BED & BREAKFAST SILVER AWARD

B&B PER ROOM PER NIGHT
s £65.00–£70.00
d £70.00–£80.00

### The Laurels

40 Hensington Road, Woodstock OX20 1JL **t** (01993) 812583 **e** stay@laurelsguesthouse.co.uk

**laurelsguesthouse.co.uk**

Fine Victorian house in Woodstock. Charmingly furnished, with an emphasis on comfort and quality. Just off town centre and a short walk from Blenheim Palace.

**open** All year except Christmas and New Year
**bedrooms** 1 double, 1 twin
**bathrooms** All en suite
**payment** Credit/debit cards, cash, cheques

Room General 10

## WOODSTOCK, Oxfordshire Map ref 2C1

★★★ GUEST HOUSE

B&B PER ROOM PER NIGHT
s £35.50–£38.50
d £60.00–£70.00

### Shepherds Hall

Witney Road, Freeland, Oxford OX29 8HQ **t** (01993) 881256

**shepherdshall.co.uk**

Well-appointed private hotel offering good food and accommodation. All rooms en suite. Ideally situated for Oxford, Woodstock and the Cotswolds, on the A4095 Woodstock to Witney road.

**open** All year except Christmas and New Year
**bedrooms** 2 double, 2 twin, 1 single
**bathrooms** All en suite
**payment** Credit/debit cards, cash, cheques

Room General P

## WROXALL, Isle of Wight Map ref 2C3

★★★ FARMHOUSE

B&B PER ROOM PER NIGHT
s £25.00–£50.00
d £50.00–£54.00

### Little Span Farm B&B

Rew Lane, Ventnor PO38 3AU **t** (01983) 852419 **e** info@spanfarm.co.uk

**spanfarm.co.uk**

**open** All year
**bedrooms** 2 double, 1 twin, 1 family
**bathrooms** All en suite
**payment** Cash, cheques

17thC stone farmhouse on working sheep farm in Area of Outstanding Natural Beauty. Short drive to sandy beaches of Shanklin, Sandown and Ventnor. Close to footpaths, cycle route, golf course and tourist attractions. Ideal for family holidays. Kennels available for dogs. English or vegetarian breakfast.

**SAT NAV** *PO38 3AU*

Room General P

## WYE, Kent Map ref 3B4

★★★★ BED & BREAKFAST

B&B PER ROOM PER NIGHT
s £30.00
d £60.00

### Mistral

3 Oxenturn Road, Wye, Ashford TN25 5BH **t** (01233) 813011 **e** geoff@chapman.invictanet.co.uk

**chapman.invictanet.co.uk**

Small bed and breakfast offering high-quality food and facilities in a central but secluded part of Wye village. Parking is available by arrangement.

**open** All year except Christmas
**bedrooms** 1 twin, 1 single
**bathrooms** 1 private
**payment** Cash, cheques

Room General P

## Gold and Silver Awards

Gold and Silver Awards are given to establishments achieving the highest levels of quality and service. You can find more information at the front of the guide, and an index to all accommodation achieving these awards at the back.

## YARMOUTH, Isle of Wight Map ref 2C3

★★★
BED & BREAKFAST

B&B PER ROOM PER NIGHT
S Min £40.00
D £60.00

### Medlars

Halletts Shute, Norton, Yarmouth PO41 0RH **t** (01983) 761541 **e** e.grey855@btinternet.com

**milford.co.uk** REAL-TIME BOOKING

**open** All year except Christmas
**bedrooms** 1 double, 1 twin
**bathrooms** 1 en suite, 1 private
**payment** Cash, cheques

Medlars is an attractive, stone-built converted barn in a quiet, rural location but within easy walking distance of Yarmouth. Well positioned for walking the excellent routes in this area. Dogs are welcome by arrangement and good, off-road parking is available.

**SAT NAV** *PO41 0RH* **ONLINE MAP**

Room General 5 P Leisure

# London

Clockwise: Buckingham Palace; Shakespeare's Globe; Tower Bridge

# Great days out

**So you think you know London? Take another look because there's always another secret to discover or something new to try, as well as inspirational itineraries to follow for weekends and days out. Just remember to leave yourself with enough time for everything (a year or more should do).**

## Culture vulture

Does Turner turn you on? The Impressionists impress? Then London is your place. With some 70 large museums and over 30 major art galleries, it's a top culture capital. The **Museum of London** is a good start for insights into local life. Experience the Great Fire of London 1666 through the eyes of survivors – what really happened? New galleries opening 2010 include the city's 21stC story.

The National Gallery

At the **National Gallery** see famous works of art by Van Gogh, Monet and da Vinci amongst an outstanding collection of Western European paintings. Nearby, **Somerset House** is bursting with Old Master and Impressionist paintings, decorative arts and treasures from the Hermitage Museum, St Petersburg. Its Admiralty Restaurant serves delicious lunches, too. And **Tate Britain**, just along the Thames, explores over 500 years of British art.

Take a boat trip to **Greenwich** for an adventure through Britain's seafaring history at the **National Maritime Museum**. And do leave time for lesser-known gems like the **Ben Uri Gallery**, **The London Jewish Museum of Art**. Or the **Royal London Hospital Archives and Museum** telling the fascinating story of the hospital and featuring people like the unfortunate 'Elephant Man'.

## Greenfingered London

Fabulous **Chelsea Flower Show** in May is a horticultural highspot of everyone's year. But at any time there are plenty of green (and every other floral colour) delights to dig into. **Kew Gardens** are the ultimate destination: over 300 acres growing more than 30,000 types of plants.

For an unusual surprise, take the train from Victoria Station to **Eltham Palace**, where 19-acre gardens combine medieval and 20thC elements. The trip to Charles Darwin's **Down House**, Orpington, also gets creative juices flowing: follow the path he paced in the beautiful gardens as he contemplated his revolutionary theories. And if you want a fragrant souvenir to take home, browse **Columbia Road Flower Market** on Sunday mornings, an absolute blaze of colour.

**why not...** climb the Monument (311 steps) in the City for superb views?

Left to right: South Bank; Westminster

**did you know...** dozens of museums and galleries are free to visit, including Tate Britain?

## Ladies who lunch

London does shopping, eating and pampering so well! And, ladies, you deserve a girls' outing. Check what's chic in **Knightsbridge** and the top designer stores on the **Kings Road**. Or perfect the quirky and vintage look shopping around **Notting Hill** and **Portobello Road**. Then enjoy a leisurely lunch with **Bateaux London Restaurant Cruisers**, watching the sights drift by, or tea at **The Ritz** or **Browns**. Dinner at **The Ivy** or **Le Caprice** sounds tempting, too.

## Sports galore

There's plenty of sport, too. London's great venues like **Wimbledon** – the **Lawn Tennis Museum** gives great insights into the world-famous championship. There's no need to wait for match days to enjoy a trip to **Chelsea Football Club**, the **Emirates Stadium** or **Lord's**. Behind-the-scenes tours bring to life soccer and cricket dreams. Take the kids, they love sport in the capital as well.

## Luvvies London

Nearly 150 theatres raise the curtain on drama, opera, dance and more. Kick off in style with a **West End** show – ask about good deals at the tkts booth in **Leicester Square**, London's official reduced theatre ticket operation. Sip pre-performance drinks at the luvvie-friendly **French House**, **Toucan** or **Dog & Duck** pub, and digest the night's entertainment at **Joe Allen**, where you might spot a thesp or two. Next day, join a back-stage tour – the **Theatre Royal**, Drury Lane is just one venue that opens its doors. And stroll along the **South Bank**, the heart of cultural cool, to see what's on at the **Southbank Centre**. Round off with a tour of the magnificent **Shakespeare's Globe**.

Tea at Harrods

## Big kids

For some family-friendly fun hop aboard the **London Eye**, rising slowly to view 55 famous landmarks across the city. Keep spirits high with a visit to the **Tower of London**, possibly the country's most haunted building – was that the scream of a ghostly nobleman being led to the executioner's block? **Hampton Court Palace** also has a host of spooks, including Henry VIII's fifth wife Catherine Howard. Who ever said history was dull?

Don't get lost in the palace's famous maze. Explore all nine decks of **HMS Belfast**, from the Captain's Bridge to the boiler and engine rooms, well below the ship's waterline. See the sick bay and operations room and imagine life on board during World War II. Who would guess you could be in a vast landscape of lagoons, lakes and ponds within 25 minutes of central London? The **London Wetland Centre** in Barnes is Europe's best urban site for watching wildlife, including hundreds of bird species. Come nose to nose with sharks and deadly stone fish at the **London Aquarium**. If you've energy to spare, let off steam in one of London's many parks. Picnic and play footie in **St James's Park** or go boating on the Serpentine in **Hyde Park**.

**why not...** explore Regent's Canal from Little Venice to the Docklands?

## The main event

London living can be pretty high octane, no more so than for event-goers. From **Chinese New Year** Celebrations to **The Proms** to lights-on for Christmas, the calendar is packed. Gather beside the Thames for spring's **Oxford and Cambridge Boat Race**, everyone likes tradition. And a summer's evening at **Kenwood House**, Hampstead, passes perfectly at a picnic concert. Hit the streets around Ladbroke Grove for the steelbands and exuberant costumes that make **Notting Hill Carnival** swing. Admire the Golden State Coach at the **Lord Mayor's Show**, processing to the Royal Courts of Justice. And there are always those impromptu smile-breakers, like street performers around **Covent Garden**. Samuel Pepys watched a Punch and Judy show here in 1662 and open-air entertainment has flourished ever since.

Left to right: Covent Garden; Hampton Court Palace

# Destinations

## Covent Garden

Designer shops such as Paul Smith and Nicole Farhi, mid range shops like Karen Millen, Monsoon and Oasis and the downright quirky such as Lush, the cosmetic maker, all have a presence here. Sample the impressive array of organic cheeses at Neal's Yard or grab a table at Carluccio's Delicatessen. Settle down for some entertainment in the Piazza: music, comedy, pavement artists and jugglers. If it's culture your after, step into the magnificently refurbished Royal Opera House for a performance or a backstage tour.

Covent Garden

## Greenwich

Stand with one foot in the East and one foot in the West astride the Greenwich Meridian, and set your watch by the red 'Time Ball' that drops each day at 1300hrs precisely and has done so for 170 years. There's a laid-back feel to Greenwich. Take time to browse the market stalls – crafts, antiques, records, bric-a-brac and, most famously, vintage clothing. Then pop into a riverside pub for lunch and some mellow jazz.

## Kew

Stroll the finest botanic gardens in the country – 400 acres and 40,000 plant varieties. The Palm House hosts a tropical jungle of plants including bananas, pawpaws and mangoes. Marvel at the giant Amazonian water lily, aloe vera and several carnivorous plants in the Princess of Wales Conservatory where ten climatic zones are recreated. You'll find activities for children and a full calendar of special events.

## Notting Hill

A colourful district filled with clubs, bars and dance venues, and now trendier than ever. Wander the celebrated Portobello Road market where over 1,500 traders compete for your custom at the Saturday antiques market. Find jewellery, silverware, paintings and more. Summertime is carnival time and the Caribbean influence has ensured the phenomenal growth of the world-famous, multi-cultural Notting Hill Carnival. Join the throng of millions – exotic costume recommended. On a quieter day, visit beautiful Holland Park, a haven of greenery with its own theatre.

## Richmond

The River Thames runs through the heart of the beautiful borough of Richmond. Arrive by summer riverboat from Westminster Pier and explore the delightful village with its riverside pubs, specialist boutiques, galleries and museums. Glimpse herds of deer in the Royal parks and step into history in Henry VIII's magnificent Hampton Court Palace, the oldest Tudor palace in England. Round off your visit with a world-class rugby match at Twickenham Stadium.

Clockwise: Kenwood House; Hyde Park; Chinese New Year

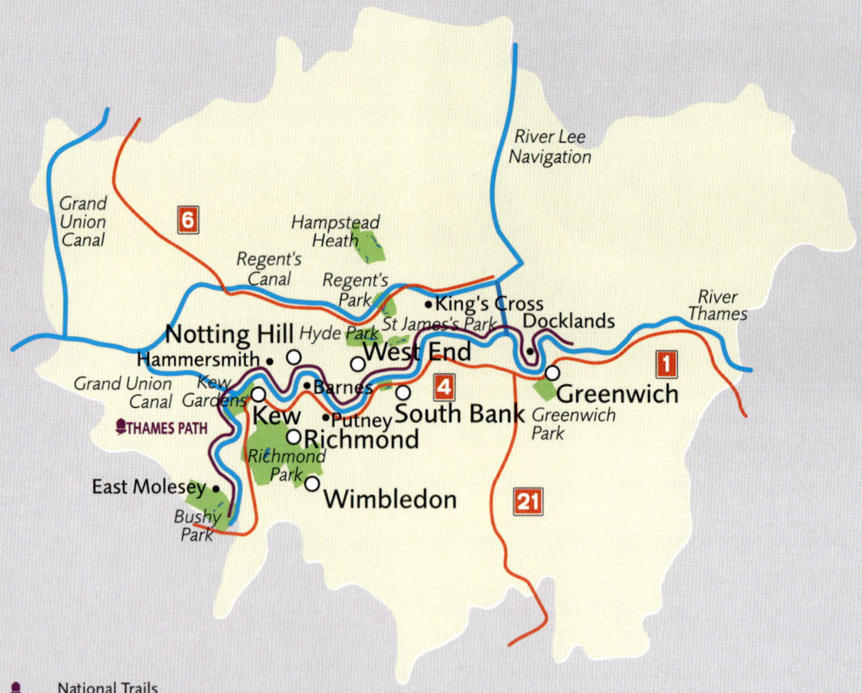


National Trails
nationaltrail.co.uk

3 Sections of the National Cycle Network
nationalcyclenetwork.org.uk

*Kew Gardens*

## South Bank

One of London's coolest quarters, the South Bank positively teems with must-see attractions and cultural highlights. Tate Modern has gained a reputation as one of the greatest modern art galleries in the world boasting works by Moore, Picasso, Dali, Warhol and Hepworth. Take in a play at the National Theatre or Shakespeare's magnificently restored Globe, and hit the heights on British Airways London Eye, the world's highest observation wheel.

## The West End

Shop in the best department stores and international designer boutiques in Oxford Street, Regent Street and Bond Street. Take lunch in a stylish eatery, and then see a major exhibition at the Royal Academy of Arts. At the heart of the West End are the landmarks of Trafalgar Square and Piccadilly Circus, and just a few minutes' stroll will take you into legendary Soho, the entertainment heart of the city, crammed with bars, pubs, clubs and restaurants.

## Wimbledon

Wimbledon village is only ten miles from the centre of London but you could be in the heart of the countryside. Enjoy the open spaces of Wimbledon Common then wander along the charming high street with its unique medieval buildings, boutiques and pavement cafés. Visit the legendary All England Club where the Lawn Tennis Museum is a must-see for fans of the sport, not to mention the chance to tour the legendary Centre Court.

**For lots more great ideas visit enjoyEngland.com/destinations**

*Clockwise: Greenwich; Notting Hill; Richmond Park*

# Visitor attractions

## Family and Fun

**Chelsea Football Club Stadium Tours**
*Fulham, SW6*
0871 984 1955
chelseafc.com
*Get behind the scenes at Stamford Bridge.*

**Emirates Stadium Tour and Museum**
*Highbury, N5*
(020) 7704 4504
arsenal.com
*Get to know Arsenal's stunning stadium.*

**HMS Belfast**
*Southwark, SE1*
(020) 7940 6300
iwm.org.uk
*A fascinating piece of British naval history.*

**London Aquarium**
*South Bank, SE1*
(020) 7967 8000
londonaquarium.co.uk
*Come face-to-face with two-metre long sharks.*

**The London Dungeon**
*Southwark, SE1*
(020) 7403 7221
thedungeons.com
*So much fun it's frightening!*

**London Eye**
*South Bank, SE1*
0870 5000 600
ba-londoneye.com
*The world's largest observation wheel.*

**London Eye River Cruise Experience**
*Westminster, SE1*
0870 500 0600
londoneye.com
*Circular cruise with fascinating live commentary.*

**London Wetland Centre**
*Barnes, SW16*
(020) 8409 4400
wwt.org.uk
*Europe's best urban site for watching wildlife.*

**Madame Tussauds and the London Planetarium**
*Marylebone, NW1*
0870 999 0046
madame-tussauds.com/london
*Meet the stars then enter the Chamber of Horrors.*

**National Maritime Museum**
*Greenwich, SE10*
(020) 8858 4422
nmm.ac.uk
*Over two million exhibits of seafaring history.*

**Royal Mews**
*St James Park, SW1*
(020) 7766 7302
royalcollection.org.uk
*One of the world's finest working stables.*

## Heritage

**Apsley House**
*Piccadilly, W1*
(020) 7499 5676
english-heritage.org.uk
*Wellington's military memorabilia and dazzling art collection.*

**Buckingham Palace**
*SW1*
(020) 7766 7300
royal.gov.uk
*HM The Queen's official London residence.*

**Chiswick House**
*W4*
(020) 8995 0508
english-heritage.org.uk
*Glorious example of 18thC British architecture.*

**Eltham Palace**
*SE9*
(020) 8294 2548
english-heritage.org.uk
*Spectacular Art Deco villa and medieval hall.*

**Hampton Court Palace**
*East Molesey, KT8*
0844 482 7777
hrp.org.uk
*Outstanding Tudor palace with famous maze.*

**Kensington Palace State Apartments**
*W8*
0844 482 7777
hrp.org.uk
*Home to the Royal Ceremonial Dress Collection.*

**Kenwood House**
*Hampstead, NW3*
(020) 8348 1286
english-heritage.org.uk
*Beautiful 18thC villa with fine interiors.*

**Tower Bridge Exhibition**
*SE1*
(020) 7403 3761
towerbridge.org.uk
*Learn all about the world's most famous bridge.*

**Tower of London**
*EC3*
0870 756 6060
hrp.org.uk
*Crown Jewels and 900 years of history.*

## Indoors

**Bateaux London Restaurant Cruisers**
*Embankment, WC2*
(020) 7695 1800
bateauxlondon.com
*Luxury dining and world-class live entertainment.*

**BBC Television Centre Tours**
*Shepherd's Bush, W12*
0870 603 0304
bbc.co.uk/tours
*Behind the scenes of world-famous television studios.*

**Ben Uri Art Gallery, London Jewish Museum of Art**
*St John's Wood, NW8*
(020) 7604 3991
benuri.org.uk
*Europe's only dedicated Jewish museum of art.*

**BFI London IMAX Cinema**
*Waterloo, SE1*
0870 787 2525
bfi.org.uk
*The ultimate big-screen experience.*

**British Museum**
*WC1*
(020) 7323 8299
britishmuseum.org
*One of the great museums of the world*

**Churchill Museum and Cabinet War Rooms**
*Westminster, SW1*
(020) 7930 6961
iwm.org.uk
*Churchill's wartime headquarters untouched since 1945.*

**Down House – Home of Charles Darwin**
*Orpington, BR6*
(01689) 859119
english-heritage.org.uk
*The great naturalist's home and workplace.*

**Hayward Gallery**
*South Bank, SE1*
0870 380 0400
hayward.org.uk
*Famous international gallery showing major exhibitions.*

**Imperial War Museum**
*Lambeth, SE1*
(020) 7416 5320
iwm.org.uk
*History of Britain at war since 1914.*

## Events 2009

**New Year's Day Parade**
London
londonparade.co.uk
**1 Jan**

**Ideal Home Show**
London
idealhomeshow.co.uk
**20 Mar - 13 Apr**

**Oxford and Cambridge Boat Race**
London
theboatrace.org
**29 Mar**

**Flora London Marathon**
London
london-marathon.co.uk
**26 Apr**

**Chelsea Flower Show**
London
rhs.org.uk
**19 - 23 May**

**Wimbledon Lawn Tennis Championships**
London
wimbledon.org/en_GB/index.html
**Jun - Jul**

**The Proms**
London
bbc.co.uk/proms
**Jul - Sep**

**Notting Hill Carnival**
London
rbkc.gov.uk
**30 - 31 Aug**

**The Mayor's Thames Festival**
London
thamesfestival.org
**Sep**

**State Opening of Parliament**
London
parliament.uk
**Oct - Nov**

**Lord Mayor's Show**
London
lordmayorsshow.org
**Nov**

**Lord's Tour (MCC)**
*St John's Wood, NW8*
(020) 7616 8595
lords.org
*Guided tour of the home of cricket.*

**Museum of London**
*EC2*
0870 444 3852
museumoflondon.org.uk
*The world's largest urban-history museum.*

**National Army Museum**
*Chelsea, SW3*
(020) 7730 0717
national-army-museum.ac.uk
*The story of the British soldier.*

**National Portrait Gallery**
*WC2*
(020) 7306 0055
npg.org.uk
*The world's largest collection of portraits.*

**Natural History Museum**
*Kensington, SW7*
(020) 7942 5000
nhm.ac.uk
*World-class collections bringing the natural world to life.*

**Royal Air Force Museum Hendon**
*NW9*
(020) 8205 2266
rafmuseum.org
*Historic aircraft from around the world.*

**Royal London Hospital Archives and Museum**
*Whitechapel, E1*
(020) 7377 7608
medicalmuseums.org
*Fascinating history of Britain's largest voluntary hospital.*

**Royal Observatory Greenwich**
*SE10*
(020) 8858 4422
nmm.ac.uk
*Explore the history of time and astronomy.*

**Science Museum**
*Kensington, SW7*
0870 870 4868
sciencemuseum.org.uk
*State-of-the-art simulators, IMAX cinema and more.*

**Somerset House**
*Strand, WC2*
(020) 7845 4600
somerset-house.org.uk
*Arts and learning in magnificent 18thC house.*

**Southbank Centre**
*SE1*
0871 663 2501
southbankcentre.co.uk
*Year-round programme encompassing all the arts.*

**Southwark Cathedral**
*SE1*
(020) 7367 6700
southwark.anglican.org/cathedral
*London's oldest Gothic church building.*

**Tate Britain**
*Millbank, SW1*
(020) 7887 8888
tate.org.uk/britain
*The greatest single collection of British art.*

**Tate Modern**
*Bankside, SE1*
(020) 7887 8888
tate.org.uk/modern
*Britain's flagship museum of modern art.*

**Victoria and Albert Museum**
**Large Visitor Attraction of Year - Gold**
*Kensington, SW7*
(020) 7942 2000
vam.ac.uk
*World-reknowned museum, 3,000 years of art and design.*

**Wimbledon Lawn Tennis Museum**
*SW19*
(020) 8946 6131
wimbledon.org/museum
*Superb memorabilia and history of the game.*

## Outdoors

**Kew Gardens (Royal Botanic Gardens)**
*Richmond, TW9*
(020) 8332 5655
kew.org
*Stunning plant collections and magnificent glasshouses.*

**ZSL London Zoo**
*Regent's Park, NW1*
(020) 7722 3333
zsl.org
*The hairiest and scariest animals on the planet.*

**ASSURANCE OF A GREAT DAY OUT**
Attractions with this sign participate in the Visitor Attraction Quality Assurance Scheme which recognises high standards in all aspects of the visitor experience.

# Regional contacts and information

For more information on accommodation, attractions, activities, events and holidays in London, contact Visit London. When you arrive at your destination, visit an Official Partner Tourist Information Centre for quality assured help, or email your request before you go. To search for attractions and Tourist Information Centres on the move just text INFO to 62233, and a web link will be sent to your mobile phone.

## London

Go to **visitlondon.com** for all you need to know about London. Look for inspirational itineraries with great ideas for weekends and short breaks.

Or call 0870 1 LONDON (0870 1 566 366) for:

- **A London visitor information pack**
- **Visitor information on London**
  Speak to an expert for information and advice on museums, galleries, attractions, riverboat trips, sightseeing tours, theatre, shopping, eating out and much more! Or simply go to visitlondon.com.
- **Accommodation reservations**

Chelsea Flower Show

## Tourist Information Centres

| | | | |
|---|---|---|---|
| **Britain & London Visitor Centre** | 1 Regent Street | 0870 156636 | blvcenquiries@visitlondon.com |
| **Croydon** | Katharine Street | (020) 8253 1009 | tic@croydon.gov.uk |
| **Greenwich** | 2 Cutty Sark Gardens | 0870 608 2000 | tic@greenwich.gov.uk |
| **Lewisham** | 199-201 Lewisham High Street | (020) 8297 8317 | tic@lewisham.gov.uk |
| **Swanley** | London Road | (01322) 614660 | touristinfo@swanley.org.uk |

# Never has a rose meant so much

Everyone has a trusted friend, someone who tells it straight. Well, that's what the Enjoy England Quality Rose does: reassures you before you check into your holiday accommodation that it will be just what you want, because it's been checked out by independent assessors. Which means you can book with confidence and get on with the real business of having a fantastic break.

enjoy**England**.com

★★★

**BED & BREAKFAST**

The **Quality Rose** is the mark of England's *official*, nationwide quality assessment scheme and covers just about every place you might want to stay, using a clear star rating system: from caravan parks to stylish boutique hotels, farmhouse B&Bs to country house retreats, self-catering cottages by the sea to comfy narrowboats perfect for getting away from it all. Think of the Quality Rose as your personal guarantee that your expectations will be met.

## Our ratings made easy

| | |
|---|---|
| ★ | Simple, practical, no frills |
| ★★ | Well presented and well run |
| ★★★ | Good level of quality and comfort |
| ★★★★ | Excellent standard throughout |
| ★★★★★ | Exceptional with a degree of luxury |

**Look no further. Just look out for the Quality Rose.**
**Find out more at** enjoy**England**.com/quality

## where to stay in
# London

For maps of inner and outer London, see the front of this guide.

A complete listing of all Enjoy England assessed accommodation covered by this guide appears at the back.

### Accommodation symbols

Symbols give useful information about services and facilities. On page 7 you can find a key to these symbols.

## INNER LONDON

## LONDON N1

★★★
GUEST ACCOMMODATION

B&B PER ROOM PER NIGHT
S £47.00–£59.00
D £67.00–£79.00

*Book for 3 nights or more and save up to 15%.*

### Kandara Guest House

68 Ockendon Road, Islington, London N1 3NW **t** (020) 7226 5721 **e** admin@kandara.co.uk

**kandara.co.uk**

**open** All year except Christmas
**bedrooms** 3 double, 1 twin, 4 single, 4 family
**payment** Credit/debit cards, cash, cheques, euros

A family-run guesthouse near the Angel, Islington. Quietly situated in a conservation area. All bedrooms and bathrooms have recently been decorated and fitted to a high standard. Ten bus routes and two underground stations provide excellent public transport services. Free overnight street parking and free cycle storage.

**SAT NAV** *N1 3NW*

Room General

## LONDON N7

★★★
GUEST ACCOMMODATION

B&B PER ROOM PER NIGHT
S £35.00–£40.00
D £50.00–£55.00

### Europa

62 Anson Road, London N7 0AA **t** (020) 7607 5935 **e** info@europahotellondon.co.uk

**europahotellondon.co.uk**

We are a listed building, over 100 years old. All rooms en suite with private facilities. We are only 15 minutes from central London.

**open** All year
**bedrooms** 12 double, 8 twin, 6 single, 7 family
**bathrooms** All en suite
**payment** Credit/debit cards, cash, cheques

Room General

## Do you have access needs?

Look for the National Accessible Scheme symbols if you have special hearing, visual or mobility needs. An index of accommodation participating in the scheme can be found at the back of this guide.

## LONDON N10

★★★
GUEST HOUSE

B&B PER ROOM PER NIGHT
S £48.00–£50.00
D £62.00–£65.00

### The Muswell Hill

73 Muswell Hill Road, London N10 3HT **t** (020) 8883 6447 **e** reception@muswellhillhotel.co.uk

**muswellhillhotel.co.uk**

A comfortable, three-storey, Edwardian corner property, close to Muswell Hill and Alexandra Palace, offering a warm, friendly service.

**open** All year except Christmas
**bedrooms** 4 double, 3 twin, 4 single, 3 family
**bathrooms** 10 en suite
**payment** Credit/debit cards, cash, cheques

Room General P

## LONDON N22

★★
BED & BREAKFAST

B&B PER ROOM PER NIGHT
S £22.00–£24.00
D £34.00–£38.00

### Pane Residence

154 Boundary Road, London N22 6AE **t** (020) 8889 3735

In a pleasant location six minutes' walk from Turnpike Lane underground station and near Alexandra Palace. Kitchen facilities available.

**open** All year
**bedrooms** 1 double, 1 single
**payment** Cash, cheques, euros

Room General P

## LONDON NW1

★★★★
GUEST ACCOMMODATION

B&B PER ROOM PER NIGHT
S £130.00–£175.00
D £130.00–£175.00

EVENING MEAL PER PERSON
£14.00–£20.00

### MIC Conferences and Accommodation

81-103 Euston Street, London NW1 2EZ **t** (020) 7380 0001 **e** sales@micentre.com

**micentre.com** GUEST REVIEWS • SPECIAL OFFERS • REAL-TIME BOOKING

**open** All year
**bedrooms** 17 double, 11 twin
**bathrooms** All en suite
**payment** Credit/debit cards, cash, cheques

Our hotel floor was completely rebuilt in 2004 and offers the highest standards and value. Contemporary, en suite double rooms feature air-conditioning, LCD TVs, desk with internet access, room safe. Twenty-four hour reception, concierge service and security for peace of mind. Full English breakfast included.

**SAT NAV** *NW1 2EZ* **ONLINE MAP**

Room General Leisure

## LONDON NW3

★★★
GUEST ACCOMMODATION

B&B PER ROOM PER NIGHT
S £40.00–£55.00
D £60.00–£75.00

*Discounts available for stays of 7 nights or more. Ask at the time of booking.*

### Dillons

21 Belsize Park, London NW3 4DU **t** (020) 7794 3360 **e** desk@dillonshotel.com

**dillonshotel.com**

**open** All year
**bedrooms** 4 double, 4 twin, 3 single, 4 family
**bathrooms** 9 en suite
**payment** Credit/debit cards, cash, cheques, euros

Located just six minutes' walk from either Swiss Cottage or Belsize Park underground stations, close to the Royal Free Hospital and convenient for Camden Market and central London. Dillons Hotel provides comfortable, reasonably priced bed and breakfast accommodation. All rooms have colour TV and many have private shower/wc.

**SAT NAV** *NW3 4DU*

Room General

## LONDON SE3

★★

**BED & BREAKFAST**

**B&B PER ROOM PER NIGHT**
S £45.00
D £70.00

# 59a Lee Road, Blackheath

London SE3 9EN **t** (020) 8318 7244 **e** ac@blackheath318.freeserve.co.uk

Charming accommodation in leafy location. Minutes from amenities of Blackheath village. Extremely convenient for historic Greenwich, central London and Docklands Light Railway. Free off-road parking. Minimum two nights' stay.

**open** All year except Christmas and New Year
**bedrooms** 1 double
**payment** Cash, cheques

Room General P

## LONDON SE6

★★★

**BED & BREAKFAST**

**B&B PER ROOM PER NIGHT**
S £35.00–£40.00
D £50.00–£55.00

# The Heathers

71 Verdant Lane, London SE6 1JD **t** (020) 8698 8340 **e** berylheath@yahoo.co.uk

**theheathersbb.com**

A clean and comfortable, family-run, home from home. Beryl and Ron will do their best to ensure you really enjoy your visit. Nothing too much trouble.

**open** All year
**bedrooms** 2 twin
**payment** Cash, cheques

Room General 5

## LONDON SE20

★★★★

**GUEST ACCOMMODATION**

**B&B PER ROOM PER NIGHT**
S £40.00–£45.00
D £60.00–£65.00

**EVENING MEAL PER PERSON**
£14.50

# Melrose House

89 Lennard Road, London SE20 7LY **t** (020) 8776 8884 **e** melrosehouse@supanet.com

**uk-bedandbreakfast.com** GUEST REVIEWS

**open** All year except Christmas and New Year
**bedrooms** 4 double, 3 twin, 1 single, 1 family
**bathrooms** 8 en suite, 1 private
**payment** Credit/debit cards, cash, euros

Superb accommodation in Victorian house with spacious, en suite bedrooms. Easy access to West End. Quiet, respectable, friendly and welcoming. Ground-floor rooms opening onto the lovely garden.

**SAT NAV** *SE20 7LY*

Room General 8 P

## LONDON SW1

★★

**GUEST ACCOMMODATION**

**B&B PER ROOM PER NIGHT**
S £45.00–£65.00
D £50.00–£75.00

# The Dover

44 Belgrave Road, London SW1V 1RG **t** (020) 7821 9085 **e** reception@dover-hotel.co.uk

**dover-hotel.co.uk** GUEST REVIEWS • SPECIAL OFFERS • REAL-TIME BOOKING

Friendly bed and breakfast hotel within minutes of Victoria station and Gatwick Express. Most rooms with satellite TV, shower/wc, telephone, hairdryer. Free Wi-Fi. Walking distance of Buckingham Palace, Big Ben and London Eye.

**open** All year
**bedrooms** 13 double, 7 twin, 5 single, 8 family
**bathrooms** 29 en suite
**payment** Credit/debit cards, cash, cheques, euros

Room General

## LONDON SW1

★★★
GUEST ACCOMMODATION

B&B PER ROOM PER NIGHT
S £50.00–£75.00
D £70.00–£110.00

# Melita House

35 Charlwood Street, London SW1V 2DU **t** (020) 7828 0471 **e** reserve@melitahotel.com

**melitahotel.com** GUEST REVIEWS • REAL-TIME BOOKING

Elegant, family-run hotel in excellent location close to Victoria station. Rooms have extensive modern facilities. Warm, friendly welcome, full English breakfast included.

**open** All year
**bedrooms** 10 double, 3 twin, 4 single, 2 family
**bathrooms** All en suite
**payment** Credit/debit cards, cash, cheques, euros

Room General Leisure

## LONDON SW1

★★★
GUEST ACCOMMODATION

B&B PER ROOM PER NIGHT
S Min £45.00

*10% discount on stays of 7 nights or more.*

# Vandon House

1 Vandon Street, London SW1H 0AH **t** (020) 7799 6780 **e** info@vandonhouse.com

**vandonhouse.com**

**bedrooms** 12 twin, 14 single, 6 family
**bathrooms** 16 en suite
**payment** Credit/debit cards, cash, cheques

Excellent-value, friendly guest accommodation in superb location. Buckingham Palace, St James's Park and Westminster Abbey lie only a few minutes away. We pride ourselves on our family atmosphere. A terrific base for exploring London. Open mid-May to end of August and two weeks over New Year.

**SAT NAV** *SW1H 0AH* **ONLINE MAP**

Room General

## LONDON SW5

★★
GUEST ACCOMMODATION

B&B PER ROOM PER NIGHT
S £40.00–£60.00
D £60.00–£76.00

# Mowbray Court

28-32 Penywern Road, London SW5 9SU **t** (020) 7370 2316 **e** mowbraycrthot@hotmail.com

**mowbraycourthotel.co.uk**

Close to Earls Court underground and West Brompton station with links to Heathrow and Gatwick airports. Good shopping available in the locality of Kensington and Knightsbridge.

**open** All year
**bedrooms** 10 double, 12 twin, 29 single, 29 family
**bathrooms** 70 en suite
**payment** Credit/debit cards, cash, cheques, euros

Room General Leisure

## LONDON W1

★★
GUEST ACCOMMODATION

B&B PER ROOM PER NIGHT
S £59.00–£79.00
D £69.00–£89.00

*Long-stay discounts on request. Most Sundays discounted. For latest long-stay and other special offers visit our website.*

# Lincoln House – Central London

33 Gloucester Place, London W1U 8HY **t** (020) 7486 7630 **e** reservations@lincoln-house-hotel.co.uk

**lincoln-house-hotel.co.uk** GUEST REVIEWS • SPECIAL OFFERS

**open** All year
**bedrooms** 6 double, 4 twin, 7 single, 7 family
**bathrooms** All en suite
**payment** Credit/debit cards, cash, cheques

A Georgian guesthouse with period character and nautical theme throughout. En suite rooms with free Wi-Fi internet. Most rooms air-conditioned. Located in the heart of London near to Oxford Street shopping, theatres, museums and exhibitions. Next to airbus stop for most airports.

**SAT NAV** *W1U 8HY* **ONLINE MAP**

Room General Leisure

## LONDON W1

★★

GUEST ACCOMMODATION

B&B PER ROOM PER NIGHT
S £35.00–£75.00
D £35.00–£85.00

### Marble Arch Inn

49-50 Upper Berkeley Street, London W1H 5QR **t** (020) 7723 7888 **e** sales@marblearch-inn.co.uk

**marblearch-inn.co.uk** GUEST REVIEWS • SPECIAL OFFERS • REAL-TIME BOOKING

Friendly bed and breakfast hotel within minutes of Hyde Park, Oxford Street, Heathrow Express. Most rooms with satellite TV, shower/wc, telephone, hairdryer. Free Wi-Fi. Very competitive prices.

**open** All year
**bedrooms** 11 double, 7 twin, 2 single, 9 family
**bathrooms** 23 en suite
**payment** Credit/debit cards, cash, cheques, euros

Room General

## LONDON W2

★★★

GUEST ACCOMMODATION

B&B PER ROOM PER NIGHT
S £40.00–£65.00
D £70.00–£89.00

*Ask for your Visit Britain discount.*

### Barry House

12 Sussex Place, London W2 2TP **t** (020) 7723 7340 **e** hotel@barryhouse.co.uk

**barryhouse.co.uk** GUEST REVIEWS • REAL-TIME BOOKING

**open** All year
**bedrooms** 4 double, 6 twin, 2 single, 6 family
**bathrooms** 14 en suite, 1 private
**payment** Credit/debit cards, cash, cheques

The family-run Barry House offers warm hospitality in a Victorian townhouse. Comfortable en suite rooms with English breakfast served each morning. Located close to the West End. Paddington Station and Hyde Park are just three minutes' walk away.

**SAT NAV** *W2 2TP* **ONLINE MAP**

Room General Leisure

## LONDON W2

★★★

GUEST ACCOMMODATION

B&B PER ROOM PER NIGHT
S £59.00
D £89.00

*5 nights for the price of 4 on selected dates/rooms. See website for details.*

### The Cardiff

5-9 Norfolk Square, London W2 1RU **t** (020) 7723 9068 **e** stay@cardiff-hotel.com

**cardiff-hotel.com**

**open** All year except Christmas
**bedrooms** 25 double, 6 twin, 25 single, 5 family
**bathrooms** 58 en suite
**payment** Credit/debit cards

Run by the Davies family since 1958, The Cardiff overlooks a quiet garden square. Located one minute from the Heathrow Express, three minutes' walk from Hyde Park and ten minutes from Oxford Street. We offer comfortable, en suite rooms with TV, telephone, tea-making facilities, hairdryer and Wi-Fi access.

**SAT NAV** *W2 1RU*

Room General

## Don't forget www.

Web addresses throughout this guide are shown without the prefix www. Please include www. in the address line of your browser. If a web address does not follow this style it is shown in full.

## LONDON W2

★★★
GUEST ACCOMMODATION

B&B PER ROOM PER NIGHT
S £48.00–£68.00
D £68.00–£85.00

*10% discount on weekly bookings.*

# Kingsway Park Hotel Hyde Park

139 Sussex Gardens, London W2 2RX **t** (020) 7723 5677 **e** info@kingswaypark-hotel.com

**kingswaypark-hotel.com** REAL-TIME BOOKING

**open** All year
**bedrooms** 6 double, 7 twin, 4 single, 5 family
**bathrooms** All en suite
**payment** Credit/debit cards, cash, cheques

Elegant, Victorian, Grade II Listed building refurbished to a high standard. Situated three minutes' walk from Paddington Station and Heathrow Express and five minutes from Hyde Park. Ten minutes to Oxford Street and Marble Arch.

**SAT NAV** *W2 2RX* **ONLINE MAP**

Room General

## LONDON W2

★★★
GUEST ACCOMMODATION

B&B PER ROOM PER NIGHT
S £45.00–£60.00
D £50.00–£66.00

# The Oxford

13-14 Craven Terrace, London W2 3QD **t** (020) 7402 6860 **e** oxfordhotel@btconnect.com

**oxfordhotellondon.co.uk**

Located in a quiet one-way street, close to underground and bus routes to Oxford Street. Five minutes' walk from Hyde Park.

**open** All year
**bedrooms** 5 double, 4 twin, 1 single, 10 family
**bathrooms** All en suite
**payment** Credit/debit cards, cash, cheques

Room General

## LONDON W2

★★★
GUEST ACCOMMODATION

B&B PER ROOM PER NIGHT
S £50.00–£75.00
D £65.00–£95.00

# Rhodes House

195 Sussex Gardens, London W2 2RJ **t** (020) 7262 5617 & (020) 7262 0537 **e** chris@rhodeshotel.com

**rhodeshotel.com** REAL-TIME BOOKING

**open** All year
**bedrooms** 3 double, 3 twin, 3 single, 9 family
**bathrooms** All en suite
**payment** Credit/debit cards, cash, cheques

All rooms with private facilities, secondary glazing, free internet access, voice mail, air-conditioning, satellite TV and DVD, telephone, refrigerator, hairdryer and tea-/coffee-making facilities. Room with jacuzzi and balcony. Friendly atmosphere. Families especially welcome. Excellent transport for sightseeing and shopping.

**SAT NAV** *W2 2RJ*

Room General P

## What do the star ratings mean?

For a detailed explanation of the quality and facilities represented by the stars, please refer to the information pages at the back of this guide.

## LONDON WC1

★★★
HOSTEL

PER PERSON PER NIGHT
BED ONLY £15.00-£25.00
B&B £15.00-£25.00

### Generator Hostel London

37 Tavistock Place, Russell Square, London WC1H 9SE **t** (020) 7388 7666
**e** london@generatorhostels.com

**generatorhostels.com**

The Generator Hostel offers a unique experience, and has established itself as the place to stay in London for young visitors. Prices include linen, breakfast, free drink and walking tour that departs daily.

**open** All year
**bedrooms** 42 single/twin, 35 triple, 103 quad, 33 dormitories. Total no of beds 845
Maximum group size 200
**bathrooms** 50 public
**meals** Breakfast, lunch and evening meals available
**payment** Credit/debit cards, cash

Room General 16 Leisure

## OUTER LONDON

## CROYDON

★★★
GUEST HOUSE

B&B PER ROOM PER NIGHT
S £40.00–£45.00
D £70.00

### The Woodstock Guest House

30 Woodstock Road, Croydon CR0 1JR **t** (020) 8680 1489 **e** woodstockhotel@tiscali.co.uk

**woodstockhotel.co.uk**

**open** All year except Christmas
**bedrooms** 1 double, 1 twin, 4 single, 2 family
**bathrooms** 2 en suite, 4 private
**payment** Credit/debit cards, cash, cheques

Located in a quiet residential area, yet only five minutes' walk to town centre and East Croydon railway station. Well-appointed and spacious rooms. High standard of housekeeping.

**SAT NAV** *CR0 1JR*

Room General 3 P Leisure

## HAMPTON

★★★
GUEST ACCOMMODATION

B&B PER ROOM PER NIGHT
S £45.00–£55.00
D £55.00–£75.00

### Houseboat Riverine

Riverine, Taggs Island, Hampton TW12 2HA **t** (020) 8979 2266 **e** malcolm@feedtheducks.com

**feedtheducks.com**

A Thames houseboat moored on Taggs Island which is just upstream from Hampton Court Palace. Easy access and private parking. Delightfully different.

**open** All year
**bedrooms** 2 double, 1 twin
**bathrooms** All en suite
**payment** Cash, cheques

Room General P Leisure

## RICHMOND

★★
GUEST HOUSE

B&B PER ROOM PER NIGHT
S £45.00–£70.00
D £75.00–£95.00

# Hobart Hall Guest House

43-47 Petersham Road, Richmond TW10 6UL **t** (020) 8940 0435 **e** hobarthall@aol.com

**hobarthall.net**

**open** All year
**bedrooms** 8 double, 5 twin, 10 single, 5 family, 1 suite
**bathrooms** 26 en suite
**payment** Credit/debit cards, cash, cheques

Built c1690. Past occupants include the Countess of Buckinghamshire and William IV. Historic setting overlooking River Thames, 200yds from Richmond Bridge. Heritage, cultural and business centres in near proximity. Heathrow, M3, M4 15 minutes. Over ground and underground trains: Waterloo 20 minutes, West End 45 minutes.

**SAT NAV** *TW10 6UL*

Room General P Leisure

## RICHMOND

★★★
BED & BREAKFAST

B&B PER ROOM PER NIGHT
S £32.50–£39.50
D £55.00–£69.00

PETS! WELCOME

# Ivy Cottage

Upper Ham Road, Ham Common, Richmond TW10 5LA **t** (020) 8940 8601 & 07742 278247 **e** taylor@dbta.freeserve.co.uk

**dbta.freeserve.co.uk**

Charming, wisteria-clad Georgian home offering exceptional views over Ham Common. Period features dating from 1760. Large garden. Self-catering an option. Good bus route and parking.

**open** All year
**bedrooms** 1 double, 1 twin, 1 single, 1 family
**bathrooms** 2 en suite, 2 private
**payment** Cash, cheques, euros

Room General 8

## RICHMOND

★★★
INN

B&B PER ROOM PER NIGHT
S £60.00–£75.00
D £70.00–£95.00

# The Red Cow

59 Sheen Road, Richmond TW9 1YJ **t** (020) 8940 2511 **e** tom@redcowpub.com

**redcowpub.com**

**open** All year
**bedrooms** 2 double, 1 twin, 1 family
**bathrooms** All en suite
**payment** Credit/debit cards, cash, cheques

Traditional Victorian inn retaining some lovely original features. Just a short walk from Richmond town centre, river, royal parks and rail links to London. Other nearby places include Heathrow Airport, Twickenham rugby ground, Hampton Court and Windsor.

**SAT NAV** *TW9 1YJ*

Room General Leisure

## SURBITON

★★
GUEST HOUSE

B&B PER ROOM PER NIGHT
S £40.00–£48.00

# The Broadway Lodge

41 The Broadway, Tolworth, Surbiton KT6 7DJ **t** (020) 8399 6555 **e** broadway.lodge@tiscali.co.uk

**broadway-stgeorgeslodge.com**

Clean and cosy bed and breakfast next to Tolworth Tower. Two miles from Kingston shopping centre and Hampton Court.

**open** All year
**bedrooms** 2 double, 3 twin, 4 single
**bathrooms** 6 en suite, 1 private
**payment** Credit/debit cards, cash, cheques

Room General 5

## SUTTON

★★
GUEST ACCOMMODATION

B&B PER ROOM PER NIGHT
S £25.00–£35.00
D £45.00–£55.00

### St Margarets Guest House

31 Devon Road, Sutton SM2 7PE **t** (020) 8643 0164 **e** margarettrotman@hotmail.com

**stmargaretsbandb.co.uk**

Family-run, established 19 years. Detached house in a quiet residential area. Long-term stays welcomed. Washing machines, fridges and microwaves available for own use.

**open** All year
**bedrooms** 1 double, 1 twin, 2 single
**bathrooms** 1 en suite
**payment** Cash, cheques

Room General P Leisure

## UPMINSTER

★★
GUEST ACCOMMODATION

B&B PER ROOM PER NIGHT
S £25.00–£35.00
D £37.50–£40.00

### Corner Farm

Fen Lane, North Ockendon, Upminster RM14 3RB **t** (01708) 851310

**corner-farm.co.uk**

Attractive, detached bungalow with view of an open field from one twin room and the family room. Breakfast is served in the farmhouse approximately 30yds from the bungalow.

**open** All year
**bedrooms** 1 twin, 1 single, 1 family, 1 suite
**bathrooms** 1 en suite
**payment** Credit/debit cards, cash, cheques

Room General P Leisure

# South West England

Bristol, Cornwall, Devon, Dorset, Gloucestershire, Isles of Scilly, Somerset, Wiltshire

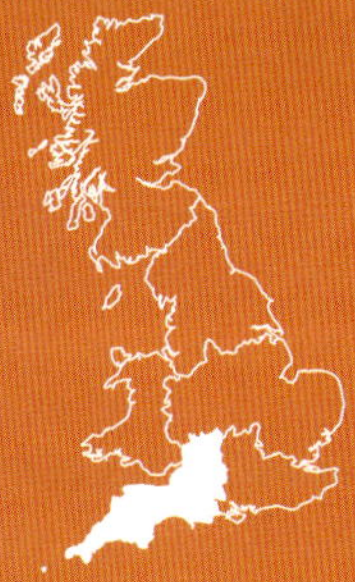



Clockwise: Porlock Bay, Somerset; Forest of Dean, Gloucestershire; Stonehenge, Wiltshire

# Great days out

## Go rock pooling in sandy coves. Indulge your love of cream teas and clotted cream fudge. Ramble along the South West Coast Path. Brave the waves surfing in Newquay. Wonder at the Cerne Abbas Giant and the stunning landscaped gardens at Stourhead. What will you do in South West England?

### Refreshing rambles

The South West is truly a walker's paradise, from the gentle **Cotswold Hills** to the wilder beauty of **Exmoor** and **Dartmoor** National Parks. Spend a day or two rambling parts of the 101-mile **Cotswold Way** through quintessential English countryside and golden-stone villages. **The Two Moors Way** over Dartmoor and Exmoor takes you through moorland, wooded valleys, farmland and coastal towns. Gee up the pace pony trekking or mountain biking – the National Parks have plenty of space for both. Then feel the sea-salted breezes along the **South West Coast Path**. It stretches for 630 miles from Somerset to Dorset, opening up dramatic views of a shoreline organically sculpted by waves. Children just love stomping 185 million years of earth history underfoot along the **Jurassic Coast**, a World Heritage Site. They could even find a dinosaur print. Who's got the biggest feet?

### Sea, surf and fun

How's this for the perfect antidote to hectic modern life? Genuine bucket-and-spade fun with the family, pure and simple. With more Blue Flag beaches than anywhere else in England, the region's sandy bays and sheltered coves are perfect getaways. Some stretches make thrilling waves for watersports: hit the hip centres of **Newquay**, **Bude**, **Croyde** and **Woolacombe**, great places to learn to surf or kitesurf. Try sailing and windsurfing in **Poole**. Devon's English Riviera – the bustling seaside towns of **Torquay**, **Paignton** and **Brixham** – is ideal for families and you can meet friendly coastal creatures like penguins and fur seals at **Living Coasts** in Torquay. Away from the beach quaint fishing villages, such as **Clovelly**, **Port Isaac** and **Beer**, are a picturesque maze of narrow streets and steep roads. And how's this for an unforgettable experience? Catch a play or musical at the open-air cliffside **Minack Theatre** at Porthcurno. The backdrop of sea vistas is breathtaking.

Torquay, Devon

### Glorious gardens

The South West's balmy subtropical climate means exotic flora flourish, creating extraordinary gardens. Delight in the **Lost Gardens of Heligan** at Pentewan, neglected for years and now brought back to life complete with magical Jungle Garden. Take a helicopter ride to **Tresco**, one of the Scilly Isles, to browse some 20,000 luxuriant plants in the **Abbey Garden**. Explore the remarkable **Eden Project**, near St Austell, which features thousands of world plants in enormous glass biomes – and children become enthralled on the interactive trails. Then enjoy the pyrotechnic seasonal displays of trees and flowers at **Westonbirt Arboretum**,

Left to right: Eden Project, Cornwall; Salisbury Cathedral, Wiltshire

**why not...** cycle along Devon's 180-mile Tarka Trail, named after Henry Williamson's Tarka the Otter?

Gloucestershire; the clipped yews and cascades at **Forde Abbey and Gardens**, Dorset; and the eye-catching tableaux of lakeside temples at **Stourhead**, Wiltshire.

## Yum yum!

Indulge yourself in the region's delicious specialities. Cornish pasties taste good washed down with a pint of sweet cider. Look out for Mendip Oggies, too: pasties made with pork, apple and cheese pastry. Devour mouthwatering scones straight from the oven and topped with rich clotted cream. And sample a different cheese every day: world-famous Cheddar, Double Gloucester, Somerset Brie, Dorset Blue Vinny and nettle-wrapped Cornish Yarg. Relish the best catches at **Rick Stein's Seafood Restaurant**, Padstow. Then finish your gourmet odyssey relaxing over a wine from **Three Choirs Vineyard**, Gloucestershire.

## Mysterious and madcap

You're in just the right area for quirky customs and intriguing places. If you look hard enough you may spot the Witch of Wookey deep in **Wookey Hole Caves** where pagan and Christian legends intermingle. Ponder the mysteries of the ancient stone circles of **Stonehenge** and **Avebury** – just how were such enormous stones transported and arranged, and why? **Chipping Campden** in Gloucestershire is the location of the Cotswolds' unique version of the Olimpick Games: contests include shin-kicking, ouch! Meanwhile **Blackawton** in Devon hosts the annual International Worm Charming Festival. Seeing is believing!

Exmoor, Somerset

## Splendid city highlights

Fill your days visiting attractions in Bristol and Bath, city neighbours yet so different. **Bristol's** maritime heritage has been channelled into the infectious vitality of the rejuvenated Harbourside of bars, eateries and sights. Clamber aboard Isambard Kingdom Brunel's **ss Great Britain**, the world's first great ocean liner. Treat the kids to an interactive science adventure at **Explore-at-Bristol** – freeze your shadow, fire a neuron, and get starry-eyed in the planetarium. Then revel in the Georgian elegance of **Bath** and tour the best-preserved Roman religious spa from the ancient world, beneath the watchful gaze of **Bath Abbey**. Dip your own toes – and more – into the natural thermal waters of the recently opened **Thermae Bath Spa**. Bliss!

**why not...** look for the Fossil Forest revealed at low tide near Little Bindon, Dorset?

Continue your journey with a trip to some of the West's other great cathedral cities. Stroll **Exeter's** historic Quayside; survey the medieval carvings of **Wells Cathedral's** majestic west front; wander the revitalised waterside of **Gloucester**; or take a guided tour of **Salisbury Cathedral**, its soaring spire the tallest in Britain.

## More great days out

If you're looking for even more inspiration for great days out, add these to your love-to list. Have a fun time uncovering the history, sights and sounds of the railway at **Steam – Museum of the Great Western Railway** in Swindon, or take the kids on a wild animal safari at **Longleat**. Take a picnic to **Corfe Castle** whose evocative hilltop ruins recall a bold past. Or potter about on a driving tour – the scenic **Royal Forest Route** through the Forest of Dean and the **Romantic Road** via **Cheltenham** and **Cirencester** spring to mind. Floating skywards in a hot-air balloon over the countryside and llama-trekking also make memorable adventures!

Clockwise: Dartmoor, Devon; St Michael's Mount, Cornwall; ss Great Britain, Bristol

# Destinations

## Bath

Set in rolling countryside, less than two hours from London, this exquisite Georgian spa city was founded by the Romans and is now a World Heritage Site. Explore the compact city centre on foot and discover a series of architectural gems including the Roman baths and Pump Room, the 15thC Abbey, and stunning Royal Crescent. Follow in the footsteps of Romans and Celts and bathe in the naturally warm waters of the Thermae Bath Spa.

Bath

## Bournemouth

Bournemouth is the perfect holiday and short-break destination, renowned for its seven miles of family-friendly, golden beaches, beautiful parks and gardens and cosmopolitan ambience. Enjoy the buzz of the town then head out and savour the beauty of the New Forest, the splendour of Dorset's spectacular World Heritage Jurassic Coastline, and the rolling countryside immortalised by Thomas Hardy.

## Bristol

In bygone times, explorers and merchants set off on epic journeys from its harbour. Nowadays, Bristol's spirit of boldness and creativity expresses itself in art, architecture and an enviable quality of life. Take in Georgian terraces, waterfront arts centres, green spaces, great shopping and top-class restaurants. The city's heritage glitters with the work of historic figures such as Isambard Kingdom Brunel, and all set against a truly classic view – the River Avon and its dramatic gorge reaching almost into the heart of the city.

## The Cotswolds

Escape to the rolling hills of the Cotswolds scattered with picturesque towns and villages built of distinctive honey-coloured limestone. Criss-cross the little bridges over the River Windrush in Bourton-on-the-Water; hunt for antiques in Stow-on-the-Wold; wander through the open-air street market of Moreton-in-Marsh and appreciate the beautifully preserved buildings in Chipping Campden and Tetbury.

## Isles of Scilly

Just 20 minutes from Cornwall you'll find over 100 islands waiting to be explored– five of them inhabited: St Mary's, Tresco, St Martin's, St Agnes and Bryher. Discover fascinating prehistoric remains, rare species of birds and plant life, historic shipwrecks and some of the best beaches in Britain. Watersports, boat trips, wonderful gardens, including Tresco Abbey Gardens, keep everyone entertained.

Left to right: Corfe Castle, Dorset
Wells Cathedral, Somerset

Bristol

## Exeter

Devon's regional capital for culture, leisure and shopping is a vibrant city, steeped in ancient history. Don't miss the superb Decorated Gothic cathedral. Stroll along the historic Quayside, once the setting for a thriving wool trade and now a bustling riverside resort. Choose from over 700 shops, join a free Red Coat-guided city tour and dine in any one of numerous acclaimed restaurants. It's also the perfect base from which to explore the sweeping National Parks of Dartmoor and Exmoor.

## Newquay

A beach paradise, stretching for seven miles, makes this one of Cornwall's premier resorts. Soaring cliffs alternate with sheltered coves, and thundering surf with secluded rock pools, smugglers' caves and soft golden sands. Whatever the weather, make a splash at Waterworld, or visit Newquay Zoo, one of the best wildlife parks in the country. Newquay offers an unforgettable holiday experience.

Clockwise: Exeter; Bournemouth; The Cotswolds

## Poole

Poole is fast becoming known as the St Tropez of the south coast with its award-winning beaches, beautiful harbour, exhilarating watersports and famous pottery. Follow the Cockle Trail around the old town to discover its seafaring and trading history. Take the ferry to Brownsea Island between March and October for wonderful walks and wildlife spotting. Or relax and enjoy alfresco dining overlooking the harbour.

## St Ives

What was once a small, thriving fishing village is now an internationally renowned haven for artists, attracted by the unique light. Explore the narrow streets and passageways and come upon countless galleries, studios and craft shops. Don't miss Tate St Ives and the Barbara Hepworth Museum. Enjoy the natural beauty of the harbour and explore Blue Flag beaches and coastal walks. Perfectly placed for all of West Cornwall's stunning scenery and famous attractions.

Tate, St Ives

## Salisbury

Nestling in the heart of southern England, Salisbury is every bit the classic English city. The majestic cathedral boasts the tallest spire in England and rises elegantly above sweeping lawns. Wander through this medieval city and you'll find first-class visitor attractions, theatre and shopping. And, of course, no trip to Salisbury would be complete without the eight-mile pilgrimage to one of the greatest prehistoric sites in the world – Stonehenge.

**For lots more great ideas visit enjoyEngland.com/destinations**

# Visitor attractions

## Family and Fun

**Babbacombe Model Village**
*Torquay, Devon*
(01803) 315315
babbacombemodelvillage.co.uk
*England in miniature in four-acre gardens.*

**The Big Sheep**
*Bideford, Devon*
(01237) 472366
thebigsheep.co.uk
*Family fun at the sheep races.*

**Blue Reef Aquarium**
*Newquay, Cornwall*
(01637) 878134
bluereefaquarium.co.uk
*Close encounters with tropical sharks and rays.*

**Bristol Zoo Gardens**
*Bristol*
(0117) 974 7399
bristolzoo.org.uk
*Over 400 exotic and endangered species.*

**Cheddar Caves & Gorge**
*Cheddar, Somerset*
(01934) 742343
cheddarcaves.com
*Britain's finest caves and deepest gorge.*

**Combe Martin Wildlife and Dinosaur Park**
*Combe Martin, Devon*
(01271) 882486
dinosaur-park.com
*A subtropical bird, animal and dinosaur paradise.*

**Dairyland Farm World**
*Summercourt, Cornwall*
(01872) 510246
dairylandfarmworld.com
*Country-life park, museum and adventure playground.*

**Devon's Crealy Great Adventure Park**
*near Exeter, Devon*
(01395) 233200
crealy.co.uk
*All-weather attractions and friendly animals.*

**Farmer Palmer's Farm Park**
*Poole, Dorset*
(01202) 622022
farmerpalmers.co.uk
*Farm activities for families with young children.*

**Kents Cavern Prehistoric Caves**
*Torquay, Devon*
(01803) 215136
kents-cavern.co.uk
*Britain's most important Stone Age caves.*

**Living Coasts**
*Torquay, Devon*
(01803) 202470
livingcoasts.org.uk
*Fascinating coastal creatures in a stunning location.*

**Longleat**
*Warminster, Wiltshire*
(01985) 844400
longleat.co.uk
*Lions, tigers and a stately home.*

**The Monkey Sanctuary Trust**
*Looe, Cornwall*
(01503) 262532
monkeysanctuary.org
*Colony of woolly monkeys.*

**National Marine Aquarium**
*Plymouth, Devon*
(01752) 600301
national-aquarium.co.uk
*Sharks and seahorses at Britain's biggest aquarium.*

**Newquay Zoo**
*Newquay, Cornwall*
(01637) 873342
newquayzoo.org.uk
*Exotic animals in subtropical lakeside gardens.*

**Noah's Ark Zoo Farm**
*Wraxall, Somerset*
(01275) 852606
noahsarkzoofarm.co.uk
*Hands-on animal experiences for all ages.*

**Paignton Zoo Environmental Park**
*Paignton, Devon*
(01803) 697500
paigntonzoo.org.uk
*Gorillas and crocodiles in 75-acre botanical gardens.*

**Pennywell - Devon's Farm and Wildlife Centre**
*Lower Dean, Devon*
(01364) 642023
pennywellfarm.co.uk
*The South West's biggest farm-activity park.*

**Woodlands Leisure Park**
*Blackawton, Devon*
(01803) 712598
woodlandspark.com
*Unique combination of indoor and outdoor attractions.*

**Wookey Hole Caves and Papermill**
*near Wells, Somerset*
(01749) 672243
wookey.co.uk
*Spectacular caves and working Victorian papermill.*

## Heritage

### The Bishop's Palace & Gardens
*Wells, Somerset*
(01749) 678691
bishopspalacewells.co.uk
*Splendid medieval palace and tranquil landscaped gardens.*

### Bowood House and Gardens
*Chippenham, Wiltshire*
(01249) 812102
bowood.org
*Wonderful 18thC Robert Adam house.*

### Corfe Castle
*Corfe Castle, Dorset*
(01929) 477063
nationaltrust.org.uk
*Majestic ruins of a former royal castle.*

### Cothay Manor & Gardens
*near Wellington, Somerset*
(01823) 672283
cothaymanor.co.uk
*Unspoilt medieval manor and romantic gardens.*

### Dunster Castle
*Dunster, Somerset*
(01643) 821314
nationaltrust.org.uk
*Romantic castle and subtropical gardens.*

### The Fashion Museum and Assembly Rooms
*Bath, Somerset*
(01225) 477789
fashionmuseum.co.uk
*Fine Georgian building with world-class dress collection.*

### Forde Abbey and Gardens
**Small Visitor Attraction of the Year – Silver**
*Forde Abbey, Dorset*
(01460) 220231
fordeabbey.co.uk
*Elegant former Cistercian monastery with gardens.*

### Lacock Abbey
*Lacock, Wiltshire*
(01249) 730459
nationaltrust.org.uk
*Fine country house with medieval cloisters.*

### Lanhydrock
*Lanhydrock, Cornwall*
(01208) 265950
nationaltrust.org.uk
*Re-built 17thC house with magnificent illustrated ceiling.*

### Lulworth Castle & Park
*Wareham, Dorset*
0845 450 1054
lulworth.com
*Idyllic castle set in extensive park.*

### Montacute House
*Montacute, Somerset*
(01935) 823289
nationaltrust.org.uk
*Renaissance manor house filled with historic treasures.*

### Old Wardour Castle
*Tisbury, Wiltshire*
(01747) 870487
english-heritage.org.uk
*Unusual hexagonal ruins of a 14thC castle.*

### Pittville Pump Room
*Cheltenham, Gloucestershire*
(01242) 523852
*Beautiful, imposing example of Regency architecture.*

### Powderham Castle
*Powderham, Devon*
(01626) 890243
powderham.co.uk
*Restored medieval castle in beautiful deer park.*

### Roman Baths
*Bath, Somerset*
(01225) 477785
romanbaths.co.uk
*Magnificent Roman temple and hot-spring baths.*

### St Michael's Mount
*Marazion, Cornwall*
(01736) 710507
stmichaelsmount.co.uk
*Rocky island filled with astonishing history.*

### Salisbury Cathedral
*Salisbury, Wiltshire*
(01722) 555120
salisburycathedral.org.uk
*Britain's finest 13thC gothic cathedral.*

### Sherborne Castle
*Sherborne, Dorset*
(01935) 813182
sherbornecastle.com
*Tudor mansion built by Sir Walter Raleigh.*

### Sudeley Castle, Gardens and Exhibition
*Winchcombe, Gloucestershire*
(01242) 602308
sudeleycastle.co.uk
*Romantic castle and restored gardens.*

### Tintagel Castle
*Tintagel, Cornwall*
(01840) 770328
english-heritage.org.uk
*Evocative ruined castle on wind-swept coast.*

### Wells Cathedral
*Wells, Somerset*
(01749) 674483
wellscathedral.org.uk
*Superb 12thC cathedral in Early English style.*

### Wilton House
*Wilton, Wiltshire*
(01722) 746714
wiltonhouse.com
*Stunning 17thC state rooms and landscaped parkland.*

## Indoors

### British Empire & Commonwealth Museum
*Bristol*
(0117) 925 4980
empiremuseum.co.uk
*Explore a dramatic history and heritage.*

### Brunel's ss Great Britain
*Bristol*
(0117) 926 0680
ssgreatbritain.org
*Experience life aboard Brunel's famous steam ship.*

### Cheltenham Art Gallery and Museum
*Cheltenham, Gloucestershire*
(01242) 237431
cheltenham.artgallery.museum
*World-renowned Arts and Crafts Movement collection.*

### The China Clay Museum
*Carthew, Cornwall*
(01726) 850362
wheal-martyn.com
*Restored clayworks in World Heritage mining landscape.*

### The Dinosaur Museum
*Dorchester, Dorset*
(01305) 269880
thedinosaurmuseum.com
*Life-sized reconstructions and hands-on displays.*

### Dorset County Museum
*Dorchester, Dorset*
(01305) 262735
dorsetcountymuseum.org
*The archeology and geology of Dorset.*

### The Dorset Teddy Bear Museum
*Dorchester, Dorset*
(01305) 266040
teddybearmuseum.co.uk
*Featuring a family of people-sized bears.*

### The Edward Jenner Museum
*Berkeley, Gloucestershire*
(01453) 810631
jennermuseum.com
*Life-story of the smallpox vaccine pioneer.*

### Explore-At-Bristol
*Bristol*
0845 345 1235
at-bristol.org.uk
*An exciting hands-on science adventure.*

### Fleet Air Arm Museum
*Yeovilton, Somerset*
(01935) 840565
fleetairarm.com
*See Europe's largest collection of naval aircraft.*

### Geevor Tin Mine
*Pendeen, Cornwall*
(01736) 788662
geevor.com
*The largest preserved mining site in Britain.*

### The Museum of East Asian Art
*Bath, Somerset*
(01225) 464640
meaa.org.uk
*Jades, bronzes and ceramics from the East.*

### National Maritime Museum Cornwall
*Falmouth, Cornwall*
(01326) 313388
nmmc.co.uk
*Enthralling exhibits for landlubbers and sailors alike.*

### STEAM - Museum of the Great Western Railway
*Swindon, Wiltshire*
(01793) 466646
swindon.gov.uk/steam
*Interactive story of pioneering rail company.*

### Tate St Ives
*St Ives, Cornwall*
(01736) 796226
tate.org.uk/stives
*International art in striking beach-front gallery.*

### The Tutankhamun Exhibition
*Dorchester, Dorset*
(01305) 269571
tutankhamun-exhibition.co.uk
*Internationally-acclaimed exhibition with perfect reconstructions.*

## Outdoors

### Abbey House Gardens
*Malmesbury, Wiltshire*
(01666) 822212
abbeyhousegardens.co.uk
*Wonderful displays featuring over 10,000 plants.*

### Eden Project
*St Austell, Cornwall*
(01726) 811911
edenproject.com
*A global garden for the 21st century.*

### Hidcote Manor Garden
*near Chipping Campden, Gloucestershire*
(01386) 438333
nationaltrust.org.uk
*Widely celebrated Arts and Crafts garden.*

### Land's End
*Sennen, Cornwall*
0871 720 0055
landsend-landmark.co.uk
*Spectacular cliffs, breathtaking vistas and multi-sensory show.*

### The Lost Gardens of Heligan
*near St Austell, Cornwall*
(01726) 845100
heligan.com
*Glorious 200-acre restored garden and pleasure grounds.*

### The Minack Theatre and Visitor Centre
*Porthcurno, Cornwall*
(01736) 810181
minack.com
*Open-air cliff-side theatre with breathtaking views.*

### Painswick Rococo Garden
*Painswick, Gloucestershire*
(01452) 813204
rococogarden.org.uk
*A flamboyant piece of English garden design.*

### Pecorama
*Beer, Devon*
(01297) 21542
peco-uk.com
*Passenger-carrying miniature railway in spectacular gardens.*

**RHS Garden Rosemoor**
*Torrington, Devon*
(01805) 624067
rhs.org.uk/rosemoor
*Enchanting 65-acre year-round garden.*

**Stonehenge and Avebury World Heritage Site**
*near Salisbury, Wiltshire*
0870 333 1181
english-heritage.org.uk
*World-famous prehistoric monument.*

**Stourhead House and Garden**
*Stourton, Wiltshire*
(01747) 841152
nationaltrust.org.uk
*Palladian mansion with world-renowned landscape gardens.*

**Thermae Bath Spa**
*Bath, Somerset*
0844 888 0848
thermaebathspa.com
*Enjoy Britain's only natural thermal waters.*

**Trelissick Garden**
*near Truro, Cornwall*
(01872) 862090
nationaltrust.org.uk
*Tender and exotic plants in tranquil garden.*

**Tresco Abbey Gardens**
*Isles of Scilly*
(01720) 424108
tresco.co.uk
*Tropical garden with species from 80 countries.*

**Westonbirt, The National Arboretum**
*Westonbirt, Gloucestershire*
(01666) 880220
forestry.gov.uk/westonbirt
*One of the world's finest tree collections.*

**Wildfowl & Wetlands Trust Slimbridge**
*Slimbridge, Gloucestershire*
(01453) 891900
wwt.org.uk
*Home to an astounding array of wildlife.*

**Willows & Wetlands Visitor Centre**
*Taunton, Somerset*
(01823) 490249
englishwillowbaskets.co.uk
*The art of willow growing and basketmaking.*

**ASSURANCE OF A GREAT DAY OUT**
Attractions with this sign participate in the Visitor Attraction Quality Assurance Scheme which recognises high standards in all aspects of the visitor experience.

## Events 2009

**Walk Scilly**
Isle of Scilly
walkscilly.co.uk
**Mar**

**Exeter Festival of South West Food & Drink**
Exeter
visitsouthwest.co.uk/exeterfoodfestival
**Apr**

**Cheese Rolling**
Brockworth
cheese-rolling.co.uk
**25 May**

**Chippenham Folk Festival**
Chippenham
chippfolk.co.uk
**22 - 25 May**

**Annual Nettle Eating Contest**
Bridport
thebottleinn.co.uk
**Jun**

**Bristol International Festival of Kites**
Bristol
kite-festival.org.uk
**Aug**

**Spirit of the Sea**
Weymouth
spiritofthesea.org.uk
**Aug**

**Falmouth Oyster Festival**
Falmouth
falmouthoysterfestival.co.uk
**Oct**

**Bath Christmas Market**
Bath
bathchristmasmarket.co.uk
**Nov - Dec**

**Tar Barrels**
Ottery St Mary
otterytourism.org.uk
**5 Nov**

**Bridgwater Guy Fawkes Carnival**
Bridgwater
bridgwatercarnival.org.uk
**6 Nov**

# Regional contacts and information

For more information on accommodation, attractions, activities, events and holidays in South West England, contact one of the following regional or local tourism organisations. Their websites have a wealth of information and many produce free publications to help you get the most out of your visit.

## South West England

Visit the following websites for further information on South West England or call **01392 360050**:

- **visitsouthwest.co.uk**
- **swcp.org.uk**
- **accessiblesouthwest.co.uk**

Publications available from South West Tourism:

- **The Trencherman's Guide to Top Restaurants in South West England**
- **Adventure South West**
  Your ultimate activity and adventure guide.
- **World Heritage Map**
  Discover our World Heritage.

Clockwise: Pedn Vounder, Cornwall; Gloucester Cathedral, Gloucestershire; Lynton, Devon

# Tourist Information Centres

When you arrive at your destination, visit an Official Partner Tourist Information Centre for quality assured help with accommodation and information about local attractions and events, or email your request before you go. To search for attractions and Tourist Information Centres on the move just text INFO to 62233, and a web link will be sent to your mobile phone. To find a Tourist Information Centre by region visit enjoyEngland.com/find-tic.

| | | | |
|---|---|---|---|
| **Avebury** | Green Street | (01672) 539425 | all.tic's@kennet.gov.uk |
| **Bath** | Abbey Church Yard | 0906 711 2000** | tourism@bathtourism.co.uk |
| **Bodmin** | Mount Folly Square | (01208) 76616 | bodmintic@visit.org.uk |
| **Bourton-on-the-Water** | Victoria Street | (01451) 820211 | bourtonvic@btconnect.com |
| **Bridport** | 47 South Street | (01308) 424901 | bridport.tic@westdorset-dc.gov.uk |
| **Bristol** | Harbourside | 0906 711 2191** | ticharbourside@destinationbristol.co.uk |
| **Brixham** | The Quay | (01803) 211 211 | holiday@torbay.gov.uk |
| **Bude** | The Crescent | (01288) 354240 | budetic@visitbude.info |
| **Burnham-on-Sea** | South Esplanade | (01278) 787852 | burnham.tic@sedgemoor.gov.uk |
| **Camelford*** | The Clease | (01840) 212954 | manager@camelfordtic.eclipse.co.uk |
| **Cartgate** | A303/A3088 Cartgate Picnic Site | (01935) 829333 | cartgate.tic@southsomerset.gov.uk |
| **Cheddar** | The Gorge | (01934) 744071 | cheddar.tic@sedgemoor.gov.uk |
| **Chippenham** | Market Place | (01249) 665970 | tourism@chippenham.gov.uk |
| **Chipping Campden** | High Street | (01386) 841206 | information@visitchippingcampden.com |
| **Christchurch** | 49 High Street | (01202) 471780 | enquiries@christchurchtourism.info |
| **Cirencester** | Market Place | (01285) 654180 | cirencestervic@cotswold.gov.uk |
| **Coleford** | High Street | (01594) 812388 | tourism@fdean.gov.uk |
| **Corsham** | 31 High Street | (01249) 714660 | enquiries@corshamheritage.org.uk |
| **Devizes** | Market Place | (01380) 729408 | all.tic's@kennet.gov.uk |
| **Dorchester** | 11 Antelope Walk | (01305) 267992 | dorchester.tic@westdorset-dc.gov.uk |
| **Falmouth** | Prince of Wales Pier | (01326) 312300 | info@falmouthtic.co.uk |
| **Frome** | Justice Lane | (01373) 467271 | frome.tic@ukonline.co.uk |
| **Glastonbury** | 9 High Street | (01458) 832954 | glastonbury.tic@ukonline.co.uk |
| **Gloucester** | 28 Southgate Street | (01452) 396572 | tourism@gloucester.gov.uk |
| **Looe*** | Fore Street | (01503) 262072 | looetic@btconnect.com |
| **Lyme Regis** | Church Street | (01297) 442138 | lymeregis.tic@westdorset-dc.gov.uk |
| **Malmesbury** | Market Lane | (01666) 823748 | malmesburyip@northwilts.gov.uk |
| **Moreton-in-Marsh** | High Street | (01608) 650881 | moreton@cotswold.gov.uk |
| **Padstow** | North Quay | (01841) 533449 | padstowtic@btconnect.com |

| | | | |
|---|---|---|---|
| **Paignton** | The Esplanade | (01803) 211 211 | holiday@torbay.gov.uk |
| **Penzance** | Station Road | (01736) 362207 | pztic@penwith.gov.uk |
| **Plymouth Mayflower** | 3-5 The Barbican | (01752) 306330 | barbicantic@plymouth.gov.uk |
| **St Ives** | The Guildhall | (01736) 796297 | ivtic@penwith.gov.uk |
| **Salisbury** | Fish Row | (01722) 334956 | visitorinfo@salisbury.gov.uk |
| **Shelton Mallet** | 70 High Street | (01749) 345258 | sheptonmallet.tic@ukonline.co.uk |
| **Sherborne** | 3 Tilton Court, Digby Road | (01935) 815341 | sherborne.tic@westdorset-dc.gov.uk |
| **Somerset** | Sedgemoor Services | (01934) 750833 | somersetvisitorcentre@somerset.gov.uk |
| **Stow-on-the-Wold** | The Square | (01451) 831082 | stowvic@cotswold.gov.uk |
| **Street** | Farm Road | (01458) 447384 | street.tic@ukonline.co.uk |
| **Stroud** | George Street | (01453) 760960 | tic@stroud.gov.uk |
| **Swanage** | Shore Road | (01929) 422885 | mail@swanage.gov.uk |
| **Swindon** | 37 Regent Street | (01793) 530328 | infocentre@swindon.gov.uk |
| **Taunton** | Paul Street | (01823) 336344 | tauntontic@tauntondeane.gov.uk |
| **Tewkesbury** | 100 Church Street | (01684) 855043 | tewkesburytic@tewkesburybc.gov.uk |
| **Torquay** | Vaughan Parade | (01803) 211 211 | holiday@torbay.gov.uk |
| **Truro** | Boscawen Street | (01872) 274555 | tic@truro.gov.uk |
| **Wadebridge** | Eddystone Road | 0870 1223337 | wadebridgetic@btconnect.com |
| **Wareham** | South Street | (01929) 552740 | tic@purbeck-dc.gov.uk |
| **Warminster** | off Station Rd | (01985) 218548 | visitwarminster@btconnect.com |
| **Wells** | Market Place | (01749) 672552 | touristinfo@wells.gov.uk |
| **Weston-super-Mare** | Beach Lawns | (01934) 888800 | westontouristinfo@n-somerset.gov.uk |
| **Weymouth** | The Esplanade | (01305) 785747 | tic@weymouth.gov.uk |
| **Winchcombe** | High Street | (01242) 602925 | winchcombetic@tewkesbury.gov.uk |
| **Yeovil** | Hendford | (01935) 845946/7 | yeoviltic@southsomerset.gov.uk |

*seasonal opening

**calls to this number are charged at premium rate

Left to right: Jurassic Coast, Dorset; Minack Theatre, Cornwall

# Quality visitor attractions

VisitBritain operates a Visitor Attraction Quality Assurance Service.

Participating attractions are visited annually by trained, impartial assessors who look at all aspects of the visit, from initial telephone enquiries to departure, customer service to catering, as well as all facilities and activities.

Only those attractions which have been assessed by Enjoy England and meet the standard receive the quality marque, your sign of a Quality Assured Visitor Attraction.

**Look out for the quality marque and visit with confidence.**

where to stay in

# South West England

All place names in the blue bands are shown on the maps at the front of this guide.

A complete listing of all Enjoy England assessed accommodation covered by this guide appears at the back.

## Accommodation symbols

Symbols give useful information about services and facilities. On page 7 you can find a key to these symbols.

## ABBOTSBURY, Dorset Map ref 2A3

★★★
GUEST ACCOMMODATION

B&B PER ROOM PER NIGHT
S £50.00–£60.00
D £70.00–£80.00

EVENING MEAL PER PERSON
£6.00–£15.00

### Swan Lodge

Rodden Row, Abbotsbury, Weymouth DT3 4JL **t** (01305) 871249

Situated on the B3157 coastal road between Weymouth and Bridport. Swan Inn public house opposite, where food is served all day in season, is under the same ownership.

**open** All year
**bedrooms** 3 double, 2 twin
**bathrooms** 4 en suite, 1 private
**payment** Credit/debit cards

Room General Leisure

## ATHELHAMPTON, Dorset Map ref 2B3

★★★★
BED & BREAKFAST
SILVER AWARD

B&B PER ROOM PER NIGHT
S £45.00–£55.00
D £70.00–£120.00

*3 nights or more: single £35-£40, double £50-£60. Children under 3: free, children under 12: £15 sharing room.*

### White Cottage

Dorchester DT2 7LG **t** (01305) 848622 **e** markjamespiper@aol.com

**freewebs.com/whitecottagebandb**

**open** All year except Christmas
**bedrooms** 1 double, 1 twin, 1 family
**bathrooms** 2 en suite, 1 private
**payment** Cash, cheques

A beautiful 300-year-old cottage, recently refurbished. Double room looks over river and hills, whereas the twin room looks over field and woodland. The new family suite has a large lounge and can sleep up to four. Each room has dressing gowns, fresh fruit and flowers and a mini-fridge. Athelhampton House 200yds.

**SAT NAV** *DT2 7LG*

Room General Leisure

## Where can I get help and advice?

Tourist Information Centres offer friendly help with accommodation and holiday ideas as well as suggestions of places to visit and things to do. You'll find contact details at the beginning of each regional section.

## AVEBURY, Wiltshire Map ref 2B2

★★★
GUEST ACCOMMODATION

B&B PER ROOM PER NIGHT
S £55.00
D £60.00

### The New Inn

Winterbourne Monkton, Swindon SN4 9NW **t** (01672) 539240 **e** enquiries@thenewinn.net

**thenewinn.net**

Bed and breakfast in 200-year-old house. Large garden and car park. Set in outstanding Wiltshire countryside only one mile from Avebury stone circle.

**open** All year except Christmas
**bedrooms** 2 double, 2 twin, 1 family
**bathrooms** All en suite
**payment** Credit/debit cards, cash, cheques

Room General

## BARNSTAPLE, Devon Map ref 1C1

★★★★
GUEST ACCOMMODATION

B&B PER ROOM PER NIGHT
S £30.00–£40.00
D £55.00–£80.00

*Romantic break: 3-night stay B&B in four-poster bed, bottle of cava, bunch of roses and box of chocolates. Total £195.*

### Lower Yelland Farm B&B

Fremington, Barnstaple EX31 3EN **t** (01271) 860101 **e** peterday@loweryellandfarm.co.uk

**loweryellandfarm.co.uk** REAL-TIME BOOKING

**open** All year
**bedrooms** 3 double, 2 twin, 2 single, 1 family
**bathrooms** All en suite
**payment** Cash, cheques

Winner of the JPC Group Golden Achievement Award for Quality and Service. The farm, built in 1658, lies adjacent to the RSPB sanctuary and Tarka Trail and borders the River Taw. Breakfast includes prize-winning home-made jams, home-made bread, eggs from our free-range chickens served in a beautiful oak-beamed lounge.

**SAT NAV** *EX31 3EN* **ONLINE MAP**

Room General Leisure

## BARNSTAPLE, Devon Map ref 1C1

★★★★
GUEST HOUSE
SILVER AWARD

B&B PER ROOM PER NIGHT
S £26.00–£29.00
D £52.00–£58.00

EVENING MEAL PER PERSON
Min £16.00

### The Spinney

Shirwell, Barnstaple EX31 4JR **t** (01271) 850282 **e** thespinney@shirwell.fsnet.co.uk

**thespinneyshirwell.co.uk**

**open** All year
**bedrooms** 1 double, 1 twin, 1 single, 2 family
**bathrooms** 3 en suite, 2 private
**payment** Credit/debit cards, cash, cheques

A former rectory, set in over an acre of grounds with views towards Exmoor. Spacious accommodation, en suite available. Centrally heated. Delicious meals cooked by chef/proprietor, served during summer months in our restored Victorian conservatory under the ancient vine. Residential licence. The Spinney is non-smoking.

**SAT NAV** *EX31 4JR*

Room General

## Don't forget www.

Web addresses throughout this guide are shown without the prefix www. Please include www. in the address line of your browser. If a web address does not follow this style it is shown in full.

For **key to symbols** see page 7

## BARNSTAPLE, Devon Map ref 1C1

★★★★
GUEST ACCOMMODATION

B&B PER ROOM PER NIGHT
S Min £50.00
D Min £90.00

EVENING MEAL PER PERSON
Min £24.50

### Westcott Barton

Middle Marwood, Barnstaple EX31 4EF **t** (01271) 812842 **e** westcott_barton@yahoo.co.uk

**westcottbarton.co.uk**

**open** All year
**bedrooms** 5 double, 2 twin
**bathrooms** 5 en suite
**payment** Cash, cheques

Historic country estate with fine example of a Saxon farmstead; ornamental gardens, streams, ponds and acres of ancient woodland. Perfect for artists, photographers, birdwatchers and naturalists. Beautiful en suite bedrooms in beamed stone cottages and our longhouse. Locally and organically sourced home-cooked breakfasts. Evening meals available on request.

**SAT NAV** *EX31 4EF*

Room General 10 P Leisure

## BATH, Somerset Map ref 2B2

★★★★★
GUEST HOUSE
GOLD AWARD

B&B PER ROOM PER NIGHT
S £55.00–£65.00
D £75.00–£88.00

*3 nights for 2/50% off second night, Nov-Feb. 4 nights for 3/50% off third night, Mar-May and Sep-Oct.*

### Athole Guest House

33 Upper Oldfield Park, Bath BA2 3JX **t** (01225) 320000 **e** info@atholehouse.co.uk

**atholehouse.co.uk** GUEST REVIEWS • SPECIAL OFFERS • REAL-TIME BOOKING

**open** All year
**bedrooms** 4 double, 1 family
**bathrooms** All en suite
**payment** Credit/debit cards, cash, cheques, euros

Large Victorian home restored to give bright, inviting, quiet bedrooms, sleek furniture, sparkling bathrooms, digital TV, Wi-Fi internet in all bedrooms, safe. Hospitality is old style. Award-winning breakfasts. Relax in our gardens, or let us help you explore the area. Secure parking behind remote-control gates or in garage. Twelve minutes' walk from centre. Free transfer from/to station.

**SAT NAV** *BA2 3JX* **ONLINE MAP**

Room General P Leisure

## BATH, Somerset Map ref 2B2

★★★★★
GUEST ACCOMMODATION
GOLD AWARD

B&B PER ROOM PER NIGHT
D £80.00–£185.00

*We offer short-break weekday packages during Dec-Feb winter season. Details available on request.*

### The Ayrlington

24-25 Pulteney Road, Bath BA2 4EZ **t** (01225) 425495 **e** mail@ayrlington.com

**ayrlington.com** SPECIAL OFFERS

**open** All year except Christmas and New Year
**bedrooms** 13 double, 1 twin
**bathrooms** All en suite
**payment** Credit/debit cards, cash, cheques

Located within an easy five-minute level walk of Bath city centre, The Ayrlington is a small, tranquil, non-smoking, luxury hotel. The Ayrlington has recently been extended and refurbished throughout – all fourteen bedrooms have an individual theme and are beautifully furnished, some with four-poster beds.

**SAT NAV** *BA2 4EZ*

Room General P Leisure

Where can I get live travel information?
For the latest travel update – call the RAC on 1740 from your mobile phone.

## BATH, Somerset Map ref 2B2

★★★★
GUEST ACCOMMODATION
SILVER AWARD

B&B PER ROOM PER NIGHT
S £65.00–£85.00
D £70.00–£100.00

# Chestnuts House

16 Henrietta Road, Bath BA2 6LY **t** (01225) 334279 **e** reservations@chestnutshouse.co.uk

**chestnutshouse.co.uk** GUEST REVIEWS · SPECIAL OFFERS

**open** All year except Christmas
**bedrooms** 3 double, 1 twin, 1 family
**bathrooms** All en suite
**payment** Credit/debit cards, cash, cheques, euros

Chestnuts House is a high quality B&B set in the heart of the city with an enclosed garden and private off-street parking. The house is built from natural stone and has five excellent en suite guest rooms and one suite, all of which are tastefully decorated and very well appointed.

**SAT NAV** *BA2 6LY* **ONLINE MAP**

Room General P Leisure

## BATH, Somerset Map ref 2B2

★★★
FARMHOUSE

B&B PER ROOM PER NIGHT
S Min £50.00
D Min £60.00

# Church Farm

Monkton Farleigh, Bradford-on-Avon BA15 2QJ **t** (01225) 858583 & 07803 966798
**e** reservations@churchfarmmonktonfarleigh.co.uk

**churchfarmmonktonfarleigh.co.uk**

Converted farmhouse barn with exceptional views in peaceful, idyllic setting. Ten minutes from Bath, ideal base for touring/walking South West England. Families/dogs welcome.

**open** All year
**bedrooms** 2 double, 1 family
**bathrooms** All en suite
**payment** Cash, cheques

Room General P Leisure

## BATH, Somerset Map ref 2B2

★★★
GUEST ACCOMMODATION

B&B PER ROOM PER NIGHT
S £35.00–£45.00
D £55.00–£65.00

# Hermitage

Bath Road, Box, Corsham SN13 8DT **t** (01225) 744187 **e** hermitagebb@btconnect.com

16thC house with heated pool in summer. Dining room with vaulted ceiling. Six miles from Bath on A4 to Chippenham, first drive on left by 30mph sign.

**open** All year except Christmas and New Year
**bedrooms** 4 double, 1 family
**bathrooms** All en suite
**payment** Cash, cheques

Room General P Leisure

## BATH, Somerset Map ref 2B2

★★★★
BED & BREAKFAST

B&B PER ROOM PER NIGHT
S £42.00–£48.00
D £65.00–£80.00

*10% discount for stays of 4 or more nights.*

# Lindisfarne Guest House

41a Warminster Road, Bath BA2 6XJ **t** (01225) 466342 **e** lindisfarne-bath@talk21.com

**bath.org/hotel/lindisfarne.htm**

**open** All year except Christmas
**bedrooms** 2 double, 1 twin
**bathrooms** All en suite
**payment** Credit/debit cards, cash, cheques

Comfortable, en suite rooms, good-quality full English breakfast and friendly proprietors. Within walking distance of pub/restaurants. About 1.5 miles from Bath city centre on regular bus route. Near walks along the Kennet and Avon canal. Easy drive to university. Large car park.

**SAT NAV** *BA2 6XJ*

Room General 8 P Leisure

## BATH, Somerset Map ref 2B2

★★★★
GUEST ACCOMMODATION

B&B PER ROOM PER NIGHT
s £80.00–£95.00
d £85.00–£140.00

*£5 off each night for stays of 3 nights or more.*

### Marlborough House

1 Marlborough Lane, Bath BA1 2NQ **t** (01225) 318175 **e** mars@manque.dircon.co.uk

**marlborough-house.net**

**open** All year except Christmas
**bedrooms** 3 double, 2 twin, 1 single, 2 family
**bathrooms** All en suite
**payment** Credit/debit cards, cash, cheques, euros

Enchanting Victorian town house in Bath's Georgian centre, exquisitely furnished and run in an elegant and friendly style, with beautiful en suite rooms featuring four-poster or antique wood beds. Both vegetarian and organic, our amazing breakfast choices include freshly prepared fruit, organic yoghurts and juices. Also speciality omelettes and Marlborough House potatoes.

**SAT NAV** *BA1 2NQ*

Room General

## BATH, Somerset Map ref 2B2

★★★
GUEST ACCOMMODATION

B&B PER ROOM PER NIGHT
s £40.00–£50.00
d £65.00–£110.00

*Reduced rates for stays of 3 nights or more – each booking assessed individually.*

### Pulteney House

14 Pulteney Road, Bath BA2 4HA **t** (01225) 460991 **e** pulteney@tinyworld.co.uk

**pulteneyhotel.co.uk** REAL-TIME BOOKING

**open** All year
**bedrooms** 7 double, 3 twin, 2 single, 5 family
**bathrooms** 16 en suite, 1 private
**payment** Credit/debit cards, cash, cheques

Large, elegant, Victorian house in picturesque, south-facing gardens with fine views of Bath Abbey. Large, private car park. Only five to ten minutes' walk from city centre. An ideal base for exploring Bath and surrounding areas. All rooms (except one) en suite with hairdryer, TV, tea/coffee facilities and radio/alarm clocks.

**SAT NAV** *BA2 4HA* **ONLINE MAP**

Room General Leisure

## BATH, Somerset Map ref 2B2

★★★★★
GUEST ACCOMMODATION
GOLD AWARD

B&B PER ROOM PER NIGHT
s Min £135.00
d Max £300.00

EVENING MEAL PER PERSON
£9.50–£40.00

### The Residence

Weston Road, Bath BA1 2XZ **t** (01225) 750180 **e** info@theresidencebath.com

**theresidencebath.com** GUEST REVIEWS • SPECIAL OFFERS • REAL-TIME BOOKING

**open** All year
**bedrooms** 5 double, 1 suite
**bathrooms** 5 en suite, 1 private
**payment** Credit/debit cards, cash, cheques, euros

The Residence is unique in Bath, offering just six rooms. It brings together the exclusivity of a private club and the service of a modern hotel within a large Georgian house near the city centre. Our aim is simple: to be the best home from home you will ever have.

**SAT NAV** *BA1 2XZ*

Room General Leisure

**Looking for a wide range of facilities?**
More stars means higher quality accommodation plus a greater range of facilities and services.

**BATH, Somerset Map ref 2B2**

★★★★
GUEST ACCOMMODATION

B&B PER ROOM PER NIGHT
S £35.00–£45.00
D £55.00–£65.00

## Walton Villa

3 Newbridge Hill, Bath BA1 3PW **t** (01225) 482792 **e** walton.villa@virgin.net

**walton.izest.com** GUEST REVIEWS

Family-run bed and breakfast, offering pretty en suite/private facilities accommodation. One mile from city centre. Off-street parking and bus service nearby.

**open** All year except Christmas and New Year
**bedrooms** 2 double, 1 twin, 1 single
**bathrooms** 3 en suite, 1 private
**payment** Credit/debit cards, cash, cheques

Room General 1 P Leisure

**BATH, Somerset Map ref 2B2**

★★★★
INN

B&B PER ROOM PER NIGHT
S £95.00–£100.00
D £120.00–£145.00

EVENING MEAL PER PERSON
£15.00–£27.50

## Wheelwrights Arms

Monkton Combe, Bath BA2 7HB **t** (01225) 722287 **e** bookings@wheelwrightsarms.co.uk

**wheelwrightsarms.co.uk** GUEST REVIEWS • SPECIAL OFFERS

Ideal centre for sightseeing, only short distance from Bath. Bedrooms are in converted 18thC carpenter's workshop. The pub was the carpenter's house originally from 1761-1850.

**open** All year
**bedrooms** 5 double, 1 twin, 1 single
**bathrooms** All en suite
**payment** Credit/debit cards, cash, cheques

Room General 1 P Leisure

**BIBURY, Gloucestershire Map ref 2B1**

★★★★
BED & BREAKFAST
GOLD AWARD

B&B PER ROOM PER NIGHT
S Min £48.00
D Min £68.00

## Cotteswold House

Arlington, Bibury, Cirencester GL7 5ND **t** (01285) 740609 **e** enquiries@cotteswoldhouse.org.uk

**cotteswoldhouse.org.uk**

**open** All year
**bedrooms** 2 double, 1 twin
**bathrooms** All en suite
**payment** Credit/debit cards, cash, cheques

Situated in this picturesque village, Cotteswold House offers high-quality accommodation in a relaxed, friendly atmosphere. Tastefully furnished bedrooms with en suite facilities, colour TV and tea/coffee. Spacious guest lounge/dining room. Cotteswold House is an ideal centre for touring the Cotswolds and surrounding area. No smoking/pets. Private parking.

**SAT NAV** *GL7 5ND*

Room General P Leisure

**BLANDFORD FORUM, Dorset Map ref 2B3**

★★★★
INN

B&B PER ROOM PER NIGHT
S £80.00–£85.00
D £105.00–£125.00

## Anvil Inn

Salisbury Road, Pimperne, Blandford Forum DT11 8UQ **t** (01258) 453431
**e** theanvil.inn@btconnect.com

**anvilinn.co.uk**

**open** All year
**bedrooms** 7 double, 2 twin, 2 single
**bathrooms** All en suite
**payment** Credit/debit cards, cash, cheques

Picturesque, family-run, 16thC thatched hotel. Beamed a la carte restaurant, mouth-watering menu, delicious desserts. Tasty bar meals and specials cooked from fresh, fine food. Meals available all day.

**SAT NAV** *DT11 8UQ*

Room General P Leisure

For **key to symbols** see page 7

## BLANDFORD FORUM, Dorset Map ref 2B3

★★★★★
GUEST ACCOMMODATION
GOLD AWARD

B&B PER ROOM PER NIGHT
s £50.00–£60.00
d £70.00–£80.00

# Farnham Farm House

Blandford Forum DT11 8DG **t** (01725) 516254 **e** info@farnhamfarmhouse.co.uk

**farnhamfarmhouse.co.uk**

**open** All year except Christmas
**bedrooms** 2 double, 1 twin
**bathrooms** All en suite
**payment** Credit/debit cards, cash, cheques

A private drive leads to this picturesque 19thC farmhouse nestling in the secluded, rolling slopes of Cranborne Chase, having flagstone floors, open fires and an acre of tranquil garden. A comfortable and relaxing base, enhanced by the addition of the Sarpenela Treatment Centre offering therapeutic massage and natural therapies.

**SAT NAV** *DT11 8DG* **ONLINE MAP**

Room General P Leisure

## BLANDFORD FORUM, Dorset Map ref 2B3

★★★★
FARMHOUSE

B&B PER ROOM PER NIGHT
s £60.00
d £60.00–£65.00

*B&B for your horse is available.*

# Lower Bryanston Farm B&B

Lower Bryanston, Blandford Forum DT11 0LS **t** (01258) 452009 **e** andrea@bryanstonfarm.co.uk

**brylow.co.uk**

**open** All year except Christmas and New Year
**bedrooms** 3 double, 1 twin, 1 family
**bathrooms** 3 en suite, 2 private
**payment** Cash, cheques

Attractive Georgian farmhouse with spacious rooms and beautiful rural views. All rooms equipped with hospitality tray, TV and DVD player. Fantastic full English breakfast. Safe off-road parking. Superb central location to explore the interesting county of Dorset. Within walking distance of Blandford. Blandford Camp and Bryanston school nearby.

**SAT NAV** *DT11 0LS*

Room General P Leisure

## BOLVENTOR, Cornwall Map ref 1C2

★★★
INN

B&B PER ROOM PER NIGHT
s £45.00–£80.00
d £70.00–£100.00

EVENING MEAL PER PERSON
£8.95–£16.50

# Jamaica Inn

Bolventor, Launceston PL15 7TS **t** (01566) 86250 **e** enquiry@jamaicainn.co.uk

**jamaicainn.co.uk**

**open** All year
**bedrooms** 15 double, 1 twin
**bathrooms** All en suite
**payment** Credit/debit cards, cash

Inspiration for Daphne du Maurier's novel. Bars, restaurant, accommodation and gift shop. Whilst here visit Daphne du Maurier's Smugglers at Jamaica Inn.

**SAT NAV** *PL15 7TS*

Room General P Leisure

### What shall we do today?

For ideas on places to visit, see the beginning of this regional section or go online at enjoyengland.com.

## BOSCASTLE, Cornwall Map ref 1B2

★★★★
GUEST ACCOMMODATION

B&B PER ROOM PER NIGHT
S £40.00–£50.00
D £50.00–£64.00

### The Old Coach House

Tintagel Road, Boscastle PL35 0AS **t** (01840) 250398 **e** jackiefarm@btinternet.com

**old-coach.co.uk**

Relax in a beautiful 300-year-old former coach house. All rooms en suite with colour TV, tea-making facilities, hairdryer etc. Friendly and helpful owners. Good parking.

**open** All year except Christmas
**bedrooms** 4 double, 2 twin, 2 family
**bathrooms** All en suite
**payment** Credit/debit cards, cash, cheques

Room General P Leisure

## BOURNEMOUTH, Dorset Map ref 2B3

★★★★
GUEST ACCOMMODATION

B&B PER ROOM PER NIGHT
S £35.00–£42.00
D £60.00–£78.00

### The Blue Palms

26 Tregonwell Road, Bournemouth BH2 5NS **t** (01202) 554968 **e** bluepalmshotel@btopenworld.com

**bluepalmshotel.com** GUEST REVIEWS · SPECIAL OFFERS

Attractive town-centre hotel with car park, patio and garden. Superb accommodation and warm, friendly service. Short walk from beaches, shops, Bournemouth International Centre, etc.

**open** All year except Christmas
**bedrooms** 5 double, 2 twin, 1 single, 2 family
**bathrooms** All en suite
**payment** Credit/debit cards, cash, cheques

Room General P

## BOURNEMOUTH, Dorset Map ref 2B3

★★★★
GUEST ACCOMMODATION

B&B PER ROOM PER NIGHT
S £35.00–£40.00
D £70.00–£80.00

### Cransley

11 Knyveton Road, East Cliff, Bournemouth BH1 3QG **t** (01202) 290067 **e** info@cransley.com

**cransley.com**

**open** All year except Christmas
**bedrooms** 6 double, 3 twin, 2 single
**bathrooms** 10 en suite, 1 private
**payment** Credit/debit cards, cash

A quiet, tree-lined road in the attractive East Cliff area of Bournemouth is the setting for this homely B&B for non-smokers. The hotel's sunny position means bedrooms are bright and welcoming. French windows lead from the sitting room and dining room to a secluded, south-facing, award-winning garden.

**SAT NAV** *BH1 3QG*

Room General 14 P

## BOURNEMOUTH, Dorset Map ref 2B3

★★★
GUEST ACCOMMODATION

B&B PER ROOM PER NIGHT
S £25.00–£35.00
D £60.00–£80.00

### Cremona

St Michaels Road, West Cliff, Bournemouth BH2 5DP **t** (01202) 290035 **e** enquiries@cremona.co.uk

**cremona.co.uk** GUEST REVIEWS

Victorian terraced town house covering three floors. Clean and comfortable, European feel throughout. Good location for the beach, gardens, town centre and Bournemouth International Centre.

**open** All year
**bedrooms** 4 double, 2 twin, 1 single, 2 family
**bathrooms** All en suite
**payment** Credit/debit cards, cash, euros

Room General Leisure

## It's all quality-assessed accommodation

Our commitment to quality involves wide-ranging accommodation assessment. Ratings and awards were correct at the time of going to press but may change following a new assessment. Please check at time of booking.

## BOURNEMOUTH, Dorset Map ref 2B3

★★★
GUEST HOUSE

B&B PER ROOM PER NIGHT
S £35.00–£65.00
D £50.00–£76.00

EVENING MEAL PER PERSON
£10.00

### The Kings Langley

1 West Cliff Road, Bournemouth BH2 5ES **t** (01202) 557349 **e** john@kingslangleyhotel.com

**kingslangleyhotel.com** GUEST REVIEWS

**open** All year
**bedrooms** 10 double, 6 twin, 4 family
**bathrooms** All en suite
**payment** Credit/debit cards, cash, cheques

Warm, friendly, family-run hotel providing excellent accommodation and traditional home-cooked food. Located just a few minutes' walk from beach, shops and entertainment. Free parking for all our guests, central heating, tea-making facilities, Sky TV and hairdrying facilities in all bedrooms.

**SAT NAV** *BH2 5ES* **ONLINE MAP**

Room General

## BOURNEMOUTH, Dorset Map ref 2B3

★★★
GUEST ACCOMMODATION

B&B PER ROOM PER NIGHT
S £20.00–£40.00
D £46.00–£60.00

### Southernhay Guest House

42 Alum Chine Road, Westbourne, Bournemouth BH4 8DX **t** (01202) 761251
**e** enquiries@southernhayhotel.co.uk

**southernhayhotel.co.uk** SPECIAL OFFERS

**open** All year
**bedrooms** 2 double, 1 twin, 1 single, 2 family
**bathrooms** 4 en suite
**payment** Cash, cheques

High-standard accommodation near beach, restaurants and shops. Full English breakfast, rooms with colour TV, radio-alarm, hairdryer and tea-/coffee-making facilities. Two-for-one golf deals.

**SAT NAV** *BH4 8DX*

Room General Leisure

## BOURNEMOUTH, Dorset Map ref 2B3

★★★★
GUEST HOUSE

B&B PER ROOM PER NIGHT
S £34.00–£55.00
D £68.00–£110.00

EVENING MEAL PER PERSON
£16.00

*Please check our website for special offers throughout the year.*

### Wood Lodge

10 Manor Road, Bournemouth BH1 3EY **t** (01202) 290891 **e** enquiries@woodlodgehotel.co.uk

**woodlodgehotel.co.uk** GUEST REVIEWS • SPECIAL OFFERS

**open** All year
**bedrooms** 5 double, 4 twin, 2 single, 4 family
**bathrooms** 14 en suite, 1 private
**payment** Credit/debit cards, cash, cheques

A beautiful, lovingly maintained English country house offering superb accommodation in the heart of Bournemouth. Set back from a tranquil, tree-lined road in idyllic, award-winning gardens. Minutes' walk to the town centre, beaches, train and coach stations. Excellent service and delicious, high-quality cooking. Relax, unwind and enjoy.

**SAT NAV** *BH1 3EY* **ONLINE MAP**

Room General Leisure

### B&B prices

Rates for bed and breakfast are shown per room per night.
Double room prices are usually based on two people sharing the room.

## BOURTON-ON-THE-WATER, Gloucestershire Map ref 2B1

★★★
INN

B&B PER ROOM PER NIGHT
S Min £40.00
D Min £50.00

### Mousetrap Inn

Lansdown, Bourton-on-the-Water GL54 2AR **t** (01451) 820579 **e** thebatesies@gmail.com

**mousetrap-inn.co.uk**

**open** All year
**bedrooms** 5 double, 4 twin, 1 suite
**bathrooms** All en suite
**payment** Credit/debit cards, cash, cheques

The Mousetrap is a delightful, traditional village inn, with its mellowed soft sandstone and old-world charm. An ideal place for country walks or visiting the many charming villages. It has a reputation for its traditional range of fresh foods and friendly atmosphere, along with a cosy bar and open fire.

**SAT NAV** *GL54 2AR*

Room General P Leisure

## BOVEY TRACEY, Devon Map ref 1D2

★★★★★
BED & BREAKFAST
GOLD AWARD

B&B PER ROOM PER NIGHT
S £50.00–£54.00
D £70.00–£78.00

*Special rates on application for stays of 4 or more nights.*

### Brookfield House

Challabrook Lane, Bovey Tracey TQ13 9DF **t** (01626) 836181 **e** enquiries@brookfield-house.com

**brookfield-house.com**

**open** February to November
**bedrooms** 2 double, 1 twin
**bathrooms** 2 en suite, 1 private
**payment** Credit/debit cards, cash, cheques

Spacious, early-Edwardian residence situated on the edge of Bovey Tracey and Dartmoor and set in two acres with panoramic moor views. Secluded tranquillity yet within easy walking distance of town. Individually decorated bedrooms, all with comfortable seating areas. Gourmet breakfasts, including home-made breads and preserves.

**SAT NAV** *TQ13 9DF*

Room General 12 P Leisure

## BOX, Wiltshire Map ref 2B2

Rating Applied For
GUEST HOUSE

B&B PER ROOM PER NIGHT
S £40.00–£50.00
D £70.00–£80.00

### Lorne House

London Road, Box, Corsham SN13 8NA **t** (01225) 742597 **e** info@lornehouse.box.co.uk

**lornehousebox.co.uk**

**open** All year except Christmas and New Year
**bedrooms** 4 double/twin
**bathrooms** All en suite
**payment** Credit/debit cards, cash, cheques

Newly refurbished B&B close to Bath with charm and character. Childhood home of the Reverend Awdry of Thomas the Tank Engine fame. Lovingly restored, individually designed bedrooms, creature comforts including flat-screen TVs. A warm and friendly welcome.

**SAT NAV** *SN13 8NA*

Room General P Leisure

Do you have access needs?
Look for the National Accessible Scheme symbols if you have special hearing, visual or mobility needs.

## BRATTON FLEMING, Devon Map ref 1C1

★★★★
BED & BREAKFAST

B&B PER ROOM PER NIGHT
S £32.00–£34.00
D £54.00–£56.00

### Sheltercombe Cottage

Bratton Fleming, Barnstaple EX32 7JL **t** (01598) 710513 **e** enquiries@sheltercombecottage.co.uk

**sheltercombecottage.co.uk**

A charming country cottage nestling in the hill at the top of a pretty North Devon village, within very easy reach of market towns, wonderful beaches and Exmoor.

**open** All year except Christmas and New Year
**bedrooms** 2 double, 1 twin
**bathrooms** 1 en suite, 2 private
**payment** Cash, cheques

Room General Leisure

## BREAM, Gloucestershire Map ref 2A1

★★★
INN

B&B PER ROOM PER NIGHT
S £40.00–£50.00
D £60.00–£70.00

EVENING MEAL PER PERSON
£6.00–£15.00

### Rising Sun

High Street, Bream, Lydney GL15 6JF **t** (01594) 564555 **e** jonjo_risingsun@msn.com

**therisingsunbream.co.uk**

A village inn dating back to 1729. Ideally situated in the Royal Forest of Dean. Real ales, home-cooked food and hearty breakfasts.

**open** All year
**bedrooms** 4 double, 1 twin
**bathrooms** All en suite
**payment** Credit/debit cards, cash, cheques

Room General P Leisure

## BREAN, Somerset Map ref 1D1

★★★★
GUEST ACCOMMODATION

B&B PER ROOM PER NIGHT
S £30.00–£40.00
D £55.00–£60.00

*Reduced rates for longer stays and singles out of season (see website for details).*

### Yew Tree House

Hurn Lane, Berrow, Nr Brean, Burnham-on-Sea TA8 2QT **t** (01278) 751382
**e** yewtree@yewtree-house.co.uk

**yewtree-house.co.uk** GUEST REVIEWS • SPECIAL OFFERS • REAL-TIME BOOKING

**open** All year except Christmas
**bedrooms** 2 double, 2 twin, 1 family, 1 suite
**bathrooms** All en suite
**payment** Credit/debit cards, cash, cheques

We warmly welcome visitors to our charming old house with its spacious rooms, modern facilities, on-site parking and gardens. We are easy to reach from the motorway and in the perfect location for a break. The house is close to the beach and ideally located for Somerset's many attractions.

**SAT NAV** *TA8 2QT* **ONLINE MAP**

Room General P Leisure

## BRIDGWATER, Somerset Map ref 1D1

★★★
INN

B&B PER ROOM PER NIGHT
S £49.50–£75.00
D £65.00–£85.00

### The Boat & Anchor Inn

Meads Crossing, Huntworth, Bridgwater TA7 0AQ **t** (01278) 662473
**e** andrea@theboatandanchor.co.uk

**theboatandanchor.co.uk**

Canalside location. Extensive beer garden. Full a la carte menu. En suite accommodation. Function room – all occasions catered for.

**open** All year
**bedrooms** 5 double, 2 twin, 2 single, 2 family
**bathrooms** All en suite
**payment** Credit/debit cards, cash, cheques

Room General P

### What do the star ratings mean?

Detailed information about star ratings can be found at the back of this guide.

## BRIDGWATER, Somerset Map ref 1D1

★★★★
BED & BREAKFAST
SILVER AWARD

B&B PER ROOM PER NIGHT
S £48.00–£55.00
D £65.00–£75.00

### Hill View

55 Liney Road, Westonzoyland, Nr Bridgwater TA7 0EU **t** (01278) 699027
**e** hillview@westonzoyland.fsbusiness.co.uk

**visit-hillview.co.uk** REAL-TIME BOOKING

Stylish, en suite non-smoking accommodation. Excellent service, comfort and hospitality. Peaceful, rural location with lovely views. Hospitality trays, TV/DVD, business facilities. Traditional breakfast, local produce whenever available. Younger children accommodated by arrangement.

**open** All year except Christmas
**bedrooms** 1 double, 1 twin
**bathrooms** All en suite
**payment** Cash, cheques, euros

Room General P Leisure

## BRIDGWATER, Somerset Map ref 1D1

★★★★
RESTAURANT WITH ROOMS

B&B PER ROOM PER NIGHT
S £49.50–£55.00
D £65.00–£75.00

### The Olive Mill

Chilton Polden Hill, Bridgwater TA7 9AH **t** (01278) 722202 **e** enquiries@theolivemill.co.uk

**theolivemill.co.uk** GUEST REVIEWS • SPECIAL OFFERS • REAL-TIME BOOKING

Mediterranean cuisine prepared and served with excellence in the heart of the West Country. Rooms with outstanding views of the Mendips.

**open** All year
**bedrooms** 7 double
**bathrooms** All en suite
**payment** Credit/debit cards, cash, cheques

Room General P Leisure

## BRIDPORT, Dorset Map ref 2A3

★★★
INN

B&B PER ROOM PER NIGHT
S Min £50.00
D Min £60.00

EVENING MEAL PER PERSON
£6.95–£9.95

### The Tiger Inn

14-16 Barrack Street, Bridport DT6 3LY **t** (01308) 427543 **e** jacquie@tigerinnbridport.co.uk

**tigerinnbridport.co.uk**

Grade II Listed freehouse pub. Town-centre location. All rooms en suite. Superb food, skittles alley. Pretty courtyard garden.

**open** All year
**bedrooms** 1 double, 1 twin, 2 family
**bathrooms** All en suite
**payment** Credit/debit cards, cash, cheques

Room General

## BRIDPORT, Dorset Map ref 2A3

★★★
BED & BREAKFAST

B&B PER ROOM PER NIGHT
S £30.00–£35.00
D £60.00–£70.00

### The Well

St Andrews Well, Bridport DT6 3DL **t** (01308) 424156 **e** thewellbandb@yahoo.co.uk

**thewellbedandbreakfast.co.uk**

The Well bed and breakfast offers high quality guest accommodation in a relaxed and friendly environment situated less than one mile from the historic market town of Bridport and two miles from the sea at West Bay.

**open** All year
**bedrooms** 1 double, 1 single, 1 family
**bathrooms** 2 en suite, 1 private
**payment** Cash, cheques

Room General P

## Remember to check when booking

Please remember that all information in this guide has been supplied by the proprietors well in advance of publication. Since changes do sometimes occur it's a good idea to check details at the time of booking.

## BRISTOL, City of Bristol Map ref 2A2

★★★
INN

B&B PER ROOM PER NIGHT
S £51.50–£87.50
D £79.00–£109.50

*Fri, Sat, Sun inclusive weekend break – single 3 nights £148, double 3 nights £228.*

### The Bowl Inn and Lilies Restaurant

16 Church Road, Almondsbury, Bristol BS32 4DT **t** (01454) 612757 **e** reception@thebowlinn.co.uk

**thebowlinn.co.uk**

**open** All year
**bedrooms** 10 double, 3 twin
**bathrooms** All en suite
**payment** Credit/debit cards, cash, cheques

Whether travelling on business or just taking a leisurely break, you will find all the comforts of modern life housed in this historic 12thC village inn. Real ales, fine wines, extensive bar fare and a la carte restaurant. Five minutes junction 16, M5.

**SAT NAV** *BS32 4DT*

Room General 4

## BRIXHAM, Devon Map ref 1D2

★★★★
GUEST ACCOMMODATION

B&B PER ROOM PER NIGHT
S £36.00–£40.00
D £64.00–£80.00

*3-day break B&B £108-£114 per person. 7-day break B&B £245-£259 per person.*

### Ranscombe House

Ranscombe Road, Brixham TQ5 9UP **t** (01803) 882337 **e** ranscombe@lineone.net

**ranscombehousehotel.co.uk**

**open** All year except Christmas and New Year
**bedrooms** 5 double, 1 twin, 1 single, 2 family
**bathrooms** All en suite
**payment** Credit/debit cards, cash, cheques, euros

A picturesque turn-of-the-19thC house standing in its own grounds and with garden and ample car park, overlooking Brixham's outer harbour and Torbay. The walk to the harbour and marina is about 300yds. Whatever the time of year, there will be a warm welcome for you.

**SAT NAV** *TQ5 9UP* **ONLINE MAP**

Room General Leisure

## BRIXTON, Devon Map ref 1C3

★★★★
GUEST ACCOMMODATION

B&B PER ROOM PER NIGHT
S £40.00–£45.00
D £55.00–£60.00

### Venn Farm

Brixton, Plymouth PL8 2AX **t** (01752) 880378 **e** info@vennfarm.co.uk

**vennfarm.co.uk**

**open** All year
**bedrooms** 2 double, 2 twin, 1 single
**bathrooms** All en suite
**payment** Credit/debit cards, cash, cheques

A 300-year-old working farm. Enjoy traditional farmhouse bed and breakfast, relax in one of the beautiful new self-contained en suite rooms converted from the original stone barns. Central for coast and country. Off-road parking.

**SAT NAV** *PL8 2AX* **ONLINE MAP**

Room General

## Using map references

Map references refer to the colour maps at the front of this guide.

## BROAD CHALKE, Wiltshire Map ref 2B3

★★★★
BED & BREAKFAST

B&B PER ROOM PER NIGHT
S £25.00–£30.00
D £50.00–£60.00

### Lodge Farmhouse Bed & Breakfast

Lodge Farmhouse, Broad Chalke, Salisbury SP5 5LU **t** (01725) 519242 **e** mj.roe@virgin.net

**lodge-farmhouse.co.uk** GUEST REVIEWS

**open** All year except Christmas and New Year
**bedrooms** 1 double, 2 twin
**bathrooms** All en suite
**payment** Credit/debit cards, cash, cheques

Peaceful brick and flint farmhouse with Wiltshire's finest views overlooking 1,000 square miles of Southern England. Comfortable and welcoming, the perfect tour base for Wessex. Lying on the Ox Drove 'green lane', a paradise for walkers and byway cyclists. For neighbouring nature reserves and archaeological sites see website.

**SAT NAV** *SP5 5LU* **ONLINE MAP**

Room General 12 P Leisure

## BROADCLYST, Devon Map ref 1D2

★★★★
BED & BREAKFAST

B&B PER ROOM PER NIGHT
S £30.00
D £50.00

### Heath Gardens

Broadclyst, Exeter EX5 3HL **t** (01392) 462311 **e** info@heathgardens.co.uk

**heathgardens.co.uk**

**open** All year
**bedrooms** 1 double, 1 twin, 1 family
**bathrooms** All en suite
**payment** Cash, cheques

A 17thC thatched cottage located on the outskirts of a village overlooking open countryside, five miles from the centre of Exeter.

**SAT NAV** *EX5 3HL*

Room General P

## BUDE, Cornwall Map ref 1C2

★★★
GUEST ACCOMMODATION

B&B PER ROOM PER NIGHT
D £56.00–£76.00

*Discounts on bookings of 4 days or more.*

### Beach House

Marine Drive, Widemouth Bay, Bude EX23 0AW **t** (01288) 361256
**e** beachhousebookings@tiscali.co.uk

**beachhousewidemouth.co.uk**

**open** Easter to end of October
**bedrooms** 8 double, 1 twin, 2 family
**bathrooms** All en suite
**payment** Credit/debit cards, cash, cheques

The Wilkins family welcome you to their unique site, with private access onto Widemouth Beach. All bedrooms are en suite, the majority with sundeck balconies. Sun lounge, new bar lounge, on-site post office, shop, surf shop and hire. Restaurant serving traditional Cornish and seafood menus. Outside dining on decked patios.

**SAT NAV** *EX23 0AW*

Room General P Leisure

## Has every property been assessed?

All accommodation in this guide has been rated for quality, or is awaiting assessment, by a professional national tourist board assessor.

## BUDE, Cornwall Map ref 1C2

★★★★
GUEST HOUSE
SILVER AWARD

B&B PER ROOM PER NIGHT
S Min £40.00
D Min £54.00

EVENING MEAL PER PERSON
Min £20.00

*Special 3-night breaks including DB&B and packed lunch – £130. With walking – £150.*

### Harefield Cottage

Upton, Bude EX23 0LY **t** (01288) 352350 **e** sales@coast-countryside.co.uk

**coast-countryside.co.uk** SPECIAL OFFERS • REAL-TIME BOOKING

**open** All year
**bedrooms** 2 double, 1 twin
**bathrooms** All en suite
**payment** Credit/debit cards, cash, cheques

Stone-built cottage with outstanding views. Luxurious and spacious en suite bedrooms, king-size beds and four-poster available. Home cooking our speciality. All diets catered for. Personal attention assured at all times. Only 250yds from the coastal footpath. One mile downhill to the National Cycle network. Hot tub available.

**SAT NAV** *EX23 0LY* **ONLINE MAP**

Room General Leisure

## BUDE, Cornwall Map ref 1C2

★★★★
GUEST ACCOMMODATION
SILVER AWARD

B&B PER ROOM PER NIGHT
D £58.00–£68.00

EVENING MEAL PER PERSON
£14.50–£19.50

### Scadghill Farm

Stibb, Bude EX23 9HN **t** (01288) 352373 **e** scadghillfarm@btconnect.com

**scadghillfarm.co.uk**

A warm welcome awaits you at our 16thC coastal working dairy farm. Delightful en suite rooms with whirlpool bath and showers, Aga-cooked food, comfort and relaxation. Footpath to Sandymouth.

**open** All year
**bedrooms** 1 double, 1 family
**bathrooms** All en suite
**payment** Cash, cheques

Room General Leisure

## BUDE, Cornwall Map ref 1C2

★★★★
GUEST HOUSE

B&B PER ROOM PER NIGHT
S £28.00–£40.00
D £48.00–£60.00

EVENING MEAL PER PERSON
£12.00–£15.00

*Special breaks – stay for 3 nights Oct-Apr and get an extra night free (excl Bank Holidays).*

### Surf Haven

31 Downs View, Bude EX23 8RG **t** (01288) 353923 **e** info@surfhaven.co.uk

**surfhaven.co.uk** GUEST REVIEWS

**open** All year
**bedrooms** 4 double, 2 twin, 3 family
**bathrooms** 7 en suite, 1 private
**payment** Credit/debit cards, cash, cheques

Surf Haven is a warm and friendly guest house. Ideally situated, overlooking the golf course and 200yds from the beach. It is just a short walk to the town with its shops and restaurants. Fresh, locally sourced and organic produce used wherever possible.

**SAT NAV** *EX23 8RG* **ONLINE MAP**

Room General Leisure

CYCLISTS WELCOME

## Fancy a cycling holiday?

For a fabulous freewheeling break, seek out accommodation participating in our Cyclists Welcome scheme. Look out for the symbol and plan your route online at nationalcyclenetwork.org.

## BUDLEIGH SALTERTON, Devon Map ref 1D2

★★★★
GUEST ACCOMMODATION
SILVER AWARD

B&B PER ROOM PER NIGHT
S £38.00–£42.00
D £79.00–£93.00

### Hansard House

3 Northview Road, Budleigh Salterton EX9 6BY **t** (01395) 442773 **e** enquiries@hansardhotel.co.uk

**hansardhousehotel.co.uk**

Adjacent to the World Heritage coastal path and only 400yds from East Devon Golf Club, this small, family-run hotel is ideally situated to enjoy the delights of Budleigh Salterton.

**open** All year
**bedrooms** 3 double, 6 twin, 2 single, 1 family
**bathrooms** All en suite
**payment** Credit/debit cards, cash, cheques, euros

Room General P Leisure

## CALLINGTON, Cornwall Map ref 1C2

★★★★
GUEST HOUSE

B&B PER ROOM PER NIGHT
S £50.00–£55.00
D £70.00–£80.00

EVENING MEAL PER PERSON
£12.95–£24.90

*Romantic DB&B packages, activity weekends for bridge players, walkers, ornithologists etc. Up to 15% discount for groups and long stays.*

### Hampton Manor

Alston, Callington PL17 8LX **t** (01579) 370494 **e** hamptonmanor@supanet.com

**hamptonmanor.co.uk**

**open** All year
**bedrooms** 2 double, 2 twin, 1 family, 1 suite
**bathrooms** 5 en suite, 1 private
**payment** Credit/debit cards, cash, cheques

Small Victorian country-house hotel set in 2.5 acres amidst tranquil countryside bordering Devon. High-quality accommodation (wheelchair access), personal service and home-cooked food (diets catered for). Forty minutes' drive from north and south coasts, historic Plymouth, Dartmoor and Bodmin Moor. The Eden Project and many well-known gardens are also nearby.

**SAT NAV** *PL17 8LX*

Room General P Leisure

## CALLINGTON, Cornwall Map ref 1C2

★★★★
FARMHOUSE

B&B PER ROOM PER NIGHT
S £30.00–£38.00
D £56.00–£64.00

### Higher Manaton

Callington PL17 8PX **t** (01579) 370460 **e** dtrewin@manaton.fsnet.co.uk

**cornwall-devon-bandb.co.uk**

**open** All year except Christmas
**bedrooms** 1 double, 1 twin, 1 family
**bathrooms** 2 en suite, 1 private
**payment** Cash, cheques

Located on the edge of the rolling hills of Bodmin Moor, we offer our guests home-cooked British food on this traditional Cornish working farm. Within easy reach of Cornish beaches and attractions such as the Eden Project and Heligan Gardens. We offer you the opportunity to relax and enjoy Cornwall at its best.

**SAT NAV** *PL17 8PX*

Room General 2 P Leisure

WALKERS WELCOME WALKERS WELCOME

## Do you like walking?

Walkers feel at home in accommodation participating in our Walkers Welcome scheme. Look out for the symbol. Consider walking all or part of a long-distance route – go online at nationaltrail.co.uk.

## CARBIS BAY, Cornwall Map ref 1B3

★★★★
GUEST ACCOMMODATION

B&B PER ROOM PER NIGHT
D £56.00–£76.00

### Beechwood House

St Ives Road, Carbis Bay, St Ives TR26 2SX **t** (01736) 795170
**e** beechwood@carbisbay.wanadoo.co.uk

**open** All year
**bedrooms** 5 double, 1 twin, 2 family
**bathrooms** All en suite
**payment** Credit/debit cards, cash, cheques

Five minutes' walk to sandy beach. Looks out over St Ives Bay. All rooms are en suite. Guests' private lounge, garden and parking. We have golf, fishing, St Michael's Mount and trips to the Isles of Scilly all within easy reach. Courtesy lift from local train or bus stations, when available. Family rates from £75.00.

**SAT NAV** *TR26 2SX*

Room General P Leisure

## CHARD, Somerset Map ref 1D2

★★★★
GUEST ACCOMMODATION

B&B PER ROOM PER NIGHT
S £35.00–£37.00
D £60.00–£65.00

### Ammonite Lodge

43 High Street, Chard TA20 1QL **t** (01460) 63839 **e** info@ammonitelodge.co.uk

**ammonitelodge.co.uk** REAL-TIME BOOKING

Grade II Listed character house in town centre on main A30. Warm welcome with every comfort, only 20 minutes from M5 motorway. Pretty garden and sumptuous breakfast. Parking at rear.

**open** All year except Christmas
**bedrooms** 3 double, 2 twin, 2 single
**bathrooms** 5 en suite, 2 private
**payment** Credit/debit cards, cash

Room General P Leisure

## CHARLTON, Wiltshire Map ref 2B2

★★★★
INN

B&B PER ROOM PER NIGHT
S £79.95
D £89.95

*Please ask for dinner, bed and breakfast rates.*

### Horse & Groom Inn

The Street, Charlton, Malmesbury SN16 9DL **t** (01666) 823904 **e** info@horseandgroominn.com

**horseandgroominn.com** SPECIAL OFFERS · REAL-TIME BOOKING

**open** All year
**bedrooms** 2 double, 1 twin, 2 family
**bathrooms** All en suite
**payment** Credit/debit cards, cash, cheques

The Horse and Groom Inn situated in the small village of Charlton is renowned for its sensational food, stylish bedrooms and glorious surroundings. Alongside its stunning interior there are five beautifully appointed, spacious en suite bedrooms, whilst outside there are extensive grounds including a gorgeous walled garden and separate children's play area.

**SAT NAV** *SN16 9DL* **ONLINE MAP**

Room General P Leisure

## CHARMINSTER, Dorset Map ref 2B3

★★★
INN

B&B PER ROOM PER NIGHT
S £28.00
D £56.00–£60.00

EVENING MEAL PER PERSON
£5.00–£10.00

### Three Compasses Inn

The Square, Charminster, Dorchester DT2 9QT **t** (01305) 263618

Traditional village inn with skittle alley set in village square. Lunch and evening meals provided.

**open** All year except Christmas
**bedrooms** 1 twin, 1 single, 1 family
**bathrooms** 1 en suite
**payment** Cash, cheques

Room General P Leisure

## CHARMOUTH, Dorset Map ref 1D2

★★★★
GUEST ACCOMMODATION

B&B PER ROOM PER NIGHT
D £60.00–£65.00

### Cliffend

Higher Sea Lane, Charmouth, Bridport DT6 6BD **t** (01297) 561047

**cliffend.org.uk**

**open** All year
**bedrooms** 2 double
**bathrooms** All en suite
**payment** Cash, cheques

Chalet bungalow situated in large garden with gate onto coastal path. Two minutes' stroll to beach. Newly refurbished rooms with sitting corner and attractive en suite facilities. Ideal for exploring this beautiful area of Dorset. A warm welcome is guaranteed. Higher price is for one night's stay only.

**SAT NAV** *DT6 6BD*

Room General **P**

## CHEDDAR, Somerset Map ref 1D1

★★
BED & BREAKFAST

B&B PER ROOM PER NIGHT
S £25.00–£30.00
D £50.00–£60.00

### Waterside

Cheddar Road, Axbridge BS26 2DP **t** (01934) 743182 **e** gillianaldridge@hotmail.com

**watersidecheddar.co.uk**

A warm and friendly welcome awaits you. Surrounded by the Mendip hills, ideal for discovering Glastonbury, Wells, Brean, Weston, Wookey Hole, or Cheddar Gorge and show caves. Children and dogs welcome.

**open** All year
**bedrooms** 1 double, 1 twin, 1 family
**bathrooms** All en suite
**payment** Cash, cheques, euros

Room General **P** Leisure

## CHEDDAR, Somerset Map ref 1D1

★★
BED & BREAKFAST

B&B PER ROOM PER NIGHT
S £30.00–£40.00
D £58.00–£60.00

EVENING MEAL PER PERSON
£12.50–£16.50

### Yew Tree Farm

Theale, Wedmore BS28 4SN **t** (01934) 712475 **e** enquiries@yewtreefarmbandb.co.uk

**yewtreefarmbandb.co.uk** SPECIAL OFFERS

17thC farmhouse near Cheddar Gorge, City of Wells, Glastonbury and Wooky Hole. Idyllic walks, fishing, golf and cycle routes. Family rooms, en suite facilities and single supplement. Superb two-/three-course home-cooked meals.

**open** All year
**bedrooms** 1 double, 1 twin, 1 family
**bathrooms** 2 en suite, 1 private
**payment** Cash, cheques, euros

Room General **P** Leisure

## CHELTENHAM, Gloucestershire Map ref 2B1

★★★★
GUEST ACCOMMODATION
SILVER AWARD

B&B PER ROOM PER NIGHT
S £50.00–£65.00
D £75.00–£120.00

*Self-catering studios within hotel also available for vacation and professional lets.*

### Butlers

Western Road, Cheltenham GL50 3RN **t** (01242) 570771 **e** info@butlers-hotel.co.uk

**butlers-hotel.co.uk** GUEST REVIEWS · REAL-TIME BOOKING

**open** All year
**bedrooms** 4 double, 1 twin, 1 single
**bathrooms** All en suite
**payment** Credit/debit cards, cash, cheques

Welcome to Butlers. Our award-winning guesthouse is situated in a central yet quiet area, and just a short stroll to the promenade and the quaint Montpellier district. The rooms are named after well-known butlers from literature and history. Facilities include free Wi-Fi Internet, guest lounge, garden and parking.

**SAT NAV** *GL50 3RN* **ONLINE MAP**

Room General 5 **P** Leisure

For **key to symbols** see page 7

## CHELTENHAM, Gloucestershire Map ref 2B1

★★★★★
GUEST ACCOMMODATION

B&B PER ROOM PER NIGHT
S £70.00–£90.00
D £75.00–£110.00

### Lypiatt House

Lypiatt Road, Cheltenham GL50 2QW **t** (01242) 224994 **e** stay@lypiatt.co.uk

**lypiatt.co.uk**

**open** All year
**bedrooms** 7 double, 3 twin
**bathrooms** All en suite
**payment** Credit/debit cards, cash, cheques, euros

Tastefully decorated and furnished detached Victorian house in own grounds with ample parking. Short walk into town.

**SAT NAV** *GL50 2QW*

Room General P Leisure

## CHELTENHAM, Gloucestershire Map ref 2B1

★★★★
GUEST ACCOMMODATION

B&B PER ROOM PER NIGHT
S £70.00–£89.00
D £70.00–£128.00

### Prestbury House

The Burgage, Prestbury, Cheltenham GL52 3DN **t** (01242) 529533
**e** enquiries@prestburyhouse.co.uk

**prestburyhouse.co.uk** GUEST REVIEWS • SPECIAL OFFERS • REAL-TIME BOOKING

A 300-year-old country manor house set in five acres of grounds, only 1.5 miles from Cheltenham town centre. Outstanding views, four-posters, two-night Cotswold breaks. See photo gallery on our website.

**open** All year except Christmas
**bedrooms** 11 double, 3 twin, 1 single
**bathrooms** All en suite
**payment** Credit/debit cards, cash, cheques, euros

Room General P Leisure

## CHILD OKEFORD, Dorset Map ref 2B3

★★★★★
BED & BREAKFAST
SILVER AWARD

B&B PER ROOM PER NIGHT
S £60.00
D £90.00

EVENING MEAL PER PERSON
£10.00–£30.00

### Manor Barn Bed & Breakfast

Upper Street, Child Okeford DT11 8EF **t** (01258) 860638 **e** carisorby@btinternet.com

**manorbarnbedandbreakfast.co.uk**

**open** All year
**bedrooms** 2 double
**bathrooms** All en suite
**payment** Credit/debit cards, cash, cheques

Ground-floor accommodation in a renovated barn with own entrance into sitting room with wood-burning stove, TV and separate eating area. A light airy corridor leads to two very comfortable and spacious en suite bedrooms. The bedrooms can be made up with either king-size or twin beds.

**SAT NAV** *DT11 8EF*

Room General 8 P

WELCOME PETS! PETS! WELCOME PETS!

## Where is my pet welcome?

Want to take your cherished companion with you on holiday? Proprietors participating in our Welcome Pets! scheme go out of their way to make special provision for you and your pet. Look out for the symbol.

## CHIPPING CAMPDEN, Gloucestershire Map ref 2B1

★★★★
INN

B&B PER ROOM PER NIGHT
s £55.00–£85.00
d £85.00–£125.00

EVENING MEAL PER PERSON
£10.00–£25.00

### The Eight Bells

Church Street, Chipping Campden GL55 6JG **t** (01386) 840371 **e** neilhargreaves@bellinn.fsnet.co.uk

**eightbellsinn.co.uk**

**open** All year except Christmas
**bedrooms** 6 double, 1 single
**bathrooms** All en suite
**payment** Credit/debit cards, cash, cheques

This unspoilt 14thC Cotswold inn features open fires in winter and candle-lit tables all year round. There is a courtyard and terraced beer garden which overlooks the church. All accommodation has recently been refurbished to a high standard, and all bedrooms are en suite. Food is of the very highest standard, and a friendly welcome awaits you.

**SAT NAV** *GL55 6JG*

Room General 10 Leisure

## CHIPPING CAMPDEN, Gloucestershire Map ref 2B1

★★★★
FARMHOUSE

B&B PER ROOM PER NIGHT
s £40.00–£60.00
d £60.00

### Manor Farm

Weston-Subedge, Chipping Campden GL55 6QH **t** (01386) 840390
**e** lucy@manorfarmbnb.demon.co.uk

**manorfarmbnb.demon.co.uk**

Luxury king-size beds, contemporary bathrooms with power showers, in a Cotswold-stone, oak-beamed farmhouse built in 1624. Village pub serves food.

**open** All year
**bedrooms** 2 double, 1 twin
**bathrooms** All en suite
**payment** Credit/debit cards, cash, cheques

Room General P Leisure

## CHOLDERTON, Wiltshire Map ref 2B2

★★★★
GUEST ACCOMMODATION

B&B PER ROOM PER NIGHT
s £54.00–£62.00
d Min £70.00

EVENING MEAL PER PERSON
£8.95–£16.00

### Parkhouse Motel

Cholderton, Salisbury SP4 0EG **t** (01980) 629256

Attractive, family-run, 17thC former coaching inn, five miles east of Stonehenge, ten miles north of Salisbury and seven miles west of Andover.

**open** All year
**bedrooms** 18 double, 6 twin, 6 single, 3 family
**bathrooms** 23 en suite
**payment** Credit/debit cards, cash, cheques, euros

Room General P Leisure

## CIRENCESTER, Gloucestershire Map ref 2B1

★★★★
GUEST ACCOMMODATION

B&B PER ROOM PER NIGHT
s Min £49.50
d Min £64.50

EVENING MEAL PER PERSON
Min £9.00

*Special group discounts are available at weekends. Ideal for clubs and societies.*

### Riverside House

Watermoor Road, Cirencester GL7 1LF **t** (01285) 647642 **e** riversidehouse@mitsubishi-cars.co.uk

**riversidehouse.org.uk** REAL-TIME BOOKING

**open** All year
**bedrooms** 13 double, 11 twin
**bathrooms** All en suite
**payment** Credit/debit cards, cash, cheques

Located 15 minutes' walk from the centre of the historic market town of Cirencester with easy access to and from M4/M5 and the Cotswolds. Riverside House is fully licensed and provides superb bed and breakfast for private and corporate guests. Built in the grounds of Mitsubishi UK headquarters.

**SAT NAV** *GL7 1LF* **ONLINE MAP**

Room General P

## CLOVELLY, Devon Map ref 1C1

★★★★
BED & BREAKFAST

B&B PER ROOM PER NIGHT
S £25.00
D Min £50.00

### Fuchsia Cottage

Higher Clovelly, Clovelly, Bideford EX39 5RR **t** (01237) 431398 **e** tom@clovelly-holidays.co.uk

**clovelly-holidays.co.uk**

Fuchsia Cottage has comfortable, ground and first-floor, en suite accommodation. Surrounded by beautiful views of sea and country. Good walking area. Ample parking.

**open** All year except Christmas
**bedrooms** 1 double, 1 twin, 2 single
**bathrooms** 2 en suite
**payment** Cash, cheques

Room General P Leisure

## COLLINGBOURNE KINGSTON, Wiltshire Map ref 2B2

★★★★
FARMHOUSE

B&B PER ROOM PER NIGHT
S £42.00–£48.00
D £60.00–£69.00

*Pleasure flights from our private airstrip over Wiltshire's ancient places, white horses and crop circles by balloon, aeroplane and helicopter.*

### Manor Farm B&B

Collingbourne Kingston, Marlborough SN8 3SD **t** (01264) 850859 **e** stay@manorfm.com

**manorfm.com** GUEST REVIEWS • SPECIAL OFFERS

**open** All year
**bedrooms** 1 double, 1 twin, 1 family
**bathrooms** 2 en suite, 1 private
**payment** Credit/debit cards, cash, cheques, euros

An attractive, Grade II Listed, period village farmhouse with comfortable and spacious rooms (all en suite/private) on a working family farm. Sumptuous traditional, vegetarian, gluten-free and other special-diet breakfasts. Beautiful countryside with superb walking and cycling from the farm. Horses and pets welcome.

**SAT NAV** *SN8 3SD* **ONLINE MAP**

Room General P Leisure

## COLYTON, Devon Map ref 1D2

★★★★
BED & BREAKFAST
SILVER AWARD

B&B PER ROOM PER NIGHT
S £32.00–£40.00
D £58.00–£60.00

### The Old Bakehouse

Lower Church Street, Colyton EX24 6ND **t** (01297) 552518 **e** france.bakehouse@hotmail.co.uk

**theoldbakehousebandb.co.uk**

A Grade II Listed 400-year-old former bakehouse recently restored. Central but quiet location. En suite accommodation. Guest lounge, restaurant (day and evening), tea garden.

**open** All year
**bedrooms** 3 double, 1 twin, 1 family
**bathrooms** All en suite
**payment** Credit/debit cards, cash, cheques

Room General P Leisure

## COLYTON, Devon Map ref 1D2

★★★★
GUEST ACCOMMODATION
SILVER AWARD

B&B PER ROOM PER NIGHT
S £40.00–£45.00
D £60.00–£70.00

*Short breaks or 'piggy' weekends and 'Introduction to Pig-Keeping' courses available.*

### Smallicombe Farm

Northleigh, Colyton EX24 6BU **t** (01404) 831310 **e** maggie_todd@yahoo.com

**smallicombe.com** SPECIAL OFFERS

**open** All year
**bedrooms** 1 double, 1 twin, 1 family
**bathrooms** All en suite
**payment** Credit/debit cards, cash, cheques

Relax in a really special place, an idyllic rural setting abounding with wildlife, yet close to the coast. Enjoy scrumptious farmhouse breakfasts including prize-winning Smallicombe sausages from our rare-breed pigs. All rooms en suite, overlooking an unspoilt valley landscape. The Garden Suite of sitting room, bedroom and bathroom is wheelchair-accessible.

**SAT NAV** *EX24 6BU* **ONLINE MAP**

Room General P Leisure

## CORFE CASTLE, Dorset Map ref 2B3

★★★
GUEST ACCOMMODATION

B&B PER ROOM PER NIGHT
D £64.00–£78.00

*Off-season special breaks available. Telephone for details.*

### Norden House

Corfe Castle, Wareham BH20 5DS **t** (01929) 480177 **e** nordenhouse@fsmail.net

**nordenhouse.com**

**open** All year except Christmas and New Year
**bedrooms** 5 double, 2 twin, 1 family
**bathrooms** All en suite
**payment** Credit/debit cards, cash, cheques

Former Georgian farmhouse in own surroundings, adjacent to working farm and campsite. At foot of Purbeck Hills in beautiful countryside, half a mile from Corfe Castle – gateway to World Heritage Site. Ideal base for walking, cycling, golf and horse-riding. Six miles from beaches. Separate proprietor accommodation.

**SAT NAV** *BH20 5DS*

Room 🛋 TV ☕ General P ✕ Leisure

## COTSWOLDS

*See under Bibury, Bourton-on-the-Water, Cheltenham, Chipping Campden, Cirencester, Guiting Power, Lechlade-on-Thames, Moreton-in-Marsh, Stow-on-the-Wold, Stroud, Tewkesbury*
*See also Cotswolds in the Central and South East England sections*

## DARTMOOR

*See under Bovey Tracey, Moretonhampstead, Tavistock, Yelverton*

## DARTMOUTH, Devon Map ref 1D3

★★★★
BED & BREAKFAST

B&B PER ROOM PER NIGHT
S £60.00–£65.00
D £60.00–£90.00

*Discounts for stays of 4 days or more.*

### Valley House

46 Victoria Road, Dartmouth TQ6 9DZ **t** (01803) 834045 **e** enquiries@valleyhousedartmouth.com

**valleyhousedartmouth.com** GUEST REVIEWS

**open** All year except Christmas
**bedrooms** 2 double, 1 twin
**bathrooms** All en suite
**payment** Cash, cheques

Receive a warm welcome to Dartmouth from Angela and Martin Cairns-Sharp. Central location, five minutes' walk to River Dart and town centre. Off-road (on-site) parking – a particular advantage in Dartmouth. Well-equipped rooms, lovely breakfasts served in dining room. Britain in Bloom prize winner 2005, 2006 and 2007.

**SAT NAV** *TQ6 9DZ* **ONLINE MAP**

Room TV ☕ General 12 P Leisure

## Country Code always follow the Country Code

- Be safe – plan ahead and follow any signs
- Leave gates and property as you find them
- Protect plants and animals, and take your litter home
- Keep dogs under close control
- Consider other people

## DEVIZES, Wiltshire Map ref 2B2

★★★★
GUEST ACCOMMODATION

B&B PER ROOM PER NIGHT
S Min £36.00
D Min £64.00

*Double en suite at single occupancy rate. Discount for 4 or more consecutive nights.*

### Rosemundy Cottage

London Road, Devizes SN10 2DS **t** (01380) 727122 **e** info@rosemundycottage.co.uk

**rosemundycottage.co.uk** GUEST REVIEWS • SPECIAL OFFERS • REAL-TIME BOOKING

**open** All year
**bedrooms** 2 double, 1 twin, 1 family
**bathrooms** All en suite
**payment** Credit/debit cards, cash, cheques

Canal-side cottage, short walk to Market Place. Fully equipped rooms, include a four-poster and a ground floor room. Sitting room with guides provided. Guest office, free Wi-Fi internet. Garden with barbecue and heated pool in summer. Wiltshire Breakfast, Kennet five-star Food Hygiene, Green Tourism Silver and Fairtrade awards. Off-road parking. Perfect for business or leisure.

**SAT NAV** *SN10 2DS* **ONLINE MAP**

Room General P Leisure

## DINTON, Wiltshire Map ref 2B3

★★★★
BED & BREAKFAST

B&B PER ROOM PER NIGHT
S £40.00–£60.00
D £55.00–£65.00

### Marshwood Farm B&B

Dinton, Salisbury SP3 5ET **t** (01722) 716334 **e** marshwood1@btconnect.com

**marshwoodfarm.co.uk**

**open** All year
**bedrooms** 1 twin, 1 family
**bathrooms** All en suite
**payment** Credit/debit cards, cash, cheques, euros

Beautiful farmhouse dating from the 17thC on working farm, surrounded by fields and woodland. Ideal location for cycling, walking and exploring the Wiltshire countryside, Salisbury, Stonehenge, Bath and many places of interest. Guests are welcome to relax in our garden and use our tennis court.

**SAT NAV** *SP3 5ET*

Room General P Leisure

## DORCHESTER, Dorset Map ref 2B3

★★★
GUEST HOUSE

B&B PER ROOM PER NIGHT
S £40.00–£60.00
D £50.00–£60.00

### Sunrise Guest House

34 London Road, Dorchester DT1 1NE **t** (01305) 262425

**sunriseguesthousedorchester.com**

**open** All year except Christmas and New Year
**bedrooms** 2 double, 1 twin
**bathrooms** All en suite
**payment** Cash, cheques

County town near Thomas Hardy's cottage. Noted for excellent food, comfort and friendly welcome. Off-road parking.

**SAT NAV** *DT1 1NE*

Room General 8 P Leisure

### B&B prices

Rates for bed and breakfast are shown per room per night.
Double room prices are usually based on two people sharing the room.

## DORCHESTER, Dorset Map ref 2B3

★★★★
GUEST ACCOMMODATION
SILVER AWARD

B&B PER ROOM PER NIGHT
S £48.00–£65.00
D £68.00–£85.00

### Yellowham Farm

Yellowham Wood, Dorchester DT2 8RW **t** (01305) 262892 **e** mail@yellowham.freeserve.co.uk

**yellowham.co.uk**

Situated in the heart of Hardy Country on the edge of the idyllic Yellowham Wood in 120 acres of farmland. Excellent base for exploring the Jurassic Coast. Peace and tranquillity guaranteed.

**open** All year
**bedrooms** 2 double, 1 twin, 1 family
**bathrooms** All en suite
**payment** Credit/debit cards, cash, cheques, euros

Room General 4 P Leisure

## DRAKEWALLS, Cornwall Map ref 1C2

★★★
GUEST HOUSE

B&B PER ROOM PER NIGHT
S £30.00–£35.00
D £40.00–£60.00

### Drakewalls House

Gunnislake PL18 9EG **t** (01822) 833617 **e** patsmyth_53@hotmail.com

**drakewallsbedandbreakfast.co.uk**

**open** All year
**bedrooms** 2 double, 1 family
**bathrooms** 1 en suite
**payment** Cash, cheques

Large, comfortable Victorian house with attractive gardens and own parking, set in the heart of the Tamar Valley. Ideal for exploring Dartmoor, Tavistock, Plymouth, etc. Within walking distance of the Tamar Valley railway line. Local produce always on the menu. A warm welcome guaranteed. Satellite TV.

**SAT NAV** *PL18 9EG*

Room General P Leisure

## EAST HARPTREE, Somerset Map ref 2A2

★★★★★
GUEST ACCOMMODATION
SILVER AWARD

B&B PER ROOM PER NIGHT
S £65.00–£75.00
D £80.00–£100.00

EVENING MEAL PER PERSON
£17.50–£25.00

### Harptree Court

East Harptree, Bristol BS40 6AA **t** (01761) 221729 **e** location.harptree@tiscali.co.uk

**harptreecourt.co.uk**

**open** All year except Christmas and New Year
**bedrooms** 2 double, 1 twin
**bathrooms** 2 en suite, 1 private
**payment** Cash, cheques

Harptree Court is a very special family-run B&B in an elegant Georgian setting in amazing gardens. Enjoy a complimentary tea on the lawn or in front of a roaring log fire. Attention to detail is notable in the bedrooms and guest sitting room, and in the welcome given to guests.

**SAT NAV** *BS40 6AA*

Room General 12 P Leisure

**EXETER, Devon Map ref 1D2**

★★★
BED & BREAKFAST

B&B PER ROOM PER NIGHT
S £35.00–£50.00
D £40.00–£60.00

## Culm Vale Country House

Culm Vale, Stoke Canon, Exeter EX5 4EG **t** (01392) 841615 **e** culmvale@hotmail.com

**culmvaleaccommodation.co.uk** REAL-TIME BOOKING

**open** All year
**bedrooms** 1 double, 1 twin, 1 family
**bathrooms** 1 en suite
**payment** Credit/debit cards, cash, cheques

Family-run bed and breakfast offering spacious, comfortable accommodation. Victorian country house set in one acre of garden, 3.5 miles from Exeter city centre. Free parking. Ideal touring base. Convenient for university, moors and coasts.

**SAT NAV** *EX5 4EG*

Room General P Leisure

**EXETER, Devon Map ref 1D2**

★★★★
GUEST ACCOMMODATION

B&B PER ROOM PER NIGHT
S £34.00–£38.00
D £52.00–£58.00

## The Grange

Stoke Hill, Exeter EX4 7JH **t** (01392) 259723 **e** dudleythegrange@aol.com

**open** All year
**bedrooms** 1 double, 1 twin
**bathrooms** All en suite
**payment** Cash, cheques, euros

Country house set in three acres of woodlands, 1.5 miles from the city centre. Ideal for holidays and off-season breaks. All rooms en suite. Off-street parking.

**SAT NAV** *EX4 7JH*

Room General P

**EXETER, Devon Map ref 1D2**

★★★
GUEST ACCOMMODATION

B&B PER ROOM PER NIGHT
S £29.00–£48.00
D £58.00–£70.00

## Park View

8 Howell Road, Exeter EX4 4LG **t** (01392) 271772 **e** enquiries@parkviewexeter.co.uk

**parkviewexeter.co.uk**

Personally managed in a Grade II Listed Georgian town house in a quiet area overlooking Bury Meadow Park. Close to city centre, Exeter University, bus and rail stations.

**open** All year except Christmas
**bedrooms** 7 double, 3 twin, 1 single, 2 family
**bathrooms** 9 en suite, 2 private
**payment** Credit/debit cards, cash, cheques

Room General P

# Check the maps for accommodation locations

Colour maps at the front pinpoint all the cities, towns and villages where you will find accommodation entries in the regional sections. Pick your location and then refer to the place index at the back to find the page number.

## EXETER, Devon Map ref 1D2

★★★★
FARMHOUSE

B&B PER ROOM PER NIGHT
S £45.00–£60.00
D £64.00–£80.00

### Rydon Farm

Woodbury, Exeter EX5 1LB **t** (01395) 232341 **e** sallyglanvill@aol.com

**rydonfarmwoodbury.co.uk** REAL-TIME BOOKING

**open** All year
**bedrooms** 1 double, 1 twin, 1 family
**bathrooms** 2 en suite, 1 private
**payment** Credit/debit cards, cash, cheques, euros

Guests return time and time again to our delightful, 16thC, Devon longhouse set amidst a 450-acre dairy farm, farmed by my husband's family for many generations. Exposed beams and inglenook fireplace. Romantic four-poster. Delicious farmhouse breakfasts using fresh, local produce. Several local pubs and restaurants. Highly recommended.

**SAT NAV** *EX5 1LB*

Room General

## EXETER, Devon Map ref 1D2

★★★
INN

B&B PER ROOM PER NIGHT
S £40.00–£50.00
D £68.50–£85.00

EVENING MEAL PER PERSON
£10.00–£20.00

*DB&B – £60 per person (min 2 people).*

### Thorverton Arms

Thorverton, Exeter EX5 5NS **t** (01392) 860205 **e** info@thethorvertonarms.co.uk

**thethorvertonarms.co.uk** SPECIAL OFFERS · REAL-TIME BOOKING

**open** All year
**bedrooms** 3 double, 1 twin, 1 single, 1 family
**bathrooms** All en suite
**payment** Credit/debit cards, cash, cheques

Traditional English country inn set in the heart of the beautiful village of Thorverton. Situated in the Exe Valley, yet only seven miles from Exeter. Comfortable en suite rooms, bar, award-winning restaurant, large south-facing garden and car park. Ideal touring base for Exmoor, Dartmoor and the Devon coasts.

**SAT NAV** *EX5 5NS* **ONLINE MAP**

Room General Leisure

## EXMOOR

*See under Lynton, Porlock*

## FALMOUTH, Cornwall Map ref 1B3

★★★★
GUEST ACCOMMODATION
SILVER AWARD

B&B PER ROOM PER NIGHT
S £40.00
D £70.00–£80.00

### The Beach House

1 Boscawen Road, Falmouth TR11 4EL **t** (01326) 210407 **e** beachhousefalmouth@hotmail.com

**beachhousefalmouth.co.uk**

A large detached residence set in its own subtropical gardens, The Beach House is in a commanding position overlooking Falmouth Bay with panoramic views towards Pendennis Castle. For those who enjoy a sense of style and calm.

**open** All year
**bedrooms** 3 double
**bathrooms** All en suite
**payment** Cash, cheques

Room General Leisure

FAMILIES WELCOME

## Looking for an ideal family break?

For accommodation offering additional facilities and services for a range of ages and family units, look out for the Families Welcome symbol. Owners of these properties will go out of their way to welcome families.

## FALMOUTH, Cornwall Map ref 1B3

★★★★
GUEST ACCOMMODATION

B&B PER ROOM PER NIGHT
S £42.00–£52.50
D £52.50–£90.00

### Chelsea House

2 Emslie Road, Falmouth TR11 4BG **t** (01326) 212230 **e** info@chelseahousehotel.com

**chelseahousehotel.com**

**open** All year
**bedrooms** 6 double, 1 twin, 1 family
**bathrooms** All en suite
**payment** Credit/debit cards, cash, cheques

Beautifully furnished en suite rooms with panoramic sea views over Falmouth Bay, some with own balcony. Parking. Short walk to town and two minutes' walk to lovely sandy, Blue Flag beach. Quiet location. Sumptuous full English breakfast using local award-winning sausages and Cornish produce.

**SAT NAV** *TR11 4BG*

Room General 7 P

## FORD, Gloucestershire Map ref 2B1

★★★★
INN

B&B PER ROOM PER NIGHT
S Min £40.00
D Min £70.00

EVENING MEAL PER PERSON
£10.00–£18.00

### The Plough

Ford, Temple Guiting, Cheltenham GL54 5RU **t** (01386) 584215 **e** info@theploughinnatford.co.uk

**theploughinnatford.co.uk**

**open** All year
**bedrooms** 1 double, 2 family
**bathrooms** All en suite
**payment** Credit/debit cards, cash, cheques

This quaint cobble-stoned building once used as a hayloft has now been converted to provide separate, comfortable accommodation. The Plough Inn at Ford makes a perfect base for exploring the Cotswolds.

**SAT NAV** *GL54 5RU*

Room General P Leisure

## FOSSEBRIDGE, Gloucestershire Map ref 2B1

★★★★
INN

B&B PER ROOM PER NIGHT
S Min £110.00
D Min £120.00

EVENING MEAL PER PERSON
£25.00–£50.00

*Special linked short breaks with Cheltenham Music, Jazz, Science festivals; also famed Giffords Circus and Royal International Air Tattoo.*

### The Inn at Fossebridge

Cheltenham GL54 3JS **t** (01285) 720721 **e** info@fossebridgeinn.co.uk

**fossebridgeinn.co.uk** REAL-TIME BOOKING

**open** All year
**bedrooms** 4 double, 3 twin, 1 family
**bathrooms** All en suite
**payment** Credit/debit cards, cash, cheques

Fully refurbished Georgian inn, with eight beautiful bedrooms. In four acres of grounds including lake, river, walks. Special Cotswolds short breaks. English-French Cuisine. Near Cirencester.

**SAT NAV** *GL54 3JS* **ONLINE MAP**

Room General P Leisure

### What if I need to cancel?

It's advisable to check the proprietor's cancellation policy at the time of booking in case you have to change your plans.

## FRAMPTON-ON-SEVERN, Gloucestershire Map ref 2B1

★★★★
INN

B&B PER ROOM PER NIGHT
S £40.00–£50.00
D £60.00–£90.00

EVENING MEAL PER PERSON
£5.95–£15.95

### The Bell

The Green, Frampton-on-Severn, Gloucester GL2 7EP **t** (01452) 740346
**e** stay@thebellatframpton.co.uk

**thebellatframpton.co.uk**

**open** All year except Christmas
**bedrooms** 2 double, 2 suites
**bathrooms** All en suite
**payment** Credit/debit cards, cash, cheques

Lying at the top of the largest green in England in the centre of the beautiful village of Frampton. The Bell has recently undergone major refurbishment and transformation and is now a contemporary-designed, welcoming pub and restaurant with gastro food. The rooms are large and well equipped, overlooking the village green.

**SAT NAV** *GL2 7EP*

Room General P Leisure

## GILLINGHAM, Dorset Map ref 2B3

★★
BED & BREAKFAST

B&B PER ROOM PER NIGHT
S £25.00–£35.00
D £50.00–£60.00

### Lyde Hill Farmhouse

Woodville, Stour Provost SP8 5LX **t** (01747) 838483

17thC stone farmhouse – lovely garden and views, good walking on the Hardy Way and Duncliffe Wood. Comfortable south-facing rooms overlooking garden. Mostly organic food. Vegetarians catered for.

**open** All year except Christmas and New Year
**bedrooms** 1 double, 1 twin
**bathrooms** 1 private
**payment** Cash, cheques

Room General 6 P Leisure

## GLASTONBURY, Somerset Map ref 2A2

Rating Applied For
GUEST ACCOMMODATION

B&B PER ROOM PER NIGHT
S £45.00–£75.00
D £60.00–£90.00

### Chindit House

23 Wells Road, Glastonbury BA6 9DN **t** (01458) 830404 **e** peter@chindit-house.co.uk

**chindit-house.co.uk** GUEST REVIEWS

**open** All year except Christmas
**bedrooms** 2 double, 2 single
**bathrooms** All en suite
**payment** Credit/debit cards, cash, cheques, euros

Centrally located, stylish, Gothic stone mansion offering the highest standards of modern luxury, comfort and hospitality. Period furnishings complement new contemporary bathrooms. A spacious guest lounge opens onto a terrace overlooking the croquet lawn in secluded grounds. Romantic, grand doubles and two elegant adjoining singles – all en suite.

**SAT NAV** *BA6 9DN* **ONLINE MAP**

Room General

## Using map references

The map references refer to the colour maps at the front of this guide. The first figure is the map number, the letter and figure that follow indicate the grid reference on the map.

## GLASTONBURY, Somerset Map ref 2A2

★★★★
BED & BREAKFAST

B&B PER ROOM PER NIGHT
D £65.00–£85.00

*B&B may also be available in some of our larger cottages – please call us with your requirements.*

### Mapleleaf Middlewick

Wick Lane, Nr Glastonbury BA6 8JW **t** (01458) 832351 **e** middlewick@btconnect.com

**middlewickholidaycottages.co.uk** REAL-TIME BOOKING

**open** All year
**bedrooms** 1 double, 1 family
**bathrooms** All en suite
**payment** Credit/debit cards, cash, cheques

Enjoy the ease and flexibility of B&B with the comfort of a cottage to yourself. Add to that, Wendy's fabulous breakfasts, an indoor heated swimming pool, steam room, treatment room, Wi-Fi and stunning views to the Mendips. All this is set amongst gardens and paddocks, a walk from Glastonbury Tor.

**SAT NAV** *BA6 8JW*

Room General P Leisure

## GLASTONBURY, Somerset Map ref 2A2

★★★
INN

B&B PER ROOM PER NIGHT
S £35.00–£55.00
D £69.00–£79.00

### Who'd A Thought It Inn

17 Northload Street, Glastonbury BA6 9JJ **t** (01458) 834460 **e** enquiries@whodathoughtit.co.uk

**whodathoughtit.co.uk**

Town-centre located traditional inn; five en suite bedrooms; extensive menus with imaginative flair; restaurant-quality food at pub prices. Excellent real ales. Please phone to reserve rooms.

**open** All year
**bedrooms** 3 double, 2 twin
**bathrooms** All en suite
**payment** Credit/debit cards, cash

Room General P

## GUITING POWER, Gloucestershire Map ref 2B1

★★★★
GUEST HOUSE
SILVER AWARD

B&B PER ROOM PER NIGHT
S Min £42.50
D Min £85.00

EVENING MEAL PER PERSON
Min £32.00

### The Guiting Guest House

Post Office Lane, Guiting Power, Cheltenham GL54 5TZ **t** (01451) 850470
**e** info@guitingguesthouse.com

**guitingguesthouse.com**

Converted 16thC Cotswold-stone farmhouse in centre of delightful village. Dining room with polished elm floor and inglenook fireplace. Some rooms have four-poster beds, all have colour TV and touches of luxury.

**open** All year
**bedrooms** 4 double, 1 twin, 1 single, 1 family
**bathrooms** 5 en suite, 2 private
**payment** Credit/debit cards, cash, cheques

Room General P Leisure

## HALWELL, Devon Map ref 1C3

★★★★★
BED & BREAKFAST
SILVER AWARD

B&B PER ROOM PER NIGHT
D £55.00–£60.00

### Orchard House

Horner, Halwell, Totnes TQ9 7LB **t** (01548) 821448 **e** helen@orchard-house-halwell.co.uk

**orchard-house-halwell.co.uk**

**open** March to November
**bedrooms** 1 double, 1 twin, 1 family
**bathrooms** All en suite
**payment** Cash, cheques

Surrounded by quiet countryside, in a beautiful valley, between Totnes and Kingsbridge, Orchard House offers three wonderfully furnished en suite bedrooms. Also guests' sitting and dining room where breakfasts are served on a large platter using local produce and home-made preserves. Large garden and private parking. Coast 15 minutes.

**SAT NAV** *TQ9 7LB*

Room General 3

## HELSTON, Cornwall Map ref 1B3

★★★
GUEST HOUSE

B&B PER ROOM PER NIGHT
S £38.00–£50.00
D £54.00–£58.00

### Mandeley Guesthouse

Clodgey Lane, Helston TR13 8PJ **t** (01326) 572550 **e** mandeley@btconnect.com

**mandeley.co.uk**

Mandeley is a family-run guesthouse offering accommodation of the highest quality. Centrally located to explore the south-west peninsula. Secure off-road car parking. Bus stop nearby.

**open** All year except Christmas
**bedrooms** 1 double, 1 twin, 1 family
**bathrooms** 2 en suite, 1 private
**payment** Credit/debit cards, cash, cheques

Room General P Leisure

## HEMYOCK, Devon Map ref 1D2

★★★★
FARMHOUSE

B&B PER ROOM PER NIGHT
D £60.00–£80.00

*Discounts on stays of 2 or more days. Telephone or see website for details.*

### Pounds Farm

Hemyock EX15 3QS **t** (01823) 680802 **e** shillingscottage@yahoo.co.uk

**poundsfarm.co.uk** GUEST REVIEWS · SPECIAL OFFERS · REAL-TIME BOOKING

**open** All year
**bedrooms** 1 double
**bathrooms** En suite
**payment** Cash, cheques

17thC stone farmhouse completely surrounded by large gardens, set in Blackdown Hills Area of Outstanding Natural Beauty. Heated outdoor pool. Open log fires. Elegant, spacious bedrooms, en suite with walk-in shower, far-reaching views. Delicious farmhouse breakfasts with free-range eggs, home-made bread, jam and marmalade. Half a mile to village pub. Easy reach of M5/A303.

**SAT NAV** *EX15 3QS* **ONLINE MAP**

Room General P Leisure

## HEYTESBURY, Wiltshire Map ref 2B2

★★★★
BED & BREAKFAST

B&B PER ROOM PER NIGHT
S £55.00–£65.00
D £60.00–£70.00

### The Resting Post

High Street, Heytesbury, Warminster BA12 0ED **t** (01985) 840204 **e** enquiries@therestingpost.co.uk

**therestingpost.co.uk**

Grade II Listed period house offering friendly, comfortable, en suite accommodation in the centre of a delightful village. There are two pubs in the village serving evening meals.

**open** All year except Christmas
**bedrooms** 2 double, 1 twin
**bathrooms** All en suite
**payment** Cash, cheques

Room General 10 Leisure

## HONITON, Devon Map ref 1D2

★★★
FARMHOUSE

B&B PER ROOM PER NIGHT
S £25.00–£30.00
D £50.00–£55.00

EVENING MEAL PER PERSON
£9.00–£13.00

*Reductions on more than one night's stay, and more reductions on weekly stays. Tea and cake on arrival.*

### Lower Luxton Farm

Honiton EX14 9PB **t** (01823) 601269 **e** lwrluxtonfm@hotmail.com

**lowerluxtonfarm.co.uk**

**open** All year
**bedrooms** 1 double, 1 family
**bathrooms** 1 en suite, 1 private
**payment** Cash, cheques

A 17thC working farm. Centre of the Blackdown Hills, overlooking the Otter Valley. Very quiet and peaceful. Ideal touring area, easy reach Sidmouth/Lyme Regis. Village inn one mile. Lovely walks watching the wildlife and seeing the wildflowers. Coarse fishing on farm. Warm welcome, excellent food and friendly family atmosphere.

**SAT NAV** *EX14 9PB*

Room General P Leisure

## ISLES OF SCILLY, Isles of Scilly Map ref 1A3

★★★★
BED & BREAKFAST

B&B PER ROOM PER NIGHT
D £68.00

### Demelza Bed & Breakfast

Demelza, Jackson's Hill, St Marys TR21 0JZ **t** (01720) 422803 **e** sibleysonscilly@tiscali.co.uk

Self-contained, centrally heated, double en suite bedroom and private use of furnished outside decking area.

**open** Easter to November
**bedrooms** 1 double
**bathrooms** En suite
**payment** Cash, cheques

Room General Leisure

## KINGSBRIDGE, Devon Map ref 1C3

★★★
GUEST ACCOMMODATION

B&B PER ROOM PER NIGHT
S £31.50–£40.00
D £53.00–£60.00

### Ashleigh House

Ashleigh Road, Kingsbridge TQ7 1HB **t** (01548) 852893 **e** reception@ashleigh-house.co.uk

**ashleigh-house.co.uk** GUEST REVIEWS

**bedrooms** 5 double, 1 twin, 2 family
**bathrooms** All en suite
**payment** Credit/debit cards, cash, cheques

This relaxed guesthouse is an ideal base for touring the South Devon Area of Outstanding Natural Beauty while having all the amenities of the town a short walk away. We offer a friendly, informal atmosphere. Breakfasts cooked to order. All rooms en suite with colour TV and beverage tray. Sun lounge. Some off-road parking.

**SAT NAV** *TQ7 1HB* **ONLINE MAP**

Room General P Leisure

## LACOCK, Wiltshire Map ref 2B2

★★★★
BED & BREAKFAST
SILVER AWARD

B&B PER ROOM PER NIGHT
S £65.00–£70.00
D £85.00–£90.00

### King John's Hunting Lodge

21 Church Street, Lacock, Chippenham SN15 2LB **t** (01249) 730313 **e** kingjohns@amserve.com

Romantic Grade II Listed property, built c1200, with tearooms and secluded garden, in National Trust village.

**open** All year except Christmas and New Year
**bedrooms** 1 double, 1 family
**bathrooms** All en suite
**payment** Credit/debit cards, cash, cheques

Room General P

## LANREATH-BY-LOOE, Cornwall Map ref 1C2

★★★★
BED & BREAKFAST

B&B PER ROOM PER NIGHT
D £65.00–£70.00

*Discounts for stays of 3 or more nights.*

### Bocaddon Farm

Looe PL13 2PG **t** (01503) 220192 **e** holidays@bocaddon.com

**bocaddon.com**

**open** All year except Christmas and New Year
**bedrooms** 1 double, 1 twin
**bathrooms** All en suite
**payment** Credit/debit cards, cash, cheques

Hidden in the centre of our dairy farm, yet within easy reach of beautiful parts of Cornwall. Enjoy the comfort of a lovely old stone farmhouse along with the luxury of recently converted, en suite bedrooms. Swim in our indoor heated pool, then indulge yourself in a really good farmhouse breakfast.

**SAT NAV** *PL13 2PG*

Room General 5 P Leisure

## LAUNCESTON, Cornwall Map ref 1C2

★★★★
BED & BREAKFAST

B&B PER ROOM PER NIGHT
S £25.00–£27.50
D £50.00–£55.00

### Oakside

South Petherwin, Launceston PL15 7JL **t** (01566) 86733 **e** janet.crossman@tesco.net

**open** All year
**bedrooms** 2 double, 1 twin
**bathrooms** 2 en suite, 1 private
**payment** Cash, cheques

Panoramic views of Bodmin Moor from farm bungalow, nestling peacefully amongst delightful surroundings, conveniently situated one minute from A30. Ideal base for touring Devon and Cornwall. Twenty-five minutes from Eden Project. English breakfasts a speciality with home-made bread and preserves. Warm welcome awaits. Cosy, well-equipped rooms. Ideal place to relax.

**SAT NAV** *PL15 7JL*

Room General P Leisure

## LAUNCESTON, Cornwall Map ref 1C2

★★★★★
BED & BREAKFAST
SILVER AWARD

B&B PER ROOM PER NIGHT
S £70.00–£90.00
D £80.00–£130.00

EVENING MEAL PER PERSON
£10.00–£14.00

*Discounts on stays of 2 or 3 days. Please see website for details.*

### Primrose Cottage

Lawhitton, Launceston PL15 9PE **t** (01566) 773645 **e** enquiry@primrosecottagesuites.co.uk

**primrosecottagesuites.co.uk**

**open** All year
**bedrooms** 2 double, 1 twin
**bathrooms** All en suite
**payment** Credit/debit cards, cash, cheques

Primrose Cottage is set in gardens and woodland leading to the River Tamar. Each luxury suite has its own sitting room, entrance and en suite facilities with beautiful views across the Tamar Valley. Five minutes from the A30 with easy access to both north and south coasts and the moors.

**SAT NAV** *PL15 9PE*

Room General 12 P Leisure

## LAUNCESTON, Cornwall Map ref 1C2

★★★★★
FARMHOUSE
SILVER AWARD

B&B PER ROOM PER NIGHT
D £30.00–£37.50

### Trevadlock Farm

Congdon Shop, Launceston PL15 7PW **t** (01566) 782239 **e** trevadlock@farming.co.uk

**trevadlock.co.uk**

Trevadlock Farm, just 1.5 miles off A30, a Grade II Listed 18thC farmhouse. Pretty en suite rooms, tea tray, hairdryer, TV. Ideal for touring Cornwall and Devon and both coasts.

**open** All year except Christmas and New Year
**bedrooms** 1 double, 1 twin
**bathrooms** All en suite
**payment** Credit/debit cards, cash, cheques

Room General P

## LECHLADE-ON-THAMES, Gloucestershire Map ref 2B1

★★★★
GUEST ACCOMMODATION

B&B PER ROOM PER NIGHT
S £45.00–£65.00
D £55.00–£75.00

### Cambrai Lodge

Oak Street, Lechlade, Lechlade-on-Thames GL7 3AY **t** (01367) 253173
**e** cambrailodge@btconnect.com

**cambrailodgeguesthouse.co.uk**

Friendly, family-run guesthouse, recently modernised, close to River Thames. One bedroom contains a king-size bed and corner bath. Ideal base for touring the Cotswolds. Garden and ample parking.

**open** All year
**bedrooms** 2 double, 2 twin, 1 suite
**bathrooms** All en suite
**payment** Cash, cheques, euros

Room General P Leisure

## LECHLADE-ON-THAMES, Gloucestershire Map ref 2B1

★★★
INN

B&B PER ROOM PER NIGHT
S £40.00–£60.00
D £45.00–£70.00

EVENING MEAL PER PERSON
£10.00–£25.00

### New Inn Hotel

Market Square, Lechlade-on-Thames GL7 3AB **t** (01367) 252296 **e** info@newinnhotel.co.uk

**newinnhotel.co.uk**

The New Inn Hotel is where a 250-year tradition of hospitality blends with 21st century comfort and Cotswold charm. On the banks of River Thames in the centre of Lechlade.

**open** All year except Christmas
**bedrooms** 10 double, 12 twin, 4 single, 2 family
**bathrooms** All en suite
**payment** Credit/debit cards, cash, cheques, euros

Room General P Leisure

## LISKEARD, Cornwall Map ref 1C2

★★★★
FARMHOUSE

B&B PER ROOM PER NIGHT
S £36.00–£40.00
D £52.00–£60.00

### Trecorme Barton

Quethiock, Liskeard PL14 3SH **t** (01579) 342646 **e** david_renfree@btinternet.com

**trecormebarton.co.uk**

Lovely, stone-built farmhouse. Wonderful views, in rolling countryside. En suite room. Near south coast and moors. Close to Eden, Cotehele and Antony House. Relaxing stay assured.

**open** March to October
**bedrooms** 1 double
**bathrooms** En suite
**payment** Cash, cheques

Room TV General 2 P Leisure

## LIZARD, Cornwall Map ref 1B3

★★★★
INN

B&B PER ROOM PER NIGHT
S £50.00–£60.00
D £70.00–£80.00

EVENING MEAL PER PERSON
£7.00–£15.00

### The Top House Inn

The Top House, Helston TR12 7NQ **t** (01326) 290974

**thetophouselizard.co.uk** SPECIAL OFFERS

Britain's most southerly inn, offering eight beautiful en suite bedrooms. After enjoying the breathtaking scenery, relax and let us provide you with excellent home-cooked food, real ales and fine wine.

**open** All year
**bedrooms** 4 double, 2 twin, 2 family
**bathrooms** All en suite
**payment** Credit/debit cards, cash, cheques

Room TV General P Leisure

## LOOE, Cornwall Map ref 1C2

★★★★
FARMHOUSE
SILVER AWARD

B&B PER ROOM PER NIGHT
S £35.00–£50.00
D £59.00–£70.00

### Bucklawren Farm

St Martin, Looe PL13 1NZ **t** (01503) 240738 **e** bucklawren@btopenworld.com

**bucklawren.co.uk**

**open** March to November
**bedrooms** 2 double, 2 twin, 2 family
**bathrooms** All en suite
**payment** Credit/debit cards, cash, cheques

Delightful farmhouse set in glorious countryside with spectacular sea views. Quiet location, situated one mile from the beach and three miles from the fishing village of Looe. An award-winning farm with all bedrooms en suite. Granary Restaurant on-site.

**SAT NAV** *PL13 1NZ*

Room TV General 5 P Leisure

## LOOE, Cornwall Map ref 1C2

★★★★
GUEST HOUSE
SILVER AWARD

B&B PER ROOM PER NIGHT
S £50.00–£60.00
D £60.00–£75.00

*Call, or visit our website for special promotions.*

### Dovers House

St Martins Road, St Martin, Looe PL13 1PB **t** (01503) 265468 **e** twhyte@btconnect.com

**dovershouse.co.uk**

**open** All year except Christmas
**bedrooms** 2 double, 1 twin, 1 family
**bathrooms** All en suite
**payment** Credit/debit cards, cash, cheques

Just a few minutes' drive from Looe harbour, Dovers House is an ideal base for exploring or visiting Cornwall's many attractions and scenic views. Looe is an old fishing port with friendly people and good inns and restaurants. Our accommodation offers twin, double and large family rooms, all with en suite. Comfortably designed to make your stay pleasant and relaxing.

**SAT NAV** *PL13 1PB*

Room General 8 P Leisure

## LYNTON, Devon Map ref 1C1

★★★★
GUEST HOUSE
SILVER AWARD

B&B PER ROOM PER NIGHT
D £50.00–£60.00

EVENING MEAL PER PERSON
£12.00–£15.00

*Beaujolais Nouveau weekend. New Year specials. Gift vouchers. 3-night DB&B.*

### The Denes Guest House

15 Longmead, Lynton EX35 6DQ **t** (01598) 753573 **e** j.e.mcgowan@btinternet.com

**thedenes.com** REAL-TIME BOOKING

**open** All year except Christmas
**bedrooms** 3 double, 2 family
**bathrooms** 4 en suite, 1 private
**payment** Credit/debit cards, cash, cheques

Peacefully located close to the Valley of Rocks, but a short walk to the heart of the village, The Denes is an ideal base to explore Exmoor, whether walking, cycling or driving. Our bedrooms are spacious, all with en suite or private facilities. Freshly cooked breakfasts and evening meals appeal to discerning appetites.

**SAT NAV** *EX35 6DQ* **ONLINE MAP**

Room General P Leisure

## LYNTON, Devon Map ref 1C1

★★★★
FARMHOUSE

B&B PER ROOM PER NIGHT
S Min £30.00
D £29.00–£34.00

EVENING MEAL PER PERSON
£16.50–£18.00

### Higher Bodley Farm

Parracombe EX31 4QN **t** (01598) 763798 **e** higherbodley@hotmail.co.uk

**higherbodleyfarm.co.uk** GUEST REVIEWS · SPECIAL OFFERS

Higher Bodley, 'where Exmoor tradition and luxury meet'. A working farm, with a truly relaxing atmosphere, set in the foothills of Exmoor, close to the stunning coastal path.

**open** All year
**bedrooms** 1 double, 1 twin, 1 suite
**bathrooms** 1 en suite, 2 private
**payment** Cash, cheques

Room SC General P Leisure

## Where can I get help and advice?

Tourist Information Centres offer friendly help with accommodation and holiday ideas as well as suggestions of places to visit and things to do. You'll find contact details at the beginning of each regional section.

**LYNTON, Devon Map ref 1C1**

★★★★
GUEST ACCOMMODATION
SILVER AWARD

B&B PER ROOM PER NIGHT
S £30.00
D £60.00–£65.00

EVENING MEAL PER PERSON
£15.50

## Kingford House

Longmead, Lynton EX35 6DQ **t** (01598) 752361 **e** tricia@kingfordhouse.co.uk

**kingfordhouse.co.uk**

Private hotel close to the Valley of Rocks. Attractive, comfortable rooms, good home-cooked meals with choice of menu. Individual attention assured.

**open** All year
**bedrooms** 3 double, 1 twin, 2 single
**bathrooms** All en suite
**payment** Cash, cheques

Room General 10 P Leisure

**LYNTON, Devon Map ref 1C1**

★★★★
GUEST ACCOMMODATION
SILVER AWARD

B&B PER ROOM PER NIGHT
S £28.00–£35.00
D £54.00–£72.00

## Longmead House

9 Longmead, Lynton EX35 6DQ **t** (01598) 752523 **e** info@longmeadhouse.co.uk

**longmeadhouse.co.uk**

**open** All year except Christmas and New Year
**bedrooms** 4 double, 1 twin, 1 single, 1 family, 1 suite
**bathrooms** All en suite
**payment** Credit/debit cards, cash, cheques

One of Lynton's best-kept secrets! Delightful Victorian house with many original features, quietly situated towards the Valley of Rocks. Beautiful gardens and croquet lawn with ample parking. Comfortable, relaxed atmosphere with warm welcome, excellent hospitality and delicious home cooking. Not to be missed.

**SAT NAV** *EX35 6DQ*

Room General P Leisure

**MALMESBURY, Wiltshire Map ref 2B2**

★★★★
FARMHOUSE

B&B PER ROOM PER NIGHT
S £30.00–£45.00
D £60.00–£70.00

## Manor Farm

Corston, Malmesbury SN16 0HF **t** (01666) 822148 **e** ross@johneavis.wanadoo.co.uk

**manorfarmbandb.co.uk**

Relax and unwind in this award-winning, 17thC Cotswold farmhouse. Ideally situated for visiting the Cotswolds, Bath and Stonehenge. Three miles north of junction 17, M4.

**open** All year except Christmas and New Year
**bedrooms** 2 double, 1 twin, 1 single, 1 family
**bathrooms** 4 en suite, 1 private
**payment** Credit/debit cards, cash, cheques

Room General 12 P

**MARAZION, Cornwall Map ref 1B3**

★★★★
GUEST ACCOMMODATION

B&B PER ROOM PER NIGHT
S £35.00–£70.00

## Rosario

The Square, Marazion TR17 0BH **t** (01736) 711998

**marazion.net**

Recently renovated Victorian house keeping most original features. Ideal for Isles of Scilly, St Michael's Mount, birdwatching or beach holidays. One-minute, level walk to pubs and eateries. Well-behaved dogs welcome.

**open** All year
**bedrooms** 2 double, 1 twin, 1 single
**bathrooms** All en suite
**payment** Cash, cheques

Room General P Leisure

### Looking for a wide range of facilities?

More stars means higher quality accommodation plus a greater range of facilities and services.

## MARKET LAVINGTON, Wiltshire Map ref 2B2

★★★
INN

B&B PER ROOM PER NIGHT
S £30.00–£50.00
D £55.00–£65.00

EVENING MEAL PER PERSON
£6.50–£20.00

WALKERS WELCOME · CYCLISTS WELCOME

### The Green Dragon

26-28 High Street, Market Lavington, Devizes SN10 4AG **t** (01380) 813235
**e** greendragonlavington@tiscali.co.uk

**greendragonlavington.co.uk** REAL-TIME BOOKING

Family-run public house, situated in the heart of the village; comfortable, non-smoking rooms; good home-cooked food. Ideal for walkers and cyclists.

**open** All year
**bedrooms** 1 double, 1 twin, 1 single, 1 family
**bathrooms** 1 en suite
**payment** Credit/debit cards, cash, cheques

Room General Leisure

## MARLBOROUGH, Wiltshire Map ref 2B2

★★★★
BED & BREAKFAST
SILVER AWARD

B&B PER ROOM PER NIGHT
S £32.50–£37.50
D £65.00–£75.00

EVENING MEAL PER PERSON
£15.00–£20.00

*Stay for 3 nights and enjoy a free dinner.*

PETS! WELCOME

### Crofton Lodge

Crofton, Marlborough SN8 3DW **t** (01672) 870328 **e** ali@croftonlodge.co.uk

**croftonlodge.co.uk**

**open** All year except Christmas and New Year
**bedrooms** 1 double, 1 twin, 1 single
**bathrooms** 1 en suite, 1 private
**payment** Cash, cheques

Comfortable, welcoming home with large gardens in hamlet next to Kennet and Avon Canal, Crofton Beam Engines and Savernake Forest. Close to Great Bedwyn and good pubs. Easy reach Marlborough and Hungerford. Excellent base for walkers and cyclists. Home grown or local produce.

**SAT NAV** *SN8 3DW*

Room General 12 Leisure

## MARTOCK, Somerset Map ref 2A3

★★★★
INN

B&B PER ROOM PER NIGHT
S Min £45.00
D Min £62.00

EVENING MEAL PER PERSON
Min £10.25

WALKERS WELCOME · CYCLISTS WELCOME

### The White Hart Hotel

East Street, Martock TA12 6JQ **t** (01935) 822005 **e** enquiries@whitehartthotelmartock.co.uk

**whiteharthotelmartock.co.uk** REAL-TIME BOOKING

Pleasant Hamstone, Grade II Listed coaching inn. Centre of Martock, seven miles from Yeovil and two miles off the A303. Top-class, fresh food served. Real ales, fine wines.

**open** All year except Christmas and New Year
**bedrooms** 5 double, 5 family
**bathrooms** All en suite
**payment** Credit/debit cards, cash, cheques, euros

Room General

## MATCHAMS, Dorset Map ref 2B3

★★★★
BED & BREAKFAST

B&B PER ROOM PER NIGHT
S £40.00–£50.00
D £60.00–£85.00

*Romantic two-night break. Sink into king-sized four-poster bed (satin sheets). Fresh flowers and bottle of bubbly in room.*

### Little Paddock B&B

Hurn Road, Matchams BH24 2BT **t** (01425) 470889 **e** enquiries@little-paddock.com

**little-paddock.com** GUEST REVIEWS · SPECIAL OFFERS · REAL-TIME BOOKING

**open** All year except Christmas
**bedrooms** 2 double, 1 twin
**bathrooms** All en suite
**payment** Credit/debit cards, cash, cheques

Small, luxurious and friendly bed and breakfast accommodation. We are well suited to catering for those looking to get away for rest and relaxation in a beautiful setting. Adults only. We have three double en suite rooms with tea-making facilities and Freeview TV. Swimming pool, sauna and jacuzzi. Near New Forest and Bournemouth beaches.

**SAT NAV** *BH24 2BT* **ONLINE MAP**

Room General Leisure

## MEVAGISSEY, Cornwall Map ref 1B3

★★★★
FARMHOUSE
SILVER AWARD

B&B PER ROOM PER NIGHT
S £32.00–£35.00
D £54.00–£58.00

### Corran Farm B&B

St Ewe, Mevagissey, St Austell PL26 6ER **t** (01726) 842159 **e** info@corranfarm.co.uk

**corranfarm.co.uk**

Quality farmhouse B&B on working farm in open countryside with own farm shop. Farm adjoins Heligan Gardens. Choice of delicious breakfast, beautiful walks, beaches, inns. Ideal for exploring Cornwall.

**open** February to November
**bedrooms** 2 double, 1 twin
**bathrooms** All en suite
**payment** Cash, cheques

Room General P

## MEVAGISSEY, Cornwall Map ref 1B3

★★★★
FARMHOUSE

B&B PER ROOM PER NIGHT
S £25.00–£30.00
D £50.00–£60.00

EVENING MEAL PER PERSON
£15.00–£18.00

### Tregilgas Farm

Gorran, St Austell PL26 6ND **t** (01726) 842342 **e** Dclemes88@aol.com

**tregilgasfarmbedandbreaksfast.co.uk**

Tregilgas Farm is central for touring. The spectacular Heligan Gardens and Eden Project are within easy reach. A warm welcome. Local produce used for breakfast.

**open** All year except Christmas and New Year
**bedrooms** 2 double, 1 twin
**bathrooms** 2 en suite, 1 private
**payment** Cash, cheques

Room General 3 P Leisure

## MILTON ABBAS, Dorset Map ref 2B3

★★★
BED & BREAKFAST

B&B PER ROOM PER NIGHT
S Min £35.00
D Min £70.00

### The Old Bank

56-57 The Street, Milton Abbas, Blandford Forum DT11 0BP **t** (01258) 880520
**e** annieaskew@yahoo.co.uk

**theoldbankmiltonabbas.co.uk**

**open** All year except Christmas and New Year
**bedrooms** 1 double, 1 single
**bathrooms** All en suite
**payment** Cheques

The Old Bank is a thatched 18thC cottage in the heart of the historic village of Milton Abbas. The cottage offers two newly refurbished bedrooms with en suites. We have superb Dorset countryside all around. Ideal for walking or for sightseeing. Heritage Coast only 15 miles away.

**SAT NAV** *DT11 0BP*

Room General P

## MILTON DAMEREL, Devon Map ref 1C2

★★★★
FARMHOUSE

B&B PER ROOM PER NIGHT
S £25.00–£32.00
D £50.00–£64.00

EVENING MEAL PER PERSON
£15.00–£20.00

### Buttermoor Farm

Milton Damerel, Holsworthy EX22 7PB **t** (01409) 261314 **e** info@buttermoorfarm.co.uk

**buttermoorfarm.co.uk**

Rediscover tranquillity. With comfortable en suite rooms, real food, gorgeous gardens and a warm welcome.

**open** All year
**bedrooms** 1 double, 1 twin
**bathrooms** All en suite
**payment** Cash, cheques

Room General P Leisure

## What shall we do today?

For ideas on places to visit, see the beginning of this regional section or go online at enjoyengland.com.

## MORETON-IN-MARSH, Gloucestershire Map ref 2B1

★★★★
FARMHOUSE

B&B PER ROOM PER NIGHT
S £35.00–£45.00
D £55.00–£59.00

### Fosseway Farm B&B

Stow Road, Moreton-in-Marsh GL56 0DS **t** (01608) 650503

Fosseway Farm is just a five-minute walk into Moreton-in-Marsh town. All rooms en suite with TV, hairdryer and refreshments. Residents' lounge, conservatory breakfast room. Individual tables.

**open** All year
**bedrooms** 1 double, 2 twin, 1 family
**bathrooms** All en suite
**payment** Credit/debit cards, cash, cheques

Room General 1 P Leisure

## MORETON-IN-MARSH, Gloucestershire Map ref 2B1

★★★
FARMHOUSE

B&B PER ROOM PER NIGHT
S Min £40.00
D Min £60.00

### New Farm

Dorn, Moreton-in-Marsh GL56 9NS **t** (01608) 650782 & 07811 646320
**e** catherinerighton@btinternet.com

**newfarmbandb.co.uk**

Old Cotswold farmhouse. Lovely large bedrooms, one with four-poster. Breakfast served with hot, crispy bread. Impressive fireplace in dining room. Ideal for touring the Cotswolds.

**open** All year
**bedrooms** 2 double, 1 twin
**bathrooms** All en suite
**payment** Cash, cheques

Room General 8 Leisure

## MORETON-IN-MARSH, Gloucestershire Map ref 2B1

★★★
FARMHOUSE

B&B PER ROOM PER NIGHT
S £45.00–£65.00
D £65.00–£80.00

*Discounts available for stays of 3 nights or more.*

### Old Farm

Dorn, Moreton-in-Marsh GL56 9NS **t** (01608) 650394 **e** info@oldfarmdorn.co.uk

**oldfarmdorn.co.uk** REAL-TIME BOOKING

**open** All year except Christmas
**bedrooms** 2 double, 1 twin
**bathrooms** All en suite
**payment** Credit/debit cards, cash, cheques

'Comfortable beds, friendly hosts and great breakfasts'. A working farm, the house dates back to the 15th century with spacious en suite bedrooms (including four-poster), guest lounge and large gardens. Local breakfast served with home-produced eggs and Old Spot sausages and bacon. Peaceful, rural location but only one mile from Moreton-in-Marsh.

**SAT NAV** *GL56 9NS*

Room General P Leisure

## MORETON-IN-MARSH, Gloucestershire Map ref 2B1

★★★★
GUEST HOUSE

B&B PER ROOM PER NIGHT
S £45.00
D £60.00–£65.00

### Treetops

London Road, Moreton-in-Marsh GL56 0HE **t** (01608) 651036 **e** treetops1@talk21.com

**treetopscotswolds.co.uk**

**open** All year except Christmas
**bedrooms** 4 double, 2 twin
**bathrooms** All en suite
**payment** Credit/debit cards, cash, cheques

Family guesthouse on the A44, set in 0.5 acres of secluded gardens. Five minutes' walk from the village centre.

**SAT NAV** *GL56 0HE*

Room General P Leisure

For **key to symbols** see page 7

## MORETONHAMPSTEAD, Devon Map ref 1C2

★★★★
FARMHOUSE

B&B PER ROOM PER NIGHT
S £40.00–£42.00
D £64.00–£76.00

### Great Sloncombe Farm

Moretonhampstead, Newton Abbot TQ13 8QF **t** (01647) 440595
**e** hmerchant@sloncombe.freeserve.co.uk

**greatsloncombefarm.co.uk**

13thC farmhouse in a magical Dartmoor valley. Meadows, woodland, wild flowers and animals. Farmhouse breakfast with freshly baked bread. Everything provided for an enjoyable break.

**open** All year
**bedrooms** 2 double, 1 twin
**bathrooms** All en suite
**payment** Credit/debit cards, cash, cheques

Room General 8 Leisure

## MORETONHAMPSTEAD, Devon Map ref 1C2

★★★★
GUEST ACCOMMODATION

B&B PER ROOM PER NIGHT
S £30.00–£40.00
D £60.00–£66.00

### Great Wooston Farm

Moretonhampstead, Newton Abbot TQ13 8QA **t** (01647) 440367 & 07798 670590
**e** info@greatwoostonfarm.com

**greatwoostonfarm.com**

Great Wooston is a peaceful haven with views across the moor and walks nearby. Two rooms en suite, one with four-poster. Excellent breakfast. Quality accommodation.

**open** All year
**bedrooms** 2 double, 1 twin
**bathrooms** 2 en suite, 1 private
**payment** Credit/debit cards, cash, cheques

Room General 8 P Leisure

## MORETONHAMPSTEAD, Devon Map ref 1C2

★★★
GUEST ACCOMMODATION

B&B PER ROOM PER NIGHT
S £22.00
D £44.00

EVENING MEAL PER PERSON
£10.00

### Little Wooston Farm

Moretonhampstead, Newton Abbot TQ13 8QA **t** (01647) 440551 **e** jeannecuming@btinternet.com

Friendly, family-run farm on outskirts of picturesque moorland village of Moretonhampstead, which is centrally situated for many Dartmoor walks. Good home-cooking. Children and pets welcome.

**open** All year
**bedrooms** 1 double, 1 single, 1 family
**payment** Cash, cheques

Room General P Leisure

## MORWENSTOW, Cornwall Map ref 1C2

★★★
INN

B&B PER ROOM PER NIGHT
S Min £46.00
D Min £78.00

EVENING MEAL PER PERSON
£8.00–£16.50

### The Bush Inn

The Bush Inn Crosstown, Morwenstow, Bude EX23 9SR **t** (01288) 331242

**bushinn-morwenstow.co.uk**

**open** All year
**bedrooms** 1 double, 2 twin
**bathrooms** All en suite
**payment** Credit/debit cards, cash, cheques

Visit our historic inn situated just off the South West Coast Path. We offer sympathetically refurbished rooms with some of the most breathtaking views in Cornwall. Open all day. We offer delicious meals freshly prepared from seasonal local produce including beef from our own farm and locally caught seafood.

**SAT NAV** *EX23 9SR*

Room General P Leisure

## B&B prices

Rates for bed and breakfast are shown per room per night.
Double room prices are usually based on two people sharing the room.

## MULLION, Cornwall Map ref 1B3

★★★★
GUEST ACCOMMODATION

B&B PER ROOM PER NIGHT
S £34.00–£40.00
D £60.00–£68.00

*5% discount for 3 nights.*

### Trenance Farmhouse

Mullion, Helston TR12 7HB **t** (01326) 240639 **e** info@trenancefarmholidays.co.uk

**trenancefarmholidays.co.uk** GUEST REVIEWS • SPECIAL OFFERS

**open** March to October
**bedrooms** 3 double, 1 twin
**bathrooms** All en suite
**payment** Credit/debit cards, cash, cheques

Welcome to our Victorian farmhouse, set in mature gardens on the outskirts of the village and only half a mile from picturesque Mullion Cove and beaches. A footpath crosses fields to the coast offering magnificent views. Bedrooms are all en suite; relax in our guest lounge; enjoy breakfast in the garden room.

**SAT NAV** *TR12 7HB*

Room General P Leisure

## NETHER STOWEY, Somerset Map ref 1D1

★★★★★
GUEST ACCOMMODATION
SILVER AWARD

B&B PER ROOM PER NIGHT
S £42.00–£92.00
D £104.00–£142.00

EVENING MEAL PER PERSON
£16.00–£24.00

### Castle of Comfort Country House

Dodington, Nether Stowey, Bridgwater TA5 1LE **t** (01278) 741264
**e** reception@castle-of-comfort.co.uk

**castle-of-comfort.co.uk** REAL-TIME BOOKING

16thC country house and restaurant nestling in the Quantock Hills with four acres of grounds. Luxurious accommodation of the highest standard.

**open** All year except Christmas and New Year
**bedrooms** 3 double, 1 twin, 1 single, 1 family
**bathrooms** All en suite
**payment** Credit/debit cards, cash, cheques

Room General P
Leisure

## NEWQUAY, Cornwall Map ref 1B2

★★
GUEST ACCOMMODATION

B&B PER ROOM PER NIGHT
S Min £24.00
D Min £48.00

### Chichester Interest Holidays

14 Bay View Terrace, Newquay TR7 2LR **t** (01637) 874216 **e** sheila.harper@virgin.net

**http://freespace.virgin.net/sheila.harper**

Comfortable, licensed, convenient for shops, beaches and gardens. Showers in most bedrooms, many extras. Walking, mineral collecting, archaeology and Cornish Heritage holidays in spring and autumn.

**open** March to October
**bedrooms** 3 double, 2 twin, 1 single, 1 family
**payment** Cash, cheques

Room General 2 P

## NEWQUAY, Cornwall Map ref 1B2

★★★
BED & BREAKFAST

B&B PER ROOM PER NIGHT
S £35.00–£40.00
D £50.00–£70.00

### Surfside B&B

35 Mount Wise, Newquay TR7 2BH **t** (01637) 872707 & 07813 330609
**e** surfsidehotel@btconnect.com

**surfsidenewquay.co.uk**

All en suite accommodation, car park, close to town, beaches, restaurants, clubs and bars. Small groups by prior arrangement only. No stag parties.

**open** All year except Christmas
**bedrooms** 4 double, 4 twin, 1 family
**bathrooms** All en suite
**payment** Credit/debit cards, cash, cheques

Room General P Leisure

## Do you have access needs?

Look for the National Accessible Scheme symbols if you have special hearing, visual or mobility needs.

## PADSTOW, Cornwall Map ref 1B2

★★★★
BED & BREAKFAST

B&B PER ROOM PER NIGHT
D £75.00–£85.00

### Garslade Guest House

52 Church Street, Padstow PL28 8BG **t** (01841) 533804 **e** garsladeguest@btconnect.com

**garslade.com**

High-standard bed and breakfast accommodation with en suite bedrooms, including one four-poster, in the old part of Padstow.

**open** All year except Christmas and New Year
**bedrooms** 4 double
**bathrooms** All en suite
**payment** Cash, cheques

Room General Leisure

## PAIGNTON, Devon Map ref 1D2

★★★★
GUEST ACCOMMODATION

B&B PER ROOM PER NIGHT
S £20.00–£25.00
D £40.00–£50.00

EVENING MEAL PER PERSON
£5.00–£10.00

### Cliveden

27 Garfield Road, Paignton TQ4 6AX **t** (01803) 557461 **e** ros.mager@btconnect.com

**clivedenguesthouse.co.uk**

Family-run guesthouse, close to all amenities, coach/rail stations, town, theatre, own car park, 100yds level walk seafront.

**open** All year
**bedrooms** 3 double, 1 twin, 1 single, 1 family
**bathrooms** 4 en suite, 2 private
**payment** Credit/debit cards, cash, cheques

Room General P Leisure

## PAIGNTON, Devon Map ref 1D2

★★★
GUEST HOUSE

B&B PER ROOM PER NIGHT
S £20.00–£24.00
D £42.00–£50.00

EVENING MEAL PER PERSON
Min £11.00

### Rockview Guest House

13 Queens Road, Paignton TQ4 6AT **t** (01803) 556702 **e** rockview@blueyonder.co.uk

**rockview.co.uk** REAL-TIME BOOKING

Rockview is a clean and friendly, family-run guesthouse within a level, short walk of the seafront, shops and stations.

**open** All year except Christmas
**bedrooms** 3 double, 2 twin, 1 single, 1 family
**bathrooms** 6 en suite, 1 private
**payment** Credit/debit cards, cash, cheques

Room General 2 P Leisure

## PAR, Cornwall Map ref 1B3

★★★★
INN

B&B PER ROOM PER NIGHT
S £40.00–£55.00
D £55.00–£70.00

EVENING MEAL PER PERSON
£8.50–£15.00

### The Royal Inn

66 Eastcliffe Road, Par PL24 2AJ **t** (01726) 815601 **e** info@royal-inn.co.uk

**royal-inn.co.uk**

Completely refurbished in 2003, The Royal offers excellent en suite accommodation at an affordable price. Four miles from Eden, close to bus and rail links, licensed bar and restaurant on site.

**open** All year except Christmas and New Year
**bedrooms** 9 double, 6 twin, 1 suite
**bathrooms** All en suite
**payment** Credit/debit cards, cash, cheques

Room General P Leisure

## PENSFORD, Somerset Map ref 2A2

★★
GUEST ACCOMMODATION

B&B PER ROOM PER NIGHT
S £27.00–£33.00
D £54.00–£66.00

WALKERS WELCOME · CYCLISTS WELCOME

### Green Acres

Stanton Wick, Pensford, Bristol BS39 4BX **t** (01761) 490397

A friendly welcome awaits you in a peaceful setting, off the A37/A368. Relax and enjoy panoramic views across Chew Valley to Dundry Hills.

**open** All year
**bedrooms** 1 double, 1 twin, 2 single, 1 family
**bathrooms** 1 en suite
**payment** Cash, cheques, euros

Room General P Leisure

## PENZANCE, Cornwall Map ref 1A3

★★★
GUEST ACCOMMODATION

B&B PER ROOM PER NIGHT
S £30.00
D £60.00

EVENING MEAL PER PERSON
Min £16.50

### Cornerways Guest House

5 Leskinnick Street, Penzance TR18 2HA **t** (01736) 364645 **e** enquiries@cornerways-penzance.co.uk

**penzance.co.uk/cornerways**

Cornerways is an attractively decorated townhouse, four minutes from car parks, bus and railway stations. We offer freshly cooked breakfast to order, and evening meal is optional. Ideal as a base for touring Cornwall.

**open** All year except Christmas
**bedrooms** 1 double, 1 twin, 2 single
**bathrooms** All en suite
**payment** Credit/debit cards, cash, cheques

Room General Leisure

## PENZANCE, Cornwall Map ref 1A3

★★★
FARMHOUSE

B&B PER ROOM PER NIGHT
S Min £28.00
D Min £56.00

EVENING MEAL PER PERSON
Min £12.00

### Menwidden Farm

Ludgvan, Penzance TR20 8BN **t** (01736) 740415 **e** coramenwidden@tiscali.co.uk

**open** March to October
**bedrooms** 4 double, 1 twin
**bathrooms** 3 en suite
**payment** Cash, cheques

Quiet farmhouse set in countryside with views towards St Michael's Mount. Centrally situated in West Cornwall. Land's End, St Ives, Lizard Peninsula and Penzance Heliport all within easy reach. Good home-cooking.

**SAT NAV** *TR20 8BN*

Room General **P** Leisure

## PENZANCE, Cornwall Map ref 1A3

★★★★★
GUEST ACCOMMODATION
GOLD AWARD

B&B PER ROOM PER NIGHT
D £95.00–£125.00

EVENING MEAL PER PERSON
£25.00–£33.00

*Special midweek breaks in early and late season.*

### The Summer House

Cornwall Terrace, Penzance TR18 4HL **t** (01736) 363744 **e** reception@summerhouse.cornwall.com

**summerhouse-cornwall.com** SPECIAL OFFERS

**open** March to October
**bedrooms** 4 double, 1 twin
**bathrooms** All en suite
**payment** Credit/debit cards, cash

Boutique B&B and two-rosette restaurant by the sea. Set in a beautiful listed building, this individually designed hotel has frequently been featured in glossy magazines in the UK and Europe. With just five bedrooms, there is a friendly, intimate atmosphere where guests unwind in the lovely public rooms and tropical walled garden.

**SAT NAV** *TR18 4HL* **ONLINE MAP**

Room General **P** Leisure

## PENZANCE, Cornwall Map ref 1A3

★★★
GUEST ACCOMMODATION

B&B PER ROOM PER NIGHT
D £46.00–£56.00

### Wymering

Regent Square, Penzance TR18 4BG **t** (01736) 362126 **e** pam@wymering.com

**wymering.com**

Small, select guesthouse situated in a peaceful Regency square, just off the beach. Town centre, promenade, bathing pool, bus, coach and train station all nearby.

**open** All year
**bedrooms** 1 double, 1 twin, 1 family, 2 suites
**bathrooms** 2 en suite, 3 private
**payment** Credit/debit cards, cash, cheques

Room General Leisure

For **key to symbols** see page 7

## PERRANPORTH, Cornwall Map ref 1B2

★★★★
GUEST HOUSE

B&B PER ROOM PER NIGHT
S £33.00–£40.00
D £66.00–£80.00

EVENING MEAL PER PERSON
£10.50–£15.00

### Tides Reach

Ponsmere Road, Perranporth TR6 0BW **t** (01872) 572188 **e** jandf.boyle@virgin.net

**tidesreachhotel.com** SPECIAL OFFERS

Charming, older style, family-run guesthouse close to shops and one minute from the beach. Dinner, bed and breakfast, and licensed bar. Private garden. Ideal base for touring Cornwall.

**open** All year except Christmas and New Year
**bedrooms** 5 double, 2 twin, 1 single, 1 family
**bathrooms** 8 en suite
**payment** Credit/debit cards, cash, cheques, euros

Room General 5 P Leisure

## PERRANPORTH, Cornwall Map ref 1B2

★★★★
INN

B&B PER ROOM PER NIGHT
S £48.00–£55.00
D £58.00–£65.00

EVENING MEAL PER PERSON
£6.95–£13.95

### The Whitehouse Inn & Luxury Lodge

Penhallow, Nr Truro, St Agnes TR4 9LQ **t** (01872) 573306 **e** whitehouseinn@btconnect.com

**whitehousecornwall.co.uk** GUEST REVIEWS

Extremely high quality en suite accommodation comprising family, disabled, double, single, twin rooms. Facilities include play areas, bar and restaurant.

**open** All year
**bedrooms** 6 double, 2 twin, 3 family, 1 suite
**bathrooms** All en suite
**payment** Credit/debit cards

Room General P Leisure

## PLYMOUTH, Devon Map ref 1C2

★★★★
GUEST ACCOMMODATION

B&B PER ROOM PER NIGHT
S £30.00–£42.00
D £44.00–£56.00

### Athenaeum Lodge

4 Athenaeum Street, The Hoe, Plymouth PL1 2RQ **t** (01752) 665005 & (01752) 670090
**e** us@athenaeumlodge.com

**athenaeumlodge.com** SPECIAL OFFERS • REAL-TIME BOOKING

**open** All year except Christmas and New Year
**bedrooms** 3 double, 2 twin, 1 single, 3 family
**bathrooms** 7 en suite
**payment** Credit/debit cards, cash, cheques

Elegant, Grade II Listed guesthouse, ideally situated on The Hoe. Centrally located for the Barbican, Theatre Royal, Plymouth Pavilions, ferry port and the National Marine Aquarium. The city centre and university are a few minutes' walk. Divers' and sailors' paradise. Excellent, central location for touring Devon and Cornwall. Wi-Fi Internet and free use of computer if required.

**SAT NAV** *PL1 2RQ* **ONLINE MAP**

Room General 5 P Leisure

## PLYMOUTH, Devon Map ref 1C2

★★★★
GUEST ACCOMMODATION

B&B PER ROOM PER NIGHT
S £40.00–£50.00
D £60.00–£70.00

### Berkeleys of St James

4 St James Place East, Plymouth PL1 3AS **t** (01752) 221654 **e** enquiry@onthehoe.co.uk

**onthehoe.co.uk**

Non-smoking Victorian town house ideally situated for seafront, Barbican, theatres, ferry port and city centre. Flexible accommodation between double/twin/triple. Excellent breakfast serving free-range, organic produce where possible.

**open** All year except Christmas and New Year
**bedrooms** 2 double, 1 twin, 1 single, 1 family
**bathrooms** 4 en suite, 1 private
**payment** Credit/debit cards, cash, cheques

Room General P

## What do the star ratings mean?

Detailed information about star ratings can be found at the back of this guide.

## PLYMOUTH, Devon Map ref 1C2

★★★★
GUEST ACCOMMODATION
SILVER AWARD

B&B PER ROOM PER NIGHT
S £46.00–£48.00
D £68.00

*Special weekend breaks Nov-Mar inclusive. Prices on application.*

### The Bowling Green

9-10 Osborne Place, Plymouth PL1 2PU **t** (01752) 209090 **e** info@bowlingreenhotel.com

**bowlingreenhotel.com** GUEST REVIEWS

**open** All year
**bedrooms** 8 double, 1 single, 3 family
**bathrooms** All en suite
**payment** Credit/debit cards, cash, cheques

Opposite Drake's bowling green, this elegant Victorian establishment has superbly appointed bedrooms offering all modern facilities. Our friendly and efficient staff will make your stay a memorable one. Centrally situated for the Barbican, Theatre Royal, leisure/conference centre, ferry port, National Marine Aquarium, with Dartmoor only a few minutes away.

**SAT NAV** *PL1 2PU*

Room General Leisure

## PLYMOUTH, Devon Map ref 1C2

★★★★
GUEST HOUSE

B&B PER ROOM PER NIGHT
S £30.00–£40.00
D £45.00–£55.00

### Brittany Guest House

28 Athenaeum Street, The Hoe, Plymouth PL1 2RQ **t** (01752) 262247
**e** enquiries@brittanyguesthouse.com

**brittanyguesthouse.co.uk**

**open** All year except Christmas and New Year
**bedrooms** 4 double, 2 twin, 2 single, 2 family
**bathrooms** All en suite
**payment** Credit/debit cards, cash, cheques, euros

Non-smoking, all rooms en suite, some 5ft beds, crisp white linen. Private car park, close to shops, bars, pavilions, seafront. Credit and debit cards taken. Run by resident proprietors.

**SAT NAV** *PL1 2RQ* **ONLINE MAP**

Room General 3 P

## PLYMOUTH, Devon Map ref 1C2

★★★★
GUEST HOUSE

B&B PER ROOM PER NIGHT
S £31.00–£46.00
D £47.00–£62.00

### Four Seasons

207 Citadel Road East, Plymouth PL1 2JF **t** (01752) 223591 **e** f.seasons@btconnect.com

**fourseasonsguesthouse.co.uk**

A non-smoking establishment, the Four Seasons is situated in the centre of an elegant Victorian terrace close to the Hoe and Barbican.

**open** All year
**bedrooms** 5 double, 2 twin
**bathrooms** 5 en suite, 2 private
**payment** Credit/debit cards, cash, cheques

Room General

## PLYMOUTH, Devon Map ref 1C2

★★★
FARMHOUSE

B&B PER ROOM PER NIGHT
S £23.00–£27.00
D £46.00–£50.00

EVENING MEAL PER PERSON
Min £12.00

### Gabber Farm

Gabber Lane, Down Thomas, Plymouth PL9 0AW **t** (01752) 862269 **e** gabberfarm@tiscali.co.uk

A courteous welcome at this farm, near coast and Mount Batten Centre. Lovely walks. Special weekly rates, especially for Senior Citizens and children. Directions provided.

**open** All year
**bedrooms** 1 double, 1 twin, 1 single, 2 family
**bathrooms** 3 en suite
**payment** Credit/debit cards, cash, cheques

Room General P Leisure

## POLZEATH, Cornwall Map ref 1B2

★★★★
GUEST HOUSE

B&B PER ROOM PER NIGHT
D £60.00–£80.00

### White Heron

Polzeath, Wadebridge PL27 6TJ **t** (01208) 863623 **e** info@whiteheronhotel.co.uk

**whiteheronhotel.co.uk**

Family-run, non-smoking, licensed establishment, 500yds from beaches. TV and tea-/coffee-making facilities in bedrooms. All rooms en suite.

**open** May to October
**bedrooms** 5 double
**bathrooms** All en suite
**payment** Credit/debit cards, cash, cheques

Room General

## PORLOCK, Somerset Map ref 1D1

★★★★
GUEST ACCOMMODATION

B&B PER ROOM PER NIGHT
S £55.00
D £80.00

EVENING MEAL PER PERSON
£28.00

### Glen Lodge

Hawkcombe, Minehead TA24 8LN **t** (01643) 863371 **e** glenlodge@gmail.com

**glenlodge.net**

Historic Victorian house with welcoming rooms, scrumptious food and views of the sea, woods and Exmoor. Ideal for exploring, relaxing, activities and more.

**open** All year except Christmas and New Year
**bedrooms** 4 double, 1 twin
**bathrooms** 1 en suite, 2 private
**payment** Cash, cheques

Room General 8 Leisure

## PORT ISAAC, Cornwall Map ref 1B2

★★★★
INN

B&B PER ROOM PER NIGHT
S £50.00–£65.00
D £70.00–£90.00

EVENING MEAL PER PERSON
£15.00–£25.00

### Cornish Arms

Pendoggett, Port Isaac PL30 3HH **t** (01208) 880263 **e** info@cornisharms.com

**cornisharms.com**

A 16thC coaching inn near to the North Cornish coast. Traditional homely pub serving fresh, home-cooked food. Daily specials board. Real ales. Close to many golf clubs and coastal path.

**open** All year
**bedrooms** 4 double, 3 family
**bathrooms** 6 en suite, 1 private
**payment** Credit/debit cards, cash, euros

Room General Leisure

## PORT ISAAC, Cornwall Map ref 1B2

★★★★
INN

B&B PER ROOM PER NIGHT
S £75.00–£110.00
D £95.00–£140.00

EVENING MEAL PER PERSON
£12.00–£30.00

*Special out-of-season breaks available – DB&B and 3 nights' B&B for the price of 2.*

### The Slipway

Harbour Front, Port Isaac PL29 3RH **t** (01208) 880264 **e** slipway@portisaachotel.com

**portisaachotel.com**

**open** All year except Christmas
**bedrooms** 7 double, 1 twin, 2 suites
**bathrooms** All en suite
**payment** Credit/debit cards, cash, cheques, euros

The Slipway Hotel is a small, friendly, family-run inn of great character. Bedrooms are stylishly furnished and many overlook the harbour. Guests can combine their stay with the delights of one of the area's finest seafood restaurants. Menus are highly imaginative, concentrating on the use of the best, locally sourced fresh fish, meat and produce.

**SAT NAV** *PL29 3RH*

Room General Leisure

## Using map references

Map references refer to the colour maps at the front of this guide.

## PORTLAND, Dorset Map ref 2B3

★★
GUEST ACCOMMODATION

B&B PER ROOM PER NIGHT
S £25.00–£45.00
D £50.00–£70.00

### Alessandria House

71 Wakeham Easton, Portland DT5 1HW **t** (01305) 822270

**open** All year
**bedrooms** 6 double, 2 twin, 3 single, 4 family
**bathrooms** 11 en suite, 1 private
**payment** Credit/debit cards, cash, cheques, euros

Friendly, good old-fashioned personal service and good value. Under the same management for 19 years, highly commended by our guests. With 15 bedrooms, two on the ground floor, and four spacious en suite family rooms. Some rooms with sea view. Quiet, desirable location. Vegetarians catered for. Free parking.

**SAT NAV** *DT5 1HW*

Room General Leisure

## PORTLAND, Dorset Map ref 2B3

★★★
BED & BREAKFAST

B&B PER ROOM PER NIGHT
D Min £54.00

### Brackenbury House

Fortuneswell, Portland DT5 1LP **t** (01305) 826509 **e** enquiries@brackenburyhouse.co.uk

**brackenburyhouse.co.uk**

Comfortable and friendly, family-run, converted manse, close to shops and eating places. Great area for sailing, diving, fishing, and also for walkers, cyclists and bird/butterfly spotters.

**open** All year except Christmas
**bedrooms** 3 double, 2 twin
**bathrooms** 3 en suite
**payment** Cash, cheques

Room General Leisure

## QUEEN CAMEL, Somerset Map ref 2A3

★★★★
GUEST ACCOMMODATION

B&B PER ROOM PER NIGHT
S £45.00–£50.00
D £60.00–£70.00

### Dairy Court

Wales, Queen Camel, Nr Yeovil BA22 7PA **t** (01935) 850003 **e** enquiries@dairycourt.com

**dairycourt.com**

A small, comfortable bed and breakfast off the beaten track, but easily accessible. Close to many lovely walks and pubs.

**open** All year
**bedrooms** 1 double, 1 single
**bathrooms** 1 en suite, 1 private
**payment** Cash, cheques

Room General P Leisure

## REDRUTH, Cornwall Map ref 1B3

★★★★
GUEST HOUSE

B&B PER ROOM PER NIGHT
S Min £38.00
D Min £56.00

EVENING MEAL PER PERSON
£12.50–£15.00

### Goonearl Cottage

Wheal Rose, Scorrier, Redruth TR16 5DF **t** (01209) 891571 **e** goonearl@onetel.com

**goonearlcottage.com** REAL-TIME BOOKING

**open** All year
**bedrooms** 4 double, 1 twin, 1 family, 1 suite
**bathrooms** 5 en suite, 2 private
**payment** Credit/debit cards, cash, cheques, euros

Family-run guesthouse; beaches close by; easy access to the whole of Cornwall; superb English breakfast.

**SAT NAV** *TR16 5DF* **ONLINE MAP**

Room General P Leisure

## RUAN HIGH LANES, Cornwall Map ref 1B3

★★★★
FARMHOUSE

B&B PER ROOM PER NIGHT
D £50.00–£60.00

### New Gonitor Farm

Ruan High Lanes, Truro TR2 5LE **t** (01872) 501345 **e** rosemary@newgonitorfarm.wanadoo.co.uk

Farmhouse B&B, rural location. Close to Eden and Heligan. Full English breakfast, tea and coffee, TV in all rooms.

**open** All year except Christmas and New Year
**bedrooms** 1 double, 1 twin
**bathrooms** All en suite
**payment** Cash, cheques

Room General P Leisure

## RUAN HIGH LANES, Cornwall Map ref 1B3

★★★
FARMHOUSE

B&B PER ROOM PER NIGHT
S £28.00–£40.00
D £56.00–£60.00

*Discounts for stays of 4 or more nights for children and for family rooms.*

### Trenona Farm Holidays

Ruan High Lanes, Truro TR2 5JS **t** (01872) 501339 **e** info@trenonafarmholidays.co.uk

**trenonafarmholidays.co.uk** REAL-TIME BOOKING

**open** March to November
**bedrooms** 1 double, 3 family
**bathrooms** 3 en suite, 1 private
**payment** Credit/debit cards, cash, cheques

Enjoy a warm welcome in our Victorian farmhouse on a working farm on the beautiful Roseland Peninsula. Our guest bedrooms have en suite or private bathrooms, and we welcome children and pets. Public footpaths lead to Veryan and the south coast (three miles).

**SAT NAV** *TR2 5JS* **ONLINE MAP**

Room General P Leisure

## RUDFORD, Gloucestershire Map ref 2B1

★★★★
GUEST ACCOMMODATION

B&B PER ROOM PER NIGHT
S Min £42.00
D Min £60.00

EVENING MEAL PER PERSON
£12.50–£15.00

### The Dark Barn Lodge

Barbers Bridge, Rudford, Gloucester GL2 8DX **t** (01452) 790412 **e** info@barbersbridge.co.uk

**barbersbridge.co.uk** GUEST REVIEWS · SPECIAL OFFERS · REAL-TIME BOOKING

**open** All year
**bedrooms** 15 double, 2 family, 1 suite
**bathrooms** All en suite
**payment** Credit/debit cards, cash, cheques

Family-run establishment, new accommodation, in quiet, rural setting. Ample floodlit parking. Internet access, complimentary use of gym and swimming pool during stay.

**SAT NAV** *GL2 8DX* **ONLINE MAP**

Room General P Leisure

## ST AGNES, Cornwall Map ref 1B3

★★★
FARMHOUSE

B&B PER ROOM PER NIGHT
S £27.50–£30.00
D £55.00–£60.00

PETS! WELCOME

### Little Trevellas Farm

Trevellas, St Agnes TR5 0XX **t** (01872) 552945 **e** velvetcrystal@xln.co.uk

A 250-year-old house on a working farm on the B3285 provides a peaceful, comfortable base for a holiday that will appeal to lovers of both coast and countryside.

**open** All year
**bedrooms** 1 double, 1 twin, 1 single
**bathrooms** All en suite
**payment** Cash, cheques

Room General P

### Has every property been assessed?

All accommodation in this guide has been rated for quality, or is awaiting assessment, by a professional national tourist board assessor.

## ST AGNES, Cornwall Map ref 1B3

★★
GUEST HOUSE

B&B PER ROOM PER NIGHT
S £22.50–£42.50
D £35.00–£55.00

EVENING MEAL PER PERSON
Min £15.00

### Penkerris

Penwinnick Road, St Agnes TR5 0PA **t** (01872) 552262 **e** info@penkerris.co.uk

**penkerris.co.uk**

**open** All year
**bedrooms** 2 double/single, 2 double/twin
**bathrooms** All en suite
**payment** Credit/debit cards, cash, cheques, euros

Penkerris is a creeper-clad Edwardian residence with a lawned garden and parking. A 'home from home' offering real food, comfortable bedrooms with all facilities (four en suite) and cosy lounge (log fires in winter). Licensed. Dramatic cliff walks and three really beautiful beaches one kilometre away. Excellent surfing, riding and gliding nearby.

**SAT NAV** *TR5 0PA*

Room General P Leisure

## ST AUSTELL, Cornwall Map ref 1B3

★★★★★
GUEST ACCOMMODATION
GOLD AWARD

B&B PER ROOM PER NIGHT
S £85.00–£120.00
D £110.00–£150.00

EVENING MEAL PER PERSON
£23.00

### Anchorage House

Nettles Corner, Boscundle, St Austell PL25 3RH **t** (01726) 814071 **e** info@anchoragehouse.co.uk

**anchoragehouse.co.uk** REAL-TIME BOOKING

**bedrooms** 2 double, 2 suites
**bathrooms** All en suite
**payment** Credit/debit cards, cash, cheques

Luxurious, national award-winning lodge with the warmth and feel of a small, private country hotel. Candlelit suppers, indoor swimming and leisure complex, huge beds, exquisite bathroom suites. In the heart of Cornwall, just minutes to the Eden Project, beach, Heligan Gardens, Fowey and Bodmin Moor. Attention to detail, elegance, comfort and flair are evident everywhere.

**SAT NAV** *PL25 3RH* **ONLINE MAP**

Room SC General 16 P Leisure

## ST AUSTELL, Cornwall Map ref 1B3

★★★★★
GUEST ACCOMMODATION
GOLD AWARD

B&B PER ROOM PER NIGHT
S £95.00–£145.00
D £110.00–£190.00

EVENING MEAL PER PERSON
Min £45.00

### Highland Court Lodge

Biscovey Road, Biscovey PL24 2HW **t** (01726) 813320 **e** enquiries@highlandcourt.co.uk

**highlandcourt.co.uk**

**open** All year
**bedrooms** 1 double, 2 twin, 1 family, 1 suite
**bathrooms** All en suite
**payment** Credit/debit cards, cash, cheques, euros

Taste of the West Gold Award 2007, Les Routiers Gold, South-West Regional Winner 2007. Idyllic, luxurious family-run country hotel with stunning views over St Austell Bay, and within walking distance of Eden Project. Two acres of beautifully landscaped grounds. Impressively equipped en suite bedrooms, lounge with deep sofas, terrace with fine views.

**SAT NAV** *PL24 2HW*

Room General P Leisure

## Where are the maps?

Colour maps can be found at the front of the guide. They pinpoint the location of all accommodation found in the regional sections.

## ST COLUMB MAJOR, Cornwall Map ref 1B2

★★★★★
FARMHOUSE
SILVER AWARD

B&B PER ROOM PER NIGHT
S £30.00–£32.00
D £60.00–£64.00

EVENING MEAL PER PERSON
£15.00–£20.00

### Pennatillie Farm

Talskiddy, St Columb Major TR9 6EF **t** (01637) 880280 **e** angelacolgrove@btconnect.com

**cornish-riviera.co.uk/pennatilliefarm.htm**

**open** March to October
**bedrooms** 2 double, 1 twin
**bathrooms** All en suite
**payment** Credit/debit cards, cash, cheques

Family dairy farm set in 450 acres of beautiful countryside. Spacious, well-appointed, en suite guest bedrooms, including a stunning four-poster (super-king-size) bedroom. Eden, the Lost Gardens of Heligan and National Trust properties are all nearby. Excellent choice on breakfast menu. Warm welcome guaranteed.

**SAT NAV** *TR9 6EF*

Room General P Leisure

## ST IVES, Cornwall Map ref 1B3

★★★★
GUEST ACCOMMODATION

B&B PER ROOM PER NIGHT
S £35.00–£80.00
D £60.00–£82.00

### Anchorage Guest House

5 Bunkers Hill, St Ives TR26 1LJ **t** (01736) 797135 **e** info@theanchoragebandb.co.uk

**theanchoragebandb.co.uk**

Built c1730, The Anchorage is located in one of the most picturesque cobbled streets in St Ives. Guests will enjoy superb breakfasts and comfortable rooms full of character. Early booking advisable.

**open** All year
**bedrooms** 3 double, 1 family
**bathrooms** 3 en suite, 1 private
**payment** Credit/debit cards, cash, cheques

Room General

## ST IVES, Cornwall Map ref 1B3

★★★★
GUEST ACCOMMODATION

B&B PER ROOM PER NIGHT
S £30.00–£55.00
D £60.00–£80.00

### Chy An Gwedhen

St Ives Road, Carbis Bay, St Ives TR26 2JN **t** (01736) 798684 **e** info@chyangwedhen.com

**chyangwedhen.com** GUEST REVIEWS

**open** All year except Christmas
**bedrooms** 3 double, 1 twin, 1 family
**bathrooms** All en suite
**payment** Credit/debit cards, cash, cheques

Gill and Mike Douglas welcome you to Chy An Gwedhen, a haven for non-smokers. Award-winning B&B, comfortable, en suite rooms, delicious choice of breakfasts. Private car park, adjacent to coastal footpath leading to Carbis Bay and St Ives' gorgeous beaches. Tate, Barbara Hepworth, wonderful restaurants within walking distance. Relaxing holiday destination.

**SAT NAV** *TR26 2JN*

Room General P Leisure

## Place index

If you know where you want to stay, the index by place name at the back of the guide will give you the page number listing accommodation in your chosen town, city or village. Check out the other useful indexes too.

## ST IVES, Cornwall Map ref 1B3

# The Grey Mullet

**GUEST HOUSE**

One of the best known and friendliest guest houses in the old fishing and artists' quarter of St Ives. Situated only 20 yards from the harbour, beaches, car parks, restaurants, pubs, shops and art galleries including the Tate Gallery and Barbara Hepworth Museum. The house though modernised to a high standard retains its "olde worlde" charm. Some private parking available. All major credit cards accepted.

**For brochure please write to:**
**Ken Weston, 2 Bunkers Hill, St Ives TR26 1LJ**
**or telephone: (01736) 796635 Email: greymulletguesthouse@lineone.net**
**www.touristnetuk.com/sw/greymullet**

## ST JUST IN ROSELAND, Cornwall Map ref 1B3

★★★★
BED & BREAKFAST

B&B PER ROOM PER NIGHT
D £80.00–£85.00

### Roundhouse Barns

Truro TR2 5JJ **t** (01872) 580038 **e** info@roundhousebarnholidays.co.uk

**roundhousebarnholidays.co.uk**

**open** All year except Christmas and New Year
**bedrooms** 2 double
**bathrooms** All en suite
**payment** Credit/debit cards, cash, cheques

Beautifully converted 17thC barn in peaceful surroundings on the Roseland Peninsula. Instant access to walks by Fal river. St Just in Roseland church with its subtropical gardens and the picturesque harbour of St Mawes are both nearby. Delightful rooms with luxury bedding. Locally sourced breakfasts. All guests welcomed with complimentary home-made Cornish cream tea.

**SAT NAV** *TR2 5JJ*

Room General 16 P Leisure

## ST MAWES, Cornwall Map ref 1B3

★★★
FARMHOUSE

B&B PER ROOM PER NIGHT
S £27.00
D £54.00

### Trenestral Farm

Ruan High Lanes, Truro TR2 5LX **t** (01872) 501259

A 200-year-old, tastefully converted barn on a mixed, family-run working farm situated on the peaceful Roseland Peninsula. All rooms en suite. Children and pets welcome.

**open** March to October
**bedrooms** 2 double, 1 twin
**bathrooms** All en suite
**payment** Cash, cheques

Room General P

## ST MAWGAN, Cornwall Map ref 1B2

★★★★
GUEST ACCOMMODATION

B&B PER ROOM PER NIGHT
S £55.00–£60.00
D £80.00–£85.00

EVENING MEAL PER PERSON
£19.50

### Dalswinton House

St Mawgan-in-Pydar, Nr Padstow TR8 4EZ **t** (01637) 860385 **e** dalswintonhouse@tiscali.co.uk

**dalswinton.com**

A former farmhouse standing in eight acres of grounds, specialising in holidays for dogs and their owners. Dog-friendly beach and coastal path 1.5 miles. Good food cooked with local ingredients.

**open** March to October
**bedrooms** 5 double, 3 twin
**bathrooms** All en suite
**payment** Credit/debit cards, cash, cheques, euros

Room General P Leisure

## What if I need to cancel?

It's advisable to check the proprietor's cancellation policy at the time of booking in case you have to change your plans.

**ST MINVER, Cornwall Map ref 1B2**

★★★
BED & BREAKFAST

B&B PER ROOM PER NIGHT
S Max £25.00
D £50.00–£65.00

## Tredower Barton

St Minver, Wadebridge PL27 6RG **t** (01208) 813501

Tredower Barton is a farm bed and breakfast set in beautiful countryside near the North Cornish coast. Good food assured.

**open** Easter to October
**bedrooms** 1 twin, 1 family
**bathrooms** All en suite
**payment** Cash, cheques

Room General P

**SALISBURY, Wiltshire Map ref 2B3**

★★
GUEST HOUSE

B&B PER ROOM PER NIGHT
S £40.00–£50.00
D £55.00–£75.00

*Special rates for extended stays of 3 weeks or more out of season. Also 4 nights for the price of 3 Oct-Apr.*

## Alabare House

15 Tollgate Road, Salisbury SP1 2JA **t** (01722) 340206 **e** bookings@alabare.org

**alabare.org** REAL-TIME BOOKING

**open** All year except Christmas
**bedrooms** 2 double, 6 twin, 2 single, 1 family
**bathrooms** 5 en suite, 1 private
**payment** Credit/debit cards, cash, cheques

This is a small oasis in the heart of Salisbury with ample off-road parking. Established as a small retreat centre, the venue is a good choice for a holiday break. There are many local places of interest, and Salisbury offers a wide variety of restaurants and shops. Online booking available.

**SAT NAV** *SP1 2JA* **ONLINE MAP**

Room TV General P Leisure

**SALISBURY, Wiltshire Map ref 2B3**

★★
BED & BREAKFAST

B&B PER ROOM PER NIGHT
S £50.00–£55.00
D £65.00–£70.00

*Reduction for stays of 3 or more nights.*

## Burcombe Manor

Burcombe Lane, Burcombe, Salisbury SP2 0EJ **t** (01722) 744288
**e** nickatburcombemanor@btinternet.com

**burcombemanor.co.uk**

**open** All year
**bedrooms** 2 double, 1 twin
**bathrooms** 2 en suite, 1 private
**payment** Credit/debit cards, cash, cheques

Burcombe Manor is set in the Nadder Valley four miles west of Salisbury. The house, built in 1865, has large, oak-floor hall, oak banisters, centrally heated bedrooms, most en suite. Guests have their own sitting room in which to plan their day. Local base to explore Wilton, Salisbury and the surrounding area.

**SAT NAV** *SP2 0EJ*

Room TV General P Leisure

## SALISBURY, Wiltshire Map ref 2B3

★★★
GUEST HOUSE

B&B PER ROOM PER NIGHT
S £39.00–£60.00
D £55.00–£75.00

### Byways House

31 Fowlers Road, Salisbury SP1 2QP **t** (01722) 328364 **e** info@bywayshouse.co.uk

**bywayshouse.co.uk**

**open** All year except Christmas and New Year
**bedrooms** 8 double, 7 twin, 4 single, 4 family
**bathrooms** 19 en suite
**payment** Credit/debit cards, cash

Attractive, large, Victorian guesthouse in quiet location alongside the city centre/restaurants. Free car parking on site. Licensed drinks lounge. Clean and comfortable en suite rooms. Special rates for long stays. Wi-Fi internet access.

**SAT NAV** *SP1 2QP*

Room General Leisure

## SALISBURY, Wiltshire Map ref 2B3

★★★
BED & BREAKFAST

B&B PER ROOM PER NIGHT
S £40.00–£45.00
D £50.00

### Highveld

44 Hulse Road, Salisbury SP1 3LY **t** (01722) 338172 **e** y.sfakianos@btopenworld.com

**salisburybedandbreakfast.com**

**open** All year
**bedrooms** 1 suite
**bathrooms** En suite
**payment** Cash, cheques

A ten-minute walk from the city centre along the River Avon to a creative home and cheerful welcome. Lovely cottage garden, quiet locality with great breakfasts and proper coffee! Upstairs sitting room with computer, TV, DVDs and videos. German, Flemish and Afrikaans spoken.

**SAT NAV** *SP1 3LY*

Room General

## SALISBURY, Wiltshire Map ref 2B3

★★★★
FARMHOUSE

B&B PER ROOM PER NIGHT
D £60.00–£65.00

*Reduction for stays of 3 or more nights.*

### Manor Farm

Burcombe Lane, Burcombe, Salisbury SP2 0EJ **t** (01722) 742177
**e** suecombes@manorfarmburcombe.fsnet.co.uk

**manorfarmburcombebandb.com**

**open** 1 March to 1 December
**bedrooms** 1 double, 1 twin
**bathrooms** All en suite
**payment** Credit/debit cards, cash, cheques

A comfortable farmhouse, warm and attractively furnished, on 1,400-acre mixed farm in a quiet, pretty village 0.25 miles off A30, west of Salisbury. Ideal base for touring this lovely area. Nearby attractions include Wilton House, Salisbury and Stonehenge. Wonderful walks, good riding. Pub with good food nearby.

**SAT NAV** *SP2 0EJ*

Room General Leisure

**Where can I get live travel information?**
For the latest travel update – call the RAC on 1740 from your mobile phone.

## SALISBURY, Wiltshire Map ref 2B3

★★★★
BED & BREAKFAST

B&B PER ROOM PER NIGHT
S £40.00–£55.00
D £55.00–£80.00

### The Old Rectory Bed & Breakfast

75 Belle Vue Road, Salisbury SP1 3YE **t** (01722) 502702 **e** stay@theoldrectory-bb.co.uk

**theoldrectory-bb.co.uk**

Victorian rectory in quiet street, a short walk from the heart of Salisbury and convenient for all attractions. Warm, welcoming atmosphere and well-appointed rooms. A relaxing bolthole. Wi-Fi internet.

**open** All year except Christmas and New Year
**bedrooms** 1 double, 1 twin, 1 single
**bathrooms** 2 en suite, 1 private
**payment** Cash, cheques

Room General 10 P Leisure

## SALISBURY PLAIN

*See under Market Lavington, Salisbury, Winterbourne Stoke*

## SAMPFORD PEVERELL, Devon Map ref 1D2

★★★★
FARMHOUSE

B&B PER ROOM PER NIGHT
D Max £60.00

### Leonard Moor House

Leonard Moor, Nr Sampford Peverell, Tiverton EX16 7EL **t** (01884) 820881 & 07813 618607
**e** sue.quick1@btinternet.com

**leonardhousebbaccommodation.com**

**open** All year
**bedrooms** 1 double, 2 twin
**bathrooms** 2 en suite, 1 private
**payment** Cash, cheques

Comfortable en suite accommodation five minutes from Tiverton Parkway station, M5 and North Devon Link Road. A traditional Devon farmhouse set in the small hamlet of Leonard Moor, near Sampford Peverell, Tiverton. Each room with en suite, tea/coffee and Freeview. Our farmhouse is cosy and well-appointed with four-course breakfasts using local produce.

**SAT NAV** *EX16 7EL*

Room General P Leisure

## SEATON, Devon Map ref 1D2

★★★★
GUEST HOUSE

B&B PER ROOM PER NIGHT
S £45.00–£55.00
D £60.00–£75.00

### Beaumont

Castle Hill, Seaton EX12 2QW **t** (01297) 20832 **e** jane@lymebay.demon.co.uk

**smoothhound.co.uk/hotels/beaumon1.html**

**open** All year except Christmas and New Year
**bedrooms** 2 double, 2 twin, 1 family
**bathrooms** All en suite
**payment** Cash, cheques

Select, Victorian, seafront, family guesthouse on World Heritage Coast. Two minutes' walk from town. Excellent walks, country parks, attractions and sporting facilities. Unrivalled views over Lyme Bay. Limited parking.

**SAT NAV** *EX12 2QW*

Room General P Leisure

enjoyEngland.com Gold AWARD

## Gold and Silver Awards

Gold and Silver Awards are given to establishments achieving the highest levels of quality and service. You can find more information at the front of the guide, and an index to all accommodation achieving these awards at the back.

enjoyEngland.com Silver AWARD

## SHAFTESBURY, Dorset Map ref 2B3

★★★★
GUEST HOUSE
SILVER AWARD

B&B PER ROOM PER NIGHT
S Min £45.00
D £75.00–£84.00

### The Retreat

47 Bell Street, Shaftesbury SP7 8AE **t** (01747) 850372 **e** info@the-retreat.org.uk

**the-retreat.org.uk**

Perfectly positioned in a quiet street, this Georgian townhouse has light and airy, individually furnished, en suite bedrooms with TV and complimentary tray. Off-road parking. 2005 winner of 'Best B&B in North Dorset'.

**open** All year
**bedrooms** 4 double, 1 twin, 1 single, 4 family
**bathrooms** All en suite
**payment** Credit/debit cards, cash, cheques

Room General P

## SHAVE CROSS, Dorset Map ref 1D2

★★★★
INN
GOLD AWARD

B&B PER ROOM PER NIGHT
S £90.00–£110.00
D Min £160.00

EVENING MEAL PER PERSON
£11.95–£28.00

### Shave Cross Inn

Bridport DT6 6HW **t** (01308) 868358 **e** roy.warburton@virgin.net

**theshavecrossinn.co.uk** GUEST REVIEWS • SPECIAL OFFERS

New luxury boutique hotel and 14thC inn in the Marshwood Vale, West Dorset, three miles from the Jurassic Coast.

**open** All year
**bedrooms** 5 double, 1 twin, 1 suite
**bathrooms** All en suite
**payment** Credit/debit cards, cash, cheques

Room General P Leisure

## SHERBORNE, Dorset Map ref 2B3

★★★★
BED & BREAKFAST

B&B PER ROOM PER NIGHT
D £55.00–£68.00

### The Alders

Sandford Orcas, Sherborne DT9 4SB **t** (01963) 220666 **e** jonsue@thealdersbb.com

**thealdersbb.com**

**open** All year
**bedrooms** 1 double, 1 twin, 1 family
**bathrooms** All en suite
**payment** Cash, cheques, euros

Secluded stone house set in old walled garden, in picturesque conservation village near Sherborne. The house is tastefully furnished, with original watercolour paintings and hand-made pottery. There is a wood-burning fire in lounge inglenook fireplace. Good breakfasts served around large farmhouse table. Excellent food available in traditional, friendly village pub.

**SAT NAV** *DT9 4SB*

Room General Leisure

## SHERBORNE, Dorset Map ref 2B3

★★★
BED & BREAKFAST

B&B PER ROOM PER NIGHT
S Min £30.00
D £50.00–£60.00

### Honeycombe View

Lower Clatcombe, Sherborne DT9 4RH **t** (01935) 814644 **e** honeycombower@talktalk.net

Delightful rural location within walking distance of Sherborne. Two comfortable en suite rooms, one in new annexe with views. Covered parking. Walkers welcome, drying facilities available.

**open** All year except Christmas and New Year
**bedrooms** 2 twin
**bathrooms** All en suite
**payment** Cash, cheques

Room General 6 P Leisure

**Looking for a wide range of facilities?**
More stars means higher quality accommodation plus a greater range of facilities and services.

## SHERBORNE, Dorset Map ref 2B3

★★★★
BED & BREAKFAST

B&B PER ROOM PER NIGHT
S £50.00–£60.00
D £65.00–£82.00

### The Pheasants B&B

24 Greenhill, Sherborne DT9 4EW **t** (01935) 815252 **e** info@thepheasants.com

**thepheasants.com**

A 300-year-old town house in the heart of historic Sherborne, a short walk from the abbey and castles. Elegant guests' lounge. Fine wines by the glass. All rooms en suite.

**open** All year except Christmas and New Year
**bedrooms** 1 double, 1 twin, 1 family
**bathrooms** All en suite
**payment** Cash, cheques

Room General Leisure

## SIDMOUTH, Devon Map ref 1D2

★★★★
GUEST HOUSE
SILVER AWARD

B&B PER ROOM PER NIGHT
D £60.00–£70.00

### Lavenders Blue

33 Sidford High Street, Sidford, Sidmouth EX10 9SN **t** (01395) 576656
**e** lavendersbluesidmouth@fsmail.net

A warm welcome awaits you at Lavenders Blue. Deluxe en suite rooms with double-size showers. Ideal location for Sidmouth and the World Heritage Site of the Jurassic Coast.

**open** All year except Christmas
**bedrooms** 4 double
**bathrooms** All en suite
**payment** Credit/debit cards, cash, cheques

Room General P

## SIDMOUTH, Devon Map ref 1D2

★★★★★
RESTAURANT WITH ROOMS
GOLD AWARD

B&B PER ROOM PER NIGHT
S £70.00–£85.00
D £110.00–£180.00

EVENING MEAL PER PERSON
£32.50–£37.50

*Bed & breakfast 3 nights for 2, low season.*

WALKERS WELCOME · CYCLISTS WELCOME

### The Salty Monk

Church Street, Sidford, Sidmouth EX10 9QP **t** (01395) 513174 **e** saltymonk@btconnect.com

**saltymonk.co.uk** GUEST REVIEWS · SPECIAL OFFERS · REAL-TIME BOOKING

**open** All year
**bedrooms** 2 double, 1 twin, 2 suites
**bathrooms** All en suite
**payment** Credit/debit cards, cash, cheques

Enjoy England Bed & Breakfast of the Year 2008. Set in award-winning gardens, The Salty Monk provides an intimate, peaceful atmosphere where you can relax and recharge. Luxurious bedrooms with crisp, Egyptian cotton bed linen, fluffy white towels and robes. Great attention to detail with warm, friendly service. Restaurant using the very best local produce.

**SAT NAV** *EX10 9QP*

Room General P Leisure

## SIDMOUTH, Devon Map ref 1D2

★★★
GUEST HOUSE

B&B PER ROOM PER NIGHT
S £20.00–£25.00
D £50.00–£60.00

### Southern Cross Guest House

High Street, Newton Poppleford, Sidmouth EX10 0DU **t** (01395) 568439
**e** timothy.flaher@btconnect.com

**southerncrossdevon.co.uk**

Fourteenth century, thatched, Grade II Listed cottage and tea room with walled rear gardens. Lunches, famous cream teas. Sidmouth, Bicton Park three miles, Exeter ten miles. Jurassic Coast nearby.

**open** All year except Christmas and New Year
**bedrooms** 3 double, 1 twin, 1 single
**bathrooms** 3 en suite
**payment** Cash, cheques

Room General P Leisure

## Do you have access needs?

Look for the National Accessible Scheme symbols if you have special hearing, visual or mobility needs. An index of accommodation participating in the scheme can be found at the back of this guide.

## SOMERTON, Somerset Map ref 2A3

★★★
GUEST ACCOMMODATION

B&B PER ROOM PER NIGHT
S £40.00–£45.00
D £50.00–£60.00

EVENING MEAL PER PERSON
£9.50–£18.00

### The White Hart Inn

Market Place, Somerton TA11 7LX **t** (01458) 272314 **e** white.hart@virgin.net

**whitehartsomerton.co.uk**

Historic town-centre coaching inn offering fine dining and newly appointed en suite accommodation. Courtyard, garden and real fires.

**open** All year
**bedrooms** 3 double, 1 twin
**bathrooms** All en suite
**payment** Credit/debit cards, cash, cheques

Room General Leisure

## STOGUMBER, Somerset Map ref 1D1

★★★★
GUEST HOUSE

B&B PER ROOM PER NIGHT
S £30.00–£44.00
D £60.00–£68.00

EVENING MEAL PER PERSON
£9.00–£30.00

*Home-cooked meals in our licensed restaurant. Special rates for full-week and midweek breaks. Residential upholstery courses.*

### Wick House

2 Brook Street, Stogumber, Taunton TA4 3SZ **t** (01984) 656422 **e** sheila@wickhouse.co.uk

**wickhouse.co.uk**

**open** All year
**bedrooms** 2 double, 3 twin
**bathrooms** All en suite
**payment** Credit/debit cards, cash, cheques

Listed family home in the picturesque village of Stogumber, situated in a designated Area of Outstanding Natural Beauty. The village nestles between the Quantock and Brendon Hills of Exmoor National Park. Offering a friendly, informal atmosphere and high standard of accommodation – perfect for escaping the stresses of the modern world.

**SAT NAV** *TA4 3SZ*

Room General Leisure

## STOW-ON-THE-WOLD, Gloucestershire Map ref 2B1

★★★
FARMHOUSE

B&B PER ROOM PER NIGHT
S £35.00–£45.00
D £48.00–£60.00

### Corsham Field Farmhouse

Bledington Road, Stow-on-the-Wold, Cheltenham GL54 1JH **t** (01451) 831750
**e** farmhouse@corshamfield.co.uk

**corshamfield.co.uk**

**open** All year except Christmas
**bedrooms** 2 double, 2 twin, 4 family
**bathrooms** 6 en suite, 2 private
**payment** Cash, cheques, euros

Traditional farmhouse with spectacular views of Cotswold countryside. Peaceful location one mile from Stow-on-the-Wold. Ideally situated for exploring all Cotswold villages, Cheltenham, Stratford-upon-Avon, Blenheim and Warwick. All rooms centrally heated with TV, tea tray and hairdryer. Relaxing guest lounge/dining room. Excellent pub food five minutes' walk.

**SAT NAV** *GL54 1JH*

Room General Leisure

## Check the maps for accommodation locations

Colour maps at the front pinpoint all the places where accommodation is featured within the regional sections of this guide. Pick your location and then refer to the place index at the back to find the page number.

## STOW-ON-THE-WOLD, Gloucestershire Map ref 2B1

★★★★
INN

B&B PER ROOM PER NIGHT
S Min £85.00
D £85.00–£110.00

EVENING MEAL PER PERSON
£8.95–£35.00

### Westcote Inn

Nether Westcote, Chipping Norton OX7 6SD **t** (01993) 830888 **e** info@westcoteinn.co.uk

**westcoteinn.co.uk** SPECIAL OFFERS

**open** All year
**bedrooms** 3 double, 1 family
**bathrooms** All en suite
**payment** Credit/debit cards, cash, cheques

Traditional Cotswold inn situated in glorious countryside with distant views, complete with all modern facilities. Traditional British food from our fine dining restaurant, or for something simpler the Tack Room menu serves fabulous pub grub in front of open fireplaces. Situated between Burford and Stow-on-the-Wold, and three miles from Kingham Station with direct trains from Paddington.

**SAT NAV** *OX7 6SD* **ONLINE MAP**

Room General Leisure

## STREET, Somerset Map ref 2A2

★★★★
BED & BREAKFAST

B&B PER ROOM PER NIGHT
S £25.00–£30.00
D £50.00–£65.00

EVENING MEAL PER PERSON
£15.00–£25.00

### Old Orchard House

Middle Brooks, Street BA16 0TU **t** (01458) 442212 **e** old.orchard.house@amserve.com

**oldorchardhouse.co.uk** SPECIAL OFFERS

Modern comfortable home in Street. Peaceful location with large garden, yet within a few minutes' drive of Clarks Village, Millfield School, Strode Theatre and Glastonbury. Wonderful.

**open** All year
**bedrooms** 2 double, 1 single
**bathrooms** 1 en suite, 2 private
**payment** Cash, cheques

Room General Leisure

## STROUD, Gloucestershire Map ref 2B1

★★★★
BED & BREAKFAST

B&B PER ROOM PER NIGHT
S £35.00–£40.00
D £55.00–£65.00

EVENING MEAL PER PERSON
£12.50

*Weekly rates on request.*

### 1 Woodchester Lodge

Southfield Road, North Woodchester, Stroud GL5 5PA **t** (01453) 872586
**e** anne@woodchesterlodge.co.uk

**woodchesterlodge.co.uk**

**open** All year except Christmas and New Year
**bedrooms** 1 double, 1 twin
**bathrooms** 1 en suite, 1 private
**payment** Credit/debit cards, cash, cheques

Historic, Victorian timber merchant's property; peaceful village setting near Cotswold Way. Attractive gardens, parking, spacious and comfortable rooms, separate TV lounge/dining room. Meals cooked by qualified chef using our own produce and eggs. Outdoor activities, scenic villages, local attractions, links to main cities: Bristol, Bath, Gloucester, Cheltenham and London.

**SAT NAV** *GL5 5PA*

Room General Leisure

## Need some ideas?

Big city buzz or peaceful panoramas? Take a fresh look at England and you may be surprised at what's right on your doorstep. Explore the diversity online at enjoyengland.com

## STROUD, Gloucestershire Map ref 2B1

★★★★
BED & BREAKFAST
SILVER AWARD

B&B PER ROOM PER NIGHT
S Min £35.00
D £56.00–£70.00

*Discounted rates for 4 or more nights.*

### Pretoria Villa

Wells Road, Eastcombe, Stroud GL6 7EE **t** (01452) 770435 **e** pretoriavilla@btinternet.com

**bedandbreakfast-cotswold.co.uk**

**open** All year except Christmas
**bedrooms** 1 double, 2 twin
**bathrooms** All en suite
**payment** Cash, cheques

Enjoy luxurious bed and breakfast in a relaxed family country house, set in peaceful secluded gardens. Spacious bedrooms with many home comforts. Guest lounge with TV. Superb breakfast served at your leisure. An excellent base from which to explore the Cotswolds. Personal service and your comfort guaranteed.

**SAT NAV** *GL6 7EE*

Room General P Leisure

## SWANAGE, Dorset Map ref 2B3

★★★★
GUEST ACCOMMODATION

B&B PER ROOM PER NIGHT
S £30.00–£50.00
D £60.00–£100.00

### The Castleton

1 Highcliffe Road, Swanage BH19 1LW **t** (01929) 423972 **e** stay@thecastleton.co.uk

**thecastleton.co.uk** GUEST REVIEWS

**open** All year except Christmas
**bedrooms** 5 double, 1 twin, 1 single, 2 family
**bathrooms** All en suite
**payment** Credit/debit cards, cash, cheques

Welcome to The Castleton, truly a 'once discovered, never forgotten' place to stay. A delightful escape from everyday life, where the welcoming nature and friendliness of your hosts add to your pleasure. The Castleton is ideally situated 100 metres from Swanage's beautiful sandy beach and a short level stroll along the seafront to the town centre with its many shops, restaurants and bars.

**SAT NAV** *BH19 1LW* **ONLINE MAP**

Room TV General 4 P Leisure

## SWINDON, Wiltshire Map ref 2B2

★★★★
GUEST ACCOMMODATION

B&B PER ROOM PER NIGHT
S £35.00–£45.00
D £52.00–£60.00

### The Lodge

1 Hunt Street, Swindon SN1 3HW **t** (01793) 526952 & (01793) 526904
**e** info@thelodgeswindon.co.uk

**thelodgeswindon.co.uk** SPECIAL OFFERS

The Lodge has eight en suite bedrooms, recently refurbished to a high standard. Quiet yet central location, secure on-site parking, Wi-Fi.

**open** All year
**bedrooms** 1 double, 1 twin, 3 single, 3 family
**bathrooms** All en suite
**payment** Credit/debit cards, cash, cheques

Room TV General P Leisure

## Where can I get help and advice?

Tourist Information Centres offer friendly help with accommodation and holiday ideas as well as suggestions of places to visit and things to do. You'll find contact details at the beginning of each regional section.

## SWINDON, Wiltshire Map ref 2B2

★★★
GUEST ACCOMMODATION

B&B PER ROOM PER NIGHT
S £33.00–£55.00
D £60.00–£75.00

### The Swandown

36/37 Victoria Road, Swindon SN1 3AS **t** (01793) 536695 **e** swandownhotel@gmail.com

**s-h-systems.co.uk/hotels/swandown**

**open** All year except Christmas and New Year
**bedrooms** 2 double, 4 twin, 6 single, 5 family
**bathrooms** 13 en suite
**payment** Credit/debit cards, cash, cheques

The Swandown is a friendly, well-maintained, family-run guest accommodation located in Swindon town centre and convenient to most amenities. Offering 17 rooms, mostly en suite, comfortably equipped with colour TV, tea-/coffee-making facilities and hairdryer. Separate TV lounge with a licensed bar and on-site parking facilities.

**SAT NAV** *SN1 3AS*

Room TV General 3 P

## TAUNTON, Somerset Map ref 1D1

★★★★
BED & BREAKFAST

B&B PER ROOM PER NIGHT
S £45.00–£48.00
D £68.00–£70.00

EVENING MEAL PER PERSON
£20.00–£24.00

### Causeway Cottage

Barbers Lane, West Buckland, Nr Taunton TA21 9JZ **t** (01823) 663458 **e** causewaybb@aol.com

**causewaycottage.co.uk**

**open** All year except Christmas and New Year
**bedrooms** 1 double, 2 twin
**bathrooms** All en suite
**payment** Cash, cheques, euros

A 200-year-old stone and beamed Somerset cottage privately tucked away with views across fields to Lofty Church. Easy access to M5, junction 26. Spacious, restful sitting room. Lesley is renowned for her cooking. Home-baked bread, free-range eggs, farm sausages for breakfast. Supper by arrangement. An informal, relaxed family home.

**SAT NAV** *TA21 9JZ*

Room General 10 Leisure

## TAVISTOCK, Devon Map ref 1C2

★★★★
GUEST ACCOMMODATION

B&B PER ROOM PER NIGHT
S £55.00–£80.00
D £65.00–£95.00

EVENING MEAL PER PERSON
Min £18.50

### Harrabeer Country House

Harrowbeer Lane, Yelverton PL20 6EA **t** (01822) 853302 **e** reception@harrabeer.co.uk

**harrabeer.co.uk** REAL-TIME BOOKING

Delightful, small, quiet country house close to Dartmoor. Finalist for a prestigious Landlady of the Year award. Specialising in food, comfort and service. Two self-catering suites available.

**open** All year except Christmas and New Year
**bedrooms** 3 double, 3 twin, 2 suites
**bathrooms** 7 en suite, 1 private
**payment** Credit/debit cards, cash, cheques

Room TV General P Leisure

## It's all quality-assessed accommodation

Our commitment to quality involves wide-ranging accommodation assessment. Ratings and awards were correct at the time of going to press but may change following a new assessment. Please check at time of booking.

## TAVISTOCK, Devon Map ref 1C2

★★★★★ GUEST ACCOMMODATION GOLD AWARD

B&B PER ROOM PER NIGHT
s £94.00
d £140.00–£150.00

*Autumn/spring breaks: 3 nights for price of 2. Special Valentine breaks. Gourmet tray suppers to order. 10% discount on 7-night stay.*

### Tor Cottage

Chillaton, Lifton PL16 0JE **t** (01822) 860248 **e** info@torcottage.co.uk

**torcottage.co.uk** REAL-TIME BOOKING

**open** All year except Christmas and New Year
**bedrooms** 3 double, 1 twin, 1 suite
**bathrooms** All en suite
**payment** Credit/debit cards, cash

Enjoy complete peace and privacy in beautiful en suite bed-sitting rooms, each with own log fire and private garden, terrace or conservatory. Streamside setting in hidden valley, 28 acres of wildlife hillsides, beautiful gardens, heated outdoor pool. Adjacent Dartmoor. Visit Devon/Cornwall coastlines, National Trust properties or the Eden Project (45-minute drive).

**SAT NAV** *PL16 0JE* **ONLINE MAP**

Room General 14 P Leisure

## TEWKESBURY, Gloucestershire Map ref 2B1

★★★ FARMHOUSE

B&B PER ROOM PER NIGHT
s £28.00–£32.00
d £50.00–£55.00

### Abbots Court Farm

Churchend, Twyning, Tewkesbury GL20 6DA **t** (01684) 292515 **e** abbotscourt@aol.com

**open** All year except Christmas and New Year
**bedrooms** 1 double, 1 twin, 2 family
**bathrooms** All en suite
**payment** Cash, cheques

Farm of 350 acres situated on the site of a monastic settlement, with private entrance to church, in a small hamlet one mile from M5/M50 junction. Bounded by the river Avon, several coarse and carp lakes available for fishing. Large dining/sitting room, excellent home-cooked food. Pool and table tennis.

**SAT NAV** *GL20 6DA*

Room General P Leisure

## TEWKESBURY, Gloucestershire Map ref 2B1

Rating Applied For BED & BREAKFAST

B&B PER ROOM PER NIGHT
s £45.00–£50.00
d £75.00–£80.00

EVENING MEAL PER PERSON
£20.00–£22.00

*Discounts on stays of 3 nights or more.*

### Green Orchard

Deerhurst Walton, Tewkesbury GL19 4BS **t** (01242) 680362 **e** wendy@green-orchard.co.uk

**green-orchard.co.uk** GUEST REVIEWS • SPECIAL OFFERS • REAL-TIME BOOKING

**open** All year
**bedrooms** 1 double, 1 suite
**bathrooms** All en suite
**payment** Cash, cheques

Recently refurbished 17thC cottage in quiet countryside. Our luxury double room en suite is on the ground floor, annexed from the main dwelling with its own entrance. The rooms are spacious with LCD TV and DVD library. The fridge contains complimentary milk, fruit juice, wine and mineral water.

**SAT NAV** *GL19 4BS* **ONLINE MAP**

Room General P Leisure

## What shall we do today?

For ideas on places to visit, see the beginning of this regional section or go online at enjoyengland.com.

## TINTAGEL, Cornwall Map ref 1B2

★★★★★
GUEST HOUSE

B&B PER ROOM PER NIGHT
S £40.00–£52.00
D £60.00–£84.00

### The Avalon

Atlantic Road, Tintagel PL34 0DD **t** (01840) 770116 **e** avalontintagel@googlemail.com

**avalon-tintagel.co.uk** GUEST REVIEWS

Perfect Tintagel village location. Recent total renovation and refurbishment. Stunning panoramic views of Tintagel Island and the sea. Car parking. Wi-Fi. Licensed. Breakfast produce local, free-range and organic whenever possible.

**open** February to November
**bedrooms** 5 double, 2 twin
**bathrooms** All en suite
**payment** Credit/debit cards, cash, cheques

Room General Leisure

## TINTAGEL, Cornwall Map ref 1B2

★★★
INN

B&B PER ROOM PER NIGHT
D £70.00–£120.00

EVENING MEAL PER PERSON
£23.00–£35.00

*Special spring, autumn and winter breaks. Please check the website for details.*

### The Mill House

Trebarwith Strand, Tintagel PL34 0HD **t** (01840) 770200 **e** management@themillhouseinn.co.uk

**themillhouseinn.co.uk** SPECIAL OFFERS • REAL-TIME BOOKING

**open** All year except Christmas
**bedrooms** 6 double, 1 twin, 1 family
**bathrooms** All en suite
**payment** Credit/debit cards, cash, cheques, euros

The 18thC Mill House nestles in an attractive woodland setting close to Trebarwith Strand surfing beach. It has a traditional bar and large restaurant set alongside the millstream serving local fish, meat and produce. There are eight stylishly furnished bedrooms. Licensed for weddings and ideal for functions and conferences.

**SAT NAV** *PL34 0HD*

Room General Leisure

## TINTINHULL, Somerset Map ref 2A3

★★★★
INN

B&B PER ROOM PER NIGHT
S £65.00–£75.00
D £80.00–£90.00

EVENING MEAL PER PERSON
£18.00–£35.00

*Enjoy fine wines and local real ales in summer in our beautiful gardens or by our roaring log fire in winter.*

### The Crown and Victoria Inn

14 Farm Street, Nr Yeovil BA22 8PZ **t** (01935) 823341 **e** info@thecrownandvictoria.co.uk

**thecrownandvictoria.co.uk**

**open** All year
**bedrooms** 4 double, 1 single
**bathrooms** All en suite
**payment** Credit/debit cards, cash, cheques

Our award-winning inn is situated in the beautiful village of Tintinhull. Open all day, seven days a week, we have an inviting lunch menu (1200-1430), or our a la carte menu is available (1830-2130). We offer a traditional Sunday roast and our delicious home-made desserts are a must.

**SAT NAV** *BA22 8PZ*

Room General

## TIVERTON, Devon Map ref 1D2

★★★
GUEST HOUSE

B&B PER ROOM PER NIGHT
S £26.00–£31.00
D £60.00–£62.00

EVENING MEAL PER PERSON
£16.00

### Bridge Guest House

23 Angel Hill, Tiverton EX16 6PE **t** (01884) 252804

**smoothhound.co.uk/hotels/bridgegh.html**

Attractive Victorian town house situated on the banks of the River Exe, with pretty riverside tea garden. Ideal for touring the heart of Devon.

**open** All year
**bedrooms** 3 double, 5 single, 2 family
**bathrooms** 6 en suite
**payment** Cash, cheques, euros

Room General Leisure

## TIVERTON, Devon Map ref 1D2

★★★★
BED & BREAKFAST

B&B PER ROOM PER NIGHT
S £27.50–£30.00
D £30.00–£32.50

### Exe-Tor

Ashley, Tiverton EX16 5PA **t** (01884) 253197 **e** jean.wynniatt@tesco.net

**open** All year
**bedrooms** 1 double, 1 twin
**bathrooms** 1 en suite, 1 private
**payment** Cash, cheques

A two-bedroom semi-bungalow in 0.33 acres of prize-winning gardens. One mile to Tiverton. Easy access to north, south, east and west Devon. There is a king-size en suite room upstairs and a twin-bedded room with private bathroom on the ground floor. Local food used as much as possible.

**SAT NAV** *EX16 5PA*

Room General 7 P

## TORQUAY, Devon Map ref 1D2

★★★★
GUEST ACCOMMODATION

B&B PER ROOM PER NIGHT
S £25.00–£30.00
D £50.00–£60.00

EVENING MEAL PER PERSON
Min £10.00

### Abingdon House

104 Avenue Road, Torquay TQ2 5LF **t** (01803) 201832 **e** abingdon-house@zen.co.uk

**abingdon-house.co.uk**

Informal, friendly bed and breakfast. Comfortable lounge and cheerful breakfast room. Small patio. Parking. Short walk to sea and all attractions. Ground-floor room suitable for the mobility-impaired and wheelchair-users.

**open** All year except Christmas
**bedrooms** 4 double, 1 twin
**bathrooms** 4 en suite, 1 private
**payment** Credit/debit cards, cash, cheques

Room General P Leisure

## TORQUAY, Devon Map ref 1D2

★★★★
GUEST ACCOMMODATION

B&B PER ROOM PER NIGHT
S £34.00–£36.00
D £68.00–£72.00

EVENING MEAL PER PERSON
£12.00–£14.00

### Coombe Court

67 Babbacombe Downs Road, Torquay TQ1 3LP **t** (01803) 327097
**e** enquiries@coombecourthotel.co.uk

**coombecourthotel.co.uk**

**open** All year except Christmas and New Year
**bedrooms** 10 double, 3 twin, 1 single, 1 family
**bathrooms** All en suite
**payment** Credit/debit cards, cash, cheques

Family-run hotel. Traditional cooking, 50yds from Babbacombe Downs. Non-smoking, no pets. Car parking for all guests.

**SAT NAV** *TQ1 3LP*

Room General 10 P

## Remember to check when booking

Please remember that all information in this guide has been supplied by the proprietors well in advance of publication. Since changes do sometimes occur it's a good idea to check details at the time of booking.

For **key to symbols** see page 7

**TORQUAY, Devon Map ref 1D2**

★★★★★ GUEST ACCOMMODATION SILVER AWARD

B&B PER ROOM PER NIGHT
S £61.00–£94.00
D £72.00–£138.00

## Haldon Priors

Meadfoot Sea Road, Torquay TQ1 2LQ **t** (01803) 213365 **e** travelstyle.ltd@talk21.com

**haldonpriors.co.uk**

**open** Easter to end of September
**bedrooms** 4 double, 1 twin, 1 family
**bathrooms** All en suite
**payment** Credit/debit cards, cash, cheques

Haldon Priors is a beautiful Victorian villa adjacent to Meadfoot Bay, set in exquisite subtropical gardens with heated outdoor pool and sauna. All rooms have everything needed to make your stay memorable, with complimentary refreshments on arrival and all the beauty of Devon on the doorstep. No smoking in hotel.

**SAT NAV** *TQ1 2LQ* **ONLINE MAP**

Room General P Leisure

**TORQUAY, Devon Map ref 1D2**

★★★★ GUEST ACCOMMODATION

B&B PER ROOM PER NIGHT
S £25.00–£40.00
D £44.00–£70.00

EVENING MEAL PER PERSON
£8.00–£15.00

## The Norwood

60 Belgrave Road, Torquay TQ2 5HY **t** (01803) 294236 **e** enquiries@norwoodhoteltorquay.co.uk

**norwoodhoteltorquay.co.uk** GUEST REVIEWS · SPECIAL OFFERS · REAL-TIME BOOKING

The Norwood Hotel is centrally located in Torquay close to seafront, shops, conference centre and station. Offers en suite, licensed facilities.

**open** All year
**bedrooms** 5 double, 3 twin, 2 family
**bathrooms** All en suite
**payment** Credit/debit cards, cash, cheques, euros

Room General P Leisure

**TORQUAY, Devon Map ref 1D2**

★★★ GUEST ACCOMMODATION

B&B PER ROOM PER NIGHT
D £40.00–£50.00

EVENING MEAL PER PERSON
£12.50

## The Sandpiper Lodge

96 Avenue Road, Torquay TQ2 5LF **t** (01803) 293293 **e** johnatsandpiper@aol.com

**sandpiperlodgehotel.co.uk**

Small, family-run, non-smoking guesthouse situated just a short level walk from the Riviera Centre and seafront.

**open** All year
**bedrooms** 3 double, 3 family
**bathrooms** All en suite
**payment** Credit/debit cards, cash, cheques

Room General P

**TORQUAY, Devon Map ref 1D2**

★★★ GUEST HOUSE

B&B PER ROOM PER NIGHT
S £20.00–£25.00
D £35.00–£40.00

## Wilsbrook Guest House

77 Avenue Road, Torquay TQ2 5LL **t** (01803) 298413 **e** thewilsbrook@hotmail.com

**wilsbrook.co.uk** REAL-TIME BOOKING

Well-established guesthouse situated close to the seafront, town centre and Riviera Centre. Private car park, en suite rooms, Freeview TV, hospitality tray in rooms and full English breakfast.

**open** All year
**bedrooms** 2 double, 1 twin, 1 single, 1 family
**bathrooms** 3 en suite
**payment** Credit/debit cards, cash

Room General 2 P

CYCLISTS WELCOME

## Fancy a cycling holiday?

For a fabulous freewheeling break, seek out accommodation participating in our Cyclists Welcome scheme. Look out for the symbol and plan your route online at nationalcyclenetwork.org.

## TOTNES, Devon Map ref 1D2

★★★★
GUEST HOUSE

B&B PER ROOM PER NIGHT
S £56.00–£76.00
D £66.00–£90.00

*3-day breaks (Nov-Mar): £4 off price of room per night.*

### The Old Forge at Totnes

Seymour Place, Totnes TQ9 5AY **t** (01803) 862174 **e** enq@oldforgetotnes.com

**oldforgetotnes.com**

**open** All year
**bedrooms** 6 double, 2 twin, 1 family, 1 suite
**bathrooms** 9 en suite, 1 private
**payment** Credit/debit cards, cash, cheques

A warm welcome assured at this delightful 600-year-old stone building with walled garden and car parking. Whirlpool spa. Extensive breakfast menu. Quiet, yet close to town and river. Coast and Dartmoor nearby, Eden Project 1.5 hours. Two-bedroomed cottage suite and family room with roof terrace available.

**SAT NAV** *TQ9 5AY*

Room General P Leisure

## TRURO, Cornwall Map ref 1B3

★★★★
GUEST HOUSE

B&B PER ROOM PER NIGHT
S £50.00–£60.00
D £70.00–£90.00

### Bissick Old Mill

Ladock, Truro TR2 4PG **t** (01726) 882557 **e** enquiries@bissickoldmill.plus.com

**bissickoldmill.co.uk**

**open** All year
**bedrooms** 1 double, 1 twin, 2 suites
**bathrooms** All en suite
**payment** Credit/debit cards, cash, cheques

17thC water mill sympathetically converted to provide well-appointed accommodation with exceptional standards throughout and a relaxing, friendly atmosphere. Top quality breakfasts prepared with fresh, local, quality ingredients. Ideal base for visiting the Eden Project, Heligan, and all of Cornwall's beautiful attractions.

**SAT NAV** *TR2 4PG*

Room General P

## TRURO, Cornwall Map ref 1B3

★★★★
BED & BREAKFAST

B&B PER ROOM PER NIGHT
S £30.00–£40.00
D £50.00–£60.00

### Palm Tree House

8 Parkins Terrace, Off St Clement Street, Truro TR1 1EJ **t** (01872) 270100
**e** bodybusiness@btconnect.com

Peaceful Victorian house and garden. Three minutes' walk from city centre. Excellent home-cooked breakfast. Free overnight parking nearby. 40 minutes by car from the Eden Project and Lost Gardens of Heligan.

**open** All year except Christmas and New Year
**bedrooms** 2 family
**bathrooms** 2 private
**payment** Credit/debit cards, cash, cheques

Room General 8 P Leisure

## TRURO, Cornwall  Map ref 1B3

★★★★
GUEST ACCOMMODATION

B&B PER ROOM PER NIGHT
S £49.00
D £69.00–£79.00

### The Townhouse Rooms

20 Falmouth Road, Truro TR1 2HX **t** (01872) 277374 **e** info@trurotownhouse.com

**trurotownhouse.com** GUEST REVIEWS

**open** All year except Christmas and New Year
**bedrooms** 8 double, 3 twin, 1 single
**bathrooms** All en suite
**payment** Credit/debit cards, cash, cheques

The Townhouse is different – relaxed, friendly, flexible – and our guests seem to love it! We aim to give you lovely rooms, real value for money and the flexibility you need to enjoy your stay. Buffet continental breakfast, home-cooked cakes with afternoon tea. Wi-Fi internet. Drying room. Secure bike lock-up. Close to all amenities.

**SAT NAV** *TR1 2HX* **ONLINE MAP**

Room General

## ULEY, Gloucestershire  Map ref 2B1

★★★
INN

B&B PER ROOM PER NIGHT
S £40.00–£60.00
D £70.00–£90.00

EVENING MEAL PER PERSON
£4.95–£13.50

### The Old Crown Inn

The Green, Dursley GL11 5SN **t** (01453) 860502 **e** info@theoldcrownuley.co.uk

**theoldcrownuley.co.uk**

Village pub set in the Cotswolds, serving good food and real ales and providing comfortable accommodation.

**open** All year except Christmas and New Year
**bedrooms** 2 double, 1 twin, 1 suite
**bathrooms** All en suite
**payment** Credit/debit cards, cash, cheques

Room General Leisure

## VERYAN, Cornwall  Map ref 1B3

★★★★
BED & BREAKFAST

B&B PER ROOM PER NIGHT
S £30.00–£32.00
D £60.00–£64.00

### Treverbyn House

Pendower Road, Veryan, Truro TR2 5QL **t** (01872) 501201 **e** holiday@treverbyn.fsbusiness.co.uk

**cornwall-online.co.uk/treverbyn/ctb.htm**

Treverbyn House occupies a commanding position in the picturesque village of Veryan, renowned for its round houses. Treverbyn House is family-run and owned by Alison and Michael Rawling and offers bed and breakfast accommodation.

**open** All year
**bedrooms** 1 double, 1 twin, 1 single
**bathrooms** All en suite
**payment** Cash, cheques

Room General Leisure

## WADEBRIDGE, Cornwall  Map ref 1B2

★★★★
GUEST ACCOMMODATION

B&B PER ROOM PER NIGHT
D £55.00–£62.00

EVENING MEAL PER PERSON
£13.50

*3-night break available at a special price.*

### Tregolls Farm

St Wenn, Bodmin PL30 5PG **t** (01208) 812154

**tregollsfarm.co.uk** GUEST REVIEWS · SPECIAL OFFERS

**open** All year except Christmas
**bedrooms** 1 double, 1 twin
**bathrooms** All en suite
**payment** Credit/debit cards, cash, cheques

Set in a picturesque valley overlooking fields of cows and sheep. Grade II Listed farmhouse with beautiful countryside views from all windows. En suite bedrooms. Farm trail links up to Saints Way footpath. Pets' corner. Eden, Helligan, Fowey and Padstow all within 25 minutes' drive.

**SAT NAV** *PL30 5PG* **ONLINE MAP**

Room General Leisure

## WELLINGTON, Somerset Map ref 1D1

★★★
BED & BREAKFAST

B&B PER ROOM PER NIGHT
S £30.00
D £55.00

# Mantle Cottage

34 Mantle Street, Wellington TA21 8AR **t** (01823) 668514 **e** dalsod@aol.com

**mantlecottage.com**

Friendly and comfortable cottage bed and breakfast in the attractive town of Wellington on the Somerset/Devon borders.

**open** All year except Christmas
**bedrooms** 2 double
**bathrooms** All en suite
**payment** Cash, cheques

Room TV General Leisure

## WELLS, Somerset Map ref 2A2

★★★
GUEST ACCOMMODATION

B&B PER ROOM PER NIGHT
S £25.00
D £50.00–£55.00

# 30 Mary Road

Mary Road, Wells BA5 2NF **t** (01749) 674031 **e** triciabailey30@hotmail.com

Comfortable, friendly, family home. Easy walking distance from city centre. Choice of breakfasts. TV in rooms. Tea/coffee. Central heating. One double has en suite toilet. Parking.

**open** February to November
**bedrooms** 2 double, 2 single
**payment** Cash, cheques, euros

Room TV SC General 3 P Leisure

## WELLS, Somerset Map ref 2A2

★★★★
FARMHOUSE

B&B PER ROOM PER NIGHT
D £70.00–£75.00

# Burnt House Farm

Burnthouse Drove, Windsor Hill BA4 4JQ **t** (01749) 840185 **e** ehparry@btinternet.com

**burnthousedrove.co.uk**

**open** All year except Christmas
**bedrooms** 1 double, 1 twin
**bathrooms** 2 private
**payment** Credit/debit cards

Rural exclusion, a short drive from Wells. Comfortable double and twin rooms with private bathroom, suitable for family or friends. Stunning views, ideal for walking and visiting Wells and Bath.

**SAT NAV** *BA4 4JQ*

Room TV General P

## WELLS, Somerset Map ref 2A2

★★★★
BED & BREAKFAST

B&B PER ROOM PER NIGHT
S £50.00–£65.00
D £65.00

# Islington Farm

Wells BA5 1US **t** (01749) 673445 **e** islingtonfarm2004@yahoo.co.uk

**islingtonfarmatwells.co.uk**

**open** All year except Christmas and New Year
**bedrooms** 1 double, 1 twin
**bathrooms** All en suite
**payment** Credit/debit cards, cash, cheques

Uniquely situated adjacent to the Bishop's Palace, a 300-year-old farmhouse surrounded by fields and parkland, just a three-minute walk from the city centre. Private parking. Quiet riverside location with choice of excellent restaurants and pubs nearby. Home-cooked breakfast with own free-range eggs.

**SAT NAV** *BA5 1US*

Room TV General P Leisure

For **key to symbols** see page 7

## WELLS, Somerset Map ref 2A2

★★★
GUEST ACCOMMODATION

B&B PER ROOM PER NIGHT
S £30.00
D £55.00

### Worth House

Worth, Wookey, Wells BA5 1LW **t** (01749) 672041 **e** margaret@wookey.eclipse.co.uk

Small country hotel, part dating back to the 16thC. Exposed beams and log fires. Two miles from Wells on the B3139.

**open** All year
**bedrooms** 3 double, 2 twin, 1 single
**bathrooms** All en suite
**payment** Cash, cheques

Room General P Leisure

## WEST BAY, Dorset Map ref 2A3

★★★★
BED & BREAKFAST

B&B PER ROOM PER NIGHT
S £35.00–£50.00
D £65.00–£70.00

*Discount for 3 or more nights.*

### Seacroft

24 Forty Foot Way, West Bay, Bridport DT6 4HD **t** (01308) 423407 **e** seacroft24@btinternet.com

**seacroftbandb.co.uk**

**open** All year
**bedrooms** 3 double, 1 family
**bathrooms** All en suite
**payment** Credit/debit cards, cash, cheques

Small and friendly bed and breakfast with private car and boat parking. Two minutes to the harbour, beach, coastal paths and Jurassic Coast. Use of garden and conservatory.

**SAT NAV** *DT6 4HD*

Room General 3 P Leisure

## WEST LOOE, Cornwall Map ref 1C3

★★★★
GUEST HOUSE

B&B PER ROOM PER NIGHT
S £33.00–£46.00
D £66.00–£96.00

EVENING MEAL PER PERSON
Min £18.00

### The Old Bridge House

The Quay, West Looe, Looe PL13 2BU **t** (01503) 263159 **e** mail@theoldbridgehousehotel.co.uk

**theoldbridgehousehotel.co.uk** GUEST REVIEWS • REAL-TIME BOOKING

A combination of location and superb views makes The Old Bridge House an ideal place for either a relaxing vacation or as a base from which to explore Cornwall's many fantastic visitor attractions.

**open** All year except Christmas
**bedrooms** 4 double, 2 twin, 2 single, 1 family
**bathrooms** All en suite
**payment** Credit/debit cards, cash, cheques

Room General 10 Leisure

## WEST LOOE, Cornwall Map ref 1C3

★★
GUEST HOUSE

B&B PER ROOM PER NIGHT
S £20.00–£28.00
D £46.00–£50.00

### Tidal Court

Church Street, West Looe, Looe PL13 2EX **t** (01503) 263695

**open** All year except Christmas
**bedrooms** 1 double, 1 twin, 1 single, 2 family
**bathrooms** 4 en suite, 1 private
**payment** Cash, cheques, euros

Small, family-run guesthouse where a warm welcome is assured. Tidal is situated in the centre of West Looe, less than one minute's walk from the harbour, quayside and ferry to East Looe. Enjoy the seaside amenities of beaches, coves, boat trips and fishing, or a stunning cliff walk to Polperro.

**SAT NAV** *PL13 2EX*

Room General Leisure

## WESTWARD HO!, Devon Map ref 1C1

★★★★
BED & BREAKFAST

B&B PER ROOM PER NIGHT
S £35.00–£45.00
D £60.00–£70.00

### Brockenhurst

11 Atlantic Way, Westward Ho!, Bideford EX39 1HX **t** (01237) 423346
**e** info@brockenhurstindevon.co.uk

**brockenhurstindevon.co.uk** SPECIAL OFFERS • REAL-TIME BOOKING

Comfortable detached house adjoining the village centre (shops, restaurants, pubs). Within sight and sound of the sea. Good walking, cycling and bus service. Vast beach.

**open** All year except Christmas and New Year
**bedrooms** 2 double, 1 twin
**bathrooms** All en suite
**payment** Credit/debit cards, cash, cheques, euros

Room General P Leisure

## WEYMOUTH, Dorset Map ref 2B3

★★★
GUEST HOUSE

B&B PER ROOM PER NIGHT
S £49.00–£59.00
D £68.00–£88.00

EVENING MEAL PER PERSON
£11.75–£14.75

### The Kinley

98 The Esplanade, Weymouth DT4 7AT **t** (01305) 782264 **e** hotelkinley@hotmail.com

**hotelkinley.co.uk**

Hotel situated along the seafront, within easy reach of the town centre. Garage for six cars. No supplement for sea view. Evening meals.

**open** All year
**bedrooms** 7 double, 1 twin, 1 family
**bathrooms** All en suite
**payment** Credit/debit cards, cash, cheques, euros

Room General P

## WEYMOUTH, Dorset Map ref 2B3

★★★★
GUEST ACCOMMODATION

B&B PER ROOM PER NIGHT
D £50.00–£85.00

EVENING MEAL PER PERSON
£10.00–£18.00

*Discounts on stays of 3 or more nights. Other special offers available throughout the year – see website for details.*

### Oaklands Edwardian Guesthouse

1 Glendinning Avenue, Weymouth DT4 7QF **t** (01305) 767081 **e** stay@oaklands-guesthouse.co.uk

**oaklands-guesthouse.co.uk** GUEST REVIEWS • SPECIAL OFFERS

**open** All year
**bedrooms** 6 double, 2 twin, 1 family
**bathrooms** 8 en suite, 1 private
**payment** Credit/debit cards, cash, cheques

Beautiful Edwardian house set in quiet, yet central location in the picturesque harbour town of Weymouth. All rooms are individually decorated and equipped to the highest standard with modern en suite or private facilities. Doubles, twins, family and a ground-floor room available. Extensive breakfast menu with vegetarian options always available.

**SAT NAV** *DT4 7QF* **ONLINE MAP**

Room General 5 P Leisure

## WEYMOUTH, Dorset Map ref 2B3

★★★★
BED & BREAKFAST

B&B PER ROOM PER NIGHT
S £57.00–£66.00
D £76.00–£88.00

### Old Harbour View

12 Trinity Road, Weymouth DT4 8TJ **t** (01305) 774633 & 07974 422241 **e** pv_1st_ind@yahoo.co.uk

Idyllic Georgian harbourside town house, offering two charming double bedrooms. Restaurants, pubs, sandy beach and ferries to the Channel Islands on its doorstep.

**open** All year except Christmas and New Year
**bedrooms** 1 double, 1 twin
**bathrooms** All en suite
**payment** Credit/debit cards, cash, cheques

Room General P Leisure

WALKERS WELCOME WELCOME WALKERS

## Do you like walking?

Walkers feel at home in accommodation participating in our Walkers Welcome scheme. Look out for the symbol. Consider walking all or part of a long-distance route – go online at nationaltrail.co.uk.

## WEYMOUTH, Dorset Map ref 2B3

★★★
GUEST ACCOMMODATION

B&B PER ROOM PER NIGHT
S £30.00–£50.00
D £50.00–£70.00

### Sou West Lodge

Rodwell Road, Weymouth DT4 8QT **t** (01305) 783749 **e** enquiry@souwestlodge.co.uk

**souwestlodge.co.uk** SPECIAL OFFERS

Family-run guest accommodation, en suite rooms with colour TV. Within easy walking distance of harbour, town centre and beach. Olympic sailing academy close by.

**open** All year except Christmas
**bedrooms** 5 double, 1 twin, 2 family
**bathrooms** All en suite
**payment** Credit/debit cards, cash, cheques

Room General Leisure

## WIMBORNE MINSTER, Dorset Map ref 2B3

★★
GUEST ACCOMMODATION

B&B PER ROOM PER NIGHT
S £35.00–£45.00
D £50.00–£70.00

### The Albion

High Street, Wimborne Minster BH21 1HR **t** (01202) 882492 **e** albioninn-wimborne@tiscali.co.uk

**albioninn-wimborne.co.uk**

The oldest-surviving coaching house in Wimborne, situated just off the town square opposite the minster. All rooms with modern facilities. Large bathroom with wc, shower and bath.

**open** All year except Christmas
**bedrooms** 1 double, 1 twin, 1 family
**payment** Credit/debit cards, cash, cheques, euros

Room General Leisure

## WINSLEY, Wiltshire Map ref 2B2

★★
BED & BREAKFAST

B&B PER ROOM PER NIGHT
S £25.00–£30.00
D £45.00–£50.00

### Conifers

4 King Alfred Way, Winsley, Bradford-on-Avon BA15 2NG **t** (01225) 722482

Semi-detached house, just over two miles from Bradford-on-Avon, seven miles from Bath. Quiet area, pleasant outlook. Friendly atmosphere. Off-road parking. Lovely garden. On bus route. Recommended pub evening meal.

**open** All year
**bedrooms** 1 double, 1 twin
**payment** Cash, cheques

Room General

## WINTERBORNE ZELSTON, Dorset Map ref 2B3

★★★
FARMHOUSE

B&B PER ROOM PER NIGHT
S £30.00–£35.00
D £30.00–£35.00

### Brook Farm

Winterborne Zelston, Blandford Forum DT11 9EU **t** (01929) 459267
**e** kerleybrookfarmzelston@yahoo.co.uk

Comfortable bed and breakfast, en suite or private facilities, on working farm in pretty peaceful hamlet between Wimborne and Bere Regis. Full English breakfast. All rooms colour TV, beverage facilities.

**open** All year except Christmas and New Year
**bedrooms** 2 double, 1 twin
**bathrooms** 2 en suite, 1 private
**payment** Cash, cheques

Room General 1

## WINTERBOURNE STOKE, Wiltshire Map ref 2B2

★★★★
BED & BREAKFAST

B&B PER ROOM PER NIGHT
S £30.00–£35.00
D £55.00–£60.00

### Scotland Lodge Farm

Winterbourne Stoke, Salisbury SP3 4TF **t** (01980) 621199 **e** william.lockwood@bigwig.net

**smoothhound.co.uk/hotels/scotlandl.html**

Warm welcome at family-run competition yard set in 46 acres. Lovely views. Stonehenge/Salisbury nearby. Conservatory for guests' use. Easy access off A303 through automatic gate. Excellent local pubs.

**open** All year except Christmas
**bedrooms** 2 double, 1 twin
**bathrooms** 3 private
**payment** Credit/debit cards, cash, cheques

Room General

### B&B prices

Rates for bed and breakfast are shown per room per night.
Double room prices are usually based on two people sharing the room.

## WOODLEIGH, Devon Map ref 1C3

★★★★
FARMHOUSE

B&B PER ROOM PER NIGHT
S £45.00–£55.00
D £60.00–£70.00

### Higher Hendham House

Woodleigh, Kingsbridge TQ7 4DP **t** (01548) 550015 **e** higherhendhamhouse@fsmail.net

**higherhendhamhouse.com**

Attractive 19thC farmhouse in quiet garden of mature trees and shrubs in glorious South Hams countryside. Three en suite bedrooms, newly refurbished. TV/DVD, beverage tray, delicious breakfasts using local produce.

**open** All year
**bedrooms** 2 double, 1 twin
**bathrooms** All en suite
**payment** Cash, cheques

Room General P

## WOOLACOMBE, Devon Map ref 1C1

★★★★
GUEST ACCOMMODATION
SILVER AWARD

B&B PER ROOM PER NIGHT
S £40.00–£50.00
D £60.00–£72.00

### Sunny Nook

Beach Road, Woolacombe EX34 7AA **t** (01271) 870964 **e** kate@sunnynook.co.uk

**sunnynook.co.uk**

A small, welcoming and friendly B&B for the more discerning guest. A real home from home. Close to Woolacombe's sandy beach, and South West Coast Path.

**open** All year except Christmas and New Year
**bedrooms** 3 double, 1 twin
**bathrooms** All en suite
**payment** Credit/debit cards, cash, cheques, euros

Room General 12 P Leisure

## YELVERTON, Devon Map ref 1C2

★★★★
GUEST ACCOMMODATION

B&B PER ROOM PER NIGHT
S £39.50–£45.00
D £70.00–£80.00

### Overcombe House

Old Station Road, Yelverton PL20 7RA **t** (01822) 853501 **e** enquiries@overcombehotel.co.uk

**overcombehotel.co.uk** REAL-TIME BOOKING

**open** All year except Christmas
**bedrooms** 4 double, 3 twin, 1 single
**bathrooms** All en suite
**payment** Credit/debit cards, cash

Offering a warm, friendly welcome in relaxed, comfortable surroundings with a substantial breakfast using local and home-made produce. Enjoying beautiful views over the village and Dartmoor. Conveniently located for exploring the varied attractions of both Devon and Cornwall, in particular Dartmoor National Park and the adjacent Tamar Valley.

**SAT NAV** *PL20 7RA* **ONLINE MAP**

WALKERS WELCOME CYCLISTS WELCOME

Room General 5 P Leisure

## YEOVIL, Somerset Map ref 2A3

★★★
BED & BREAKFAST

B&B PER ROOM PER NIGHT
S £35.00–£45.00
D £60.00–£70.00

### Pendomer House

Nr Yeovil BA22 9PB **t** (01935) 862785 **e** enquiries@pendomerhouse.co.uk

**pendomerhouse.co.uk**

Pendomer House is a lovely old rectory, only three miles from Yeovil, but set in a stunning position. Comfortable and very peaceful.

**open** All year
**bedrooms** 1 double, 1 twin, 1 family
**bathrooms** All en suite
**payment** Cash, cheques

Room General Leisure

## Do you have access needs?

Look for the National Accessible Scheme symbols if you have special hearing, visual or mobility needs.

For **key to symbols** see page 7

# The Channel Islands

Jersey, Guernsey, Herm, Sark and Alderney

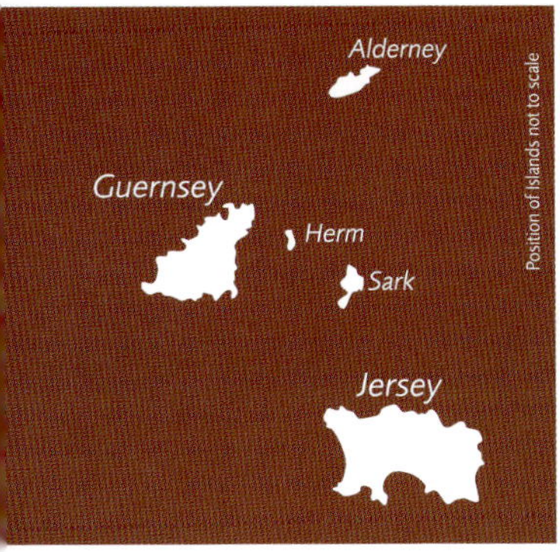




Clockwise: St Ouens Bay, Jersey; Alderney; St Peters Port, Guernsey

# Great days out

## The Channel Islands combine the spirit of Britain with the heart of Old Normandy in a rare fusion of English and French. Ancient customs blend with global commerce, beach and country living, the modern, the cosmopolitan and the homespun. Welcome to five distinct islands, two cultures and one memorable holiday.

### Rock pools to rural treasures

Enjoy beautiful, safe sandy beaches, secret coves and rock pools, rugged harbours, stunning cliffs and fantastic flora and fauna. Inland, each island has a country character that follows the rhythm of the seasons. Sleepy lanes, private gardens, nature reserves and migrating birds are just some of the rural treasures waiting to surprise you. Take the charming Heritage Walk from **Samarès Manor** on Jersey, or spot the rare Aquatic Warbler on the wetland reserve at **La Claire Mare** on Guernsey. And with a temperate climate offering more warmth and sunshine than elsewhere in the British Isles, you'll find the islands in bloom all year round.

Bonne Nuit Bay, Jersey

### Frontline history

Roll back the years to uncover Channel Island history, beginning with Neolithic Man and some of the oldest manmade structures in Europe: visit **La Hougue Bie** on Jersey, an extraordinary burial chamber and focal point for religious activity or Guernsey's Dehus Dolmen to see mysterious carvings. Twentieth-century turmoil also left its mark when the islands became bulwarks in Europe's WWII Atlantic Wall. Get a taste of daily life under occupation in the superbly preserved **Jersey War Tunnels** built by forced labour and now home to a gripping exhibition. Train your sights with the very rangefinders used by German forces in Guernsey's **Pleinmont Observation Tower**, or wander through a skilfully recreated wartime street scene at the **German Occupation Museum**.

### Five lives

Each of the five islands has a distinctive personality – explore and you'll be charmed by their open welcome.

Guernsey is a heady mix of dazzling scenery and the best of contemporary living. Take inspiring walks or spend lazy days on wonderful beaches. Then explore the bustling harbour town of **St Peter Port** and let its tapestry of architectural styles tell the story of the region's changing fortunes. Here bistros, restaurants and boutiques jostle for your attention while, in the harbour, ferries are readied to take you to the sister islands. Wander through the museums at **Castle Cornet** and witness the firing of the noon day gun.

In Jersey, culture vultures will discover history at every turn, walkers will be captivated by breathtaking natural beauty and families can relax without a care on pristine beaches. In St Helier, take the Castle Ferry to the rocky islet where Sir Walter Raleigh built **Elizabeth Castle** and witness the 12-noon 'call to arms'

Left to right: Dehus Dolmen, Guernsey; Creux, Guernsey

**did you know...** these low-duty islands are a shopper's paradise – treat yourself!

and the firing of the castle cannon. Learn bygone skills and catch up with gossip from the time of Charles II at **Hamptonne**, a country life museum, or explore local marine ecology and learn how tides work, at the **Discovery Pier**. Jersey is also the ideal place to clear your head – come and indulge in some exhilarating outdoor sports, or simply live the life.

**Herm**, a tranquil island idyll that's easily reached from Guernsey by ferry, is a favourite with visitors and locals alike. No wonder: as soon as you step off the boat, the stresses of the modern world evaporate. **Alderney**, the closest island to France, feels more remote, although quickly accessible by air. Now you're in a paradise for nature lovers, where varied and rare wildlife from blonde hedgehogs to gannets share the invigorating landscapes. Refresh in the restaurants and lively pubs of the capital, **St Anne's**. Another day, step back in time in traffic-free **Sark** whose superb coastal views and picturesque rural interior can be best experienced on foot, by hired bicycle or horse and trap.

## Best of two cultures

Throughout history, the islands have taken the best of Gallic and British culture: taste it now in the delicious cuisine, whether a casual snack of a fresh crab sandwich in a country pub or luxury seafood in a Michelin-starred restaurant. Norman Law, street names, surnames and local patois – a form of ancient French – give a romantic air. English conversation, the main language, extends a contemporary welcome. Stamps and currency, distinct from mainland Britain, also add to the islands' special sense of place.

Herm

## Small islands, big attractions

Jersey, just 45 square miles, is packed with things to do, from shopping in the colourful town of **St Helier** to visiting the internationally famed **Durrell Wildlife Conservation Trust** to see exotic and endangered species. Delve into the island's past and rich maritime heritage at award-winning museums, unlock the secrets of **Mont Orgueil Castle**, Gorey. And plenty of attractions provide fun-filled family days out, like **Jersey Pottery** and **The Living Legend** adventure and leisure village.

Guernsey, too, embraces a wide range of must-sees, from the tiny wildlife preserve and remains of a 12th-century priory on **Lihou Island**, to museums, family activity and craft centres, quaint tearooms and top quality restaurants. Take in the extraordinary decoration of **Victor Hugo House**, where the writer of Les Misérables spent 14 years in exile, or discover the fate of ships wrecked on the infamous Hanois reefs on the rocky west coast at **Fort Grey and Shipwreck Museum**. Find out what life was like 100 years ago at the **National Trust of Guernsey Folk and Costume Museum** and thrill to the momentous events that **Castle Cornet** has witnessed.

**why not...** island hop to see some of the most beautiful scenery in Europe?

## Walks to water-skiing

Feeling active? The islands are made for walkers! How about a slow stroll across the sands, or an energetic hike along cliff-top paths and into rocky coves. And the perfect way of taking in all the sights, sounds and smells is from the seat of a bicycle. Rent one or bring your own, enjoy a leisurely scenic ride for a few miles or gear yourself up for a more challenging route. Anglers, of course, are spoilt for choice – there's never a bad time to fish in the Channel Islands because such a wide variety of species flourish in the waters: bass to ballan wrasse, grey mullet to good old reliable garfish; something for every season.

Check the calendar for year-round high-level events like motor sports, powerboating, athletics and bowling. Watch classic cars tackle a twisting, scenic route across the island at the **Jersey Festival of Motoring** in June, then set sail for Guernsey's **Rocquaine Regatta** in August and the **Jersey Regatta** in September. Don't forget to save some energy, though – you'll need it to complete the famous Around Island Walk during Jersey's **Autumn Walking Week**. If you are looking for something a little more unusual, Guernsey hosts an **Underwater Cycling Race** in September where you can marvel at cyclists in full diving kit taking to the local outdoor bathing pools on specially modified bikes! Raise your pulse in Jersey wakeboarding, water-skiing, on banana rides, speedboat trips and ocean kayaks, or in Guernsey take an exhilarating rib ride!

Left to right: Fort Grey, Guernsey; St Brelades Bay, Jersey

# Destinations

## Alderney

With its rich and varied wildlife Alderney remains almost totally unaffected by the outside world, and is a paradise for nature lovers. Pull on your boots and discover over 30 miles of walks over cliffs and golden bays, across exposed commons, past Victorian fortresses and World War II batteries and alongside a scenic and challenging golf course. St Anne, the capital town, is a pretty community of colour-washed houses, cobbled streets and shops. Its magnificent church, known as 'the cathedral of the Channel Islands' is a must-see, and there are plenty of welcoming pubs and restaurants in which to relax and soak up the atmosphere.

## Guernsey

Just seventy miles by fast ferry, or a short flight from mainland England, you'll find a heady mix of stunning scenery and the best of contemporary living. From its capital of St Peter Port – often regarded as the prettiest harbour in Europe – its miles of golden beaches, clear blue sea and breathtaking cliff walks to its early spring, superb seafood and fascinating history, Guernsey is the perfect mix of Continental and natural beauty.

St Peter Port, the island's capital, is a bustling harbour town in which a tapestry of architectural styles tells the story of the region's changing fortunes.

Enjoy a wide choice of dining experiences, where unsurprisingly fresh fish is in abundance. Shopping in St Peter Port is an experience not to be missed: electronic and photographic equipment, jewellery and perfume are all good, low-duty buys, and, of course, the famous Guernsey jumper. Small boutiques offer exclusive clothes, shoes and leather goods, whilst the Old Quarter is the place to find antiques. For a memorable excursion, take a trip to one of Guernsey's sister islands (Alderney, Herm or Sark) – frequent ferries run from St Peter Port harbour. And planes fly to Alderney regularly.

## Herm

Disover this unspoiled paradise of sand dunes, long golden beaches, hidden bays, cliffwalks and seabreeze-combed common, just twenty minutes by boat from Guernsey. Allow yourself time to spend at least a couple of hours on Shell Beach, where clear waters lap the white sand made from millions of tiny shell fragments. It's easy to visit Herm in a day, but to really appreciate the island's charm, consider an overnight stay.

Shell Beach, Herm

# The Channel Islands

Left to right: St Peter Port, Guernsey; Bluebell Valley, Guernsey; St Aubin, Jersey

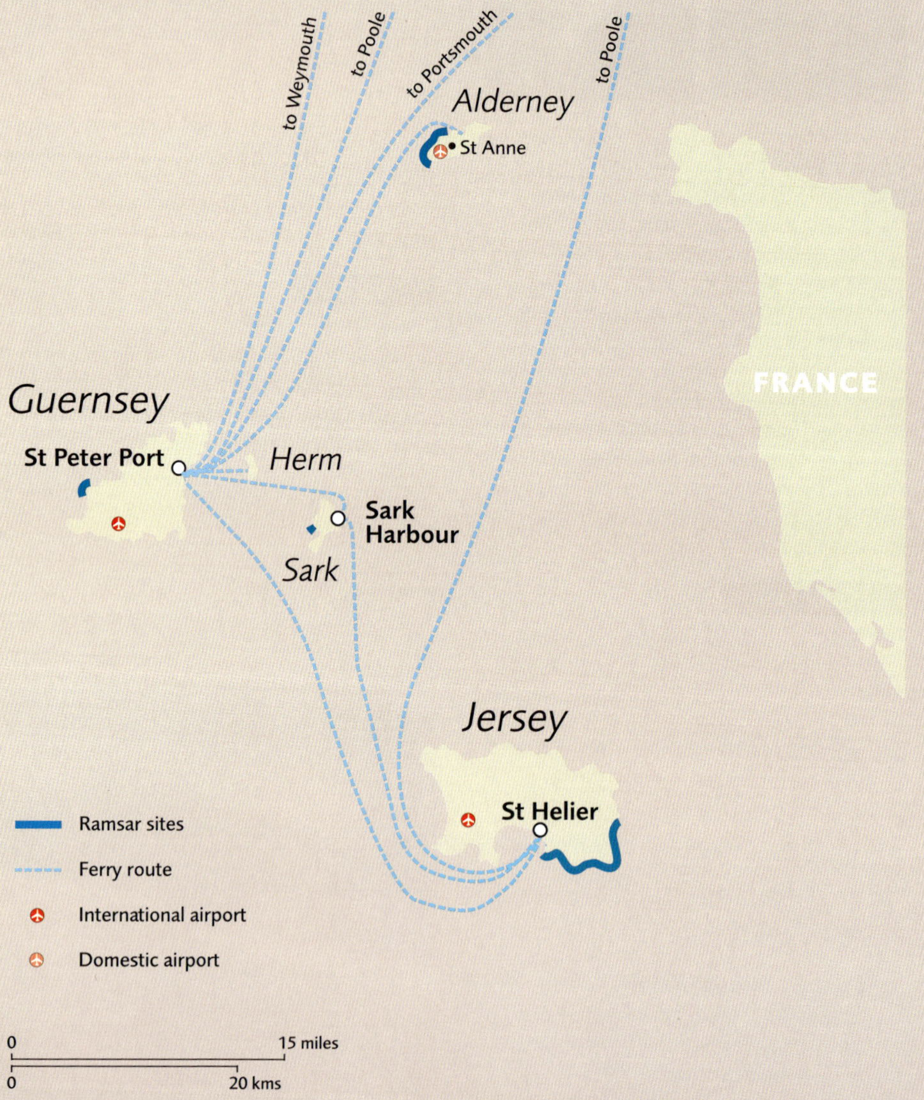

## Jersey

Clear water and beaches surround some 45 miles of coastline – the island's greatest natural treasure. Sweeping bays in the south give way to dramatic cliffs in the north offering spectacular scenery and stunning vistas. If food is your passion your taste buds are in for a real treat with over 170 eateries featuring Jersey's delicious local produce, top chefs and gourmet delights from around the world.

The streets of St Helier buzz with life. By day shop 'til you drop, dine al fresco whilst watching exciting street theatre or take a nautical jaunt with an appointed Blue Badge guide around the town's historic harbours. There are lots of attractions to explore, too. By night, linger in the warm evening sun in Royal Square, join theatre-goers at the Jersey Opera House or enjoy live music in one of the town's many pubs.

## Sark

The picturesque island of Sark is the perfect escape. Traffic-free and overflowing with natural beauty, the island is easily reached by ferry from Guernsey. Take advantage of this walkers' paradise and follow one of the many coastal walks. Experience peace and tranquillity, admire wildflowers and seabirds, and feel like you have been transported to another world. If you wish to stay a little longer, there are a number of hotels and good restaurants to choose from.

Hog's Back, Sark

For lots more great ideas go to visitbritain.com/destinations, visitguernsey.com and jersey.com

Clockwise: St Martin's Parish Church, Guernsey; St Lawrence, Jersey; Portelet Bay, Jersey; Rousse Tower, Guernsey

# Visitor attractions

## Family and Fun

**aMaizin! Maze and Adventure Park**
*St Peter, Jersey*
(01534) 482116
jerseyleisure.com
*Award-winning attraction featuring maize maze, activities and entertainment.*

**Discovery Pier**
*Gorey, Jersey*
(01534) 617704
eco-active.je
*Interactive fun bringing Jersey's marine ecology to shore.*

**Guernsey Aquarium**
*St Peter Port, Guernsey*
(01481) 723301
visitguernsey.com
*Local, European and tropical marine life.*

**Jersey Goldsmiths and Lion Park**
*St Lawrence, Jersey*
(01534) 482098
jerseygoldsmiths.com
*Gold and gemstones set among beautiful lakes and gardens.*

**La Mare Wine Estate**
*St Mary, Jersey*
(01534) 481178
lamarewineestate.com
*Vineyards, winery and visitor centre with children's activities.*

**The Living Legend**
*St Peter, Jersey*
(01534) 485496
jerseyslivinglegend.co.je
*Adventure and leisure village packed with family fun.*

**Oatlands Village**
*St Sampson, Guernsey*
(01481) 244282
*Watch craftspeople at work, plus shops and café.*

**Samarès Manor**
*St Clement, Jersey*
(01534) 870551
samaresmanor.com
*Historic house, splendid gardens, crafts and children's activities.*

## Heritage

**Castle Cornet**
*St Peter Port, Guernsey*
(01481) 721657
museums.gov.gg
*Ancient harbour fortress containing maritime and military museums.*

**Elizabeth Castle**
*St Helier, Jersey*
(01534) 723971
jerseyheritage.com
*16thC stronghold with daily call to arms.*

**German Occupation Museum**
*Forest, Guernsey*
(01481) 238205
visitguernsey.com
*Life during the WWII featuring authentic occupation street.*

**Jersey Museum and Art Gallery**
*St Helier, Jersey*
(01534) 633300
jerseyheritage.com
*Discover the history, traditions and culture of Jersey.*

**Jersey War Tunnels**
*St Lawrence, Jersey*
(01534) 860808
jerseywartunnels.com
*Gripping glimpse of life on Jersey under occupation.*

**La Hougue Bie**
*St Saviour, Jersey*
(01534) 853823
jerseyheritage.com
*One of the finest burial mounds in Europe.*

**La Vallette Underground Military Museum**
*St Peter Port, Guernsey*
(01481) 722300
visitguernsey.com
*Military museum housed in air-conditioned German tunnel complex.*

**The Little Chapel**
*St Andrews, Guernsey*
(01481) 237200
thelittlechapel.org
*Possibly the smallest chapel in the world.*

**Mont Orgueil Castle**
*Gorey, Jersey*
(01534) 853292
jerseyheritage.com
*Superbly preserved castle, the jewel in Jersey's crown.*

**Pleinmont Observation Tower**
*Torteval, Guernsey*
(01481) 238205
visitguernsey.com
*Naval observation tower used by the Germans 1942-45.*

**Victor Hugo House**
*St Peter Port, Guernsey*
(01481) 721911
visitguernsey.com
*Where the famous writer spent 14 years in exile.*

## Indoors

**Fort Grey & Shipwreck Museum**
*Rocquaine, Guernsey*
(01481) 265036
museums.gov.gg
*Martello tower housing museum with many salvaged artefacts.*

**Guernsey Museum and Art Gallery**
*St Peter Port, Guernsey*
(01481) 726518
museums.gov.gg
*The island's natural and human history plus exhibitions.*

**The Guernsey Tapestry**
*St Peter Port, Guernsey*
(01481) 727106
guernseytapestry.org.gg
*Tells the 1,000-year story of Guernsey in a remarkable tapestry.*

**Jersey Pottery**
*Gorey, Jersey*
(01534) 850850
jerseypottery.com
*Decorate your own pottery at this famous attraction.*

**Maritime Museum and Occupation Tapestry**
*St Helier, Jersey*
(01534) 811043
jerseyheritage.com
*Interactive museum and famous tapestry commemorating wartime Jersey.*

**National Trust of Guernsey Folk and Costume Museum**
*Castel, Guernsey*
(01481) 255384
nationaltrust-gsy.org.gg
*Exhibitions and displays of old Guernsey life.*

## Outdoors

**Durrell Wildlife**
*Trinity, Jersey*
(01534) 860000
durrell.org
*World-famous sanctuary for exotic and endangered species.*

**Hamptonne**
*St Lawrence, Jersey*
(01534) 863955
jerseyheritage.com
*Superbly restored farm buildings recreate rural life.*

**La Claire Mare**
*St Pierre du Bois, Guernsey*
(01481) 725093
societe.org.gg
*Nature reserve featuring wet grassland and reedbeds.*

**Le Vaux de Monel and La Varde Rock**
*Rocquaine, Guernsey*
nationaltrust-gsy.org.gg
*Naturalised garden with panoramic views over Rocquaine Bay.*

**Lihou Island**
*St Pierre du Bois, Guernsey*
(01481) 266294
lihouisland.com
*Unspoilt bird sanctuary reached by tidal causeway.*

## Events 2009

**Liberation Day**
Various venues, Jersey
jersey.com/liberation
**9 May 2009**

**World Jersey Cheese Festival**
Trinity, Jersey
jerseycheese.com
**23 - 25 May 2009**

**Seafood Festival**
Various venues, Guernsey
goodfoodguernsey.gg
**1 - 31 Jul 2009**

**Out of the Blue Maritime Festival**
St Helier, Jersey
jersey.com
**4 - 5 Jul 2009**

**Battle of Flowers Carnival**
St Helier, Jersey
battleofflowers.com
**13 - 14 Aug 2009**

**Battle of Britain Week**
Various venues, Guernsey
visitguernsey.com
**7 - 13 Sep 2009**

**International Chess Festival**
Vale, Guernsey
visitguernsey.com
**18 - 24 Oct 2009**

**Guernsey Jazz Festival**
St Peter Port, Guernsey
dukeofrichmond.com
**30 Oct - 1 Nov 2009**

**La Fête dé Noué**
Various venues, Jersey
jersey.com
**28 Nov - 14 Dec 2009**

# Regional contacts and information

For more information on accommodation, attractions, activities, events and holidays in the Channel Islands, contact one of the following tourism organisations. Their websites have a wealth of information and publications to help you get the most out of your visit.

## Guernsey

Guernsey Information Centre
North Esplanade, St Peter Port
Guernsey GY1 3AN
**t** (01481) 723552
**t** 0800 028 5353 (information pack request)
**e** enquiries@visitguernsey.com
**w** visitguernsey.com

## Alderney

States of Alderney
PO Box 1
Alderney
GY9 3AA
**t** (01481) 822811

## Jersey

Jersey Tourism
Liberation Place
St Helier
Jersey
JE1 1BB
**t** (01534) 448800
**e** info@jersey.com
**w** jersey.com

Free publications available to order from Jersey Tourism include:

- **What's on**
- **Jersey Map**
- **Walking Guide**

Clockwise: Liberation Day, Guernsey; Regatta, Guernsey; La Fête dé Noué, Jersey

# Help before you go

When it comes to your next break, the first stage of your journey could be closer than you think.

You've probably got a Tourist Information Centre nearby which is there to serve the local community – as well as visitors. Knowledgeable staff will be happy to help you, wherever you're heading.

Many Tourist Information Centres can provide you with maps and guides, and it's often possible to book accommodation and travel tickets too.

You'll find the address of your nearest centre in your local phone book, or look in the regional sections in this guide for a list of Tourist Information Centres.

where to stay in

# The Channel Islands

For the location of the accommodation listed, refer to the maps at the front of this guide.

## Accommodation symbols

Symbols give useful information about services and facilities. On page 7 you can find a key to these symbols.

**GUERNSEY Map 6**

★★★★
GUEST ACCOMMODATION

B&B PER ROOM PER NIGHT
S £35.00–£45.00
D £30.00–£35.00

## Auberge du Val

Sous L'eglise, St Saviour GY7 9FX **t** (01481) 263862 **e** aubduval@guernsey.net

A warm welcome awaits you at this 150-year-old farmhouse sitting in three acres of its own grounds, in a beautiful trout-streamed, wooded valley. Restaurant serving unusual dishes.

**open** All year except Christmas
**bedrooms** 4 double, 2 twin, 2 family
**bathrooms** All en suite
**payment** Credit/debit cards, cash, cheques, euros

Room General

**GUERNSEY Map 6**

★★★★
BED & BREAKFAST

B&B PER ROOM PER NIGHT
D £60.00–£70.00

## Hill Crest Cottage Bed & Breakfast

St Clair Hill, St Sampsons GY2 4DS **t** (01481) 240 635 **e** sgcgold@yahoo.co.uk

**hillcrestguernsey.co.uk**

Lovely guesthouse with all comforts. 100% satisfied customers to date.

**open** All year
**bedrooms** 1 double, 1 twin
**bathrooms** 1 en suite, 1 private
**payment** Credit/debit cards, cash, cheques

Room General P Leisure

**GUERNSEY Map 6**

★★★
GUEST HOUSE

B&B PER ROOM PER NIGHT
S £29.00–£37.00
D £60.00–£74.00

## St Georges

21 St Georges Esplanade, St Peter Port GY1 2BG **t** (01481) 721027 **e** stgeorges@guernsey.net

**stgeorges-guernsey.com**

Twenty en suite rooms, eight with sea view of neighbouring islands Herm and Sark. Tea-making facilities, TV (nine channels), DVD, Wi-Fi, in-house computer. Ground-floor rooms. Full English breakfast.

**open** All year
**bedrooms** 4 double, 6 twin, 2 single, 8 family
**bathrooms** All en suite
**payment** Credit/debit cards, cash, cheques

Room General Leisure

### What do the star ratings mean?

Detailed information about star ratings can be found at the back of this guide.

## JERSEY Map 6

★★★
GUEST HOUSE

B&B PER ROOM PER NIGHT
S £25.00–£37.00
D £50.00–£74.00

EVENING MEAL PER PERSON
£10.00

### Fairholme

Roseville Street, St Helier JE2 4PL **t** (01534) 732194 **e** fairholme@localdial.com

**fairholmejersey.com**

Victorian town house, located in the tranquil Havre des Pas district of St Helier. Home-cooked meals on offer, with lobster and crab as specialities. Bicycles and fishing gear available to hire.

**open** All year except Christmas and New Year
**bedrooms** 7 double, 7 twin, 1 single
**bathrooms** All en suite
**payment** Credit/debit cards, cash, cheques, euros

Room General Leisure

## JERSEY Map 6

★★★
GUEST ACCOMMODATION

B&B PER ROOM PER NIGHT
S £30.00–£80.00
D £47.00–£80.00

### St Magloire Guest House

Rue Du Crocquet, St Aubin JE3 8BZ **t** (01534) 741302 **e** stmagloireguesthouse@jerseymail.co.uk

**stmagloireguesthouse.com**

Located a short stroll from the golden sands of St Aubins Bay, charming country/coastal walks, cycle routes, sea sports, only minutes away from golf courses and the quaint village of St Aubin.

**open** All year
**bedrooms** 4 double, 3 twin, 5 family
**bathrooms** All en suite
**payment** Credit/debit cards, cash, cheques

Room TV General Leisure

## JERSEY Map 6

★★★
GUEST HOUSE

B&B PER ROOM PER NIGHT
S £34.50–£48.00
D £49.00–£76.00

### Villa d'Oro Guest House

La Grande Route de St Laurent, St Lawrence JE3 1NJ **t** (01534) 862262 **e** stay@villadorojersey.com

**villadorojersey.com** GUEST REVIEWS · SPECIAL OFFERS

In the heart of the Jersey countryside and perfectly located for exploring beautiful Jersey by foot, cycle or car. Charming B&B with pub, shop and parish church all but next door.

**open** All year except Christmas and New Year
**bedrooms** 6 double, 2 twin, 4 single
**bathrooms** All en suite
**payment** Credit/debit cards, cash, cheques

Room TV General P Leisure

## Help before you go

When it comes to your next break, the first stage of your journey could be closer than you think.

You've probably got a Tourist Information Centre nearby which is there to serve the local community – as well as visitors. Knowledgeable staff will be happy to help you, wherever you're heading.

Many Tourist Information Centres can provide you with maps and guides, and it's often possible to book accommodation and travel tickets too.

You'll find the address of your nearest centre in your local phone book, or look in the regional sections in this guide for a list of Tourist Information Centres.

# Enjoy England assessed accommodation

On the following pages you will find an exclusive listing of all bed and breakfast accommodation in England that has been assessed for quality by Enjoy England.

The information includes brief contact details for each place to stay, together with its star rating, classification and quality award if appropriate. The listing also shows if an establishment has a National Accessible rating or participates in the Welcome schemes: Cyclists Welcome, Walkers Welcome, Welcome Pets! and Families Welcome (see the front of the guide for further information).

Accommodation is listed by region and then alphabetically by place name. Establishments may be located in, or a short distance from, the places in the blue bands.

More detailed information on all the properties shown in bold can be found in the regional sections (where establishments have paid to have their details included). To find these entries please refer to the property index at the back of this guide.

The list which follows was compiled slightly later than the regional sections. For this reason you may find that, in a few instances, a rating and quality award may differ between the two sections. This list contains the most up-to-date information and was correct at the time of going to press.

# NORTHERN ENGLAND

## ABBEYSTEAD
Lancashire

**Greenbank Farmhouse, Lancaster** ★★★
*Bed & Breakfast*
Abbeystead, Lancaster
LA2 9BA
t (01524) 792063
e tait@greenbankfarmhouse.freeserve.co.uk
w greenbankfarmhouse.co.uk

## ACCRINGTON
Lancashire

**Norwood Guest House**
★★★★ *Guest House*
**SILVER AWARD**
349 Whalley Road, Accrington
BB5 5DF
t (01254) 398132
e stuart@norwoodguesthouse.co.uk
w norwoodguesthouse.co.uk

## ACKLAM
North Yorkshire

**Trout Pond Barn** ★★★★
*Farmhouse*
Acklam Malton, Malton
YO17 9RG
t (01653) 658468
e troutpondbarn@aol.com
w troutpondbarn.co.uk

## ADDINGHAM
West Yorkshire

**Beck House Farm** ★★★★
*Bed & Breakfast*
**SILVER AWARD**
Moorside Lane, Addingham, Ilkley LS29 9JX
t (01943) 830397
e cathandave@tiscali.co.uk
w beckhousefarm.co.uk

---

**The Crown Inn** ★★★★ *Inn*
136 Main Street, Addingham, Ilkley LS29 0NS
t (01943) 830278
e mariawells350@tiscali.co.uk
w thecrowninnaddingham.co.uk

---

**Lumb Beck Farmhouse Bed and Breakfast** ★★★★
*Bed & Breakfast*
**SILVER AWARD**
Moorside Lane, Addingham Moorside, Ilkley LS29 9JX
t (01943) 830400
e croft-lumbbeck@tiscali.co.uk

## AINTREE
Merseyside

**A Church View Guest House**
★★ *Bed & Breakfast*
7 Church Avenue, Liverpool
L9 4SG
t (0151) 525 8166

## ALDBROUGH
East Riding of Yorkshire

**West Carlton Country Guest House** ★★★★ *Guest House*
**GOLD AWARD**
Carlton Road, Aldbrough, Hornsea HU11 4RB
t (01964) 527724
e caroline_maltas@hotmail.com
w west-carlton.co.uk

## ALDERLEY EDGE
Cheshire

**Mayfield Bed & Breakfast @ Sheila's** ★★★
*Bed & Breakfast*
Wilmslow Road, Alderley Edge
SK9 7QW
t (01625) 583991 & 07703 289663

## ALDFIELD
North Yorkshire

**Bay Tree Farm** ★★★★
*Farmhouse* **GOLD AWARD**
Aldfield, Ripon HG4 3BE
t (01765) 620394
e val@btfarm.entadsl.com
w baytreefarm.co.uk

## ALLENDALE
Northumberland

**Deneholme** ★★★
*Guest Accommodation*
The Dene, Hexham NE47 9PX
t (01434) 618579
e info@deneholme.co.uk
w deneholme.co.uk

---

**High Keenley Fell Farm**
★★★★ *Farmhouse*
Allendale NE47 9NU
t (01434) 618344
e camaclean@btinternet.com
w highkeenleyfarm.co.uk

---

**Keenley Thorn Farmhouse**
★★★★ *Bed & Breakfast*
**SILVER AWARD**
Keenley Thorn, Allendale
NE47 9NU
t (01434) 683248
e keithfairless@aol.com
w keenleythornfarmhouse.co.uk

---

**Struthers Farm** ★★★★
*Farmhouse*
Catton, Hexham NE47 9LP
t (01434) 683580

---

**Thornley House** ★★★★
*Bed & Breakfast*
Thornley Gate NE47 9NH
t (01434) 683255
e enquiries@thornleyhouse.co.uk
w thornleyhouse.co.uk

## ALNMOUTH
Northumberland

**Alnmouth Golf Club** ★★★
*Guest Accommodation*
Foxton Hall, Alnwick NE66 3BE
t (01665) 830231
e secretary@alnmouthgolfclub.com
w alnmouthgolfclub.com

---

**Beech Lodge** ★★★★
*Bed & Breakfast*
**SILVER AWARD**
8 Alnwood, Alnwick NE66 3NN
t (01665) 830709
e beechlodge@hotmail.com
w welcomenorthumberland.co.uk

---

**Bilton Barns Farmhouse**
★★★★ *Farmhouse*
**SILVER AWARD**
Bilton NE66 2TB
t (01665) 830427
e dorothy@biltonbarns.com
w biltonbarns.com

---

**Hope and Anchor Inn** ★★★
*Inn*
44 Northumberland Street, Alnmouth NE66 2RA
t (01665) 830363
e info@hopeandanchorholidays.co.uk
w hopeandanchorholidays.co.uk

---

**Nether Grange**
Rating Applied For
*Guest Accommodation*
Marine Road, Alnmouth
NE66 2RZ
t (020) 8511 1534

---

**Sefton House** ★★★★
*Guest House*
15 Argyle Street, Alnmouth
NE66 2SB
t (01665) 833174
e simoneneri@aol.com
w seftonhousealnmouth.com

---

**Westlea** ★★★★
*Guest Accommodation*
**SILVER AWARD**
29 Riverside Road, Alnmouth
NE66 2SD
t (01665) 830730
e ritaandray77@btinternet.com

## ALNWICK
Northumberland

**Aln House** ★★★★
*Guest Accommodation*
**SILVER AWARD**
South Road, Alnwick NE66 2NZ
t (01665) 602265
e enquiries@alnhouse.co.uk
w alnhouse.co.uk

---

**Alndyke Bed and Breakfast**
★★★★ *Farmhouse*
**SILVER AWARD**
Alnmouth Road, Alnwick
NE66 3PB
t (01665) 510252
e laura@alndyke.co.uk
w alndyke.co.uk

---

**Alnwick Lodge** ★★★
*Guest Accommodation*
West Cawledge Park, Alnwick
NE66 2HJ
t (01665) 604363 & (01665) 603377
e bookings@alnwicklodge.com
w alnwicklodge.com

---

**Aydon House** ★★★
*Guest Accommodation*
South Road, Alnwick
NE66 2NT
t (01665) 602218
w smoothhound.co.uk/hotels/aydon

---

**Bailiffgate Bed and Breakfast** ★★★
*Guest Accommodation*
1 Bailiffgate, Alnwick NE66 1LZ
t (01665) 602078
e will@wakefield.onyxnet.co.uk
w alnwickaccommodation.com

---

**Beaconsfield B&B** ★★★
*Bed & Breakfast*
3 Beaconsfield Terrace, Alnwick NE66 1XB
t (01665) 604912
e enquiries@beaconsfieldbb.co.uk
w beaconsfieldbb.co.uk

---

**Boulmer Village B&B**
★★★★ *Bed & Breakfast*
21 Boulmer Village, Boulmer
NE66 3BS
t (01665) 577262
e hazel_campbell@btopenworld.com

---

**Brunton House** ★★★
*Bed & Breakfast*
Brunton, Embleton NE66 3HQ
t (01665) 589198
e victoriajolliffe@tiscali.co.uk
w bruntonhouse.co.uk

---

**Castle Gate Guest House**
★★★ *Bed & Breakfast*
23 Bondgate Without, Alnwick
NE66 1PR
t (01665) 602657 & 07706 113434
e tracy@amfr.co.uk

---

**Castleview B & B** ★★★★
*Bed & Breakfast*
1b Bailiffgate, Alnwick
NE66 1LZ
t (01665) 606227
e enquiries@castleviewalnwick.co.uk
w castleviewalnwick.co.uk

---

**Charlton House** ★★★★
*Guest Accommodation*
2 Aydon Gardens, South Road, Alnwick NE66 2NT
t (01665) 605185
w s-h-systems.co.uk

---

**Courtyard Garden** ★★★★
*Bed & Breakfast*
**SILVER AWARD**
Prudhoe Street, Alnwick
NE66 1UW
t (01665) 603393
e maureenpeter10@btinternet.com
w courtyardgarden-alnwick.com

---

**Crosshills House** ★★★★
*Guest House*
40 Blakelaw Road, Alnwick
NE66 1BA
t (01665) 602518
e crosshillshouse@hotmail.com
w crosshillshouse.ntb.org.uk/

**The Georgian Guest House**
★★★ *Guest House*
3 Hotspur Street, Alnwick
NE66 1QE
**t** (01665) 602398
**e** enquiries@georgianguesthouse.co.uk
**w** georgianguesthouse.co.uk

**Green Batt House** ★★★
*Guest Accommodation*
Green Batt NE66 1TY
**t** 07985 490327
**e** gbannex@aol.com

**Hawkhill Farmhouse** ★★★★
*Farmhouse*
Lesbury NE66 3PG
**t** (01665) 830380
**e** stay@hawkhillfarmhouse.com
**w** hawkhillfarmhouse.com

**Limetree Cottage** ★★★★
*Bed & Breakfast*
38 Eglingham Village, Eglingham NE66 2TX
**t** (01665) 578322
**e** viwhillis@aol.com

**Linhope House** ★★★★★
*Guest House*
South Street, Alnwick
NE66 1AH
**t** (01665) 603904
**e** linhopehouse@aol.com
**w** linhopehouse.co.uk

**The Masons Arms Country Inn** ★★★★ *Inn*
Stamford Cott NE66 3RX
**t** (01665) 577275
**e** bookings@masonsarms.net
**w** masonsarms.net

**Norfolk** ★★★★
*Bed & Breakfast*
**SILVER AWARD**
41 Blakelaw Road, Alnwick
NE66 1BA
**t** (01665) 602892
**w** norfolkhouse-alnwick.co.uk

**Percy Terrace Bed and Breakfast** ★★★
*Bed & Breakfast*
3 Percy Terrace, Alnwick
NE66 1AF
**t** (01665) 606867
**e** bookings@alnwick-bedandbreakfast.co.uk
**w** alnwick-bedandbreakfast.co.uk/

**Prudhoe Croft** ★★★★
*Bed & Breakfast*
**SILVER AWARD**
11 Prudhoe Street, Alnwick
NE66 1UW
**t** (01665) 606197
**e** prudhoecroft@supanet.com
**w** prudhoecroft.co.uk

**The Queens Head Hotel**
★★★★ *Inn*
25 Market Street, Alnwick
NE66 1SS
**t** (01665) 604691
**e** stay@alnwickqueensheadhotel.co.uk
**w** alnwickqueensheadhotel.co.uk

**Redfoot Lea Bed & Breakfast**
★★★★ *Bed & Breakfast*
**SILVER AWARD**
Redfoot Lea, Greensfield Moor Farm, Alnwick NE66 2HH
**t** (01665) 603891
**e** info@redfootlea.co.uk
**w** redfootlea.co.uk

**Reighamsyde** ★★★★
*Bed & Breakfast*
Alnwick Moor, Alnwick
NE66 2AJ
**t** (01665) 602535
**e** reighamsyde@aol.com

**Rooftops** ★★★★
*Guest Accommodation*
**SILVER AWARD**
14 Blakelaw Road, Alnwick
NE66 1AZ
**t** (01665) 604201
**e** rooftops.alnwick@tiscali.co.uk
**w** rooftops.ntb.org.uk

**Ros View** ★★★★
*Bed & Breakfast*
14 Mill Hill, Chatton NE66 5PA
**t** (01668) 215289
**e** info@coastal-accommodation.co.uk
**w** coastal-accommodation.co.uk

**Roseworth** ★★★★
*Bed & Breakfast*
Alnmouth Road, Alnwick
NE66 2PR
**t** (01665) 603911
**e** roseworth@tiscali.co.uk
**w** roseworthalnwick.co.uk

**The Shepherds Rest** ★★ *Inn*
Alnwick Moor, Alnwick
NE66 2AH
**t** (01665) 510809
**e** robert@rlaybourn.wanadoo.co.uk
**w** the-shepherds-rest.co.uk

**Tate House Bed & Breakfast**
★★★ *Bed & Breakfast*
11 Bondgate Without, Alnwick
NE66 1PR
**t** (01665) 604661
**e** bookings@stayinalnwick.co.uk
**w** stayinalnwick.co.uk

**Tower Restaurant and Accommodation** ★★★★
*Restaurant with Rooms*
10 Bondgate Within, Alnwick
NE66 1TD
**t** (01665) 603888
**e** roylhardy@o2.co.uk
**w** tower-alnwick.co.uk

**West Acre House** ★★★★★
*Guest Accommodation*
**GOLD AWARD**
West Acres, Alnwick
NE66 2QA
**t** (01665) 510374 & 07746 038180
**e** info@westacrehouse.co.uk
**w** westacrehouse.co.uk

## ALSTON
### Cumbria

**Rosemount Cottage** ★★★★
*Guest Accommodation*
**SILVER AWARD**
Rosemount, Burgh-by-Sands, Carlisle CA5 6AN
**t** (01228) 576440
**e** tweentown@aol.com
**w** rosemountcottage.co.uk

**YHA Alston** ★★★ *Hostel*
The Firs, Alston CA9 3RW
**t** (01434) 381509

## ALWINTON
### Northumberland

**Rose and Thistle** ★★★★ *Inn*
Alwinton NE65 7BQ
**t** (01669) 650226
**e** stay@roseandthistlealwinton.com
**w** roseandthistlealwinton.com

## AMBLE
### Northumberland

**Amble Guesthouse** ★★★
*Guest Accommodation*
16 Leazes Street, Amble
NE65 0AL
**t** (01665) 714661
**e** stephmclaughlin@aol.com
**w** theamblein.co.uk

**Harbour Guest House** ★★★
*Guest House*
24 Leazes Street, Amble
NE65 0AA
**t** (01665) 710381
**e** info@ambleharbourguesthouse.co.uk
**w** ambleharbourguesthouse.co.uk

**No 20** ★★★ *Bed & Breakfast*
Marine House, Marine Road, Amble NE65 0BB
**t** (01665) 711965
**e** moe2@hotmail.co.uk
**w** numbertwenty.co.uk

## AMBLE-BY-THE-SEA
### Northumberland

**Coquetside** ★★★★
*Bed & Breakfast*
16 Broomhill Street, Amble-by-the-Sea NE65 0AN
**t** (01665) 710352

**Togston Hall Farmhouse**
★★★ *Guest Accommodation*
North Togston, Amble
NE65 0HR
**t** (01665) 712699
**e** togstonhallfarmhouse@yahoo.co.uk

## AMBLESIDE
### Cumbria

**2 Cambridge Villas** ★★★★
*Guest House*
Church Street, Ambleside
LA22 9DL
**t** (015394) 32142
**e** charles@black475.fsnet.co.uk
**w** 2cambridgevillas.co.uk

**3 Cambridge Villas** ★★★★
*Guest House*
Church Street, Ambleside
LA22 9DL
**t** (015394) 32307
**e** cambridgevillas3@aol.com
**w** 3cambridgevillas.co.uk

**Amboseli Lodge** ★★★★
*Bed & Breakfast*
**SILVER AWARD**
Rothay Road, Ambleside
LA22 0EE
**t** (015394) 31110
**e** enquiries@amboselilodge.co.uk
**w** amboselilodge.co.uk

**Barnes Fell Guest House**
★★★★ *Guest House*
**GOLD AWARD**
Low Gale, Ambleside
LA22 0BB
**t** (015394) 33311
**e** info@barnesfell.co.uk
**w** barnesfell.co.uk

**Brantfell House** ★★★★
*Guest House*
Rothay Road, Ambleside
LA22 0EE
**t** (015394) 32239
**e** brantfell@kencomp.net
**w** brantfell.co.uk

**Chapel House** ★★★
*Guest House*
Kirkstone Road, Ambleside
LA22 9DZ
**t** (015394) 33143
**e** info@chapelhouse-ambleside.co.uk
**w** chapelhouse-ambleside.co.uk

**Claremont House** ★★★
*Guest House*
Compston Road, Ambleside
LA22 9DJ
**t** (015394) 33448
**e** enquiries@claremontambleside.co.uk
**w** claremontambleside.co.uk

**Compston House American-Style B&B** ★★★★
*Guest House*
Compston Road, Ambleside
LA22 9DJ
**t** (015394) 32305
**e** stay@compstonhouse.co.uk
**w** compstonhouse.co.uk

**Crow How Country House**
★★★★
*Guest Accommodation*
**SILVER AWARD**
Rydal Road, Ambleside
LA22 9PN
**t** (015394) 32193
**e** stay@crowhow.co.uk
**w** crowhow.co.uk

**Dower House** ★★★★
*Bed & Breakfast*
Wray Castle, Low Wray, Ambleside LA22 0JA
**t** (015394) 33211

**Easedale Lodge Guest House**
★★★★ *Guest House*
**GOLD AWARD**
Compston Road, Ambleside
LA22 9DJ
**t** (015394) 32112
**e** enquiries@easedaleambleside.co.uk
**w** easedaleambleside.co.uk


Look out for establishments participating in the National Accessible Scheme

**Elder Grove ★★★★**
*Guest Accommodation*
SILVER AWARD
Lake Road, Ambleside
LA22 0DB
t (015394) 32504
e info@eldergrove.co.uk
w eldergrove.co.uk

**Far Nook ★★★★**
*Bed & Breakfast*
GOLD AWARD
Rydal Road, Ambleside
LA22 9BA
t (015394) 31605
w farnook.co.uk

**Fern Cottage ★★★★**
*Bed & Breakfast*
SILVER AWARD
6 Waterhead Terrace,
Ambleside LA22 0HA
t (015394) 33007
e hibbertsally@hotmail.com
w ferncottageguesthouse.co.uk

**Ferndale Lodge ★★★**
*Guest House*
Lake Road, Ambleside
LA22 0DB
t (015394) 32207
e stay@ferndalelodge.co.uk
w ferndalelodge.co.uk

**Fisherbeck ★★★★**
*Guest Accommodation*
SILVER AWARD
Lake Road, Ambleside
LA22 0DH
t (015394) 33215
e email@fisherbeckhotel.co.uk
w fisherbeckhotel.co.uk

**Foxghyll ★★★★**
*Bed & Breakfast*
Under Loughrigg, Ambleside
LA22 9LL
t (015394) 33292
e foxghyll@hotmail.com
w foxghyll.co.uk

**Freshfields Guest House**
★★★★ *Guest House*
SILVER AWARD
Wansfell Road, Ambleside
LA22 0EG
t (015394) 34469
e info@freshfieldsguesthouse.co.uk
w freshfieldsguesthouse.co.uk

**The Gables ★★★★**
*Guest Accommodation*
Church Walk, Ambleside
LA22 9DJ
t (015394) 33272
e info@thegables-ambleside.co.uk
w thegables-ambleside.co.uk

**High Wray Farm B&B**
★★★★ *Farmhouse*
SILVER AWARD
High Wray, Ambleside
LA22 0JE
t (015394) 32280
e sheila@highwrayfarm.co.uk
w highwrayfarm.co.uk

**Highfield Bed & Breakfast**
★★★★ *Bed & Breakfast*
Lake Road, Ambleside
LA22 0DB
t (015394) 32671
e info@highfield-ambleside.co.uk
w highfield-ambleside.co.uk

**Hillsdale in Ambleside**
★★★★
*Guest Accommodation*
Church Street, Ambleside
LA22 0BT
t (015394) 33174
e stay@hillsdaleambleside.co.uk
w hillsdaleambleside.co.uk

**Holme Lea Guest House**
★★★ *Guest House*
Church Street, Ambleside
LA22 0BT
t (015394) 32114
e enquiries@holmeleaguesthouse.co.uk
w holmeleaguesthouse.co.uk

**Holmeshead Farm ★★★★**
*Farmhouse*
Skelwith Fold, Ambleside
LA22 0HU
t (015394) 33048
e info@holmesheadfarm.co.uk
w holmesheadfarm.co.uk

**Kingswood 'Bee & Bee'**
★★★★ *Guest House*
GOLD AWARD
Old Lake Road, Ambleside
LA22 0AE
t (015394) 34081
e info@kingswood-guesthouse.co.uk
w kingswood-guesthouse.co.uk

**Lacet House ★★★★**
*Guest House*
Kelsick Road, Ambleside
LA22 0EA
t (015394) 34342
e lacethouse@aol.com
w lacethouse.co.uk

**Lake District Backpackers Hostel ★** *Backpackers*
High Street, Windermere
LA23 1AH
t (015394) 46374
e enquiries@lakedistrictbackpackers.co.uk
w lakedistrictbackpackers.co.uk

**Lancrigg Vegetarian Country House ★★★**
*Guest Accommodation*
Easedale, Grasmere LA22 9QN
t (015394) 35317
e info@lancrigg.co.uk
w lancrigg.co.uk

**Lattendales Guest House**
★★★★ *Guest House*
Compston Road, Ambleside
LA22 9DJ
t (015394) 32368
e info@lattendales.co.uk
w lattendales.co.uk

**Lyndale Guest House ★★★**
*Guest Accommodation*
Low Fold, Lake Road,
Ambleside LA22 0DN
t (015394) 34244
e alison@lyndale-guesthouse.co.uk
w lyndale-guesthouse.co.uk

**Meadowbank ★★★**
*Guest Accommodation*
Rydal Road, Ambleside
LA22 9BA
t (015394) 32710
e enquiries@meadowbank.org.uk

**Melrose Guest House**
★★★★
*Guest Accommodation*
Church Street, Ambleside
LA22 0BT
t (015394) 32500
e relax@melrose-guesthouse.co.uk
w melrose-guesthouse.co.uk

**Norwood House ★★★★**
*Guest Accommodation*
SILVER AWARD
Church Street, Ambleside
LA22 0BT
t (015394) 33349
e mail@norwoodhouse.net
w norwoodhouse.net

**The Old Vicarage ★★★★**
*Guest Accommodation*
Vicarage Road, Ambleside
LA22 9DH
t (015394) 33364
e info@oldvicarageambleside.co.uk
w oldvicarageambleside.co.uk

**Park House Guest House In Ambleside ★★★★**
*Guest House*
Compston Road, Ambleside
LA22 9DJ
t (015394) 31107
e mail@loughrigg.plus.com
w parkhouseguesthouse.co.uk

**Red Bank ★★★★★**
*Bed & Breakfast*
SILVER AWARD
Wansfell Road, Ambleside
LA22 0EG
t (015394) 34637
e info@red-bank.co.uk
w red-bank.co.uk

**Riverside ★★★★**
*Guest Accommodation*
SILVER AWARD
Under Loughrigg, Rothay Bridge, Ambleside LA22 9LJ
t (015394) 32395
e info@riverside-at-ambleside.co.uk
w riverside-at-ambleside.co.uk

**Rothay Garth ★★★★**
*Guest Accommodation*
Rothay Road, Ambleside
LA22 0EE
t (015394) 32217
e book@rothay-garth.co.uk
w rothay-garth.co.uk

**Rothay House ★★★**
*Guest Accommodation*
Rothay Road, Ambleside
LA22 0EE
t (015394) 32434
e email@rothay-house.com
w rothay-house.com

**Rysdale Guest House**
★★★★
*Guest Accommodation*
Rothay Road, Ambleside
LA22 0EE
t (015394) 32140
e info@rysdalehotel.co.uk
w rysdalehotel.co.uk

**Smallwood House ★★★★**
*Guest Accommodation*
Compston Road, Ambleside
LA22 9DJ
t (015394) 32330
e enq@smallwoodhotel.co.uk
w smallwoodhotel.co.uk

**Thorneyfield Guest House**
★★★★ *Guest House*
Compston Road, Ambleside
LA22 9DJ
t (015394) 32464
e info@thorneyfield.co.uk
w thorneyfield.co.uk

**Tock How Farm ★★★★**
*Farmhouse*
High Wray, Ambleside
LA22 0JF
t (015394) 36106
e info@tock-how-farm.com
w tock-how-farm.com

**Walmar ★★★** *Guest House*
Lake Road, Ambleside
LA22 0DB
t (015394) 32454
e walmar.ambleside@tiscali.co.uk
w walmar-ambleside.co.uk

**Wateredge Inn ★★★★** *Inn*
Waterhead Bay, Ambleside
LA22 0EP
t (015394) 32332
e stay@wateredgeinn.co.uk
w wateredgeinn.co.uk

**Waterwheel Guesthouse**
★★★★ *Bed & Breakfast*
SILVER AWARD
3 Bridge Street, Ambleside
LA22 9DU
t (015394) 33286
e info@waterwheelambleside.co.uk
w waterwheelambleside.co.uk

**Wordsworths Guest House**
★★★★
*Guest Accommodation*
Lake Road, Ambleside
LA22 0DB
t (015394) 32095
e anna@wordsworthsguesthouse.co.uk
w wordsworthsguesthouse.co.uk

## AMOTHERBY North Yorkshire

**Cherry Tree B&B ★★★★**
*Bed & Breakfast*
4 Cherry Tree Walk,
Amotherby, Malton YO17 6TR
t (01653) 690825
e cherrytreeamotherby@googlemail.com
w 4cherrytree.googlepages.com

## AMPLEFORTH North Yorkshire

**Carr House Farm ★★★**
*Farmhouse*
Ampleforth, Helmsley
YO62 4ED
t (01347) 868526
e stay@carrhousefarm.co.uk
w carrhousefarm.co.uk

**Daleside** ★★★★★
*Bed & Breakfast*
**GOLD AWARD**
East End, Ampleforth, Helmsley YO62 4DA
t (01439) 788266
e dalesidepaul@hotmail.com

**Shallowdale House** ★★★★★
*Guest Accommodation*
**GOLD AWARD**
West End, Ampleforth, Helmsley YO62 4DY
t (01439) 788325
e phillip@shallowdalehouse.co.uk
w shallowdalehouse.co.uk

### APPLEBY-IN-WESTMORLAND
Cumbria

**Bank End House** ★★★★
*Bed & Breakfast*
Appleby-in-Westmorland CA16 6LH
t (017683) 52050
e jackiellane@hotmail.com

**Broom House** ★★★★
*Guest Accommodation*
**SILVER AWARD**
Long Marton, Appleby-in-Westmorland CA16 6JP
t (017683) 61318
e sandra@bland01.freeserve.co.uk
w broomhouseappleby.co.uk

**Royal Oak** ★★★★ *Inn*
45 Bongate, Appleby-in-Westmorland CA16 6UN
t (017683) 51463
e jan@royaloakappleby.co.uk
w royaloakappleby.com

### ARKENGARTHDALE
North Yorkshire

**Chapel Farmhouse** ★★★★
*Bed & Breakfast*
Whaw, Arkengarthdale, Reeth DL11 6RT
t (01748) 884062
e chapelfarmbb@aol.com

**The Charles Bathurst Inn** ★★★★ *Inn*
Arkengarthdale, Reeth DL11 6EN
t (01748) 884567
e info@cbinn.co.uk
w cbinn.co.uk

### ARNSIDE
Cumbria

**Arnside YHA** ★★★ *Hostel*
Oakfield Lodge, Redhills Road, Arnside LA5 0AT
t (01524) 761781
e arnside@yha.org.uk
w yha.org.uk

**Number 43** ★★★★★
*Guest House* **SILVER AWARD**
The Promenade, Arnside LA5 0AA
t (01524) 762761
e lesley@no43.org.uk
w no43.org.uk

**The Willowfield** ★★★★
*Guest Accommodation*
53 The Promenade, Arnside LA5 0AD
t (01524) 761354
e info@willowfield.uk.com
w willowfield.uk.com

### ARTHINGTON
West Yorkshire

**The Wharfedale Inn & Restaurant** ★★★★ *Inn*
Arthington Lane, Arthington, Otley LS21 1NL
t (0113) 284 2921
e david@thewharfedale.co.uk
w thewharfedale.co.uk

### ASHTON-UNDER-LYNE
Greater Manchester

**Lynwood** ★★★★
*Guest Accommodation*
3 Richmond Street, Ashton-under-Lyne OL6 7TX
t (0161) 330 5358

### ASKRIGG
North Yorkshire

**Apothecary's House** ★★★★
*Guest Accommodation*
**SILVER AWARD**
Main Street, Askrigg, Leyburn DL8 3HT
t (01969) 650626
e bookings@apothecaryhouse.co.uk
w apothecaryhouse.co.uk

**Helm** ★★★★★
*Guest Accommodation*
**GOLD AWARD**
Askrigg, Leyburn DL8 3JF
t (01969) 650443
e holiday@helmyorkshire.com
w helmyorkshire.com

**Home Farm** ★★★ *Farmhouse*
Stalling Busk, Askrigg, Leyburn DL8 3DH
t (01969) 650360

**Milton House** ★★★★
*Guest Accommodation*
Leyburn Road, Askrigg, Leyburn DL8 3HJ
t (01969) 650217

**Stoney End** ★★★★★
*Guest Accommodation*
**SILVER AWARD**
Worton, Askrigg, Leyburn DL8 3ET
t (01969) 650652
e pmh@stoneyend.co.uk
w stoneyend.co.uk

**Thornsgill House** ★★★★
*Guest Accommodation*
Moor Road, Askrigg, Leyburn DL8 3HH
t (01969) 650617
e stay@thornsgill.co.uk
w thornsgill.co.uk

### AUSTWICK
North Yorkshire

**Austwick Hall** ★★★★★
*Guest Accommodation*
**SILVER AWARD**
Austwick, Settle LA2 8BS
t (01524) 251794
e austwickhall@austwick.org
w austwickhall.co.uk

**The Dalesbridge Centre** ★★★ *Group Hostel*
Settle LA2 8AZ
t (01524) 251021
e info@dalesbridge.co.uk
w dalesbridge.co.uk

**Pengarth** ★★★★
*Bed & Breakfast*
Austwick, Settle LA2 8BD
t (01524) 251073
e jishreid@austwick.org
w pengarthaustwick.co.uk

**Wood View** ★★★★
*Guest House*
The Green, Austwick LA2 8BB
t (015242) 51190
e woodview@austwick.org
w woodviewbandb.com

### AYSGARTH
North Yorkshire

**Cornlee** ★★★★ *Guest House*
Aysgarth, Leyburn, Aysgarth Falls DL8 3AE
t (01969) 663779
e cornlee.aysgarth@btinternet.com
w cornlee.co.uk

**Field House** ★★★★
*Bed & Breakfast*
Aysgarth, Aysgarth Falls DL8 3AB
t (01969) 663556
e rosfieldhouse@btinternet.com
w fieldhouse-aysgarth.co.uk

**Heather Cottage Guesthouse** ★★★★
*Bed & Breakfast*
**SILVER AWARD**
Heather Cottage, Aysgarth, Leyburn DL8 3AH
t (01969) 663229
e hcind@btinternet.com
w heathercottage.co.uk

**Stow House Country House** ★★★★
*Guest Accommodation*
**SILVER AWARD**
Aysgarth Falls, Aysgarth DL8 3SR
t (01969) 663635
e info@stowhouse.co.uk
w stowhouse.co.uk

**Thornton Lodge** ★★★★★
*Guest Accommodation*
**SILVER AWARD**
Thornton Rust, Leyburn DL8 3AP
t (01969) 663375
e enquiries@thorntonlodgenorth yorkshire.co.uk
w thorntonlodgenorth yorkshire.co.uk

**Wensleydale Farmhouse** ★★★★
*Guest Accommodation*
Aysgarth, Aysgarth Falls DL8 3SR
t (01969) 663534
e stay@wensleydale-farmhouse.co.uk
w wensleydale-farmhouse.co.uk

**Wheatsheaf Inn** ★★★ *Inn*
Main Street, Carperby, Nr Aygarth DL8 4DF
t (01969) 663216
e wheatsheaf@paulmit.globalnet.uk
w wheatsheafinwensleydale.co.uk

**Yoredale House** ★★★★
*Guest House*
Aysgarth, Leyburn, Aysgarth Falls DL8 3AE
t (01969) 663423
e info@yoredalehouse.com
w yoredalehouse.com

### BACUP
Lancashire

**Rossbrook House** ★★★★
*Guest Accommodation*
New Line, Bacup OL13 0BY
t (01706) 878187
e rossbkhouse@aol.com
w a1touristguide.com/rossbrookhouse

### BAILDON
West Yorkshire

**Ford House Farm Bed and Breakfast** ★★★★
*Guest Accommodation*
**SILVER AWARD**
Ford House, Buck Lane, Bradford BD17 7RW
t (01274) 584489
e fordhousefarm@hotmail.com
w fordhousefarmbedandbreakfast.co.uk

**Langbar House** ★★★★
*Bed & Breakfast*
8 Temple Rhydding Drive, Bradford BD17 5PU
t (01274) 599900
e enquiry@langbarhouse.co.uk
w langbarhouse.co.uk

### BAILIFF BRIDGE
West Yorkshire

**The Lodge at Birkby Hall** ★★★★ *Bed & Breakfast*
**SILVER AWARD**
Birkby Lane, Brighouse HD6 4JJ
t (01484) 400321
e thelodge@birkbyhall.co.uk
w birkbyhall.co.uk

### BAINBRIDGE
North Yorkshire

**Hazel's Roost** ★★★
*Bed & Breakfast*
Bainbridge, Leyburn DL8 3EH
t (01969) 650400
e hazel@hazelsroost.co.uk

### BAINTON
East Riding of Yorkshire

**Wolds Village Luxury Guest Accommodation** ★★★★
*Guest Accommodation*
**SILVER AWARD**
Manor Farm, Bainton, Driffield YO25 9EF
t (01377) 217698
e sally@woldsvillage.co.uk
w woldsvillage.co.uk

### BALDERSDALE
Durham

**Blackton Grange** ★★★★
*Group Hostel*
Baldersdale, Romaldkirk DL12 9UP
t (01833) 650629
e manager@blacktongrange.com
w blacktongrange.com

### BAMBURGH
Northumberland

**Glenander Bed & Breakfast**
★★★★ *Bed & Breakfast*
**SILVER AWARD**
27 Lucker Road, Bamburgh
NE69 7BS
**t** (01668) 214336
**e** enquiries@glenander.com
**w** glenander.com

**The Sunningdale** ★★★
*Guest Accommodation*
21-23 Lucker Road, Bamburgh
NE69 7BS
t (01668) 214334
e enquiries@sunningdale-hotel.com
w sunningdale-hotel.com

### BAMPTON
Cumbria

**Mardale Inn @ St Patricks Well** ★★★★ *Inn*
Bampton, Penrith CA10 2RQ
t (01931) 713244
e info@mardaleinn.co.uk
w mardaleinn.co.uk

### BAMPTON GRANGE
Cumbria

**Crown & Mitre Inn** ★★★★
*Inn*
Bampton Grange, Penrith
CA10 2QR
t (01931) 713225
e info@crown-and-mitre.co.uk
w crown-and-mitre.co.uk

### BARDON MILL
Northumberland

**Gibbs Hill Farm** ★★★★
*Farmhouse*
Once Brewed NE47 7AP
t (01434) 344030
e val@gibbshillfarm.co.uk
w gibbshillfarm.co.uk

**Gibbs Hill Farm Hostel** ★★★
*Hostel*
Bardon Mill NE47 7AP
t (01434) 344030
e val@gibbshillfarm.co.uk
w gibbshillfarm.co.uk

**Maple Lodge Bed and Breakfast** ★★★★
*Bed & Breakfast*
Birkshaw, Bardon Mill NE47 7JL
t (01434) 344365
e tonyarmstrong@tiscali.co.uk
w maplelodge-hadrianswall.co.uk

**Montcoffer** ★★★★★
*Guest Accommodation*
**GOLD AWARD**
Bardon Mill NE47 7HZ
t (01434) 344138
e john-dehlia@talk21.com
w montcoffer.co.uk

**Once Brewed YHA** ★★★
*Hostel*
Once Brewed, Military Road,
Hexham NE47 7AN
t (01434) 344360
e oncebrewed@yha.org.uk
w yha.org.uk

**Strand Cottage Bed and Breakfast** ★★★★
*Bed & Breakfast*
The Strand, 2 Main Road
(A69), Hexham NE47 7BH
t (01434) 344643
e stay@strand-cottage.co.uk
w strand-cottage.co.uk

**Twice Brewed Inn** ★★★ *Inn*
Bardon Mill, Hexham
NE47 7AN
**t** (01434) 344534
**e** info@twicebrewedinn.co.uk
**w** twicebrewedinn.co.uk

**Vallum Lodge** ★★★★
*Guest House*
Military Road, Bardon Mill
NE47 7AN
t (01434) 344248
e stay@vallum-lodge.co.uk
w vallum-lodge.co.uk

### BARLEY
Lancashire

**The Pendle Inn** ★★★★ *Inn*
Barley, Burnley BB12 9JX
t (01282) 614808
e yoken@tiscali.co.uk
w pendleinn.co.uk

### BARLOW
North Yorkshire

**Berewick House** ★★★★
*Guest House* **SILVER AWARD**
Park Lane, Barlow, Selby
YO8 8EW
t (01757) 617051
e wilson.guesthouse@berewick.co.uk
w berewick.co.uk

### BARMBY MOOR
East Riding of Yorkshire

**Alder Carr House** ★★★
*Bed & Breakfast*
York Road, Barmby Moor, York
YO42 4HU
t (01759) 380566

**Mohair Farm (Newlands Farm)** ★★★ *Bed & Breakfast*
York Road, Barmby Moor, York
YO42 4HU
t (01759) 380308

### BARNACRE
Lancashire

**Kenlis Arms** ★★ *Inn*
Kenlis Road, Preston PR3 1GD
t (01995) 603307
e andreadjarvis@tiscali.co.uk
w kenlisarmsgarstang.co.uk

### BARNARD CASTLE
Durham

**33 Newgate** ★★★
*Guest Accommodation*
Barnard Castle DL12 8NJ
t (01833) 690208
e peter.whittaker@tinyworld.co.uk
w barnard-castle.co.uk

**Crich House Bed & Breakfast** ★★★★
*Guest Accommodation*
**SILVER AWARD**
94 Galgate, Barnard Castle
DL12 8BJ
**t** (01833) 630357
**e** info@crich-house.co.uk
**w** crich-house.co.uk

**Greta House** ★★★★★
*Bed & Breakfast*
**GOLD AWARD**
89 Galgate, Barnard Castle
DL12 8ES
t (01833) 631193
e kathchesman@btinternet.com
w gretahouse.co.uk

**The Homelands** ★★★★
*Guest Accommodation*
**GOLD AWARD**
85 Galgate, Barnard Castle
DL12 8ES
t (01833) 638757
e enquiries@homelandsguesthouse.co.uk
w homelandsguesthouse.co.uk

**Kirkstone** ★★★★
*Bed & Breakfast*
Barnard Castle DL12 8QS
t (01833) 690497
e dstonekirk@aol.com

**Marwood House** ★★★★
*Bed & Breakfast*
98 Galgate, Barnard Castle
DL12 8BJ
t (01833) 637493
e marwoodhouse@yahoo.co.uk
w marwoodhouse.co.uk

**Strathmore Lawn East** ★★★★
*Guest Accommodation*
81 Galgate, Barnard Castle
DL12 8ES
t (01833) 637061
e strathmorelawn@aol.com
w strathmorelawneast.co.uk

### BARRASFORD
Northumberland

**Barrasford Arms Camping Barn** *Camping Barn*
Barrasford NE48 4AA
t (01434) 681237
e barrasfordarmshotel@yahoo.co.uk
w barrasfordarms.com

### BARROW-IN-FURNESS
Cumbria

**November House B&B**
★★★★ *Bed & Breakfast*
**SILVER AWARD**
Hawcoat Lane, Barrow-in-Furness LA14 4HE
**t** (01229) 827247
**e** november-house@tiscali.co.uk
**w** novemberhouse.co.uk

### BARROWFORD
Lancashire

**Holmefield Gardens Bed & Breakfast** ★★★★
*Bed & Breakfast*
57 Holmefield Gardens,
Barrowford BB9 8NW
t (01282) 606984
e jayjay2@talktalk.net

**Merok Bed & Breakfast**
★★★★ *Bed & Breakfast*
**SILVER AWARD**
124 Wheatley Lane Road,
Barrowford BB9 6QW
t (01282) 612888
e pat@duxbury124.freeserve.co.uk

### BARTON
Cheshire

**Higher Farm Bed & Breakfast** ★★★★
*Guest Accommodation*
**SILVER AWARD**
Higher Farm, Barton SY14 7HU
t (01829) 782422
e info@higherfarm.co.uk
w higherfarm.co.uk

### BARTON-LE-STREET
North Yorkshire

**Barn Owl Cottage** ★★★
*Bed & Breakfast*
Barton-le-Street, Malton
YO17 6QB
t (01653) 628329

### BASHALL EAVES
Lancashire

**The Red Pump Inn** ★★★★
*Guest Accommodation*
Clitheroe Road, Bashall Eaves,
Clitheroe BB7 3DA
t (01254) 826227
e info@theredpumpinn.co.uk
w theredpumpinn.co.uk

### BASSENTHWAITE
Cumbria

**Herdwick Croft Guest House**
★★★★
*Guest Accommodation*
**SILVER AWARD**
Bassenthwaite, Keswick
CA12 4RD
t (017687) 76241
e info@herdwick-croft.co.uk
w herdwick-croft.co.uk

**Highside Farm** ★★★★
*Farmhouse* **SILVER AWARD**
Bassenthwaite, Keswick
CA12 4QG
t (017687) 76952
e info@highside.co.uk
w highside.co.uk

**Link House by Bassenthwaite Lake** ★★★★
*Guest House*
Bassenthwaite Lake, Keswick
CA13 9YD
t (017687) 76291
e info@link-house.co.uk
w link-house.co.uk

**Ouse Bridge House** ★★★★
*Guest House*
Dubwath, Bassenthwaite Lake,
Bassenthwaite CA13 9YD
**t** (017687) 76322
**e** enquiries@ousebridge.com
**w** ousebridge.com

**Skiddaw House YHA**
*Bunkhouse*
Skiddaw House, Keswick
CA12 4QX
t (01697) 478325

### BEADNELL
Northumberland

**Beach Court** ★★★★★
*Guest Accommodation*
**SILVER AWARD**
Harbour Road, Beadnell
NE67 5BJ
t (01665) 720225
e info@beachcourt.com
w beachcourt.com

**Low Dover Beadnell Bay** ★★★★★
*Guest Accommodation*
**SILVER AWARD**
Harbour Road, Beadnell
NE67 5BJ
t (01665) 720291
e enquiries@lowdover.co.uk
w lowdover.co.uk

**Shepherds Cottage** ★★★★
*Guest Accommodation*
Beadnell NE67 5AD
t (01665) 720497
e shepherds.cott@tiscali.co.uk
w shepherdscottagebeadnell.co.uk

### BEAL
Northumberland

**Brock Mill Farmhouse** ★★★
*Guest Accommodation*
Brock Mill, Beal, Berwick-upon-Tweed TD15 2PB
**t (01289) 381283 & 07889 099517**
**e brockmillfarmhouse@btinternet.com**
**w lindisfarne.org.uk/brock-mill-farmhouse**

### BEAMISH
Durham

**Malling House** ★★★
*Guest House*
1 Oakdale Terrace, Newfield
DH2 2SU
t (0191) 370 2571
e wendy@kafs.wanadoo.co.uk
w mallingguesthouse.freeserve.co.uk

### BEDALE
North Yorkshire

**The Castle Arms Inn** ★★★★
*Inn*
Bedale DL8 2TB
t (01677) 470270
e castlearms@aol.com
w thecastlearms.co.uk

**Elmfield House** ★★★★
*Guest House* **SILVER AWARD**
Bedale DL8 1NE
t (01677) 450558
e stay@elmfieldhouse.co.uk
w elmfieldhouse.co.uk

**Mill Close Farm** ★★★★★
*Farmhouse* **GOLD AWARD**
Patrick Brompton DL8 1JY
t (01677) 450257
e pat@millclose.co.uk
w millclose.co.uk

### BEEFORD
East Riding of Yorkshire

**Pinderhill Farm Bed & Breakfast** ★★★★ *Farmhouse*
Beverley Road, Beeford, Driffield YO25 8AE
t (01262) 488645

### BEETHAM
Cumbria

**Barn Close/North West Birds** ★★★ *Bed & Breakfast*
Barn Close, Beetham, Milnthorpe LA7 7AL
t (015395) 63191
e anne@nwbirds.co.uk
w nwbirds.co.uk

### BELFORD
Northumberland

**Detchant Farm** ★★★
*Farmhouse*
Detchant, Belford NE70 7PF
t (01668) 213261
e stay@detchantfarm.co.uk
w detchantfarm.co.uk

**Easington Farm** ★★★★
*Farmhouse* **SILVER AWARD**
Easington, Belford NE70 7EG
t (01668) 213298
e oates925@btinternet.com
w easingtonfarm.co.uk

**The Farmhouse Guest House** ★★★★
*Guest Accommodation*
**SILVER AWARD**
24 West Street, Belford
NE70 7QE
t (01668) 213083
e farmhouseguesthouse@hotmail.com
w thefarmhouseguesthouse belford.co.uk

**Seafields** ★★★★
*Bed & Breakfast*
7 Cragside Avenue, Belford
NE70 7NA
t (01668) 213502
e seafields.bryden@tiscali.co.uk
w seafieldsbelford.co.uk

### BELL BUSK
North Yorkshire

**Tudor House** ★★★★
*Guest House*
Bell Busk, Skipton BD23 4DT
t (01729) 830301
e bellbusk.hitch@virgin.net
w tudorbellbusk.co.uk

### BELLINGHAM
Northumberland

**Bridgeford Farm** ★★★★
*Farmhouse*
Bellingham NE48 2HU
t (01434) 220940
e info@bridgefordfarmbandb.co.uk
w bridgefordfarmbandb.co.uk

**Lyndale Guest House**
★★★★ *Guest House*
Riverside Walk, Bellingham
NE48 2AW
t (01434) 220361
e lyndaleguesthouse@hotmail.com
w lyndaleguesthouse.co.uk

**YHA Bellingham Bunkhouse**
Rating Applied For
*Bunkhouse*
Demesne Farm, Bellingham
NE48 2BS
t (01434) 220258

### BELMONT
Durham

**Moor End House Bed and Breakfast** ★★★★
*Guest House*
7-8 Moor End Terrace, Belmont
DH1 1BJ
t (0191) 384 2796
e marybnb@hotmail.com
w moorenddurham.co.uk

### BEN RHYDDING
West Yorkshire

**Farmhouse at Wharfedale Grange** ★★★★
*Bed & Breakfast*
**SILVER AWARD**
Ben Rhydding Drive, Ben Rhydding, Ilkley LS29 8BG
t (01943) 604204
e sandrine@pickard.co.uk
w ilkleybedandbreakfast.co.uk

### BERWICK-UPON-TWEED
Northumberland

**Alannah House** ★★★★
*Bed & Breakfast*
**SILVER AWARD**
**84 Church Street, Berwick-upon-Tweed TD15 1DU**
**t (01289) 307252**
**e steven@berwick1234.freeserve.co.uk**
**w alannahhouse.com**

**Bankhead Villa Bed & Breakfast** ★★★★
*Guest Accommodation*
Chainbridge, Berwick-upon-Tweed TD15 2XT
t (01289) 386201
e patrickandnina@btconnect.com

**Ben More House** ★★★
*Bed & Breakfast*
51 Church Street, Berwick-upon-Tweed TD15 1EE
t (01289) 309274
e bookings@benmorehouse.com
w benmorehouse.com

**Berwick Backpackers**
★★★★ *Backpackers*
**56 Bridge Street, Berwick-upon-Tweed TD15 1AQ**
**t (01289) 331481**
**e bkbackpacker@aol.com**
**w berwickbackpackers.co.uk**

**Bridge View** ★★★★
*Guest Accommodation*
14 Tweed Street, Berwick-upon-Tweed TD15 1NG
t (01289) 308098
e lyndda@tiscali.co.uk
w bridgeviewberwick.com

**Canty's Brig Riverside Bed & Breakfast** ★★★
*Bed & Breakfast*
Canty's Brig Riverside Bed and Breakfast, Berwick-upon-Tweed TD15 1SY
t (01289) 386451
e paulbrooke@hotmail.com
w cantysbrig.co.uk

**Cara House** ★★★★
*Guest Accommodation*
44 Castlegate, Berwick-upon-Tweed TD15 1JT
t (01289) 302749
e pam@carahouse.co.uk
w carahouse.co.uk

**The Cat Inn** ★★★ *Inn*
**Great North Road, Cheswick, Berwick-upon-Tweed TD15 2RL**
**t (01289) 387251**

**Clovelly House** ★★★★
*Bed & Breakfast*
**SILVER AWARD**
58 West Street, Berwick-upon-Tweed TD15 1AS
t (01289) 302337
e vivroc@clovelly53.freeserve.co.uk
w clovelly53.freeserve.co.uk

**Dervaig Guest House**
★★★★ *Guest House*
1 North Road, Berwick-upon-Tweed TD15 1PW
t (01289) 307378
e dervaig@talk21.com
w dervaigguesthouse.co.uk

**Elizabethan Townhouse**
★★★ *Guest Accommodation*
8 Sidey Court, Marygate
TD15 1DR
t (01289) 304580
e eliztownhouse@aol.com

**Fairholm** ★★★★
*Guest Accommodation*
East Ord TD15 2NS
t (01289) 305370
e bethiawelsh@ukonline.com
w welcometofairholm.com

**Four North Road** ★★★★
*Guest Accommodation*
**SILVER AWARD**
4 North Road, Berwick-upon-Tweed TD15 1PL
t (01289) 306146
e sandra@thorntonfour.freeserve.co.uk
w fournorthroad.co.uk

**Friendly Hound Cottage**
★★★★ *Bed & Breakfast*
Ford Common, Berwick-upon-Tweed TD15 2QD
t (01289) 388554
e friendlyhound@hotmail.co.uk
w friendlyhoundcottage.co.uk

**Granary Guest House**
★★★★★ *Guest House*
**SILVER AWARD**
11 Bridge Street, Berwick-upon-Tweed TD15 1ES
t (01289) 304403
e pamwaddell@btinternet.com
w granaryguesthouse.co.uk

**Ladythorne Guest House**
★★★★ *Guest House*
**Cheswick, Berwick-upon-Tweed TD15 2RW**
**t (01289) 387382**
**e valparker@ladythorne.wanadoo.co.uk**
**w ladythorne.wanadoo.co.uk**

**Mansergh House** ★★★
*Bed & Breakfast*
Church Street, Berwick-upon-Tweed TD15 1DU
t (01289) 302297
e manserghhouse@aol.co.uk
w manserghhouse.co.uk

**Meadow Hill Guest House**
★★★★ *Guest House*
Duns Road, Berwick-upon-Tweed TD15 1UB
t (01289) 306325
e christineabart@aol.com
w meadow-hill.co.uk

**Miranda's Guest House** ★★
*Guest House*
43 Church Street, Berwick-upon-Tweed TD15 1EE
t (01289) 306483
e mirandasberwick@aol.com

**No 1 Sallyport** ★★★★★
*Guest House* **GOLD AWARD**
Off Bridge Street, Berwick-upon-Tweed TD15 1EZ
t (01289) 308827
e info@sallyport.co.uk
w sallyport.co.uk

**No 4 Ravensdowne** ★★★★
*Guest Accommodation*
4 Ravensdowne, Berwick-upon-Tweed TD15 1HX
t (01289) 308082
e fourravensdowne@hotmail.co.uk
w berwick-accomodation.co.uk

**The Old Vicarage Guest House Farm** ★★★★
*Guest House* **SILVER AWARD**
24 Church Road, Berwick-upon-Tweed TD15 2AN
t (01289) 306909 & 07730 234236
e stay@oldvicarageberwick.co.uk
w oldvicarageberwick.co.uk

**Orkney House** ★★
*Bed & Breakfast*
37 Woolmarket, Berwick-upon-Tweed TD15 1DH
t (01289) 331710
e orkneyguesthouse@yahoo.com

**Ravensdowne Guest House** ★★★★
*Guest Accommodation*
40 Ravensdowne, Berwick-upon-Tweed TD15 1DQ
t (01289) 306992
e bookings@40ravensdowne.co.uk
w 40ravensdowne.co.uk

**Tweed View House** ★★★★
*Bed & Breakfast*
16 Railway Street, Berwick-upon-Tweed TD15 1NF
t (01289) 302864

**The Walls** ★★★★
*Bed & Breakfast*
8 Quay Walls, Berwick-upon-Tweed TD15 1HB
t (01289) 330233
e info@thewallsberwick.com
w thewallsberwick.com

**West Coates** ★★★★★
*Bed & Breakfast*
**GOLD AWARD**
30 Castle Terrace, Berwick-upon-Tweed TD15 1NZ
t (01289) 309666
e karenbrownwestcoates@yahoo.com
w westcoates.co.uk

**Whyteside House** ★★★★
*Guest Accommodation*
**SILVER AWARD**
46 Castlegate, Berwick-upon-Tweed TD15 1JT
t (01289) 331019
e albert.whyte@onetel.net
w secretkingdom.com/whyte/side.htm

### BETCHTON
### Cheshire

**Yew Tree Farm Bed and Breakfast** ★★★★
*Bed & Breakfast*
Love Lane, Betchton CW11 4TD
t (01477) 500626
e jshollinshead@btinternet.com

### BEVERLEY
### East Riding of Yorkshire

**6 St Mary's Close** ★★
*Bed & Breakfast*
Beverley HU17 7AY
t (01482) 868837

**Beck View Guest House** ★★★★
*Guest Accommodation*
1a Blucher Lane, Beverley HU17 0PT
t (01482) 882332
e beckviewhouse@aol.com
w beckviewguesthouse.co.uk

**Beverley Friary YHA** ★★★
*Hostel*
Friar's Lane, Beverley HU17 0DF
t 0870 770 5696
e beverleyfriary@yha.org.uk
w yha.org.uk

**Burton Mount Country House** ★★★★★
*Guest Accommodation*
**GOLD AWARD**
Malton Road, Cherry Burton, Beverley HU17 7RA
t (01964) 550541
e pg@burtonmount.co.uk
w burtonmount.co.uk

**Eastgate Guest House** ★★★★
*Guest Accommodation*
7 Eastgate, Beverley HU17 0DR
t (01482) 868464
e dodd@dodd.karoo.co.uk

**The Inn on the Bar** ★★★
*Guest House*
8 North Bar Without, Beverley HU17 7AA
t (01482) 868137

**Market Cross** ★★★
*Guest Accommodation*
14 Lairgate, Beverley HU17 8EE
t (01482) 882573

**Minster Garth Guest House** ★★★★ *Guest House*
2 Keldgate, Beverley HU17 8HY
t (01482) 882402
e minstergarth@yahoo.co.uk
w beverleybedandbreakfast.com

**Newbegin Guest House** ★★★★ *Bed & Breakfast*
Newbegin, Beverley HU17 8EG
t (01482) 872320

**Number One** ★★★
*Bed & Breakfast*
1 Woodlands, Beverley HU17 8BT
t (01482) 862752
e neilandsarah@mansle.karoo.co.uk
w number-one-bedandbreakfast-beverley.co.uk

**Potts of Flemingate Guest Accommodation** ★★★
*Bed & Breakfast*
18 Flemingate, Beverley HU17 0NR
t (01482) 862586
e pottsofflemingate@hotmail.com
w pottsofflemingate.co.uk

**Rudstone Walk Country B&B** ★★★★
*Guest Accommodation*
South Cave, Beverley HU15 2AH
t (01430) 422230
e office@rudstone-walk.co.uk
w rudstone-walk.co.uk

**Trinity Guest House** ★★★★
*Guest House*
Trinity Lane, Beverley HU17 0AR
t (01482) 869537
e info@trinity-house.net
w trinity-house.net

**Westfield Bed and Breakfast** ★★ *Bed & Breakfast*
13 Westfield Avenue, Beverley HU17 7HA
t (01482) 860212

### BIRKENHEAD
### Merseyside

**Shrewsbury Lodge** ★★★
*Guest Accommodation*
Shrewsbury Lodge Hotel, 31 Shrewsbury Road, Prenton CH43 2JB
t (0151) 652 4029
e info@shrewsbury-hotel.com
w shrewsbury-hotel.com

**Villa Venezia** ★★★
*Guest Accommodation*
14-16 Prenton Road West, Birkenhead CH42 9PN
t (0151) 608 9212
e enquiry@veneziapizzeria.co.uk
w veneziapizzeria.co.uk

### BIRTLEY
### Tyne and Wear

**The Bowes Incline** ★★★★
*Inn*
Northside, Eighton Banks DH3 1RF
t (0191) 410 2233
e info@bowesinclinehotel.co.uk
w bowesinclinehotel.co.uk

### BISHOP AUCKLAND
### Durham

**Parkhead Station** ★★★
*Guest Accommodation*
Stanhope Moor, Stanhope DL13 2ES
t (01388) 526434
e parkheadstation@aol.com
w parkheadstation.co.uk

### BISHOP THORNTON
### North Yorkshire

**Dukes Place** ★★★★
*Guest Accommodation*
Fountains Abbey Road, Bishop Thornton, Harrogate HG3 3JY
t (01765) 620229
e enquiries@dukesplace-courtyard.co.uk
w dukesplace-courtyard.co.uk

### BISHOP WILTON
### East Riding of Yorkshire

**High Belthorpe** ★★★
*Farmhouse*
Thorny Lane, Bishop Wilton, Driffield YO42 1SB
t (01759) 368238
e meg@holidaysfordogs.plus.com
w holidayswithdogs.com

### BLACKFORD
### Cumbria

**Mount Farm Bed & Breakfast** ★★★★ *Farmhouse*
Blackford, Carlisle CA6 4ER
t (01228) 674641
e judith.wilson11@btinternet.com
w mount-farm.co.uk

### BLACKPOOL
### Lancashire

**Abbey Lodge** ★★★★
*Guest Accommodation*
31 Palatine Road, Blackpool FY1 4BX
t (01253) 624721
e info@abbeyhotel-blackpool.co.uk
w abbeyhotel-blackpool.co.uk

**The Aberford** ★★
*Guest Accommodation*
12-14 Yorkshire Street, Blackpool FY1 5BG
t (01253) 625026
e info@aberfordhotel.co.uk
w aberfordhotel.co.uk

**Adelaide House** ★★★
*Guest Accommodation*
66-68 Adelaide Street, Blackpool FY1 4LA
t (01253) 625172
e info@adelaidehousehotel.com
w adelaidehousehotel.com

**Alanco** ★★★ *Guest House*
2-4 General Street, Blackpool FY1 1RW
t (01253) 863447

**The Allendale** ★★★
*Guest House*
104 Albert Road, Blackpool FY1 4PR
t (01253) 623268
e info@allendale-hotel.co.uk
w allendale-hotel.co.uk

**Almeria** ★★★
*Guest Accommodation*
61 Hornby Road, Blackpool FY1 4QJ
t (01253) 294757
e almeria61@hotmail.co.uk

**Amethyst**
Rating Applied For
*Guest House*
Palatine Road, Blackpool
FY1 4BY
**t** (01253) 622127
**e** info@amethysthotelblackpool.co.uk
**w** amethysthotelblackpool.co.uk

**Arabella ★★★** *Guest House*
102 Albert Road, Blackpool
FY1 4PR
**t** (01253) 623189
**e** graham.waters3@virgin.net
**w** thearabella.co.uk

**Ardsley Guest Accommodation ★★★**
*Guest Accommodation*
20 Woodfield Road, Blackpool
FY1 6AX
**t** (01253) 345419
**e** christineglass@gmail.com
**w** ardsleyblackpool.co.uk

**Arendale ★★★**
*Guest Accommodation*
23 Gynn Avenue, Blackpool
FY1 2LD
**t** (01253) 351044
**e** arendale@zetnet.co.uk
**w** arendalehotel.co.uk

**Arncliffe ★★★** *Guest House*
24 Osborne Road, Blackpool
FY4 1HJ
**t** (01253) 345209
**e** arncliffehotel@talk21.com
**w** blackpool-internet.co.uk/homearncliffe.html

**The Ascot ★★★**
*Guest Accommodation*
7 Alexandra Road, Blackpool
FY1 6BU
**t** (01253) 346439
**e** info@ascothotel.co.uk
**w** ascothotel.co.uk

**Ash Lodge ★★★**
*Guest House*
**131 Hornby Road, Blackpool**
**FY1 4JG**
**t (01253) 627637**
**e admin@ashlodgehotel.co.uk**
**w ashlodgehotel.co.uk**

**Astoria ★★★**
*Guest Accommodation*
118-120 Albert Road,
Blackpool FY1 4PN
**t** (01253) 621321
**e** enquiries@astoria-hotel.co.uk
**w** astoria-hotel.co.uk

**The Avenue ★★★**
*Guest House*
56 Reads Avenue, Blackpool
FY1 4DE
**t** (01253) 626146
**e** info@blackpooluk.co.uk
**w** blackpooluk.co.uk

**The Bambi ★★★**
*Guest Accommodation*
27 Bright Street, Blackpool
FY4 1BS
**t** (01253) 343756
**e** bambihotel@hotmail.co.uk

**Bamford House ★★★**
*Guest House*
28 York Street, Blackpool
FY1 5AQ
**t** (01253) 622433
**e** info@bamfordhotelblackpool.co.uk
**w** bamfordhotelblackpool.co.uk

**Baron ★★★★**
*Guest Accommodation*
296 North Promenade,
Blackpool FY1 2EY
**t** (01253) 622729

**Beachwood Guest House**
★★★ *Guest Accommodation*
30 Moore Street, Blackpool
FY4 1DA
**t** (01253) 401951
**e** beachwood.guesthouse@virgin.net
**w** beachwoodhotel.co.uk

**The Beauchief ★★★**
*Guest Accommodation*
48 King Edward Avenue,
Blackpool FY2 9TA
**t** (01253) 353314
**e** beauchief2hotel@amserve.com
**w** smoothhound.co.uk/hotels/beauchief

**The Beaucliffe ★★★**
*Guest Accommodation*
20-22 Holmfield Road,
Blackpool FY2 9TB
**t** (01253) 351663

**Belgrave 21 ★★★**
*Guest House*
21 Barton Avenue, Blackpool
FY1 6AP
**t** (01253) 346792
**e** belgrave21@fsmail.net
**w** belgrave21.co.uk

**The Berkswell ★★★**
*Guest Accommodation*
8 Withnell Road, Blackpool
FY4 1HF
**t** (01253) 341374 & 0800 977 4723
**e** theberkswell@yahoo.com
**w** berkswellhotel.co.uk

**The Berwick ★★★★**
*Guest Accommodation*
**23 King Edward Avenue,**
**Blackpool FY2 9TA**
**t (01253) 351496**
**e theberwickhotel@btconnect.com**
**w theberwickhotel.co.uk**

**Berwyn ★★★★**
*Guest Accommodation*
1-2 Finchley Road, Blackpool
FY1 2LP
**t** (01253) 352896
**e** stay@berwynhotel.co.uk
**w** berwynhotel.co.uk

**Beverley Dean ★★★**
*Guest Accommodation*
25 Dean Street, South Shore
FY4 1AU
**t** (01253) 344426
**e** admin@beverleydean.co.uk
**w** beverleydean.co.uk

**The Bianca ★★★**
*Guest House*
25 Palatine Road, Blackpool
FY1 4BX
**t** (01253) 752824
**w** hotelbianca.co.uk

**Blackpool's Wimbourne**
★★★ *Guest House*
10 Moore Street, Blackpool
FY4 1DB
**t** (01253) 347272
**e** info@wimbourneblackpool.co.uk
**w** wimbourneblackpool.co.uk

**Boltonia ★★★**
*Guest Accommodation*
124-126 Albert Road,
Blackpool FY1 4PN
**t** (01253) 620248
**e** info@boltoniahotel.co.uk
**w** boltoniahotel.co.uk

**Bracondale Guest House**
★★★★ *Guest House*
14 Warley Road, Blackpool
FY1 2JU
**t** (01253) 351650
**e** bracondale-hotel@btconnect.com
**w** nosmokingblackpool.co.uk

**The Brayton ★★★**
*Guest Accommodation*
7-8 Finchley Road, Blackpool
FY1 2LP
**t** (01253) 351645
**e** blackpool@the-brayton-hotel.com
**w** the-brayton-hotel.com

**Brincliffe ★★★**
*Guest Accommodation*
168-170 Queens Promenade,
Blackpool FY2 9JN
**t** (01253) 351654
**e** susan@brincliffehotel.co.uk
**w** brincliffehotel.co.uk

**Briny View ★★**
*Guest Accommodation*
2 Woodfield Road, Blackpool
FY1 6AX
**t** (01253) 346584
**e** brinyviewhotel@aol.com
**w** brinyviewhotel.co.uk

**The Brioni ★★★**
*Guest Accommodation*
324 Queens Promenade,
Blackpool FY2 9AB
**t** (01253) 351988
**e** hamlinheros@aol.com
**w** brionihotelblackpool.co.uk

**Brooklands ★★★**
*Guest Accommodation*
28-30 King Edward Avenue,
Blackpool FY2 9TA
**t** (01253) 351479
**e** brooklandhotel@btinternet.com
**w** brooklands-hotel.com

**Burleigh ★★★**
*Guest Accommodation*
47 Osborne Road, Blackpool
FY4 1HQ
**t** (01253) 343737
**e** paulandnett@hotmail.com

**Cardoh Lodge ★★★**
*Guest House*
**21 Hull Road, Blackpool**
**FY1 4QB**
**t (01253) 627755**

**Caroldene ★★**
*Guest Accommodation*
12 Woodfield Road, Blackpool
FY1 6AX
**t** (01253) 346963
**e** caroldenehotel2003@yahoo.co.uk
**w** http://caroldenehotel.mysite.wanadoo-members.co.uk

**Castlemere**
Rating Applied For
*Guest Accommodation*
13 Shaftesbury Avenue,
Blackpool FY2 9QQ
**t** (01253) 352430
**e** sue@hotelcastlemere.co.uk
**w** hotelcastlemere.co.uk

**Cliff Head Seafront Guest House ★★★** *Guest House*
174 Queens Promenade,
Blackpool FY2 9JN
**t** (01253) 591086
**e** cliffheadhotelblackpool@yahoo.co.uk
**w** cliffheadhotelblackpool.com

**Clovelly ★★★★**
*Guest Accommodation*
22 St Chads Road, Blackpool
FY1 6BP
**t** (01253) 346087
**e** kamess2557@aol.com
**w** clovellyhotel.com

**Collingwood ★★★★**
*Guest Accommodation*
8-10 Holmfield Road, Blackpool
FY2 9SL
**t** (01253) 352929
**e** enquiries@collingwoodhotel.co.uk
**w** collingwoodhotel.co.uk

**Colyndene ★★★**
*Guest Accommodation*
53 Reads Avenue, Blackpool
FY1 4DG
**t** (01253) 295282
**e** reception@colyndenehotel.fsnet.co.uk
**w** blackpool-holidays.com/colyndene/colyndene.htm

**Corona ★★★**
*Guest Accommodation*
18 Clifton Drive, Blackpool
FY4 1NX
**t** (01253) 342586
**e** coronablackpool@aol.com
**w** thecoronahotel.com

**Courtney's of Gynn Square ★★★★**
*Guest Accommodation*
1 Warbreck Hill Road,
Blackpool FY2 9SP
**t** (01253) 352179
**e** courtneyshotel@aol.com
**w** courtneysofgynnsquare.co.uk

**The Craimar ★★★**
*Guest Accommodation*
32 Hull Road, Blackpool
FY1 4QB
**t** (01253) 622185
**e** thecraimar@sky.com
**w** craimarhotel.co.uk

**The Crescent** ★★★
*Guest Accommodation*
70 Hornby Road, Blackpool
FY1 4QJ
**t** (01253) 624388
**e** freda.youde@homecall.co.uk
**w** crescentblackpool.com

**Cumbrian Guest House**
★★★ *Guest House*
81 Hornby Road, Blackpool
FY1 4QP
**t** (01253) 623677
**e** john@johnbuchanan04.wanadoo.co.uk
**w** blackpool-holidays.con/cumbrian/cumbrian.htm

**David & Wahn's Sea View Guest House** ★★★
*Guest House*
10 Nelson Road, Blackpool
FY1 6AS
**t** (01253) 402316
**e** david_hague1234@hotmail.com
**w** seaview-blackpool.co.uk

**Denely Guest Accommodation** ★★★
*Guest House*
15 King Edward Avenue, Blackpool FY2 9TA
**t** (01253) 352757
**e** denely@tesco.net
**w** denelyhotel.co.uk

**Deneside**
Rating Applied For
*Guest Accommodation*
27 Albert Road, Blackpool
FY1 4TA
**t** (01253) 620703
**e** booking@denesidehotel.co.uk
**w** denesidehotel.co.uk

**The Derwent** ★★★
*Guest House*
42 Palatine Road, Blackpool
FY1 4BY
**t** (01253) 620004
**e** chris@derwenthotelblackpool.co.uk
**w** derwenthotelblackpool.co.uk

**The Dudley** ★★★
*Guest Accommodation*
67 Dickson Road, Blackpool
FY1 2BX
**t** (01253) 620281
**e** dudley.hotel@btconnect.com
**w** dudley-hotel.co.uk

**The Dudley** ★★★★
*Guest Accommodation*
3 Alexandra Road, South Shore, Blackpool FY1 6BU
**t** (01253) 346827

**Dunromin** ★★★
*Guest House*
27 Palatine Road, Blackpool
FY1 4BX
**t** (01253) 620543
**e** info@dunrominhotel.co.uk
**w** dunrominhotel.co.uk

**The Edelweiss**
Rating Applied For
*Guest House*
36 St Chads Road, Blackpool
FY1 6BP
**t** (01253) 341265
**e** edelweissstchads@aol.com
**w** edelweisshotel.co.uk

**Edenfield Guest House**
★★★★ *Guest House*
17 Cocker Street, Blackpool
FY1 2BY
**t** (01253) 624009
**e** info@edenfieldguesthouse.com
**w** edenfieldguesthouse.com

**Ellan Vannin** ★★★
*Guest House*
6 Gynn Avenue, Blackpool
FY1 2LD
**t** (01253) 351784
**e** seaside@blueyonder.co.uk
**w** the-ellan-vannin.co.uk

**Everglades** ★★★
*Guest House*
14 Barton Avenue, Blackpool
FY1 6AP
**t** (01253) 343093
**e** info@evergladesblackpool.co.uk
**w** evergladesblackpool.co.uk

**The Fairhaven**
Rating Applied For
*Guest Accommodation*
46 Palatine Road, Blackpool
FY1 4BY
**t** (01772) 536600
**w** fairhavenhotelblackpool.co.uk

**The Fame** ★★★
*Guest Accommodation*
363 Promenade, Blackpool
FY1 6BJ
**t** (01253) 346615
**e** hotelfame@hotmail.co.uk
**w** hotelfame.com

**Feng Shui House** ★★★
*Guest Accommodation*
661 New South Promenade, Blackpool FY4 1RN
**t** (01253) 342266
**e** kate_burns@btconnect.com
**w** classic-feng-shui.com

**The Fern Royd** ★★★
*Guest Accommodation*
35 Holmfield Road, Blackpool
FY2 9TE
**t** (01253) 351066
**e** fernroyd@btconnect.com
**w** thefernroyd.co.uk

**Four Seasons Blackpool**
Rating Applied For
*Guest House*
60 Reads Avenue, Blackpool
FY1 4DE
**t** (01253) 752171
**e** info@fourseasonsblackpool.co.uk
**w** fourseasonsblackpool.co.uk

**Gleneagles** ★★
*Guest Accommodation*
9 Bairstow Street, Blackpool
FY1 5BN
**t** (01253) 623771
**e** gleneagles99@hotmail.com

**Gleneagles** ★★★★
*Guest Accommodation*
75 Albert Road, Blackpool
FY1 4PW
**t** (01253) 295266
**e** gleneaglesblackpool@tiscali.co.uk
**w** gleneagles-hotel.com

**Glenholme** ★★★
*Guest Accommodation*
44 Alexandra Road, Blackpool
FY1 6BU
**t** (01253) 345823
**e** glenholme44@yahoo.co.uk
**w** glenholmehotel.co.uk

**The Glenmere** ★★★
*Guest Accommodation*
7 Gynn Avenue, Blackpool
FY1 2LD
**t** (01253) 351259
**e** glenmerebandb@aol.com
**w** glenmereguesthouse.co.uk

**Glenwalden**
Rating Applied For
*Guest Accommodation*
382 Promenade, Blackpool
FY1 2LB
**t** (01253) 353332
**e** glenwalden@btinternet.com
**w** glenwaldenhotelblackpool.co.uk/

**The Golden Sands** ★★★★
*Guest Accommodation*
20 Gynn Avenue, Blackpool
FY1 2LD
**t** (01253) 352285
**e** info@thegoldensands.co.uk
**w** thegoldensands.co.uk

**Granville** ★★★
*Guest Accommodation*
12 Station Road, South Shore, Blackpool FY4 1BE
**t** (01253) 343012
**e** wilft@granvillehotelf.s.net.co.uk
**w** thegranvillehotel.co.uk

**Hadley** ★★★
*Guest Accommodation*
225 Promenade, Blackpool
FY1 5DL
**t** (01253) 621197
**e** admin@hadley-hotel.com
**w** hadley-hotel.com

**The Happy Return** ★★★
*Guest Accommodation*
17-19 Hull Road, Blackpool
FY1 4QB
**t** (01253) 622596
**e** happyreturn@yahoo.co.uk
**w** happyreturnhotel.co.uk

**Hartshead** ★★★
*Guest Accommodation*
17 King Edward Avenue, Blackpool FY2 9TA
**t** (01253) 353133 & (01253) 357111
**e** info@hartshead-hotel.co.uk
**w** hartshead-hotel.co.uk

**Hatton** ★★★
*Guest Accommodation*
10 Banks Street, Blackpool
FY1 1RN
**t** (01253) 624944
**e** hattonhotel@hotmail.com
**w** hattonhotel.co.uk

**Holmsdale** ★★★
*Guest House*
6-8 Pleasant Street, Blackpool
FY1 2JA
**t** (01253) 621008
**e** stay@holmsdalehotel-blackpool.com
**w** holmsdalehotel-blackpool.com

**Holmside House** ★★★
*Guest House*
24 Barton Avenue, Blackpool
FY1 6AP
**t** (01253) 346045
**e** holmsidehotel@fsnet.co.uk
**w** holmsidehotel.fsnet.co.uk

**Homecliffe** ★★★★
*Guest Accommodation*
5-6 Wilton Parade, Blackpool
FY1 2HE
**t** (01253) 625147
**e** enquiry@homecliffehotel.com
**w** homecliffehotel.com

**Hornby Villa** ★★★
*Guest Accommodation*
130 Hornby Road, Blackpool
FY1 4QS
**t** (01253) 624959
**e** thehornbyvilla@aol.com
**w** hornbyvillahotel.com

**The Hurstmere** ★★★
*Guest Accommodation*
5 Alexandra Road, Blackpool
FY1 6BU
**t** (01253) 345843
**e** stay@thehurstmerehotel.com
**w** thehurstmerehotel.com

**The Inglewood** ★★★
*Guest Accommodation*
18 Holmfield Road, Blackpool
FY2 9TB
**t** (01253) 351668
**e** enquiries@theinglewoodhotel.com
**w** theinglewoodhotel.com

**Karen Annes Guest House**
★★★ *Guest House*
4 Barton Avenue, Blackpool
FY1 6AP
**t** (01253) 346719
**e** karen@karen-annes.freeserve.co.uk
**w** karenanneshotel.com

**Kendal Private Guest Accommodation** ★★★
*Guest Accommodation*
76 Withnell Road, Blackpool
FY4 1HE
**t** (01253) 348209
**e** doberman4@icliff.wanadoo.co.uk

**The Kimberley** ★★★★
*Guest House*
25 Gynn Avenue, Blackpool
FY1 2LD
**t** (01253) 352264
**e** thekimberley@btconnect.com
**w** kimberleyguesthouse.com

**The King Edward** ★★★
*Guest Accommodation*
44 King Edward Avenue, Blackpool FY2 9TA
**t** (01253) 352932
**e** enquiries@kingedwardhotel.co.uk
**w** kingedwardhotel.co.uk

**Kings Court ★★★**
*Guest Accommodation*
34 King Edward Avenue, Blackpool FY2 9TA
**t** (01253) 593312
**e** chris@kingscourthotel.freeserve.co.uk
**w** blackpoolkingscourthotel.co.uk

**Kingscliff ★★★**
*Guest Accommodation*
78 Hornby Road, Blackpool FY1 4QJ
**t** (01253) 620200
**e** kingscliff.blackpool@virgin.net
**w** kingscliffhotel.co.uk

**Kirkstall House ★★★**
*Guest Accommodation*
25 Hull Road, Blackpool FY1 4QB
**t** (01253) 623077
**e** rooms@kirkstallhotel.co.uk
**w** kirkstallhotel.co.uk

**Langroyd ★★★**
*Guest Accommodation*
Station Road, Blackpool FY4 1EU
**t** (01253) 342263
**e** langroyd@tiscali.co.uk
**w** langroydhotel.co.uk

**The Lawton ★★★**
*Guest Accommodation*
58 Charnley Road, Blackpool FY1 4PF
**t** (01253) 753471
**e** lawtonhotel@lycos.co.uk
**w** thelawtonhotel.co.uk

**Leawood**
Rating Applied For
*Guest Accommodation*
72 Hornby Road, Blackpool FY1 4QJ
**t** (01253) 627327

**Llanryan Guest House ★★★**
*Guest Accommodation*
37 Reads Avenue, Blackpool FY1 4DD
**t** (01253) 628446
**e** keith@llanryan.co.uk
**w** llanryan.co.uk

**Lynbar Guesthouse ★★★**
*Guest House*
32 Vance Road, Blackpool FY1 4QD
**t** (01253) 294504
**e** enquiries@lynbarhotel.co.uk
**w** lynbarhotel.co.uk

**Lynmoore Guest House ★★★** *Guest Accommodation*
25 Moore Street, Blackpool FY4 1DA
**t** (01253) 349888
**e** stay@lynmooreblackpool.freeserve.co.uk
**w** lynmooreblackpool.co.uk

**Mackintosh ★★★**
*Guest Accommodation*
5 Gynn Avenue, Blackpool FY1 2LD
**t** (01253) 352296

**Manchester House ★★★**
*Guest Accommodation*
77 Withnell Road, Blackpool FY4 1HE
**t** (01253) 342637
**e** heathgeorge9@aol.com
**w** hotels-blackpoolpleasurebeach.co.uk

**The Manor Grove ★★**
*Guest House*
24 Leopold Grove, Blackpool FY1 4LD
**t** (01253) 625577
**e** themanorgrove@blueyonder.co.uk
**w** themanorgrove.co.uk

**The Marina ★★★**
*Guest House*
30 Gynn Avenue, Blackpool FY1 2LD
**t** (01253) 352833
**e** robinglockhart@hotmail.com
**w** smoothhound.co.uk/hotels/marinagh

**Marlow Lodge ★★★**
*Guest Accommodation*
76 Station Road, Blackpool FY4 1EU
**t** (01253) 341580
**e** info@marlowlodge.co.uk
**w** marlowlodge.co.uk

**The Middleton ★★★**
*Guest Accommodation*
55 Holmfield Road, Blackpool FY2 9RU
**t** (01253) 354559
**e** info@middleton-hotel.co.uk
**w** middleton-hotel.co.uk

**The Montclair ★★★**
*Guest House*
95 Albert Road, Blackpool FY1 4PW
**t** (01253) 625860
**e** chrissbowen@aol.com
**w** hotelmontclair.co.uk

**Newholme Guest House ★★★** *Guest House*
2 Wilton Parade, Blackpool FY1 2HE
**t** (01253) 624010
**e** newholmehotel@aol.com
**w** newholme.biz

**The Northdene ★★★**
*Guest House*
19 Gynn Avenue, Blackpool FY1 2LD
**t** (01253) 353005
**e** phil@tackler.org.uk
**w** northdene.co.uk

**Norville House ★★★**
*Guest Accommodation*
44 Warbreck Hill Road, Blackpool FY2 9SU
**t** (01253) 352714
**e** norvillehouse@btconnect.com
**w** norvillehousehotel.co.uk

**The Norwood ★★★**
*Guest Accommodation*
35 Hull Road, Blackpool FY1 4QB
**t** (01253) 621118
**e** norwood35@msn.com
**w** thenorwood.co.uk

**Novello Hotel**
Rating Applied For
*Guest House*
11 Hornby Road, Blackpool FY1 4QG
**t** (01253) 293474
**w** novellohotel.co.uk

**Number One ★★★★★**
*Bed & Breakfast*
**GOLD AWARD**
1 St Lukes Road, Blackpool FY4 2EL
**t** (01253) 343901
**e** info@numberoneblackpool.com
**w** numberoneblackpool.com

**Number One South Beach ★★★★★**
*Guest Accommodation*
**GOLD AWARD**
4 Harrowside West, Blackpool FY4 1NW
**t** (01253) 343900
**e** info@numberonesouthbeach.com
**w** numberoneblackpool.com/southbeach

**Oban House ★★★**
*Guest Accommodation*
63 Holmfield Road, Blackpool FY2 9RU
**t** (01253) 352413
**e** obanhousehotel@aol.com
**w** obanhousehotel.co.uk

**Osborne**
Rating Applied For
*Guest Accommodation*
31 St Chads Road, Blackpool FY1 6BP
**t** (01253) 346093
**e** stayosborne@tiscali.co.uk

**The Osprey ★★★**
*Guest House*
27 Charnley Road, Blackpool FY1 4PE
**t** (01253) 621684
**e** dinesh@theospreyhotel.com
**w** theospreyhotel.com

**Pembroke**
Rating Applied For
*Guest Accommodation*
17 Banks Street, Blackpool FY1 1RN
**t** (01253) 625069
**e** pembroke@xln.co.uk
**w** pembrokehotelblackpool.com

**The Pembroke ★★★★**
*Guest Accommodation*
11 King Edward Avenue, Blackpool FY2 9TD
**t** (01253) 351306
**e** info@neartheprom.com
**w** neartheprom.com

**Penrhyn ★★★**
*Guest Accommodation*
38 King Edward Avenue, Blackpool FY2 9TA
**t** (01253) 352762
**e** annettepenrhyn@yahoo.co.uk
**w** penrhynhotel.com

**The Pilatus ★★★**
*Guest Accommodation*
10 Willshaw Road, Blackpool FY2 9SH
**t** (01253) 352470
**e** enquiries@pilatushotel.co.uk
**w** pilatushotel.co.uk

**The Poldhu ★★★**
*Guest Accommodation*
330 Queens Promenade, Blackpool FY2 9AB
**t** (01253) 356918
**e** info@poldhu-hotel.co.uk
**w** poldhu-hotel.co.uk

**The Raffles Guest Accommodation ★★★★**
*Guest Accommodation*
73-77 Hornby Road, Blackpool FY1 4QJ
**t** (01253) 294713
**e** enquiries@raffleshotelblackpool.fsworld.co.uk
**w** raffleshotelblackpool.co.uk

**Rio Rita ★★★**
*Guest Accommodation*
49 Withnell Road, Blackpool FY4 1HE
**t** (01253) 345203
**e** rioritahotel@btconnect.com
**w** rioritahotel.co.uk

**The Rockcliffe ★★★**
*Guest Accommodation*
248 Promenade, Blackpool FY1 1RZ
**t** (01253) 623476
**e** stay@rockcliffehotel.com
**w** rockcliffehotel.co.uk

**Rossdene House ★★★★**
*Guest Accommodation*
12 Gynn Avenue, Blackpool FY1 2LD
**t** (01253) 351714
**e** scott@rossdenehotel.wanadoo.co.uk
**w** rossdenehouse.com

**Royal Seabank ★★★**
*Guest Accommodation*
219-222 Promenade, Blackpool FY1 5DL
**t** (01253) 622717

**Rutland ★★★**
*Guest Accommodation*
330 Promenade, Blackpool FY1 2JG
**t** (01253) 622791
**e** enquiries@rutland-hotel.co.uk
**w** rutland-hotel.co.uk

**The Rutlands ★★★**
*Guest Accommodation*
13 Hornby Road, Blackpool FY1 4QG
**t** (01253) 623067
**w** rutlandshotel.co.uk

**St Ives Blackpool ★★★**
*Guest Accommodation*
10 King George Avenue, Blackpool FY2 9SN
**t** (01253) 352122
**e** enquiries@stiveshotel-blackpool.co.uk
**w** stiveshotel-blackpool.co.uk

**Salmar Bed & Breakfast ★★★** *Guest Accommodation*
138 Albert Road, Blackpool FY1 4PL
**t** (01253) 623183
**e** thesalmar@btconnect.com
**w** blackpoolseaside accommodation.com

**Seabreeze Guest House** ★★★★
*Guest Accommodation*
1 Gynn Avenue, Blackpool
FY1 2LD
**t** (01253) 351427
**e** info@vbreezy.co.uk
**w** vbreezy.co.uk

---

**Shepperton Hotel**
Rating Applied For
*Guest Accommodation*
74 Station Road, Blackpool
FY4 1HJ
**t** (01253) 343600

---

**Sheron House** ★★★★
*Guest House*
21 Gynn Avenue, Blackpool
FY1 2LD
**t** (01253) 354614
**e** sheronhousehotel@btconnect.com
**w** sheronhouse.co.uk

---

**Silversands** ★★★
*Guest Accommodation*
3 Burlington Road West,
Blackpool FY4 1NL
**t** (01253) 341459
**e** info@silversandshotel.com
**w** silversandshotel.com

---

**The South Beach** ★★★
*Guest Accommodation*
**367 Promenade, Blackpool**
**FY1 6BJ**
**t (01253) 342250**
**e info@southbeachhotel.co.uk**
**w southbeachhotel.co.uk**

---

**South Lea** ★★★ *Guest House*
4 Willshaw Road, Blackpool
FY2 9SH
**t** (01253) 351940
**e** info@southlea.co.uk
**w** southlea.co.uk

---

**Stafford House** ★★★
*Guest Accommodation*
8 Woodfield Road, Blackpool
FY1 6AX
**t** (01253) 346727
**e** staffordhousehotel@hotmail.co.uk
**w** staffordhousehotel.co.uk

---

**The Strathdon** ★★★★
*Guest Accommodation*
28 St Chads Road, Blackpool
FY1 6BP
**t** (01253) 343549
**e** stay@strathdonhotel.com
**w** strathdonhotel.com

---

**Strathmere**
Rating Applied For
*Guest Accommodation*
84 Reads Avenue, Blackpool
FY1 4DE
**t** (01253) 621896
**e** jane.strathmere@tiscali.co.uk

---

**Sunny Cliff** ★★★★
*Guest Accommodation*
98 Queens Promenade,
Blackpool FY2 9NS
**t** (01253) 351155

---

**Sunnymede** ★★★
*Guest Accommodation*
50 King Edward Avenue,
Blackpool FY2 9TA
**t** (01253) 352877
**e** enquiries@hotelsunnymede.fsnet.co.uk
**w** sunnymedehotel.co.uk

---

**Sunnyside** ★★★
*Guest Accommodation*
36 King Edward Avenue,
Blackpool FY2 9TA
**t** (01253) 352031
**e** david@sunnysidehotel.com
**w** sunnysidehotel.com

---

**Sunset** ★★★
*Guest Accommodation*
45 Palatine Road, Blackpool
FY1 4BX
**t** (01253) 628369
**e** ruth@sunsethotel.wanadoo.co.uk
**w** sunsethotel.net

---

**The Sunset Guest House** ★★★★
*Guest Accommodation*
5 Banks Street, Blackpool
FY1 1RN
**t** (01253) 624949
**e** thesunsethotel@msn.com
**w** thesunsethotelblackpool.com/

---

**Surrey House** ★★★
*Guest Accommodation*
9 Northumberland Avenue,
Blackpool FY2 9SB
**t** (01253) 351743
**e** coursemanager1@aol.com
**w** surreyhousehotel.com

---

**Tamarind Cove** ★★★
*Guest Accommodation*
56 Hornby Road, Blackpool
FY1 4QJ
**t** (01253) 624319

---

**Tower View** ★★★
*Guest House*
31 Bethesda Road, Blackpool
FY1 5DT
**t** (01253) 620391
**e** postmaster@blackpooltowerview.co.uk
**w** blackpooltowerview.co.uk

---

**The Trafalgar** ★★★
*Guest House*
106 Albert Road, Blackpool
FY1 4PR
**t** (01253) 625000
**e** enquiries@trafalgarhotel.co.uk
**w** trafalgarhotel.co.uk

---

**Tregenna**
Rating Applied For
*Guest Accommodation*
115 Albert Road, Blackpool
FY1 4PW
**t** (01253) 624151
**e** tregennahotel@hotmail.co.uk
**w** tregennahotel.info

---

**Tudor Rose Original** ★★★★
*Guest House*
5 Withnell Road, Blackpool
FY4 1HF
**t** (01253) 343485
**e** tudor_rose@onetel.com
**w** tudorroseblackpool.com

---

**The Valentine** ★★★
*Guest Accommodation*
**35 Dickson Road, Blackpool**
**FY1 2AT**
**t (01253) 622775**
**e anthony@anthonypalmer.orangehome.co.uk**
**w valentinehotelblackpool.co.uk**

---

**The Vidella** ★★★
*Guest Accommodation*
80-82 Dickson Road, Blackpool
FY1 2BU
**t** (01253) 621201
**e** info@videllahotel.com
**w** videllahotel.com

---

**The Waterford** ★★★★
*Guest Accommodation*
**GOLD AWARD**
2 Gynn Avenue, Blackpool
FY1 2LD
**t** (01253) 351946
**e** thewaterford@btconnect.com
**w** thewaterfordblackpool.co.uk

---

**Waverley** ★★★
*Guest Accommodation*
95 Reads Avenue, Blackpool
FY1 4DG
**t** (01253) 621633
**e** waverleyrooms@aol.com
**w** thewaverleyhotel.net

---

**The Wescoe** ★★★
*Guest House*
14 Dean Street, Blackpool
FY4 1AU
**t** (01253) 342772
**e** wescoeblackpool@yahoo.co.uk
**w** thewescoeblackpool.com

---

**Westcliffe** ★★★
*Guest Accommodation*
46 King Edward Avenue,
Blackpool FY2 9TA
**t** (01253) 352943
**e** westcliffehotel@aol.com
**w** westcliffehotel.com

---

**Westdean** ★★★
*Guest Accommodation*
59 Dean Street, Blackpool
FY4 1BP
**t** (01253) 342904
**e** westdeanhotel@aol.com
**w** westdeanhotel.com

---

**Westfield Lodge** ★★★
*Guest Accommodation*
14 Station Road, Blackpool
FY4 1BE
**t** (01253) 342468
**e** joycerobinson@btconnect.com
**w** westfieldhotel.co.uk

---

**Wilford Guest House** ★★★
*Guest Accommodation*
55 Station Road, Blackpool
FY4 1EU
**t** (01253) 344329
**e** enquiries@wilfordhotel.co.uk
**w** wilfordhotel.co.uk

---

**The Wilton** ★★★
*Guest Accommodation*
108-112 Dickson Road,
Blackpool FY1 2HF
**t** (01253) 627763
**e** wiltonhotel@supanet.com
**w** wiltonhotel.co.uk

---

**Windsor** ★★★★
*Guest Accommodation*
21 King Edward Avenue,
Blackpool FY2 9TA
**t** (01253) 353735
**e** enquiries@windsorblackpool.co.uk
**w** windsorblackpool.co.uk

---

**Windsor Carlton Guest Accommodation** ★★★★
*Guest Accommodation*
6 Warley Road, Blackpool
FY1 2JU
**t** (01253) 354924
**e** info@windsorcarlton.com
**w** windsorcarlton.com

---

**Woodfield** ★★★
*Guest Accommodation*
31-33 Woodfield Road,
Blackpool FY1 6AX
**t** (01253) 346304
**e** bookings@thewoodfield.com
**w** thewoodfield.com

---

**Wynnstay** ★★★
*Guest House*
64 Hornby Road, Blackpool
FY1 4QJ
**t** (01253) 627601
**e** info@wynnstayhotel.co.uk
**w** wynnstayhotel.co.uk

---

**Wyvern Hotel**
Rating Applied For
*Guest Accommodation*
9 Alexandra Road, Blackpool
FY1 6BU
**t** (01253) 404130
**e** t.eagle@btconnect.com
**w** wyvernhotel.com

## BLAXTON
South Yorkshire

**Barnside Cottage** ★★★
*Bed & Breakfast*
Mosham Road, Blaxton,
Doncaster DN9 3AZ
**t** (01302) 770315
**e** info@barnside.net
**w** barnside.net

---

**Beech Grove Lodge** ★★★★
*Guest Accommodation*
**SILVER AWARD**
Station Road, Blaxton,
Doncaster DN9 3AF
**t** (01302) 771771
**e** enquiries@beechgrovelodge.co.uk
**w** beechgrovelodge.co.uk

---

**New Farm House Bed and Breakfast** ★★★
*Bed & Breakfast*
Bank End Road, Doncaster
DN9 3AN
**t** (01302) 770072
**w** newfarmhouse.com

## BLENCARN
Cumbria

**Lakes and Dales Accommodation** ★★★★
*Bed & Breakfast*
Midtown Farm, Blencarn,
Penrith CA10 1TX
**t** (01768) 879091
**e** info@lakesanddales.co.uk
**w** lakesanddales.co.uk

## BLUNDELLSANDS
Merseyside

**Blundellsands Guesthouse** ★★★★
*Guest Accommodation*
**SILVER AWARD**
9 Elton Avenue, Liverpool
L23 8UN
**t** (0151) 924 6947
**e** bsbb@blueyonder.co.uk
**w** blundellsands.info

### BOLTBY
North Yorkshire

**Willow Tree Cottage Bed and Breakfast ★★★★**
*Guest Accommodation*
Willow Tree Cottage Bed and Breakfast, Boltby, Thirsk YO7 2DY
**t** (01845) 537406
**e** townsend.sce@virgin.net

### BOLTON
Cumbria

**Tarka House ★★★★**
*Guest Accommodation*
Appleby-in-Westmorland CA16 6AW
**t** (017683) 61422

### BOLTON
Greater Manchester

**Archangelos Bed & Breakfast ★★★**
*Guest Accommodation*
82 Pennine Road, Horwich, Bolton BL6 7HW
**t** (01204) 692303
**e** enquiries@archangelos.co.uk
**w** archangelos.co.uk

**Highgrove Guest House ★★★** *Guest House*
63 Manchester Road, Bolton BL2 1ES
**t** (01204) 384928
**e** thehighgrove@btconnect.com
**w** highgroveguesthouse.co.uk

### BOLTON-BY-BOWLAND
Lancashire

**Middle Flass Lodge ★★★★**
*Guest House*
Forest Becks Brow, Clitheroe BB7 4NY
**t** (01200) 447259
**e** middleflasslodge@btconnect.com
**w** middleflasslodge.co.uk

### BOLTONGATE
Cumbria

**Boltongate Old Rectory ★★★★★**
*Guest Accommodation*
**GOLD AWARD**
**Enjoy England Awards for Excellence Winner**
The Old Rectory, Boltongate, Wigton CA7 1DA
**t** (01697) 371647
**e** boltongate@talk21.com
**w** boltongateoldrectory.com

### BOOT
Cumbria

**Eskdale YHA ★★★** *Hostel*
Holmrook CA19 1TH
**t** (01946) 723219

### BOOTLE
Merseyside

**Regent Maritime Hotel ★★**
*Guest Accommodation*
58-68 Regent Road, Liverpool L20 8DB
**t** (0151) 922 4090
**e** info@regentmaritimehotel.com
**w** regentmaritimehotel.com

### BORROWDALE
Cumbria

**Ashness Farm ★★★★**
*Farmhouse*
Borrowdale, Keswick CA12 5UN
**t** (017687) 77361
**e** enquiries@ashnessfarm.co.uk
**w** ashnessfarm.co.uk

**Derwentwater YHA ★★★**
*Hostel*
Barrow House, Keswick CA12 5UR
**t** (017687) 77246

**Dinah Hoggus Camping Barn**
*Camping Barn*
Thorneythwaite Farm, Borrowdale, Keswick CA12 5XQ
**t** (017687) 77237

**Hazel Bank Country House ★★★★★** *Guest House*
**GOLD AWARD**
Rosthwaite, Borrowdale, Keswick CA12 5XB
**t** (017687) 77248
**e** enquiries@hazelbankhotel.co.uk
**w** hazelbankhotel.co.uk

**Seatoller Farm ★★★★**
*Farmhouse*
Borrowdale, Keswick CA12 5XN
**t** (017687) 77232

### BOSTON SPA
West Yorkshire

**Four Gables ★★★★★**
*Guest Accommodation*
**SILVER AWARD**
Oaks Lane, Boston Spa, Wetherby LS23 6DS
**t** (01937) 845592
**e** info@fourgables.co.uk
**w** fourgables.co.uk

### BOWBURN
Durham

**Prince Bishop Guest House ★★★** *Guest House*
1 Oxford Terrace, Bowburn DH6 5AX
**t** (0191) 377 8703
**e** enquiries@durhamguesthouse.co.uk
**w** durhamguesthouse.co.uk

### BOWNESS-ON-SOLWAY
Cumbria

**The Old Chapel ★★★**
*Bed & Breakfast*
Bowness-on-Solway, Wigton CA7 5BL
**t** (01697) 351126
**e** oldchapelbowness@hotmail.com
**w** oldchapelbownessonsolway.com

**Wallsend House, The Old Rectory ★★★★**
*Guest Accommodation*
Church Lane, Bowness-on-Solway CA7 5AF
**t** (01697) 351055
**e** bandb@wallsend.net
**w** wallsend.net

### BRADFORD
West Yorkshire

**Ivy Guest House ★★**
*Guest House*
3 Melbourne Place, Bradford BD5 0HZ
**t** (01274) 727060
**e** enquiries@ivyguesthousebradford.com
**w** ivyguesthousebradford.com

**New Beehive Inn ★★**
*Guest Accommodation*
171 Westgate, Bradford BD1 3AA
**t** (01274) 721784
**e** newbeehiveinn.t21@btinternet.com
**w** newbeehiveinn.co.uk

**Norland Guest House ★★★**
*Guest Accommodation*
695 Great Horton Road, Bradford BD7 4DU
**t** (01274) 571698
**w** norlandguesthouse.gbr.cc

**Woodlands Guest House ★★★★**
*Guest Accommodation*
2 The Grove, Shelf, Halifax HX3 7PD
**t** (01274) 677533
**e** suewood45@hotmail.com
**w** woodlands-yorkshire.com

### BRAITHWAITE
Cumbria

**Coledale Inn ★★★** *Inn*
Braithwaite, Keswick CA12 5TN
**t** (017687) 78272
**e** info@coledale-inn.com
**w** coledale-inn.co.uk

**Howe View**
Rating Applied For
*Bed & Breakfast*
Braithwaite, Keswick CA12 5SZ
**t** (017687) 78593
**e** info@howeview.co.uk
**w** howeview.co.uk

**Middle Ruddings ★★★** *Inn*
Braithwaite, Keswick CA12 5RY
**t** (017687) 78436
**e** middleruddings@btconnect.com
**w** middle-ruddings.co.uk

### BRAMPTON
Cumbria

**Bankshead Camping Barn**
*Camping Barn*
Bankshead Farm, Banks, Brampton CA8 2BX
**t** (01697) 73198

**Blacksmiths Arms ★★★★**
*Inn*
Talkin, Brampton CA8 1LE
**t** (01697) 73452
**e** blacksmithsarmstalkin@yahoo.co.uk
**w** blacksmithstalkin.co.uk

**Low Rigg Farm ★★★★**
*Farmhouse*
Walton, Brampton CA8 2DX
**t** (01697) 73233
**e** lowrigg@toucansurf.com
**w** lowriggfarm.com

**Quarry Side ★★★★**
*Bed & Breakfast*
Banks, Brampton CA8 2JH
**t** (01697) 72538
**e** elizabeth.harding@btinternet.com

**Scarrowhill House ★★★★**
*Bed & Breakfast*
Scarrow Hill House, Denton Mill, Brampton CA8 2QU
**t** (01697) 746759 & 07789 950322
**e** ianmac2949@aol.com
**w** scarrowhillhouse.co.uk

**South View ★★★★**
*Guest Accommodation*
Banks, Brampton CA8 2JH
**t** (01697) 72309

**Vallum Barn ★★★★**
*Bed & Breakfast*
**SILVER AWARD**
Irthington, Carlisle CA6 4NN
**t** (01697) 742478
**e** vallumbarn@tinyworld.co.uk
**w** vallumbarn.co.uk

**Walton High Rigg ★★★**
*Farmhouse*
Walton, Brampton CA8 2AZ
**t** (01697) 72117
**e** mounsey_highrigg@hotmail.com
**w** waltonhighrigg.co.uk

### BRANCEPETH
Durham

**Nafferton Farm ★★★★**
*Farmhouse*
Brancepeth, Durham DH7 8EF
**t** (0191) 378 0538
**e** sndfell@aol.com
**w** nafferton-farm.co.uk

### BRIDGE HEWICK
North Yorkshire

**The Black A Moor Inn ★★★★** *Inn*
Boroughbridge Road, Bridge Hewick, Ripon HG4 5AA
**t** (01765) 603511

### BRIDLINGTON
East Riding of Yorkshire

**Ashford House ★★★**
*Guest House*
94 Trinity Road, Bridlington YO15 2HF
**t** (01262) 675849
**e** ashfordhousebrid@tiscali.co.uk
**w** ashfordhousebridlington.co.uk

**Balmoral House ★★★★**
*Guest Accommodation*
21 Marshall Avenue, Bridlington YO15 2DT
**t** (01262) 676678
**e** enquiry@thebalmoralhouse.co.uk
**w** balmoralhouse.co.uk

**The Bay Court ★★★★**
*Guest Accommodation*
**SILVER AWARD**
35a Sands Lane, Bridlington YO15 2JG
**t** (01262) 676288
**e** bay.court@virgin.net
**w** baycourt.co.uk

**The Bay Ridge** ★★★
*Guest Accommodation*
11-13 Summerfield Road, Bridlington YO15 3LF
t (01262) 673425
e bayridgehotel@aol.com
w bayridgehotel.co.uk

**Blantyre House** ★★★
*Guest House*
21 Pembroke Terrace, Bridlington YO15 3BX
t (01262) 400660
e info@blantyreguesthouse.co.uk
w blantyreguesthouse.co.uk

**Bluebell Guest House** ★★★
*Guest House*
3 St Annes Road, Bridlington YO15 2JB
t (01262) 675163
e enquiries@thebluebellguesthouse.co.uk
w thebluebellguesthouse.co.uk

**Bosville Arms Country Inn & Restaurant** ★★★ *Inn*
Main Street, Rudston, Driffield YO25 4UB
t (01262) 420259
e bosvillearms@aol.com

**Bradfield House**
Rating Applied For
*Guest House*
Horsforth Avenue, Bridlington YO15 3DF
t (01262) 672457

**Brentwood House** ★★★
*Guest House*
42 Princess Street, Bridlington YO15 2RB
t (01262) 608739
e info@brentwoodhouse.co.uk
w brentwoodhouse.co.uk

**Broadfield** ★★★
*Guest Accommodation*
18 Shaftesbury Road, Bridlington YO15 3NW
t (01262) 677379
e broadfieldhotel@talktalk.net
w broadfieldbridlington.co.uk

**The Brockton** ★★★★
*Guest House*
4 Shaftesbury Road, Bridlington YO15 3NP
t (01262) 673967
e brocktonhotel@yahoo.co.uk
w thebrockton.co.uk

**Charleston Guest House**
★★★ *Guest House*
12 Vernon Road, Bridlington YO15 2HQ
t (01262) 676228
e charlestongh@aol.com

**Chatley Court** ★★★
*Guest Accommodation*
54-56 Windsor Crescent, Bridlington YO15 3JA
t (01262) 674666
e chatlycourt@aol.com
w chatleycourt.co.uk

**The Crescent** ★★★
*Guest House*
12 The Crescent, Bridlington YO15 2NX
t (01262) 401015

**Cromer Guest House** ★★★
*Guest House*
78 Trinity Road, Bridlington YO15 2HF
t (01262) 679452
w cromerguesthouse.co.uk

**Doriam Guest House** ★★★
*Guest Accommodation*
35 Windsor Crescent, Bridlington YO15 3HX
t (01262) 672513

**Dulverton Court** ★★★
*Guest Accommodation*
17 Victoria Road, Bridlington YO15 2BW
t (01262) 672600
e joangbrid@aol.com

**Glen Alan Guest House**
★★★★ *Guest House*
21 Flamborough Road, Bridlington YO15 2HU
t (01262) 674650
e tonymaddison@aol.com
w glenalanhotel.co.uk

**The Grantlea Guest House**
★★★ *Guest House*
2 South Street, Bridlington YO15 3BY
t (01262) 400190
e enquiries@grantlea-guest-house.co.uk
w grantlea-guest-house.co.uk

**Harmony Guesthouse** ★★★
*Guest House*
38 Marshall Avenue, Bridlington YO15 2DS
t (01262) 603867
e enquiries@harmonyguesthouse.co.uk
w harmonyguesthouse.co.uk

**Ivanhoe Guest House** ★★★
*Guest House*
63 Cardigan Road, Bridlington YO15 3JS
t (01262) 675983 & (01262) 675983
e enquiries@ivanhoeguesthouse.co.uk
w ivanhoeguesthouse.co.uk

**The Jasmine Guest House**
★★★ *Guest House*
27-29 Richmond Street, Bridlington YO15 3DL
t (01262) 676608
e jasmineguesthouse@btinternet.com
w jasmineguesthouse.com

**Leeds House**
Rating Applied For
*Guest House*
40 Windsor Crescent, Bridlington YO15 3HY
t (01262) 674227

**Lincoln House** ★★★★
*Bed & Breakfast*
43 Wellington Road, Bridlington YO15 2AX
t (01262) 679595
e lincolnhousebrid@fsmail.net
w lincolnhousebridlington.co.uk

**The London Guest House**
★★★★
*Guest Accommodation*
1 Royal Crescent, York Road, Bridlington YO15 2PF
t (01262) 675377
e londonhotelbrid@yahoo.co.uk
w londonhotelbrid.co.uk

**Longcroft Lodge** ★★★★
*Guest House*
100 Trinity Road, Bridlington YO15 2HF
t (01262) 672180
e longcroft_hotel@hotmail.com

**The Marina** ★★★★
*Guest House*
8 Summerfield Road, Bridlington YO15 3LF
t (01262) 677138
e themarina8@hotmail.com
w themarina-bridlington.com

**Maryland Bed & Breakfast**
★★★★
*Guest Accommodation*
66 Wellington Road, Bridlington YO15 2AZ
t (01262) 671088
e ann@maryland.me.uk
w maryland.me.uk

**The Mayville Guest House**
★★★ *Guest Accommodation*
74 Marshall Avenue, Bridlington YO15 2DS
t (01262) 674420
e mayville@fedaye.fsnet.co.uk
w mayvilleguesthouse.co.uk

**Mont Millais** ★★★
*Guest Accommodation*
64 Trinity Road, Bridlington YO15 2HF
t (01262) 601890
w montmillais.co.uk

**The Mount** ★★★★
*Guest Accommodation*
2 Roundhay Road, Bridlington YO15 3JY
t (01262) 672306
e mounthotel01@btconnect.com
w mounthotelbridlington.co.uk

**Number 7 Guest House**
★★★★
*Guest Accommodation*
7 South Street, Bridlington YO15 3BY
t (01262) 601249
e number-seven@tiscali.co.uk
w numbersevenguesthouse.com

**Park View** ★★★★
*Guest Accommodation*
9-11 Tennyson Avenue, Bridlington YO15 2EU
t (01262) 672140

**The Promenade** ★★★
*Guest Accommodation*
121 Promenade, Bridlington YO15 2QN
t (01262) 602949
e m-abbott_@tiscali.co.uk
w thepromenadehotel.co.uk

**Providence Place** ★★★★
*Guest House*
11 North View Terrace, Bridlington YO15 2QP
t (01262) 603840
e enquiries@providenceplace.info
w providenceplace.info

**Rags Restaurant with rooms**
★★★★
*Restaurant with Rooms*
South Pier, Bridlington YO15 3AN
t (01262) 400355
e ragshotel@tesco.net
w ragshotel.co.uk

**Ridings Guest House** ★★★
*Guest House*
100 Windsor Crescent, Bridlington YO15 3JA
t (01262) 671744
e susan.potter7@tesco.net
w ridingsguesthouse.co.uk

**Rivendell Guest House**
★★★★
*Guest Accommodation*
19 Sands Lane, Bridlington YO15 2JG
t (01262) 679189
e rivendellhoteld@hotmail.co.uk
w rivendellhotel.net

**Rosebery House** ★★★★
*Guest Accommodation*
1 Belle Vue, Tennsyon Ave, Bridlington YO15 2ET
t (01262) 670336
e zexuc@btinternet.com

**Sandringham House** ★★★
*Guest House*
11 The Crescent, Bridlington YO15 2NX
t (01262) 672064
e sandringham-hotel@talk21.com

**The Sandsend** ★★★
*Guest House*
8 Sands Lane, Bridlington YO15 2JE
t (01262) 673265

**Sea View House** ★★★★
*Guest House*
54 South Marine Drive, Bridlington YO15 3JN
t (01262) 677775
e judybebber@hotmail.com

**The Seacourt** ★★★★
*Guest Accommodation*
**SILVER AWARD**
76 South Marine Drive, Bridlington YO15 3NS
t (01262) 400872
e seacourt.hotel@tiscali.co.uk
w seacourt-hotel.co.uk

**Seawinds Guest House**
★★★ *Guest Accommodation*
48 Horsforth Avenue, Bridlington YO15 3DF
t (01262) 676330
e alan@seawinds.co.uk
w seawinds.co.uk

**Southdowne** ★★★★
*Guest House*
78 South Marine Drive, Bridlington YO15 3NS
t (01262) 673270

**Spinnaker House** ★★★★
*Guest Accommodation*
19/20 Pembroke Terrace, Bridlington YO15 3BX
**t** (01262) 678440

**Stonmar Guest House** ★★★
*Guest House*
15 Flamborough Road, Bridlington YO15 2HU
**t** (01262) 674580
**e** info@stonmar.co.uk
**w** stonmar.co.uk

**The Trinity** ★★★
*Guest Accommodation*
9 Trinity Road, Bridlington YO15 2EZ
**t** (01262) 670444
**e** davcazz@aol.com
**w** bridlingtontrinityhotel.co.uk

**Vernon Villa** ★★★★
*Guest Accommodation*
2 Vernon Road, Bridlington YO15 2HQ
**t** (01262) 670661
**e** vernonvillaguesthouse@yahoo.co.uk

**Victoria House** ★★★
*Guest Accommodation*
25/27 Victoria Road, Bridlington YO15 2AT
**t** (01262) 673871
**e** contact@victoriahotelbridlington.co.uk
**w** victoriahotelbridlington.co.uk

**The Waverley** ★★★
*Guest House*
105 Cardigan Road, Bridlington YO15 3LP
**t** (01262) 671040
**e** info@waverley-bridlington.co.uk
**w** waverley-bridlington.co.uk

**White Lodge Guest House** ★★★ *Guest Accommodation*
9 Neptune Terrace, Neptune Street, Bridlington YO15 3DE
**t** (01262) 670903
**e** caitlyn.greene@btinternet.com
**w** whitelodgeguesthouse.co.uk

**Winston House** ★★★
*Guest Accommodation*
5/6 South Street, Bridlington YO15 3BY
**t** (01262) 670216
**e** winstonhouse@tiscali.co.uk

## BRIGNALL
Durham

**Lily Hill Farm** ★★★★
*Farmhouse*
Brignall, Barnard Castle DL12 9SF
**t** (01833) 627254
**e** karenerrington@yahoo.co.uk
**w** lilyhillfarm.co.uk

## BRISCO
Cumbria

**Crossroads House** ★★★★
*Bed & Breakfast*
**GOLD AWARD**
Brisco, Carlisle CA4 0QZ
**t** (01228) 528994
**e** viv@crossroadshouse.co.uk
**w** crossroadshouse.co.uk

## BROMPTON-ON-SWALE
North Yorkshire

**Brompton-on-Swale Camping Barn** *Bunkhouse*
Village Farm, 24 Richmond Road, Richmond DL10 7HE
**t** (01748) 818326
**e** info@ytb.org.uk
**w** yha.org.uk

## BROOMPARK
Durham

**My Way Guest House** ★★★
*Guest House*
West Farm, Broompark Village DH7 7RW
**t** (0191) 375 0874
**e** info@mywayguesthouse.co.uk
**w** mywayguesthouse.co.uk

## BROUGH
Cumbria

**River View** ★★★★
*Bed & Breakfast*
Brough CA17 4BZ
**t** (017683) 41894
**e** riverviewbb@btinternet.com
**w** riverviewbb.co.uk

## BROUGHTON IN FURNESS
Cumbria

**Dower House** ★★★
*Guest Accommodation*
High Duddon, Duddon Bridge, Broughton-in-Furness LA20 6ET
**t** (01229) 716279
**e** info@dowerhouse.biz
**w** dowerhouse.biz

**Fell End** *Camping Barn*
Fell End Barn, Thornthwaite, Woodland Hall, Woodland, Broughton-in-Furness LA20 6DF
**t** (01229) 716340

**Low Hall Farm** ★★★★
*Farmhouse*
Kirkby-in-Furness, Broughton in Furness LA17 7TR
**t** (01229) 889220
**e** enquiries@low-hall.co.uk
**w** low-hall.co.uk

## BRUERA
Cheshire

**Churton Heath Farm Bed & Breakfast** ★★★★
*Bed & Breakfast*
**GOLD AWARD**
Churton Heath Farm, Chapel Lane CH3 6EW
**t** (01244) 620420
**e** info@churtonheathfarm.co.uk
**w** churtonheathfarm.co.uk

## BUCKDEN
North Yorkshire

**Low Raisgill** ★★★★
*Bed & Breakfast*
Buckden, Skipton BD23 5JQ
**t** (01756) 760351

**Nethergill Farm** ★★★★
*Farmhouse*
Oughtershaw, Skipton BD23 5JS
**t** (01756) 761126
**e** fiona.clark@nethergill.co.uk
**w** nethergill.co.uk

**The White Lion Inn** ★★★
*Inn*
Cray, Skipton BD23 5JB
**t** (01756) 760262
**e** admin@whitelioncray.com
**w** whitelioncray.com

## BULMER
North Yorkshire

**Grange Farm** ★★★
*Farmhouse*
Castle Howard, Bulmer, York, Malton YO60 7BN
**t** (01653) 618376
**e** grangefarm3@yahoo.co.uk
**w** grangefarmbulmer.co.uk

## BURGH-BY-SANDS
Cumbria

**Highfield Farm** ★★★★
*Farmhouse*
Boustead Hill,, Burgh-by-Sands, Carlisle CA5 6AA
**t** (01228) 576060
**e** info@highfield-holidays.co.uk
**w** highfield-holidays.co.uk

**Hillside Farm** ★★★
*Bed & Breakfast*
Boustead Hill, Burgh-by-Sands, Carlisle CA5 6AA
**t** (01228) 576398
**e** ruddshillside1@btinternet.com
**w** hadrianswalkbnb.co.uk

## BURNLEY
Lancashire

**Ormerod** ★★★
*Guest Accommodation*
123 Ormerod Road, Burnley BB11 3QW
**t** (01282) 423255

**Thorneyholme Farm Cottage** ★★★★
*Guest Accommodation*
Barley New Road, Roughlee BB12 9LH
**t** (01282) 612452

## BURNT YATES
North Yorkshire

**High Winsley Farm** ★★★★
*Farmhouse*
Brimham Rocks Road, Burnt Yates, Pateley Bridge HG3 3EP
**t** (01423) 770376
**e** highwinsley@aol.com

**The New Inn** ★★★★ *Inn*
Pateley Bridge Road, Burnt Yates, Pateley Bridge HG3 3EG
**t** (01423) 771070
**e** newinnharrogate@btconnect.com
**w** thenewinnburtyates.co.uk

## BURSCOUGH
Lancashire

**The Farm**
Rating Applied For
*Farmhouse*
71 Martin Lane, Burscough L40 0RT
**t** (01704) 894889
**e** freda.neale@ic24.net
**w** thefarmburscough.co.uk

## BURY
Greater Manchester

**Ashbury Guest House** ★★★
*Guest Accommodation*
235 Rochdale Road, Bury BL9 7BX
**t** (0161) 762 9623
**e** glyniswoodall@btinternet.com

**Castle Guest House** ★★★
*Guest Accommodation*
7 Wellington Street, Bolton BL8 2AL
**t** (0161) 797 3396
**e** alanrusselluk@aol.com
**w** guesthousebury.co.uk

**Pennine View Guest House** ★★★ *Guest Accommodation*
8 Hunstanton Drive, Brandlesholme BL8 1EG
**t** (0161) 763 1249
**e** j.mckeon@tinyworld.co.uk

## BURYTHORPE
North Yorkshire

**Low Penhowe** ★★★★★
*Bed & Breakfast*
**GOLD AWARD**
Burythorpe, Malton YO17 9LU
**t** (01653) 658336
**e** lowpenhowe@btinternet.com
**w** bedandbreakfastyorkshire.co.uk

## BUTTERMERE
Cumbria

**Buttermere YHA** ★★★
*Hostel*
King George Vi Memorial Hostel, Cockermouth CA13 9XA
**t** (017687) 70245

**Cragg Barn** *Camping Barn*
Cragg Farm, Cockermouth CA13 9XA
**t** (017687) 70204

## BYRNESS
Northumberland

**Forest View** ★★★ *Hostel*
Otterburn Green, Byrness Village NE19 1TS
**t** (01830) 520425
**e** joycetaylor1703@hotmail.co.uk
**w** yha.org.uk

## CALDBECK
Cumbria

**Swaledale Watch** ★★★★
*Guest House* **SILVER AWARD**
Whelpo, Caldbeck CA7 8HQ
**t** (01697) 478409
**e** nan.savage@talk21.com
**w** swaledale-watch.co.uk

**YHA Caldbeck**
Rating Applied For
*Hostel*
Fellside Centre, Fellside, Witon CA7 8HA
**t** (017687) 72816

### CALDY
Merseyside

**Cheriton Guest House**
★★★★ *Bed & Breakfast*
151 Caldy Road, Caldy
CH48 1LP
t (0151) 625 5271
e cheriton151@hotmail.com
w cheritonguesthouse.co.uk

### CALTON
North Yorkshire

**Newfield Hall** ★★★★
*Guest Accommodation*
Skipton BD23 4AA
t (020) 8511 1534

### CARLETON
Cumbria

**Birklands House** ★★★★
*Bed & Breakfast*
**SILVER AWARD**
Carleton, Carlisle CA4 0BU
t (01228) 511837
e info@birklandshouse.co.uk
w birklandshouse.co.uk

**River Forge Bed & Breakfast**
★★★★ *Bed & Breakfast*
**SILVER AWARD**
River Forge, Carleton, Carlisle
CA4 8LE
t (01228) 523569
e bookings@river-forge.co.uk
w river-forge.co.uk

### CARLISLE
Cumbria

**Abberley House** ★★★★
*Bed & Breakfast*
33 Victoria Place, Carlisle
CA1 1HP
t (01228) 521645
e booking@abberleyhouse.co.uk
w abberleyhouse.co.uk

**Abbey Court** ★★★★
*Guest Accommodation*
24 London Road, Carlisle
CA1 2EL
t (01228) 528696
e abbeycourt@virgin.net

**Ashbourne House** ★★★
*Guest House*
11 Lazonby Terrace, Carlisle
CA1 2PZ
t (01228) 523500
e ashbournehouse@hotmail.co.uk

**Ashleigh House** ★★★★
*Guest House*
46 Victoria Place, Carlisle
CA1 1EX
t (01228) 521631

**Cartref Guest House** ★★★★
*Guest House* **SILVER AWARD**
44 Victoria Place, Carlisle
CA1 1EX
t (01228) 522077

**Cherry Grove** ★★★★
*Guest Accommodation*
87 Petteril Street, Carlisle
CA1 2AW
t (01228) 541942
w cherrygroveguesthouse.co.uk

**Cornerways Guest House**
★★★★
*Guest Accommodation*
107 Warwick Road, Carlisle
CA1 1EA
t (01228) 521733
e info@cornerwaysbandb.co.uk
w cornerwaysbandb.co.uk

**Courtfield Guest House**
★★★★ *Guest House*
**SILVER AWARD**
169 Warwick Road, Carlisle
CA1 1LP
t (01228) 522767
e mdawes@courtfieldhouse.fsnet.co.uk

**East View Guest House**
★★★★
*Guest Accommodation*
110 Warwick Road, Carlisle
CA1 1JU
t (01228) 522112
e eastviewgh@hotmail.co.uk
w eastviewguesthouse.co.uk

**Fernlee Guest House**
★★★★ *Guest House*
**SILVER AWARD**
9 St Aidans Road, Carlisle
CA1 1LT
t (01228) 511930

**Hazeldean Guest House**
★★★ *Guest House*
Orton Grange, Wigton Road,
Carlisle CA5 6LA
t (01228) 711953
e hazeldean1@btopenworld.com
w smoothhound.co.uk/hotels/hazeldean

**Howard Lodge Guest House**
★★★★
*Guest Accommodation*
90 Warwick Road, Carlisle
CA1 1JU
t (01228) 529842
e chrltdavi@aol.com
w howard-lodge.co.uk

**Kate's Guest House**
Rating Applied For
*Guest House*
6 Lazonby Terrace, London
Road, Carlisle CA1 2PZ
t (01228) 539577
e katesguesthouse@hotmail.com

**Knockupworth Hall** ★★★★
*Bed & Breakfast*
Burgh Road, Carlisle CA2 7RF
t (01228) 523531
e knockupworthdi@aol.com
w knockupworthdi.co.uk

**Langleigh House** ★★★★
*Guest House*
6 Howard Place, Carlisle
CA1 1HR
t (01228) 530440
e langleighhouse@aol.com
w langleighhouse.co.uk

**Lynebank House**
Rating Applied For
*Guest Accommodation*
Westlinton, Carlisle CA6 6AA
t (01228) 792820
e info@lynebank.co.uk
w lynebank.co.uk

**Number Thirty One**
★★★★★ *Guest House*
**GOLD AWARD**
31 Howard Place, Carlisle
CA1 1HR
t (01228) 597080
e pruirving@aol.com
w number31.co.uk

**Old Brewery Residences**
★★★ *Hostel*
Bridge Lane, Caldewgate,
Carlisle CA2 5SR
t (01228) 597352
e deec@impacthousing.org.uk
w impacthousing.org.uk

**Townhouse B&B** ★★★★
*Guest Accommodation*
153 Warwick Road, Carlisle
CA1 1LU
t (01228) 598782
e townhouse@christine60.freesereve.co.uk
w townhousebandb.com

**University of Cumbria – Carlisle** ★★★★ *Campus*
Fusehill Street, Carlisle
CA1 2HH
t (015394) 30232
e zoe.rome@cumbria.ac.uk
w conferencescumbria.co.uk

**Vallum House** ★★★
*Guest House*
73 Burgh Road, Carlisle
CA2 7NB
t (01228) 521860
e denmar39@tiscali.co.uk
w vallumhousehotel.co.uk

**White Lea Guest House**
★★★★ *Bed & Breakfast*
191 Warwick Road, Carlisle
CA1 1LP
t (01228) 533139

### CARLTON
North Yorkshire

**Abbots Thorn** ★★★★
*Guest Accommodation*
Carlton in Coverdale, Leyburn
DL8 4AY
t (01969) 640620
e abbotsthorn@virgin.net
w abbotsthorn.co.uk

### CARLTON
West Yorkshire

**Foxwood** ★★★★
*Guest Accommodation*
Carr Lane, Carlton, Wakefield
WF3 3RT
t (0113) 282 4786

### CARNFORTH
Lancashire

**Capernwray House** ★★★★
*Guest Accommodation*
**SILVER AWARD**
Borrans Lane, Capernwray
LA6 1AE
t (01524) 732363
e thesmiths@capernwrayhouse.com
w capernwrayhouse.com

**Dale Grove** ★★★★
*Bed & Breakfast*
162 Lancaster Road, Carnforth
LA5 9EF
t (01524) 733382
e stevenage3@btinternet.com

**Grisedale Farm** ★★★★
*Farmhouse*
Leighton Hall, Carnforth
LA5 9ST
t (01524) 734360
e ailsarobinson@btconnect.com
w grisedalefarm.co.uk

**Longlands Inn and Restaurant** ★★★★ *Inn*
Tewitfield, Carnforth LA6 1JH
t (01524) 781256
e info@longlandshotel.co.uk
w longlandshotel.co.uk

### CARTMEL
Cumbria

**Bank Court Cottage** ★★★
*Bed & Breakfast*
The Square, Cartmel, Grange-over-Sands LA11 6QB
t (015395) 36593

**Cavendish Arms** ★★★ *Inn*
Cavendish Street, Cartmel
LA11 6QA
t (015395) 36240
e info@thecavendisharms.co.uk
w thecavendisharms.co.uk

**Hill Farm B&B For Country Lovers** ★★★★★
*Bed & Breakfast*
**GOLD AWARD**
Cartmel, Grange-over-Sands
LA11 7SS
t (015395) 36477
e hillfarmbb@btinternet.com
w hillfarmbb.co.uk

**Priors Yeat** ★★★★
*Bed & Breakfast*
Aynsome Road, Cartmel,
Grange-over-Sands LA11 6PR
t (015395) 35178
e priorsyeat@hotmail.com
w priorsyeat.co.uk

### CASTLE CARROCK
Cumbria

**The Weary at Castle Carrock**
★★★★
*Restaurant with Rooms*
**SILVER AWARD**
Castle Carrock, Brampton
CA8 9LU
t (01228) 670230
e relax@theweary.com
w theweary.com

### CASTLE HOWARD
North Yorkshire

**Ganthorpe Gate Farm** ★★★
*Farmhouse*
Ganthorpe, Terrington, York
YO60 6QD
t (01653) 648269
e millgate001@msn.com
w ganthorpegatefarm.co.uk

**Lowry's Restaurant and Bed & Breakfast** ★★★
*Guest House*
Malton Road, Slingsby, Malton
YO62 4AF
t (01653) 628417
e dgwilliams@onetel.com

**CASTLESIDE**
**Durham**

**Bee Cottage Guesthouse**
★★★★ *Guest House*
Castleside, Nr Consett
DH8 9HW
**t** (01207) 508224
**e** beecottage68@aol.com
**w** beecottage.co.uk

**Dene View** ★★★★
*Guest Accommodation*
15 Front Street, Castleside
DH8 9AR
**t** (01207) 502925
**e** catherine@deneview.co.uk
**w** deneview.co.uk

**CATTERICK BRIDGE**
**North Yorkshire**

**St Giles Farm** ★★★★
*Farmhouse*
Catterick Bridge, Richmond
DL10 7PH
**t** (01748) 811372
**e** janethor@aol.co.uk

**CHAIGLEY**
**Lancashire**

**Moorhead House Farm** ★★
*Guest Accommodation*
Thornley Road, Chaigley
BB7 3LY
**t** (01995) 61108

**CHAPEL ALLERTON**
**West Yorkshire**

**Green House** ★★★
*Bed & Breakfast*
5 Bank View, Chapel Allerton,
Leeds LS7 2EX
**t** (0113) 268 1380

**CHATTON**
**Northumberland**

**South Hazelrigg Farmhouse**
★★★★ *Farmhouse*
**SILVER AWARD**
**Enjoy England Awards for Excellence Winner**
Chatton, Alnwick NE66 5RZ
**t** (01668) 215216 &
07710 346076
**e** sed@hazelrigg.fsnet.co.uk
**w** farmhousebandb.co.uk

**CHEADLE**
**Greater Manchester**

**Curzon House** ★★
*Bed & Breakfast*
3 Curzon Road, Heald Green,
Cheadle, Stockport SK8 3LN
**t** (0161) 436 2804
**e** curzonhouse@aol.com
**w** smoothhound.co.uk

**CHEADLE HULME**
**Greater Manchester**

**Spring Cottage Guest House**
★★★ *Guest House*
60 Hulme Hall Road, Cheadle
Hulme, Stockport SK8 6JZ
**t** (0161) 485 1037

**CHESTER**
**Cheshire**

**Ba Ba Guest House** ★★★★
*Guest Accommodation*
65 Hoole Road, Hoole CH2 3NJ
**t** (01244) 315047
**e** reservations@babaguesthouse.co.uk
**w** babaguesthouse.co.uk

**Bawn Lodge**
Rating Applied For
*Guest House*
10 Hoole Road, Hoole
CH2 3NH
**t** (01244) 324971
**e** info@bawnlodge.co.uk
**w** bawnlodge.co.uk

**Bowman Lodge** ★★★
*Guest Accommodation*
52 Hoole Road, Chester
CH2 3NL
**t** (01244) 342208
**e** info@bowmanlodge.co.uk
**w** bowmanlodge.co.uk

**Buckingham House**
Rating Applied For
*Guest Accommodation*
38 Hough Green, Chester
CH4 8JQ
**t** (01244) 681600
**e** info@buckinghamhousechester.co.uk
**w** buckinghamhousechester.co.uk

**Chester Backpackers** ★★
*Backpackers*
67 Boughton, Chester
CH3 5AF
**t** (01244) 400185

**Chester Brooklands** ★★★★
*Guest Accommodation*
8 Newton Lane, Chester
CH2 3RB
**t** (01244) 348856
**e** enquiries@chester-bandb.co.uk
**w** chester-bandb.co.uk

**Chester Town House**
★★★★ *Guest House*
23 King Street, Chester
CH1 2AH
**t** (01244) 350021
**e** davidbellis@chestertownhouse.co.uk
**w** chestertownhouse.co.uk

**Craigleith Lodge** ★★★★
*Guest Accommodation*
56 Hoole Road, Chester
CH2 3NL
**t** (01244) 318740
**e** welcome@craigleithlodge.co.uk
**w** craigleithlodge.co.uk

**Derry Raghan Lodge** ★★★★
*Guest Accommodation*
54 Hoole Road, Chester
CH2 3NL
**t** (01244) 318740
**e** welcome@derryraghanlodge.co.uk
**w** derryraghanlodge.co.uk

**Eastern Guest House** ★★★
*Bed & Breakfast*
Eastern Pathway, Chester
CH4 7AQ
**t** (01244) 680104

**Golborne Manor** ★★★★
*Bed & Breakfast*
Platts Lane, Hatton Heath,
Chester CH3 9AN
**t** (01829) 770310 &
07774 695268
**e** info@golbornemanor.co.uk
**w** golbornemanor.co.uk

**The Golden Eagle** ★★★ *Inn*
Castle Street, Chester
CH1 2DS
**t** (01244) 321098
**e** pipadee@tiscali.co.uk

**Grosvenor Place**
Rating Applied For
*Guest Accommodation*
2 Grosvenor Place, Chester
CH1 2DE
**t** (01244) 324455
**e** info@grosvenorplacechester.co.uk
**w** grosvenorplacechester.co.uk

**Grove Villa** ★★★★
*Bed & Breakfast*
18 The Groves, Chester
CH1 1SD
**t** (01244) 349713
**e** grovevilla18@btinternet.com
**w** grovevillachester.com

**Halcyon Guest House** ★★★
*Guest House*
18 Eaton Road, Handbridge
CH4 7EN
**t** (01244) 676159
**e** eric.owen@tiscali.co.uk

**Hameldaeus** ★★★
*Bed & Breakfast*
9 Lorne Street, Chester
CH1 4AE
**t** (01244) 374913
**e** joyce_brunton@tiscali.co.uk

**Homeleigh Guest House**
★★★ *Guest Accommodation*
14 Hough Green, Chester
CH4 8JG
**t** (01244) 676761
**e** colin-judy@tiscali.co.uk
**w** homeleighchester.co.uk

**Kilmorey Lodge** ★★★
*Guest Accommodation*
50 Hoole Road, Chester
CH2 3NL
**t** (01244) 324306
**e** kilmoreylodge@aol.com
**w** smoothhound.co.uk/hotels/kilmorey

**Kings Guesthouse** ★★★★
*Guest House*
14 Eaton Road, Handbridge
CH4 7EN
**t** (01244) 671249
**e** kings@kingsguesthouse.co.uk
**w** kingsguesthouse.co.uk/

**Laburnum House** ★★★
*Guest House*
2 St Anne Street, Chester
CH1 3HS
**t** (01244) 380313
**e** info@laburnumhousechester.co.uk
**w** laburnumhousechester.co.uk

**Laurels** ★★★★
*Bed & Breakfast*
14 Selkirk Road, Curzon Park
CH4 8AH
**t** (01244) 679682
**e** halandpam@talktalk.net
**w** visitchester.com

**Lavender Lodge Bed and Breakfast** ★★★★
*Guest Accommodation*
46 Hoole Road, Chester
CH2 3NL
**t** (01244) 323204
**e** bookings@lavenderlodgechester.co.uk
**w** lavenderlodgechester.co.uk

**The Limes** ★★★★
*Guest Accommodation*
12 Hoole Road, Chester
CH2 3NJ
**t** (01244) 328239
**e** malveena.hall@talktalk.net
**w** limes-chester.co.uk

**Lloyds Guest House** ★
*Guest Accommodation*
108 Brook Street, Chester
CH1 3DH
**t** (01244) 325838
**e** info@lloydsofchesterhotel.co.uk
**w** lloydsofchesterhotel.co.uk/

**Mitchell's of Chester Guest House** ★★★★★
*Guest House* **SILVER AWARD**
28 Hough Green, Chester
CH4 8JQ
**t** (01244) 679004
**e** mitoches@dialstart.net
**w** mitchellsofchester.com

**Newton Hall Farm Bed & Breakfast** ★★★★ *Farmhouse*
Tattenhall, Chester CH3 9NE
**t** (01829) 770153
**e** saarden@btinternet.com
**w** newtonhallfarm.co.uk

**Recorder House** ★★★★
*Guest Accommodation*
19 City Walls, Chester
CH1 1SB
**t** (01244) 326580
**e** reservations@recorderhotel.co.uk
**w** recorderhotel.co.uk

**Sycamore House Bed & Breakfast** ★★★★
*Bed & Breakfast*
8 Queens Park Road, Chester
CH4 7AD
**t** (01244) 675417
**e** helen.speke@btinternet.com
**w** visitchester.com

**Tentry Heys** ★★★
*Bed & Breakfast*
Queens Park Road, Chester
CH4 7AD
**t** (01244) 677857

**Tower House**
Rating Applied For
*Bed & Breakfast*
14 Dee Hills Park, Chester
CH3 5AR
**t** (01244) 341936
**e** sueheather62@hotmail.com

**Willow Run Bed & Breakfast**
★★★★ *Bed & Breakfast*
**SILVER AWARD**
Barrow Lane, Tarvin Sands
CH3 8JF
**t** (01829) 749142
**e** willowrun@btconnect.com
**w** willowrun.co.uk

### CHESTER-LE-STREET Durham

**Hollycroft** ★★★★
*Bed & Breakfast*
11 The Parade, Chester-le-Street DH3 3LR
t (0191) 388 7088
e staydurham@talktalk.net
w staydurham.co.uk

**Low Urpeth Farm** ★★★★
*Farmhouse* **SILVER AWARD**
Ouston, Chester-le-Street DH2 1BD
t (0191) 410 2901
e stay@lowurpeth.co.uk
w lowurpeth.co.uk

### CHIPPING Lancashire

**Chipping Camping Barn**
*Camping Barn*
Forest of Bowland, Chipping PR3 2GQ
t (01995) 61209
w yha.org.uk

**Clark House Farm** ★★★★
*Farmhouse*
Chipping PR3 2GQ
t (01995) 61209
e fpr@agriplus.net
w clarkhousefarm.com

### CHOLMONDELEY Cheshire

**Manor Farm Bed & Breakfast** ★★★★ *Farmhouse*
Egerton, Cholmondeley SY14 8AW
t (01829) 720261
e manorfarmbandb@btconnect.com
w egertonmanorfarm.co.uk

### CHOPPINGTON Northumberland

**The Swan at Choppington** ★★★ *Inn*
Choppington NE62 5TG
t (01670) 826060
e enquiries@theswanchoppington.co.uk
w theswanchoppington.co.uk

### CHORLEY Lancashire

**Inglewood B&B** ★★★
*Guest Accommodation*
19 Southport Road, Chorley PR7 1LB
t 07792 957168
e gorsesam@aol.com
w inglewoodboutiquebandb.co.uk

**Parr Hall Farm** ★★★★
*Guest Accommodation*
Parr Lane, Eccleston, Chorley PR7 5SL
t (01257) 451917
e enquiries@parrhallfarm.com
w parrhallfarm.com

### CLIFTON Cumbria

**The White House Experience Guest House** ★★★★
*Guest Accommodation*
Clifton, Penrith CA10 2EL
t (01768) 865115
e info@thewhitehouseexperience.co.uk
w thewhitehouseexperience.co.uk

### CLITHEROE Lancashire

**Bayley Arms** ★★★★ *Inn*
Avenue Road, Hurst Green, Clitheroe, Nr Blackburn BB7 9QB
t (01254) 826478
e sales@bayleyarms.co.uk
w bayleyarms.co.uk

**Rakefoot Farm** ★★★★
*Farmhouse*
Thornley Road, Chaigley BB7 3LY
t (01995) 61332
e info@rakefootfarm.co.uk

**The Rowan Tree**
Rating Applied For
*Bed & Breakfast*
10 Railway View Road, Clitheroe BB7 2HE
t (01200) 427115
w the-rowan-tree.org.uk

**Waddow Hall** ★★★
*Group Hostel*
Waddington Road, Waddington, Clitheroe BB7 3LD
t (01200) 423186

**York House Bed & Breakfast** ★★★★ *Bed & Breakfast*
York House, York Street, Clitheroe BB7 2DL
t (01200) 429519
e brindle_susan@hotmail.com
w yorkhousebandb.co.uk

### CLOUGHTON North Yorkshire

**Blacksmiths Arms** ★★★ *Inn*
High Street, Cloughton, Scarborough YO13 0AE
t (01723) 870244
e enquiries@blacksmithsarmsinn.co.uk
w blacksmithsarmsinn.co.uk

**Cober Hill** ★★★
*Guest Accommodation*
Newlands Road, Cloughton, Scarborough YO13 0AR
t (01723) 870310
e enquiries@coberhill.co.uk
w coberhill.co.uk

### COCKERMOUTH Cumbria

**Cockermouth YHA** ★★
*Hostel*
Double Mills, Fern Bank Road, Cockermouth CA13 0DS
t (01900) 822561
e cockermouth@yha.org.uk

**Croft Guesthouse** ★★★★
*Guest House*
6-8 Challoner Street, Cockermouth CA13 9QS
t (01900) 827533
e info@croft-guesthouse.com
w croft-guesthouse.com

**Graysonside** ★★★★★
*Guest Accommodation*
**GOLD AWARD**
Lorton Road, Cockermouth CA13 9TQ
t (01900) 822351
e stay@graysonside.co.uk
w graysonside.co.uk

**The Old Homestead** ★★★★
*Farmhouse*
Byresteads Farm, Cockermouth CA13 9TW
t (01900) 822223
e info@byresteads.co.uk
w byresteads.co.uk

**Rose Cottage** ★★★★
*Guest House*
Lorton Road, Cockermouth CA13 9DX
t (01900) 822189
e bookings@rosecottageguest.co.uk
w rosecottageguest.co.uk

### COLDEN West Yorkshire

**Riverdene House** ★★★★
*Bed & Breakfast*
Smithy Lane, Jack Bridge, Hebden Bridge HX7 7HN
t (01422) 847447

### COLLINGHAM West Yorkshire

**Tilworth** ★★ *Bed & Breakfast*
2 Green Lane, Collingham, Wetherby LS22 5DE
t (01937) 572254
e joan@tilworth.fsnet.co.uk

### COLNE Lancashire

**The Alma Inn**
Rating Applied For
*Guest Accommodation*
Emmott Lane, Colne BB8 7EG
t (01282) 863447
e janice.waters@btconnect.com

**Blakey Hall Farm** ★★★★
*Farmhouse* **SILVER AWARD**
Red Lane, Colne BB8 9TD
t (01282) 863121
e blakeyhall@hotmail.com
w blakeyhallfarm.co.uk

**Higher Wanless Farm** ★★★★ *Farmhouse*
Red Lane, Colne BB8 7JP
t (01282) 865301
e info@stayinlancs.co.uk
w stayinlancs.co.uk

**Middle Beardshaw Head Farm** ★★★
*Guest Accommodation*
Burnley Road, Trawden BB8 8PP
t (01282) 865257
e ursula@mann1940.freeserve.co.uk
w smoothhound.co.uk/a11504

**Rowan House B&B** ★★★
*Guest Accommodation*
Harrison Drive, Colne BB8 9SJ
t (01282) 870937
e antony.hartley1@ntlworld.com
w rowanhousebandb.com

**Rye Flatt Farmhouse** ★★★★
*Bed & Breakfast*
20 School Lane, Colne BB8 7JB
t (01282) 871565
e info@rye-flatt.co.uk
w rye-flatt.co.uk

**Stable Cross** ★★★ *Hostel*
Knotts Lane, Colne BB8 8AD
t (01282) 863229
e alicermann@aol.com

**Wayside Barn Bed & Breakfast**
Rating Applied For
*Guest Accommodation*
Greenfield Road, Colne BB8 9PE
t (01282) 865077
e velma.brads@virgin.net

### CONGLETON Cheshire

**Cloud House Farm** ★★★★
*Farmhouse*
Toft Green, Congleton CW12 3QF
t (01260) 226272

**Coppice Edge Bed & Breakfast** ★★★★
*Bed & Breakfast*
Blackfirs Lane, Somerford CW12 4QQ
t (01260) 270605
e nicole@somerford24.freeserve.co.uk
w coppice-edge.co.uk

**HP Bed & Breakfast** ★★★
*Bed & Breakfast*
Norfolk Road, Congleton CW12 1NY
t (01260) 279887
e hpbedandbreakfast@hotmail.com

**Sandhole Farm** ★★★★
*Guest Accommodation*
Manchester Road (A34), Hulme Walfield CW12 2JH
t (01260) 224419
e veronica@sandholefarm.co.uk
w sandholefarm.co.uk

**The Woodlands** ★★★★
*Guest Accommodation*
Quarry Wood Farm, Wood Street, Mow Cop ST7 3PF
t (01782) 518877

**Yew Tree Farm B&B** ★★★★
*Farmhouse*
North Rode, Congleton CW12 2PF
t (01260) 223569
e yewtreebb@hotmail.com
w yewtreebb.co.uk

### CONISTON Cumbria

**Beech Tree House** ★★★★
*Guest House*
Yewdale Road, Coniston LA21 8DX
t (015394) 41717

**Coniston Coppermines YHA** ★★★ *Hostel*
Coniston Coppermines, Coppermines House, Coniston LA21 8HP
t (015394) 41261
e coppermines@yha.org.uk
w yha.org.uk

**Coniston Lodge** ★★★★★
*Guest Accommodation*
**GOLD AWARD**
Station Road, Coniston LA21 8HH
t (015394) 41201
e info@coniston-lodge.com
w coniston-lodge.com

**Coniston YHA** ★★★ *Hostel*
Holly How, Far End, Coniston LA21 8DD
t (015394) 41323

**Crown Inn** ★★★★ *Inn*
Tilberthwaite Avenue, Coniston LA21 8ED
t (015394) 41243
e info@crown-hotel-coniston.com
w crown-hotel-coniston.com

**Lakeland House** ★★★
*Guest Accommodation*
Tilberthwaite Avenue, Coniston LA21 8ED
t (015394) 41303
e info@lakelandhouse.com
w lakelandhouse.com

**Oaklands** ★★★★
*Guest House*
Yewdale Road, Coniston LA21 8DX
**t** (015394) 41245
**e** judithzeke@oaklandsguesthouse.fsnet.co.uk
**w** oaklandsconiston.co.uk

**The Old Rectory** ★★★★
*Guest House* **SILVER AWARD**
Torver, Coniston LA21 8AX
t (015394) 41353
e enquiries@theoldrectoryhotel.com
w theoldrectoryhotel.com

**Orchard Cottage** ★★★★
*Bed & Breakfast*
18 Yewdale Road, Coniston LA21 8DU
t (015394) 41319
e enquiries@conistonholidays.co.uk
w conistonholidays.co.uk

**Thwaite Cottage** ★★★★
*Bed & Breakfast*
Waterhead, Coniston LA21 8AJ
t (015394) 41367
e m@thwaitcot.freeserve.co.uk
w thwaitcot.freeserve.co.uk

**Wilson Arms** ★★★ *Inn*
Torver, Coniston LA21 8BB
t (015394) 41237
e wilsonarms@tesco.net

**Yew Tree Farm** ★★★★★
*Farmhouse* **SILVER AWARD**
Coniston LA21 8DP
**t** (015394) 41433
**e** info@yewtree-farm.com
**w** yewtree-farm.com

**Yewdale Inn** ★★★ *Inn*
Yewdale Road, Coniston LA21 8DU
**t** (015394) 41280
**e** mail@yewdalehotel.com
**w** yewdalehotel.com

## CONSETT
### Durham

**Hownsgill Bunkhouse** ★★★
*Hostel*
Hownsgill Farm, Consett DH8 9AA
t (01207) 503597
e hownsgill_bunkhouse@hotmail.co.uk
w c2cstopoff.co.uk

**St Ives Bed & Breakfast** ★★
*Bed & Breakfast*
22 St Ives Road, Leadgate DH8 7PY
t (01207) 580173

**Wharnley Burn Farm** ★★★
*Bed & Breakfast*
Castleside, Consett DH8 9AY
t (01207) 508374

## CORBRIDGE
### Northumberland

**2 The Crofts** ★★★★
*Bed & Breakfast*
Newcastle Road, Corbridge NE45 5LW
t (01434) 633046
e welcome@2thecrofts.co.uk
w 2thecrofts.co.uk

**5 Dilston West Cottages**
★★★★ *Bed & Breakfast*
Dilston, Corbridge NE45 5RL
t (01434) 632464
e liz.nev@hotmail.co.uk

**Broxdale** ★★★★
*Bed & Breakfast*
Station Road, Corbridge NE45 5AY
**t** (01434) 632492
**e** mike@broxdale.co.uk

**Dilston Mill** ★★★★
*Bed & Breakfast*
Corbridge NE45 5QZ
t (01434) 633493
e susan@dilstonmill.com
w dilstonmill.com

**Dyvels Inn**
Rating Applied For
*Inn*
Station Road, Corbridge NE45 5AY
t (01434) 633633
e thedyvelsinn@googlemail.com

**Fellcroft** ★★★★
*Bed & Breakfast*
Station Road, Corbridge NE45 5AY
**t** (01434) 632384
**e** tove.brown@ukonline.co.uk

**The Hayes** ★★★
*Guest Accommodation*
Newcastle Road, Corbridge NE45 5LP
**t** (01434) 632010
**e** camon@surfree.co.uk
**w** hayes-corbridge.co.uk

**Low Fotherley Farmhouse Bed and Breakfast** ★★★★
*Farmhouse*
Low Fotherley Farm, Riding Mill NE44 6BB
t (01434) 682277
e hugh@lowfotherley.fsnet.co.uk
w westfarm.freeserve.co.uk

**Norgate** ★★★★
*Bed & Breakfast*
7 Leazes Terrace, Corbridge NE45 5HS
t (01434) 633736
e norgatecorbridge@btinternet.com
w norgatecorbridge.co.uk

**Priorfield** ★★★★
*Bed & Breakfast*
**SILVER AWARD**
Hippingstones Lane, Corbridge NE45 5JP
t (01434) 633179
e nsteenberg@btinternet.com
w priorfieldbedandbreakfast.co.uk

**Prospect House B&B**
Rating Applied For
*Bed & Breakfast*
Ladycutter Lane, Corbridge NE45 5RR
t (01434) 633551
e susanwalne@hotmail.co.uk

**Riggsacre** ★★★★★
*Bed & Breakfast*
**GOLD AWARD**
Appletree Lane, Corbridge NE45 5DN
t (01434) 632617
e atclive@supanet.com
w riggsacrebandb.co.uk

**Town Barns** ★★★★
*Bed & Breakfast*
**SILVER AWARD**
Off Trinity Terrace, Corbridge NE45 5HP
t (01434) 633345

## CORNHILL-ON-TWEED
### Northumberland

**The Coach House at Crookham** ★★★★
*Guest Accommodation*
**SILVER AWARD**
Cornhill-on-Tweed TD12 4TD
t (01890) 820293
e stay@coachhousecrookham.com
w coachhousecrookham.com

**The Old School House B&B**
★★★★★ *Bed & Breakfast*
**SILVER AWARD**
Tillmouth Park, Tillmouth TD12 4UT
t (01890) 882463
e noelhodgson@btinternet.com
w tillmouthschoolhouse.co.uk

## COTEHILL
### Cumbria

**The Green Bed & Breakfast**
★★★★ *Bed & Breakfast*
The Green, Cotehill, Carlisle CA4 0EA
t (01228) 561824
e thegreenbb@uwclub.net

## COTHERSTONE
### Durham

**Glendale** ★★★
*Bed & Breakfast*
Cotherstone, Barnard Castle DL12 9UH
t (01833) 650384
w barnard-castle.co.uk

## COTTINGHAM
### East Riding of Yorkshire

**Kenwood House**
Rating Applied For
*Bed & Breakfast*
7 Newgate Street, Cottingham, Hull HU16 4DY
t (01482) 847558

**Newholme Guest House**
★★★ *Guest House*
47 Thwaite Street, Cottingham, Hull HU16 4QX
t (01482) 849879
e lorraine.headley@hotmail.com

## COXWOLD
### North Yorkshire

**The Abbey Country Restaurant with Rooms**
Rating Applied For
*Restaurant with Rooms*
Byland Abbey, York YO61 4BD
t (01347) 868204
e abbeyinn@english-heritage.org.uk
w bylandabbeyinn.com

**Newburgh House** ★★★★★
*Bed & Breakfast*
Newburgh, Coxwold, Thirsk YO61 4AS
t (01347) 868177
e info@newburghhouse.com
w newburghhouse.com

## CRASTER
### Northumberland

**Cottage Inn** ★★★
*Guest Accommodation*
Dunstan Village NE66 3SZ
t (01665) 576658
e enquiries@cottageinnhotel.co.uk
w cottageinnhotel.co.uk

**Harbour Lights** ★★★★
*Bed & Breakfast*
Whin Hill, Craster NE66 3TP
t (01665) 576062
e info@harbourlights-craster.co.uk
w harbourlights-craster.co.uk

**Howick Scar Farmhouse**
★★★ *Farmhouse*
Craster, Alnwick NE66 3SU
**t** (01665) 576665
**e** stay@howickscar.co.uk
**w** howickscar.co.uk


Look out for establishments participating in the National Accessible Scheme

**Stonecroft** ★★★★
*Bed & Breakfast*
**SILVER AWARD**
Dunstan, Craster NE66 3SZ
**t** (01665) 576433
**e** sally@stonestaff.freeserve.co.uk
**w** stonecroft-craster.co.uk

## CRAYKE
North Yorkshire

**The Durham Ox** ★★★★
*Restaurant with Rooms*
West Way, Crayke, Easingwold YO61 4TE
**t** (01347) 821506
**e** enquiries@thedurhamox.com
**w** thedurhamox.com

**Hazelwood Farm Bed and Breakfast** ★★★★ *Farmhouse*
**SILVER AWARD**
Mosswood Lane, Crayke, Easingwold YO61 4TQ
**t** (01347) 824654
**e** amcanespie@toucansurf.com
**w** hazelwoodfarm.net

**The Hermitage** ★★★
*Bed & Breakfast*
Mill Lane, Crayke YO61 4TD
**t** (01347) 821635

## CROFTON
West Yorkshire

**Redbeck Motel Ltd** ★★
*Guest Accommodation*
Doncaster Road, Crofton, Wakefield WF4 1RR
**t** (01924) 862730
**e** enquiries@redbeckmotel.co.uk
**w** redbeckmotel.co.uk

## CROOK
Durham

**Dowfold House** ★★★★
*Bed & Breakfast*
Low Jobs Hill, Crook DL15 9AB
**t** (01388) 762473
**e** enquiries@dowfoldhouse.co.uk
**w** dowfoldhouse.co.uk

## CROPTON
North Yorkshire

**High Farm Bed & Breakfast** ★★★★ *Farmhouse*
**SILVER AWARD**
High Farm, Cropton, Pickering YO18 8HL
**t** (01751) 417461
**e** highfarmcropton@aol.com
**w** hhml.com/bb/highfarmcropton.htm

**New Inn and Cropton Brewery** ★★★ *Inn*
Cropton, Pickering YO18 8HH
**t** (01751) 417330
**e** info@croptonbrewery.co.uk
**w** croptonbrewery.com

## CROSBY-ON-EDEN
Cumbria

**Bluebell Camping Barn**
Rating Applied For
*Bunkhouse*
Crosby House, Crosby-on-Eden, Carlisle CA6 4QZ
**t** (01228) 573600
**e** joanneharper1@aol.com

## CROSBY RAVENSWORTH
Cumbria

**Crake Trees Manor** ★★★★★
*Guest Accommodation*
**GOLD AWARD**
Crosby Ravensworth, Penrith CA10 3JG
**t** (01931) 715205
**e** ruth@craketreesmanor.co.uk
**w** craketreesmanor.co.uk

## CROSSGATE MOOR
Durham

**The Lodge (Formerly The Pot and Glass)** ★★★★ *Inn*
Newcastle Road, Durham DH1 4HX
**t** (0191) 386 4556
**e** info@thelodge.durhamcity.net
**w** thelodge.durhamcity.net

## CROW EDGE
South Yorkshire

**The Dog and Partridge Inn** ★★★★ *Inn*
Bord Hill, Flouch, Barnsley S36 4HH
**t** (01226) 763173
**e** info@dogandpartridgeinn.co.uk
**w** dogandpartridgeinn.co.uk

## CUDDINGTON
Cheshire

**Acorn House Bed and Breakfast** ★★
*Bed & Breakfast*
34 Forest Close, Cuddington CW8 2EE
**t** (01606) 881714
**e** alanbridge02@aol.com

## CULGAITH
Cumbria

**Laurel House** ★★★★
*Bed & Breakfast*
**SILVER AWARD**
Culgaith, Penrith CA10 1QL
**t** (01768) 88638
**e** laurelhouse@fsmail.net
**w** laurelhousecumbria.co.uk

## CUNDALL
North Yorkshire

**Cundall Lodge Farm** ★★★★★ *Farmhouse*
**SILVER AWARD**
Cundall, Harrogate YO61 2RN
**t** (01423) 360203
**e** info@lodgefarmbb.co.uk
**w** lodgefarmbb.co.uk

## CUSWORTH
South Yorkshire

**The Cottage**
Rating Applied For
*Guest Accommodation*
Village Street, Doncaster DN5 7TR
**t** (01302) 786616
**e** joolsbon@yahoo.com

## DACRE BANKS
North Yorkshire

**Dalriada** ★★★
*Bed & Breakfast*
Cabin Lane, Dacre Banks, Pateley Bridge HG3 4EE
**t** (01423) 780512

**Gate Eel Farm** ★★★★
*Guest House*
Dacre Banks, Pateley Bridge HG3 4ED
**t** (01423) 781707
**e** diandpeterdriver@aol.co

**The Royal Oak Inn** ★★★★
*Inn*
Oak Lane, Dacre Banks, Harrogate, Pateley Bridge HG3 4EN
**t** (01423) 780200
**e** steve@the-royaloak-dacre.co.uk
**w** the-royaloak-dacre.co.uk

## DALBY
North Yorkshire

**South Moor Farm** ★★★★
*Farmhouse*
Dalby Forest Drive, Scarborough YO13 0LW
**t** (01751) 460285
**e** tbg@southmoorfarm.co.uk
**w** southmoorfarm.co.uk

## DALTON
North Yorkshire

**Dunsa Manor** ★★★★
*Guest Accommodation*
Dalton, Richmond DL11 7HE
**t** 07817 028237
**e** shaheenburnett@btinternet.com
**w** dunsamanor.com

## DALTON-LE-DALE
Durham

**The Chapel House B&B** ★★★ *Bed & Breakfast*
Stockton Road, Dalton-le-Dale SR7 8RG
**t** (0191) 581 2626
**e** gina.ryder@talktalk.net
**w** thechapelhousebandb.co.uk

## DANBY
North Yorkshire

**Botton Grove Farm** ★★★
*Farmhouse*
Danby Head, Danby YO21 2NH
**t** (01287) 660284
**e** judytait@bottongrove.freeserve.co.uk
**w** http://mysite.wanadoo-members.co.uk/botton_grove_farm/

**Duke of Wellington Inn** ★★★★ *Inn*
West Lane, Danby YO21 2LY
**t** (01287) 660351
**e** landlord@dukeofwellington.freeserve.co.uk
**w** danby-dukeofwellington.co.uk

**The Fox & Hounds Inn** ★★★★ *Inn*
45 Brook Lane, Ainthorpe, Whitby YO21 2LD
**t** (01287) 660218
**e** info@foxandhounds-ainthorpe.com
**w** foxandhounds-ainthorpe.com

**Great Fryupdale Outdoorcentre** ★★★
*Group Hostel*
Danby, Whitby YO21 2NP
**t** (01947) 893333
**e** enquiries@eastbarnby.co.uk
**w** eastbarnby.co.uk

**Rowantree Farm** ★★★★
*Farmhouse*
Fryup Road, Ainthorpe, Whitby YO21 2LE
**t** (01287) 660396
**e** krbsatindall@aol.com
**w** rowantreefarm.co.uk

## DARLINGTON
Tees Valley

**Boot & Shoe** ★★★ *Inn*
Church Row, Darlington DL1 5QD
**t** (01325) 287501
**e** enquiries@bootandshoe.com
**w** bootandshoe.com

**Clow Beck House** ★★★★★
*Guest Accommodation*
**GOLD AWARD**
**Enjoy England Awards for Excellence Winner**
Monk End, Croft on Tees, Darlington DL2 2SW
**t** (01325) 721075
**e** heather@clowbeckhouse.co.uk
**w** clowbeckhouse.co.uk

**The Greenbank** ★★★
*Guest Accommodation*
90 Greenbank Road, Darlington DL3 6EL
**t** (01325) 462624
**e** mikedalton1805@yahoo.co.uk

**Harewood Lodge** ★★★
*Guest House*
40 Grange Road, Darlington DL1 5NP
**t** (01325) 358152
**e** harewood.lodge@ntlworld.com
**w** harewood-lodge.co.uk

**Seafield House Bed and Breakfast** ★★★★
*Guest Accommodation*
18 Northumberland Street, Alnmouth NE66 2RJ
**t** (01665) 833256
**e** stay@seafieldhouse.co.uk
**w** seafieldhouse.co.uk

## DEIGHTON
North Yorkshire

**Grimston House** ★★★★
*Guest Accommodation*
Deighton House, York YO19 6HB
**t** (01904) 728328
**e** pat_wright@btinternet.com
**w** grimstonhouse.com

**Rush Farm** ★★★
*Guest Accommodation*
York Road, Deighton, York YO19 6HQ
**t** (01904) 728459
**e** david@rushfarm.co.uk
**w** rushfarm.co.uk

## DENSHAW
Greater Manchester

**Cherry Clough Farm House Accommodation** ★★★★
*Farmhouse*
Cherry Clough Farm, Denshaw OL3 5UE
**t** (01457) 874369
**e** info@cherryclough.co.uk
**w** cherryclough.co.uk

### DENT
Cumbria

**The George and Dragon**
★★★ *Inn*
Main Street, Dent, Sedbergh LA10 5QL
t (015396) 25256
e mail@thegeorgeanddragondent.co.uk
w thegeorgeanddragondent.co.uk

**Stone Close Tea Room & Guest House** ★★★
*Bed & Breakfast*
Main Street, Dent, Sedbergh LA10 5QL
t (015396) 25231
e stoneclose@btinternet.com
w dentdale.com

### DINNINGTON
South Yorkshire

**Throapham House Bed & Breakfast** ★★★★★
*Guest Accommodation*
**GOLD AWARD**
Oldcotes Road, Throapham, Dinnington S25, Rotherham S25 2QS
t (01909) 562208
e enquiries@throapham-house.co.uk
w throapham-house.co.uk

### DISLEY
Cheshire

**The Grey Cottage** ★★★
*Bed & Breakfast*
20 Jackson's Edge Road, Disley SK12 2JE
t (01663) 763286
e carol.greycottage@talk21.com

### DONCASTER
South Yorkshire

**The Balmoral** ★★★
*Guest Accommodation*
129 Thorne Road, Doncaster DN2 5BH
t (01302) 364385
e thebalmoralhotel@blueyonder.co.uk

**The Caribbean** ★★★
*Guest Accommodation*
87-89 Thorne Road, Doncaster DN1 2ES
t (01302) 364605
e dene@caribbean-hotel.co.uk
w caribbean-hotel.co.uk

**Earlesmere Guest House**
★★★ *Guest House*
Thorne Road, Doncaster DN2 5BL
t (01302) 368532
e earlesmere84@yahoo.co.uk

**Holly Guest House**
Rating Applied For
*Guest Accommodation*
18-20 Kings Road, Doncaster DN1 2LX
t (01302) 562436

**The Lyntone Guest House**
★★★ *Guest Accommodation*
24 Avenue Road, Wheatley, Doncaster DN2 4AQ
t (01302) 361586

**Oaklands Guest House** ★★
*Guest House*
36 Christ Church Road, Doncaster DN1 2QL
t (01302) 369875

**Park Inn** ★★★ *Inn*
232 Carrhouse Road, Doncaster DN4 5DS
t (01302) 364008

**Rock Farm** ★★★ *Farmhouse*
Hooton Pagnell, Doncaster DN5 7BT
t (01977) 642200 & 07785 916186
e info@rockfarm.info
w rockfarm.info

**Rockingham Arms** ★★★ *Inn*
Bennetthorpe, Doncaster DN2 6AA
t (01302) 360980
e info@rockinghamarms.co.uk
w rockinghamarms.co.uk

**Wheatley Hotel** ★★★ *Inn*
Thorne Road, Doncaster DN2 5DR
t (01302) 364092

**Windsor House** ★★★★
*Guest Accommodation*
7 Windsor Road, Town Moor, Doncaster DN2 5BS
t (01302) 768768
e ianmgell@aol.com
w windsorhousedoncaster.com

**The Woodborough** ★★★
*Guest Accommodation*
2 Belle-Vue Avenue, Belle-Vue, Doncaster DN4 5DX
t (01302) 361381
e mail@woodboroughhotel.co.uk
w woodboroughhotel.co.uk

### DOWNHAM
Lancashire

**New Hey** *Camping Barn*
Twiston Lane, Downham, Clitheroe BB7 4DF
t (01200) 441667

### DOWNHOLME
North Yorkshire

**Walburn Hall** ★★★★
*Farmhouse* **SILVER AWARD**
Downholme, Richmond DL11 6AF
t (01748) 822152
e walburnhall@farmersweekly.net

### DRIFFIELD
East Riding of Yorkshire

**Blacksmiths Cottage Country Guest House** ★★★
*Guest House*
Driffield Road, Kilham, Driffield YO25 4SN
t (01262) 420624
e rob@blacksmiths.orangehome.co.uk
w smoothhound.co.uk

### DRINGHOUSES
North Yorkshire

**The Racecourse Centre**
★★★★ *Group Hostel*
Tadcaster Road, Dringhouses, York YO24 1QG
t (01904) 620911
e info@racecoursecentre.co.uk
w racecoursecentre.co.uk

### DUFTON
Cumbria

**Brow Farm Bed & Breakfast**
★★★★ *Farmhouse*
**SILVER AWARD**
Dufton, Appleby-in-Westmorland CA16 6DF
t (017683) 52865
e stay@browfarm.com
w browfarm.com

**Dufton YHA** ★★★★ *Hostel*
Redstones, Dufton, Appleby-in-Westmorland CA16 6DB
t (017683) 51236
e dufton@yha.org.uk

### DUKINFIELD
Greater Manchester

**Barton Villa Guest House**
★★★ *Guest House*
Crescent Road, Dukinfield, Stockport SK16 4EY
t (0161) 330 3952
e harrott4@aol.com
w bartonvilla.co.uk

### DUNGWORTH
South Yorkshire

**Rickett Field Guest Accommodation** ★★★★
*Guest Accommodation*
Dungworth, Sidling Hollow, Sheffield S6 6HA
t (0114) 285 1218
e sshepherd@sky.com
w rickettfieldfarm.co.uk

**The Royal** ★★★★ *Inn*
Main Road, Dungworth, Bradfield, Sheffield S6 6HF
t (0114) 285 1213
e joanne@royalhotel-dungworth.co.uk
w royalhotel-dungworth.co.uk

### DUNSOP BRIDGE
Lancashire

**Root Farm House** ★★★★
*Bed & Breakfast*
Dunsop Bridge, Clitheroe BB7 3BB
t (01200) 448214
w roothouse.co.uk

**Wood End Farm** ★★★★
*Farmhouse*
Dunsop Bridge, Clitheroe BB7 3BE
t (01200) 448223

### DUNSWELL
East Riding of Yorkshire

**The Ship's Quarters** ★★★
*Inn*
Beverley High Road, Dunswell, Hull HU6 0AJ
t (01482) 859160
w theshipsquarters.co.uk

### DURHAM

**60 Albert Street** ★★★★
*Bed & Breakfast*
**SILVER AWARD**
Western Hill, Durham DH1 4RJ
t (0191) 386 0608
e laura@sixtyalbertstreet.co.uk
w sixtyalbertstreet.co.uk

**66 Claypath** ★★
*Bed & Breakfast*
Durham DH1 1QT
t (0191) 384 3193
e richard@66claypath.co.uk
w 66claypath.co.uk

**The Avenue Inn** ★★ *Inn*
Avenue Street, High Shincliffe DH1 2PT
t (0191) 386 5954
e info@theavenue.biz
w theavenue.biz

**The Bridge** ★★★ *Inn*
40 North Road, Durham DH1 4SE
t (0191) 386 8090
e thebridgehotel@fsmail.net
w bridgehoteldurham.co.uk

**Broom Farm Guest House**
★★★★ *Guest House*
Front Street, Broompark DH7 7QX
t (0191) 386 4755
e liz.welsh@tiscali.co.uk
w broomfarmguesthouse.co.uk

**Burnhope Lodge Guest House** ★★★ *Guest House*
1 Wrights Way, Burnhope DH7 0DL
t (01207) 529596

**Castle View Guest House**
★★★★
*Guest Accommodation*
4 Crossgate, Durham DH1 4PS
t (0191) 386 8852
e castle_view@hotmail.com
w castle-view.co.uk

**Cathedral View Town House**
★★★★
*Guest Accommodation*
**SILVER AWARD**
212 Gilesgate, Durham DH1 1QN
t (0191) 386 9566
e cathedralview@hotmail.com
w cathedralview.com

**College of St. Hild & St. Bede** ★★
*Guest Accommodation*
St Hild's Lane, Durham DH1 1SZ
t (0191) 334 8568
e p.c.oates@durham.ac.uk
w dur.ac.uk

**Collingwood College** ★★★
*Guest Accommodation*
South Road, Durham DH1 3LT
t (0191) 334 5000
e cwd.reception@durham.ac.uk
w dur.ac.uk

**The Court Inn** ★★★ *Inn*
Court Lane, Durham DH1 3AW
t (0191) 384 7350
w courtinn.co.uk

**Cuthberts Rest** ★★★
*Bed & Breakfast*
42 Oswald Court, Durham DH1 3DJ
t (0191) 384 0405

**Durham Castle**
Rating Applied For
*Campus*
Palace Green, Durham
DH1 3RW
**t** (0191) 334 4106
**e** castle.reception@durham.ac.uk
**w** durhamcastle.com

**Durham YHA** ★★ *Hostel*
St Chad's College, University of Durham, Durham DH1 3RH
**t** (0191) 334 3358
**e** st-chads.www@durham.ac.uk
**w** dur.ac.uk

**Farnley Tower and Gourmet Spot Restaurant** ★★★★
*Guest Accommodation*
The Avenue, Durham
DH1 4DX
**t** (0191) 375 0011
**e** enquiries@farnley-tower.co.uk
**w** farnley-tower.co.uk

**The Gables** ★★★
*Guest Accommodation*
Front Street, Haswell Plough
DH6 2EW
**t** (0191) 526 2982
**e** jmgables@aol.com
**w** the-gables-durham.co.uk

**Garden House** ★★★ *Inn*
North Road, Durham DH1 4NQ
**t** (0191) 384 3460

**Hatfield College** ★★
*Guest Accommodation*
North Bailey, Durham
DH1 3RQ
**t** (0191) 334 2633
**e** hatfield.reception@durham.ac.uk
**w** dur.ac.uk

**Hatfield College, Melville Building** ★★★★
*Guest Accommodation*
North Bailey, Durham
DH1 3RQ
**t** (0191) 334 2633
**e** hatfield.reception@durham.ac.uk
**w** dur.ac.uk

**Hillrise Guest House** ★★★
*Guest Accommodation*
13 Durham Road West, Bowburn, Durham DH6 5AU
**t** (0191) 377 0302
**e** enquiries@hill-rise.com
**w** hill-rise.com

**Moorcroft Bed and Breakfast** ★★★
*Bed & Breakfast*
Moor End, Belmont DH1 1BJ
**t** (0191) 386 7677
**e** moorcroft.dur@hotmail.co.uk

**St Aidan's College** ★★★
*Guest Accommodation*
Durham University, Windmill Hill DH1 3LJ
**t** (0191) 334 5769
**e** aidans.reception@durham.ac.uk
**w** dur.ac.uk

**St Chad's College** ★★
*Guest Accommodation*
18 North Bailey, Durham
DH1 3RH
**t** (0191) 334 3358
**e** St-Chads.www@durham.ac.uk
**w** dur.ac.uk/StChads

**St Johns College** ★★
*Guest Accommodation*
3 South Bailey, Durham
DH1 3RJ
**t** (0191) 334 3877
**e** s.l.hobson@durham.ac.uk
**w** durham.ac.uk/st-johns.college

**Seven Stars Inn** ★★★ *Inn*
High Street North, Shincliffe
DH1 2NU
**t** (0191) 384 8454
**e** reservations@sevenstarsinn.co.uk
**w** sevenstarsinn.co.uk

**Triermayne** ★★★★
*Bed & Breakfast*
Nevilles Cross Bank, Durham
DH1 4JP
**t** (0191) 384 6036
**e** annjamesdh1@yahoo.co.uk

**Van Mildert College** ★★★
*Guest Accommodation*
Mill Hill Lane, Durham
DH1 3LH
**t** (0191) 334 7100
**e** van-mildert.college@durham.ac.uk
**w** dur.ac.uk

**Victoria Inn** ★★★ *Inn*
86 Hallgarth Street, Durham
DH1 3AS
**t** (0191) 386 5269
**w** victoriainn-durhamcity.co.uk

**The Victorian Town House** ★★★★
*Guest Accommodation*
**SILVER AWARD**
2 Victoria Terrace, Durham
DH1 4RW
**t** 05601 459168
**e** thevictoriantownhouse-durham@yahoo.co.uk
**w** durhambedandbreakfast.co.uk

### EARBY
Lancashire

**Earby Youth Hostel** ★★★
*Hostel*
9-11 Birch Hall Lane, Barnoldswick BB18 6JX
**t** (01282) 842349
**e** earby@yha.org.uk
**w** yha.org.uk

### EASINGTON
Tees Valley

**Boulby Grange** ★★★★
*Bed & Breakfast*
Easington, Saltburn-by-the-Sea
TS13 4UW
**t** (01287) 640769
**e** jonjg526@hotmail.com
**w** boulbygrange.co.uk

**The Grapes Inn** ★★★ *Inn*
Easington, Saltburn-by-the-Sea
TS13 4TP
**t** (01287) 640461
**e** thegrapesinn@supanet.com

**Townend Farm B & B**
★★★★ *Bed & Breakfast*
**SILVER AWARD**
Whitby Road, Easington
TS13 4NE
**t** (01287) 640444
**e** info@townendfarm.co.uk
**w** townendfarm.co.uk

### EASINGWOLD
North Yorkshire

**Thornton Lodge Farm**
★★★★ *Farmhouse*
Thornton Hill, Easingwold
YO61 3QA
**t** (01347) 821306
**e** enquiries@thorntonlodgefarm.co.uk
**w** thorntonlodgefarm.co.uk

### EASTGATE-IN-WEARDALE
Durham

**Rose Hill Farm** ★★★★
*Farmhouse* **SILVER AWARD**
Rose Hill, Eastgate DL13 2LB
**t** (01388) 517209
**e** info@rosehillfarmbb.co.uk
**w** rosehillfarmbb.co.uk

### EBBERSTON
North Yorkshire

**Studley House Farm** ★★★★
*Bed & Breakfast*
**SILVER AWARD**
67 Main Street, Ebberston, Pickering YO13 9NR
**t** (01723) 859285
**e** brenda@yorkshireancestors.com
**w** studleyhousefarm.co.uk

### EDENTHORPE
South Yorkshire

**Beverley Inn** ★★★ *Inn*
117 Thorne Road, Edenthorpe, Doncaster DN3 2JE
**t** (01302) 882724
**e** beverleyinn@hotmail.co.uk
**w** beverleyinnandhotel.co.uk

### EDMUNDBYERS
Durham

**Edmundbyers YHA** ★★★
*Hostel*
Edmundbyers, Consett
DH8 9NL
**t** (01207) 255651
**e** edmundbyers@yha.org.uk
**w** yha.org.uk

**Punchbowl Inn** ★★★ *Inn*
Edmundbyers, Consett
DH8 9NL
**t** (01207) 255555

### EGREMONT
Cumbria

**Horse and Groom Court**
*Bunkhouse*
Market Place, Egremont
CA22 2AE
**t** (01946) 758198
**e** info@horseandgroomcourt.co.uk
**w** horseandgroomcourt.co.uk

### EGTON BRIDGE
North Yorkshire

**Broom House** ★★★★
*Guest House* **SILVER AWARD**
Egton Bridge, Whitby
YO21 1XD
**t** (01947) 895279
**e** mw@broom-house.co.uk
**w** egton-bridge.co.uk

### ELLINGHAM
Northumberland

**The Pack Horse Inn** ★★★
*Inn*
Ellingham, Chathill NE67 5HA
**t** (01665) 589292
**e** graham_c_simpson@hotmail.co.uk
**w** packhorseinn-ellingham.co.uk

### ELLINGSTRING
North Yorkshire

**Hollybreen, Masham** ★★★
*Guest Accommodation*
Ellingstring, Masham HG4 4PW
**t** (01677) 460216
**e** dales.accommodation@virgin.net
**w** dalesaccommodation.org.uk

### ELTERWATER
Cumbria

**Elterwater Park Country Guest House** ★★★★
*Guest House*
Skelwith Bridge, Ambleside
LA22 9NP
**t** (015394) 32227
**e** enquiries@elterwater.com
**w** elterwater.com

**Elterwater YHA** ★★★ *Hostel*
Elterwater, Ambleside
LA22 9HX
**t** 0870 770 5816
**w** yha.org.uk

### EMBLETON
Northumberland

**Blue Bell Inn** ★★★ *Inn*
W T Stead Road, Embleton
NE66 3UP
**t** (01665) 576573

**Four Winds B&B** ★★★
*Bed & Breakfast*
31 Woodstead, Embleton
NE66 3XY
**t** (01665) 576668
**e** billdawnmcd@hotmail.com

**The Sportsman Inn** ★★ *Inn*
6 Sea Lane, Embleton
NE66 3XF
**t** (01665) 576588
**e** stay@sportsmanhotel.co.uk
**w** sportsmanhotel.co.uk

### EMBSAY
North Yorkshire

**Bondcroft Farm** ★★★★
*Farmhouse*
Skipton BD23 6SF
**t** (01756) 793371
**e** bondcroftfarm@bondcroftfarm.yorks.net
**w** bondcroft.yorks.net

## ENNERDALE
Cumbria

**Black Sail YHA** ★ *Hostel*
Ennerdale Road, Cleator Moor, Egremont CA23 3AY
t 07711 108450
e blacksail@yha.org.uk

**Ennerdale YHA** ★★★★
*Hostel*
Cat Crag, Ennerdale, Cockermouth CA23 3AX
t 0870 770 8868
e ennerdale@yha.org.uk
w yha.org.uk

**High Gillerthwaite**
*Camping Barn*
Ennerdale, Cleator CA23 3AX
t (017687) 72645

## ESHOTT
Northumberland

**Eshott Hall** ★★★★★
*Guest Accommodation*
**SILVER AWARD**
Morpeth NE65 9EN
t (01670) 787777
e thehall@eshott.co.uk
w eshott.com

## FACEBY
North Yorkshire

**Four Wynds Bed and Breakfast** ★★★
*Bed & Breakfast*
Faceby, Wallhill, Stokesley TS9 7BZ
t (01642) 701315

## FAR SAWREY
Cumbria

**Fair Rigg at Far Sawrey**
★★★★★ *Bed & Breakfast*
**SILVER AWARD**
Far Sawrey, Hawkshead, Sawrey LA22 0LW
t (015394) 42532
e enquiries@fair-rigg.com
w fair-rigg.com

## FARNWORTH
Greater Manchester

**Fernbank Guest House**
★★★★ *Bed & Breakfast*
61 Rawson Street, Farnworth, Bolton BL4 7RJ
t (01204) 708832

## FEARBY
North Yorkshire

**The Black Swan**
Rating Applied For
*Inn*
Fearby, Masham HG4 4NF
t (01765) 689477
e info@blackswan-masham.co.uk
w blackswan-masham.co.uk

## FENCE
Lancashire

**Grains Barn Farm** ★★★★★
*Bed & Breakfast*
**SILVER AWARD**
Barrowford Road, Fence BB12 9QQ
t (01282) 601320
e stay@grainsbarnfarm.com
w grainsbarnfarm.com

## FENHAM
Tyne and Wear

**The Brighton** ★★
*Guest Accommodation*
47-49 Brighton Grove, Newcastle-upon-Tyne NE4 5NS
t (0191) 273 3600
e wendyhaldane@aol.com

## FENWICK
Northumberland

**The Manor House** ★★★★
*Bed & Breakfast*
7 The Village, Fenwick TD15 2PQ
t (01289) 381016
e katemoore@homecall.co.uk
w manorhousefenwick.co.uk

## FILEY
North Yorkshire

**Abbot's Leigh Guest House**
★★★★ *Guest House*
7 Rutland Street, Filey YO14 9JA
t (01723) 513334
e abbots.leigh@btinternet.com
w fileybedandbreakfast.com

**Athol House** ★★★★
*Guest Accommodation*
67 West Avenue, Filey YO14 9AX
t (01723) 515189
e atholhouse@tiscali.co.uk
w athol-guesthouse.co.uk

**Binton Guest House** ★★★★
*Guest House*
25 West Avenue, Filey YO14 9AX
t (01723) 513753
e jag25@tiscali.co.uk

**Cherries** ★★★★
*Guest House*
59 West Avenue, Filey YO14 9AX
t (01723) 513299
e cherriesfiley@talktalk.net
w cherriesfiley.co.uk

**The Edwardian Guest House**
★★★★
*Guest Accommodation*
2 Brooklands, Filey YO14 9BA
t (01723) 514557
e johnwinn.ok@talk21.com

**The Forge Guest House**
★★★★
*Guest Accommodation*
23 Rutland Street, Filey YO14 9JA
t (01723) 512379
e theforge2@btinternet.com
w theforgefiley.com

**The Gables Guest House**
★★★★ *Guest House*
2a Rutland Street, Filey YO14 9JB
t (01723) 514750
e thegablesfiley@aol.com
w thegablesfiley.co.uk

**Sea Brink** ★★★
*Guest Accommodation*
3 The Beach, Filey YO14 9LA
t (01723) 513257
e anntindall@aol.com
w seabrinkhotel.co.uk

**The Seafield** ★★★★
*Guest Accommodation*
9 Rutland Street, Filey YO14 9JA
t (01723) 513715
e seafield1@btconnect.com
w seafieldguesthouse.co.uk

## FIR TREE
Durham

**Greenhead Country House** ★★★★
*Guest Accommodation*
Green Head, Fir Tree DL15 8BL
t (01388) 763143
e info@thegreenheadhotel.co.uk
w thegreenheadhotel.co.uk

## FLAXBY
North Yorkshire

**Herons Keep B&B** ★★
*Bed & Breakfast*
Shortsill Lane, Flaxby, Knaresborough HG5 0RT
t (01423) 860353
e buck_kath@yahoo.co.uk

## FORD
Northumberland

**Hay Farm House** ★★★★
*Guest Accommodation*
**SILVER AWARD**
Ford and Etal Estate, Cornhill-on-Tweed TD12 4TR
t (01890) 820647
e tinahayfarm@tiscali.co.uk
w hayfarm.co.uk

## FOREST-IN-TEESDALE
Durham

**Langdon Beck YHA** ★★★★
*Hostel*
Forest-in-Teesdale, Barnard Castle DL12 0XN
t (01833) 622228
e langdonbeck@yha.org.uk
w yha.org.uk

## FORTON
Lancashire

**New Holly** ★★★★ *Inn*
A6 Lancaster Road, Forton PR3 0BL
t (01524) 793500
e stay@newholly.co.uk
w newholly.co.uk

## FOULRIDGE
Lancashire

**Hare & Hounds Foulridge**
★★★ *Inn*
Skipton Old Road, Foulridge, Colne BB8 7PD
t (01282) 864235
e cherylcrabtree@btconnect.com
w hare&houndsfoulridge.co.uk

## FROSTERLEY
Durham

**Newlands Hall** ★★★★
*Farmhouse*
Frosterley DL13 2SH
t (01388) 529233
e carol@newlandshall.co.uk
w newlandshall.co.uk

## FRYUP
North Yorkshire

**Crossley Side Farm** ★★★★
*Farmhouse*
Fryup, Whitby YO21 2NR
t (01287) 660313
e fryupruth@aol.com
w crossley-side-farm.co.uk

**Furnace Farm** ★★★★
*Farmhouse*
Fryup, Whitby YO21 2AP
t (01947) 897271
e furnacefarm@hotmail.com

## FULFORD
North Yorkshire

**Pinfold Cottage B&B** ★★★★
*Guest House*
145-147 Main Street, Fulford, York YO10 4PR
t (01904) 634683
e pinfoldcottage@aol.com
w pinfoldcottageyork.co.uk

## FYLINGTHORPE
North Yorkshire

**Boggle Hole YHA** ★★★
*Hostel*
Mill Beck, Fylingthorpe, Whitby YO22 4UQ
t 0870 770 5704
e bogglehole@yha.org.uk
w yha.org.uk

**Croft Farm** ★★★★
*Farmhouse*
Fylingthorpe, Whitby YO22 4PW
t (01947) 880231
e croftfarmbb@aol.com
w croft-farm.com

## GARFORTH
West Yorkshire

**Myrtle House** ★★★
*Guest House*
31 Wakefield Road, Garforth, Leeds LS25 1AN
t (0113) 286 6445

## GARSTANG
Lancashire

**Ashdene** ★★★
*Guest Accommodation*
Parkside Lane, Nateby, Garstang PR3 0JA
t (01995) 602676
e ashdene@supanet.com
w ashdenebedandbreakfast.gbr.cc

**Guys Thatched Hamlet**
★★★★
*Guest Accommodation*
Canalside, St Michael's Road, Bilsborrow, Preston PR3 0RS
t (01995) 640010
e info@guysthatchedhamlet.com
w guysthatchedhamlet.com

## GARSTON
Merseyside

**Aplin House** ★
*Guest Accommodation*
35 Clarendon Road, Garston L19 6PJ
t (0151) 427 5047


Look out for establishments participating in the National Accessible Scheme

## GATESHEAD
Tyne and Wear

**Alexandra Guest House**
★★★ *Guest House*
377 Alexandra Road, Gateshead NE8 4HY
**t** (0191) 478 1105

**The Bewick** ★★★
*Guest House*
145 Prince Consort Road, Gateshead NE8 4DS
**t** (0191) 477 1809
**e** welcome@bewick-hotel.com
**w** bewick-hotel.com

**Park Farm**
Rating Applied For
*Guest Accommodation*
Banesley Lane, Ravensworth, Tyne & Wear NE11 0HS
**t** (0191) 482 4870
**e** parkfarmhotel@hotmail.co.uk
**w** park-farm-hotel.co.uk

**The Riding Farm House**
★★★★ *Farmhouse*
**SILVER AWARD**
Riding Lane, Beamish NE11 0JA
**t** (0191) 370 1868
**e** stay@ridingfarmbedandbreakfast.co.uk
**w** ridingfarmbedandbreakfast.co.uk

**Shaftesbury Guest House**
★★★ *Guest House*
245 Prince Consort Road, Gateshead NE8 4DT
**t** (0191) 478 2544
**e** shaftesbury.hotel@hotmail.com

## GIGGLESWICK
North Yorkshire

**The Black Horse** ★★★★ *Inn*
Church Street, Giggleswick, Settle BD24 0BE
**t** (01729) 822506

**The Harts Head Inn ★★★★**
***Inn***
**Belle Hill, Giggleswick, Settle BD24 0BA**
**t (01729) 822086**
**e info@hartsheadinn.co.uk**
**w hartsheadinn.co.uk**

**Tipperthwaite Barn** ★★★★
*Bed & Breakfast*
Giggleswick, Settle BD24 0DZ
**t** (01729) 823146
**e** stay@tipperthwaitebarn.co.uk
**w** tipperthwaitebarn.co.uk

## GILDERSOME
West Yorkshire

**End Lea** ★★★★ *Guest House*
39 Town Street, Gildersome, Leeds LS27 7AX
**t** (0113) 252 1661
**e** pat_mcbride@talktalk.net

## GILLAMOOR
North Yorkshire

**Manor Farm** ★★★
*Farmhouse*
Main Street, Gillamoor, Kirkbymoorside YO62 7HX
**t** (01751) 432695
**e** gibson.manorfarm@btopenworld.com
**w** manorfarmgillamoor.co.uk

**Royal Oak Inn** ★★★★ *Inn*
Main Street, Gillamoor, Kirkbymoorside YO62 7HX
**t** (01751) 431414
**e** mcgill473@btinternet.com

## GILSLAND
Cumbria

**Birdoswald YHA** ★★★★
*Hostel*
Birdoswald Roman Fort, Brampton CA8 7DD
**t** 0870 770 8868

**Brookside Villa** ★★★★
*Bed & Breakfast*
Gilsland, Brampton CA8 7DA
**t** (01697) 747300
**e** brooksidevilla@hotmail.co.uk
**w** brooksidevilla.com

**Bush Nook Guest House**
★★★★ *Guest House*
**SILVER AWARD**
Upper Denton, Gilsland, Brampton CA8 7AF
**t** (01697) 747194
**e** info@bushnook.co.uk
**w** bushnook.co.uk

**Gilsland Spa ★★★★**
***Guest Accommodation***
**Gilsland, Brampton CA8 7AR**
**t (01697) 747203**
**w gilslandspa.co.uk**

**Hadrian's Wall Residential Study Centre** ★★★★
*Group Hostel*
Birdoswald Roman Fort, Gilsland, Brampton CA8 7DD
**t** (01697) 747602
**e** birdoswald.romanfort@english-heritage.org.uk
**w** english-heritage.org.uk

**The Hill on the Wall**
★★★★★
*Guest Accommodation*
**SILVER AWARD**
Gilsland, Brampton CA8 7DA
**t** (01697) 747214
**e** info@hadrians-wallbedandbreakfast.com
**w** hadrians-wallbedandbreakfast.com

**Slack House Farm** ★★★★
*Farmhouse*
Gilsland, Brampton CA8 7DB
**t** (01697) 747351
**e** slackhousefarm@lineone.net
**w** slackhousefarm.co.uk

**Willowford Farm B&B**
★★★★ *Farmhouse*
Willowford, Gilsland, Brampton CA8 7AA
**t** (01697) 747962
**e** stay@willowford.co.uk
**w** willowford.co.uk

## GISBURN
Lancashire

**Foxhill Barn** ★★★★
*Bed & Breakfast*
Great Todber Farm, Howgill Lane, Gisburn BB7 4JL
**t** (01200) 415906
**e** peter@foxhillbarn.co.uk
**w** foxhillbarn.co.uk

## GLAISDALE
North Yorkshire

**Beggar's Bridge Bed & Breakfast** ★★★★
*Bed & Breakfast*
Station House, Glaisdale, Whitby YO21 2QL
**t** (01947) 897409
**e** info@beggarsbridge.co.uk
**w** beggarsbridge.co.uk

**Egton Banks Farm** ★★★★
*Farmhouse*
Glaisdale, Whitby YO21 2QP
**t** (01947) 897289
**e** egtonbanksfarm@agriplus.net
**w** egtonbanksfarm.agriplus.net

## GLENRIDDING
Cumbria

**Helvellyn YHA** ★★ *Hostel*
Greenside, Glenridding, Ullswater CA11 0QR
**t** (017684) 82269
**e** helvellyn@yha.org.uk
**w** yha.org.uk

**Swirral Barn** *Camping Barn*
Greenside Mine, Penrith CA11 0PL
**t** (017687) 79242

## GOATHLAND
North Yorkshire

**The Beacon Guest House**
Rating Applied For
*Guest Accommodation*
Goathland, Whitby YO22 5AN
**t** (01947) 896409
**e** stewartkatz@hotmail.com
**w** touristnetuk.com/ne/beacon.

**Fairhaven Country Guest House ★★★★** ***Guest House***
**The Common, Goathland, Whitby YO22 5AN**
**t (01947) 896361**
**e enquiries@fairhavencountryguesthouse.co.uk**
**w fairhavencountryguesthouse.co.uk**

**Heatherdene** ★★★★
*Guest House* **SILVER AWARD**
Goathland, Whitby YO22 5AN
**t** (01947) 896334
**e** tony.sanchez@diageo.com
**w** heatherdenehotel.co.uk

## GOLDSBOROUGH
North Yorkshire

**Bay Horse Inn** ★★★★ *Inn*
Main Street, Goldsborough, Harrogate HG5 8NW
**t** (01423) 862212
**e** bayhorseinn@btinternet.com
**w** edirectory.co.uk/bayhorseinn/

## GOODSHAW
Lancashire

**The Old White Horse**
★★★★
*Guest Accommodation*
**SILVER AWARD**
211 Goodshaw Lane, Goodshaw BB4 8DD
**t** (01706) 215474
**e** johnandmaggie54@hotmail.com
**w** theoldwhitehorse.co.uk

## GOOLE
East Riding of Yorkshire

**The Briarcroft Hotel** ★★★
*Guest Accommodation*
49-51 Clifton Gardens, Goole DN14 6AR
**t** (01405) 763024
**e** briarcrofthotel@aol.com
**w** briarcrofthotel.co.uk

## GOOSNARGH
Lancashire

**White Moss Gate** ★★★★
*Bed & Breakfast*
Bed & Breakfast, Horns Lane, Preston PR3 2NE
**t** (01772) 782262
**e** frandewhurst@fsmail.net

## GRANGE-OVER-SANDS
Cumbria

**Elton Guest House** ★★★★
*Guest House*
Windermere Road, Grange-over-Sands LA11 6EQ
**t** (015395) 32838
**e** info@eltonprivatehotel.co.uk
**w** eltonprivatehotel.co.uk

**Greenacres Country Guesthouse ★★★★**
***Guest House***
**Lindale, Grange-over-Sands LA11 6LP**
**t (015395) 34578**
**e greenacres.lindale@googlemail.com**
**w greenacres-lindale.co.uk**

**The Lymehurst ★★★★**
***Guest Accommodation***
**Kents Bank Road, Grange-over-Sands LA11 7EY**
**t (015395) 33076**
**e enquiries@lymehurst.co.uk**
**w lymehurst.co.uk**

**Mayfields** ★★★★
*Bed & Breakfast*
30 Mayfield Road, Whitby YO21 1LX
**t** (01947) 603228
**e** mayfield30@btconnect.com
**w** bandbwhitby.co.uk

## GRANTLEY
North Yorkshire

**St Georges Court ★★★★**
***Farmhouse***
**Old Home Farm, Ripon HG4 3PJ**
**t (01765) 620618**
**e stgeorgescourt@bronco.co.uk**
**w stgeorges-court.co.uk**

## GRASMERE
Cumbria

**Beck Allans Guest House**
★★★★ *Guest House*
**SILVER AWARD**
College Street, Grasmere LA22 9SZ
**t** (015394) 35563
**e** mail@beckallans.com
**w** beckallans.com

**Chestnut Villa** ★★★
*Guest Accommodation*
Keswick Road, Grasmere, Ambleside LA22 9RE
**t** (015394) 35218

**Dunmail House** ★★★★★
*Bed & Breakfast*
Keswick Road, Grasmere
LA22 9RE
**t** (015394) 35256
**e** info@dunmailhouse.com
**w** dunmailhouse.com

**Grasmere Butharlyp Howe YHA** ★★★★ *Hostel*
Easdale Road, Grasmere
LA22 9QG
**t** 0870 770 5836
**e** grasmere@yha.org.uk
**w** yha.org.uk

**Grasmere Independent Hostel** ★★★★ *Hostel*
Broadrayne Farm, Ambleside
LA22 9RU
**t** (015394) 35055

**Heron Beck Guest House** ★★★★
*Guest Accommodation*
**GOLD AWARD**
Grasmere LA22 9RB
**t** (015394) 35272
**e** info@heronbeck.com
**w** heronbeck.com

**How Foot Lodge** ★★★
*Guest House*
Town End, Grasmere
LA22 9SQ
**t** (015394) 35366
**e** enquiries@howfoot.co.uk
**w** howfoot.co.uk

**Lake View Country House** ★★★★ *Guest House*
**GOLD AWARD**
Lake View Drive, Grasmere
LA22 9TD
**t** (015394) 35384
**e** info@lakeview-grasmere.com
**w** lakeview-grasmere.com

**Riversdale** ★★★★
*Guest House* **GOLD AWARD**
White Bridge, Grasmere
LA22 9RH
**t** (015394) 35619
**e** info@riversdalegrasmere.co.uk
**w** riversdalegrasmere.co.uk

**The Travellers Rest Inn** ★★★ *Inn*
Grasmere LA22 9RR
**t** 05006 00725
**e** stay@lakedistrictinns.co.uk
**w** lakedistrictinns.co.uk

**YHA Grasmere (Thorney How)** ★ *Hostel*
Easedale Road, Ambleside
LA22 9QG
**t** (015394) 35316

## GRASSINGTON
North Yorkshire

**Craiglands Guest House** ★★★★ *Bed & Breakfast*
Brooklyn, Threshfield, Skipton
BD23 5ER
**t** (01756) 752093
**e** craiglands@talk21.com
**w** craiglandsguesthouse.co.uk

**Foresters Arms** ★★★ *Inn*
20 Main Street, Grassington, Skipton BD23 5AA
**t** (01756) 752349
**e** theforesters@totalise.co.uk

**Grassington Lodge** ★★★★★
*Guest Accommodation*
**GOLD AWARD**
8 Wood Lane, Grassington, Skipton BD23 5LU
**t** (01756) 752518
**e** relax@grassingtonlodge.co.uk
**w** grassingtonlodge.co.uk

**Grove House** ★★★★
*Bed & Breakfast*
1 Moor Lane, Grassington, Skipton BD23 5BD
**t** (01756) 753364
**e** fraser.turner@btinternet.com
**w** grovehousegrassington.co.uk

**New Laithe House** ★★★★
*Guest Accommodation*
Wood Lane, Grassington, Skipton BD23 5LU
**t** (01756) 752764
**e** enquiries@newlaithehouse.co.uk
**w** newlaithehouse.co.uk

**Raines Close Guest House** ★★★★ *Guest House*
13 Station Road, Grassington
BD23 5LS
**t** (01756) 752678
**e** raines.close@btinternet.com
**w** rainesclose.co.uk

**Scar Croft** ★★★
*Bed & Breakfast*
Chapel Street, Grassington
BD23 5BE
**t** (01756) 752455
**e** dianemackridge@gmail.com
**w** scarcroft.net

**Springroyd House** ★★★
*Guest Accommodation*
8a Station Road, Grassington, Skipton BD23 5NQ
**t** (01756) 752473
**e** springroydhouse@hotmail.com
**w** springroydhouse.co.uk

**Station House** ★★★
*Bed & Breakfast*
Station Road, Threshfield, Grassington BD23 5ES
**t** (01756) 752667
**e** info@stationhousegrassington.co.uk
**w** yorkshirenet.co.uk/stayat/stationhouse

**Yew Tree House** ★★★★
*Bed & Breakfast*
**GOLD AWARD**
Scar Street, Grassington, Skipton BD23 5AS
**t** (01756) 753075
**e** julie@badgergate.com
**w** yewtreehouse.org

## GREAT AYTON
North Yorkshire

**Bridge Guest House** ★★
*Guest House*
Bridge Street, Great Ayton, Stokesley TS9 6NP
**t** (01642) 725236
**e** john@walton2505.freeserve.co.uk
**w** greataytonaccommodation.co.uk

**The Kings Head at Newton under Roseberry** ★★★★
*Guest Accommodation*
**SILVER AWARD**
The Green, Newton under Roseberry, Middlesbrough
TS9 6QR
**t** (01642) 722318
**e** info@kingsheadhotel.co.uk
**w** kingsheadhotel.co.uk

**Royal Oak** ★★★ *Inn*
123high Street, Great Ayton, Stokesley TS9 6BW
**t** (01642) 722361
**e** info@royaloak-hotel.co.uk
**w** royaloak-hotel.co.uk

**Susie D's B & B** ★★★
*Guest Accommodation*
Crossways, 116 Newton Road, Stokesley TS9 6DL
**t** (01642) 724351
**e** info@susieds.com
**w** susieds.com

**Travellers Rest** ★★★★
*Bed & Breakfast*
97 High Street, Great Ayton
TS9 6NF
**t** (01642) 724523
**w** travellersrest.info

## GREAT ECCLESTON
Lancashire

**The Cartford Inn** ★★★★ *Inn*
Cartford Lane, Little Eccleston, Nr Great Eccleston PR3 0YP
**t** (01995) 670166
**e** info@thecartfordinn.co.uk
**w** thecartfordinn.co.uk

## GREENHEAD
Northumberland

**Four Wynds** ★★★
*Bed & Breakfast*
Longbyre, Greenhead
CA8 7HN
**t** (01697) 747972
**e** info@four-wynds-guest-house.co.uk
**w** four-wynds-guest-house.co.uk

**Holmhead Camping Barn**
*Camping Barn*
Thirlwall Castle Farm, Brampton CA8 7HY
**t** (01697) 747402
**e** holidays@holmhead.com
**w** holmhead.com

**Holmhead Guest House** ★★★★ *Guest House*
Holmhead, Hadrian's Wall
CA8 7HY
**t** (01697) 747402
**e** holidays@holmhead.com
**w** holmhead.com

**YHA Greenhead** ★ *Hostel*
Station Road, Brampton
CA8 7HG
**t** (01697) 747401
**e** greenhead@yha.org.uk
**w** yha.org.uk

## GRINTON
North Yorkshire

**The Bridge Inn** ★★★ *Inn*
Grinton, Reeth DL11 6HH
**t** (01748) 884224
**e** atkinbridge@btinternet.com
**w** bridgeinngrinton.co.uk

**Grinton Lodge YHA** ★★★★
*Hostel*
Richmond DL11 6HS
**t** (01748) 884206
**e** grinton@yha.org.uk
**w** yha.org.uk

## GUILDEN SUTTON
Cheshire

**Roseville** ★★★★★
*Bed & Breakfast*
**SILVER AWARD**
Belle Vue Lane, Chester
CH3 7EJ
**t** (01244) 300602
**e** traceyandjerry@tiscali.co.uk

## GUISBOROUGH
Tees Valley

**The Fox and Hounds** ★★★
*Inn*
Slapewath, Guisborough
TS14 6PX
**t** (01287) 632964
**e** info@thefoxandhound.co.uk
**w** thefoxandhound.co.uk

**Fox Inn** ★★★ *Inn*
Bow Street, Guisborough
TS14 6BP
**t** (01287) 632958
**e** val.baines@btconnect.com

**Three Fiddles** ★★ *Inn*
34 Westgate, Guisborough
TS14 6BA
**t** (01287) 632417
**e** jill@hendersoncampbell.co.uk

## GUISELEY
West Yorkshire

**Lyndhurst** ★★★
*Bed & Breakfast*
Oxford Road, Guiseley, Leeds
LS20 9AB
**t** (01943) 879985
**w** guisley.co.uk/lyndhurst

## HACKFORTH
North Yorkshire

**Ainderby Myers Farm** ★★★
*Farmhouse*
Bedale DL8 1PF
**t** (01609) 748668

## HALEBARNS
Greater Manchester

**Oaklands Farm** ★★★
*Bed & Breakfast*
Shay Lane, Hale Barns
WA15 8SN
**t** (0161) 980 4111

### HALIFAX West Yorkshire

**Field House** ★★★★
*Guest Accommodation*
Staups Lane, Stump Cross, Halifax HX3 6XW
t (01422) 355457
e stayatfieldhouse@yahoo.co.uk
w fieldhouse-bb.co.uk

**Rose Cottage** ★★★★★
*Guest Accommodation*
**SILVER AWARD**
Shibden Fold, Halifax HX3 6XP
t (01422) 365437
e reservations@shibden-fold.co.uk
w shibden-fold.co.uk

**Travis Guest House** ★★★
*Guest Accommodation*
8 West Parade, Halifax HX1 2TA
t (01422) 365727

### HALLBANKGATE Cumbria

**Belted Will Inn** ★★★ *Inn*
Hallbankgate, Brampton CA8 2NJ
t (01697) 746236
e stephenbeltedwill@yahoo.co.uk
w beltedwill.co.uk

### HALTWHISTLE Northumberland

**Ashcroft Guest House**
★★★★ *Guest House*
**GOLD AWARD**
Lanty's Lonnen, Ashcroft NE49 0DA
t (01434) 320213
e info@ashcroftguesthouse.co.uk
w ashcroftguesthouse.co.uk

**Burnhead Bed and Breakfast**
★★★★ *Bed & Breakfast*
Cawfields NE49 9PJ
t (01434) 320841
e enquiries@burnheadbedandbreakfast.co.uk
w burnheadbedandbreakfast.co.uk

**Chare Close Bed & Breakfast**
★★★★ *Bed & Breakfast*
Chare Close, Castle Hill NE49 0EE
t (01434) 322789
e chareclose@btinternet.com
w chareclose.com

**The Grey Bull** ★★★★
*Guest Accommodation*
Main Street, Haltwhistle NE49 0DL
t (01434) 321991
e reception@greybullhotel.co.uk
w greybullhotel.co.uk

**Hall Meadows** ★★★★
*Bed & Breakfast*
Main Street, Haltwhistle NE49 0AZ
t (01434) 321021
e richardhumes@tiscali.co.uk
w hallmeadows.co.uk

**Melkridge Farm Bed & Breakfast**
Rating Applied For
*Bed & Breakfast*
Melkridge Farm, Melkridge NE49 0LT
t (01434) 322933
e melkridgefarm@yahoo.co.uk
w melkridgefarm.com

**The Mount** ★★★
*Bed & Breakfast*
Comb Hill NE49 9NS
t (01434) 321075
e the-mount@talk21.com
w themountbb.co.uk

**Oakey Knowe Farm** ★★★
*Farmhouse*
Oakey Knowe, Haltwhistle NE49 0NB
t (01434) 320648
e garlinegoldens@aol.com

**Saughy Rigg Farm** ★★★★
*Guest House*
Twice Brewed, Haltwhistle NE49 9PT
t (01434) 344120
e info@saughyrigg.co.uk
w saughyrigg.co.uk

**Wydon Farm Bed and Breakfast** ★★★★ *Farmhouse*
Wydon Farm, Haltwhistle NE49 0LG
t (01434) 321702
e stay@wydon-haltwhistle.co.uk
w wydon-haltwhistle.co.uk

### HAMSTERLEY Durham

**Dale End** ★★★★
*Bed & Breakfast*
**SILVER AWARD**
Hamsterley DL13 3PT
t (01388) 488091
e info@dale-endhamsterleybandb.co.uk
w dale-endhamsterleybandb.co.uk

**Hamsterley B&B** ★★★★
*Bed & Breakfast*
**SILVER AWARD**
Fern Lea, Hamsterley DL13 3PT
t (01388) 488056 & 07710 908735

**Hamsterley Forest B and B**
★★★★ *Bed & Breakfast*
Redford, Hamsterley Forest DL13 3NL
t (01388) 488420
e jst_ayhope@yahoo.co.uk
w hamsterleyforestbandb.com

### HARBOTTLE Northumberland

**Bonny Barn** *Camping Barn*
Harbottle NE65 7DG
t (01669) 650476
e rosemary@bonnybarn.co.uk
w bonnybarn.co.uk

**The Byre Vegetarian B&B**
★★★★ *Bed & Breakfast*
**SILVER AWARD**
Harbottle NE65 7DG
t (01669) 650476
e rosemary@the-byre.co.uk
w the-byre.co.uk

**Parsonside Bed & Breakfast**
★★★★ *Bed & Breakfast*
Newton Farm, Harbottle, Morpeth NE65 7DP
t (01669) 650275
e carolyn.graham@harbottle.net

### HARRAS MOOR Cumbria

**The Georgian House** ★★★★
*Guest Accommodation*
9-11 Church Street, Whitehaven CA28 7AY
t (01946) 696611
e stephanie@thegeorgianhousehotel.net
w thegeorgianhousehotel.net

### HARROGATE North Yorkshire

**17 Peckfield Close** ★★★
*Guest Accommodation*
Hampsthwaite, Pateley Bridge HG3 2ES
t (01423) 770765

**18 Park Parade** ★★★★★
*Bed & Breakfast*
**SILVER AWARD**
Harrogate HG1 5AF
t (01423) 563800
e why@globalnet.co.uk
w parkparade.co.uk

**Acacia** ★★★★
*Bed & Breakfast*
**GOLD AWARD**
3 Springfield Avenue, Harrogate HG1 2HR
t (01423) 560752
e dee@acaciaharrogate.co.uk
w acaciaharrogate.co.uk

**Acomb Lodge** ★★★
*Guest House*
6 Franklin Road, Harrogate HG1 5EE
t (01423) 563599

**Acorn Lodge** ★★★★
*Guest Accommodation*
1 Studley Road, Harrogate HG1 5JU
t (01423) 525630
e info@acornlodgehotel.com
w acornlodgehotel.com

**Alamah Guest House**
★★★★ *Guest House*
88 Kings Road, Harrogate HG1 5JX
t (01423) 502187 & (01423) 502187
e alamahguesthouse@btconnect.com

**Alderside Guest House**
★★★ *Bed & Breakfast*
11 Belmont Road, Harrogate HG2 0LR
t (01423) 529400

**Alvera Court** ★★★★
*Guest Accommodation*
76 Kings Road, Harrogate HG1 5JX
t (01423) 505735
e reception@alvera.co.uk
w alvera.co.uk

**Applewood House** ★★★★
*Guest Accommodation*
**GOLD AWARD**
55 St Georges Road, Harrogate HG2 9BP
t (01423) 544549
e applewood@teamknight.com
w applewoodhouse.co.uk

**Arden House** ★★★★
*Guest Accommodation*
69-71 Franklin Road, Harrogate HG1 5EH
t (01423) 509224
e enquiries@ardenhousehotel.co.uk
w ardenhousehotel.co.uk

**Argyll House** ★
*Guest Accommodation*
80 Kings Road, Harrogate HG1 5JX
t (01423) 567166
e argyll.harrogate@btopenworld.com

**Ash Grove Guesthouse**
★★★★ *Guest House*
72 Kings Road, Harrogate HG1 5JR
t (01423) 569970
e admin@ash-grove.co.uk
w ash-grove.co.uk

**Ashbrooke House** ★★★★
*Guest Accommodation*
140 Valley Drive, Harrogate HG2 0JS
t (01423) 564478
e ashbrooke@harrogate.com
w harrogate.com/ashbrooke

**Ashley House** ★★★★
*Guest House*
36-40 Franklin Road, Harrogate HG1 5EE
t (01423) 507474
e keith@ashleyhousehotel.com
w ashleyhousehotel.com

**Askern Guest House** ★★★
*Guest House*
3 Dragon Parade, Harrogate HG1 5BZ
t (01423) 523057
e info@askernhouse.co.uk
w askernhouse.co.uk

**Aston** ★★
*Guest Accommodation*
7-9 Franklin Mount, Harrogate HG1 5EJ
t (01423) 564262
e astonhotel@btinternet.com

**Azalea Court Guest House**
★★★ *Guest Accommodation*
56-58 Kings Road, Harrogate HG1 5JR
t (01423) 560424

**Barkers Guest House** ★★★
*Guest Accommodation*
204 Kings Road, Harrogate HG1 5JG
t (01423) 568494
e eebarkeruk@yahoo.co.uk

**Baytree House ★★★★**
*Guest House*
98 Franklin Road, Harrogate
HG1 5EN
**t** (01423) 564493
**e** info@baytreeharrogate.co.uk

**Belmont Guest House**
★★★★ *Guest House*
86 Kings Road, Harrogate
HG1 5JX
**t** (01423) 528086
**e** belmontharrogate@btinternet.com
**w** belmont-harrogate.co.uk

**The Bijou ★★★★★**
*Guest Accommodation*
**SILVER AWARD**
17 Ripon Road, Harrogate
HG1 2JL
**t** (01423) 567974
**e** info@thebijou.co.uk
**w** thebijou.co.uk

**Bowes Green Farm ★★★★**
*Farmhouse* **SILVER AWARD**
Colber Lane, Bishop Thornton, Harrogate HG3 3JX
**t** (01423) 770114

**Brookfield House ★★★★**
*Guest House* **SILVER AWARD**
5 Alexandra Road, Harrogate
HG1 5JS
**t** (01423) 506646
**e** office@brookfieldhousehotel.co.uk
**w** brookfieldhousehotel.co.uk

**Brooklands ★★★★**
*Guest House*
5 Valley Drive, Harrogate
HG2 0JJ
**t** (01423) 564609
**e** brooklandsbb@supanet.com

**Central House Farm ★★★★**
*Farmhouse* **SILVER AWARD**
Haverah Park, Beckwithshaw, Pateley Bridge HG3 1SQ
**t** (01423) 566050
**e** jayne@centralhousefarm.freeserve.co.uk
**w** centralhousefarm.co.uk

**Cold Cotes ★★★★★**
*Guest Accommodation*
**GOLD AWARD**
Cold Cotes Road, Felliscliffe, Harrogate HG3 2LW
**t** (01423) 770937
**e** info@coldcotes.com
**w** coldcotes.com

**Conference View Guest House ★★★**
*Guest Accommodation*
74 Kings Road, Harrogate
HG1 5JR
**t** (01423) 563075
**e** admin@conferenceview.co.uk
**w** conferenceview.co.uk

**Coppice Guest House**
★★★★ *Guest House*
9 Studley Road, Harrogate
HG1 5JU
**t** (01423) 569626
**e** coppice@harrogate.com
**w** harrogate.com/coppice

**Dragon House ★★★★**
*Guest House*
6 Dragon Parade, Harrogate
HG1 5DA
**t** (01423) 569888
**e** marie@dragonhousehotel.com
**w** dragonhousehotel.com

**Franklin View ★★★★**
*Guest Accommodation*
**SILVER AWARD**
19 Grove Road, Harrogate
HG1 5EW
**t** (01423) 541388
**e** jennifer@franklinview.com
**w** franklinview.com

**Garden House ★★★★**
*Guest Accommodation*
14 Harlow Moor Drive, Harrogate HG2 0JX
**t** (01423) 503059
**e** gardenhouse@harrogate.com
**w** harrogate.com/gardenhouse

**Geminian Guest House**
★★★★ *Guest House*
11-13 Franklin Road, Harrogate
HG1 5ED
**t** (01423) 523347
**e** info@geminian.org.uk
**w** geminian.org.uk

**Glenayr ★★★**
*Guest Accommodation*
19 Franklin Mount, Harrogate
HG1 5EJ
**t** (01423) 504259
**e** liz-glenayr@boltblue.com
**w** glenayr.co.uk

**Hollins House ★★★**
*Guest House*
17 Hollins Road, Harrogate
HG1 2JF
**t** (01423) 503646
**e** hollinshouse@tiscali.co.uk
**w** hollinshouse.co.uk

**Kingsway ★★★**
*Guest Accommodation*
36 Kings Road, Harrogate
HG1 5JW
**t** (01423) 562179
**e** tanya@kingswayhotel.com
**w** kingswayhotel.com

**Knabbs Ash ★★★★**
*Farmhouse* **GOLD AWARD**
Skipton Road, Kettlesing, Felliscliffe, Harrogate HG3 2LT
**t** (01423) 771040
**e** sheila@knabbsash.co.uk
**w** knabbsash.co.uk

**Lamont House ★★★★**
*Guest Accommodation*
12 St Lamont House Marys Walk, Harrogate HG2 0LW
**t** (01423) 567143
**e** lamonthouse@btinternet.com

**Lavender House ★★★★**
*Guest Accommodation*
**SILVER AWARD**
94 Franklin Road, Harrogate
HG1 5EN
**t** (01423) 549949 & 07732 422478
**e** lavenderhouse@ntlworld.com
**w** lavenderhouseharrogate.co.uk

**Murray House ★★★★**
*Guest Accommodation*
67 Franklin Road, Harrogate
HG1 5EH
**t** (01423) 505857
**e** enquiries@murray-house.com
**w** murray-house.co.uk

**Ye Olde Coach House**
★★★★
*Guest Accommodation*
2 Strawberry Dale Terrace, Harrogate HG1 5EQ
**t** (01423) 500302
**e** yeoldecoachhouse@btinternet.com

**Scotia Guest House ★★**
*Guest House*
66 Kings Road, Harrogate
HG1 5JR
**t** (01423) 504361
**e** enquiries@scotiahotel.co.uk
**w** scotiahotel.co.uk

**Sherwood ★★★★**
*Guest Accommodation*
7 Studley Road, Harrogate
HG1 5JU
**t** (01423) 503033
**e** sherwood@harrogate.com
**w** sherwood-hotel.com

**Spring Lodge ★★★**
*Guest House*
22 Spring Mount, Harrogate
HG1 2HX
**t** (01423) 506036
**e** dv22harrogate@aol.com
**w** spring-lodge.co.uk

**The Welford ★★★**
*Guest House*
27 Franklin Road, Harrogate
HG1 5ED
**t** (01423) 566041
**e** judith.mudd@btopenworld.com
**w** the-welford.co.uk

## HARTLEPOOL
### Tees Valley

**Brafferton Guest House ★★**
*Guest House*
159/161 Stockton Road, Hartlepool TS25 1SL
**t** (01429) 273875
**e** sales@braffertonguesthouse.co.uk
**w** braffertonguesthouse.co.uk

**Chimneys**
Rating Applied For
*Guest Accommodation*
East Street, Blackhall TS27 4HA
**t** (0191) 587 0401
**e** info@chimneyshotel.com
**w** chimneyshotel.com

**The Douglas ★★★**
*Guest House*
2 Grange Road, Hartlepool
TS26 8JA
**t** (01429) 272038
**e** info@douglas-hotel.co.uk
**w** douglas-hotel.co.uk

**The Oakroyd ★★★**
*Guest Accommodation*
133 Park Road, Hartlepool
TS26 9HT
**t** (01429) 864361
**e** mandyoakroydhotel@hotmail.com

**Ocean View Guest House**
★★★ *Guest House*
2 The Cliff, Seaton Carew
TS25 1AB
**t** (01429) 271983
**e** 2thecliff@tiscali.co.uk
**w** oceanviewguesthouse.co.uk

**The York House ★★★★**
*Guest Accommodation*
185 York Road, Hartlepool
TS26 9EE
**t** 0845 500 5566
**e** info@theyorkhotel.co.uk
**w** theyorkhotel.co.uk

## HARTOFT
### North Yorkshire

**Robin's Nest ★★★★**
*Bed & Breakfast*
**SILVER AWARD**
Duks Ley Farm, Hartoft, Pickering YO18 8RR
**t** (01751) 417651
**e** pennyleask@btinternet.com

## HARTWITH
### North Yorkshire

**Brimham Lodge ★★★**
*Farmhouse*
Brimham Rocks Road, Hartwith, Pateley Bridge
HG3 3HE
**t** (01423) 771770
**e** neil.clarke@virgin.net
**w** brimhamlodge.co.uk

## HARWOOD DALE
### North Yorkshire

**The Grainary ★★★★**
*Farmhouse*
Harwood Dale, Scarborough
YO13 0DT
**t** (01723) 870026
**e** grainary@btopenworld.com
**w** grainary.co.uk

**Thirley Banks Cottage**
★★★★ *Farmhouse*
Harwood Dale, Scarborough
YO13 0DR
**t** (01723) 871404
**e** info@thirleybanks.co.uk
**w** thirleybanks.co.uk

## HAWES
### North Yorkshire

**Cocketts 1688 ★★★★**
*Guest Accommodation*
Market Place, Hawes DL8 3RD
**t** (01969) 667312
**e** enquiries@cocketts.co.uk
**w** cocketts.co.uk

**East House ★★★★**
*Guest Accommodation*
Gayle, Leyburn DL8 3RZ
**t** (01969) 667405
**e** lornaward@lineone.net
**w** easthouse-hawes.com

**Ebor House ★★★★**
*Guest Accommodation*
Burtersett Road, Hawes
DL8 3NT
**t** (01969) 667337
**e** eborhousehawes@yahoo.co.uk
**w** eborhouse.co.uk

**FairView House** ★★★★
*Guest House*
Burtersett Road, Hawes
DL8 3NP
t (01969) 667348
e info@fairview-hawes.co.uk
w fairview-hawes.co.uk

**Hawes YHA** ★★★ *Hostel*
Lancaster Terrace, Hawes
DL8 3LQ
t (01969) 667368
e hawes@yha.org.uk
w yha.org.uk

**Herriots** ★★★★
*Guest Accommodation*
Main Street, Hawes DL8 3QW
t (01969) 667536
e info@herriotsinhawes.co.uk
w herriotsinhawes.co.uk

**Laburnum House** ★★★
*Guest House*
The Holme, Hawes DL8 3QR
t (01969) 667717
e info@stayatlaburnumhouse.co.uk
w stayatlaburnumhouse.co.uk

**The Old Dairy Farm**
★★★★★
*Guest Accommodation*
**SILVER AWARD**
Widdale, Hawes DL8 3LX
t (01969) 667070
w olddairyfarm.co.uk

**Rookhurst Country House**
★★★★★ *Guest House*
**GOLD AWARD**
West End, Gayle, Hawes
DL8 3RT
t (01969) 667454
e enquiries@rookhurst.co.uk
w rookhurst.co.uk

**South View** ★★★
*Bed & Breakfast*
Gayle Lane, Hawes DL8 3RW
t (01969) 667447
e carol@bell3630.freeserve.co.uk

**Springbank House** ★★★
*Guest Accommodation*
Spring Bank, Hawes DL8 3NW
t (01969) 667376

**Thorney Mire Barn B&B**
★★★★★
*Guest Accommodation*
**GOLD AWARD**
Appersett, Hawes DL8 3LU
t (01969) 666122
e stay@thorneymirebarn.co.uk
w thorneymirebarn.co.uk

**Thorney Mire House** ★★★★
*Bed & Breakfast*
Appersett, Hawes DL8 3LU
t (01969) 667159
e sylvia.turner2@virgin.net
w thorneymire.yorks.net

**White Hart Inn** ★★★ *Inn*
Main Street, Hawes DL8 3QL
t (01969) 667259
e sasencas@aol.com
w whiteharthawes.co.uk

## HAWKSHAW
Greater Manchester

**Loe Lodge** ★★★★★
*Guest Accommodation*
Redisher Lane, Hawkshaw,
Bury BL8 4HX
t (01204) 888860
e loelodge@btinternet.com
w loelodge.co.uk

## HAWKSHEAD
Cumbria

**Crosslands Farm** ★★★★
*Farmhouse*
Rusland, Hawkshead LA22 8JU
t (01229) 860242
e enquiries@crosslandsfarm.co.uk
w crosslandsfarm.co.uk

**The Drunken Duck Inn**
★★★★★ *Inn*
**GOLD AWARD**
Barngates, Ambleside
LA22 0NG
t (015394) 36347

**Hawkshead YHA** ★★★
*Hostel*
Esthwaite Lodge, Ambleside
LA22 0QD
t (015394) 36293

**Ivy House & Restaurant**
★★★ *Guest House*
Main Street, Hawkshead
LA22 0NS
t (015394) 36204
e ivyhousehotel@btinternet.com
w ivyhousehotel.com

**Walker Ground Manor**
★★★★ *Bed & Breakfast*
**SILVER AWARD**
Vicarage Lane, Hawkshead
LA22 0PD
t (015394) 36219
e info@walkerground.co.uk
w walkerground.co.uk

**Yewfield Vegetarian Guest House** ★★★★★
*Guest Accommodation*
**SILVER AWARD**
Hawkshead Hill, Hawkshead,
Ambleside LA22 0PR
t (015394) 36765
e derek.yewfield@btinternet.com
w yewfield.co.uk

## HAWKSHEAD HILL
Cumbria

**Summer Hill Country House**
★★★★
*Guest Accommodation*
**GOLD AWARD**
Hawkshead Hill, Ambleside
LA22 0PP
t (015394) 36180
e info@summerhillcountryhouse.com
w summerhillcountryhouse.com

## HAWKSWICK
North Yorkshire

**Warren House B & B** ★★★★
*Bed & Breakfast*
Warren House, Skipton
BD23 5PU
t (01756) 770375
e info@warren-house.net
w warren-house.net

## HAWNBY
North Yorkshire

**Easterside Farm** ★★★★
*Farmhouse*
Hawnby, Helmsley YO62 5QT
t (01439) 798277
e info@eastersidefarm.co.uk
w eastersidefarm.co.uk

## HAWORTH
West Yorkshire

**Aitches Guest House**
★★★★ *Guest House*
11 West Lane, Haworth
BD22 8DU
t (01535) 642501
e aitches@talk21.com
w aitches.co.uk

**The Apothecary Guest House** ★★ *Guest House*
86 Main Street, Haworth,
Keighley BD22 8DP
t (01535) 643642
e Nicholasapt@aol.com
w theapothecaryguesthouse.co.uk

**Ashmount Guest House**
★★★★★ *Guest House*
**SILVER AWARD**
Mytholmes Lane, Haworth
BD22 8EZ
t (01535) 645726
e info@ashmounthaworth.co.uk
w ashmounthaworth.co.uk

**Bridge House B&B** ★★★
*Bed & Breakfast*
Bridge House, Bridgehouse
Lane, Haworth BD22 8PA
t (01535) 642372
e claire@bridgehouselane.co.uk
w bridgehouselane.co.uk

**The Bronte** ★★★
*Guest Accommodation*
Lees Lane, Haworth, Keighley
BD22 8RA
t (01535) 644112
e bookings@bronte-hotel.co.uk
w bronte-hotel.co.uk

**Haworth Tea Rooms and Guest House** ★★★
*Guest House*
68 Main Street, Haworth
BD22 8DP
t (01535) 644278
w haworthtearooms.co.uk

**Haworth YHA** ★★★ *Hostel*
Longlands Drive, Lees Lane,
Haworth BD22 8RT
t (01535) 642234
e haworth@yha.org.uk
w yha.org.uk

**Heathfield Bed & Breakfast**
★★★★
*Guest Accommodation*
1 Bronte Street, Haworth
BD22 8EE
t (01535) 640606
e ray.trudy@heathfield-haworth.co.uk
w heathfield-haworth.co.uk

**The Manor Guest House**
★★★★★ *Guest House*
**SILVER AWARD**
Sutton Drive, Cullingworth,
Bradford BD13 5BQ
t (01535) 274374
e michelecotter@btinternet.com
w cullingworthmanor.co.uk

**The Old Registry** ★★★★
*Guest Accommodation*
**SILVER AWARD**
2-4 Main Street, Haworth
BD22 8DA
t (01535) 646503
e enquiries@theoldregistryhaworth.co.uk
w theoldregistryhaworth.co.uk

**Park Top House** ★★★★
*Guest Accommodation*
1 Rawdon Road, Haworth
BD22 8DX
t (01535) 646102
e vannessa@parktophouse.co.uk
w parktophouse.co.uk

**Rosebud Cottage** ★★★★
*Guest Accommodation*
1 Belle Isle Road, Haworth
BD22 8QQ
t (01535) 640321
e info@rosebudcottage.co.uk
w rosebudcottage.co.uk

**Woodlands Grange** ★★★
*Guest House*
Belle Isle, Haworth BD22 8PB
t (01535) 646814
e woodlandsgrange@hotmail.com
w woodlandsgrange.com

## HAYDON BRIDGE
Northumberland

**Grindon Cartshed** ★★★★
*Bed & Breakfast*
Haydon Bridge, Hexham
NE47 6NQ
t (01434) 684273
e cartshed@grindon.force9.co.uk
w grindon-cartshed.co.uk

**Hadrian Lodge** ★★★
*Guest Accommodation*
Hindshield Moss, North Road,
Haydon Bridge NE47 6NF
t (01434) 684867
e hadrian-lodge@btconnect.com
w hadrianlodge.co.uk

**Old Repeater Station** ★★★
*Hostel*
Military Road, Grindon
NE47 6NQ
t (01434) 688668
e les.gibson@tiscali.co.uk
w hadrians-wall-bedandbreakfast.co.uk

**The Reading Rooms** ★★★★
*Bed & Breakfast*
2 Church Street, Haydon
Bridge NE47 6JQ
t (01434) 688802
e thereadingrooms@aol.com
w thereadingroomshaydonbridge.co.uk

**Shaftoe's ★★★★**
*Guest House*
4 Shaftoe Street, Haydon Bridge NE47 6BJ
**t** (01434) 684664
**e** bookings@shaftoes.co.uk
**w** shaftoes.co.uk

## HAZEL GROVE
### Greater Manchester

**Bramdene ★★**
*Bed & Breakfast*
1 Delamere Close, Hazel Grove, Stockport SK7 4NP
**t** (0161) 483 4066

## HEADINGLEY
### West Yorkshire

**Oak Villa ★★★**
*Guest Accommodation*
55-57 Cardigan Road, Leeds LS6 1DW
**t** (0113) 275 8439
**e** oakvillahotel@msn.com
**w** oakvillahotel.co.uk

## HEADS NOOK
### Cumbria

**Croft House ★★★★**
*Farmhouse* **SILVER AWARD**
Newbiggin, Brampton, Carlisle CA8 9DH
**t** (01768) 896695
**e** info@crofthousecumbria.co.uk
**w** crofthousecumbria.co.uk

## HEALAUGH
### North Yorkshire

**Riddings Farm ★★★★**
*Farmhouse*
Reeth DL11 6UR
**t** (01748) 884267

## HEBDEN
### North Yorkshire

**Court Croft ★★★**
*Bed & Breakfast*
Church Lane, Hebden, Skipton BD23 5DX
**t** (01756) 753406

## HEBDEN BRIDGE
### West Yorkshire

**b@r Place ★★★★**
*Guest Accommodation*
10 Crown Street, Hebden Bridge HX7 8EH
**t** (01422) 842814
**e** intouch@barplace.co.uk
**w** barplace.co.uk

**Holme House ★★★★★**
*Bed & Breakfast*
**GOLD AWARD**
New Road, Hebden Bridge HX7 8AD
**t** (01422) 847588
**e** mail@holmehousehebdenbridge.co.uk
**w** holmehousehebdenbridge.co.uk

**Mount Skip Bed & Breakfast**
**★★★★** *Bed & Breakfast*
1 Mount Road, Wadsworth, Hebden Bridge HX7 8PH
**t** (01422) 842903
**e** mountskipbandb@hotmail.com

## HEDDON-ON-THE-WALL
### Northumberland

**Heddon Lodge ★★★★**
*Bed & Breakfast*
**SILVER AWARD**
38 Heddon Banks, Heddon-on-the-Wall NE15 0BU
**t** (01661) 854042

**Houghton North Farm**
**★★★★** *Hostel*
Heddon-on-the-Wall NE15 0EZ
**t** (01661) 854364 & 07708 419911
**e** wjlaws@btconnect.com
**w** houghtonnorthfarm.co.uk

## HELLIFIELD
### North Yorkshire

**Chapel Farm B&B ★★★★**
*Bed & Breakfast*
**SILVER AWARD**
Gisburn Road, Hellifield, Settle BD23 4LA
**t** (01729) 851158
**e** info@chapelfarmbandb.com
**w** chapelfarmbandb.com

## HELMSLEY
### North Yorkshire

**Carlton Lodge ★★★★**
*Guest House* **SILVER AWARD**
Bondgate, Helmsley YO62 5EY
**t** (01439) 770557
**e** admin@carlton-lodge.com
**w** carlton-lodge.com

**The Crown Inn ★★★★** *Inn*
21 Market Place, Helmsley YO62 5BJ
**t** (01439) 770297
**e** info@tchh.co.uk
**w** tchh.co.uk

**The Feathers ★★★** *Inn*
Market Place, Helmsley YO62 5BH
**t** (01439) 770275
**e** reservations@feathershotelhelmsley.co.uk
**w** feathershotelhelmsley.co.uk

**Griff Farm Bed & Breakfast**
**★★★★** *Farmhouse*
Griff Farm, York, Helmsley YO62 5EN
**t** (01439) 771600
**e** j.fairburn@farmline.com

**Helmsley YHA ★★★** *Hostel*
Carlton Lane, Helmsley YO62 5HB
**t** (01439) 770433
**e** helmsley@yha.org.uk
**w** yha.org.uk

**The Inn at Hawnby ★★★★**
*Inn*
Hill Top, Hawnby, Helmsley YO62 5QS
**t** (01439) 798202
**e** info@innathawnby.co.uk
**w** innathawnby.co.uk

**Laskill Grange ★★★★**
*Farmhouse*
Near Hawnby, Helmsley YO62 5NB
**t** (01439) 798268
**e** laskillgrange@tiscali.co.uk
**w** laskillgrange.co.uk

**No 54 ★★★★★** *Guest House*
54 Bondgate, Helmsley YO62 5EZ
**t** (01439) 771533
**e** lizzie@no54.co.uk
**w** no54.co.uk

**Oldstead Grange ★★★★★**
*Guest Accommodation*
**GOLD AWARD**
Oldstead, Coxwold, Helmsley YO61 4BJ
**t** (01347) 868634
**e** anne@yorkshireuk.com
**w** yorkshireuk.com

**Redroofs ★★★★**
*Bed & Breakfast*
3 Carlton Road, Helmsley YO62 5HD
**t** (01439) 770175
**e** babenm@globalnet.co.uk
**w** redroofs-helmsley.co.uk

**Stilworth House ★★★★**
*Bed & Breakfast*
**SILVER AWARD**
1 Church Street, Helmsley YO62 5AD
**t** (01439) 771072
**e** carol@stilworth.co.uk
**w** stilworth.co.uk

**West View Cottage ★★★★**
*Bed & Breakfast*
**GOLD AWARD**
Pockley, Helmsley YO62 7TE
**t** (01439) 770526
**e** westviewcottage@tiscali.co.uk
**w** westviewcottage.info

## HEPTONSTALL
### West Yorkshire

**Poppyfields House ★★★**
*Bed & Breakfast*
29 Slack Top, Heptonstall, Hebden Bridge HX7 7HA
**t** (01422) 843636
**e** poppyfieldshouse29@yahoo.co.uk

## HESKET NEWMARKET
### Cumbria

**Denton House ★★★★**
*Guest House*
Hesket Newmarket, Wigton, Caldbeck CA7 8JG
**t** (01697) 478415
**e** dentonhnm@aol.com
**w** dentonhouseguesthouse.co.uk

**Hudscales Camping Barn**
*Camping Barn*
Hudscales Farm, Hesket Newmarket, Caldbeck CA7 8JZ
**t** (017687) 72645
**e** info@lakelandcampingbarns.co.uk
**w** lakelandcampingbarns.co.uk

## HESKIN
### Lancashire

**Farmers Arms ★★★** *Inn*
85 Wood Lane, Heskin PR7 5NP
**t** (01257) 451276
**e** info@farmersarms.co.uk
**w** farmersarms.co.uk

## HESLEDEN
### Durham

**The Ship Inn ★★★★** *Inn*
**SILVER AWARD**
Main Street, High Hesleden TS27 4QD
**t** (01429) 836453
**e** sheila@theshipinn.net
**w** theshipinn.net

## HESSLE
### East Riding of Yorkshire

**Redcliffe House Luxury B&B**
**★★★★** *Guest House*
Redcliff Road, Hessle, Hull HU13 0HA
**t** (01482) 648655
**e** sally.skiba@hotmail.com
**w** redcliffehouse.co.uk

## HETTON
### North Yorkshire

**Angel Inn ★★★★★**
*Restaurant with Rooms*
Hetton, Skipton BD23 6LT
**t** (01756) 730263
**e** info@angelhetton.co.uk
**w** angelhetton.co.uk

## HEXHAM
### Northumberland

**Anick Grange Farmhouse B&B ★★★★** *Farmhouse*
Anick Grange, Hexham NE46 4LP
**t** (01434) 603807
**e** julie@anickgrange.fsnet.co.uk
**w** anickgrange.com

**Dukesfield Hall Farm**
**★★★★** *Bed & Breakfast*
Steel NE46 1SH
**t** (01434) 673634
**e** catherineswallow@btinternet.com
**w** dukesfieldhall.co.uk

**Fairshaw Rigg ★★★★**
*Bed & Breakfast*
**SILVER AWARD**
Lowgate NE46 2NW
**t** (01434) 602630
**e** kathryn.shrimpton@btinternet.com
**w** fairshawrigg.co.uk

**Hallbank Guest House**
**★★★★★** *Guest House*
Hallbank House, Hallgate NE46 1XA
**t** (01434) 605567
**e** hallbank@freenetname.co.uk
**w** hallbankguesthouse.com

**HallBarns B&B ★★★★**
*Farmhouse*
Simonburn, Hexham NE48 3AQ
**t** (01434) 681419 & 07788 998959
**e** enquiries@hallbarns-simonburn.co.uk
**w** hallbarns-simonburn.co.uk

**High Reins ★★★★**
*Bed & Breakfast*
Leazes Lane, Hexham NE46 3AT
**t** (01434) 603590
**e** walton45@hotmail.com
**w** highreins.co.uk

**Kitty Frisk House** ★★★★
*Bed & Breakfast*
**SILVER AWARD**
Corbridge Road, Hexham
NE46 1UN
t (01434) 601533
e alan@kittyfriskhouse.co.uk
w kittyfriskhouse.co.uk

**Loughbrow House ★★★★**
*Guest Accommodation*
Dipton Mill Road, Hexham
NE46 1RS
t (01434) 603351
e patricia@loughbrow.fsnet.co.uk
w loughbrow.fsnet.co.uk

**Oakwood Cottage** ★★★★
*Bed & Breakfast*
Oakwood NE46 4LE
t (01434) 602013
e sturner@oakwoodcottage.com
w oakwoodcottage.com

**Rye Hill Farm** ★★★★
*Farmhouse*
Slaley, Hexham NE47 0AH
t (01434) 673259
e info@ryehillfarm.co.uk
w ryehillfarm.co.uk

**Station Inn** ★★ *Inn*
Station Road, Hexham
NE46 1EZ
t (01434) 603155
e info@stationinnhexham.co.uk
w stationinnhexham.co.uk

**Woodley Field** ★★★★
*Bed & Breakfast*
Allendale Road, Hexham
NE46 2NB
t (01434) 601600
e woodleyfield@btinternet.com
w woodleyfield.co.uk

### HIGH BENTHAM
North Yorkshire

**The Coach House** ★★★★
*Inn*
16 Main Street, High Bentham, Ingleton LA2 7HE
t (01524) 262305
e info@coachhousebentham.co.uk
w coachhousebentham.co.uk

### HIGH LORTON
Cumbria

**Swinside End Farm** ★★★★
*Farmhouse* **SILVER AWARD**
Scales, High Lorton, Cockermouth CA13 9UA
t (01900) 85136
e karen@swinsideendfarm.co.uk
w swinsideendfarm.co.uk

**Terrace Farm** ★★★★
*Farmhouse*
High Lorton, Cockermouth
CA13 9TX
t (01900) 85278
w terracefarm.co.uk

### HIGH STITTENHAM
North Yorkshire

**Hall Farm** ★★★★ *Farmhouse*
High Stittenham, Sheriff Hutton, Malton YO60 7TW
t (01347) 878461
e hallfarm@btinternet.com
w hallfarm.btinternet.co.uk

### HIGHER BEBINGTON
Merseyside

**The Bebington Hotel** ★★★
*Guest Accommodation*
Bebington Hotel, 24 Town Lane, Wirral CH63 5JG
t (0151) 645 0608
e vaghena@aol.com
w thebebingtonhotel.co.uk

### HOLLYM
East Riding of Yorkshire

**Plough Inn** ★★ *Inn*
Northside Road, Hollym, Withernsea HU19 2RS
t (01964) 612049
e the.plough.inn@btconnect.com
w theploughinnhollym.co.uk

### HOLMBRIDGE
West Yorkshire

**Corn Loft House B&B** ★★★
*Guest Accommodation*
146 Woodhead Road, Holmbridge, Holmfirth
HD9 2NL
t (01484) 683147

### HOLMES CHAPEL
Cheshire

**Bridge Farm Bed & Breakfast** ★★★★ *Farmhouse*
Blackden, Holmes Chapel
CW4 8BX
t (01477) 571202
e stay@bridgefarm.com
w bridgefarm.com

**Padgate Guest House**
★★★★ *Bed & Breakfast*
**SILVER AWARD**
Twemlow Lane, Cranage
CW4 8EX
t (01477) 534291
e lyndaboagmunroe@yahoo.co.uk
w padgateguesthouse.co.uk

### HOLMFIRTH
West Yorkshire

**Ash House B&B** ★★★
*Bed & Breakfast*
240 Dunford Road, Holmfirth
HD9 2SJ
t (01484) 688244
e accommodation@swcch.co.uk
w summerwineclassics.co.uk

**Elephant and Castle** ★★★
*Guest Accommodation*
Hollowgate, Huddersfield
HD9 2DG
t (01484) 683178

**The Huntsman Inn** ★★★★
*Guest Accommodation*
Greenfield Road, Holmfirth
HD9 3XF
t (01484) 850705
e kempsterpk@aol.com
w the-huntsman-inn.com

**Sunnybank Guesthouse**
★★★★★
*Guest Accommodation*
**GOLD AWARD**
78 Upperthong Lane, Holmfirth
HD9 3BQ
t (01484) 684857
e info@sunnybankguesthouse.co.uk
w sunnybankguesthouse.co.uk

**Uppergate Farm B&B**
★★★★
*Guest Accommodation*
**SILVER AWARD**
Uppergate, Hepworth, Holmfirth HD9 1TG
t (01484) 681369
e info@uppergatefarm.co.uk
w uppergatefarm.co.uk

### HOLMPTON
East Riding of Yorkshire

**Elmtree Farm** ★★★
*Bed & Breakfast*
Holmpton, Withernsea
HU19 2QR
t (01964) 630957
e cft-mcox@supanet.com
w bandbatelmtreefarm.com

**Rysome Garth** ★★★★
*Guest Accommodation*
Holmpton, Withernsea
HU19 2QR
t (01964) 631248
e amandapannett@neoeon.com

### HOLY ISLAND
Northumberland

**The Bungalow** ★★★★
*Guest Accommodation*
Chare Ends, Holy Island
TD15 2SE
t (01289) 389308
e bungalow@lindisfarne.org.uk
w lindisfarne.org.uk/bungalow

**Cafe Beangoose B & B** ★★
*Bed & Breakfast*
Selby House, Market Square, Holy Island TD15 2RX
t (01289) 389083
e enquiries@cafebeangoose.co.uk
w cafebeangoose.co.uk

**The Lindisfarne on Holy Island** ★★★
*Guest Accommodation*
Holy Island TD15 2SQ
t (01289) 389273
e lindisfarnehotel@btconnect.com
w lindisfarne.org.uk/lindisfarne.htm

**The Ship** ★★★ *Inn*
Marygate, Holy Island
TD15 2SJ
t (01289) 389311
e the_ship_inn@btconnect.com
w theshipinn-holyisland.co.uk

### HOOLE
Cheshire

**Chester Stone Villa**
★★★★★
*Guest Accommodation*
3 Stone Place, Hoole CH2 3NR
t (01244) 345014
e enquiries@chesterstonevilla.co.uk
w stonevillahotel.co.uk

**Hamilton Court** ★★★★
*Guest Accommodation*
5/7 Hamilton Street, Hoole
CH2 3JG
t (01244) 345387
e hamiltoncourth@aol.com
w smoothhound.co.uk/hotels/hamilton

**Holly House Guest House**
★★★★ *Guest House*
1 Stone Place, Hoole CH2 3NR
t (01244) 328967
e marinacassidy@yahoo.com
w hollyhouseguesthouse.co.uk

### HORNSEA
East Riding of Yorkshire

**Earlham House Guest House**
★★★★ *Bed & Breakfast*
**SILVER AWARD**
59a Eastgate, Hornsea
HU18 1NB
t (01964) 537809
e info@earlhamhouse.com
w earlhamhouse.com

**Sandhurst Guest House**
★★★ *Guest House*
3 Victoria Avenue, Hornsea
HU18 1NH
t (01964) 534653
e rhodes@hornsea15.fsnet.co.uk
w sandhurstguesthouse.co.uk

**Wentworth House** ★★★★
*Guest House*
12 Seaside Road, Aldbrough, Hornsea HU11 4RX
t (01964) 527246
e enquiry@wentworthhousehotel.com
w wentworthhousehotel.com

### HOWICK
Northumberland

**The Old Rectory** ★★★★
*Guest Accommodation*
Howick, Craster NE66 3LE
t (01665) 577590
e stay@oldrectoryhowick.co.uk
w oldrectoryhowick.co.uk

### HUBBERHOLME
North Yorkshire

**Church Farm** ★★★★
*Farmhouse*
Hubberholme, Skipton
BD23 5JE
t (01756) 760240
e gwhuck@hubberholme.fsnet.co.uk

### HUDDERSFIELD
West Yorkshire

**Cambridge Lodge** ★★★
*Guest Accommodation*
4 Clare Hill, Huddersfield
HD1 5BS
t (01484) 519892
e cambridge.lodge.hudd@btconnect.com
w cambridgelodge.co.uk

**Castle View Guest House**
★★★★★
*Guest Accommodation*
**GOLD AWARD**
148 Ashes Lane, Castle Hill, Huddersfield HD4 6TE
t (01484) 307460
e info@castleviewyorkshire.co.uk
w castleviewyorkshire.co.uk

**Croppers Arms** ★★★★
*Guest Accommodation*
136 Westbourne Road, Huddersfield HD1 4LF
t (01484) 421522
e enquiries@greystone.co.uk
w croppersarms.co.uk

**Elm Crest** ★★★★
*Guest House* **SILVER AWARD**
2 Queens Road, Huddersfield
HD2 2AG
t (01484) 530990
e ginette@elmcrest.biz
w elmcrest.biz

**Holmcliffe Guest House**
★★★★ *Guest House*
16 Mountjoy Road, Edgerton,
Huddersfield HD1 5PZ
t (01484) 429598
e j.wilcockson1@ntlworld.com

**Huddersfield Central Lodge**
★★★★
*Guest Accommodation*
**SILVER AWARD**
11-15 Beast Market,
Huddersfield HD1 1QF
t (01484) 515551
e enquiries@centrallodge.com
w centrallodge.com

**Manor Mill Cottage** ★★★★
*Bed & Breakfast*
21 Linfit Lane, Kirkburton,
Huddersfield HD8 0TY
t (01484) 604109
e manormill@paskham.
freeserve.co.uk

**The Old Co-Op** ★★★★★
*Bed & Breakfast*
**SILVER AWARD**
96 The Village, Thurstonland,
Huddersfield HD4 6XF
t (01484) 663621
e contact@theoldco-op.com
w theoldco-op.com

**Storthes Hall Park** ★★★
*Campus*
Storthes Hall Lane,
Huddersfield HD8 0WA
t (01484) 488820
w campusdigs.com

**Woods End Bed & Breakfast**
★★★★
*Guest Accommodation*
46 Inglewood Avenue,
Huddersfield HD2 2DS
t (01484) 513580 &
07730 030993
e jmsm2306@hotmail.com
w the-woods-end.co.uk

## HULL
### East Riding of Yorkshire

**Acorn Guest House** ★★★
*Guest House*
719 Beverley Road, Hull
HU6 7JN
t (01482) 853248
e janet_the_acorn@yahoo.co.
uk
w smoothhound.co.uk/hotels/
acornhull

**The Admiral Guest House**
★★ *Bed & Breakfast*
234 The Boulevard, Hull
HU3 3ED
t (01482) 329664

**Allandra House** ★★
*Guest Accommodation*
5 Park Avenue, Princes
Avenue, Hull HU5 3EN
t (01482) 493349
e macklin2003@macklin2003.
karoo.co.uk
w allandrahotel.co.uk

**Cornerbrook Guest House**
★★★★ *Guest House*
1 Desmond Avenue, Beverley
Road, Hull HU6 7JY
t (01482) 474272
e cornerbrookhouse@
cornerbrookhouse.karoo.co.uk

**The Earlsmere Guest House**
★★★ *Guest House*
76-78 Sunny Bank, Hull
HU3 1LQ
t (01482) 341977
e su@earlsmerehotel.karoo.
co.uk
w earlsmerehotel.karoo.net

**The Endsleigh Centre**
Rating Applied For
*Campus*
481 Beverley Road, Hull
HU6 7LJ
t (01482) 342779
e endsleigh@endsleigh.karoo.
co.uk
w endsleighcentre.org.uk

**The Hornbeams** ★★★★★
*Bed & Breakfast*
**SILVER AWARD**
373 Saltshouse Road, Hull
HU8 9HS
t (01482) 718630
e info@the-hornbeams.co.uk
w the-hornbeams.co.uk

## HUMSHAUGH
### Northumberland

**Carraw Bed and Breakfast**
★★★★ *Guest House*
**SILVER AWARD**
Carraw Farm, Military Road,
Hexham NE46 4DB
t (01434) 689857
e relax@carraw.co.uk
w carraw.co.uk

**Greencarts** ★★★ *Farmhouse*
Humshaugh NE46 4BW
t (01434) 681320
e sandra@greencarts.co.uk
w greencarts.co.uk

## HURST GREEN
### Lancashire

**The Fold** ★★★★
*Bed & Breakfast*
15 Smithy Row, Hurst Green
BB7 9QA
t (01254) 826252
e derek.harwood1@virgin.net

## HUTTON-LE-HOLE
### North Yorkshire

**The Barn Hotel and Tea
Rooms** ★★★★ *Guest House*
Hutton-le-Hole, York
YO62 6UA
t (01751) 417311

**Burnley House** ★★★★
*Guest House* **SILVER AWARD**
Hutton-le-Hole,
Kirkbymoorside YO62 6UA
t (01751) 417548
e info@burnleyhouse.co.uk
w burnleyhouse.co.uk

## HUTTON SESSAY
### North Yorkshire

**Burtree Country Guest
House** ★★★★ *Guest House*
York Road, Hutton Sessay,
Thirsk YO7 3AY
t (01845) 501333
e info@burtreecountryhouse.
co.uk
w burtreecountryhouse.co.uk

## HUXLEY
### Cheshire

**Higher Huxley Hall**
★★★★★
*Guest Accommodation*
**SILVER AWARD**
Red Lane, Huxley CH3 9BZ
t (01829) 781484
e enquiries@huxleyhall.co.uk
w huxleyhall.co.uk

## ILKLEY
### West Yorkshire

**The Coach House** ★★★★
*Bed & Breakfast*
28 Parish Ghyll Road, Ilkley
LS29 9NE
t (01943) 605091
e amelia@28parishghyllrd.co.
uk
w 28parishghyllrd.co.uk

**Ilkley Riverside** ★★★
*Guest Accommodation*
Riverside Gardens, Bridge
Lane, Ilkley LS29 9EU
t (01943) 607338
e enquiries@ilkley-
riversidehotel.com
w ilkley-riversidehotel.com

**Moorland View Bed and
Breakfast**
Rating Applied For
*Bed & Breakfast*
Moorland View, 4 Manor Rise,
Ilkley LS29 8QL
t (01943) 816 483
e bandb@moorlandviewilkley.
co.uk
w moorlandviewilkley.co.uk

**One Tivoli Place** ★★★★
*Guest Accommodation*
1 Tivoli Place, Ilkley LS29 8SU
t (01943) 600328
e enquiries@tivoliplace.co.uk
w tivoliplace.co.uk

**Roberts Family Bed and
Breakfast** ★★
*Bed & Breakfast*
63 Skipton Road, Ilkley
LS29 9HF
t (01943) 817542
e ilkleybb@blueyonder.co.uk

## INGLETON
### North Yorkshire

**The Dales Guest House**
★★★ *Guest House*
Main Street, Ingleton LA6 3HH
t (01524) 241401
e dalesgh@hotmail.com

**Gatehouse Farm** ★★★★
*Farmhouse*
Westhouse, Ingleton LA6 3NR
t (01524) 241458
e gatehousefarm@ktdinternet.
com

**Ingleborough View Guest
House** ★★★★ *Guest House*
Main Street, Ingleton LA6 3HH
t (01524) 241523
e stay@ingleboroughview.
com
w ingleboroughview.com

**Inglenook Guest House**
★★★★
*Guest Accommodation*
20 Main Street, Ingleton
LA6 3HJ
t (01524) 241270
e inglenook20@hotmail.com
w inglenookguesthouse.com

**Ingleton YHA** ★★★★ *Hostel*
Greta Tower, Sammy Lane,
Ingleton LA6 3EG
t (01524) 241444
w yha.org.uk

**New Butts Farm** ★★★
*Guest House*
High Bentham, Ingleton
LA2 7AN
t (01524) 241238

**The Pines Country House**
★★★★ *Guest House*
New Road, Ingleton LA6 3HN
t (01524) 241252
e pinesingleton@aol.com
w pinesingleton.com

**Riverside Lodge** ★★★★
*Guest House*
24 Main Street, Ingleton
LA6 3HJ
t (01524) 241359
e info@riversideingleton.co.uk
w riversideingleton.co.uk

**Springfield Country Guest
House** ★★★★
*Guest Accommodation*
26 Main Street, Ingleton,
Carnforth LA6 3HJ
t (015242) 41280
w destination-england.co.uk/
springfield.html

**Thorngarth Country Guest
House** ★★★★ *Guest House*
New Road, Ingleton LA6 3HN
t (01524) 241295
e davidegregory@
btopenworld.com
w thorngarth.co.uk

**Wheatsheaf Inn** ★★★★ *Inn*
22 High Street, Ingleton
LA6 3AD
t (01524) 241275
e info@wheatsheaf-ingleton.
co.uk

## INGRAM
### Northumberland

**Reaveley Farmhouse B&B**
★★★★ *Bed & Breakfast*
Ingram Valley NE66 4LS
t (01665) 578268 &
07766 834504
e reaveleyfarm@aol.com
w reaveleyfarmhouse.co.uk

## INGS
Cumbria

**The Hill** ★★★★
*Guest Accommodation*
**SILVER AWARD**
Ings, Windermere LA8 9QQ
t (01539) 822217
e thehill@ktdinternet.com
w thehillonline.co.uk

**Meadowcroft Country Guest House**
Rating Applied For
*Guest House*
Ings, Windermere LA8 9PY
t (01539) 821171
e info@meadowcroft-guesthouse.com
w meadowcroft-guesthouse.com

## INSKIP
Lancashire

**Chesham Hill B&B** ★★★
*Farmhouse*
Pinfold Lane, Inskip, Preston PR4 0UA
t (01995) 679424
w cheshamhillfarm.co.uk

## IRESHOPEBURN
Durham

**Slack House Farm** ★★★
*Farmhouse*
Ireshopeburn DL13 1HL
t (01388) 537292
w fleecewithaltitude.co.uk

## IRTHINGTON
Cumbria

**Newtown Farm** ★★★
*Farmhouse*
Newtown, Irthington, Carlisle CA6 4NX
t (01697) 72768
e susangrice@tiscali.co.uk
w newtownfarmbedandbreakfast.co.uk

## JARROW
Tyne and Wear

**Bede's Well Guest House**
★★★ *Guest House*
146 Bede Burn Road, Jarrow NE32 5AU
t (0191) 428 4794
e paulkelly.bedeswell@virgin.net
w bedeswellguesthouse.co.uk

## JESMOND
Tyne and Wear

**The Adelphi** ★★★
*Guest House*
63 Fern Avenue, Newcastle-upon-Tyne NE2 2QU
t (0191) 281 3109
e maxinecalvert@blueyonder.co.uk
w adelphihotelnewcastle.co.uk

## KELLAH
Northumberland

**Kellah Farm B & B** ★★★★
*Farmhouse* **SILVER AWARD**
Kellah NE49 0JL
t (01434) 320816
e teasdale@ukonline.co.uk
w kellah.co.uk

## KENDAL
Cumbria

**Beech House** ★★★★★
*Guest House* **SILVER AWARD**
40 Greenside, Kendal LA9 4LD
t (01539) 720385
e stay@beechhouse-kendal.co.uk
w beechhouse-kendal.co.uk

**Burrow Hall** ★★★★
*Bed & Breakfast*
Plantation Bridge, Kendal LA8 9JR
t (01539) 821711
e burrow.hall@virgin.net
w burrowhall.co.uk

**The Glen** ★★★★
*Guest House*
Oxenholme, Kendal LA9 7RF
t (01539) 726386 & 07743 604599
e greenintheglen@btinternet.com
w glen-kendal.co.uk

**Hillside Bed & Breakfast**
★★★★
*Guest Accommodation*
4 Beast Banks, Kendal LA9 4JW
t (01539) 722836
e info@hillside-kendal.co.uk
w hillside-kendal.co.uk

**Kendal Arms and Hotel** ★★
*Inn*
72 Milnthorpe Road, Kendal LA9 5HG
t (01539) 720956

**Lyndhurst Guest House**
★★★ *Guest Accommodation*
8 South Road, Kendal LA9 5QH
t (01539) 723819
e stay@lyndhurst-kendal.co.uk
w lyndhurst-kendal.co.uk

**Riversleigh Guest House**
★★★ *Guest House*
49 Milnthorpe Road, Kendal LA9 5QG
t (01539) 726392

**Sonata Guest House** ★★★★
*Guest Accommodation*
19 Burneside Road, Kendal LA9 4RL
t (01539) 732290
e chris@sonataguesthouse.freeserve.co.uk
w sonataguesthouse.co.uk

**Sundial House** ★★★
*Guest Accommodation*
51 Milnthorpe Road, Kendal LA9 5QG
t (01539) 724468
e suemcleod2000@yahoo.co.uk
w sundialguesthousekendal.co.uk

**YHA Kendal** ★★★ *Hostel*
118 Highgate, Kendal LA9 4HE
t 0870 770 5892
e kendal@yha.org.uk
w yha.org.uk

## KERMINCHAM
Cheshire

**The Fields Farm** ★★★★
*Farmhouse*
Forty Acre Lane, Crewe CW4 8DY
t (01477) 571224
w theenglishdiningroom.co.uk

## KESWICK
Cumbria

**Abacourt House** ★★★★
*Guest Accommodation*
**SILVER AWARD**
26 Stanger Street, Keswick CA12 5JU
t (017687) 72967
e abacourt@btinternet.com
w abacourt.co.uk

**Acorn House** ★★★★
*Guest House* **SILVER AWARD**
Ambleside Road, Keswick CA12 4DL
t (017687) 72553
e info@acornhousehotel.co.uk
w acornhousehotel.co.uk

**Allerdale House** ★★★★
*Guest House* **SILVER AWARD**
1 Eskin Street, Keswick CA12 4DH
t (017687) 73891
e allerdalehouse@btinternet.com
w allerdale-house.co.uk

**Amble House Guest House**
★★★★ *Guest House*
**SILVER AWARD**
23 Eskin Street, Keswick CA12 4DQ
t (017687) 73288
e info@amblehouse.co.uk
w amblehouse.co.uk

**The Anchorage**
Rating Applied For
*Guest House*
14 Ambleside Road, Keswick CA12 4DL
t (017687) 72813
e anchorage.keswick@btopenworld.com
w anchorage-keswick.co.uk

**Appletrees** ★★★★
*Guest House*
The Heads, Keswick CA12 5ER
t (017687) 80400
e john@armstrong2001.fsnet.co.uk
w appletreeskeswick.com

**Avondale Guest House**
★★★★
*Guest Accommodation*
20 Southey Street, Keswick CA12 4EF
t (017687) 72735
e enquiries@avondaleguesthouse.com
w avondaleguesthouse.com

**Badgers Wood** ★★★★
*Guest House* **SILVER AWARD**
30 Stanger Street, Keswick CA12 5JU
t (017687) 72621
e ctb@badgers-wood.co.uk
w badgers-wood.co.uk

**Beckside** ★★★ *Guest House*
5 Wordsworth Street, Keswick CA12 4HU
t (017687) 73093
e info@beckside-keswick.co.uk
w beckside-keswick.co.uk

**Beckstones Farm Guest House** ★★★ *Guest House*
Thornthwaite, Keswick CA12 5SQ
t (017687) 78510
e enquiries@beckstonesfarm.co.uk
w beckstonesfarm.co.uk

**Berkeley Guest House**
★★★★ *Guest House*
The Heads, Keswick CA12 5ER
t (017687) 74222
e reception@berkeley-keswick.com
w berkeley-keswick.com

**Bluestones** ★★★★
*Guest House*
7 Southey Street, Keswick CA12 4EG
t (017687) 74237
e mjr@bluestonesguesthouse.co.uk
w bluestonesguesthouse.co.uk

**Braemar Guest House**
★★★★ *Guest House*
**SILVER AWARD**
21 Eskin Street, Keswick CA12 4DQ
t (017687) 73743
e enquiries@braemar-guesthouse.co.uk
w braemar-guesthouse.co.uk

**Bramblewood Cottage Guest House** ★★★★
*Guest House*
2 Greta Street, Keswick CA12 4HS
t (017687) 75918
e info@bramblewoodkeswick.com
w bramblewoodkeswick.com

**Brookfield** ★★★★
*Guest House*
Penrith Road, Keswick CA12 4LJ
t (017687) 72867
e info@brookfield-keswick.co.uk
w brookfield-keswick.co.uk

**Brundholme Guest House**
★★★★ *Guest House*
The Heads, Keswick CA12 5ER
t (017687) 73305
e barbara@brundholme.co.uk
w brundholme.co.uk

**Burleigh Mead** ★★★★
*Guest House*
The Heads, Keswick CA12 5ER
t (017687) 75935
e info@burleighmead.co.uk
w burleighmead.co.uk

**Burnside B&B** ★★★★
*Bed & Breakfast*
**SILVER AWARD**
Penrith Road, Keswick CA12 4LJ
t (017687) 72639
e stay@burnside-keswick.co.uk
w burnside-keswick.co.uk

**The Cartwheel** ★★★
*Guest House*
5 Blencathra Street, Keswick
CA12 4HW
**t** (017687) 73182
**e** info@thecartwheel.co.uk
**w** thecartwheel.co.uk

**Castlefell** ★★★
*Bed & Breakfast*
31 The Headlands, Keswick
CA12 5EQ
**t** (017687) 72849
**e** castlefell31@tiscali.co.uk
**w** castlefell.co.uk

**Charnwood Guest House**
★★★★ *Guest House*
6 Eskin Street, Keswick
CA12 4DH
**t** (017687) 74111

**Cherry Trees Guest House**
★★★★ *Guest House*
16 Eskin Street, Keswick
CA12 4DQ
**t** (017687) 71048
**e** info@cherrytrees-keswick.co.uk
**w** cherrytrees-keswick.co.uk

**Cumbria House** ★★★★
*Guest House*
1 Derwentwater Place,
Ambleside Road, Keswick
CA12 4DR
**t** (017687) 73171
**e** mavisandpatrick@cumbriahouse.co.uk
**w** cumbriahouse.co.uk

**Damson Lodge** ★★★★
*Bed & Breakfast*
Eskin Street, Keswick
CA12 4DQ
**t** (017687) 75547
**e** damsonlodge@yahoo.co.uk
**w** damsonlodge.co.uk

**Dolly Waggon** ★★★
*Guest Accommodation*
17 Helvellyn Street, Keswick
CA12 4EN
**t** (017687) 73593
**e** info@dollywaggon.co.uk
**w** dollywaggon.co.uk

**Dunsford Guest House**
★★★★ *Guest House*
**SILVER AWARD**
16 Stanger Street, Keswick
CA12 5JU
**t** (017687) 75059
**e** enquiries@dunsford.net
**w** dunsford.net

**Easedale House** ★★★★
*Guest House*
1 Southey Street, Keswick
CA12 4HL
**t** (017687) 72710
**e** info@easedalehouse.com
**w** easedalehouse.com

**Eden Green Guest House**
★★★★ *Guest House*
20 Blencathra Street, Keswick
CA12 4HP
**t** (017687) 72077
**e** enquiries@edengreenguesthouse.com
**w** edengreenguesthouse.com

**The Edwardene** ★★★★
*Guest Accommodation*
**SILVER AWARD**
26 Southey Street, Keswick
CA12 4EF
**t** (017687) 73586
**e** info@edwardenehotel.com
**w** edwardenehotel.com

**Ellas Crag** ★★★★
*Guest House* **SILVER AWARD**
Newlands Valley, Keswick
CA12 5TS
**t** (017687) 78217
**e** info@ellascrag.co.uk
**w** ellascrag.co.uk

**Ellergill Guest House**
★★★★ *Guest House*
22 Stanger Street, Keswick
CA12 5JU
**t** (017687) 73347
**e** stay@ellergill.co.uk
**w** ellergill.co.uk

**Fell House** ★★★★
*Guest House*
28 Stanger Street, Keswick
CA12 5JU
**t** (017687) 72669

**Fisher-Gill Camping Barn**
*Camping Barn*
Stybeck Farm, Thirlmere,
Keswick CA12 4TN
**t** (017687) 73232
**e** stybeckfarm@farming.co.uk
**w** members.farmline.com/stybeckfarm

**Gill Brow Farm** ★★★
*Farmhouse*
Newlands Valley, Keswick
CA12 5TS
**t** (017687) 78270
**e** wilson_gillbrow@hotmail.com
**w** gillbrow-keswick.co.uk

**Glencoe Guest House**
★★★★ *Guest House*
21 Helvellyn Street, Keswick
CA12 4EN
**t** (017687) 71016
**e** enquiries@glencoeguesthouse.co.uk
**w** glencoeguesthouse.co.uk

**Glendale Guest House**
★★★★ *Guest House*
**SILVER AWARD**
7 Eskin Street, Keswick
CA12 4DH
**t** (017687) 73562
**e** info@glendalekeswick.co.uk
**w** glendalekeswick.co.uk

**Goodwin House Guest House** ★★★★
*Guest Accommodation*
29 Southey Street, Keswick
CA12 4EE
**t** (017687) 74634
**e** enquiries@goodwinhouse.co.uk
**w** goodwinhouse.co.uk

**The Grange Country House**
★★★★★ *Guest House*
**SILVER AWARD**
Manor Brow, Ambleside Road,
Keswick CA12 4BA
**t** (017687) 72500
**e** info@grangekeswick.com
**w** grangekeswick.com

**Grassmoor Guest House**
★★★★ *Guest House*
10 Blencathra Street, Keswick
CA12 4HP
**t** (017687) 74008
**e** info@grassmoor-keswick.co.uk
**w** grassmoor-keswick.co.uk

**Greystones**
Rating Applied For
*Guest Accommodation*
Ambleside Road, Keswick
CA12 4DP
**t** (017687) 73108
**e** enquiries@greystoneskeswick.co.uk
**w** greystoneskeswick.co.uk

**Hawcliffe House** ★★★★
*Guest House*
30 Eskin Street, Keswick
CA12 4DG
**t** (017687) 73250
**e** diane@hawcliffehouse.co.uk
**w** hawcliffehouse.co.uk

**Hazeldene** ★★★★
*Guest Accommodation*
The Heads, Keswick CA12 5ER
**t** (017687) 72106
**e** info@hazeldene-hotel.co.uk
**w** hazeldene-hotel.co.uk

**Hedgehog Hill Guesthouse**
★★★★ *Guest House*
18 Blencathra Street, Keswick
CA12 4HP
**t** (017687) 80654
**e** keith@hedgehoghill.co.uk
**w** hedgehoghill.co.uk

**Howe Keld** ★★★★
*Guest Accommodation*
**GOLD AWARD**
5-7 The Heads, Keswick
CA12 5ES
**t** (017687) 72417
**e** david@howekeld.co.uk
**w** howekeld.co.uk

**Hunters Way Guest House**
★★★★ *Guest House*
4 Eskin Street, Keswick
CA12 4DH
**t** (017687) 72324
**e** huntersway@btconnect.com
**w** hunterswaykeswick.co.uk

**Keswick Park** ★★★★
*Guest Accommodation*
**SILVER AWARD**
33 Station Road, Keswick
CA12 4NA
**t** (017687) 72072
**e** enquiries@keswickparkhotel.com
**w** keswickparkhotel.com

**Keswick YHA** ★★★★ *Hostel*
Station Road, Keswick
CA12 5LH
**t** (017687) 72484

**Lakeland View** ★★★★
*Bed & Breakfast*
13 High Hill, Keswick
CA12 5NY
**t** (017687) 72555
**e** lakelandview@aol.com
**w** lakelandview.net

**Larry's Lodge** ★★★★
*Guest House*
39 Eskin Street, Keswick
CA12 4DG
**t** (017687) 73965
**e** suendave@larryslodge.co.uk
**w** larryslodge.co.uk

**Laurel Bank** ★★★★
*Bed & Breakfast*
Penrith Road, Keswick
CA12 4LJ
**t** (017687) 73006
**e** info@laurelbankkeswick.co.uk
**w** laurelbankkeswick.co.uk

**Leonard's Field House**
★★★★ *Guest House*
3 Leonard Street, Keswick
CA12 4EJ
**t** (017687) 74170
**e** enquiries@leonardsfieldhouse.com
**w** leonardsfieldhouse.com

**Lincoln Guest House** ★★★
*Guest House*
23 Stanger Street, Keswick
CA12 5JX
**t** (017687) 72597
**e** info@lincolnguesthouse.com
**w** lincolnguesthouse.com

**Lindisfarne House** ★★★★
*Guest House*
21 Church Street, Keswick
CA12 4DX
**t** (017687) 73218
**e** alison230@btinternet.com
**w** lindisfarnehouse.com

**Linnett Hill** ★★★★
*Guest House*
4 Penrith Road, Keswick
CA12 4HF
**t** (017687) 73109
**e** info@linnetthillhotel.com
**w** linnetthillhotel.com

**Littletown Farm** ★★★
*Farmhouse*
Newlands, Keswick CA12 5TU
**t** (017687) 78353
**e** info@littletownfarm.co.uk
**w** littletownfarm.co.uk

**Lyndhurst** ★★★★
*Guest House*
22 Southey Street, Keswick
CA12 4EF
**t** (017687) 72303
**e** stay@lyndhurstkeswick.co.uk
**w** lyndhurstkeswick.co.uk

**Lynwood Guest House**
★★★★ *Guest House*
12 Ambleside Road, Keswick
CA12 4DL
**t** (017687) 72081
**e** info@lynwood-keswick.co.uk
**w** lynwood-keswick.co.uk

**Newlands Fell Guesthouse**
★★★ *Guest House*
Newlands Valley, Keswick
CA12 5TS
**t** (017687) 78477
**e** kelly.wood8@btinternet.com
**w** lakedistrict-bandb.co.uk

**The Paddock** ★★★★
*Guest House*
Wordsworth Street, Keswick
CA12 4HU
t (017687) 72510
e val@thepaddock.info
w thepaddock.info

**Parkfield Guest House** ★★★★
*Guest Accommodation*
**SILVER AWARD**
The Heads, Keswick CA12 5ES
t (017687) 72328
e enquiries@parkfieldkeswick.co.uk
w parkfield-keswick.co.uk

**Ravensworth House** ★★★★
*Guest Accommodation*
**SILVER AWARD**
29 Station Street, Keswick
CA12 5HH
t (017687) 72476
e info@ravensworth-hotel.co.uk
w ravensworth-hotel.co.uk

**Rickerby Grange Country House** ★★★★ *Guest House*
Portinscale, Keswick CA12 5RH
t (017687) 72344
e stay@rickerbygrange.co.uk
w rickerbygrange.co.uk

**Rivendell** ★★★★
*Guest House*
23 Helvellyn Street, Keswick
CA12 4EN
t (017687) 73822
e info@rivendellguesthouse.com
w rivendellguesthouse.com

**Sandon Guesthouse** ★★★★
*Guest House*
13 Southey Street, Keswick
CA12 4EG
t (017687) 73648
e enquiries@sandonguesthouse.com
w sandonguesthouse.com

**Seven Oaks** ★★★★
*Guest House*
7 Acorn Street, Keswick
CA12 4EA
t (017687) 72088
e info@sevenoaks-keswick.co.uk
w sevenoaks-keswick.co.uk

**Shemara Guest House**
★★★★ *Guest House*
27 Bank Street, Keswick
CA12 5JZ
t (017687) 73936
e info@shemara.uk.com
w shemara.uk.com

**Skiddaw Grove Country Guest House** ★★★★
*Guest House*
Vicarage Hill, Keswick
CA12 5QB
t (017687) 73324
e info@skiddawgrove.co.uk
w skiddawgrove.co.uk

**Springs Farm Guesthouse**
★★★ *Guest House*
Springs Farm, Springs Road, Keswick CA12 4AN
t (017687) 72144
e info@springsfarmcumbria.co.uk
w springsfarmcumbria.co.uk

**Squirrel Lodge** ★★★★
*Guest House*
43 Eskin Street, Keswick
CA12 4DG
t (017687) 71189
e enquiries@squirrellodge.co.uk
w squirrellodge.co.uk

**Stonegarth Guest House**
★★★★ *Guest House*
2 Eskin Street, Keswick
CA12 4DH
t (017687) 72436
e info@stonegarth.com
w stonegarth.com

**Sweeneys Bar, Restaurant and Rooms** ★★★★
*Restaurant with Rooms*
20 Lake Road, Keswick
CA12 5BX
t 05006 00725
e stay@lakedistrictinns.co.uk
w lakedistrictinns.co.uk

**The Swinside Inn** ★★★ *Inn*
Newlands, Keswick CA12 5UE
t (017687) 78253
e info@theswinsideinn.com
w theswinsideinn.com

**Swiss Court Guest House**
★★★ *Guest House*
25 Bank Street, Keswick
CA12 5JZ
t (017687) 72637
e enquiries@swisscourt.co.uk
w swisscourt.co.uk

**Tarn Hows** ★★★★
*Guest House* **SILVER AWARD**
3-5 Eskin Street, Keswick
CA12 4DH
t (017687) 73217
e enquiries@tarnhows.co.uk
w tarnhows.co.uk

**Thornleigh Guest House**
★★★★ *Guest House*
23 Bank Street, Keswick
CA12 5JZ
t (017687) 72863
e thornleigh@btinternet.com
w thornleighguesthouse.co.uk

**Watendlath Guest House**
★★★★ *Guest House*
15 Acorn Street, Keswick
CA12 4EA
t (017687) 74165
e info@watendlathguesthouse.co.uk
w watendlathguesthouse.co.uk

**West View Guest House**
★★★★ *Guest House*
The Heads, Keswick CA12 5ES
t (017687) 73638
e info@westviewkeswick.co.uk
w westviewkeswick.co.uk

**Whitehouse** ★★★★
*Guest Accommodation*
**SILVER AWARD**
15 Ambleside Road, Keswick
CA12 4DL
t (017687) 73176
e whitehousekeswick@hotmail.com
w whitehouse.co.uk

## KETTLESING
North Yorkshire

**Green Acres** ★★★★
*Bed & Breakfast*
**GOLD AWARD**
Sleights Lane, Kettlesing, Pateley Bridge HG3 2LE
t (01423) 771524
e christine@yorkshiredalesbb.com
w yorkshiredalesbb.com

## KETTLEWELL
North Yorkshire

**Kettlewell YHA** ★★★ *Hostel*
Whernside House, Westgate, Skipton BD23 5QU
t (01756) 760232
e kettlewell@yha.org.uk
w yha.org.uk

**Lynburn** ★★★
*Bed & Breakfast*
Kettlewell, Skipton BD23 5RF
t (01756) 760803
e lorna@lthornborrow.fsnet.co.uk

**Pennycroft Guest House**
★★★★ *Guest House*
Far Lane, Kettlewell, Skipton
BD23 5QY
t (01756) 760845
e pennycroft123@tiscali.co.uk
w pennycroft.co.uk

## KIELDER
Northumberland

**Kielder YHA** ★★★★ *Hostel*
Butteryhaugh, Kielder
NE48 1HQ
t 0870 770 5898
e kielder@yha.org.uk
w yha.org.uk

**Twenty Seven** ★★
*Bed & Breakfast*
27 Castle Drive, Kielder, Hexham NE48 1EQ
t (01434) 250462 & (01434) 250366
e twentyseven@staykielder.co.uk
w staykielder.co.uk

## KIELDER WATER
Northumberland

**The Pheasant Inn (by Kielder Water)** ★★★★ *Inn*
**SILVER AWARD**
Stannersburn, Hexham
NE48 1DD
t (01434) 240382
e enquiries@thepheasantinn.com
w thepheasantinn.com

## KILBURN
North Yorkshire

**Church Farm** ★★★
*Farmhouse*
Kilburn, Thirsk YO61 4AH
t (01347) 868318
e churchfarmkilburn@yahoo.co.uk

## KILDALE
North Yorkshire

**Kildale Camping Barn**
*Camping Barn*
Park Farm, Kildale, Stokesley
YO21 2RN
t (01642) 722847
e parkfarm_2000@yahoo.co.uk
w kildalebarn.co.uk

## KILNWICK PERCY
East Riding of Yorkshire

**Paws-A-While** ★★★★
*Farmhouse*
Kilnwick Percy, Pocklington
YO42 1UF
t (01759) 301168
e paws.a.while@lineone.net
w pawsawhile.net

## KIRBY HILL
North Yorkshire

**Shoulder of Mutton** ★★★
*Inn*
Kirby Hill, Reeth DL11 7JH
t (01748) 822772
e info@shoulderofmutton.net
w shoulderofmutton.net

## KIRBY MISPERTON
North Yorkshire

**Beansheaf** ★★★★ *Inn*
Malton Road, Kirby Misperton, Malton YO17 6UE
t (01653) 668614
e enquiries@beansheafhotel.com
w beansheafhotel.com

## KIRKBURTON
West Yorkshire

**The Woodman Inn** ★★★★
*Inn*
Thunderbridge Lane, Kirkburton, Huddersfield
HD8 0PX
t (01484) 605778
e thewoodman@connectfree.co.uk
w woodman-inn.co.uk

## KIRKBY
Merseyside

**Greenbank Guest House** ★★
*Bed & Breakfast*
193 Rowan Drive, Liverpool
L32 0SG
t (0151) 546 9971

## KIRKBY
North Yorkshire

**Dromonby Hall Farm** ★★★
*Bed & Breakfast*
Busby Lane, Kirkby-in-Cleveland, Stokesley TS9 7AP
t (01642) 712312
e pat@dromonby.co.uk
w dromonby.co.uk

## KIRKBY-IN-CLEVELAND
North Yorkshire

**Dromonby Grange Farm**
★★★★ *Farmhouse*
Busby Lane, Kirkby-in-Cleveland, Stokesley TS9 7AR
**t** (01642) 712227
**e** jehugill@aol.com

## KIRKBY LONSDALE
Cumbria

**Copper Kettle Restaurant & Guest House** ★★
*Guest Accommodation*
3-5 Market Street, Kirkby Lonsdale, Carnforth LA6 2AU
**t** (015242) 71714

**High Green Farm** ★★★★
*Guest Accommodation*
Middleton in Lonsdale, Carnforth, Kirkby Lonsdale LA6 2NA
**t** (01524) 276256
**e** nora@highgreenfarm.com
**w** highgreenfarm.com

**The Pheasant Inn** ★★★ *Inn*
Casterton, Kirkby Lonsdale LA6 2RX
**t** (01524) 271230
**e** info@pheasantinn.co.uk
**w** pheasantinn.co.uk

**Ullathorns Farm** ★★★★
*Guest Accommodation*
Middleton, Kirkby Lonsdale, Carnforth LA6 2LZ
**t** (015242) 76214 & 07800 990689
**e** pauline@ullathorns.co.uk
**w** ullathorns.co.uk

## KIRKBY STEPHEN
Cumbria

**Augill Castle** ★★★★★
*Guest Accommodation*
**GOLD AWARD**
Brough, Kirkby Stephen CA17 4DE
**t** (017683) 41937
**e** enquiries@augillcastle.co.uk
**w** stayinacastle.com

**Ing Hill Lodge** ★★★★
*Bed & Breakfast*
Mallerstang Dale, Kirkby Stephen CA17 4JT
**t** (017683) 71153
**e** tony.sawyer@ing-hill-lodge.co.uk
**w** ing-hill-lodge.co.uk

**Kirkby Stephen YHA** ★★
*Hostel*
Market Street, Kirkby Stephen CA17 4QQ
**t** (017683) 71793

**Riddlesay Farm** ★★★★
*Farmhouse*
Soulby, Kirkby Stephen CA17 4PX
**t** (017683) 71474
**e** mrarmstrong@btinternet.com

**Westview** ★★★★
*Bed & Breakfast*
Ravenstonedale, Kirkby Stephen CA17 4NG
**t** (015396) 23415

## KIRKBYMOORSIDE
North Yorkshire

**Brickfields Farm** ★★★★★
*Farmhouse* **SILVER AWARD**
Kirkby Mills, Kirkbymoorside YO62 6NS
**t** (01751) 433074
**e** janet@brickfieldsfarm.co.uk
**w** brickfieldsfarm.co.uk

**The Cornmill** ★★★★
*Guest House* **SILVER AWARD**
Kirby Mills, Kirkbymoorside, York YO62 6NP
**t** (01751) 432000
**e** cornmill@kirbymills.demon.co.uk
**w** kirbymills.demon.co.uk

**Ely Cottage** ★★★★★
*Bed & Breakfast*
**SILVER AWARD**
26 Kirby Mills, Keldholme, Kirkbymoorside YO62 6NN
**t** (01751) 432824

**Farndale** *Camping Barn*
Oak House, High Farndale, York YO62 7LH
**t** (01751) 433053
**e** pipmead@aol.com
**w** yha.org.uk

**Feversham Arms Inn** ★★★★
*Inn*
Church Houses, Helmsley YO62 7LF
**t** (01751) 433206
**e** fevershamfarndale@hotmail.com

**George & Dragon** ★★★★
*Inn*
Market Place, Kirkbymoorside YO62 6AA
**t** (01751) 433334
**e** reception@georgeanddragon.net
**w** georgeanddragon.net

## KIRKNEWTON
Northumberland

**Hethpool House Bed and Breakfast** ★★★
*Bed & Breakfast*
Hethpool, Kirknewton NE71 6TW
**t** (01668) 216232
**e** eildon@hethpoolhouse.co.uk
**w** hethpoolhouse.co.uk

## KIRKSTALL
West Yorkshire

**Abbey Guest House**
Rating Applied For
*Guest House*
44 Vesper Road, Leeds LS5 3NX
**t** (0113) 278 5580
**e** abbeyleeds@ntlworld.com

## KIRKWHELPINGTON
Northumberland

**Cornhills Farmhouse**
★★★★ *Bed & Breakfast*
**SILVER AWARD**
Kirkwhelpington NE19 2RE
**t** (01830) 540232
**e** cornhills@northumberlandfarmhouse.co.uk
**w** northumberlandfarmhouse.co.uk

## KNARESBOROUGH
North Yorkshire

**Ebor Mount** ★★★
*Guest House*
18 York Place, Knaresborough HG5 0AA
**t** (01423) 863315

**Gallon House** ★★★★★
*Guest House*
47 Kirkgate, Knaresborough HG5 8BZ
**t** (01423) 862102
**e** gallon-house@ntlworld.com
**w** gallon-house.co.uk

**General Tarleton Inn**
★★★★★
*Restaurant with Rooms*
Boroughbridge Road, Ferrensby, Knaresborough HG5 0PZ
**t** (01423) 340284
**e** gti@generaltarleton.co.uk
**w** generaltarleton.co.uk

**Holly Corner Bed & Breakfast** ★★★★
*Guest Accommodation*
3 Coverdale Drive, High Bond End, Knaresborough HG5 9BW
**t** (01423) 864204
**e** hollycorner3@aol.com
**w** holly-corner.co.uk

**The Mitre** ★★★★★ *Inn*
**SILVER AWARD**
4 Station Road, Knaresborough HG5 9AA
**t** (01423) 868948
**e** office@themitreinn.co.uk
**w** themitreinn.co.uk

**Old Royal Oak** ★★★★ *Inn*
7 Market Place, Knaresborough HG5 8AL
**t** (01423) 865880
**e** thebarns@theroyaloak.demon.co.uk
**w** theoldroyaloak-knaresborough.co.uk

**Watergate Lodge** ★★★★
*Guest Accommodation*
Watergate Haven, Ripley Road, Knaresborough HG5 9BU
**t** (01423) 864627
**e** info@watergatehaven.com
**w** watergatehaven.com

## KNOTTINGLEY
West Yorkshire

**Wentvale Court** ★★★★
*Guest House*
Great North Road, Knottingley, Pontefract WF11 8PF
**t** (01977) 676714
**e** wentvale1@btconnect.com
**w** wentvalecourt.co.uk

## KNUTSFORD
Cheshire

**The Dog Inn** ★★★★ *Inn*
Well Bank Lane, Over Peover WA16 8UP
**t** (01625) 861421
**e** info@doginn-overpeover.co.uk
**w** doginn-overpeover.co.uk

**Moat Hall Motel** ★★★
*Guest Accommodation*
Chelford Road, Marthall, Knutsford WA16 8SU
**t** (01625) 860367
**e** val@moathall.fsnet.co.uk
**w** moat-hall-motel.co.uk

## LACH DENNIS
Cheshire

**Melvin Holme Farm** ★★
*Bed & Breakfast*
Pennys Lane, Lach Dennis CW9 7SJ
**t** (01606) 330008

## LAKESIDE
Cumbria

**The Knoll Country House**
★★★★★
*Guest Accommodation*
**SILVER AWARD**
Lakeside, Newby Bridge, Ulverston LA12 8AU
**t** (015395) 31347

## LAMBRIGG
Cumbria

**Wythmoor Camping Barn**
*Camping Barn*
Wythmoor Farm, Lambrigg, Kendal LA8 0DH
**t** (01946) 758198
**e** info@lakelandcampingbarns.co.uk
**w** lakelandcampingbarns.co.uk

## LANCASTER
Lancashire

**Edenbreck House** ★★★★
*Bed & Breakfast*
Sunnyside Lane, Lancaster LA1 5ED
**t** (01524) 32464
**e** edenbreckhouse@aol.com
**w** edenbreckhouse.com

**Lancaster Town House**
★★★ *Guest Accommodation*
11-12 Newton Terrace, Caton Road, Lancaster LA1 3PB
**t** (01524) 65527
**e** hedge-holmes@talk21.com
**w** lancastertownhouse.com

**Low House Farm** ★★★★
*Farmhouse*
Claughton, Lancaster LA2 9LA
**t** (01524) 221260 & 07870 635854
**e** shirley@lunevalley.freeserve.co.uk
**w** lowhousefarm.co.uk

**Middle Holly Cottage**
★★★★
*Guest Accommodation*
Middle Holly, Forton PR3 1AH
**t** (01524) 792399
**e** mhcottage@btconnect.com
**w** middlehollycottage.co.uk


Look out for establishments participating in the National Accessible Scheme

**Old Station House** ★★★★
*Guest Accommodation*
25 Meeting House Lane, Lancaster LA1 1TX
**t** (01524) 381060
**e** oldstationhouse@hotmail.com

**Penny Street Bridge, Lancaster** ★★★★
*Guest Accommodation*
**SILVER AWARD**
Penny Street, Lancaster LA1 1XT
**t** (01524) 599900
**e** info@pennystreetbridge.co.uk
**w** pennystreetbridge.co.uk

**The Shakespeare Bed & Breakfast** ★★★★
*Guest House*
96 St Leonardgate, Lancaster LA1 1NN
**t** (01524) 841041
**e** theshakespearelancaster@talktalk.net

**University of Cumbria** ★★
*Campus*
Bowerham Road, Lancaster LA1 3JD
**t** (01524) 384460
**e** conferences.lancaster@ucsm.ac.uk
**w** ucsm.ac.uk

## LANCHESTER
### Durham

**Kings Head** ★★★
*Guest Accommodation*
Station Road, Lanchester DH7 0EX
**t** (01207) 520054

## LANERCOST
### Cumbria

**Abbey Mill** ★★★★
*Bed & Breakfast*
Brampton CA8 2HG
**t** (01697) 742746
**e** tony@abbeymill.mc.uk

## LANGDALE
### Cumbria

**Britannia Inn** ★★★ *Inn*
Elterwater, Langdale, Ambleside, Langdale LA22 9HP
**t** (015394) 37210
**e** info@britinn.co.uk
**w** britinn.co.uk

**Three Shires Inn** ★★★★ *Inn*
Little Langdale, Langdale LA22 9NZ
**t** (015394) 37215
**e** enquiry@threeshiresinn.co.uk
**w** threeshiresinn.co.uk

## LEALHOLM
### North Yorkshire

**High Park Farm** ★★★★
*Farmhouse*
Lealholm, Whitby YO21 2AQ
**t** (01947) 897416
**e** highparkfarm@btinternet.com

## LEEDS
### West Yorkshire

**Avalon Guest House** ★★★★
*Guest House*
132 Woodsley Road, Leeds LS2 9LZ
**t** (0113) 243 2545
**e** info@woodsleyroad.com
**w** avalonguesthouseleeds.co.uk

**City Centre Guest House**
★★ *Guest House*
51a New Briggate, Leeds LS2 8JD
**t** (0113) 242 9019
**e** info@leedscitycentrehotel.com
**w** citycentrehotelleeds.co.uk

**The Glengarth** ★★★
*Guest House*
162 Woodsley Road, Leeds LS2 9LZ
**t** (0113) 245 7940
**e** info@woodsleyroad.com
**w** glengarthhotel.co.uk

**Headingley Lodge** ★★★
*Guest Accommodation*
Headingley Stadium, St Michael's Lane, Leeds LS6 3BR
**t** (0113) 278 5323
**e** tamsin_lee@talk21.com
**w** headingleylodge.co.uk

**Hinsley Hall** ★★★
*Guest Accommodation*
62 Headingley Lane, Leeds LS6 2BX
**t** (0113) 261 8000
**e** info@hinsley-hall.co.uk
**w** hinsley-hall.co.uk

**Manxdene Private Hotel** ★★
*Guest Accommodation*
154 Woodsley Road, Leeds LS2 9LZ
**t** (0113) 243 2586
**e** manxdenehotel@leedscity.wanadoo.co.uk

**The Moorlea** ★★
*Guest Accommodation*
146 Woodsley Road, Leeds LS2 9LZ
**t** (0113) 243 2653
**e** themoorleahotel@aol.com

**New Masons Arms** ★★★ *Inn*
26 Aberford Road, Leeds LS26 8JR
**t** (0113) 282 2334

**Number 23** ★★
*Bed & Breakfast*
23 St Chads Rise, Far Headingley, Leeds LS6 3QE
**t** (0113) 275 7825

**St Michael's Guest House**
★★★ *Guest House*
5 St Michael's Villas, Cardigan Road, Leeds LS6 3AF
**t** (0113) 275 5557
**e** stmichaels-guesthouse@hotmail.co.uk
**w** stmichaels-guesthouse.co.uk

**University of Leeds** ★★
*Campus*
Conference Office, University House, University of Leeds, Leeds LS2 9JT
**t** (0113) 233 6100
**e** david@universallyleeds.co.uk
**w** leeds.ac.uk/conference

**Wheelgate Guest House** ★★
*Guest House*
7 Kirkgate, Sherburn-in-Elmet, Leeds LS25 6BH
**t** (01977) 682231
**e** wheelgate01@btconnect.com
**w** smoothhound.co.uk/hotels/wheelgate

## LEEMING BAR
### North Yorkshire

**Little Holtby** ★★★★
*Bed & Breakfast*
**SILVER AWARD**
Leeming Bar, Northallerton, Bedale DL7 9LH
**t** (01609) 748762
**e** littleholtby@yahoo.co.uk
**w** littleholtby.co.uk

## LESBURY
### Northumberland

**Swallowdale Cottage**
★★★★ *Bed & Breakfast*
Longhoughton Road, Lesbury NE66 3AT
**t** (01665) 830389
**e** swallowdale@fsmail.net
**w** swallowdale.org.uk

## LEVISHAM
### North Yorkshire

**The Moorlands Country House** ★★★★★
*Guest House* **GOLD AWARD**
Main Street, Levisham, Pickering YO18 7NL
**t** (01751) 460229
**e** ronaldoleonardo@aol.com
**w** moorlandslevisham.co.uk

## LEYBURN
### North Yorkshire

**Clyde House** ★★★★
*Guest Accommodation*
**SILVER AWARD**
5 Railway Street, Leyburn DL8 5AY
**t** (01969) 623941
**e** lucia.fisher1@btinternet.com
**w** clydehouseleyburn.co.uk

**Dales Haven Guest House**
★★★★ *Guest House*
Market Place, Leyburn DL8 5BJ
**t** (01969) 623814
**e** info@daleshaven.co.uk
**w** daleshaven.co.uk

**Eastfield Lodge**
Rating Applied For
*Guest House*
1 St Matthews Terrace, Leyburn DL8 5EL
**t** (01969) 623196
**e** paula@eastfieldlodge.co.uk
**w** eastfieldlodge.co.uk

**The Grove** ★★★
*Guest House*
8 Grove Square, Leyburn DL8 5AE
**t** (01969) 622569
**e** info@grove-hotel.com
**w** grove-hotel.com

**The Old Vicarage** ★★★★
*Guest Accommodation*
West Witton, Leyburn DL8 4LX
**t** (01969) 622108
**e** grant.chumphreys@btinernet.com
**w** dalesbreaks.co.uk

**Street Head Inn** ★★★★ *Inn*
Newbiggin-in-Bishopdale, Leyburn DL8 3TE
**t** (01969) 663282
**e** joanne.fawcett@virgin.net
**w** streetheadinn.co.uk

**Sunnyridge, Argill Farm**
★★★ *Farmhouse*
Harmby, Leyburn DL8 5HQ
**t** (01969) 622478
**e** richah@freenet.co.uk

**Waterford House** ★★★★★
*Guest Accommodation*
**GOLD AWARD**
19 Kirkgate, Leyburn DL8 4PG
**t** (01969) 622090
**e** info@waterfordhousehotel.co.uk
**w** waterfordhousehotel.co.uk

**West Close Farmhouse**
★★★★
*Guest Accommodation*
**SILVER AWARD**
Melmerby-in-Coverdale, Leyburn DL8 4TW
**t** (01969) 640275
**e** thompson@westclose.wanadoo.co.uk
**w** westclosefarmhouse.co.uk

## LEYLAND
### Lancashire

**Smithy Lodge Guest House**
★★★★
*Guest Accommodation*
310 Dunkirk Lane, Leyland PR26 7SN
**t** (01772) 457650
**e** enquiries@smithy-lodge.co.uk
**w** smithy-lodge.co.uk

## LINTON
### North Yorkshire

**Linton Laith**
Rating Applied For
*Guest Accommodation*
The Grange, Skipton-on-Swale BD23 5HH
**t** (01756) 752230
**e** stay@lintonlaithe.co.uk
**w** lintonlaithe.co.uk

## LITHERLAND
### Merseyside

**Litherland Park Bed & Breakfast** ★★
*Bed & Breakfast*
34 Litherland Park, Litherland L21 9HP
**t** (0151) 928 1085
**e** bevaharper@yahoo.co.uk

## LITTLE BOLLINGTON
### Greater Manchester

**Bollington Hall Farm** ★★
*Bed & Breakfast*
Park Lane, Little Bollington, Altrincham WA14 4TJ
**t** (0161) 928 1760

## LITTLE BUDWORTH
### Cheshire

**Akesmere Farm** ★★★
*Farmhouse*
Chester Road, Little Budworth CW6 9ER
**t** (01829) 760348
**e** akesmerefarm@hotmail.com

**Elm Cottage Bed & Breakfast ★★★**
*Guest Accommodation*
Chester Lane, Winsford CW7 2QJ
**t** (01829) 760544
**e** chris@elmcottagecp.co.uk
**w** elmcottagecp.co.uk

## LITTLE CRAKEHALL
North Yorkshire

**Crakehall Watermill ★★★★**
*Bed & Breakfast*
Little Crakehall, Bedale DL8 1HU
**t** (01677) 423240
**e** stay@crakehallwatermill.co.uk
**w** crakehallwatermill.co.uk

## LITTLEBOROUGH
Greater Manchester

**Hollingworth Lake B&B ★★★★★**
*Guest Accommodation*
**SILVER AWARD**
164 Smithy Bridge Road, Littleborough OL15 0DB
**t** (01706) 376583
**w** b-visible.co.uk/businesses/32/hollingworthlakeb+b.htm

**Leighton House B&B**
★★★★ *Guest House*
1 Leighton Avenue, Littleborough, Rochdale OL15 0BW
**t** (01706) 378113

**Swing Cottage ★★★**
*Guest House*
31 Lakebank, Hollingworth Lake, Littleborough OL15 0DQ
**t** (01706) 379094
**e** swingcottage@aol.com
**w** hollingworthlake.com

## LIVERPOOL
Merseyside

**Aachen ★★★**
*Guest Accommodation*
89-91 Mount Pleasant, Liverpool L3 5TB
**t** (0151) 709 3477
**e** enquiries@aachenhotel.co.uk
**w** aachenhotel.co.uk

**Beechmount ★★★★**
*Guest Accommodation*
Beech Mount, Liverpool L7 0HL
**t** (0151) 264 9189
**e** reservations@beechmountexecutive.co.uk

**Blenheim Lakeside ★★★**
*Guest Accommodation*
37 Aigburth Drive, Sefton Park L17 4JE
**t** (0151) 727 7380
**e** enquiries@blenheimlakesidehotel.co.uk
**w** blenheimlakesidehotel.co.uk

**Feathers ★★★★**
*Guest Accommodation*
117-125 Mount Pleasant, Liverpool L3 5TF
**t** (0151) 709 9655
**e** feathershotel@feathers.uk.com
**w** feathers.uk.com

**Greenbank Sports Academy**
★★★ *Hostel*
Greenbank Lane, Liverpool L17 1AG
**t** (0151) 280 7757
**w** greenbanksportsacademy.co.uk

**Holme-Leigh Guest House**
★★★ *Guest Accommodation*
93 Woodcroft Road, Wavertree, Liverpool L15 2HG
**t** (0151) 734 2216
**e** info@holmeleigh.com
**w** holmeleigh.com

**International Inn ★★★**
*Hostel*
4 South Hunter Street, Off Hardman Street, Liverpool L1 9JG
**t** (0151) 709 8135
**e** info@internationalinn.co.uk
**w** internationalinn.co.uk

**Lord Nelson ★★**
*Guest Accommodation*
Hotham Street, Liverpool L3 5PD
**t** (0151) 709 5161
**e** reservations@lordnelsonliverpool.com
**w** lordnelsonliverpool.com

**Mulberry Court ★★** *Campus*
Liverpool University Mulberry Court, Liverpool L7 7EZ
**t** (0151) 794 6444

**Parkview**
Rating Applied For
*Guest Accommodation*
239-241 Netherfield Road North, Liverpool L5 3PN
**t** (0151) 207 2444
**e** dwyerjohn@btinternet.com

**The Penny Lane**
Rating Applied For
*Guest House*
Elm Hall Drive, Liverpool L18 1LF
**t** (0151) 735 0160

**Racquet Club ★★★★**
*Restaurant with Rooms*
Hargreaves Building, 5 Chapel Street, Liverpool L3 9AG
**t** (0151) 236 6676
**e** into@racquetclub.org.uk
**w** racquetclub.org.uk

**Real McCoy Guest House**
★★ *Bed & Breakfast*
126 Childwall Park Avenue, Childwall L16 0JH
**t** 07971 161542
**e** ann557@btinternet.com

**Roscoe & Gladstone Hall – Liverpool University ★★**
*Campus*
Greenbank Halls of Residence, Liverpool L17 1AH
**t** (0151) 794 6402

**Throstles Nest ★★★★**
*Guest Accommodation*
344 Scotland Road, Kirkdale L5 5AQ
**t** (0151) 207 9797
**e** kvmcmul@aol.com
**w** throstlesnesthotel.co.uk

**Victoria Hall ★★★** *Campus*
29 Hatton Garden, Liverpool L3 2EZ
**t** (0151) 907 7000
**e** liverpool@victoriahall.com
**w** victoriahall.com

**YHA Liverpool ★★★★**
*Hostel*
25 Tabley Street, Off Wapping, Liverpool L1 8EE
**t** 0870 770 5924
**e** liverpool@yha.org.uk
**w** yha.org.uk

## LIVERSEDGE
West Yorkshire

**Geordie Pride Lodge ★★★★**
*Guest Accommodation*
112 Roberttown Lane, Liversedge, Batley WF15 7LY
**t** (01924) 412044
**e** geordiehotel@aol.com

**Heirloom Carriage Driving B&B ★★** *Bed & Breakfast*
9 Windsor Drive, Norristhorpe WF15 7RA
**t** (01924) 235120

## LOCKTON
North Yorkshire

**Farfields Farmhouse ★★★★**
*Farmhouse*
Lockton, Pickering YO18 7NQ
**t** (01751) 460239
**e** stay@farfieldsfarm.co.uk
**w** farfieldsfarm.co.uk

**YHA Lockton ★★★★** *Hostel*
The Old School, Lockton YO18 7PY
**t** (01751) 460376
**e** lockton@yha.org.uk
**w** yha.org.uk

## LOFTHOUSE
North Yorkshire

**Studfold Farm Activity Centre ★★★** *Group Hostel*
Studfold Farm, Lofthouse, Pateley Bridge HG3 5SG
**t** (01423) 755399
**e** ianwalker@studfold.fsnet.co.uk
**w** studfoldfarm.co.uk

## LONDESBOROUGH
East Riding of Yorkshire

**Towthorpe Grange ★★**
*Bed & Breakfast*
Towthorpe Lane, Londesborough, Driffield YO43 3LB
**t** (01430) 873814
**e** towthorpegrange@hotmail.com

## LONDONDERRY
North Yorkshire

**Tatton Lodge ★★★**
*Guest House*
Londonderry, Northallerton, Bedale DL7 9NF
**t** (01677) 422222
**e** enquiries@tattonlodge.co.uk
**w** tattonlodge.co.uk

## LONGFRAMLINGTON
Northumberland

**The Angler's Arms ★★★★**
*Inn*
Weldon Bridge NE65 8AX
**t** (01665) 570655
**e** johnyoung@anglersarms.fsnet.co.uk
**w** anglersarms.com

**Coquet Bed & Breakfast**
★★★★ *Farmhouse*
**SILVER AWARD**
Elyhaugh Farm, Longframlington NE65 8BE
**t** (01665) 570305
**e** stay@coquetbb.co.uk
**w** coquetbb.co.uk

**Lee Farm ★★★★★**
*Farmhouse* **GOLD AWARD**
Rothbury NE65 8JQ
**t** (01665) 570257
**e** engs@leefarm.co.uk
**w** leefarm.co.uk

## LONGHORSLEY
Northumberland

**The Baronial ★★★**
*Guest House*
Longhorsley NE65 8TD
**t** (01670) 788378
**w** thebaronial.co.uk

**Thistleyhaugh Farm**
★★★★★ *Farmhouse*
**GOLD AWARD**
Morpeth NE65 8RG
**t** (01665) 570629
**e** thistleyhaugh@hotmail.com
**w** thistleyhaugh.co.uk

## LONGHOUGHTON
Northumberland

**Chestnut Tree House**
★★★★
*Guest Accommodation*
7 Crowlea Road, Longhoughton NE66 3AN
**t** (01665) 577153
**e** janetholtuk@btinternet.com

**Number One ★★★★**
*Bed & Breakfast*
1 Springfield, Longhoughton NE66 3NT
**t** (01665) 577811
**e** christine.wilson@numberonespringfield.co.uk
**w** numberonespringfield.co.uk

**Swallows' Rest ★★★★**
*Bed & Breakfast*
**SILVER AWARD**
8 The Croft, Longhoughton NE66 3DD
**t** (01665) 577425
**e** stay@swallows-rest.co.uk
**w** swallows-rest.co.uk

## LONGRIDGE
Lancashire

**The Corporation Arms**
★★★★ *Inn*
Lower Road, Longridge PR3 2YJ
**t** (01772) 782644
**e** corporationarmss@yahoo.co.uk
**w** corporationarms.co.uk

**Oak Lea** ★★★★
*Guest Accommodation*
Clitheroe Road, Knowle Green
PR3 2YS
**t** (01254) 878486
**e** tandm.mellor@tiscali.co.uk

## LONGTHWAITE
Cumbria

**Borrowdale YHA** ★★★★
*Hostel*
Longthwaite, Keswick
CA12 5XE
**t** (017687) 77257

## LONGTON
Lancashire

**Willow Cottage** ★★★★
*Bed & Breakfast*
**SILVER AWARD**
Longton by Pass, Longton
PR4 4RA
**t** (01772) 617570
**e** willow.cottage@btconnect.com
**w** lancashirebedandbreakfast.co.uk

## LONGTOWN
Cumbria

**Briar Lea Guest House** ★★★★
*Guest Accommodation*
Brampton Road, Longtown, Carlisle CA6 5TN
**t** (01228) 791538
**e** info@briarleahouse.co.uk
**w** briarleahouse.co.uk

---

**Craigburn Farmhouse**
★★★★ *Farmhouse*
Penton, Longtown CA6 5QP
**t** (01228) 577214
**e** louiselawson@hotmail.com
**w** criagburnfarmhouse.co.uk

## LOUGHRIGG
Cumbria

**Langdale YHA** ★★ *Hostel*
High Close, Loughrigg, Langdale LA22 9HJ
**t** 0870 770 5908
**e** langdale@yha.org.uk
**w** yha.org.uk

## LOW ROW
North Yorkshire

**Low Row Camping Barn/ Bunkhouse** *Bunkhouse*
Low Whita Farm, Richmond
DL11 6NT
**t** (01748) 884601
**e** rwcclarkson@aol.com

---

**Rowleth End Guest House**
★★★★ *Guest House*
**SILVER AWARD**
Low Row, Richmond DL11 6PY
**t** (01748) 886327
**e** stay@upperswale.co.uk
**w** upperswale.co.uk

---

**Summer Lodge** ★★★★
*Farmhouse*
Summer Lodge Farm, Low Row, Reeth DL11 6NP
**t** (01748) 886504

## LOWER BARTLE
Lancashire

**Crow Tree Villa** ★★
*Guest Accommodation*
Bartle Lane, Bartle PR4 0RU
**t** (01772) 690101
**e** crowtreevilla@talktalk.net

## LOWER WITHINGTON
Cheshire

**Chapel Cottage** ★★★
*Bed & Breakfast*
Dicklow Cob, Lower Withington SK11 9EA
**t** (01477) 571489
**e** barbara.hides2@virgin.net

## LOWESWATER
Cumbria

**Askhill Farm** ★★★★
*Farmhouse*
Loweswater, Cockermouth
CA13 0SU
**t** (01946) 861640
**e** askhillfarm@aol.com
**w** countrycaravans.co.uk/askhillfarm

---

**Swallow** *Camping Barn*
Waterend Farm, Loweswater, Cockermouth CA13 0SU
**t** (01946) 758198
**e** info@lakelandcampingbarns.co.uk
**w** lakecampingbarns.co.uk

## LOWICK
Northumberland

**Black Bull Inn** ★★★ *Inn*
2-4 Main Street, Berwick-upon-Tweed TD15 2UA
**t** (01289) 388228
**e** johnneilscott06@aol.com

---

**Burn House Bed & Breakfast**
★★★★ *Bed & Breakfast*
**SILVER AWARD**
Lowick Common, Lowick
TD15 2UG
**t** (01289) 388457
**e** margaretsoutter@btinternet.com
**w** burn-house.co.uk

---

**The Old Drapery** ★★★
*Bed & Breakfast*
50 Main Street, Lowick
TD15 2UA
**t** (01289) 388592
**e** davidlaidle@onetel.com

---

**Primrose Cottage** ★★★★
*Bed & Breakfast*
Main Street, Lowick TD15 2UA
**t** (01289) 388900
**e** info@primrosecottagelowick.co.uk
**w** primrosecottagelowick.co.uk

## LOWICK GREEN
Cumbria

**Pomona Bed & Breakfast**
★★★★ *Bed & Breakfast*
Lowick Green, Ulverston, Coniston LA12 8DX
**t** (01229) 885399
**e** steve@pomonalakedistrict.co.uk
**w** pomonalakedistrict.co.uk

## LOXLEY
South Yorkshire

**Barnfield House** ★★★★
*Guest Accommodation*
**SILVER AWARD**
Loxley Road, Loxley, Sheffield
S6 6RW
**t** (0114) 233 6365
**e** enquiries@barnfieldhouse.com
**w** barnfieldhouse.com

## LUDDENDENFOOT
West Yorkshire

**Rockcliffe West** ★★★★
*Bed & Breakfast*
Burnley Road, Luddendenfoot, Halifax HX2 6HL
**t** (01422) 882151
**e** rockcliffe.b.b@virgin.net
**w** rockcliffewest.co.uk

## LUPTON
Cumbria

**The Plough Inn** ★★★ *Inn*
Cow Brow, Lupton, Kirkby Lonsdale LA6 1PJ
**t** (015395) 67227
**e** ploughhotel@totalise.co.uk
**w** theplough-lupton.co.uk

## LYTHAM ST ANNES
Lancashire

**The Breverton** ★★★
*Guest Accommodation*
64 Orchard Road, Lytham St Annes FY8 1PJ
**t** (01253) 726179

---

**Cornubia** ★★★★
*Bed & Breakfast*
**SILVER AWARD**
13 Derbe Road, St Annes-on-Sea FY8 1NJ
**t** (01253) 640834
**e** cornubia@lycos.co.uk

---

**The Endsleigh** ★★★
*Guest Accommodation*
315 Clifton Drive South, St Annes-on-Sea FY8 1HN
**t** (01253) 725622
**e** endsleighhotel@hotmail.com
**w** howarthhouse.co.uk

---

**Fairmile** ★★★
*Guest Accommodation*
9 St Annes Road East, St Anne's FY8 1TA
**t** (01253) 728375
**w** hotellink/lytham/fairmile

---

**The Queens Inn** ★★★ *Inn*
Central Beach, Lytham FY8 5LB
**t** (01253) 737316
**e** enquiries@the-queens-lytham.co.uk
**w** the-queens-lytham.co.uk

---

**The Strathmore** ★★★
*Guest Accommodation*
305 Clifton Drive South, St Annes-on-Sea FY8 1HN
**t** (01253) 725478

---

**Tudor House** ★★★
*Guest House*
32 St Davids Road South, St Annes FY8 1TJ
**t** (01253) 722444
**e** stay@tudorhouse.uk.com
**w** tudorhouse.uk.com

## MACCLESFIELD
Cheshire

**Astle Farm East** ★★
*Farmhouse*
Chelford, Macclesfield
SK10 4TA
**t** (01625) 861270
**e** gill.farmhouse@virgin.net

---

**Carr House Farm Bed & Breakfast** ★★ *Farmhouse*
Mill Lane, Macclesfield
SK10 4LG
**t** (01625) 828337
**e** isobel@carrhousefarm.com
**w** carrhousefarm.com

---

**Moorhayes House** ★★★
*Guest Accommodation*
27 Manchester Road, Tytherington, Macclesfield
SK10 2JJ
**t** (01625) 433228
**e** helen@moorhayes.co.uk
**w** moorhayes.co.uk

---

**Red Oaks Farm B&B** ★★★★
*Farmhouse* **SILVER AWARD**
Charter Road, Bollington
SK10 5NU
**t** (01625) 574280
**e** bb@redoaksfarm.co.uk
**w** redoaksfarm.co.uk

---

**The Ryles Arms** ★★★★ *Inn*
Hollin Lane, Higher Sutton
SK11 0NN
**t** (01260) 252244
**e** info@rylesarms.com
**w** rylesarms.com

## MACCLESFIELD FOREST
Cheshire

**The Stanley Arms Bed & Breakfast** ★★★★ *Inn*
Macclesfield Forest, Wildboarclough SK11 0AR
**t** (01260) 252414
**e** thestanleyarms@btconnet.com
**w** stanleyarms.com

## MALHAM
North Yorkshire

**Malham YHA** ★★★ *Hostel*
Skipton BD23 4DE
**t** (01729) 830321
**e** malham@yha.org.uk
**w** yha.org.uk

---

**Miresfield Farm** ★★★
*Guest House*
Malham, Skipton BD23 4DA
**t** (01729) 830414
**e** chris@miresfield.freeserve.co.uk
**w** miresfield-farm.com

## MALHAM MOOR
North Yorkshire

**High Trenhouse** ★★★★
*Guest Accommodation*
Malham Moor, Settle
BD24 9PR
**t** (01729) 830322
**e** bernadette@changeandinnovation.com
**w** high-trenhouse.co.uk

## MALTBY
South Yorkshire

**The Cottages Guest House**
★★ *Guest House*
1, 3 & 5 Bligh Road, Maltby, Rotherham S66 8HX
**t** (01709) 813382

## MALTON
North Yorkshire

**The George** ★★★ *Inn*
19 Yorkersgate, Malton
YO17 7AA
**t** (01653) 692884

**Manor Farm** ★★★
*Farmhouse*
Malton YO17 8RN
t (01944) 728268
e info@manorfarmonline.co.uk
w manorfarmonline.co.uk

**Mill House Bed & Breakfast** ★★★ *Farmhouse*
East Knapton, Malton YO17 8JA
t (01944) 728026
e carol@millhouse822.freeserve.co.uk

**Red House** ★★★★
*Bed & Breakfast*
**SILVER AWARD**
Wharram, Malton YO17 9TL
t (01944) 768185
e elaineatredhouse@hotmail.com

### MANCHESTER
Greater Manchester

**Abbey Lodge** ★★★
*Bed & Breakfast*
501 Wilbraham Road, Chorlton M21 0UJ
t (0161) 862 9266
e info@abbey-lodge.co.uk
w abbey-lodge.co.uk

**The Hatters** ★★ *Hostel*
50 Newton Street, Manchester M1 2EA
t (0161) 236 9500
e manchester@hattersgroup.com
w hattersgroup.com

**Hilton Chambers**
Rating Applied For
*Hostel*
15 Hilton Street, Manchester M1 1JJ
t (0161) 236 4414
e hilton@hattersgroup.com
w hattersgroup.com

**The Ivy Mount Guest House** ★ *Guest Accommodation*
35 Half Edge Lane, Manchester M30 9AY
t (0161) 789 1756
e ivymount1@tiscali.co.uk
w ivymountguesthouse.co.uk/

**Luther King House** ★★★
*Guest Accommodation*
Brighton Grove, Wilmslow Road, Manchester M14 5JP
t (0161) 224 6404
e reception@lkh.co.uk
w lkh.co.uk

**Manchester YHA** ★★★★
*Hostel*
Potato Wharf, Castlefield M3 4NB
t 0870 770 5950
e manchester@yha.org.uk
w yha.org.uk

**Monroe's Guest House and Bar** ★★ *Inn*
38 London Road, Manchester M1 1PE
t (0161) 236 0564

**Seasons Guest House** ★★★
*Guest Accommodation*
803 Altrincham Road, Manchester M23 9AH
t (0161) 945 3232
e seasons803@fsmail.net
w seasonsguesthouse.co.uk

**Stay Inn – Manchester** ★★★
*Guest Accommodation*
55 Blackfriars Road, Salford, Manchester M3 7DB
t (0161) 907 2277
e info@stayinn.co.uk
w stayinn.co.uk

**Victoria Hall** ★★★ *Campus*
28 Higher Cambridge Street, Manchester M15 6AA
t (0161) 908 7000
e manchester.hcs@victoriahall.com
w victoriahall.com

**Victoria Hall** ★★★ *Campus*
281 Upper Brook Street, Manchester M13 0FZ
t (0161) 908 7000
w victoriahall.com

### MAPPLEWELL
South Yorkshire

**The Grange** ★★★
*Guest House*
29 Spark Lane, Mapplewell, Barnsley S75 6AA
t (01226) 380078
e hwje454@aol.com

### MARKET WEIGHTON
East Riding of Yorkshire

**Arras Farmhouse** ★★★
*Farmhouse*
Arras, Market Weighton, Driffield YO43 4RN
t (01430) 872404

**Red House** ★★★★
*Guest Accommodation*
North Cliffe, Market Weighton, Beverley YO43 4XB
t (01430) 827652
e simon.lyn@virgin.net
w redhousenorthcliffe.co.uk

### MARPLE BRIDGE
Greater Manchester

**Forge Bank Mill** ★★
*Bed & Breakfast*
1 Longhurst Lane, Marple Bridge, Stockport SK6 5AE
t (0161) 427 9345
w forgebankmill.com

### MARRICK
North Yorkshire

**Marrick Moor B&B** ★★★★
*Bed & Breakfast*
Marrick Moor House, Marrick, Richmond DL11 7LF
t (01748) 884065
e info@marrickmoorbedandbreakfast.co.uk
w marrickmoorbedandbreakfast.co.uk

### MASHAM
North Yorkshire

**Garden House** ★★★★
*Guest Accommodation*
1 Park Street, Masham, Ripon HG4 4HN
t (01765) 689989
e suefurbymasham@gmail.com

**Glasshouse B&B (Uredale Glass)** ★★★★
*Guest Accommodation*
42 Market Place, Masham, Ripon HG4 4EF
t (01765) 689780
e info@uredale.co.uk

**Park House** ★★★★★
*Guest Accommodation*
**SILVER AWARD**
Jervaulx, Ripon HG4 4PH
t (01677) 460184
e ba123@btopenworld.com

**Warren House Farm** ★★★★
*Farmhouse*
High Ellington, Masham, Ripon HG4 4PP
t (01677) 460244
e cathebroadley@msn.com

### MAULDS MEABURN
Cumbria

**Trainlands B&B** ★★★
*Farmhouse*
Maulds Meaburn, Penrith CA10 3HX
t (017683) 51249
e enquire@trainlands.co.uk
w trainlands.co.uk

### MENSTON
West Yorkshire

**Chevin End Guest House** ★★★ *Guest House*
West Chevin Road, Menston, Ilkley LS29 6BE
t (01943) 876845
w chevinendguesthouse.co.uk

### MIDDLEHAM
North Yorkshire

**The Priory** ★★★★
*Guest House*
West End, Middleham, Leyburn DL8 4QG
t (01969) 623279
e priory.guesthouse@virgin.net

### MIDDLESBROUGH
Tees Valley

**Chadwicks Guest House** ★★
*Guest House*
Clairville Road, Middlesbrough TS4 2HN
t (01642) 287235
e chadwickguesthouse@hotmail.com
w chadwickguesthouse.com

### MIDDLETON
Greater Manchester

**Three Gates Farm** ★★★★
*Bed & Breakfast*
Stakehill Lane, Middleton, Manchester M24 2RT
t (0161) 653 8314
e info@threegatesfarmbandb.co.uk
w threegatesfarmbandb.co.uk

### MIDDLETON-IN-TEESDALE
Durham

**Belvedere House** ★★★★
*Bed & Breakfast*
54 Market Place, Middleton-in-Teesdale DL12 0QH
t (01833) 640884
e belvedere@thecoachhouse.net
w thecoachhouse.net

**Brunswick House** ★★★★
*Guest House* **SILVER AWARD**
55 Market Place, Middleton-in-Teesdale DL12 0QH
t (01833) 640393
e enquiries@brunswickhouse.net
w brunswickhouse.net

**Grove Lodge** ★★★★
*Guest Accommodation*
**GOLD AWARD**
Hude, Middleton-in-Teesdale DL12 0QW
t (01833) 640798
w grovelodgeteesdale.co.uk

**Holwick** *Camping Barn*
Middleton-in-Teesdale DL12 0NJ
t (01833) 640506

**Wemmergill Hall Farm** ★★★★ *Farmhouse*
Lunedale, Middleton-in-Teesdale DL12 0PA
t (01833) 640379
e enquiries@wemmergill-farm.co.uk
w wemmergill-farm.co.uk

### MIDDLEWICH
Cheshire

**Hopley House** ★★★
*Guest Accommodation*
Wimboldsley, Middlewich CW10 0LN
t (01270) 526292
e margery@hopleyhouse.co.uk
w hopleyhouse.co.uk

### MIDGLEY
West Yorkshire

**Midgley Lodge Motel** ★★★★
*Guest Accommodation*
Bar Lane, Midgley, Wakefield WF4 4JJ
t (01924) 830069
e midgleylodgemotel@tiscali.co.uk
w midgleylodgemotel.co.uk

### MIDHOPESTONES
South Yorkshire

**Ye Olde Mustard Pot** ★★★★ *Inn*
Mortimer Road, Sheffield S36 4GW
t (01226) 761155
e reservations@mustardpot.co.uk
w yeoldemustardpot.co.uk

### MILBURN
Cumbria

**Low Howgill Farm** ★★★★
*Bed & Breakfast*
Low Howgill, Milburn, Appleby-in-Westmorland CA10 1TL
t (017683) 61595
e jane@low-howgill.co.uk
w lowhowgill.f9.co.uk

**Slakes Farm** ★★★
*Farmhouse*
Milburn, Appleby-in-Westmorland CA16 6DP
t (017683) 61385
e oakleaves@slakesfarm.wanadoo.co.uk
w slakesfarm.co.uk

## MILNTHORPE
Cumbria

**The Cross Keys** ★★★★ *Inn*
1 Park Road, Milnthorpe
LA7 7AB
**t** (015395) 62115
**e** stay@thecrosskeyshotel.co.uk
**w** thecrosskeyshotel.co.uk

## MINSHULL VERNON
Cheshire

**Higher Elms Farm Bed & Breakfast** ★★★ *Farmhouse*
Cross Lane, Minshull Vernon
CW1 4RG
**t** (01270) 522252

## MOHOPE
Northumberland

**YHA Ninebanks** ★★★★
*Hostel*
Orchard House, Mohope
NE47 8DQ
**t** (01434) 345288
**e** ninebanks@yha.org.uk
**w** yha.ninebanks.org.uk

## MOORSHOLM
Tees Valley

**Green Ghyl** ★★★★
*Bed & Breakfast*
10 Recreation View,
Moorsholm TS12 3HZ
**t** (01287) 669050
**e** info@greenghyl.co.uk
**w** greenghyl.co.uk

## MORECAMBE
Lancashire

**Ashley Guest House** ★★★
*Guest House*
371 Marine Road East,
Morecambe LA4 5AH
**t** (01524) 412034
**e** info@ashleyhotel.co.uk
**w** ashleyhotel.co.uk

**The Balmoral** ★★★
*Guest House*
34 Marine Road West,
Morecambe LA3 1BZ
**t** (01524) 418526
**e** info@balmoralhotelmorecambe.co.uk
**w** balmoralhotelmorecambe.co.uk

**Berkeley Guest House, Morecambe** ★★★
*Guest House*
39 Promenade West,
Morecambe LA3 1BZ
**t** (01524) 418201
**e** donval4144@hotmail.com
**w** hotelmorecambe.co.uk

**Broadwater** ★★★
*Guest Accommodation*
356 Marine Road East,
Morecambe LA4 5AQ
**t** (01524) 411333
**e** broadwaterhotel@aol.com

**The Clifton** ★★★
*Guest Accommodation*
Marine Road West,
Morecambe LA3 1BZ
**t** (01524) 411573
**e** clifton.hotel@btinternet.com
**w** hotel-clifton.co.uk

**Highview** ★★★★
*Guest Accommodation*
235 Heysham Road, Heysham
LA3 1NN
**t** (01524) 424991
**e** wynconway4@tiscali.co.uk

**The Kerswell Guest House** ★★ *Guest House*
36 Marine Road West,
Morecambe LA3 1BZ
**t** (01524) 418427
**e** martine.meah@blueyonder.co.uk
**w** kerswellhotel.co.uk

**Morecambe Bay Guest House** ★★★★ *Guest House*
35 Marine Road West,
Morecambe LA3 1BZ
**t** (01524) 426593
**e** info@morecambebayguesthouse.co.uk
**w** morecambebayguesthouse.co.uk

**The Park** ★★★
*Guest Accommodation*
91 Regent Road, Morecambe
LA3 1AF
**t** (01524) 414979
**e** lesjak@talktalk.net
**w** parkhotel.moonfruit.co.uk

**Sea Crest** ★★★
*Guest Accommodation*
9-13 West End Road,
Morecambe LA4 4DJ
**t** (01524) 411006
**e** seacrest-hotel@tiscali.co.uk
**w** seacrest-hotel.co.uk/seacreasthotel.asp

**Silverwell** ★★★ *Guest House*
20 West End Road,
Morecambe LA4 4DL
**t** (01524) 410532
**e** sverwll@aol.com
**w** silverwellguesthouse.co.uk

**The Townhouse** ★★★★
*Guest Accommodation*
78 Thornton Road, Morecambe
LA4 5PJ
**t** (01524) 412762
**e** enquiries@townhousemorecambe.co.uk
**w** townhousemorecambe.co.uk

**The Westleigh** ★★★
*Guest House*
9 Marine Road West,
Morecambe LA3 1BS
**t** (01524) 418352
**e** info@westleighbay.co.uk
**w** westleighbay.co.uk

**The Wimslow** ★★★
*Guest House*
374 Marine Road East,
Morecambe LA4 5AH
**t** (01524) 417804
**e** morecambewimslow@aol.com
**w** wimslowhotel.co.uk

**Yacht Bay View** ★★★
*Guest House*
359 Marine Road East,
Morecambe LA4 5AQ
**t** (01524) 414481
**e** yachtbayview@hotmail.com
**w** yachtbay.co.uk

## MORPETH
Northumberland

**Castle View B & B** ★★★★
*Guest House*
6 Dacre Street, Morpeth
NE61 1HW
**t** (01670) 514140
**e** info@castleviewbedandbreakfast.co.uk
**w** castleviewbedandbreakfast.co.uk

**Chestnut House** ★★★
*Guest House*
2 Dacre Street, Morpeth
NE61 1HW
**t** (01670) 518777
**e** enquiries@chestnuthouse.net
**w** chestnuthouse.net

**Cottage View Guesthouse** ★★ *Guest House*
6 Staithes Lane, Morpeth
NE61 1TD
**t** (01670) 518550
**e** bookings@cottageview.co.uk
**w** cottageview.co.uk

**Cottingburn House B&B** ★★★ *Bed & Breakfast*
40 Bullers Green, Morpeth
NE61 1DE
**t** (01670) 503195
**e** veeherbert@hotmail.com
**w** cottingburnhouse.co.uk

**Kington** ★★★
*Bed & Breakfast*
East Linden, Longhorsley,
Morpeth NE65 8TH
**t** (01670) 788554
**e** clivetaylor.services@tiscali.co.uk
**w** kington-longhorsley.com

**Lansdown House** ★★★★
*Bed & Breakfast*
90 Newgate Street, Morpeth
NE61 1BU
**t** (01670) 511129
**w** lansdownhouse.co.uk

**Morpeth Court** ★★★★
*Guest Accommodation*
Castle Bank, Morpeth
NE61 1YJ
**t** (01670) 517217
**e** carol_edmundson@hotmail.com
**w** morpethcourt.com

**Newminster Cottage** ★★★
*Bed & Breakfast*
High Stanners, Morpeth
NE61 1QL
**t** (01670) 503124
**e** enquiries@newminster-cottage.co.uk
**w** newminster-cottage.co.uk

**Northumberland Cottage** ★★★★ *Guest House*
Chevington Moor, Chevington
NE61 3BA
**t** (01670) 783339
**e** info@northumberland-cottage.co.uk
**w** northumberland-cottage.co.uk

**Queens Head** ★★★
*Guest Accommodation*
Bridge Street, Morpeth
NE61 1NB
**t** (01670) 512083
**w** queensheadmorpeth.co.uk

**River Cottage** ★★★★
*Bed & Breakfast*
Mouldhaugh Farm, Felton
NE65 9NP
**t** (01670) 787081
**e** easells@clara.co.uk
**w** river-cottage-bandb.co.uk

**Riverside Guest House** ★★★ *Guest House*
77 Newgate Street, Morpeth
NE61 1BX
**t** (01670) 515026
**e** elaine.riverside@virgin.net
**w** riverside-guesthouse.co.uk

**Stepping Stones B&B** ★★★
*Guest Accommodation*
75 Newgate Street, Morpeth
NE61 1BX
**t** (01670) 517869
**e** steppingstonesbb@aol.com
**w** steppingstonesbedandbreakfast.co.uk

## MOSSER
Cumbria

**Mosser Heights** ★★★★
*Farmhouse*
Mosser, Cockermouth
CA13 0SS
**t** (01900) 822644
**e** amandavickers1@aol.com

## MOTTRAM ST ANDREW
Cheshire

**Goose Green Farm Bed & Breakfast** ★★★ *Farmhouse*
Oak Road, Mottram St Andrew
SK10 4RA
**t** (01625) 828814
**e** info@goosegreenfarm.com
**w** goosegreenfarm.com

## MUKER
North Yorkshire

**Muker Village Stores & Tea Shop** ★★★★ *Bed & Breakfast*
The Village Stores, Muker,
Richmond DL11 6QG
**t** (01748) 886409
**e** mukerteashop@btinternet.com
**w** mukervillage.co.uk

## MUNCASTER
Cumbria

**Muncaster Coachman's Quarters** ★★★★
*Guest Accommodation*
Muncaster Castle, Muncaster,
Ravenglass CA18 1RQ
**t** (01229) 717614
**e** info@muncaster.co.uk
**w** muncaster.co.uk

**Muncaster Country Guest House** ★★★★ *Guest House*
Muncaster, Ravenglass
CA18 1RD
**t** (01229) 717693
**e** donandsheila@muncastercountryguesthouse.com
**w** muncastercountryguesthouse.com

### MUNGRISDALE
Cumbria

**Near Howe Guest House**
★★★★
*Guest Accommodation*
Mungrisdale, Penrith
CA11 0SH
**t** (017687) 79678
**e** enquiries@nearhowe.co.uk
**w** nearhowe.co.uk

### NANTWICH
Cheshire

**Coole Hall Farm Bed and Breakfast** ★★★★ *Farmhouse*
**SILVER AWARD**
Hankelow, Crewe CW3 0JD
**t** (01270) 811232
**e** goodwin200@hotmail.com

**Hamilton House Bed and Breakfast** ★★★
*Bed & Breakfast*
Station Road, Hampton Heath
SY14 8JF
**t** (01948) 820421
**e** hamiltonhouse5@hotmail.com
**w** hamiltonhousecheshire.co.uk

**Outlanes Farmhouse Bed & Breakfast** ★★★
*Guest Accommodation*
The Outlanes, Church Minshull
CW5 6DX
**t** (01270) 522284
**e** robert.parton@theoutlanes.com
**w** theoutlanes.com

**Stoke Grange Farm** ★★★★
*Farmhouse*
Chester Road, Nantwich
CW5 6BT
**t** (01270) 625525
**e** stokegrange@freeuk.com
**w** stokegrangefarm.co.uk

### NATEBY
Cumbria

**The Black Bull** ★★★★ *Inn*
Nateby, Kirkby Stephen
CA17 4JP
**t** (017683) 71588
**e** enquiries@blackbullnateby.co.uk

### NAWTON
North Yorkshire

**Little Manor Farm** ★★★★
*Farmhouse*
Highfield Lane, Nawton,
Kirkbymoorside YO62 7TH
**t** (01439) 771672
**e** penny-avison@tiscali.co.uk

### NELSON
Lancashire

**Lovett House Guest House**
★★★ *Guest House*
6 Howard Street, Nelson
BB9 7SZ
**t** (01282) 697352
**e** lovetthouse@ntlworld.com
**w** lovetthouse.co.uk

### NEW BRANCEPETH
Durham

**Alum Waters Guest House**
★★★★ *Bed & Breakfast*
Unthank Farmhouse, Alum
Waters DH7 7JJ
**t** (0191) 373 0628
**e** tony@alumwaters.freeserve.co.uk
**w** alumwatersgh.co.uk

### NEW BRIGHTON
Merseyside

**Sherwood Guest House**
★★★ *Guest House*
55 Wellington Road, New
Brighton CH45 2ND
**t** (0151) 639 5198
**e** info@sherwoodguesthouse.com
**w** sherwoodguesthouse.com

### NEW HUTTON
Cumbria

**1 Ashes Barn** ★★★★
*Guest Accommodation*
**SILVER AWARD**
New Hutton, Kendal LA8 0AS
**t** (01539) 729215
**e** gillian@gillianwray.co.uk
**w** ashesbarn.co.uk

### NEWBIGGIN-BY-THE-SEA
Northumberland

**Captain's Lodge B & B**
★★★★ *Bed & Breakfast*
2 Haven View, Newbiggin-by-the-Sea NE64 6NR
**t** (01670) 810082
**e** captains.lodge@btinternet.com

**Seaton House** ★★
*Bed & Breakfast*
20 Seaton Avenue, Newbiggin-by-the-Sea NE64 6UX
**t** (01670) 816057

### NEWBIGGIN-ON-LUNE
Cumbria

**Bents Camping Barn**
*Camping Barn*
Bents Farm, Newbiggin-on-Lune, Kirkby Stephen
CA17 4NX
**t** (01946) 758198
**e** info@lakelandcampingbarns.co.uk
**w** lakelandcampingbarns.co.uk

**Tranna Hill** ★★★★
*Guest Accommodation*
Newbiggin-on-Lune, Kirkby
Stephen CA17 4NY
**t** (015396) 23227 &
07989 892368
**e** enquiries@trannahill.co.uk
**w** trannahill.co.uk

### NEWBROUGH
Northumberland

**Allerwash Farmhouse**
★★★★★ *Bed & Breakfast*
**GOLD AWARD**
Allerwash, Hexham NE47 5AB
**t** (01434) 674574
**e** angela@allerwash.co.uk
**w** allerwash.co.uk

**Carr Edge Farm** ★★★★
*Farmhouse*
Newbrough NE47 5EA
**t** (01434) 674788
**e** stay@carredge.co.uk
**w** carredge.co.uk

**Westfield Bed and Breakfast**
★★★★ *Bed & Breakfast*
Newbrough, Hexham
NE47 5AR
**t** (01434) 674241
**e** byhexham@aol.com
**w** westfieldbandb.co.uk

### NEWBY WISKE
North Yorkshire

**Well House** ★★★★
*Guest Accommodation*
Newby Wiske, Thirsk DL7 9EX
**t** (01609) 772253
**e** info@wellhouse-newbywiske.co.uk
**w** wellhouse-newbywiske.co.uk

### NEWCASTLE UPON TYNE
Tyne and Wear

**Albatross** ★★ *Backpackers*
51 Grainger Street, Newcastle-upon-Tyne NE1 5JE
**t** (0191) 233 1330
**e** info@albatrossnewcastle.co.uk
**w** albatrossnewcastle.com

**The Avenue** ★★★
*Guest House*
2 Manor House Road,
Newcastle-upon-Tyne NE2 2LU
**t** (0191) 281 1396
**e** avenue.hotel@amserve.com

**Brandling Guest House**
★★★ *Guest House*
4 Brandling Park, Newcastle-upon-Tyne NE2 4QA
**t** (0191) 281 3175
**e** johncatto@btconnect.com
**w** brandlingguesthouse.co.uk

**Clifton House** ★★★
*Guest Accommodation*
46 Clifton Road, Off Grainger
Park Road, Newcastle upon
Tyne NE4 6XH
**t** (0191) 273 0407
**e** cliftonhousehotel@hotmail.com
**w** cliftonhousehotel.com

**The Dene** ★★★
*Guest Accommodation*
38-42 Grosvenor Road,
Newcastle-upon-Tyne NE2 2RP
**t** (0191) 281 1502
**e** denehotel@ukonline.co.uk

**Greenholme** ★★★
*Bed & Breakfast*
40 South View, Newcastle-upon-Tyne NE5 2BP
**t** (0191) 267 4828 &
07910 529089
**e** info@greenholmeguesthouse.co.uk
**w** greenholmeguesthouse.co.uk

**Jesmond Park** ★★★
*Guest House*
74-76 Queens Road,
Newcastle-upon-Tyne NE2 2PR
**t** (0191) 281 2821
**e** vh@jespark.fsnet.co.uk
**w** jesmondpark.com

**The Keelman's Lodge**
★★★★
*Guest Accommodation*
Grange Road, Newcastle upon
Tyne NE15 8NL
**t** (0191) 267 1689 &
(0191) 414 0156
**e** admin@biglampbrewers.co.uk
**w** keelmanslodge.co.uk

**The Lynnwood** ★★
*Guest House*
1 Lynnwood Terrace,
Newcastle-upon-Tyne NE4 6UL
**t** (0191) 273 3497
**e** davidreynolds07@aol.com
**w** thelynnwood.co.uk

**Newcastle YHA** ★★ *Hostel*
107 Jesmond Road, Newcastle-upon-Tyne NE2 1NJ
**t** (0191) 281 2570
**e** newcastle@yha.org.uk
**w** yha.org.uk

**Northumbria University**
★★★ *Campus*
Claude Gibb Hall and Camden
Court, University Precinct,
Northumberland Road,
Newcastle-upon-Tyne
NE1 8SG
**t** (0191) 227 4717
**e** rc.conferences@northumbria.ac.uk
**w** northumbria.ac.uk/conferences

**Stonehaven Lodge** ★★★
*Guest House*
Prestwick Road Ends,
Ponteland, Newcastle upon
Tyne NE20 9BX
**t** (01661) 872363
**e** stonehavenlodge@hotmail.co.uk

### NEWCHURCH
Lancashire

**Old Earth House** ★★★★
*Bed & Breakfast*
33 Newchurch in Pendle,
Newchurch Village BB12 9JR
**t** (01282) 698812
**e** isolde@healey7809.fsnet.co.uk

### NEWLANDS
Cumbria

**Catbells Camping Barn**
*Camping Barn*
Low Skelgill Farm, Keswick
CA12 5UE
**t** (017687) 78453

**YHA Hawse End**
Rating Applied For
*Hostel*
Hawse End Cottage,
Portinscale CA12 5UE
**t** (017687) 72816

### NEWTON-ON-RAWCLIFFE
North Yorkshire

**Elm House Farm** ★★★★
*Farmhouse*
Newton-on-Rawcliffe, Pickering
YO18 8QA
**t** (01751) 473223
**w** elmhousefarm.co.uk

**Swan Cottage** ★★★★
*Bed & Breakfast*
Newton-on-Rawcliffe, Pickering YO18 8QA
t (01751) 472502
e swancottagenewton@yahoo.co.uk

### NEWTON-ON-THE-MOOR
Northumberland

**The Old School** ★★★★★
*Bed & Breakfast*
**GOLD AWARD**
Newton-on-the-Moor, Alnwick NE65 9JY
t (01665) 575767
e info@northumberlandbedandbreakfast.co.uk
w theoldschool.eu

### NIBTHWAITE
Cumbria

**Lakeside YMCA National Centre** ★★★ *Hostel*
Lakeside, Newby Bridge LA12 8BD
t (015395) 39012
e sales@lakesideymca.co.uk
w lakesideymca.co.uk

### NORTH CAVE
East Riding of Yorkshire

**Albion House** ★★
*Bed & Breakfast*
18 Westgate, North Cave, Beverley HU15 2NJ
t (01430) 422958
e info@hawleys.info
w hawleys.info

### NORTH FERRIBY
East Riding of Yorkshire

**B & B @103** ★★★
*Bed & Breakfast*
103 Ferriby High Road, North Ferriby, Hull HU14 3LA
t (01482) 633637
e info@bnb103.co.uk
w bnb103.co.uk

### NORTH SHIELDS
Tyne and Wear

**No 61, Guest House & Tea Rooms** ★★★★ *Guest House*
No 61, Front Street, Tynemouth NE30 4BT
t (0191) 257 3687
e no.61@btconnect.com
w no61.co.uk

### NORTH STAINLEY
North Yorkshire

**The Staveley Arms** ★★★★
*Inn*
North Stainley, Ripon HG4 3HT
t (01765) 635439

### NORTH SUNDERLAND
Northumberland

**The Old Manse** ★★★★
*Bed & Breakfast*
9 North Lane, North Sunderland NE68 7UQ
t (01665) 720521
e info@theoldemanse.com
w theoldemanse.com

**The Olde School House**
★★★ *Guest House*
17 North Lane, North Sunderland NE68 7UQ
t (01665) 720760
e theoldeschoolhouse@hotmail.co.uk
w theoldeschoolhouse.co.uk

**Regal House** ★★★★
*Bed & Breakfast*
6 Regal Close, North Sunderland NE68 7US
t (01665) 720008
e julieashford1@btinternet.com
w regalhouse-seahouses.co.uk

**St Cuthbert's House**
Rating Applied For
*Guest House*
192 Main Street, North Sunderland NE68 7UB
t (01665) 720456
e stay@stcuthbertshouse.com
w stcuthbertshouse.com

### NORTHALLERTON
North Yorkshire

**Alverton Guest House** ★★★
*Guest House*
26 South Parade, Northallerton DL7 8SG
t (01609) 776207
e alvertonguesthse@btconnect.com
w alvertonguesthouse.com

**Elmscott** ★★★★
*Bed & Breakfast*
**SILVER AWARD**
10 Hatfield Road, Northallerton DL7 8QX
t (01609) 760575
e elmscott@btinternet.com
w elmscottbedandbreakfast.co.uk

**Lovesome Hill Farm** ★★★★
*Farmhouse* **SILVER AWARD**
Northallerton DL6 2PB
t (01609) 772311
e pearsonlhf@care4free.net
w lovesomehillfarm.co.uk

**Lovesome Hill Farm**
*Bunkhouse*
Lovesome Hill, Northallerton DL6 2PB
t (01609) 772311

### NORTHWICH
Cheshire

**Ash House Farm** ★★★★
*Farmhouse*
Chapel Lane, Acton Bridge CW8 3QS
t (01606) 852717
e sue_schofield40@hotmail.com
w ashhousefarm.co.uk

**Parkdale Guest House** ★★★
*Guest Accommodation*
140 Middlewich Road, Rudheath CW9 7DS
t (01606) 45228
e srb7@btinernet.com

**The Poplars** ★★★★
*Farmhouse*
Norley Lane, Crowton CW8 2RR
t (01928) 788083
e thepoplarsbandb@aol.com
w the-poplarsbandb.co.uk/

### NORTON
North Yorkshire

**Brambling Fields B&B**
★★★★ *Bed & Breakfast*
Brambling Fields, Scarborough Road, Malton YO17 8EE
t (01653) 698510

**The Union Inn** ★★★ *Inn*
46 Commercial Street, Norton, Malton YO17 9ES
t (01653) 692945

### NUNNINGTON
North Yorkshire

**Sunley Court** ★★★
*Farmhouse*
Muscoates, Nunnington, Helmsley YO62 5XQ
t (01439) 748233
e sunleycourt@tiscali.co.uk

### OLD BEWICK
Northumberland

**Old Bewick Farmhouse**
★★★★★ *Bed & Breakfast*
Old Bewick NE66 4DZ
t (01668) 217372
e oldbewickfarmhse@aol.com
w oldbewick.co.uk

### OLD TRAFFORD
Greater Manchester

**Lancashire County Cricket Club & Old Trafford Lodge**
★★★ *Guest Accommodation*
Talbot Road, Old Trafford, Manchester M16 0PX
t (0161) 874 3333
e lodge@lccc.co.uk
w lccc.co.uk

### OLDHAM
Greater Manchester

**Boothstead Farm** ★★★★
*Guest Accommodation*
Rochdale Road, Denshaw, Oldham OL3 5UE
t (01457) 878622
e boothsteadfarm@tiscali.co.uk

**Grains Bar Farm** ★★★
*Guest Accommodation*
Ripponden Road, Oldham OL1 4SX
t (0161) 624 0303
e info@grainsbarhotel.co.uk

### OSMOTHERLEY
North Yorkshire

**Chequers Tea-Room** ★★★★
*Guest Accommodation*
Chequers Tearoom, Chequer Farm, Northallerton DL6 3QB
t (01609) 883710
e mcemma1@yahoo.co.uk
w chequersosmotherley.co.uk

**Osmotherley YHA** ★★★
*Hostel*
Cote Ghyll, Osmotherley, Northallerton DL6 3AH
t (01609) 883575
e osmotherley@yha.org.uk
w yha.org.uk

**Vane House** ★★★★
*Guest Accommodation*
11a North End, Osmotherley, Northallerton DL6 3BA
t (01609) 883448
e allan@vanehouse.co.uk
w coast2coast.co.uk/vanehouse

### OTLEY
West Yorkshire

**Scaife Hall Farm** ★★★★
*Farmhouse* **GOLD AWARD**
Hardisty Hill, Blubberhouses, Harrogate LS21 2PL
t (01943) 880354
e christine.a.ryder@btinternet.com
w scaifehallfarm.co.uk

**Wood Top Farm** ★★★★
*Farmhouse*
Off Norwood Edge, Lindley, Otley LS21 2QS
t (01943) 464010
e mailwoodtop@aol.com

### OTTERBURN
Northumberland

**Butterchurn Guest House**
★★★★ *Guest House*
Main Street, Otterburn NE19 1NP
t (01830) 520585
e keith@butterchurn.freeserve.co.uk
w butterchurnguesthouse.co.uk

**Dunns Houses Farmhouse Bed and Breakfast** ★★★★
*Farmhouse*
Dunns Houses Farm, Otterburn NE19 1LB
t (01830) 520677
e dunnshouses@hotmail.com
w northumberlandfarmholidays.co.uk

### OULTON
Cheshire

**New Farm Bed and Breakfast** ★★★★
*Guest Accommodation*
Long Lane, Wettenhall CW7 4DW
t (01270) 528213
e info@newfarmbbandcaravanpark.co.uk
w newfarmbbandcaravanpark.co.uk/index.htm

### OVER ALDERLEY
Cheshire

**Lower Harebarrow Farm Bed & Breakfast** ★★
*Bed & Breakfast*
Alderley Road, Over Alderley SK10 4SW
t (01625) 829882
w lowerharebarrowfarm.co.uk/

### OVER KELLET
Lancashire

**Chapel Lodge**
Rating Applied For
*Guest Accommodation*
The Chapel, Kirkby Lonsdale Road, Over Kellet LA6 1DS
t (01524) 720660
e jandnhammond@supanet.com

### OVER SILTON
North Yorkshire

**Greystone Farm** ★★★★
*Farmhouse*
Over Silton, Thirsk YO7 2LH
t (01609) 883468
e greystone@freenet.co.uk

### OVINGHAM
### Northumberland

**Dukes Cottages Bed and Breakfast ★★★★**
*Bed & Breakfast*
2 Dukes Cottages, Main Road, Ovingham NE42 6AD
**t** (01661) 832566
**e** info@dukescottages.co.uk
**w** dukescottages.co.uk

### OVINGTON
### Durham

**The Four Alls ★★★** *Inn*
Ovington, Richmond DL11 7BP
**t** (01833) 627302
**e** john.stroud@virgin.net
**w** thefouralls-teesdale.co.uk

### OVINGTON
### Northumberland

**Evenwood Cottage ★★★★**
*Bed & Breakfast*
Ovington, Prudhoe NE42 6DN
**t** (01661) 832259
**e** stuartoram@btinternet.com
**w** evenwoodcottage.co.uk

### OXENHOPE
### West Yorkshire

**Springfield Guest House**
★★★★ *Guest House*
Springfield, Shaw Lane, Haworth BD22 9QL
**t** (01535) 643951
**e** best_bb_uk@msn.com
**w** s-h-systems.co.uk

### PATELEY BRIDGE
### North Yorkshire

**Bewerley Hall Farm ★★★**
*Farmhouse*
Bewerley, Pateley Bridge HG3 5JA
**t** (01423) 711636
**e** bewerleyhallfm@orange.net
**w** bewerleyhallfarm.co.uk

---

**High Green Farm ★★★★**
*Bed & Breakfast*
**SILVER AWARD**
Wath Road, Wath, Pateley Bridge HG3 5PJ
**t** (01423) 715958
**e** info@highgreen.co.uk
**w** highgreen-nidderdale.co.uk

---

**Lyndale Guest House ★★★**
*Guest House*
King Street, Pateley Bridge HG3 5AT
**t** (01423) 712657
**e** lyndale.guesthouse@talktalk.net

---

**Talbot House ★★★**
*Guest House*
27 High Street, Pateley Bridge HG3 5AL
**t** (01423) 711597
**e** reservations@talbothouse.co.uk
**w** talbothouse.co.uk

### PATRICK BROMPTON
### North Yorkshire

**Neesham Cottage ★★★★**
*Bed & Breakfast*
Patrick Brompton, Bedale DL8 1LN
**t** (01677) 450271
**e** info@neeshamcottage.co.uk
**w** neeshamcottage.co.uk

### PATRINGTON
### East Riding of Yorkshire

**Mill Lodge ★★★**
*Guest Accommodation*
Station Road, Patrington, Withernsea HU12 0NG
**t** (01964) 630782
**e** milllodge@mail.com
**w** milllodge.com

### PATTERDALE
### Cumbria

**Deepdale Hall Farmhouse**
★★★★ *Farmhouse*
Deepdale Hall, Patterdale, Ullswater CA11 0NR
**t** (017684) 82369
**e** brown@deepdalehall.freeserve.co.uk
**w** deepdalehall.co.uk

---

**Patterdale YHA ★★** *Hostel*
Goldrill House, Penrith CA11 0NW
**t** (017684) 82394

### PENISTONE
### South Yorkshire

**Cubley Hall Inn ★★★★** *Inn*
Mortimer Road, Penistone, Barnsley S36 9DF
**t** (01226) 766086
**e** cubley.hall@ukonline.co.uk
**w** cubleyhall.co.uk

### PENRITH
### Cumbria

**Blue Swallow Guest House**
★★★★ *Guest House*
11 Victoria Road, Penrith CA11 8HR
**t** (01768) 866335
**e** blueswallow@tiscali.co.uk
**w** blueswallow.co.uk

---

**Bracken Bank Lodge ★★★★**
*Guest Accommodation*
Lazonby, Penrith CA10 1AX
**t** (01768) 898241
**e** info@brackenbank.co.uk
**w** brackenbank.co.uk

---

**Brandelhow Guest House**
★★★★ *Guest House*
1 Portland Place, Penrith CA11 7QN
**t** (01768) 864470
**e** enquiries@brandelhowguesthouse.co.uk
**w** brandelhowguesthouse.co.uk

---

**Caledonia Guest House**
★★★★
*Guest Accommodation*
8 Victoria Road, Penrith CA11 8HR
**t** (01768) 864482
**e** ian.rhind1@virgin.net
**w** caledoniaguesthouse.co.uk

---

**Glendale Guest House**
★★★★ *Guest House*
4 Portland Place, Penrith CA11 7QN
**t** (01768) 210061
**e** glendaleguesthouse@yahoo.co.uk
**w** glendaleguesthouse.com

---

**The Limes Country Guest House ★★★** *Guest House*
Redhills, Penrith CA11 0DT
**t** (01768) 863343
**e** jdhanton@aol.com
**w** members.aol.com/jdhanton/index.htm

---

**Little Blencowe Farm ★★★**
*Farmhouse*
Blencow, Penrith CA11 0DG
**t** (017684) 83338 & 07745 460186
**e** bef@littleblencowe.wanadoo.co.uk

---

**Norcroft Guest House**
★★★★ *Guest House*
Graham Street, Penrith CA11 9LQ
**t** (01768) 862365
**e** info@norcroft-guesthouse.co.uk
**w** norcroft-guesthouse.co.uk

---

**The Old School ★★★★★**
*Guest House* **SILVER AWARD**
Newbiggin, Stainton, Penrith CA11 0HT
**t** (017684) 83709
**e** info@theold-school.com
**w** theold-school.com

---

**Roundthorn Country House**
★★★★★
*Guest Accommodation*
**SILVER AWARD**
Beacon Edge, Roundthorn, Penrith CA11 8SJ
**t** (01768) 863952
**e** info@roundthorn.co.uk
**w** roundthorn.co.uk

### PETERLEE
### Durham

**The Bell ★★★** *Guest House*
Sunderland Road, Horden SR8 4PF
**t** (0191) 586 3863
**e** bar-is.thebell@unicombox.co.uk

---

**Crawford's Guest House ★★**
*Bed & Breakfast*
8 Warwick Place, Peterlee SR8 2EZ
**t** (0191) 518 0996
**e** angiechilton@yahoo.com

---

**Manor House ★★★★**
*Bed & Breakfast*
Southside, Easington Village SR8 3AX
**t** (0191) 527 2141
**e** danmullaney3009@hotmail.com
**w** manorhousebandb.net

### PICKERING
### North Yorkshire

**17 Burgate ★★★★★**
*Guest House* **GOLD AWARD**
Pickering YO18 7AU
**t** (01751) 473463
**e** info@17burgate.co.uk
**w** 17burgate.co.uk

---

**Apricot Lodge ★★★★★**
*Bed & Breakfast*
**SILVER AWARD**
25 Crossgate Lane, Pickering YO18 7EX
**t** (01751) 477744
**e** apricotlodge@beeb.net
**w** apricotlodge.com

---

**Artisan House**
Rating Applied For
*Guest Accommodation*
Eastgate, Pickering YO18 7DU
**t** (01751) 477226

---

**Ashfield House Bed & Breakfast ★★★★**
*Bed & Breakfast*
Ashfield House, Ruffa Lane, Pickering YO18 7HN
**t** (01751) 477429
**e** info@ashfield-house.co.uk
**w** ashfield-house.co.uk

---

**August Guest House ★★★★**
*Guest House*
3 Plane Trees, Rosedale, Pickering YO18 8RF
**t** (01751) 417328
**e** mary@augustguesthouse.co.uk
**w** augustguesthouse.co.uk

---

**Barker Stakes Farm ★★★★**
*Farmhouse*
Lendals Lane, Pickering YO18 8EE
**t** (01751) 476759
**e** info@barkerstakesfarm.com
**w** barkerstakesfarm.com

---

**Bramwood Guest House**
★★★★ *Guest House*
**SILVER AWARD**
19 Hallgarth, Pickering YO18 7AW
**t** (01751) 474066
**e** enquiries@bramwoodguesthouse.co.uk
**w** bramwoodguesthouse.co.uk

---

**Bridge House ★★★★**
*Bed & Breakfast*
**SILVER AWARD**
8 Bridge Street, Pickering YO18 8DT
**t** (01751) 477234
**e** kgbridgehouse@tiscali.co.uk
**w** pickeringuk.net/bridgehouse

---

**Cawthorne House ★★★★**
*Guest House* **SILVER AWARD**
42 Eastgate, Pickering YO18 7DU
**t** (01751) 477364
**e** info@cawthornehouse.co.uk
**w** cawthornehouse.co.uk

---

**Costa House ★★★★**
*Bed & Breakfast*
**SILVER AWARD**
12 Westgate, Pickering YO18 8BA
**t** (01751) 474291
**e** ruth.leeming@virgin.net

---

**Eleven Westgate ★★★★**
*Bed & Breakfast*
**SILVER AWARD**
Eden House, Pickering YO18 8BA
**t** (01751) 475111
**e** info@elevenwestgate.co.uk
**w** elevenwestgate.co.uk

---

**Five Acre View ★★★★**
*Farmhouse*
Rosedale Abbey, Pickering YO18 8RE
**t** (01751) 417830
**e** fiveacreview@aol.com
**w** fiveacreview.co.uk

**Givendale Head Farm**
★★★★ *Farmhouse*
Ebberston, Snainton, Pickering YO13 9PU
t (01723) 859383
e sue.gwilliam@talk21.com
w givendaleheadfarm.co.uk

**The Hawthornes** ★★★★
*Bed & Breakfast*
High Back Side, Middleton, Pickering YO18 8PB
t (01751) 474755
e paulaappleby@btinternet.com
w the-hawthornes.com

**Keld Farm Bed and Breakfast** ★★★
*Bed & Breakfast*
Newton-on-Rawcliffe, Pickering YO18 8QA
t (01751) 474039

**Kirkham Garth Bed and Breakfast** ★★★
*Bed & Breakfast*
Kirkham Garth, Whitby Road, Pickering YO18 7AT
t (01751) 474931
e kirkhamgarth@hotmail.co.uk
w kirkhamgarth.co.uk

**No 9 B&B** ★★★★
*Bed & Breakfast*
**SILVER AWARD**
9 Thornton Road, Pickering YO18 7HZ
t (01751) 476533
e info@no9pickering.co.uk
w no9pickering.co.uk

**The Old Vicarage** ★★★★★
*Guest Accommodation*
**GOLD AWARD**
Toftly View, Pickering YO18 8QD
t (01751) 476126
e oldvic@toftlyview.co.uk
w toftlyview.co.uk

**Rains Farm Bed & Breakfast**
★★★★ *Farmhouse*
**SILVER AWARD**
Rains Farm, Allerston, Pickering YO18 7PQ
t (01723) 859333
e rainsholidays@btconnect.com
w rains-farm-holidays.co.uk

**Tangalwood** ★★★★
*Bed & Breakfast*
Roxby Road, Thornton Dale, Pickering YO18 7SX
t (01751) 474688

**Vivers Mill** ★★★★
*Guest House*
Mill Lane, Pickering YO18 8DJ
t (01751) 473640
e viversmill@talk21.com
w viversmill.co.uk

**Wildsmith House** ★★★★
*Bed & Breakfast*
**SILVER AWARD**
Marton, Sinnington, Kirkbymoorside YO62 6RD
t (01751) 432702
e wildsmithhouse@btinternet.com

### PIERCEBRIDGE
Tees Valley

**Holme House** ★★★
*Farmhouse*
Piercebridge, Darlington DL2 3SY
t (01325) 374280
e graham.holmehouse@gmail.com

### PITY ME
Durham

**The Lambton Hounds Inn**
Rating Applied For
*Inn*
Front Street, Pity Me DH1 5DE
t (0191) 386 4742
e lambtonhounds@aol.com
w lambtonhounds.com

### PONTEFRACT
West Yorkshire

**Tower House Executive Guest House** ★★★★★
*Guest House* **SILVER AWARD**
21 Bondgate, Pontefract WF8 2JP
t (01977) 699988
e towerhouse.guesthouse@virgin.net
w towerhouseguesthouse.com

### POOLEY BRIDGE
Cumbria

**The Pooley Bridge Inn** ★★★
*Inn*
Pooley Bridge, Lake Ullswater, Penrith CA10 2NN
t (017684) 86215
e stay@pooleybridgeinn.co.uk
w pooleybridgeinn.co.uk

### PORT CARLISLE
Cumbria

**Brockelrigg** ★★★★★
*Bed & Breakfast*
**SILVER AWARD**
Port Carlisle, Wigton CA7 5BU
t (01697) 351953
e mu.atkinson@btopenworld.com
w brockelrigg.co.uk

**Hesket House** ★★★★
*Guest Accommodation*
Port Carlisle, Wigton CA7 5BU
t (01697) 351876
e stay@heskethouse.com
w heskethouse.com

### PORTINSCALE
Cumbria

**Derwent Bank**
Rating Applied For
*Guest Accommodation*
Derwentwater, Keswick CA12 5TY
t (020) 8511 1534

**Lakeview** ★★★★
*Guest House* **SILVER AWARD**
Portinscale, Keswick CA12 5RD
t (017687) 71122
e sandkmuir@aol.com
w lakeviewkeswick.co.uk

**Powe House** ★★★★
*Guest House* **SILVER AWARD**
Portinscale, Keswick CA12 5RW
t (017687) 73611
e andrewandhelen@powehouse.com
w powehouse.com

### POULTON-LE-FYLDE
Lancashire

**The Shard Riverside Inn**
★★★★ *Inn*
Old Bridge Lane, Hambleton FY6 9BT
t (01253) 700208
e info@shardriversideinn.co.uk
w shardriversideinn.co.uk

### POWBURN
Northumberland

**Cheviot View** ★★★★
*Bed & Breakfast*
Powburn NE66 4HL
t (01665) 578306
e cheviotview@hotmail.co.uk
w wcheviotview.com

**Crawley Farmhouse** ★★★
*Farmhouse*
Powburn NE66 4JA
t (01665) 578413
e crawleyfarmhouse@hotmail.co.uk

**Low Hedgeley Farm**
★★★★★ *Farmhouse*
**SILVER AWARD**
Powburn, Alnwick NE66 4JD
t (01665) 578815

### PREESALL
Lancashire

**Grassendale** ★★★
*Bed & Breakfast*
Green Lane, Preesall, Poulton-le-Fylde FY6 0NS
t (01253) 812331
e rondeyo@aol.com

### PRESTBURY
Cheshire

**Artizana Suite** ★★★★★
*Bed & Breakfast*
The Village, Prestbury SK10 4DG
t (01625) 827582
e enquiries@artizana.co.uk
w artizana.co.uk/suite

### PRESTON
East Riding of Yorkshire

**Little Weghill Farm** ★★★★
*Farmhouse* **SILVER AWARD**
Weghill Road, Preston, Hull HU12 8SX
t (01482) 897650
e info@littleweghillfarm.co.uk
w littleweghillfarm.co.uk

### PRESTON
Lancashire

**Ye Horns Inn** ★★★★
*Guest Accommodation*
Horns Lane, Goosnargh PR3 2FJ
t (01772) 865230
e info@yehornsinn.co.uk
w yehornsinn.co.uk

**Little Stubbins Bed & Breakfast** ★★★★
*Bed & Breakfast*
Stubbins Lane, Preston PR3 0PL
t (01995) 640376
e littlestubbins@aol.com
w littlestubbins.co.uk

### PRESTON-UNDER-SCAR
North Yorkshire

**Hawthorn Cottage** ★★★★
*Bed & Breakfast*
Preston-under-Scar, Leyburn DL8 4AQ
t (01969) 624492
e helen@ricduffield.com
w hawthorn-wensleydale.com

### PRESTWICH
Greater Manchester

**The Church Inn – Bury** ★★★
*Inn*
Church Lane, Prestwich, Manchester M25 1AJ
t (0161) 798 6727
e tom.gribben@virgin.net

### PUDSEY
West Yorkshire

**Lynnwood House** ★★★
*Guest House*
18 Alexandra Road, Uppermoor, Leeds LS28 8BY
t (0113) 257 1117
w lynnwoodhouse.co.uk

### QUEBEC
Durham

**Hamsteels Hall** ★★★★
*Farmhouse*
Hamsteels Lane, Quebec DH7 9RS
t (01207) 520388
e june@hamsteelshall.co.uk
w hamsteelshall.co.uk

### RAINOW
Cheshire

**Common Barn Farm B&B**
★★★★ *Bed & Breakfast*
Smith Lane, Rainow, Macclesfield SK10 5XJ
t (01625) 574878
e g_greengrass@hotmail.com
w commonbarnfarm.co.uk

**Harrop Fold Farm Bed & Breakfast** ★★★★★
*Farmhouse* **SILVER AWARD**
Macclesfield Road, Rainow SK10 5UU
t (01625) 560085
e stay@harropfoldfarm.co.uk
w harropfoldfarm.co.uk

### RAMSHAW
Northumberland

**The Bridge Inn** ★★★ *Inn*
1 Gordon Lane, Ramshaw DL14 0NS
t (01388) 832509
e thebridgeinnramshaw@hotmail.com
w thebridgeinnramshaw.com

### RASKELF
North Yorkshire

**Old Black Bull Inn** ★★★ *Inn*
Raskelf, Easingwold YO61 3LF
t (01347) 821431
e info@northyorkshotel.co.uk

**The Old Farmhouse** ★★★★
*Bed & Breakfast*
North End, Raskelf, Easingwold YO61 3LF
t (01347) 821491
e oldfarmhouse4bb@aol.com
w theoldfarmhouseraskelfyork.co.uk

## RASTRICK
West Yorkshire

**Elder Lea House** ★★★★★
*Guest Accommodation*
**GOLD AWARD**
Clough Lane, Rastrick, Halifax HD6 3QH
**t** (01484) 717832
**e** elderleahouse@blueyonder.co.uk

## RATHMELL
North Yorkshire

**Littlebank Guest House** ★★★★★ *Guest House*
**SILVER AWARD**
Littlebank Farm, Rathmell, Settle BD24 0AJ
**t** (01729) 822330
**e** richardlord495@hotmail.com
**w** littlebankbandb.co.uk

## RAVENGLASS
Cumbria

**Rosegarth**
Rating Applied For
*Guest House*
Main Street, Ravenglass CA18 1SQ
**t** (01229) 717275
**e** rosegarth1@yahoo.co.uk
**w** rosegarth1.fsnet.co.uk

## RAVENSTONEDALE
Cumbria

**A Corner of Eden** ★★★★
*Guest Accommodation*
**GOLD AWARD**
Low Stennerskeugh, Ravenstonedale, Kirkby Stephen CA17 4LL
**t** (015396) 23370
**e** enquiries@acornerofeden.co.uk
**w** acornerofeden.co.uk

**Coldbeck House** ★★★★★
*Bed & Breakfast*
**GOLD AWARD**
Ravenstonedale, Kirkby Stephen CA17 4LW
**t** (015396) 23407
**e** belle@coldbeckhouse.co.uk
**w** coldbeckhouse.co.uk

## REASEHEATH
Cheshire

**Reaseheath College**
Rating Applied For
*Campus*
Nantwich CW5 6DF
**t** (01270) 625131
**e** enquiries@reaseheath.ac.uk
**w** reaseheath.ac.uk

## REDCAR
Tees Valley

**A 2 Z Guest House** ★
*Guest House*
71 Station Road, Redcar TS10 1RD
**t** (01642) 775533
**e** babsredcar@yahoo.co.uk
**w** a2zguesthouse.co.uk

**All Welcome In** ★★
*Guest Accommodation*
81 Queen Street, Redcar TS10 1BG
**t** (01642) 484790
**e** patredcar2004@yahoo.co.uk
**w** allwelcomein.co.uk

**Armada Guest House** ★★★
*Guest House*
28-30 Henry Street, Redcar TS10 1BJ
**t** (01642) 471710
**e** info@armadaguesthouse.co.uk
**w** armadaguesthouse.co.uk

**The Kastle View** ★★
*Guest House*
55 Newcomen Place, Redcar TS10 1DB
**t** (01642) 489313

**Springdale House** ★★★★
*Bed & Breakfast*
3 Nelson Terrace, Redcar TS10 1RX
**t** (01642) 297169
**e** reservations@springdalehouse.co.uk
**w** springdalehouse.co.uk

**Tudor Lodge**
Rating Applied For
*Guest Accommodation*
7 Turner Street, Redcar TS10 1AY
**t** (01642) 474883

## REDMIRE
North Yorkshire

**The Old Town Hall B & B**
Rating Applied For
*Bed & Breakfast*
Leyburn DL8 4ED
**t** (01969) 625641
**e** enquiries@theoldtownhall.co.uk
**w** theoldtownhall.co.uk

## REETH
North Yorkshire

**Cambridge House** ★★★★
*Guest House* **SILVER AWARD**
Arkengarthdale Road, Reeth DL11 6QX
**t** (01748) 884633
**e** info@cambridgehousereeth.co.uk
**w** cambridgehousereeth.co.uk

**Hackney House** ★★★
*Guest Accommodation*
Reeth DL11 6TW
**t** (01748) 884302
**e** hackneyhse@tinyworld.co.uk

**Ivy Cottage** ★★★
*Guest Accommodation*
The Green, Reeth DL11 6SF
**t** (01748) 884418
**e** ivycottagereeth@supanet.com
**w** ivycottagereeth.co.uk

**Springfield House** ★★★★
*Guest Accommodation*
Quaker Close, Reeth DL11 6UY
**t** (01748) 884634
**e** denise@guy426.fsnet.co.uk

## RIBCHESTER
Lancashire

**Riverside Barn** ★★★★★
*Guest Accommodation*
**SILVER AWARD**
Riverside, Ribchester PR3 3XS
**t** (01254) 878095
**e** relax@riversidebarn.co.uk
**w** riversidebarn.co.uk

## RICCALL
North Yorkshire

**Dairymans of Riccall** ★★★★
*Guest Accommodation*
14 Kelfield Road, Riccall, York YO19 6PG
**t** (01757) 248532
**e** bookings@dairymansriccall.co.uk
**w** dairymansriccall.co.uk

**South Newlands Farm** ★★★
*Guest Accommodation*
Selby Road, Riccall, York YO19 6QR
**t** (01757) 248203
**e** southnewlandsfarm@yahoo.co.uk
**w** southnewlands.co.uk

**White Rose Villa** ★★★★
*Bed & Breakfast*
33 York Road, Riccall, York YO19 6QG
**t** (01757) 248115
**e** whiterosevilla@btinternet.com
**w** whiterosevilla-info.com

## RICHMOND
North Yorkshire

**Beechfield** ★★★★
*Bed & Breakfast*
16 Beechfield Road, Richmond DL10 4PN
**t** (01748) 824060
**e** thelmaj@tiscali.co.uk
**w** beechfieldrichmond.co.uk

**The Buck Inn** ★★★ *Inn*
27-29 Newbiggin, Richmond DL10 4DX
**t** (01748) 822259
**e** info@thebuck-richmond.co.uk
**w** thebuck-richmond.co.uk

**Emmanuel Guest House**
★★★ *Guest Accommodation*
41 Maison Dieu, Richmond DL10 7AU
**t** (01748) 823584
**e** margaretpsimson@msn.com

**Frenchgate Guest House** ★★★★
*Guest Accommodation*
66 Frenchgate, Richmond DL10 7AG
**t** (01748) 823421 & 07889 768696
**e** info@66frenchgate.co.uk

**Mount Pleasant Farm**
★★★★ *Farmhouse*
**SILVER AWARD**
Whashton, Richmond DL11 7JP
**t** (01748) 822784
**e** info@mountpleasantfarmhouse.co.uk
**w** mountpleasantfarmhouse.co.uk

**New Skeeby Grange**
★★★★★ *Bed & Breakfast*
**SILVER AWARD**
Sedbury Lane, Skeeby, Richmond DL10 5ED
**t** (01748) 822276
**e** gandmf@tiscali.co.uk
**w** newskeebygrange.co.uk

**Nuns Cottage** ★★★★
*Guest Accommodation*
5 Hurgill Road, Richmond DL10 4AR
**t** (01748) 822809
**e** the.flints@ukgateway.net
**w** nunscottage.co.uk

**The Old Brewery Guest House** ★★★ *Guest House*
29 The Green, Richmond DL10 4RG
**t** (01748) 822460
**e** info@oldbreweryguesthouse.com
**w** oldbreweryguesthhouse.com

**The Old Dairy** ★★★★
*Guest Accommodation*
Low Row, Reeth DL11 6PE
**t** (01748) 886215
**e** theolddairy@swaledale.org
**w** theolddairy-swaledale.co.uk

**Pottergate Guest House**
★★★ *Guest House*
4 Pottergate, Richmond DL10 4AB
**t** (01748) 823826

**The Restaurant on the Green**
★★★ *Guest Accommodation*
5-7 Bridge Street, Richmond DL10 4RW
**t** (01748) 826229
**e** accom.bennett@talk21.com
**w** coast2coast.co.uk/restaurantonthegreen

**Richmond Camping Barn**
*Camping Barn*
East Applegarth Farm, Westfields, Richmond DL10 4SD
**t** (01748) 822940

**Rosedale Bed & Breakfast**
★★★★ *Guest House*
2 Pottergate, Richmond DL10 4AB
**t** (01748) 823926
**e** gary53uk@hotmail.com
**w** richmondbedandbreakfast.co.uk

**Strawberry House B&B**
★★★★ *Bed & Breakfast*
49 Maison Dieu, Richmond DL10 7AU
**t** (01748) 829741
**e** wfohalloran@yahoo.co.uk

**Victoria House** ★★★★
*Guest Accommodation*
3 Terrace Gardens, Linden Close, Richmond DL10 7AL
**t** (01748) 824830

**West End Guest House** ★★★★
*Guest Accommodation*
45 Reeth Road, Richmond DL10 4EX
**t** (01748) 824783
**e** guesthouse@stayatwestend.com
**w** stayatwestend.com

**Whashton Springs Farm**
★★★★ *Farmhouse*
**SILVER AWARD**
Whashton, Reeth DL11 7JS
**t** (01748) 822884
**e** whashtonsprings@btconnect.com
**w** whashtonsprings.co.uk

**The White House** ★★★★
*Bed & Breakfast*
Gilling Road, Richmond DL10 5AA
**t** (01748) 825491

**Willance House** ★★★★
*Guest House*
24 Frenchgate, Richmond DL10 7AG
**t** (01748) 824467
**e** willancehouse@hotmail.co.uk
**w** willancehouse.com

## RIDING MILL
### Northumberland

**Shepherds Dene Retreat Dene** ★★
*Guest Accommodation*
Riding Mill NE44 6AF
**t** (01434) 682212
**w** shepherdsdene.co.uk

## RIEVAULX
### North Yorkshire

**Barn Close Farm** ★★★★
*Farmhouse*
Old Byland, Helmsley YO62 5LH
**t** (01439) 798321

## RIPLEY
### North Yorkshire

**Slate Rigg Farm** ★★★★
*Farmhouse*
Birthwaite Lane, Ripley HG3 3JQ
**t** (01423) 770135
**e** slateriggfarm@hotmail.com
**w** slate-rigg-farm.co.uk

## RIPON
### North Yorkshire

**Bishopton Grove House**
★★★ *Guest Accommodation*
Bishopton, Ripon HG4 2QL
**t** (01765) 600888

**Box Tree Cottages** ★★★★
*Guest House*
Coltsgate Hill, Ripon HG4 2AB
**t** (01765) 698006
**e** boxtreecottages@gmail.com
**w** boxtreecottages.com

**Crescent Lodge** ★★★★
*Guest Accommodation*
42 North Street, Ripon HG4 1EN
**t** (01765) 609589
**e** simpgry@aol.com
**w** crescent-lodge.com

**Fountain Guest House**
★★★★
*Guest Accommodation*
25 North Road, Ripon HG4 1JP
**t** (01765) 606012
**e** reservations@fountainhouseripon.co.uk
**w** fountainhouseripon.co.uk

**Mallard Grange** ★★★★★
*Farmhouse* **SILVER AWARD**
Aldfield, Fountainsabbey, Ripon HG4 3BE
**t** (01765) 620242
**e** maggie@mallardgrange.co.uk
**w** mallardgrange.co.uk

**The Old Coach House**
★★★★★
*Guest Accommodation*
2 Stable Cottages, North Stainley, Ripon HG4 3HT
**t** (01765) 634900
**e** enquiries@oldcoachhouse.info
**w** oldcoachhouse.info

**Ravencroft B&B** ★★★★
*Bed & Breakfast*
Moorside Avenue, Ripon HG4 1TA
**t** (01765) 602543
**e** guestmail@btopenworld.com
**w** ravencroftbandb.com

**River Side Guest House**
★★★ *Guest Accommodation*
20-21 Iddesleigh Terrace, Ripon HG4 1QW
**t** (01765) 603864
**e** christopher.pearson3@virgin.net

**The Royal Oak** ★★★★ *Inn*
36 Kirkgate, Ripon HG4 1PB
**t** (01765) 602284
**e** info@royaloakripon.co.uk
**w** royaloakripon.co.uk

**Sharow Cross House**
★★★★★ *Guest House*
**GOLD AWARD**
Dishforth Road, Sharow, Ripon HG4 5BQ
**t** (01765) 609866
**e** sharowcrosshouse@btinternet.com
**w** sharowcrosshouse.com

**The White Horse** ★★★ *Inn*
61 North Street, Ripon HG4 1EN
**t** (01765) 603622
**e** david.bate13@btopenworld.com
**w** white-horse-ripon.co.uk

## RIPPONDEN
### West Yorkshire

**Over The Bridge** ★★★★
*Bed & Breakfast*
**SILVER AWARD**
Bridge End, Ripponden, Halifax HX6 4DF
**t** (01422) 820226
**e** enquiries@over-the-bridge.co.uk
**w** over-the-bridge.co.uk

**Thurst House Farm** ★★★★
*Guest Accommodation*
Ripponden, Sowerby Bridge, Halifax HX6 4NN
**t** (01422) 822820
**e** thursthousefarm@bushinternet.com

## RISEBOROUGH
### North Yorkshire

**Cliff Farm** *Camping Barn*
Cliff Farm Holidays, Camping Barn, Kirkbymoorside YO62 6SS
**t** (01751) 473792
**e** jean.scaling@btinternet.com
**w** clifffarmholidays.com

## ROBIN HOOD'S BAY
### North Yorkshire

**Lee-Side** ★★★★
*Guest Accommodation*
**SILVER AWARD**
Mount Pleasant South, Robin Hood's Bay, Whitby YO22 4RQ
**t** (01947) 881143
**e** lee-side@rhbay.co.uk
**w** lee-side.rhbay.co.uk

## ROCHDALE
### Greater Manchester

**Fernhill Barn B & B** ★★★★
*Guest Accommodation*
Fernhill Lane, Lanehead, Rochdale OL12 6BW
**t** (01706) 355671
**e** info@fernhillbarn.com
**w** fernhillbarn.com

**Moss Lodge** ★★★★★
*Guest Accommodation*
**SILVER AWARD**
Kings Road, Rochdale OL16 5HW
**t** (01706) 350555
**e** info@mosslodgehotel.com
**w** mosslodgehotel.com

## ROMALDKIRK
### Durham

**Hollin Croft** ★★★★
*Bed & Breakfast*
**SILVER AWARD**
Romaldkirk DL12 9EL
**t** (01833) 650192
**e** enquiries@hollincroft.co.uk
**w** hollincroft.co.uk

**Mill Riggs Cottage** ★★★
*Bed & Breakfast*
Romaldkirk, Barnard Castle DL12 9EW
**t** (01833) 650392

## ROMANBY
### North Yorkshire

**Bridge End** ★★★
*Bed & Breakfast*
159 Chantry Road, Northallerton DL7 8JJ
**t** (01609) 772655

## ROSEDALE ABBEY
### North Yorkshire

**Sevenford House** ★★★★
*Bed & Breakfast*
**SILVER AWARD**
Rosedale Abbey, Pickering YO18 8SE
**t** (01751) 417283
**e** sevenford@aol.com
**w** sevenford.com

## ROSEDALE EAST
### North Yorkshire

**Ann's Cottage** ★★★★
*Bed & Breakfast*
**SILVER AWARD**
Hill Yard Cottage, Rosedale East, Pickering YO18 8RH
**t** (01751) 417646
**e** ann@annscottagerosedale.co.uk
**w** annscottagerosedale.co.uk

## ROSSENDALE
### Lancashire

**Glen Valley Guesthouse** ★★
*Guest House*
634 Bacup Road, Waterfoot BB4 7AW
**t** (01706) 222637
**e** glenvalleyhouse@aol.com
**w** glenvalleyguesthouse.co.uk

**Horncliffe Mount Farm B&B**
★★★★ *Bed & Breakfast*
Lomas Lane, Rawtenstall BB4 6HU
**t** (01706) 220227
**e** info@horncliffemountfarm.co.uk
**w** horncliffemountfarm.co.uk

**Middle Carr Farm** ★★★★
*Bed & Breakfast*
**SILVER AWARD**
Off Hall Carr Road, Rossendale BB4 6BS
**t** (01706) 225353
**e** info@middlecarrfarm.co.uk
**w** middlecarrfarm.co.uk

**No 678** ★★★★ *Guest House*
Burnley Road East, Whitewell Bottom BB4 9NT
**t** (01706) 215884
**e** info@no678.co.uk
**w** no678.co.uk

**One 3 One**
Rating Applied For
*Guest Accommodation*
Haslingden Old Road, Rossendale BB4 8RR
**t** (01772) 536600
**w** one3one.co.uk

**Peers Clough Farm** ★★★
*Guest Accommodation*
Peers Clough Road, Lumb BB4 9NG
**t** (01706) 210552
**e** peerscloughfarm@hotmail.com
**w** peerscloughfarm.co.uk

## ROTHBURY
### Northumberland

**The Chirnells** ★★★★
*Farmhouse*
Thropton NE65 7JE
**t** (01669) 621507
**e** thechirnells@aol.com

**Farm Cottage Guest House**
★★★★★ *Guest House*
**GOLD AWARD**
Thropton NE65 7NA
**t** (01669) 620831
**e** joan@farmcottageguesthouse.co.uk
**w** farmcottageguesthouse.co.uk

**The Haven** ★★★★
*Guest Accommodation*
Back Crofts, Rothbury NE65 7YA
**t** (01669) 620577
**e** the.haven.rothbury@talk21.com
**w** thehavenrothbury.co.uk

**Katerina's Guest House**
★★★★ *Guest House*
**SILVER AWARD**
Sun Buildings, Rothbury
NE65 7TQ
**t** (01669) 620691
**e** cath@katerinasguesthouse.co.uk
**w** katerinasguesthouse.co.uk

**Lorbottle West Steads**
★★★★ *Farmhouse*
Thropton NE65 7JT
**t** (01665) 574672
**e** info@lorbottle.com
**w** lorbottle.com

**The Queens Head** ★★★ *Inn*
Townfoot NE65 7SR
**t** (01669) 620470
**e** enqs@queensheadrothbury.com
**w** queensheadrothbury.com

**Silverton House** ★★★★
*Bed & Breakfast*
**SILVER AWARD**
Silverton Lane, Rothbury
NE65 7RJ
**t** (01669) 621395
**e** maggie@silvertonhouse.wanadoo.co.uk
**w** silvertonhouse.co.uk

**Springfield House** ★★★★
*Guest House*
Townfoot NE65 7SP
**t** (01669) 621277
**e** enquiries@springfieldguesthouse.co.uk
**w** springfieldguesthouse.co.uk

**Tosson Tower Farm B&B**
★★★★★ *Farmhouse*
**GOLD AWARD**
Great Tosson, Rothbury
NE65 7NW
**t** (01669) 620228
**e** stay@tossontowerfarm.com
**w** tossontowerfarm.com

**Wagtail Farm** ★★★★
*Farmhouse*
Rothbury NE65 7PL
**t** (01669) 620367
**e** wagtail@tinyworld.co.uk
**w** wagtailfarm.info

### ROTHERHAM
### South Yorkshire

**Fitzwilliam Arms** ★★★
*Guest Accommodation*
Taylors Lane, Parkgate,
Rotherham S62 6EE
**t** (01709) 522744
**w** fitzwilliam-arms-hotel.co.uk

### ROUGHLEE
### Lancashire

**Dam Head Barn** ★★★★
*Guest Accommodation*
Dam Head Farm, Nelson
BB9 6MX
**t** (01282) 617190
**e** sagarbarn@btinternet.com

### ROWELTOWN
### Cumbria

**Low Luckens Organic Resource Centre** ★★★
*Hostel*
Low Luckens, Roweltown,
Carlisle CA6 6LJ
**t** (01697) 748186
**e** lowluckensorc@hotmail.com
**w** lowluckensfarm.co.uk

### RUNSWICK BAY
### North Yorkshire

**Ellerby** ★★★★ *Inn*
**SILVER AWARD**
Ryeland Lane, Ellerby,
Saltburn-by-the-Sea TS13 5LP
**t** (01947) 840342
**e** david@ellerbyhotel.co.uk
**w** ellerbyhotel.co.uk

**The Firs** ★★★★ *Guest House*
26 Hinderwell Lane, Runswick
Bay, Nr Whitby TS13 5HR
**t** (01947) 840433
**e** mandy.shackleton@talk21.com
**w** the-firs.co.uk

**The Runswick Bay** ★★★ *Inn*
Hinderwell Lane, Runswick
Bay, Saltburn-by-the-Sea
TS13 5HR
**t** (01947) 841010
**e** therunswickbayhotel@btopenworld.com
**w** therunswickbayhotel.co.uk

### RUSHYFORD
### Durham

**Garden House** ★★★★
*Bed & Breakfast*
Windlestone Park,
Windlestone DL17 0LZ
**t** (01388) 720217
**e** info@gardenhousedurham.co.uk
**w** gardenhousedurham.co.uk

### RUSWARP
### North Yorkshire

**Esk View Cottage** ★★★★
*Bed & Breakfast*
The Carrs, Ruswarp, Whitby
YO21 1RL
**t** (01947) 605658
**e** enquiries@eskviewcottage.co.uk
**w** eskviewcottage.com

**Ruswarp Hall** ★★★
*Guest Accommodation*
4-6 High Street, Ruswarp,
Whitby YO21 1NH
**t** (01947) 602801
**e** colinscarth@aol.com
**w** ruswarphallhotel.co.uk

### RYDAL
### Cumbria

**Cote How Organic Guest House** ★★★★ *Guest House*
Rydal, Ambleside LA22 9LW
**t** (015394) 32765
**e** info@cotehow.co.uk
**w** bedbreakfastlakedistrict.com

**Nab Cottage** ★★★
*Guest House*
Rydal, Grasmere, Ambleside
LA22 9SD
**t** (015394) 35311
**e** tim@nabcottage.com
**w** rydalwater.com

### RYTON
### Tyne and Wear

**A1 Hedgefield House** ★★★
*Guest Accommodation*
Stella Road, Blaydon-on-Tyne
NE21 4LR
**t** (0191) 413 7373
**e** david@hedgefieldhouse.co.uk
**w** hedgefieldhouse.co.uk

### SABDEN
### Lancashire

**Cobden Farm Bed and Breakfast** ★★★★ *Farmhouse*
Off Whalley Road, Sabden
BB7 9ED
**t** (01282) 776285
**e** enquiries@cobdenfarm.co.uk
**w** cobdenfarm.co.uk

**The Shippon at Wiswell Moor Farm** ★★★★
*Bed & Breakfast*
1 The Barn, Clerk Hill Road,
Clitheroe BB7 9FR
**t** (01254) 822389

### ST BEES
### Cumbria

**Fleatham House** ★★★★★
*Guest Accommodation*
High House Road, St Bees
CA27 0BX
**t** (01946) 822341
**e** fleathamhouse@aol.com
**w** fleathamhouse.com

**Stonehouse Farm** ★★★★
*Farmhouse*
133 Main Street, St Bees
CA27 0DE
**t** (01946) 822224
**e** csmith.stonehouse@btopenworld.com
**w** stonehousefarm.net

### ST JOHNS-IN-THE-VALE
### Cumbria

**St John's in the Vale**
*Camping Barn*
Low Bridge End Farm, St Johns-in-the-Vale, Keswick CA12 4TS
**t** (01946) 758198
**e** info@campingbarn.com
**w** campingbarn.com

### SALE
### Greater Manchester

**The Belforte House** ★★★
*Guest Accommodation*
7-9 Broad Road, Sale M33 2AE
**t** (0161) 973 8779
**e** belfortehotel@aol.com
**w** belfortehousehotel.co.uk

### SALTBURN-BY-THE-SEA
### Tees Valley

**The Arches** ★★★★
*Guest House*
Low Farm, Ings Lane, Brotton,
Saltburn-by-the-Sea TS12 2QX
**t** (01287) 677512
**e** hotel@gorallyschool.co.uk
**w** thearcheshotel.co.uk

**Diamond Guest House**
★★★★ *Guest House*
9 Diamond Street, Saltburn-by-the-Sea TS12 1EB
**t** (01287) 207049
**e** diamondhouse9@ntlworld.com
**w** diamondguesthouse.co.uk

**The Rose Garden** ★★★★
*Bed & Breakfast*
20 Hilda Place, Saltburn-by-the-Sea TS12 1BP
**t** (01287) 622947
**e** enquiries@therosegarden.co.uk
**w** therosegarden.co.uk

**Sea Holly Guest House**
Rating Applied For
*Bed & Breakfast*
17 Pearl Street, Saltburn-by-the-Sea TS12 1DU
**t** (01287) 207284
**e** info@seahollyguesthouse.co.uk
**w** seahollyguesthouse.co.uk

**Victorian Guest House**
★★★★ *Bed & Breakfast*
1 Oxford Street, Saltburn-by-the-Sea TS12 1LG
**t** (01287) 625237
**e** sueandstew@saltburn-accommodation.co.uk
**w** saltburn-accommodation.co.uk

### SALTNEY
### Cheshire

**Garden Gate Guest House**
★★ *Guest Accommodation*
8 Chester Street, Saltney
CH4 8BJ
**t** (01244) 682306
**e** dollywal@msn.com

### SANDBACH
### Cheshire

**Bagmere Bank Farm Luxury Bed and Breakfast** ★★★★
*Bed & Breakfast*
**SILVER AWARD**
Brereton Park, Brereton
CW11 1RX
**t** (01477) 537503

### SANDSIDE
### Cumbria

**Plantation Cottage** ★★★★
*Bed & Breakfast*
Arnside Road, Sandside,
Milnthorpe LA7 7JU
**t** (01524) 762069

### SANDWITH
### Cumbria

**Tarn Flatt Barn** *Camping Barn*
Sandwith, Whitehaven, St Bees
CA28 9UX
**t** (01946) 758198
**e** stay@tarnflattfarm.co.uk
**w** lakelandcampingbarns.co.uk

### SAWDON
### North Yorkshire

**Foxholm** ★★★★
*Bed & Breakfast*
Foxholm, Main Street, Sawdon,
Scarborough YO13 9DY
**t** (01723) 859743
**e** info@foxholmsawdon.co.uk
**w** foxholmsawdon.co.uk

### SAWREY
### Cumbria

**Beechmount Country House**
★★★★★ *Bed & Breakfast*
**SILVER AWARD**
Sawrey, Hawkshead LA22 0JZ
**t** (015394) 36356
**e** beechmount@btinternet.com
**w** beechmountcountryhouse.co.uk

**Buckle Yeat Guest House**
★★★★ *Guest House*
Nr Sawrey, Ambleside
LA22 0LF
**t** (015394) 36446
**e** info@buckle-yeat.co.uk
**w** buckle-yeat.co.uk

**West Vale Country House & Restaurant** ★★★★★
*Guest Accommodation*
**GOLD AWARD**
Far Sawrey, Hawkshead
LA22 0LQ
**t** (015394) 42817
**e** enquiries@westvalecountryhouse.co.uk
**w** westvalecountryhouse.co.uk

## SCALBY
North Yorkshire

**Scalby Hayes B&B** ★★★★
*Bed & Breakfast*
**SILVER AWARD**
1 Scalby Hayes, Barmoor Lane, Scarborough YO13 0PG
**t** (01723) 362588
**e** ktulley@scalby.plus.com
**w** scalbyhayes.co.uk

## SCARBOROUGH
North Yorkshire

**Aartswood Guest House** ★★
*Guest House*
27-29 Trafalgar Square, Scarborough YO12 7PZ
**t** (01723) 360689
**e** william@aartswood.wanadoo.co.uk
**w** yorkshirecoast.co.uk/aartswood

**The Acacia** ★★★
*Guest House*
37 Esplanade Road, Scarborough YO11 2AT
**t** (01723) 373270
**e** acaciahotel@live.co.uk
**w** acaciahotel.co.uk

**Adene** ★★★
*Guest Accommodation*
39 Esplanade Road, Scarborough YO11 2AT
**t** (01723) 373658
**e** harvey@adenehotel.fsnet.co.uk

**The Admiral** ★★★
*Guest Accommodation*
13 West Square, Scarborough YO11 1TW
**t** (01723) 375084
**e** sandy.theadmiral@btinternet.com
**w** theadmiralhotel.co.uk

**The Ainsley** ★★★
*Guest Accommodation*
4 Rutland Terrace, Queens Parade, Scarborough YO12 7JB
**t** (01723) 364832
**e** info@theainsleyhotel.co.uk
**w** theainsleyhotel.co.uk

**Ainsley Court Guest House**
★★★★ *Guest House*
112 North Marine Road, Scarborough YO12 7JA
**t** (01723) 500352
**e** lynn@ainsleycourt.co.uk
**w** ainsleycourt.co.uk

**The Alexander** ★★★★
*Guest Accommodation*
**SILVER AWARD**
33 Burniston Road, Scarborough YO12 6PG
**t** (01723) 363178
**e** enquiries@alexanderhotelscarborough.co.uk
**w** alexanderhotelscarborough.co.uk

**Alexandra House** ★★★★
*Guest House*
21 West Street, Scarborough YO11 2QR
**t** (01723) 503205
**e** info@scarborough-alexandra.co.uk
**w** scarborough-alexandra.co.uk

**The Almar** ★★★
*Guest Accommodation*
116 Columbus Ravine, Scarborough YO12 7QZ
**t** (01723) 372887
**e** bevandphill@rendellp.fsnet.co.uk
**w** thealmar.co.uk

**Amrock Guest House** ★★★
*Guest House*
11 Victoria Park Avenue, Scarborough YO12 7TR
**t** (01723) 374423
**e** info@amrock.co.uk
**w** amrock.co.uk

**Ashburton** ★★★★
*Guest Accommodation*
43 Valley Road, Scarborough YO11 2LX
**t** (01723) 374382
**e** stay@ashburtonhotel.co.uk
**w** ashburtonhotel.co.uk

**Atlanta** ★★★★
*Guest Accommodation*
60-62 Columbus Ravine, Scarborough YO12 7QU
**t** (01723) 360996
**e** info@atlanta-hotel.co.uk
**w** atlanta-hotel.co.uk

**Blands Cliff Lodge** ★★★
*Guest Accommodation*
Blands Cliff, Scarborough YO11 1NR
**t** (01723) 363653 & (01723) 363653
**e** tonight@yorkshire-coast.co.uk

**Brambles Lodge** ★★★
*Guest Accommodation*
156-158 Filey Road, Scarborough YO11 3AA
**t** (01723) 374613
**e** nightingales22@aol.com
**w** accommodation.uk.net/brambleslodge.htm

**Brontes Guest House** ★★★
*Guest House*
135 Columbus Ravine, Scarborough YO12 7QZ
**t** (01723) 362934
**e** ericwatson@talktalk.net
**w** brontesguesthouse.co.uk

**The Castle by the Sea**
★★★★ *Guest House*
Mulgrave Place, Scarborough YO11 1HZ
**t** (01723) 365166
**e** john.cresswell@btconnect.com
**w** thecastlebythesea.co.uk

**Catania** ★★★★ *Guest House*
141 Queens Parade, Scarborough YO12 7HU
**t** (01723) 364516
**e** catania@yorkshire.net
**w** hotelcatania.co.uk

**The Cavendish** ★★★★
*Guest Accommodation*
53 Esplanade Road, Scarborough YO11 2AT
**t** (01723) 362108
**e** anne@cavendishscarborough.co.uk
**w** cavendishscarborough.co.uk

**The Clarence Gardens** ★★★
*Guest Accommodation*
Blenheim Terrace, Scarborough YO12 7HF
**t** (01723) 374884
**e** enquiries@clarencegardens.force9.co.uk
**w** clarencegardenshotel.net

**Cliffside** ★★★ *Guest House*
79-81 Queens Parade, Scarborough YO12 7HH
**t** (01723) 361087
**e** cliffside@fsmail.net
**w** yorkshirecoast.co.uk/cliffside

**The Cordelia** ★★★★
*Guest Accommodation*
51 Esplanade Road, Scarborough YO11 2AT
**t** (01723) 363393
**e** melanie.watson@btconnect.com

**The Croft** ★★★
*Guest Accommodation*
87 Queens Parade, Scarborough YO12 7HY
**t** (01723) 373904
**e** information@crofthotel.co.uk
**w** crofthotel.co.uk

**Derwent House** ★★★
*Guest House*
6 Rutland Terrace, Queens Parade, Scarborough YO12 7JB
**t** (01723) 373880
**e** info@derwenthousehotel.co.uk
**w** derwenthousehotel.co.uk

**Dolphin Guest House** ★★★
*Guest House*
151 Columbus Ravine, Scarborough YO12 7QZ
**t** (01723) 341914
**e** dolphinguesthouse@btinternet.com
**w** thedolphin.info

**Donnington House** ★★★
*Guest House*
13 Givendale Road, Scarborough YO12 6LE
**t** (01723) 374394
**e** bookings@donningtonhotel.co.uk
**w** donningtonhotel.co.uk

**Douglas Guest House** ★★★
*Guest House*
153 Columbus Ravine, Scarborough YO12 7QZ
**t** (01723) 371311
**e** stay@douglasguesthouse.co.uk

**The Ellenby** ★★★★
*Guest House*
95-97 Queens Parade, Scarborough YO12 7HY
**t** (01723) 372916
**e** johnfail@aol.com
**w** theellenby.co.uk

**The Empire** ★★★
*Guest House*
39 Albemarle Crescent, Scarborough YO11 1XX
**t** (01723) 373564
**e** gillian@empire1939.wanadoo.co.uk

**Esplanade Gardens Guest House** ★★★
*Guest Accommodation*
24 Esplanade Gardens, Scarborough YO11 2AP
**t** (01723) 360728
**e** kerry@khubbard.fsnet.co.uk
**w** esplanadegardens scarborough.co.uk

**The Gordon** ★★★★
*Guest House*
Ryndleside, Scarborough YO12 6AD
**t** (01723) 362177
**e** sales@gordonhotel.co.uk
**w** gordonhotel.co.uk

**Green Gables** ★★★
*Guest House*
West Bank, Scarborough YO12 4DX
**t** (01723) 361005

**Greno Seafront Guest House**
★★★★ *Guest House*
25 Blenheim Terrace, Queens Parade, Scarborough YO12 7HD
**t** (01723) 375705

**Harmony Country Lodge**
★★★★ *Guest House*
80 Limestone Road, Burniston, Scarborough YO13 0DG
**t** 0800 298 5840
**e** tony@harmonylodge.net
**w** harmonycountrylodge.co.uk

**The Headlands** ★★★
*Guest House*
16 Weydale Avenue, Scarborough YO12 6AX
**t** (01723) 373717
**e** info@theheadlandshotel.co.uk
**w** theheadlandshotel.co.uk

**The Helaina** ★★★★
*Guest Accommodation*
**SILVER AWARD**
14 Blenheim Terrace, Scarborough YO12 7HF
**t** (01723) 375191
**e** info@hotelhelaina.co.uk

**Howdale** ★★★★
*Guest House*
121 Queen's Parade, Scarborough YO12 7HU
**t** (01723) 372696
**e** mail@howdalehotel.co.uk
**w** howdalehotel.co.uk

**Jadellas** ★★★ *Guest House*
72 Columbus Ravine,
Scarborough YO12 7QU
**t** (01723) 378811
**e** john@johnhowe.wanadoo.co.uk
**w** jadellashotelscarborough.co.uk

**The Kensington** ★★★★
*Guest House*
66 Columbus Ravine,
Scarborough YO12 7QU
**t** (01723) 368117
**e** info@kensingtonguesthouse.co.uk
**w** kensingtonguesthouse.co.uk

**Kenways Guest House** ★★★
*Guest House*
9 Victoria Park Avenue,
Scarborough YO12 7TR
**t** (01723) 365757
**e** info@kenwaysguesthouse.co.uk
**w** kenwaysguesthouse.co.uk

**Killerby Cottage Farm**
★★★★ *Bed & Breakfast*
**SILVER AWARD**
Killerby Lane, Cayton,
Scarborough YO11 3TP
**t** (01723) 581236
**e** val@stainedglasscentre.co.uk
**w** smoothhound.co.uk/hotels/killerby

**The Kimberley** ★★★★
*Guest House*
131 Queens Parade,
Scarborough YO12 7HY
**t** (01723) 372734
**e** kimberleyhotel@hotmail.com
**w** kimberleyseafronthotel.co.uk

**The Kingsway** ★★★★
*Guest House*
58 Columbus Ravine,
Scarborough YO12 7QU
**t** (01723) 372948
**e** info@kingswayhotelscarborough.co.uk
**w** kingswayhotelscarborough.co.uk

**Levante** ★★★ *Guest House*
118 Columbus Ravine,
Scarborough YO12 7QZ
**t** (01723) 372366

**The Lincoln** ★★★
*Guest House*
112 Columbus Ravine,
Scarborough YO12 7QZ
**t** (01723) 500897
**e** enquiries@lincolnhotel.net
**w** lincolnhotel.net

**Lonsdale Villa** ★★★★
*Guest Accommodation*
Lonsdale Road, Scarborough
YO11 2QY
**t** (01723) 363383
**e** enquiries@lonsdalevilla.com
**w** lonsdalevilla.com

**Lyncris Manor** ★★★★
*Guest Accommodation*
45 Northstead Manor Drive,
Scarborough YO12 6AF
**t** (01723) 361052
**e** lyncris@manorhotel.fsnet.co.uk
**w** manorhotel.fsnet.co.uk

**Lyness Guest House** ★★★
*Guest House*
145 Columbus Ravine,
Scarborough YO12 7QZ
**t** (01723) 375952
**e** info@lynessguesthousescarborough.co.uk
**w** lynessguesthousescarborough.co.uk

**The Lynton** ★★★
*Guest House*
104 Columbus Ravine,
Scarborough YO12 7QZ
**t** (01723) 374240
**e** paul.watson6@btconnect.com
**w** thelyntonscarborough.co.uk

**The Lysander** ★★★★
*Guest House*
22 Weydale Avenue,
Scarborough YO12 6AX
**t** (01723) 373369
**e** info@lysanderhotel.co.uk
**w** lysanderhotel.co.uk

**Marine View Guest House**
★★★ *Guest House*
34 Blenheim Terrace,
Scarborough YO12 7HD
**t** (01723) 361864
**e** info@marineview.co.uk
**w** marineview.co.uk

**Maynard** ★★★ *Guest House*
16 Esplanade Gardens,
Scarborough YO11 2AW
**t** (01723) 372289
**e** info@maynardhotel.co.uk
**w** maynardhotel.co.uk

**Moseley Lodge** ★★★★
*Guest House*
26 Avenue Victoria, South Cliff,
Scarborough YO11 2QT
**t** (01723) 360564
**e** holidays@moseleylodge.co.uk
**w** moseleylodge.co.uk

**The Mount House** ★★★★
*Guest Accommodation*
33 Trinity Road, South Cliff,
Scarborough YO11 2TD
**t** (01723) 362967
**e** bookings@mounthouse-hotel.co.uk
**w** mounthouse-hotel.co.uk

**The Mountview** ★★★★
*Guest House*
32 West Street, Scarborough
YO11 2QP
**t** (01723) 500608
**e** info@mountview-hotel.co.uk
**w** mountview-hotel.co.uk

**The Newlands** ★★★
*Guest House*
80 Columbus Ravine,
Scarborough YO12 7QU
**t** (01723) 367261
**e** newlandshotel@btconnect.com
**w** thenewlandshotel.co.uk

**The Norlands** ★★★★
*Guest Accommodation*
10 Weydale Avenue,
Scarborough YO12 6BA
**t** (01723) 362606
**e** info@norlandshotel.co.uk
**w** norlandshotel.co.uk

**Parmelia** ★★★
*Guest Accommodation*
17 West Street, Scarborough
YO11 2QN
**t** (01723) 361914
**e** parmelia.hotel@btconnect.com
**w** parmeliahotel.co.uk

**The Philmore** ★★★★
*Guest House*
126 Columbus Ravine,
Scarborough YO12 7QZ
**t** (01723) 361516
**e** info@philmorehotel.co.uk
**w** philmorehotel.co.uk

**Phoenix Court** ★★★★
*Guest House*
8-9 Rutland Terrace, Queens
Parade, Scarborough YO12 7JB
**t** (01723) 501150
**e** info@hotel-phoenix.co.uk
**w** hotel-phoenix.co.uk

**The Phoenix Guest House**
★★★ *Guest House*
157 Columbus Ravine,
Scarborough YO12 7QZ
**t** (01723) 368319

**Powys Lodge Guest House**
★★★★ *Guest House*
2 Westbourne Road, South
Cliff, Scarborough YO11 2SP
**t** (01723) 374019
**e** info@powyslodge.co.uk
**w** powyslodge.co.uk

**Princess Court Guest House**
★★★★
*Guest Accommodation*
11 Princess Royal Terrace,
Scarborough YO11 2RP
**t** (01723) 501922
**e** irvin@princesscourt.co.uk
**w** princesscourt.co.uk

**Raincliffe**
Rating Applied For
*Guest House*
21 Valley Road, Scarborough
YO11 2LY
**t** (01723) 373541
**e** enquiries@raincliffehotel.co.uk
**w** raincliffehotel.co.uk

**The Redcliffe** ★★★★
*Guest Accommodation*
18 Prince of Wales Terrace,
South Bay, Scarborough
YO11 2AL
**t** (01723) 372310
**e** b.m.bean@daisybroadband.co.uk
**w** theredcliffehotel.com

**Riviera Town House** ★★★★
*Guest Accommodation*
**SILVER AWARD**
St Nicholas Cliff, Scarborough
YO11 2ES
**t** (01723) 372277
**e** info@riviera-scarborough.co.uk
**w** riviera-scarborough.co.uk

**Robyn's Guest House** ★★★
*Guest House*
139 Columbus Ravine,
Scarborough YO12 7QZ
**t** (01723) 374217
**e** info@robynsguesthouse.co.uk
**w** robynsguesthouse.co.uk

**Rose Dene** ★★★
*Guest Accommodation*
106 Columbus Ravine,
Scarborough YO12 7QZ
**t** (01723) 374252
**e** sandra@rose-denehotel.co.uk
**w** rosedenehotel.co.uk

**Sawdon Heights** ★★★★
*Farmhouse* **SILVER AWARD**
Scarborough YO13 9EB
**t** (01723) 859321
**e** info@sawdonheights.com
**w** sawdonheights.com

**The Scarborough Travel and Holiday Lodge** ★★★
*Guest Accommodation*
33 Valley Road, Scarborough
YO11 2LX
**t** (01723) 363537
**e** enquiries@scarborough-lodge.co.uk
**w** scarborough-lodge.co.uk

**Scarborough YHA** ★★★
*Hostel*
The White House, Burniston
Road, Scarborough YO13 0DA
**t** 0870 770 6022
**e** scarborough@yha.org.uk
**w** yha.org.uk

**Selomar** ★★★★
*Guest House*
23 Blenheim Terrace,
Scarborough YO12 7HD
**t** (01723) 364964
**e** info@selomarhotel.co.uk
**w** selomarhotel.co.uk

**The Sheridan** ★★★
*Guest Accommodation*
108 Columbus Ravine,
Scarborough YO12 7QZ
**t** (01723) 372094
**e** kimarfhoteljp@aol.com
**w** thesheridanhotel.co.uk

**Smugglers Rock Country House** ★★★★
*Guest Accommodation*
Staintondale Road, Ravenscar,
Scarborough YO13 0ER
**t** (01723) 870044
**e** info@smugglersrock.co.uk
**w** smugglersrock.co.uk

**The Stuart House** ★★★★
*Guest House*
1 & 2 Rutland Terrace, Queens
Parade, Scarborough YO12 7JB
**t** (01723) 373768
**e** h.graham@btconnect.com
**w** thestuarthousehotel.com

**Sunningdale** ★★★★
*Guest House*
105 Peasholm Drive,
Scarborough YO12 7NB
**t** (01723) 372041
**e** sunningdale@yorkshire.net
**w** sunningdale-scarborough.co.uk

**Sylvern House** ★★★★
*Guest House*
25 New Queen Street,
Scarborough YO12 7HJ
**t** (01723) 360952
**e** sylvernhotel@aol.com
**w** smoothhound.co.uk/hotels/sylvern

**Tall Storeys** ★★★★
*Guest Accommodation*
**SILVER AWARD**
Old Town, 131 Longwestgate, Scarborough YO11 1RQ
**t** (01723) 373696
**e** gordon@gordonking.demon.co.uk
**w** tallstoreyshotel.co.uk

**The Terrace** ★★ *Guest House*
69 Westborough, Scarborough YO11 1TS
**t** (01723) 374937
**e** theterracehotel@btinternet.com
**w** smoothhound.co.uk/a13751

**The Thoresby** ★★★
*Guest House*
53 North Marine Road, Scarborough YO12 7EY
**t** (01723) 365715

**Toulson Court** ★★★★
*Guest Accommodation*
100 Columbus Ravine, Scarborough YO12 7QZ
**t** (01723) 503218
**e** toulsoncourt@scarborough.co.uk
**w** toulsoncourt.scarborough.co.uk

**Victoria Seaview** ★★★★
*Guest Accommodation*
125 Queens Parade, Scarborough YO12 7HY
**t** (01723) 362164
**e** info@victoriaseaviewhotel.co.uk
**w** victoriaseaviewhotel.co.uk

**Villa Marina** ★★★★
*Guest House*
59 Northstead Manor Drive, Scarborough YO12 6AF
**t** (01723) 361088

**West Lodge** ★★ *Guest House*
38 West Street, Scarborough YO11 2QP
**t** (01723) 500754

**The Wharncliffe** ★★★★
*Guest Accommodation*
26 Blenheim Terrace, Scarborough YO12 7HD
**t** (01723) 374635
**e** info@thewharncliffescarborough.co.uk
**w** thewharncliffescarborough.co.uk

**White Rails** ★★★★
*Guest House*
128 Columbus Ravine, Scarborough YO12 7QZ
**t** (01723) 362800
**e** info@whiterailshotel.co.uk
**w** whiterailshotel.co.uk

**The Whiteley** ★★★★
*Guest Accommodation*
99-101 Queens Parade, Scarborough YO12 7HY
**t** (01723) 373514
**e** whiteleyhotel@bigfoot.com
**w** yorkshire-coast.co.uk/whiteley

**Willow Dene** ★★★
*Guest House*
110 Columbus Ravine, Scarborough YO12 7QZ
**t** (01723) 365173
**e** andy@willowdenehotel.com
**w** willowdenehotel.com

## SCORTON
Lancashire

**The Priory Inn, Scorton**
★★★ *Guest Accommodation*
The Square, Scorton PR3 1AU
**t** (01524) 791255
**e** collinsonjulie@aol.com
**w** theprioryscorton.co.uk

## SCOTBY
Cumbria

**Willowbeck Lodge** ★★★★★
*Guest Accommodation*
**GOLD AWARD**
Lambley Bank, Scotby, Carlisle CA4 8BX
**t** (01228) 513607
**e** info@willowbeck-lodge.com
**w** willowbeck-lodge.com

## SCREMERSTON
Northumberland

**Northumbrian Wigwam Village** *Camping Barn*
Borewell Farm, Scremerston TD15 2RJ
**t** (01289) 307107
**e** info@northumbrianwigwams.com
**w** northumbrianwigwams.com

## SEAHOUSES
Northumberland

**Fairfield** ★★★
*Bed & Breakfast*
102 Main Street, Seahouses NE68 7TP
**t** (01665) 721736
**e** jen2col@fairfield1.fsnet.co.uk

**Gun Rock** ★★★
*Bed & Breakfast*
15 St Aidans, Seahouses NE68 7SS
**t** (01665) 721980
**e** judy.oxley@unn.ac.uk

**Holly Trees**
Rating Applied For
*Bed & Breakfast*
4 James Street, Seahouses NE68 7YB
**t** (01665) 721942
**e** margaret.tucker4@btinternet.com

**Leeholme** ★★★
*Bed & Breakfast*
93 Main Street, Seahouses NE68 7TS
**t** (01665) 720230
**e** lisaevans67@tiscali.co.uk

**Railston House** ★★★★
*Guest Accommodation*
**SILVER AWARD**
133 Main Street,, North Sunderland NE68 7TS
**t** (01665) 720912
**e** twgrundy@btinternet.com
**w** railstonhouse.com

**Rowena** ★★★
*Guest Accommodation*
99 Main Street, North Sunderland NE68 7TS
**t** (01665) 721309

**Spindrift** ★★★★
*Bed & Breakfast*
Kings Field, Seahouses NE68 7PA
**t** (01665) 721677
**e** suewilkinson321@msn.com
**w** spindrift-seahouses.co.uk

**Springwood** ★★★★
*Bed & Breakfast*
**SILVER AWARD**
South Lane, North Sunderland NE68 7UL
**t** (01665) 720320
**e** marian@slatehall.freeserve.co.uk
**w** slatehallridingcentre.com

## SEATOLLER
Cumbria

**Honister Hause YHA** ★★
*Hostel*
Seatoller, Keswick CA12 5XN
**t** (017687) 77267

## SEATON CAREW
Tees Valley

**Altonlea Lodge Guest House**
★★★★ *Guest House*
The Green, Seaton Carew TS25 1AT
**t** (01429) 271289
**e** enquiries@altonlea.co.uk
**w** altonlea.co.uk

**The Norton** ★★★
*Guest House*
1a The Green, Seaton Carew TS25 1AR
**t** (01429) 268317
**e** sue@thenortonhotel.com
**w** thenortonhotel.com

## SEDBERGH
Cumbria

**Dalesman Country Inn**
★★★★ *Inn*
Main Street, Sedbergh LA10 5BN
**t** (015396) 21183
**e** info@thedalesman.co.uk
**w** thedalesman.co.uk

**High Roans** ★★★★
*Bed & Breakfast*
Guldrey Lane, Sedbergh LA10 5DS
**t** (015396) 21440
**e** gandkmilburn@lineone.net
**w** highroans.co.uk

**Howgills Bunk Barn** ★★★
*Hostel*
Castlehaw Farm, Castlehaw Lane, Sedbergh LA10 5BA
**t** (015396) 21000
**e** cobblesedbergh@yahoo.co.uk
**w** howgillsbunkbarn.co.uk

**St Mark's** ★★★★
*Guest Accommodation*
Cautley, Sedbergh LA10 5LZ
**t** (015396) 20287
**e** saint.marks@btinternet.com
**w** saintmarks.uk.com

**Thorns Hall**
Rating Applied For
*Guest Accommodation*
Cautley Road, Sedbergh LA10 5LE
**t** (020) 8511 1534

## SEDGEFIELD
Durham

**Todds House Farm** ★★★
*Farmhouse*
Sedgefield, Stockton-on-Tees TS21 3EL
**t** (01740) 620244
**e** mail@toddshousefarm.co.uk
**w** toddshousefarm.co.uk

## SELBY
North Yorkshire

**Hazeldene Guest House**
★★★ *Guest House*
32-34 Brook Street, Selby YO8 4AR
**t** (01757) 704809
**e** info@hazeldene-selby.co.uk
**w** hazeldene-selby.co.uk

**The Old Vicarage** ★★★★
*Guest Accommodation*
Main Street, Kellington, Selby DN14 0NE
**t** (01977) 661119
**e** enquiries@theoldvicarageyorkshire.co.uk
**w** theoldvicarageyorkshire.co.uk

**The Willows** ★★★
*Guest House*
Cockret Close, Selby YO8 4BS
**t** (01757) 701271
**e** thewillowsguesthouse@hotmail.co.uk

## SETTLE
North Yorkshire

**Halsteads Barn** ★★★★★
*Bed & Breakfast*
**SILVER AWARD**
Mewith, Bentham, Settle LA2 7AR
**t** (01524) 262641
**e** info@halsteadsbarn.co.uk
**w** halsteadsbarn.co.uk

**Mainsfield** ★★★★
*Bed & Breakfast*
**SILVER AWARD**
Stackhouse Lane, Giggleswick, Settle BD24 0DL
**t** (01729) 823549
**e** mainsfield_bb@btopenworld.com
**w** mainsfieldguesthouse.co.uk

**Maypole Inn** ★★★ *Inn*
Maypole Green, Long Preston, Skipton BD23 4PH
**t** (01729) 840219
**e** robert@maypole.co.uk
**w** maypole.co.uk

**Oast Guest House** ★★★
*Guest House*
5 Penyghent View, Settle BD24 9JJ
**t** (01729) 822989
**e** stay@oastguesthouse.co.uk
**w** oastguesthouse.co.uk

**The Plough Inn at Wigglesworth** ★★★ *Inn*
The Plough Inn, Wigglesworth, Settle BD23 4RJ
**t** (01729) 840243
**e** sue@ploughinn.info
**w** ploughinn.info

**Scar Close Farm ★★★★**
*Farmhouse*
Feizor, Austwick, Ingleton
LA2 8DF
t (01729) 823496
e yeadonjohn@yahoo.co.uk
w scarclosefarmhouse.co.uk

**Settle Lodge ★★★★**
*Guest House*
Duke Street, Settle BD24 9AS
t (01729) 823258
e eddie@settlelodge.co.uk
w settlelodge.co.uk

**Whitefriars Country Guest House ★★★★**
*Guest Accommodation*
Church Street, Settle BD24 9JD
t (01729) 823753
e info@whitefriars-settle.co.uk
w whitefriars-settle.co.uk

## SEWERBY
East Riding of Yorkshire

**Marton Hall Hotel and Brasserie ★★★★**
*Restaurant with Rooms*
Marton Hall, Church Lane, Bridlington YO15 1DS
t (01262) 401010
e info@martonhall.com
w martonhall.com

**The Poplars Motel ★★★**
*Guest Accommodation*
45 Jewison Lane, Sewerby, Bridlington YO15 1DX
t (01262) 677251
w the-poplars.co.uk

## SHAROW
North Yorkshire

**Half Moon Inn ★★★** *Inn*
Sharow Lane, Sharow, Ripon
HG4 5BP
t (01765) 600291
e info@halfmoonsharow.co.uk
w halfmoonsharow.co.uk

## SHEFFIELD
South Yorkshire

**Beighton Bed & Breakfast**
★★★ *Bed & Breakfast*
48-50 High Street, Beighton, Sheffield S20 1EA
t (0114) 269 2004
e beightonbandb@aol.com

**Coniston Guest House ★★★**
*Guest House*
90 Beechwood Road, Hillsborough, Sheffield S6 4LQ
t (0114) 233 9680
e conistonguest@freeuk.com
w conistonguesthouse.co.uk

**Etruria House ★★★**
*Guest House*
91 Crookes Road, Sheffield
S10 5BD
t (0114) 266 2241
e etruria@waitrose.com

**Gulliver's Bed And Breakfast**
★★★ *Guest Accommodation*
167 Ecclesall Road South, Sheffield S11 9PN
t (0114) 262 0729

**Ivory House ★★★**
*Guest Accommodation*
34 Wostenholm Road, Sheffield S7 1LJ
t (0114) 255 1853
e ivoryhousehotel@amserve.com

**Loadbrook Cottages ★★★★**
*Bed & Breakfast*
Game Lane, Loadbrook, Sheffield S6 6GT
t (0114) 233 1619
e alisoncolver@hotmail.com
w smoothhound.co.uk/hotels/load

**The Noose and Gibbet ★** *Inn*
97 Broughton Lane, Attercliffe, Sheffield S9 2DE
t (0114) 261 7182

**The Old Crown Inn**
Rating Applied For
*Inn*
Scotland Street, Sheffield
S3 7BS
t (0114) 278 6058
e jmfftt@aol.com
w sheffieldbandb.co.uk

**Parson House Farm ★★★**
*Guest Accommodation*
Longshaw, Sheffield S11 7TZ
t (01433) 631017
e deb_bel@hotmail.co.uk
w parsonhouse.co.uk

**Psalter House ★★★★**
*Bed & Breakfast*
17 Clifford Road, Sheffield
S11 9AQ
t (0114) 255 7758
w smoothhound.co.uk/hotels/psalter

**Tyndale ★★★**
*Guest Accommodation*
164 Millhouses Lane, Sheffield
S7 2HE
t (0114) 236 1660

## SHELLEY
West Yorkshire

**Three Acres Inn and Restaurant ★★★★**
*Restaurant with Rooms*
Roydhouse, Shelley HD8 8LR
t (01484) 602606
e 3acres@globalnet.co.uk
w 3acres.com

## SHIBDEN
West Yorkshire

**Ploughcroft Cottage ★★★**
*Guest Accommodation*
53 Ploughcroft Lane, Halifax
HX3 6TX
t (01422) 341205
e ploughcroft.cottage@care4free.net
w ploughcroftcottage.com

## SHIPLEY
West Yorkshire

**Clifton Lodge Guest House**
★★★ *Guest House*
75 Kirkgate, Shipley BD18 3LU
t (01274) 580509
e cliftonlodge75@hotmail.com

## SHOTLEY BRIDGE
Durham

**The Manor House Inn**
★★★★ *Inn* **SILVER AWARD**
Carterway Heads DH8 9LX
t (01207) 255268
w manorhouse-a68.co.uk/

## SIDDINGTON
Cheshire

**Golden Cross Farm ★★★**
*Farmhouse*
Siddington, Macclesfield
SK11 9PJ
t (01260) 224358

## SILLOTH
Cumbria

**Nith View Guest House**
★★★★
*Guest Accommodation*
1 Pine Terrace, Skinburness Road, Silloth CA7 4DT
t (01697) 332860
e enquiries@nithview-guesthouse.co.uk
w nithview-guesthouse.co.uk

## SILSDEN
West Yorkshire

**Pickersgill Manor Farm**
★★★★ *Farmhouse*
**SILVER AWARD**
Low Lane, Silsden, Haworth
BD20 9JH
t (01535) 655228
e pickersgillmanorfarm@tiscali.co.uk
w dalesfarmhouse.co.uk

## SILVERDALE
Lancashire

**The Silverdale Inn ★★★**
*Guest Accommodation*
Shore Road, Silverdale LA5 0TP
t (01524) 701206
e silverdalehotel9@aol.com

## SIMONBURN
Northumberland

**Simonburn Guest House ★★**
*Guest Accommodation*
1 The Mains, Simonburn
NE48 3AW
t (01434) 681321
e ann@simonburntearoom.com
w simonburntearooms.com

## SINNINGTON
North Yorkshire

**Green Lea ★★★★**
*Bed & Breakfast*
Main Street, Sinnington, Pickering YO62 6SH
t (01751) 432008

## SKEEBY
North Yorkshire

**Ewden House ★★★★**
*Guest Accommodation*
Sedbury Lane, Skeeby, Richmond DL10 5ED
t (01748) 824473
e bb@ewdenhouse.com
w richmond.org/stayat/edenhouse

## SKELTON
Tees Valley

**Westerland's Guest House**
★★ *Bed & Breakfast*
27 East Parade, Skelton-in-Cleveland TS12 2BJ
t (01287) 650690

## SKIPSEA
East Riding of Yorkshire

**Village Farm ★★★★**
*Guest Accommodation*
**SILVER AWARD**
Back Street, Skipsea, Driffield
YO25 8SW
t (01262) 468479
e info@villagefarmskipsea.co.uk
w villagefarmskipsea.co.uk

## SKIPTON
North Yorkshire

**Carlton House ★★★★**
*Guest Accommodation*
46 Keighley Road, Skipton
BD23 2NB
t (01756) 700921
e carltonhouse@rapidial.co.uk
w carltonhouse.rapidial.co.uk

**Chinthurst ★★★★★**
*Guest House* **SILVER AWARD**
Otley Road, Skipton BD23 1EX
t (01756) 799264
e info@chinthurst.co.uk
w chinthurst.co.uk

**Cononley Hall Bed & Breakfast ★★★★★**
*Bed & Breakfast*
**SILVER AWARD**
Main Street, Cononley, Skipton
BD20 8LJ
t (01535) 633923
e cononleyhall@madasafish.com
w cononleyhall.co.uk

**Craven Heifer Inn ★★★** *Inn*
Grassington Road, Skipton
BD23 3LA
t (01756) 792521
e john@cravenheifer.co.uk
w cravenheifer.co.uk

**Cravendale Guest House**
★★★ *Guest House*
57 Keighley Road, Skipton
BD23 2LX
t (01756) 795129

**Dalesgate Lodge ★★★★**
*Guest Accommodation*
69 Gargrave Road, Skipton
BD23 1QN
t (01756) 790672
e dalesgatelodge@hotmail.com

**Highfield House**
Rating Applied For
*Guest House*
58 Keighley Road, Skipton
BD23 2NB
t (01756) 793182
e highfield.skipton@fsmail.net
w highfieldguesthouse.co.uk

**The Masons Arms Inn ★★★**
*Inn*
Barden Road, Eastby, Skipton
BD23 6SN
t (01756) 792754
e info@masonsarmseastby.co.uk
w masonsarmseastby.co.uk

**Napier's Restaurant & Accommodation ★★★★**
*Restaurant with Rooms*
Chapel Hill, Skipton BD23 1NL
t (01756) 799688
e info@accommodation-skipton.co.uk
w restaurant-skipton.co.uk

**Newton Grange ★★★★**
*Bed & Breakfast*
Bank Newton, Gargrave, Skipton BD23 3NT
t (01756) 748140 & (01756) 796016
e bookings@banknewton.fsnet.co.uk
w cravencountryconnections.co.uk

**Skipton Park Guest'otel Ltd**
★★★★ *Guest House*
2 Salisbury Street, Skipton
BD23 1NQ
t (01756) 700640
e skiptonpark@btconnect.com
w skiptonpark.co.uk

**The Woolly Sheep** ★★★ *Inn*
38 Sheep Street, Skipton
BD23 1HY
t (01756) 700966
w timothytaylor.co.uk/woollysheep

## SLAGGYFORD
Northumberland

**Yew Tree Chapel** ★★★★
*Guest Accommodation*
Slaggyford CA8 7NH
t (01434) 382525
e info@yewtreechapel.co.uk
w yewtreechapel.co.uk

## SLAIDBURN
Lancashire

**Slaidburn YHA** ★★★ *Hostel*
Church Street, Slaidburn
BB7 3ER
t (01282) 842349
e slaidburn@yha.org.uk
w yha.org.uk

## SLAITHWAITE
West Yorkshire

**The Mistal Bed and Breakfast** ★★★★★
*Guest Accommodation*
**SILVER AWARD**
The Mistal, Cop Hill Side,
Huddersfield HD7 5XA
t (01484) 845404
e carolineandphil1@tiscali.co.uk
w themistal.co.uk

**Weirside Bed & Breakfast**
★★★★
*Guest Accommodation*
Weirside Bungalow,
Huddersfield HD7 6BU
t (01484) 840601
e david.elder3@btinternet.com
w marsdenbedandbreakfast.com

## SLALEY
Northumberland

**Flothers Farm** ★★★
*Bed & Breakfast*
Slaley NE47 0BJ
t (01434) 673240
e flothers@ecosse.net
w flothers.co.uk

**The Travellers Rest** ★★★★
*Inn* **SILVER AWARD**
Hexham NE46 1TT
t (01434) 673231
e info@1travellersrest.com
w 1travellersrest.com

## SLEDMERE
East Riding of Yorkshire

**Life Hill Farm B&B** ★★★★
*Farmhouse* **GOLD AWARD**
Sledmere, Driffield YO25 3EY
t (01377) 236224
e info@lifehillfarm.co.uk
w lifehillfarm.co.uk

**The Triton Inn** ★★★★ *Inn*
Sledmere YO25 3XQ
t (01377) 236644
e thetritoninn@sledmere644.fsnet.co.uk
w sledmere.fsbusiness.co.uk

## SLEIGHTS
North Yorkshire

**Hedgefield Guest House**
★★★★ *Guest House*
47 Coach Road, Sleights,
Whitby YO22 5AA
t (01947) 810647
e hedgefieldguesthouse@tiscali.co.uk
w hedgefieldguesthouse.co.uk

**The Lawns** ★★★★★
*Guest Accommodation*
**GOLD AWARD**
73 Carr Hill Lane, Briggswath,
Whitby YO21 1RS
t (01947) 810310
e lorton@onetel.com

**The Salmon Leap** ★★ *Inn*
Coach Road, Sleights, Whitby
YO22 5AA
t (01947) 810233
e adrianmee@ukonline.co.uk
w salmonleaphotel.co.uk

## SLYNE
Lancashire

**Slyne Lodge** ★★★★ *Inn*
92 Main Road, Slyne LA2 6AZ
t (01524) 825035
e slynelodge@btconnect.com
w slynelodge.co.uk

## SNEATON
North Yorkshire

**Wilson Arms** ★★★ *Inn*
Beacon Way, Whitby
YO22 5HS
t (01947) 602552

## SOUTH CHARLTON
Northumberland

**Middle Croft** ★★★★
*Bed & Breakfast*
4 Ditchburn Road, South
Charlton NE66 2JU
t (01665) 579212
e lorna@middlecroft.co.uk
w middlecroft.co.uk

## SOUTH SHIELDS
Tyne and Wear

**Ainsley Guest House** ★★★
*Guest House*
59 Ocean Road, South Shields
NE33 2JJ
t (0191) 454 3399
e info@ainsleyguesthouse.co.uk
w ainsleyguesthouse.co.uk

**Atlantis Guest House** ★★★
*Guest House*
55 Ocean Road, South Shields
NE33 2JJ
t (0191) 455 6070
e hani.gazia@btinternet.com
w atlantisguesthouse.com

**Beaches Guest House** ★★★
*Guest House*
81 Ocean Road, South Shields
NE33 2JJ
t (0191) 456 3262
e jdocchar@yahoo.co.uk
w smoothhound.co.uk

**Beechwood Guest House**
★★★ *Guest House*
119 Ocean Road, South Shields
NE33 2JL
t (0191) 454 1829
e ask@beechwoodguesthouse.com
w beechwoodguesthouse.com

**Britannia Guesthouse**
★★★★ *Guest House*
54/56 Julian Avenue, South
Shields NE33 2EW
t (0191) 456 0896
e cbgh56@hotmail.com
w britanniaguesthouse.co.uk

**Clifton Guest House** ★★★
*Guest House*
101 Ocean Road, South Shields
NE33 2JL
t (0191) 455 1965
e info@thecliftonguesthouse.com
w thecliftonguesthouse.com

**Forest Guest House** ★★★★
*Guest House*
117 Ocean Road, South Shields
NE33 2JL
t (0191) 454 8160
e enquiries@forestguesthouse.com
w forestguesthouse.com

**The Magpies Nest** ★★★
*Guest House*
75 Ocean Road, South Shields
NE33 2JJ
t (0191) 455 2361
e christine.taylor3@btinternet.com
w magpies-nest.co.uk

**Marina Guest House** ★★★
*Guest Accommodation*
32 Sea View Terrace, South
Shields NE33 2NW
t (0191) 456 1998
e austin.mercer@sky.com

**Once Upon a Tyne** ★★
*Guest House*
55 Beach Road, South Shields
NE33 2QU
t (0191) 454 3119
e liveonce@once-tyne.co.uk
w once-tyne.co.uk

**Saraville Guest House** ★★★
*Guest House*
103 Ocean Road, South Shields
NE33 2JL
t (0191) 454 1169
e emma@saraville.freeserve.co.uk
w geocities.com/saravillehouse

## SOUTHPORT
Merseyside

**Aaron Guest House** ★★★
*Guest House*
18 Bath Street, Southport
PR9 0DA
t (01704) 530283
e info@theaaron.co.uk
w theaaron.co.uk

**The Adelphi Guest House**
★★★ *Guest Accommodation*
39 Bold Street, Southport
PR9 0ED
t (01704) 544947
e gromad@aol.com
w adelphihotelsouthport.co.uk

**Alexandra & Victoria**
★★★★
*Guest Accommodation*
38 The Promenade, Southport
PR8 1QU
t (01704) 530072
e info@alexandraandvictoriahotel.com
w alexandraandvictoriahotel.com

**Allenby** ★★★
*Guest Accommodation*
56 Bath Street, Southport
PR9 0DH
t (01704) 532953

**Ambassador Town House**
★★★★
*Guest Accommodation*
**SILVER AWARD**
13 Bath Street, Southport
PR9 0DP
t (01704) 543998
e rooms@ambassadortownhouse.com
w ambassadorsouthport.com

**Andora** ★★★
*Guest Accommodation*
25 Bath Street, Southport
PR9 0DP
t (01704) 530214
e enquiries@andorahotel.com
w andorahotel.com

**Bayona Guest House** ★★★
*Guest Accommodation*
71 Bath Street, Southport
PR9 0DN
t (01704) 543166
e johnandlyn@bayona.freeserve.co.uk
w bayonasouthport.com

**Braemar** ★★★★
*Guest Accommodation*
4 Bath Street, Southport
PR9 0DA
t (01704) 535838
e jackiewilbraham@aol.com
w braemarhotelsouthport.com

**Carleton House** ★★★★
*Guest House*
17 Alexandra Road, Southport
PR9 0NB
t (01704) 538035
e enquiries@thecarleton.co.uk
w thecarleton.co.uk

**Carlton Lodge** ★★★★
*Guest Accommodation*
43 Bath Street, Southport
PR9 0DP
t (01704) 542290
e christinecoppack@xln.co.uk
w carltonlodgesouthport.co.uk

**Crescent House** ★★★
*Guest Accommodation*
27 Bath Street, Southport
PR9 0DP
t (01704) 530339
e enquiries@crescenthousehotel.co.uk
w crescenthousehotel.co.uk/index.htm

**Fairfield House** ★★★
*Guest Accommodation*
83 The Promenade, Southport
PR9 0JN
t (01704) 530137
e jclulee@toucansurf.com

**Gables ★★★**
*Guest Accommodation*
110 Leyland Road, Southport
PR9 0JG
**t** (01704) 535554
**e** info@gableshotel.co.uk
**w** gableshotel.co.uk

**Garden Court Guest House**
Rating Applied For
*Guest House*
22 Bank Square, Southport
PR9 0DG
**t** (01704) 530219
**e** davidheppenstall@btinternet.com
**w** gardencourtsouthport.co.uk

**The Heidi ★★★** *Guest House*
43 Bold Street, Southport
PR9 0ED
**t** (01704) 531273
**e** claudia@the-heidi.co.uk
**w** the-heidi.co.uk

**Ivydene Guest House**
★★★★ *Guest House*
46 Talbot Street, Southport
PR8 1HS
**t** (01704) 544760
**e** book@ivydene-southport.com
**w** ivydene-southport.com

**Lynwood House ★★★★**
*Guest Accommodation*
11a Leicester Street, Southport
PR9 0ER
**t** (01704) 540794
**e** info@lynwoodhotel.com
**w** lynwoodhotel.com

**Le Maitre ★★★★**
*Guest Accommodation*
69 Bath Street, Southport
PR9 0DN
**t** (01704) 530394
**e** enquiries@hotel-lemaitre.co.uk
**w** hotel-lemaitre.co.uk

**Norland ★★★**
*Guest Accommodation*
11 Bath Street, Southport
PR9 0DP
**t** (01704) 530890

**The Norwood Guest House ★★★★**
*Guest Accommodation*
62 Bath Street, Southport
PR9 0DH
**t** (01704) 500536
**e** thenorwood@aol.com
**w** thenorwood.com

**Pajaree's Ban Thai & Restaurant ★★**
*Guest Accommodation*
78-80 King Street, Southport
PR8 1LG
**t** (01704) 544462
**e** thai-hotel@pajarees.co.uk
**w** pajarees.co.uk

**Penkelie ★★**
*Guest Accommodation*
34 Bold Street, Southport
PR9 0ED
**t** (01704) 538510
**e** info@penkeliehotel.co.uk
**w** penkeliehotel.co.uk

**Sandown ★★★**
*Guest Accommodation*
21 Bath Street, Southport
PR9 0DP
**t** (01704) 530416
**e** enolan2@btconnect.com
**w** sandownhotel-southport.co.uk

**Sandy Brook Farm ★★★**
*Farmhouse*
52 Wyke Cop Road, Scarisbrick, Southport PR8 5LR
**t** (01704) 880337 & 07719 468712
**e** sandybrookfarm@lycos.co.uk
**w** sandybrookfarm.co.uk

**Seaview Hotel ★★★★**
*Guest Accommodation*
28 Bath Street, Southport
PR9 0DA
**t** (01704) 530874
**e** seaview-hotel@hotmail.co.uk
**w** freewebs.com/seaview-hotel

**Sunnybank ★★**
*Guest Accommodation*
19 Bath Street, Southport
PR9 0DP
**t** (01704) 530209
**e** sunnybankhotel@tiscali.co.uk
**w** 4hotels.co.uk/uk/hotels/sunnybankhotel.html

**The Victorian ★★★**
*Guest Accommodation*
52 Avondale Road North, Southport PR9 0NE
**t** (01704) 530755
**e** reception@victorianhotel.co.uk
**w** victorianhotel.co.uk

**The Warwick ★★★**
*Guest Accommodation*
39 Bath Street, Southport
PR9 0DP
**t** (01704) 530707
**e** enquiries@thewarwickhotel.co.uk
**w** thewarwickhotel.co.uk

**The Waterford ★★★★**
*Guest Accommodation*
**SILVER AWARD**
37 Leicester Street, Southport
PR9 0EX
**t** (01704) 530559
**e** reception@waterford-hotel.co.uk
**w** waterford-hotel.co.uk

**Windsor Lodge ★★★**
*Guest Accommodation*
37 Saunders Street, Southport
PR9 0HJ
**t** (01704) 530070

### SOWERBY
North Yorkshire

**Long Acre Bed and Breakfast ★★★★**
*Bed & Breakfast*
86a Topcliffe Road, Sowerby, Thirsk YO7 1RY
**t** (01845) 522360
**e** dawsonlongacre@aol.com
**w** longacrethirsk.co.uk

### SPEKE
Merseyside

**Gateway Lodge ★★★**
*Guest Accommodation*
1 Speke Church Road, Speke
L24 3TA
**t** (0151) 284 4801
**e** info@gatewaylodge.com
**w** gatewaylodgeuk.com

### SPENNYMOOR
Durham

**Highview Country House**
★★★★ *Guest House*
Kirk Merrington, Spennymoor
DL16 7JT
**t** (01388) 811006
**e** jayne@highviewcountryhouse.co.uk
**w** highviewcountryhouse.com

### SPITTAL
Northumberland

**Caroline House ★★★**
*Bed & Breakfast*
Main Street, Spittal TD15 1RD
**t** (01289) 307595
**e** carolinehouse@hotmail.com
**w** carolinehouse.net

**Marlborough House ★★★★**
*Bed & Breakfast*
133 Main Street, Berwick-upon-Tweed TD15 1RP
**t** (01289) 305293
**e** seaside133@onetel.com
**w** marlboroughhouse.info

**The Roxburgh Guest House**
★★ *Guest House*
117 Main Street, Spittal
TD15 1RP
**t** (01289) 306266
**e** roxburghhotel@aol.com
**w** roxburghguesthouse.co.uk

### SPROTBROUGH
South Yorkshire

**The Old Rectory ★★★★**
*Guest House* **SILVER AWARD**
Boat Lane, Sprotbrough, Doncaster DN5 7LU
**t** (01302) 858561
**w** theoldrectorydoncaster.co.uk

### STAINBURN
Cumbria

**Falconwood ★★★★★**
*Bed & Breakfast*
**GOLD AWARD**
Moor Road, Stainburn, Workington CA14 1XW
**t** (01900) 602563
**e** info@lakedistrict-bedandbreakfast.co.uk
**w** lakedistrict-bedandbreakfast.co.uk

### STAINTONDALE
North Yorkshire

**Island House ★★★★**
*Farmhouse*
Staintondale, Scarborough
YO13 0EB
**t** (01723) 870249
**e** roryc@tinyworld.co.uk
**w** islandhousefarm.co.uk

### STAITHES
North Yorkshire

**Brooklyn ★★★**
*Bed & Breakfast*
Browns Terrace, Staithes
TS13 5BG
**t** (01947) 841396
**e** m.heald@tesco.net
**w** brooklynuk.com

**Grinkle Lodge ★★★★★**
*Guest Accommodation*
**GOLD AWARD**
Snipe Lane, Easington
TS13 4UD
**t** (01287) 644701
**e** grinklelodge@yahoo.co.uk
**w** grinklelodge.co.uk

### STAMFORD BRIDGE
East Riding of Yorkshire

**High Catton Grange ★★★★**
*Farmhouse* **SILVER AWARD**
High Catton, Stamford Bridge, York YO41 1EP
**t** (01759) 371374
**e** foster-s@sky.com
**w** highcattongrange.co.uk

### STANBURY
West Yorkshire

**Ponden Guest House**
★★★★ *Guest House*
Ponden House, Stanbury, Haworth BD22 0HR
**t** (01535) 644154
**e** brenda.taylor@pondenhouse.co.uk
**w** pondenhouse.co.uk

### STANDISH
Greater Manchester

**The Crown at Worthington**
★★★ *Inn*
Platt Lane, Standish WN1 2XF
**t** 0800 068 6678
**e** reservations@thecrownatworthington.co.uk
**w** thecrownatworthington.co.uk

### STANHOPE
Durham

**Horsley Hall ★★★★★**
*Guest Accommodation*
**SILVER AWARD**
Eastgate DL13 2LJ
**t** (01388) 517239
**e** hotel@horsleyhall.co.uk
**w** horsleyhall.co.uk

### STANLEY
Durham

**Bushblades Farm ★★★**
*Farmhouse*
Harperley, Stanley DH9 9UA
**t** (01207) 232722

**Oak Tree Inn ★★** *Inn*
Front Street, Tantobie, Stanley
DH9 9RF
**t** (01207) 235445

**South Causey Inn ★★★** *Inn*
Beamish Burn Road, Stanley
DH9 0LS
**t** (01207) 235555
**e** southcausey@hotmail.com
**w** southcausey.co.uk

## STANNINGTON Northumberland

**Cheviot View Farmhouse Bed & Breakfast** ★★★★
*Farmhouse* **SILVER AWARD**
North Shotton Farm, Morpeth NE61 6EU
t (01670) 789231
e julie.phili@btconnect.com
w cheviotviewfarmhouse.co.uk

## STANNINGTON South Yorkshire

**Robin Hood Inn** ★★★★ *Inn*
**SILVER AWARD**
Greaves Lane, Little Matlock, Sheffield S6 6BG
t 07768 754424
e enquiries@robinhoodloxley.co.uk
w robin-hood-loxley.co.uk

## STAPE North Yorkshire

**High Muffles** ★★★★
*Bed & Breakfast*
**SILVER AWARD**
Pickering YO18 8HP
t (01751) 417966
e candrew840@aol.com
w highmuffles.co.uk

**Rawcliffe House Farm**
★★★★ *Farmhouse*
**SILVER AWARD**
Stape, Pickering YO18 8JA
t (01751) 473292
e stay@rawcliffehousefarm.co.uk
w rawcliffehousefarm.co.uk

**Seavy Slack** ★★★★
*Farmhouse* **SILVER AWARD**
Stape, Pickering YO18 8HZ
t (01751) 473131

## STARTFORTH Durham

**Startforth House Bed & Breakfast** ★★★★
*Bed & Breakfast*
**SILVER AWARD**
Church Bank, Startforth DL12 9AE
t (01833) 631126
e joan@startforthhouse.co.uk
w startforthhouse.co.uk

## STAVELEY Cumbria

**The Eagle and Child Inn**
★★★ *Inn*
Kendal Road, Staveley LA8 9LP
t (01539) 821320
e info@eaglechildinn.co.uk
w eaglechildinn.co.uk

## STAVELEY North Yorkshire

**Staveley Grange** ★★★★★
*Guest Accommodation*
**SILVER AWARD**
Main Street, Staveley HG5 9LD
t (01423) 340265
e staveleygrange@onetel.com

## STILLINGFLEET North Yorkshire

**Harmony House** ★★★★
*Guest Accommodation*
The Green, Stillingfleet, York YO19 6SH
t (01904) 720933
e harmony.house@virgin.net
w harmonyhouseyork.com

## STIRTON North Yorkshire

**Tarn House Country Inn**
★★★★
*Guest Accommodation*
Skipton BD23 3LQ
t (01756) 794891
e tarnhse@aol.co.uk
w tarnhouse.co.uk

## STOCKSFIELD Northumberland

**Locksley, Bed & Breakfast**
★★★★ *Bed & Breakfast*
**SILVER AWARD**
45 Meadowfield Road, Stocksfield NE43 7PY
t (01661) 844778
e josie@locksleybedandbreakfast.co.uk
w locksleybedandbreakfast.co.uk

**Old Ridley Hall** ★★★
*Guest Accommodation*
Stocksfield NE43 7RU
t (01661) 842816
e josephinealdridge@oldridleyhall.force9.co.uk
w oldridley.co.uk

## STOCKTON-ON-TEES Tees Valley

**Ashton**
Rating Applied For
*Guest House*
88 Yarm Road, Stockton-on-Tees TS18 3PQ
t (01642) 679044
e ron@theashton.co.uk
w theashton.co.uk

**The Garrick** ★★ *Inn*
Yarm Lane, Stockton-on-Tees TS18 1ES
t (01642) 350360

**The Parkwood** ★★★ *Inn*
64-66 Darlington Road, Stockton-on-Tees TS18 5ER
t (01642) 587933
e theparkwoodhotel@aol.co.uk
w theparkwoodhotel.com

**The Stockton Arms Hotel**
Rating Applied For
*Inn*
24 Darlington Road, Stockton-on-Tees TS18 5BH
t (01642) 571900
e andy701968@hotmail.com
w thestocktonarmshotel.co.uk

## STOKESLEY North Yorkshire

**Willow Cottage** ★★★★
*Bed & Breakfast*
**SILVER AWARD**
67 Levenside, Stokesley TS9 5BH
t (01642) 710795
e sue@willowcottagestokesley.co.uk
w willowcottagestokesley.co.uk

## STONEGRAVE North Yorkshire

**Manor Cottage Bed and Breakfast** ★★★★
*Bed & Breakfast*
Stonegrave, Helmsley YO62 4LJ
t (01653) 628599
e gideon.v@virgin.net
w http://business.virgin.net/gideon.v/index.html

## STONYHURST Lancashire

**Alden Cottage – B&B**
★★★★
*Guest Accommodation*
**GOLD AWARD**
Kemple End, Birdy Brow BB7 9QY
t (01254) 826468
e carpenter@aldencottage.f9.co.uk
w fp.aldencottage.f9.co.uk

## SUNDERLAND Tyne and Wear

**Abingdon Guest House**
★★★ *Guest House*
5 St Georges Terrace, Sunderland SR6 9LX
t (0191) 514 0689
e karen@abingdonguesthouse.co.uk
w abingdonguesthouse.co.uk

**Acorn Guest House** ★★★
*Guest House*
10 Mowbray Road, Sunderland SR2 8EN
t (0191) 514 2170
e theacornguesthouse@hotmail.com

**April Guest House** ★★★★
*Guest House*
12 St Georges Terrace, Sunderland SR6 9LX
t (0191) 565 9550
e hilda@dickinson2772.fslife.co.uk
w aprilguesthouse.com

**Areldee Guest House** ★★★
*Guest House*
18 Roker Terrace, Sunderland SR6 9NB
t (0191) 514 1971
e peter@areldeeguesthouse.freeserve.co.uk

**The Ashborne** ★★★
*Guest House*
7 St Georges Terrace, Sunderland SR6 9LX
t (0191) 565 3997
e ashborneguesthouse@btinternet.com
w ashborne-guesthouse.co.uk

**Balmoral Guest House** ★★★
*Guest House*
3 Roker Terrace, Sunderland SR6 9NB
t (0191) 565 9217
e thebalmoral@supanet.com
w thebalmoral.supanet.com

**Belmont Guest House** ★★★
*Guest House*
8 St Georges Terrace, Roker SR6 9LX
t (0191) 567 2438
e belmontguesthouse@freedomnames.co.uk
w belmontguesthouse.com

**Braeside Holiday Guest House** ★★★ *Guest House*
26 Western Hill, Sunderland SR2 7PH
t (0191) 565 4801
e george@the20thhole.co.uk
w the20thhole.co.uk

**The Chaise Guest House**
★★★ *Guest House*
5 Roker Terrace, Sunderland SR6 9NB
t (0191) 565 9218
e thechaise@aol.com
w activereservations.com/hotel/en/hotels-in-sunderland/ah-116306.html

**Felicitations** ★★★
*Bed & Breakfast*
94 Ewesley Road, High Barnes, Sunderland SR4 7RJ
t (0191) 522 0960
e felicitations_uk@talk21.com
w felicitations.biz

**Lemonfield Guesthouse**
★★★★ *Guest House*
Sea Lane, Sunderland SR6 8EE
t (0191) 529 3018
e gary@lemonfieldhotel.com
w lemonfieldhotel.com

**Mayfield Guesthouse** ★★★
*Guest House*
Sea Lane, Sunderland SR6 8EE
t (0191) 529 3345
e enquiries@themayfieldguesthouse.co.uk
w themayfieldguesthouse.co.uk

**St George's Guest House**
★★★ *Guest House*
6 St Georges Terrace, Sunderland SR6 9LX
t (0191) 514 0689
e karen@abingdonguesthouse.co.uk
w abingdonguesthouse.co.uk

**Terrace Guest House** ★★★
*Guest House*
2 Roker Terrace, Sunderland SR6 9NB
t (0191) 565 0132
e thebalmoral@supanet.com
w thebalmoral.supanet.com

## SWARLAND Northumberland

**East House** ★★★★
*Farmhouse*
East House Farm, Guyzance NE65 9AH
t (01665) 513022
e easthousebandb@tesco.net

**Swarland Old Hall** ★★★★★
*Farmhouse* **GOLD AWARD**
Alnwick NE65 9HU
t (01670) 787642
e proctor@swarlandoldhall.fsnet.co.uk
w swarlandoldhall.co.uk

## SWINITHWAITE North Yorkshire

**Temple Farmhouse B& B**
★★★★ *Farmhouse*
Temple Farm, Aysgarth, Aysgarth Falls DL8 4UJ
t (01969) 663246
e stay@templefarmhouse.co.uk
w templefarmhouse.co.uk

## TALKIN
Cumbria

**Hullerbank** ★★★★
*Farmhouse*
Talkin, Brampton CA8 1LB
t (01697) 746668
e info@hullerbank.freeserve.co.uk
w hullerbankbnb.co.uk

## TARPORLEY
Cheshire

**Foresters Arms** ★★★ *Inn*
92 High Street, Tarporley CW6 0AX
t (01829) 733151
e foresters-arms@btconnect.com
w theforesters.co.uk

**Hill House Farm Bed & Breakfast** ★★★★ *Farmhouse*
**SILVER AWARD**
Rushton, Tarporley CW6 9AU
t (01829) 732238
e info@hillhousefarm-cheshire.com
w hillhousefarm-cheshire.co.uk/

## TARSET
Northumberland

**Snabdough Farm** ★★★★
*Farmhouse*
Tarset, Hexham NE48 1LB
t (01434) 240239

## TATTENHALL
Cheshire

**Carriages** ★★★ *Inn*
New Russia Hall, Chester Road, Gateshead CH3 9AH
t (01829) 770958

**Fernlea Cottage Bed & Breakfast** ★★★★
*Bed & Breakfast*
Chester Road, Hatton Heath CH3 9AQ
t (01829) 770807
e stevegb@talktalk.net
w fernleacottage.co.uk/

**Ford Farm Bed & Breakfast**
★★★ *Farmhouse*
Newton Lane, Tattenhall CH3 9NE
t (01829) 770307
w fordfarmcheshire.co.uk

## TEBAY
Cumbria

**Primrose Cottage** ★★★★
*Guest Accommodation*
Orton Road, Tebay CA10 3TL
t (015396) 24791
e info@primrosecottagecumbria.co.uk
w primrosecottagecumbria.co.uk

## THIRSK
North Yorkshire

**Borrowby Mill, Bed and Breakfast** ★★★★
*Guest Accommodation*
**SILVER AWARD**
Borrowby, Nr Thirsk YO7 4AW
t (01845) 537717
e markandvickipadfield@btinternet.com
w borrowbymill.co.uk

**The Gallery** ★★★★
*Bed & Breakfast*
18 Kirkgate, Thirsk YO7 1PQ
t (01845) 523767
e kathryn@gallerybedandbreakfast.co.uk
w gallerybedandbreakfast.co.uk

**Laburnum House** ★★★★
*Bed & Breakfast*
**SILVER AWARD**
31 Topcliffe Road, Sowerby, Thirsk YO7 1RX
t (01845) 524120
e ronturnbull38@aol.com
w smoothhound.co.uk/hotels/laburnumhse

**Manor House Cottage**
★★★★
*Guest Accommodation*
Hag Lane, South Kilvington, Thirsk YO7 2NY
t (01845) 527712
e info@manor-house-cottage.co.uk
w manor-house-cottage.co.uk

**The Old Rectory** ★★★★
*Bed & Breakfast*
South Kilvington, Thirsk YO7 2NL
t (01845) 526153
e ocfenton@freenet.co.uk

**Oswalds Restaurant with Rooms** ★★★★
*Restaurant with Rooms*
Front Street, Sowerby, Thirsk YO7 1JF
t (01845) 523655
e bookings@oswaldsrestaurantwith rooms.co.uk
w oswaldsrestaurantwith rooms.co.uk

**The Poplars** ★★★★
*Guest House* **SILVER AWARD**
Carlton Miniott, Thirsk YO7 4LX
t (01845) 522712
e amanda@thepoplarsthirsk.com
w thepoplarsthirsk.com

**St James House B&B** ★★★★
*Guest Accommodation*
35-37 St James Green, Thirsk YO7 1AQ
t (01845) 526565
e barry@stjameshousethirsk.co.uk
w stjameshousethirsk.co.uk

**Station House** ★★★
*Guest Accommodation*
Station Road, Thirsk YO7 4LS
t (01845) 522063
e stationhousejones@tiscali.co.uk

**Town Pasture Farm** ★★★★
*Farmhouse*
Thirsk YO7 2DY
t (01845) 537298

## THIXENDALE
North Yorkshire

**The Cross Keys** ★★★ *Inn*
Thixendale, Malton YO17 9TG
t (01377) 288272

## THORALBY
North Yorkshire

**Bishopdale** *Bunkhouse*
The Old School Bunkhouse, Leyburn DL8 3TB
t (01629)592683

**The George Inn** ★★★★ *Inn*
Thoralby, Leyburn DL8 3SU
t (01969) 663256
e chm@thegeorge.tv
w thegeorge.tv

**The Old Barn** ★★★★
*Guest Accommodation*
**SILVER AWARD**
Thoralby, Leyburn DL8 3SZ
t (01969) 663590
e holidays@dalesbarn.co.uk
w dalesbarn.co.uk

## THORNABY
Tees Valley

**Sporting Lodge Inn Middlesbrough** ★★★★ *Inn*
Low Lane, Stainton Village, Middlesbrough TS17 9LW
t (01642) 578100
e sophie@sportinglodgeinns.co.uk
w sportinglodgeinns.co.uk

## THORNE
South Yorkshire

**Thorne Central Guest House**
★★★ *Guest House*
11a Queen Street, Thorne, Doncaster DN8 5AA
t (01405) 818358
e panksy63@aol.com
w thornecentralguesthouse.co.uk

## THORNTHWAITE
Cumbria

**Jenkin Hill Cottage** ★★★★
*Guest Accommodation*
**SILVER AWARD**
Thornthwaite, Keswick CA12 5SG
t (017687) 78443
e bookings@jenkinhill.co.uk
w jenkinhill.co.uk

## THORNTON
West Yorkshire

**Ann's Farmhouse** ★★★
*Farmhouse*
New Farm, Thornton Road, Bradford BD13 3QE
t (01274) 833214
e yorkshirefarmer@hotmail.co.uk

## THORNTON-CLEVELEYS
Lancashire

**Four Seasons Guest House**
★★ *Guest Accommodation*
9 Cambridge Road, Thornton-Cleveleys FY5 1EP
t (01253) 853537
e fourseasonsguesthouse@talktalk.net

## THORNTON DALE
North Yorkshire

**Banavie** ★★★★
*Bed & Breakfast*
Roxby Road, Thornton Dale, Pickering YO18 7SX
t (01751) 474616
e info@banavie.uk.com
w banavie.uk.com

**Bridgefoot Guest House**
★★★★ *Guest House*
Pickering YO18 7RR
t (01751) 474749
e enquire@bridgefoot-house.co.uk
w bridgefoot-house.co.uk

**Cherry Garth** ★★★★
*Bed & Breakfast*
**SILVER AWARD**
Church Hill, Pickering YO18 7QH
t (01751) 473404
e claire@cherrygarthholidays.com
w cherrygarthholidays.com

**New Inn**
Rating Applied For
*Inn*
Maltongate, Pickering YO18 7LF
t (01751) 474226
e newinntld@aol.com

**Warrington Guest House**
★★★ *Guest House*
Whitbygate, Thornton Dale, Pickering YO18 7RY
t (01751) 475028
e jonathan@warringtonhouse.co.uk
w warringtonhouse.co.uk

## THORNTON-LE-MOOR
North Yorkshire

**The Black Swan** ★★★★ *Inn*
Main Street, Thornton-le-Moor, Northallerton DL7 9DN
t (01609) 774444
e woodys@thornton-le-moor.co.uk

## THORNTON WATLASS
North Yorkshire

**The Buck Inn** ★★★ *Inn*
Thornton Watlass, Ripon, Bedale HG4 4AH
t (01677) 422461
e innwatlass1@btconnect.com
w buckwatlass.co.uk

## THRELKELD
Cumbria

**The Bungalows Country Guest House** ★★★★
*Bed & Breakfast*
Sunnyside, Threlkeld, Keswick CA12 4SD
t (017687) 79679
e paulsunley@msn.com
w thebungalows.co.uk

**Horse and Farrier Inn**
★★★★ *Inn*
Threlkeld, Keswick CA12 4SQ
t (017687) 79688
e info@horseandfarrier.com
w horseandfarrier.com

**Scales Farm Country Guest House** ★★★★ *Guest House*
**SILVER AWARD**
Scales, Threlkeld, Penrith CA12 4SY
t (017687) 79660
e scales@scalesfarm.com
w scalesfarm.com

### THROPTON
Northumberland

**Rockwood House** ★★★★
*Bed & Breakfast*
Thropton NE65 7NA
t (01669) 620989
e chris@howey7618.freeserve.co.uk

**Thropton Demesne Farmhouse B&B** ★★★★★
*Guest House*
Thropton NE65 7LT
t (01669) 620196
e thropton_demesne@yahoo.co.uk
w throptondemesne.co.uk

### THRUSCROSS
North Yorkshire

**West End Outdoor Centre**
★★★ *Hostel*
West End, Summerbridge, Harrogate HG3 4BA
t (01943) 880207
e m.verity@virgin.net
w westendoutdoorcentre.co.uk

### THURNHAM
Lancashire

**The Stork**
Rating Applied For
*Inn*
Corricks Lane, Conder Green LA2 0AN
t (01524) 751234
e thestorkinn@hotmail.com
w thestorkinn.co.uk

### THURSTONLAND
West Yorkshire

**Ackroyd House** ★★★★★
*Bed & Breakfast*
**SILVER AWARD**
13 Top of the Bank, Thurstonland, Holmfirth HD4 6XZ
t (01484) 660169
e enquiries@ackroydhouse.co.uk
w ackroydhouse.co.uk

### THWAITES BROW
West Yorkshire

**Golden View Guest House**
★★★ *Guest Accommodation*
21 Golden View Drive, Thwaites Brow, Haworth BD21 4SN
t (01535) 662138
e info@goldenview.supanet.com
w goldenview.supanet.com

### TICKHILL
South Yorkshire

**Hannah's Guest House**
★★★ *Guest House*
72 Sunderland Street, Tickhill, Doncaster DN11 9EG
t (01302) 752233
e hannahsguesthouse@tiscali.co.uk
w hannahsguesthouse.com

### TODMORDEN
West Yorkshire

**Kilnhurst Old Hall** ★★★★★
*Guest Accommodation*
**SILVER AWARD**
Kilnhurst Lane, Todmorden OL14 6AX
t (01706) 814289
e kilnhurst@aol.com

**Mankinholes YHA** ★★★★
*Hostel*
Mankinholes, Todmorden OL14 6HR
t (01706) 812340
e mankinholes@yha.org.uk
w yha.org.uk

**Woodleigh Hall**
Rating Applied For
*Bed & Breakfast*
Ewood Lane, Todmorden OL14 7DF
t (01706) 814664
e mauricerheath@btinternet.net

### TOLLERTON
North Yorkshire

**Angel Inn House** ★★★★
*Bed & Breakfast*
York Road, Tollerton, York YO61 1QZ
t (01347) 833019
e enquiries@angelinnhouse.co.uk
w angelinnhouse.co.uk

### TRAWDEN
Lancashire

**Trawden** *Camping Barn*
Middle Beardshaw Head Farm, Burnley Road, Colne BB8 8PP
t (01282) 865257

### TRIANGLE
West Yorkshire

**The Dene** ★★★★
*Guest Accommodation*
Triangle, Halifax HX6 3EA
t (01422) 823562
e knoble@uk2.net

### TRIMDON GRANGE
Durham

**Polemonium Plantery**
★★★★ *Bed & Breakfast*
28 Sunnyside Terrace, Trimdon Grange, Trimdon Station TS29 6HF
t (01429) 881529
e bandb@polemonium.co.uk
w polemonium.co.uk

### TROUTBECK
Cumbria

**Gill Head Farm** ★★★★
*Farmhouse*
Troutbeck, Penrith CA11 0ST
t (017687) 79652
e enquiries@gillheadfarm.co.uk
w gillheadfarm.co.uk

**High Fold Guest House**
★★★★ *Guest House*
Troutbeck, Windermere LA23 1PG
t (015394) 32200
e info@highfoldbedandbreakfast.co.uk
w highfoldbedandbreakfast.co.uk

**Troutbeck Inn** ★★★ *Inn*
Troutbeck, Penrith CA11 0SJ
t (017684) 83635

**YHA Windermere** ★★★
*Hostel*
Bridge Lane, Troutbeck, Windermere LA23 1LA
t (015394) 43543
e windermere@yha.org.uk
w yha.org.uk

### TURTON
Greater Manchester

**Clough Head Farm** ★★★★
*Bed & Breakfast*
Broadhead Road, Turton BL7 0JN
t (01254) 704758
e ethelhoughton@hotmail.co.uk
w cloughheadfarm.co.uk

### TWEEDMOUTH
Northumberland

**Ford Castle** ★★★
*Group Hostel*
Ford Village TD15 2PX
t (01890) 820257
e fordcastle@northumberland.gov.uk

**West Sunnyside House**
★★★★ *Bed & Breakfast*
**SILVER AWARD**
Tweedmouth TD15 2QH
t (01289) 305387
e kjamieson58@aol.com
w westsunnysidehouse.co.uk

### TYNEMOUTH
Tyne and Wear

**Martineau Guest House**
★★★★ *Guest House*
**SILVER AWARD**
57 Front Street, Tynemouth NE30 4BX
t (0191) 296 0746
e martineau.house@ukgateway.net
w martineau-house.co.uk

### ULLSWATER
Cumbria

**Elm House** ★★★★
*Guest House* **SILVER AWARD**
High Street, Pooley Bridge, Ullswater CA10 2NH
t (017684) 86334
e enquiries@stayullswater.co.uk
w stayullswater.co.uk

**Knotts Mill Country Lodge**
★★★ *Guest House*
Watermillock, Penrith CA11 0JN
t (017684) 86699
e relax@knottsmill.com
w knottsmill.com

**Land Ends Country Lodge**
★★★ *Guest House*
Watermillock, Ullswater CA11 0NB
t (017684) 86438
e infolandends@btinternet.com
w landends.co.uk

**Mosscrag Guest House**
★★★ *Guest House*
Glenridding, Penrith, Ullswater CA11 0PA
t (017684) 82500
e info@mosscrag.co.uk
w mosscrag.co.uk

**Tymparon Hall** ★★★★
*Farmhouse*
Newbiggin, Penrith CA11 0HS
t (017684) 83236
e margaret@tymparon.freeserve.co.uk
w tymparon.freeserve.co.uk

**Whitbarrow Farm** ★★★★
*Farmhouse* **SILVER AWARD**
Berrier, Penrith CA11 0XB
t (017684) 83366
e mary@whitbarrowfarm.co.uk
w whitbarrowfarm.co.uk

### ULVERSTON
Cumbria

**St Marys Mount Manor House** ★★★★★
*Guest Accommodation*
Belmont, Ulverston LA12 7HD
t (01229) 583372
e gerry.bobbett@virgin.net
w stmarysmount.co.uk

**Virginia House** ★★★★
*Guest House*
24 Queen Street, Ulverston LA12 7AF
t (01229) 584844
e virginia@ulverstonhotels.wanadoo.co.uk
w ulverstonhotels.com

### UNDERBARROW
Cumbria

**Tranthwaite Hall** ★★★★
*Farmhouse*
Underbarrow, Kendal LA8 8HG
t (015395) 68285
e stay@tranthwaitehall.co.uk
w tranthwaitehall.co.uk

### UTKINTON
Cheshire

**Yew Tree Farm Bed & Breakfast** ★★ *Farmhouse*
Fishers Green, Utkinton CW6 0JG
t (01829) 732441

### WADDINGTON
Lancashire

**Peter Barn Country House**
★★★★
*Guest Accommodation*
Cross Lane, Waddington BB7 3JH
t (01200) 428585
e jean@peterbarn.co.uk

**The Waddington Arms**
★★★★ *Inn*
Clitheroe Road, Waddington BB7 3HP
t (01200) 423262
e info@waddingtonarms.co.uk
w waddingtonarms.co.uk

### WALKINGTON
East Riding of Yorkshire

**The Barn House** ★★★★★
*Guest Accommodation*
18a East End, Walkington, Beverley HU17 8RY
t (01482) 880542
e info@barnhouse-walkington.co.uk
w barnhouse-walkington.co.uk

## WALL
Northumberland

**The Hadrian Wall Inn** ★★★
*Inn*
Wall, Hexham NE46 4EE
**t** (01434) 681232
**e** david.lindsay13@btinternet.com
**w** hadrianhotel.com

**Tantallon House** ★★★★
*Bed & Breakfast*
**SILVER AWARD**
Gilsland, Brampton CA8 7DA
**t** (01697) 747111
**e** info@tantallonhouse.co.uk
**w** hadrians-wall-bed-and-breakfast.co.uk

## WALLSEND
Tyne and Wear

**The Dorset Arms** ★★ *Inn*
Dorset Avenue, Wallsend NE28 8DX
**t** (0191) 209 9754
**e** info@dorsetarmshotel.co.uk
**w** dorsetarmshotel.co.uk

## WALSDEN
West Yorkshire

**Birks Clough** ★★★
*Guest House*
Hollingworth Lane, Todmorden OL14 6QX
**t** (01706) 814438
**e** mstorah@mwfree.net

## WALTON
Cumbria

**Centurion Inn** ★★★★ *Inn*
Walton, Brampton CA8 2DH
**t** (01697) 72438
**e** bookings@centurioninn.com
**w** centurioninn.com

**Sandysike Bunkhouse**
*Bunkhouse*
Sandysike, Walton, Brampton CA8 2DU
**t** (01697) 72330
**e** sandysike@talk21.com
**w** nationaltrail.co.uk/hadrianswall/accommodation.asp

## WARK
Northumberland

**Battlesteads Country Inn & Restaurant** ★★★★ *Inn*
**SILVER AWARD**
Wark, Hexham NE48 3LS
**t** (01434) 230209
**e** info@battlesteads.com
**w** battlesteads.com

## WARKWORTH
Northumberland

**Beck 'N' Call** ★★★★
*Bed & Breakfast*
Birling West Cottage, Warkworth NE65 0XS
**t** (01665) 711653
**e** beck-n-call@lineone.net
**w** beck-n-call.co.uk

**Fairfield House** ★★★★★
*Guest House* **SILVER AWARD**
16 Station Road, Warkworth NE65 0XP
**t** (01665) 714455
**e** mandy@fairfield-guesthouse.com
**w** fairfield-guesthouse.com

**Magdalene House** ★★★★
*Bed & Breakfast*
Maudlin Farm, Warkworth NE65 0TL
**t** (01665) 711539

**Morwick House Bed and Breakfast** ★★★★
*Guest Accommodation*
Beal Bank, Warkworth NE65 0TB
**t** (01665) 712101
**e** morwickhouse@tiscali.co.uk
**w** morwickhouse.co.uk

**Number 28** ★★★★
*Bed & Breakfast*
28 Castle Street, Warkworth NE65 0UL
**t** (01665) 712869
**e** johnross57@aol.com

**The Old Manse** ★★★★
*Bed & Breakfast*
20 The Butts, Alnwick NE65 0SS
**t** (01665) 710850
**e** a.coulter1@btinternet.com
**w** oldmanse.info

**Roxbro House** ★★★★
*Bed & Breakfast*
**GOLD AWARD**
5 Castle Terrace, Alnwick NE65 0UP
**t** (01665) 711416
**e** info@roxbrohouse.co.uk
**w** roxbrohouse.co.uk

**Tower House B&B** ★★★★
*Bed & Breakfast*
47 Castle Street, Warkworth NE65 0UN
**t** (01665) 714375
**e** tower.1@tiscali.co.uk
**w** towerhousebandb.co.uk/

**West View Lodge** ★★★★
*Bed & Breakfast*
35 Watershaugh Road, Warkworth NE65 0TX
**t** (01665) 711532
**e** smgunn@aol.com

**Westrigg Bed and Breakfast**
★★★★ *Bed & Breakfast*
30 Watershaugh Road, Warkworth NE65 0TX
**t** (01665) 711410
**e** katiemorwick@yahoo.com

## WARRINGTON
Cheshire

**New House Farm Cottages**
★★ *Bed & Breakfast*
Hatton Lane, Hatton, Warrington WA4 4BZ
**t** (01925) 730567
**e** newhousefarmcottages@goggle.com
**w** newhousefarmcottages.co.uk

**Tall Trees Lodge** ★★★
*Guest Accommodation*
Tarporley Road, Lower Whitley, Warrington WA4 4EZ
**t** (01928) 790824 & (01928) 715117
**e** booking@talltreeslodge.co.uk
**w** talltreeslodge.co.uk

## WARTHILL
North Yorkshire

**Snowball Plantation** ★★
*Group Hostel*
Stockton-on-Forest, York YO19 5XS
**t** (01904) 410084
**w** snowballplantation.org.uk

## WASDALE
Cumbria

**Murt** *Camping Barn*
Nether Wasdale, Wasdale CA20 1ET
**t** (01946) 758198
**e** info@lakelandcampingbarns.co.uk
**w** lakelandcampingbarns.co.uk

**Wastwater YHA** ★★★
*Hostel*
Wasdale Hall, Wasdale CA20 1ET
**t** 0870 770 6082
**e** wastwater@yha.org.uk
**w** yha.org.uk

## WASHINGTON
Tyne and Wear

**Ye Olde Cop Shop** ★★★★
*Guest House*
6 The Green, Washington NE38 7AB
**t** (0191) 416 5333
**e** yeoldecopshop@btopenworld.com

**The Victoria Inn** ★★★ *Inn*
Oxclose Road, Washington NE38 7DJ
**t** (0191) 417 2526
**e** carling2@aol.com
**w** victoriainnwashington.com

## WATERHEAD
Cumbria

**Ambleside YHA** ★★★ *Hostel*
Waterhead, Ambleside LA22 0EU
**t** 0870 770 5908
**e** ambleside@yha.org.uk
**w** yha.org.uk

## WATERHOUSES
Durham

**Ivesley** ★★★★ *Farmhouse*
Waterhouses DH7 9HB
**t** (0191) 373 4324
**e** ivesley@msn.com
**w** ridingholidays-ivesley.co.uk

## WATERLOO
Merseyside

**Marlborough Hotel** ★★★
*Guest House*
21 Crosby Road South, Liverpool L22 1RG
**t** (0151) 928 7709

## WATERMILLOCK-ON-ULLSWATER
Cumbria

**Mellfell House Farm B&B**
★★★★ *Farmhouse*
Watermillock-on-Ullswater, Penrith CA11 0LS
**t** (017684) 86295
**e** ben@mellfell.co.uk
**w** mellfell.co.uk

## WEAVERTHORPE
North Yorkshire

**Blue Bell Inn** ★★★★
*Restaurant with Rooms*
**SILVER AWARD**
Main Street, Weaverthorpe, Malton YO17 8EX
**t** (01944) 738204
**e** bluebellinn@hotmail.co.uk
**w** bluebellweaverthorpe.com

## WEETON
North Yorkshire

**Arthington Lodge** ★★★★
*Farmhouse*
Wescoe Hill, Weeton, Harrogate LS17 0EZ
**t** (01423) 734102
**e** arthingtonlodge@btinternet.com

## WELBURN
North Yorkshire

**The Barley Basket** ★★★
*Bed & Breakfast*
Main Road, York YO60 7DX
**t** (01653) 618352
**e** marianlacey@btinternet.com

**Welburn Lodge** ★★★★
*Bed & Breakfast*
**SILVER AWARD**
Castle Howard Station Road, Welburn, Malton YO60 7EW
**t** (01653) 618885
**e** stay@welburnlodge.com

## WELTON
Cumbria

**Lakelynn** ★★★
*Bed & Breakfast*
Warnell, Welton, Carlisle CA5 7HW
**t** (01697) 476239
**e** banks@lakelynn-welton.fsnet.co.uk

## WELTON
East Riding of Yorkshire

**Green Dragon** ★★★★ *Inn*
Cowgate, Welton, Hull HU15 1NB
**t** (01482) 666700

## WENSLEY
North Yorkshire

**Wensley House** ★★★★
*Guest House*
Wensley, Leyburn DL8 4HL
**t** (01969) 624866

## WENSLEYDALE
North Yorkshire

**Ivy Dene Guesthouse** ★★★
*Guest House*
Main Street, West Witton, Leyburn DL8 4LP
**t** (01969) 622785
**e** info@ivydeneguesthouse.co.uk
**w** yorkshirenet.co.uk/stayat/ivydene/

## WEST DERBY
Merseyside

**Blackmoor Bed & Breakfast**
★★★ *Bed & Breakfast*
160 Blackmoor Drive, West Derby L12 9EF
**t** (0151) 291 1407

## WEST KIRBY
### Merseyside

**21 Park House Guesthouse**
★★★★ *Guest House*
21 Park Road, West Kirby
CH48 4DN
**t** (0151) 625 4665
**e** enquiries@21parkhouse.co.uk
**w** 21parkhouse.co.uk

**At Peel Hey** ★★★★
*Guest House* **SILVER AWARD**
Frankby Road, Frankby, Wirral
CH48 1PP
**t** (0151) 677 9077
**e** enquiries@peelhey.co.uk
**w** peelhey.co.uk

**Caldy Warren Cottage**
★★★★★ *Bed & Breakfast*
42 Caldy Road, West Kirby,
Wirral CH48 2HQ
**t** (0151) 625 8740
**e** office@warrencott.demon.co.uk
**w** warrencott.demon.co.uk

## WEST WITTON
### North Yorkshire

**The Old Star** ★★★
*Guest Accommodation*
Main Street, West Witton,
Leyburn DL8 4LU
**t** (01969) 622949
**e** enquiries@theoldstar.com
**w** theoldstar.com

## WEST WOODBURN
### Northumberland

**Bay Horse Inn** ★★★ *Inn*
West Woodburn NE48 2RX
**t** (01434) 270218
**e** enquiry@bayhorseinn.org
**w** bayhorseinn.org

**Brandy Bank House** ★★★★
*Guest House*
West Woodburn NE48 2RA
**t** (01434) 270210
**e** brandybankhse@btinternet.com
**w** brandybankhse.com

**Yellow House Farm B&B**
Rating Applied For
*Bed & Breakfast*
West Woodburn, Hexham
NE48 2SB
**t** (01434) 270070
**e** avril@yellowhousebandb.co.uk
**w** yellowhousebandb.co.uk

## WESTERDALE
### North Yorkshire

**Westerdale** *Bunkhouse*
Broadgate Farm, Westerdale,
Whitby YO21 2DE
**t** (01287) 660259

## WESTGATE-IN-WEARDALE
### Durham

**Lands Farm** ★★★★
*Farmhouse* **SILVER AWARD**
Westgate DL13 1SN
**t** (01388) 517210
**e** barbara@landsfarm.fsnet.co.uk

## WESTOW
### North Yorkshire

**Ryedale Vineyards Bed & Breakfast** ★★★★ *Farmhouse*
Farfield Farm, Malton
YO60 7LS
**t** 07837 979789
**e** bandb@thevinehouse.fsnet.co.uk

## WETHERAL
### Cumbria

**Acorn Bank** ★★★★★
*Guest Accommodation*
Wetheral, Carlisle CA4 8JG
**t** (01228) 561434
**e** enquiry@acornbank.co.uk
**w** acornbank.co.uk

## WETHERBY
### West Yorkshire

**Broadleys** ★★★★
*Bed & Breakfast*
39 North Street, Wetherby
LS22 6NU
**t** (01937) 585866

**Linton Close** ★★★★
*Bed & Breakfast*
**SILVER AWARD**
2 Wharfe Grove, Wetherby
LS22 6HA
**t** (01937) 582711

**Prospect House** ★★
*Guest House*
8 Caxton Street, Wetherby
LS22 6RU
**t** (01937) 582428

**The Royal Oak** ★★★★
*Bed & Breakfast*
60 North Street, Wetherby
LS22 6NR
**t** (01937) 580508
**e** a.johnston11@btconnect.com

**Swan Guest House** ★★★★
*Guest House*
38 North Street, Wetherby
LS22 6NN
**t** (01937) 582381
**e** info@swanguesthouse.co.uk
**w** swanguesthouse.co.uk

## WHALLEY
### Lancashire

**Whalley Abbey** ★★★★
*Guest Accommodation*
The Sands, Whalley, Clitheroe
BB7 9SS
**t** (01254) 828400
**e** office@whalleyabbey.org
**w** whalleyabbey.co.uk

## WHICKHAM
### Tyne and Wear

**A1 Summerville Guest House** ★★★ *Guest House*
33 Orchard Road, Whickham
NE16 4TG
**t** (0191) 488 3388
**e** info@a1summerville.co.uk
**w** a1summerville.co.uk

**East Byermoor Guest House**
★★★★ *Guest House*
**SILVER AWARD**
Fellside Road, Newcastle-upon-Tyne NE16 5BD
**t** (01207) 272687
**e** byermoor@talktalkbusiness.net
**w** eastbyermoor.co.uk

## WHITBY
### North Yorkshire

**Arches Guest House** ★★★★
*Guest House*
The Arches, 8, Havelock Place,
Whitby YO21 3ER
**t** 0800 915 4256 &
0800 915 4256
**e** archeswhitby@freeola.com
**w** whitbyguesthouses.co.uk

**Argyle House** ★★★★
*Guest Accommodation*
18 Hudson Street, Whitby
YO21 3EP
**t** (01947) 602733
**e** argyle-house@fsmail.net
**w** argyle-house.co.uk

**Ashford Guest House** ★★★
*Guest House*
8 Royal Crescent, Whitby
YO21 3EJ
**t** (01947) 602138
**e** info@ashfordguesthouse.co.uk
**w** ashfordguesthouse.co.uk

**The Avalon** ★★
*Guest Accommodation*
13-14 Royal Crescent, Whitby
YO21 3EJ
**t** (01947) 820313
**e** info@avalonhotelwhitby.co.uk
**w** avalonhotelwhitby.co.uk

**Boulmer Guest House** ★★★
*Guest House*
23 Crescent Avenue, Whitby
YO21 3ED
**t** (01947) 604284
**e** boulmerguesthouse@tiscali.co.uk

**Bramblewick** ★★★★
*Guest House*
3 Havelock Place, Whitby
YO21 3ER
**t** (01947) 604504
**e** bramblewick@havelockplace.wanadoo.co.uk
**w** bramblewick.co.uk

**The Captain's Lodge** ★★★★
*Guest House*
3 Crescent Avenue, Whitby
YO21 3EF
**t** (01947) 601178

**Corner Guest House** ★★★★
*Guest House*
3-4 Crescent Place, Whitby
YO21 3HE
**t** (01947) 602444
**e** awpicknett@yahoo.co.uk
**w** thecornerguesthouse.com

**Crescent Lodge** ★★★★
*Guest Accommodation*
27 Crescent Avenue, Whitby
YO21 3EW
**t** (01947) 820073
**e** arthurcrescentlodge@telco4u.net

**Cross Butts Stable Restaurant with Rooms**
★★★★
*Restaurant with Rooms*
**SILVER AWARD**
Guisborough Road, Whitby
YO21 1TL
**t** (01947) 820986

**Ellie's Guest House** ★★★★
*Guest Accommodation*
4 Langdale Terrace, Whitby
YO21 3EE
**t** (01947) 600022
**e** info@elliesguesthouse.co.uk
**w** elliesguesthouse.co.uk

**Esklet Guest House** ★★★★
*Guest Accommodation*
22 Crescent Avenue, Whitby
YO21 3ED
**t** (01947) 605663
**e** esklet@axis-connect.com
**w** esklet.com

**The Florence Guest House**
★★★★ *Guest House*
4 Broomfield Terrace, Whitby
YO21 1QP
**t** (01947) 605083
**e** enquiries@florence-guesthouse.co.uk
**w** florence-guesthouse.co.uk

**The Full English** ★★★★
*Guest House*
9 John Street, Whitby
YO21 3ET
**t** (01947) 604021
**e** garybevang@aol.com
**w** thefullenglishwhitby.com

**Glendale Guest House**
★★★★ *Guest House*
16 Crescent Avenue, Whitby
YO21 3ED
**t** (01947) 604242
**w** glendalewhitby.co.uk

**Glenora** ★★★★ *Guest House*
8 Upgang Lane, Whitby
YO21 3EA
**t** (01947) 605363
**e** glenora.whitby@btopenworld.com
**w** glenora.users.btopenworld.com

**Gramarye Suites B&B**
★★★★ *Bed & Breakfast*
**SILVER AWARD**
15 Coach Road, Sleights,
Whitby YO22 5AA
**t** (01947) 811656
**e** gramaryesuites@btinternet.com
**w** gramaryesuites.co.uk

**The Grove** ★★★★
*Guest House*
36 Bagdale, Whitby YO21 1QL
**t** (01947) 603551
**e** angelaswales@btconnect.com
**w** smoothhound.co.uk/hotels/grove2

**Hailwood House** ★★★★
*Bed & Breakfast*
25a Crescent Avenue, Whitby
YO21 3ED
**t** (01947) 602704
**e** hailwoodhouse@yahoo.co.uk

**Havelock Guest House**
★★★ *Guest House*
30 Hudson Street, Whitby
YO21 3EP
**t** (01947) 602295

**Haven Crest** ★★★★
*Guest Accommodation*
**SILVER AWARD**
137 Upgang Lane, Whitby
YO21 3JW
**t** (01947) 605187
**e** enquiries@havencrest.co.uk
**w** havencrest.co.uk

**The Haven Guest House**
★★★★ *Guest House*
4 East Crescent, Whitby
YO21 3HD
**t** (01947) 603842
**e** info@thehavenwhitby.co.uk
**w** thehavenwhitby.co.uk

**High Tor Guest House**
★★★★ *Guest House*
7 Normanby Terrace, Whitby
YO21 3ES
**t** (01947) 602507
**e** hightorguesthouse@hotmail.com
**w** hightorguesthousewhitby.co.uk

**Hillcrest Guest House**
★★★★ *Guest House*
9 Prospect Hill, Whitby
YO21 1QE
**t** (01947) 606604
**e** hillcrestgh@btinternet.com
**w** hillcrestguesthouse.org.uk

**Khyber Mount Guest House**
★★★ *Guest Accommodation*
9 East Crescent, Whitby
YO21 3HD
**t** (01947) 602125
**e** khybermount@hotmail.com
**w** khybermount.co.uk

**The Langley** ★★★★★
*Guest Accommodation*
**SILVER AWARD**
Royal Crescent, West Cliff, Whitby YO21 3EJ
**t** (01947) 604250
**e** langleyhotel@hotmail.com
**w** langleyhotel.com

**Larpool Hall** ★★★★
*Guest Accommodation*
Larpool Drive, Whitby
YO22 4ND
**t** 0845 470 7558
**e** reservations@hfholidays.co.uk
**w** hfholidays.co.uk

**Lavinia House** ★★★★
*Guest Accommodation*
3 East Crescent, Whitby
YO21 3HD
**t** (01947) 602945
**e** info@laviniahouse.co.uk
**w** laviniahouse.co.uk

**The Leeway** ★★★★
*Guest Accommodation*
1 Havelock Place, Whitby
YO21 3ER
**t** (01947) 602604
**e** enquiries@theleeway.co.uk
**w** theleeway.co.uk

**Netherby House** ★★★★
*Guest Accommodation*
**SILVER AWARD**
Coach Road, Sleights, Whitby
YO22 5EQ
**t** (01947) 810211
**e** info@netherby-house.co.uk
**w** netherby-house.co.uk

**Number Five** ★★★★
*Guest House*
5 Havelock Place, Whitby
YO21 3ER
**t** (01947) 606361

**Number Seven Guest House**
★★★★
*Guest Accommodation*
7 East Crescent, Whitby
YO21 3HD
**t** (01947) 606019
**e** number7.whitbytown@btinternet.com
**w** numbersevenwhitby.co.uk

**The Olde Ford** ★★★★
*Guest Accommodation*
**SILVER AWARD**
1 Briggswath, Whitby
YO21 1RU
**t** (01947) 810704
**e** gray.theoldeford@btinternet.com
**w** theoldeford.com/contact.htm

**Pannett House** ★★★★
*Guest Accommodation*
14 Normanby Terrace, Whitby
YO21 3ES
**t** (01947) 603261
**e** info@pannetthouse.co.uk
**w** pannetthouse.co.uk

**Partridge Nest Farm** ★★★
*Farmhouse*
Eskdaleside, Sleights, Whitby
YO22 5ES
**t** (01947) 810450
**e** barbara@partridgenestfarm.com
**w** partridgenestfarm.com

**Prospect Villa Guest House**
★★★ *Guest House*
13 Prospect Hill, Whitby
YO21 1QE
**t** (01947) 603118
**e** prospectvillawhitby@hotmail.com
**w** prospectvillahotel.co.uk

**Queensland** ★★★★
*Guest Accommodation*
2 Crescent Avenue, Whitby
YO21 3EQ
**t** (01947) 604262
**e** info@queensland.co.uk
**w** queensland.co.uk

**Riviera** ★★★★ *Guest House*
4 Crescent Terrace, West Cliff, Whitby YO21 3EL
**t** (01947) 602533
**e** info@rivierawhitby.com
**w** rivierawhitby.com

**Rosslyn House** ★★★★
*Guest House*
11 Abbey Terrace, Whitby
YO21 3HQ
**t** (01947) 604086
**e** rosslyn_gh@btconnect.com
**w** guesthousewhitby.co.uk

**The Rothbury** ★★★★
*Bed & Breakfast*
2 Ocean Road, Whitby
YO21 3HY
**t** (01947) 606282
**e** therothbury@f2s.com
**w** therothbury.co.uk

**Ryedale House** ★★★★
*Guest Accommodation*
Coach Road, Sleights, Whitby
YO22 5EQ
**t** (01947) 810534
**w** ryedalehouse.co.uk

**The Seacliffe** ★★★★
*Guest Accommodation*
12 North Promenade, Whitby
YO21 3JX
**t** (01947) 603139
**e** stay@seacliffehotel.com
**w** seacliffehotel.com

**Seacrest Guest House** ★★★
*Guest House*
10 Crescent Avenue, Whitby
YO21 3ED
**t** (01947) 605541
**e** axby18@dsi.pipex.com
**w** seacrest.org.uk

**Sneaton Castle Centre**
★★★★
*Guest Accommodation*
Sneaton Castle, Whitby
YO21 3QN
**t** (01947) 600051
**e** sneaton@globalnet.co.uk
**w** sneatoncastle.co.uk

**Sneaton Castle Centre** ★★★
*Hostel*
Castle Road, Whitby
YO21 3QN
**t** (01947) 600051
**e** sneaton@globalnet.co.uk
**w** sneatoncastle.co.uk

**Storrbeck Guest House**
★★★★ *Bed & Breakfast*
**SILVER AWARD**
9 Crescent Avenue, Whitby
YO21 3ED
**t** (01947) 605468
**e** storrbeck@bigfoot.com
**w** storrbeckguesthouse.co.uk

**Sunnyvale House** ★★★★
*Guest House*
12 Normanby Terrace, Whitby
YO21 3ES
**t** (01947) 820389
**e** sunnyvalehouse@hotmail.co.uk
**w** sunnyvalehouse.co.uk

**Wentworth House** ★★★
*Guest House*
27 Hudson Street, Whitby
YO21 3EP
**t** (01947) 602433
**e** info@whitbywentworth.co.uk
**w** whitbywentworth.co.uk

**The Wheeldale** ★★★★
*Guest House*
11 North Promenade, Whitby
YO21 3JX
**t** (01947) 602365
**e** enquiries@wheeldale-hotel.co.uk
**w** wheeldalewhitby.co.uk

**Whitby YHA** ★★★★ *Hostel*
East Cliff, Whitby YO22 4JT
**t** (01947) 602878

**White Linen Guest House**
★★★★
*Guest Accommodation*
24 Bagdale, Whitby YO21 1QS
**t** (01947) 603635
**e** info@whitelinenguesthouse.co.uk
**w** whitelinenguesthouse.co.uk

**The Willows** ★★★★
*Guest House*
35 Bagdale, Whitby YO21 1QL
**t** (01947) 600288
**e** martindyer74@hotmail.com
**w** thewillowsguesthouse.co.uk

**York House** ★★★★
*Guest House*
3 Back Lane, High Hawsker, Whitby YO22 4LW
**t** (01947) 880314
**e** admin@york-house-hotel.co.uk
**w** york-house-hotel.co.uk

## WHITEGATE
Cheshire

**Beechtree Farm Bed and Breakfast** ★★★
*Bed & Breakfast*
Daleford Lane, Whitegate
CW8 2BW
**t** (01606) 301140
**e** marylspann@btinternet.com
**w** cheshire.homestay.googlepages.com/home

## WHITEHAVEN
Cumbria

**Moresby Hall** ★★★★★
*Guest House* **GOLD AWARD**
Moresby, Whitehaven
CA28 6PJ
**t** (01946) 696317
**e** info@moresbyhall.co.uk
**w** moresbyhall.co.uk

## WHITESTAKE
Lancashire

**Whitestake Farm** ★★★★★
*Bed & Breakfast*
**SILVER AWARD**
Pope Lane, Whitestake PR4 4JR
**t** (01772) 619392
**e** enquiries@gardenofedenspa.co.uk
**w** gardenofedenspa.co.uk

## WHITEWELL
Lancashire

**The Inn at Whitewell**
★★★★★ *Inn*
**GOLD AWARD**
Dunsop Road, Whitewell
BB7 3AT
**t** (01200) 448222
**e** reception@innatwhitewell.com
**w** innatwhitewell.com

## WHITFIELD
Northumberland

**The Elk's Head** ★★★ *Inn*
Whitfield NE47 8HD
**t** (01434) 345282
**e** elkshead@amserve.com
**w** elkshead.co.uk

## WHITLEY BAY
Tyne and Wear

**Avalon** ★★★
*Guest Accommodation*
26-28 South Parade, Whitley Bay NE26 2RG
**t** (0191) 251 0080
**e** info@theavalon.co.uk
**w** theavalon.co.uk

**The Cara** ★★★ *Guest House*
9 The Links, Whitley Bay
NE26 1PS
**t** (0191) 253 0172
**e** info@caraguesthouse.co.uk
**w** caraguesthouse.co.uk

**The Chedburgh** ★★★
*Guest Accommodation*
12 Esplanade, Whitley Bay
NE26 2AH
**t** (0191) 253 0415
**e** chedburghhotel@aol.com
**w** chedburgh-hotel.co.uk

**Esplanade Lodge** ★★★
*Guest House*
1 Linden Terrace, Esplanade
NE26 2AA
**t** (0191) 251 7557
**e** esplanadelodge@hotmail.com
**w** esplanadelodge.co.uk

**Lighthouse Guest House**
Rating Applied For
*Guest Accommodation*
20 North Parade, Whitley Bay
NE26 1PA
**t** (0191) 252 2319

**Lindsay Guest House**
★★★★ *Guest House*
50 Victoria Avenue, Whitley Bay NE26 2BA
**t** (0191) 252 7341
**e** info@lindsayguesthouse.co.uk
**w** lindsayguesthouse.co.uk

**The Marlborough** ★★★★
*Guest Accommodation*
20-21 East Parade, Whitley Bay
NE26 1AP
**t** (0191) 251 3628
**e** reception@marlborough-hotel.com
**w** marlborough-hotel.com

**The Northumbria**
Rating Applied For
*Guest Accommodation*
51-52 Victoria Avenue, Whitley Bay NE26 2BA
**t** (0191) 252 5265
**e** northumbriahotel@btconnect.com

**Oaktree Lodge** ★★★★
*Guest House*
15 Esplanade, Whitley Bay
NE26 2AH
**t** (0191) 252 8587
**e** oaktreelodge@aol.com
**w** oaktree-lodge.co.uk

**York House** ★★★★
*Guest Accommodation*
106-110 Park Avenue, Whitley Bay NE26 1DN
**t** (0191) 252 8313
**e** reservations@yorkhousehotel.com
**w** yorkhousehotel.com

## WHITTINGHAM
Northumberland

**Callaly Cottage B&B and Massage Therapy** ★★★★
*Bed & Breakfast*
Callaly Cottage, Whittingham
NE66 4TA
**t** (01665) 574684
**e** callalycottage@talktalk.net
**w** callaly.alnwick.org.uk

## WHITWORTH
Lancashire

**Hindle Pastures** ★★★★
*Guest Accommodation*
**SILVER AWARD**
Highgate Lane, Whitworth
OL12 0TS
**t** (01706) 643310
**e** hindlepastures@tiscali.co.uk
**w** hindlepastures.co.uk

**The Red Lion** ★★★ *Inn*
Whitworth Square, Whitworth
OL12 8PY
**t** (01706) 861441
**e** redlionwhitworth@hotmail.co.uk
**w** redlionwhitworth.co.uk

## WHIXLEY
North Yorkshire

**Little Orchard** ★★★
*Guest Accommodation*
High Street, Whixley, York
YO26 8AW
**t** (01423) 330615

## WIGGLESWORTH
North Yorkshire

**Cowper Cottage** ★★★★
*Bed & Breakfast*
**SILVER AWARD**
Cowper Terrace, Wigglesworth, Settle
BD23 4RP
**t** (01729) 840598

## WIKE
West Yorkshire

**Wike Ridge Farm** ★★★★
*Guest Accommodation*
Wike Ridge Lane, Leeds
LS17 9JF
**t** (0113) 266 1190

## WILBERFOSS
East Riding of Yorkshire

**Cuckoo Nest Farm** ★★★
*Farmhouse*
York Road, Wilberfoss, York
YO41 5NL
**t** (01759) 380365

## WILDBOARCLOUGH
Cheshire

**Underbank Camping Barn**
*Camping Barn*
Wildboarclough, Macclesfield
SK11 0BL
**t** 0870 770 6113

## WILMSLOW
Cheshire

**Heatherlea Guest House**
★★★★
*Guest Accommodation*
106 Lacey Green, Wilmslow
SK9 4BN
**t** (01625) 522872
**e** info@heatherleaguesthouse.com
**w** heatherleaguesthouse.com

## WILTON
North Yorkshire

**The Old Forge** ★★★★
*Guest Accommodation*
Wilton, Pickering YO18 7JY
**t** (01751) 477399

## WINCLE
Cheshire

**Hill Top Farm Bed and Breakfast** ★★★★ *Farmhouse*
Wincle, Macclesfield
SK11 0QH
**t** (01260) 227257
**e** hilltopfarm_bb@hotmail.co.uk
**w** hill-top-farm.co.uk/welcome-to-hill-top-farm-b-b/

## WINDERMERE
Cumbria

**1 Park Road** ★★★★
*Guest House*
Windermere LA23 2AW
**t** (015394) 42107
**e** enquiries@1parkroad.com
**w** 1parkroad.com

**All Seasons Guest House**
★★★ *Guest Accommodation*
3 High Street, Windermere
LA23 1AF
**t** (015394) 48515
**e** info@allseasonsrest.co.uk
**w** allseasonsrest.co.uk

**Annisgarth B&B** ★★★
*Bed & Breakfast*
48 Craig Walk, Bowness-on-Windermere, Windermere
LA23 2JT
**t** (015394) 43866
**e** sharron@annisgarth.com
**w** annisgarth.co.uk

**Applegarth Villa & JR's Restaurant** ★★★★
*Guest Accommodation*
College Road, Windermere
LA23 1BU
**t** (015394) 43206
**e** info@lakesapplegarth.co.uk
**w** lakesapplegarth.co.uk

**Archway Guesthouse**
★★★★ *Guest House*
13 College Road, Windermere
LA23 1BU
**t** (015394) 45613
**e** stay@archwaywindermere.co.uk
**w** archwaywindermere.co.uk

**Ashleigh Guest House**
★★★★
*Guest Accommodation*
11 College Road, Windermere
LA23 1BU
**t** (015394) 42292
**e** enquiries@ashleighhouse.com
**w** ashleighhouse.com

**Autumn Leaves Guest House**
★★★ *Guest Accommodation*
29 Broad Street, Windermere
LA23 2AB
**t** (015394) 48410
**e** info@autumnleavesguesthouse.co.uk
**w** autumnleavesguesthouse.co.uk

**Beaumont House** ★★★★★
*Guest House*
Holly Road, Windermere
LA23 2AF
**t** (015394) 47075
**e** thebeaumonthotel@btinternet.com
**w** lakesbeaumont.co.uk

**Beckmead House** ★★★
*Guest Accommodation*
5 Park Avenue, Windermere
LA23 2AR
**t** (015394) 42757
**e** beckmead_house@yahoo.com
**w** beckmead.co.uk

**Beckside Cottage** ★★★
*Guest Accommodation*
4 Park Road, Windermere
LA23 2AW
**t** (015394) 42069
**e** info@becksidewindermere.co.uk
**w** becksidewindermere.co.uk

**Beech House**
Rating Applied For
*Guest House*
11 Woodland Road, Windermere LA23 2AE
**t** (015394) 88985
**e** info@beech-house.com
**w** beech-house.com

**Beechwood** ★★★★
*Guest Accommodation*
**GOLD AWARD**
South Craig, Beresford Road, Bowness-on-Windermere, Windermere LA23 2JG
**t** (015394) 43403
**e** enquiries@beechwoodlakes.co.uk
**w** beechwoodlakes.co.uk

**Belsfield House** ★★★★
*Guest House*
Kendal Road, Bowness-on-Windermere, Windermere
LA23 3EQ
**t** (015394) 45823
**e** enquiries@belsfieldhouse.co.uk
**w** belsfieldhouse.co.uk

**Bowfell Cottage** ★★★
*Bed & Breakfast*
Middle Entrance Drive, Bowness-on-Windermere, Windermere LA23 3JY
**t** (015394) 44835

**Braemount House** ★★★★
*Guest Accommodation*
**SILVER AWARD**
Sunny Bank Road, Windermere
LA23 2EN
**t** (015394) 45967
**e** enquiries@braemount-house.co.uk
**w** braemount-house.co.uk

**Brendan Chase** ★★★
*Guest House*
1 College Road, Windermere
LA23 1BU
**t** (015394) 45638
**e** brendanchase@aol.com
**w** placetostaywindermere.co.uk

**Briscoe Lodge Guest House**
★★★ *Guest House*
26 Ellerthwaite Road, Windermere LA23 2AH
**t** (015394) 42928
**e** stay@briscoelodge.co.uk
**w** briscoelodge.co.uk

**Brook House ★★★**
*Guest House*
30 Ellerthwaite Road, Windermere LA23 2AH
**t** (015394) 44932
**e** stay@brookhouselakes.co.uk
**w** brookhouselakes.co.uk

**Brooklands ★★★**
*Guest Accommodation*
Ferry View, Bowness-on-Windermere, Windermere LA23 3JB
**t** (015394) 42344
**e** enquiries@brooklandsguesthouse.net
**w** brooklandsguesthouse.net

**Cambridge House ★★★★**
*Guest House*
9 Oak Street, Windermere LA23 1EN
**t** (015394) 43846
**e** oak.lakes@btinternet.com
**w** cambridge-house.net

**Clifton House ★★★**
*Guest House*
28 Ellerthwaite Road, Windermere LA23 2AH
**t** (015394) 44968
**e** info@cliftonhse.co.uk
**w** cliftonhse.co.uk

**College House ★★★★**
*Guest House*
15 College Road, Windermere LA23 1BU
**t** (015394) 45767
**e** clghse@aol.com
**w** college-house.com

**The Cranleigh ★★★**
*Guest House*
Kendal Road, Bowness-on-Windermere, Windermere LA23 3EW
**t** (015394) 43293
**e** enquiries@thecranleigh.com
**w** thecranleigh.com

**Crompton House ★★★**
*Guest House*
Lake Road, Windermere LA23 2EQ
**t** (015394) 43020

**Denecrest ★★★**
*Guest House*
Woodland Road, Windermere LA23 2AE
**t** (015394) 44979
**e** denecrest@btconnect.com
**w** denecrest.com

**Denehurst Guest House**
★★★★ *Guest House*
**SILVER AWARD**
40 Queens Drive, Windermere LA23 2EL
**t** (015394) 44710
**e** denehurst@btconnect.com
**w** denehurst-guesthouse.co.uk

**Dunvegan Guest House**
★★★★
*Guest Accommodation*
Broad Street, Windermere LA23 2AB
**t** (015394) 43502
**e** bryan.twaddle@btinternet.com
**w** dunveganguesthouse.co.uk

**Eastbourne Guest House**
★★★★★ *Guest House*
Biskey Howe Road, Bowness-on-Windermere, Windermere LA23 2JR
**t** (015394) 88657
**e** stay@eastbourne-windermere.co.uk
**w** eastbourne-windermere.co.uk

**Elim Lodge ★★★**
*Guest House*
Biskey Howe Road, Bowness-on-Windermere LA23 2JP
**t** (015394) 47299
**e** enquiries@elimlodge.co.uk
**w** elimlodge.co.uk

**Ellerbrook House ★★★★**
*Guest House*
3 Park Avenue, Windermere LA23 2AR
**t** (015394) 88014
**e** information@ellerbrook.co.uk
**w** ellerbrook.co.uk

**Ellerthwaite Lodge ★★★★**
*Guest Accommodation*
New Road, Windermere LA23 2LA
**t** (015394) 45115
**e** info@ellerthwaitelodge.co.uk
**w** ellerthwaitelodge.com

**Fair Rigg ★★★★**
*Guest House* **SILVER AWARD**
Ferry View, Bowness-on-Windermere, Windermere LA23 3JB
**t** (015394) 43941
**e** stay@fairrigg.co.uk
**w** fairrigg.co.uk

**Fairfield House and Gardens**
★★★★ *Guest House*
**SILVER AWARD**
Brantfell Road, Bowness Bay LA23 3AE
**t** (015394) 46565
**e** relax@the-fairfield.co.uk
**w** the-fairfield.co.uk

**Fir Trees ★★★★**
*Guest House*
Lake Road, Windermere LA23 2EQ
**t** (015394) 42272
**e** enquiries@fir-trees.com
**w** fir-trees.com

**Firgarth ★★★** *Guest House*
Ambleside Road, Windermere LA23 1EU
**t** (015394) 46974
**e** enquiries@firgarth.com
**w** firgarth.com

**Greenriggs Guest House**
★★★ *Guest House*
8 Upper Oak Street, Windermere LA23 2LB
**t** (015394) 42265
**e** greenriggs@tiscali.co.uk
**w** greenriggs.com

**Heatherbank ★★★**
*Guest Accommodation*
13 Birch Street, Windermere LA23 1EG
**t** (015394) 46503
**e** heatherbank@btinternet.com
**w** heatherbank.com

**High View ★★★★★**
*Bed & Breakfast*
**SILVER AWARD**
Sun Hill Lane, Troutbeck Bridge, Windermere LA23 1HJ
**t** (015394) 44618
**e** info@accommodationlakedistrict.com
**w** accommodationlakedistrict.com

**Hilton House ★★★★**
*Guest House*
New Road, Windermere LA23 2EE
**t** (015394) 43934
**e** enquiries@hiltonhouse-guesthouse.co.uk
**w** hiltonhouse-guesthouse.co.uk

**Holly Lodge ★★★★**
*Guest Accommodation*
6 College Road, Windermere LA23 1BX
**t** (015394) 43873
**e** enquiries@hollylodge20.co.uk
**w** hollylodge20.co.uk

**Holly-Wood Guest House**
★★★★ *Guest House*
Holly Road, Windermere LA23 2AF
**t** (015394) 42219
**e** info@hollywoodguesthouse.co.uk
**w** hollywoodguesthouse.co.uk

**Holmlea Guest House ★★★**
*Guest House*
Kendal Road, Bowness-on-Windermere, Windermere LA23 3EW
**t** (015394) 42597
**e** info@holmleaguesthouse.co.uk
**w** holmleaguesthouse.co.uk

**Ivy Bank ★★★★**
*Guest House* **SILVER AWARD**
Holly Road, Windermere LA23 2AF
**t** (015394) 42601
**e** ivybank@clara.co.uk
**w** ivy-bank.co.uk

**Kays Cottage ★★★★**
*Guest House*
7 Broad Street, Windermere LA23 2AB
**t** (015394) 44146
**e** rooms@kayscottage.co.uk
**w** kayscottage.co.uk

**Kenilworth Guest House**
★★★★
*Guest Accommodation*
Holly Road, Windermere LA23 2AF
**t** (015394) 44004
**e** busby@kenilworth-lake-district.co.uk
**w** kenilworth-lake-district.co.uk

**Kirkwood Guest House**
★★★★ *Guest House*
Prince's Road, Windermere LA23 2DD
**t** (015394) 43907
**e** info@kirkwood51.co.uk
**w** kirkwood51.co.uk

**Lake View Guest House & Coffee Shop ★★★**
*Guest Accommodation*
2 Belsfield Terrace, Bowness-on-Windermere, Windermere LA23 3EQ
**t** (015394) 47098
**e** lakeview@dsl.pipex.com
**w** lakeview-guesthouse.co.uk

**Lakes Lodge ★★★**
*Guest Accommodation*
1 High Street, Windermere LA23 1AF
**t** (015394) 42751
**e** admin@lakes-hotel.com
**w** lakes-hotel.com

**Langdale View Guest House**
★★★ *Guest House*
114 Craig Walk, Off Helm Road, Bowness LA23 3AX
**t** (015394) 44076
**e** enquiries@langdaleview.co.uk
**w** langdaleview.co.uk

**Latimer House ★★★★**
*Guest House*
Lake Road, Bowness-on-Windermere, Windermere LA23 2JJ
**t** (015394) 46888
**e** enquiries@latimerhouse.co.uk
**w** latimerhouse.co.uk

**Laurel Cottage ★★★★**
*Guest Accommodation*
Park Road, Windermere LA23 2BJ
**t** (015394) 43053
**e** info@laurelcottagewindermere.co.uk
**w** laurelcottagewindermere.co.uk

**Laurel Cottage Bowness**
★★★★ *Guest House*
Kendal Road, Bowness-on-Windermere, Windermere LA23 3EF
**t** (015394) 45594
**e** enquiries@laurelcottage-bnb.co.uk
**w** laurelcottage-bnb.co.uk

**Lindisfarne Guest House**
★★★★ *Guest House*
Sunny Bank Road, Windermere LA23 2EN
**t** (015394) 46295
**e** enquiries@lindisfarne-house.co.uk
**w** lindisfarne-house.co.uk

**Lingmoor Guesthouse ★★★**
*Guest House*
7 High Street, Windermere LA23 1AF
**t** (015394) 44947
**e** info@lingmoor-guesthouse.co.uk
**w** lingmoor-guesthouse.co.uk

**Lingwood Lodge ★★★★**
*Guest House* **SILVER AWARD**
Birkett Hill, Bowness-on-Windermere, Windermere LA23 3EZ
**t** (015394) 44680
**e** stay@lingwoodlodge.co.uk
**w** lingwoodlodge.co.uk

**Lonsdale House** ★★★★
*Guest House* **SILVER AWARD**
Lake Road, Bowness-on-Windermere, Windermere
LA23 2JJ
t (015394) 43348
e info@lonsdale-hotel.co.uk
w lonsdale-hotel.co.uk

**Lynwood** ★★★★
*Guest House*
Broad Street, Windermere
LA23 2AB
t (015394) 42550
e enquiries@lynwood-guest-house.co.uk
w lynwood-guest-house.co.uk

**Meadfoot Guest House** ★★★★
*Guest Accommodation*
New Road, Windermere
LA23 2LA
t (015394) 42610
e queries@meadfoot-guesthouse.co.uk
w meadfoot-guesthouse.co.uk

**Melbourne Guest House** ★★★ *Guest Accommodation*
2-3 Biskey Howe Road, Bowness-on-Windermere, Windermere LA23 2JP
t (015394) 43475
e info@melbournecottage.co.uk
w melbournecottage.co.uk

**Millbeck Guest House** ★★★★ *Bed & Breakfast*
44 Ellerthwaite Road, Windermere LA23 2BS
t (015394) 45 392
e hpwhiteuk@aol.com

**Mylne Bridge House** ★★★★
*Guest House* **SILVER AWARD**
Brookside, Lake Road, Windermere LA23 2BX
t (015394) 43314
e stay@mylnebridgehouse.co.uk
w mylnebridgehouse.co.uk

**New Hall Bank** ★★★★
*Guest House*
Fallbarrow Road, Windermere
LA23 3DJ
t (015394) 43558
e info@newhallbank.co.uk
w newhallbank.com

**Newstead** ★★★★★
*Guest House*
New Road, Windermere
LA23 2EE
t (015394) 44485
e info@newstead-guesthouse.co.uk
w newstead-guesthouse.co.uk

**Oakfold House** ★★★★
*Guest House* **GOLD AWARD**
Beresford Road, Bowness
LA23 2JG
t (015394) 43239
e oakfoldhouse@fsmail.net
w oakfoldhouse.co.uk

**Oldfield House** ★★★★
*Guest House* **SILVER AWARD**
Oldfield Road, Windermere
LA23 2BY
t (015394) 88445
e info@oldfieldhouse.co.uk
w oldfieldhouse.co.uk

**Orrest Cottage Bed & Breakfast** ★★★
*Bed & Breakfast*
17 Church Street, Windermere
LA23 1AQ
t (015394) 88722
e orrestcottage@uwclub.net
w orrestcottage.co.uk

**Park Beck** ★★★ *Guest House*
3 Park Road, Windermere
LA23 2AW
t (015394) 44025

**Ravenscroft** ★★★★
*Bed & Breakfast*
**SILVER AWARD**
Lake Road, Windermere
LA23 2EQ
t (015394) 47046
e book@lakesguesthouse.co.uk
w lakesguesthouse.co.uk

**The Ravensworth** ★★★★
*Guest House*
Ambleside Road, Windermere
LA23 1BA
t (015394) 43747
e info@theravensworth.com
w theravensworth.co.uk

**Rayrigg Villa Guest House** ★★★ *Guest House*
Ellerthwaite Square, Windermere LA23 1DP
t (015394) 88342
e rayriggvilla@etherway.net
w rayriggvilla.co.uk

**Rocklea** ★★★★ *Guest House*
Brookside, Lake Road, Windermere LA23 2BX
t (015394) 45326
e info@rocklea.co.uk
w rocklea.co.uk

**Rockside Guest House** ★★★★ *Guest House*
25 Church Street, Windermere
LA23 1AQ
t (015394) 45343
e info@rockside-guesthouse.co.uk
w rockside-guesthouse.co.uk

**Rosemount** ★★★
*Guest House*
Lake Road, Windermere
LA23 2EQ
t (015394) 43739
e stay@lakedistrictguesthouse.com
w lakedistrictguesthouse.com

**St John's Lodge** ★★★
*Guest Accommodation*
Lake Road, Windermere
LA23 2EQ
t (015394) 43078
e mail@st-johns-lodge.co.uk
w st-johns-lodge.co.uk

**Southview House & Indoor Pool** ★★★★ *Guest House*
**SILVER AWARD**
Cross Street, Windermere
LA23 1AE
t (015394) 42951
e stay@southviewwindermere.co.uk
w southviewwindermere.co.uk

**Squirrel Bank** ★★★★
*Bed & Breakfast*
Ferry View, Crook Road, Bowness-on-Windermere
LA23 3JB
t (015394) 43329
e soar@squirrelbank.co.uk
w squirrelbank.co.uk

**Stockghyll Cottage** ★★★★
*Bed & Breakfast*
Rayrigg Road, Bowness-on-Windermere, Windermere
LA23 1BN
t (015394) 43246
e stay@stockghyllcottage.co.uk
w stockghyllcottage.co.uk

**Storrs Gate House** ★★★★★
*Guest House* **SILVER AWARD**
Longtail Hill, Bowness-on-Windermere, Windermere
LA23 3JD
t (015394) 43272
e enquiries@storrsgatehouse.co.uk
w storrsgatehouse.co.uk

**Tarn Rigg Guest House** ★★★★ *Guest House*
Thornbarrow Road, Windermere LA23 2DG
t (015394) 88777
e info@tarnrigg-guesthouse.co.uk
w tarnrigg-guesthouse.co.uk

**Thornbank House** ★★★★
*Guest House*
4 Thornbarrow Road, Windermere LA23 2EW
t (015394) 43724
e enquiries@thornbankwindermere.co.uk
w thornbankwindermere.co.uk

**Watermill Inn** ★★★★ *Inn*
Ings, Kendal, Windermere
LA8 9PY
t (01539) 821309
e info@watermillinn.co.uk
w watermillinn.co.uk

**The Waverley** ★★★
*Guest House*
College Road, Windermere
LA23 1BX
t (015394) 45026
e info@waverleyhotel.com
w waverleyhotel.com

**The Westbourne** ★★★★
*Guest House* **SILVER AWARD**
Biskey Howe Road, Bowness-on-Windermere, Windermere
LA23 2JR
t (015394) 43625
e westbourne@btinternet.com
w westbourne-lakes.co.uk

**Westbury House** ★★★
*Guest House*
27 Broad Street, Windermere
LA23 2AB
t (015394) 46839
e stay@windermerebnb.co.uk
w windermerebnb.co.uk

**Wheatlands Lodge** ★★★★★
*Guest Accommodation*
Old College Lane, Windermere
LA23 1BY
t (015394) 43789
e info@warzecha.plus.com
w wheatlandslodge-windermere.co.uk

**White Lodge** ★★★★
*Guest House*
Lake Road, Bowness-on-Windermere, Windermere
LA23 2JJ
t (015394) 43624
e enquiries@whitelodgehotel.com
w whitelodgehotel.com

**The White Rose** ★★★
*Guest Accommodation*
Broad Street, Windermere
LA23 2AB
t (015394) 45180
e whiteroselakes01@tiscali.co.uk
w whiteroselakes.co.uk

## WINGATES
Northumberland

**Pele Cottage** ★★★★
*Bed & Breakfast*
Wingates, Morpeth NE65 8RW
t (01670) 788320
e jane@pelecottage.co.uk
w pelecottage.co.uk

**South Farm** ★★★★★
*Farmhouse*
Wingates NE65 8RW
t (01670) 788562
e stay@southfarmwingates.co.uk
w southfarmwingates.co.uk

## WINSFORD
Cheshire

**Clivehall Farm** ★★★★
*Farmhouse*
Clive Lane, Wimsford
CW7 3PA
t (01606) 592505
e mail@clivehallfarm.co.uk
w clivehallfarm.co.uk

**The Winsford Lodge** ★★★
*Guest House*
85-87 Station Road, Winsford
CW7 3DE
t (01606) 862008
w winsfordlodge.co.uk/

## WIRRAL
Merseyside

**Mere Brook House**
Rating Applied For
*Bed & Breakfast*
Thornton Common Road, Wirral CH63 0LU
t (0151) 342 8237
e lorna@merebrookhouse.co.uk
w merebrookhouse.co.uk

**Pendragon House** ★★★★
*Guest House* **SILVER AWARD**
1 Bertram Drive, Wirral
CH47 0LG
t (0151) 632 5344
e pendragonhousehoylake@uwclub.net
w pendragonhouseuk.com

## WITTON GILBERT
Durham

**The Coach House** ★★★★
*Guest Accommodation*
Stobbilee House, Witton Gilbert DH7 6TW
t (0191) 373 6132
e suzanne@cronin.org.uk
w stobbilee.com

**WITTON-LE-WEAR**
**Durham**

**Witton Camping Barn**
*Camping Barn*
Witton Castle Estate, Witton-le-Wear DL14 0DE
t (01388) 488230
w wittoncastle.co.uk

**WOLD NEWTON**
**East Riding of Yorkshire**

**The Wold Cottage** ★★★★★
*Farmhouse* **GOLD AWARD**
Wold Newton, Driffield
YO25 3HL
t (01262) 470696
e katrina@woldcottage.com
w woldcottage.com

**WOMBLETON**
**North Yorkshire**

**Rockery Cottage** ★★★★
*Bed & Breakfast*
**SILVER AWARD**
Main Street, Wombleton, Helmsley YO62 7RX
t (01751) 432257
e enquiries@rockerycottage.co.uk
w rockerycottage.co.uk

**WOOLER**
**Northumberland**

**Belmont House Bed and Breakfast** ★★★★
*Bed & Breakfast*
Belmont House, 15 Glendale Road, Wooler NE71 6DN
t (01668) 283769
e susan@belmonthouse.org
w belmonthouse.org

**Cheviot View**
Rating Applied For
*Bed & Breakfast*
24 High Street, Wooler
NE71 6BY
t (01668) 281612
e info@cheviotview.co.uk

**Firwood** ★★★★★
*Bed & Breakfast*
**GOLD AWARD**
Middleton Hall, Wooler
NE71 6RD
t (01668) 283699
e welcome@firwoodhouse.co.uk
w firwoodhouse.co.uk

**The Hemmel Wooler**
★★★★ *Bed & Breakfast*
Way To Wooler Farm, Wooler
NE71 6AQ
t (01668) 283165
e j.staden@btopenworld.com
w thehemmelwooler.co.uk

**Mounthooly**
Rating Applied For
*Bunkhouse*
College Valley, Kirknewton
NE71 6DX
t (01668) 216358
e pauline@college-valley.co.uk
w college-valley.co.uk

**The Old Manse** ★★★★★
*Guest Accommodation*
**GOLD AWARD**
New Road, Chatton NE66 5PU
t (01668) 215343
e chattonbb@aol.com
w oldmansechatton.co.uk

**Rockliffe House** ★★★★
*Bed & Breakfast*
6 Glendale Road, Wooler
NE71 6DN
t (01668) 283992
e info@rockliffehouse.co.uk
w rockliffehouse.co.uk

**Tilldale House** ★★★★
*Guest Accommodation*
**SILVER AWARD**
34/40 High Street, Wooler
NE71 6BG
t (01668) 281450
e tilldalehouse@freezone.co.uk
w tilldalehouse.co.uk

**Tillside B&B** ★★★★
*Bed & Breakfast*
**SILVER AWARD**
1 The Peth, Wooler NE71 6NB
t (01668) 281252
e info@redteegolfbreaks.co.uk
w tillside-wooler.co.uk

**Wooler YHA** ★★★ *Hostel*
30 Cheviot Street, Wooler
NE71 6LW
t 0870 770 6100
e wooler@yha.org.uk
w yha.org.uk

**WORKINGTON**
**Cumbria**

**Morven Guest House** ★★★
*Guest Accommodation*
Siddick Road, Siddick, Workington CA14 1LE
t (01900) 602118 & 07718 864 7196
e cnelsonmorven@aol.com
w morvenguesthouse.com

**Old Ginn House** ★★★★ *Inn*
Moor Road, Great Clifton, Workington CA14 1TS
t (01900) 64616
e enquiries@oldginnhouse.co.uk
w oldginnhouse.co.uk

**WORSTON**
**Lancashire**

**Angram Green Farmhouse B&B** ★★★★ *Farmhouse*
Worston, Clitheroe BB7 1QB
t (01200) 441441
w angramgreenfarm.co.uk

**The Calf's Head** ★★★★
*Guest Accommodation*
Worston, Clitheroe BB7 1QA
t (01200) 441218
e info@calfshead.co.uk
w calfshead.co.uk

**WORTLEY**
**South Yorkshire**

**Wortley Hall** ★★★
*Guest Accommodation*
Wortley Village, Sheffield, Barnsley S35 7DB
t (0114) 288 2100
e info@wortleyhall.org.uk
w wortleyhall.org.uk

**WYCOLLER**
**Lancashire**

**Parson Lee Farm** ★★★
*Farmhouse*
Trawden, Wycoller BB8 8SU
t (01282) 864747
e pathodgson@hotmail.com
w parsonleefarm.co.uk

**WYKEHAM**
**North Yorkshire**

**Downe Arms Hotel** ★★★
*Inn*
Main Road, Wykeham, Scarborough YO13 9QB
t (01723) 862471
e info@downarmshotel.co.uk
w downarmshotel.co.uk

**WYLAM**
**Northumberland**

**Wormald House** ★★★★
*Bed & Breakfast*
Main Road, Wylam NE41 8DN
t (01661) 852529
e jr.craven@tiscali.co.uk
w wormaldhouse.co.uk

**YEADON**
**West Yorkshire**

**Willow Cottage B&B** ★★★★
*Guest Accommodation*
Willow Cottage, Ivegate, Leeds LS19 7RE
t (0113) 250 1189
e info@willowcottage.org.uk
w willowcottage.org.uk

**YORK**
**North Yorkshire**

**23 St Marys** ★★★★
*Guest House* **SILVER AWARD**
Bootham, York YO30 7DD
t (01904) 622738
e stmarys23@hotmail.com
w 23stmarys.co.uk

**Abbey Guest House** ★★★★
*Guest House*
13-14 Earlsborough Terrace, Marygate YO30 7BQ
t (01904) 627782
e info@abbeyghyork.co.uk
w abbeyghyork.co.uk

**Abbeyfields Guest House** ★★★★
*Guest Accommodation*
19 Bootham Terrace, York
YO30 7DH
t (01904) 636471
e enquire@abbeyfields.co.uk
w abbeyfields.co.uk

**Abbingdon Guest House**
★★★ *Guest House*
60 Bootham Crescent, York
YO30 7AH
t (01904) 621761
e info@abbingdonyork.co.uk
w abbingdonyork.co.uk

**The Acer Guest House**
★★★★ *Guest House*
52 Scarcroft Hill, York
YO24 1DE
t (01904) 653839
e info@acerhotel.co.uk
w acerhotel.co.uk

**Acres Dene Guest House**
★★★ *Guest House*
87 Fulford Road, York
YO10 4BD
t (01904) 647482
e stay@acresdene.co.uk
w acresdene.co.uk

**Airden House** ★★★★
*Guest House*
1 St Mary's, Bootham, York
YO30 7DD
t (01904) 638915
e info@airdenhouse.co.uk
w airdenhouse.co.uk

**Alcuin Lodge Guest House**
★★★★ *Guest House*
15 Sycamore Place, Bootham, York YO30 7DW
t (01904) 632222
e info@alcuinlodge.com
w alcuinlodge.com

**Alexander House** ★★★★★
*Guest Accommodation*
**GOLD AWARD**
94 Bishopthorpe Road, York
YO23 1JS
t (01904) 625016
e info@alexanderhouseyork.co.uk
w alexanderhouseyork.co.uk

**Amber House** ★★★★
*Bed & Breakfast*
36 Bootham Crescent, Bootham, York YO30 7AH
t (01904) 620275
e info@amberhouse-york.co.uk
w amberhouse-york.co.uk

**Ambleside Guest House**
★★★ *Guest House*
62 Bootham Crescent, Bootham YO30 7AH
t (01904) 637165
e ambles@globalnet.co.uk
w ambleside-gh.co.uk

**The Apple House** ★★★★
*Guest House*
74-76 Holgate Road, York
YO24 4AB
t (01904) 625081
e pamelageorge1@yahoo.co.uk
w applehouseyork.co.uk

**Ardmore Guest House** ★★★
*Guest House*
31 Claremont Terrace, Gillygate, York YO31 7EJ
t (01904) 622562
w ardmoreyork.co.uk

**Arnot House** ★★★★★
*Bed & Breakfast*
**GOLD AWARD**
17 Grosvenor Terrace, York
YO30 7AG
t (01904) 641966
e kim.robbins@virgin.net
w arnothouseyork.co.uk

**Ascot House** ★★★★
*Guest Accommodation*
**SILVER AWARD**
80 East Parade, York
YO31 7YH
**t** (01904) 426826
**e** admin@ascothouseyork.com
**w** ascothouseyork.com

**Ascot Lodge** ★★★★
*Guest Accommodation*
112 Acomb Road, York
YO24 4EY
**t** (01904) 798234
**e** info@ascotlodge.com
**w** ascotlodge.com

**The Ashberry** ★★★★
*Guest Accommodation*
103 The Mount, York
YO24 1AX
**t** (01904) 647339
**e** kevlyon@ashberryhotel.co.uk
**w** ashberryhotel.co.uk

Avondale Guest House
★★★ *Guest Accommodation*
61 Bishopthorpe Road, York
YO23 1NX
t (01904) 633989
e kaleda@avondaleguesthouse.co.uk
w avondaleguesthouse.co.uk

Bar Convent ★★★
*Guest Accommodation*
17 Blossom Street, York
YO24 1AQ
t (01904) 643238
e info@bar-convent.org.uk
w bar-convent.org.uk

**Barbican House** ★★★★
*Guest Accommodation*
**SILVER AWARD**
20 Barbican Road, York
YO10 5AA
**t** (01904) 627617
**e** info@barbicanhouse.com
**w** barbicanhouse.com

Barclay Lodge ★★
*Guest Accommodation*
19/21 Gillygate, York
YO31 7EA
t (01904) 633274
e info@barclaylodge.co.uk
w barclaylodge.co.uk

Barrington House ★★★★
*Guest Accommodation*
15 Nunthorpe Avenue, Scarcroft Road, York YO23 1PF
t (01904) 634539
e info@barringtonhouse.net
w barringtonhouse.net

Bay Tree Guest House
★★★★ *Guest House*
92 Bishopthorpe Road, York
YO1 6HQ
t (01904) 659462
e info@baytree-york.co.uk
w baytree-york.co.uk

Beckett Guest House ★★★
*Guest Accommodation*
58 Bootham Crescent, York
YO30 7AH
t (01904) 644728
e nova@woko.freeserve.co.uk
w becketthotel.co.uk

Beech House ★★★★
*Guest Accommodation*
SILVER AWARD
6-7 Longfield Terrace, Bootham, York YO30 7DJ
t (01904) 634581
e beechhouse-york@hotmail.co.uk
w beechhouse-york.co.uk

**The Bentley Guest House** ★★★★
*Guest Accommodation*
25 Grosvenor Terrace, Bootham, York YO30 7AG
**t** (01904) 644313
**e** enquiries@bentleyofyork.com
**w** bentleyofyork.com

Bishopgarth Guest House
★★★ *Guest House*
3 Southlands Road, York
YO23 1NP
t (01904) 635220
e bishopgarth@btconnect.com
w bishopgarth.co.uk

**Bishops** ★★★★★
*Guest Accommodation*
**SILVER AWARD**
135 Holgate Road, York
YO24 4DF
**t** (01904) 628000
**e** enquiries@bishopshotel.co.uk
**w** bishopshotel.co.uk

The Bloomsbury ★★★★
*Guest House* SILVER AWARD
127 Clifton, York YO30 6BL
t (01904) 634031
e thebloomsbury@btinternet.com
w bloomsburyhotel.co.uk

Blossoms York ★★★
*Guest Accommodation*
28 Clifton, York YO30 6AE
t (01904) 652391
e reception@blossomsyork.co.uk
w blossomsyork.co.uk

Bootham Gardens Guesthouse ★★★★
*Guest House*
47 Bootham Crescent, York
YO30 7AJ
t (01904) 625911
e guesthouse@hotmail.co.uk
w bootham-gardens-guesthouse.co.uk

Bootham Guest House ★★★★
*Guest Accommodation*
56 Bootham Crescent, York
YO30 7AH
t (01904) 672123
e boothamguesthouse1@hotmail.com
w boothamguesthouse.com

Bootham Park ★★★★
*Guest Accommodation*
9 Grosvenor Terrace, Bootham, York YO30 7AG
t (01904) 644262
e boothampark@aol.com
w boothamparkhotel.co.uk

Bowen House ★★★★
*Guest House*
4 Gladstone St, Huntington Rd, York YO31 8RF
t (01904) 636881
e info@bowenhouseyork.com
w bowenhouseyork.com

Bowmans Guest House
★★★★ *Guest House*
SILVER AWARD
33 Grosvenor Terrace, York
YO30 7AG
t (01904) 622204
e info@bowmansguesthouse.co.uk
w bowmansguesthouse.co.uk

The Brentwood ★★★★
*Guest Accommodation*
54 Bootham Crescent, York
YO30 7AH
t (01904) 636419
e brentwoodps@aol.com
w thebrentwoodofyork.com

Briar Lea Guest House ★★★
*Guest Accommodation*
8 Longfield Terrace, Bootham, York YO30 7DJ
t (01904) 635061
e briarleahouse@msn.com
w briarlea.co.uk

Bronte Guest House ★★★★
*Guest Accommodation*
22 Grosvenor Terrace, Bootham, York YO30 7AG
t (01904) 621066
e enquiries@bronte-guesthouse.com
w bronte-guesthouse.com

Bull Lodge Guest House
★★★ *Guest House*
37 Bull Lane, Lawrence Street, York YO10 3EN
t (01904) 415522
e stay@bulllodge.co.uk
w bulllodge.co.uk

Burton Villa Guest House
★★★ *Guest House*
24 Haxby Road, York YO31 8JX
t (01904) 626364
e burtonvilla@supanet.com
w burtonvilla.com

**Carlton House** ★★★★
*Guest Accommodation*
134 The Mount, York
YO24 1AS
**t** (01904) 622265
**e** etb@carltonhouse.co.uk
**w** carltonhouse.co.uk

Carousel Guest House ★★
*Guest House*
83 Eldon Street, York
YO31 7NH
t (01904) 646709
e w_zhuang@hotmail.com

The Cavalier ★★★
*Guest House*
39 Monkgate, York YO31 7PB
t (01904) 636615
e julia@cavalier.co.uk
w cavalierhotel.co.uk

Chelmsford Place Guest House ★★★ *Guest House*
85 Fulford Road, York
YO10 4BD
t (01904) 624491
e chelmsfordplace@btinternet.com
w chelmsfordplace.co.uk

City Guest House ★★★★
*Guest Accommodation*
68 Monkgate, York YO31 7PF
t (01904) 622483
e info@cityguesthouse.co.uk
w cityguesthouse.co.uk

Claxton Hall Cottage Guest House ★★★★
*Bed & Breakfast*
Malton Road, York YO60 7RE
t (01904) 468697
e claxcott@aol.com
w claxtonhallcottage.com

Coach House ★★★★
*Guest Accommodation*
20-22 Marygate, York
YO30 7BH
t (01904) 652780
e info@coachhousehotel-york.com
w coachhousehotel-york.com

Cooks Guest House ★★★
*Guest House*
120 Bishopthorpe Road, York
YO23 1JX
t (01904) 652519
e jennieslcook@hotmail.co.uk
w cooksguesthouse.co.uk

Crescent Guest House ★★
*Guest House*
77 Bootham, York YO30 7DQ
t (01904) 623216

Crook Lodge ★★★★
*Guest Accommodation*
SILVER AWARD
26 St Marys, Bootham, York
YO30 7DD
t (01904) 655614
e crooklodge@hotmail.com
w crooklodge.co.uk

Crossways Guest House
★★★★ *Guest House*
23 Wiggington Road, York
YO31 8HJ
t (01904) 637250
e enquiries@crossways-york.co.uk
w crossways-york.co.uk

**Cumbria House** ★★★
*Guest House*
2 Vyner Street, York YO31 8HS
**t** (01904) 636817
**e** candj@cumbriahouse.freeserve.co.uk
**w** cumbriahouse.com

**Curzon Lodge and Stable Cottages** ★★★★
*Guest House*
23 Tadcaster Road, York
YO24 1QG
**t** (01904) 703157
**e** admin@curzonlodge.com
**w** smoothhound.co.uk/hotels/curzon.html

**Dairy Guest House** ★★★★
*Guest House*
3 Scarcroft Road, York
YO23 1ND
**t** (01904) 639367
**e** stay@dairyguesthouse.co.uk
**w** dairyguesthouse.co.uk

Dalescroft Guest House
★★★ *Guest House*
10 Southlands Road, York
YO23 1NP
t (01904) 626801
e info@dalescroft-york.co.uk
w dalescroft-york.co.uk

**Elliotts** ★★★★ *Guest House*
2 Sycamore Place, Bootham, York YO30 7DW
**t** (01904) 623333
**e** elliotshotel@aol.com
**w** elliottshotel.co.uk

**Farthings Guest House**
★★★★ *Guest House*
5 Nunthorpe Avenue, York YO23 1PF
**t** (01904) 653545
**e** stay@farthingsyork.co.uk
**w** farthingsyork.co.uk

**Feversham Lodge** ★★★★
*Guest Accommodation*
**SILVER AWARD**
1 Feversham Crescent, Off Wigginton Road, York YO31 8HQ
**t** (01904) 623882
**e** bookings@fevershamlodge.co.uk
**w** fevershamlodge.co.uk

**Foss Bank Guest House**
★★★★ *Guest House*
16 Huntington Road, York YO31 8RB
**t** (01904) 635548
**w** fossbank.co.uk

**Four Seasons** ★★★★★
*Guest Accommodation*
7 Stpeters Grove, Bootham, York YO30 6AQ
**t** (01904) 622621
**e** roe@fourseasons.supanet.com
**w** fourseasons-hotel.co.uk

**Fourposter Lodge** ★★★
*Guest House*
68-70 Heslington Road, York YO10 5AU
**t** (01904) 651170
**e** fourposter.lodge@virgin.net
**w** fourposterlodge.co.uk

**Friars Rest Guest House**
★★★ *Guest House*
81 Fulford Road, York YO10 4BD
**t** (01904) 629823
**e** friarsrest@btinernet.com
**w** friarsrest.co.uk

**Galtres Lodge** ★★
*Guest Accommodation*
54 Low Petergate, York YO1 7HZ
**t** (01904) 622478
**e** info@galtreslodgehotel.co.uk
**w** galtreslodgehotel.co.uk

**Georgian House** ★★
*Guest Accommodation*
35 Bootham, York YO30 7BT
**t** (01904) 622874
**e** york1e45@aol.com
**w** georgianhouse.co.uk

**Glade Farm** ★★★★
*Bed & Breakfast*
Riccall Road, Escrick, Selby YO19 6ED
**t** (01904) 728098
**e** victorialeaf@hotmail.com

**Goldsmiths Guest House**
★★★★
*Guest Accommodation*
18 Longfield Terrace, York YO30 7DJ
**t** (01904) 655738
**e** susan@goldsmith18.freeserve.co.uk
**w** goldsmithsguesthouse.co.uk

**Grange Lodge Guest House**
★★★ *Guest Accommodation*
52 Bootham Crescent, York YO30 7AH
**t** (01904) 621137
**e** grangeldg@aol.com
**w** grange-lodge.com

**Greenside** ★★★
*Guest House*
124 Clifton, York YO30 6BQ
**t** (01904) 623631
**e** greenside@surfree.co.uk
**w** greensideguesthouse.co.uk

**Gregory's** ★★★★
*Guest Accommodation*
**SILVER AWARD**
160 Bishopthorpe Road, York YO23 1LF
**t** (01904) 627521
**e** gregorys.york@virgin.net
**w** gregorysofyork.co.uk

**The Groves** ★★★
*Guest Accommodation*
St Peters Grove, York YO30 6AQ
**t** (01904) 559777
**e** admin@ecsyork.co.uk
**w** ecsyork.co.uk

**The Hazelwood** ★★★★
*Guest Accommodation*
**SILVER AWARD**
24-25 Portland Street, York YO31 7EH
**t** (01904) 626548
**e** reservations@thehazelwoodyork.com
**w** thehazelwoodyork.com

**Heworth Court** ★★★★
*Guest Accommodation*
Heworth Green, York YO31 7TQ
**t** (01904) 425156
**e** hotel@heworth.co.uk
**w** heworth.co.uk

**Heworth Guest House**
★★★★ *Guest House*
126 East Parade, Heworth, York YO31 7YG
**t** (01904) 426384
**e** chris@yorkcity.co.uk
**w** yorkbandb.co.uk

**Hillcrest Guest House**
Rating Applied For
*Guest House*
110 Bishopthorpe Road, York YO23 1JX
**t** (01904) 653160
**e** info@hillcrest-guest-house.co.uk
**w** hillcrest-guest-house.co.uk

**Holgate Bridge** ★★★
*Guest Accommodation*
106 Holgate Rd, York YO24 4BB
**t** (01904) 635971
**e** info@holgatebridge.co.uk
**w** holgatebridge.co.uk

**The Hollies Guest House**
★★★★ *Guest House*
141 Fulford Road, York YO10 4HG
**t** (01904) 634279
**e** hayleycarlyle@hotmail.com

**Holly Cottage B&B**
Rating Applied For
*Bed & Breakfast*
194 Malton Road, York YO32 9TD
**t** (01904) 424223
**e** carol@carolz.plus.com
**w** hollycottageyork.co.uk

**Holly Lodge** ★★★★
*Guest Accommodation*
206 Fulford Road, York YO10 4DD
**t** (01904) 646005
**e** geoff@thehollylodge.co.uk
**w** thehollylodge.co.uk

**Holme – Lea – Manor**
★★★★ *Guest House*
18 St Peters Grove, Clifton, York YO30 6AQ
**t** (01904) 623529
**e** holmelea@btclick.com
**w** holmelea.co.uk

**Huntington House** ★★★
*Group Hostel*
18 Huntington Road, York YO31 8RB
**t** (01904) 622755
**e** pp@huntingtonhouse.demon.co.uk
**w** huntingtonhouse.demon.co.uk

**The Lighthorseman** ★★★★
*Inn*
124 Fulford Road, Fishergate YO10 4BE
**t** (01904) 624818
**e** janinerobinson03@aol.com
**w** lighthorseman.co.uk

**Limes** ★★★★ *Guest House*
**SILVER AWARD**
135 Fulford Road, York YO10 4HE
**t** (01904) 624548
**e** queries@limeshotel.co.uk
**w** limeshotel.co.uk

**Linden Lodge** ★★★★
*Guest Accommodation*
6 Nunthorpe Avenue, York YO23 1PF
**t** (01904) 620107
**e** lindenlodgehotel@btinternet.com
**w** lindenlodgehotel.co.uk

**Manor Guest House** ★★★★
*Guest Accommodation*
Main Street, Linton-on-Ouse YO30 2AY
**t** (01347) 848391
**e** manorguesthouse@tiscali.co.uk
**w** manorguesthouse.co.uk

**Midway House** ★★★★
*Guest Accommodation*
145 Fulford Road, York YO10 4HG
**t** (01904) 659272
**e** info@midwayhouseyork.co.uk
**w** midwayhouseyork.co.uk

**Minster View Guest House**
★★★ *Guest House*
2 Grosvenor Terrace, Bootham, York YO30 7AG
**t** (01904) 655034
**e** julieholborn@aol.com
**w** minsterviewyork.com

**Monkgate Guest House**
★★★ *Guest House*
65 Monkgate, York YO31 7PA
**t** (01904) 655947
**e** 65monkgate@btconnect.com
**w** monkgateguesthouse.com

**Mont-Clare Guest House**
★★★ *Guest House*
32 Claremont Terrace, Gillygate, York YO31 7EJ
**t** (01904) 651011
**e** info@mont-clare.co.uk
**w** mont-clare.co.uk

**Moorgarth Guest House**
★★★ *Guest House*
158 Fulford Road, York YO10 4DA
**t** (01904) 636768
**w** moorgarthyork.co.uk

**Moorland House** ★★★
*Guest Accommodation*
1a Moorland Road, Fulford, York YO10 4HF
**t** (01904) 629354
**e** g.metcalfe@tesco.net
**w** moorlandhouseyork.co.uk

**Mowbray House** ★★★
*Bed & Breakfast*
34 Haxby Road, York YO31 8JX
**t** (01904) 637710
**e** carol@mowbrayhouse.co.uk
**w** mowbrayhouse.co.uk

**No 40** ★★★★
*Bed & Breakfast*
40 Queen Anne's Rd, Bootham, York YO30 7AA
**t** (01904) 655509
**e** dilys.no40bbyork@btinternet.com
**w** no40bbyork.co.uk

**Northolme Guest House**
★★★ *Guest House*
114 Shipton Road, Rawcliffe, York YO30 5RN
**t** (01904) 639132
**e** g.liddle@tesco.net
**w** northolmeguesthouse.co.uk

**Oaklands Guest House**
★★★★
*Guest Accommodation*
351 Strensall Road, Earswick, York YO32 9SW
**t** (01904) 768443
**e** mavmo@oaklands5.fsnet.co.uk

**Orillia House** ★★★★
*Guest Accommodation*
89 The Village, Stockton-on-Forest, York YO32 9UP
**t** (01904) 400600
**e** orillia@globalnet.co.uk

**Palm Court** ★★★★
*Guest Accommodation*
17 Huntington Road, York YO31 8RB
**t** (01904) 639387
**e** helencoll_2000@hotmail.com
**w** thepalmcourt.org.uk

**The Papillon** ★★
*Guest House*
43 Gillygate, York YO31 7EA
**t** (01904) 636505
**e** papillonhotel@btinternet.com
**w** btinternet.com/~papillonhotel

**Park View** ★★★★
*Guest House*
34 Grosvenor Terrace, Bootham, York YO30 7AG
**t** (01904) 620437
**e** theparkviewyork@aol.com
**w** theparkviewyork.co.uk

**Park View – Haxby Road**
Rating Applied For
*Guest Accommodation*
22 Haxby Road, York YO31 8JX
**t** (01904) 611396
**e** ahmforh@aol.com
**w** parkviewguesthouse.co.uk

**Queen Annes Guest House**
★★★ *Guest Accommodation*
24 Queen Annes Road, Bootham, York YO30 7AA
**t** (01904) 629389
**e** queen.annes@btopenworld.com
**w** queen-annes-guesthouse.co.uk

**St George's** ★★★
*Guest Accommodation*
6 St Georges Place, York YO24 1DR
**t** (01904) 625056
**e** sixstgeorg@aol.com
**w** stgeorgesyork.com

**St Marys Guest House**
★★★★
*Guest Accommodation*
17 Longfield Terrace, Bootham, York YO30 7DJ
**t** (01904) 626972
**e** stmaryshotel@talk21.com
**w** stmaryshotel.co.uk

**St Raphael Guesthouse**
★★★★
*Guest Accommodation*
44 Queen Annes Road, York YO30 7AF
**t** (01904) 645028
**e** info@straphaelguesthouse.co.uk
**w** straphaelguesthouse.co.uk

**Skelton Grange Farmhouse**
★★★★
*Guest Accommodation*
Orchard View, Skelton, York YO30 1YQ
**t** (01904) 470780
**e** susie@skelton-farm.co.uk
**w** skelton-farm.co.uk

**Southlands Guest House**
★★★★
*Guest Accommodation*
69 Nunmill Street, York YO23 1NT
**t** (01904) 675966
**e** enquiries@southlands-guest.co.uk
**w** southlands-guesthouse.co.uk

**Stanley House** ★★★
*Guest House*
Stanley Street, York YO31 8NW
**t** (01904) 637111
**e** stanleyhouseyork@hotmail.com
**w** stanleyhouseyork.co.uk

**Staymor Guest House**
★★★★ *Guest House*
2 Southlands Road, York YO23 1NP
**t** (01904) 626935
**e** kathwilson@lineone.net
**w** staymorguesthouse.com

**The Steer Inn** ★★★ *Inn*
Hull Road, Wilberfoss, York YO41 5PF
**t** (01759) 380600
**e** reception@thesteerinn.co.uk
**w** thesteerinn.co.uk

**Sycamore Guest House**
★★★ *Guest House*
19 Sycamore Place, York YO30 7DW
**t** (01904) 624712
**e** mail@thesycamore.co.uk
**w** guesthousesyork.co.uk

**Tree Tops** ★★★ *Guest House*
21 St Marys, Bootham, York YO30 7DD
**t** (01904) 629494
**e** treetopsguesthouseyork@yahoo.co.uk
**w** treetopsguesthouse.co.uk

**Turnberry House** ★★★★
*Guest House*
143 Fulford Road, York YO10 4HG
**t** (01904) 658435
**e** turnberry.house@virgin.net
**w** turnberryhouse.com

**Tyburn House** ★★★
*Guest Accommodation*
11 Albermarle Road, The Mount, York YO23 1EN
**t** (01904) 655069
**e** york@tyburnhotel.freeserve.co.uk

**Warrens** ★★★★
*Guest Accommodation*
30-32 Scarcroft Road, York YO23 1NF
**t** (01904) 643139
**e** info@warrenshotel.co.uk
**w** warrenshotel.co.uk

**Wellgarth House** ★★★
*Guest Accommodation*
Wetherby Road, Rufforth, York YO23 3QB
**t** (01904) 738592 & 07711 252577
**w** wellgarthhouse.co.uk

**The Windmill** ★★★★ *Inn*
Hull Road, Dunnington, York YO19 5LP
**t** (01904) 481898
**e** j.saggers@btopenworld.com
**w** thewindmilldunnington.co.uk

**Wood Farm** ★★★★
*Farmhouse*
York YO30 1BU
**t** (01904) 470333
**e** email@woodfarmbedandbreakfast.co.uk
**w** woodfarmbedandbreakfast.co.uk

**YHA York International**
★★★ *Hostel*
42 Water End, Clifton, York YO30 6LP
**t** (01904) 653147
**e** york@yha.org.uk
**w** yha.org.uk

**York House** ★★★★
*Guest Accommodation*
62 Heworth Green, York YO31 7TQ
**t** (01904) 427070
**e** yorkhouse.bandb@tiscali.co.uk
**w** yorkhouseyork.co.uk

**York Lodge Guest House**
★★★ *Guest Accommodation*
64 Bootham Crescent, Bootham, York YO30 7AH
**t** (01904) 654289
**e** yorkldg@aol.com
**w** york-lodge.com

**The York Priory** ★★★★
*Guest House*
126 Fulford Road, York YO10 4BE
**t** (01904) 625280
**e** reservations@priory-hotelyork.co.uk
**w** priory-hotelyork.co.uk

## CENTRAL ENGLAND

### AB KETTLEBY
Leicestershire

**White Lodge Farm Bed & Breakfast** ★★★★ *Farmhouse*
Nottingham Road, Ab Kettleby, Melton Mowbray LE14 3JB
**t** (01664) 822286

### ACLE
Norfolk

**The Kings Head Inn** ★★★
*Inn*
The Street, Norwich NR13 3DY
**t** (01493) 750204
**e** info@kingsheadinnacle.co.uk
**w** kingsheadinnacle.co.uk

### ACTON
Suffolk

**Barbies** ★★
*Guest Accommodation*
25 Clay Hall Place, Sudbury CO10 0BT
**t** (01787) 373702
**w** tiscover.co.uk

### ALBRIGHTON
Shropshire

**Boningale Manor** ★★★★
*Bed & Breakfast*
Holyhead Road, Boningale, Albrighton, Wolverhampton WV7 3AT
**t** (01902) 373376
**e** boningalemanor@aol.com
**w** boningalemanor.com

**Parkside Farm** ★★★★
*Farmhouse* **SILVER AWARD**
Holyhead Road, Albrighton WV7 3DA
**t** (01902) 372310
**e** margaret@parksidefarm.com
**w** parksidefarm.com

### ALBURGH
Norfolk

**Dove Restaurant** ★★★★
*Restaurant with Rooms*
Holbrook Hill, Alburgh, Harleston IP20 0EP
**t** (01986) 788315

### ALCESTER
Warwickshire

**The Globe** ★★★★
*Guest Accommodation*
54 Birmingham Road, Alcester B49 5EG
**t** (01789) 763287
**e** globe_hotel@btconnect.com
**w** theglobehotel.com

**Sambourne Hall Farm**
★★★★ *Farmhouse*
Wike Lane, Sambourne, Studley B96 6NZ
**t** (01527) 852151

### ALDBOROUGH
Norfolk

**Butterfly Cottage** ★★★★
*Guest House*
The Green, Aldborough, Norwich NR11 7AA
**t** (01263) 768198 & (01263) 761689
**e** butterflycottage@btopenworld.com
**w** butterflycottage.com

### ALDEBURGH
Suffolk

**Marygold** ★★★★
*Bed & Breakfast*
Beaconsfield Road, Aldeburgh IP15 5HF
**t** (01728) 453323
**e** bandb@marygoldaldeburgh.co.uk
**w** tiscover.co.uk

**Oak** ★★★★ *Bed & Breakfast*
111 Saxmundham Road, Aldeburgh IP15 5JF
**t** (01728) 453503
**e** info@ppaskletting.co.uk
**w** ppaskletting.co.uk

**Sanviv** ★★★ *Bed & Breakfast*
59 Fairfield Road, Aldeburgh IP15 5JN
**t** (01728) 453107

**Toll House** ★★★★
*Guest House*
50 Victoria Road, Aldeburgh IP15 5EJ
**t** (01728) 453239
**e** tollhouse@fsmail.net
**w** tollhouse.travelbugged.com

## ALDEBY Norfolk

**Old Vicarage** ★★★
*Bed & Breakfast*
Rectory Road, Aldeby, Beccles NR34 0BJ
**t** (01502) 678229
**e** butler@beccles33.freeserve.co.uk
**w** tiscover.co.uk

## ALDERTON Northamptonshire

**Magnolia** ★★★★
*Bed & Breakfast*
Church Lane, Alderton NN12 7LP
**t** (01327) 811479
**e** bandb@magnolia.me.uk
**w** magnolia.me.uk

## ALDHAM Essex

**Caterpillar Cottage** ★★★★
*Bed & Breakfast*
Ford Street, Aldham, Colchester CO6 3PH
**t** (01206) 240456
**w** smoothhound.co.uk/hotels/caterpillar

## ALDWARK Derbyshire

**Lydgate Farmhouse Bed & Breakfast** ★★★★ *Farmhouse*
Aldwark, Grange Mill, Matlock DE4 4HW
**t** (01629) 540720
**e** jjlomas@btinternet.com

## ALDWINCLE Northamptonshire

**Pear Tree Farm** ★★★★
*Farmhouse*
Main Street, Aldwincle, Kettering NN14 3EL
**t** (01832) 720614
**e** beverley@peartreefarm.net
**w** peartreefarm.net

## ALFORD Lincolnshire

**Alford Bed & Breakfast** ★★★ *Bed & Breakfast*
27 Chauntry Road, Alford LN13 9HH
**t** (01507) 462751
**e** nick.ofarrell@virgin.net
**w** lincolnshire-isntboring.co.uk

**The White Horse Hotel** ★★
*Inn*
29 West Street, Alford LN13 9DG
**t** (01507) 462218
**e** the.white.horse.hotel@unicombox.co.uk
**w** whitehorsealford.com

## ALL STRETTON Shropshire

**All Stretton Bunk House**
*Bunkhouse*
Batch Valley, All Stretton SY6 6JW
**t** (01694) 722593
**e** frankiegoode@zoom.co.uk

## ALPHETON Suffolk

**Amicus** ★★★★
*Bed & Breakfast*
Old Bury Road, Alpheton, Sudbury CO10 9BT
**t** (01284) 828579
**e** stanleyburcham@aol.com

## ALSTONEFIELD Staffordshire

**Alstonefield YHA** ★★★
*Hostel*
Overdale, Lode Lane, Ashbourne DE6 2FZ
**t** (01335) 310206
**w** yha.org.uk

**Gateham Cottage and the Coach House** *Camping Barn*
Gateham Grange, Alstonefield, Ashbourne DE6 2FT
**t** (01335) 310349
**e** gateham.grange@btinternet.com
**w** cressbrook.co.uk/hartingt/gateham/

## ALTON Staffordshire

**Alverton Motel** ★★★★
*Guest Accommodation*
Denstone Lane, Alton, Alton Towers Area ST10 4AX
**t** (01538) 702265
**e** enquiries@alvertonmotel.co.uk

**Bank House** ★★★★
*Guest Accommodation*
Smithy Bank, Alton, Alton Towers Area ST10 4AD
**t** (01538) 702524
**e** gemma@alton-bandb.co.uk
**w** alton-bandb.co.uk

**Bulls Head Inn** ★★★ *Inn*
High Street, Alton, Stoke-on-Trent ST10 4AQ
**t** (01538) 702307
**e** janet@thebullsheadalton.co.uk
**w** altontowers-bedandbreakfast.co.uk

**Fields Farm** ★★★★
*Bed & Breakfast*
Chapel Lane, Threapwood Alton, Stoke-on-Trent ST10 4QZ
**t** (01538) 752721 & 07850 310381
**e** pat.massey@fieldsfarmbb.co.uk
**w** fieldsfarmbb.co.uk

**Hillside Farm** ★★★
*Bed & Breakfast*
Alton Road, Uttoxeter ST14 5HG
**t** (01889) 590760
**w** smoothhound.co.uk/hotels/hillside.html

**The Malthouse** ★★★★
*Guest Accommodation*
Malthouse Road, Alton, Alton Towers Area ST10 4AG
**t** (01538) 703273
**e** enquiries@the-malthouse.com

**The Mousehole** ★★★★
*Bed & Breakfast*
Cotton Lane, Cotton, Alton Towers Area ST10 3DS
**t** (01538) 703351
**w** themouseholebandb.co.uk

**Peakstones Inn** ★★★ *Inn*
Cheadle Road, Alton, Alton Towers Area ST10 4DH
**t** (01538) 755776
**e** info@peakstones.co.uk
**w** peakstones-inn.co.uk

**Trough Ivy House** ★★★★
*Bed & Breakfast*
Farley, Alton Towers Area ST10 3BQ
**t** (01538) 702683
**e** info@troughivyhouse.co.uk
**w** troughivyhouse.co.uk

**Tythe Barn House** ★★★
*Guest Accommodation*
Denstone Lane, Alton Towers Area ST10 4AX
**t** (01538) 702852
**w** tythebarnhouse.co.uk

**The Warren** ★★★★
*Guest Accommodation*
**SILVER AWARD**
Battlesteads, Alton Towers Area ST10 4BG
**t** (01538) 702493
**e** annettebas@tinyworld.co.uk
**w** thewarren-bb.com

**Windy Arbour** ★★★★
*Guest House*
Hollis Lane, Denstone, Uttoxeter ST14 5HP
**t** (01889) 591013
**e** stay@windyarbour.co.uk
**w** windyarbour.co.uk

## ALVASTON Derbyshire

**Grace Guest House** ★
*Guest House*
1063 London Road, Alvaston, Derby DE24 8PZ
**t** (01332) 571051

**The Maryland B&B** ★★★
*Guest House*
1083 London Road, Alvaston, Derby DE24 8PZ
**t** (01332) 754892
**e** themaryland7@yahoo.co.uk

## ALVECHURCH Worcestershire

**Alcott Farm** ★★★ *Farmhouse*
Icknield Street, Weatheroak, Alvechurch B48 7EH
**t** (01564) 824051
**e** alcottfarm@btinternet.com
**w** alcottfarm.co.uk

**Woodlands Bed and Breakfast** ★★★★
*Bed & Breakfast*
Coopers Hill, Alvechurch, Nr Bromsgrove B48 7BX
**t** (0121) 445 6772
**e** john.impey@gmail.com
**w** woodlandsbedandbreakfast.com

## ALVESTON Warwickshire

**YHA Hemmingford House**
★★★★ *Hostel*
Alveston, Stratford-upon-Avon CV37 7RG
**t** 0870 770 6052
**e** stratford@yha.org.uk
**w** yha.org.uk

## AMBERGATE Derbyshire

**The Lord Nelson Inn** ★★★
*Inn*
Bullbridge, Ambergate, Ripley DE56 2EW
**t** (01773) 852037
**e** lord.nelson_inn@unicombox.co.uk
**w** thelordnelson.fsworld.co.uk

## ANSTEY Hertfordshire

**Anstey Grove Barn** ★★★★
*Farmhouse*
The Grove, Buntingford SG9 0BJ
**t** (01763) 848828
**e** enquiries@ansteygrovebarn.co.uk
**w** ansteygrovebarn.co.uk

## ARDLEIGH Essex

**Malting Farm** ★★★★
*Bed & Breakfast*
Malting Farm Lane, Ardleigh, Colchester CO7 7QG
**t** (01206) 230207

**Old Shields Farm** ★★★★
*Bed & Breakfast*
Waterhouse Lane, Ardleigh, Colchester CO7 7NE
**t** (01206) 230251 & 07831 278036
**e** ruthemarshall@btinternet.com
**w** oldsheildsbedandbreakfast.co.uk

**Park Cottage** ★★★★
*Bed & Breakfast*
**SILVER AWARD**
Bromley Road, Ardleigh, Colchester CO7 7SJ
**t** (01206) 230170
**e** parkcottage@talktalk.net
**w** parkcottage.org

## ARKESDEN Essex

**Parsonage Farm** ★★★★
*Guest Accommodation*
Arkesden, Saffron Walden CB11 4HB
**t** (01799) 550306
**e** danijaud@aol.com
**w** tiscover.co.uk

## ARLEY Worcestershire

**Tudor Barn** ★★★★
*Bed & Breakfast*
**GOLD AWARD**
Nib Green, Arley, Bewdley DY12 3LY
**t** (01299) 400129
**e** tudorbarn@aol.com
**w** tudor-barn.co.uk

**ARTHINGWORTH**
**Northamptonshire**

**The Bull's Head** ★★★ *Inn*
Kelmarsh Road, Arthingworth LE16 8JZ
**t** (01858) 525637
**e** thebullshead@btconnect.com
**w** thebullsheadonline.co.uk

**ASH MAGNA**
**Shropshire**

**Ash Hall Bed and Breakfast**
★★ *Bed & Breakfast*
Ash Magna, Whitchurch SY13 4DL
**t** (01948) 663151
**w** stmem.com/ashhall/

**ASHBOURNE**
**Derbyshire**

**2 Spencer Close** ★★★
*Guest Accommodation*
Ashbourne DE6 1BU
**t** (01335) 343718
**e** annburtonibu@hotmail.co.uk

**Bentley Brook Inn** ★★★ *Inn*
Fenny Bentley, Ashbourne DE6 1LF
**t** (01335) 350278
**e** all@bentleybrookinn.co.uk
**w** bentleybrookinn.co.uk

**Cross Farm** ★★★★
*Bed & Breakfast*
Main Road, Ellastone, Ashbourne DE6 2GZ
**t** (01335) 324668
**e** info@cross-farm.co.uk
**w** cross-farm.co.uk

**Holly Meadow Farm** ★★★★
*Farmhouse* **SILVER AWARD**
Pinfold Lane, Bradley, Ashbourne DE6 1PN
**t** (01335) 370261 & 07970 922856
**e** babette_lawton@yahoo.com
**w** hollymeadowfarm.co.uk

**The Lilacs** ★★★★
*Guest Accommodation*
Mayfield Road, Ashbourne DE6 2BJ
**t** (01335) 343749

**Manor Barn**
Rating Applied For
*Bed & Breakfast*
The Green, Ashbourne DE6 1JB
**t** (01335) 345063
**e** kaylivesey@yahoo.co.uk

**Mona Villas Bed and Breakfast** ★★★★
*Bed & Breakfast*
1 Mona Villas, Church Lane, Ashbourne DE6 2JS
**t** (01335) 343773
**e** info@mona-villas.fsnet.co.uk

**Newton House** ★★★
*Guest Accommodation*
Buxton Road, Ashbourne DE6 1EX
**t** (020) 8511 1534

**Omnia Somnia** ★★★★★
*Guest Accommodation*
**GOLD AWARD**
The Coach House, The Firs, Ashbourne DE6 1HF
**t** (01335) 300145
**e** alan@omniasomnia.co.uk
**w** omniasomnia.co.uk

**Overfield Farm** ★★★★
*Farmhouse*
Tissington, Ashbourne DE6 1RA
**t** (01335) 390285
**e** info@overfieldfarm.co.uk
**w** overfieldfarm.co.uk

**Shirley Hall** ★★★★
*Farmhouse* **SILVER AWARD**
Shirley, Ashbourne DE6 3AS
**t** (01335) 360820
**e** ian@iancrabtree.wanadoo.co.uk

**Stanshope Hall** ★★★★
*Guest Accommodation*
Stanshope, Ashbourne DE6 2AD
**t** (01335) 310278
**e** naomi@stanshope.demon.co.uk
**w** stanshope.net

**Tan Mill Farm** ★★★★
*Farmhouse*
Mappleton Road, Ashbourne DE6 2AA
**t** (01335) 342387
**e** tanmill@ashbourne-town.com

**White Cottage** ★★★★
*Bed & Breakfast*
Wyaston, Ashbourne DE6 2DR
**t** (01335) 345503
**e** jackie@previll.fsnet.co.uk
**w** whitecottage-bandb.co.uk

**ASHBY-DE-LA-ZOUCH**
**Leicestershire**

**Clockmakers House B&B** ★★★★
*Guest Accommodation*
8 Lower Church Street, Ashby-de-la-Zouch LE65 1AB
**t** (01530) 417974
**e** mike@clockmakershouse.com
**w** clockmakershouse.com

**Holywell Guest House** ★★
*Guest House*
58 Burton Road, Ashby-de-la-Zouch LE65 2LN
**t** (01530) 412005

**Measham House Farm**
★★★★ *Bed & Breakfast*
Gallows Lane, Measham, Ashby-de-la-Zouch DE12 7HD
**t** (01530) 270465
**e** dilovett@meashamhouse.freeserve.co.uk
**w** meashamhouse.co.uk

**ASHFORD IN THE WATER**
**Derbyshire**

**A Woodland View** ★★★★
*Bed & Breakfast*
John Bank Lane, Ashford-in-the-Water, Bakewell DE45 1PY
**t** (01629) 813008
**e** woodview@neilellis.free-online.co.uk
**w** woodlandviewbandb.co.uk

**The Ashford Arms** ★★★★
*Inn*
1 Church Street, Ashford-in-the-Water, Bakewell DE45 1QB
**t** (01629) 812725
**e** enquiries@ashford-arms.co.uk
**w** ashford-arms.co.uk

**Chy-an-Dour** ★★★★
*Guest Accommodation*
**SILVER AWARD**
Vicarage Lane, Ashford-in-the-Water, Bakewell DE45 1QN
**t** (01629) 813162
**w** smoothhound.co.uk

**River Cottage** ★★★★★
*Guest Accommodation*
**SILVER AWARD**
The Duke's Drive, Ashford-in-the-Water, Bakewell DE45 1QP
**t** (01629) 813327
**e** info@rivercottageashford.co.uk
**w** rivercottageashford.co.uk

**ASHOVER**
**Derbyshire**

**Old School Farm** ★★★★
*Farmhouse*
Uppertown, Ashover, Chesterfield S45 0JF
**t** (01246) 590813
**e** dawn@ja8ty.wanadoo.co.uk

**ASHPERTON**
**Herefordshire**

**Pridewood** ★★★
*Guest Accommodation*
Ashperton, Ledbury HR8 2SF
**t** (01531) 670416
**e** julia@pridewoodbandb.co.uk
**w** pridewoodbandb.co.uk

**ASHWELL**
**Hertfordshire**

**The Three Tuns** ★★★ *Inn*
6 High Street, Baldock SG7 5NL
**t** (01462) 742107
**e** info@tuns.co.uk

**ASSINGTON**
**Suffolk**

**The Case Restaurant with Rooms** ★★★★
*Restaurant with Rooms*
**SILVER AWARD**
Further Street, Assington, Sudbury CO10 5LD
**t** (01787) 210483
**e** rooms@thecaserestaurantwith rooms.co.uk
**w** thecaserestaurantwith rooms.co.uk

**ASTLEY**
**Worcestershire**

**Woodhampton House**
★★★★ *Bed & Breakfast*
Weather Lane, Astley, Stourport-on-Severn DY13 0SF
**t** (01299) 826510
**e** pete-a@sally-a.freeserve.co.uk
**w** woodhamptonhouse.co.uk

**ASTON CANTLOW**
**Warwickshire**

**Tudor Rose Cottage** ★★★
*Bed & Breakfast*
29 Chapel Lane, Aston Cantlow, Stratford-upon-Avon B95 6HU
**t** (01789) 488315
**e** wendywithspaniels@tiscali.co.uk

**ASTON MUNSLOW**
**Shropshire**

**Chadstone** ★★★★★
*Bed & Breakfast*
**SILVER AWARD**
Aston Munslow, Craven Arms SY7 9ER
**t** (01584) 841675
**e** chadstone.lee@btinternet.com
**w** chadstonebandb.co.uk

**ATCHAM**
**Shropshire**

**Mad Jack's** ★★★★
*Restaurant with Rooms*
15 St Mary's Street, Shrewsbury SY1 1EQ
**t** (01743) 358870
**e** admin@madjacks.uk.com
**w** madjacks.uk.com

**ATHERSTONE**
**Warwickshire**

**Manor Farm Bed & Breakfast**
★★★ *Bed & Breakfast*
Main Road, Ratcliffe Culey, Hinckley CV9 3NY
**t** (01827) 712269
**e** janetrivett@btinternet.com

**ATTERBY**
**Lincolnshire**

**East Farm Farmhouse Bed and Breakfast** ★★★★
*Bed & Breakfast*
East Farm, Atterby, Bishop Norton LN8 2BJ
**t** (01673) 818917

**ATTLEBOROUGH**
**Norfolk**

**Home Farm Bed and Breakfast** ★★★★ *Farmhouse*
Stow Bedon, Attleborough NR17 1BZ
**t** (01953) 483592
**e** valerie.dove@virgin.net
**w** homefarm-bandb.co.uk

**AYLMERTON**
**Norfolk**

**Driftway Guest House**
★★★★ *Bed & Breakfast*
**SILVER AWARD**
The Close, Norwich NR11 8PX
**t** (01263) 838589
**e** dawn@sparrowsnorfolkholidaycottages.co.uk
**w** sparrowsnorfolkholidaycottages.co.uk

**AYLSHAM**
**Norfolk**

**Bure Valley Farm Stays**
★★★★ *Farmhouse*
Bune Valley Farm, Burgh Road, Norwich NR11 6TZ
**t** (01263) 732177
**e** burevalleyfarm@btconnect.com
**w** burevalleyfarmstays.co.uk

**Old Pump House** ★★★★★
*Guest Accommodation*
**GOLD AWARD**
Holman Road, Aylsham
NR11 6BY
**t** (01263) 733789
**e** theoldpumphouse@btconnect.com
**w** theoldpumphouse.com

**Pink House Bed & Breakfast**
★★★★ *Bed & Breakfast*
Wickmere, Norwich NR11 7AL
**t** (01263) 577678
**e** info@pinkhousebb.co.uk
**w** pinkhousebb.co.uk

### AYLTON
### Herefordshire

**Newbridge Farm Park** ★★★
*Bed & Breakfast*
Ledbury HR8 2QG
**t** (01531) 670780
**e** wayne@newbridgefarmpark.com
**w** newbridgefarmpark.com

### BADBY
### Northamptonshire

**Meadows Farm** ★★★★
*Farmhouse*
Newnham Lane, Badby
NN11 3AA
**t** (01327) 703302

### BADINGHAM
### Suffolk

**Colston Hall** ★★★★
*Farmhouse* **SILVER AWARD**
Badingham, Woodbridge
IP13 8LB
**t** (01728) 638375
**e** enquiries@colstonhall.com
**w** colstonhall.com

### BADSEY
### Worcestershire

**Orchard House** ★★
*Guest Accommodation*
99 Bretforton Road, Badsey, Evesham WR11 7XQ
**t** (01386) 831245

### BAKEWELL
### Derbyshire

**2 Lumford Cottages** ★★★
*Bed & Breakfast*
Off Holme Lane, Bakewell
DE45 1GG
**t** (01629) 813273

**Bolehill Farm** ★★★★
*Bed & Breakfast*
**SILVER AWARD**
Monyash Road, Bakewell
DE45 1QW
**t** (01629) 812359
**e** infobb8@bolehillfarm.co.uk
**w** bolehillbb.co.uk

**Castle Cliffe Guest House**
★★★★
*Guest Accommodation*
Monsal Head, Bakewell
DE45 1NL
**t** (01629) 640258
**e** relax@castle-cliffe.com
**w** castle-cliffe.com

**Castle Hill Farm House**
★★★★ *Bed & Breakfast*
**SILVER AWARD**
Castle Mount Crescent, Baslow Road, Bakewell DE45 1AA
**t** (01629) 813168
**e** christine@castlehillfarmhouse.co.uk
**w** castlehillfarmhouse.co.uk

**Dale View** ★★★★
*Guest Accommodation*
Ashford Road, Bakewell
DE45 1GL
**t** (01629) 813832
**e** enquiries@dale-view.com
**w** dale-view.com

**The Garden Room** ★★★★
*Guest Accommodation*
**SILVER AWARD**
1 Park Road, Bakewell
DE45 1AX
**t** (01629) 814299
**e** the.garden.room@talk21.com
**w** smoothhound.co.uk/hotels/thegarden

**The Haven** ★★★★
*Guest Accommodation*
Haddon Road, Bakewell
DE45 1AW
**t** (01629) 812113
**e** contact@visitbakewell.com
**w** visitbakewell.com

**Housley Cottage** ★★★★
*Bed & Breakfast*
Housley, Nr Foolow, Hope Valley S32 5QB
**t** (01433) 631505
**e** kevin@housleycottages.co.uk
**w** housleycottages.co.uk

**Mandale House** ★★★★
*Farmhouse*
Haddon Grove, Over Haddon, Bakewell DE45 1JF
**t** (01629) 812416
**e** julia.finney@virgin.net
**w** mandalehouse.co.uk

**Meadow View** ★★★★
*Bed & Breakfast*
Coombs Road, Bakewell
DE45 1AQ
**t** (01629) 812961

**Melbourne House & Easthorpe** ★★★★
*Guest Accommodation*
Buxton Road, Bakewell
DE45 1DA
**t** (01629) 815357
**e** melbournehouse@supanet.com
**w** bakewell-accommodation.co.uk

**Normanhurst Bed & Breakfast**
Rating Applied For
*Bed & Breakfast*
Ashford Road, Bakewell
DE45 1GL
**t** (01629) 812317

**River Walk Bed & Breakfast**
★★★★ *Bed & Breakfast*
3 New Lumford, Bakewell
DE45 1GH
**t** (01629) 812459
**e** jean.davies22@btinternet.com
**w** riverwalkbedandbreakfast.co.uk

**West Lawn**
Rating Applied For
*Bed & Breakfast*
Aldern Way, Bakewell
DE45 1AJ
**t** (01629) 812243
**e** couplandallan@hotmail.com
**w** westlawn.co.uk

**Westmorland House** ★★★★
*Guest Accommodation*
Park Road, Bakewell DE45 1AX
**t** (01629) 812932
**e** lesley@westmorlandhouse.co.uk
**w** westmorlandhouse.co.uk

**Willow Croft** ★★★★
*Guest Accommodation*
Station Road, Great Longstone, Bakewell DE45 1TS
**t** (01629) 640576
**w** smoothhound.co.uk

**Wilmadah** ★★★★
*Bed & Breakfast*
The Square, Middleton-by-Youlgreave, Bakewell
DE45 1LS
**t** (01629) 636303

### BALDERTON
### Nottinghamshire

**Newark Lodge Guest House**
★★★★★ *Guest House*
**SILVER AWARD**
5 Bullpit Road, Balderton, Newark NG24 3PT
**t** (01636) 703999
**e** coolspratt@aol.com

### BALSALL COMMON
### West Midlands

**Camp Farm** ★★★
*Bed & Breakfast*
Hob Lane, Balsall Common, Coventry CV7 7GX
**t** (01676) 533804

**G & G B & B** ★★★★
*Bed & Breakfast*
68 Needlers End Lane, Balsall Common, Coventry CV7 7AB
**t** (01676) 532847
**e** gillymatthew68@hotmail.com
**w** gillyandgrant.co.uk

**Willow House** ★★★★
*Bed & Breakfast*
64 Needlers End Lane, Balsall Common, Coventry CV7 7AB
**t** (01676) 533901
**e** christine@glowbox.demon.co.uk
**w** glowbox.demon.co.uk/willowhouse.htm

### BAMFORD
### Derbyshire

**Pioneer House** ★★★★
*Bed & Breakfast*
**SILVER AWARD**
Station Road, Bamford, Hope Valley S33 0BN
**t** (01433) 650638
**e** pioneerhouse@yahoo.co.uk
**w** pioneerhouse.co.uk

**Yorkshire Bridge Inn**
★★★★ *Inn* **SILVER AWARD**
Ashopton Road, Bamford, Hope Valley S33 0AZ
**t** (01433) 651361
**e** info@yorkshire-bridge.co.uk
**w** yorkshire-bridge.co.uk

### BARDNEY
### Lincolnshire

**The Black Horse** ★★★
*Guest House*
16 Wragby Road, Bardney
LN3 5XL
**t** (01526) 398900
**e** black-horse@lineone.net
**w** blackhorsebardney.co.uk

### BARFORD
### Warwickshire

**Machado Gallery** ★★★
*Bed & Breakfast*
9 Wellesbourne Road, Barford, Stratford-upon-Avon CV35 8EL
**t** (01926) 624061
**e** machadogallery@barford.org.uk
**w** machadogallery.co.uk

**Westham House B&B**
★★★★ *Bed & Breakfast*
**SILVER AWARD**
Westham Lane, Barford, Warwick CV35 8DP
**t** (01926) 624148
**e** westham_house@hotmail.com
**w** westhamhouse.co.uk

### BARHAM
### Cambridgeshire

**Ye Olde Globe & Chequers**
Rating Applied For
*Guest Accommodation*
Main Street, Barham, Huntingdon PE28 5AB
**t** (01480) 890247
**e** cheryllgroveprice@btinternet.com
**w** globeandchequers.co.uk

### BARKSTON
### Lincolnshire

**Kelling House** ★★★★
*Bed & Breakfast*
17 West Street, Barkston
NG32 2NL
**t** (01400) 251440
**e** sue.evans7@btopenworld.com
**w** kellinghouse.co.uk

### BARLBOROUGH
### Derbyshire

**Stone Croft** ★★★★
*Bed & Breakfast*
15 Church Street, Barlborough, Chesterfield S43 4ER
**t** (01246) 810974
**w** stone-croft.co.uk

### BARLEYTHORPE
### Rutland

**Barleythorpe Conference Centre** ★★★
*Guest Accommodation*
Barleythorpe, Oakham
LE15 7ED
**t** (01572) 723711
**e** info@eef-eastmids.org.uk
**w** barleythorpe.com

### BARLOW
### Derbyshire

**Nestfield Cottages** ★★★★
*Bed & Breakfast*
Nesfield, Dronfield S18 7TB
**t** (01246) 559786
**e** nesfieldcottage@tiscali.co.uk

**Woodview Cottage** ★★★★
*Bed & Breakfast*
Millcross Lane, Barlow, Dronfield S18 7TA
t (0114) 289 0724
e richard.collis@virgin.net

### BARNSDALE
Rutland

**Lakeside Guest Accommodation** ★★★★
*Guest Accommodation*
Stamford Road, Barnsdale, Oakham LE15 8AB
t (01572) 722422
e robwaddington@onetel.com
w thelodgebarnsdale.co.uk

### BARONS CROSS
Herefordshire

**Lavender House** ★★★★
*Bed & Breakfast*
**SILVER AWARD**
1 Richmond Villas, Barons Cross Road, Leominster HR6 8RS
t (01568) 617559
e lavenderhouse@fsmail.net
w lavenderhouse.012webpages.com

### BARROW-ON-TRENT
Derbyshire

**5 Nook Cottages** ★★★★
*Bed & Breakfast*
**SILVER AWARD**
The Nook, Barrow-on-Trent, Derby DE73 7NA
t (01332) 702050
e nookcottage@nookcottage.com
w nookcottage.com

### BARROW UPON SOAR
Leicestershire

**Hunting Lodge** ★★★★ *Inn*
38 South Street, Barrow upon Soar, Loughborough LE12 8LZ
t (01509) 412337
w probablythebestpubintheworld.com

### BARTLOW
Cambridgeshire

**Westoe Farm** ★★★★★
*Bed & Breakfast*
**SILVER AWARD**
Bartlow, Cambridge CB21 4PR
t (01223) 892731
e enquire@bartlow.u-net.com
w westoefarm.co.uk

### BARTON UNDER NEEDWOOD
Staffordshire

**The Shoulder of Mutton**
Rating Applied For
*Inn*
16 Main Street, Barton-under-Needwood DE13 8AA
t (01283) 712568
e rcspurrier@yahoo.co.uk
w shoulderofmutton.com

### BASILDON
Essex

**38 Kelly Road** ★★★★
*Guest Accommodation*
Bowers Gifford, Basildon SS13 2HL
t (01268) 726701
e patricia.jenkinson@tesco.net

**Frasers** ★★★★
*Guest Accommodation*
5 Maltings Road, Wickford SS11 7RF
t (01268) 561700 & 07876 717353
e frasers@battlesbridge.com
w battlesbridge.com/guesthouse.php

### BASLOW
Derbyshire

**Bubnell Cliff Farm** ★★★★
*Farmhouse*
Wheatlands Lane, Baslow, Bakewell DE45 1RF
t (01246) 582454
e c.k.mills@btinternet.com
w bubnellcliff.co.uk

### BAWDSEY
Suffolk

**Bawdsey Manor** ★★★
*Guest Accommodation*
Bawdsey IP12 3AZ
t (01394) 411633
e info@bawdseymanor.co.uk
w bawdseymanor.co.uk

### BAYSTON HILL
Shropshire

**Chatford House** ★★★★
*Bed & Breakfast*
**SILVER AWARD**
Chatford, Bayston Hill, Shrewsbury SY3 0AY
t (01743) 718301
e b&b@chatfordhouse.co.uk
w chatfordhouse.co.uk

### BECCLES
Suffolk

**Catherine House** ★★★★
*Guest Accommodation*
2 Ringsfield Road, Beccles NR34 9PQ
t (01502) 716428
w catherinehouse.net

**Eveleigh House** ★★★★
*Bed & Breakfast*
**SILVER AWARD**
49 London Road, Beccles NR34 9YR
t (01502) 715214
e bookings@eveleighhouse.com
w eveleighhouse.com

**Pinetrees** ★★★★
*Guest Accommodation*
Park Drive, Beccles NR34 7DQ
t (01502) 470796
e info@pinetrees.net
w pinetrees.net

**Saltgate House** ★★★★
*Guest Accommodation*
5 Saltgate, Beccles NR34 9AN
t (01502) 710889
e cazjohns@aol.com
w saltgatehouse.co.uk

### BEDFORD
Bedfordshire

**Church Farm** ★★★★
*Bed & Breakfast*
**SILVER AWARD**
High Street, Bedford MK44 3EB
t (01234) 870234
e churchfarm@amserve.net

**Cornfields** ★★★★
*Restaurant with Rooms*
**SILVER AWARD**
Wilden Road, Roothams Green, Bedford MK44 2NJ
t (01234) 378990
e reservations@cornfieldsrestaurant.co.uk
w cornfieldsrestaurant.co.uk

### BEESTON
Norfolk

**Holmdene Farm** ★★★
*Farmhouse*
Syers Lane, Beeston, King's Lynn PE32 2NJ
t (01328) 701284
e holmdenefarm@farmersweekly.net
w holmdenefarm.co.uk

### BEESTON
Nottinghamshire

**Hylands** ★★★ *Guest House*
Queens Road, Beeston, Nottingham NG9 1JB
t (0115) 925 5472
e hyland.hotel@btconnect.com
w accommodation.uk.net/hylands.htm

### BEESTON REGIS
Norfolk

**Sheringham View Cottage** ★★★★ *Bed & Breakfast*
**SILVER AWARD**
Cromer Road, Sheringham NR26 8RX
t (01263) 820300
e info@sheringhamview.co.uk
w sheringhamview.co.uk

### BELPER
Derbyshire

**Amber Hills** ★★★★
*Guest Accommodation*
Whitehouse Farm, Belper Lane, Belper DE56 2UJ
t (01773) 824080
e veronica.cooke1@tesco.net
w amberhills.co.uk

**The Cedars** ★★★★
*Guest Accommodation*
Field Lane, Belper DE56 1DD
t (01773) 824157
e cedars@derbyshire-holidays.com
w derbyshire-holidays.com/cedars

**Hill Top Farm Bed & Breakfast** ★★★★
*Bed & Breakfast*
Hill Top Farm, 80 Ashbourne Road, Belper DE56 2LF
t (01773) 550338

### BELTON IN RUTLAND
Rutland

**Old Rectory – Belton in Rutland** ★★★ *Farmhouse*
4 New Road, Belton in Rutland, Oakham LE15 9LE
t (01572) 717279
e bb@iepuk.com
w theoldrectorybelton.co.uk

### BENNIWORTH
Lincolnshire

**Glebe Farm** ★★★★
*Farmhouse* **SILVER AWARD**
Church Lane, Benniworth, Market Rasen LN8 6JP
t (01507) 313231
e info@glebe-farm.com
w glebe-farm.com

### BENTHALL
Shropshire

**Hilltop House** ★★★★
*Guest House*
Bridge Road, Benthall, Ironbridge TF12 5RB
t (01952) 884441
e info@hilltop-house.co.uk
w hilltop-house.co.uk

### BESTHORPE
Nottinghamshire

**Lord Nelson Inn** ★★★★ *Inn*
Main Road, Besthorpe, Newark NG23 7HR
t (01636) 892265
e enquiries@thelordnelsoninn.plus.com

### BEWDLEY
Worcestershire

**Kateshill House** ★★★★★
*Bed & Breakfast*
**GOLD AWARD**
Red Hill, Bewdley DY12 2DR
t (01299) 401563
e info@kateshillhouse.co.uk
w kateshillhouse.co.uk

**The Old Town Hall**
Rating Applied For
*Bed & Breakfast*
Wyre Hill, Bewdley DY12 2UE
t (01299) 409465
e theoldtownhall@btinternet.com
w bewdley-oldtownhall-bandb.co.uk

**Woodcolliers Arms** ★★★
*Inn*
76 Welch Gate, Bewdley DY12 2AU
t (01299) 400589
e roger@woodcolliers.co.uk
w woodcolliers.co.uk

### BEYTON
Suffolk

**Bear Inn** ★★★★
*Guest Accommodation*
Tostock Road, Beyton, Bury St Edmunds IP30 9AG
t (01359) 270249
w thebearinn.net

### BIDDULPH
Staffordshire

**Chapel Croft Guest House** ★★★★ *Guest House*
Newtown Road, Biddulph Park, Stoke-on-Trent ST8 7SW
t (01782) 511013
e enquiries@chapelcroft.com
w chapelcroft.com

**Garden Cottage** ★★★★
*Bed & Breakfast*
Halls Road, Biddulph, Stoke-on-Trent ST8 6DB
t (01782) 510835
e pchood@talktalk.net
w gardencottagebiddulph.co.uk

### BIDFORD-ON-AVON
Warwickshire

**Brookleys Bed & Breakfast**
★★★★ *Bed & Breakfast*
Honeybourne Road, Bidford-on-Avon, Stratford-upon-Avon B50 4PD
**t** (01789) 772785
**e** brookleyschris@aol.com
**w** brookleys.co.uk

**Fosbroke House** ★★★★
*Guest House*
4 High Street, Bidford-on-Avon, Stratford-upon-Avon B50 4BU
**t** (01789) 772327
**e** mark@swiftvilla.fsnet.co.uk
**w** smoothhound.co.uk/hotels/fosbroke

**The Harbour** ★★★★
*Bed & Breakfast*
20 Salford Road, Bidford-on-Avon, Stratford-upon-Avon B50 4EN
**t** (01789) 772975
**e** peter@theharbour-gh.com
**w** theharbour-gh.com

### BIGGIN-BY-HARTINGTON
Derbyshire

**The Kings at Ivy House**
★★★★★
*Guest Accommodation*
**GOLD AWARD**
Biggin-by-Hartington, Newhaven, Buxton SK17 0DT
**t** (01298) 84709
**e** kings.ivyhouse@lineone.net
**w** thekingsativyhouse.co.uk

### BIGGLESWADE
Bedfordshire

**Old Warden Guesthouse**
★★★ *Bed & Breakfast*
Shop & Post Office, Old Warden SG18 9HQ
**t** (01767) 627201
**e** owgh@idnet.co.uk

### BILDESTON
Suffolk

**Silwood Barns** ★★★★
*Bed & Breakfast*
**SILVER AWARD**
Consent Lane, Bildeston, Ipswich IP7 7SB
**t** (01449) 741370
**e** neilashwell@aol.com
**w** lalaproducts.com

### BILLERICAY
Essex

**Badgers Rest** ★★★★
*Bed & Breakfast*
**GOLD AWARD**
2 Mount View, Billericay CM11 1HB
**t** (01277) 625384

### BILLINGHAY
Lincolnshire

**119 Walcott Road** ★★★
*Bed & Breakfast*
Lincoln LN4 4EW
**t** (01526) 861661
**e** chucriesue@btinternet.com

**Old Mill Crafts B&B** ★★★
*Bed & Breakfast*
8 Mill Lane, Billinghay LN4 4ES
**t** (01526) 861996

### BIRCH
Essex

**Woodview B&B** ★★★
*Bed & Breakfast*
Mill Lane, Birch, Colchester CO2 0NH
**t** (01206) 331956

### BIRCHOVER
Derbyshire

**Birchover** *Camping Barn*
Barn Farm, Birchover, Matlock DE4 2BL
**t** (01629) 650245

**Poppy Cottage** ★★★★
*Bed & Breakfast*
Main Street, Birchover, Matlock DE4 2BN
**t** (01629) 650847
**e** alison@poppycottagebandb.co.uk
**w** poppycottagebandb.co.uk

### BIRMINGHAM
West Midlands

**Alden Bed & Breakfast**
★★★ *Bed & Breakfast*
7 Elmdon Road, Marston Green, Birmingham B37 7BS
**t** (0121) 684 2851
**e** powellalden@aol.com

**Central Guest House** ★★★
*Guest House*
1637 Coventry Road, Yardley, Birmingham B26 1DD
**t** (0121) 706 7757
**e** stay@centralguesthouse.com
**w** centralguesthouse.com

**Clay Towers** ★★★★
*Bed & Breakfast*
51 Frankley Beeches Road, Northfield, Birmingham B31 5AB
**t** (0121) 628 0053
**e** john@claytowers.co.uk

**Elmdon Guest House** ★★★
*Guest Accommodation*
2369 Coventry Road, Sheldon, Birmingham B26 3PN
**t** (0121) 688 1720 & (0121) 742 1626
**e** elmdonhouse@blueyonder.co.uk
**w** elmdonguesthouse.co.uk

**Rollason Wood** ★★
*Guest Accommodation*
130 Wood End Road, Erdington, Birmingham B24 8BJ
**t** (0121) 373 1230
**e** rollwood@globalnet.co.uk
**w** rollasonwoodhotel.co.uk

**Springfield Guest House**
★★★★ *Guest House*
69 Coventry Road, Coleshill, Birmingham B46 3EA
**t** (01675) 465695

### BIRTSMORTON
Worcestershire

**The Birches** ★★★★
*Bed & Breakfast*
Birts Street, Birtsmorton, Malvern WR13 6AW
**t** (01684) 833821
**e** katherine-thebirches@hotmail.co.uk

### BISHOP'S CASTLE
Shropshire

**Broughton Farm B&B** ★★★
*Farmhouse*
Broughton Farm, Bishop's Castle SY15 6SZ
**t** (01588) 638393
**e** broughtonfarm@micro-plus-web.net
**w** virtual-shropshire.co.uk

**Inn on the Green** ★★★★ *Inn*
Wentnor, Bishop's Castle SY9 5EF
**t** (01588) 650105
**e** sempleaj@aol.com
**w** theinnonthegreen.net

**Magnolia** ★★★★
*Bed & Breakfast*
**GOLD AWARD**
3 Montgomery Road, Bishop's Castle SY9 5EZ
**t** (01588) 638098
**e** magnoliabishopscastle@yahoo.co.uk
**w** magnoliabishopscastle.co.uk

### BISHOP'S STORTFORD
Hertfordshire

**33 Harrisons** ★★
*Bed & Breakfast*
Birchanger Place, Bishop's Stortford CM23 5QT
**t** (01279) 815012
**e** annieadams@harrisons33bb.plus.com
**w** harrisons33bb.plus.com

**Acer Cottage** ★★★
*Bed & Breakfast*
17 Windhill, Bishop's Stortford CM23 2NE
**t** (01279) 834797
**e** admill@ntlworld.com
**w** acercottage.co.uk

**AJ Bed and Breakfast** ★★
*Bed & Breakfast*
5 Ascot Close, Bishop's Stortford CM23 5BP
**t** (01279) 652228
**e** aandjbnb@tesco.net
**w** aandjbandb.co.uk

**Aldburys Farm** ★★★★
*Bed & Breakfast*
Boxley Lane, Hatfield Broad Oak, Bishop's Stortford CM22 7JX
**t** (01279) 718282
**e** aldbury@supanet.com
**w** a1tourism.com/uk/aldbury.html

**Ascot B&B** ★★★
*Bed & Breakfast*
6 Ascot Close, Bishop's Stortford CM23 5BP
**t** (01279) 651027
**e** derek@derekfox1.wanadoo.co.uk

**Avery House** ★★★★
*Bed & Breakfast*
52 Thorley Hill, Bishop's Stortford CM23 3NA
**t** (01279) 658311
**e** jacki-ross.accommodation@virgin.net
**w** averyhouse.co.uk

**Coral's B & B** ★★★★
*Bed & Breakfast*
Shire House, 14 Cannons Mill Lane, Bishop's Stortford CM23 2BN
**t** (01279) 508544
**e** shirehouse@coralsbnb.co.uk
**w** coralsbnb.co.uk

**Lancasters** ★★★★
*Guest Accommodation*
Market Square, Bishop's Stortford CM23 3UU
**t** (01279) 501307
**e** linda@lancasterguesthouse.com
**w** lancastersguesthouse.com

**Marie's Bed and Breakfast**
★★★★ *Bed & Breakfast*
26 Heath Row, Bishop's Stortford CM23 5DE
**t** (01279) 833870
**e** mariesbandb@hotmail.com
**w** mariesbedandbreakfast.co.uk

**Oakfields** ★★★★
*Bed & Breakfast*
26 Kestral Gardens, Bishop's Stortford CM23 4LU
**t** (01279) 506014
**e** nicola@oakfieldsbedandbreakfast.co.uk
**w** oakfieldsbedandbreakfast.co.uk

**Phoenix Lodge** ★★★
*Guest House*
91 Dunmow Road, Bishop's Stortford CM23 5HF
**t** (01279) 659780
**e** phoenixlodge@ntlworld.com
**w** phoenixlodge.co.uk

### BLAKENEY
Norfolk

**Navestock Bed and Breakfast** ★★★★
*Bed & Breakfast*
Cley Road, Blakeney NR25 7NL
**t** (01263) 740998
**w** tiscover.co.uk

### BLAXHALL
Suffolk

**Blaxhall YHA** ★★★ *Hostel*
Heath Walk, Blaxhall, Woodbridge IP12 2EA
**t** 0870 770 5702
**e** blaxhall@yha.org.uk
**w** yha.org.uk

### BLETSOE
Bedfordshire

**Bourne End Farm**
Rating Applied For
*Farmhouse*
Bourne End, Bletsoe, Bedford MK44 1QS
**t** (01234) 783184
**e** bourneendbandb@btconnect.com
**w** highfield-farm.co.uk

**North End Barns** ★★★★
*Farmhouse*
Risley Road, Bletsoe, Bedford MK44 1QT
**t** (01234) 781320
**w** northendbarns.co.uk

## BLICKLING
Norfolk

**Buckinghamshire Arms**
★★★★ *Inn*
Blickling, Aylsham NR11 6NF
t (01263) 732133
w bucks-arms.co.uk/

## BOBBINGTON
Staffordshire

**Red Lion Inn** ★★★★ *Inn*
Six Ashes Road, Bobbington, Stourbridge DY7 5DU
t (01384) 221237
e bookings@redlioninn.co.uk
w redlioninn.co.uk

## BOCKING
Essex

**Fennes View** ★★★★
*Bed & Breakfast*
131 Church Street, Bocking, Braintree CM7 5LF
t (01376) 326080

## BOLNHURST
Bedfordshire

**Old School House** ★★★★
*Bed & Breakfast*
**SILVER AWARD**
School Lane, Bolnhurst, Bedford MK44 2EN
t (01234) 376754
e enquiries@breakfastinbeds.co.uk
w breakfastinbeds.co.uk

## BONSALL
Derbyshire

**The Old Schoolhouse** ★★★
*Bed & Breakfast*
The Dale, Bonsall, Matlock DE4 2AY
t (01629) 826017
e lydia.art@btinternet.com
w oldschoolhousebonsall.co.uk

## BOSTON
Lincolnshire

**Bramley House** ★★★
*Guest House*
267 Sleaford Road, Boston PE21 7PQ
t (01205) 354538

---

**Fairfield Guest House** ★★★
*Guest House*
101 London Road, Boston PE21 7EN
t (01205) 362869

---

**Haven Guest House** ★★★★
*Bed & Breakfast*
49 Robin Hoods Walk, Boston PE21 9EX
t (01205) 364076

---

**Park Lea Guest House** ★★★
*Guest Accommodation*
85 Norfolk Street, Boston PE21 6PE
t (01205) 356309
e park.lea@btopenworld.com
w park-lea.co.uk/

---

**Plummers Place Guest House** ★★★★
*Guest Accommodation*
Plummers Place, Freiston Shore, Boston PE22 0LY
t (01205) 761490
e frei24@btopenworld.com
w plummersplace.co.uk

---

**Y-Not Guesthouse** ★★★
*Guest Accommodation*
10 Langrick Road, Boston PE21 8HT
t (01205) 367422
e margaret@emcgarry.orangehome.co.uk

## BOTTESFORD
Leicestershire

**The Thatch Restaurant** ★★★★
*Restaurant with Rooms*
**SILVER AWARD**
26 High Street, Bottesford, Melton Mowbray NG13 0AA
t (01949) 842330
e the.thatch@btconnect.com
w thethatchbottesford.co.uk

## BOURNE
Lincolnshire

**Maycroft Cottage Bed and Breakfast** ★★★★
*Guest Accommodation*
**SILVER AWARD**
6 Edenham Road, Hanthorpe, Bourne PE10 0RB
t (01778) 571689
e enquiries@maycroftcottage.co.uk
w maycroftcottage.co.uk

---

**Mill House** ★★★★
*Bed & Breakfast*
64 North Road, Bourne PE10 9BU
t (01778) 422278
e pat.stratford@googlemail.com
w millhouse.healerwoman.com/

## BRACKLEY
Northamptonshire

**Astwell Mill** ★★★★
*Farmhouse*
Helmdon, Brackley NN13 5QU
t (01295) 760507
e astwell01@aol.com
w astwellmill.co.uk

---

**Floral Hall Guest House**
★★★ *Bed & Breakfast*
50 Valley Road, Brackley NN13 7DQ
t (01280) 702950
e floralhallguesthouse@talk21.com

---

**Hill Farm** ★★★★ *Farmhouse*
Halse, Brackley NN13 6DY
t (01280) 703300 & 07860 865146
e j.g.robinson@btconnect.com

---

**Manor Grange** ★★★★
*Bed & Breakfast*
Cottisford, Brackley NN13 5SW
t (01280) 847770
e triciahazan@manor-grange.com
w manor-grange.com

---

**The Old Surgery** ★★★★
*Bed & Breakfast*
**SILVER AWARD**
Pebble Lane, Brackley NN13 7DA
t (01280) 705090
e jaymaddison@aol.com

---

**Yew Tree House** ★★★★
*Bed & Breakfast*
The Green, Hinton-in-the-Hedges, Brackley NN13 5NG
t (01280) 700547

## BRADFIELD COMBUST
Suffolk

**Church Farm Bed and Breakfast** ★★★★ *Farmhouse*
Bradfield Combust, Bury St Edmunds IP30 0LW
t (01284) 386333
e ruth@churchfarm-bandb.co.uk
w churchfarm-bandb.co.uk

## BRADLEY
Derbyshire

**Yeldersley Old Hall Farm**
★★★★ *Farmhouse*
**SILVER AWARD**
Yeldersley Lane, Bradley, Ashbourne DE6 1PH
t (01335) 344504
e janethindsfarm@yahoo.co.uk
w yeldersleyoldhallfarm.co.uk

## BRADNOP
Staffordshire

**Middle Farm** ★★★
*Guest Accommodation*
Apesford, Bradnop, Leek ST13 7EX
t (01538) 382839
e susan@middlefarmbandb.co.uk
w middlefarmbandb.co.uk

## BRADWELL
Derbyshire

**Travellers Rest** ★★★ *Inn*
Brough Lane End, Brough, Hope Valley S33 9HG
t (01433) 620363
e elliottstephen@btconnect.com
w travellers-rest.net

## BRAINTREE
Essex

**Brook Farm** ★★★★
*Farmhouse*
Braintree Road, Braintree CM7 4BX
t (01371) 850284

---

**Hare and Hounds** ★★★★
*Inn*
104 High Garrett, Braintree CM7 5NT
t (01376) 324430
e handhpub@hotmail.com
w hare-and-hounds.com

---

**The Old House** ★★★
*Guest House*
Braintree CM7 9AS
t (01376) 550457
e old_house@talk21.com
w theoldhousebraintree.co.uk

## BRAMPTON
Derbyshire

**Brampton Guest House**
★★★ *Guest House*
75 Old Road, Off Chatsworth Road, Chesterfield S40 2QU
t (01246) 276533
e enquiries@brampton-guesthouse.co.uk
w brampton-guesthouse.co.uk

## BRAMPTON ABBOTTS
Herefordshire

**Brampton Cottage** ★★★
*Bed & Breakfast*
Brampton Abbotts, Ross-on-Wye HR9 7JD
t (01989) 562459
e caroline-keen@btconnect.co.uk

## BRAMSHALL
Staffordshire

**Bowmore House** ★★★★
*Farmhouse*
Stone Road, Bramshall, Uttoxeter ST14 8SH
t (01889) 564452
e glovatt@furoris.com

## BRANCASTER
Norfolk

**Ship Inn** ★★★ *Inn*
Main Road, Brancaster PE31 8AP
t (01485) 210333
e mike.ali.ship@btinternet.com
w shipinnbrancaster.co.uk

## BRATTLEBY
Lincolnshire

**Robindale Bed & Breakfast**
★★★★ *Bed & Breakfast*
Back Lane, Brattleby, Lincoln LN1 2SQ
t (01522) 730712
e robindale@robindale.co.uk
w robindale.co.uk

## BRAUNSTON
Northamptonshire

**Braunston Manor Hotel** ★★★★
*Guest Accommodation*
**SILVER AWARD**
High Street, Daventry NN11 7HS
t (01788) 890267
e maureen.hume@yahoo.co.uk
w braunstonmanor.com

---

**The Old Workshop** ★★★★
*Bed & Breakfast*
The Wharf, Daventry NN11 7JQ
t (01788) 891421
e info@the-old-workshop.com
w the-old-workshop.com

## BREEDON ON THE HILL
Leicestershire

**Holly Bush Inn** ★★★★ *Inn*
1 Melbourne Lane, Breedon-on-the-Hill, Ashby-de-la-Zouch DE73 1AT
t (01332) 862359

---

**Underhill Cottage** ★★★
*Bed & Breakfast*
9-11 Main Street, Breedon-on-the-Hill, Castle Donington DE73 8AN
t (01332) 865630
e beniceberg@aol.com
w t-multimedia.net/underhillcottage

## BRENTWOOD
Essex

**Brentwood Guesthouse**
★★★ *Guest Accommodation*
Rose Valley, Brentwood
CM14 4HJ
t (01277) 262713
e info@brentwoodguesthouse.com
w brentwoodguesthouse.com

## BRETBY
Derbyshire

**Bretby Conference Centre**
★★★ *Guest Accommodation*
Ashby Road, Bretby, Burton-on-Trent DE15 0YZ
t (01283) 553440
e enquiries@bretbycc.co.uk
w bretbycc.co.uk

## BRIDGNORTH
Shropshire

**Bulls Head Inn** ★★★★ *Inn*
Chelmarsh, Bridgnorth
WV16 6BA
t (01746) 861469
e bull_chelmarsh@btconnect.com
w bullsheadchelmarsh.co.uk

**Churchdown House**
★★★★★ *Bed & Breakfast*
**SILVER AWARD**
14 East Castle Street, Bridgnorth WV16 4AL
t (01746) 761236
e churchdownhouse@tiscali.co.uk
w churchdownhouse.co.uk

**The Croft** ★★★★
*Guest Accommodation*
10/11 St Mary's Street, Bridgnorth WV16 4DW
t (01746) 762416
e crofthotel@aol.com
w crofthotelbridgnorth.co.uk

**Dinney Farm** ★★★★
*Farmhouse*
Chelmarsh, Bridgnorth
WV16 6AU
t (01746) 861070
e info@thedinney.co.uk
w thedinney.co.uk

**The Golden Lion** ★★★
*Guest Accommodation*
83 High Street, Bridgnorth
WV16 4DS
t (01746) 762016
e jeff@goldenlionbridgnorth.co.uk
w goldenlionbridgnorth.co.uk

**The Old House** ★★★★
*Bed & Breakfast*
Hilton, Bridgnorth WV15 5PJ
t (01746) 716560
e enquiries@oldhousehilton.co.uk
w oldhousehilton.co.uk

**The Severn Arms** ★★★★
*Guest Accommodation*
3 Underhill Street, Bridgnorth
WV16 4BB
t (01746) 764616
e thesevernarms@aol.com

**The Swan**
Rating Applied For
*Inn*
Knowle Sands, Bridgnorth
WV16 5JL
t (020) 8777 3636
e tu@bcinns.co.uk

## BRIGG
Lincolnshire

**Albert House** ★★★★
*Guest Accommodation*
23 Bigby Street, Brigg
DN20 8ED
t (01652) 658081
e jeancwalker@yahoo.co.uk
w albert-house.co.uk

**Beldon House** ★★★★
*Guest Accommodation*
Wrawby Road, Brigg
DN20 8DL
t (01652) 653517
e info@beldonhouse.co.uk

**Holcombe Guest House**
★★★★ *Guest House*
34 Victoria Road, Barnetby
DN38 6JR
t 07850 764002
e holcombe.house@virgin.net
w holcombeguesthouse.co.uk

## BRIGHTLINGSEA
Essex

**Paxton Dene** ★★★★
*Guest Accommodation*
**SILVER AWARD**
Church Road, Brightlingsea, Colchester CO7 0QT
t (01206) 304560
e holben@btinternet.com
w paxtondenebedandbreakfast.co.uk

## BRIMFIELD
Herefordshire

**Mill Hill House B&B** ★★
*Bed & Breakfast*
Wyson Lane, Brimfield, Ludlow, Mortimer Country
SY8 4NW
t (01584) 711509
e info@millhillhouseludlow.co.uk
w millhillhouseludlow.co.uk

## BROADWAY
Worcestershire

**The Bell at Willersey** ★★★★
*Guest Accommodation*
The Bell Inn, Willersey, Broadway WR12 7PJ
t (01386) 858405
e enq@bellatwillersey.fsnet.co.uk
w the-bell-willersey.com

**Burhill Farm** ★★★★★
*Farmhouse* **SILVER AWARD**
Buckland, Broadway
WR12 7LY
t (01386) 858171
e burhillfarm@yahoo.co.uk
w burhillfarm.co.uk

**Dove Cottage** ★★★★
*Bed & Breakfast*
**SILVER AWARD**
Colletts Fields, Broadway
WR12 7AT
t (01386) 859085
e delia.dovecottage@ukonline.co.uk
w broadway-cotswolds.co.uk

**Farncombe Estate Centre**
★★★★
*Guest Accommodation*
Broadway WR12 7LJ
t (01386) 854100
e visit@farncombeestate.co.uk
w farncombeestate.co.uk

**Lowerfield Farm** ★★★★
*Farmhouse*
Willersey Fields, Broadway
WR11 7HF
t (01386) 858273
e info@lowerfieldfarm.com
w lowerfieldfarm.com

**The Old Stationhouse**
★★★★ *Guest House*
**SILVER AWARD**
Station Drive, Broadway
WR12 7DF
t (01386) 852659
e oldstationhouse@eastbankbroadway.fsnet.co.uk
w broadway-cotswolds.co.uk

**The Olive Branch Guest House** ★★★★
*Guest Accommodation*
**SILVER AWARD**
78 High Street, Broadway
WR12 7AJ
t (01386) 853440
e davidpam@theolivebranch-broadway.com
w theolivebranch-broadway.com

**Sheepscombe House**
★★★★ *Bed & Breakfast*
**GOLD AWARD**
Snowshill, Broadway
WR12 7JU
t (01386) 853769
e reservations@snowshill-broadway.co.uk
w broadway-cotswolds.co.uk/sheepscombe.html

**Small Talk Lodge** ★★★★
*Guest House*
32 High Street, Broadway
WR12 7DP
t (01386) 858953
e bookings@smalltalklodge.co.uk
w smalltalklodge.co.uk

**Southwold Guest House**
★★★★ *Guest House*
Station Road, Broadway
WR12 7DE
t (01386) 853681
e alyson@cotswolds-broadway-southwold.co.uk
w cotswolds-broadway-southwold.co.uk

**Whiteacres** ★★★★
*Guest Accommodation*
**SILVER AWARD**
Station Road, Broadway
WR12 7DE
t (01386) 852320
e whiteacres@btinternet.com
w whiteacres-cotswolds.co.uk

**Windrush House** ★★★★
*Guest House* **GOLD AWARD**
Station Road, Broadway
WR12 7DE
t (01386) 853577
e evan@broadway-windrush.co.uk
w broadway-windrush.co.uk

## BROBURY
Herefordshire

**Brobury House & Gardens**
★★★★ *Bed & Breakfast*
Brobury, Bredwardine, Hereford HR3 6BS
t (01981) 500229
e enquiries@broburyhouse.co.uk
w broburyhouse.co.uk

## BROCKDISH
Norfolk

**Grove Thorpe** ★★★★★
*Bed & Breakfast*
**GOLD AWARD**
Grove Road, Diss IP21 4JR
t (01379) 668305
e grovethorpe@btinternet.com
w grovethorpe.co.uk

## BROMSGROVE
Worcestershire

**The Durrance** ★★★★
*Farmhouse* **SILVER AWARD**
Berry Lane, Upton Warren, Bromsgrove B61 9EL
t (01562) 777533
e helenhirons@thedurrance.co.uk
w thedurrance.co.uk

**Overwood** ★★★★
*Bed & Breakfast*
Woodcote Lane, Woodcote Green, Bromsgrove B61 9EE
t (01562) 777193
e info@overwood.net
w overwood.net

**Wellington Lodge** ★★★★
*Guest Accommodation*
49 Wellington Road, Bromsgrove B60 2AX
t (01527) 570433
e info@wellington-lodge.co.uk
w welling-lodge.co.uk

## BROOKE
Norfolk

**Hillside Farm** ★★★★
*Farmhouse*
Welbeck Road, Brooke, Norwich NR15 1AU
t (01508) 550260
e carrieholl@tinyworld.co.uk
w hillside-farm.com

**Old Vicarage** ★★★★
*Guest Accommodation*
**SILVER AWARD**
48 The Street, Brooke
NR15 1JU
t (01508) 558329
w tiscover.co.uk

## BROOKMANS PARK
Hertfordshire

**Stewards Cottage** ★★★★
*Bed & Breakfast*
60 Bell Lane, Bell Bar, Hatfield
AL9 7AY
t 07076 42091
e info@stewardscottagebandb.co.uk
w stewardscottagebandb.co.uk

## BROSELEY
Shropshire

**Broseley House** ★★★★
*Guest House* **SILVER AWARD**
1 The Square, Broseley, Ironbridge TF12 5EW
t (01952) 882043
e info@broseleyhouse.co.uk
w broseleyhouse.co.uk

**Coalport YHA** ★★★ *Hostel*
c/o John Rose Building, High Street, Telford TF8 7HT
t 0870 770 5882
e ironbridge@yha.org.uk
w yha.org.uk

**The Lion** ★★★★
*Guest Accommodation*
High Street, Broseley, Telford TF12 5EZ
t (01952) 881128
e lionhotelshrops@aol.com
w lionhotelshropshire.co.uk

**Rock Dell** ★★★★
*Bed & Breakfast*
**SILVER AWARD**
30 Ironbridge Road, Broseley TF12 5AJ
t (01952) 883054
e rockdell@ukgateway.net
w rock-dell.co.uk

## BRUNDALL
Norfolk

**Braydeston House** ★★★★
*Bed & Breakfast*
9 The Street, Brundall, Norwich NR13 5JY
t (01603) 713123
e ann@braydeston.freeserve.co.uk

**Breckland B&B** ★★★★
*Bed & Breakfast*
**12 Strumpshaw Road, Brundall NR13 5PA**
**t (01603) 712122**
**e brecklandbandb@hotmail.co.uk**
**w breckland-bandb.co.uk**

## BUNGAY
Suffolk

**Earsham Park Farm** ★★★★
*Farmhouse* **GOLD AWARD**
Old Railway Road, Earsham, Bungay NR35 2AQ
t (01986) 892180
e bobbie@earsham-parkfarm.co.uk
w earsham-parkfarm.co.uk

## BUNTINGFORD
Hertfordshire

**Buckland Bury Farm** ★★
*Guest Accommodation*
Buckland Bury, Buckland, Buntingford SG9 0PY
**t 07760 227366**
**e bucklandbury@shrubbsfarm.demon.co.uk**
**w tiscover.co.uk**

**Chipping Hall Farm** ★★★★
*Bed & Breakfast*
Chipping Hall, Buntingford SG9 0PH
t (01763) 271514
e stay@chippinghall.co.uk
w chippinghall.com

## BURNHAM DEEPDALE
Norfolk

**Deepdale Backpackers Hostel** ★★★★ *Hostel*
Main Road, Burnham Deepdale PE31 8DD
t (01485) 210256
e info@deepdalefarm.co.uk
w deepdalefarm.co.uk

**Deepdale Granary Group Hostel** ★★★ *Group Hostel*
Deepdale Farms, Main Road, King's Lynn PE31 8DD
t 07776 254019
e info@deepdalefarm.co.uk
w deepdalefarm.co.uk

## BURNHAM MARKET
Norfolk

**Wood Lodge** ★★★★
*Bed & Breakfast*
Millwood, Herring's Lane, King's Lynn PE31 8DP
t (01328) 730152
e philip.roll@btinternet.com

## BURNHAM-ON-CROUCH
Essex

**Mangapp Manor** ★★★★
*Bed & Breakfast*
**SILVER AWARD**
Mangapp Chase, Burnham-on-Crouch CM0 8QQ
t 07769 676735
e kewilsdon@yahoo.co.uk
w mangappmanor.co.uk

**The Oyster Smack Motel**
★★★ *Guest Accommodation*
112 Station Road, Burnham-on-Crouch CM0 8HR
t (01621) 782141
e info@theoystersmack.co.uk
w theoystersmack.co.uk

**The Railway Hotel** ★★★★
*Inn* **SILVER AWARD**
**Station Road, Burnham-on-Crouch CM0 8BQ**
**t (01621) 786868**
**w therailwayhotelburnham.co.uk**

## BURNHAM THORPE
Norfolk

**Whitehall Farm** ★★★★
*Farmhouse* **SILVER AWARD**
**Burnham Thorpe PE31 8HN**
**t (01328) 738416**
**e barrysoutherland@aol.com**
**w tiscover.co.uk**

## BURTON DASSETT
Warwickshire

**Caudle Hill Farm** ★★★★
*Farmhouse* **GOLD AWARD**
Burton Dassett, Southam, Leamington Spa CV47 2AB
t (01295) 770255
e janeperry@another.com
w caudlehillfarm.co.uk

## BURTON UPON TRENT
Staffordshire

**A511 B&B** ★★★
*Guest Accommodation*
20 Station Road, Hatton DE65 5EL
t (01283) 815996
e rod@invictaindustrial.co.uk

**New Inn Farm** ★★★
*Bed & Breakfast*
Burton Road, Needwood, Burton-on-Trent DE13 9PB
t (01283) 575435

**Redmoor Accommodation**
★★ *Bed & Breakfast*
6 Redmoor Close, Winshill, Burton-on-Trent DE15 0HZ
t (01283) 531977
e petervyze@btinternet.com

## BURWELL
Cambridgeshire

**Chestnut House** ★★★★
*Bed & Breakfast*
14a High Street, Burwell, Cambridge CB5 0HB
t (01638) 742996

## BURY ST EDMUNDS
Suffolk

**Brambles Lodge** ★★★★
*Bed & Breakfast*
**SILVER AWARD**
**Welham Lane, Risby, Bury St Edmunds IP28 6QS**
**t (01284) 810701**

**Brighthouse Farm** ★★★★
*Farmhouse*
Melford Road, Lawshall, Bury St Edmunds IP29 4PX
t (01284) 830385
e info@brighthousefarm.fsnet.co.uk
w brighthousefarm.fsnet.co.uk

**Dunston Guesthouse** ★★★
*Guest House*
**8 Springfield Road, Bury St Edmunds IP33 3AN**
**t (01284) 767981**
**w dunstonguesthouse.co.uk**

**The Glen B&B** ★★★★
*Guest House*
Eastgate Street, Bury St Edmunds IP33 1YR
t (01284) 755490
e rallov@aol.com
w smoothhound.co.uk

**Hilltop** ★★ *Bed & Breakfast*
Bury St Edmunds IP33 3XB
t (01284) 767066
e bandb@hilltop22br.freeserve.co.uk
w hilltop22br.freeserve.co.uk

**Manorhouse** ★★★★★
*Bed & Breakfast*
**GOLD AWARD**
The Green, Beyton, Bury St Edmunds IP30 9AF
t (01359) 270960
e manorhouse@beyton.com
w beyton.com

**Ounce House** ★★★★★
*Guest Accommodation*
**SILVER AWARD**
Northgate Street, Bury St Edmunds IP33 1HP
t (01284) 761779
e enquiries@ouncehouse.co.uk
w ouncehouse.co.uk

**Regency House** ★★★★
*Guest Accommodation*
3 Looms Lane, Bury St Edmunds IP33 1HE
t (01284) 764676

**Sanctuary B&B** ★★★★
*Bed & Breakfast*
1 Kings Road, Bury St Edmunds IP33 3DE
t 07756 940372
e allison814@btinternet.com

**Sycamore House** ★★★★
*Guest Accommodation*
23 Northgate Street, Bury St Edmunds IP33 1HP
t (01284) 755828
e me.chalkley@btinternet.com

**The Wallow** ★★★★
*Bed & Breakfast*
Mount Road, Bury St Edmunds IP31 2QU
t (01284) 788055
e info@thewallow.co.uk
w thewallow.co.uk

**Westbank House B & B** ★★
*Guest Accommodation*
Westbank Place, 116a Westley Road, Bury St Edmunds IP33 3SD
t (01284) 753874
e grahampaske@tiscali.co.uk
w westbank-house.co.uk

## BUTTERTON
Staffordshire

**Butterton A** *Camping Barn*
Feens Farm, Wetton Road, Leek ST13 7ST
t (01538) 304185

**Butterton B** *Camping Barn*
Fenns Farm, Wetton Road, Leek ST13 7ST
t (01538) 304185

**Coxon Green Farm** ★★★★
*Farmhouse* **SILVER AWARD**
Butterton, Leek ST13 7TA
t (01538) 304221
e coxongreen@butterton.fsnet.co.uk

**Stoop House Farm**
Rating Applied For
*Farmhouse*
Butterton, Leek ST13 7SY
t (01538) 304486

## BUXTON
Derbyshire

**9 Green Lane B&B** ★★★★
*Guest Accommodation*
**SILVER AWARD**
Green Lane, Buxton SK17 9DP
t (01298) 73731
e book@9greenlane.co.uk
w 9greenlane.co.uk

**Abbey Guest House** ★★★
*Guest Accommodation*
43 South Avenue, Buxton SK17 6NQ
t (01298) 26419
e aghbuxton@aol.com

**Braemar** ★★★★
*Guest Accommodation*
10 Compton Road, Buxton SK17 9DN
t (01298) 78050
e buxtonbraemar@supanet.com
w cressbrook.co.uk/buxton/braemar

**Buxton Hilbre** ★★★
*Bed & Breakfast*
8 White Knowle Road, Buxton SK17 9NH
t (01298) 22358
e min.hilbre@virgin.net

**Compton House Guest House (Buxton)** ★★★
*Guest House*
4 Compton Road, Buxton
SK17 9DN
t (01298) 26926
e comptonhousesk17@aol.com
w cressbrook.co.uk/buxton/compton

**Corbar Bank** ★★★★
*Guest Accommodation*
Corbar Road, Buxton
SK17 6RQ
t (01298) 22664
e thecrabbs@ntlworld.com

**Cotesfield Farm** ★★
*Farmhouse*
Parsley Hay, Buxton SK17 0BD
t (01298) 83256

**Devonshire Arms** ★★★ *Inn*
Peak Forest, Buxton SK17 8EJ
t (01298) 23875
e fiona.clough@virgin.net
w devarms.com

**Devonshire Lodge Guest House** ★★★★
*Guest Accommodation*
**SILVER AWARD**
2 Manchester Road, Buxton
SK17 6SB
t (01298) 71487
e enquiries@devonshirelodgeguesthouse.co.uk
w devonshirelodgeguesthouse.co.uk

**Fairhaven Guest House**
★★★ *Guest Accommodation*
1 Dale Terrace, Buxton
SK17 6LU
t (01298) 24481
e paul@fairhavenguesthouse.freeserve.co.uk

**Fernydale Farm** ★★★★
*Farmhouse* **SILVER AWARD**
Earl Sterndale, Nr Buxton
SK17 0BS
t (01298) 83236
e wjnadin@btconnect.com
w fernydalefarmbandb.co.uk

**Grendon Guest House**
★★★★★ *Guest House*
**GOLD AWARD**
Bishops Lane, Buxton
SK17 6UN
t (01298) 78831
e grendonguesthouse@hotmail.com
w grendonguesthouse.co.uk

**Grosvenor House** ★★★★
*Guest House* **SILVER AWARD**
Broad Walk, Buxton SK17 6JE
t (01298) 72439
e grosvenor.buxton@btopenworld.com
w grosvenorbuxton.co.uk

**Hawthorn Farm Guest House** ★★★ *Guest House*
Fairfield Road, Buxton
SK17 7ED
t (01298) 23230
e hawthornfarm@btconnect.com

**Kingscroft Guest House**
★★★★ *Guest House*
**SILVER AWARD**
10 Green Lane, Buxton
SK17 9DP
t (01298) 22757

**Lakenham Guest House**
★★★★ *Guest House*
11 Burlington Road, Buxton
SK17 9AL
t (01298) 79209
e enquiries@lakenhambuxton.co.uk
w lakenhambuxton.co.uk

**Linden Lodge** ★★★★
*Bed & Breakfast*
31 Temple Road, Buxton
SK17 9BA
t (01298) 27591
e info@lindentreelodge.co.uk
w lindentreelodge.co.uk

**Lowther Guest House**
★★★★
*Guest Accommodation*
7 Hardwick Square West, Buxton SK17 6PX
t (01298) 71479
e lowtherguesthouse@hotmail.co.uk
w lowtherguesthouse.co.uk

**Netherdale Guest House**
★★★★ *Guest House*
16 Green Lane, Buxton
SK17 9DP
t (01298) 23896
w smoothhound.co.uk/hotels/netherdale

**The Old Manse** ★★★★
*Guest House*
6 Clifton Road, Buxton
SK17 6QL
t (01298) 25638
e info@oldmanse.co.uk
w oldmanse.co.uk

**The Place**
Rating Applied For
*Restaurant with Rooms*
9-11 Market Street, Buxton
SK17 6JY
t (01298) 214565
e eatstay@theplacebuxton.orangehome.co.uk
w theplacebuxton.co.uk.

**Roseleigh** ★★★★
*Guest House* **SILVER AWARD**
19 Broad Walk, Buxton
SK17 6JR
t (01298) 24904
e enquiries@roseleighhotel.co.uk
w roseleighhotel.co.uk

**Southmead**
Rating Applied For
*Bed & Breakfast*
Bishops Lane, Buxton
SK17 6UN
t (01298) 24029
e hardie@southmead-guesthouse.co.uk
w southmead-guesthouse.co.uk

**Staden Grange Country House Hotel** ★★★★
*Guest Accommodation*
Staden Lane, Buxton SK17 9RZ
t (01298) 24965
e stadengrangehotel@yahoo.co.uk
w stadengrangehotel.co.uk

**Stoneridge Guest House**
★★★★
*Guest Accommodation*
**SILVER AWARD**
9 Park Road, Buxton SK17 6SG
t (01298) 26120
e duncan@stoneridge.co.uk
w stoneridge.co.uk

**Westlands** ★★★★★
*Guest Accommodation*
**SILVER AWARD**
Bishops Lane, Burbage, Buxton
SK17 6UN
t (01298) 71122
e enquiries@westlandshouse.co.uk
w westlandshouse.co.uk

## BYFIELD
Northamptonshire

**Glebe Farm Bed and Breakfast** ★★
*Bed & Breakfast*
61 Church Street, Byfield, Daventry NN11 6XN
t (01327) 260512

## CADEBY
Leicestershire

**Bosworth Accommodation**
★★★★ *Guest House*
Cadeby Lane, Market Bosworth CV13 0BA
t (01455) 292259
e info@bosworthaccommodation.co.uk
w bosworthaccommodation.co.uk

## CAENBY CORNER
Lincolnshire

**Ermine Lodge Bed and Breakfast** ★★★★
*Bed & Breakfast*
**SILVER AWARD**
Ermine Lodge, Caenby Corner
LN8 2AR
t (01673) 878152 & 07771 740722
e info@erminelodgebandb.com
w erminelodgebandb.com

## CAISTOR
Lincolnshire

**Little Hen Bed & Breakfast**
★★★★ *Bed & Breakfast*
Brocklesby Hilltop Cottage, Brigg Road, Grasby DN38 6AQ
t (01652) 629005
e polly@littlehen.co.uk
w littlehen.co.uk

## CALDECOTE
Warwickshire

**Hill House Country Guest House** ★★★★ *Guest House*
Off Mancetter Road, Nuneaton
CV10 0RS
t (024) 7639 6685

## CALDECOTT
Rutland

**Meadow Farm B&B** ★★
*Farmhouse*
The Green, Caldecott, Market Harborough LE16 8RR
t (01536) 770343
e meadowfarm5@hotmail.com
w meadowfarmcaldecott.co.uk

**Old Plough – Caldecott**
★★★★
*Guest Accommodation*
41 Main Street, Caldecott, Uppingham LE16 8RS
t (01536) 772031
e comfort@oldplough-rutland.co.uk
w oldplough-rutland.co.uk

## CALVER
Derbyshire

**Valley View Guest House**
★★★★ *Guest House*
**SILVER AWARD**
Smithy Knoll Road, Calver, Hope Valley S32 3XW
t (01433) 631407
e sue@a-place-2-stay.co.uk
w a-place-2-stay.co.uk

## CAMBRIDGE
Cambridgeshire

**77 Grantchester Meadows**
★★★★ *Bed & Breakfast*
Grantchester Meadows, Cambridge CB3 9JL
t (01223) 316363

**A and B Guesthouse** ★★★
*Guest House*
124 Tenison Road, Cambridge
CB1 2DP
t (01223) 315702
e abguest@hotmail.com

**Acorn Guesthouse** ★★★★
*Guest House*
154 Chesterton Road, Cambridge CB4 1DA
t (01223) 353888
e info@acornguesthouse.co.uk
w acornguesthouse.co.uk

**Alexander Bed And Breakfast** ★★★★
*Bed & Breakfast*
56 St Barnabas Road, Cambridge CB1 2DE
t (01223) 525725
e enquiries@beesley-schuster.co.uk
w beesley-schuster.co.uk

**Allenbell** ★★★★
*Bed & Breakfast*
517a Coldham Lane, Cambridge CB1 3JS
t (01223) 210353
e sandragailturner@hotmail.com
w allenbell.co.uk

**Alpha Milton Guesthouse**
★★★ *Guest House*
61-63 Milton Road, Cambridge
CB4 1XA
t (01223) 311625
e info@alphamilton.com
w alphamilton.com

**Antonys Bed And Breakfast**
★★ *Guest Accommodation*
4 Huntingdon Road, Cambridge CB3 0HH
t (01223) 357444

**Arbury Lodge Guesthouse**
★★★★ *Guest House*
82 Arbury Road, Cambridge
CB4 2JE
t (01223) 364319
e arbury-lodge@btconnect.com
w arburylodgeguesthouse.co.uk

**Archway House** ★★★★
*Bed & Breakfast*
52 Gilbert Road, Cambridge
CB4 3PE
**t** (01223) 575314
**e** archway52@ntlworld.com
**w** archwayhousebandb.co.uk

**At Woodhaven** ★★★★
*Bed & Breakfast*
245 Milton Road, Cambridge
CB4 1XQ
**t** (01223) 226108
**e** woodhavencambridge@btinternet.com
**w** stayatwoodhaven.co.uk

**Autumn House** ★★★★
*Bed & Breakfast*
710 Newmarket Road, Cambridge CB5 8RS
**t** (01223) 575122
**e** us@autumnhousecambridge.co.uk
**w** autumnhousecambridge.co.uk

**Avalon** ★★★★
*Bed & Breakfast*
62 Gilbert Road, Cambridge
CB4 3PD
**t** (01223) 353071
**e** avalonbandb@hotmail.co.uk

**Avondale** ★★★
*Bed & Breakfast*
35 Highfields Road, Caldecote
CB3 7NX
**t** (01954) 210746
**e** avondalecambs@amserve.com
**w** tiscover.co.uk

**Aylesbray Lodge Guesthouse** ★★★★
*Guest House*
5 Mowbray Road, Cambridge
CB1 7SR
**t** (01223) 240089
**e** stay@aylesbray.com
**w** aylesbray.com

**Bridge Guest House** ★★★
*Guest House*
151 Hills Road, Cambridge
CB2 2RJ
**t** (01223) 247942
**e** bghouse@gmail.com
**w** bridgeguesthouse.co.uk

**Cam Guesthouse** ★★★★
*Guest House*
17 Elizabeth Way, Cambridge
CB4 1DD
**t** (01223) 354512
**e** camguesthouse@btinternet.com
**w** camguesthouse.co.uk

**Cambridge City Tenison Towers** ★★★★
*Guest Accommodation*
148 Tenison Road, Cambridge
CB1 2DP
**t** (01223) 363924
**e** info@cambridgecitytenisontowers.com
**w** cambridgecitytenisontowers.com

**Cambridge Guesthouse**
★★★★ *Guest House*
201a Milton Road, Cambridge
CB4 1XG
**t** (01223) 423239
**w** thecambridgeguesthouse.co.uk

**Cambridge Lodge** ★★★★
*Guest Accommodation*
139 Huntingdon Road, Cambridge CB3 0DQ
**t** (01223) 352833
**e** cambridge.lodge@btconnect.com
**w** smoothhound.co.uk/hotels/cambridge

**Cambridge YHA** ★★ *Hostel*
97 Tenison Road, Cambridge
CB1 2DN
**t** (01223) 354601

**Canterbury House** ★★★★
*Bed & Breakfast*
69 Canterbury Street, Cambridge CB4 3QG
**t** (01223) 300053
**w** canterburyhouse.co.uk

**Carlton Lodge** ★★★
*Guest House*
245 Chesterton Road, Cambridge CB4 1AS
**t** (01223) 367792
**e** info@carltonlodge.co.uk
**w** carltonlodge.co.uk

**Carolina B&B** ★★★★
*Bed & Breakfast*
138 Perne Road, Cambridge
CB1 3NX
**t** (01223) 247015
**e** carolina.amabile@tesco.net
**w** carolinaguesthouse.co.uk

**City Centre North Bed And Breakfast** ★★★★
*Bed & Breakfast*
328a Histon Road, Cambridge
CB4 3HT
**t** (01223) 312843
**e** gscambs@tiscali.co.uk
**w** citycentrenorth.co.uk

**The Conifers** ★★★★
*Bed & Breakfast*
**SILVER AWARD**
213 Histon Road, Cambridge
CB4 3HL
**t** (01223) 311784
**e** enquiry@the-conifers.net
**w** the-conifers.net

**Fenners** ★★
*Guest Accommodation*
142-146 Tenison Road, Cambridge CB1 2DP
**t** (01229) 360246
**e** enquiries@fennershotel.co.uk
**w** fennershotel.co.uk

**Finches Bed and Breakfast**
★★★★ *Bed & Breakfast*
**SILVER AWARD**
144 Thornton Road, Girton, Cambridge CB3 0ND
**t** (01223) 276653
**e** enquiry@finches-bnb.com
**w** finches-bnb.com

**Granta House** ★★★
*Bed & Breakfast*
53 Eltisley Avenue, Newnham
CB3 9JQ
**t** (01223) 560466
**e** tj.dathan@ntlworld.com
**w** tiscover.co.uk

**Hamilton Lodge** ★★★
*Guest House*
156 Chesterton Road, Cambridge CB4 1DA
**t** (01223) 365664

**Harry's Bed and Breakfast**
★★★★ *Guest House*
39 Milton Road, Cambridge
CB4 1XA
**t** (01223) 503866
**e** cjmadden@ntlworld.com
**w** welcometoharrys.co.uk

**Hawthorn House** ★★★★
*Bed & Breakfast*
10 Hawthorn Way, Cambridge
CB4 1AX
**t** (01223) 364483
**e** hawthornhouse@hotmail.co.uk

**Hobsons House** ★★★
*Bed & Breakfast*
96 Barton Road, Cambridge
CB3 9LH
**t** (01223) 304906
**e** hilltout@yahoo.co.uk

**Home From Home** ★★★★
*Bed & Breakfast*
78 Milton Road, Cambridge
CB4 1LA
**t** (01223) 323555
**e** homefromhome2@btconnect.com
**w** accommodationincambridge.com

**Iceni House Bed And Breakfast** ★★★★
*Guest House*
171 Coleridge Road, Cambridge CB1 3PN
**t** (01223) 708967
**e** paragon.holdings@ntlworld.com
**w** icenihouse.co.uk

**June's Bed & Breakfast**
★★★ *Bed & Breakfast*
78 Arbury Road, Cambridge
CB4 2JE
**t** (01223) 572034
**e** j.nayar1@ntlworld.com

**Kirkwood Guesthouse**
★★★★ *Guest House*
Cambridge CB4 1DA
**t** (01223) 306283
**e** info@kirkwoodhouse.co.uk
**w** kirkwoodhouse.co.uk

**Lantern House** ★★★★
*Guest House*
174 Chesterton Road, Cambridge CB4 1DA
**t** (01223) 359980
**e** lanternhouse@msn.com
**w** lanternguesthouse.co.uk

**Leverton House** ★★★★
*Guest House*
732-734 Newmarket Road, Cambridge CB5 8RS
**t** (01223) 292094
**e** wendy.ison@ntlworld.com
**w** levertonhouse.co.uk

**The Poplars** ★★★★
*Bed & Breakfast*
12 East Drive, Highfields Caldecote, Cambridge
CB23 7NZ
**t** (01954) 210396
**e** thepoplars@onetel.com
**w** tiscover.co.uk

**Railway Lodge Guest House**
★★★ *Guest House*
150 Tenison Road, Cambridge
CB1 2DP
**t** (01223) 467688
**e** railwaylodge@cambridge-guesthouse-accommodation.co.uk
**w** cambridge-guesthouse-accommodation.co.uk

**Rock View** ★★★
*Bed & Breakfast*
99 Cherry Hinton Road, Cambridge CB1 7BS
**t** (01223) 573455
**e** rockviewguesthouse@yahoo.co.uk
**w** rockviewguesthouse.co.uk

**Somerset House** ★★★
*Bed & Breakfast*
Cambridge CB4 1XE
**t** (01223) 505131
**e** somersetbedandbreakfast@msn.com
**w** bedandbreakfastcambridge.net

**Southampton Guest House**
★★★ *Guest House*
7 Elizabeth Way, Cambridge
CB4 1DE
**t** (01223) 357780
**e** southamptonhouse@btinternet.com
**w** southamptonguesthouse.com

**The Three Hills**
Rating Applied For
*Inn*
Ashdon Road, Bartlow, Cambridge CB1 6PW
**t** (01223) 891259
**e** threehills@rhubarb-inns.co.uk
**w** rhubarb-inns.co.uk

**Tudor Cottage** ★★★★
*Bed & Breakfast*
292 Histon Road, Cambridge
CB4 3HS
**t** (01223) 565212
**e** email@tudor-cottage.net
**w** tudorcottageguesthouse.co.uk

**Upton House** ★★★★
*Bed & Breakfast*
**SILVER AWARD**
11b Grange Road, Cambridge
CB3 9AS
**t** (01223) 323201
**e** tom.challis@talk21.com

**Vicarage** ★★★
*Bed & Breakfast*
15 St Pauls Road, Cambridge
CB1 2EZ
**t** (01223) 315832
**e** debbie.beckett2@googlemail.com

**Victoria Guest House**
★★★★ *Guest House*
57 Arbury Road, Cambridge
CB4 2JB
**t** (01223) 350086
**e** info@victoria-guesthouse.co.uk
**w** cambridge-accommodation.com

**Warkworth House** ★★★★
*Guest House*
Warkworth Terrace, Cambridge CB1 1EE
t (01223) 363682
e enquiries@warkworthhouse.co.uk
w warkworthhouse.co.uk

**Woodfield House** ★★★★
*Bed & Breakfast*
Madingley Road, Coton CB23 7PH
t (01954) 210265
e wendy-john@wsadler.freeserve.co.uk
w tiscover.co.uk

**Woodview Bed & Breakfast** ★★★★ *Bed & Breakfast*
Great Cambourne, Cambridge CB3 6GF
t (01954) 710338
e woodviewcambridge@tiscali.co.uk

**Worth House** ★★★★
*Guest House* **SILVER AWARD**
152 Chesterton Road, Cambridge CB4 1DA
t (01223) 316074
e enquiry@worth-house.co.uk
w worth-house.co.uk

### CAMMERINGHAM Lincolnshire

**Field View B&B** ★★★★
*Bed & Breakfast*
Back Lane, Cammeringham LN1 2SH
t (01522) 730193
e info@fieldviewbandb.com
w fieldviewbandb.com

### CAMPSEA ASHE Suffolk

**The Dog & Duck** ★★★
*Guest Accommodation*
Station Road, Woodbridge IP13 0PT
t (01728) 748439

### CANNOCK Staffordshire

**Hillside Bed & Breakfast** ★★★★ *Bed & Breakfast*
29 Littleworth Hill, Cannock WS12 1NS
t (01543) 425886
e hillsidebandb@hotmail.co.uk

### CARDINGTON Shropshire

**Upper Shadymoor Farm** ★★★★ *Farmhouse*
Stapleton, Dorrington, Shrewsbury SY5 7LB
t (01743) 718670
e kevan@shadymoor.co.uk
w shadymoor.co.uk

**Woodside Farm** ★★★★
*Farmhouse*
Cardington, Church Stretton SY6 7LB
t (01694) 771314
w virtual-shropshire.co.uk

### CARLTON Suffolk

**Willow Tree Cottage** ★★★★
*Bed & Breakfast*
3 Belvedere Close, Kelsale, Saxmundham IP17 2RS
t (01728) 602161

### CARSINGTON Derbyshire

**Breach Farm** ★★★★
*Farmhouse*
Carsington, Matlock, Wirksworth DE4 4DD
t (01629) 540265
w breachfarm.co.uk

### CASEWICK Lincolnshire

**Lindsey Cottage** ★★★★
*Bed & Breakfast*
Greatford Road, Uffington, Stamford PE9 4ST
t (01780) 752975
e smb@lindseycottage01.fsbusiness.co.uk

### CASTLE ACRE Norfolk

**Willow Cottage Tea Rooms** ★★★★
*Guest Accommodation*
Stocks Green, Castle Acre, King's Lynn PE32 2AE
t (01760) 755551
e info@willowcottage.biz
w broadland.com

### CASTLE DONINGTON Leicestershire

**Castletown House** ★★★★
*Guest Accommodation*
4 High Street, Castle Donington DE74 2PP
t (01332) 812018
e info@castletownhouse.com
w castletownhouse.com

**Scot's Corner Guest House** ★★★ *Bed & Breakfast*
82 Park Lane, Castle Donington DE74 2JG
t (01332) 811226
e linda.deary@ntlworld.com
w scots-corner.com

### CASTLETON Derbyshire

**Bargate Cottage** ★★★★
*Bed & Breakfast*
Bargate Street, Bargate, Hope Valley S33 8WG
t (01433) 620201

**Cheshire House** ★★★
*Bed & Breakfast*
How Lane, Castleton, Hope Valley S33 8WJ
t (01433) 623225
e sue_cheshirehouse@btinternet.com
w cheshire-house.co.uk

**Cheshire Mews** ★★★★
*Guest Accommodation*
How Lane, Castleton, Hope Valley S33 8WJ
t 07977 998881
e kslack@btconnect.com
w cheshiremews-castleton.co.uk

**Dunscar Farm Bed & Breakfast** ★★★★
*Guest Accommodation*
Castleton, Hope Valley S33 8WA
t (01433) 620483
e janet@dunscarfarm.co.uk
w dunscarfarm.co.uk

**Hillside House** ★★★★
*Bed & Breakfast*
Pindale Road, Hope Valley S33 8WU
t (01433) 620312
w peakdistrictnationalpark.com

**Ye Olde Cheshire Cheese Inn** ★★★ *Inn*
How Lane, Castleton, Hope Valley S33 8WJ
t (01433) 620330
e info@cheshirecheeseinn.co.uk
w cheshirecheeseinn.co.uk

**Ye Olde Nag's Head** ★★★
*Inn*
Cross Street, Castleton, Hope Valley S33 8WH
t (01433) 620248
e info@yeoldenagshead.co.uk
w yeoldenagshead.co.uk

**Ramblers Rest** ★★★
*Guest Accommodation*
Back Street, Mill Bridge, Hope Valley S33 8WR
t (01433) 620125
e mary@ramblersrest.wanadoo.co.uk
w ramblersrest-castleton.co.uk

**Swiss House** ★★★
*Guest Accommodation*
How Lane, Castleton, Hope Valley S33 8WJ
t (01433) 621098
e info@swiss-house.co.uk
w swiss-house.co.uk

**YHA Castleton Hall** ★★★
*Hostel*
Castle Street, Castleton, Hope Valley S33 8WG
t (01433) 620235
e castleton@yha.org.uk
w yha.org.uk

### CATESBY Northamptonshire

**Long Furlong Farm** ★★★
*Farmhouse*
Catesby, Daventry NN11 6LW
t (01327) 264770
e haighfamily@waitrose.com

### CATFIELD Norfolk

**The Limes** ★★★★
*Bed & Breakfast*
Limes Road, Great Yarmouth NR29 5DG
t (01692) 581221
e info@thelimesatcatfield.com
w thelimesatcatfield.com

### CAVENDISH Suffolk

**Embleton House** ★★★★
*Guest Accommodation*
**SILVER AWARD**
Melford Road, Cavendish, Sudbury CO10 8AA
t (01787) 280447
e silverned@aol.com
w embletonhouse.co.uk

### CHADDESDEN Derbyshire

**Green Gables** ★★★
*Guest House*
19 Highfield Lane, Chaddesden, Derby DE21 6PG
t (01332) 672298
e enquiries@greengablesuk.co.uk
w greengablesuk.co.uk

### CHAPEL-EN-LE-FRITH Derbyshire

**Forest Lodge** ★★★★
*Bed & Breakfast*
58 Manchester Road, Chapel-en-le-Frith, High Peak SK23 9TH
t (01298) 812854
e noreen@forestlodge.org.uk
w forestlodge.org.uk

**High Croft** ★★★★★
*Guest House* **SILVER AWARD**
Manchester Road, Chapel-en-le-Frith, High Peak SK23 9UH
t (01298) 814843
e elaine@highcroft-guesthouse.co.uk
w highcroft-guesthouse.co.uk

**Rushop Hall B&B** ★★★★
*Farmhouse*
Rushup Lane, Rushup, High Peak SK23 0QT
t (01298) 813323
e neil@rushophall.com
w rushophall.com

**Slack Hall Farm** ★★★★
*Farmhouse*
Castleton Road, Chapel-en-le-Frith, High Peak SK23 0QS
t (01298) 812845

### CHAPEL ST LEONARDS Lincolnshire

**South Sands Guest House** ★★★ *Guest House*
35 South Road, Chapel St Leonards PE24 5TL
t (01754) 873066
e info@south-sands.co.uk

### CHEADLE Staffordshire

**Ley Fields Farm** ★★★★
*Farmhouse* **SILVER AWARD**
Leek Road, Cheadle, Alton Towers Area ST10 2EF
t (01538) 752875
e leyfieldsfarm@aol.com
w leyfieldsfarm.co.uk

**The Manor** ★★★
*Guest House*
Watt Place, Cheadle, Alton Towers Area ST10 1NZ
t (01538) 753450
e enquiries@themanor-cheadle.com
w themanor-cheadle.com

**Park View Guest House** ★★★ *Guest House*
15 Mill Road, Cheadle, Alton Towers Area ST10 1NG
t (01538) 755412
e stewart@parkviewguesthouse.fsworld.co.uk
w theparkviewguesthouse.co.uk

**Rakeway House Farm B&B**
★★★★ *Farmhouse*
Rakeway Road, Cheadle, Alton Towers Area ST10 1RA
**t** (01538) 755295
**e** enquiries@rakewayhousefarm.co.uk
**w** rakewayhousefarm.co.uk

### CHEDDLETON Staffordshire

**Brook House Farm** ★★★
*Farmhouse*
Brookhouse Lane, Cheddleton, Leek ST13 7DF
**t** (01538) 360296

**The Garden House** ★★★★
*Bed & Breakfast*
150 Cheadle Road, Cheddleton, Leek ST13 7BD
**t** (01538) 361449
**e** pearl@garden-house.org
**w** garden-house.org

**Mosslee Grange Bed and Breakfast** ★★★
*Bed & Breakfast*
Basford Green, Cheddleton, Leek ST13 7ES
**t** 07969 463685
**e** mossleegrange@supanet.com
**w** freewebs.com/mossleegrangebedandbreakfast

### CHEDGRAVE Norfolk

**Chedgrave House B & B**
★★★★ *Bed & Breakfast*
2 Norwich Road, Chedgrave, Norwich NR14 6HB
**t** (01508) 521095
**e** june@chedgrave-house.freeserve.co.uk
**w** chedgravehouse.co.uk

**Little Willows** ★★★★
*Bed & Breakfast*
Willow Cottage, Nursery Road, Norwich NR14 6BF
**t** (01508) 528525
**e** info@littlewillows.co.uk
**w** littlewillows.co.uk

### CHEDISTON Suffolk

**Oak Lodge** ★★★★
*Guest Accommodation*
Chediston Green, Halesworth IP19 0BB
**t** (01986) 785268
**e** oaklodgebandb@btconnect.com

### CHELLASTON Derbyshire

**The Lawns** ★★★ *Inn*
High Street, Chellaston, Derby DE73 1TB
**t** (01332) 701553

### CHELMARSH Shropshire

**Hampton House** ★★★★
*Guest Accommodation*
Hampton Loade, Chelmarsh, Bridgnorth WV16 6BN
**t** (01746) 861436
**w** stmem.com/hampton-house

**The Unicorn Inn** ★★ *Inn*
Hampton Loade, Chelmarsh, Bridgnorth WV16 6BN
**t** (01746) 861515
**e** kenunicorninn@aol.com
**w** http://freespace.virginnet.co.uk/unicorninn.bridgnorth

### CHELMORTON Derbyshire

**Church Inn** ★★★★ *Inn*
Buxton SK17 9SL
**t** (01298) 85319

### CHELMSFORD Essex

**Aarandale** ★★★
*Guest House*
9 Roxwell Road, Chelmsford CM1 2LY
**t** (01245) 251713
**e** aarandaleuk@aol.com
**w** aarandale.com

**Chatton Park House Bed & Breakfast** ★★★★★
*Bed & Breakfast*
**GOLD AWARD**
Chatton NE66 5RA
**t** (01668) 215507
**e** enquiries@chattonpark.com
**w** chattonpark.com

**Compasses Motel** ★★★ *Inn*
141 Broomfield Road, Chelmsford CM1 1RY
**t** (01245) 292051

**Sherwood** ★★★
*Bed & Breakfast*
Cedar Avenue West, Chelmsford CM1 2XA
**t** (01245) 257981
**e** jeremy.salter@btclick.com

**Wards Farm** ★★
*Bed & Breakfast*
Loves Green, Highwood Road, Chelmsford CM1 3QJ
**t** (01245) 248812
**e** alsnbrtn@aol.com

### CHELVESTON Northamptonshire

**Middle Farm Villa B&B**
★★★★ *Bed & Breakfast*
The Green, Chelveston, Wellingborough NN9 6AJ
**t** (01933) 625541
**e** middlefarmvilla@aol.com

**Sunburrow**
Rating Applied For
*Bed & Breakfast*
15 Hillside, Wellingborough NN9 6AQ
**t** (01933) 624383
**e** baxter941@btinternet.com

### CHERRY HINTON Cambridgeshire

**Old Rosemary Branch** ★★
*Bed & Breakfast*
Church End, Cherry Hinton, Cambridge CB1 3LF
**t** (01223) 247161
**e** saa30@cam.ac.uk
**w** theoldrosemarybranch.co.uk

### CHESHUNT Hertfordshire

**YHA Lee Valley Village**
★★★★ *Hostel*
Windmill Lane, Cheshunt, Waltham Cross EN8 9AJ
**t** (01992) 628392
**e** leevalley@yha.org.uk
**w** yha.org.uk

### CHESTERFIELD Derbyshire

**Abigails Guest House** ★★★
*Guest House*
62 Brockwell Lane, Chesterfield S40 4EE
**t** (01246) 279391
**e** gail@abigails.fsnet.co.uk
**w** abigailsguesthouse.co.uk

**Acorns Guest House** ★★★
*Guest House*
56 Sheffield Road, Chesterfield S41 7LS
**t** (01246) 233602

**Anis Louise Guest House**
★★★★ *Guest House*
34 Clarence Road, Chesterfield S40 1LN
**t** (01246) 235412
**e** anislouise@gmail.com
**w** anislouiseguesthouse.co.uk

**Batemans Mill Country Inn & Restaurant** ★★★★ *Inn*
**SILVER AWARD**
Mill Lane, Old Tupton, Chesterfield S42 6AE
**t** (01246) 862296
**e** info@batemansmill.co.uk
**w** batemansmill.co.uk

**Clarendon Guest House**
★★★ *Guest Accommodation*
32 Clarence Road, Chesterfield S40 1LN
**t** (01246) 235004

### CHEVELEY Cambridgeshire

**1eleven Bed & Breakfast**
★★★★ *Bed & Breakfast*
**SILVER AWARD**
111 High Street, Cheveley, Newmarket CB8 9DG
**t** (01638) 731177
**e** richard@1elevenbandb.co.uk
**w** 1elevenbandb.co.uk

**Old Farmhouse** ★★★★
*Bed & Breakfast*
165 High Street, Cheveley, Newmarket CB8 9DG
**t** (01638) 730771 & 07909 970047
**e** amrobinson@clara.co.uk
**w** cheveleybandb.co.uk

### CHINLEY Derbyshire

**Moseley House Farm** ★★★
*Farmhouse*
Maynestone Road, Chinley, High Peak SK23 6AH
**t** (01663) 750240
**e** moseleyhouse@supanet.com
**w** smoothhound.co.uk/hotels/moseleyhouse

**The Old Hall Inn** ★★★★ *Inn*
Whitehough, Chinley, Stockport SK23 6EJ
**t** (01663) 750529
**e** info@old-hall-inn.co.uk
**w** old-hall-inn.co.uk

### CHIPPENHAM Cambridgeshire

**Maltings Yard Cottage**
★★★★ *Bed & Breakfast*
20 High Street, Chippenham, Newmarket CB7 5PP
**t** (01638) 720110
**e** alanblazfm@aol.com

### CHORLEYWOOD Hertfordshire

**Ashburton Country House**
★★★★★ *Bed & Breakfast*
**SILVER AWARD**
48 Berks Hill, Chorleywood, Rickmansworth WD3 5AH
**t** (01923) 285510
**e** info@ashburtonhouse.co.uk
**w** ashburtonhouse.co.uk

### CHURCH STRETTON Shropshire

**Acton Scott Farm B&B** ★★★
*Farmhouse*
Acton Scott, Church Stretton SY6 6QN
**t** (01694) 781260
**e** shrops@actonscottfarm.co.uk
**w** actonscottfarm.co.uk

**Brookfields Guest House**
★★★★★ *Guest House*
**SILVER AWARD**
Watling Street North, Church Stretton SY6 7AR
**t** (01694) 722314
**e** paulangie@brookfields51.fsnet.co.uk
**w** churchstretton-guesthouse.co.uk

**Highcliffe** ★★★
*Bed & Breakfast*
Madeira Walk, Church Stretton SY6 6JQ
**t** (01694) 722908
**w** stmem.com/highcliffe

**Highlands Bed and Breakfast** ★★★★
*Bed & Breakfast*
Hazler Road, Church Stretton SY6 7AF
**t** (01694) 723737
**e** info@highlandsbandb.co.uk
**w** highlandsbandb.co.uk

**Jinlye Guest House**
★★★★★ *Guest House*
**GOLD AWARD**
Castle Hill, All Stretton, Church Stretton SY6 6JP
**t** (01694) 723243
**e** info@jinlye.co.uk
**w** jinlye.co.uk

**Juniper Cottage** ★★★★
*Bed & Breakfast*
**SILVER AWARD**
All Stretton, Church Stretton SY6 6HG
**t** (01694) 723427
**e** colinmcintyre@ukonline.co.uk

**Mynd House** ★★★★
*Guest House* **SILVER AWARD**
Little Stretton, Church Stretton SY6 6RB
**t** (01694) 722212
**e** info@myndhouse.co.uk
**w** myndhouse.co.uk

**Old Rectory House** ★★★
*Bed & Breakfast*
Burway Road, Church Stretton SY6 6DW
**t** (01694) 724462
**e** smamos@btinternet.com
**w** oldrectoryhouse.co.uk

**Rheingold** ★★★★
*Guest Accommodation*
9 The Bridleways, Church Stretton SY6 7AN
**t** (01694) 723969
**w** rheingold-b-and-b.co.uk

**Sayang House** ★★★★
*Bed & Breakfast*
Hope Bowdler, Church Stretton SY6 7DD
**t** (01694) 723981
**e** madegan@aol.com
**w** sayanghouse.co.uk

**Victoria House** ★★★★
*Guest Accommodation*
48 High Street, Church Stretton SY6 6BX
**t** (01694) 723823
**e** victoriahouse@fsmail.net
**w** bedandbreakfast-shropshire.co.uk

## CLACTON-ON-SEA
Essex

**Adelaide Guesthouse** ★★★
*Guest House*
24 Wellesley Road, Clacton-on-Sea CO15 3PP
**t** (01255) 435628
**e** adelaide_guesthouse@yahoo.co.uk
**w** adelaide-guesthouse.co.uk

**Beam Guest House** ★★★★
*Guest House*
26 Nelson Road, Clacton-on-Sea CO15 1LU
**t** (01255) 433992
**e** beamguesthouse@talk21.com
**w** clacton-on-sea.net

**The Chudleigh** ★★★★
*Guest Accommodation*
13 Agate Road, Marine Parade West, Clacton-on-Sea CO15 1RA
**t** (01255) 425407
**e** reception@chudleighhotel.com
**w** tiscover.co.uk/chudleigh-hotel

**Le'Vere House** ★★★
*Guest Accommodation*
Clacton-on-Sea CO15 1RA
**t** (01255) 423044
**e** kemphotel@aol.com
**w** leverehotel.co.uk

**Pond House Farmhouse Bed and Breakfast** ★★★★
*Farmhouse* **GOLD AWARD**
Earls Hall Farm, Clacton-on-Sea CO16 8BP
**t** (01255) 820458
**e** brenda_lord@farming.co.uk
**w** earlshallfarm.info

## CLAPHAM
Bedfordshire

**Narly Oak Lodge** ★★★★
*Bed & Breakfast*
The Baulk, Green Lane, Bedford MK41 6AA
**t** (01234) 350353
**e** mollie.foster07@btinternet.com
**w** narlyoaklodge.com

## CLARE
Suffolk

**The Bell** ★★★★ *Inn*
Market Hill, Sudbury CO10 8NN
**t** (01787) 277741
**e** info@thebellhotel-clare.com
**w** thebellhotel-clare.com

## CLAXBY
Lincolnshire

**Swallows Barn** ★★★★
*Bed & Breakfast*
St Mary's Lane, Claxby (West Lindsey) LN8 3YX
**t** (01673) 828626
**e** swallowsbarn@btinternet.com
**w** swallowsbarn.co.uk

## CLAY CROSS
Derbyshire

**Blanches Guesthouse**
★★★★ *Bed & Breakfast*
172 Market Street, Clay Cross, Chesterfield S45 9LY
**t** (01246) 861163
**e** info@blanchesguesthouse.co.uk
**w** blanchesguesthouse.co.uk

## CLEE STANTON
Shropshire

**Timberstone B&B** ★★★★
*Bed & Breakfast*
Clee Stanton, Ludlow SY8 3EL
**t** (01584) 823519
**e** enquiry@timberstone.co.uk
**w** timberstoneludlow.co.uk

## CLEETHORPES
North East Lincolnshire

**Acer House** ★★★
*Bed & Breakfast*
14 Queens Parade, Cleethorpes DN35 0DF
**t** (01472) 200289

**Arlana Guest House** ★★★
*Guest House*
53 Princes Road, Cleethorpes DN35 8AW
**t** (01472) 699689
**e** colleen.waters@ntlworld.com
**w** arlanaguesthouse.co.uk

**Ginnie's Guest House** ★★★
*Guest House*
27 Queen's Parade, Cleethorpes DN35 0DF
**t** (01472) 694997
**e** enquiries@ginnies.co.uk
**w** ginnies.co.uk

**Gladson Guest House** ★★★
*Guest Accommodation*
14 Isaacs Hill, Cleethorpes DN35 8AD
**t** (01472) 694858
**e** enquiries@gladsonguesthouse.co.uk
**w** gladsonguesthouse.co.uk

**Tudor Terrace Guest House**
★★★★ *Guest House*
11 Bradford Avenue, Cleethorpes DN35 0BB
**t** (01472) 600800
**e** tudor.terrace@ntlworld.com
**w** tudorterrace.co.uk

**The Vines B&B** ★★★
*Guest Accommodation*
15 Isaacs Hill, Cleethorpes DN35 8JU
**t** (01472) 690524
**e** stevhw3@aol.com

## CLEHONGER
Herefordshire

**The Old Vicarage** ★★★★
*Guest House*
Church Road, Old Clehonger, Hereford HR2 9SE
**t** (01432) 371343
**e** info@theoldvicarage.uk.com
**w** theoldvicarage.uk.com

## CLENCHWARTON
Norfolk

**Kismet Lodge Bed and Breakfast** ★★★★
*Guest Accommodation*
15 Willow Drive, Clenchwarton, King's Lynn PE34 4EN
**t** (01553) 761409
**e** kismetlodgebb@aol.com
**w** bed-and-breakfast-kismet-lodge.co.uk

## CLENT
Worcestershire

**Tall Trees Cottage** ★★★★
*Guest Accommodation*
Tall Trees, Thicknall Lane, Stourbridge DY9 0HN
**t** (01562) 883883
**e** talltreescottage@btconnect.com
**w** talltreescottage.co.uk

## CLEOBURY MORTIMER
Shropshire

**Broome Park Farm** ★★★
*Farmhouse*
Catherton Road, Cleobury Mortimer DY14 0LB
**t** (01299) 270647
**e** catherine@broomeparkfarm.co.uk
**w** broomeparkfarm.co.uk

**Clod Hall** ★★ *Bed & Breakfast*
Milson, Cleobury Mortimer DY14 0BJ
**t** (01584) 781421
**w** stmem.com/clod-hall

**Cox's Barn** ★★★★
*Farmhouse*
Bagginswood, Cleobury Mortimer DY14 8LS
**t** (01746) 718415
**e** iain.thompson12@btopenworld.com
**w** stmem.com/coxs-barn

**Woodview B&B** ★★★★
*Guest Accommodation*
**GOLD AWARD**
Mawley Oak, Cleobury Mortimer DY14 9BA
**t** (01299) 271422
**w** woodviewcountryvilla.co.uk

## CLEVELODE
Worcestershire

**Severnside Bed & Breakfast**
★★★★ *Bed & Breakfast*
Clevelode, Malvern WR13 6PD
**t** (01684) 311894
**e** info@severn-side.co.uk
**w** severn-side.co.uk

## CLIFFORD
Herefordshire

**Cottage Farm** ★★
*Bed & Breakfast*
Middlewood, Dorstone, Golden Valley HR3 5SX
**t** (01497) 831496
**e** cottagefarm@fsmail.net
**w** golden-valley.co.uk/cottagefarm

## CLIFTON
Derbyshire

**Stone Cottage** ★★★
*Guest Accommodation*
Green Lane, Clifton, Ashbourne DE6 2BL
**t** (01335) 343377
**e** info@stone-cottage.fsnet.co.uk
**w** stone-cottage.fsnet.co.uk

## CLIFTON UPON TEME
Worcestershire

**Pitlands Farm** ★★★★
*Farmhouse*
Clifton upon Teme, Tenbury Wells WR6 6DX
**t** (01886) 812220
**e** pitlandsfarmholidays@btopenworld.com
**w** pitlandsfarm.co.uk

## CLOWS TOP
Worcestershire

**Colliers Hill Guest House & Conference Centre** ★★★★
*Bed & Breakfast*
Colliers Hill, Bayton DY14 9NZ
**t** (01299) 832247
**e** info@collierhill.co.uk
**w** colliershill.co.uk

## CLUN
Shropshire

**Clun Mill Youth Hostel** ★★
*Hostel*
The Mill, Clun, Craven Arms SY7 8NY
**t** (01588) 640582
**e** reservations@yha.org.uk
**w** yha.org.uk

**Crown House (Old Stables and Saddlery)** ★★★★
*Bed & Breakfast*
Crown House, Clun, Craven Arms SY7 8JW
**t** (01588) 640780
**e** crownhouseclun@talk21.com
**w** smoothhound.co.uk/hotels/crownhouse

**Llanhedric Farm** ★★★★
*Farmhouse*
Clun, Craven Arms SY7 8NG
t (01588) 640203
e maryandhugh@btconnect.com
w llanhedricfarm.co.uk

**New House Farm** ★★★★★
*Farmhouse* **GOLD AWARD**
Clun, Craven Arms SY7 8NJ
t (01588) 638314
e sarah@bishopscastle.co.uk
w new-house-clun.co.uk

**The Old Farmhouse** ★★★★
*Guest House*
Woodside, Clun SY7 0JB
t (01588) 640695
e helen@vuan1.freeserve.co.uk
w theoldfarmhousebandb.co.uk

**Springhill Farm** ★★★
*Farmhouse*
Clun, Craven Arms SY7 8PE
t (01588) 640337
e info.springhillfarm@gmail.com
w springhill-farm.org.uk

**Thomas Cottage** ★★★★
*Bed & Breakfast*
Church Bank, Clun SY7 8LP
t (01588) 640029
e info@thomascottageclun.co.uk
w thomascottageclun.co.uk

**The White Horse Inn** ★★★
*Inn*
The Square, Clun SY7 8JA
t (01588) 640305
e jack@whi-clun.co.uk
w whi-clun.co.uk

## COALBROOKDALE Shropshire

**Springhill B&B** ★★★★
*Guest Accommodation*
2 School Road, Coalbrookdale, Ironbridge TF8 7DY
t (01952) 433225
e info@springhillbandb.co.uk
w springhillbandb.co.uk

## COALPORT Shropshire

**Ironbridge Youth Hostel (YHA)** ★★★ *Group Hostel*
John Rose Building, High Street, Telford TF8 7HT
t (01952) 588755
e ironbridge@yha.org.uk
w yha.org.uk

**The Shakespeare Inn**
★★★★ *Inn*
High Street, Coalport, Telford TF8 7HT
t (01952) 580675
w shakespeare-inn.co.uk

## COCKFIELD Suffolk

**The Old Manse Barn** ★★★★
*Guest Accommodation*
**SILVER AWARD**
Chapel Road, Cockfield, Bury St Edmunds IP30 0HE
t (01284) 828120
e bookings@theoldmansebarn.co.uk
w theoldmansebarn.co.uk

## COLCHESTER Essex

**17 Roman Road** ★★★★
*Bed & Breakfast*
Colchester CO1 1UR
t (01206) 768898
e marianne.gilbert@btinternet.com
w 17romanroad.co.uk

**Apple Blossom House**
★★★★
*Guest Accommodation*
8 Guildford Road, Colchester CO1 2YL
t (01206) 512303
e patricia.appleblossom@virgin.net

**Beacon Guest House** ★★
*Bed & Breakfast*
12 Berrimans Close, Colchester CO4 3XF
t (01206) 794501
e hannahmulvey@aol.com

**Charlie Brown's** ★★★★
*Bed & Breakfast*
**SILVER AWARD**
60 East Street, Colchester CO1 2TS
t (01206) 517541
e info@charliebrownsbedandbreakfast.co.uk
w charliebrownsbedandbreakfast.co.uk

**Corner House** ★★★
*Bed & Breakfast*
36 West Stockwell Street, Colchester CO1 1HS
t 07737 533879
e anneminns@googlemail.com
w cornerhouse-bb.co.uk

**Four Sevens Guest House**
★★★ *Guest Accommodation*
28 Inglis Road, Colchester CO3 3HU
t (01206) 546093
e calypsod@hotmail.com

**Fridaywood Farm** ★★★★
*Farmhouse* **SILVER AWARD**
Bounstead Road, Colchester CO2 0DF
t (01206) 573595
e lochorem8@aol.com

**Greenview House**
Rating Applied For
*Bed & Breakfast*
St Johns Green, Colchester CO2 7HA
t (01206) 570847
e greenviewhouse@btinternet.com

**Myland Pear Tree B & B**
Rating Applied For
*Bed & Breakfast*
53 Mile End Road, Colchester CO4 5BU
t (01206) 853204
e ek@mylandpeartree.co.uk
w mylandpeartree.co.uk

**Nutcrackers** ★★★
*Bed & Breakfast*
6 Mayberry Walk, Colchester CO2 8PS
t (01206) 543085
e nutcrackers@btinternet.com

**Old Courthouse Inn** ★★★★
*Inn*
Harwich Road, Great Bromley, Colchester CO7 7JG
t (01206) 250322
e oldcourthouseinn@btinternet.com
w theoldcourthouseinn.co.uk

**Park Hall Country House**
★★★★★
*Guest Accommodation*
**GOLD AWARD**
Clay Lane, St Osyth, Clacton-on-Sea CO16 8HG
t (01255) 820922
e trish@parkhall.fslife.co.uk
w parkhall.info

**Rutland House Bed and Breakfast** ★★★★
*Bed & Breakfast*
**SILVER AWARD**
121 Lexden Road, Colchester CO3 3RD
t (01206) 573437
e rutland121@aol.com
w rutlandhousebandb.co.uk

**Rye Farm** ★★★★ *Farmhouse*
Rye Lane, Layer-de-la-Haye, Colchester CO2 0JL
t (01206) 734350
e peterbunting@btconnect.com
w buntingp.fsbusiness.co.uk

**Scheregate Guesthouse** ★★
*Guest House*
36 Osborne Street, Via St John's Street, Colchester CO2 7DB
t (01206) 573034

**University of Essex**
Rating Applied For
*Campus*
Wivenhoe Park, Colchester CO4 3SQ
t (01206) 872358
e conferences@essex.ac.uk

## COLESHILL Warwickshire

**Grimscote Manor**
Rating Applied For
*Guest Accommodation*
Grimstock Hill, Lichfield Road, Birmingham B46 1LH
t (01675) 464222
e grimscotemanor@hotmail.co.uk

**Merrimoles Bed & Breakfast**
★★★★ *Bed & Breakfast*
Back Lane, Shustoke, Coleshill, Birmingham B46 2AW
t (01675) 481158
e stella@merrimoles.co.uk
w merrimoles.co.uk

**Ye Olde Station Guest House** ★★★ *Guest House*
Church Road, Shustoke, Coleshill, Birmingham B46 2AX
t (01675) 481736
e patr@freeuk.com

**The Railway Guest House**
Rating Applied For
*Guest Accommodation*
Station Road, Birmingham B46 2JA
t (01675) 463909
e railwayguesthouse@btinternet.com
w therailwayguesthouse.co.uk

## COLSTERWORTH Lincolnshire

**The Stables** ★★★★
*Guest House*
Stainby Rd, Colsterworth NG33 5JB
t (01476) 861057
e thestablesbb@aol.com
w stablesbandb.co.uk

## COLTISHALL Norfolk

**Bridge House** ★★★★
*Guest House*
Coltishall, Norwich NR12 7AA
t (01603) 737323
e bhbookings@talktalk.net
w bridgehouse-coltishall.co.uk

**Hedges Guesthouse** ★★★★
*Guest Accommodation*
Tunstead Road, Coltishall NR12 7AL
t (01603) 738361
e info@hedgesbandb.co.uk
w hedgesbandb.co.uk

**Old Railway Station** ★★★★
*Bed & Breakfast*
Station Road, Norwich NR12 7JG
t (01603) 737069
e info@theoldrailwaystation.co.uk
w theoldrailwaystation.co.uk

**Seven Acres House**
★★★★★ *Bed & Breakfast*
**SILVER AWARD**
Great Hautbois, Coltishall NR12 7JZ
t (01603) 736737
e william@hautbois.plus.com
w norfolkbroadsbandb.com

## COLTON Staffordshire

**Colton House** ★★★★★
*Guest House* **SILVER AWARD**
Bellamour Way, Colton, Rugeley WS15 3LL
t (01889) 578580
e mail@coltonhouse.com
w coltonhouse.com

## CONINGSBY Lincolnshire

**The Leagate Inn** ★★★★ *Inn*
Leagate Road, Coningsby LN4 4RS
t (01526) 342370
e theleagateinn@hotmail.com
w the-leagate-inn.co.uk/

### CONISHOLME
Lincolnshire

**Wickham House ★★★★★**
*Guest Accommodation*
**SILVER AWARD**
Church Lane, Conisholme LN11 7LX
t (01507) 358465
e cizekann@hotmail.com
w wickham-house.co.uk

### CORBY
Northamptonshire

**Home Farm ★★★**
*Bed & Breakfast*
Main Street, Sudborough, Kettering NN14 3BX
t (01832) 730488
e bandbhomefarmsud@aol.com
w homefarmsudborough.co.uk

**Manor Farm Guest House ★★★★**
*Guest Accommodation*
Station Road, Rushton, Kettering NN14 1RL
t (01536) 710305
w rushtonmanorfarm.co.uk

### COTON IN THE ELMS
Derbyshire

**Fern Cottage**
Rating Applied For
*Bed & Breakfast*
Mill Street, Coton in the Elms, Swadlincote DE12 8ES
t (01283) 763306
e hjacherry@yahoo.co.uk

### COTTESMORE
Rutland

**Tithe Barn ★★★★**
*Guest Accommodation*
Clatterpot Lane, Cottesmore, Oakham LE15 7DW
t (01572) 813591
e jp@thetithebarn.co.uk
w tithebarn-rutland.co.uk

### COUGHTON
Warwickshire

**Coughton Lodge ★★★★**
*Guest House*
Coughton, Alcester B49 5HU
t (01789) 764600
e enquiries@coughtonlodge.co.uk
w coughtonlodge.co.uk

### COVENTRY
West Midlands

**Acacia Guest House ★★★★**
*Guest House*
11 Park Road, Coventry CV1 2LE
t (024) 7663 3622
e acaciaguesthouse@hotmail.com

**Ashdowns Guest House**
**★★★** *Guest House*
12 Regent Street, Earlsdon, Coventry CV1 3EP
t (024) 7622 9280

**Ashleigh House ★★★**
*Guest House*
17 Park Road, Coventry CV1 2LH
t (024) 7622 3804

**Barnacle Hall ★★★★★**
*Bed & Breakfast*
**GOLD AWARD**
Shilton Lane, Shilton, Coventry CV7 9LH
t (024) 7661 2629
e rose@barnaclehall.co.uk
w barnaclehall.co.uk

**Bede Guest House ★★★**
*Bed & Breakfast*
250 Radford Road, Radford, Coventry CV6 3BU
t (024) 7659 7837
e bedehouse@aol.com
w bedeguesthouse.co.uk

**Bourne Brook Lodge ★★★★**
*Bed & Breakfast*
Mill Lane, Fillongley, Coventry CV7 8EE
t (01676) 541898
w bournebrooklodge.co.uk

**Highcroft Guest House**
**★★★** *Guest House*
65 Barras Lane, Coundon, Coventry CV1 4AQ
t (024) 7622 8157
e deepakcov@hotmail.com

**Merlyn Guest House ★★★**
*Guest House*
105 Holyhead Road, Coundon, Coventry CV1 3AD
t (024) 7622 2800
e info@merlynguesthouse.co.uk
w merlynguesthouse.co.uk

**Mount Guest House ★★★**
*Guest House*
9 Coundon Road, Coventry CV1 4AR
t (024) 7622 5998
e enquiries@guesthousecoventry.com
w guesthousecoventry.com

**Spire View Guest House**
**★★★** *Guest House*
36 Park Road, Coventry CV1 2LD
t (024) 7625 1602
e bookings@spireviewguesthouse.co.uk
w spireviewguesthouse.co.uk

### CRANFIELD
Bedfordshire

**Croft End Bed And Breakfast ★★★**
*Guest Accommodation*
10 Hotch Croft, Cranfield, Bedford MK43 0BN
t (01234) 750753
e chambers120@btinternet.com

### CRANWELL
Lincolnshire

**Byards Leap Bed & Breakfast ★★★**
*Bed & Breakfast*
Byards Leap Cottage, Cranwell NG34 8EY
t (01400) 261537
e info@byardsleapcottage.co.uk
w byardsleapcottage.co.uk

**Byards Leap Lodge ★★★★**
*Guest Accommodation*
**SILVER AWARD**
Byards Leap, Cranwell NG34 8EY
t (01400) 261375
e byards.leap@virgin.net
w byards-leap-lodge.co.uk

### CRANWELL VILLAGE
Lincolnshire

**Oxenford Farm ★★★★**
*Bed & Breakfast*
Cranwell NG34 8DE
t (01400) 261369
e oldblackie50@hotmail.com
w oxenfordfarm.co.uk

### CREATON
Northamptonshire

**Highgate House – A Sundial Group Venue ★★★★**
*Guest Accommodation*
Grooms Lane, Creaton, Northampton NN6 8NN
t (01604) 731999
e highgate@sundialgroup.com
w sundialgroup.com

### CREETING ST MARY
Suffolk

**Hungercut Hall Bed and Breakfast ★★★★**
*Guest Accommodation*
Coddenham Road, Creeting St Mary, Ipswich IP6 8NX
t (01449) 721323
e info@hungercuthall.co.uk
w hungercuthall.co.uk

### CRESSBROOK
Derbyshire

**Cressbrook Hall ★★★★**
*Guest Accommodation*
Cressbrook, Buxton SK17 8SY
t (01298) 871289
e stay@cressbrookhall.co.uk
w cressbrookhall.co.uk

**The Old Hay Barn ★★★★★**
*Guest Accommodation*
The Barns, Cressbrook, Buxton SK17 8SY
t (01298) 873503
e dcmacb@aol.com
w cressbrook.co.uk/tidza/oldhaybarn

### CROMER
Norfolk

**Albury House ★★★★**
*Guest House*
20 Alfred Road, Cromer NR27 9AN
t (01263) 515011
e vicky@albury-house.co.uk
w albury-house.co.uk

**Cambridge House ★★★★**
*Guest Accommodation*
Sea Front, Cromer NR27 9HD
t (01263) 512085
w cambridgecromer.co.uk

**Captains House ★★★★★**
*Guest Accommodation*
**GOLD AWARD**
5 The Crescent, Cromer NR27 9EX
t (01263) 515434
e captainshouse@aol.com
w captains-house.co.uk

**Grove Guesthouse ★★★★**
*Guest Accommodation*
95 Overstrand Road, Cromer NR27 0DJ
t (01263) 512412
e enquiries@thegrovecromer.co.uk
w thegrovecromer.co.uk

**Incleborough House Luxury Bed and Breakfast ★★★★★**
*Bed & Breakfast*
**GOLD AWARD**
Lower Common, East Runton, Cromer NR27 9PG
t (01263) 515939
e enquiries@incleboroughhouse.co.uk
w incleboroughhouse.co.uk

**Knoll Guesthouse ★★★**
*Guest Accommodation*
23 Alfred Road, Cromer NR27 9AN
t (01263) 512753
e ian@knollguesthouse.co.uk
w tiscover.co.uk

**Shrublands Farm ★★★★**
*Farmhouse*
Northrepps, Cromer NR27 0AA
t (01263) 579297

### CROPSTON
Leicestershire

**Horseshoe Cottage Farm**
**★★★★★** *Bed & Breakfast*
**GOLD AWARD**
Hallgates Reservoir Road, Cropston, Leicester LE7 7GQ
t (0116) 235 0038
e lindajee@ljee.freeserve.co.uk
w horseshoecottagefarm.com

### CROPTHORNE
Worcestershire

**Cropvale Farm Bed and Breakfast ★★★★** *Farmhouse*
**GOLD AWARD**
Smokey Lane, Cropthorne, Pershore WR10 3NF
t (01386) 861925
e cropvale@hotmail.com
w cropvalefarm.co.uk

**Oaklands Farmhouse**
**★★★★★** *Bed & Breakfast*
**GOLD AWARD**
Bricklehampton, Pershore WR10 3JT
t (01386) 861716
e barbara-stewart@lineone.net
w oaklandsfarmhouse.co.uk

### CROSS HOUSES
Shropshire

**Upper Brompton Farm**
**★★★★** *Bed & Breakfast*
**SILVER AWARD**
Cross Houses, Shrewsbury SY5 6LE
t (01743) 761629
e philippa@upperbrompton.orangehome.co.uk
w upperbromptonfarm.co.uk

### CROWDEN
Derbyshire

**Crowden Youth Hostel**
**★★★★** *Hostel*
Crowden, Glossop SK13 1HZ
t (01457) 852135

**CROWLAND**
**Lincolnshire**

**The Abbey** ★★★ *Inn*
21 East Street, Crowland
PE6 0EN
t (01733) 210200
e bruce.upson@btopenworld.com

**CROWLE**
**Worcestershire**

**Sunbrae Bed and Breakfast**
★★★★ *Bed & Breakfast*
**GOLD AWARD**
Wadborough Road, Stoulton, Worcester WR7 4RF
t (01905) 841129
e rita@sunbrae.co.uk
w sunbrae.co.uk

**CROXTON**
**Lincolnshire**

**Croxton House** ★★★
*Guest Accommodation*
Croxton DN39 6YD
t (01652) 688306
e info@croxtonhousebedandbreakfast.co.uk

**CUBBINGTON**
**Warwickshire**

**Bakers Cottage** ★★★★
*Bed & Breakfast*
52-54 Queen Street, Cubbington, Leamington Spa CV32 7NA
t (01926) 772146

**CULFORD**
**Suffolk**

**47 Benyon Gardens** ★★★
*Bed & Breakfast*
Culford, Bury St Edmunds IP28 6EA
t (01284) 728763

**CUMBERWORTH**
**Lincolnshire**

**Muffins** ★★★★
*Bed & Breakfast*
Willloughby Road, Cumberworth LN13 9LF
t (01507) 490068
e jean.robert@btopenworld.com
w muffins-cumberworth.co.uk/

**CURDWORTH**
**West Midlands**

**The Old School House Hotel**
★★★★ *Guest House*
Kingsbury Road, Sutton Coldfield B76 9DR
t (01675) 470177
e vicki@oldschoolhousehotel.co.uk
w oldschoolhousehotel.co.uk

**CUTTHORPE**
**Derbyshire**

**Cowclose Farm** ★★★★
*Bed & Breakfast*
Overgreen, Cutthorpe, Chesterfield S42 7BA
t (01246) 272948
e cowclosebarn@hotmail.co.uk
w cowclosebarn.com

**DANBURY**
**Essex**

**Wych Elm** ★★★
*Bed & Breakfast*
Mayes Lane, Danbury, Chelmsford CM3 4NJ
t (01245) 222674
e axonwychelm@tiscali.co.uk
w wychelmb-b.co.uk

**DARLEY ABBEY**
**Derbyshire**

**The Coach House** ★★
*Guest Accommodation*
185a Duffield Road, Derby DE22 1JB
t (01332) 551795

**DARLEY BRIDGE**
**Derbyshire**

**Square and Compass**
★★★★ *Inn*
Station Road, Darley Dale, Matlock DE4 2EQ
t (01629) 733255
e info@thesquareandcompass.co.uk
w thesquareandcompass.co.uk

**DAVENTRY**
**Northamptonshire**

**Drayton Lodge** ★★★★
*Farmhouse*
Staverton Road, Daventry NN11 4NL
t (01327) 702449
e ann.spicer@farming.co.uk
w draytonlodge.com

**The Mill House** ★★
*Bed & Breakfast*
West Farndon NN11 3TX
t (01327) 261727
e josephinelincoln53@amserve.com
w millhousebandb.co.uk

**Threeways House** ★★★★
*Bed & Breakfast*
Everdon NN11 3BL
t (01327) 361631
e threewayshouse@googlemail.com
w threewayshouse.com/

**DAWLEY**
**Shropshire**

**Hartfield Guest House**
★★★★
*Guest Accommodation*
Pool Hill Road, Horsehay, Telford TF4 3AS
t (01952) 505626
e enquiries@hartfieldguesthouse.co.uk
w hartfieldguesthouse.co.uk

**DEEPDALE**
**Lincolnshire**

**West Wold Farmhouse**
★★★★ *Guest House*
Deepdale, Barton-upon-Humber DN18 6ED
t (01652) 633293
e westwoldfarm@aol.com

**DEEPING ST NICHOLAS**
**Lincolnshire**

**St Nicholas House** ★★★★
*Guest Accommodation*
**SILVER AWARD**
Main Road, Deeping St Nicholas PE11 3HA
t (01775) 630484
e stnicholashouse@f2s.com
w stnicholashouse.co.uk

**DENSTONE**
**Staffordshire**

**Heywood Hall** ★★★★
*Guest Accommodation*
College Road, Denstone, Alton Towers Area ST14 5HR
t (01889) 591747
e johmccann@aol.com
w heywoodhall.co.uk

**Manor House Farm** ★★★★
*Farmhouse* **SILVER AWARD**
Quixhill Lane, Prestwood, Uttoxeter ST14 5DD
t (01889) 590415
e cm_ball@yahoo.co.uk
w 4posteraccom.com

**The Riddings** ★★★★
*Farmhouse*
Uttoxeter ST14 5HW
t (01889) 590008
e caberley@hotmail.co.uk

**Rowan Lodge** ★★★★
*Guest Accommodation*
Stubwood Lane, Denstone, Alton Towers Area ST14 5HU
t (01889) 590913
e rowanlodge@hotmail.com
w rowanlodge.co.uk

**DENVER**
**Norfolk**

**Westhall Cottages** ★★★
*Bed & Breakfast*
20-22 Sluice Road, Downham Market PE38 0DY
t (01366) 382987
w tiscover.co.uk

**DEOPHAM**
**Norfolk**

**Park Farm**
Rating Applied For
*Farmhouse*
Park Lane, Wymondham NR18 9HL
t (01953) 602289
e parkfarmbb@yahoo.co.uk

**DERBY**
**Derbyshire**

**Bonehill Farm** ★★★
*Bed & Breakfast*
Etwall Road, Mickleover, Derby DE3 0DN
t (01332) 513553
e bonehillfarm@hotmail.com
w bonehillfarm.co.uk

**Braeside Guest House**
★★★★ *Guest House*
113 Derby Road, Risley, Derby DE72 3SS
t (0115) 939 5885
e bookings@braesideguesthouse.co.uk
w braesideguesthouse.co.uk

**Chuckles Guest House** ★★★
*Bed & Breakfast*
48 Crompton Street, Derby DE1 1NX
t (01332) 367193
e enquire@chucklesguesthouse.co.uk
w chucklesguesthouse.co.uk

**Crompton Coach House**
★★★ *Guest Accommodation*
45 Crompton Street, Derby DE1 1NX
t (01332) 365735
e enquiries@coachhousederby.co.uk
w coachhousederby.co.uk

**East Midlands Hostel**
Rating Applied For
*Hostel*
100a Douglas Street, Derby DE23 8LJ
t (01332) 233192
e booking@emhotel.co.uk
w emhotel.co.uk

**Red Setters Guest House**
★★★ *Guest Accommodation*
85 Curzon Street, Derby DE1 1LN
t (01332) 362770
e michael.swann2@btopenworld.com
w derbycity.com/michael/redset.html

**Rose and Thistle Guest House** ★★★
*Guest Accommodation*
21 Charnwood Street, Derby DE1 2GU
t (01332) 344103

**Thornhill Lodge Guest House** ★★★★ *Guest House*
**SILVER AWARD**
Thornhill Road, Derby DE22 3LX
t (01332) 345318
e info@thornhill-lodge.com
w thornhill-lodge.com

**DEREHAM**
**Norfolk**

**Greenbanks** ★★★★
*Guest Accommodation*
Wendling, Dereham NR19 2AB
t (01362) 687747
e jenny@greenbankshotel.co.uk
w greenbankshotel.co.uk

**Hunters Hall** ★★★★
*Farmhouse*
Park Farm, Swanton Morley, Dereham NR20 4JU
t (01362) 637457
e office@huntershall.com
w huntershall.com

**DERSINGHAM**
**Norfolk**

**Ashdene House** ★★★★
*Guest Accommodation*
**SILVER AWARD**
60 Hunstanton Road, Dersingham, King's Lynn PE31 6HQ
t (01485) 540395
e mail@ashdene-house.co.uk
w ashdene-house.co.uk

**Barn House Bed And Breakfast** ★★★★
*Guest Accommodation*
14 Station Road, Dersingham, King's Lynn PE31 6PP
t (01485) 543086
e tom@d14mxs.wanadoo.co.uk
w smoothhound.co.uk/hotels/barnho

**The Corner House** ★★★★
*Bed & Breakfast*
**SILVER AWARD**
2 Sandringham Road, Dersingham, King's Lynn PE31 6LL
t (01485) 543532
e the_corner_house@btinternet.com

**Holkham Cottage** ★★★★
*Guest Accommodation*
34 Hunstanton Road, Dersingham, King's Lynn PE31 6HQ
t (01485) 544562
e holkham.cottage@btinternet.com

**St Jude's** ★★★
*Bed & Breakfast*
12 Sandringham Road, Dersingham, King's Lynn PE31 6LL
t (01485) 541755
e st.judes@uwclub.net
w glavenvalley.co.uk

**Tall Trees** ★★★★
*Bed & Breakfast*
7 Centre Vale, Dersingham, King's Lynn PE31 6JR
t (01485) 542638
e frostytrees@tiscali.co.uk
w talltrees-norfolk.co.uk

**The White House** ★★★★
*Guest House*
44 Hunstanton Road, Dersingham, King's Lynn PE31 6HQ
t (01485) 541895
e firesafe@ukonline.co.uk

## DICKLEBURGH Norfolk

**Moor View**
Rating Applied For
*Bed & Breakfast*
Semere Green Lane, Diss IP21 4NT
t (01603) 700438
w moor-view.com

## DIDDLEBURY Shropshire

**Larkfield Farm** ★★
*Bed & Breakfast*
Diddlebury, Craven Arms SY7 9DH
t (01584) 841575
e larkfieldfarm@hotmail.co.uk

## DIGBY Lincolnshire

**Digby Manor Bed & Breakfast** ★★★★
*Bed & Breakfast*
**SILVER AWARD**
The Manor, North Street, Digby LN4 3LY
t (01526) 322064
e gilltown@lineone.net
w digbymanor.com

**Woodend Bed & Breakfast**
★★★ *Bed & Breakfast*
Woodend Farm, The Lodge, Digby LN4 3NG
t (01526) 860347

## DILWYN Herefordshire

**Sollars Barn** ★★★★
*Bed & Breakfast*
Dilwyn, Leominster HR4 8JJ
t (01544) 388260

## DISEWORTH Leicestershire

**Lady Gate Guest House**
★★★★ *Guest House*
**SILVER AWARD**
47 The Green, Diseworth, Castle Donington DE74 2QN
t (01332) 811565
e ladygateguesthouse@tiscali.co.uk
w ladygateguesthouse.co.uk

## DISS Norfolk

**Dickleburgh Hall** ★★★★★
*Bed & Breakfast*
**GOLD AWARD**
Semere Green Lane, Diss IP21 4NT
t (01379) 741259
e johntaylor05@btinternet.com
w dickhall.co.uk

**The Old Rectory Hopton**
★★★★★ *Bed & Breakfast*
**GOLD AWARD**
Hopton, Diss IP22 2QX
t (01953) 688135
e llewellyn.hopton@btinternet.com
w theoldrectoryhopton.com

**Strenneth** ★★★★
*Guest Accommodation*
**SILVER AWARD**
Airfield Road, Fersfield Common, Fersfield, Diss IP22 2BP
t (01379) 688182
e pdavey@strenneth.co.uk
w strenneth.co.uk

## DOCKING Norfolk

**Jubilee Lodge** ★★★★
*Guest Accommodation*
Station Road, Docking PE31 8LS
t (01485) 518473
e eghoward62@hotmail.com
w jubilee-lodge.com

## DODDINGTON Cambridgeshire

**Fenview Lodge** ★★★★
*Guest Accommodation*
15 Brickmakers Arms Lane, Doddington, March PE15 0TR
t (01354) 740103
e info@fenviewlodge.co.uk
w fenviewlodge.co.uk

## DONINGTON Lincolnshire

**Browntoft House** ★★★★
*Guest Accommodation*
**SILVER AWARD**
Browntoft Lane, Donington PE11 4TQ
t (01775) 822091
e finchedward@hotmail.com
w browntofthouse.co.uk

## DORRINGTON Shropshire

**Meadowlands** ★★★
*Bed & Breakfast*
Lodge Lane, Frodesley, Shrewsbury SY5 7HD
t (01694) 731350
e meadowlands.t21@btinternet.com
w meadowlands.co.uk

## DORSTONE Herefordshire

**Highfield** ★★★★ *Farmhouse*
**SILVER AWARD**
The Bage, Dorstone, Golden Valley HR3 5SU
t (01497) 831431
e book@highfieldbandb.com
w highfieldbandb.com

## DOVERCOURT Essex

**The Hive Bed and Breakfast**
Rating Applied For
*Bed & Breakfast*
81 Parkeston Road, Dovercourt Bay, Harwich CO12 4HE
t (01255) 503316
e bumbles.debbie@virgin.net
w thehiveharwich.co.uk

**Homebay** ★★★
*Guest Accommodation*
9 Bay Road, Dovercourt, Harwich CO12 3JZ
t (01255) 504428
e sydiej9@btinternet.com

## DOVERIDGE Derbyshire

**Ashmore Bed & Breakfast**
★★★★
*Guest Accommodation*
Derby Road, Doveridge, Ashbourne DE6 5JU
t (01889) 569620
e ashmorecottage@btinternet.com
w ashmorecottage.co.uk

## DOWNHAM MARKET Norfolk

**Chestnut Villa** ★★★
*Guest Accommodation*
44 Railway Road, Downham Market PE38 9EB
t (01366) 384099
e chestnutvilla@talk21.com
w chestnutvilla-downham.com

**Station Villa** ★★★★
*Bed & Breakfast*
11 Bennett Street, Downham Market PE38 9EE
t (01366) 386663
e downhampost@tiscali.co.uk
w archiesholidays.com

## DOWNTON ON THE ROCK Shropshire

**Old Downton Lodge** ★★★★
*Restaurant with Rooms*
Ludlow SY8 2HU
t (01568) 770820
e jayne@olddowntonlodge.co.uk
w olddowntonlodge.co.uk

## DRAYCOTT Derbyshire

**Hilltop Farm**
Rating Applied For
*Guest Accommodation*
Nottingham Road, Derby DE72 3PD
t (01332) 874902
e info@hilltopfarmbandb.co.uk
w hilltopfarmbandb.co.uk

## DRAYTON Norfolk

**West Lodge (vegetarian guesthouse)**
Rating Applied For
*Guest House*
24 Fakenham Road, Norwich NR8 6PR
t (01603) 861191
e info@vegetarian-bedandbreakfast-norwich.co.uk
w vegetarian-bedandbreakfast-norwick.co.uk

## DROITWICH Worcestershire

**Foxbrook** ★★★
*Guest Accommodation*
238a Worcester Road, Droitwich Spa WR9 8AY
t (01905) 772414

**Middleton Grange** ★★★★
*Guest Accommodation*
**SILVER AWARD**
Ladywood Road, Salwarpe, Droitwich Spa WR9 0AH
t (01905) 451678
e salli@middletongrange.com
w middletongrange.com

**The Old Farmhouse**
★★★★★
*Guest Accommodation*
**SILVER AWARD**
Hadley Heath, Ombersley, Droitwich Spa WR9 0AR
t (01905) 620837
e judylambe@theoldfarmhouse.uk.com
w theoldfarmhouse.uk.com

## DUNCHURCH Warwickshire

**The Old Thatched Cottage of Dunchurch** ★★★★
*Guest Accommodation*
Southam Road, Dunchurch, Rugby CV22 6NG
t (01788) 810417

## DUNMOW Essex

**Puttocks Farm B & B** ★★★★
*Farmhouse*
Philpot End, Great Dunmow CM6 1JQ
t (01371) 872377
e roger@puttocksfarm.com
w puttocksfarm.com

**Westpoint** ★★★
*Bed & Breakfast*
Aythorpe Roding, Dunmow, Great Dunmow CM6 1PU
t (01279) 876462
e barbara@westpointbandb.co.uk
w westpointbandb.co.uk

## EARDISLAND Herefordshire

**Lawton Bury Farm B & B**
★★★★ *Farmhouse*
**SILVER AWARD**
Lawton, Leominster HR6 9AX
t (01568) 709285
e elaine@lyke5502.freeserve.co.uk
w visitlawtonbury.co.uk


Look out for establishments participating in the National Accessible Scheme

**Moat Edge** ★★★★
*Bed & Breakfast*
6 St Marys Walk, Leominster HR6 9BB
t (01544) 388097
e moatedge@btinternet.com
w moatedge.co.uk

### EARL SOHAM
Suffolk

**Bridge House** ★★★★
*Guest Accommodation*
**SILVER AWARD**
Earl Soham, Woodbridge IP13 7RT
t (01728) 685473
e bridgehouse46@hotmail.com

### EARLS COLNE
Essex

**Greenlands Farm** ★★★★
*Bed & Breakfast*
**SILVER AWARD**
Lamberts Lane, Earls Colne, Colchester CO6 2LE
t (01787) 224895
e david@greenlandsfarm.freeserve.co.uk
w greenlandsfarm.co.uk

**Riverside Lodge** ★★★
*Guest Accommodation*
40 Lower Holt Street, Earls Colne, Colchester CO6 2PH
t (01787) 223487
e bandb@riversidelodge-uk.com
w riversidelodge-uk.com

### EARLSWOOD
West Midlands

**The Limes Country Lodge**
★★★ *Guest House*
Forshaw Heath Road, Earlswood, Solihull B94 5JZ
t (0121) 780400
e info@thelimes.biz
w thelimes.biz

### EAST BARKWITH
Lincolnshire

**The Grange** ★★★★
*Farmhouse* **SILVER AWARD**
Torrington Lane, East Barkwith, Market Rasen LN8 5RY
t (01673) 858670
e sarahstamp@farmersweekly.net
w thegrange-lincolnshire.co.uk

### EAST BARSHAM
Norfolk

**White Horse Inn** ★★★★ *Inn*
Fakenham Road, East Barsham, Fakenham NR21 0LH
t (01328) 820645

### EAST BERGHOLT
Suffolk

**Rosemary** ★★★
*Guest Accommodation*
Rectory Hill, East Bergholt, Colchester CO7 6TH
t (01206) 298241

### EAST CARLETON
Norfolk

**Majority Cottage** ★★★★
*Guest Accommodation*
**GOLD AWARD**
Wymondham Road, East Carleton, Norwich NR14 8JB
t (01508) 571198
e richard@majoritycottage.co.uk
w totaltravel.co.uk/link.asp?fid=609048

### EAST HADDON
Northamptonshire

**East Haddon Lodge** ★★★
*Farmhouse*
Main Street, East Haddon, Northampton NN6 8BU
t (01604) 770240

### EAST HYDE
Bedfordshire

**Hyde Mill** ★★★★
*Bed & Breakfast*
Lower Luton Road, East Hyde, Luton LU2 9PX
t (01582) 712641
e info@hydemill.co.uk
w hydemill.co.uk

### EAST LANGTON
Leicestershire

**West Langton Lodge** ★★★
*Guest Accommodation*
Melton Road, East Langton, Market Harborough LE16 7TG
t (01858) 545450
e lindsay@westlangtonlodge.co.uk
w westlangtonlodge.co.uk

### EAST MERSEA
Essex

**Bromans Farm** ★★★★
*Bed & Breakfast*
Bromans Lane, East Mersea, Colchester CO5 8UE
t (01206) 383235
e bromansfarm@btopenworld.com

### EASTHOPE WOOD
Shropshire

**Easthope Wood Farm**
Rating Applied For
*Bed & Breakfast*
Easthope Wood, Much Wenlock TF13 6DL
t (01694) 771562
e easthopewood@talktalk.net

### EASTNOR
Herefordshire

**Hill Farmhouse Bed and Breakfast** ★★★ *Farmhouse*
Eastnor, Ledbury HR8 1EF
t (01531) 632827

### ECCLESHALL
Staffordshire

**Cobblers Cottage** ★★★★
*Guest Accommodation*
Kerry Lane, Eccleshall, Stafford ST21 6EJ
t (01785) 850116

**The George Inn** ★★ *Inn*
Castle Street, Eccleshall, Stafford ST21 6DF
t (01785) 850300
e information@thegeorgeinn.freeserve.co.uk
w thegeorgeinn.freeserve.co.uk

### ECKINGTON
Worcestershire

**Harrowfields Bed and Breakfast** ★★★★
*Bed & Breakfast*
**SILVER AWARD**
Harrowfields, Cotheridge Lane, Eckington WR10 3BA
t (01386) 751053
e susie@harrowfields.co.uk
w harrowfields.co.uk

**Myrtle Cottage** ★★★★
*Bed & Breakfast*
Jarvis Street, Eckington, Pershore WR10 3AS
t (01386) 750893
e veronica@myrtle-cottage.com
w myrtle-cottage.com

### EDALE
Derbyshire

**Edale** *Camping Barn*
Cotefield Farm, Ollerbrook, Hope Valley S33 7ZG
t (01433) 670273

**Edale YHA** ★★ *Hostel*
Rowland Cote, Nether Booth, Hope Valley S33 7ZH
t 0870 770 5808

**Stonecroft Country Guest House** ★★★★
*Bed & Breakfast*
**GOLD AWARD**
Stonecroft, Grindsbrook, Hope Valley S33 7ZA
t (01433) 670262
e stonecroftedale@btconnect.com
w stonecroftguesthouse.co.uk

### EDINGTHORPE
Norfolk

**Church Farm Barn** ★★★★★
*Bed & Breakfast*
**SILVER AWARD**
Rectory Road, Edingthorpe, North Walsham NR28 9TN
t (01692) 651014
e andywkerr@tiscali.co.uk
w churchfarmbarn.com

### EDWINSTOWE
Nottinghamshire

**Sherwood Forest YHA**
★★★★ *Hostel*
Forest Corner, Mansfield NG21 9RN
t (01623) 825794

### ELLINGTON
Cambridgeshire

**Thorpe Lodge Farm** ★★★★
*Farmhouse*
Ellington, Huntingdon PE28 0AP
t (01480) 810266
e tl.farm@tiscali.co.uk
w thorpelodgefarm.co.uk

### ELMESTHORPE
Leicestershire

**Badgers Mount** ★★★★
*Guest Accommodation*
**SILVER AWARD**
6 Station Road, Elmesthorpe, Hinckley LE9 7SG
t (01455) 848161
e info@badgersmount.com
w badgersmount.com

### ELMSTEAD
Essex

**Pheasant Lodge** ★★★★
*Bed & Breakfast*
**SILVER AWARD**
Balls Farm, Tye Road, Colchester CO7 7BB
t (01206) 822514
e lyndaevans@aol.com
w ballsfarm.net

### ELMSWELL
Suffolk

**Elmswell Hall B&B** ★★★★
*Farmhouse* **SILVER AWARD**
Elmswell Hall, Bury St Edmunds IP30 9EN
t (01359) 240215
e kate@elmswellhall.freeserve.co.uk
w elmswellhall.co.uk

**Kiln Farm** ★★★★
*Guest House*
Kiln Lane, Elmswell, Bury St Edmunds IP30 9QR
t (01359) 240442
e davejankilnfarm@btinternet.com

**Mulberry Farm** ★★★★
*Farmhouse* **SILVER AWARD**
Ashfield Road, Elmswell, Bury St Edmunds IP30 9HG
t (01359) 244244
e mulberryfarm@tesco.net

### ELSING
Norfolk

**Bartles Lodge**
Rating Applied For
*Guest House*
Church Street, Elsing, Dereham NR20 3EA
t (01362) 637177
e bartleslodge@yahoo.co.uk
w bartleslodge.co.uk/

### ELTON
Derbyshire

**Elton Guest House**
Rating Applied For
*Bed & Breakfast*
Moor Lane, Elton, Matlock DE4 2DA
t (01629) 650217
e jenny.hirst@w3z.co.uk
w eltonholidays.com

**Hawthorn Cottage** ★★★★★
*Guest Accommodation*
**SILVER AWARD**
Well Street, Elton, Matlock DE4 2BY
t (01629) 650372
w hawthorncottage-elton.co.uk

**Homestead Farm** ★★★★
*Farmhouse*
Main Street, Elton, Matlock DE4 2BW
t (01629) 650359
e jeanniecarson@hotmail.co.uk

### ELY
Cambridgeshire

**29 Waterside** ★★★
*Bed & Breakfast*
Ely CB7 4AU
t (01353) 614329
e info@29waterside.org.uk
w 29waterside.org.uk

**57 Lynn Road** ★★★★
*Bed & Breakfast*
Ely CB6 1DD
t (01353) 663685
e marting7vgh@aol.com

**9 Willow Walk** ★★★★
*Bed & Breakfast*
Ely CB7 4AT
t (01353) 664205

**96 Lynn Road** ★★★★
*Guest Accommodation*
**SILVER AWARD**
Ely CB6 1DE
t (01353) 665044
e phvenn@hotmail.com

**Anchor Inn** ★★★★
*Restaurant with Rooms*
Sutton Gault, Sutton CB6 2BD
t (01353) 778537
e anchorinn@popmail.bta.com
w anchorsuttongault.co.uk

**Bowmount House** ★★★★
*Bed & Breakfast*
**SILVER AWARD**
Ely CB6 3WP
t (01353) 669943
e pauljacton@hotmail.com

**Casa Nostra Guesthouse**
★★★ *Guest House*
6 Black Bank Road, Little Downham, Ely CB6 2UA
t (01353) 862495
e info@woodfenlodge.co.uk
w casanostraguesthouse.co.uk

**Coach House at Cathedral House** ★★★★
*Bed & Breakfast*
17 St Mary's Street, Ely CB7 4ER
t (01353) 662124
e farndale@cathedralhouse.co.uk

**The Grove** ★★★★
*Bed & Breakfast*
**SILVER AWARD**
Bury Lane, Sutton Gault, Ely CB6 2BD
t (01353) 777196
e stella.f.anderson@btopenworld.com

**Harvest House** ★★★★
*Bed & Breakfast*
122b St Johns Road, Ely CB6 3BW
t (01353) 663517

**Hill House Farm** ★★★★
*Farmhouse* **GOLD AWARD**
9 Main Street, Coveney, Ely CB6 2DJ
t (01353) 778369
e info@hillhousefarm-ely.co.uk
w hillhousefarm-ely.co.uk

**Little Haven** ★★★★
*Bed & Breakfast*
36 Wissey Way, Ely CB6 2WW
t (01353) 615492

**The Nyton** ★★★
*Guest Accommodation*
7 Barton Road, Ely CB7 4HZ
t (01353) 662459
e nytonhotel@yahoo.co.uk
w thenytonhotel.co.uk

**The Old School B & B**
★★★★ *Bed & Breakfast*
The Old School, School Lane, Coveney, Ely CB6 2DB
t (01353) 777087
e info@theoldschoolbandb.co.uk
w theoldschoolbandb.co.uk

**Post House** ★★
*Bed & Breakfast*
12a Egremont Street, Ely CB6 1AE
t (01353) 667184
e info@posthouse-ely.co.uk
w posthouse-ely.co.uk

**Riverside Inn** ★★★★
*Guest House*
8 Annesdale, Ely CB7 4BN
t (01353) 661677
e info@riversideinn-ely.co.uk
w riversideinn-ely.co.uk

**Spinney Abbey** ★★★★
*Farmhouse*
Stretham Road, Wicken CB7 5XQ
t (01353) 720971
e spinney.abbey@tesco.net
w spinneyabbey.co.uk

**Sycamore House** ★★★★
*Guest Accommodation*
91 Cambridge Road, Ely CB7 4HX
t (01353) 662139
e info@sycamorehouse.gb.com
w sycamorehouse.gb.com

**Walnut House** ★★★★
*Bed & Breakfast*
**SILVER AWARD**
Ely CB7 4JN
t (01353) 661793
e walnuthouse1@aol.com
w ely.org.uk/walnuthouse

**Willow Fen Cottage** ★★
*Bed & Breakfast*
4 Prickwillow Road, Ely CB7 4QP
t (01353) 665591

### EMPINGHAM
Rutland

**Shacklewell Lodge** ★★★★
*Bed & Breakfast*
Stamford Road, Empingham, Oakham LE15 8QQ
t (01780) 460646
e shacklewell@hotmail.com

### ENDON
Staffordshire

**Hollinhurst Farm** ★★★
*Farmhouse*
Park Lane, Endon, Stoke-on-Trent ST9 9JB
t (01782) 502633
e joan.hollinhurst@btconnect.com

### EPPING
Essex

**The Coach House** ★★★★
*Guest Accommodation*
**SILVER AWARD**
Wintry Park House, Thornwood Road, Epping CM16 6SZ
t (01992) 577407
e k13abb@aol.com
w wintrypanc.co.uk

**Forest Lodge Motel** ★★★
*Guest Accommodation*
Wakes Arms, Epping New Road, Epping CM16 5HW
t (01992) 815759
e enquiries@forest-lodge-motel.co.uk
w forest-lodge-motel.co.uk

### EPWORTH
Lincolnshire

**Albion House** ★★★
*Bed & Breakfast*
Albion Hill, Epworth DN9 1HD
t (01472) 872451
e albionhousebandb@aol.com
w albionhousebedandbreakfast.co.uk

**Wisteria Cottage Bed and Breakfast** ★★★★
*Bed & Breakfast*
10 Belton Road, Epworth DN9 1JL
t (01427) 873988
e enquiries@wisteriacottage.org.uk
w wisteriacottage.org.uk

### ERPINGHAM
Norfolk

**Saracens Head Inn** ★★★★
*Restaurant with Rooms*
**SILVER AWARD**
Wolterton, Aylsham, Norwich NR11 7LZ
t (01263) 768909
e saracenshead@wolterton.freeserve.co.uk
w saracenshead-norfolk.co.uk

### ETWALL
Derbyshire

**The Barn Retreat** ★★★
*Guest Accommodation*
Tara Centre, Ashe Hall, Derby DE65 6HT
t 07875 250716
e relax@thebarnretreat.co.uk
w thebarnretreat.co.uk

### EWYAS HAROLD
Herefordshire

**The Old Rectory – Ewyas Harold** ★★★★
*Bed & Breakfast*
**SILVER AWARD**
Ewyas Harold, Hereford, Golden Valley HR2 0EY
t (01981) 240498
e jenny.juckes@btopenworld.com
w theoldrectory.org.uk

### EYAM
Derbyshire

**Bretton Cottage** ★★★★★
*Bed & Breakfast*
**SILVER AWARD**
Bretton, Eyam, Hope Valley S32 5QD
t (01433) 631076
e andrew@metcalfeandco.co.uk
w peakholidayhomes.com

**Crown Cottage** ★★★★
*Guest Accommodation*
Main Road, Eyam, Hope Valley S32 5QW
t (01433) 630858
e janet@eatonfold.demon.co.uk
w crown-cottage.co.uk

**YHA Bretton** *Bunkhouse*
Bretton, Eyam, Hope Valley S32 5QD
t 0870 770 5720
e bretton@yha.org.uk
w yha.org.uk

**YHA Eyam** ★★★ *Hostel*
Hawkhill Road, Eyam, Hope Valley S32 5QP
t (01433) 630335
e eyam@yha.org.uk
w yha.org.uk

### EYDON
Northamptonshire

**Crockwell Farm** ★★★★
*Farmhouse*
Eydon, Daventry NN11 3QA
t (01327) 361358
e info@crockwellfarm.co.uk
w crockwellfarm.co.uk

### EYE
Suffolk

**Bull Auberge** ★★★★★
*Restaurant with Rooms*
**SILVER AWARD**
Ipswich Road, Yaxley, Eye IP23 8BZ
t (01379) 783604
w the-auberge.co.uk

**Camomile Cottage** ★★★★
*Bed & Breakfast*
**SILVER AWARD**
Brome Avenue, Langton Green, Eye IP23 7HW
t (01379) 873528
e aly@camomilecottage.co.uk
w camomilecottage.co.uk

**Rookery House Bed and Breakfast** ★★★
*Bed & Breakfast*
Rookery House, Eye IP23 7AR
t (01379) 873155

**The White Horse Inn**
★★★★ *Inn*
Stoke Ash, Eye IP23 7ET
t (01379) 678222
e mail@whitehorse-suffolk.co.uk
w whitehorse-suffolk.co.uk

### EYE KETTLEBY
Leicestershire

**Old Guadaloupe B&B**
★★★★ *Farmhouse*
Old Guadaloupe, Kirby Lane, Melton Mowbray LE14 2TS
t 07989 960588
e sue@suelomas.orangehome.co.uk
w oldguadaloupeb&b.co.uk

### FAIRFIELD
Derbyshire

**Barms Farm** ★★★★★
*Bed & Breakfast*
**SILVER AWARD**
Fairfield Common, Buxton SK17 7HW
t (01298) 77723
e enquiries@barmsfarm.co.uk
w barmsfarm.co.uk

## FAKENHAM Norfolk

**Abbott Farm** ★★★
*Farmhouse*
Walsingham Road, Binham NR21 0AW
**t** (01328) 830519
**e** abbot.farm@btinternet.com
**w** abbottfarm.co.uk

**Erikas Bed And Breakfast**
★★★★ *Bed & Breakfast*
3 Gladstone Road, Fakenham NR21 9BZ
**t** (01328) 863058
**w** erikasbandb.co.uk

**Highfield Farm** ★★★★
*Farmhouse* **SILVER AWARD**
Highfield Lane, Great Ryburgh, Fakenham NR21 7AL
**t** (01328) 829249
**e** elizabethsavory@waitrose.com
**w** broadland.com/highfield

**Holly Lodge** ★★★★★
*Bed & Breakfast*
**GOLD AWARD**
Thursford Green, Fakenham NR21 0AS
**t** (01328) 878465
**e** info@hollylodgeguesthouse.co.uk
**w** hollylodgeguesthouse.co.uk

**The Old Brick Kilns Guesthouse** ★★★★
*Bed & Breakfast*
Little Barney Lane, Barney, Fakenham NR21 0NL
**t** (01328) 878305
**e** enquiries@old-brick-kilns.co.uk
**w** old-brick-kilns.co.uk

**Rosemary Cottage** ★★★
*Guest Accommodation*
The Street, West Raynham, Fakenham NR21 7AD
**t** (01328) 838318
**e** francoisew@btinternet.com
**w** tiscover.co.uk

## FAZELEY Staffordshire

**Hollies Guest House** ★★★
*Guest House*
Atherstone Street, Tamworth B78 3RF
**t** (01827) 283550
**e** thehollies-tamworth@hotmail.co.uk
**w** thehollies-tamworth.com

## FECKENHAM Worcestershire

**Orchard House** ★★★★
*Bed & Breakfast*
**SILVER AWARD**
Berrow Hill Lane, Feckenham, Redditch B96 6QJ
**t** (01527) 821497
**w** orchardhouse-bb.co.uk

**The Steps** ★★★★
*Bed & Breakfast*
6 High Street, Feckenham, Redditch B96 6HS
**t** (01527) 892678
**e** jenny@thesteps.co.uk
**w** thesteps.co.uk

## FEERING Essex

**Old Wills Farm** ★★★★
*Farmhouse* **SILVER AWARD**
Little Tey Road, Feering, Colchester CO5 9RP
**t** (01376) 570259
**e** janecrayston@btconnect.com

## FELIXSTOWE Suffolk

**Burlington House** ★★★★
*Bed & Breakfast*
7 Beach Road West, Felixstowe IP11 2BH
**t** (01394) 282051
**w** tiscover.co.uk

**Castle Lodge** ★★★★
*Guest House* **SILVER AWARD**
Chevalier Road, Felixstowe IP11 7EY
**t** (01394) 282149
**w** castlelodgefelixstowe.co.uk

**Dolphin** ★★
*Guest Accommodation*
41 Beach Station Road, Felixstowe IP11 2EY
**t** (01394) 282261
**w** tiscover.co.uk

**Dorincourt Guesthouse** ★★
*Guest House*
Undercliff Road West, Felixstowe IP11 2AH
**t** (01394) 270447
**w** tiscover.co.uk

**The Grafton Guesthouse**
★★★★
*Guest Accommodation*
13 Sea Road, Felixstowe IP11 2BB
**t** (01394) 284881
**e** info@grafton-house.com
**w** grafton-house.com

**The Norfolk Guest House**
★★★★ *Guest House*
1-3 Holland Road, Felixstowe IP11 2BA
**t** (01394) 283160
**e** thenorfolk@btconnect.com
**w** thenorfolk.com

**Ranevale** ★★★★
*Bed & Breakfast*
96 Ranelagh Road, Felixstowe IP11 7HU
**t** (01394) 270001
**e** joy.s@btclick.com

## FENNY BENTLEY Derbyshire

**Cairn Grove** ★★★★
*Guest Accommodation*
Ashes Lane, Fenny Bentley, Ashbourne DE6 1LD
**t** (01335) 350538
**e** cairngrove@supanet.com
**w** cairngrove.co.uk

**Millfields** ★★★
*Bed & Breakfast*
Fenny Bentley, Ashbourne DE6 1LA
**t** (01335) 350454
**e** millfieldsbandb@hotmail.com
**w** millfieldsbandb.co.uk

## FENNY COMPTON Warwickshire

**The Grange** ★★★ *Farmhouse*
The Stable, Fenny Compton, Southam CV47 2YB
**t** (01295) 770590

## FENSTANTON Cambridgeshire

**Orchard House** ★★★
*Bed & Breakfast*
6a Hilton Road, Fenstanton, Huntingdon PE28 9LH
**t** (01480) 469208
**e** ascarrow@aol.com

## FERNHILL HEATH Worcestershire

**Dilmore House** ★★★★
*Bed & Breakfast*
**SILVER AWARD**
254 Droitwich Road, Fernhill Heath, Worcester WR3 7UL
**t** (01905) 451543
**e** dilmorehouse@tiscali.co.uk
**w** dilmorehouse.co.uk

**Heathside** ★★★★
*Guest House*
172 Droitwich Road, Fernhill Heath, Worcester WR3 7UA
**t** (01905) 458245
**e** info@heathsideguesthouse.co.uk
**w** heathsideguesthouse.co.uk

## FIELD DALLING Norfolk

**Old Plough House B&B**
Rating Applied For
*Bed & Breakfast*
59 Holt Road, Field Dalling, Holt NR25 7AS
**t** (01328) 830017
**e** pmwallace1@yahoo.co.uk
**w** oldploughhouse.co.uk

## FILLONGLEY Warwickshire

**Grooms Cottage** ★★★★
*Farmhouse* **SILVER AWARD**
Manor House Farm, Green End Road, Fillongley, Coventry CV7 8DS
**t** (01676) 540256

## FISHMORE Shropshire

**Acorn Place**
Rating Applied For
*Bed & Breakfast*
Fishmore, Ludlow SY8 3DP
**t** (01584) 875295
**e** info@acornplace.co.uk
**w** acornplace.co.uk

## FISKERTON Lincolnshire

**The Old Tannery at Diamond House** ★★★★
*Bed & Breakfast*
Ferry Road, Fiskerton LN3 4HU
**t** (01522) 595956
**e** oldtannerydiamondhouse@btinternet.com

## FLAGG Derbyshire

**Knotlow Farm**
Rating Applied For
*Guest Accommodation*
Buxton SK17 9QP
**t** (01298) 85313
**e** enquiries@knotlowfarm.co.uk
**w** knotlowfarm.co.uk

## FLATFORD MILL Suffolk

**Granary** ★★★
*Guest Accommodation*
Flatford, East Bergholt, Colchester CO7 6UL
**t** (01206) 298111
**e** b&b@derektripp.plus.com
**w** granaryflatford.co.uk

## FORDHAM Cambridgeshire

**Annes Bed And Breakfast**
★★★★ *Bed & Breakfast*
158 Mildenhall Road, Fordham, Ely CB7 5NS
**t** (01638) 720514
**e** annes.bnb@btinternet.com

## FORTON Staffordshire

**The Swan At Forton**
Rating Applied For
*Inn*
Eccleshall Road, Newport TF10 8BY
**t** (020) 8777 3636
**e** tu@bcinns.co.uk

## FOWNHOPE Herefordshire

**Bark Cottage** ★★★★
*Bed & Breakfast*
Fownhope, Hereford HR1 4PE
**t** (01432) 860344
**e** arthur@wyeleisure.com

## FRAMLINGHAM Suffolk

**High House Farm** ★★★
*Farmhouse*
Cransford, Woodbridge IP13 9PD
**t** (01728) 663461
**e** info@highhousefarm.co.uk
**w** highhousefarm.co.uk

## FRECKENHAM Suffolk

**The Golden Boar Inn** ★★★★
*Inn*
The Street, Freckenham, Bury St Edmunds IP28 8HZ
**t** (01638) 723000

## FRINTON-ON-SEA Essex

**Russell Lodge** ★★★
*Bed & Breakfast*
47 Hadleigh Road, Frinton-on-Sea CO13 9HQ
**t** (01255) 675935 & 07891 899824
**e** stay@russell-lodge.fsnet.co.uk
**w** russell-lodge.fsnet.co.uk

**Uplands Guesthouse** ★★★
*Guest Accommodation*
41 Hadleigh Road, Frinton-on-Sea CO13 9HQ
**t** (01255) 674889
**e** info@uplandsguesthouse.co.uk
**w** uplandsguesthouse.com

### FRISTON
Suffolk

**Old School** ★★★★
*Guest Accommodation*
**SILVER AWARD**
Aldeburgh Road, Friston, Saxmundham IP17 1NP
t (01728) 688173
e oldschool@fristonoldschool.freeserve.co.uk
w fristonoldschool.co.uk

### FRITTON
Norfolk

**Decoy Barn Bed & Breakfast** ★★★★ *Bed & Breakfast*
Beccles Road, Great Yarmouth NR31 9AB
t (01493) 488222
w decoybarn.co.uk

### FURNEUX PELHAM
Hertfordshire

**The White House** ★★★★
*Bed & Breakfast*
East End, Furneux Pelham, Buntingford SG9 0JU
t 07976 436611
e white_house_bb@yahoo.co.uk
w bbwhitehouse.co.uk

### GAINSBOROUGH
Lincolnshire

**The Beckett Arms** ★★★ *Inn*
25 High Street, Corringham DN21 5QP
t (01427) 838201

---

**Blyton (Sunnyside) Ponds** ★★★ *Bed & Breakfast*
Sunnyside Farm, Station Road, Blyton, Gainsborough DN21 3LE
t (01427) 628240
e blytonponds@msn.com
w blytonponds.co.uk

### GAMLINGAY
Cambridgeshire

**The Emplins** ★★★
*Bed & Breakfast*
Church Street, Gamlingay, Sandy SG19 3ER
t (01767) 650581

### GARBOLDISHAM
Norfolk

**Ingleneuk Lodge**
Rating Applied For
*Guest House*
Hopton Road, Diss IP22 2RQ
t (01953) 681541
e rodmid@dsl.pipex.com
w ingleneuklodge.co.uk

### GAYTON LE MARSH
Lincolnshire

**Westbrook House B & B** ★★★★ *Bed & Breakfast*
Westbrook House, Gayton-le-Marsh, Alford LN13 0NW
t (01507) 450624
e westbrook_house@hotmail.com
w bestbookwestbrook.co.uk

### GLOSSOP
Derbyshire

**Avondale** ★★★★
*Guest House*
28 Woodhead Road, Glossop SK13 7RH
t (01457) 853132
e margaret@avondale28.plus.com
w avondale-guesthouse.co.uk

---

**Norfolk Arms** ★★★★
*Guest Accommodation*
Norfolk Square, Glossop SK13 8BP
t (01457) 851940

---

**Windy Harbour Farm** ★★★
*Guest Accommodation*
Woodhead Road, Glossop SK13 7QE
t (01457) 853107
e graham@windyharbourfarm.fsnet.co.uk
w peakdistrict-hotel.co.uk

### GNOSALL
Staffordshire

**Leys House** ★★★★
*Bed & Breakfast*
Quarry Lane, Gnosall, Stafford ST20 0BZ
t (01785) 822532
e proffitt.gnosall@virgin.net

### GOADBY
Leicestershire

**The Hollies** ★★★
*Bed & Breakfast*
Goadby, Leicester LE7 9EE
t (0116) 259 8301

### GOLDHANGER
Essex

**Brent Cottage** ★★★★
*Bed & Breakfast*
18 Fish Street, Goldhanger, Maldon CM9 8AT
t (01621) 788275
e brentcottage@hotmail.com

### GOULCEBY
Lincolnshire

**Thorngate Bed and Breakfast** ★★★★
*Bed & Breakfast*
Watery Lane, Goulceby, Louth LN11 9UR
t (01507) 343270
e johnhamp@waitrose.com
w johnhamp.com

### GRANGEMILL
Derbyshire

**Middlehills Farm** ★★★
*Guest Accommodation*
Grangemill, Matlock DE4 4HY
t (01629) 650368
e enquiry@middlehills.demon.co.uk

### GRANTHAM
Lincolnshire

**The Cedars** ★★★★
*Bed & Breakfast*
Low Road, Barrowby, Grantham NG32 1DL
t (01476) 563400
e pbcbennett@mac.com

---

**The Red House** ★★★★
*Guest House*
74 North Parade, Grantham NG31 8AN
t (01476) 579869
e enquiry@red-house.com
w red-house.com/

---

**York House** ★★★★
*Bed & Breakfast*
Bourne Road, Colsterworth NG33 5JE
t (01476) 861955
e rkyorkhouse@dsl.pipex.com
w yorkhousebnb.co.uk/

### GREAT BADDOW
Essex

**Homecroft** ★★★
*Guest Accommodation*
Southend Road, Great Baddow, Chelmsford CM2 7AD
t (01245) 475070
e jesse@pryke.fsbusiness.co.uk
w tiscover.co.uk

---

**Rothmans** ★★
*Bed & Breakfast*
22 High Street, Great Baddow, Chelmsford CM2 7HQ
t 07786 234302
e pjaspbury@ukonline.co.uk
w rothmansbedandbreakfast.co.uk

### GREAT BEALINGS
Suffolk

**Apple Tree Cottage** ★★★
*Bed & Breakfast*
Boot Street, Woodbridge IP13 6PB
t (01473) 738997
w appletreebedandbreakfast.co.uk

### GREAT BRICETT
Suffolk

**Riverside Cottage** ★★★★
*Bed & Breakfast*
The Street, Great Bricett, Ipswich IP7 7DQ
t (01473) 658266
e chasmhorne@aol.com
w riversidecottagebandb.co.uk

### GREAT CRESSINGHAM
Norfolk

**The Olde Windmill Inn**
Rating Applied For
*Inn*
Water End, Great Cressingham, Thetford IP25 6NN
t (01760) 756232
e halls232@aol.com
w oldewindmillinn.co.uk

---

**The Vines** ★★★★
*Bed & Breakfast*
The Street, Great Cressingham, Thetford IP25 6NL
t (01760) 756303
e stay@thevines.fsbusiness.co.uk
w thevines.fsbusiness.co.uk

### GREAT DALBY
Leicestershire

**Dairy Farm** ★★★ *Farmhouse*
8 Burrough End, Great Dalby, Melton Mowbray LE14 2EW
t (01664) 562783
e dairyfarm@tesco.net
w dairy-farm.co.uk

### GREAT DUNMOW
Essex

**Harwood Guest House** ★★★★ *Guest House*
52 Stortford Road, Great Dunmow CM6 1DN
t (01371) 874627
e info@harwoodguesthouse.com
w harwoodguesthouse.com

---

**Homelye Farm** ★★★★
*Guest Accommodation*
Homelye Chase, Braintree Road, Great Dunmow CM6 3AW
t (01371) 872127
e homelye@btconnect.com
w homelyefarm.co.uk

---

**Mallards** ★★★★
*Bed & Breakfast*
Star Lane, Dunmow, Great Dunmow CM6 1AY
t (01371) 872641
e millersmallardsdunmow@tesco.net

### GREAT EASTON
Essex

**The Swan Inn** ★★★★ *Inn*
**SILVER AWARD**
The Endway, Great Easton, Great Dunmow CM6 2HG
t (01371) 870359
e theswangreateaston@tiscali.co.uk
w swangreateaston.co.uk

### GREAT ELLINGHAM
Norfolk

**Home Cottage Farm** ★★★★
*Farmhouse*
Penhill Road, Great Ellingham, Attleborough NR17 1LS
t (01953) 483734
e maureenhcf@waitrose.com
w bandbinuk.co.uk

### GREAT HORMEAD
Hertfordshire

**Brick House Farm Bed And Breakfast** ★★★★ *Farmhouse*
**SILVER AWARD**
Great Hormead, Buntingford SG9 0PB
t (01763) 289356
e helen@brickhousefarm.net
w brickhousefarm.net

### GREAT LEIGHS
Essex

**Acorns Bed & Breakfast** ★★★★ *Bed & Breakfast*
3 Woodview Drive, Great Leighs, Chelmsford CM3 1NW
t (01245) 361403
e kathryn@acornsbedandbreakfast.com
w acornsbedandbreakfast.co.uk

### GREAT OAKLEY
Essex

**Zig Zag Cottage** ★★★★
*Bed & Breakfast*
**GOLD AWARD**
8 Queen Street, Great Oakley, Harwich CO12 5AS
t (01255) 880968
e ziza.lifestyle@zigzagcottage.com
w zigzagcottage.com

## GREAT SNORING
Norfolk

**Top Farm** ★★★★ *Farmhouse*
Thursford Road, Great Snoring NR21 0HW
t (01328) 820351
e davidperowne@aol.com
w tiscover.co.uk

## GREAT WILBRAHAM
Cambridgeshire

**Kettles Cottage** ★★★★
*Bed & Breakfast*
30 High Street, Great Wilbraham, Cambridge CB21 5JD
t (01223) 880801
e enquiries@kettlescottage.co.uk
w kettlescottage.co.uk

## GREAT WOLFORD
Warwickshire

**The Old Coach House**
★★★★★ *Bed & Breakfast*
**SILVER AWARD**
Great Wolford, Shipston-on-Stour CV36 5NQ
t (01608) 674152
e theoldcoachhouse@thewolfords.net
w theoldecoachhouse.co.uk

## GREAT YARMOUTH
Norfolk

**Anglia House** ★★★
*Guest House*
56 Wellesley Road, Great Yarmouth NR30 1EX
t (01493) 844395
e angliahouse@aol.com

**Barnard House** ★★★★
*Bed & Breakfast*
**SILVER AWARD**
2 Barnard Crescent, Great Yarmouth NR30 4DR
t (01493) 855139
e enq@barnardhouse.com
w barnardhouse.com

**Barons Court** ★★★★
*Guest Accommodation*
5 Norfolk Square, Great Yarmouth NR30 1EE
t (01493) 843987
e info@baronscourthotel.co.uk
w baronscourthotel.co.uk

**Beaumont House** ★★★★
*Guest House* **SILVER AWARD**
52 Wellesley Road, Great Yarmouth NR30 1EX
t (01493) 843957
e info@beaumonthousehotel.com
w beaumonthousehotel.com

**Belvedere** ★★★
*Guest House*
90 North Denes Road, Great Yarmouth NR30 4LN
t (01493) 844200
e info@stayatbelvedere.co.uk
w stayatbelvedere.co.uk

**The Bromley** ★★★★
*Guest House*
Great Yarmouth NR30 2HG
t (01493) 842321
e info@bromleyhotel.co.uk
w bromleyhotel.co.uk

**Cavendish House** ★★★
*Guest Accommodation*
19-20 Princes Road, Great Yarmouth NR30 2DG
t (01493) 843148
e cavendishhousehotel@yahoo.co.uk
w cavendishhousehotel.com

**Chateau** ★★★
*Guest Accommodation*
1 North Drive, Great Yarmouth NR30 1ED
t (01493) 859052
e info@chateau-gy.fsbusiness.co.uk
w chateau-gy.fsbusiness.co.uk

**Chatsworth** ★★★
*Guest Accommodation*
32 Wellesley Road, Great Yarmouth NR30 1EU
t (01493) 842890
w chatsworthfamilyhotel.co.uk

**The Chimes** ★★★★
*Guest House*
48 Wellesley Road, Great Yarmouth NR30 1EX
t (01493) 844610
e dilys.jones1@ntlworld.com
w thechimes.co.uk

**The Cleasewood**
Rating Applied For
*Guest Accommodation*
55 Wellesley Road, Great Yarmouth NR30 1EX
t (01493) 843960

**Copperfields Guest House**
Rating Applied For
*Guest House*
16 Trafalgar Road, Great Yarmouth NR30 2LD
t (01493) 856679
e bauervrnn@aol.com
w copperfieldsguesthouse.com

**Dene House** ★★★★
*Guest House*
89 North Denes Road, Great Yarmouth NR30 4LW
t (01493) 844181
e denehouse@btinternet.com
w denehouse-greatyarmouth.com

**The Fjaerland** ★★★★
*Guest Accommodation*
24-25 Trafalgar Road, Great Yarmouth NR30 2LD
t (01493) 856339
w fjaerland.co.uk

**The Kensington** ★★★★
*Guest Accommodation*
29 North Drive, Great Yarmouth NR30 4EW
t (01493) 844145
e frontdesk@kensington-hotel.co.uk
w kensington-hotel.co.uk

**Kentville Guest House** ★★★
*Guest House*
5 Kent Square, Great Yarmouth NR30 2EX
t (01493) 844783

**Kilbrannan Guest House**
★★★ *Guest House*
14 Trafalgar Road, Great Yarmouth NR30 2LD
t (01493) 850383

**Lea Hurst Guesthouse** ★★★
*Guest House*
117 Wellesley Road, Great Yarmouth NR30 2AP
t (01493) 843063
e info@theleahurst.co.uk
w theleahurst.co.uk

**Little Emily** ★★★
*Guest House*
18 Princes Road, Great Yarmouth NR30 2DG
t (01493) 842515
e little-emily@hotmail.co.uk
w littleemily.co.uk

**Lynden Guest House** ★★★
*Guest House*
102 Wellesley Road, Great Yarmouth NR30 2AR
t (01493) 844693

**Maluth Lodge** ★★★★
*Guest Accommodation*
40 North Denes Road, Great Yarmouth NR30 4LU
t (01493) 304652
e enquiries@maluthlodge.co.uk
w maluthlodge.co.uk

**The Maryland** ★★★
*Guest House*
Great Yarmouth NR30 1EX
t (01493) 844409
e lucy@themaryland.co.uk
w themaryland.co.uk

**Merivon Guest House**
★★★★
*Guest Accommodation*
6 Trafalgar Road, Great Yarmouth NR30 2LD
t (01493) 844419
w tiscover.co.uk

**No 78** ★★★★
*Guest Accommodation*
78 Marine Parade, Great Yarmouth NR30 2DH
t (01493) 850001
e info@no78.co.uk
w no78.co.uk

**Royston House** ★★★
*Guest House*
Great Yarmouth NR30 1DY
t (01493) 844680
e enquiries@roystonhotel.com
w roystonhotel.com

**The Ryecroft** ★★★
*Guest House*
91 North Denes Road, Great Yarmouth NR30 4LW
t (01493) 844015
e info@ryecroftguesthouse.co.uk
w ryecroftguesthouse.co.uk

**Sandy Acres** ★★★★
*Guest Accommodation*
80-81 Salisbury Road, Great Yarmouth NR30 4LB
t (01493) 856553
e enquiries@sandyacres.co.uk
w sandyacres.co.uk

**The Shrewsbury Guest House** ★★★
*Guest Accommodation*
9 Trafalgar Road, Great Yarmouth NR30 2LD
t (01493) 844788
e shrewsbury.guesthouse@virgin.net
w shrewsburyguesthouse.co.uk

**Silverstone House** ★★★
*Guest Accommodation*
Great Yarmouth NR30 1EU
t (01493) 844862
e silverstonehouse@yahoo.co.uk
w silverstone-house.co.uk

**The Southern** ★★★★
*Guest Accommodation*
46 Queens Road, Great Yarmouth NR30 3JR
t (01493) 843313
e sally@southernhotel.co.uk
w southernhotel.co.uk

**Spindrift Guesthouse** ★★★
*Guest House*
Great Yarmouth NR30 1EU
t (01493) 843772
e spindrifthotel@btinternet.com

**Sunnydene** ★★★★
*Guest House*
83-84 North Denes Road, Great Yarmouth NR30 4LW
t (01493) 843554
e info@sunnydenehotel.co.uk
w sunnydenehotel.co.uk

**Trevi Guest House** ★★★
*Guest House*
57 Wellesley Road, Great Yarmouth NR30 1EX
t (01493) 842821
w treviguesthouse.co.uk

**Trotwood** ★★★
*Guest Accommodation*
2 North Drive, Great Yarmouth NR30 1ED
t (01493) 843971
e ian.irons@btconnect.com
w trotwood.fsbusiness.co.uk

**Woods End** ★★★
*Guest House*
49 Wellesley Road, Great Yarmouth NR30 1EX
t (01493) 842229
e woodsend1@bushinternet.com

## GREAT YELDHAM
Essex

**The White Hart** ★★★★
*Restaurant with Rooms*
**SILVER AWARD**
Poole Street, Halstead CO9 4HJ
t (01787) 237250
w whitehartyeldham.co.uk

## GRIMSTON
Norfolk

**The Old Bell Guesthouse**
★★★★ *Guest House*
1 Gayton Road, King's Lynn PE32 1BG
t (01485) 601156

## GRINDON
Staffordshire

**Summerhill Farm Bed and Breakfast** ★★★ *Farmhouse*
Grindon, Leek ST13 7TT
t (01538) 304264
e info@summerhillfarm.co.uk
w summerhillfarm.co.uk

## GRINGLEY ON THE HILL
Nottinghamshire

**Gringley Hall** ★★★★
*Guest Accommodation*
Mill Road, Gringley-on-the-Hill
DN10 4QT
**t** (01777) 817262
**e** dulce@gringleyhall.fsnet.co.uk

## GUYHIRN
Cambridgeshire

**Oliver Twist Country Inn**
★★★★ *Inn*
High Road, Guyhirn, Wisbech
PE13 4EA
**t** (01945) 450523
**e** enjoy@theolivertwist.com
**w** theolivertwist.com

## HABROUGH
North East Lincolnshire

**Church Farm** ★★★★
*Guest Accommodation*
**SILVER AWARD**
Immingham Road, Habrough
DN35 8JU
**t** (01469) 576190

## HACKTHORN
Lincolnshire

**Honeyholes** ★★★
*Farmhouse*
South Farm, Hackthorn
LN2 3PW
**t** (01673) 861868
**e** dgreen8234@aol.com

## HADLEIGH
Suffolk

**Edge Hall** ★★★★★
*Guest Accommodation*
2 High Street, Hadleigh,
Ipswich IP7 5AP
**t** (01473) 822458
**e** r.rolfe@edgehall.co.uk
**w** edgehall.co.uk

## HAINFORD
Norfolk

**Haynford Lodge B&B** ★★
*Guest Accommodation*
Hall Road, Haynford, Norwich
NR10 3LX
**t** (01603) 898844
**e** info@haynfordlodge.co.uk
**w** haynfordlodge.co.uk

## HALESWORTH
Suffolk

**The Angel** ★★★★ *Inn*
Thoroughfare, Halesworth
IP19 8AH
**t** (01986) 873365
**e** hotel@angel-halesworth.co.uk
**w** angel-halesworth.co.uk

---

**Fen-Way Guest House**
★★★★ *Bed & Breakfast*
Fen-Way, School Lane,
Halesworth IP19 8BW
**t** (01986) 873574

---

**Rumburgh Farm** ★★★★
*Farmhouse*
Rumburgh, Halesworth
IP19 0RU
**t** (01986) 781351
**e** binder@rumburghfarm.co.uk
**w** rumburghfarm.co.uk

---

**Valley Farm Vineyards**
★★★★ *Bed & Breakfast*
**SILVER AWARD**
Rumburgh Road, Wissett,
Halesworth IP19 0JJ
**t** (01986) 785535
**e** valleyfarmvineyards@tiscali.co.uk
**w** valleyfarmvineyards.com

## HALSTEAD
Essex

**The Limes B & B @ Hedingham Antiques** ★★★
*Bed & Breakfast*
100 Swan Street, Sible
Hedingham, Halstead
CO9 3HP
**t** (01787) 460360
**e** patricia@patriciapatterson.wanadoo.co.uk

---

**The White Hart** ★★★ *Inn*
15 High Street, Halstead
CO9 2AA
**t** (01787) 475657
**w** innpubs.co.uk

## HANDSACRE
Staffordshire

**Olde Peculiar (The)** ★★★★
*Inn*
The Green, Handsacre,
Lichfield WS15 4DP
**t** (01543) 491891
**e** corinne.odonnell@ntlworld.com

## HANLEY
Staffordshire

**The Northwood Hotel** ★★★
*Guest Accommodation*
146 Keelings Road,
Northwood, Stoke-on-Trent
ST1 6QA
**t** (01782) 279729
**e** northwoodhotel@gmail.com
**w** cityhotels.org.uk

## HANLEY CASTLE
Worcestershire

**The Chestnuts** ★★★★
*Bed & Breakfast*
**SILVER AWARD**
Gilberts End, Hanley Castle
WR8 0AS
**t** (01684) 311219
**e** heather@chestnutshp.co.uk
**w** chestnutshp.co.uk

---

**Gilberts End Farm B&B**
★★★★ *Bed & Breakfast*
Gilberts End, Hanley Castle,
Upton-upon-Severn WR8 0AR
**t** (01684) 311392
**e** chrissy.bacon@onetel.net
**w** gilbertsendfarm.co.uk

## HANLEY SWAN
Worcestershire

**Blackmore Gardens** ★★★★
*Guest Accommodation*
Worcester WR8 0EF
**t** (01684) 311931
**e** stay@blackmore-gardens.co.uk
**w** blackmore-gardens.co.uk

---

**Meadowbank** ★★★★
*Bed & Breakfast*
**SILVER AWARD**
Picken End, Hanley Swan
WR8 0DQ
**t** (01684) 310917
**e** dave@meadowbankhs.freeserve.co.uk
**w** http://mysite.freeserve.com/meadowbank

## HANWOOD
Shropshire

**Caer-Urfa** ★★★★
*Bed & Breakfast*
46 Woodlands Avenue,
Hanwood, Shrewsbury
SY5 8NG
**t** (01743) 861120
**e** caer-urfa@hotmail.co.uk
**w** caer-urfa.co.uk

## HARDWICK
Cambridgeshire

**Wallis Farm** ★★★★
*Farmhouse*
98 Main Street, Hardwick,
Aylesbury CB23 7QU
**t** (01954) 210347
**e** enquiries@wallisfarmhouse.co.uk
**w** wallisfarmhouse.co.uk

## HARDWICK, HAY ON WYE
Herefordshire

**Hardwicke Green** ★★★★
*Bed & Breakfast*
Hardwicke, Hay-on-Wye
HR3 5HA
**t** (01497) 831051
**e** info@hardwickegreen.co.uk
**w** hardwickegreen.co.uk

## HARLESTON
Norfolk

**Weston House Farm** ★★★★
*Farmhouse*
Mendham, Harleston IP20 0PB
**t** (01986) 782206
**e** holden@farmline.com
**w** westonhousefarm.co.uk

## HARLEY
Shropshire

**Rowley Farm** ★★ *Farmhouse*
Harley, Shrewsbury SY5 6LX
**t** (01952) 727348
**e** bedandbreakfast@rowleyfarm.fsnet.co.uk
**w** stmem.com/rowley-farm

## HARLOW
Essex

**Harlow International Hostel**
★★ *Hostel*
13 School Lane, Harlow
CM20 2QD
**t** (01279) 421702
**e** mail@h-i-h.co.uk
**w** h-i-h.co.uk

---

**The Old Granary** ★★★★
*Guest Accommodation*
Holts Farm, Theshers Bush,
High Laver, Harlow CM17 0NS
**t** (01279) 438377
**e** info@holtsfarm.co.uk
**w** holtsfarm.co.uk

## HARRINGTON
Northamptonshire

**Church Farm Lodge** ★★★★
*Guest Accommodation*
Harrington NN6 9NU
**t** (01536) 713320
**e** info@churchfarmlodge.com
**w** churchfarmlodge.com

## HARSTON
Cambridgeshire

**Beech Farm Bed & Breakfast**
Rating Applied For
*Guest Accommodation*
Beech Farm, 34 Church Street,
Cambridge CB22 7NR
**t** (01223) 871563
**e** jackie@beechfarm.demon.co.uk
**w** beechfarmcambridge.com

## HARTINGTON
Derbyshire

**Bank Top Farm** ★★★★
*Farmhouse*
Pilsbury Lane, Hartington
SK17 0AD
**t** (01298) 84205
**e** jane@banktopfarm.orangehome.co.uk
**w** banktophartington.freeserve.co.uk

---

**The Hayloft** ★★★★
*Guest Accommodation*
Sennilow Farm, Church Street,
Buxton SK17 0AW
**t** (01298) 84358
**e** hartington.hayloft@ii2.com
**w** hartingtonhayloft.co.uk

---

**Wolfscote Grange Farm**
★★★★ *Farmhouse*
Hartington, Buxton SK17 0AX
**t** (01298) 84342
**e** wolfscote@btinternet.com
**w** wolfscotegrangecottages.co.uk

---

**YHA Hartington Hall**
★★★★ *Hostel*
Hartington, Buxton SK17 0AT
**t** 0870 770 5848
**w** yha.org.uk

## HARWICH
Essex

**Paston Lodge** ★★★
*Guest Accommodation*
Una Road, Parkeston, Harwich
CO12 4PP
**t** (01255) 551390
**e** harwichb.b@pastonlodge.co.uk

---

**Stingray Freehouse** ★★★
*Guest Accommodation*
56 Church Street, Harwich
CO12 3DS
**t** (01255) 503507
**e** enquiries@thestingray.co.uk
**w** thestingray.co.uk

---

**Woodview Cottage** ★★★★
*Bed & Breakfast*
**SILVER AWARD**
Wrabness Road, Ramsey,
Harwich CO12 5ND
**t** (01255) 886413
**e** annec@zetnet.co.uk
**w** woodview-cottage.co.uk

## HATFIELD
Hertfordshire

**University of Hertfordshire de Havilland** ★★★ *Campus*
Fielder Centre, Hatfield
Business Park, Hatfield
AL10 9FL
**t** (01707) 284841

### HATFIELD BROAD OAK
Essex

**Bury House** ★★★
*Bed & Breakfast*
High Street, Bishop's Stortford CM22 7HQ
**t** (01279) 718259
**e** bswan@buryhouse.wanadoo.co.uk
**w** tiscover.co.uk

**Cottage** ★★ *Bed & Breakfast*
Dunmow Road, Hatfield Broad Oak, Bishop's Stortford CM22 7JJ
**t** (01279) 718230
**e** elizabeth.britton@virgin.net
**w** tiscover.co.uk

### HATFIELD HEATH
Essex

**Friars Farm** ★★★★
*Farmhouse* **SILVER AWARD**
Friars Lane, Bishop's Stortford CM22 7AP
**t** (01279) 730244

**Oaklands** ★★★★
*Bed & Breakfast*
Bishop's Stortford CM22 7AD
**t** (01279) 730240
**e** langman544@btinternet.com

### HATHERSAGE
Derbyshire

**Abney Camping Barn**
*Camping Barn*
Abney, Hathersage, Hope Valley S32 1AH
**t** (01433) 650481
**w** independenthostelguide.co.uk

**Cannon Croft** ★★★★
*Bed & Breakfast*
**GOLD AWARD**
Cannonfields, Hathersage, Hope Valley S32 1AG
**t** (01433) 650005
**e** soates@cannoncroft.fsbusiness.co.uk
**w** cannoncroft.fsbusiness.co.uk

**The Plough Inn** ★★★★ *Inn*
**SILVER AWARD**
Leadmill Bridge, Hathersage, Hope Valley S32 1BA
**t** (01433) 650319

**Polly's B&B** ★★★★
*Bed & Breakfast*
Moorview Cottage, Cannonfields, Hope Valley S32 1AG
**t** (01433) 650110

**YHA Hathersage** ★★ *Hostel*
The Hollies, Castleton Road, Hope Valley S32 1EH
**t** 0870 770 5852
**w** yha.org.uk

### HAUGHLEY
Suffolk

**Haughley House** ★★★★★
*Guest Accommodation*
**SILVER AWARD**
Haughley, Stowmarket IP14 3NS
**t** (01449) 673398
**e** bowden@keme.co.uk
**w** haughleyhouse.co.uk

**Red House Farm** ★★★★
*Farmhouse*
Haughley, Stowmarket IP14 3QP
**t** (01449) 673323
**e** mary@redhousefarmhaughley.co.uk
**w** farmstayanglia.co.uk

### HAUXTON
Cambridgeshire

**Dorset House** ★★★★
*Guest Accommodation*
35 Newton Road, Little Shelford, Cambridge CB2 5HL
**t** (01223) 844440
**e** dorsethouse@btopenworld.com

### HAXEY
Lincolnshire

**The Loco** ★★★★ *Inn*
31-33 Church Street, Haxey DN9 2HY
**t** (01427) 752879
**e** info@thelocohaxey.co.uk
**w** thelocohaxey.co.uk

### HEACHAM
Norfolk

**Holly House** ★★★
*Guest Accommodation*
3 Broadway, Heacham, King's Lynn PE31 7DF
**t** (01485) 572935
**e** enquiries@hollyhouseheacham.co.uk
**w** hollyhouseheacham.co.uk

**Saint Annes Guest House** ★★★★
*Guest Accommodation*
53 Neville Road, Heacham, King's Lynn PE31 7HB
**t** (01485) 570021
**e** elaine@stannesguesthouse.co.uk

**The Wheatsheaf Inn** ★★★★
*Guest House*
5 Lynn Road, Heacham PE31 7HU
**t** (01485) 570282
**e** gooch@wheatsheafheacham.fsnet.co.uk
**w** heacham-on-line.co.uk/wheatsheafheacham

### HEATH
Derbyshire

**Stainsby Mill Farm** ★★★
*Farmhouse*
Stainsby, Heath, Chesterfield S44 5RW
**t** (01246) 850288

### HELHOUGHTON
Norfolk

**Woodfarm House** ★★★★★
*Bed & Breakfast*
**SILVER AWARD**
Broomsthorpe Road, Fakenham NR21 7BT
**t** (01485) 528586
**e** booking@woodfarm-house.com
**w** woodfarm-house.com

### HELLESDON
Norfolk

**Cairdean** ★★★★
*Bed & Breakfast*
71 Middletons Lane, Hellesdon, Norwich NR6 5NS
**t** (01603) 419041
**e** info@cairdean.co.uk
**w** cairdean.co.uk

**Old Corner Shop Guesthouse** ★★★
*Bed & Breakfast*
26 Cromer Road, Norwich NR6 6LZ
**t** (01603) 419000
**e** info@theoldcornershopguesthouse.co.uk
**w** theoldcornershopguesthouse.co.uk

### HEMEL HEMPSTEAD
Hertfordshire

**47 Crescent Road** ★★
*Bed & Breakfast*
Hemel Hempstead HP2 4AJ
**t** (01442) 255137

**Marsh Farm** ★★★★
*Bed & Breakfast*
Ledgemore Lane, Great Gaddesden HP2 6HA
**t** (01442) 252517
**e** nicky@bennett-baggs.com
**w** marshfarm.org.uk

### HEMINGFORD ABBOTS
Cambridgeshire

**Riverside House** ★★★
*Bed & Breakfast*
Common Lane, Hemingford Abbots, Huntingdon PE28 9AN
**t** (01480) 468993
**e** caroline@carolinecatering.co.uk
**w** carolinecatering.co.uk

### HEREFORD
Herefordshire

**Alberta Guest House** ★★★
*Guest House*
7-13 Newtown Road, Hereford HR4 9LH
**t** (01432) 270313
**e** albertaguesthouse@amserve.com
**w** thealbertaguesthouse.co.uk

**The Bowens Country House Hotel** ★★★★
*Guest Accommodation*
Fownhope, Hereford HR1 4PS
**t** (01432) 860430
**e** thebowenshotel@aol.com
**w** thebowenshotel.co.uk

**Brandon Lodge** ★★★★
*Guest Accommodation*
**SILVER AWARD**
Ross Road, Grafton, Hereford HR2 8BH
**t** (01432) 355621
**e** info@brandonlodge.co.uk
**w** brandonlodge.co.uk

**Charades** ★★★ *Guest House*
34 Southbank Road, Hereford HR1 2TJ
**t** (01432) 269444
**e** stay@charadeshereford.co.uk
**w** charadeshereford.co.uk

**Graiseley House** ★★★★
*Bed & Breakfast*
180 Whitecross Road, Hereford HR4 0DJ
**t** (01432) 358289
**e** janespearpoint@yahoo.co.uk
**w** graiseleyhouse.co.uk

**Hedley Lodge** ★★★★
*Guest Accommodation*
Belmont Abbey, Abergavenny Road, Hereford HR2 9RZ
**t** (01432) 374747
**e** hedley@belmontabbey.org.uk
**w** hedleylodge.com

**Heron House** ★★★
*Bed & Breakfast*
Canon Pyon Road, Portway, Hereford HR4 8NG
**t** (01432) 761111
**e** info@theheronhouse.com
**w** theheronhouse.com

**Hopbine House** ★★★
*Guest House*
Roman Road, Hereford HR1 1LE
**t** (01432) 268722
**e** info@hopbine.com
**w** hopbine.com

**Old Rectory** ★★★★
*Guest Accommodation*
**SILVER AWARD**
Byford, Hereford HR4 7LD
**t** (01981) 590218
**e** info@cm-ltd.com
**w** smoothhound.co.uk/hotels/oldrectory2

### HERTFORD
Hertfordshire

**Castle Moat House** ★★★★
*Bed & Breakfast*
25 Castle Street, Hertford SG14 1HH
**t** (01992) 584004
**e** thornton25@ntlworld.com

**Hertford Boutique B&B** ★★★★ *Bed & Breakfast*
10 Cowbridge, Hertford SG14 1PQ
**t** (01992) 300717
**e** j.ardley@hotmail.co.uk

### HEVINGHAM
Norfolk

**Marsham Arms Inn** ★★★★
*Inn*
Holt Road, Hevingham NR10 5NP
**t** (01603) 754268
**e** info@marshamarms.co.uk
**w** marshamarms.co.uk

### HEYDON
Cambridgeshire

**The End Cottage** ★★★★
*Guest Accommodation*
Fowlmere Road, Heydon, Royston SG8 8PZ
**t** (01763) 838212
**e** d-macfadyen@amserve.com

### HICKLING
Norfolk

**Black Horse Cottage** ★★★
*Bed & Breakfast*
The Green, Norwich NR12 0YA
**t** (01692) 598691
**e** info@blackhorsecottage.com
**w** blackhorsecottage.com

**The Dairy Barns ★★★★**
*Farmhouse* **GOLD AWARD**
Lound Farm, Hickling, Norwich NR12 0BE
**t** (01692) 598243
**e** enquiries@dairybarns.co.uk
**w** dairybarns.co.uk

## HIGHAM
Derbyshire

**The Crown Inn ★★** *Inn*
Main Road, Higham, Alfreton DE55 6EH
**t** (01773) 832310

## HIGHAM ON THE HILL
Warwickshire

**Bed & Breakfast at Vale Farm ★★★★** *Farmhouse*
Stoke Golding Lane, Higham-on-the-Hill, Hinckley CV13 6ES
**t** 07977 915272
**e** prestons@valefarm.eleven.com
**w** valefarm-bed-and-breakfast.co.uk

## HILDERSHAM
Cambridgeshire

**The Pear Tree Inn**
Rating Applied For
*Guest Accommodation*
High Street CB21 6BU
**t** (01223) 891680
**e** peartreeinn@btconnect.com
**w** peartreecambridge-bb.co.uk

## HILTON
Derbyshire

**Tudor Rose ★★★★**
*Guest Accommodation*
Main Street, Derby DE65 5FF
**t** (01283) 734564
**e** hilton-tudor-rose@tiscali.co.uk
**w** hilton-tudor-rose.co.uk

## HIMBLETON
Worcestershire

**Court Farm ★★★★**
*Farmhouse*
Himbleton, Droitwich WR9 7LG
**t** (01905) 391254
**e** penelopewesner@courtfarm.info
**w** courtfarm.info

---

**Phepson Farm ★★★★**
*Guest Accommodation*
Himbleton, Droitwich Spa WR9 7JZ
**t** (01905) 391205
**e** info@phepsonfarm.co.uk
**w** phepsonfarm.co.uk

## HINDRINGHAM
Norfolk

**Field House ★★★★★**
*Bed & Breakfast*
**GOLD AWARD**
Moorgate Road, Hindringham NR21 0PT
**t** (01328) 878726
**e** stay@fieldhousehindringham.co.uk
**w** fieldhousehindringham.co.uk

## HINTLESHAM
Suffolk

**College Farm ★★★★**
*Farmhouse* **SILVER AWARD**
Hintlesham, Ipswich IP8 3NT
**t** (01473) 652253
**e** bandb@collegefarm.plus.com
**w** collegefarm.net

## HINTON IN THE HEDGES
Northamptonshire

**The Old Rectory ★★★**
*Bed & Breakfast*
Hinton-in-the-Hedges, Brackley NN13 5NG
**t** (01280) 706807
**e** lavinia@lavinia.demon.co.uk
**w** northamptonshire.co.uk/hotels/oldrectory.htm

---

**Two Hoots ★★★★**
*Bed & Breakfast*
The Green, Hinton-in-the-Hedges, Brackley NN13 5NG
**t** (01280) 701220
**e** louiewithers@aol.com
**w** northamptonshire.co.uk/hotels/twohoots.htm

## HITCHAM
Suffolk

**Stanstead Hall ★★**
*Farmhouse*
Hares Road, Hitcham, Ipswich IP7 7NY
**t** (01449) 740 270
**e** stanstead@btinternet.com

## HITCHIN
Hertfordshire

**East Tithe Barn**
Rating Applied For
*Farmhouse*
New Wellbury Farmhouse, Hitchin SG5 3BP
**t** (01462) 768627
**e** veronicaalvarez@compuserve.com

---

**Honeysuckle Cottage**
Rating Applied For
*Guest Accommodation*
25 High Street, Great Offley, Hitchin SG5 3AP
**t** (01462) 768050

## HOARWITHY
Herefordshire

**The Old Mill ★★★★**
*Bed & Breakfast*
Hoarwithy, Hereford HR2 6QH
**t** (01432) 840602
**e** carol.probert@virgin.net

## HOCKLEY HEATH
West Midlands

**Eden End Bed & Breakfast ★★★** *Guest House*
Eden End, Stratford Road, Solihull B94 6NN
**t** (01564) 783372
**e** bedandbreakfast@edenend.com
**w** edenend.com

---

**Illshaw Heath Farm ★★★★**
*Farmhouse*
Kineton Lane, Hockley Health B94 6RX
**t** (01564) 782214
**e** janetandtony@amserve.com

## HOLBEACH
Lincolnshire

**Cackle Hill House ★★★★**
*Bed & Breakfast*
**SILVER AWARD**
Cackle Hill Lane, Holbeach PE12 8BS
**t** (01406) 426721
**e** cacklehillhouse@farming.co.uk

## HOLBECK
Nottinghamshire

**Browns ★★★★★**
*Bed & Breakfast*
**GOLD AWARD**
The Old Orchard Cottage, Holbeck, Worksop S80 3NF
**t** (01909) 720659
**e** browns@holbeck.fsnet.co.uk
**w** brownsholbeck.co.uk

## HOLLINGTON
Derbyshire

**Reevsmoor ★★★★**
*Bed & Breakfast*
Hoargate Lane, Hollington, Ashbourne DE6 3AG
**t** (01335) 330318
**w** smoothhound.co.uk

## HOLLYBUSH
Worcestershire

**Bank Cottage ★★★**
*Bed & Breakfast*
The Common, Hollybush, Ledbury HR8 1ET
**t** (01531) 650683
**e** hpwhite@bloomberg.net
**w** bankcottage.net

## HOLMESFIELD
Derbyshire

**Carpenter House ★★★★**
*Bed & Breakfast*
Cordwell Lane, Millthorpe, Chesterfield S18 7WH
**t** (0114) 289 0307

## HOLT
Norfolk

**Byfords ★★★★★**
*Guest Accommodation*
**GOLD AWARD**
1-3 Shirehall Plain, Holt NR25 6BG
**t** (01263) 711400
**e** queries@byfords.org.uk
**w** byfords.org.uk

---

**Hempstead Hall ★★★★**
*Farmhouse*
Hempstead, Holt NR25 6TN
**t** (01263) 712224

---

**Holm Oaks ★★★★**
*Bed & Breakfast*
83a Cromer Road, Holt NR25 6DY
**t** (01263) 711061
**w** glavenvalley.co.uk

---

**Kadina ★★★★**
*Bed & Breakfast*
**SILVER AWARD**
Holt NR25 6QX
**t** (01263) 710116
**e** enquiries@kadinanorfolk.co.uk
**w** kadinanorfolk.co.uk

---

**Three Corners ★★**
*Bed & Breakfast*
12 Kelling Close, Holt NR25 6RU
**t** (01263) 713389
**e** ronvcox@aol.com
**w** tiscover.co.uk

## HOLTON ST MARY
Suffolk

**Stratford House ★★★★**
*Bed & Breakfast*
Stubbins Lane, Holton St Mary, Colchester CO7 6NT
**t** (01206) 298246

## HONINGTON
Suffolk

**North View Guesthouse ★★★** *Guest Accommodation*
North View, Malting Row, Honington IP31 1RE
**t** (01359) 269423

---

**Willow Bed And Breakfast ★★★★** *Bed & Breakfast*
Ixworth Road, Honington, Bury St Edmunds IP31 1QY
**t** (01359) 269600
**e** celialawrence@talk21.com

## HOPE
Derbyshire

**Causeway House B&B ★★★**
*Bed & Breakfast*
Back Street, Castleton, Hope Valley S33 8WE
**t** (01433) 623291
**e** steynberg@btinternet.com
**w** causewayhouse.co.uk

---

**Poachers Arms ★★★★** *Inn*
**SILVER AWARD**
Castleton Road, Hope Valley S33 6SB
**t** (01433) 620380
**e** btissington95@aol.com
**w** poachersarms.co.uk

---

**Underleigh House ★★★★★**
*Guest Accommodation*
**GOLD AWARD**
Off Edale Road, Hope, Hope Valley S33 6RF
**t** (01433) 621372
**e** info@underleighhouse.co.uk
**w** underleighhouse.co.uk

---

**Woodbine B&B ★★★**
*Guest House*
18 Castleton Road, Hope Valley S33 6RD
**t** 07778 113882

## HOPE BAGOT
Shropshire

**Croft Cottage B&B ★★★★**
*Bed & Breakfast*
Cumberley Lane, Hope Bagot, Ludlow SY8 3LJ
**t** (01584) 890664
**e** shropshiretourism@croftcottagebedandbreakfast.co.uk
**w** croftcottagebedandbreakfast.co.uk

## HOPE VALLEY
Derbyshire

**The Chequers Inn** ★★★★
*Inn* **SILVER AWARD**
Froggatt Edge, Hope Valley
S32 3ZJ
**t** (01433) 630231
**e** info@chequers-froggatt.com
**w** chequers-froggatt.com

**The Rambler Country House Hotel** ★★★ *Inn*
Edale, Hope Valley S33 7ZA
t (01433) 670268

**The Rising Sun** ★★★★ *Inn*
**SILVER AWARD**
Thornhill Moor, Bamford, Hope Valley S33 0AL
t (01433) 651323
e info@the-rising-sun.org
w the-rising-sun.org

## HOPTON HEATH
Shropshire

**Hopton House** ★★★★
*Bed & Breakfast*
**GOLD AWARD**
Hopton Heath, Craven Arms
SY7 0QD
t (01547) 530885
e info@shropshirebreakfast.co.uk
w shropshirebreakfast.co.uk

## HORNCASTLE
Lincolnshire

**Bank Cottage Guest House**
★★★★ *Guest House*
16 Bank Street, Horncastle
LN9 5BW
**t** (01507) 526666
**e** horncastleinfo@e-lindsey.gov.uk
**w** bankcottage-guesthouse.com

**Mizpah Villa** ★★★★
*Guest Accommodation*
9 Low Toynton Road, Horncastle LN9 5LL
t (01507) 523917
e mizpahvilla@googlemail.co.uk

**Oak House** ★★★★
*Bed & Breakfast*
26 Harrison Close, Horncastle
LN9 5ER
t (01507) 522096

## HORNING
Norfolk

**Gable Cottage** ★★★★
*Guest Accommodation*
61 Lower Street, Horning
NR12 8AA
t (01692) 631239
e gablecottage61@aol.com
w tiscover.co.uk

**The Moorhen** ★★★★
*Bed & Breakfast*
45 Lower Street, Horning, Norwich NR12 8AA
t (01692) 631444
e themoorhenhorning@tiscali.co.uk
w themoorhenhorning.co.uk

## HORSEHEATH
Cambridgeshire

**Chequer Cottage** ★★★★
*Bed & Breakfast*
43 Streetly End, Horseheath, Cambridge CB1 6RP
t (01223) 891522
e stay@chequercottage.com
w chequercottage.com

## HORSLEY
Derbyshire

**Horsley Lodge** ★★★★
*Guest Accommodation*
**SILVER AWARD**
Smalley Mill Road, Horsley, Derby DE21 5BL
**t** (01332) 780838
**e** enquiries@horsleylodge.co.uk
**w** horsleylodge.co.uk

## HOVETON
Norfolk

**The Vineries Bed & Breakfast** ★★★★
*Guest Accommodation*
72 Stalham Road, Hoveton, Norwich NR12 8DU
t (01603) 782514
e enquiries@thevineries.com
w thevineries.com

## HOW CAPLE
Herefordshire

**The Falcon House** ★★★★
*Guest Accommodation*
How Caple, Hereford, Ross-on-Wye HR1 4TF
t (01989) 740223
e falcon.house@gmail.com
w thefalconhouse.co.uk

## HOWE
Norfolk

**Rectory Barn Bed and Breakfast** ★★★★
*Bed & Breakfast*
Howe Green, Howe, Norwich
NR15 1HD
t (01508) 558176
e d.cuddon@btinternet.com
w rectorybarnbandb.co.uk

## HULME END
Staffordshire

**The Manifold Inn** ★★★★
*Inn*
Hulme End, Buxton SK17 0EX
t (01298) 84537
e info@themanifoldinn.co.uk
w themanifoldinn.co.uk

**Raikes Farm** ★★★★
*Farmhouse*
Hulme End, Hartington, Buxton
SK17 0HJ
t (01298) 84344

## HUNDON
Suffolk

**The Plough Inn**
Rating Applied For
*Inn*
Brockley Green, Sudbury
CO10 8DT
**t** (01440) 786789
**e** info@theploughhundon.co.uk
**w** theploughhundon.co.uk

## HUNSTANTON
Norfolk

**Ashleigh Lodge** ★★★
*Guest Accommodation*
Austin Street, Hunstanton
PE36 6AL
t (01485) 533247
e nick.bishop1@tesco.net
w ashleighlodge.co.uk

**The Bays Guesthouse**
★★★★★ *Guest House*
**SILVER AWARD**
31 Avenue Road, Hunstanton
PE36 5BW
t (01485) 532079
e enquiries@thebays.co.uk
w thebays.co.uk

**Belgrave House** ★★★★
*Guest Accommodation*
49 Northgate, Hunstanton
PE36 6DS
t (01485) 533007
e belgrave-house@btconnect.com
w belgrave-housebb.co.uk

**The Burleigh** ★★★★
*Guest Accommodation*
7 Cliff Terrace, Hunstanton
PE36 6DY
t (01485) 533080
e reservations@theburleigh.com
w theburleigh.com

**Burlington House** ★★★★
*Bed & Breakfast*
**SILVER AWARD**
3 Austin Street, Hunstanton
PE36 6AJ
t (01485) 533366

**Cori House Bed & Breakfast**
★★★★ *Bed & Breakfast*
Hunstanton PE36 5HA
t (01485) 533034
e corihousebandb@yahoo.co.uk
w corihouse.co.uk

**Deepdene House** ★★★★
*Guest House* **SILVER AWARD**
29 Avenue Road, Hunstanton
PE36 5BW
t (01485) 532460
e deepdenehouse@btopenworld.com
w deepdenehouse.co.uk

**Ellinbrook House** ★★★★
*Guest Accommodation*
37 Avenue Road, Hunstanton
PE36 5HW
t (01485) 532022
e ellinbrookhouse@aol.com
w ellinbrookhouse.co.uk

**Eton Lodge** ★★★★
*Bed & Breakfast*
47 Greevegate, Hunstanton
PE36 6AF
t (01485) 533783
w bbinhunstanton.co.uk

**The Gables** ★★★★
*Guest Accommodation*
Austin Street, Hunstanton
PE36 6AW
t (01485) 532514

**Garganey House** ★★★
*Guest House*
46 Northgate, Hunstanton
PE36 6DR
t (01485) 533269
e garganey1.@f.s.net.co.uk

**Gate Lodge** ★★★★
*Guest Accommodation*
**GOLD AWARD**
2 Westgate, Hunstanton
PE36 5AL
t (01485) 533549
e lynn@gatelodge-guesthouse.co.uk
w gatelodge-guesthouse.co.uk

**Glenberis Bed And Breakfast** ★★★★
*Bed & Breakfast*
**SILVER AWARD**
6 St Edmunds Avenue, Hunstanton PE36 6AY
t (01485) 533663
e glenberis.hunstanton@ntlworld.com

**Hunstanton Yha** ★★★
*Hostel*
15 Avenue Road, Hunstanton
PE36 5BW
t (01485) 532061
e hunstanton@yha.org.uk
w yha.org.uk

**Kiama Cottage Guesthouse**
★★★★
*Guest Accommodation*
23 Austin Street, Hunstanton
PE36 6AN
t (01485) 533615
e kiamacottage@btopenworld.com

**The King William IV Country Inn & Restaurant** ★★★★ *Inn*
**SILVER AWARD**
Heacham Road, Sedgeford, Hunstanton PE36 5LU
**t** (01485) 571765
**e** info@thekingwilliamsedgeford.co.uk
**w** thekingwilliamsedgeford.co.uk

**Lakeside Guesthouse**
★★★★
*Guest Accommodation*
Waterworks Road, Old Hunstanton, Hunstanton
PE36 6JE
t (01485) 533763
w oldwaterworks.co.uk

**Linksway Country House**
★★★★
*Guest Accommodation*
**SILVER AWARD**
Golf Course Road, Old Hunstanton, Hunstanton
PE36 6JE
t (01485) 532209
e linksway-hotel@totalise.co.uk
w linkswayhotel.com

**The Lodge** ★★★★ *Inn*
Old Hunstanton, Hunstanton
PE36 6HX
**t** (01485) 532896
**e** thelodge@norfolk-hotels.co.uk
**w** norfolk-hotels.co.uk

**Miramar Guesthouse ★★★**
*Guest House*
7 Boston Square, Hunstanton PE36 6DT
t (01485) 532902

**Peacock House ★★★★**
*Guest Accommodation*
**SILVER AWARD**
28 Park Road, Hunstanton PE36 5BY
t (01485) 534551
e peacockhouse@onetel.com
w peacockhouse-hunstanton.co.uk

**Queensbury House ★★★**
*Bed & Breakfast*
Glebe Avenue, Hunstanton PE36 6BS
t (01485) 534320
w tiscover.co.uk

**Rosamaly Guesthouse ★★★★**
*Guest Accommodation*
14 Glebe Avenue, Hunstanton PE36 6BS
t (01485) 534187
e rosamaly@supanet.com
w allhotelsnet.com/europe/rosamaly-guesthouse.asp

**Rose Fitt House ★★★★**
*Guest Accommodation*
**SILVER AWARD**
40 Northgate, Hunstanton PE36 6DR
t (01485) 534776
e andrea.rosefitt@btinternet.com
w rose-fitt-house-hunstanton.co.uk

**The Shellbrooke ★★★★**
*Guest House*
9 Cliff Terrace, Hunstanton PE36 6DY
t (01485) 532289
e info@theshellbrooke.co.uk
w theshellbrooke.co.uk

**Sunningdale ★★★★**
*Guest House*
3-5 Avenue Road, Hunstanton PE36 5BW
t (01485) 532562
e reception@sunningdalehotel.com
w sunningdalehotel.com

## HUNTINGDON
Cambridgeshire

**Bramble Corner ★★**
*Guest Accommodation*
9 Rectory Road, Bluntisham, Huntingdon PE28 3LN
t (01487) 842646
e info@bramblecorner.co.uk
w bramblecorner.co.uk

**Braywood House ★★★**
*Guest House*
27 St Peters Road, Huntingdon PE29 7AA
t (01480) 459782
e admin@braywood.org.uk
w braywood.org.uk

## ICKLETON
Cambridgeshire

**Shepherds Cottage ★★★★**
*Bed & Breakfast*
Grange Road, Ickleton, Saffron Walden CB10 1TA
t (01799) 531171
e simon.casement@btinternet.com

## IDRIDGEHAY
Derbyshire

**Millbank House ★★★**
*Guest Accommodation*
Idridgehay, Wirksworth, Matlock DE56 2SH
t (01629) 823161
e cmjones123@hotmail.co.uk

## ILAM
Staffordshire

**Beechenhill Farm B&B**
**★★★★** *Farmhouse*
**SILVER AWARD**
Beechenhill Farm, Ilam DE6 2BD
t (01335) 310274
e beechenhill@btinternet.com
w beechenhill.co.uk

**Ilam Hall YHA ★★★** *Hostel*
Ilam Hall, Ashbourne DE6 2AZ
t 0870 770 5879
e ilam@yha.org.uk
w yha.org.uk

**Throwley Hall Farm B&B**
**★★★★** *Farmhouse*
Throwley Hall Farm, Ilam, Ashbourne DE6 2BB
t (01538) 308202
e throwleyhall@btinternet.com
w throwleyhallfarm.co.uk

## ILKETSHALL ST LAWRENCE
Suffolk

**Buckland House**
Rating Applied For
*Guest Accommodation*
Halesworth Road, Ilketshall St Lawrence, Beccles NR34 8LB
t (01986) 781413
e info@buckland-house.co.uk
w buckland-house.co.uk

## INGHAM
Suffolk

**Ingham Lodge B&B ★★★★**
*Bed & Breakfast*
Dairy Lane, Ingham, Bury St Edmunds IP31 1HT
t (01284) 729642
e bandb@inghamlodge.net
w inghamlodge.net

## INGOLDISTHORPE
Norfolk

**Pencob House ★★★★**
*Bed & Breakfast*
**SILVER AWARD**
56 Hill Road, Ingoldisthorpe, King's Lynn PE31 6NZ
t (01485) 543882
e pencob@supanet.com

## IPSWICH
Suffolk

**Bramshaw ★★★★**
*Guest House*
77 Bucklesham Road, Ipswich IP3 8TR
t (01473) 712379
e gill.mann@btinternet.com
w tiscover.co.uk

**Carlton ★★**
*Guest Accommodation*
41-43 Berners Street, Ipswich IP1 3LT
t (01473) 254955
e carltonhotel@hotmail.com
w carlton-ipswich.co.uk

**Gables of Park Road ★★★**
*Guest House*
17 Park Road, Ipswich IP1 3SX
t (01473) 254252
e enquiries@gablesofparkroad.co.uk
w gablesofparkroad.co.uk

**Lattice Lodge Guest House**
**★★★★** *Guest House*
**SILVER AWARD**
Ipswich IP4 4EP
t (01473) 712474
e latticelodge@btconnect.com
w latticelodge.co.uk

**Melverley Heights Guest House ★★★★** *Guest House*
**SILVER AWARD**
62 Tuddenham Road, Ipswich IP4 2SP
t (01473) 253524
e enquiries@melverleyheights.co.uk
w melverleyheights.co.uk

**Queenscliffe Bed And Breakfast ★★★★**
*Bed & Breakfast*
2 Queenscliffe Road, Ipswich IP2 9AS
t (01473) 686810
e queenscliffe@supanet.com

**Sidegate Guesthouse**
**★★★★** *Guest House*
**SILVER AWARD**
121 Sidegate Lane, Ipswich IP4 4JB
t (01473) 728714
e bookings@sidegateguesthouse.co.uk
w sidegateguesthouse.co.uk

## IRONBRIDGE
Shropshire

**Bird In Hand Inn ★★★** *Inn*
Waterloo Street, Ironbridge, Telford TF8 7HG
t (01952) 432226
e bird1774@aol.com

**Bridge House ★★★★★**
*Guest Accommodation*
**SILVER AWARD**
Buildwas Road, Ironbridge, Telford TF8 7BN
t (01952) 432105
e the-bridgehouse@bt.com
w smoothhound.co.uk

**Bridge View Bed & Breakfast**
**★★★** *Guest House*
10 Tontine Hill, Ironbridge, Telford TF8 7AL
t (01952) 684249
e jayne@eleys-ironbridge.co.uk
w eleys-ironbridge.co.uk

**The Calcutts House ★★★★**
*Guest Accommodation*
Calcutts Road, Jackfield, Ironbridge, Telford TF8 7LH
t (01952) 882631
e info@calcuttshouse.co.uk
w calcuttshouse.co.uk

**Coalbrookdale Villa Guest House ★★★★**
*Guest Accommodation*
**SILVER AWARD**
Paradise, Coalbrookdale, Telford TF8 7NR
t (01952) 433450
e coalbrookdalevilla@currantbun.com
w coalbrookdale.f9.co.uk

**Golden Ball Inn ★★★★** *Inn*
1 Newbridge Road, Ironbridge, Telford TF8 7BA
t (01952) 432179
e info@goldenballinn.com
w goldenballinn.co.uk

**The Library House ★★★★★**
*Guest Accommodation*
**GOLD AWARD**
11 Severn Bank, Ironbridge TF8 7AN
t (01952) 432299
e info@libraryhouse.com
w libraryhouse.com

**The Malthouse ★★★★** *Inn*
The Wharfage, Ironbridge, Telford TF8 7NH
t (01952) 433712

**The Meadow Inn**
Rating Applied For
*Inn*
29 Buildwas Road, Telford TF8 7BJ
t (020) 8777 3636
e tu@bcinns.co.uk

**The Meadow Lodge ★★★★**
*Inn*
29 Buildwas Road, Ironbridge, Telford TF8 7BJ
t (01952) 432632

**The Old Rectory at Broseley**
**★★★★★** *Guest House*
**SILVER AWARD**
46 Ironbridge Road, Broseley TF12 5AF
t (01952) 883399
e info@theoldrectoryatbroseley.co.uk
w theoldrectoryatbroseley.co.uk

**Post Office House ★★★**
*Guest Accommodation*
6 The Square, Ironbridge, Telford TF8 7AQ
t (01952) 433201

**Severn Lodge ★★★★★**
*Bed & Breakfast*
**SILVER AWARD**
New Road, Ironbridge, Telford TF8 7AU
t (01952) 432148

**The Swan ★★★★** *Inn*
The Wharfage, Ironbridge TF8 7NH
t (01952) 432306
e enquiries@malthousepubs.co.uk
w malthousepubs.co.uk

**Tontine** ★★★ *Inn*
The Square, Ironbridge, Telford TF8 7AL
t (01952) 432127
e tontinehotel@tiscali.co.uk
w tontine-ironbridge.com

**Wharfage Cottage** ★★★
*Bed & Breakfast*
17 The Wharfage, Ironbridge, Telford TF8 7AW
t (01952) 432721
e info@wharfagecottage.co.uk
w wharfagecottage.co.uk

**Woodville B&B** ★★★★
*Bed & Breakfast*
4a The Woodlands, Ironbridge TF8 7PA
t (01952) 433343
e enquiries@enjoywoodville.com
w enjoywoodville.com

### KELSALE
Suffolk

**Hill House** ★★★★
*Bed & Breakfast*
Kelsale, Saxmundham IP17 2NZ
t (01728) 602940
e smp@hillhousekelsale.co.uk
w hillhousekelsale.co.uk

### KELVEDON
Essex

**Highfields Farm B & B**
★★★★ *Farmhouse*
Highfields Lane, Kelvedon CO5 9BJ
t (01376) 570334
e highfieldsfarm@farmersweekly.net
w highfieldsfarm.co.uk

**Swan House** ★★★
*Bed & Breakfast*
3 Swan Street, Kelvedon CO5 9NG
t (01376) 573768
e dnspiers@lineone.net
w swan-house.co.uk

### KENILWORTH
Warwickshire

**Abbey Guest House** ★★★★
*Guest House*
41 Station Road, Kenilworth CV8 1JD
t (01926) 512707
e the.abbey@btinternet.com
w abbeyguesthouse.com

**Avondale B&B** ★★★★
*Bed & Breakfast*
18 Moseley Road, Kenilworth CV8 2AQ
t (01926) 859072

**Castle Laurels Guest House**
★★★★ *Guest House*
22 Castle Road, Kenilworth CV8 1NG
t (01926) 856179
e reception@castlelaurels.co.uk
w castlelaurels.co.uk

**Enderley Guest House**
★★★★ *Guest House*
20 Queens Road, Kenilworth CV8 1JQ
t (01926) 855388
e enderleyguesthouse@supanet.com
w enderleyguesthouse.com

**Ferndale House** ★★★★
*Guest House*
45 Priory Road, Kenilworth CV8 1LL
t (01926) 853214
e info@kenilworth-guesthouse-accommodation.com
w kenilworth-guesthouse-accommodation.com

**Grounds Farm** ★★★★
*Bed & Breakfast*
Kenilworth CV8 1PP
t (01926) 864542
e zoe@groundsfarm.com
w groundsfarm.com

**Loweridge Guest House**
★★★★★ *Guest House*
**GOLD AWARD**
Hawkesworth Drive, Kenilworth CV8 2GP
t (01926) 859522
e info@loweridgeguesthouse.co.uk
w loweridgeguesthouse.co.uk

**Quince House** ★★★★
*Guest Accommodation*
29 Moseley Road, Kenilworth CV8 2AR
t (01926) 858652
w quincehouse.co.uk

**Victoria Lodge** ★★★★
*Guest Accommodation*
**SILVER AWARD**
180 Warwick Road, Kenilworth CV8 1HU
t (01926) 512020
e info@victorialodgehotel.co.uk
w victorialodgehotel.co.uk

### KESSINGLAND
Suffolk

**The Old Rectory Bed & Breakfast** ★★★★★
*Bed & Breakfast*
157 Church Road, Lowestoft NR33 7SQ
t (01502) 742188
e theoldrectory_kessingland@hotmail.co.uk

### KETTERING
Northamptonshire

**Dairy Farm** ★★★ *Farmhouse*
Cranford St Andrew, Kettering NN14 4AQ
t (01536) 330273

### KETTLEBASTON
Suffolk

**Box Tree Farm** ★★★★
*Farmhouse* **SILVER AWARD**
Kettlebaston, Ipswich IP7 7PZ
t (01449) 741318
e junecarpenter@btinternet.com
w boxtreefarm.350.com

### KETTLEBURGH
Suffolk

**Church Farm** ★★★
*Farmhouse*
Kettleburgh, Woodbridge IP13 7LF
t (01728) 723532
e jbater@suffolkonline.net
w churchfarmkettleburgh.co.uk

### KEXBY
Lincolnshire

**The Grange** ★★★ *Farmhouse*
Kexby, Gainsborough DN21 5PJ
t (01427) 788265

### KEYWORTH
Nottinghamshire

**Vine Lodge** ★★★★
*Bed & Breakfast*
8 Highbury Road, Keyworth, Nottingham NG12 5JB
t (0115) 937 3944
e enquiries@vine-lodge.co.uk
w vine-lodge.co.uk

### KIDDERMINSTER
Worcestershire

**Bewdley Hill House** ★★★★
*Guest House*
8 Bewdley Hill, Kidderminster DY11 6BS
t (01562) 60473
e info@bewdleyhillhouse.co.uk
w bewdleyhillhouse.co.uk

**The Brook House** ★★★★
*Bed & Breakfast*
**SILVER AWARD**
Hemming Way, Chaddesley Corbett, Kidderminster DY10 4SF
t (01562) 777453
e enquiries@thebrookhouse.co.uk
w thebrookhouse.co.uk

**Collingdale** ★★★
*Guest House*
197 Comberton Road, Kidderminster DY10 1UE
t (01562) 515460
e collingdale@sharvell.fsnet.co.uk

**Garden Cottages** ★★★★
*Guest House* **GOLD AWARD**
Crossway Green, Hartlebury, Stourport-on-Severn DY13 9SL
t (01299) 250626
e accommodation@gardencottages.co.uk
w gardencottages.co.uk

**Hollies Farm Cottage B&B**
★★★★ *Farmhouse*
Hollies Lane, Franche, Kidderminster DY11 5RW
t (01562) 745677
e info@holliesfarmcottage.co.uk
w holliesfarmcottage.co.uk

### KIMBOLTON
Herefordshire

**Lower Bache House** ★★★★
*Bed & Breakfast*
Kimbolton, Leominster HR6 0ER
t (01568) 750304
e leslie.wiles@care4free.net
w smoothhound.co.uk/hotels/lowerbache

### KINGS CAPLE
Herefordshire

**Ruxton Farm** ★★★★
*Farmhouse*
Kings Caple, Hereford HR1 4TX
t (01432) 840493

### KING'S CLIFFE
Northamptonshire

**19 West Street** ★★★★
*Bed & Breakfast*
Kings Cliffe, Peterborough PE8 6XB
t (01780) 470365
e kjhl_dixon@hotmail.com
w kingjohnhuntinglodge.co.uk

### KINGS LANGLEY
Hertfordshire

**67 Hempstead Road** ★★
*Bed & Breakfast*
King's Langley WD4 8BS
t (01923) 400453
e ian.macpherson17@ntlworld.com

### KING'S LYNN
Norfolk

**Beeches Guesthouse**
★★★★
*Guest Accommodation*
2 Guanock Terrace, King's Lynn PE30 5QT
t (01553) 766577
e kelvin.sellers@virgin.net
w beechesguesthouse.co.uk

**Fairlight Lodge** ★★★★
*Guest Accommodation*
79 Goodwins Road, King's Lynn PE30 5PE
t (01553) 762234
e enquiries@fairlightlodge.co.uk
w fairlightlodge.co.uk

**King's Lynn YHA** ★★ *Hostel*
Thoresby College, College Lane, King's Lynn PE30 1JB
t 0870 770 5902

**Maranatha Guesthouse**
★★★ *Guest House*
115-117 Gaywood Road, King's Lynn PE30 2PU
t (01553) 774596
e maranathaguesthouse@yahoo.co.uk
w maranathaguesthouse.co.uk

**Marsh Farm** ★★★★
*Farmhouse*
Wolferton, King's Lynn PE31 6HB
t (01485) 540265
e info@marshfarmbedandbreakfast.co.uk
w marshfarmbedandbreakfast.co.uk

**Old Rectory** ★★★★
*Guest Accommodation*
33 Goodwins Road, King's Lynn PE30 5QX
t (01553) 768544
e clive@theoldrectory-kingslynn.com
w theoldrectory-kingslynn.com

### KINGSLAND
Herefordshire

**The Corners Inn** ★★★★ *Inn*
Kingsland, Leominster HR6 9RY
t (01568) 708385
w cornersinn.co.uk

## KINGSTHORNE Herefordshire

**Pullastone** ★★★★
*Bed & Breakfast*
Kingsthorn, Hereford, Hereford HR2 8AQ
t (01981) 540450
e info@pullastone.com
w pullastone.com

## KINGTON Herefordshire

**Arrow Weir House** ★★★★
*Bed & Breakfast*
Kingswood Road, Kington HR5 3HD
t (01544) 231780
e info@arrowweirhouse.co.uk
w arrowweirhouse.co.uk

**Kington Youth Hostel**
★★★★ *Hostel*
Victoria Road, Kington HR5 3BX
t (01544) 232745
e kington@yha.org.uk
w yha.org.uk

## KINNERLEY Shropshire

**Meadowbank Lodge** ★★★★
*Bed & Breakfast*
**SILVER AWARD**
Dovaston, Kinnerley, Oswestry SY10 8DP
t (01691) 682023
e meadowbanklodge@hotmail.com
w meadowbanklodge.co.uk

## KIRBY CANE Norfolk

**Butterley House** ★★★★
*Bed & Breakfast*
Leet Hill Farm, Kirby Cane, Bungay NR35 2HJ
t (01508) 518301

## KIRKBY-ON-BAIN Lincolnshire

**Rose Cottage** ★★★★
*Guest Accommodation*
Wharf Lane, Kirkby-on-Bain LN10 6YW
t (01526) 354932
e info@rosecottagebandb.net
w rosecottagebandb.net

## KIRMINGTON Lincolnshire

**Blink Bonny Bed and Breakfast** ★★★ *Guest House*
Grimsby Road, Kirmington DN39 6YQ
t (01652) 680610
e info@blinkbonnybedandbreakfast.co.uk
w blinkbonnybedandbreakfast.co.uk

## KISLINGBURY Northamptonshire

**The Nook** ★★ *Farmhouse*
5 The Green, Northampton NN7 4AH
t (01604) 830326

**Olde Red Lion** ★★ *Inn*
15 High Street, Kislingbury NN7 4AG
t (01604) 830219
w theolderedlion.com

## KNAPTOFT Leicestershire

**Bruntingthorpe Farmhouse B&B** ★★★★ *Farmhouse*
Knaptoft House Farm & The Greenway, Bruntingthorpe Road, Lutterworth LE17 6PR
t (0116) 247 8388
e info@knaptofthousefarm.com
w knaptoft.co.uk

## KNEBWORTH Hertfordshire

**Goldhill** ★★★★
*Bed & Breakfast*
10 Deards End Lane, Knebworth SG3 6NL
t (01438) 813230
e tengoldhill@hotmail.com
w maryharris.co.uk

## KNIGHTWICK Worcestershire

**The Talbot** ★★★★ *Inn*
Bromyard Road, Knightwick, Worcester WR6 5PH
t (01886) 821235
e info@the-talbot.co.uk
w the-talbot.co.uk

## KNIPTON Leicestershire

**Manners Arms** ★★★★
*Restaurant with Rooms*
Croxton Road, Knipton, Grantham NG32 1RH
t (01476) 879222
e info@mannersarms.com
w mannersarms.com

## KNOWLE West Midlands

**Ivy House Guest House**
★★★ *Guest House*
Warwick Road, Heronfield, Knowle B93 0EB
t (01564) 770247
e john@ivy-guest-house.freeserve.co.uk

## LAKENHEATH Suffolk

**Paradise Lodge** ★★★★
*Guest Accommodation*
Highbridge Gravel Road, Lakenheath, Brandon IP27 9HD
t (01842) 862963
w paradiselodgefishery.co.uk

## LANGHAM Essex

**Oak Apple Farm** ★★★★
*Bed & Breakfast*
Greyhound Hill, Langham, Colchester CO4 5QF
t (01206) 272234
e oak_apple_farm@btinternet.com
w smoothhound.co.uk/hotels/oak

## LANGHAM Norfolk

**Home Close** ★★★★
*Guest Accommodation*
North Street, Holt NR25 7DG
t (01328) 830348
e patallen@lineone.net
w homecloselangham.co.uk

## LANGWORTH Lincolnshire

**The Blackbirds** ★★★
*Guest House*
Wragby Road, Langworth LN3 5DH
t (01522) 754404
e matthew.nellist@theblackbirds.co.uk
w theblackbirds.co.uk

**Ferry House Farm** ★★★
*Bed & Breakfast*
Low Barlings, Langworth LN3 5DG
t (01522) 751939
e ifleet@barlings.demon.co.uk
w barlings.demon.co.uk

## LARLING Norfolk

**Angel Inn** ★★★★ *Inn*
Larling, Norwich NR16 2QU
t (01953) 717963
w tiscover.co.uk

## LATCHINGDON Essex

**Crouch Valley Lodge** ★★★
*Guest Accommodation*
Burnham Road, Latchingdon CM3 6EX
t (01621) 740770
e reservations@crouchvalley.com
w crouchvalley.com

## LAVENHAM Suffolk

**Angel Gallery** ★★★★
*Bed & Breakfast*
17 Market Place, Lavenham, Sudbury CO10 9QZ
t (01787) 248417
e angel-gallery@gofornet.co.uk
w lavenham.co.uk

**Brett Farm** ★★★★
*Bed & Breakfast*
The Common, Sudbury, Lavenham CO10 9PG
t (01787) 248533
e brettfarmbandb@aol.com
w brettfarm.com

**Erindor** ★★★★
*Bed & Breakfast*
36 High Street, Lavenham, Sudbury CO10 9PY
t (01787) 249198
w erindor.co.uk

**Guinea House Bed & Breakfast** ★★★★
*Bed & Breakfast*
**SILVER AWARD**
16 Bolton Street, Lavenham, Sudbury CO10 9RG
t (01787) 249046
e gdelucy@aol.com
w guineahouse.co.uk

**Lavenham Priory** ★★★★★
*Bed & Breakfast*
**GOLD AWARD**
Water Street, Lavenham, Sudbury CO10 9RW
t (01787) 247404
e mail@lavenhampriory.co.uk
w lavenhampriory.co.uk

**Old Convent** ★★★★
*Bed & Breakfast*
**SILVER AWARD**
The Street, Kettlebaston, Ipswich IP7 7QA
t (01449) 741557
e holidays@kettlebaston.fsnet.co.uk
w kettlebaston.fsnet.co.uk

## LAXTON Nottinghamshire

**Lilac Farm** ★★★
*Guest House*
Laxton, Newark NG22 0NX
t (01777) 870376
e na@na.com

**Manor Farm** ★★★
*Farmhouse*
Moorhouse Road, Laxton, Newark NG22 0NU
t (01777) 870417

## LEA MARSTON West Midlands

**Reindeer Park Lodge**
Rating Applied For
*Bed & Breakfast*
Kingsbury Road, Sutton Coldfield B76 0DE
t (01675) 470811

## LEADENHAM Lincolnshire

**George Hotel** ★★★ *Inn*
20 High Street, Leadenham LN5 0PN
t (01400) 272251
e thegeorge.hotel@btconnect.com
w thegeorgeatleadenham.co.uk

## LEAMINGTON SPA Warwickshire

**Avenue Lodge Guest House**
★★★ *Guest House*
61 Avenue Road, Royal Leamington Spa, Leamington Spa CV31 3PF
t (01926) 338555
e avenue_lodge@yahoo.co.uk
w avenue-lodge.co.uk

**Braeside Bed & Breakfast**
★★★★ *Bed & Breakfast*
26 Temple End, Harbury, Nr Royal Leamington Spa CV33 9NE
t (01926) 613402
e rosemary@braesidebb.co.uk
w braesidebb.co.uk

**Buckland Lodge** ★★★
*Guest House*
35 Avenue Road, Royal Leamington Spa, Leamington Spa CV31 3PG
t (01926) 423843
e info@buckland-lodge.co.uk
w buckland-lodge.co.uk

**Bungalow Farm** ★★★★
*Bed & Breakfast*
Windmill Hill, Cubbington, Leamington Spa CV32 7LW
t (01926) 423276
e sheila@bungalowfarm.co.uk
w bungalowfarm.co.uk

**Charnwood Guest House**
★★★ *Guest House*
47 Avenue Road, Leamington Spa CV31 3PF
**t** (01926) 831074
**e** ray@charnwoodguesthouse.com
**w** charnwoodguesthouse.com

**The Coach House** ★★★★
*Farmhouse* **SILVER AWARD**
Snowford Hall Farm, Hunningham, Royal Leamington Spa CV33 9ES
**t** (01926) 632297
**e** the_coach_house@lineone.net
**w** http://website.lineone.net/~the_coach_house

**Corkill B&B** ★★★
*Bed & Breakfast*
27 Newbold Street, Royal Leamington Spa, Leamington Spa CV32 4HN
**t** (01926) 336303
**e** mrscorkill@aol.com

**Hedley Villa Guest House**
★★★ *Guest House*
31 Russell Terrace, Royal Leamington Spa, Leamington Spa CV31 1EZ
**t** (01926) 424504
**e** hedley_villa@hotmail.com
**w** hedleyvillaguesthouse.co.uk

**No 8 Clarendon Crescent**
★★★★ *Bed & Breakfast*
**SILVER AWARD**
Royal Leamington Spa, Leamington Spa CV32 5NR
**t** (01926) 429840
**e** lawson@lawson71.fsnet.co.uk
**w** 8clarendoncrescent.co.uk

**Victoria Park Lodge** ★★★★
*Guest House*
12 Adelaide Road, Leamington Spa CV31 3PW
**t** (01926) 424195
**e** info@victoriaparkhotelleamingtonspa.co.uk
**w** victoriaparkhotelleamingtonspa.co.uk

**York House Guest House**
★★★★ *Guest House*
9 York Road, Royal Leamington Spa, Leamington Spa CV31 3PR
**t** (01926) 424671
**e** reservations@yorkhousehotel.biz
**w** yorkhousehotel.biz

## LEDBURY
Herefordshire

**Brook House** ★★★★
*Bed & Breakfast*
Birtsmorton, Malvern WR13 6AF
**t** (01531) 650664
**e** marydowding@onetel.com
**w** brookhousemalvern.co.uk

**Orchard Cottage** ★★★
*Bed & Breakfast*
Bromyard Road, Ledbury HR8 1LG
**t** (01531) 635107

**Russet House** ★★★★
*Guest Accommodation*
Belle Orchard, Ledbury HR8 1DD
**t** (01531) 630060
**e** info@russethousebnb.co.uk
**w** russethousebnb.co.uk

**The Talbot** ★★★ *Inn*
New Street, Ledbury HR8 2DX
**t** (01531) 632963
**e** talbot@wadworth.co.uk
**w** visitledbury.co.uk/talbot

## LEEK
Staffordshire

**The Green Man** ★★★
*Guest Accommodation*
38 Compton, Leek ST13 5NH
**t** (01538) 388084
**e** diannemoir@btconnect.com
**w** greenman-guesthouse.co.uk

**The Hatcheries** ★★★
*Bed & Breakfast*
Church Lane, Leek ST13 5EX
**t** (01538) 399552
**e** jan@l33k.wanadoo.co.uk
**w** thehatcheries.co.uk

**Peak Weavers Hotel** ★★★★
*Guest House*
21 King Street, Leek ST13 5NW
**t** (01538) 383729
**e** info@peakweavershotel.co.uk
**w** peakweavershotel.co.uk

**White Hart B&B** ★★★★
*Guest Accommodation*
1 & 3 Stockwell Street, Leek ST13 6DH
**t** (01538) 372122
**e** info@whiteharttearoom.co.uk
**w** whiteharttearoom.co.uk

## LEICESTER
Leicestershire

**Abinger Guest House** ★★★
*Guest House*
175 Hinckley Road, Leicester LE3 0TF
**t** (0116) 255 4674
**e** abinger@btinternet.com
**w** leicesterguest.co.uk

**Castle Park** ★★★
*Guest Accommodation*
12 Millstone Lane, Leicester LE1 5JN
**t** (0116) 251 1000
**e** castleparkhotel@tiscali.co.uk
**w** castleparkhotel.com

**Glenfield Lodge** ★
*Guest Accommodation*
4 Glenfield Road, Leicester LE3 6AP
**t** (0116) 262 7554
**e** glenleic@aol.com
**w** glenfieldlodge.co.uk

**The Haynes** ★★★★
*Guest House*
185 Uppingham Road, Leicester LE5 4BQ
**t** (0116) 276 8973
**e** hayneshotel@yahoo.co.uk

**University of Leicester Conference Centr** ★★★
*Campus*
Stoughton Drive South, Leicester, Oadby LE2 2ND
**t** (0116) 271 9933
**e** conferences@le.ac.uk
**w** le.ac.uk/conference

**Wondai B&B** ★★★
*Bed & Breakfast*
47-49 Main Street, Newtown Linford, Leicester LE6 0AE
**t** (01530) 242728

## LEIGH SINTON
Worcestershire

**Chirkenhill Farm** ★★★★
*Farmhouse*
Sherridge Road, Leigh Sinton, Malvern WR13 5DE
**t** (01886) 832205
**e** chirkenhillbandb@tiscali.co.uk
**w** chirkenhill.co.uk

## LEINTHALL STARKES
Herefordshire

**Marlbrook Hall** ★★★★
*Farmhouse*
Elton, Ludlow, Mortimer Country SY8 2HR
**t** (01568) 770230
**e** valemorgan@hotmail.com
**w** marlbrookhall.co.uk

## LEINTWARDINE
Herefordshire

**Caradoc** ★★★★
*Bed & Breakfast*
49 Watling Street, Leintwardine, Ludlow SY7 0LL
**t** (01547) 540238
**e** robinandsue@amserve.com
**w** caradoc.org.uk

**Kinton Thatch** ★★★★
*Bed & Breakfast*
Kinton, Leintwardine, Mortimer Country SY7 0LT
**t** (01547) 540611
**w** tuckedup.com/stayat/795/kinton_thatch.php

**Lower Buckton Country House** ★★★★
*Bed & Breakfast*
**SILVER AWARD**
Buckton, Leintwardine, Wigmore & Lingen,, Mortimer Country SY7 0JU
**t** (01547) 540532
**e** carolyn@lowerbuckton.co.uk
**w** lowerbuckton.co.uk

**Lower House** ★★★★
*Guest Accommodation*
Adforton, Leintwardine, Mortimer Country SY7 0NF
**t** (01568) 770223
**e** reservations@sy7.com
**w** sy7.com

**Upper Buckton** ★★★★★
*Farmhouse*
Leintwardine, Ludlow SY7 0JU
**t** (01547) 540634

**Walford Court** ★★★★
*Farmhouse*
Walford, Leintwardine, Mortimer Country SY7 0JT
**t** (01547) 540570
**e** enquiries@romanticbreak.com
**w** romanticbreak.com

## LEISTON
Suffolk

**Field End** ★★★★
*Guest House* **SILVER AWARD**
1 Kings Road, Leiston IP16 4DA
**t** (01728) 833527
**w** fieldendbedandbreakfast.co.uk

## LEOMINSTER
Herefordshire

**Copper Hall** ★★★★
*Bed & Breakfast*
134 South Street, Leominster HR6 8JN
**t** (01568) 611622
**e** sccrick@copperhall.freeserve.co.uk
**w** smoothhound.co.uk/hotels/copper

**The Farmhouse** ★★★★
*Bed & Breakfast*
Aymestrey, Mortimer Country HR6 9ST
**t** (01568) 708075
**e** farmbreakfasts@tesco.net

**Highfield** ★★★★
*Bed & Breakfast*
Newtown, Ivington Road, Leominster HR6 8QD
**t** (01568) 613216
**e** info@stay-at-highfield.co.uk
**w** stay-at-highfield.co.uk

**Ryelands** ★★★★★
*Bed & Breakfast*
**GOLD AWARD**
Ryelands Road, Leominster HR6 8QB
**t** (01568) 617575
**e** info@ryelandsbandb.co.uk
**w** ryelandsbandb.co.uk

**YHA Leominster** ★★★★
*Hostel*
The Priory, Leominster HR6 8EQ
**t** (01568) 620517
**e** leominster@yha.org.uk
**w** yha.org.uk

## LESSINGHAM
Norfolk

**The Star Inn** ★★★ *Inn*
Star Inn, School Road, Lessingham, Norwich NR12 0DN
**t** (01692) 580510
**e** info@thestarlessingham.co.uk
**w** thestarlessingham.co.uk

## LEVINGTON
Suffolk

**Lilac Cottage** ★★★★
*Bed & Breakfast*
Levington Green, Ipswich IP10 0LE
**t** (01473) 659509
**e** lenandjo.wenham@btinternet.com

## LICHFIELD
Staffordshire

**32 Beacon Street** ★★★★
*Bed & Breakfast*
Lichfield WS13 7AJ
**t** (01543) 262378
**e** liz&ray.allen@service-deli.com

**Altair House** ★★
*Bed & Breakfast*
21 Shakespeare Avenue, Lichfield WS14 9BE
**t** (01543) 252900

**Bogey Hole (The)** ★★★★
*Guest House*
21-23 Dam Street, Lichfield WS13 6AE
**t** (01543) 264303

**Coppers End Guest House** ★★★★ *Guest House*
Walsall Road, Muckley Corner, Lichfield WS14 0BG
**t** (01543) 372910
**e** info@coppersendguesthouse.co.uk
**w** coppersendguesthouse.co.uk

**Davolls Cottage** ★★★★
*Bed & Breakfast*
156 Woodhouses Road, Burntwood WS7 9EL
**t** (01543) 671250

**The Maples** ★★
*Bed & Breakfast*
38 Balmoral Close, Lichfield WS14 9SP
**t** (01543) 255645
**e** javincen@tiscali.co.uk

**Old Rectory** ★★★★
*Bed & Breakfast*
**GOLD AWARD**
Mavesyn Ridware, Lichfield WS15 3QE
**t** (01543) 490792
**e** sandra@oldrectory-mavesyn.co.uk
**w** oldrectory-mavesyn.co.uk

**Poppies** ★★★★
*Bed & Breakfast*
6 Millbrook Drive, Lichfield WS14 0JL
**t** (01543) 480652
**e** bill.whitney@btinternet.com

**Spires View** ★★★
*Bed & Breakfast*
4 Friary Road, Lichfield WS13 6QL
**t** (01543) 306424
**e** tarra@spiresviewbnb.co.uk
**w** spiresviewbnb.co.uk

## LIGHTHORNE
Warwickshire

**Church Hill Farm B & B** ★★★★ *Farmhouse*
Lighthorne, Warwick CV35 0AR
**t** (01926) 651251
**e** sue@churchhillfarm.co.uk
**w** churchhillfarm.co.uk

## LILLESHALL
Shropshire

**Lilleshall National Sports Centre** ★★★ *Campus*
Lilleshall Hall, Lilleshall, Newport TF10 9AT
**t** (01952) 603003
**e** enquiries@lilleshall.co.uk
**w** lilleshallnsc.co.uk

## LINCOLN
Lincolnshire

**202 Guesthouse** ★★★★
*Guest Accommodation*
202 West Parade, Lincoln LN2 1RN
**t** (01522) 878642
**e** steve-omeara@btinternet.com
**w** 202guesthouse.co.uk

**Aaron Whisby Guest House** ★★★ *Guest House*
262 West Parade, Lincoln LN1 1LY
**t** (01522) 526930
**e** aaron-whisby@hotmail.co.uk
**w** aaron-whisby.webeden.co.uk

**Creston Villa Guest House** ★★★★★ *Guest House*
**SILVER AWARD**
27 St Catherines, Lincoln LN5 8LW
**t** (01522) 872511
**e** info@crestonvilla.co.uk
**w** crestonvilla.co.uk

**Crossfell**
Rating Applied For
*Bed & Breakfast*
16 Worcester Close, Lincoln LN6 3LW
**t** (01522) 683538
**e** crossfellbandb@yahoo.co.uk

**Damon's Motel** ★★★★
*Guest Accommodation*
997 Doddington Road, Lincoln LN6 3SE
**t** (01522) 887733
**e** motel@damons.co.uk
**w** damons.co.uk

**Duke William Inn** ★★★ *Inn*
44 Bailgate, Lincoln LN1 3AP
**t** (01522) 533351
**e** enquiries@dukewilliam.com
**w** dukewilliam.com

**Goodlane B&B** ★★★
*Bed & Breakfast*
31 Good Lane, Lincoln LN1 3EH
**t** (01522) 542994 & 07778 061494
**e** sue@goodlane.co.uk
**w** goodlane.co.uk

**Hamiltons** ★★
*Guest Accommodation*
2 Hamilton Road, Lincoln LN5 8ED
**t** (01522) 528243
**w** hamiltonhotel.co.uk

**Ivory Guest House** ★★★★
*Guest Accommodation*
258 West Parade, Lincoln LN1 1LY
**t** (01522) 887868
**e** ivoryguesthouse@hotmail.co.uk

**Lincoln YHA** ★ *Hostel*
77 South Park, Lincoln LN5 8ES
**t** (01522) 522076
**e** lincoln@yha.org.uk
**w** yha.org.uk

**Manor Farm Stables B+B** ★★★★ *Bed & Breakfast*
Manor Farm, Broxholme LN1 2NG
**t** (01522) 704220
**e** pfieldson@lineone.net
**w** manorfarmstables.co.uk

**The Old Bakery Restaurant with Rooms** ★★★★
*Restaurant with Rooms*
**SILVER AWARD**
26/28 Burton Road, Lincoln LN1 3LB
**t** (01522) 576057
**e** enquiries@theold-bakery.co.uk
**w** theold-bakery.co.uk

**Old Rectory Guest House** ★★★ *Guest House*
19 Newport, Lincoln LN1 3DQ
**t** (01522) 514774

**The Old Vicarage** ★★★★
*Guest Accommodation*
**SILVER AWARD**
East Street, Nettleham, Lincoln LN2 2SL
**t** (01522) 750819
**e** susan@oldvic.net
**w** oldvic.net

**Savill Guest House** ★★★★
*Guest Accommodation*
203 Yarborough Road, Lincoln LN1 3NQ
**t** (01522) 523261
**e** info@savillguesthouse.co.uk
**w** savillguesthouse.co.uk

**Welbeck Cottage B&B** ★★★★ *Bed & Breakfast*
19 Meadow Lane, South Hykeham, Lincoln LN6 9PF
**t** (01522) 692669
**e** maggied@hotmail.co.uk

**Wheelwright's Cottage B&B** ★★★★ *Bed & Breakfast*
Wheelwright's Cottage, Haddington LN5 9EF
**t** (01522) 788154
**e** dawn.dunning2@btopenworld.com
**w** wheelwrightsbnb.co.uk

## LINGEN
Herefordshire

**Willey Lane Farm** ★★★★
*Farmhouse*
Lower Willey, Presteigne LD8 2LU
**t** (01544) 267148
**e** juliamurray@willeylane.co.uk
**w** willeylane.co.uk

## LINGWOOD
Norfolk

**Station House**
Rating Applied For
*Bed & Breakfast*
26 Station Road, Norwich NR13 4AZ
**t** (01603) 715872
**w** stationhouse.line.com

## LINTON
Derbyshire

**The Manor** ★★★★
*Guest Accommodation*
**SILVER AWARD**
Hillside Road, Linton, Swadlincote DE12 6RA
**t** (01283) 761177
**e** themanor@ukonline.co.uk

## LITCHAM
Norfolk

**Hanworth House** ★★★★
*Guest Accommodation*
Pound Lane, King's Lynn PE32 2QR
**t** (01328) 701172
**e** cfstewart@breathemail.net
**w** hanworthhouse.com

## LITTLE BEALINGS
Suffolk

**Timbers** ★★★
*Guest Accommodation*
Martlesham Road, Little Bealings, Woodbridge IP13 6LY
**t** (01473) 622713
**w** tiscover.co.uk

## LITTLE BYTHAM
Lincolnshire

**The Willoughby Arms** ★★★★ *Inn*
Station Road, Little Bytham, Stamford NG33 4RA
**t** (01780) 410276
**e** lkulme@tiscali.co.uk

## LITTLE CAWTHORPE
Lincolnshire

**The Royal Oak Inn – The Splash** ★★★★ *Inn*
Watery Lane, Little Cawthorpe, Louth LN11 8LZ
**t** (01507) 600750
**e** info@royaloaksplash.co.uk
**w** royaloaksplash.co.uk

## LITTLE COMPTON
Warwickshire

**The Old School** ★★★★★
*Guest Accommodation*
**SILVER AWARD**
Little Compton, Moreton-in-Marsh GL56 0SL
**t** (01608) 674588
**e** wendy@theoldschoolbedandbreakfast.com
**w** theoldschoolbedandbreakfast.com

## LITTLE COWARNE
Herefordshire

**The Three Horseshoes Inn** ★★★ *Inn*
Little Cowarne, Bromyard HR7 4RQ
**t** (01885) 400276

## LITTLE CRESSINGHAM
Norfolk

**Sycamore House B&B** ★★★★
*Guest Accommodation*
Sycamore House, Little Cressingham, Thetford IP25 6NE
**t** (01953) 881887
**e** j.wittridge@btinternet.com

## LITTLE DOWNHAM
Cambridgeshire

**Bury House Bed And Breakfast** ★★★
*Bed & Breakfast*
11 Main Street, Little Downham, Ely CB6 2ST
t (01353) 698766
e p.ambrose@amserve.com

## LITTLE EASTON
Essex

**Roslyns** ★★★★
*Bed & Breakfast*
**SILVER AWARD**
Duck Street, Little Easton, Great Dunmow CM6 2JF
t (01371) 852177
e clare@roslynsbandb.co.uk
w roslynsbandb.co.uk

## LITTLE HALLINGBURY
Hertfordshire

**SWAY** ★★★★
*Bed & Breakfast*
Wrights Green, Bishop's Stortford CM22 7RH
t (01279) 723572
e caroleedwards112@aol.com
w swayaccommodation.co.uk/tariff.htm

## LITTLE INKBERROW
Worcestershire

**Perrymill Farm** ★★★
*Bed & Breakfast*
Inkberrow, Worcester WR7 4JQ
t (01386) 792177
e alexander@perrymill.com

## LITTLE NESS
Shropshire

**Hollies Farm** ★★★
*Bed & Breakfast*
Valeswood, Little Ness, Shrewsbury SY4 2LH
t (01939) 261046
e janetwakefield@btinternet.com

## LITTLE SAMPFORD
Essex

**Bush Farm** ★★★★
*Guest Accommodation*
**SILVER AWARD**
Bush Lane, Little Sampford, Saffron Walden CB10 2RY
t (01799) 586636
e angelabushfarm@yahoo.co.uk

## LITTLE SHELFORD
Cambridgeshire

**Ayah-Villa**
Rating Applied For
*Guest Accommodation*
157 Shelford Road, Cambridge CB2 5EU
t (01223) 844818
e admin@ayah-villa.co.uk
w ayah-villa.co.uk

## LITTLE STAUGHTON
Bedfordshire

**Robins Reach**
Rating Applied For
*Bed & Breakfast*
Top End, Little Staughton, St Neots MK44 2BY
t (01234) 376889
e bnb@robinsreach.co.uk
w robinsreach.co.uk

## LITTLE WALSINGHAM
Norfolk

**The Old Bakehouse Tea Room & Guesthouse**
Rating Applied For
*Guest Accommodation*
33 High Street, Little Walsingham, Walsingham NR22 6BZ
t (01328) 820454
e theoldbakehouse guesthouse@yahoo.co.uk
w glavenvalley.co.uk/oldbakehouse

## LITTLE WALTHAM
Essex

**Channels Lodge** ★★★★
*Guest Accommodation*
**GOLD AWARD**
Belsteads Farm Lane, Little Waltham, Chelmsford CM3 3PT
t (01245) 441547
e info@channelslodge.co.uk
w channelslodge.co.uk

---

**Little Belsteads** ★★★★
*Bed & Breakfast*
Back Lane, Little Waltham, Chelmsford CM3 3PP
t (01245) 360249

## LITTLEPORT
Cambridgeshire

**Glebe House** ★★★★
*Bed & Breakfast*
**SILVER AWARD**
Littleport, Ely CB6 1RG
t (01353) 862924
e info@glebehouseuk.co.uk
w glebehouseuk.co.uk

---

**Killiney House** ★★★★★
*Bed & Breakfast*
**GOLD AWARD**
18 Barkhams Lane, Littleport, Ely CB6 1NN
t (01353) 860404
e enquiries@killineyhouse.co.uk
w killineyhouse.co.uk

## LITTON
Derbyshire

**Ashleigh B&B**
Rating Applied For
*Bed & Breakfast*
Ashleigh, Buxton SK17 8QU
t (01298) 873135
e peterbrown459@hotmail.com

---

**Beacon House** ★★★★
*Farmhouse*
Litton, Tideswell, Buxton SK17 8QP
t (01298) 871752
e laurajane117@hotmail.com

---

**Hall Farm House** ★★★★
*Bed & Breakfast*
**SILVER AWARD**
Litton, Buxton SK17 8QP
t (01298) 872172
e jfscott@waitrose.com
w users.waitrose.com/~jfscott

## LODDON
Norfolk

**Hall Green Farm B&B** ★★★★
*Guest Accommodation*
Norton Road, Loddon NR14 6DT
t (01508) 522039
e hallgreenfarm@hotmail.com
w hallgreenfarm.co.uk

## LONG BUCKBY
Northamptonshire

**Murcott Mill** ★★★★
*Farmhouse*
Murcott, Long Buckby, Northampton NN6 7QR
t (01327) 842236
e carrie.murcottmill@virgin.net
w murcottmill.com

## LONG CLAWSON
Leicestershire

**Elms Farm** ★★★★
*Bed & Breakfast*
52 East End, Long Clawson, Melton Mowbray LE14 4NG
t (01664) 822395
e elmsfarm@whittard.net
w whittard.net

## LONG COMPTON
Warwickshire

**Butlers Road Farm** ★★★
*Farmhouse*
Long Compton, Shipston-on-Stour CV36 5JZ
t (01608) 684262
e eileen@butlersroad.com
w butlersroadfarm.co.uk

## LONG MELFORD
Suffolk

**Denmark House** ★★★★
*Bed & Breakfast*
Hall Street, Long Melford, Sudbury CO10 9JD
t (01787) 378798
e info@denmarkhousebb.co.uk
w denmarkhousebb.co.uk

---

**High Street Farmhouse** ★★★★ *Bed & Breakfast*
**SILVER AWARD**
High Street, Long Melford, Sudbury CO10 9BD
t (01787) 375765
e mail@gallopingchef.co.uk
w highstreetfarmhouse.co.uk

## LONG STRATTON
Norfolk

**Greenacres Farm** ★★★★
*Bed & Breakfast*
Wood Green, Long Stratton NR15 2RR
t (01508) 530261
e greenacresfarm@tinyworld.co.uk
w abreakwithtradition.co.uk

## LONGDON
Staffordshire

**Grand Lodge** ★★★★
*Bed & Breakfast*
Horsey Lane, Rugeley WS15 4LW
t (01543) 686103
e grandlodge@edbroemt.demon.co.uk

## LONGNOR
Staffordshire

**Nab End Camping Barn**
*Camping Barn*
Nab End Farm, Hollinsclough, Buxton SK17 0RJ
t (01298) 83225
e david@nabendfarm.co.uk
w nabendfarm.co.uk

---

**Spring Cottage B&B** ★★★★
*Guest Accommodation*
Leek Road, Longnor, Buxton SK17 0PA
t (01298) 83101
e garry.roe1@btopenworld.com

## LONGTOWN
Herefordshire

**Olchon Cottage Farm** ★★★
*Farmhouse*
Mountain Road, Longtown, Golden Valley HR2 0NS
t (01873) 860233
e ivy@olchon.wanadoo.co.uk

## LOUGHBOROUGH
Leicestershire

**Charnwood Lodge** ★★★★
*Guest House*
136 Leicester Road, Loughborough LE11 2AQ
t (01509) 211120
e reservations@charnwoodlodge.com
w charnwoodlodge.com

---

**Forest Rise Hotel** ★★★
*Guest House*
55-57 Forest Road, Loughborough LE11 3NW
t (01509) 215928

---

**Garendon Park** ★★★
*Guest House*
92 Leicester Road, Loughborough LE11 2AQ
t (01509) 236557
e info@garendonparkhotel.co.uk
w morningtonweb.com/garendon

---

**Highbury Guest House** ★★★★ *Guest House*
146 Leicester Road, Loughborough LE11 2AQ
t (01509) 230545
e cosmo@thehighburyguesthouse.co.uk
w thehighburyguesthouse.co.uk

---

**Lane End Cottage** ★★★★
*Bed & Breakfast*
**SILVER AWARD**
School Lane, Woodhouse, Loughborough LE12 8UJ
t (01509) 890706
e maryj.hudson@btinternet.com

---

**The Mountsorrel** ★★★★
*Guest House*
217 Loughborough Road, Mountsorrel, Loughborough LE12 7AR
t (01509) 412627
e info@mountsorrelhotel.co.uk
w mountsorrelhotel.co.uk

**New Life Guest House**
★★★★ *Guest House*
121 Ashby Road, Loughborough LE11 3AB
t (01509) 216699
e jean-of-newlife@ntlworld.com
w smoothhound.co.uk/hotels/newlife

**Peachnook Guest House** ★★
*Guest Accommodation*
154 Ashby Road, Loughborough LE11 3AG
t (01509) 264390

## LOUGHTON
Essex

**9 Garden Way** ★★
*Bed & Breakfast*
Loughton IG10 2SF
t (020) 8508 6134

**Forest Edge** ★★★
*Bed & Breakfast*
61 York Hill, Loughton IG10 1HZ
t (020) 8508 9834
e arthur@catterallarthur.fsnet.co.uk

## LOUTH
Lincolnshire

**Masons Arms** ★★★ *Inn*
Cornmarket, Louth LN11 9PY
t (01507) 609525
e justin@themasons.co.uk
w themasons.co.uk

**Nutty Cottage Guest House**
★★★★ *Bed & Breakfast*
Nutty Cottage, Legbourne Road, Louth LN11 8LQ
t (01507) 601766
e janeandmike23@tiscali.co.uk

**The Old Rectory, Stewton**
★★★★ *Bed & Breakfast*
Stewton, Louth LN11 8SF
t (01507) 328063
e ajp100@postmaster.co.uk
w louthbedandbreakfast.co.uk

**The Travellers Bed and Breakfast** ★★★★
*Guest House*
The Travellers Hotel, Upgate, Louth LN11 9HG
t (01507) 602765
e cj.sowter@btinternet.com
w thetravellers.yourfreehosting.net/

## LOWER LOXLEY
Staffordshire

**The Grange** ★★★★
*Bed & Breakfast*
Uttoxeter ST14 8RZ
t (01889) 502021
e mary.grange@hotmail.co.uk

## LOWESTOFT
Suffolk

**Britten House** ★★★★★
*Guest House*
Kirkley Cliff Road, Lowestoft NR33 0DB
t (01502) 573950
e ann_ceresa@yahoo.com
w brittenhouse.co.uk

**Fairways Bed and Breakfast**
★★★★ *Bed & Breakfast*
288 Normanston Drive, Oulton Broad, Lowestoft NR32 2PS
t (01502) 582756
e info@fairwaysbb.co.uk
w fairwaysbb.co.uk

**Homelea Guest House** ★★★
*Guest House*
Marine Parade, Lowestoft NR33 0QN
t (01502) 511640
e maroulla.keith@googlemail.com
w homeleaguesthouse.co.uk

**Lorne Guest House** ★★★
*Guest House*
4 Pakefield Road, Lowestoft NR33 0HS
t (01502) 568972
w tiscover.co.uk

**Saint Catherines House**
★★★ *Bed & Breakfast*
186 Denmark Road, Lowestoft NR32 2EN
t (01502) 500951
w tiscover.co.uk

**The Sandcastle** ★★★★
*Guest House* **SILVER AWARD**
35 Marine Parade, Lowestoft NR33 0QN
t (01502) 511799
e susie@thesandcastle.co.uk
w thesandcastle.co.uk

## LOXLEY
Warwickshire

**Elm Cottage** ★★★
*Bed & Breakfast*
Stratford Road, Loxley, Stratford-upon-Avon CV35 9JW
t (01789) 840609

**Loxley Guest House**
Rating Applied For
*Guest Accommodation*
Stratford Road, Warwick CV35 9JN
t (01789) 840092
e enquiries@loxleyguesthouse.co.uk
w loxleyguesthouse.co.uk

## LUDHAM
Norfolk

**Broadland Bed and Breakfast** ★★★★
*Bed & Breakfast*
West End Lodge, Norwich Road, Great Yarmouth NR29 5PB
t (01692) 678420
e westendlodge@btinternet.com
w bedbreakfast-norfolkbroads.co.uk

## LUDLOW
Shropshire

**Bromley Court** ★★★★
*Bed & Breakfast*
18-20 Lower Broad Street, Ludlow SY8 1PQ
t (01584) 876996 & 07809 699665
e phil@ludlowhotels.com
w ludlowhotels.com

**The Bull** ★★★
*Guest Accommodation*
14 The Bull Ring, Ludlow SY8 1AD
t (01584) 873611
e info@bull-ludlow.co.uk
w bull-ludlow.co.uk

**Cecil Guest House** ★★★
*Guest House*
Sheet Road, Ludlow SY8 1LR
t (01584) 872442

**The Church Inn** ★★★★ *Inn*
The Buttercross, Ludlow SY8 1AW
t (01584) 872174
e reception@thechurchinn.com
w thechurchinn.com

**The Clive Bar and Restaurant With Rooms**
★★★★★
*Restaurant with Rooms*
**SILVER AWARD**
Bromfield, Ludlow SY8 2JR
t (01584) 856565 & (01584) 856665
e info@theclive.co.uk
w theclive.co.uk

**DeGreys** ★★★★★
*Guest Accommodation*
**SILVER AWARD**
5-6 Broad Street, Ludlow SY8 1NG
t (01584) 872764
e degreys@btopenworld.com
w degreys.co.uk

**Elm Lodge B&B** ★★★★
*Bed & Breakfast*
Elm Lodge, Fishmore, Ludlow SY8 3DP
t (01584) 872308
e info@elm-lodge.org.uk
w elm-lodge.org.uk

**Hen & Chickens Guest House** ★★★★ *Guest House*
103 Old Street, Ludlow SY8 1NU
t (01584) 874318
e charlotte@henandchickensgh.biz
w henandchickensgh.biz

**Henwick House** ★★★
*Bed & Breakfast*
Gravel Hill, Ludlow SY8 1QU
t (01584) 873338
e info@henwickhouse.co.uk
w henwickhouse.co.uk

**Longlands** ★★★★
*Farmhouse*
Woodhouse Lane, Richards Castle, Ludlow SY8 4EU
t (01584) 831636
e iankemsley@aol.com

**Mill House** ★★★★
*Bed & Breakfast*
Squirrel Lane, Lower Ledwyche, Ludlow SY8 4JX
t (01584) 872837
e millhousebnb@btopenworld.com
w virtual-shropshire.co.uk

**The Mount Guest House**
★★★★ *Guest House*
61 Gravel Hill, Ludlow SY8 1QS
t (01584) 874084
e rooms@themountludlow.co.uk
w themountludlow.co.uk

**Mr Underhill's** ★★★★★
*Restaurant with Rooms*
**GOLD AWARD**
Dinham Weir, Ludlow SY8 1EH
t (01584) 874431
w mr-underhills.co.uk

**Mulberry House** ★★★★
*Guest Accommodation*
10 Corve Street, Ludlow SY8 1DA
t (01584) 876765
e bookings@tencorvestreet.co.uk
w tencorvestreet.co.uk

**Nelson Cottage** ★★★★
*Bed & Breakfast*
Rocks Green, Ludlow SY8 2DS
t (01584) 878108
e info@ludlow.uk.com
w ludlow.uk.com

**Ravenscourt Manor**
★★★★★ *Bed & Breakfast*
**GOLD AWARD**
Woofferton, Ludlow SY8 4AL
t (01584) 711905
e elizabeth@ravenscourtmanor.plus.com
w smoothhound.co.uk/hotels/ravenscourt

**The White House** ★★★
*Bed & Breakfast*
No 4 Brand Lane, Ludlow SY8 1NN
t (01584) 875592
e karendan@enta.net
w 4brandlane.co.uk

## LUTON
Bedfordshire

**32 Blundell Road** ★★
*Guest Accommodation*
Luton LU3 1SH
t (01582) 651689
e patrick.hayes.4.@ntlworld.com

## LUTTERWORTH
Leicestershire

**Ashlawn House** ★★★★
*Guest Accommodation*
Church Lane, Dunton Bassett, Lutterworth LE17 5JZ
t (01455) 208277
e kate@ashlawnhouse.com
w ashlawnhouse.com

## LYONSHALL
Herefordshire

**Penrhos Farm** ★★★★
*Guest Accommodation*
Lyonshall, Kington HR5 3LH
t (01544) 231467
e sallyatpenrhos@aol.com
w penrhosfarm.co.uk

## MABLETHORPE
Lincolnshire

**The Cannon Guest House**
★★★ *Guest House*
7 Waterloo Road, Mablethorpe LN12 1JR
t (01507) 473148
e info@cannon-guesthouse.co.uk
w cannon-guesthouse.co.uk

**Colours Guest House**
★★★★ *Guest House*
Queens Park Close, Mablethorpe LN12 2AS
t (01507) 473427
e info@coloursguesthouse.co.uk
w coloursguesthouse.co.uk

**The Cross Guest House & Touring Park** ★★★★
*Guest Accommodation*
Alford Road, Mablethorpe LN12 1PX
**t** (01507) 477708
**e** reception@thecrossguesthouse.co.uk
**w** thecrossguesthouse.co.uk

**May House** ★★★★
*Bed & Breakfast*
40 Long Acre, Mablethorpe LN12 1JF
**t** (01507) 473664
**e** mablethorpe@btinternet.com

**Myrtle Lodge** ★★★
*Guest House*
60 Victoria Road, Mablethorpe LN12 2AJ
**t** (01507) 472228
**e** info@myrtlelodge.co.uk
**w** myrtlelodge.co.uk

## MADLEY
Herefordshire

**Shenmore Cottage** ★★★★
*Guest Accommodation*
Upper Shenmore, Madley, Hereford HR2 9NX
**t** (01981) 250507

## MAESBURY MARSH
Shropshire

**White House Vegetarian Bed & Breakfast** ★★★★
*Bed & Breakfast*
Maesbury Marsh, Oswestry SY10 8JA
**t** (01691) 658524
**e** whitehouse@maesburymarsh.co.uk
**w** maesburymarsh.co.uk

## MALDON
Essex

**Anchor Guesthouse** ★★★
*Guest House*
7 Church Street, Maldon CM9 5HW
**t** (01621) 853711
**w** tiscover.co.uk

**Limburn House** ★★★★
*Bed & Breakfast*
Wycke Hill, Maldon CM9 6SH
**t** (01621) 851392
**w** limburnhouse.co.uk

**The Limes Guesthouse**
★★★★ *Guest House*
21 Market Hill, Maldon CM9 4PZ
**t** (01621) 850350
**e** maldonlimes@ukonline.co.uk
**w** smoothhound.co.uk

**The Star House Bed And Breakfast** ★★★
*Guest Accommodation*
72 Wantz Road, Maldon CM9 5DE
**t** 07789 113954
**e** starhouse@btinternet.com

**Tatoi Bed & Breakfast**
★★★★ *Bed & Breakfast*
31 Acacia Drive, Maldon CM9 6AW
**t** (01621) 853841 & 07860 162328
**e** diana.rogers2@btinternet.com

## MALTBY LE MARSH
Lincolnshire

**Farmhouse Bed and Breakfast** ★★★ *Farmhouse*
10 Watermill Lane, Toynton All Saints, Spilsby PE23 5AG
**t** (01790) 753416
**e** tojenwills@farmhouse10.fsnet.co.uk

**Old Mill House B&B** ★★★★
*Guest Accommodation*
**SILVER AWARD**
Main Road, Alford LN13 0JP
**t** (01507) 450504
**e** pwbreeds@onetel.net
**w** oldmillmaltby.co.uk

## MALVERN
Worcestershire

**The Brambles** ★★★★
*Guest Accommodation*
**SILVER AWARD**
173 Wells Road, Malvern Wells WR14 4HE
**t** (01684) 572994
**e** bren.lawler@talk21.com
**w** thebramblesmalvern.com

**Cannara Guest House**
★★★★ *Guest House*
**SILVER AWARD**
147 Barnards Green Road, Malvern WR14 3LT
**t** (01684) 564418
**e** info@cannara.co.uk
**w** cannara.co.uk

**Clevelands** ★★★
*Bed & Breakfast*
**SILVER AWARD**
41 Alexandra Road, Malvern WR14 1HE
**t** (01684) 572164
**e** jonmargstocks@aol.com
**w** malvernbandbconsortium.co.uk

**Como House** ★★★
*Guest Accommodation*
Como Road, Malvern WR14 2TH
**t** (01684) 561486
**e** kevin@comohouse.co.uk
**w** comohouse.co.uk

**Copper Beech House**
★★★★ *Guest House*
32 Avenue Road, Malvern WR14 3BJ
**t** (01684) 565013
**e** enquiries@copperbeechhouse.co.uk
**w** copperbeechhouse.co.uk

**Cowleigh Park Farm** ★★★★
*Guest Accommodation*
Cowleigh Road, Malvern WR13 5HJ
**t** (01684) 566750
**e** cowleighpark@ukonline.co.uk
**w** cowleighparkfarm.co.uk

**Edgeworth** ★★★
*Bed & Breakfast*
4 Carlton Road, Malvern WR14 1HH
**t** (01684) 572565
**e** garlandsidney@yahoo.co.uk

**The Elms** ★★★
*Bed & Breakfast*
52 Guarlford Road, Malvern WR14 3QP
**t** (01684) 573466
**e** jili_holland@yahoo.co.uk

**Grassendale House** ★★★
*Guest Accommodation*
3 Victoria Road, Malvern WR14 2TD
**t** (01684) 893348
**e** hilarymurray@hotmail.co.uk
**w** grassendale.com

**Guarlford Grange** ★★★
*Bed & Breakfast*
**SILVER AWARD**
11 Guarlford Road, Malvern WR14 3QW
**t** (01684) 575996
**e** guarlfordgrange@msn.com

**Harmony House Malvern**
★★★ *Bed & Breakfast*
184 West Malvern Road, Malvern WR14 4AZ
**t** (01684) 891650
**e** catherine@harmonymalvern.com
**w** harmonyhousemalvern.com

**Hidelow House** ★★★★
*Bed & Breakfast*
**SILVER AWARD**
Acton Green, Acton Beauchamp, Bromyard WR6 5AH
**t** (01886) 884547
**e** hwv@hidelow.co.uk
**w** hidelow.co.uk

**Kingfisher Bed & Breakfast**
★★★★ *Bed & Breakfast*
Kingfisher Barn, Merebrook Farm, Hanley Swan WR8 0DX
**t** (01684) 311922
**e** info@kingfisher-barn.co.uk
**w** kingfisher-barn.co.uk

**Montrose House** ★★★
*Guest Accommodation*
23 Graham Road, Malvern WR14 2HU
**t** (01684) 572335
**e** info@themontrosehotel.co.uk
**w** themontrosehotel.co.uk

**The Old Coach House**
★★★★ *Bed & Breakfast*
208 Wells Road, Malvern Wells, Malvern WR14 4HD
**t** (01684) 564382
**w** coachhousemalvern.co.uk

**The Old Croque** ★★★★
*Bed & Breakfast*
**SILVER AWARD**
221 Wells Road, Malvern WR14 4HF
**t** (01684) 564522
**e** griffiths@theoldcroque.co.uk
**w** theoldcroque.co.uk

**Orchid House** ★★★★
*Bed & Breakfast*
**SILVER AWARD**
19 St Wulstans Drive, Upper Welland, Malvern WR14 4JA
**t** (01684) 568717
**e** sally@oml.demon.co.uk
**w** orchidmalvern.co.uk

**Rosendale Bed & Breakfast**
★★★★ *Bed & Breakfast*
The View, 66 Worcester Road, Malvern WR14 1NU
**t** (01684) 566159

**Thornbury House** ★★★★
*Guest House*
16 Avenue Road, Great Malvern WR14 3AR
**t** (01684) 572278
**e** thornburyhousehotel@compuserve.com
**w** thornburyhouse-hotel.co.uk

**Treherne House** ★★★★
*Bed & Breakfast*
**SILVER AWARD**
54 Guarlford Road, Malvern WR14 3QP
**t** (01684) 572445
**e** relax@trehernehouse.co.uk
**w** trehernehouse.co.uk

## MANNINGTREE
Essex

**Curlews** ★★★★
*Bed & Breakfast*
**SILVER AWARD**
Station Road, Bradfield, Manningtree CO11 2UP
**t** (01255) 870890
**e** margherita@curlewsaccommodation.co.uk
**w** curlewsacccommodation.co.uk

**Dry Dock** ★★★
*Bed & Breakfast*
Dry Dock Quay Street, Manningtree CO11 1AU
**t** (01206) 392620

**Emsworth House** ★★★★
*Bed & Breakfast*
Station Road, Ship Hill, Bradfield, Manningtree CO11 2UP
**t** (01255) 870860
**e** emsworthhouse@hotmail.com
**w** emsworthhouse.co.uk

## MANSFIELD
Nottinghamshire

**Blue Barn Farm** ★★★
*Farmhouse*
Langwith, Mansfield NG20 9JD
**t** (01623) 742248
**e** bluebarnfarm@supanet.com
**w** bluebarnfarm-notts.co.uk

## MANTON
Rutland

**Broccoli Bottom** ★★★★
*Bed & Breakfast*
**SILVER AWARD**
Wing Road, Manton, Oakham LE15 8SZ
**t** 07702 437102
**e** sally@udale.wanadoo.co.uk
**w** http://broccolibottom.mysite.wanadoo-members.co.uk

## MARCH
Cambridgeshire

**Causeway Guest House**
★★★ *Guest House*
6 The Causeway, March PE15 9NT
**t** (01354) 650823
**w** causewayguesthouse.co.uk

**Willows Motel** ★★★
*Guest Accommodation*
Elm Road, March PE15 8PS
**t** (01354) 661292
**e** info@willowsmotel.co.uk
**w** willowsmotel.co.uk

### MARCHINGTON
Staffordshire

**Forest Hills Guest House**
★★★★
*Guest Accommodation*
Moisty Lane, Marchington, Uttoxeter ST14 8JY
t (01283) 820447

### MARKET BOSWORTH
Leicestershire

**Dixie Arms** ★★★ *Inn*
6 Main Street, Market Bosworth CV13 0JW
t (01455) 290218
e enquiries@dixiearmshotel.co.uk
w dixiearmshotel.co.uk

**The Granary** ★★★
*Bed & Breakfast*
Hall Farm Hall Lane, Osbaston, Market Bosworth CV13 0BW
t (01455) 291621
e thegranary@hallfarmosbaston.co.uk

### MARKET DRAYTON
Shropshire

**Brooklands B&B** ★★★★
*Bed & Breakfast*
Adderley Road, Market Drayton TF9 3SW
t (01630) 695988
e brooklandsdirect@btinternet.com

**Crofton** ★★★★
*Bed & Breakfast*
80 Rowan Road, Market Drayton TF9 1RR
t (01630) 655484
e ericrussell@f2s.com
w stmem.com/crofton

**The Hermitage** ★★★
*Guest House*
44 Stafford Street, Market Drayton TF9 1JB
t (01630) 658508
e info@thehermitagebb.co.uk
w thehermitagebb.co.uk

### MARKET HARBOROUGH
Leicestershire

**Honeypot Lane Bed & Breakfast** ★★★★
*Bed & Breakfast*
32 Honeypot Lane, Husbands Bosworth, Lutterworth LE17 6LY
t (01858) 880836
e bandb@honeypotlane.co.uk
w honeypotlane.co.uk

**Hunters Lodge** ★★★★
*Bed & Breakfast*
Gumley, Market Harborough LE16 7RT
t (0116) 279 3744
e info@hunterslodgefoxton.co.uk
w hunterslodgefoxton.co.uk

**Langton Brook Farm** ★★★★
*Farmhouse*
Langton Road, Great Bowden, Market Harborough LE16 7EZ
t (01858) 545730
e mervyn@langtonbrookfarm.freeserve.co.uk
w langtonbrookfarm.com

### MARKET RASEN
Lincolnshire

**Beechwood Guest House**
★★★★ *Guest House*
54 Willingham Road, Market Rasen LN8 3DX
t (01673) 844043
e beechwoodgh@aol.com
w beechwoodguesthouse.co.uk

**Little Owls** ★★★★
*Farmhouse*
North End Farm, Thornton Road, North Owersby, Market Rasen LN8 3PP
t (01673) 828116
e askus@littleowls.com
w littleowls.com

**Redhurst B&B** ★★★
*Bed & Breakfast*
Redhurst, Holton cum Beckering, Market Rasen LN8 5NG
t (01673) 857927
w redhurstbandb.com

**Waveney Cottage** ★★★★
*Bed & Breakfast*
Willingham Road, Market Rasen LN8 3DN
t (01673) 843236
e jane@waveneycottage.co.uk
w waveneycottage.co.uk

### MARSHAM
Norfolk

**The Plough Inn** ★★★★ *Inn*
Old Norwich Road, Aylsham, Norwich NR10 5PS
t (01263) 735000
e enq@ploughinnmarsham.co.uk
w ploughinnmarsham.co.uk

### MARSTON MORETAINE
Bedfordshire

**Twin Lodge** ★★★★
*Bed & Breakfast*
177 Lower Shelton Road, Bedford MK43 0LP
t (01234) 767597
e pwillsmore@waitrose.com
w twinlodge.co.uk

**The White Cottage** ★★★★
*Guest House*
Marston Hill, Bedford MK43 0QJ
t (01234) 751766
e stay@thewhitecottage.frbusiness.co.uk
w thewhitecottage.net

### MARTIN
Lincolnshire

**The Stables Studio** ★★★★
*Bed & Breakfast*
94 High Street, Martin LN4 3QT
t (01526) 378528
e stablesstudio@homecall.co.uk
w stablesstudio.co.uk

### MARTIN HUSSINGTREE
Worcestershire

**Knoll Farm Bed and Breakfast** ★★★★ *Farmhouse*
Ladywood Rd, Martin Hussingtree, Worcester WR3 7SX
t (01905) 455565
e knollfarmwr3@hotmail.com
w knollfarm.co.uk

### MATHON
Herefordshire

**Weobley Cross Cottage**
★★★★ *Bed & Breakfast*
**SILVER AWARD**
South End Lane, Mathon, Malvern WR13 5PB
t (01684) 541488
e anne@hanleyinteriors.co.uk
w bedandbreakfastmalvernhills.co.uk

### MATLOCK
Derbyshire

**B&B Yew Tree Cottage**
★★★★ *Bed & Breakfast*
**SILVER AWARD**
The Knoll, Tansley, Matlock DE4 5FP
t (01629) 583862
e enquiries@yewtreecottagebb.co.uk
w yewtreecottagebb.co.uk

**Cascades Gardens** ★★★★★
*Guest Accommodation*
**SILVER AWARD**
Clatterway Hill, Bonsall, Matlock DE4 2AH
t (01629) 822464
e info@cascadesgardens.com
w cascadesgardens.com

**Ellen House** ★★★★
*Bed & Breakfast*
37 Snitterton Road, Matlock DE4 3LZ
t (01629) 55584
e anne.ellenhouse@w3z.co.uk
w ellenhousebandbmatlock.co.uk

**Packhorse Farm Bungalow**
★★★★ *Bed & Breakfast*
Foxholes Lane, Tansley, Matlock DE4 5LF
t (01629) 582781

**Riverbank House** ★★★★
*Guest House* **SILVER AWARD**
Derwent Avenue, Off Olde English Road, Matlock DE4 3LX
t (01629) 582593
e bookings@riverbankhouse.co.uk
w riverbankhouse.co.uk

**Robertswood Country House** ★★★★★
*Guest Accommodation*
**GOLD AWARD**
Farley Hill, Matlock DE4 3LL
t (01629) 55642
e robertswoodhouse@aol.com
w robertswood.co.uk

**Rosegarth** ★★★★
*Bed & Breakfast*
57 Dimple Road, Matlock DE4 3JX
t (01629) 56294
e john@crich.ndo.co.uk
w rosegarthmatlock.co.uk

**Sheriff Lodge** ★★★★
*Guest House* **GOLD AWARD**
Dimple Road, Matlock DE4 3JX
t (01629) 760760
e info@sherifflodge.co.uk
w sherifflodge.co.uk

**Town Head Farmhouse**
★★★★ *Guest House*
**SILVER AWARD**
70 High Street, Bonsall, Matlock DE4 2AR
t (01629) 823762
w townheadfarmhouse.co.uk

### MATLOCK BATH
Derbyshire

**Ashdale Guest House** ★★★
*Guest Accommodation*
92 North Parade, Matlock Bath, Matlock DE4 3NS
t (01629) 57826
e ashdale@matlockbath.fsnet.co.uk
w ashdaleguesthouse.co.uk

**The Firs** ★★★
*Guest Accommodation*
180 Dale Road, Matlock DE4 3PS
t (01629) 582426
e bernhard@thefirs180.demon.co.uk

**Fountain Villa** ★★★★
*Guest Accommodation*
86 North Parade, Matlock Bath, Matlock DE4 3NS
t (01629) 56195
e enquiries@fountainvilla.co.uk
w fountainvilla.co.uk

**Sunnybank Guest House**
★★★★
*Guest Accommodation*
**SILVER AWARD**
37 Clifton Road, Matlock Bath, Matlock DE4 3PW
t (01629) 584621
e sunnybankmatlock@aol.com
w visitpeakdistrictbedandbreakfast.co.uk

### MEDBOURNE
Leicestershire

**Homestead House** ★★★★
*Bed & Breakfast*
**SILVER AWARD**
5 Ashley Road, Medbourne, Market Harborough LE16 8DL
t (01858) 565724
e june@homesteadhouse.co.uk
w homesteadhouse.co.uk

### MELTON CONSTABLE
Norfolk

**Lowes Farm** ★★★
*Guest Accommodation*
Edgefield, Melton Constable NR24 2EX
t (01263) 712317
e davidhudson@tiscali.co.uk
w tiscover.co.uk

### MELTON MOWBRAY
Leicestershire

**Beckmill Guest House**
Rating Applied For
*Guest Accommodation*
44 Kings Road, Melton Mowbray LE13 1QF
t (01664) 852881
e lesleyfarrow476@btinternet.com
w beckmill.co.uk

**Hall Farm** ★★★★ *Farmhouse*
1 Main Street, Holwell, Melton Mowbray LE14 4SZ
t (01664) 444275
e enquiries@hallfarmholwell.co.uk
w hallfarmholwell.co.uk

**Hillside House** ★★★★
*Bed & Breakfast*
27 Melton Road, Burton Lazars, Melton Mowbray LE14 2UR
**t** (01664) 566312
**e** hillhs27@aol.com
**w** hillside-house.co.uk

**The Lodge** ★★★★
*Bed & Breakfast*
Melton Road, Scalford, Melton Mowbray LE14 4UB
**t** (01664) 444205
**e** rchfel@aol.com
**w** geocities.com/thelodgebandb

## MEOLE BRACE
Shropshire

**Meole Brace Hall** ★★★★★
*Guest Accommodation*
**SILVER AWARD**
Meole Brace, Shrewsbury SY3 9HF
**t** (01743) 235566
**e** hathaway@meolebracehall.co.uk
**w** meolebracehall.co.uk

## MEPPERSHALL
Bedfordshire

**Old Joe's** ★★ *Bed & Breakfast*
90 Fildyke Road, Meppershall, Shefford SG17 5LU
**t** (01462) 815585 & 07831 111062
**e** cih@freenet.co.uk

## MERIDEN
West Midlands

**Barnacle Farm** ★★★★
*Farmhouse*
Back Lane, Meriden, Coventry CV7 7LD
**t** (024) 7646 8875

**Bonnifinglas Guest House** ★★★ *Guest House*
3 Berkswell Road, Meriden, Coventry CV7 7LB
**t** (01676) 523193
**e** bookings@bonnifinglas.co.uk
**w** bonnifinglas.co.uk

## MICHAELCHURCH ESCLEY
Herefordshire

**The Grove Farm** ★★★★
*Farmhouse*
Michaelchurch Escley, Golden Valley HR2 0PT
**t** (01981) 510229
**e** lyn229@hotmail.com

## MIDDLETON
Derbyshire

**Castle Farm Camping Barn**
*Camping Barn*
Middleton-by-Youlgreave, Bakewell DE45 1LS
**t** (01629) 636746

## MIDDLETON
Northamptonshire

**Valley View** ★★★
*Bed & Breakfast*
3 Camsdale Walk, Middleton, Market Harborough LE16 8YR
**t** (01536) 770874

## MIDDLETON-BY-YOULGREAVE
Derbyshire

**Castle Farm** ★★★★
*Farmhouse*
Middleton-by-Youlgreave, Bakewell DE45 1LS
**t** (01629) 636746

**Smerrill Grange Farm** ★★★
*Farmhouse*
Middleton-by-Youlgrave, Bakewell DE45 1LQ
**t** (01629) 636232

## MIDDLETON CHENEY
Northamptonshire

**Gate House B&B** ★★★★
*Bed & Breakfast*
65 Main Road, Banbury OX17 2LU
**t** (01295) 711723
**e** info@gatehousemc.com
**w** gatehousemc.com

## MILLER'S DALE
Derbyshire

**YHA Ravenstor** ★★★ *Hostel*
Millers Dale, Buxton SK17 8SS
**t** 0870 770 6008
**e** ravenstor@yha.org.uk
**w** yha.org.uk

## MILLTHORPE, HOLMESFIELD
Derbyshire

**Cordwell House** ★★★★
*Bed & Breakfast*
Cordwell Lane, Millthorpe, Dronfield S18 7WH
**t** (0114) 289 0271

## MILSON
Shropshire

**Woodlands Barn** ★★★★
*Bed & Breakfast*
Church Court, Milson,, Near Cleobury Mortimer DY14 0AU
**t** (01299) 272983
**e** rjw261@btopenworld.com

## MILTON
Cambridgeshire

**Ambassador Lodge** ★★★★
*Guest Accommodation*
37 High Street, Milton, Cambridge CB24 6DF
**t** (01223) 860168
**e** ambassadorlodge@yahoo.co.uk
**w** ambassadorlodge.co.uk

## MILTON BRYAN
Bedfordshire

**Town Farm** ★★★★
*Farmhouse*
South End, Milton Bryan, Milton Keynes MK17 9HS
**t** (01525) 210001
**e** townfarm@tesco.net

## MINSTERLEY
Shropshire

**Holly House B&B** ★★★★
*Bed & Breakfast*
Bromlow, Minsterley SY5 0EA
**t** (01743) 891435
**e** paul.jaques1@btinternet.com
**w** stmem.com/hollyhouseb&b

## MOIRA
Leicestershire

**YHA National Forest**
Rating Applied For
*Hostel*
Enterprise Glade, 48 Bath Lane, Swadlincote DE12 6BD
**t** 0870 770 6141
**e** nationalforest@yha.org.uk

## MONNINGTON-ON-WYE
Herefordshire

**Dairy House Farm** ★★★★
*Farmhouse*
Monnington-on-Wye, Golden Valley HR4 7NL
**t** (01981) 500143
**e** pearson-greg@clara.co.uk
**w** dairyhousefarm.org

## MONSAL HEAD
Derbyshire

**Ruskins** ★★★★
*Guest Accommodation*
Monsal Head, Bakewell DE45 1NL
**t** (01629) 640125
**e** office@peakescapes.com
**w** peakescapes.com/ruskins.html

## MONYASH
Derbyshire

**Arbor Low B&B** ★★★
*Farmhouse*
Arbor Low, Upper Oldhams Farm, Bakewell DE45 1JS
**t** (01629) 636337
**e** nicola@arborlow.co.uk
**w** arborlow.co.uk

## MORVILLE
Shropshire

**Hannigans Farm** ★★★★
*Farmhouse*
Morville, Bridgnorth WV16 4RN
**t** (01746) 714332
**e** hannigansfarm@btinternet.com
**w** hannigans-farm.co.uk

**Hurst Farm** ★★★★
*Farmhouse*
Morville, Bridgnorth WV16 4TF
**t** (01746) 714375
**e** info@cottagefishingholidays.co.uk
**w** cottagefishingholidays.co.uk

## MOULTON
Suffolk

**37 Newmarket Road** ★★★★
*Bed & Breakfast*
Newmarket Road, Moulton, Newmarket CB8 8QP
**t** (01638) 750362
**e** dkbowes@waitrose.com

## MUCH BIRCH
Herefordshire

**The Old School** ★★★★
*Bed & Breakfast*
Much Birch, Hereford HR2 8HJ
**t** (01981) 541317
**e** carolannedixon@btinternet.com
**w** oldschoolbb.co.uk

## MUCH HADHAM
Hertfordshire

**Wheatcroft** ★★★★
*Bed & Breakfast*
Hadham Cross, Much Hadham SG10 6AP
**t** (01279) 842206

## MUCH WENLOCK
Shropshire

**Carnewydd** ★★★
*Bed & Breakfast*
Farley Road, Much Wenlock TF13 6NB
**t** (01952) 728418
**e** clive.ship@sca.com

**Danywenallt** ★★★
*Bed & Breakfast*
Farley Road, Much Wenlock TF13 6NB
**t** 07974 081618
**e** merlibobs@tiscali.co.uk
**w** stmem.com/danywenallt

**Old Quarry Cottage** ★★★★
*Bed & Breakfast*
**SILVER AWARD**
Brockton, Much Wenlock TF13 6JR
**t** (01746) 785596
**e** triciawebb@oldquarrycottage.co.uk
**w** oldquarrycottage.co.uk

**Talbot Inn** ★★★ *Inn*
High Street, Much Wenlock TF13 6AA
**t** (01952) 727077
**e** the_talbot_inn@hotmail.com
**w** the-talbot-inn.com

**Wenlock Pottery & Craft Centre** ★★★★
*Bed & Breakfast*
Shineton Street, Much Wenlock TF13 6HT
**t** (01952) 727600
**e** wenlockpots@btopenworld.com
**w** wenlockpottery.co.uk

**Wilderhope Manor YHA** ★★
*Hostel*
The John Cadbury Memorial Hostel, Much Wenlock TF13 6EG
**t** 0870 770 6090
**e** wilderhope@yha.org.uk
**w** yha.org.uk

## MUCKTON
Lincolnshire

**The Old Rectory** ★★★★
*Bed & Breakfast*
South Willingham LN8 6NG
**t** (01507) 313584
**e** paul&maureen@the-old-rectory.info
**w** uniquevenues.org.uk

## MUMBY
Lincolnshire

**Brambles** ★★★★
*Guest Accommodation*
Occupation Lane, Alford LN13 9JU
**t** (01507) 490174
**e** suescrimshaw@btinternet.com

### MUNDESLEY
Norfolk

**The Durdans ★★★★**
*Guest Accommodation*
36 Trunch Road, Mundesley, Norwich NR11 8JX
**t** (01263) 722225
**e** info@thedurdans.co.uk
**w** thedurdans.co.uk

**Overcliff Lodge ★★★★**
*Guest House*
46 Cromer Road, Mundesley NR11 8DB
**t** (01263) 720016
**e** overclifflodge@btinternet.com
**w** overclifflodge.co.uk

### MUNDFORD
Norfolk

**Colveston Manor ★★★★**
*Farmhouse*
Mundford, Thetford IP26 5HU
**t** (01842) 878218
**e** mail@colveston-manor.co.uk
**w** colveston-manor.co.uk

### MUNDHAM
Norfolk

**Grange Farm Bed & Breakfast ★★★★**
*Bed & Breakfast*
Grange Road, Norwich NR14 6EP
**t** (01508) 550027
**e** info@grangefarmcottage.rest.org.uk
**w** grangefarmcottage.rest.org.uk

### MUNSTONE
Herefordshire

**Munstone House ★★★★**
*Guest House*
Munstone, Hereford HR1 3AH
**t** (01432) 267122
**w** munstonehouse.co.uk

### NARBOROUGH
Norfolk

**Mill View Rooms ★★★★**
*Bed & Breakfast*
Main Road, King's Lynn PE32 1TE
**t** (01760) 338005
**e** narfish@supanet.com
**w** millviewbandb.co.uk

### NASSINGTON
Northamptonshire

**Fairlands ★★★★**
*Bed & Breakfast*
35 Church Street, Nassington, Peterborough PE8 6QG
**t** (01780) 783603
**e** enquiries@fairlandsbandb.co.uk
**w** fairlandsbandb.co.uk

**The Queens Head**
Rating Applied For
*Inn*
54 Station Road, Peterborough PE8 6QB
**t** (01780) 784006
**e** info@queensheadnassington.co.uk
**w** queensheadnassington.co.uk

**Sunnyside ★★★**
*Bed & Breakfast*
62 Church Street, Nassington, Peterborough PE8 6QG
**t** (01780) 782864

### NAYLAND
Suffolk

**Gladwins Farm ★★★★**
*Farmhouse*
Harpers Hill, Nayland CO6 4NU
**t** (01206) 262261
**e** gladwinsfarm@aol.com
**w** gladwinsfarm.co.uk

**The Steam Mill House**
★★★★ *Bed & Breakfast*
**SILVER AWARD**
1 Fen Street, Nayland, Colchester CO6 4HT
**t** (01206) 262818
**e** brendaassing@tiscali.co.uk
**w** thesteammillhouse.com

**White Hart Inn ★★★★★**
*Restaurant with Rooms*
**GOLD AWARD**
High Street, Nayland CO6 4JF
**t** (01206) 263382
**e** nayhart@aol.com
**w** whitehart-nayland.co.uk

### NEATISHEAD
Norfolk

**Regency Guesthouse**
★★★★ *Guest House*
**SILVER AWARD**
The Street, Neatishead, Norwich NR12 8AD
**t** (01692) 630233
**e** regencywrigley@btopenworld.com
**w** go2norfolk.co.uk

### NETHER HEYFORD
Northamptonshire

**Heyford Bed and Breakfast**
★★ *Guest House*
27 Church Street, Nether Heyford NN7 3LH
**t** (01327) 340872
**e** info@heyfordguesthouse.co.uk
**w** heyfordguesthouse.co.uk

### NETTLETON
Lincolnshire

**Nettleton Lodge Inn ★★★**
*Guest Accommodation*
Off Moortown Road (B1205), Nettleton LN7 6HX
**t** (01472) 851829
**e** pubinthewood@btinternet.com
**w** visitlincolnshire.com

### NEW BALDERTON
Nottinghamshire

**Bridge House ★★★★**
*Guest Accommodation*
**SILVER AWARD**
4 London Road, New Balderton, Newark-on-Trent NG24 3AJ
**t** (01636) 674663
**e** info@arnoldsbandb.co.uk
**w** arnoldsbandb.co.uk

### NEW BUCKENHAM
Norfolk

**Pump Court Bed and Breakfast ★★★★**
*Bed & Breakfast*
Church Street, New Buckenham, Norwich NR16 2BA
**t** (01953) 861039
**e** enquiries@pump-court.co.uk
**w** pump-court.co.uk

### NEW MILLS
Derbyshire

**Pack Horse Inn ★★★★** *Inn*
Mellor Road, New Mills, High Peak SK22 4QQ
**t** (01663) 742365
**e** info@packhorseinn.co.uk
**w** packhorseinn.co.uk

### NEW WALTHAM
North East Lincolnshire

**Peaks Top Farm ★★★★**
*Farmhouse*
Hewitts Avenue, New Waltham, Grimsby DN36 4RS
**t** (01472) 812941
**e** lmclayton@tinyworld.co.uk

### NEWARK
Nottinghamshire

**Brecks Cottage Bed and Breakfast ★★★★**
*Guest Accommodation*
Green Lane, Newark NG23 6LZ
**t** (01636) 822445

**Crosshill House Bed and Breakfast ★★★★**
*Guest Accommodation*
**SILVER AWARD**
Crosshill House, Laxton, Newark NG22 0NT
**t** (01777) 871953

**Ivy Farm B&B ★★★**
*Farmhouse*
Newark Road, Barnby in the Willows, Newark NG24 2SL
**t** (01636) 672568
**e** clare@ivyfarnewark.co.uk
**w** ivyfarmnewark.co.uk

### NEWCASTLE-UNDER-LYME
Staffordshire

**Graythwaite Guest House ★★★★**
*Guest Accommodation*
106 Lancaster Road, Newcastle-under-Lyme, Newcastle ST5 1DS
**t** (01782) 612875
**e** info@thegraythwaite.co.uk
**w** thegraythwaite.co.uk

### NEWGATE STREET
Hertfordshire

**Mulberry Lodge ★★★★**
*Guest Accommodation*
Newgate Street, Epping Green, Hertford SG13 8NQ
**t** (01707) 879652
**e** boookings@mulberrylodge.org.uk
**w** mulberrylodge.org.uk

### NEWMARKET
Suffolk

**Birdcage Walk ★★★★**
*Guest Accommodation*
**GOLD AWARD**
2 Birdcage Walk, Newmarket CB8 0NE
**t** (01638) 669456
**e** patmerry@btinternet.com
**w** birdcagewalk.co.uk

**Byerley House ★★★★**
*Bed & Breakfast*
Warrington Street, Newmarket CB8 8BA
**t** (01638) 667870
**e** bobbie@sportsdays.co.uk
**w** byerleyhouse.com

**Laurel ★★★** *Bed & Breakfast*
40 Green Road, Newmarket CB8 9BA
**t** (01638) 664461

**Meadow House ★★★★**
*Guest Accommodation*
2a High Street, Burwell, Cambridge CB25 0HB
**t** (01638) 741926
**e** hilary@themeadowhouse.co.uk
**w** themeadowhouse.co.uk

**Rosery ★★★★**
*Guest Accommodation*
15 Church Street, Exning, Newmarket CB8 7EH
**t** (01638) 577312
**e** roseryhotel@tiscali.co.uk
**w** roseryhotel.co.uk

**Sandhurst ★★★**
*Guest Accommodation*
14 Cardigan Street, Newmarket CB8 8HZ
**t** (01638) 667483 & 07714 347130
**e** crighton@rousnewmarket.freeserve.co.uk
**w** sandhurstbandb.mysite.orange.co.uk

**The Walnuts ★★★**
*Guest House*
22 Exning Road, Newmarket CB8 0AB
**t** (01638) 664121
**e** walnutsguesthouse@btinternet.com
**w** walnuts-guesthouse.co.uk

### NEWPORT
Shropshire

**Lane End Farm ★★★★**
*Bed & Breakfast*
Chetwynd, Newport TF10 8BN
**t** (01952) 550337
**e** janicepark854@aol.com
**w** stmem.com/laneendfarm

**Offley Grove Farm ★★★**
*Farmhouse*
Adbaston, Stafford ST20 0QB
**t** (01785) 280205
**e** enquiries@offleygrovefarm.co.uk
**w** offleygrovefarm.co.uk

**Pear Tree Farmhouse**
★★★★ *Bed & Breakfast*
Farm Grove, Newport TF10 7PX
**t** (01952) 811193
**e** philgreen@peartreefarm.co.uk
**w** peartreefarmhouse.co.uk

**Red Gables Country B&B**
★★★★ *Bed & Breakfast*
**SILVER AWARD**
Longford, Newport TF10 8LN
**t** (01952) 811118
**e** sandracorbett@red-gables.com
**w** red-gables.com

**Sambrook Manor** ★★★★
*Farmhouse*
Sambrook, Newport TF10 8AL
**t** (01952) 550256
**e** sambrookmanor@btconnect.com
**w** sambrookmanor.co.uk

### NEWTON SOLNEY
Derbyshire

**The Unicorn Inn** ★★★ *Inn*
Repton Road, Burton-on-Trent DE15 0SG
**t** (01283) 703324
**e** unicorn.newtonsolney@barbox.net
**w** unicorn-inn.co.uk

### NEWTON ST MARGARETS
Herefordshire

**Marises Barn** ★★★★
*Guest Accommodation*
Newton St Margarets, Hereford HR2 0QG
**t** (01981) 510101
**e** marisesbandb@aol.com
**w** marisesbarn.co.uk

### NORTH COTES
Lincolnshire

**Fleece Inn** ★★★ *Inn*
Lock Road, North Cotes DN36 5UP
**t** (01472) 388233

### NORTH FAMBRIDGE
Essex

**Ferry Boat Inn** ★★★ *Inn*
Ferry Road, North Fambridge, Chelmsford CM3 6LR
**t** (01621) 740208
**e** enquiries@ferryboatinn.net
**w** ferryboatinn.net

### NORTH HYKEHAM
Lincolnshire

**The Gables Guest House**
★★★★ *Guest House*
546 Newark Road, North Hykeham, Lincoln LN6 9NG
**t** (01522) 829102
**e** info@gablesguesthouse.com
**w** gablesguesthouse.com

### NORTH KILWORTH
Leicestershire

**Old Rectory** ★★★★
*Bed & Breakfast*
**SILVER AWARD**
Church Street, North Kilworth, Lutterworth LE17 6EZ
**t** (01858) 881130
**e** info@oldrectorybandb.co.uk
**w** oldrectorybandb.co.uk

### NORTH KYME
Lincolnshire

**Old Coach House Motel**
★★★★
*Guest Accommodation*
1 Church Lane, North Kyme LN4 4DJ
**t** (01526) 861465
**e** barbara@motel-plus.co.uk
**w** motel-plus.co.uk

### NORTH LOPHAM
Norfolk

**Church Farm House**
★★★★★
*Guest Accommodation*
**GOLD AWARD**
Church Road, North Lopham, Diss IP22 2LP
**t** (01379) 687270
**e** hosts@bassetts.demon.co.uk
**w** churchfarmhouse.org

### NORTH SOMERCOTES
Lincolnshire

**Leslie Cottage Bed and Breakfast** ★★★★
*Bed & Breakfast*
Jubilee Road, North Somercotes LN11 7LH
**t** (01507) 358734
**e** lesliecottage@msn.com
**w** lesliecottage.co.uk

### NORTH WALSHAM
Norfolk

**Bradfield House** ★★★★
*Bed & Breakfast*
19 Station Road, North Walsham NR28 0DZ
**t** (01692) 404352
**e** info@bradfieldhouse.com
**w** bradfieldhouse.com

### NORTH WOOTTON
Norfolk

**Red Cat** ★★★ *Inn*
Station Road, North Wootton, King's Lynn PE30 3QH
**t** (01553) 631244
**e** enquiries@redcathotel.com
**w** redcathotel.com

### NORTHAMPTON
Northamptonshire

**Coton Lodge** ★★★★★
*Bed & Breakfast*
West Haddon Road, Guilsborough, Northampton NN6 8QE
**t** (01604) 740215
**e** jo@cotonlodge.co.uk
**w** cotonlodge.co.uk

**Lake House Bed and Breakfast** ★★★★
*Bed & Breakfast*
Brixworth Hall Park, Brixworth, Northampton NN6 9DE
**t** (01604) 880280
**e** rosemarytuckley@talktalk.net
**w** brixworthlakehouse.com

**The Poplars** ★★★★
*Guest Accommodation*
**SILVER AWARD**
Cross Street, Moulton NN3 7RZ
**t** (01604) 643983
**e** info@thepoplarshotel.com
**w** thepoplarshotel.com

**Roade House Restaurant and Hotel** ★★★★
*Restaurant with Rooms*
**SILVER AWARD**
16 High Street, Roade, Northampton NN7 2NW
**t** (01604) 863372

### NORTHREPPS
Norfolk

**The Stables Church Farm**
★★★★
*Guest Accommodation*
**SILVER AWARD**
Church Farm, Northrepps NR27 0LG
**t** (01263) 579790
**w** tiscover.co.uk

### NORTON DISNEY
Lincolnshire

**Brills Farm** ★★★★
*Farmhouse* **SILVER AWARD**
Brills Hill, Norton Disney, Lincoln LN6 9JN
**t** (01636) 892311
**e** admin@brillsfarm-bedandbreakfast.co.uk
**w** brillsfarm-bedandbreakfast.co.uk

**River Farm House B&B**
★★★★ *Bed & Breakfast*
Clay Lane, Norton Disney LN6 9JS
**t** (01522) 788600
**e** amandajane500@aol.com
**w** pyrah.com/riverfarmhouse

### NORTON LINDSEY
Warwickshire

**Saddlebow Cottage** ★★★★
*Guest House*
Norton Lindsey, Warwick CV35 8JN
**t** (01926) 842083
**e** info@saddlebowcottage.co.uk
**w** saddlebowcottage.co.uk

### NORWICH
Norfolk

**3 Chalk Hill Road B&B** ★★★
*Bed & Breakfast*
3 Chalk Hill Road, Norwich NR1 1SL
**t** (01603) 619188
**e** moira@beauvillage.com
**w** beauvillage.com

**38 St Giles B&B**
Rating Applied For
*Guest Accommodation*
38 St Giles, Norwich NR2 1LL
**t** (01603) 662944
**e** cheeseman695@aol.com
**w** 38stgiles.co.uk

**Arbor Linden Lodge** ★★★★
*Guest House*
Linden House, 557 Earlham Road, Norwich NR4 7HW
**t** (01603) 451303
**e** info@guesthousenorwich.com
**w** guesthousenorwich.com

**Arrandale Lodge**
Rating Applied For
*Guest Accommodation*
431 Earlham Road, Norwich NR4 7HL
**t** (01603) 250150
**e** info@arrandalelodge.co.uk
**w** arrandalelodge.co.uk

**Beaufort Lodge** ★★★★
*Guest House* **SILVER AWARD**
62 Earlham Road, Norwich NR2 3DF
**t** (01603) 627928
**e** beaufortlodge@aol.com
**w** beaufortlodge.com

**Becklands** ★★★★
*Guest Accommodation*
105 Holt Road, Norwich NR10 3AB
**t** (01603) 898582
**e** becklands@aol.com
**w** becklandsguesthouse.com

**Belmonte And The Light Bar**
★★★ *Guest Accommodation*
60-62 Prince of Wales Road, Norwich NR1 1LT
**t** (01603) 622533
**e** hotelbelmonte@hotmail.com
**w** hotelbelmonte.com

**The Blue Boar Inn** ★★★★
*Inn*
259 Wroxham Road, Norwich NR7 8RL
**t** (01603) 426802
**e** blueboar@btconnect.com
**w** blueboarnorwich.co.uk

**Blue Cedar Lodge Guesthouse** ★★★
*Guest House*
391 Earlham Road, Norwich NR2 3RQ
**t** (01603) 458331

**Broadview Lodge** ★★★★
*Campus*
University of East Anglia, Earlham Road, Norwich NR4 7TL
**t** (01603) 591918
**e** guestsuite@uea.ac.uk
**w** uea.ac.uk/conferences

**Butterfly Guest House** ★★★
*Guest House*
240 Thorpe Road, Norwich NR1 1TW
**t** (01603) 437740

**By Appointment** ★★★★
*Restaurant with Rooms*
**GOLD AWARD**
25-29 St Georges Street, Norwich NR3 1AB
**t** (01603) 630730
**e** puttii@tiscali.co.uk
**w** byappointmentnorwich.co.uk

**Cavell House** ★★★★
*Bed & Breakfast*
The Common, Swardeston, Norwich NR14 8DZ
**t** (01508) 578195
**e** joljean.harris@virgin.net

**Chestnut Grove** ★★★★
*Guest House*
129 Newmarket Road, Norwich NR4 6SZ
**t** (01603) 451932
**e** bookings@chestnutgrovebb.co.uk

**Church Farm Guesthouse**
★★★★
*Guest Accommodation*
Church Street, Horsford, Norwich NR10 3DB
**t** (01603) 898020
**e** churchfarm.guesthouse@btinternet.com
**w** btinternet.com

**Cottage** ★★★★
*Guest Accommodation*
Rectory Lane, Norwich
NR16 1QU
t (01953) 789226
w thecottagenorfolk.co.uk

**Earlham Guesthouse** ★★★
*Guest House*
147 Earlham Road, Norwich
NR2 3RG
t (01603) 454169
e info@earlham-guesthouse.co.uk
w earlham-guesthouse.co.uk

**Eaton Bower** ★★★★
*Bed & Breakfast*
20 Mile End Road, Norwich
NR4 7QY
t (01603) 462204
e eaton_bower@hotmail.com
w eatonbower.co.uk

**Edmar Lodge** ★★★
*Guest Accommodation*
64 Earlham Road, Norwich
NR2 3DF
t (01603) 615599
e mail@edmarlodge.co.uk
w edmarlodge.co.uk

**Gilman Lodge Guest House**
★★★★★ *Guest House*
**SILVER AWARD**
221 Sprowston Road, Norwich
NR3 4HZ
t (01603) 447716
e gilman.lodge@ntlworld.com
w gilmanlodge.co.uk

**Ivy Dene** ★★ *Guest House*
12 Earlham Road, Norwich
NR2 3DB
t (01603) 762567
e theivydene@hotmail.co.uk

**Manor Barn House** ★★★★
*Guest Accommodation*
Back Lane, Rackheath, Norwich
NR13 6NN
t (01603) 783543
e jane.roger@manorbarnhouse.co.uk
w manorbarnhouse.co.uk

**Marlborough House** ★★★
*Guest House*
22 Stracey Road, Norwich
NR1 1EZ
t (01603) 628005

**Oakbrook House, South Norfolk's Guest House**
★★★ *Guest Accommodation*
Frith Way, Norwich NR15 2HE
t (01379) 677359
e oakbrookhouse@btinternet.com
w oakbrookhouse.co.uk

**Old Lodge** ★★★★
*Bed & Breakfast*
**SILVER AWARD**
New Road, Bawburgh, Norwich
NR9 3LZ
t (01603) 742798
e peggy@theoldlodge.freeserve.co.uk
w theoldlodge.co.uk

**Park View**
Rating Applied For
*Bed & Breakfast*
22 Harvey Lane, Norwich
NR7 0BN
t (01603) 700438
e sueno6p@aol.com
w number-6.co.uk

**Saint Edmundsbury** ★★★
*Guest House*
The Street, Old Costessey,
Norwich NR8 5DG
t (01603) 745959
e info@stedmundsbury.co.uk
w stedmundsbury.co.uk

**Wedgewood House** ★★★
*Guest Accommodation*
42 St Stephens Road, Norwich
NR1 3RE
t (01603) 625730
e stay@wedgewoodhouse.co.uk
w wedgewoodhouse.co.uk

**Wensum Guest House** ★★★
*Guest House*
225 Dereham Road, Norwich
NR2 3TF
t (01603) 621069
e info@wensumguesthouse.co.uk
w wensumguesthouse.co.uk

### NOTTINGHAM
Nottinghamshire

**The Acorn** ★★★
*Guest House*
4 Radcliffe Road, West Brigford
NG2 5FW
t (0115) 981 1297
e reservations@acorn-hotel.co.uk
w acorn-hotel.co.uk

**Andrews Private Hotel**
★★★ *Guest Accommodation*
310 Queens Road, Beeston,
Nottingham NG9 1JA
t (0115) 925 4902
e andrews.hotel@ntlworld.com
w s-h-systems.co.uk

**Elm Bank Lodge** ★★★
*Bed & Breakfast*
9 Elm Bank, Mapperley Park,
Nottingham NG3 5AJ
t (0115) 962 5493
e elmbanklodge@aol.com

**Greenwood Lodge City Guesthouse** ★★★★★
*Guest House* **GOLD AWARD**
5 Third Avenue, Sherwood
Rise, Nottingham NG7 6JH
t (0115) 962 1206

**Nelson and Railway Inn**
★★★ *Inn*
Station Road, Kimberley,
Nottingham NG16 2NR
t (0115) 938 2177

**Orchard Cottage** ★★★★
*Bed & Breakfast*
Trowell Moor, Nottingham
NG9 3PQ
t (0115) 928 0933
e orchardcottage.bandb@virgin.net
w orchardcottages.org

**P and J Hotel** ★★★
*Guest Accommodation*
Derby Road, Nottingham
NG7 2DP
t (0115) 978 3998
e enquiries@pj-hotel.co.uk
w pj-hotel.co.uk

**Yew Tree Grange** ★★★★
*Guest House*
2 Nethergate, Clifton Village,
Nottingham NG11 8NL
t (0115) 984 7562

### OAKAMOOR
Staffordshire

**Dimmingsdale YHA** ★★
*Hostel*
Little Ranger, Dimmingsdale,
Stoke-on-Trent ST10 3AS
t 0870 770 5794
e dimmingsdale@yha.org.uk
w yha.org.uk

**Ribden Farm** ★★★★
*Farmhouse*
Three Lows, Oakamoor, Alton
Towers Area ST10 3BW
t (01538) 702830
w ribden.fsnet.co.uk

**Tenement Farm Guest House** ★★★★ *Farmhouse*
Ribden, Oakamoor, Alton
Towers Area ST10 3BW
t (01538) 702333
e stanleese@aol.com
w tenementfarm.co.uk

### OAKENGATES
Shropshire

**Chellow Dene** ★★
*Bed & Breakfast*
Park Road, Malinslee, Telford
TF4 2AY
t (01952) 505917
e weh5@blueyonder.co.uk

### OAKHAM
Rutland

**17 Northgate** ★★★★
*Bed & Breakfast*
Oakham LE15 6QR
t (01572) 759271
e dane@danegould.wanadoo.co.uk
w 17northgate.co.uk

**Mayfield B&B** ★★★★
*Bed & Breakfast*
19 Ashwell Road, Oakham
LE15 6QG
t (01572) 756656
e sgbruce@onetel.com

### OASBY
Lincolnshire

**The Pinomar** ★★★★
*Bed & Breakfast*
Mill Lane, Oasby NG32 3ND
t (01529) 455400
e joturner@pinomar.fsnet.co.uk

### ODSEY
Cambridgeshire

**The Jester**
Rating Applied For
*Inn*
116 Station Road, Baldock
SG7 5RS
t (020) 8777 3636
e tu@bcinns.co.uk

### OFFCHURCH
Warwickshire

**Mill House** ★★★★
*Bed & Breakfast*
Offchurch Lane, Offchurch,
Leamington Spa CV33 9AP
t (01926) 427296
e info@millhouse-offchurch.co.uk
w millhouse-offchurch.co.uk

### OLD
Northamptonshire

**Wold Farm** ★★★★
*Farmhouse* **SILVER AWARD**
Harrington Road, Old NN6 9RJ
t (01604) 781258
w woldfarm.co.uk/

### OLD CATTON
Norfolk

**Catton Old Hall** ★★★★★
*Guest Accommodation*
**SILVER AWARD**
Lodge Lane, Old Catton,
Norwich NR6 7HG
t (01603) 419379
e enquiries@catton-hall.co.uk
w catton-hall.co.uk

### ORLETON
Worcestershire

**Rosecroft** ★★★★★
*Bed & Breakfast*
**SILVER AWARD**
Orleton, Ludlow SY8 4HN
t (01568) 780565
e gailanddavid@rosecroftorleton.freeserve.co.uk

### ORSETT
Essex

**Jays Lodge** ★★★★
*Guest Accommodation*
Chapel Farm, Baker Street,
Grays RM16 3LJ
t (01375) 891663
e info@jayslodge.co.uk
w jayslodge.co.uk

### OSBOURNBY
Lincolnshire

**Barn Gallery** ★★★★
*Bed & Breakfast*
**SILVER AWARD**
18 West Street, Osbournby
NG34 0DS
t (01529) 455631
e enquiries@barngallery.co.uk
w barngallery.co.uk

### OSGATHORPE
Leicestershire

**Royal Oak House** ★★★
*Guest House*
20 Main Street, Osgathorpe,
Coalville LE12 9TA
t (01530) 222443

### OSWESTRY
Shropshire

**BJ's** ★★ *Bed & Breakfast*
87 Llwyn Road, Oswestry
SY11 1EW
t (01691) 650205
e barbara@williams87.fsnet.co.uk

**Harthill** ★★★
*Bed & Breakfast*
80 Welsh Walls, Oswestry
SY11 1RW
t (01691) 679024
e thecatmurs@lineone.net

**Llwyn Guest House ★★**
*Bed & Breakfast*
5 Llwyn Terrace, Beatrice Street, Oswestry SY11 1HR
**t** (01691) 670746

**The Old Rectory Selattyn**
★★★ *Guest Accommodation*
Glyn Road, Selattyn, Oswestry SY10 7DH
**t** (01691) 659708
**e** maggie.barnes.b@btinternet.com

**Railway Cottage ★★**
*Bed & Breakfast*
51 Gobowen Road, Oswestry SY11 1HU
**t** (01691) 654851

**Yew Tree House**
Rating Applied For
*Bed & Breakfast*
Lower Frankton, Oswestry SY11 4PB
**t** (01691) 622126
**e** info@yewtreebandb.co.uk
**w** yewtreebandb.co.uk

### OULTON
Suffolk

**Laurel Farm ★★★★**
*Bed & Breakfast*
Hall Lane, Oulton, Lowestoft NR32 5DL
**t** (01502) 568724
**e** info@laurelfarm.co.uk
**w** laurelfarm.com

### OULTON BROAD
Suffolk

**The Mill House Bed and Breakfast ★★★★**
*Guest House* **SILVER AWARD**
53 Bridge Road, Oulton Broad, Lowestoft NR32 3LN
**t** (01502) 565038
**e** penny@themillhousebedandbreakfast.co.uk
**w** themillhousebedandbreakfast.co.uk

### OUNDLE
Northamptonshire

**2 Benefield Road ★★★★**
*Bed & Breakfast*
Peterborough PE8 4ET
**t** (01832) 273953

**Ashworth House ★★★★**
*Bed & Breakfast*
75 West Street, Oundle PE8 4EJ
**t** (01832) 275312
**e** sue@ashworthhouse.co.uk
**w** ashworthhouse.co.uk

**Castle Farm Guesthouse**
★★★★ *Guest House*
Fotheringhay, Peterborough PE8 5HZ
**t** (01832) 226200

**Lilford Lodge Farm ★★★★**
*Farmhouse*
Barnwell, Oundle, Peterborough PE8 5SA
**t** (01832) 272230
**e** trudy@lilford-lodge.demon.co.uk
**w** lilford-lodge.demon.co.uk

**The Rowan House ★★★★**
*Bed & Breakfast*
45 Hillfield Road, Oundle, Peterborough PE8 4QR
**t** (01832) 273252

### OVERSTRAND
Norfolk

**Cliff Cottage Bed and Breakfast ★★★**
*Bed & Breakfast*
18 High Street, Overstrand NR27 0AB
**t** (01263) 578179
**e** roymin@btinternet.com
**w** cliffcottagebandb.com

**Danum House ★★★**
*Guest Accommodation*
22 Pauls Lane, Overstrand NR27 0PE
**t** (01263) 579327
**w** tiscover.co.uk

### OXHILL
Warwickshire

**Stable Croft ★★★★**
*Bed & Breakfast*
Green Lane, Oxhill, Warwick CV35 0RB
**t** (01295) 680055
**e** pam@stablecroft.co.uk
**w** stablecroft.co.uk

### OXTON
Nottinghamshire

**Far Baulker Farm**
Rating Applied For
*Guest Accommodation*
Old Rufford Road, Oxton NG25 0RQ
**t** (01623) 882375
**e** j.esam@virgin.net
**w** farbaulkerfarm.info

### PAPPLEWICK
Nottinghamshire

**Forest Farm ★★** *Farmhouse*
Mansfield Road, Papplewick NG15 8FL
**t** (0115) 963 2310

### PARTNEY
Lincolnshire

**The Red Lion Inn ★★★★** *Inn*
Spilsby PE23 4PG
**t** (01790) 752271
**w** redlioninnpartney.co.uk

### PEMBRIDGE
Herefordshire

**Lowe Farm B & B ★★★★**
*Farmhouse* **GOLD AWARD**
Lowe Farm, Pembridge, Leominster HR6 9JD
**t** (01544) 388395
**e** williams_family@lineone.net
**w** bedandbreakfastlowefarm.co.uk

### PENTNEY
Norfolk

**Little Abbey Farm ★★★★**
*Farmhouse* **SILVER AWARD**
Low Road, Pentney, King's Lynn PE32 1JF
**t** (01760) 337348
**e** enquiries@littleabbeyfarm.co.uk
**w** littleabbeyfarm.co.uk

### PENTRICH
Derbyshire

**Coney Grey Farm ★★**
*Farmhouse*
Chesterfield Road, Pentrich, Ripley DE5 3RJ
**t** (01773) 833179

### PERRY
Cambridgeshire

**West Perry B&B**
Rating Applied For
*Bed & Breakfast*
38 West Perry, Perry, Huntingdon PE28 0BX
**t** (01480) 810225
**e** dianahickling@tesco.net
**w** westperrybandb.co.uk

### PERSHORE
Worcestershire

**Anchor Inn & Restaurant**
★★★ *Inn*
Cotheridge Lane, Eckington, Nr Pershore WR10 3BA
**t** (01386) 750356
**e** anchoreck@aol.com
**w** anchoreckington.co.uk

**Arbour House ★★★★**
*Bed & Breakfast*
**SILVER AWARD**
Main Road, Wyre Piddle, Pershore WR10 2HU
**t** (01386) 555833
**e** liz@arbour-house.com
**w** arbour-house.com

**The Star Inn ★★★** *Inn*
23 Bridge Street, Pershore WR10 1AJ
**t** (01386) 552704
**e** info@thestarinnpershore.com
**w** thestarinnpershore.com

**Tibbitts Farm ★★★★**
*Farmhouse*
Russell Street, Great Comberton, Pershore WR10 3DT
**t** (01386) 710210
**e** jennynewbury@btinternet.com
**w** farmstayuk.co.uk

### PETERBOROUGH
Cambridgeshire

**Aragon House ★★★**
*Guest House*
75-77 London Road, Peterborough PE2 9BS
**t** (01733) 563718
**e** aragonhouse@tiscali.co.uk
**w** aragonhouse.co.uk

**The Brandon ★★★**
*Guest Accommodation*
161 Lincoln Road, Peterborough PE1 2PW
**t** (01733) 568631
**e** enquiries@brandonhotel.co.uk

**Graham Guesthouse ★★★**
*Guest House*
296 Oundle Road, Peterborough PE2 9QA
**t** (01733) 567824

**Longueville Guesthouse**
★★★★ *Guest House*
Oundle Road, Orton Longueville, Peterborough PE2 7DA
**t** (01733) 233442
**e** maureen.glover@ntlworld.com

**Park Road Guesthouse**
★★★ *Guest House*
67 Park Road, Peterborough PE1 2TN
**t** (01733) 562220
**e** booking@parkrdguesthouse.co.uk
**w** parkrdguesthouse.co.uk

### PINWALL
Leicestershire

**The Red Lion ★★★** *Inn*
Main Road, Atherstone CV9 3NB
**t** (01827) 712223
**e** redlionpinwall@btconnect.com

### PLESHEY
Essex

**Bury Farm ★★★★**
*Bed & Breakfast*
**SILVER AWARD**
Bury Road, Pleshey, Chelmsford CM3 1HB
**t** (01245) 237234
**e** anne@oates.u-net.com
**w** burybarncottage.co.uk

### POLSTEAD
Suffolk

**Polstead Lodge ★★★★**
*Bed & Breakfast*
Mill Street, Polstead CO6 5AD
**t** (01206) 262196
**e** howards@polsteadlodge.freeserve.co.uk
**w** polsteadlodge.com

### PONTRILAS
Herefordshire

**Station House ★★★**
*Bed & Breakfast*
Station Approach, Pontrilas, Golden Valley HR2 0EH
**t** (01981) 240564
**e** gwrstation04@tesco.net

### PRIESTCLIFFE
Derbyshire

**Highfield B & B**
Rating Applied For
*Bed & Breakfast*
Buxton SK17 9TN
**t** (0118) 930 2504
**e** theslackies@tiscali.co.uk

### PRIORS HARDWICK
Warwickshire

**Hill Farm ★★★** *Farmhouse*
Lower End, Priors Hardwick, Southam CV47 7SP
**t** (01327) 260338
**e** simon.darbishire@farming.co.uk
**w** stayathillfarm.co.uk

### PULHAM MARKET
Norfolk

**Old Bakery ★★★★★**
*Guest Accommodation*
**GOLD AWARD**
The Old Bakery, Church Walk, Pulham Market IP21 4SL
**t** (01379) 676492
**e** info@theoldbakery.net
**w** theoldbakery.net

## PULVERBATCH
### Shropshire

**Lane Farmhouse B&B ★★★**
*Farmhouse*
Wilderley, Pulverbatch, Shrewsbury SY5 8DF
t (01743) 718935
e info@lanefarmhouse.co.uk
w lanefarmhouse.co.uk

## QUARNFORD
### Staffordshire

**Gradbach Mill YHA ★★★**
*Group Hostel*
Gradbach, Buxton SK17 0SU
t (01260) 227625
e gradbachmill@yha.org.uk
w yha.org.uk

## RACKHEATH
### Norfolk

**Barn Court ★★★**
*Guest Accommodation*
6 Back Lane, Rackheath, Norwich NR13 6NN
t (01603) 782536
e barncourtbb@hotmail.com

**Hill Farm Lodge ★★★★**
*Bed & Breakfast*
Wroxham Road, Rackheath, Norwich NR13 6NE
t (01603) 720093
e patandclive.marshall@virgin.net
w hillfarmlodge.co.uk

## RADFORD SEMELE
### Warwickshire

**Hill Cottage ★★★**
*Guest House*
78 Southam Road, Radford Semele, Leamington Spa CV31 1UA
t (01926) 427636
e hillcott78@aol.com

## RAMSEY
### Cambridgeshire

**Shire Lodge ★★★★**
*Bed & Breakfast*
Warboys Road, Bury, Huntingdon PE26 2NU
t (01487) 711927
e s.turner4@homecall.co.uk
w shirelodge.com

## RAMSEY
### Essex

**Roborough ★★★**
*Bed & Breakfast*
Church Hill, Ramsey, Harwich CO12 5EU
t (01255) 880417

## RATCLIFFE CULEY
### Leicestershire

**Barn Farm Bed & Breakfast**
★★ *Farmhouse*
Sibson Road, Ratcliffe Culey, Hinckley CV9 3PH
t (01827) 713338

## RATLINGHOPE
### Shropshire

**Bridges Youth Hostel (Long Mynd)** ★★ *Hostel*
Ratlinghope, Shrewsbury SY5 0SP
t (01588) 650656
w yha.org.uk

## REARSBY
### Leicestershire

**Manor Farm ★★★**
*Farmhouse*
Brookside, Rearsby, Melton Mowbray LE7 4YB
t (01664) 424239
e timpalmer@ukfarming.co.uk
w farmstayuk.co.uk

## REDDITCH
### Worcestershire

**White Hart Inn ★★★** *Inn*
157 Evesham Road, Redditch B97 5EJ
t (01527) 545442
e enquiries@whitehartredditch.co.uk

## RENDHAM
### Suffolk

**Rendham Hall ★★★**
*Farmhouse*
Rendham, Saxmundham IP17 2AW
t (01728) 663440
e dc.strachan@onetel.com
w farmstayanglia.co.uk/database/page.php?farmno=nsfh65

## RETFORD
### Nottinghamshire

**The Barns Country Guest House, The ★★★★**
*Guest House*
Morton Farm, Babworth, Retford DN22 8HA
t (01777) 706336
e enquiries@thebarns.co.uk
w thebarns.co.uk

**Bolham Manor ★★★★**
*Bed & Breakfast*
**SILVER AWARD**
Off Tiln Lane, Retford DN22 9JG
t (01777) 703528
e pamandbutch@bolham-manor.com
w bolham-manor.com/

## REYDON
### Suffolk

**Ridge Bed And Breakfast**
★★★★ *Bed & Breakfast*
14 Halesworth Road, Reydon IP18 6NH
t (01502) 724855
e jules.heal@btinternet.com
w southwold.ws/ridge

## RICKINGHALL
### Suffolk

**Grangers ★★★★**
*Bed & Breakfast*
Garden House Lane, Rickinghall, Diss IP22 1EA
t (01379) 897210
e jan@grangersbandb.co.uk

## RIDGEWELL
### Essex

**The White Horse Inn**
★★★★ *Inn*
Mill Road, Ridgewell, Halstead CO9 4SG
t (01440) 785532
e enquries@ridgewellwhitehorse.com
w ridgewellwhitehorse.com

## RIPLEY
### Derbyshire

**B&B at The Latte Lounge**
★★ *Guest Accommodation*
15 Church Street, Ripley DE5 3BU
t (01773) 512000
e misscagarner@hotmail.com

**Bowling Green Bed & Breakfast ★★**
*Bed & Breakfast*
Blacksmiths Croft, Ripley DE5 8JL
t (01773) 742921

**Hellinside ★★**
*Bed & Breakfast*
1/3 Whitegates, Codnor, Ripley DE5 9QD
t (01773) 742750
e hellinside@aol.com

## RISBY
### Suffolk

**Highwaymans B&B**
Rating Applied For
*Guest Accommodation*
Heath Barn Farm, Risby, Bury St Edmunds IP28 6QP
t (01284) 810283
e info@highwaymans.co.uk
w highwaymans.co.uk

## ROSS-ON-WYE
### Herefordshire

**Broome Farm ★★★★**
*Bed & Breakfast*
Peterstow, Ross-on-Wye HR9 6QG
t (01989) 562824
e broomefarm@tesco.net
w broomefarmhouse.co.uk

**Linden House ★★★**
*Guest House*
14 Church Street, Ross-on-Wye HR9 5HN
t (01989) 565373
e pat@lindenguesthouse.com
w lindenguesthouse.com

**Lumleys B & B ★★★★**
*Bed & Breakfast*
**SILVER AWARD**
Kerne Bridge, Bishop Wood, Ross-on-Wye HR9 5TQ
t (01600) 890040
e helen@lumleys.force9.co.uk
w lumleys.force9.co.uk

**Norton House ★★★★**
*Guest Accommodation*
**GOLD AWARD**
Whitchurch, Ross-on-Wye HR9 6DJ
t (01600) 890046
e su@norton.wyenet.co.uk
w norton-house.com

**Sunnymount ★★★★**
*Guest Accommodation*
Ryefield Road, Ross-on-Wye HR9 5LU
t (01989) 563880
e sunnymount@tinyworld.co.uk

**Walnut Tree Cottage**
★★★★ *Guest House*
**SILVER AWARD**
Symonds Yat West, Symonds Yat HR9 6BN
t (01600) 890828
e enquiries@walnuttreehotel.co.uk
w walnuttreehotel.co.uk

**The White House Guest House ★★★** *Guest House*
Wye Street, Ross-on-Wye HR9 7BX
t (01989) 763572
e whitehouseross@aol.com
w whitehouseross.com

## ROUGHAM GREEN
### Suffolk

**Oak Farm Barn ★★★★**
*Bed & Breakfast*
**SILVER AWARD**
Rougham, Bury St Edmunds IP30 9JU
t (01359) 270014
e oakfarmbarn@tiscali.co.uk
w oakfarmbarn.co.uk

## ROWSLEY
### Derbyshire

**The Old Station House**
★★★★ *Bed & Breakfast*
4 Chatsworth Road, Rowsley, Matlock DE4 2EJ
t (01629) 732987
e enquiries@oldstationhousebandborg.uk
w oldstationhousebandb.org.uk

## ROYDON
### Essex

**Riverside Guesthouse**
★★★★
*Guest Accommodation*
218 High Street, Roydon, Harlow CM19 5EQ
t (01279) 792332
e info@riversideguesthouse.biz
w riversideguesthouse.biz

## ROYSTON
### Hertfordshire

**Hall Farm ★★★★**
*Guest Accommodation*
Hall Lane, Great Chishill Nr Royston SG8 8SH
t (01763) 838263
e wisehall@tiscali.co.uk
w hallfarmbb.co.uk

**New Farm ★★★** *Farmhouse*
Chrishall, Royston SG8 8RJ
t (01763) 838282
e nfwiseman@waitrose.com

## RUCKLAND
### Lincolnshire

**Woody's Top Youth Hostel**
★★★ *Hostel*
Woody's Top, Ruckland, Louth LN11 8RQ
t 0870 770 8868
e woodystop@yha.org.uk
w yha.org.uk

## RUGBY
### Warwickshire

**The Carlton ★★★★**
*Guest Accommodation*
130 Railway Terrace, Rugby CV21 3HE
t (01788) 560211
e carlton-hotel@btconnect.com
w thecarltonrugby.com

**Courtyard ★★★★**
*Guest House*
Toft House, Toft, Rugby CV22 6NR
t (01788) 810540

**Diamond House** ★★★
*Guest House*
28-30 Hillmorton Road, Rugby CV22 5AA
t (01788) 572701
e diamondhouse2830@aol.com
w diamondhousehotel.co.uk

**Lawford Hill Farm** ★★★★
*Farmhouse* **SILVER AWARD**
Lawford Heath Lane, Lawford Heath, Rugby CV23 9HG
t (01788) 542001
e lawford.hill@talk21.com
w lawfordhill.co.uk

**Village Green** ★★★★
*Guest Accommodation*
The Green, Dunchurch, Rugby CV22 6NX
t (01788) 813434
e info@villagegreenhotel.co.uk
w villagegreenhotel.co.uk

**White Lion Inn** ★★★ *Inn*
Coventry Road, Pailton, Rugby CV23 0QD
t (01788) 832359
w whitelionpailton.co.uk

## RUGELEY Staffordshire

**Park Farm** ★★ *Farmhouse*
Hawksyard, Armitage Lane, Rugeley WS15 1ED
t (01889) 583477

## RUSHTON SPENCER Staffordshire

**Heaton House Farm** ★★★★
*Farmhouse*
Rushton Spencer, Macclesfield SK11 0RD
t (01260) 226203
e mick@heatonhouse.fsnet.co.uk
w heatonhousefarm.co.uk

## RUSKINGTON Lincolnshire

**Sunnyside Farm** ★★★
*Farmhouse*
Leasingham Lane, Ruskington, Sleaford NG34 9AH
t (01526) 833010
e sunnyside_farm@btinternet.com
w sunnysidefarm.co.uk

## SAFFRON WALDEN Essex

**Ashleigh House** ★★★
*Guest Accommodation*
7 Farmadine Grove, Saffron Walden CB11 3DR
t (01799) 513611
e info@ashleighhouse.dabsol.co.uk
w ashleighhouse.dabsol.co.uk

**Bell House** ★★★★
*Bed & Breakfast*
Castle Street, Saffron Walden CB10 1BD
t (01799) 527857

**Buriton House** ★★★★
*Bed & Breakfast*
Station Road, Newport CB11 3PL
t (01799) 542237
e buriton_house@hotmail.com
w tiscover.co.uk

**Chapmans** ★★
*Bed & Breakfast*
30 Lambert Cross, Saffron Walden CB10 2DP
t (01799) 527287

**The Cricketers** ★★★★ *Inn*
**SILVER AWARD**
Wicken Road, Clavering, Saffron Walden CB11 4QT
t (01799) 550442
e info@thecricketers.co.uk
w thecricketers.co.uk

**Redgates Farmhouse**
★★★★ *Bed & Breakfast*
Redgates Lane, Ashdon Road, Saffron Walden CB10 2LP
t (01799) 516166
w tiscover.co.uk

**Rockells Farm** ★★★★
*Farmhouse*
Duddenhoe End, Saffron Walden CB11 4UY
t (01763) 838053
e evert.westerhuis@tiscali.co.uk
w rockellsfarm.co.uk

**Rowley Hill Lodge** ★★★★
*Bed & Breakfast*
**SILVER AWARD**
Little Walden Road, Little Walden, Saffron Walden CB10 1UZ
t (01799) 525975
e rhlbandb@onetel.com

**Saffron Walden YHA** ★★
*Hostel*
2 Myddylton Place, Saffron Walden CB10 1BB
t (01799) 523117
e saffron@yha.org.uk
w yha.org.uk

**Victoria House** ★★
*Bed & Breakfast*
10 Victoria Avenue, Saffron Walden CB11 3AE
t (01799) 525923
w tiscover.co.uk

## ST ALBANS Hertfordshire

**16 York Road** ★★★
*Bed & Breakfast*
St Albans AL1 4PL
t (01727) 853647
w tiscover.co.uk

**178 London Road** ★★★
*Bed & Breakfast*
St Albans AL1 1PL
t (01727) 846726
e bookings_178londonroad@btconnect.com
w 178londonroad.co.uk

**2 The Limes** ★★
*Bed & Breakfast*
Spencer Gate, St Albans AL1 4AT
t (01727) 831080
e hunter.mitchell@virgin.net

**22 Ardens Way** ★★★★
*Bed & Breakfast*
Marshalswick, St Albans AL4 9UJ
t (01727) 861986
e beteddickens@btinternet.com

**36 Potters Field** ★★
*Bed & Breakfast*
St Albans AL3 6LJ
t (01727) 766840
e manners_smith@ntlworld.com

**5 Approach Road** ★
*Bed & Breakfast*
St Albans AL1 1SP
t 07944 837533
e eileenvkent@aol.com

**7 Marlborough Gate** ★★★
*Bed & Breakfast*
St Albans AL1 3TX
t (01727) 865498
e michael.jameson@btinternet.com

**Avona** ★★★ *Bed & Breakfast*
478 Hatfield Road, St Albans AL4 0SX
t (01727) 842216
e murchu@ntlworld.com

**Braemar House** ★★★★
*Bed & Breakfast*
89 Salisbury Avenue, St Albans AL1 4TY
t (01727) 839641
e slatersbraemar@btinternet.com
w braemar-st-albans.co.uk

**Carousel Guest House** ★★★
*Bed & Breakfast*
122 Hatfield Road, St Albans AL1 4HY
t (01727) 850004
e sandra.woodland@ntlworld.com

**Fern Cottage** ★★★★
*Bed & Breakfast*
116 Old London Road, St Albans AL1 1PU
t (01727) 834200
e bookinginfo@ferncottage.uk.net
w ferncottage.uk.net

**The Greens** ★★★★
*Bed & Breakfast*
56 Sandpit Lane, St Albans AL1 4BW
t (01727) 856799
e yvonnegreen@talktalk.net

**Margarets B&B** ★★
*Bed & Breakfast*
16 Broomleys, St Albans AL4 9UR
t (01727) 862421

**Oaktree House** ★★★★
*Bed & Breakfast*
512 Hatfield Road, St Albans AL4 0SX
t (01727) 857521

**Park House** ★★
*Bed & Breakfast*
30 The Park, St Albans AL1 4RY
t (01727) 811910
e nora@parkhouseonline.co.uk

**Riverside** ★★★★
*Bed & Breakfast*
**SILVER AWARD**
24 Minister Court, St Albans AL2 2NF
t (01727) 758780
e ellispatriciam@ntlworld.com

**Tresco** ★★★ *Bed & Breakfast*
76 Clarence Road, St Albans AL1 4NG
t (01727) 864880
e pat_leggatt@hotmail.com
w geocities.com/patleggatt/index.htm

**White House** ★★
*Bed & Breakfast*
28 Salisbury Avenue, St Albans AL1 4TU
t (01727) 861017

## ST IVES Cambridgeshire

**Cheriton House** ★★★★★
*Guest Accommodation*
**SILVER AWARD**
Mill Street, Houghton PE28 2AZ
t (01480) 464004
e sales@cheritonhousecambs.co.uk
w cheritonhousecambs.co.uk

**Forty Winks** ★★★★
*Bed & Breakfast*
3 Laburnum Way, St Ives PE27 3YW
t (01480) 465117
e 40winks@waitrose.com

**The Old Ferry Boat Inn**
Rating Applied For
*Guest Accommodation*
Back Lane, St Ives PE27 4TG
t (01462) 436411
e 8638@greeneking.co.uk
w oldenglish.co.uk

## ST NEOTS Cambridgeshire

**Nags Head** ★★★★
*Guest Accommodation*
2 Berkley Street, Eynesbury, St Neots PE19 2NA
t (01480) 476812
e nags.stneots@btconnect.com
w stneots.co.uk/nagshead/main.htm

## ST OWENS CROSS Herefordshire

**The New Inn** ★★★ *Inn*
St Owens Cross, Ross-on-Wye HR2 8LQ
t (01989) 730274
e info@newinn.biz
w newinn.biz

## SANDY Bedfordshire

**Highfield Farm** ★★★★★
*Farmhouse* **SILVER AWARD**
Tempsford Road, Great North Road, Sandy SG19 2AQ
t (01767) 682332
e margaret@highfield-farm.co.uk
w highfield-farm.co.uk

**Pantiles** ★★★★
*Bed & Breakfast*
6 Swaden, Sandy SG19 2DA
t (01767) 680668
e pantilesbandb@live.com
w thepantilesbandb.co.uk

**The Tythe Barn** ★★★★
*Bed & Breakfast*
Drove Road, Gamlingay, Sandy SG19 2HT
t (01767) 650156
e thetythebarn@supanet.com
w tythebb.co.uk

**Village Farm** ★★★★
*Farmhouse*
Thorncote Green, Sandy
SG19 1PU
t (01767) 627345

### SAWBRIDGEWORTH Hertfordshire

**7 Church Walk** ★★
*Bed & Breakfast*
Sawbridgeworth CM21 9BJ
t (01279) 723233
e kent@sawbridgeworth.co.uk
w ourbedandbreakfast.co.uk

### SAWTRY Cambridgeshire

**A1 Bed And Breakfast** ★★
*Guest Accommodation*
5 High Street, Sawtry,
Huntingdon PE28 5SR
t (01487) 830201
e john.pat@a1bedandbreakfast.co.uk
w a1bedandbreakfast.co.uk

### SAXILBY Lincolnshire

**Orchard Cottage** ★★★★
*Bed & Breakfast*
3 Orchard Lane, Saxilby
LN1 2HT
t (01522) 703192
e margaretallen@orchardcottage.org.uk
w smoothhound.co.uk/hotels/orchardcot

### SAXLINGHAM THORPE Norfolk

**Foxhole Farm** ★★★★
*Bed & Breakfast*
Saxlingham Thorpe, Norwich
NR15 1UG
t (01508) 499226
e foxholefarm@hotmail.com
w tiscover.co.uk

### SAXMUNDHAM Suffolk

**The Bell** ★★★★
*Restaurant with Rooms*
31 High Street, Saxmundham
IP17 1AF
t (01728) 602331
e enquiries@bellhotel-saxmundham.co.uk
w bellhotel-saxmundham.co.uk

**Georgian Guest House**
★★★★★ *Guest House*
**SILVER AWARD**
6 North Entrance,
Saxmundham IP17 1AY
t (01728) 603337
e enquiries@thegeorgian-house.com
w thegeorgian-house.com

**Honeypot Lodge** ★★★★
*Bed & Breakfast*
Aldecar Lane, Benhall Green,
Saxmundham IP17 1HN
t (01728) 602449
e enquiries@honeypotlodge.co.uk
w saxmundham.info

**Moat House Farm** ★★★★
*Bed & Breakfast*
**GOLD AWARD**
Rendham Road, Carlton,
Saxmundham IP17 2QN
t (01728) 602228
e sally@goodacres.com
w goodacres.com

### SCALDWELL Northamptonshire

**The Old House Bed and Breakfast** ★★★★
*Bed & Breakfast*
East End, Scaldwell NN6 9LB
t (01604) 880359
e mrsv@scaldwell43.fsnet.co.uk
w the-oldhouse.co.uk

### SCAMBLESBY Lincolnshire

**The Paddock at Scamblesby**
★★★★ *Bed & Breakfast*
**SILVER AWARD**
Old Main Road, Scamblesby,
Louth LN11 9XG
t 07787 998906
e steve@thepaddockatscamblesby.co.uk
w thepaddockatscamblesby.co.uk

### SCOTTER Lincolnshire

**Ivy Lodge** ★★★★
*Guest Accommodation*
4 Messingham Road, Scotter
DN21 3UQ
t (01724) 763723
e bandb@ivylodgehotel.co.uk
w ivylodgehotel.co.uk

### SCULTHORPE Norfolk

**Manor Farm Bed & Breakfast**
★★★★ *Farmhouse*
**SILVER AWARD**
Manor Farm, Sculthorpe,
Fakenham NR21 9NJ
t (01328) 862185
e carol@manorfarmbandb.fsworld.co.uk
w manorfarmbandb.com

**Sculthorpe Mill** ★★★ *Inn*
Lynn Road, Fakenham
NR21 9QG
t (01328) 856161
e elainesbarnett@hotmail.com
w sculthorpemill.co.uk

### SCUNTHORPE Lincolnshire

**The Beverley** ★★★★
*Guest Accommodation*
55 Old Brumby Street,
Scunthorpe DN16 2AJ
t (01724) 282212
w beverleyhotelscunthorpe.co.uk

**Cocked Hat** ★★★ *Inn*
Ferry Road, Scunthorpe
DN15 8LQ
t (01724) 841538

**Cosgrove Guest House**
★★★ *Guest House*
33-35 Wells Street, Scunthorpe
DN15 6HL
t (01724) 279405

**Kirks Korner** ★★
*Guest Accommodation*
12 Scotter Road, Scunthorpe
DN15 8DR
t (01724) 855344
e paul.kirk1@ntlworld.com

**The Normanby** ★★★
*Guest House*
9-11 Normanby Road,
Scunthorpe DN15 6NU
t (01724) 289982
e jonormanby@yahoo.co.uk

### SEVERN STOKE Worcestershire

**Roseland Bed & Breakfast**
★★★★ *Bed & Breakfast*
Clifton, Severn Stoke,
Worcester WR8 9JF
t (01905) 371463
e guy@roselandworcs.demon.co.uk
w roselandworcs.demon.co.uk

### SHALFORD Essex

**Lynton House** ★★★
*Bed & Breakfast*
**SILVER AWARD**
Lynton, Church End, Braintree
CM7 5EZ
t (01371) 850975
e lynton-house@hotmail.co.uk
w lynton-house.co.uk

### SHEEN Staffordshire

**Sheen Bunkhouse** *Bunkhouse*
Peak Stones, Buxton SK17 0ES
t (01298) 84501
e grahambelfield@fsmail.net

### SHENTON Leicestershire

**Top House Farm** ★★★
*Farmhouse*
Shenton, Hinckley CV13 6DP
t (01455) 212200
e eileen_clarke@btconnect.com

### SHEPSHED Leicestershire

**Croft Guest House** ★★★
*Guest House*
21 Hall Croft, Shepshed,
Loughborough LE12 9AN
t (01509) 505657
e js@croftguesthouse.demon.co.uk
w croftguesthouse.demon.co.uk

**Grange Courtyard** ★★★★★
*Guest Accommodation*
**SILVER AWARD**
Forest Street, Shepshed,
Loughborough LE12 9DA
t (01509) 600189
e info@thegrangecourtyard.co.uk
w thegrangecourtyard.co.uk

### SHERINGHAM Norfolk

**Alverstone** ★★★
*Bed & Breakfast*
33 The Avenue, Sheringham
NR26 8DG
t (01263) 825527
w alverstone-sheringham.co.uk

**Ashcroft House Bed And Breakfast** ★★★★
*Bed & Breakfast*
15 Morris Street, Sheringham
NR26 8JY
t (01263) 822225
e carol@fenn1465.freeserve.co.uk
w tiscover.co.uk

**Bench Mark House**
★★★★★
*Guest Accommodation*
**SILVER AWARD**
32 Morley Road, Sheringham
NR26 8JE
t (01263) 823551
e benchmark.house@btinternet.com
w bench-markhouse.co.uk

**Camberley Guesthouse**
★★★★
*Guest Accommodation*
62 Cliff Road, Sheringham
NR26 8BJ
t (01263) 823101
e graham@gsimmo.co.uk
w camberleyguesthouse.co.uk

**Claremont Bed and Breakfast** ★★★★
*Bed & Breakfast*
49 Holway Road, Sheringham
NR26 8HP
t (01263) 821889
e claremontbb@googlemail.com
w claremont-sheringham.co.uk

**Cleat House** ★★★★★
*Bed & Breakfast*
**SILVER AWARD**
7 Montague Road, Sheringham
NR26 8LN
t (01263) 822765
e stay@cleathouse.co.uk
w cleathouse.co.uk

**Fairlawns** ★★★★★
*Guest House* **SILVER AWARD**
26 Hooks Hill Road,
Sheringham NR26 8NL
t (01263) 824717
w fairlawns-sheringham.co.uk

**The Melrose** ★★★
*Guest House*
9 Holway Road, Sheringham
NR26 8HN
t (01263) 823299
e jparsonage@btconnect.com
w themelrosesheringham.co.uk

**Myrtle House** ★★★
*Bed & Breakfast*
27 Nelson Road, Sheringham
NR26 8BU
t (01263) 823889
e enquiries@myrtlehouse-sheringham.co.uk
w myrtlehouse-sheringham.co.uk

**No 1 Bistro Bar B&B** ★★★
*Inn*
1 High Street, Sheringham
NR26 8JP
t (01263) 820368
e enquiries@no1sheringham.co.uk
w no1sheringham.co.uk

**Olivedale** ★★★★
*Guest Accommodation*
**SILVER AWARD**
20 Augusta Street, Sheringham
NR26 8LA
t (01263) 825871
e olivedale@btinternet.com
w olivedale.co.uk

**Pentland Lodge**
Rating Applied For
*Guest House*
51 The Avenue, Sheringham
NR26 8DQ
t (01263) 823533
e gelhanky@hotmail.com
w pentlandlodge.co.uk

**Sheringham Lodge** ★★★★
*Guest House*
Cromer Road, Sheringham
NR26 8RS
t (01263) 821954
e mikewalker19@hotmail.com
w sheringhamlodge.co.uk

**Sheringham YHA** ★★ *Hostel*
1 Cremers Drift, Sheringham
NR26 8HX
t 0870 770 6024
e sheringham@yha.org.uk
w yha.org.uk

**The Sun Deck**
Rating Applied For
*Bed & Breakfast*
10 Holway Road, Sheringham
NR26 8HN
t (01263) 823489
e andrewsparish@tiscali.co.uk

**Sunrays B&B** ★★★★
*Bed & Breakfast*
**SILVER AWARD**
29 Holt Road, Sheringham
NR26 8NB
t 07749 402309
e elainesunrays@btinternet.com
w tiscover.co.uk

**Viburnham House B&B** ★★★★
*Guest Accommodation*
**SILVER AWARD**
Augusta Street, Sheringham
NR26 8LB
t (01263) 822528
e viburnhamhouse@aol.com
w viburnhamhouse.co.uk

**White Lodge** ★★★★
*Bed & Breakfast*
28 Holt Road, Sheringham
NR26 8NB
t (01263) 822901
e peter-rowland@startline2000.fsnet.co.uk

## SHIFNAL Shropshire

**Odfellows – The Wine Bar** ★★★ *Inn*
Market Place, Shifnal
TF11 9AU
t (01952) 461517
e odfellows@odley.co.uk

## SHINGLE STREET Suffolk

**Lark Cottage** ★★★★
*Bed & Breakfast*
Shingle Street, Nr Woodbridge
IP12 3BE
t (01394) 411292

## SHIRLEY Derbyshire

**Thatched Cottage**
Rating Applied For
*Guest Accommodation*
Ashbourne DE6 3AS
t (01335) 360950
e sylandjohn@btinternet.com

## SHIRLEY West Midlands

**Baltimore House** ★★
*Bed & Breakfast*
12 Brampton Crescent, Shirley, Solihull B90 3SY
t (0121) 744 9100
e egeeborall@aol.com

## SHOBY Leicestershire

**Shoby Lodge Farmhouse** ★★★★ *Farmhouse*
**SILVER AWARD**
Shoby, Asfordby, Melton Mowbray LE14 3PF
t (01664) 812156

## SHOTLEY Suffolk

**Hill House Farm Bed & Breakfast** ★★★★ *Farmhouse*
**SILVER AWARD**
Wades Lane, Shotley, Ipswich
IP9 1EW
t 07887 941921
e hazel@wrinchfarmstay.co.uk
w wrinchfarmstay.co.uk

## SHREWSBURY Shropshire

**Abbey Court House** ★★★★
*Guest House*
134 Abbey Foregate, Shrewsbury SY2 6AU
t (01743) 364416
e info@abbeycourt.biz
w abbeycourt.biz

**Anton Guest House** ★★★★
*Bed & Breakfast*
1 Canon Street, Monkmoor, Shrewsbury SY2 5HG
t (01743) 359275
e antonguesthouse@btconnect.com
w antonhouse.com

**Avonlea** ★★ *Bed & Breakfast*
33 Coton Crescent, Coton Hill, Shrewsbury SY1 2NZ
t (01743) 359398
w stmem.com/avonlea

**Castlecote Guest House** ★★★ *Guest Accommodation*
77 Monkmoor Road, Shrewsbury SY2 5AT
t (01743) 245473
e soniataplin@yahoo.co.uk
w stmem.com/castlecoteguesthouse

**Castlegates House** ★★★★★
*Bed & Breakfast*
**SILVER AWARD**
Castle Gates, Shrewsbury
SY1 2AT
t (01743) 362395
e rachel-castlegates@hotmail.co.uk

**Charnwood** ★★★★
*Bed & Breakfast*
110 London Road, Shrewsbury
SY2 6PP
t (01743) 359196
e charnwoodguesthouse@tiscali.co.uk
w charnwoodguesthouse.co.uk

**College Hill Guest House** ★★★ *Guest Accommodation*
11 College Hill, Shrewsbury
SY1 1LZ
t (01743) 365744
w stmem.com/collegehillhouse

**Ferndell B&B** ★★★★
*Bed & Breakfast*
14 Underdale Road, Abbey Foregate, Shrewsbury SY2 5DL
t (01743) 344949
e ferndell@tiscali.co.uk
w ferndellbandb.co.uk

**Grove Farm House**
Rating Applied For
*Guest Accommodation*
Condover, Shrewsbury
SY5 7BH
t (01743) 718544
e liz@grovefarmhouse.com
w grovefarmhouse.com

**Kingsland Bed & Breakfast** ★★★ *Bed & Breakfast*
47 Kennedy Road, Shrewsbury
SY3 7AA
t (01743) 355990
e kate@kingslandbandb.com
w kingslandbandb.com

**Lyth Hill House** ★★★★
*Bed & Breakfast*
**GOLD AWARD**
28 Old Coppice, Lyth Hill, Shrewsbury SY3 0BP
t (01743) 874660
e bnb@lythhillhouse.com
w lythhillhouse.com

**North Farm** ★★★★
*Farmhouse*
Eaton Mascot, Shrewsbury
SY5 6HF
t (01743) 761031
e northfarm@btinternet.com
w northfarm.co.uk

**The Old Post Office Inn** ★★★ *Inn*
1 Milk Street, Shrewsbury
SY1 1SZ
t (01743) 236019
e info@oldpostofficepub.co.uk
w oldpostofficepub.co.uk

**The Old Station** ★★★★
*Guest House*
Leaton, Bomere Heath, Shrewsbury SY4 3AP
t (01939) 290905
e langley.cm@virgin.net
w theoldstationshropshire.co.uk

**Ye Olde Bucks Head Inn** ★★★ *Inn*
Frankwell, Shrewsbury SY3 8JR
t (01743) 369392
e adminbucksheadinn@tesco.net
w bucksheadinn.co.uk

**Prynce's Villa Guest House**
Rating Applied For
*Bed & Breakfast*
15 Monkmoor Rd, Shrewsbury
SY2 5AG
t (01743) 356217
e lawrence.wyatt@virgin.net
w stmem.com/pryncesvilla

**Rest-a-while Guest House** ★★ *Bed & Breakfast*
36 Coton Crescent, Coton Hill, Shrewsbury SY1 2NZ
t (01743) 240969
e restawhilebb@yahoo.co.uk
w virtual-shropshire.co.uk

**Sandford House** ★★★★
*Guest Accommodation*
St Julians Friars, Shrewsbury
SY1 1XL
t (01743) 343829
e sandfordhouse@lineone.net
w sandfordhouse.co.uk

**The Stiperstones Guest House** ★★★
*Guest Accommodation*
18 Coton Crescent, Coton Hill, Shrewsbury SY1 2NZ
t (01743) 246720
e thestiperstones@aol.com
w thestiperstones.com

**Sydney House** ★★★
*Guest Accommodation*
Coton Crescent, Shrewsbury
SY1 2LJ
t (01743) 354681
e sydneyhouse@sydneyhousehotel.co.uk
w sydneyhousehotel.co.uk

**Trevellion House Bed & Breakfast** ★★★★
*Bed & Breakfast*
1 Bradford Street, Monkmoor, Shrewsbury SY2 5DP
t (01743) 249582
e soniataplin@yahoo.co.uk
w stmem.com/1-bradford-street

## SIBTON Suffolk

**Park Farm** ★★★★
*Farmhouse* **SILVER AWARD**
Yoxford Road, Sibton, Saxmundham IP17 2LZ
t (01728) 668324
e mail@sibtonparkfarm.co.uk
w sibtonparkfarm.co.uk

**Sibton White Horse Inn** ★★★★ *Inn*
Halesworth Road, Sibton, Saxmundham IP17 2JJ
t (01728) 660337
e info@sibtonwhitehorseinn.co.uk
w sibtonwhitehorseinn.co.uk

## SILVERSTONE Northamptonshire

**Pembury House** ★★★★
*Guest Accommodation*
6 Brackley Road, Silverstone
NN12 8UA
t (01327) 858743
e joyce@pembury.f2s.com
w pembury.f2s.com

## SKEGNESS Lincolnshire

**Amber House ★★★**
*Guest House*
19 Scarbrough Avenue, Skegness PE25 2SZ
t (01754) 766503
e info@theamberhotel.co.uk
w theamberhotel.co.uk

**Beachlands Quality Guest Accommodation ★★★**
*Guest Accommodation*
58 Scarborough Avenue, Skegness PE25 2TB
t (01754) 764106

**Belmont Guest House ★★**
*Guest House*
30 Grosvenor Road, Skegness PE25 2DB
t (01754) 765439
e info@belmont-guesthouse.co.uk
w belmontguesthouse.co.uk

**The Chalfonts ★★★**
*Guest Accommodation*
41 Beresford Avenue, Skegness PE25 3JF
t (01754) 766374
e info@chalfontshotel.com
w chalfontshotel.com

**Chatsworth ★★★**
*Guest Accommodation*
15-16 North Parade, Skegness PE25 2UB
t (01754) 764177
e info@chatsworthhotel.co.uk
w chatsworthskegness.co.uk

**Clarence House ★★★★**
*Guest House*
32 South Parade, Skegness PE25 3HW
t (01754) 765588
e colin-rita@lineone.net
w clarence-house-hotel.co.uk

**The Craigside ★★★**
*Guest Accommodation*
26 Scarborough Avenue, Skegness PE25 2SY
t (01754) 763307
e info@craigside-hotel.co.uk
w craigside-hotel.co.uk

**The Eastleigh ★★★★**
*Guest Accommodation*
60 Scarborough Avenue, Skegness PE25 2TB
t (01754) 764605
e info@eastleigh-skegness.co.uk
w eastleigh-skegness.co.uk

**Fairfax Hotel**
Rating Applied For
*Guest Accommodation*
36 Drummond Road, Skegness PE25 3EB
t (01754) 763690
w fairfax-hotel.com

**The Fountaindale ★★★★**
*Guest Accommodation*
69 Sandbeck Avenue, Skegness PE25 3JS
t (01754) 762731
e info@fountaindale-hotel.co.uk
w fountaindale-hotel.co.uk

**The Grafton Guest House**
★★★ *Guest Accommodation*
15 Seaview Road, Skegness PE25 1BW
t (01574) 766158
e thegraftonhotelskegness@fsmail.net
w grafton-skegness.co.uk

**Grosvenor House ★★★**
*Guest Accommodation*
North Parade, Skegness PE25 2TE
t (01754) 763376
w grosvenorhotelskegness.co.uk

**Halcyon Guest House ★★★**
*Guest House*
29 Park Avenue, Skegness PE25 2TF
t (01754) 763914
e info@halcyon-guesthouse.co.uk
w halcyon-guesthouse.co.uk

**Hoylake Guest House ★★★**
*Guest House*
23 Hoylake Drive, Skegness PE25 1AB
t (01754) 765695
e chazsmith@supanet.com
w hoylakeguesthouse.co.uk

**The Karema ★★★**
*Guest House*
17 Sunningdale Drive, Skegness PE25 1BB
t (01754) 764440
e info@karema.co.uk
w karema.co.uk

**The Kildare ★★★**
*Guest Accommodation*
80 Sandbeck Avenue, Skegness PE25 3JS
t (01754) 762935
e info@kildare-hotel.co.uk
w kildare-hotel.co.uk

**Knighton Lodge ★★★**
*Guest House*
9 Trafalgar Avenue, Skegness PE25 3EU
t (01754) 764354
e info@knighton-lodge.co.uk
w knighton-lodge.co.uk

**Linroy Guesthouse ★★★**
*Guest House*
26 Lumley Avenue, Skegness PE25 2AT
t (01754) 763924
e info@linroy.co.uk
w linroy.co.uk

**The Lyndsay Guest House**
★★★★ *Guest House*
13 Scarborough Avenue, Skegness PE25 2SZ
t (01754) 765565
e lindagjones@btinternet.com
w lyndsayguesthouse.co.uk

**The Mayfair ★★★**
*Guest Accommodation*
10 Saxby Avenue, Skegness PE25 3JZ
t (01754) 764687
e info@mayfair-skegness.co.uk
w mayfair-skegness.co.uk

**Mickleton Guest House**
★★★ *Guest House*
6 North Parade Extension, Skegness PE25 1BX
t (01754) 763862
w mickleton-guesthouse.co.uk

**North Parade Seafront Accommodation ★★★**
*Guest Accommodation*
20 North Parade, Skegness PE25 2UB
t (01754) 762309
e juleebunce@aol.com
w north-parade-hotel.co.uk

**The Northdale ★★★**
*Guest Accommodation*
12 Firbeck Avenue, Skegness PE25 3JY
t (01754) 610554
e info@northdale-hotel.co.uk
w northdale-hotel.co.uk

**Palm Court Hotel ★★★**
*Guest House*
74 South Parade, Skegness PE25 3HP
t (01754) 767711
e palmcourtskegness@yahoo.co.uk
w palmcourtskegness.co.uk

**The Queen's ★★★★**
*Guest Accommodation*
49 Scarborough Avenue, Skegness PE25 2TD
t (01754) 762073

**The Quorn ★★★**
*Guest Accommodation*
11 North Parade, Skegness PE25 2UB
t (01754) 763508
e reservations@quornhotel.net
w quornhotel.net

**Roosevelt Lodge ★★★**
*Guest Accommodation*
59 Drummond Road, Skegness PE25 3EQ
t (01754) 766548
e skegnessinfo@e-lindsey.gov.uk

**The Rufford ★★★**
*Guest Accommodation*
Rufford Hotel, 5 Saxby Avenue, Skegness PE25 3JZ
t (01754) 763428
e steve@srain.wanadoo.co.uk
w ruffordhotel-skegness.com

**The Sandgate ★★★**
*Guest House*
44 Drummond Road, Skegness PE25 3EB
t (01754) 762667
e info@sandgate-hotel.co.uk
w sandgate-hotel.co.uk

**Sherwood Lodge ★★★**
*Guest House*
100 Drummond Road, Skegness PE25 3EH
t (01754) 762548
e info@sherwood-skegness.co.uk
w sherwood-skegness.co.uk

**The Singlecote ★★★**
*Guest House*
34 Drummond Road, Skegness PE25 3EB
t (01754) 764698
e mark87evans@yahoo.co.uk
w singlecotehotel.com

**Southwold ★★★**
*Guest House*
16 Sea View Road, Skegness PE25 1BW
t (01754) 611335
e info@southwold-hotel.co.uk
w southwold-hotel.co.uk

**Stoneleigh ★★★★**
*Guest House* **SILVER AWARD**
67 Sandbeck Avenue, Skegness PE25 3JS
t (01754) 769138
e info@stoneleighskegness.com
w stoneleigh-hotel.com

**Thisledome Guest House**
★★★ *Guest House*
5 Glentworth Crescent, Skegness PE25 2TG
t (01754) 612212
e info@thisledome.com
w thisledome.com

**Tudor Lodge Guest House**
★★★ *Guest House*
61-63 Drummond Road, Skegness PE25 3EQ
t (01754) 766487
e info@thetudorlodge.co.uk
w thetudorlodge.co.uk

**Westdene ★★★**
*Guest House*
1 Trafalgar Avenue, Skegness PE25 3EU
t (01754) 765168
e westdenehotel@aol.com
w westdenehotel.co.uk

**The White Lodge ★★★**
*Guest Accommodation*
129 Drummond Road, Skegness PE25 3DW
t (01754) 764120
e info@white-lodge.co.uk
w white-lodge.co.uk

**The Woodthorpe ★★★★**
*Guest House*
64 South Parade, Skegness PE25 1DL
t (01754) 763452
e info@woodthorpe-hotel.co.uk
w woodthorpe-hotel.co.uk

## SKENDLEBY Lincolnshire

**Old Post Office B&B ★★★★**
*Bed & Breakfast*
Old Post Office, Spilsby PE23 4QE
t (01754) 890588
e reg@equitable-life.com
w theoldpostofficebandb.co.uk

## SLEAFORD Lincolnshire

**The Barn**
Rating Applied For
*Bed & Breakfast*
Spring Lane, Folkingham NG34 0SJ
t (01529) 497199
e sjwright@farming.co.uk
w thebarnspringlane.co.uk

**Farthings Guest House**
★★★★ *Bed & Breakfast*
35 Northgate, Sleaford NG34 7BS
t (01529) 302354
e farthingsguesthouse@btopenworld.com


Look out for establishments participating in the National Accessible Scheme

### SMISBY
Derbyshire

**Forest Court Accommodation** ★★
*Guest Accommodation*
Anwell Lane, Smisby LE65 2TA
t (01530) 411711

**Hillside Lodge Bed & Breakfast** ★★★★
*Bed & Breakfast*
Derby Road, Smisby, Ashby-de-la-Zouch LE65 2RG
t (01530) 416411
e barbaraball2000@yahoo.co.uk
w hillsidelodge.co.uk

### SNELSTON
Derbyshire

**Oldfield House** ★★★★★
*Guest Accommodation*
**GOLD AWARD**
Snelston, Ashbourne DE6 2EP
t (01335) 324510
e s-jarvis@tiscali.co.uk

### SNETTERTON
Norfolk

**Holly House Guest House**
★★★★★ *Guest House*
**GOLD AWARD**
Holly House, Snetterton, Norwich NR16 2LG
t (01953) 498051
e jeffstonell@aol.com
w hollyhouse-guesthouse.co.uk

### SNETTISHAM
Norfolk

**The Queen Victoria** ★★★★
*Inn*
19 Lynn Road, Snettisham, King's Lynn PE31 7LW
t (01485) 541344
e bobwarburton@talk21.com
w queenvictoriasnettisham.co.uk

**Twitchers Retreat** ★★★★
*Bed & Breakfast*
**SILVER AWARD**
9 Beach Road, Snettisham, King's Lynn PE31 7RA
t (01485) 543581
e twitchers.retreat@googlemail.com
w twitchers-retreat.co.uk

### SOHAM
Cambridgeshire

**Greenbank** ★★
*Bed & Breakfast*
111 Brook Street, Soham, Ely CB7 5AE
t (01353) 720929

### SOLIHULL
West Midlands

**Acorn Guest House** ★★★
*Guest House* **SILVER AWARD**
**29 Links Drive, Solihull B91 2DJ**
**t (0121) 705 5241**
**e acorn.wood@btinternet.com**
**w acorn-guest-house.com**

**Chelsea Lodge** ★★★★
*Bed & Breakfast*
**SILVER AWARD**
48 Meriden Road, Hampton-in-Arden B92 0BT
t (01675) 442408
e chelsealodgebnb@aol.com

**No 6 Gillott Close** ★★★★
*Bed & Breakfast*
Gillott Close, Solihull B91 2QY
t (0121) 709 2279
e tcsolihull@blueyonder.co.uk

**Ravenhurst Guest House**
★★★ *Guest House*
56 Lode Lane, Solihull B91 2AW
t (0121) 705 5754
e ravenhurstaccom@aol.com

### SOUTH COCKERINGTON
Lincolnshire

**West View Bed & Breakfast**
★★★★ *Bed & Breakfast*
**SILVER AWARD**
South View Lane, South Cockerington, Louth LN11 7ED
**t (01507) 327209 & 07855 291185**
**e enquiries@west-view.co.uk**
**w west-view.co.uk**

### SOUTH CREAKE
Norfolk

**Valentine House** ★★★
*Bed & Breakfast*
62 Back Street, South Creake NR21 9PG
t (01328) 823413
e ros@valentinehouse.co.uk
w valentinehouse.co.uk

### SOUTH HYKEHAM
Lincolnshire

**Hall Farm House** ★★★★
*Farmhouse*
Meadow Lane, South Hykeham LN6 9PF
t (01522) 686432
e carol@hallfarmhouse.fsworld.co.uk
w hallfarmhouselincoln.co.uk

### SOUTH LUFFENHAM
Rutland

**Coach House Inn** ★★★★ *Inn*
Stamford Road, South Luffenham, Oakham LE15 8NT
t (01780) 720166
e lord345@aol.com

### SOUTH SCARLE
Nottinghamshire

**Greystones** ★★★★
*Bed & Breakfast*
**SILVER AWARD**
Main Street, South Scarle, Newark NG23 7JH
t (01636) 893969
e greystonesguests@tiscali.co.uk
w greystonesguests.co.uk

### SOUTH WALSHAM
Norfolk

**Leeward Bed and Breakfast**
★★★★ *Bed & Breakfast*
5 Broad Lane, South Walsham, Norwich NR13 6EE
t (01603) 270491
e a.horsfield@tiscali.co.uk
w http://mysite.wanadoo-members.co.uk/stayawhileinnorfolk

**Old Hall Farm** ★★★★
*Guest Accommodation*
**Newport Road, South Walsham, Norwich NR13 6DS**
**t (01603) 270271**
**e veronica@oldhallfarm.co.uk**
**w oldhallfarm.co.uk**

### SOUTH WILLINGHAM
Lincolnshire

**The Old Chapel Bed & Breakfast** ★★★★
*Bed & Breakfast*
The Old Chapel, Barkwith Road, South Willingham LN8 6NN
t (01507) 313395
e oldch03@yahoo.co.uk
w theoldchapelbnb.co.uk

### SOUTH WITHAM
Lincolnshire

**Blue Cow Inn and Brewery**
★★ *Inn*
29 High St, South Witham NG33 5QB
t (01572) 768432
e richard@thirlwell.fslife.co.uk
w thebluecowinn.co.uk

### SOUTHAM
Warwickshire

**Wormleighton Hall** ★★★★
*Farmhouse* **GOLD AWARD**
Wormleighton, Southam, Banbury CV47 2XQ
t (01295) 770234
e wormleightonbb-bookings@yahoo.co.uk
w wormleightonhall.com

### SOUTHEND-ON-SEA
Essex

**Arosa Guesthouse**
Rating Applied For
*Guest House*
184 Eastern Esplanade, Thorpe Bay, Southend-on-Sea SS1 3AA
t (01702) 585416
e sam_arosa@yahoo.co.uk
w arosaguesthouse.co.uk

**Gleneagles** ★★★★
*Guest Accommodation*
Clifftown Parade, Southend-on-Sea SS1 1DP
t (01702) 333635
w thegleneagleshotel.co.uk

**The Moorings B&B**
Rating Applied For
*Bed & Breakfast*
172 Eastern Esplanade, Southend-on-Sea SS1 3AA
t (01702) 587575
e mail@themooringsbedandbreakfast.com
w themooringsbedandbreakfast.com

**Pier View Guest House**
Rating Applied For
*Guest House*
5 Royal Terrace, Southend-on-Sea SS1 1DY
t (01702) 437900
e info@pierviewguesthouse.co.uk
w pierviewguesthouse.co.uk

**Pleasant Court Guest House**
★★ *Guest House*
66 Pleasant Road, Southend-on-Sea SS1 2HJ
t (01702) 467079
e tinapapworth@aol.com
w smoothhound.co.uk/hotels/pleasant-court

### SOUTHMINSTER
Essex

**New Moor Farm** ★★★★
*Farmhouse*
Tillingham Road, Southminster CM0 7DS
t (01621) 772840

### SOUTHWOLD
Suffolk

**Brendas B & B** ★★★
*Bed & Breakfast*
3 Strickland Place, Southwold IP18 6HN
t (01502) 722403
w tiscover.co.uk

**Newlands Country House**
★★★★
*Guest Accommodation*
72 Halesworth Road, Southwold IP18 6NS
t (01502) 722164
e info@newlandsofsouthwold.co.uk
w tiscover.co.uk

**Poplar Hall** ★★★★
*Bed & Breakfast*
**Frostenden Corner, Frostenden, Southwold NR34 7JA**
**t (01502) 578549**
**e poplarhall@tiscali.co.uk**
**w southwold.ws/poplar-hall**

### SPALDING
Lincolnshire

**Saville Lodge** ★★★★
*Bed & Breakfast*
11 King's Road, Spalding PE11 1QB
t (01775) 722244
e patriciabarnes@fsmail.net

**White Lodge Guest House**
★★★★★ *Guest House*
10 Helmergate, Spalding PE11 2DR
t (01775) 719002
e whitelodge@lincmail.co.uk
w whitelodge-guesthouse.com

### SPALDWICK
Cambridgeshire

**Chestnut View** ★★★★
*Guest House*
8-10 High Street, Spaldwick, Huntingdon PE28 0TD
t (01480) 890216
e joyceleach@hotmail.com
w chestnutview-bedbreakfast.co.uk

### SPELLBROOK
Hertfordshire

**Margray Guesthouse** ★★★
*Bed & Breakfast*
London Road, Spellbrook, Bishop's Stortford CM23 4BA
t (01279) 600138
e margalf@talktalk.net
w margrayguesthouse.co.uk

### SPEXHALL
Suffolk

**St Peter's House B&B**
Rating Applied For
*Bed & Breakfast*
Church Road, Halesworth IP19 0RQ
t (01986) 874275
e steve@stevemurray.demon.co.uk
w stpetersspexhall.co.uk

## SPILSBY
Lincolnshire

**Spye House ★★★★**
*Bed & Breakfast*
**SILVER AWARD**
Main Road, West Keal, Spilsby PE23 4BE
**t** (01790) 752102
**e** spye.house@btinternet.com

## SPORLE
Norfolk

**Corfield House ★★★★**
*Guest Accommodation*
**SILVER AWARD**
Sporle, King's Lynn PE32 2EA
**t** (01760) 723636
**e** info@corfieldhouse.co.uk
**w** corfieldhouse.co.uk

## SPROUGHTON
Suffolk

**Finjaro ★★★★** *Guest House*
Valley Farm Drive, Hadleigh Road, Sproughton, Ipswich IP8 3EL
**t** (01473) 652581
**e** jan@finjaro.freeserve.co.uk
**w** s-h-systems.co.uk

## SPROWSTON
Norfolk

**Driftwood Lodge ★★★**
*Bed & Breakfast*
102 Wroxham Road, Sprowston, Norwich NR7 8EX
**t** (01603) 444908
**e** info@driftwoodlodge.co.uk
**w** driftwoodlodge.co.uk

## STAFFORD
Staffordshire

**Amerton Farm ★★★**
*Farmhouse*
Amerton, Stowe-by-Chartley, Stafford ST18 0LA
**t** (01889) 270294
**w** amertonfarm.co.uk

**Cedarwood ★★★★**
*Bed & Breakfast*
**SILVER AWARD**
46 Weeping Cross, Stafford ST17 0DS
**t** (01785) 662981

**Littywood House ★★★★**
*Bed & Breakfast*
Bradley, Stafford ST18 9DW
**t** (01785) 780234
**e** suebusby@amserve.com
**w** littywood.co.uk

**Park Farm, Stafford ★★★**
*Farmhouse*
Weston Road, Stafford ST18 0BD
**t** (01785) 240257
**e** parkfarm12@hotmail.com

**Rooks Nest Farm ★★★**
*Farmhouse*
Weston Bank, Weston, Stafford ST18 0BA
**t** (01889) 270624
**e** info@rooksnest.co.uk
**w** rooksnest.co.uk

**Wyndale Guest House ★★★**
*Guest House*
199 Corporation Street, Stafford ST16 3LQ
**t** (01785) 223069
**e** wyndale@aol.com
**w** wyndaleguesthouse.co.uk

## STALHAM
Norfolk

**Bramble House ★★★★**
*Guest Accommodation*
**GOLD AWARD**
Cat's Common, Norwich Road, Smallburgh NR12 9NS
**t** (01692) 535069
**e** bramblehouse07@btinternet.com
**w** bramblehouse.com

## STAMFORD
Lincolnshire

**4 Camphill Cottages ★★★★**
*Bed & Breakfast*
Little Casterton, Stamford PE9 4BE
**t** (01780) 763661

**5 Rock Terrace ★★★★**
*Bed & Breakfast*
Scotgate, Stamford PE9 2YJ
**t** (01780) 755475
**e** averdieckguest@talk21.com

**Candlesticks ★★★**
*Restaurant with Rooms*
1 Church Lane, Stamford PE9 2JU
**t** (01780) 764033
**e** pinto@breathemail.com
**w** candlestickshotel.co.uk

**Dolphin Guesthouse ★★**
*Guest House*
12 East Street, Stamford PE9 1QE
**t** (01780) 757515
**e** mik@mikdolphin.demon.co.uk

**Elm Guest House B&B ★★★★**
*Guest Accommodation*
New Cross Road, Stamford PE9 1AJ
**t** (01780) 764210
**e** inf@elmguesthouse.co.uk
**w** elmguesthouse.co.uk

**Gwynne House ★★★**
*Bed & Breakfast*
Kings Road, Stamford PE9 1HD
**t** (01780) 762210
**e** john@johng.demon.co.uk
**w** gwynnehouse.co.uk

**The Oak Inn ★★★** *Inn*
48 Stamford Road, Easton-on-the-Hill, Stamford PE9 3PA
**t** (01780) 752286
**e** graham@theoakinn.co.uk
**w** sgmcatering.co.uk

**Park Farm ★★★★**
*Bed & Breakfast*
**SILVER AWARD**
Careby, Stamford PE9 4EA
**t** (01780) 410515
**e** enquiries@parkfarmcareby.co.uk
**w** parkfarmcareby.co.uk

**Rock Lodge ★★★★★**
*Guest Accommodation*
**GOLD AWARD**
1 Empingham Road, Stamford PE9 2RH
**t** (01780) 481758
**e** philipsagar@innpro.co.uk
**w** rock-lodge.co.uk

**The Royal Oak ★★★★** *Inn*
High Street, Duddington, Stamford PE9 3QE
**t** (01780) 444267
**e** royaloak@pe93qe.freeserve.co.uk
**w** theroyaloakduddington.co.uk

**Spires View ★★★★**
*Bed & Breakfast*
North Street, Stamford PE9 1AA
**t** (01780) 764419

**Stamford Lodge Guest House ★★★★** *Guest House*
66 Scotgate, Stamford PE9 2YB
**t** (01780) 482932
**e** info@stamfordlodge.co.uk
**w** stamfordlodge.co.uk

**Ufford Farm ★★★**
*Farmhouse*
Main Street, Ufford, Stamford PE9 3BH
**t** (01780) 740220
**e** vergette@ufford1.freeserve.co.uk

## STANDON
Hertfordshire

**The Granary – Mill End Farm ★★★★**
*Guest Accommodation*
Mill End Farm, Standon, Ware SG11 1LR
**t** (01920) 823955
**e** tricia@thegranaryatmillendfarm.co.uk
**w** thegranaryatmillendfarm.co.uk

## STANFORD
Bedfordshire

**Green Man ★★★★** *Inn*
Southill Road, Stanford SG18 9JD
**t** (01462) 812293
**e** info@greenmanstanford.co.uk
**w** stanfordgreenman.co.uk

## STANSTED
Essex

**The Cottage ★★★★**
*Guest Accommodation*
**SILVER AWARD**
71 Birchanger Lane, Birchanger, Bishop's Stortford CM23 5QA
**t** (01279) 812349
**e** bookings@thecottagebirchanger.co.uk
**w** thecottagebirchanger.co.uk

**High Trees ★★**
*Bed & Breakfast*
Parsonage Road, Bishop's Stortford CM22 6QX
**t** (01279) 871306
**e** jeanhightrees@aol.com
**w** stansted-bandb.co.uk

**The Laurels ★★★★**
*Guest Accommodation*
84 St Johns Road, Stansted CM24 8JS
**t** (01279) 813023
**e** info@thelaurelsstansted.co.uk
**w** thelaurelsstansted.co.uk

**The White House ★★★★**
*Guest Accommodation*
Smiths Green, Takeley CM22 6NR
**t** (01279) 870257
**e** enquiries@whitehousestansted.co.uk
**w** whitehousestansted.co.uk

## STANSTED MOUNTFITCHET
Essex

**Chimneys ★★★★**
*Guest House* **SILVER AWARD**
44 Lower Street, Stansted CM24 8LR
**t** (01279) 813388

## STANTON-BY-BRIDGE
Derbyshire

**Ivy House Farm ★★★★**
*Guest Accommodation*
**SILVER AWARD**
Ingleby Road, Stanton-by-Bridge, Derby DE73 7HT
**t** (01332) 863152
**e** info@ivy-house-farm.com
**w** ivy-house-farm.com

## STANTON IN PEAK
Derbyshire

**Congreave Farm ★★★★**
*Farmhouse* **GOLD AWARD**
Congreave, Bakewell DE4 2NF
**t** (01629) 732063
**e** deborah@matsam16.freeserve.co.uk
**w** matsam16.freeserve.co.uk

## STANWAY
Essex

**The Loft ★★★**
*Bed & Breakfast*
Frederick House, New Road, Stanway, Colchester CO3 0HU
**t** (01206) 516006

## STEBBING
Essex

**Motts Cottage ★★★★**
*Bed & Breakfast*
High Street, Stebbing, Dunmow CM6 3SE
**t** (01371) 856633
**e** dianekittow@hotmail.com
**w** mottsbedandbreakfast.co.uk

## STEEPLE
Essex

**The Star Inn ★★★★** *Inn*
The Street, Steeple, Southminster CM0 7LF
**t** (01621) 772646
**e** info@starinnsteeple.co.uk
**w** starinnsteeple.co.uk

## STOKE-BY-NAYLAND
Suffolk

**The Angel Inn ★★★★** *Inn*
Polstead Street, Colchester CO6 4SA
**t** (01206) 263245
**e** info@theangelinn.net

## STOKE HEATH
Worcestershire

**Avoncroft Guest House ★★★★** *Guest House*
77 Redditch Road, Bromsgrove B60 4JP
**t** (01527) 832819
**e** reservations@avoncroftguesthouse.co.uk
**w** avoncroftguesthouse.co.uk

### STOKE HOLY CROSS
Norfolk

**Highfields Farm** ★★★
*Bed & Breakfast*
Chandler Road, Upper Stoke Holy Cross, Norwich NR14 8RQ
t (01508) 493247
e valgolding@lineone.net
w highfieldsfarm.org.uk

**Salamanca Farm** ★★★
*Farmhouse*
118 Norwich Road, Norwich NR14 8QJ
t (01508) 492322
w tiscover.co.uk

### STOKE-ON-TRENT
Staffordshire

**Cedar Tree Cottage** ★★★★
*Bed & Breakfast*
**SILVER AWARD**
41 Longton Road, Trentham, Stoke-on-Trent ST4 8ND
t (01782) 644751
e n.portas@btinternet.com

**The Corrie Guest House**
★★★★ *Guest House*
13 Newton Street, Basford, Stoke-on-Trent ST4 6JN
t (01782) 614838
e info@thecorrie.co.uk
w thecorrie.co.uk

**The Hollies** ★★★
*Bed & Breakfast*
Clay Lake, Stoke-on-Trent ST9 9DD
t (01782) 503252

**L Beez Guest House** ★★
*Guest Accommodation*
46 Leek Road, Stoke-on-Trent ST4 2AR
t (01782) 846727

**Reynolds Hey** ★★★★
*Guest Accommodation*
Park Lane, Endon, Stoke-on-Trent ST9 9JB
t (01782) 502717
e reynoldshey@hotmail.com
w reynoldshey.co.uk

**Shawgate Farm Guest House**
★★★★ *Guest House*
Shay Lane, Foxt, Alton Towers Area ST10 2HN
t (01538) 266590
e ken@shawgatefarm.co.uk
w shawgatefarm.co.uk

**Sneyd Arms Hotel** ★★ *Inn*
Tower Square, Stoke-on-Trent ST6 5AA
t (01782) 826722
w thesneydarms.co.uk

**Verdon Guest House** ★★
*Guest House*
44 Charles Street, Stoke-on-Trent ST1 3JY
t (01782) 264244
w verdonguesthouse.co.uk

### STOKE ST MILBOROUGH
Shropshire

**Stoke Court Bed & Breakfast**
★★★★ *Farmhouse*
Stoke St Milborough, Ludlow SY8 2EQ
t (01584) 823203
e margaret@stokecourtfarm.co.uk
w stokecourtfarm.co.uk

### STONE
Staffordshire

**Mayfield House** ★★★
*Bed & Breakfast*
112 Newcastle Road, Stone ST15 8LG
t (01785) 811446

### STOTTESDON
Worcestershire

**Hardwicke Farm Bed & Breakfast** ★★★★ *Farmhouse*
**SILVER AWARD**
Stottesdon, Cleobury Mortimer DY14 8TN
t (01746) 718220
e althea@hardwickefarm.plus.com
w hardwickefarm.co.uk

### STOURBRIDGE
West Midlands

**The Willows B&B** ★★★
*Bed & Breakfast*
4 Brook Road, Stourbridge DY8 1NH
t (01384) 396964
e trickard@blueyonder.co.uk

### STOURPORT-ON-SEVERN
Worcestershire

**Baldwin House** ★★★★
*Guest House*
8 Lichfield Street, Stourport-on-Severn DY13 9EU
t (01299) 877221
e philpam@dialstart.net
w smoothhound.co.uk

**Victoria Villa Bed & Breakfast** ★★★★
*Guest House*
4 Lion Hill, Stourport-on-Severn DY13 9HD
t (01299) 824017
e bookings@victoriavilla.co.uk
w victoriavilla.co.uk

### STOW
Lincolnshire

**Belle Vue Farm** ★★★★
*Bed & Breakfast*
21 Church Road, Stow LN1 2DE
t (01427) 788981
e claxtons@bellevuefarm21.fsnet.co.uk

### STOWMARKET
Suffolk

**Bays Farm** ★★★★★
*Guest Accommodation*
**GOLD AWARD**
Forward Green, Stowmarket IP14 5HU
t (01449) 711286
e info@baysfarmsuffolk.co.uk
w baysfarmsuffolk.co.uk

**Step House** ★★★★
*Bed & Breakfast*
**SILVER AWARD**
Hockey Hill, Wetheringsett, Stowmarket IP14 5PL
t (01449) 766476
e info@thestephouse.co.uk
w thestephouse.co.uk

**Three Bears Cottage** ★★★
*Guest Accommodation*
Mulberry Tree Farm, Middlewood Green, Stowmarket IP14 5EU
t (01449) 711707
w aristoclassics.com

**Verandah House** ★★★★
*Guest House*
29 Ipswich Road, Stowmarket IP14 1BD
t (01449) 676104
e info@verandahhouse.co.uk
w verandahhouse.co.uk

### STRAGGLETHORPE
Lincolnshire

**Brant House** ★★★★★
*Bed & Breakfast*
Stragglethorpe, Lincoln LN5 0QZ
t (01400) 272626
e branthouse@aol.com
w branthouse.co.uk

### STRATFORD-UPON-AVON
Warwickshire

**Adelphi Guest House** ★★★
*Guest House*
39 Grove Road, Stratford-upon-Avon CV37 6PB
t (01789) 204469
e info@adelphi-guesthouse.com
w adelphi-guesthouse.com

**Ambleside Guest House**
★★★★ *Guest House*
41 Grove Road, Stratford-upon-Avon CV37 6PB
t (01789) 297239
e ruth@amblesideguesthouse.com
w amblesideguesthouse.com

**Arden Park Guest House**
★★★★ *Guest House*
6 Arden Street, Stratford-upon-Avon CV37 6PA
t (01789) 262126
e mark@ardenparkhotel.co.uk
w ardenparkhotel.co.uk

**Arrandale Guest House**
★★★ *Bed & Breakfast*
208 Evesham Road, Stratford-upon-Avon CV37 9AS
t (01789) 267112
w arrandale.netfirms.com

**Ashgrove House** ★★★★
*Guest House*
37 Grove Road, Stratford-upon-Avon CV37 6PB
t (01789) 297278
e info@ashgrovehousestratford.co.uk
w ashgrovehousestratford.co.uk

**Avonlea** ★★★★
*Guest House*
47 Shipston Road, Stratford-upon-Avon CV37 7LN
t (01789) 205940
e avonlea-stratford@lineone.net
w avonlea-stratford.co.uk

**Avonpark House** ★★★★
*Guest House*
123 Shipston Road, Stratford-upon-Avon CV37 7LW
t (01789) 417722
e avonparkhouse@sky.com
w avonparkhouse.com

**Bradbourne House** ★★★★
*Guest House*
44 Shipston Road, Stratford-upon-Avon CV37 7LP
t (01789) 204178
e ian@bradbourne-house.co.uk
w bradbourne-house.co.uk

**Broadlands Guest House**
★★★★ *Guest House*
**SILVER AWARD**
23 Evesham Place, Stratford-upon-Avon CV37 6HT
t (01789) 299181
e philandjohn@broadlandsguesthouse.co.uk
w broadlandsguesthouse.co.uk

**Brook Lodge Guest House**
★★★★ *Guest House*
192 Alcester Road, Stratford-upon-Avon CV37 9DR
t (01789) 295988
e brooklodgeguesthouse@btinternet.com
w brook-lodge.co.uk

**Broom Hall Inn** ★★★ *Inn*
Bidford Road, Broom, Alcester B50 4HE
t (01789) 773757

**Carlton Guest House** ★★★
*Guest House*
22 Evesham Place, Stratford-upon-Avon CV37 6HT
t (01789) 293548

**Caterham House** ★★★★
*Guest House*
58-59 Rother Street, Stratford-upon-Avon CV37 6LT
t (01789) 267309
e caterhamhousehotel@btconnect.com
w caterhamhouse.co.uk

**Church Farm** ★★★
*Farmhouse*
Dorsington, Stratford-upon-Avon CV37 8AX
t (01789) 720471
e chfarmdorsington@aol.com
w churchfarmstratford.co.uk

**Church Farmhouse** ★★★★
*Bed & Breakfast*
Welford Road, Long Marston, Stratford-upon-Avon CV37 8RH
t (01789) 720275
e wiggychurchfarm@hotmail.com
w churchfarmhouse.co.uk

**Courtland** ★★★★
*Guest House*
12 Guild Street, Stratford-upon-Avon CV37 6RE
t (01789) 292401
e info@courtlandhotel.co.uk
w courtlandhotel.co.uk

**Craig Cleeve House** ★★★★
*Guest House*
67-69 Shipston Road, Stratford-upon-Avon CV37 7LW
t (01789) 296573
e craigcleeve@aol.com
w craigcleeve.com

**Curtain Call** ★★★
*Guest House*
142 Alcester Road, Stratford-upon-Avon CV37 9DR
t (01789) 267734
e curtaincall@onetel.com
w curtaincallguesthouse.co.uk

**Cymbeline House** ★★★
*Guest House*
24 Evesham Place, Stratford-upon-Avon CV37 6HT
t (01789) 292958
e linda@cymbelineguesthouse.co.uk
w cymbelinehouse.co.uk

**Drybank Farm** ★★★★
*Farmhouse*
Fosseway, Ettington, Stratford-upon-Avon CV37 7PD
t (01789) 740476
e drybank@btinternet.com
w drybank.co.uk

**The Emsley Guest House**
★★★★ *Guest House*
4 Arden Street, Stratford-upon-Avon CV37 6PA
t (01789) 299557
e val@theemsley.co.uk
w theemsley.co.uk

**Faviere Guest House**
★★★★ *Guest House*
127 Shipston Road, Stratford-upon-Avon CV37 7LW
t (01789) 293764
e reservations@faviere.com
w faviere.com

**Folly Farm Cottage** ★★★★
*Bed & Breakfast*
**GOLD AWARD**
Back Street, Ilmington, Chipping Campden CV36 4LJ
t (01608) 682425
e bruceandpam@follyfarm.co.uk
w follyfarm.co.uk

**Green Gables** ★★★
*Bed & Breakfast*
47 Banbury Road, Stratford-upon-Avon CV37 7HW
t (01789) 205557
e jke985@aol.com
w stratford-upon-avon.co.uk

**Green Haven** ★★★★
*Guest House*
217 Evesham Road, Stratford-upon-Avon CV37 9AS
t (01789) 297874
e info@green-haven.co.uk
w green-haven.co.uk

**Halford Bridge Inn** ★★★★
*Inn*
Fosseway, Halford, Stratford-upon-Avon CV36 5BN
t (01789) 748217
e su@thehalfordbridge.co.uk
w thehalfordbridge.co.uk

**Hampton Lodge Guest House** ★★★
*Guest Accommodation*
38 Shipston Road, Stratford-upon-Avon CV37 7LP
t (01789) 299374
e hamptonlodge.info@btopenworld.com
w hamptonlodge.co.uk

**Heron Lodge** ★★★★
*Guest House*
260 Alcester Road, Stratford-upon-Avon CV37 9JQ
t (01789) 299169
e chrisandbob@heronlodge.com
w heronlodge.com

**The Houndshill** ★★★ *Inn*
Banbury Road, Ettington, Stratford-upon-Avon CV37 7NS
t (01789) 740267

**The Howard Arms** ★★★★★
*Inn* **SILVER AWARD**
Lower Green, Ilmington, Shipston-on-Stour CV36 4LT
t (01608) 682226
e info@howardarms.com
w howardarms.com

**The Hunters Moon Guest House** ★★★ *Guest House*
150 Alcester Road, Stratford-upon-Avon CV37 9DR
t (01789) 292888
e thehuntersmoon@ntlworld.com
w huntersmoonguesthouse.com

**Ingon Bank Farm** ★★★
*Bed & Breakfast*
Warwick Road, Stratford-upon-Avon CV37 0NY
t (01789) 292642
w ingonbankfarmbandb.co.uk

**Larkrise Cottage** ★★★
*Bed & Breakfast*
Upper Billesley, Stratford-upon-Avon CV37 9RA
t (01789) 268618
e alanbailey17@hotmail.com
w larkrisecottage.co.uk

**Linhill Guest House** ★★★
*Guest House*
35 Evesham Place, Stratford-upon-Avon CV37 6HT
t (01789) 292879
e linhill@bigwig.net
w linhillguesthouse.co.uk

**Melita** ★★★★
*Guest Accommodation*
37 Shipston Road, Stratford-upon-Avon CV37 7LN
t (01789) 292432
e info@melitaguesthouse.co.uk
w melitaguesthouse.co.uk

**Midway Guest House** ★★★
*Guest House*
182 Evesham Road, Stratford-upon-Avon CV37 9BS
t (01789) 204154
e mealing@midway182.fsnet.co.uk
w stratford-upon-avon.co.uk

**Mil-Mar** ★★★★ *Guest House*
96 Alcester Road, Stratford-upon-Avon CV37 9DP
t (01789) 267095
e milmar@btinternet.com
w mil-mar.co.uk

**Minola Guest House** ★★★
*Guest House*
25 Evesham Place, Stratford-upon-Avon CV37 6HT
t (01789) 293573

**Penryn Guest House** ★★★★
*Guest House* **SILVER AWARD**
126 Alcester Road, Stratford-upon-Avon CV37 9DP
t (01789) 293718
e penrynhouse@btinternet.com
w penrynguesthouse.co.uk

**The Poplars** ★★★ *Farmhouse*
Mansell Farm, Newbold-on-Stour, Stratford-upon-Avon CV37 8BZ
t (01789) 450540
e judith@poplars-farmhouse.co.uk
w poplars-farmhouse.co.uk

**The Queens Head** ★★ *Inn*
54 Ely Street, Stratford-upon-Avon CV37 6LN
t (01789) 204914

**Quilt & Croissants** ★★★
*Guest House*
33 Evesham Place, Stratford-upon-Avon CV37 6HT
t (01789) 267629
e rooms@quilt-croissants.demon.co.uk
w quiltcroissants.co.uk

**Shakespeare's View**
★★★★★ *Bed & Breakfast*
**GOLD AWARD**
Kings Lane, Snitterfield, Stratford-upon-Avon CV37 0QB
t (01789) 731824
e shakespeares.view@btinternet.com
w shakespeares.view.btinternet.co.uk

**Sunnydale Guest House**
★★★★ *Guest House*
64 Shipston Road, Stratford-upon-Avon CV37 7LP
t (01789) 295166
e helena.kim@ntlworld.com
w sunny-dale.co.uk

**Victoria Spa Lodge** ★★★★
*Guest House* **SILVER AWARD**
Bishopton Lane, Bishopton, Stratford-upon-Avon CV37 9QY
t (01789) 267985
e ptozer@victoriaspalodge.demon.co.uk
w victoriaspa.co.uk

**Virginia Lodge** ★★★
*Guest House*
12 Evesham Place, Stratford-upon-Avon CV37 6HT
t (01789) 292157 & (01789) 266605
e enquiries@virginialodge.co.uk
w virginialodge.co.uk

**White-Sails** ★★★★★
*Guest House* **GOLD AWARD**
85 Evesham Road, Stratford-upon-Avon CV37 9BE
t (01789) 264326
e enquiries@white-sails.co.uk
w white-sails.co.uk

**Woodstock Guest House**
★★★★ *Guest House*
30 Grove Road, Stratford-upon-Avon CV37 6PB
t (01789) 299881
e jackie@woodstock-house.co.uk
w woodstock-house.co.uk

## STRETTON ON DUNSMORE
Warwickshire

**Home Farm (A45)** ★★★★
*Bed & Breakfast*
**SILVER AWARD**
152 London Road (A45), Stretton-on-Dunsmore, Rugby CV23 9HZ
t (024) 7654 1211
e info@homefarma45.co.uk
w homefarma45.co.uk

## SUDBURY
Suffolk

**The Black Boy** ★★★ *Inn*
7 Market Hill, Sudbury CO10 2EA
t (01787) 379046

**Hill Lodge** ★★★
*Guest Accommodation*
8 Newton Road, Sudbury CO10 2RL
t (01787) 377568
e enquiries@hilllodgehotel.co.uk
w hilllodgehotel.co.uk

**Hillview Studio** ★★★
*Bed & Breakfast*
58 Clarence Road, Sudbury CO10 1NJ
t (01787) 374221 & 07779 854199
e sooteapot@hotmail.com

**Millhouse Bed & Breakfast**
★★★★ *Bed & Breakfast*
Nayworth Cottages, Cross Street, Sudbury CO10 2DS
t (01787) 881173
e mills@travelandleisure.co.uk
w millhouse-sudbury.co.uk

**St David's Hall** ★★★★
*Bed & Breakfast*
**SILVER AWARD**
40a Friars Street, Sudbury CO10 2AG
t (01787) 373044
e stdavidshall@tiscali.co.uk

**West House** ★★
*Bed & Breakfast*
59 Ballingdon Street, Sudbury CO10 2DA
t (01787) 375033
e aitken@westhousebb.fsnet.co.uk

## SUTTON-ON-SEA
Lincolnshire

**Bacchus** ★★★★ *Inn*
17 High Street, Sutton-on-Sea LN12 2EY
t (01507) 441204
e enquiries@bacchushotel.co.uk
w bacchushotel.co.uk

## SUTTON-ON-TRENT
Nottinghamshire

**Fiveways** ★★ *Bed & Breakfast*
Barrel Hill Road, Sutton-on-Trent, Newark NG23 6PT
t (01636) 822086
e enquiries@experiencenottinghamshire.com

**Orchard End B & B** ★★★★
*Bed & Breakfast*
Carlton Lane, Newark NG23 6PH
t (01636) 821015
e alanpetrie@vodafoneemail.co.uk
w orchard-end.co.uk

**Woodbine Farmhouse** ★★
*Bed & Breakfast*
Ingram Lane, Sutton-on-Trent, Newark NG23 6PD
t (01636) 822549
e bandb@woodbinefarmhouse.co.uk

## SUTTON ST NICHOLAS
Herefordshire

**Pool House** ★★★★
*Guest Accommodation*
Sutton St Nicholas, Hereford HR1 3AY
t (01432) 880494
e poolhouse@herefordbedandbreakfast.co.uk
w herefordbedandbreakfast.co.uk

## SWADLINCOTE
Derbyshire

**Ferne Cottage** ★★
*Bed & Breakfast*
5 Black Horse Hill, Appleby Magna, Ashby-de-la-Zouch DE12 7AQ
t (01530) 271772
e gbirdapplebymag@aol.com

**Manor Farm** ★★★★
*Farmhouse*
Coton in the Elms, Swadlincote DE12 8EP
t (01283) 760340
e cath@manorfarmbb.co.uk
w manorfarmbb.co.uk

## SWAFFHAM
Norfolk

**Lydney House** ★★★★
*Guest House*
Norwich Road, Swaffham PE37 7QS
t (01760) 723355
e rooms@lydney-house.demon.co.uk
w lydney-house.demon.co.uk

**Repton House** ★★★★
*Bed & Breakfast*
11 Oaks Drive, Swaffham PE37 7ER
t (01760) 336399
e booking@reptonhouse.com
w reptonhouse.com

## SWAFFHAM BULBECK
Cambridgeshire

**B&B at Martin House**
★★★★ *Bed & Breakfast*
**SILVER AWARD**
1 Station Road, Swaffham Bulbeck, Cambridge CB25 0NB
t (01223) 813115
e sally@martinhousebb.co.uk
w martinhousebb.co.uk

**Black Horse** ★★★ *Inn*
35 High Street, Cambridge CB5 0HP
t (01223) 811366
e blackhorsepubandmotel@hotmail.com
w a1tourism.com/uk/blackhorse.html

## SWANNINGTON
Leicestershire

**Hillfield House** ★★★★
*Bed & Breakfast*
52 Station Hill, Swannington, Coalville LE67 8RH
t (01530) 837414
e molly@hillfieldhouse.co.uk
w hillfieldhouse.co.uk

## SWANTON ABBOTT
Norfolk

**Pheasant Cottage** ★★★★★
*Guest Accommodation*
Long Common Lane, Norwich NR10 5BH
t (01692) 538169
e mail@pheasantcottage.freeserve.co.uk
w pheasantcottage.com

## SWANTON MORLEY
Norfolk

**Carricks at Castle Farm**
★★★★★
*Guest Accommodation*
**SILVER AWARD**
Castle Farm, Elsing Road, Dereham NR20 4JT
t (01362) 638302
e jean@castlefarm-swanton.co.uk
w carricksatcastlefarm.co.uk

**Frogs Hall Farm** ★★★★★
*Guest Accommodation*
**SILVER AWARD**
Frogs Hall Lane, Woodgate, Swanton Morley, Dereham NR20 4NX
t (01362) 638355
e mail@frogshallfarm.co.uk
w frogshallfarm.co.uk

## SWINESHEAD
Lincolnshire

**The Wheatsheaf** ★★★ *Inn*
Market Place, Swineshead PE20 3LJ
t (01205) 820349
e carl@smoke-screen.co.uk
w wheatsheafhotel.co.uk

## SWINFORD
Leicestershire

**Ravendale House** ★★★★
*Bed & Breakfast*
Firtree Lane, Swinford, Lutterworth LE17 6BH
t (01788) 860442
e info@ravendalehousebandb.co.uk
w ravendalehousebandb.co.uk

## SWINHOPE
Lincolnshire

**Hoe Hill House** ★★★★
*Bed & Breakfast*
Swinhope, Market Rasen LN8 6HX
t (01472) 399366
e wardhealing@hotmail.com
w hoehill.co.uk

## SYMONDS YAT EAST
Herefordshire

**Garth Cottage** ★★★★
*Guest Accommodation*
**SILVER AWARD**
Symonds Yat East, Ross-on-Wye HR9 6JL
t (01600) 890364
e val.eden@virgin.net

## TACHBROOK MALLORY
Warwickshire

**Tachbrook Mallory House**
★★★★ *Bed & Breakfast*
Oakley Wood Road, Royal Leamington Spa, Leamington Spa CV33 9QE
t (01926) 451450
e tmhouse@btinternet.com
w tachbrookmalloryhouse.co.uk

## TADDINGTON
Derbyshire

**The Old Bake & Brewhouse, Blackwell Hall** ★★★★
*Farmhouse*
Blackwell in the Peak, Taddington, Buxton SK17 9TQ
t (01298) 85271
e christine.gregory@btinternet.com
w peakdistrictfarmhols.co.uk

**Taddington Camping Barn**
*Camping Barn*
The Woodlands, Taddington, Buxton SK17 9UD
t (01298) 85730

## TAKELEY
Essex

**Crossroads B and B** ★★
*Bed & Breakfast*
2 Hawthorn Close, Bishop's Stortford CM22 6SD
t (01279) 870619
e ajcaiger884@aol.com
w tiscover.co.uk

**Jan Smiths Bandb** ★★★★
*Bed & Breakfast*
The Cottage, Jacks Lane, Takeley, Bishop's Stortford CM22 6NT
t (01279) 870603
e smiths-residence@fsmail.net
w thecottagebnbjackslane.co.uk

**Little Bullocks Farm** ★★★★
*Guest Accommodation*
Bullocks Lane, Hope End, Stansted CM22 6TA
t (01279) 870464
e julie@waterman-farm.demon.co.uk
w littlebullocksfarm.co.uk

**Oak Lodge Bed And Breakfast** ★★★★
*Bed & Breakfast*
**SILVER AWARD**
Oak Lodge, Jacks Lane, Takeley, Bishop's Stortford CM22 6NT
t (01279) 871667
e oaklodgebb@aol.com
w oaklodgebb.com

**Pussy Willow** ★★★★
*Bed & Breakfast*
**SILVER AWARD**
Mill House, The Street, Bishop's Stortford CM22 6QR
t (01279) 871609
e enquiries@thepussywillow.co.uk

**Tap Hall** ★★★
*Bed & Breakfast*
15 The Street, Bishop's Stortford CM22 6QS
t (01279) 871035
e info@taphall.com
w a1tourism.com/uk/tap-hall.html

## TAMWORTH
Staffordshire

**Belmont Guest House**
★★★★ *Guest House*
56 Upper Gungate, Tamworth B79 8AA
t (01827) 62585
w belmont-tamworth.co.uk

**Chestnuts Country Guest House** ★★★★ *Guest House*
**SILVER AWARD**
Watling Street, Grendon, Atherstone CV9 2PZ
t (01827) 331355
e ccltd@aol.com
w thechestnutshotel.com

**Middleton House Farm**
★★★★
*Guest Accommodation*
**SILVER AWARD**
Tamworth Road, Middleton, Tamworth B78 2BD
t (01827) 873474

**The Peel Aldergate** ★★★★
*Guest Accommodation*
13-14b Aldergate, Tamworth B79 7DL
t (01827) 67676

## TANWORTH-IN-ARDEN
Warwickshire

**Grange Farm** ★★★★
*Farmhouse* **SILVER AWARD**
Forde Hall Lane, Tanworth-in-Arden, Solihull B94 5AX
t (01564) 742911
e enquiries@grange-farm.com
w grange-farm.com

**Mows Hill Farm** ★★★★
*Farmhouse* **SILVER AWARD**
Mows Hill Road, Kemps Green, Solihull B94 5PP
t (01564) 784312
e mowshill@farmline.com
w b-and-bmowshill.co.uk

## TARRINGTON
Herefordshire

**Swan House** ★★★★
*Guest Accommodation*
Tarrington, Ledbury HR1 4EU
t (01432) 890203
e parrylizzy@aol.com
w swanhousetarrington.co.uk

**TATTERSHALL**
**Lincolnshire**

**Castle Lodge B&B ★★★★**
*Bed & Breakfast*
11 Sleaford Road, Lincoln LN4 4LR
**t** (01526) 343293
**e** peter.hopkin@virgin.net
**w** castlelodge.net

**TEAN**
**Staffordshire**

**Granary Room**
Rating Applied For
*Guest Accommodation*
Blythe Farm House, Riverside Road, Stoke-on-Trent ST10 4JW
**t** (01538) 724061
**e** irene@blythefarmhouse.co.uk
**w** blythefarmhouse.co.uk

**TEIGH**
**Rutland**

**Old Rectory ★★★★**
*Bed & Breakfast*
Main Street, Teigh, Oakham LE15 7RT
**t** (01572) 787681
**e** torowen@btinternet.com

**TELFORD**
**Shropshire**

**Grove House Bed and Breakfast ★★★★**
*Guest Accommodation*
1 Stafford Street, St Georges, Telford TF2 9JW
**t** (01952) 616140
**w** virtual-shropshire.co.uk

**The Mill House ★★★★**
*Bed & Breakfast*
Shrewsbury Road, High Ercall, Telford TF6 6BE
**t** (01952) 770394
**e** cjpy@lineone.net
**w** ercallmill.co.uk

**The Mount ★★★★**
*Guest Accommodation*
**SILVER AWARD**
Dawley Road, Arleston Hill, Lawley, Telford TF1 2LZ
**t** (01952) 503102
**e** pam@mountguesthouse.co.uk
**w** mountguesthouse.co.uk

**The Old Orleton ★★★★★**
*Inn* **SILVER AWARD**
Holyhead Road, Wellington TF1 2HA
**t** (01952) 255011
**e** info@theoldorleton.com
**w** theoldorleton.com

**The Stanage ★★★★**
*Bed & Breakfast*
Dawley Road, Lawley Village, Telford TF4 2PG
**t** (01952) 507742
**e** hazelbexon@yahoo.co.uk
**w** bedandbreakfastintelford.co.uk

**Stone House ★★★★**
*Guest Accommodation*
Shifnal Road, Priorslee, Telford TF2 9NN
**t** (01952) 290119
**e** stonehousegh@aol.com
**w** stonehouseguesthouse.co.uk

**West Ridge B&B ★★★★**
*Bed & Breakfast*
**SILVER AWARD**
Kemberton, Shifnal, Telford TF11 9LB
**t** (01952) 580992
**e** westridgebb@tiscali.co.uk
**w** westridgebb.com

**Willow House ★★★**
*Guest Accommodation*
137 Holyhead Road, Wellington, Telford TF1 2DH
**t** (01952) 223817
**e** info@telfordguesthouse.co.uk
**w** telfordguesthouse.co.uk

**TENBURY WELLS**
**Worcestershire**

**Fountain ★★★★** *Inn*
Oldwood, St Michaels, Tenbury Wells WR15 8TB
**t** (01584) 810701
**e** enquiries@fountain-hotel.co.uk
**w** fountain-hotel.co.uk

**Millbrook ★★★★**
*Bed & Breakfast*
Eastham, Tenbury Wells WR15 8NP
**t** (01584) 781720
**e** keithoddy@millbrook01584.co.uk
**w** millbrook01584.co.uk

**TERRINGTON ST JOHN**
**Norfolk**

**The White House ★★★★**
*Bed & Breakfast*
**SILVER AWARD**
Main Road, Terrington St John, Wisbech PE14 7RR
**t** (01945) 880741
**e** fieldcarol@hotmail.com
**w** thewhitehousebnb.co.uk

**TETFORD**
**Lincolnshire**

**Tetford Country Cottages ★★★** *Bed & Breakfast*
East Road, Horncastle LN9 6QQ
**t** (01507) 533276
**e** contact@tetfordcountrycottages.co.uk
**w** tetfordcountrycottages.co.uk

**THAXTED**
**Essex**

**Crossways Guesthouse ★★★★** *Bed & Breakfast*
**SILVER AWARD**
32 Town Street, Thaxted, Great Dunmow CM6 2LA
**t** (01371) 830348
**e** info@crosswaysthaxted.co.uk
**w** crosswaysthaxted.co.uk

**The Farmhouse Inn ★★★**
*Guest Accommodation*
Monk Street, Dunmow CM6 2NR
**t** (01371) 830864
**e** info@farmhouseinn.org
**w** farmhouseinn.org

**THEBERTON**
**Suffolk**

**Alders ★★★**
*Guest Accommodation*
Potters Street, Theberton, Leiston IP16 4RL
**t** (01728) 831790

**Lupin Cottage ★★★**
*Bed & Breakfast*
Church Road, Theberton, Leiston IP16 4SF
**t** (01728) 830531

**THETFORD**
**Norfolk**

**Glebe Country House Bed & Breakfast ★★★★**
*Guest Accommodation*
**SILVER AWARD**
Elveden, Thetford IP24 3TL
**t** (01842) 890027
**e** deirdre@jrudderham.freeserve.co.uk
**w** glebecountryhouse.co.uk

**Wereham House ★★★★**
*Guest Accommodation*
24 White Hart Street, Thetford IP24 1AD
**t** (01842) 761956
**e** mail@werehamhouse.co.uk
**w** werehamhouse.co.uk

**THOMPSON**
**Norfolk**

**Chequers Inn ★★★★** *Inn*
Griston Road, Thompson IP24 1PX
**t** (01953) 483360
**e** richard@chequers-inn.wanadoo.co.uk
**w** thompson-chequers.co.uk

**THORNDON**
**Suffolk**

**Moat Farm ★★★★**
*Farmhouse* **SILVER AWARD**
Thorndon, Eye IP23 7LX
**t** (01379) 678437
**e** bookings@moatfarm.co.uk
**w** moatfarm.co.uk

**THORNHAM**
**Norfolk**

**Rushmeadow ★★★★**
*Bed & Breakfast*
Main Road, Thornham PE36 6LZ
**t** (01485) 512372
**e** rushmeadow@sky.com
**w** rushmeadow.com

**THORNHAM MAGNA**
**Suffolk**

**The Four Horseshoes ★★★★** *Inn*
Wickham Road, Eye IP23 8HD
**t** (01379) 678777

**Red House ★★★★**
*Guest Accommodation*
**SILVER AWARD**
Thornham Magna, Eye IP23 8HH
**t** (01379) 783336
**e** ladyhenniker@tiscali.co.uk

**Thornham Hall ★★★★★**
*Guest Accommodation*
**SILVER AWARD**
Thornham Magna, Eye IP23 8HA
**t** (01379) 783314
**e** thornhamhall@aol.com
**w** thornhamhall.com

**THORNTON CURTIS**
**Lincolnshire**

**Pine Lodge Bed and Breakfast ★★★★**
*Bed & Breakfast*
Laurel Lane, Thornton Curtis DN39 6XJ
**t** 07880 601476

**Thornton Hunt Inn ★★★★**
*Inn*
17 Main Street, Thornton Curtis, Nr Ulceby DN39 6XW
**t** (01469) 531252
**e** peter@thornton-inn.co.uk
**w** thornton-inn.co.uk

**THORPE**
**Derbyshire**

**Hillcrest House ★★★★**
*Guest House*
Dovedale, Thorpe, Ashbourne DE6 2AW
**t** (01335) 350436
**e** info@hillcresthousedovedale.co.uk
**w** hillcresthousedovedale.co.uk

**The Old Orchard ★★★**
*Bed & Breakfast*
Thorpe, Ashbourne DE6 2AW
**t** (01335) 350410
**w** theoldorchardguesthouse.co.uk

**THORPE BAY**
**Essex**

**Beaches ★★★★**
*Guest House*
192 Eastern Esplanade, Thorpe Bay, Southend-on-Sea SS1 3AA
**t** (01702) 586124
**e** mark@beachesguesthouse.co.uk
**w** beachesguesthouse.co.uk

**THORPE MARKET**
**Norfolk**

**Manorwood ★★★★**
*Bed & Breakfast*
Church Road, Thorpe Market, Norwich NR11 8UA
**t** (01263) 834938

**THORPE MORIEUX**
**Suffolk**

**Elm Tree Farm ★★★★**
*Bed & Breakfast*
Bury Road, Thorpe Morieux, Bury St Edmunds IP30 0NT
**t** (01284) 827053
**e** liz.conibear@virgin.net
**w** elmtreefarmlodge.co.uk

**THURLBY**
**Lincolnshire**

**6 The Pingles ★★★★**
*Guest Accommodation*
**SILVER AWARD**
Thurlby PE10 0EX
**t** (01778) 394517

**Thurlby YHA ★★★** *Hostel*
Capstone, 16 High Street, Bourne PE10 0EE
**t** (01778) 425588

**THURLEIGH**
**Bedfordshire**

**The Windmill** ★★★★
*Bed & Breakfast*
Milton Road, Thurleigh, Bedford MK44 2DF
**t** (01234) 771016
**e** wendy.armitage1@talk21.com
**w** thewindmill.uk.com

**THURMASTON**
**Leicestershire**

**Aaron Lodge** ★★★
*Guest Accommodation*
3 Coppice Court, Thurmaston, Leicester LE4 8PJ
**t** (0116) 269 4494
**e** info@aaronlodgeguesthouse.co.uk
**w** aaronlodgeguesthouse.co.uk

**THURSTON**
**Suffolk**

**The Fox & Hounds** ★★★★
*Inn*
Barton Road, Bury St Edmunds IP31 3QT
**t** (01359) 232228
**e** thurstonfox@btinternet.com
**w** thurstonfoxandhounds.co.uk

**TIBSHELF**
**Derbyshire**

**Rosvern House** ★★★
*Bed & Breakfast*
High Street, Tibshelf, Alfreton DE55 5NY
**t** (01773) 874800
**e** sara.byard@orange.net

**TICKNALL**
**Derbyshire**

**The Staff of Life** ★★★★
*Guest Accommodation*
7 High Street, Ticknall, Derby DE73 7JH
**t** (01332) 862479
**e** reservations@thestaffoflife.co.uk
**w** thestaffoflife.co.uk

**TIDESWELL**
**Derbyshire**

**Jaret House** ★★★★
*Guest Accommodation*
Queen Street, Tideswell, Buxton SK17 8JZ
**t** (01298) 872470
**e** info@jarethouse.co.uk
**w** jarethouse.co.uk

**TIMBERLAND**
**Lincolnshire**

**Clifton Coach House** ★★★★
*Guest Accommodation*
Clifton House, Church Lane, Timberland LN4 3SB
**t** (01526) 378810
**e** paul.j.hutson@btopenworld.com

**TINWELL**
**Rutland**

**Old Village Hall** ★★★★
*Bed & Breakfast*
Main Road, Tinwell, Stamford PE9 3UD
**t** (01780) 763900
**e** theoldvillagehall@hotmail.com

**TISSINGTON**
**Derbyshire**

**Bassett Wood Farm** ★★★★
*Farmhouse*
Tissington, Ashbourne DE6 1RD
**t** (01335) 350254
**e** janet@bassettwood.freeserve.co.uk

**TOFT**
**Cambridgeshire**

**Meadowview** ★★★★
*Bed & Breakfast*
3 Brookside, Toft, Cambridge CB23 2RJ
**t** (01223) 263395
**e** carol@meadowview.co.uk
**w** meadowview.co.uk

**TOLLESBURY**
**Essex**

**Fernleigh** ★★★
*Bed & Breakfast*
16 Woodrolfe Farm Lane, Tollesbury, Maldon CM9 8SX
**t** (01621) 868245
**e** gillwillson@onetel.com

**TOLLESHUNT MAJOR**
**Essex**

**Wicks Manor Farm** ★★★★
*Farmhouse*
Witham Road, Tolleshunt Major, Maldon CM9 8JU
**t** (01621) 860629
**e** rhowie@aspects.net
**w** wicksmanor.co.uk

**TOPPESFIELD**
**Essex**

**Harrow Hill Cottage** ★★★
*Bed & Breakfast*
Harrow Hill, Toppesfield CO9 4LX
**t** (01787) 237425
**w** tiscover.co.uk

**TOTTENHILL**
**Norfolk**

**Andel Lodge** ★★★★
*Restaurant with Rooms*
48 Lynn Road, Tottenhill, King's Lynn PE33 0RH
**t** (01553) 810256
**e** reservations@andellodge.co.uk
**w** andellodge.co.uk

**TOWCESTER**
**Northamptonshire**

**Home Farm** ★★★★
*Guest Accommodation*
Caldecote, Towcester NN12 8AG
**t** (01327) 352651
**e** gisela@giselasbedandbreakfast.com
**w** giselasbedandbreakfast.com

**Potcote** ★★★★★
*Guest Accommodation*
**SILVER AWARD**
Towcester NN12 8LP
**t** (01327) 830224
**e** timbeckbrown@aol.com
**w** potcote.co.uk

**Slapton Manor Accommodation** ★★★★
*Farmhouse* **SILVER AWARD**
Slapton Manor, Slapton NN12 8PF
**t** (01327) 860344
**e** accommodation@slaptonmanor.co.uk

**TRUMPINGTON**
**Cambridgeshire**

**Bishops Bed And Breakfast** ★★★★ *Bed & Breakfast*
80 Bishops Road, Trumpington, Cambridge CB2 2NH
**t** (01223) 840045
**e** valneilm@yahoo.co.uk
**w** geocities.com/valneilm

**TRUSTHORPE**
**Lincolnshire**

**The Ramblers Guest House** ★★★★ *Guest House*
Sutton Road, Trusthorpe LN12 2PY
**t** (01507) 441171
**e** mail@theramblers.info
**w** theramblers.info

**TUGFORD**
**Shropshire**

**Tugford Farm B&B** ★★★★
*Farmhouse*
Tugford Farm, Craven Arms SY7 9HS
**t** (01584) 841259
**e** tugfordfarm@yahoo.co.uk
**w** tugford.com

**TUNSTALL**
**Norfolk**

**Manor House** ★★★★
*Farmhouse* **SILVER AWARD**
Tunstall Road, Halvergate, Norwich NR13 3PS
**t** (01493) 700279
**e** smore@fsmail.net

**TUNSTALL**
**Staffordshire**

**The Victoria** ★★★
*Guest Accommodation*
4 Roundwell Street, Tunstall, Stoke-on-Trent ST6 5JJ
**t** (01782) 835964
**e** victoriahoteltunstall@hotmail.com

**TUTBURY**
**Staffordshire**

**Woodhouse Farm Bed and Breakfast** ★★★ *Farmhouse*
Fauld, Tutbury, Burton-on-Trent DE13 9HR
**t** (01283) 812185
**e** woodhousetutbury@aol.com
**w** woodhousebandb.co.uk

**UCKINGHALL**
**Worcestershire**

**Ivydene House Bed and Breakfast** ★★★★★
*Bed & Breakfast*
**SILVER AWARD**
Ivydene House, Uckinghall GL20 6ES
**t** (01684) 592453
**e** rosemaryg@fsmail.net
**w** ivydenehouse.net

**UFFORD**
**Suffolk**

**Strawberry Hill** ★★★★
*Bed & Breakfast*
Loudham Lane, Lower Ufford, Woodbridge IP13 6ED
**t** (01394) 460252
**e** strawberryhilly@yahoo.co.uk
**w** smoothhound.co.uk/hotels/strawber

**UGGESHALL**
**Suffolk**

**Bankside** ★★★★
*Bed & Breakfast*
The Hills, Southwold NR34 8EN
**t** (01502) 578047
**e** liz@bankside19.fsnet.co.uk
**w** banksidebandb.co.uk

**ULCEBY**
**Lincolnshire**

**Gillingham Court**
Rating Applied For
*Bed & Breakfast*
Spruce Lane, Ulceby DN39 6UL
**t** (01469) 588427
**e** gillinghamrest@supanet.com
**w** gillinghamcourt.co.uk

**ULLESTHORPE**
**Leicestershire**

**The Chequers Country Inn** ★★★ *Inn*
Main Street, Lutterworth LE17 5BT
**t** (01455) 209214
**w** chequerscountryinn.com

**UPPER BENEFIELD**
**Northamptonshire**

**Benefield Wheatsheaf Hotel** ★★★★ *Inn*
Main Street, Upper Benefield PE8 5AN
**t** (01832) 205400

**UPPER COLWALL**
**Worcestershire**

**Little Kings Hill** ★★★★
*Bed & Breakfast*
Walwyn Road, Upper Colwall, Malvern WR13 6PL
**t** (01684) 540589
**e** littlekingshill@btinternet.com

**UPPER SAPEY**
**Herefordshire**

**Tippins Farm** ★★★★
*Farmhouse*
Upper Sapey, Bromyard WR6 6XT
**t** (024) 7669 6909
**e** tippinsfarm@btinternet.com
**w** tippinsfarm.co.uk

**UPPER SHERINGHAM**
**Norfolk**

**Lodge Cottage** ★★★★
*Guest Accommodation*
Lodge Hill, Upper Sheringham NR26 8TJ
**t** (01263) 821445
**e** stay@visitlodgecottage.com
**w** visitlodgecottage.com

**UPPINGHAM**
**Rutland**

**Crown Inn** ★★★ *Inn*
19 High Street East, Uppingham LE15 9PY
**t** (01572) 822302
**e** thecrownrutland@aol.com

**Grange Farm B&B** ★★★★
*Farmhouse*
Seaton, Rutland, Uppingham LE15 9HT
**t** (01572) 747664
**w** seatongrange.co.uk

**Spanhoe Lodge** ★★★★★
*Guest Accommodation*
**GOLD AWARD**
Harringworth Road, Laxton, Corby NN17 3AT
**t** (01780) 450328
**e** jennie.spanhoe@virgin.net
**w** spanhoelodge.co.uk

## UPTON Leicestershire

**Upton Barn Restaurant & Accommodation** ★★
*Guest Accommodation*
Manor Farm, Upton, Market Bosworth CV13 6JX
**t** (01455) 212374
**e** info@uptonbarn.co.uk
**w** uptonbarn.co.uk

## UPTON Warwickshire

**Uplands House** ★★★★★
*Bed & Breakfast*
Upton, Banbury, Stratford-upon-Avon OX15 6HJ
**t** (01295) 678663
**e** poppy@cotswolds-uplands.co.uk
**w** cotswolds-uplands.co.uk

## UPTON SNODSBURY Worcestershire

**Bants** ★★★★ *Inn*
Worcester Road, Upton Snodsbury WR7 4NN
**t** (01905) 381282
**e** info@bants.co.uk
**w** bants.co.uk

## UPTON UPON SEVERN Worcestershire

**Sunnyside Bed & Breakfast**
★★★★ *Bed & Breakfast*
Station Road, Ripple GL20 6EY
**t** (01684) 592461
**e** sunnysideripple@btinternet.com
**w** sunnysidebandb.co.uk

**Tiltridge Farm & Vineyard**
★★★★ *Farmhouse*
**SILVER AWARD**
Upper Hook Road, Upton-upon-Severn WR8 0SA
**t** (01684) 592906
**e** sandy@tiltridge.com
**w** tiltridge.com

## VOWCHURCH Herefordshire

**New Barns Farm** ★★★★
*Farmhouse*
Vowchurch, Golden Valley HR2 0QA
**t** (01981) 250250
**e** lloydnewbarns@tiscali.co.uk
**w** golden-valley.co.uk/newbarns

**The Old Vicarage** ★★★★
*Guest Accommodation*
**SILVER AWARD**
Vowchurch, Hereford, Golden Valley HR2 0QD
**t** (01981) 550357
**w** golden-valley.co.uk/vicarage

**Upper Gilvach Farm** ★★★★
*Farmhouse* **SILVER AWARD**
Newton St Margarets, Vowchurch, Golden Valley HR2 0QY
**t** (01981) 510618
**e** ruth@uppergilvach.freeserve.co.uk
**w** golden-valley.co.uk/gilvach

**Yew Tree House** ★★★★
*Bed & Breakfast*
**GOLD AWARD**
Vowchurch, Hereford HR2 9PF
**t** (01981) 251195
**e** enquiries@yewtreehouse-hereford.co.uk
**w** yewtreehouse-hereford.co.uk

## WADESMILL Hertfordshire

**The Feathers inn**
Rating Applied For
*Guest Accommodation*
Cambridge Road, Ware SG12 0TN
**t** (01920) 462606
**w** feathersinn.com

## WADSHELF Derbyshire

**Temperance House Farm**
★★★★ *Bed & Breakfast*
**SILVER AWARD**
Bradshaw Lane, Wadshelf, Chesterfield S42 7BT
**t** (01246) 566416
**w** temperancehousefarm.co.uk

## WAINFLEET Lincolnshire

**Willow Farm** ★★★
*Farmhouse*
Thorpe Fendykes, Skegness PE24 4QH
**t** (01754) 830316
**e** willowfarmhols@aol.com
**w** willowfarmholidays.co.uk

## WAKES COLNE Essex

**Rosebank** ★★★★
*Bed & Breakfast*
Station Road, Wakes Colne, Colchester CO6 2DS
**t** (01787) 223552
**e** barbaralynn@btconnect.com

## WALBERSWICK Suffolk

**Troy** ★★★★ *Bed & Breakfast*
Church Field, Southwold IP18 6TG
**t** (01502) 723387
**w** visit.walberswick.com

## WALDRINGFIELD Suffolk

**Thatched Farm** ★★★★
*Bed & Breakfast*
Woodbridge Road, Waldringfield, Woodbridge IP12 4PW
**t** (01473) 811755
**e** mailus@thatchedfarm.co.uk
**w** thatchedfarm.co.uk

## WALSALL West Midlands

**Lyndon House Hotel** ★★★
*Inn*
Upper Rushall Street, Walsall WS1 2HA
**t** (01922) 612511
**e** bookings@lyndonhousehotel.co.uk
**w** lyndonhousehotel.com

## WALSINGHAM Norfolk

**St Felix**
Rating Applied For
*Bed & Breakfast*
2a Knight Street, Walsingham NR22 6DA
**t** (01328) 820117
**e** th@paston.co.uk

## WALTHAM-ON-THE-WOLDS Leicestershire

**Royal Horseshoes** ★★★ *Inn*
Melton Road, Waltham-on-the-Wolds, Melton Mowbray LE14 4AJ
**t** (01664) 464289
**e** the_roy.noble@btconnect.com

## WALTON-ON-THE-NAZE Essex

**Bufo Villae Guest House**
★★★★
*Guest Accommodation*
31 Beatrice Road, Walton-on-the-Naze CO14 8HJ
**t** (01255) 672644
**e** bufovillae@btinternet.com
**w** bufovillae.co.uk

## WANGFORD Suffolk

**The Angel Inn** ★★★★ *Inn*
High Street, Beccles NR34 8RL
**t** (01502) 578636
**e** info@angelinnwangford.co.uk
**w** angelinnwangford.co.uk

**Fluff Cottage** ★★★★
*Bed & Breakfast*
1 High Street, Beccles NR34 8RL
**t** (01502) 578997
**w** tiscover.co.uk

**The Plough Inn** ★★★★
*Guest Accommodation*
London Road, Wangford, Southwold, Beccles NR34 8AZ
**t** (01353) 698000
**e** enquiries@the-plough.biz
**w** the-plough.biz

## WANSFORD Cambridgeshire

**Stoneacre Guest House**
★★★★ *Guest House*
Elton Road, Wansford, Peterborough PE8 6JT
**t** (01780) 783283
**w** stoneacreguesthouse.co.uk

## WARE Hertfordshire

**Barbaras B&B** ★★
*Guest Accommodation*
6 High Oak Road, Ware SG12 7PG
**t** (01920) 484796
**e** truttb@aol.com

## WARMINGTON Warwickshire

**Springfield House** ★★★★
*Bed & Breakfast*
School Lane, Warmington, Banbury OX17 1DD
**t** (01295) 690286
**e** jenny.handscombe@virgin.net
**w** springfieldbb.net

## WARWICK Warwickshire

**Agincourt Lodge** ★★★★
*Guest House*
36 Coten End, Warwick CV34 4NP
**t** (01926) 499399
**e** enquiries@agincourtlodge.co.uk
**w** agincourtlodge.co.uk

**Apothecary's Bed and Breakfast** ★★★★
*Bed & Breakfast*
The Old Dispensary, Stratford Road, Stratford-upon-Avon CV35 9RN
**t** (01789) 470060
**e** bandbapothecary@aol.com
**w** apothecarysbandb.co.uk

**Ashburton Guest House**
★★★ *Guest House*
74 Emscote Road, Warwick CV34 5QG
**t** (01926) 499133
**e** lordnelsonnb@btconnect.com

**Austons Down** ★★★★
*Bed & Breakfast*
Saddle Bow Lane, Claverdon, Stratford-upon-Avon CV35 8PQ
**t** (01926) 842068
**e** lmh@austonsdown.com
**w** austonsdown.com

**Avon Guest House** ★★★★
*Guest House*
7 Emscote Road, Warwick CV34 4PH
**t** (01926) 491367
**e** info@avonguesthouse.co.uk
**w** avonguesthouse.co.uk

**Cambridge Villa** ★★★
*Guest House*
20a/B Emscote Road, Warwick CV34 4PP
**t** (01926) 491169
**e** cambridgevilla_warwick@yahoo.co.uk

**Chesterfields Guest House**
★★★ *Guest House*
84 Emscote Road, Warwick CV34 5QT
**t** (01926) 774864
**e** jchapman@chesterfields.freeserve.co.uk
**w** smoothhound.co.uk

**Croft Guesthouse** ★★★★
*Guest House*
Haseley Knob, Warwick CV35 7NL
**t** (01926) 484447
**e** david@croftguesthouse.co.uk
**w** croftguesthouse.co.uk

**Jersey Villa Guest House** ★★
*Guest House*
69 Emscote Road, Warwick
CV34 5QR
t (01926) 730336
e info@jerseyvillaguesthouse.co.uk
w jerseyvillaguesthouse.co.uk

**Longbridge Farm** ★★★★
*Bed & Breakfast*
Longbridge, Warwick
CV34 6RB
t (01926) 401857
e paul.preston@longbridge.demon.co.uk

**Park Cottage** ★★★★
*Guest Accommodation*
**SILVER AWARD**
113 West Street, Warwick
CV34 6AH
t (01926) 410319
e janet@parkcottagewarwick.co.uk
w parkcottagewarwick.co.uk

**Peacock Lodge** ★★★
*Bed & Breakfast*
97 West Street, Warwick
CV34 6AH
t (01926) 419480

**The Seven Stars Guest Accommodation** ★★★★
*Bed & Breakfast*
**SILVER AWARD**
Friars Street, Warwick
CV34 6HD
t (01926) 492658
e thesevenstars@btinternet.com

**Shrewley Pools Farm**
★★★★ *Farmhouse*
**SILVER AWARD**
Haseley, Warwick CV35 7HB
t (01926) 484315
e cathydodd@hotmail.com
w s-h-systems.co.uk

**Warwick Lodge** ★★★
*Guest House*
82 Emscote Road, Warwick
CV34 5QJ
t (01926) 492927

**Westham Guest House**
★★★ *Guest House*
76 Emscote Road, Warwick
CV34 5QG
t (01926) 491756
e westham.house@ntlworld.com
w westhambedandbreakfast.co.uk

## WATERDEN
Norfolk

**Old Rectory** ★★★★
*Bed & Breakfast*
Waterden, Little Walsingham
NR22 6AT
t (01328) 823298
w tiscover.co.uk

## WATERHOUSES
Staffordshire

**Leehouse Farm** ★★★★
*Bed & Breakfast*
**SILVER AWARD**
Leek Road, Waterhouses, Leek
ST10 3HW
t (01538) 308439

## WATERS UPTON
Shropshire

**Groom's Cottage** ★★★★
*Bed & Breakfast*
Waters Upton, Telford
TF6 6NP
t (01952) 541869
e kbright44@btinternet.com
w grooms-cottage.co.uk

## WELFORD-ON-AVON
Warwickshire

**Bridgend Guest House**
★★★★ *Bed & Breakfast*
Binton Road, Welford-on-Avon, Stratford-upon-Avon
CV37 8PW
t (01789) 750900
e bridgendhouse@aol.com
w stratford-upon-avon.co.uk

## WELL
Lincolnshire

**Wellbeck House** ★★
*Bed & Breakfast*
Well LN13 9EE
t (01507) 462453

## WELLAND
Worcestershire

**North Farm** ★★★
*Guest Accommodation*
Hancocks Lane, Welland, Malvern WR13 6LG
t (01684) 574365

**The Pheasant Inn** ★★ *Inn*
Drake Street, Welland, Malvern WR13 6LP
t (01684) 310400
e thepheasantwelland@yahoo.co.uk
w thepheasantwelland.co.uk

## WELLESBOURNE
Warwickshire

**Meadow Cottage** ★★★
*Bed & Breakfast*
36 Church Walk, Wellesbourne, Warwick
CV35 9QT
t (01789) 840220
e thomas.harland@virgin.net
w meadowcottagebandb.co.uk

## WELLINGTON
Shropshire

**Clairmont** ★★★★
*Guest Accommodation*
54 Haygate Road, Wellington
TF1 1QN
t (01952) 414214
e info@clairmontguesthouse.co.uk
w clairmontguesthouse.co.uk

**Potford House** ★★★
*Bed & Breakfast*
Little Bolas, Wellington, Telford
TF6 6PS
t (01952) 541362
e dsadler@potford.fsnet.co.uk
w shropshirebedandbreakfast.com

## WELLINGTON HEATH
Herefordshire

**Hope End House** ★★★★★
*Guest Accommodation*
**GOLD AWARD**
Hope End, Ledbury HR8 1JQ
t (01531) 635890
e info@hopeendhouse.com
w hopeendhouse.com

## WELLS-NEXT-THE-SEA
Norfolk

**Admiral House** ★★★★
*Bed & Breakfast*
**SILVER AWARD**
6 Southgate Close, Wells-next-the-Sea NR23 1HG
t 07768 892526
e info@admiralhouse-wells.co.uk
w admiralhouse-wells.co.uk

**Arch House** ★★★★
*Guest Accommodation*
50 Mill Road, Wells-next-the-Sea NR23 1DB
t (01328) 710112
e enquiries@archhouse.co.uk
w archhouse.co.uk

**Boxwood Guest House**
★★★★ *Guest House*
**SILVER AWARD**
Northfield Lane, Wells-next-the-Sea NR23 1JZ
t (01328) 711493

**The Cobblers** ★★★★
*Guest House*
Standard Road, Wells-next-the-Sea NR23 1JU
t (01328) 710155
e info@cobblers.co.uk
w cobblers.co.uk

**Glebe Barn** ★★★★
*Bed & Breakfast*
The Glebe, Wells-next-the-Sea
NR23 1AZ
t (01328) 711809
e glebebarn@aol.com
w tiscover.co.uk

**Machrimore** ★★★★
*Bed & Breakfast*
**GOLD AWARD**
Burnt Street, Wells-next-the-Sea NR23 1HS
t (01328) 711653
e enquiries@machrimore.co.uk
w machrimore.co.uk

**Meadow View Guest House**
★★★★
*Guest Accommodation*
**GOLD AWARD**
53 High Street, Wighton, Wells-next-the-Sea NR23 1PF
t (01328) 821527
e bookings@meadowview.net
w meadow-view.net

**Normans** ★★★★★
*Guest Accommodation*
**GOLD AWARD**
Standard Road, Wells-next-the-Sea NR23 1JW
t (01328) 710657
w thenormansatwells.co.uk

**Old Custom House** ★★★★
*Guest Accommodation*
East Quay, Wells-next-the-Sea
NR23 1LD
t (01328) 711463
e bb@eastquay.co.uk
w eastquay.co.uk

**Wells-next-the-Sea YHA**
★★★★ *Hostel*
Church Plain, Wells-next-the-Sea NR23 1EQ
t (01328) 711748
e wellsnorfolk@yha.org.uk
w yha.org.uk

## WELWYN
Hertfordshire

**Catbells** ★★★★
*Bed & Breakfast*
40 Firs Walk, Tewin Wood, Welwyn AL6 0NZ
t (01438) 798412

## WENNINGTON
Cambridgeshire

**Wennington Lodge Bed and Breakfast** ★★ *Farmhouse*
Abbots Ripton, Huntingdon
PE28 2LP
t (01487) 773276
w wennington-lodge.co.uk

## WENTWORTH
Cambridgeshire

**Desiderata** ★★★
*Bed & Breakfast*
44 Main Street, Wentowrth, Ely
CB6 3QG
t (01353) 776131
e chips.1@virgin.net
w mgraham.net

## WEOBLEY
Herefordshire

**Garnstone House** ★★★
*Bed & Breakfast*
Weobley, Hereford, Kington
HR4 8QP
t (01544) 318943
e macleod@garnstonehouse.co.uk
w garnstonehouse.co.uk

## WESSINGTON
Derbyshire

**Crich Lane Farm** ★★★★
*Farmhouse*
Moorwood Moor Lane, Wessington, Alfreton
DE55 6DU
t (01773) 835186
e crichlanefarm@w3z.co.uk
w crichlanefarm.co.uk

## WEST BRIDGFORD
Nottinghamshire

**Firs Guesthouse** ★★★
*Guest House*
96 Radcliffe Road, West Bridgford, Nottingham
NG2 5HH
t (0115) 981 0199
e firs.hotel@btinternet.com

## WEST MERSEA
Essex

**The Victory at Mersea**
Rating Applied For
*Guest Accommodation*
92 Coast Road, Mersea Island, Colchester CO5 8LS
t (01206) 382907
e tydies@aol.com
w victoryatmersea.com

## WEST RUDHAM
Norfolk

**Oyster House** ★★★★
*Bed & Breakfast*
**SILVER AWARD**
Lynn Road, Nest Rudham, King's Lynn PE31 8RW
t (01485) 528327
e oyster-house@tiscali.co.uk
w oysterhouse.co.uk

### WEST RUNTON
Norfolk

**The Old Barn** ★★★★
*Bed & Breakfast*
**SILVER AWARD**
Cromer Road, West Runton NR27 9QT
**t** (01263) 838285
**w** theoldbarnnorfolk.co.uk

### WESTBOROUGH
Lincolnshire

**The Old Tavern** ★★★★
*Bed & Breakfast*
**SILVER AWARD**
Bakers Lane, Westborough, Newark NG23 5HL
**t** (01400) 281071
**e** enquiries@theoldtavern.co.uk
**w** theoldtavern.co.uk

### WESTCLIFF-ON-SEA
Essex

**Pavilion** ★★
*Guest Accommodation*
1 Trinity Avenue, Westcliff-on-Sea SS0 7PU
**t** (01702) 332767
**w** tiscover.co.uk

**Retreat Guesthouse** ★★★
*Guest Accommodation*
12 Canewdon Road, Westcliff-on-Sea, Southend-on-Sea SS0 7NE
**t** (01702) 348217
**e** retreatguesthouse.co.uk@tinyworld.co.uk
**w** a1tourism.com/uk/retreat1.html

**Rose House** ★★★
*Guest House*
21-23 Manor Road, Westcliff-on-Sea SS0 7SR
**t** (01702) 341959

### WESTHOPE
Shropshire

**Ward Farm Bed & Breakfast**
★★★★ *Farmhouse*
Ward Farm, Westhope, Craven Arms SY7 9JL
**t** (01584) 861601
**e** contact@wardfarm.co.uk
**w** wardfarm.co.uk

### WESTHORPE
Suffolk

**Moat Hill Farm B&B** ★★★★
*Bed & Breakfast*
Church Road, Westhorpe, Stowmarket IP14 4SZ
**t** (01449) 780165
**e** moathillb&b@talktalk.net

### WESTON HILLS
Lincolnshire

**The Beeches** ★★★★
*Guest Accommodation*
Austendyke Road, Weston Hills PE12 6BZ
**t** (01406) 370345
**e** info@visitthefens.co.uk

### WESTON-ON-TRENT
Derbyshire

**The Willows** ★★★★
*Guest Accommodation*
**SILVER AWARD**
Trent Lane, Weston-on-Trent, Derby DE72 2BT
**t** (01332) 702525
**e** stay@willowsinweston.co.uk
**w** willowsinweston.co.uk

### WESTON UNDER WETHERLEY
Warwickshire

**Wethele Manor Farm**
★★★★★
*Guest Accommodation*
Weston-under-Wetherley, Royal Leamington Spa, Leamington Spa CV33 9BZ
**t** (01926) 831772
**e** simonmoreton@wethelemanor.com
**w** wethelemanor.com

### WETHERSFIELD
Essex

**Church Hill House** ★★★★
*Bed & Breakfast*
**SILVER AWARD**
High Street, Wethersfield, Braintree CM7 4BY
**t** (01371) 850342
**e** clubley@churchhillhouse.co.uk
**w** churchhillhouse.co.uk

### WETTON
Staffordshire

**The Old Chapel** ★★★★
*Guest Accommodation*
**SILVER AWARD**
Wetton, Ashbourne DE6 2AF
**t** (01335) 310450
**e** lynne.imeson@tiscali.co.uk

### WHALEY BRIDGE
Derbyshire

**Springbank Guest House (Whaley Bridge)** ★★★★
*Guest House* **SILVER AWARD**
3 Reservoir Road, Whaley Bridge, High Peak SK23 7BL
**t** (01663) 732819
**e** margot@whaleyspringbank.co.uk
**w** whaleyspringbank.co.uk

### WHATSTANDWELL
Derbyshire

**Riverdale Guest House**
★★★★ *Bed & Breakfast*
Middle Lane, Crich Carr, Matlock DE4 5EG
**t** (01773) 853905
**e** riverdale@clara.co.uk
**w** riverdaleguesthouse.co.uk

### WHEATHAMPSTEAD
Hertfordshire

**The Crosskeys** ★★★ *Inn*
Gustard Wood, Wheathampstead, St Albans AL4 8LA
**t** (01582) 832165

### WHEPSTEAD
Suffolk

**The Old Pear Tree** ★★★★
*Bed & Breakfast*
Whepstead, Bury St Edmunds IP29 4UD
**t** (01284) 850470
**e** jenny@theoldpeartree.co.uk
**w** theoldpeartree.itgo.com

### WHISSENDINE
Rutland

**Conifers Bed & Breakfast**
★★★★ *Bed & Breakfast*
37 Main Street, Whissendine, Oakham LE15 7ES
**t** (01664) 474141
**e** karentaylor@ukgo.com
**w** conifers.ukgo.com

### WHISTON
Staffordshire

**Whiston Hall Mansion Court Guest House** ★★★
*Guest House*
Whiston Hall Golf Club, Black Lane, Alton Towers Area ST10 2HZ
**t** (01538) 266260
**e** enquiries@whistonhall.com
**w** whistonhall.com

### WHITCHURCH
Shropshire

**Sedgeford House** ★★★★
*Bed & Breakfast*
Sedgeford, Whitchurch SY13 1EX
**t** (01948) 665598
**e** sedgefordhousebandb@tesco.net
**w** sedgefordhouse.com

### WHITE NOTLEY
Essex

**Elms Farm** ★★★★
*Bed & Breakfast*
Green Lane, White Notley, Witham CM8 1RB
**t** (01376) 321559

### WHITFIELD
Northamptonshire

**Chestnut View** ★★
*Bed & Breakfast*
Mill Lane, Whitfield, Brackley NN13 5TQ
**t** (01280) 850246

### WHITNEY-ON-WYE
Herefordshire

**Rhydspence Inn** ★★★★ *Inn*
Whitney-on-Wye, Hay-on-Wye HR3 6EU
**t** (01497) 831262
**e** info@rhydspence-inn.co.uk
**w** rhydspence-inn.co.uk

### WHITTINGTON
Shropshire

**Fitzwarine House** ★★★
*Bed & Breakfast*
Castle Street, Whittington SY11 4DF
**t** (01691) 680882
**e** fitzwarinehouse@supanet.com
**w** fitzwarinehouse.co.uk

### WHITTINGTON
Staffordshire

**Peel Farm Bed & Breakfast**
★★★★ *Farmhouse*
Fisherwick Road, Whittington, Lichfield WS14 9JJ
**t** (01543) 433461
**e** accommodation@peelfarm.co.uk
**w** peelfarm.co.uk

### WHITTINGTON
Worcestershire

**Edgefield Bed and Breakfast**
Rating Applied For
*Guest Accommodation*
Old Road, Whittington, Worcester WR5 2RL
**t** (01905) 356635
**e** lizpowell@edgefield-bandb.co.uk
**w** edgefield-bandb.co.uk

### WHITTLESEY
Cambridgeshire

**Whitmore House** ★★★★
*Bed & Breakfast*
31 Whitmore Street, Whittlesey, Peterborough PE7 1HE
**t** (01733) 203088

### WICKHAMFORD
Worcestershire

**Longacres Bed & Breakfast**
★★★ *Bed & Breakfast*
Longdon Hill, Wickhamford, Evesham WR11 7RP
**t** (01386) 442575
**e** eveshambandb@tiscali.co.uk

### WIGMORE
Herefordshire

**Pear Tree Farm** ★★★★
*Guest Accommodation*
**GOLD AWARD**
Wigmore, Mortimer Country HR6 9UR
**t** (01568) 770140
**e** info@peartree-farm.co.uk
**w** peartree-farm.co.uk

### WILNECOTE
Staffordshire

**Villa Marie** ★★★★
*Bed & Breakfast*
63 Quarry Hill, Wilnecote, Tamworth B77 5BW
**t** (01827) 250966

### WILTON
Herefordshire

**Benhall Farmhouse** ★★★★
*Bed & Breakfast*
**SILVER AWARD**
Wilton, Ross-on-Wye HR9 6AG
**t** (01989) 563900
**e** info@benhallfarm.co.uk
**w** benhallfarm.co.uk

### WIMBISH
Essex

**Beeholme House** ★★★★★
*Bed & Breakfast*
**SILVER AWARD**
Howlett End, Saffron Walden CB10 2XP
**t** (01799) 599458
**e** beeholme@btinternet.com
**w** wolseylodges.com

**Fieldview Bed and Breakfast**
★★★★ *Bed & Breakfast*
Howlett End, Wimbish CB10 2XW
**t** (01799) 599616
**e** mfludre@aol.com
**w** fieldview.eu

**Newdegate House** ★★★★
*Guest Accommodation*
**SILVER AWARD**
Howlett End, Wimbish, Saffron Walden CB10 2XW
**t** (01799) 599748
**e** jacky@newdegate.co.uk

## WINGFIELD Suffolk

**Gables Farm** ★★★★
*Bed & Breakfast*
**SILVER AWARD**
Earsham Street, Wingfield, Diss IP21 5RH
**t** (01379) 586355 & 07824 445464
**e** enquiries@gablesfarm.co.uk
**w** gablesfarm.co.uk

## WINSTER Derbyshire

**Brae Cottage** ★★★★
*Guest Accommodation*
**SILVER AWARD**
East Bank, Winster, Matlock DE4 2DT
**t** (01629) 650375

## WINTERTON-ON-SEA Norfolk

**Tower Cottage** ★★★★
*Bed & Breakfast*
Black Street, Winterton-on-Sea, Great Yarmouth NR29 4AP
**t** (01493) 394053
**e** towercottage@talktalk.net
**w** towercottage.co.uk

## WIRKSWORTH Derbyshire

**Avondale Farm** ★★★★
*Guest Accommodation*
**SILVER AWARD**
Grangemill, Matlock DE4 4HT
**t** (01629) 650820
**e** avondale@tinyworld.co.uk
**w** avondalefarm.co.uk

**The Glenorchy Centre** ★★
*Group Hostel*
West Derbyshire United Reformed Church, Coldwell Street, Wirksworth DE4 4FB
**t** (01629) 824323
**w** glenorchycentre.org.uk

**Manor Barn** ★★★★
*Guest Accommodation*
**SILVER AWARD**
Hopton, Carsington, Wirksworth DE4 4DF
**t** (01629) 540686
**e** yvonneevans55@hotmail.co.uk
**w** manor-barn.co.uk

**The Old Lock-Up** ★★★★★
*Guest Accommodation*
**GOLD AWARD**
North End, Wirksworth DE4 4FG
**t** (01629) 826272
**e** wheeler@theoldlockup.co.uk
**w** theoldlockup.co.uk

## WISBECH Cambridgeshire

**4 Union Place** ★★★
*Bed & Breakfast*
Wisbech PE13 1HB
**t** (01945) 588160

**Marmion House** ★★★
*Guest Accommodation*
11-19 Lynn Road, Wisbech PE13 3DD
**t** (01945) 582822
**w** a1tourism.com/uk/marmionhouse.html

## WISHAW Warwickshire

**Ash House** ★★★★
*Bed & Breakfast*
The Gravel, Wishaw, Sutton Coldfield B76 9QB
**t** (01675) 475782
**e** kate@rectory80.freeserve.co.uk

## WISSETT Suffolk

**Wissett Lodge** ★★★★
*Farmhouse*
Lodge Lane, Wissett, Halesworth IP19 0JQ
**t** (01986) 873173
**e** mail@wissettlodge.co.uk
**w** wissettlodge.co.uk

## WISTANSWICK Shropshire

**Marsh Farm Bed & Breakfast** ★★★★ *Bed & Breakfast*
Marsh Farm, Wistanswick, Market Drayton TF9 2BB
**t** (01630) 638520
**e** wiz.light@talk21.com
**w** marshfarmbandb.co.uk

## WISTOW Cambridgeshire

**Pointers Guest House** ★★★★ *Farmhouse*
Pointers, Wistow, Huntingdon PE28 2QH
**t** (01487) 822366
**e** ew@pointers-guest-house.co.uk
**w** pointers-guest-house.co.uk

## WITCHFORD Cambridgeshire

**The Woodlands** ★★★★
*Guest House*
Grunty Fen Road, Witchford, Ely CB6 2JE
**t** (01353) 663746
**e** info@woodlandsbandb.co.uk
**w** woodlandsbandb.co.uk

## WITHAM Essex

**Chestnuts** ★★★
*Bed & Breakfast*
8 Octavia Drive, Witham Lodge, Witham CM8 1HQ
**t** (01376) 515990
**e** janetmoya@aol.com

## WITHERLEY Warwickshire

**The Old House Bed & Breakfast** ★★★★
*Guest House*
Watling Street, Witherley, Hinckley CV9 1RD
**t** (01827) 715634
**e** enquiries@theoldhousebandb.co.uk
**w** theoldhousebandb.co.uk

## WIX Essex

**Periwinkle Cottage** ★★★★
*Bed & Breakfast*
**SILVER AWARD**
Colchester Road, Wix, Nr Harwich CO11 2PD
**t** (01255) 870167
**w** tiscover.co.uk

## WOLSTON Warwickshire

**Lords Hill Farm, Farmhouse B&B** ★★★★ *Farmhouse*
Lords Hill Farm, Coalpit Lane, Coventry CV8 3GB
**t** (024) 76544430
**e** jane@lordshillfarm.co.uk
**w** lordshillfarm.co.uk

## WOODBRIDGE Suffolk

**Cherry Tree Inn** ★★★★
*Guest Accommodation*
73 Cumberland Street, Woodbridge IP12 4AG
**t** (01394) 384627
**e** info@thecherrytreepub.co.uk
**w** thecherrytreepub.co.uk

**The Coach House** ★★★★
*Bed & Breakfast*
121 Ipswich Road, Woodbridge IP12 4BY
**t** (01394) 385918
**e** rita@thecoachhouse-woodbridge.co.uk
**w** thecoachhouse-woodbridge.co.uk

**Deben Lodge** ★★
*Bed & Breakfast*
Melton Road, Woodbridge IP12 1NH
**t** (01394) 382740
**w** smoothhound.co.uk

**Fir Tree Lodge** ★★★★
*Bed & Breakfast*
**SILVER AWARD**
25 Moorfield Road, Woodbridge IP12 4JN
**t** 07968 346029
**e** nights@debenaccom.com
**w** debenaccom.com

**Hill House** ★★★★
*Bed & Breakfast*
30 Market Hill, Woodbridge IP12 4LU
**t** (01394) 383890
**e** sarenkaknight@tiscali.co.uk
**w** hillhousewoodbridge.com

**Mill View House** ★★★
*Bed & Breakfast*
33 Mill View Close, Woodbridge IP12 4HR
**t** (01394) 383010
**e** millview.house@btinternet.com

**Moat Barn** ★★★★
*Bed & Breakfast*
Dallinghoo Road, Bredfield, Woodbridge IP13 6BD
**t** (01473) 737520
**w** moatbarn.co.uk

**Pond Farm B & B** ★★★
*Bed & Breakfast*
Pond Farm, Fingal Street, Woodbridge IP13 7PD
**t** (01728) 628565
**e** enquiries@pond-farm.co.uk
**w** pond-farm.co.uk

**St Anne's School House** ★★★★ *Bed & Breakfast*
**SILVER AWARD**
Crown Place, Woodbridge IP12 1BU
**t** (01394) 386942
**e** sash@justsuffolk.com

## WOODHALL SPA Lincolnshire

**Chaplin House** ★★★★
*Guest Accommodation*
**SILVER AWARD**
92 High Street, Martin LN4 3QT
**t** (01526) 378795
**e** info@chaplin-house.co.uk
**w** chaplin-house.co.uk

**Kirkstead Old Mill Cottage** ★★★★
*Guest Accommodation*
**SILVER AWARD**
Tattershall Road, Woodhall Spa LN10 6UQ
**t** (01526) 353637
**e** barbara@woodhallspa.com
**w** woodhallspa.com

**The Limes** ★★★
*Bed & Breakfast*
Tattershall Road, Woodhall Spa LN10 6TW
**t** (01526) 352219

**Newlands** ★★★★
*Bed & Breakfast*
56 Woodland Drive, Woodhall Spa LN10 6YG
**t** (01526) 352881

**Oglee Guest House** ★★★★
*Guest Accommodation*
16 Stanhope Avenue, Woodhall Spa LN10 6SP
**t** (01526) 353512
**e** ogleeguesthouse@gmail.com

**Pitchaway** ★★★★
*Guest House*
The Broadway, Woodhall Spa LN10 6SQ
**t** (01526) 352969
**e** info@pitchaway.co.uk
**w** pitchaway.co.uk

**The Vale** ★★★
*Bed & Breakfast*
50 Tor-O-Moor Road, Woodhall Spa LN10 6SB
**t** (01526) 353022
**e** margot.mills@hotmail.co.uk

**Village Limits Motel** ★★★★
*Guest Accommodation*
Stixwould Road, Woodhall Spa LN10 6UJ
**t** (01526) 353312
**e** info@villagelimits.co.uk
**w** villagelimits.co.uk

## WOODHAM MORTIMER Essex

**Chase Farm Bed & Breakfast** ★★★ *Bed & Breakfast*
Hyde Chase, Maldon CM9 6TN
**t** (01245) 223268

## WOODHURST Cambridgeshire

**Fullards Farm** ★★★★
*Farmhouse*
South Street, Woodhurst, Huntingdon PE28 3BW
**t** (01487) 824356
**e** fullards@btopenworld.com
**w** fullardsfarm.co.uk

**The Raptor Foundation** ★★★ *Guest Accommodation*
The Heath, St Ives Road, Huntingdon PE28 3BT
**t** (01487) 741140
**e** heleowl@aol.com
**w** raptorfoundation.org.uk

**WOODNEWTON**
Northamptonshire

**Bridge Cottage** ★★★★
*Bed & Breakfast*
Oundle Road, Woodnewton
PE8 5EG
**t** (01780) 470779 &
07979 644864
**e** enquiries@bridgecottage.
net
**w** bridgecottage.net

**WOODSTON**
Cambridgeshire

**White House Guesthouse**
★★★ *Guest House*
White House, 318 Oundle
Road, Peterborough PE2 9QP
**t** (01733) 566650
**e** helmorgan@lineone.com
**w** tiscover.co.uk

**WOOFFERTON**
Shropshire

**Orchard House** ★★★★
*Bed & Breakfast*
**SILVER AWARD**
Ashford Bowdler, Ludlow
SY8 4DJ
**t** (01584) 831270
**e** judith@orchard-barn.co.uk
**w** orchard-barn.co.uk

**WOOLLEY**
Cambridgeshire

**New Manor Farm** ★★★★
*Farmhouse*
Ellington Road, Woolley,
Huntingdon PE28 5BH
**t** (01480) 890092
**e** newmanor.farm@virgin.net
**w** new-manor-farm.co.uk

**WOOLPIT**
Suffolk

**Bull Inn and Restaurant**
★★★ *Inn*
The Street, Woolpit, Bury St
Edmunds IP30 9SA
**t** (01359) 240393
**e** info@bullinnwoolpit.co.uk
**w** bullinnwoolpit.co.uk

**Grange Farm** ★★★★
*Farmhouse*
Woolpit, Bury St Edmunds
IP30 9RG
**t** (01359) 241143
**e** grangefarm@btinternet.com
**w** farmstayanglia.co.uk/
grangefarm/

**WOONTON**
Herefordshire

**Rose Cottage – Woonton**
★★★★
*Guest Accommodation*
**SILVER AWARD**
Woonton, Hereford, Kington
HR3 6QW
**t** (01544) 340459
**e** tessa.plummer@ukonline.co.
uk
**w** rosecottagewoonton.co.uk

**WORCESTER**
Worcestershire

**The Barn House** ★★★
*Farmhouse*
Broadwas in Teme, Worcester
WR6 5NS
**t** (01886) 888733 &
07778 274328
**e** info@barnhouseonline.co.uk
**w** barnhouseonline.co.uk

**The Croft** ★★★★
*Bed & Breakfast*
25 Station Road, Fernhill Heath,
Worcester WR3 7UJ
**t** (01905) 453482
**e** thecroft@janetandbrian.
wanadoo.co.uk

**De-Bury House** ★★★
*Bed & Breakfast*
3 The Bullring, St Johns,
Worcester WR2 5AA
**t** (01905) 425532
**w** de-bury.co.uk

**Green Farm** ★★★★
*Farmhouse*
Crowle Green, Worcester
WR7 4AB
**t** (01905) 381807
**e** thegreenfarm@btinternet.
com
**w** thegreenfarm.co.uk

**Hill Farm House** ★★★★
*Bed & Breakfast*
**SILVER AWARD**
Dormston Lane, Dormston,
Worcester WR7 4JS
**t** (01386) 793159
**e** jim@hillfarmhouse.co.uk
**w** hillfarmhouse.co.uk

**Holland House** ★★★
*Bed & Breakfast*
210 London Road, Worcester
WR5 2JT
**t** (01905) 353939
**e** beds@holland-house.me.uk
**w** holland-house.me.uk

**Laburnum Villa** ★★★★
*Bed & Breakfast*
243 Ombersley Road,
Worcester WR3 7BY
**t** (01905) 755572
**e** laburnumvilla@tiscali.co.uk
**w** laburnumvilla.com

**The Manor Coach House**
Rating Applied For
*Guest Accommodation*
Hindlip Lane, Hindlip,
Worcester WR3 8SJ
**t** (01905) 456457
**e** info@manorcoachhouse.co.
uk
**w** manorcoachhouse.co.uk

**Oldbury Farm** ★★★★
*Farmhouse* **SILVER AWARD**
Lower Broadheath, Worcester
WR2 6RQ
**t** (01905) 421357
**e** janejordan@oldburyfarm.
freeserve.co.uk
**w** smoothhound.co.uk/hotels/
oldburyfarm

**Osborne House** ★★★
*Guest Accommodation*
17 Chestnut Walk, Worcester
WR1 1PR
**t** (01905) 22296
**e** enquiries@osborne-house.
co.uk
**w** osborne-house.co.uk

**Shrubbery Guest House**
★★★ *Guest House*
38 Barbourne Road, Worcester
WR1 1HU
**t** (01905) 24871

**WORMELOW**
Herefordshire

**Lyston Villa** ★★★
*Bed & Breakfast*
Wormelow, Hereford HR2 8EL
**t** (01981) 540130
**e** sue@lystonvilla.co.uk
**w** lystonvilla.co.uk

**WORSTEAD**
Norfolk

**Hall Farm Guesthouse**
★★★★
*Guest Accommodation*
**SILVER AWARD**
Sloley Road, North Walsham
NR28 9RS
**t** (01692) 536124
**e** lowehall@aol.com
**w** hallfarmguesthouse.co.uk

**WORTHAM**
Suffolk

**Rookery Farm** ★★★★
*Farmhouse* **SILVER AWARD**
Old Bury Road, Wortham, Diss
IP22 1RB
**t** (01379) 783236
**e** russell.ling@ukgateway.net
**w** tiscover.co.uk

**WRAWBY**
Lincolnshire

**Mowden House** ★★★★
*Guest Accommodation*
Barton Road, Wrawby
DN20 8SQ
**t** (01652) 652145
**e** dr@prabhakaran.fsnet.co.uk

**WRENTHAM**
Suffolk

**Five Bells** ★★★ *Inn*
Southwold Road, Wrentham
NR34 7JF
**t** (01502) 675249
**e** victoriapub@aol.com
**w** five-bells.com

**WROXHAM**
Norfolk

**58 Norwich Road** ★★★★
*Bed & Breakfast*
Wroxham, Norwich NR12 8RX
**t** (01603) 783998

**Coach House** ★★★★
*Bed & Breakfast*
**SILVER AWARD**
96 Norwich Road, Norwich
NR12 8RY
**t** (01603) 784376
**e** info@coachhousewroxham.
co.uk
**w** coachhousewroxham.co.uk

**Wroxham Park Lodge**
★★★★ *Bed & Breakfast*
142 Norwich Road, Wroxham,
Norwich NR12 8SA
**t** (01603) 782991
**e** parklodge@computer-assist.
net
**w** wroxhamparklodge.com

**WYMONDHAM**
Norfolk

**Elm Lodge Bed & Breakfast**
Rating Applied For
*Bed & Breakfast*
Downham Grove,
Wymondham NR18 0SN
**t** (01953) 607501
**e** elm.lodge@btinternet.com
**w** smoothhound.co.uk/hotels/
elmlodge

**Witch Hazel** ★★★★
*Bed & Breakfast*
**SILVER AWARD**
55 Church Lane, Wicklewood,
Wymondham NR18 9QH
**t** (01953) 602247
**e** witchhazel@tiscali.co.uk
**w** witchhazel-norfolk.co.uk

**YOULGREAVE**
Derbyshire

**The Farmyard Inn** ★★★
*Guest Accommodation*
Main Street, Youlgrave,
Bakewell DE45 1UW
**t** (01629) 636221

**The Old Bakery** ★★★
*Bed & Breakfast*
Church Street, Youlgrave,
Bakewell DE45 1UR
**t** (01629) 636887

**YHA Youlgreave** ★★★
*Hostel*
Fountain Square, Youlgreave,
Bakewell DE45 1UR
**t** (01629) 636518
**w** yha.org.uk

**YOXALL**
Staffordshire

**The Golden Cup** ★★★★ *Inn*
Main Street, Yoxall, Burton-on-
Trent DE13 8NQ
**t** (01543) 472295
**e** rchltrner@aol.com
**w** thegoldencup.com

**YOXFORD**
Suffolk

**Chapel Cottage** ★★★★
*Bed & Breakfast*
**SILVER AWARD**
High Street, Yoxford,
Saxmundham IP17 3HP
**t** (01728) 667096
**e** info@chapelcottage-
yoxford.co.uk
**w** chapelcottage-yoxford.co.uk

**The Griffin** ★★★ *Inn*
Yoxford, Saxmundham
IP17 3EP
**t** (01728) 668229
**e** enquiries@thegriffin.co.uk
**w** thegriffin.co.uk

# SOUTH EAST ENGLAND

## ABINGDON
### Oxfordshire

**Abbey Guest House** ★★★★
*Guest House*
136 Oxford Road, Abingdon
OX14 2AG
t (01235) 537020
e info@abbeyguest.com
w abbeyguest.com

**Kingfisher Barn** ★★★★
*Guest Accommodation*
Rye Farm, Abingdon
OX14 3NN
t (01235) 537538
e info@kingfisherbarn.com
w kingfisherbarn.com

## ABINGER COMMON
### Surrey

**Leylands Farm** ★★★★
*Guest Accommodation*
**SILVER AWARD**
Leylands Lane, Abinger
Common RH5 6JU
t (01306) 730115 &
07818 422881
e annieblf@btopenworld.com
w leylandsfarm.co.uk

## ADDERBURY
### Oxfordshire

**The Bell Inn** ★★★ *Inn*
High Street, Adderbury,
Banbury OX17 3LS
t (01295) 810338
e info@the-bell.com
w the-bell.com

The Red Lion
Rating Applied For
*Guest Accommodation*
The Green, Banbury
OX17 3NG
t (01295) 810269
w redlion-adderbury.com

## ALBURY
### Surrey

**Barn Cottage** ★★★★
*Bed & Breakfast*
Farley Green, Albury GU5 9DN
t (01483) 202571
e bookings@barn-cottage.com
w barn-cottage.com

## ALDERMASTON
### Berkshire

**The Hinds Head** ★★★★ *Inn*
Wasing Lane, Aldermaston
RG7 4LX
t (0118) 971 2194
e hindshead@fullers.co.uk
w fullersinns.co.uk

## ALDINGBOURNE
### West Sussex

**Limmer Pond House** ★★★
*Bed & Breakfast*
Church Road, Aldingbourne
PO20 3TU
t (01243) 543210

## ALDINGTON
### Kent

**Fostums** ★★★★
*Guest Accommodation*
**SILVER AWARD**
Roman Road, Aldington
TN25 7EP
t (01233) 720996
e fax@fostums.co.uk
w fostums.co.uk

Hogben Farm ★★★★
*Farmhouse*
Church Lane, Aldington,
Ashford TN25 7EH
t (01233) 720219
e ros@hogbenfarm.co.uk
w hogbenfarm.co.uk

## ALDWORTH
### Berkshire

**Fieldview Cottage** ★★★★
*Bed & Breakfast*
Bell Lane, Aldworth, Reading
RG8 9SB
t (01635) 578964
e hunt@fieldvu.freeserve.co.uk

## ALFRISTON
### East Sussex

**Alfriston Youth Hostel** ★★
*Hostel*
Frog Firle, Alfriston, Polegate
BN26 5SD
t 0870 770 5666
e alfriston@yha.org.uk

**Rose Cottage** ★★★★
*Bed & Breakfast*
North Street, Alfriston
BN26 5UQ
t (01323) 871534
e hd.rosecottage@btinternet.com
w rosecott.uk.com

**Wingrove House** ★★★★★
*Restaurant with Rooms*
High Street, Alfriston
BN26 5TD
t (01323) 870276
e info@wingrovehousehotel.com
w wingrovehousehotel.com

## ALRESFORD
### Hampshire

**Haygarth** ★★★
*Bed & Breakfast*
Val Ramshaw, 82 Jacklyns
Lane, Alresford SO24 9LJ
t (01962) 732715 &
07986 372895

## ALTON
### Hampshire

**Boundary House** ★★★★
*Bed & Breakfast*
**SILVER AWARD**
Gosport Road, Lower
Farringdon GU34 3DH
t (01420) 587076
e boundarys@messages.co.uk
w boundaryhouse.co.uk

**The Granary** ★★★★
*Farmhouse* **GOLD AWARD**
Stubbs Farm, South Hay
GU35 9NR
t (01420) 474906
e info@stubbsfarm.co.uk
w stubbsfarm.co.uk

**Neatham Barn** ★★★★
*Bed & Breakfast*
Holybourne, Neatham, Alton
GU34 4NP
t (01420) 544215
e neathambarn@f2s.com
w neathambarn.com

**St Mary's Hall** ★★★★
*Bed & Breakfast*
18 Albert Road, Alton
GU34 1LP
t (01420) 88269
e joanmossop@stmaryshall.com
w stmaryshall.com

**Shepherds Court** ★★★★
*Guest Accommodation*
**SILVER AWARD**
Whitehouse Farm, Selborne
Road, Alton GU34 3HL
t (01420) 83847
e info@shepherdscourt.co.uk
w shepherdscourt.co.uk

**West End Farm** ★★★★
*Farmhouse*
Upper Froyle, Alton GU34 4JG
t (01420) 22130
e westend@hampshirebedandbreakfast.co.uk
w hampshirebedandbreakfast.co.uk

## ALVERSTONE GARDEN VILLAGE
### Isle of Wight

**Bluebell Wood Bed & Breakfast** ★★★★
*Bed & Breakfast*
**SILVER AWARD**
13 Woodside Avenue,
Alverstone Garden Village,
Sandown PO36 0JD
t (01983) 401869

## AMBERLEY
### West Sussex

**Brook Green Arundel** ★★
*Bed & Breakfast*
Hog Lane, Amberley, Arundel
BN18 9NQ
t (01798) 831275

## AMERSHAM
### Buckinghamshire

**St Catherins** ★★★
*Bed & Breakfast*
9 Parkfield Avenue, Amersham
HP6 6BE
t (01494) 728125
e jellio@talktalk.net
w st-catherins-bandb.co.uk

## ANDOVER
### Hampshire

**The Amberley** ★★★
*Guest Accommodation*
70 Weyhill Road, Andover
SP10 3NP
t (01264) 352224
e amberleyand@fsbdial.co.uk

**Amport Inn** ★★★ *Inn*
Amport, Andover SP11 8AE
t (01264) 710371

**Church Mews Guest House**
★★ *Guest House*
2 Chantry Street, Andover
SP10 1DE
t (01264) 324323
e edmund@churchmews.co.uk

**May Cottage** ★★★★
*Bed & Breakfast*
**SILVER AWARD**
Thruxton, Andover SP11 8LZ
t (01264) 771241
e info@maycottage-thruxton.co.uk
w maycottage-thruxton.co.uk

**Salisbury Road Bed & Breakfast** ★★★★
*Bed & Breakfast*
99 Salisbury Road, Andover
SP10 2LN
t (01264) 362638
e jenny@andoveraccommodation.co.uk
w andoveraccommodation.co.uk

## ARDLEY
### Oxfordshire

**The Old Post Office** ★★★
*Bed & Breakfast*
Church Road, Ardley, Bicester
OX27 7NP
t (01869) 345958
e mail@theoldpostofficeardley.co.uk
w theoldpostofficeardley.co.uk

## ARRETON
### Isle of Wight

**Arreton Manor** ★★★★★
*Bed & Breakfast*
**GOLD AWARD**
Main Road, Arreton PO30 3AA
t (01983) 522604
e arreton@arretonmanor.co.uk
w arretonmanor.co.uk

## ARUNDEL
### West Sussex

**Arundel House Restaurant & Rooms** ★★★★★
*Restaurant with Rooms*
**GOLD AWARD**
11 High Street, Arundel
BN18 9AD
t (01903) 882136 &
(01903) 882136
e mail@arundelhouseonline.co.uk
w arundelhouseonline.co.uk

**Burpham Country House**
★★★★ *Guest House*
(Formerly The Old Parsonage),
The Street, Arundel BN18 9RJ
t (01903) 882160
e info@burphamcountryhouse.com
w burphamcountryhouse.com

**Pindars** ★★★★
*Guest Accommodation*
**SILVER AWARD**
Lyminster, Littlehampton
BN17 7QF
**t** (01903) 882628
**e** pindars@btinternet.com
**w** pindars.co.uk

**Sandfield House** ★★★
*Bed & Breakfast*
Lyminster Road, Wick
BN17 7PG
**t** (01903) 724129
**e** francesfarrerbrown@btconnect.com
**w** visitsussex.org

**The Townhouse** ★★★★
*Restaurant with Rooms*
**SILVER AWARD**
65 High Street, Arundel
BN18 9AJ
**t** (01903) 883847
**e** enquiries@thetownhouse.co.uk
**w** thetownhouse.co.uk

**Woodpeckers** ★★★★
*Bed & Breakfast*
15 Dalloway Road, Arundel
BN18 9HJ
**t** (01903) 883948

### ASCOT
### Berkshire

**Tanglewood** ★★★
*Bed & Breakfast*
Tanglewood Birch Lane, Long Hill Road Chavey Down, Ascot
SL5 8RF
**t** (01344) 882528
**e** beer.tanglewood@btinternet.com
**w** tanglewood-ascot.co.uk/index.html

### ASCOTT-UNDER-WYCHWOOD
### Oxfordshire

**College Farm** ★★★★
*Farmhouse*
Ascott-under-Wychwood
OX7 6AL
**t** (01993) 831900
**e** sally@college-farm.com

**Meadowbank House** ★★★★
*Bed & Breakfast*
Shipton Road, Chipping Norton
OX7 6AG
**t** (01993) 830612
**e** ingrid@meadowbank-ascott.co.uk
**w** meadowbank-ascott.co.uk

**The Swan At Ascott**
Rating Applied For
*Inn*
Ascott-under-Wychwood
OX7 6AY
**t** (01993) 832332
**e** ricky_lait_uk@yahoo.com
**w** swanatascott.com

### ASH
### Kent

**Great Weddington**
★★★★★ *Bed & Breakfast*
Weddington, Ash, Canterbury
CT3 2AR
**t** (01304) 813407
**e** traveltale@aol.com
**w** greatweddington.co.uk

### ASHFORD
### Kent

**Dean Court Farm** ★★★
*Guest Accommodation*
Challock Lane, Westwell, Ashford TN25 4NH
**t** (01233) 712924

**The New Flying Horse**
★★★★ *Inn*
Upper Bridge Street, Wye
TN25 5AN
**t** (01233) 812297
**e** newflyhorse@shepherdneame.co.uk
**w** newflyinghorsewye.co.uk

**Sue & Jim's Bed & Breakfast**
★★ *Guest Accommodation*
31 Birling Road, Ashford
TN24 8BD
**t** (01233) 643069
**e** susan.mclaren1@ntlworld.com
**w** sueandjimsbandb.co.uk

### ASHURST
### Hampshire

**Forest Gate Lodge** ★★★★
*Guest Accommodation*
161 Lyndhurst Road, Ashurst, Lyndhurst SO40 7AW
**t** (023) 8029 3026
**e** forestgatelodge161@hotmail.co.uk
**w** forestgatelodge.co.uk

**Kingswood Cottage** ★★★★
*Bed & Breakfast*
**SILVER AWARD**
10 Woodlands Road, Ashurst
SO40 7AD
**t** (023) 8029 2582
**e** kingswoodcottage@yahoo.co.uk
**w** kingswoodcottage.co.uk

### ASTON ABBOTTS
### Buckinghamshire

**Windmill Hill Barns** ★★★★
*Bed & Breakfast*
Moat Lane, Aston Abbotts
HP22 4NF
**t** (01296) 681714

### ASTON UPTHORPE
### Oxfordshire

**Middle Fell** ★★★★
*Guest Accommodation*
Moreton Road, Aston Upthorpe OX11 9ER
**t** (01235) 850207
**e** middlefell@ic24.net
**w** middlefell.co.uk

### AWBRIDGE
### Hampshire

**Crofton Country Bed and Breakfast** ★★★★★
*Bed & Breakfast*
**SILVER AWARD**
Kents Oak, Awbridge
SO51 0HH
**t** (01794) 340333
**e** pauline@croftonbandb.com
**w** croftonbandb.com

**Woodpeckers B&B** ★★★★
*Farmhouse* **SILVER AWARD**
1 The Prophets, Newtown
SO51 0GJ
**t** (01794) 342400
**e** woodpeckersbandb@aol.com
**w** woodpeckersbandb.co.uk

### AYLESBURY
### Buckinghamshire

**26 King Edward Avenue**
Rating Applied For
*Guest Accommodation*
King Edward Avenue, Aylesbury HP21 7JD
**t** (01296) 338673

**74 Friarscroft Way** ★★
*Bed & Breakfast*
Aylesbury HP20 2TF
**t** (01296) 489439

**Applecroft** ★★★
*Bed & Breakfast*
187 Aylesbury Road, Aylesbury
HP22 5DS
**t** (01296) 485345
**e** marie.archer@applecroftbb.co.uk
**w** applecroftbb.co.uk

**Ardenwood Bed & Breakfast**
Rating Applied For
*Guest Accommodation*
The Malt House, 45 Walton Road, Aylesbury HP21 7SR
**t** (01296) 484482
**e** james@ardenwoodbandb.co.uk
**w** ardenwoodbandb.co.uk

**Bay Lodge Guest House** ★★
*Guest House*
47 Tring Road, Aylesbury
HP20 1LD
**t** (01296) 331404
**e** blodge47@hotmail.com
**w** bay-lodge.co.uk

**The Cottage B&B** ★★★★
*Bed & Breakfast*
Pitchcott Road, Oving
HP22 4HR
**t** (01296) 641891
**e** thegeorges@btinternet.com

**Lakeside Bed & Breakfast**
★★★★ *Bed & Breakfast*
9/10 Osprey Walk, Aylesbury
HP19 0FF
**t** (01296) 331351
**e** sil@waitrose.com

**The Old Forge Barn** ★★★
*Bed & Breakfast*
Ridings Way, Cublington
LU7 0LW
**t** (01296) 681194
**e** waples@ukonline.co.uk

**Olympic Lodge** ★★★
*Guest Accommodation*
Stoke Mandeville Stadium, Guttmann Road, Stoke Mandeville HP21 9PP
**t** (01296) 461121
**e** stoke.mandeville@leisureconnection.co.uk
**w** olympic-lodge.co.uk

**Tanamera** ★★★★
*Bed & Breakfast*
**SILVER AWARD**
37 Bishopstone Village, Bishopstone, Aylesbury
HP17 8SH
**t** (01296) 748551
**e** tanamera@tesco.net

**Town House** ★★★
*Guest House*
35 Tring Road, Aylesbury
HP20 1LD
**t** (01296) 395295
**w** yell.com

### AYLESFORD
### Kent

**Wickham Lodge** ★★★★★
*Guest Accommodation*
**GOLD AWARD**
High Street, Aylesford
ME20 7AY
**t** (01622) 717267
**e** wickhamlodge@aol.com
**w** wickhamlodge.co.uk

### BALCOMBE
### West Sussex

**Rocks Lane Cottage** ★★★★
*Bed & Breakfast*
Rocksl Lane, Balcombe, Haywards Heath RH17 6JG
**t** (01444) 811245
**e** angelaparry@talktalk.net

### BAMPTON
### Oxfordshire

**The Granary** ★★★
*Bed & Breakfast*
Main Street, Bampton
OX18 2SH
**t** (01367) 810266

**Wheelgate House Bed & Breakfast** ★★★★
*Bed & Breakfast*
Market Square, Bampton
OX18 2JH
**t** (01993) 851151
**e** wheelgatehouse@hotmail.co.uk
**w** wheelgatehouse.co.uk

### BANBURY
### Oxfordshire

**Amberley Guesthouse** ★★
*Guest Accommodation*
151 Middleton Road, Banbury
OX16 3QS
**t** (01295) 255797
**e** amberley151@netscape.net

**Ark Guesthouse** ★★★
*Guest Accommodation*
Warwick Road, Banbury
OX16 2AN
**t** (01295) 254498

**Ashlea Guesthouse** ★★
*Guest Accommodation*
58 Oxford Road, Banbury
OX16 9AN
**t** (01295) 250539
**e** billyboland@tiscali.co.uk

**Avonlea Guesthouse** ★★★
*Guest Accommodation*
41 Southam Road, Banbury
OX16 7EP
**t** (01295) 267837
**e** whitforddebbie@hotmail.com
**w** avonleaguesthouse.co.uk

**Babington Barn** ★★★
*Bed & Breakfast*
Williamscot, Banbury
OX17 1AD
**t** (01295) 750546
**e** info@thomasmartin.co.uk

**Banbury Cross B&B** ★★★★
*Guest House* **SILVER AWARD**
1 Broughton Road, Banbury
OX16 9QB
**t** (01295) 266048
**e** michelle@scars1.freeserve.co.uk
**w** banburycrossbandb.co.uk

**Cotefields Bed & Breakfast**
★★ *Bed & Breakfast*
Oxford Road, Bodicote, Banbury OX15 4AQ
t (01295) 264977
e tony.stockford@ic24.net or cheapbed@yahoo.com
w bedandbreakfastcotefields.co.uk

**Easington House** ★★★★
*Guest House*
50 Oxford Road, Banbury OX16 9AN
t (01295) 270181
e enquiries@easingtonhouse.co.uk
w easingtonhouse.co.uk

**Hanwell House** ★★★★
*Bed & Breakfast*
2 Lapsley Drive, Banbury OX16 1EJ
t (01295) 263001
e hanwell.house@googlemail.com
w hanwellhouse.com

**Prospect House** ★★★
*Guest Accommodation*
Oxford Road, Banbury OX16 9AN
t (01295) 268749

**St Martins House** ★★★★
*Bed & Breakfast*
Warkworth, Banbury OX17 2AG
t (01295) 712684

**Treetops Guest House**
Rating Applied For
*Guest Accommodation*
28 Dashwood Road, Banbury OX16 5HD
t (01295) 254444

**White Cross House** ★★★★
*Bed & Breakfast*
7 Broughton Road, Banbury OX16 9QB
t (01295) 277932
e marian@kedwards50.fsnet.co.uk

## BARHAM
Kent

**The Duke of Cumberland**
★★★★ *Inn*
The Street, Canterbury CT4 6NY
t (01227) 831396
e info@dukeofcumberland.co.uk
w dukeofcumberland.co.uk

## BARNHAM
West Sussex

**Downhills** ★★
*Bed & Breakfast*
87 Barnham Road, Barnham PO22 0EQ
t (01243) 553104

**Saxby**
Rating Applied For
*Guest Accommodation*
Yapton Road, Barnham PO22 0BQ
t (01243) 552996
e saxby-bandb@tiscali.co.uk
w saxbybandb.co.uk

## BARTON ON SEA
Hampshire

**Grandco Lodge** ★★★★
*Bed & Breakfast*
**SILVER AWARD**
29 Marine Drive East, Barton-on-Sea BH25 7DU
t (01425) 610541
w explorethenewforest.co.uk/grandcolodge.htm

**Pebble Beach** ★★★★
*Restaurant with Rooms*
Marine Drive, Barton-on-Sea BH25 7DZ
t (01425) 627777
e mail@pebblebeach-uk.com
w pebblebeach-uk.com

## BARTON STACEY
Hampshire

**Riverside Cottage** ★★★★
*Guest Accommodation*
Bransbury, Barton Stacey SO21 3QJ
t 07973 215407
e csdryden.clark@btinternet.com

## BASINGSTOKE
Hampshire

**Arundel (Old Basing)** ★★
*Bed & Breakfast*
25 Linden Avenue, Old Basing RG24 7HS
t (01256) 327282
e dianapcole@aol.com

**The Haven** ★★
*Bed & Breakfast*
8 Newnham Lane, Old Basing RG24 7AT
t (01256) 462892

**Millfield House** ★★★★
*Guest Accommodation*
**SILVER AWARD**
1a Little Basing, Bartons Lane, Basingstoke RG24 8AX
t (01256) 474513
e info@millfieldhouse.co.uk
w millfieldhouse.co.uk

**Wessex House** ★★★
*Guest House*
120 Winchester Road, Basingstoke RG21 8YW
t (01256) 325202
e wessexhouse@gmail.com
w wessexhousebandb.co.uk

## BATTLE
East Sussex

**A White Lodge** ★★★★
*Bed & Breakfast*
**SILVER AWARD**
42 Hastings Road, Battle TN33 0TE
t 07714 270373
e janewhitelodge2@msn.com
w bedandbreakfastbattle.co.uk

**Acacia House** ★★★★
*Bed & Breakfast*
Starrs Green Lane, Battle TN33 0TD
t (01424) 772416
e acacia.house@beamingmail.com
w battlebedandbreakfast.co.uk

**The Annex Cottage** ★★★★
*Bed & Breakfast*
Woodmans, Whatlington, Battle TN33 0NN
t (01424) 870342

**Heather Hill** ★★★★★
*Guest Accommodation*
94 Hastings Road, Battle TN33 0TQ
t (01424) 774746
e battlebb@battlebedandbreakfast.com
w battlebedandbreakfast.com

**Tollgate Farm House**
★★★★
*Guest Accommodation*
**SILVER AWARD**
North Trade Road, Battle TN33 0HS
t (01424) 777436
e christinemhowe@hotmail.com
w tollgatefarmhouse.co.uk

## BEARSTED
Kent

**Cherwell** ★★★★
*Guest Accommodation*
88 Ashford Road, Maidstone ME14 4LT
t (01622) 738278
e anna.cherwell@btinternet.com
w cherwellbandb.co.uk

## BEAULIEU
Hampshire

**Dale Farm House** ★★★★
*Guest Accommodation*
Manor Road, Applemore Hill, Dibden, Southampton SO45 5TJ
t (023) 8084 9632
w dalefarmhouse.co.uk

**Leygreen Farm House**
★★★★ *Bed & Breakfast*
Lyndhurst Road, Beaulieu SO42 7YP
t (01590) 612355

## BEMBRIDGE
Isle of Wight

**Breakfast at Tiffany's**
★★★★ *Bed & Breakfast*
40 Forelands Road, Bembridge PO35 5XW
t (01983) 874665
e tiffanyrichardbandb@hotmail.com
w tiffanysbandb.com

## BENENDEN
Kent

**The Holt** ★★★★
*Bed & Breakfast*
**SILVER AWARD**
New Pond Road, Benenden TN17 4EL
t (01580) 240414
e kate@theholt.org
w theholt.org

## BENSON
Oxfordshire

**Brookside** ★★★★
*Bed & Breakfast*
Brook Street, Benson OX10 6LJ
t (01491) 838289
e clivefolley@btinternet.com

**Fyfield Manor** ★★★★
*Bed & Breakfast*
**GOLD AWARD**
Benson, Wallingford OX10 6HA
t (01491) 835184
e chris_fyfield@hotmail.co.uk
w fyfieldmanor.co.uk

## BENTLEY
Hampshire

**Pittersfield** ★★★★
*Bed & Breakfast*
Hole Lane, Bentley GU10 5LT
t (01420) 22414
e jenefer@pittersfield.wanadoo.co.uk

## BETHERSDEN
Kent

**Anderson Potters Farm**
★★★ *Bed & Breakfast*
Brissenden Lane, Bethersden TN26 3JX
t (01233) 820341
e pottersfarms@aol.com
w pottersfarm.co.uk

**The Old Stables** ★★★★
*Guest Accommodation*
**SILVER AWARD**
Wissenden, Bethersden, Ashford TN26 3EL
t (01233) 820597
e pennygillespie@theoldstables.co.uk
w theoldstables.co.uk

## BEXHILL-ON-SEA
East Sussex

**Arden House** ★★★★
*Bed & Breakfast*
**SILVER AWARD**
28 Manor Road, Bexhill-on-Sea TN40 1SP
t (01424) 225068
e info@ardenhousebexhill.co.uk
w ardenhousebexhill.co.uk

**Arosa** ★★★★
*Guest Accommodation*
6 Albert Road, Bexhill-on-Sea TN40 1DG
t (01424) 212574
e info@arosahotel.co.uk
w arosahotel.co.uk

**Barkers B&B** ★★★
*Bed & Breakfast*
16 Magdalen Road, Bexhill-on-Sea TN40 1SB
t (01424) 218969

**Barrington** ★★★★
*Guest Accommodation*
14 Wilton Road, Bexhill-on-Sea TN40 1HY
t (01424) 210250

**Buenos Aires** ★★★★
*Guest House*
24 Albany Road, Bexhill-on-Sea TN40 1BZ
t (01424) 212269
e buenosairesguesthouse@hotmail.com
w buenosairesguesthouse.com

**Carols Bed and Breakfast**
★★★★ *Bed & Breakfast*
109 de la Warr Road, Bexhill-on-Sea TN40 2JN
t (01424) 222503
e enquiries@carols-bed-and-breakfast.co.uk
w carols-bed-and-breakfast.co.uk

**Cobwebs** ★★★★
*Guest Accommodation*
26 Collington Avenue, Bexhill-on-Sea TN39 3QA
t (01424) 213464
e kobwebs@waitrose.com

**Collington Lodge ★★★★**
*Guest House*
41 Collington Avenue, Bexhill-on-Sea TN39 3PX
t (01424) 210024
e info@collingtonlodge.co.uk
w collingtonlodge.co.uk

**Dunselma ★★★★**
*Guest Accommodation*
**SILVER AWARD**
25 Marina, Bexhill-on-Sea TN40 1BP
t (01424) 734144
e stay@dunselma.co.uk
w dunselma.co.uk

**Eve's Bed and Breakfast ★★★★**
*Guest Accommodation*
20 Hastings Road, Bexhill-on-Sea TN40 2HH
t (01424) 733268
e eve@bandb.wanadoo.co.uk

**Manor Barn Ensuite Chalets**
★★★ *Bed & Breakfast*
Ninfield Road, Lunsford Cross TN39 5JJ
t (01424) 893018
e bsgillingham@yahoo.co.uk

**The Old Manse ★★★★★**
*Bed & Breakfast*
**SILVER AWARD**
Terminus Avenue, Bexhill-on-Sea TN39 3LS
t (01424) 216151
e debbie.march@virgin.net
w theoldmansebexhill.co.uk

**The Old Vicarage ★★★★**
*Bed & Breakfast*
**GOLD AWARD**
5 Brassey Road, Bexhill-on-Sea TN40 1LD
t (01424) 213498
e oldvicaragebexhill@hotmail.com

**Park Lodge ★★★★**
*Guest Accommodation*
16 Egerton Road, Bexhill-on-Sea TN39 3HH
t (01424) 216547
e info@parklodgehotel.co.uk
w parklodgehotel.co.uk

**The Wiltons ★★★★**
*Guest Accommodation*
33 Wilton Road, Bexhill-on-Sea TN40 1HX
t (01424) 212748
e email@the-wiltons.com
w the-wiltons.com

**The York ★★★** *Inn*
92 London Road, Bexhill-on-Sea TN39 4AE
t (01424) 224275

## BIDDENDEN Kent

**Barclay Farmhouse**
★★★★★ *Bed & Breakfast*
**GOLD AWARD**
Woolpack Corner, Biddenden TN27 8BQ
t (01580) 292626
e info@barclayfarmhouse.co.uk
w barclayfarmhouse.co.uk

**Birchley 5 Star Bed & Breakfast ★★★★★**
*Guest Accommodation*
**GOLD AWARD**
Fosten Lane, Biddenden, Ashford TN27 8DZ
t (01580) 291413
e bookings@birchleyhouse.co.uk
w birchleyhouse.co.uk

**Heron Cottage ★★★★**
*Guest Accommodation*
Biddenden, Ashford TN27 8HH
t (01580) 291358
w heroncottage.info

**Tudor Cottage ★★★★**
*Guest Accommodation*
25 High Street, Biddenden, Ashford TN27 8AL
t (01580) 291913
e suemorris.biddenden@virgin.net
w tudorcottagebiddenden.co.uk

**Whitfield Farm ★★★★**
*Guest Accommodation*
**SILVER AWARD**
Dashmonden Lane, Biddenden, Ashford TN27 8BZ
t (01580) 291092
e enquiries@whitfieldfarm.co.uk
w whitfieldfarm.co.uk

## BILSINGTON Kent

**Willow Farm B&B ★★**
*Guest Accommodation*
Bilsington, Ashford TN25 7JJ
t (01233) 721700
e renee@willowfarmenterprises.co.uk
w willowfarmenterprises.co.uk

## BINSTEAD Isle of Wight

**Newnham Farm ★★★★★**
*Farmhouse* **SILVER AWARD**
Newnham Lane, Binstead PO33 4ED
t (01983) 882423
e di@newnhamfarm.co.uk
w newnhamfarm.co.uk

## BIRDHAM West Sussex

**Croftside Cottage ★★★★**
*Bed & Breakfast*
Main Road, Birdham, Chichester PO20 7HS
t (01243) 512864
e info@croftside.com
w croftside.com

## BISHOPSTONE Buckinghamshire

**Standalls Farm ★★**
*Bed & Breakfast*
Bishopstone, Aylesbury HP17 8SL
t (01296) 612687
e rogergoodchild@tesco.net

## BLACKBOYS East Sussex

**Blackboys Youth Hostel ★★**
*Hostel*
Gun Road, Blackboys, Uckfield TN22 5HU
t (01825) 890607
e blackboys@yha.org.uk

**Rangers Cottage ★★★★**
*Bed & Breakfast*
Terminus Road, Blackboys, Uckfield TN22 5LX
t (01825) 890463
e rangers.cottage@btinternet.com

## BLACKTHORN Oxfordshire

**Lime Trees Farm ★★★★**
*Farmhouse*
Lower Road, Blackthorn OX25 1TG
t (01869) 248435
e caroline@limetreesfarm.co.uk
w limetreesfarm.co.uk

## BLADBEAN Kent

**Molehills ★★★★**
*Guest Accommodation*
Bladbean, Canterbury CT4 6LU
t (01303) 840051
e molehills84@hotmail.com
w molehillsbedbreakfast.co.uk

## BLADON Oxfordshire

**Park House Tearoom**
★★★★ *Bed & Breakfast*
26 Park Street, Bladon OX20 1RW
t (01993) 813888
e info@parkhouseantiques.co.uk
w parkhouseantiques.co.uk/bandb

## BLOXHAM Oxfordshire

**Virginia House ★★★**
*Bed & Breakfast*
1 High Street, Banbury OX15 4LX
t (01295) 720596
e virginia.house@btopenworld.com
w virginiahousebloxham.co.uk

## BODIAM East Sussex

**Elms Farm**
Rating Applied For
*Guest Accommodation*
1 The Elms, Robertsbridge TN32 5UT
t (01580) 830494

## BOGNOR REGIS West Sussex

**Alderwasley Cottage**
★★★★ *Bed & Breakfast*
**SILVER AWARD**
Off West Street, Bognor Regis PO21 1XH
t (01243) 821339
e alderwasley@btinternet.com
w alderwasleycottage.co.uk

**Bognor Regis Campus University College Chichester ★–★★** *Campus*
Accommodation Office, Upper Bognor Road, Bognor Regis PO21 1HR
t (01243) 812140
w ucc.ac.uk

**Hayleys Corner ★★**
*Bed & Breakfast*
14 Limmer Lane, Bognor Regis PO22 7EJ
t (01243) 826139
e hayleyscornerbandb@yahoo.co.uk

**Homestead Guest House**
★★★ *Guest House*
90 Aldwick Road, Bognor Regis PO21 2PD
t (01243) 823443

**Jubilee Guest House ★★★**
*Guest Accommodation*
5 Gloucester Road, Bognor Regis PO21 1NU
t (01243) 863016
e jubileeguesthouse@tiscali.co.uk
w jubileeguesthouse.com

**Regis Lodge ★★★**
*Guest Accommodation*
3 Gloucester Road, Bognor Regis PO21 1NU
t (01243) 827110
e frank.regislodge@btinternet.com
w regislodge.co.uk

**Sea Crest ★★★**
*Guest Accommodation*
19 Nyewood Lane, Aldwick PO21 2QB
t (01243) 821438
e seacrest.19@btinternet.com
w visitsussex.org

**Selwood Lodge ★★★**
*Guest House*
93 Victoria Drive, Bognor Regis PO21 2DZ
t (01243) 865071
e mail@selwoodlodge.com
w selwoodlodge.com

**Swan Guest House ★★★★**
*Guest Accommodation*
17 Nyewood Lane, Aldwick PO21 2QB
t (01243) 826880
e swanhse@globalnet.co.uk
w swanguesthousebognor.co.uk

**Trevali Guest House ★★★★**
*Guest Accommodation*
Belmont Street, Bognor Regis PO21 1LE
t (01243) 862203
e info@trevaliguesthouse.co.uk
w trevaliguesthouse.co.uk

**Tudor Cottage Guest House**
★★★ *Bed & Breakfast*
194 Chichester Road, Bognor Regis PO21 5BJ
t (01243) 821826
e tudorcottage@supernet.com

**The White Horse Pub & B&B**
Rating Applied For
*Bed & Breakfast*
39 Chichester Road, Bognor Regis PO21 2XH
t (01243) 864523
e whitehorselive@aol.com
w thewhitehorse.org

**White Horses Felpham**
★★★★ *Bed & Breakfast*
Clyde Road, Felpham, Bognor Regis PO22 7AH
t (01243) 824320
e info@whitehorsesfelpham.co.uk
w whitehorsesfelpham.co.uk

## BOLNEY
West Sussex

**Bramble Cottage ★★★★**
*Bed & Breakfast*
The Street, Bolney, Haywards Heath RH17 5PG
t (01444) 881643
e enquiries@bramblecottagebb.co.uk
w bramblecottagebb.co.uk

Broxmead Paddock ★★★★
*Bed & Breakfast*
Broxmead Lane, Bolney, Haywards Heath RH17 5RG
t (01444) 881458
e broxmeadpaddock@hotmail.com
w broxmeadpaddock.eclipse.co.uk

## BONCHURCH
Isle of Wight

**The Lake ★★★**
*Guest Accommodation*
Shore Road, Bonchurch, Ventnor PO38 1RF
t (01983) 852613
e enquiries@lakehotel.co.uk
w lakehotel.co.uk

**Winterbourne Country House ★★★★★**
*Guest House* **SILVER AWARD**
Bonchurch Village Road, Ventnor PO38 1RQ
t (01983) 852535
e info@winterbournehouse.co.uk
w winterbournehouse.co.uk

## BORDEN
Kent

Holly House Bed & Breakfast
★★★★ *Bed & Breakfast*
SILVER AWARD
Wises Lane, Borden ME9 8LR
t (01795) 426953
e jane.leefrost@talktalk.net
w hollyhousebandb.org.uk

## BORDON
Hampshire

Groomes ★★★★★
*Guest Accommodation*
GOLD AWARD
Frith End, Bordon GU35 0QR
t (01420) 489858
e pete@groomes.co.uk
w groomes.co.uk

## BOSHAM
West Sussex

Good Hope ★★★★
*Bed & Breakfast*
SILVER AWARD
Delling Lane, Bosham, Chichester PO18 8NR
t (01243) 572487
e goodhope_bosham@yahoo.co.uk
w visitsussex.org

## BOUGHTON
Kent

The Lees ★★★
*Bed & Breakfast*
Horselees Road, Boughton-under-Blean, Faversham ME13 9TG
t (01227) 751332
e keith@theleesbb.co.uk
w theleesbb.fsnet.co.uk

## BOUGHTON MONCHELSEA
Kent

Wierton Hall Farm ★★★
*Guest Accommodation*
East Hall Hill, Maidstone ME17 4JU
t (01622) 743535
e lorraine@aspentreeservices.co.uk
w wiertonhallfarm.co.uk

## BOURNE END
Buckinghamshire

Hollands Farm ★★★★
*Farmhouse*
Hedsor Road, Bourne End SL8 5EE
t (01628) 520423
e info@hollands-farm.co.uk
w hollands-farm.co.uk

Lower Martins ★★★★
*Bed & Breakfast*
Coldmoorholme Lane, Bourne End SL8 5PS
t (01628) 521730
e marianiwills@supanet.com
w marianiwills.supanet.com

## BOXGROVE
West Sussex

Brufords ★★★★
*Guest Accommodation*
66/66a The Street, Boxgrove, Chichester PO18 0EE
t (01243) 774085
e room4me@brufords.org
w brufords.org

## BOXLEY
Kent

Styles House ★★
*Guest Accommodation*
Style Cottage, Styles Lane, Maidstone ME14 3DZ
t (01622) 757567
e sue@stylescottage.co.uk
w stylescottage.co.uk

## BRACKNELL
Berkshire

The Admirals Inn ★★★
*Guest Accommodation*
27 Stoney Road, Bracknell RG42 1XY
t (01344) 483052
e cunninghambarry@tiscali.co.uk
w theadmiralsinnguesthouse.com

Elizabeth House ★★★★
*Guest Accommodation*
Rounds Hill, Wokingham Road, Bracknell RG42 1PB
t (01344) 868480
e res@lizhotel.co.uk
w lizhotel.co.uk

Tenterden ★★★
*Guest Accommodation*
Rounds Hill, Wokingham Road, Bracknell RG42 1PB
t (01344) 483052
e cunninghambarry@tiscali.co.uk
w tenterdenguesthouse.co.uk

## BRADWELL
Buckinghamshire

YHA Bradwell Village ★★
*Hostel*
Manor Farm, Vicarage Road, Milton Keynes MK13 9AG
t 0870 770 5716
e bradwellvillage@yha.org.uk
w yha.org.uk

## BRAMSHAW
Hampshire

Wych Green Cottage
★★★★ *Bed & Breakfast*
Bramshaw, Lyndhurst SO43 7JF
t (023) 8081 2561
e suniverseone@aol.com
w newforest-uk.com

## BRASTED
Kent

**The Mount House ★★★★**
*Bed & Breakfast*
Brasted, Westerham TN16 1JB
t (01959) 563617
e diana@themounthouse.com
w themounthouse.com

The Orchard House ★★
*Bed & Breakfast*
Brasted Chart, Westerham TN16 1LR
t (01959) 563702
e david.godsal@tesco.net

## BREDE
East Sussex

**2 Stonelink Cottages ★★**
*Bed & Breakfast*
Stubb Lane, Brede, Rye TN31 6BL
t (01424) 882943 & 07802 573612
e stonelinkC@aol.com
w visit-rye.co.uk

Brede Court Country House
★★★★ *Guest House*
Brede Hill, Brede TN31 6EJ
t (01424) 883105
e bredecrt@globalnet.co.uk
w bredecourt.co.uk

The Mill House ★★★★
*Bed & Breakfast*
SILVER AWARD
Pottery Lane, Rye TN31 6EA
t (01424) 883096
e michaelt@euphonyzone.com
w themillhousebandb.co.uk

## BRENCHLEY
Kent

Hononton Cottage ★★★★
*Bed & Breakfast*
GOLD AWARD
Palmers Green Lane, Brenchley TN12 7BJ
t (01892) 722483
e marston.brenchley@tinyworld.co.uk
w smoothhound.co.uk/hotels/hononton

## BRIGHSTONE
Isle of Wight

Brighstone Tea Rooms Bed & Breakfast ★★★★
*Guest Accommodation*
Main Road, Brighstone PO30 4AH
t (01983) 740370
w brighstone-tearooms-bb.co.uk

**Chilton Farm B&B ★★★★**
*Farmhouse*
Chilton Farm, Chilton Lane, Newport PO30 4DS
t (01983) 740338
e info@chiltonfarm.co.uk
w chiltonfarm.co.uk

The Lodge Brighstone
★★★★
*Guest Accommodation*
Main Road, Brighstone PO30 4DJ
t (01983) 741272
e paul@thelodgebrighstone.com
w thelodgebrighstone.com

## BRIGHTLING
East Sussex

Orchard Barn ★★★
*Bed & Breakfast*
3 Twelve Oaks Cottages, Brightling TN32 5HS
t (01424) 838263

## BRIGHTON & HOVE
East Sussex

The Abbey ★★★
*Guest Accommodation*
14-19 Norfolk Terrace, Brighton BN1 3AD
t (01273) 778771
e reception@abbeyhotel.biz
w abbeyhotel.biz

**Adelaide House ★★★★**
*Guest Accommodation*
51 Regency Square, Brighton BN1 2FF
t (01273) 205286
e info@adelaidehotel.co.uk
w adelaidehotel.co.uk

Amblecliff
Rating Applied For
*Guest Accommodation*
35 Upper Rock Gardens, Brighton BN2 1QF
t (01273) 681161
e reservations@amblecliff.co.uk
w amblecliff.co.uk

Amherst ★★★★
*Guest Accommodation*
2 Lower Rock Gardens, Brighton BN2 1PG
t (01273) 670131
e info@amhersthotel.co.uk
w amhersthotel.co.uk

**Andorra Guest Accommodation ★★★**
*Guest Accommodation*
15-16 Oriental Place, Brighton BN1 2LJ
t (01273) 321787
w andorrahotelbrighton.co.uk

**Atlantic Seafront ★★★**
*Guest Accommodation*
16 Marine Parade, Brighton
BN2 1TL
**t** (01273) 695944
**e** majanatlantic@hotmail.com
**w** atlantichotelbrighton.co.uk

**Aymer Guest House ★★★★**
*Guest Accommodation*
13 Aymer Road, Hove
BN3 4GB
**t** (01273) 271165
**e** michelle@aymerguesthouse.co.uk
**w** aymerguesthouse.co.uk

**Blanch House ★★★★**
*Guest Accommodation*
17 Atlingworth Street, Brighton
BN2 1PL
**t** (01273) 603504
**e** info@blanchhouse.co.uk
**w** blanchhouse.co.uk

**Brightonwave ★★★★**
*Guest Accommodation*
**GOLD AWARD**
10 Madeira Place, Brighton
BN2 1TN
**t** (01273) 676794
**e** info@brightonwave.co.uk
**w** brightonwave.co.uk

**Brightside ★★★★**
*Guest Accommodation*
4 Shirley Road, Hove BN3 6NN
**t** (01273) 552557

**The Cavalaire ★★★★**
*Guest Accommodation*
**SILVER AWARD**
34 Upper Rock Gardens,
Brighton BN2 1QF
**t** (01273) 696899
**e** welcome@cavalaire.co.uk
**w** cavalaire.co.uk

**Chatsworth House ★★**
*Guest House*
9 Salisbury Road, Hove
BN3 3AB
**t** (01273) 737360

**Christina Guest House ★★★**
*Guest House*
20 St Georges Terrace,
Brighton BN2 1JH
**t** (01273) 690862
**e** christinaguesthouse@yahoo.co.uk
**w** christinaguesthouse brighton.co.uk

**The Claremont ★★★★★**
*Guest Accommodation*
13 Second Avenue, Hove,
Brighton BN3 2LL
**t** (01273) 735161
**e** info@theclaremont.eu
**w** theclaremont.eu

**Cosmopolitan ★★★**
*Guest Accommodation*
29-31 New Steine, Brighton
BN2 1PD
**t** (01273) 682461
**e** cosmopolitan2@btconnect.com
**w** cosmopolitanhotel.co.uk

**Hudsons ★★★★**
*Guest Accommodation*
22 Devonshire Place, Brighton
BN2 1QA
**t** (01273) 683642
**e** info@hudsonshotel.com
**w** hudsonsinbrighton.co.uk

**Lansdowne Guest House ★★★★**
*Guest Accommodation*
21 Lansdowne Road, Hove
BN3 1FE
**t** 07803 484775
**e** lansdowneguesthouse@hotmail.co.uk

**Leona House ★★★★**
*Guest Accommodation*
**SILVER AWARD**
74 Middle Street, Brighton
BN1 1AL
**t** (01273) 327309
**e** hazel.eastman@btconnect.com
**w** leonahousebrighton.com

**Lichfield House ★★★★**
*Guest Accommodation*
30 Waterloo Street, Hove
BN3 1AN
**t** (01273) 777740
**e** bookings@fieldhousehotels.co.uk
**w** fieldhousehotels.co.uk

**The Neo ★★★★**
*Guest Accommodation*
19 Oriental Place, Brighton
BN1 2LL
**t** (01273) 711104
**e** info@neohotel.com
**w** neohotel.com

**One Broad Street**
Rating Applied For
*Guest Accommodation*
1 Broad Street, Brighton
BN2 1TJ
**t** (01273) 699227
**e** onebroadst@btconnect.com

**Russell Guest House ★★★**
*Guest Accommodation*
19 Russell Square, Brighton
BN1 2EE
**t** (01273) 327969
**e** info@therussell.co.uk
**w** therussell.co.uk

**Sandpiper Guest House**
★★★ *Guest Accommodation*
11 Russell Square, Brighton
BN1 2EE
**t** (01273) 328202
**e** sandpiper@brighton.co.uk

**Sea Breeze ★★★★**
*Guest House* **SILVER AWARD**
12a Upper Rock Gardens,
Brighton BN2 1QE
**t** (01273) 818886
**e** info@seabreezebrighton.com
**w** seabreezebrighton.com

**Sea Spray ★★★★**
*Guest Accommodation*
25 New Steine, Brighton
BN2 1PD
**t** (01273) 680332
**e** seaspray@brighton.co.uk
**w** seaspraybrighton.co.uk

**Seafield House ★★★★**
*Guest Accommodation*
23 Seafield Road, Hove
BN3 2TP
**t** (01273) 777740
**e** enquiries@fieldhousehotels.co.uk
**w** fieldhousehotels.co.uk

**The Townhouse Brighton ★★★★**
*Guest Accommodation*
19 New Steine, Brighton
BN2 1PD
**t** (01273) 607456
**e** info@thetownhousebrighton.com
**w** thetownhousebrighton.com

**The Twenty One**
Rating Applied For
*Guest Accommodation*
21 Charlotte Street, Brighton
BN2 1AG
**t** (01273) 686450
**e** enquiries@thetwentyone.co.uk
**w** thetwentyone.co.uk

**University of Brighton**
★★-★★★ *Campus*
Conference Office, Room 228,
Brighton BN2 4AT
**t** (01273) 600900
**e** conferences@brighton.ac.uk
**w** brighton.ac.uk/conferences

**Whitburn Lodge ★★★★**
*Guest House*
12 Montpelier Road, Brighton
BN1 2LQ
**t** (01273) 729005
**e** info@whitburnlodge.com
**w** whitburnlodge.com

## BRILL
Buckinghamshire

**Poletrees Farm ★★★★**
*Farmhouse*
Ludgersall Road, Aylesbury
HP18 9TZ
**t** (01844) 238276

## BRIZE NORTON
Oxfordshire

**The Priory ★★★**
*Guest Accommodation*
Manor Farm, Manor Road,
Brize Norton OX18 3NA
**t** (01993) 843062
**e** mail@priorymanor.wanadoo.co.uk
**w** priorymanor.co.uk

## BROAD OAK
East Sussex

**Hazelhurst B&B ★★★★**
*Guest Accommodation*
**SILVER AWARD**
Chitcombe Road, Rye
TN31 6EU
**t** (01424) 883411
**e** bookings@hazelhurstbroadoak.co.uk
**w** hazelhurstbroadoak.co.uk

## BROADSTAIRS
Kent

**Anchor House ★★★★**
*Guest House*
10 Chandos Road, Broadstairs
CT10 1QP
**t** (01843) 863347
**e** stay@anchorhouse.net
**w** anchorhouse.net

**Anchor Lodge ★★★★**
*Bed & Breakfast*
**SILVER AWARD**
57 Dumpton Park Drive,
Broadstairs CT10 1RH
**t** (01843) 602564
**e** enquiries@anchorlodge.net
**w** anchorlodge.net

**Bay Tree Broadstairs ★★★★**
*Guest Accommodation*
12 Eastern Esplanade,
Broadstairs CT10 1DR
**t** (01843) 862502

**Burrow House ★★★★★**
*Guest Accommodation*
Granville Road, Broadstairs
CT10 1QD
**t** (01843) 601817
**e** gavincox@aol.com
**w** burrowhouse.com

**Cintra ★★★**
*Guest Accommodation*
24 Victoria Parade, Broadstairs
CT10 1QL
**t** (01843) 862253
**e** visit@cintrabb.com
**w** cintrabb.com

**Copperfields Guest House**
★★★★ *Guest House*
**SILVER AWARD**
Queens Road, Broadstairs
CT10 1NU
**t** (01843) 601247
**e** copperfieldsbb@btinternet.com
**w** copperfieldsbb.co.uk

**The Devonhurst ★★★★**
*Guest Accommodation*
**SILVER AWARD**
Eastern Esplanade, Broadstairs
CT10 1DR
**t** (01843) 863010
**e** info@devonhurst.co.uk
**w** devonhurst.co.uk

**The Hanson ★★★**
*Guest Accommodation*
41 Belvedere Road, Broadstairs
CT10 1PF
**t** (01843) 868936
**e** hotelhanson@tiscali.co.uk
**w** hansonhotel.co.uk

**Merriland ★★★★**
*Guest House*
13 The Vale, Broadstairs
CT10 1RB
**t** (01843) 861064
**e** merrilandhotel@aol.com

**Number 68 ★★★★**
*Guest Accommodation*
**SILVER AWARD**
68 West Cliff Road, Broadstairs
CT10 1PY
**t** (01843) 609459
**e** number68@btinternet.com
**w** number68.co.uk

**South Lodge Guest House**
★★★★ *Guest House*
**SILVER AWARD**
19 The Vale, Broadstairs
CT10 1RB
**t** (01843) 600478
**e** reservations@visitsouthlodge.co.uk
**w** visitsouthlodge.co.uk

**Torwood House ★★★★★**
*Bed & Breakfast*
41 West Cliff Road, Broadstairs
CT10 1PU
**t** (01843) 863953
**e** enquiries@torwoodhouse.co.uk
**w** torwoodhouse.co.uk

**Viking** ★★★★
*Guest Accommodation*
**SILVER AWARD**
West Cliff Avenue, Broadstairs
CT10 1QA
**t** (01843) 862375
**e** viking-guesthouse@tiscali.co.uk

### BROCKENHURST
Hampshire

**Goldenhayes** ★★
*Bed & Breakfast*
9 Chestnut Road, Brockenhurst
SO42 7RF
**t** (01590) 623743

### BROOKLAND
Kent

**The Royal Oak** ★★★★ *Inn*
High Street, Brookland,
Romney Marsh TN29 9QR
**t** (01797) 344215
**e** dzrj@btinternet.com
**w** royaloakbrookland.co.uk

### BUCKINGHAM
Buckinghamshire

**Churchwell** ★★
*Bed & Breakfast*
23 Church Street, Buckingham
MK18 1BY
**t** (01280) 815415
**w** churchwell.co.uk

**Folly Farm** ★★★★
*Farmhouse*
Buckingham Road, Adstock
MK18 2HS
**t** (01296) 712413

**Huntsmill Farm B&B** ★★★★
*Bed & Breakfast*
Shalstone, Nr Buckingham
MK18 5ND
**t** (01280) 704852 & 07970 871104
**e** fiona@huntsmill.com
**w** huntsmill.com

**Radclive Dairy Farm** ★★★★
*Farmhouse*
Radclive Road, Buckingham
MK18 4AA
**t** (01280) 813433
**e** rosalind.fisher@radclivedairyfarm.co.uk
**w** radclivedairyfarm.co.uk

### BURFORD
Oxfordshire

**Barley Park** ★★★★
*Bed & Breakfast*
**SILVER AWARD**
Shilton Road, Burford
OX18 4PD
**t** (01993) 823573
**e** barley_park@hotmail.com
**w** burford-bed-and-breakfast.co.uk

**Cotland House B&B** ★★★★
*Guest Accommodation*
Fulbrook Hill, Burford
OX18 4BH
**t** (01993) 822382
**e** info@cotlandhouse.com
**w** otlandhouse.com

**Courtlands B&B** ★★★★
*Bed & Breakfast*
6 Courtlands Road, Shipton-under-Wychwood OX7 6DF
**t** (01993) 830551
**e** jeanandjohn@cotswoldsbandb.com
**w** cotswoldsbandb.com

**The Highway**
Rating Applied For
*Inn*
117 High Street, Burford
OX18 4RG
**t** (01993) 823661
**e** enquiries@thehighwayhotel.co.uk
**w** thehighwayhotel.co.uk

**Westview House** ★★★★
*Bed & Breakfast*
**GOLD AWARD**
151 The Hill, Burford
OX18 4RE
**t** (01993) 824723
**e** titcombe@aol.com
**w** westview-house.co.uk

### BURGESS HILL
West Sussex

**Daisy Lodge B&B** ★★★
*Guest Accommodation*
26 Royal George Road, Burgess Hill RH15 9SE
**t** (01444) 870570
**e** daisylodge@btinternet.com

**Meadows** ★★★★
*Bed & Breakfast*
87 Meadow Lane, Burgess Hill
RH15 9JD
**t** (01444) 248421
**e** bsayers@hotmail.co.uk

**St Owens** ★★★★
*Bed & Breakfast*
11 Silverdale Road, Burgess Hill
RH15 0ED
**t** (01444) 236435
**e** nevillebaker@btinternet.com
**w** visitsussex.org

**Wellhouse** ★★★★
*Guest Accommodation*
**SILVER AWARD**
Wellhouse Lane, Burgess Hill
RH15 0BN
**t** (01444) 233231
**e** amhallen@onetel.com
**w** visitsussex.org

### BURLEY
Hampshire

**The Burley Inn** ★★★ *Inn*
The Cross, Ringwood
BH24 4AB
**t** (01425) 403448
**e** info@theburleyinn.co.uk
**w** theburleyinn.co.uk

**Burley YHA** ★★ *Hostel*
Cottesmore House, Cott Lane,
Ringwood BH24 4BB
**t** (01425) 403233

**Holmans** ★★★★
*Bed & Breakfast*
**GOLD AWARD**
Bisterne Close, Burley,
Ringwood BH24 4AZ
**t** (01425) 402307
**e** holmans@talktalk.net

**Wayside Cottage** ★★★★
*Bed & Breakfast*
27 Garden Road, Burley,
Ringwood BH24 4EA
**t** (01425) 403414
**e** jwest@wayside-cottage.co.uk
**w** wayside-cottage.co.uk

**The White Buck Inn** ★★★
*Inn*
Bisterne Close, Burley
BH24 4AT
**t** (01425) 402264
**e** whitebuck@fullers.co.uk
**w** fullersinns.co.uk

### BURMARSH
Kent

**Haguelands Farmhouse** ★★★★★
*Guest Accommodation*
**GOLD AWARD**
Haguelands Farm, Burmarsh,
Romney Marsh TN29 0JR
**t** (01303) 872273
**e** info@aaclifton.ltd.uk
**w** haguelandsfarm.co.uk

### BURNHAM
Buckinghamshire

**Servants Quarters** ★★
*Bed & Breakfast*
Hitcham Vale, Parliament Lane,
Slough SL1 8NT
**t** (01628) 660618
**e** judy@v21.me.uk

### BURY
West Sussex

**The Barn at Penfolds**
★★★★ *Bed & Breakfast*
**GOLD AWARD**
The Street, Bury, Pulborough
RH20 1PA
**t** (01798) 831496

### BUSCOT WICK
Oxfordshire

**Weston Farm** ★★★★
*Farmhouse*
Buscot Wick, Faringdon
SN7 8DJ
**t** (01367) 252222
**e** andrewwoof@btconnect.com
**w** country-accom.co.uk/weston-farm

### CADNAM
Hampshire

**Kingsbridge House** ★★★★
*Guest Accommodation*
Southampton Road, Cadnam,
Lyndhurst SO40 2NH
**t** (023) 8081 1161
**e** linda@kingsbridgehouse.plus.com
**w** kingsbridge-house.co.uk

**Twin Oaks Guest House**
★★★★ *Guest House*
**SILVER AWARD**
Southampton Road, Cadnam,
New Forest SO40 2NQ
**t** (023) 8081 2305
**e** enquiries@twinoaks-guesthouse.co.uk

### CANTERBURY
Kent

**Abberley House** ★★★
*Bed & Breakfast*
115 Whitstable Road,
Canterbury CT2 8EF
**t** (01227) 450265
**e** r.allcorn@discovercanterbury.co.uk
**w** discovercanterbury.co.uk

**Acacia Lodge & Tanglewood**
★★★★
*Guest Accommodation*
39-40 London Road,
Canterbury CT2 8LF
**t** (01227) 769955
**e** acacialodge39@yahoo.com
**w** acacialodge.co.uk

**Alexandra House** ★★★★
*Guest Accommodation*
1 Roper Road, Canterbury
CT2 7EH
**t** (01227) 786617
**e** alexandrahouse2@aol.com
**w** alexandrahouse.net

**Alicante Guest House**
★★★★
*Guest Accommodation*
4 Roper Road, Canterbury
CT2 7EH
**t** (01227) 766277

**Ann's House** ★★★
*Guest House*
63 London Road, Canterbury
CT2 8JZ
**t** (01227) 768767
**e** info@annshousecanterbury.co.uk
**w** annshousecanterbury.co.uk

**Ashley Guest House** ★★
*Bed & Breakfast*
9 London Road, Canterbury
CT2 8LR
**t** (01227) 455863

**Bluebells Guest House** ★★★
*Guest House*
248 Wincheap, Canterbury
CT1 3TY
**t** (01227) 478842
**e** canterburybluebells@yahoo.co.uk
**w** smoothhound.co.uk/hotels/bluebells

**Bower Farm House** ★★★★
*Bed & Breakfast*
**SILVER AWARD**
Bossingham Road, Stelling
Minnis, Canterbury CT4 6BB
**t** (01227) 709430
**e** anne@bowerbb.freeserve.co.uk
**w** bowerfarmhouse.co.uk

**Canterbury YHA** ★★ *Hostel*
54 New Dover Road,
Canterbury CT1 3DT
**t** (01227) 462911
**e** canterbury@yha.org.uk
**w** yha.org.uk

**Carena House** ★★★
*Guest House*
250 Wincheap, Canterbury
CT1 3TY
**t** (01227) 765630
**e** carena.house@btconnect.com
**w** carenaguesthouse.co.uk

**Castle House** ★★★★
*Guest Accommodation*
**SILVER AWARD**
28 Castle Street, Canterbury
CT1 2PT
**t** (01227) 761897
**e** enquiries@castlehousehotel.co.uk
**w** castlehousehotel.co.uk

**Chaucer Lodge ★★★**
*Guest House*
62 New Dover Road, Canterbury CT1 3DT
t (01227) 459141
e enquiries@chaucerlodge.co.uk
w chaucerlodge.co.uk

**The City of Canterbury ★★★★**
*Guest Accommodation*
27 St Thomas Hill, Canterbury CT2 8HW
t (01227) 457455
e t.mills@talktalk.net
w thecityofcanterbury.co.uk

**Clare Ellen Guest House**
**★★★★** *Guest House*
9 Victoria Road, Canterbury CT1 3SG
**t** (01227) 760205
**e** enquiry@clareellenguesthouse.co.uk
**w** clareellenguesthouse.co.uk

**Four Seasons Guest Accommodation ★★★**
*Guest Accommodation*
77 Sturry Road, Canterbury CT1 1BU
t (01227) 787078
e fourseasonsbnb@aol.com
w fourseasonscanterbury.co.uk

**Greyfriars House ★★★**
*Guest House*
6 Stour Street, Canterbury CT1 2NR
t (01227) 456255
e christine@greyfriars-house.co.uk
w greyfriars-house.co.uk

**Harriet House ★★★★**
*Guest Accommodation*
**SILVER AWARD**
3 Broad Oak Road, Canterbury CT2 7PL
t (01227) 457363
e merryjb@supanet.com
w harriethouse.co.uk

**Hornbeams ★★★★**
*Farmhouse*
Jesses Hill, Kingston, Canterbury CT4 6JD
**t** (01227) 830119
**e** bandb@hornbeams.co.uk
**w** hornbeams.co.uk

**Iffin Farm House ★★★★**
*Guest Accommodation*
Iffin Lane, Canterbury CT4 7BE
t (01227) 462776
e info@iffin.co.uk
w iffinfarmhouse.co.uk

**Kent Hospitality ★★★**
*Campus*
Tanglewood, Giles Lane, The University, Canterbury CT2 7LX
t (01227) 828000
e hospitality-enquiry@kent.ac.uk
w kent.ac.uk/hospitality/

**Kings Head ★★★** *Inn*
204 Wincheap, Canterbury CT1 3RY
t (01227) 462885
e thekingshead@wincheap.wanadoo.co.uk
w smoothhound.co.uk/hotels/thekingshead

**Kingsbridge Villa ★★★★**
*Guest House*
15 Best Lane, Canterbury CT1 2JB
t (01227) 766415
e info@canterburyguesthouse.com
w canterburyguesthouse.com

**Kingsmead House ★★★**
*Bed & Breakfast*
68 St Stephens Road, Canterbury CT2 7JF
t (01227) 760132
e john@kingsmeadhouse.com
w kingsmeadhouse.com

**Magnolia House ★★★★★**
*Guest Accommodation*
**GOLD AWARD**
36 St Dunstans Terrace, Canterbury CT2 8AX
**t** (01227) 765121
**e** info@magnoliahousecanterbury.co.uk
**w** magnoliahousecanterbury.co.uk

**The Millers Arms ★★★★** *Inn*
2 Mill Lane, St Radigunds CT1 2AW
t (01227) 456057
w shepherd-neame.co.uk

**Oak Cottage ★★★★**
*Guest Accommodation*
**SILVER AWARD**
Elmsted, Ashford TN25 5JT
**t** (01233) 750272
**e** oakcottage@invictanet.co.uk
**w** oakcottage-elmsted.co.uk

**The Old Kent Barn ★★★★★**
*Bed & Breakfast*
**GOLD AWARD**
Smersole Farm, Swingfield, Dover CT15 7HF
t (01303) 844270
e hilaryjanesimmons@zoom.co.uk
w theoldkentbarn.co.uk

**The Plantation ★★★★**
*Bed & Breakfast*
Iffin Lane, Canterbury CT4 7BD
t (01227) 472104
e plantation@lycos.co.uk
w theplantation.biz

**Renville Oast ★★★★**
*Bed & Breakfast*
Bridge, Canterbury CT4 5AD
t (01227) 830215
e renville.oast@virgin.net
w renvilleoast.co.uk

**Thanington ★★★★★**
*Guest Accommodation*
**SILVER AWARD**
140 Wincheap, Canterbury CT1 3RY
t (01227) 453227
e enquiries@thanington-hotel.co.uk
w thanington-hotel.co.uk

**Tudor House ★★★**
*Guest Accommodation*
6 Best Lane, Canterbury CT1 2JB
t (01227) 765650
e tudor.house@hotmail.co.uk

**White Horse Inn ★★★★**
*Guest Accommodation*
The Street, Boughton-under-Blean, Faversham ME13 9AX
t (01227) 751700
e whitehorse@shepherd-neame.co.uk
w shepherd-neame.co.uk

**Wincheap Guest House**
**★★★** *Guest House*
94 Wincheap, Canterbury CT1 3RS
t (01227) 762309
e wincheapguesthouse@tiscali.co.uk
w wincheapguesthouse.com

**The Woolpack Inn ★★★★**
*Inn*
The Street, Chilham CT4 8DL
t (01227) 730351
e woolpack@shepherdneame.co.uk
w woolpackchilham.co.uk

**Yorke Lodge ★★★★★**
*Guest Accommodation*
50 London Road, Canterbury CT2 8LF
**t** (01227) 451243
**e** info@yorkelodge.com
**w** yorkelodge.com

## CAPEL
### Surrey

**Nightless Copse ★★★★**
*Bed & Breakfast*
Rusper Road, Capel RH5 5HE
t (01306) 713247
e bb@nightlesscopse.co.uk
w nightlesscopse.co.uk

## CARISBROOKE
### Isle of Wight

**Alvington Manor Farm ★★★**
*Guest Accommodation*
Manor Farm Lane, Off Calbourne Road, Carisbrooke PO30 5SP
t (01983) 523463
e info@islandbreaks.co.uk

## CARTERTON
### Oxfordshire

**The Jays ★★★★**
*Bed & Breakfast*
23 The Crescent, Carterton OX18 3SJ
t (01993) 843301
e info@thejays-carterton.co.uk
w thejays-carterton.co.uk

## CASSINGTON
### Oxfordshire

**Burleigh Farm ★★★★**
*Farmhouse*
Bladon Road, Nr Cassington, Oxford OX29 4EA
**t** (01865) 881352
**e** cook_jane@btconnect.com
**w** oxfordcity.co.uk/accom/burleighfarm

## CASTLETHORPE
### Buckinghamshire

**A Village B & B ★★**
*Guest Accommodation*
Manor Farm House, South Street, Milton Keynes MK19 7EL
t (01908) 510216
e manorfarmhouse@aol.com
w mkweb.co.uk

## CATHERINGTON
### Hampshire

**Flowerdown ★★★**
*Bed & Breakfast*
82 Downhouse Road, Catherington PO8 0TY
t (023) 9259 8029
e madeingb@btinternet.com

**Lone Barn ★★★★**
*Bed & Breakfast*
**SILVER AWARD**
Catherington, Waterlooville PO8 0SF
t (023) 9263 2911
e marchburn@ukonline.co.uk
w lonebarn.net

## CHALFONT ST GILES
### Buckinghamshire

**Gorelands Corner ★★★★**
*Bed & Breakfast*
Gorelands Lane, Chalfont St Giles HP8 4HQ
t (01494) 872689
e bickfordcsg@onetel.com

**The Ivy House ★★★★** *Inn*
London Road, Chalfont St Giles HP8 4RS
t (01494) 872184

**The White Hart Inn ★★★★**
*Inn*
Three Households, Chalfont St Giles HP8 4LP
t (01494) 872441
e enquiries@thewhitehartstgiles.co.uk

## CHALFONT ST PETER
### Buckinghamshire

**Hebron ★★★**
*Bed & Breakfast*
128 Rickmansworth Lane, Chalfont St Peter SL9 0RQ
t (01494) 873533
e sheppee@btinternet.com

## CHALGROVE
### Oxfordshire

**Cornerstones ★★**
*Bed & Breakfast*
1 Cromwell Close, Chalgrove, Oxford OX44 7SE
**t** (01865) 890298
**e** corner.stones@virgin.net
**w** http://freespace.virgin.net/corner.stones

## CHARLBURY
### Oxfordshire

**Banbury Hill Farm ★★★★**
*Guest Accommodation*
Enstone Road, Charlbury OX7 3JH
t (01608) 810314
e beds@gfwiddows.f9.co.uk
w charlburyoxfordaccom.co.uk

**Bull ★★★★** *Inn*
Sheep Street, Charlbury OX7 3RR
t (01608) 810689
e info@bullinn-charlbury.com
w bullinn-charlbury.com


Look out for establishments participating in the National Accessible Scheme

## CHARLWOOD
Surrey

**Trumbles Guest House**
★★★★
*Guest Accommodation*
Stan Hill, Charlwood RH6 0EP
**t** (01293) 863418
**e** info@trumbles.co.uk
**w** trumbles.co.uk

## CHART SUTTON
Kent

**Chart Hill Cottage B&B**
Rating Applied For
*Guest Accommodation*
Chart Road, Maidstone
ME17 3RG
**t** (01622) 844397
**e** maggiet@gotadsl.co.uk
**w** charthillcottage.co.uk

**White House Farm** ★★★★
*Farmhouse* **SILVER AWARD**
Green Lane, Maidstone
ME17 3ES
**t** (01622) 842490
**e** info@whitehousefarm-kent.co.uk
**w** whitehousefarm-kent.co.uk

## CHATHAM
Kent

**Normandy House** ★★★
*Guest Accommodation*
Maidstone Road, Chatham
ME4 6JE
**t** (01634) 843047

**Officers Hill** ★★★★★
*Bed & Breakfast*
**GOLD AWARD**
7 College Road, The Historic Dockyard, Chatham ME4 4QX
**t** (01634) 828436
**e** gmchambers@btopenworld.com

**Ship & Trades** ★★★
*Guest Accommodation*
Maritime Way, St Marys Island
ME4 3ER
**t** (01634) 895200
**e** ship&trades@shepherd-neame.co.uk
**w** shepherd-neame.co.uk

## CHATTENDEN
Kent

**Windwhistle** ★★★★
*Guest Accommodation*
Lodge Hill Lane, Chattenden, Rochester ME3 8NY
**t** (01634) 252859

## CHECKENDON
Oxfordshire

**Larchdown Farm** ★★★★
*Guest Accommodation*
**SILVER AWARD**
Whitehall Lane, Checkendon
RG8 0TT
**t** (01491) 682282
**e** larchdown@onetel.com
**w** larchdown.com

## CHELWOOD GATE
East Sussex

**Holly House** ★★★★
*Guest House*
Beaconsfield Road, Chelwood Gate, East Grinstead RH17 7LF
**t** (01825) 740484
**e** deebirchell@hollyhousebnb.demon.co.uk
**w** hollyhousebnb.demon.co.uk

**Laurel Cottage** ★★★
*Bed & Breakfast*
Baxters Lane, Chelwood Gate, Haywards Heath RH17 7LU
**t** (01825) 740547
**e** smartin@chelwood.fsnet.co.uk
**w** visitsussex.org

## CHERITON
Hampshire

**Old Kennetts Cottage**
★★★★ *Bed & Breakfast*
Cheriton, Alresford SO24 0PX
**t** (01962) 771863
**e** dglssmith@aol.com

## CHESHAM
Buckinghamshire

**49 Lowndes Avenue** ★★★
*Bed & Breakfast*
Chesham HP5 2HH
**t** (01494) 792647
**e** bbormelowndes@tiscali.co.uk

**Katsina** ★★ *Bed & Breakfast*
Broomstick Lane, Botley, Chesham HP5 1XU
**t** (01494) 773110

## CHICHESTER
West Sussex

**21 Brandyhole Lane** ★★
*Guest Accommodation*
Brandy Hole Lane, Chichester
PO19 5RL
**t** (01243) 528201
**e** anne@anneparry.me.uk

**5a Little London** ★★★
*Bed & Breakfast*
Little London, Chichester
PO19 1PH
**t** (01243) 788405

**Anna's** ★★★ *Bed & Breakfast*
27 Westhampnett Road, Chichester PO19 7HW
**t** (01243) 788522
**e** judiths@fsmail.net
**w** annasofchichester.co.uk

**Apiary Cottage** ★★★
*Bed & Breakfast*
Compton, Chichester
PO18 9EX
**t** (023) 9263 1306

**Brandram House** ★★★
*Bed & Breakfast*
200 Whyke Road, Chichester
PO19 7AQ
**t** (01243) 781335
**e** brandramhouse@boltblue.com
**w** brandramhouse.co.uk

**Cherry End** ★★★★
*Bed & Breakfast*
3 Clydesdale Avenue, Chichester PO19 7PW
**t** (01243) 531397
**e** cherryendbb@yahoo.co.uk
**w** cherryend.2ya.com

**The Cottage** ★★★
*Bed & Breakfast*
22b Westhampnett Road, Chichester PO19 7HW
**t** (01243) 774979
**e** mbc.technical@virgin.net

**Fox Goes Free** ★★★ *Inn*
Charlton, Chichester
PO18 0HU
**t** (01243) 811461
**e** thefoxgoesfree.always@virgin.net
**w** thefoxgoesfree.com

**Friary Close** ★★★★
*Bed & Breakfast*
**SILVER AWARD**
Friary Lane, Chichester
PO19 1UF
**t** (01243) 527294
**e** mail@friaryclose.co.uk
**w** friaryclose.co.uk

**Kia-ora** ★★★ *Bed & Breakfast*
Main Road, Nutbourne, Chichester PO18 8RT
**t** (01243) 572858
**e** ruthiefp@tiscali.co.uk

**Litten House** ★★★
*Bed & Breakfast*
148 St Pancras, Chichester
PO19 7SH
**t** (01243) 774503
**e** victoria@littenho.demon.co.uk
**w** littenho.demon.co.uk

**Longmeadow** ★★
*Bed & Breakfast*
Pine Grove, Chichester
PO19 3PN
**t** (01243) 782063
**e** bbeeching@lineone.net
**w** longmeadowguesthouse.com

**Old Store Guest House**
★★★★
*Guest Accommodation*
Stane Street, Halnaker, Chichester PO18 0QL
**t** (01243) 531977
**e** info@theoldstoreguesthouse.com
**w** theoldstoreguesthouse.com

**Pen Cottage** ★★★
***Bed & Breakfast***
**The Drive, Summersdale, Chichester PO19 5QA**
**t (01243) 783667**
**e monicaandcolinkaye@talktalk.net**
**w visitsussex.org/pencottage**

**Sherwood House** ★★★
*Bed & Breakfast*
Drayton Lane, Shopwyke, Chichester PO20 2BN
**t** (01243) 778005
**e** tony@sherwoodbb.co.uk
**w** sherwoodbb.co.uk

**Spooners** ★★★★
*Bed & Breakfast*
1 Maplehurst Road, Chichester
PO19 6QL
**t** (01243) 528467
**e** sue-spooner@tiscali.co.uk

**West Faldie** ★★★★
*Bed & Breakfast*
**SILVER AWARD**
Lavant, Chichester PO18 0BW
**t** (01243) 527450
**e** hilary@mitten.fsnet.co.uk

**Woodstock House** ★★★★
***Guest House*** **SILVER AWARD**
**Charlton, Chichester**
**PO18 0HU**
**t (01243) 811666**
**e info@woodstockhousehotel.co.uk**
**w woodstockhousehotel.co.uk**

## CHIDDINGSTONE
Kent

**Hoath House** ★★★
***Guest Accommodation***
**Chiddingstone, Edenbridge**
**TN8 7DB**
**t (01342) 850362**
**e janestreatfeild@hoath-house.freeserve.co.uk**
**w hoathhouse.co.uk**

## CHIEVELEY
Berkshire

**Thatched House B&B**
★★★★ *Bed & Breakfast*
**SILVER AWARD**
High Street, Chieveley
RG20 8TE
**t** (01635) 248295
**e** s.malty@btinternet.com
**w** mychieveley.co.uk/info/thatchedhousebandb

## CHILCOMB
Hampshire

**Complyns B&B** ★★★★
*Bed & Breakfast*
Chilcomb, Winchester
SO21 1HT
**t** (01962) 861600
**w** complyns.co.uk

## CHILGROVE
West Sussex

**Chilgrove Farm** ★★★★
*Bed & Breakfast*
Chilgrove, Chichester
PO18 9HU
**t** (01243) 519436
**e** simonrenwick@aol.com
**w** chilgrovefarmbedandbreakfast.co.uk

## CHILHAM
Kent

**Castle Cottage Chilham Bed & Breakfast** ★★★★
*Bed & Breakfast*
School Hill, Canterbury
CT4 8DE
**t** (01227) 730330
**e** l.frankel@btinternet.com
**w** castlecottagechilham.co.uk

## CHINEHAM
Hampshire

**Ashfields, 51A Reading Road** ★★★
***Guest Accommodation***
**Chineham, Basingstoke**
**RG24 8LT**
**t (01256) 324629**

## CHINNOR
Oxfordshire

**The Croft** ★★★★
***Bed & Breakfast***
**Chinnor Hill, Chinnor**
**OX39 4BS**
**t (01844) 353654**
**e beth@acornhomesltd.co.uk**
**w bethatthecroft.co.uk**

**Manor Farm Cottage**
★★★★ *Bed & Breakfast*
Henton OX39 4AE
**t** (01844) 353301
**e** dixonhenton@aol.com
**w** manorfarmcottage.info

## CHIPPING NORTON
### Oxfordshire

**The Forge** ★★★★
*Guest Accommodation*
**SILVER AWARD**
Church Road, Chipping Norton OX7 6NJ
**t** (01608) 658173
**e** enquiries@cotswolds-accommodation.com
**w** cotswolds-accommodation.com

---

**Rectory Farm** ★★★★★
*Farmhouse* **SILVER AWARD**
Golden Lane, Chipping Norton OX7 5YZ
**t** (01608) 643209
**e** colston@rectoryfarm75.freeserve.co.uk
**w** rectoryfarm.info

## CHIPSTEAD
### Kent

**Windmill Farm** ★★★★
*Guest Accommodation*
Chevening Road, Sevenoaks TN13 2SA
**t** (01732) 452054

## CHURT
### Surrey

**The Retreat** ★★★★
*Bed & Breakfast*
New Farm Cottage, Frensham Lane, Farnham GU10 2QG
**t** (01252) 792998
**e** suzy.johnson@tiscali.co.uk

## CLIFFE WOODS
### Kent

**Orchard Cottage** ★★★★
*Guest Accommodation*
**SILVER AWARD**
11 View Road, Cliffe Woods, Rochester ME3 8JQ
**t** (01634) 222780

## CLIFTONVILLE
### Kent

**The Bay Guest House** ★★
*Guest Accommodation*
23 Fort Crescent, Margate CT9 1HX
**t** (01843) 290889
**e** thebaymargate@btinternet.com
**w** bayguesthouse.com

## CLIMPING
### West Sussex

**Derwent House**
Rating Applied For
*Bed & Breakfast*
Climping Street, Climping BN17 5RQ
**t** (01903) 726204
**e** jonshorrock@yahoo.co.uk
**w** derwent-house.co.uk

## COLD ASH
### Berkshire

**2 Woodside** ★★★★
*Bed & Breakfast*
Woodside, Cold Ash, Thatcham RG18 9JF
**t** (01635) 860028
**e** anita.rhiggs@which.net

## COLEMANS HATCH
### East Sussex

**Gospel Oak** ★★★
*Bed & Breakfast*
Sandy Lane, Colemans Hatch, Hartfield TN7 4ER
**t** (01342) 823840
**e** lindah@thehatch.freeserve.co.uk

## COLWELL BAY
### Isle of Wight

**Rockstone Cottage** ★★★★
*Guest House*
Colwell Chine Road, Colwell Bay, Freshwater PO40 9NR
**t** (01983) 753723
**e** enquiries@rockstonecottage.co.uk
**w** rockstonecottage.co.uk

## COLWORTH
### West Sussex

**Glencroft** ★★★★
*Bed & Breakfast*
**SILVER AWARD**
Colworth, Chichester PO20 2DS
**t** (01243) 532929
**e** glencroft.b_and_b@btinternet.com
**w** glencroft.biz

## COOKSBRIDGE
### East Sussex

**Lower Tulleys Wells Farm**
★★★ *Guest Accommodation*
Beechwood Lane, Cooksbridge, Lewes BN7 3QG
**t** (01273) 472622
**e** jmpnzr@aol.com

## COOLING
### Kent

**The Horseshoe and Castle**
★★★★ *Inn*
Main Road, Cooling ME3 8DJ
**t** (01634) 221691
**e** horseshoe.castle@btconnect.com
**w** horseshoeandcastle.co.uk

## COPTHORNE
### West Sussex

**The Gatwick Grove Guest House** ★★★★ *Guest House*
Copthorne Common, Copthorne, Gatwick RH10 3LA
**t** (01342) 719463
**e** info@thegatwickgrove.co.uk
**w** thegatwickgrove.co.uk

## COWDEN
### Kent

**Southernwood House**
★★★★ *Bed & Breakfast*
Church Street, Edenbridge TN8 7JE
**t** (01342) 850880
**e** info@southernwoodhouse.org.uk
**w** southernwoodhouse.org.uk

---

**White Horse Inn** ★★★ *Inn*
Holtye, Cowden, Edenbridge TN8 7ED
**t** (01342) 850640
**e** whitehorse@greatpubs.net
**w** greatpubs.net/whitehorse

## COWES
### Isle of Wight

**Anchorage Guest House**
★★★★
*Guest Accommodation*
23 Mill Hill Road, Cowes PO31 7EE
**t** (01983) 247975
**e** peterandjenni@anchoragecowes.co.uk
**w** anchoragecowes.co.uk

---

**Endeavour House**
Rating Applied For
*Bed & Breakfast*
47 Mill Hill Road, Cowes PO31 7EG
**t** (01983) 297406
**e** enquiries@endeavourhousecowes.co.uk
**w** endeavourhousecowes.co.uk

---

**Halcyone Villa** ★★★
*Guest Accommodation*
Grove Road, West Cowes PO31 7JP
**t** (01983) 291334
**e** sandraonwight@btinternet.com

## CRANBROOK
### Kent

**Bargate House** ★★★★
*Guest Accommodation*
Angley Road, Cranbrook TN17 2PQ
**t** (01580) 714254
**e** pennylane@bargatehouse.co.uk
**w** bargatehouse.co.uk

---

**Bull Farm Oast** ★★★★
*Bed & Breakfast*
**SILVER AWARD**
Corner Bishops Lane, Glassonbury Road, Cranbrook TN17 2ST
**t** (01580) 714140
**e** b+b@bullfarmoast.co.uk
**w** bullfarmoast.co.uk

---

**Guernsey Cottage** ★★★
*Guest Accommodation*
Wilsley Green, Cranbrook TN17 2LG
**t** (01580) 712542
**e** grahamstarkey@waitrose.com

---

**Hallwood Farm Oast**
★★★★★ *Farmhouse*
**SILVER AWARD**
Hallwood Farm, Hawkhurst Road, Cranbrook TN17 2SP
**t** (01580) 712416
**e** email@hallwoodfarm.co.uk
**w** hallwoodfarm.co.uk

---

**Tilsden House** ★★★★
*Bed & Breakfast*
Tilsden Lane, Cranbrook TN17 3PJ
**t** (01580) 714226
**e** pauldean67@aol.com
**w** tilsdenhouse.co.uk

---

**Tolehurst Barn** ★★★★
*Guest Accommodation*
Cranbrook Road, Frittenden TN17 2BP
**t** (01580) 714385
**e** info@tolehurstbarn.co.uk
**w** tolehurstbarn.co.uk

## CRANLEIGH
### Surrey

**Long Copse** ★★★
*Guest Accommodation*
Pitch Hill, Ewhurst GU6 7NN
**t** (01483) 277458
**e** shhandley@btinternet.com

## CROCKHAM HILL
### Kent

**Pootings Oast** ★★★
*Bed & Breakfast*
Pootings Road, Crockham Hill TN8 6SD
**t** (01732) 866235
**e** alanwhitlock@hotmail.com

## CROSS-IN-HAND
### East Sussex

**High Brow** ★★★★
*Bed & Breakfast*
**SILVER AWARD**
Back Lane, Cross-in-Hand, Heathfield TN21 0QD
**t** (01435) 868406
**e** jrossm@gmail.com
**w** smoothhound.co.uk/hotels/high-brow

## CROSSBUSH
### West Sussex

**April Cottage** ★★★★
*Bed & Breakfast*
**SILVER AWARD**
Crossbush Lane, Arundel BN18 9PQ
**t** (01903) 885401
**e** april.cott@btinternet.com
**w** april-cottage.co.uk

## CROWBOROUGH
### East Sussex

**Bathurst** ★★★★
*Bed & Breakfast*
Fielden Road, Crowborough TN6 1TR
**t** (01892) 665476
**e** annslender1@hotmail.com

---

**Braemore** ★★★★
*Bed & Breakfast*
**SILVER AWARD**
Eridge Road, Crowborough TN6 2SS
**t** (01892) 665700

---

**Yew House Bed & Breakfast**
★★★★
*Guest Accommodation*
**SILVER AWARD**
Crowborough Hill, Crowborough TN6 2EA
**t** (01892) 610522
**e** yewhouse@yewhouse.com
**w** yewhouse.com

## CRUNDALE
### Kent

**The Man of Kent** ★★★★
*Bed & Breakfast*
Denwood Street, Crundale CT4 7EF
**t** (01227) 730743
**e** lewisgerol@hotmail.com

## CUBLINGTON
### Buckinghamshire

**Manor Farm B&B** ★★★
*Bed & Breakfast*
Whitchurch Road, Cublington, Leighton Buzzard LU7 0LP
**t** (01296) 681107

## CUCKFIELD
West Sussex

**Highbridge Mill ★★★★**
*Bed & Breakfast*
**SILVER AWARD**
Cuckfield Road, Haywards Heath RH17 5AE
**t** (01444) 450881
**w** highbridgemill.com

## DANEHILL
East Sussex

**New Glenmore ★★★★**
*Guest Accommodation*
Sliders Lane, Furners Green, Uckfield TN22 3RU
**t** (01825) 790783
**e** alan.robinson@bigfoot.com

## DEAL
Kent

Beachbrow ★★★
*Guest Accommodation*
29 Beach Street, Deal CT14 6HY
t (01304) 374338
e info@beachbrow-hotel.com
w beachbrow-hotel.com

By The Beach ★★
*Bed & Breakfast*
55 The Marina, Deal CT14 6NP
t (01304) 366511
e info@bythebeachindeal.co.uk
w bythebeachindeal.co.uk

**Ilex Cottage ★★★★**
*Guest Accommodation*
Temple Way, Worth, Deal CT14 0DA
**t** (01304) 617026
**e** info@ilexcottage.com
**w** ilexcottage.com

Keep House ★★★
*Guest Accommodation*
1 Deal Castle Road, Deal CT14 7BB
t (01304) 368162
e keephouse@talk21.com
w keephouse.co.uk

Kings Head Public House
★★★ *Inn*
9 Beach Street, Deal CT14 7AH
t (01304) 368194

The Malvern ★★★
*Guest House*
5-7 Ranelagh Road, Deal CT14 7BG
t (01304) 372944
e reception@themalvernguesthouse.com
w themalvernguesthouse.com

Number One B and B
★★★★
*Guest Accommodation*
GOLD AWARD
1 Ranelagh Road, Deal CT14 7BG
t (01304) 364459
e enquiries@numberonebandb.co.uk
w numberonebandb.co.uk

The Roast House Lodge
★★★ *Guest Accommodation*
224 London Road, Deal CT14 9PW
t (01304) 380824
e theroasthouse@amserve.com

St Crispin Inn ★★★★ *Inn*
The Street, Worth, Deal CT14 0DF
t (01304) 612081
w stcrispininn.com

## DEDDINGTON
Oxfordshire

Hill Barn ★★★
*Bed & Breakfast*
Banbury Road, Deddington OX15 0TS
t (01869) 338631
e hillbarn-bb@supanet.com
w hillbarn-bb.co.uk

Stonecrop Guesthouse ★★
*Guest Accommodation*
Hempton Road, Deddington OX15 0QH
t (01869) 338335

## DENNER HILL
Buckinghamshire

Rickyard Cottage ★★★★
*Bed & Breakfast*
Denner Hill HP16 0HZ
t (01494) 488388
e richard@rickyard.plus.com
w rickyardcottage.co.uk

## DETLING
Kent

**Wealden Hall ★★★★**
*Bed & Breakfast*
Pilgrims Way, Detling, Maidstone ME14 3JY
**t** (01622) 739622 & 07934 489041
**e** johnwatson@wealdenhall.net
**w** wealdenhall.net

## DIDCOT
Oxfordshire

Prospect House ★★★
*Bed & Breakfast*
Upton OX11 9HU
t (01235) 850268

## DINTON
Buckinghamshire

Dinton Cottage ★★★
*Guest Accommodation*
Biggs Lane, Dinton HP17 8UH
t (01296) 748270
e lesley@dintoncottage.co.uk
w dintoncottage.co.uk

## DODDINGTON
Kent

Palace Farm Hostel ★★★
*Hostel*
Doddington, Sittingbourne ME9 0AU
t (01795) 886200
e info@palacefarm.com
w palacefarm.com

Palace Farmhouse ★★★
*Guest Accommodation*
Chequers Hill, Doddington, Sittingbourne ME9 0AU
t (01795) 886820

## DORKING
Surrey

Ballantrae ★★★
*Bed & Breakfast*
55 Ashcombe Road, Dorking RH4 1LZ
t (01306) 875873
e morris@mabadanfsnet.co.uk

**Broomhill ★★★**
*Bed & Breakfast*
15 Broomfield Park, Dorking RH4 3QQ
**t** (01306) 885565
**e** suzanne.willis@virgin.net

Bulmer Farm ★★★★
*Guest Accommodation*
Holmbury St Mary, Dorking RH5 6LG
t (01306) 731871
e enquiries@bulmerfarm.co.uk
w bulmerfarm.co.uk

Claremont Cottage ★★★★
*Bed & Breakfast*
Rose Hill, Dorking RH4 2ED
t (01306) 885487
e claremontcott@btinternet.com
w claremontcott.co.uk

**Denbies Farmhouse ★★★★**
*Farmhouse* **SILVER AWARD**
Denbies Wine Estate, London Road, Dorking RH5 6AA
**t** (01306) 876777
**e** bandb@denbiesvineyard.co.uk
**w** denbiesvineyard.co.uk

Fairdene Guest House ★★★
*Guest Accommodation*
Moores Road, Dorking RH4 2BG
t (01306) 888337
e zoe.richardson@ntlworld.com

Stylehurst Farm ★★★★
*Bed & Breakfast*
SILVER AWARD
Weare Street, Capel RH5 5JA
t (01306) 711259
e rosemary.goddard@virgin.net
w stylehurstfarm.com

Tanners Hatch YHA ★ *Hostel*
Off Ranmore Road, Dorking RH5 6BE
t (01306) 877964
e tanners@yha.org.uk
w yha.org.uk

The Waltons ★★★★
*Guest Accommodation*
5 Rose Hill, Dorking RH4 2EG
t (01306) 883127
e thewaltons@rosehill5.demon.co.uk
w a1tourism.com/uk/walt.html

## DOVER
Kent

Alkham Court Farmhouse B&B ★★★★★ *Farmhouse*
GOLD AWARD
Meggett Lane, South Alkham, Dover CT15 7DG
t (01303) 892056
e wendy.burrows@alkhamcourt.co.uk
w alkhamcourt.co.uk

Amanda Guest House ★★★
*Guest House*
4 Harold Street, Dover CT16 1SF
t (01304) 201711
e amandaguesthouse@hotmail.com
w amandaguesthouse.homestead.com

Blakes of Dover ★★★★
*Guest Accommodation*
52 Castle Street, Dover CT16 1PJ
t (01304) 202194
w blakesofdover.com

Castle House ★★★★
*Guest House*
Castle Hill Road, Dover CT16 1QW
t (01304) 201656
e dimechr@aol.com
w castle-guesthouse.co.uk

Chrislyn's ★★★★
*Bed & Breakfast*
104 Maison Dieu Road, Dover CT16 1RU
t (01304) 203317

Clare House ★★★
*Guest House*
167 Folkestone Road, Dover CT17 9SJ
t (01304) 204553
e stay@clarehouse-dover.co.uk
w clarehouse-dover.co.uk

**Colret House ★★★★**
*Bed & Breakfast*
**SILVER AWARD**
The Green, Coldred, Dover CT15 5AP
**t** (01304) 830388
**e** jackiecolret@aol.com
**w** colrethouse.co.uk

Dover's Restover ★★★
*Guest Accommodation*
69 Folkestone Road, Dover CT17 9RZ
t (01304) 206031
e enquiries@doversrestover.co.uk
w doversrestover.co.uk

**East Lee Guest House**
★★★★ *Guest House*
**SILVER AWARD**
108 Maison Dieu Road, Dover CT16 1RT
**t** (01304) 210176
**e** elgh@eclipse.co.uk
**w** eastlee.co.uk

Frith Lodge ★★★
*Bed & Breakfast*
14 Frith Road, Dover CT16 2PY
t (01304) 208139
e stay@frithlodge.co.uk
w frithlodge.co.uk

Hubert House Guest & Coffee House ★★★★
*Guest House*
Castle Hill Road, Dover CT16 1QW
t (01304) 202253
e huberhouse@btinternet.com
w huberthouse.co.uk

Lenox House ★★★★
*Bed & Breakfast*
27 Granville Road, St Margarets Bay, Dover CT15 6DS
t (01304) 853253

Loddington House ★★★★
*Guest Accommodation*
SILVER AWARD
14 East Cliff, Dover CT16 1LX
t (01304) 201947
e loddingtonhotel@btconnect.com
w loddingtonhousehotel.co.uk

**Longfield Guest House**
★★★ *Guest Accommodation*
203 Folkestone Road, Dover CT17 9SL
**t** (01304) 204716
**e** res@longfieldguesthouse.co.uk
**w** longfieldguesthouse.co.uk

**Maison Dieu Guest House**
★★★★ *Guest House*
89 Maison Dieu Road, Dover CT16 1RU
**t** (01304) 204033
**e** info@maisondieu.co.uk
**w** maisondieu.com

**The Norman Guest House**
★★★ *Guest House*
75 Folkestone Road, Dover CT17 9RZ
**t** (01304) 207803
**e** the.norman@btconnect.com
**w** thenorman-guesthouse.co.uk

**Number One Guest House**
★★★★ *Guest House*
1 Castle Street, Dover CT16 1QH
**t** (01304) 202007
**e** res@number1guesthouse.co.uk
**w** number1guesthouse.co.uk

**Number Twenty- Four Bed & Breakfast** ★★★★
*Bed & Breakfast*
24 East Cliff, Marine Parade, Dover CT16 1LU
**t** (01304) 330549
**e** number24dover@aol.com

**Westbank Guest House**
★★★★ *Guest House*
239-241 Folkestone Road, Dover CT17 9LL
**t** (01304) 201061
**e** thewestbank@btconnect.com
**w** thewestbankguesthouse.co.uk

## DUCKLINGTON
Oxfordshire

**Ducklington Farm** ★★★
*Farmhouse*
Course Hill Lane, Ducklington OX29 7YL
**t** (01993) 772175
**e** strainge@ducklingtonfarm.co.uk
**w** countryaccom.co.uk

## DUMMER
Hampshire

**Oakdown Farm Bungalow**
★★★ *Farmhouse*
Oakdown Farm, Dummer, Basingstoke RG23 7LR
**t** (01256) 397218

## DYMCHURCH
Kent

**Waterside Guest House**
★★★★
*Guest Accommodation*
15 Hythe Road, Dymchurch, Romney Marsh TN29 0LN
**t** (01303) 872253
**e** info@watersideguesthouse.co.uk
**w** watersideguesthouse.co.uk

## EARNLEY
West Sussex

**Millstone** ★★★★
*Bed & Breakfast*
**GOLD AWARD**
Clappers Lane, Earnley, Chichester PO20 7JJ
**t** (01243) 670116
**e** m.harrington193@btinternet.com
**w** visitsussex.org

## EAST ASHLING
West Sussex

**The Dairy Farm** ★★★★
*Bed & Breakfast*
**SILVER AWARD**
East Ashling, Chichester PO18 9AR
**t** (01243) 575544
**e** david.ash1@virgin.net

**Horse & Groom** ★★★★ *Inn*
East Ashling, Chichester PO18 9AX
**t** (01243) 575339
**e** info@thehorseandgroomchichester.co.uk
**w** thehorseandgroomchichester.co.uk

## EAST COWES
Isle of Wight

**Crossways House** ★★★★
*Guest Accommodation*
**SILVER AWARD**
Crossways Road, East Cowes PO32 6LJ
**t** (01983) 298282
**e** enquiries@bedbreakfast-cowes.co.uk
**w** bedbreakfast-cowes.co.uk

**Wisteria House** ★★★★
*Bed & Breakfast*
191 York Avenue, East Cowes PO32 6BE
**t** (01983) 295999
**e** philgillan@hotmail.co.uk

## EAST GRINSTEAD
West Sussex

**Coach House** ★★★
*Bed & Breakfast*
Courtlands, Chilling Street, East Grinstead RH19 4JF
**t** (01342) 810512
**e** friends@mmarshall.vispa.com
**w** visitsussex.org

**Gothic House** ★★★★
*Guest Accommodation*
55 High Street, East Grinstead RH19 3DD
**t** (01342) 301910
**e** info@gothichouse55.com
**w** gothichouse55.com

**Saxons** ★★★★
*Guest Accommodation*
Horsted Lane, Sharpthorne, East Grinstead RH19 4HY
**t** (01342) 810821
**e** saxonsbandb@btinternet.com
**w** saxons.freeuk.com

## EAST HAGBOURNE
Oxfordshire

**Hagbourne Mill Farm** ★★★
*Bed & Breakfast*
East Hagbourne, Didcot OX11 9EA
**t** (01235) 813140
**e** corderoy@hagmill.freeserve.co.uk

## EAST HENDRED
Oxfordshire

**A Monks Court** ★★★
*Bed & Breakfast*
Newbury Road, East Hendred, Wantage OX12 8LG
**t** (01235) 833797

**Cowdrays** ★★★
*Bed & Breakfast*
Cat Street, East Hendred, Wantage OX12 8JT
**t** (01235) 833313

## EAST PRESTON
West Sussex

**Roselea Cottage** ★★★
*Bed & Breakfast*
2 Elm Avenue, East Preston BN16 1HJ
**t** (01903) 786787
**e** roselea.cottage@tesco.net
**w** roseleacottage.co.uk

## EAST WELLOW
Hampshire

**Country Views B & B**
★★★★ *Bed & Breakfast*
Willowbend, Dunwood Hill, Shootash SO51 6FD
**t** (01794) 514735
**e** sue@countryviewsbandb.freeserve.co.uk
**w** countryviewsbandb.freeserve.co.uk

## EAST WITTERING
West Sussex

**Stubcroft Farm**
Rating Applied For
*Guest Accommodation*
Stubcroft Lane, East Wittering, Chichester PO20 8PJ
**t** (01243) 671469
**e** mail@stubcroft.com
**w** stubcroft.com

## EASTBOURNE
East Sussex

**The Berkeley** ★★★★★
*Guest Accommodation*
3 Lascelles Terrace, Eastbourne BN21 4BJ
**t** (01323) 645055
**e** info@theberkeley.net
**w** theberkeley.net/

**The Birling Gap** ★★★
*Guest Accommodation*
Birling Gap, Seven Sisters Cliffs, Eastbourne BN20 0AB
**t** (01323) 423197
**e** reception@birlinggaphotel.co.uk
**w** birlinggaphotel.co.uk

**Boyne House** ★★★★
*Guest Accommodation*
12 St Aubyn's Road, Eastbourne BN22 7AS
**t** (01323) 430245

**Bramble Guest House**
★★★★ *Guest House*
16 Lewes Road, Eastbourne BN21 2BT
**t** (01323) 722343
**e** bramble@eastbourneguesthouse.co.uk
**w** brambleguesthouse.co.uk

**Brayscroft House** ★★★★
*Guest House* **GOLD AWARD**
13 South Cliff Avenue, Eastbourne BN20 7AH
**t** (01323) 647005
**e** brayscroft@hotmail.com
**w** brayscrofthotel.co.uk

**Cambridge House** ★★★
*Guest House*
6 Cambridge Road, Eastbourne BN22 7BS
**t** (01323) 721100
**e** rochester11@btinternet.com
**w** cambridgehouseeastbourne.co.uk

**The Cherry Tree** ★★★★
*Guest House*
15 Silverdale Road, Lower Meads, Eastbourne BN20 7AJ
**t** (01323) 722406
**e** lynda@cherrytree-eastbourne.co.uk
**w** cherrytree-eastbourne.co.uk

**Cromwell House**
Rating Applied For
*Guest House*
23 Cavendish Place, Eastbourne BN21 3EJ
**t** (01323) 725288
**e** info@cromwell-house.co.uk
**w** cromwell-house.co.uk

**Ebor Lodge** ★★★★
*Guest House*
71 Royal Parade, Eastbourne BN22 7AQ
**t** (01323) 640792
**e** info@eborlodge.co.uk
**w** eborlodge.co.uk

**The Gladwyn** ★★★★
*Guest House*
16 Blackwater Road, Eastbourne BN21 4JD
**t** (01323) 733142
**e** contact@thegladwyn.com
**w** thegladwyn.com

**Guest House Pavilion**
★★★★ *Guest House*
**SILVER AWARD**
60 Royal Parade, Eastbourne BN22 7AQ
**t** (01323) 736988
**e** info@hotelpavilion.co.uk
**w** hotelpavilion.co.uk

**The Guesthouse East**
★★★★
*Guest Accommodation*
**SILVER AWARD**
13 Hartington Place, Eastbourne BN21 3BS
**t** (01323) 722774
**e** fiona.bugler1@btinternet.com
**w** theguesthouseeastbourne.co.uk

**Loriston Guest House**
★★★★
*Guest Accommodation*
**GOLD AWARD**
17 St Aubyns Road, Eastbourne BN22 7AS
**t** (01323) 726193
**e** loriston@btconnect.com

**La Mer** ★★★ *Guest House*
7 Marine Road, Eastbourne
BN22 7AU
**t** (01323) 724926
**e** penalope@tiscali.co.uk
**w** lamer-guesthouse.com

**Nirvana** ★★★ *Guest House*
32 Redoubt Road, Eastbourne
BN22 7DL
**t** (01323) 722603
**e** eastbournenirvana@btinternet.com

**Ocklynge Manor** ★★★★★
*Guest Accommodation*
**GOLD AWARD**
Mill Road, Eastbourne
BN21 2PG
**t** (01323) 734121
**e** ocklyngemanor@hotmail.com
**w** ocklyngemanor.co.uk

**The Pier** ★★★★
*Guest Accommodation*
2-4 Grand Parade, Eastbourne
BN21 3EH
**t** (01323) 649544

**The Reymar** ★★★
*Guest Accommodation*
2 Cambridge Road, Eastbourne
BN22 7BS
**t** (01323) 724649
**e** info@reymar.co.uk
**w** reymarhotel.co.uk

**St Omer** ★★★★
*Guest House*
13 Royal Parade, Eastbourne
BN22 7AR
**t** (01323) 722152
**e** stomerhotel@hotmail.com
**w** st-omer.co.uk

**Southcroft** ★★★★
*Guest House* **SILVER AWARD**
15 South Cliff Avenue,
Eastbourne BN20 7AH
**t** (01323) 729071
**e** southcroft@eastbourne34.freeserve.co.uk
**w** southcrofthotel.co.uk

## EASTCHURCH
### Kent

**Dunmow House** ★★★★
*Guest Accommodation*
9 Church Road, Eastchurch,
Sheerness ME12 4DG
**t** (01795) 880576
**e** mep4@btinternet.com

## EASTERGATE
### West Sussex

**Eastmere House (B&B)**
★★★ *Bed & Breakfast*
Eastergate Lane, Eastergate
PO20 3SJ
**t** (01243) 544204
**e** bernardlane@hotmail.com
**w** eastmere.com

**Mount Pleasant House**
★★★★ *Bed & Breakfast*
**SILVER AWARD**
Level Mare Lane, Eastergate,
Chichester PO20 3SB
**t** (01243) 545368

## EASTLEIGH
### Hampshire

**Carinya B & B** ★★★
*Bed & Breakfast*
38 Sovereign Way, Eastleigh
SO50 4SA
**t** (023) 8061 3128
**e** carinya38@talktalk.net

## EDENBRIDGE
### Kent

**Mowshurst Farm House**
★★★★ *Bed & Breakfast*
**SILVER AWARD**
Swan Lane, Edenbridge
TN8 6AH
**t** (01732) 862064
**w** mowshurstfarmhouse.co.uk

**Starborough Manor** ★★★★
*Guest Accommodation*
**GOLD AWARD**
Marsh Green Road, Marsh
Green TN8 5QY
**t** (01732) 862152
**e** lynn@starboroughmanor.co.uk
**w** starboroughmanor.co.uk

## EDGCOTT
### Buckinghamshire

**Perry Manor Farm** ★★
*Farmhouse*
Buckingham Road, Edgcott
HP18 0TR
**t** (01296) 770257

## EFFINGHAM
### Surrey

**Cornerways Cottage** ★★★
*Bed & Breakfast*
Orestan Lane, Effingham
KT24 5SN
**t** (01372) 451990
**e** carolinegatford@fsmail.net

**Sir Douglas Haig** ★★ *Inn*
The Street, Effingham
KT24 5LU
**t** (01372) 456886
**e** sirdouglashaig@fullers.co.uk
**w** fullersinns.co.uk

## EGHAM
### Surrey

**Royal Holloway University of London** ★★-★★★★
*Campus*
Egham Hill, Egham TW20 0EX
**t** (01784) 443045
**e** sales-office@rhul.ac.uk
**w** rhul.ac.uk/fm

## ELMSTED
### Kent

**Elmsted Court Farm** ★★★★
*Guest Accommodation*
Elmsted, Ashford TN25 5JN
**t** (01233) 750269
**e** carol@elmsted-court-farm.co.uk
**w** elmsted-court-farm.co.uk

## ELSTEAD
### Surrey

**Anstey's Bed and Breakfast**
★★★ *Bed & Breakfast*
10 Springhill, Elstead GU8 6EL
**t** (01252) 706995
**e** nickyanstey@aol.com
**w** hometown.aol.co.uk/nickyanstey/bedandbreakfast.html

**Puttenham Camping Barn**
*Camping Barn*
Woolford Lane, Elstead
GU8 6LL
**t** (01629) 592682

## EPWELL
### Oxfordshire

**Yarnhill Farm** ★★★
*Farmhouse*
Shenington Road, Epwell,
Banbury OX15 6JA
**t** (01295) 780250
**e** bedandbreakfast@yarnhillfarm.freeserve.co.uk

## EVERTON
### Hampshire

**Glenhurst B & B** ★★★★
*Bed & Breakfast*
86 Wainsford Road, Everton,
Lymington SO41 0UD
**t** (01590) 644256

**Trees Cottage B&B** ★★★★
*Bed & Breakfast*
East Lane, Everton SO41 0JL
**t** (01590) 641622
**e** sidcrowton@yahoo.com

## EWELME
### Oxfordshire

**Mays Farm** ★★★★
*Bed & Breakfast*
Ewelme, Wallingford
OX10 6QF
**t** (01491) 641294
**e** trish.passmore@btinternet.com

## EWHURST
### Surrey

**Malricks** ★★★
*Bed & Breakfast*
The Street, Ewhurst GU6 7RH
**t** (01483) 277575
**e** malricks@tesco.net
**w** http://malricks.mysite.wanadoo-members.co.uk

**Rumbeams Cottage** ★★★
*Bed & Breakfast*
The Green, Ewhurst GU6 7RR
**t** (01483) 268627
**e** joanna@joannacadman.com

## EWHURST GREEN
### East Sussex

**Clouds Bed and Breakfast**
★★★★★ *Bed & Breakfast*
**SILVER AWARD**
9 Dagg Lane, Ewhurst Green
TN32 5RD
**t** (01580) 830677
**e** jandfwouters@aol.com
**w** cloudsbedandbreakfast.co.uk

## FAIRLIGHT
### East Sussex

**Fairlight Cottage** ★★★★
*Guest Accommodation*
Warren Road, Fairlight
TN35 4AG
**t** (01424) 812545
**e** fairlightcottage@supanet.com

## FAREHAM
### Hampshire

**Bridge House** ★★★
*Bed & Breakfast*
1 Waterside Gardens,
Wallington, Fareham
PO16 8SD
**t** (01329) 287775
**e** maryhb8@aol.com

**Catisfield Cottage Guest House** ★★
*Guest Accommodation*
1 Catisfield Lane, Fareham
PO15 5NW
**t** (01329) 843301

**Seven Sevens Guest House**
★★★ *Guest Accommodation*
56 Hill Head Road, Hill Head
PO14 3JL
**t** (01329) 662408
**e** red.reed77@amserve.com

**Trafalgar Guest House** ★★★
*Guest Accommodation*
63 High Street, Fareham
PO16 7BG
**t** (01329) 235010
**e** enquiries@trafalgarguesthouse.co.uk
**w** trafalgarguesthouse.co.uk

**Travelrest Solent Gateway**
★★★ *Guest Accommodation*
22 The Avenue, Fareham
PO14 1NS
**t** (01329) 232175
**e** solentreservations@travelrest.co.uk
**w** travelrest.co.uk/fareham

## FARNBOROUGH
### Hampshire

**Langfords Bed & Breakfast**
★★ *Bed & Breakfast*
165 Cheyne Way, Cove
GU14 8SD
**t** (01252) 547311
**e** bookings@langfordsbandb.co.uk
**w** langfordsbandb.co.uk

## FARNHAM
### Surrey

**High Wray** ★★★
*Bed & Breakfast*
73 Lodge Hill Road, Lower
Bourne GU10 3RB
**t** (01252) 715589
**e** alexine@highwray73.co.uk
**w** highwray73.co.uk

**Princess Royal Lodge**
★★★★ *Inn*
Guildford Road, Runfold
GU10 1NX
**t** (01252) 782243
**e** princessroyal@fullers.co.uk
**w** fullersinns.co.uk

**St Gallen** ★★★★
*Bed & Breakfast*
Old Frensham Road, Lower
Bourne GU10 3PT
**t** (01252) 793412
**e** cary_wilkins@cw1999.freeserve.co.uk

## FAVERSHAM
Kent

**Barnsfield** ★★★
*Guest Accommodation*
Fostall, Hernhill, Faversham
ME13 9JG
**t** (01227) 750973
**e** barnsfield@yahoo.com
**w** barnsfield.co.uk

**Brenley Farm House** ★★★★
*Farmhouse*
Brenley Lane, Boughton-under-Blean, Faversham ME13 9LY
**t** (01227) 751203
**e** maggie@brenley.freeserve.co.uk

**Fairlea** ★★★★
*Bed & Breakfast*
27 Preston Avenue, Faversham
ME13 8NH
**t** (01795) 539610
**e** davidfairlie@supanet.com

**Gladstone House** ★★
*Guest Accommodation*
**SILVER AWARD**
60 Newton Road, Faversham
ME13 8DZ
**t** (01795) 536432
**e** maryjmackay@hotmail.com
**w** gladstoneguesthouse.com

**Leaveland Court** ★★★★
*Guest Accommodation*
Leaveland, Faversham
ME13 0NP
**t** (01233) 740596
**e** info@leavelandcourt.co.uk
**w** leavelandcourt.co.uk

**March Cottage** ★★★
*Guest Accommodation*
5 Preston Avenue, Faversham
ME13 8NH
**t** (01795) 536514
**e** sarah@marchcottagebandb.co.uk
**w** marchcottagebandb.co.uk

**The Railway Hotel** ★★★★
*Inn*
Preston Street, Faversham
ME13 8PE
**t** (01795) 533173
**w** shepherd-neame.co.uk

**The Sun Inn** ★★★ *Inn*
10 West Street, Faversham
ME13 7JE
**t** (01795) 535098
**w** shepherd-neame.co.uk

**Tenterden House** ★★★
*Guest Accommodation*
209 The Street, Boughton
ME13 9BL
**t** (01227) 751593
**e** platham@tesco.net
**w** faversham.org/tenterdenhouse

## FAWLEY
Hampshire

**Walcot Guest House** ★★★★
*Guest House*
Blackfield Road, Fawley
SO45 1ED
**t** (023) 8089 1344
**e** stephenjbrown@tiscali.co.uk
**w** walcothousehotel.com

## FIFIELD
Berkshire

**Victoria Cottage** ★★
*Bed & Breakfast*
2 Victoria Cottages, Fifield Road, Fifield SL6 2NZ
**t** (01628) 623564

## FINDON
West Sussex

**John Henry's Inn** ★★★★ *Inn*
The Forge, Nepcote Lane, Worthing BN14 0SE
**t** (01903) 877277
**e** findev@btopenworld.com
**w** john-henrys.com

## FINGLESHAM
Kent

**Orchard Lodge** ★★★★
*Guest Accommodation*
The Street, Finglesham, Deal
CT14 0NA
**t** (01304) 620192
**e** hutsonbob@aol.com
**w** orchardlodge.co.uk

## FITTLEWORTH
West Sussex

**Old Post Office** ★★★★
*Bed & Breakfast*
Fittleworth, Pulborough
RH20 1JE
**t** (01798) 865315
**e** sue.moseley@ukgateway.net
**w** visitsussex.org

**Swan Inn** ★★★★ *Inn*
Lower Street, Fittleworth, Petworth RH20 1EN
**t** (01798) 865429
**e** hotel@swaninn.com
**w** swaninn.com

## FIVE OAK GREEN
Kent

**Ivy House** ★★
*Bed & Breakfast*
Five Oak Green, Tonbridge
TN12 6RB
**t** (01892) 832041

## FLEET
Hampshire

**Copperfield Bed & Breakfast**
★★★ *Bed & Breakfast*
16 Glen Road, Fleet GU51 3QR
**t** (01252) 616140
**e** bill@copperfieldbnb.co.uk
**w** copperfieldbnb.co.uk

**Tinkers Furze** ★★★★
*Bed & Breakfast*
Gough Road, Fleet GU51 4LL
**t** (01252) 615995

**Tundry House** ★★★★
*Bed & Breakfast*
Dogmersfield, Near Hook
RG27 8SZ
**t** (01252) 614677
**e** sally@tundry.co.uk
**w** tundryhouse.co.uk

## FLIMWELL
Kent

**Forest Edge Motel** ★★★
*Guest Accommodation*
Rosaem House, London Road, Wadhurst TN5 7PL
**t** (01580) 879222
**w** forestedgemotel.co.uk

## FOLKESTONE
Kent

**Garden Lodge** ★★★★
*Guest Accommodation*
324 Canterbury Road, Densole, Folkestone CT18 7BB
**t** (01303) 893147
**e** stay@garden-lodge.com
**w** garden-lodge.com

**Kentmere Guest House**
★★★ *Guest House*
76 Cheriton Road, Folkestone
CT20 1DG
**t** (01303) 259661
**e** enquiries@kentmere-guesthouse.co.uk
**w** kentmere-guesthouse.co.uk

**The Rob Roy Guest House**
★★★ *Guest House*
227 Dover Road, Folkestone
CT19 6NH
**t** (01303) 253341
**e** robroy.folkestone@ntlworld.com
**w** therobroyguesthouse.co.uk

**Seacliffe** ★★★
*Guest Accommodation*
3 Wear Bay Road, Folkestone
CT19 6AT
**t** (01303) 254592
**e** sheila_foot@yahoo.com

**Sunny Lodge Guest House**
★★★ *Guest Accommodation*
85 Cheriton Road, Folkestone
CT20 2QL
**t** (01303) 251498
**e** linda.dowsett@btclick.com
**w** s-h-systems.co.uk

**Windsor Hotel** ★★
*Guest Accommodation*
5-6 Langhorne Gardens, Folkestone CT20 2EA
**t** (01303) 251348
**e** windsorhotel_folkestone@hotmail.com

## FONTWELL
West Sussex

**Park Cottage** ★★★★
*Bed & Breakfast*
London Road, Fontwell
BN18 0SG
**t** (01243) 544133

**Woodacre** ★★★★
*Guest Accommodation*
Arundel Road, Fontwell
BN18 0QP
**t** (01243) 814301
**e** wacrebb@aol.com
**w** woodacre.co.uk

## FORDINGBRIDGE
Hampshire

**Broomy** ★★★★
*Bed & Breakfast*
Ogdens SP6 2PY
**t** (01425) 653264

**Snowtalia Lodge**
Rating Applied For
*Bed & Breakfast*
Ringwood Road, Fordingbridge
SP6 2EY
**t** (01425) 655114
**e** bookings@snowtalialodge.co.uk
**w** snowtalialodge.co.uk

**The Three Lions** ★★★★
*Restaurant with Rooms*
Stuckton, Fordingbridge
SP6 2HF
**t** (01425) 652489
**e** the3lions@btinternet.com
**w** thethreelionsrestaurant.co.uk

## FOREST ROW
East Sussex

**The Brambletye Inn** ★★★
*Inn*
The Square, Forest Row
RH18 5EZ
**t** (01342) 824144
**e** brambletye.hotel@fullers.co.uk
**w** fullersinns.co.uk

## FORTON
Hampshire

**The Barn House B&B**
★★★★★ *Bed & Breakfast*
**SILVER AWARD**
Andover SP11 6NU
**t** (01264) 720544
**e** hello@thebarnhousebandb.co.uk
**w** thebarnhousebandb.co.uk

## FRAMFIELD
East Sussex

**Beggars Barn** ★★★★
*Guest Accommodation*
**SILVER AWARD**
Barn Lane, Framfield, Uckfield
TN22 5RX
**t** (01825) 890868
**e** caroline@beggarsbarn.co.uk
**w** beggarsbarn.co.uk

## FREEFOLK
Hampshire

**The Old Rectory** ★★★
*Bed & Breakfast*
Freefolk, Whitchurch
RG28 7NW
**t** (01256) 895408
**w** theoldrectoryfreefolk.co.uk

## FRESHWATER
Isle of Wight

**Braewood** ★★★★
*Bed & Breakfast*
Afton Road, Freshwater
PO40 9TP
**t** (01983) 759910
**e** enquiries@braewood-iow.co.uk
**w** braewood-iow.co.uk

**Freshwater Bay House**
★★★★
*Guest Accommodation*
Freshwater Bay, Freshwater
PO40 9RB
**t** (020) 8511 1534

**Heather Cottage B&B**
★★★★ *Bed & Breakfast*
Afton Road, Freshwater Bay
PO40 9TP
**t** (01983) 754319
**e** heathercottbb@aol.com

**The Old Traidcraft Shop B&B**
Rating Applied For
*Guest Accommodation*
119 School Green Road, Freshwater PO40 9AZ
**t** (01983) 752451
**e** ctjmurph@hotmail.com

**The Orchards ★★★★**
*Bed & Breakfast*
Princes Road, Freshwater
PO40 9ED
**t** (01983) 753795
**e** paulagerrish@vodafoneemail.co.uk
**w** theorchardsbandb.co.uk

**Seahorses ★★★★**
*Guest Accommodation*
Victoria Road, Freshwater
PO40 9PP
**t** (01983) 752574
**e** seahorses-iow@tiscali.co.uk
**w** seahorsesisleofwight.com

## FROXFIELD GREEN
Hampshire

**The Trooper Inn ★★★★** *Inn*
Froxfield, Petersfield
GU32 1BD
**t** (01730) 827293
**e** troopersec@btconnect.com
**w** trooperinn.com

## FULBROOK
Oxfordshire

**Star Cottage ★★★★**
*Bed & Breakfast*
**SILVER AWARD**
Meadow Lane, Burford
OX18 4BW
**t** (01993) 822032
**e** peterwyatt@tesco.net

## GARSINGTON
Oxfordshire

**Hill Copse Cottage ★★★**
*Bed & Breakfast*
Wheatley Road, Garsington
OX44 9DT
**t** (01865) 361478

## GATCOMBE
Isle of Wight

**Freewaters ★★★★**
*Guest Accommodation*
**SILVER AWARD**
New Barn Lane, Gatcombe
PO30 3EQ
**t** (01983) 721439
**e** john@pitstopmodels.demon.co.uk
**w** colourpointdesign.co.uk/freewaters

**Little Gatcombe Farm**
**★★★★** *Bed & Breakfast*
**SILVER AWARD**
Newbarn Lane, Gatcombe
PO30 3EQ
**t** (01983) 721580
**e** anita@littlegatcombefarm.co.uk
**w** littlegatcombefarm.co.uk

## GATWICK
West Sussex

**The Lawn Guest House**
**★★★★** *Guest House*
**SILVER AWARD**
30 Massetts Road, Horley
RH6 7DF
**t** (01293) 775751
**e** info@lawnguesthouse.co.uk
**w** lawnguesthouse.co.uk

**Southbourne Guest House Gatwick ★★★★**
*Guest House*
34 Massetts Road, Horley
RH6 7DS
**t** (01293) 771991
**e** reservations@southbournegatwick.com
**w** southbournegatwick.com

## GILLINGHAM
Kent

**Medway YHA ★★★** *Hostel*
351 Capstone Road, Gillingham
ME7 3JE
**t** (01634) 400788
**e** medway@yha.org.uk
**w** yha.org.uk

**Ramsey House ★★★★**
*Guest Accommodation*
228a Barnsole Road,
Gillingham ME7 4JB
**t** (01634) 854193

## GODALMING
Surrey

**24 Croft Road ★★★**
*Guest Accommodation*
Croft Road, Godalming
GU7 1BY
**t** (01483) 429982
**e** enquiries@no24croftroad.orangehome.co.uk

**Combe Ridge ★★★**
*Bed & Breakfast*
Pook Hill, Chiddingfold,
Godalming GU8 4XR
**t** (01428) 682607
**e** brendaessex@btinternet.com

**Heath Hall Farm ★★★**
*Farmhouse*
Bowlhead Green, Godalming
GU8 6NW
**t** (01428) 682808
**e** heathhallfarm@btinternet.com
**w** heathhallfarm.co.uk

**Heath House ★★★★**
*Bed & Breakfast*
**SILVER AWARD**
Alldens Lane, Godalming
GU8 4AP
**t** (01483) 416961
**e** info@heathhouse.eu
**w** heathhouse.eu

**Highview ★★**
*Bed & Breakfast*
**SILVER AWARD**
39 Nightingale Road,
Godalming GU7 2HU
**t** (01483) 861974
**e** highview@which.net
**w** highview-bedbreakfast.co.uk

## GODSHILL
Hampshire

**Croft Cottage ★★★**
*Bed & Breakfast*
Southampton Road, Godshill,
Fordingbridge SP6 2LE
**t** (01425) 657955
**e** croftcottage@btopenworld.com
**w** croftcottagenewforest.co.uk

## GODSHILL
Isle of Wight

**Koala Cottage Retreat**
**★★★★★** *Bed & Breakfast*
**GOLD AWARD**
Church Hollow, Godshill
PO38 3DR
**t** (01983) 842031
**e** info@koalacottage.co.uk
**w** koalacottage.co.uk

## GOLFORD
Kent

**Tollgate Farm B&B**
Rating Applied For
*Bed & Breakfast*
Tollgate Farm, Cranbrook
TN17 3NX
**t** (01580) 712864
**e** enquiry@tollgate-farm.co.uk
**w** tollgate-farm.co.uk

## GOODWOOD
West Sussex

**The Coach House ★★★★**
*Bed & Breakfast*
**SILVER AWARD**
1 Pilleygreen Lodge,
Goodwood, Chichester
PO18 0QE
**t** (01243) 811467 & 07776 417709
**e** enquiries@coachhousegoodwood.co.uk
**w** coachhousegoodwood.co.uk

## GRAFFHAM
West Sussex

**Brook Barn ★★★★**
*Bed & Breakfast*
**SILVER AWARD**
Selham Road, Graffham,
Petworth GU28 0PU
**t** (01798) 867356
**e** brookbarn@hotmail.com
**w** visitsussex.org

**Withy ★★★★★**
*Bed & Breakfast*
**SILVER AWARD**
Graffham, Petworth GU28 0PY
**t** (01798) 867000
**e** jacquelinewoods@hotmail.com
**w** withy.uk.com

## GRAFTY GREEN
Kent

**Foxes Earth Bed & Breakfast**
**★★★★**
*Guest Accommodation*
**SILVER AWARD**
Headcorn Road, Grafty Green
ME17 2AP
**t** (01622) 858350
**e** foxesearth@btinternet.com
**w** foxesearthbedandbreakfast.co.uk

**Who'd A Thought It ★★★★**
*Guest Accommodation*
Headcorn Road, Grafty Green,
Maidstone ME17 2AR
**t** (01622) 858951
**e** joe@whodathoughtit.com
**w** whodathoughtit.com

## GRAVESEND
Kent

**Briars Court B & B ★★★★**
*Bed & Breakfast*
90 Windmill Street, Gravesend
DA12 1LH
**t** (01474) 363788
**e** bandb@briarscourt.co.uk
**w** briarscourt.co.uk

**Eastcourt Oast ★★**
*Guest Accommodation*
**SILVER AWARD**
Church Lane, Gravesend
DA12 2NL
**t** (01474) 823937
**e** mary@eastcourtoast.co.uk
**w** eastcourtoast.co.uk

## GREAT BOOKHAM
Surrey

**Selworthy ★★**
*Bed & Breakfast*
310 Lower Road, Bookham
KT23 4DW
**t** (01372) 453952
**e** bnb.selworthy@btinternet.com

## GREAT MISSENDEN
Buckinghamshire

**Forge House ★★★★**
*Bed & Breakfast*
10 Church Street, Great
Missenden HP16 0AX
**t** (01494) 867347

## GREATSTONE
Kent

**White Horses Cottage**
**★★★★**
*Guest Accommodation*
**SILVER AWARD**
180 The Parade, Greatstone
TN28 8RS
**t** (01797) 366626
**e** whitehorses@tesco.net
**w** horses-cottage.co.uk

## GREENHAM
Berkshire

**Cumorah Guest Accommodation ★★★★**
*Guest Accommodation*
7 Spa Meadow Close,
Greenham RG19 8ST
**t** (01635) 34464
**e** pam@cumorah.co.uk
**w** cumorah.co.uk

## GUESTLING
East Sussex

**Mount Pleasant Farm**
**★★★★** *Bed & Breakfast*
White Hart Hill, Guestling
TN35 4LR
**t** (01424) 813108
**e** angelajohn@mountpleasantfarm.fsbusiness.co.uk
**w** mountpleasantfarm.fsbusiness.co.uk

## GUILDFORD
Surrey

**Abeille House ★★★★**
*Bed & Breakfast*
119 Stoke Road, Guildford
GU1 1ET
**t** (01483) 532200
**e** abeille.house119@ntlworld.com
**w** abeillehouse.co.uk

**Amberley** ★★★
*Bed & Breakfast*
Maori Road, Guildford
GU1 2EL
**t** (01483) 573198
**e** amberleyjoyners@connectfree.co.uk

**Bluebells** ★★★
*Bed & Breakfast*
21 Coltsfoot Drive, Guildford
GU1 1YH
**t** (01483) 826124
**e** hughes.a@ntlworld.com
**w** bluebellsbedandbreakfast.co.uk

**Cherry Trees** ★★★★
*Bed & Breakfast*
Gomshall Lane, Shere
GU5 9HE
**t** (01483) 202288

**East Woodhay** ★★★
*Bed & Breakfast*
86a Epsom Road, Guildford
GU1 2DH
**t** (01483) 575986
**e** eastwoodhaybandb@hotmail.co.uk

**Guildford YMCA** ★★★★
*Hostel*
Bridge Street, Guildford
GU1 4SB
**t** (01483) 532555
**e** accom@guildfordymca.org.uk
**w** guildfordymca.org.uk

**Holroyd Arms Pubotel** ★★
*Inn*
36 Aldershot Road, Guildford
GU2 8AF
**t** (01483) 560215
**w** infotel.co.uk/900988.htm

**The Homestead BNB** ★★
*Bed & Breakfast*
75 Bray Road, Guildford
GU2 7LJ
**t** (01483) 828663
**w** thehomesteadbnb.co.uk

**The Laurels** ★★★
*Bed & Breakfast*
Dagden Road, Shalford
GU4 8DD
**t** (01483) 565753

**Lavender House B&B** ★★
*Bed & Breakfast*
4 Medlar Close, Guildford
GU1 1LS
**t** 07709 760000
**e** ayse.stevenson@ntlworld.com

**Littlefield Manor** ★★★
*Farmhouse*
Littlefield Common, Guildford
GU3 3HJ
**t** (01483) 233068
**e** john@littlefieldmanor.co.uk
**w** littlefieldmanor.co.uk

**Matchams** ★★
*Guest Accommodation*
35 Boxgrove Avenue,
Guildford GU1 1XQ
**t** (01483) 567643

**The Old Malt House** ★★★
*Bed & Breakfast*
Bagshot Road, Worplesdon
GU3 3PT
**t** (01483) 232152

**Patcham** ★★ *Bed & Breakfast*
44 Farnham Road, Guildford
GU2 4LS
**t** (01483) 570789

**Plaegan House** ★★★★
*Bed & Breakfast*
**SILVER AWARD**
96 Wodeland Avenue,
Guildford GU2 4LD
**t** (01483) 822181 &
07961 919430
**e** froxanephillips@yahoo.co.uk
**w** plaeganhouse.co.uk

**Portofino** ★★★★
*Bed & Breakfast*
1a Glendale Drive, Guildford
GU4 7HX
**t** (01483) 573735
**e** nahid.mcneil@gmail.com

**Stoke House** ★★★
*Guest House*
113 Stoke Road, Guildford
GU1 1ET
**t** (01483) 453025 &
07714 339588
**e** bookings@stokehouse.net
**w** stokehouse.net

**Yew Tree House** ★★★★
*Bed & Breakfast*
2 The Paddock, Guildford
GU1 2RQ
**t** (01483) 573735
**e** rooms@yewtreehouse.info
**w** yewtreehouse.info

## GURNARD
Isle of Wight

**Hillbrow House** ★★★★
*Guest Accommodation*
Tuttons Hill, Cowes PO31 8JA
**t** (01983) 297240
**e** hill-brow@btconnect.com

**The Woodvale** ★★★★ *Inn*
1 Princes Esplanade, Gurnard
PO31 8LE
**t** (01983) 292037
**e** info@the-woodvale.co.uk
**w** the-woodvale.co.uk

## HADDENHAM
Buckinghamshire

**New Hadden** ★★★
*Bed & Breakfast*
3a High Street, Haddenham,
Aylesbury HP17 8ES
**t** (01844) 291347

## HADLOW
Kent

**Ferndale House** ★★★★
*Bed & Breakfast*
Maidstone Road, Hadlow
TN11 0DN
**t** (01732) 850876
**e** mikenanniereynolds@btopenworld.com

## HAILEY
Oxfordshire

**Hunters Close Farm** ★★★★
*Bed & Breakfast*
Middletown, Witney
OX29 9UB
**t** (01993) 772332
**e** huntersclose@yahoo.co.uk
**w** huntersclosefarm.co.uk

## HAILSHAM
East Sussex

**The Corn Exchange** ★★★
*Inn*
19 High Street, Hailsham
BN27 1AL
**t** (01323) 442290
**e** jason@thechapmansgroup.co.uk
**w** cornexchangehailsham.co.uk

**Hailsham Grange** ★★★★★
*Guest Accommodation*
**SILVER AWARD**
Vicarage Road, Hailsham
BN27 1BL
**t** (01323) 844248
**e** noel-hgrange@amserve.com
**w** hailshamgrange.co.uk

**Longleys Farm Cottage**
★★★ *Guest Accommodation*
Harebeating Lane, Hailsham
BN27 1ER
**t** (01323) 841227
**e** longleysfarmcottagebb@dsl.pipex.com
**w** longleysfarmcottage.co.uk

**Windesworth** ★★★★
*Bed & Breakfast*
Carters Corner, Hailsham
BN27 4HT
**t** (01323) 847178
**e** windesworth.bedandbreakfast@virgin.net
**w** visitsussex.org

## HALE
Hampshire

**Finches Hatch** ★★★
*Bed & Breakfast*
Forest Road, Hale SP6 2NP
**t** (01725) 510529
**e** suesutherland@ssla.demon.co.uk
**w** fincheshatch.co.uk

## HALLAND
East Sussex

**Beechwood B&B** ★★★★★
*Guest Accommodation*
Eastbourne Road, Halland,
Lewes BN8 6PS
**t** (01825) 840937
**e** chyland1956@aol.com
**w** beechwoodbandb.co.uk

## HAMBLEDON
Hampshire

**Forestside** ★★★
*Bed & Breakfast*
Hambledon, Waterlooville
PO7 4RA
**t** (023) 9263 2672

## HAMBROOK
West Sussex

**Willowbrook Riding Centre**
★★ *Bed & Breakfast*
Hambrook Hill South,
Hambrook, Chichester
PO18 8UJ
**t** (01243) 572683
**e** info@willowbrook-stables.co.uk

## HANSLOPE
Buckinghamshire

**Woad Farm** ★★★ *Farmhouse*
Tathall End, Hanslope
MK19 7NE
**t** (01908) 510985
**e** s.stacey@btconnect.com

## HARTFIELD
East Sussex

**Dorset House** ★★★
*Bed & Breakfast*
Withyham, Hartfield TN7 4BD
**t** (01892) 770035
**e** meg@rosneathengineering.co.uk
**w** dorset-house.co.uk

## HASLEMERE
Surrey

**Deerfell** ★★★★
*Bed & Breakfast*
Blackdown, Haslemere
GU27 3BU
**t** (01428) 653409
**e** deerfell@tesco.net
**w** deerfell.co.uk

**Sheps Hollow** ★★★
*Bed & Breakfast*
Henley Common, Henley,
Haslemere GU27 3HB
**t** (01428) 653120
**e** bizzielizziebee@msn.com
**w** tuckedup.com/accommodation/840/sheps-hollow.php

**Strathire** ★★★★
*Bed & Breakfast*
Grayswood Road, Haslemere
GU27 2BW
**t** (01428) 642466

**The Wheatsheaf Inn** ★★★
*Inn*
Grayswood Road, Haslemere
GU27 2DE
**t** (01428) 644440
**e** ken@thewheatsheafgrayswood.co.uk

## HASTINGS
East Sussex

**Castle Hill Guest House**
★★★★ *Bed & Breakfast*
113 Castle Hill Road, Hastings
TN34 3RD
**t** (01424) 720787
**e** castlehillbnb@yahoo.co.uk
**w** castlehillguesthouse.co.uk

**Churchills** ★★★
*Guest Accommodation*
3 St Helens Crescent, Hastings
TN34 2EN
**t** (01424) 439359
**e** enquiries@churchillshotelhastings.co.uk
**w** churchillshotelhastings.co.uk

**Croft Place** ★★★★
*Guest Accommodation*
2 The Croft, Hastings
TN34 3HH
**t** (01424) 433004
**e** lorraine@croftplace.co.uk
**w** croftplace.co.uk

**The Elms** ★★★ *Guest House*
9 St Helens Park Road,
Hastings TN34 2ER
**t** (01424) 429979
**e** jmktbriggs@btinternet.com

**Europa Guest Accommodation** ★★★
*Guest Accommodation*
2 Carlisle Parade, Hastings
TN34 1JG
**t** (01424) 717329
**e** info@europahotelhastings.co.uk
**w** europahotelhastings.co.uk

**Four Winds** ★★★★
*Bed & Breakfast*
Parsonage Lane, Westfield TN35 4SH
t (01424) 752585
e stewarts@4-winds.fsnet.co.uk
w 4-winds.org

**Lavender & Lace** ★★★★
*Bed & Breakfast*
106 All Saints Street, Hastings TN34 3BE
t (01424) 716290
e lavenderlace1066@btinternet.com
w lavenderlace1066.co.uk

**The Lindum** ★★★★
*Guest Accommodation*
1a Carlisle Parade, Hastings TN34 1JG
t (01424) 434070
e hotellindum@aol.com
w hotellindum.co.uk

**The Lookout** ★★★★
*Bed & Breakfast*
**GOLD AWARD**
Pett Level TN35 4EQ
t (01424) 812070

**Minstrel's Rest** ★★★★
*Bed & Breakfast*
21 Greville Road, Hastings TN35 5AL
t (01424) 443500
e minstrelsrest@hotmail.com

**The Old Town Guest House**
Rating Applied For
*Guest Accommodation*
1a George Street, Hastings TN34 3EG
t (01424) 423342 & 07870 163818
e sophiew84@hotmail.com

**Seaspray** ★★★★
*Guest Accommodation*
**SILVER AWARD**
54 Eversfield Place, St Leonards-on-Sea, Hastings TN37 6DB
t (01424) 436583
e jo@seaspraybb.co.uk
w seaspraybb.co.uk

**South Riding Guest House**
★★★ *Guest House*
96 Milward Road, Hastings TN34 3RT
t (01424) 420805

**Summerfields House**
★★★★
*Guest Accommodation*
Bohemia Road, Hastings TN34 1EX
t (01424) 718142
e liz.summerfields@btinternet.com
w summerfieldshouse.co.uk

**Swan House** ★★★★★
*Guest Accommodation*
**SILVER AWARD**
1 Hill Street, Old Town, Hastings TN34 3HU
t (01424) 430014
e res@swanhousehastings.co.uk
w swanhousehastings.co.uk

## HAVANT
Hampshire

**High Towers** ★★★
*Bed & Breakfast*
14 Portsdown Hill Road, Bedhampton PO9 3JY
t (023) 9247 1748
e hightowers14@aol.com
w hightowers.co.uk

## HAWKLEY
Hampshire

**Scotland Farm Countryside Bed and Breakfast** ★★★★
*Farmhouse* **SILVER AWARD**
Upland Lane, Hawkley GU33 6NH
t (01730) 827473
e admin@scotlandfarm.com
w scotlandfarm.com

## HAYLING ISLAND
Hampshire

**16 Charleston Close** ★★
*Bed & Breakfast*
Hayling Island PO11 0JY
t (023) 9246 2527

**Ann's Cottage** ★★
*Bed & Breakfast*
45 St Andrews Road, Hayling Island PO11 9JN
t (023) 9246 7048
e ann.jay@virgin.net

**The Coach House** ★★★★
*Guest Accommodation*
**SILVER AWARD**
Church Lane, Northney PO11 0SB
t (023) 9246 6266
e jenny.stenning1@btinternet.com
w wakeup.to/coachhouse

**Copsewood House** ★★★★
*Bed & Breakfast*
Copse Lane, Hayling Island PO11 0QD
t (023) 9246 9294
e jillgoulding@hotmail.com
w copsewoodhouse.piczo.com

**White House** ★★★★
*Bed & Breakfast*
250 Havant Road, Hayling Island PO11 0LN
t (023) 9246 3464
e info@whitehousehayling.co.uk
w whitehousehayling.co.uk/

## HAYWARDS HEATH
West Sussex

**Copyhold Hollow Bed & Breakfast** ★★★★
*Bed & Breakfast*
**GOLD AWARD**
Copyhold Lane, Borde Hill, Haywards Heath RH16 1XU
t (01444) 413265
e vs@copyholdhollow.co.uk
w copyholdhollow.co.uk

**Oakfield Cottage** ★★★★
*Guest Accommodation*
Brantridge Lane, Staplefield, Haywards Heath RH17 6JR
t (01444) 401121
e joydougoakfield@btinternet.com
w smoothhound.co.uk/hotels/oakfieldcottage

**The Old Forge** ★★★
*Bed & Breakfast*
16 Lucastes Avenue, Haywards Heath RH16 1JH
t (01444) 451905

## HEADCORN
Kent

**Curtis Farm** ★★★★
*Guest Accommodation*
Waterman Quarter, Headcorn TN27 9JJ
t (01622) 890393
e curtis.farm@btopenworld.com
w curtis-farm-kent.co.uk

**Four Oaks** ★★★★
*Guest Accommodation*
Four Oaks Road, Headcorn TN27 9PB
t (01622) 891224
e info@fouroaks.uk.com
w fouroaks.uk.com

**Wilderness Bed & Breakfast**
★★★★ *Bed & Breakfast*
Waterman Quarter, Headcorn TN27 9JJ
t (01622) 891757
e vhonychurch@toucansurf.com
w wildernessbandb.co.uk

## HEADINGTON
Oxfordshire

**YHA Oxford** ★★★★ *Hostel*
2a Botley Road, Oxford OX2 0AB
t (01865) 727275
e oxford@yha.org.uk
w yha.org.uk

## HEATHFIELD
East Sussex

**Iwood Bed & Breakfast**
★★★★
*Guest Accommodation*
**GOLD AWARD**
Mutton Hall Lane, Heathfield TN21 8NR
t (01435) 863918
e iwoodbb@aol.com
w iwoodbb.com

**Woodbine Farm** ★★★★
*Bed & Breakfast*
Cross in Hand, Heathfield TN21 0QA
t (01435) 867458
e poppyflower668@hotmail.com
w woodbine-farm.co.uk

## HEDGE END
Hampshire

**Lakeside B & B** ★★★★
*Bed & Breakfast*
48 Stag Drive, Hedge End SO30 2QN
t (01489) 780618
e enquiries@lakesidebandb.co.uk
w lakesidebandb.co.uk

## HENFIELD
West Sussex

**1 The Laurels** ★★★★
*Bed & Breakfast*
Martyn Close, Henfield BN5 9RQ
t (01273) 493518
e malc.harrington@lineone.net
w no1thelaurels.co.uk

**The George** ★★★★ *Inn*
High Street, Henfield BN5 9DB
t (01273) 492296
e info@thegeorgehotel.net
w thegeorgehotel.net

## HENLEY-ON-THAMES
Oxfordshire

**61 Deanfield Road** ★★★
*Guest Accommodation*
Henley-on-Thames RG9 1UU
t (01491) 576784
e susan@bushells.co.uk

**Abbottsleigh** ★★★
*Guest Accommodation*
107 St Marks Road, Henley-on-Thames RG9 1LP
t (01491) 572982
e abbottsleigh@hotmail.com

**Alushta** ★★★★
*Guest Accommodation*
**SILVER AWARD**
23 Queen Street, Henley-on-Thames RG9 1AR
t (01491) 636041
e sdr@alushta.co.uk
w alushta.co.uk

**Amanchris** ★★★★
*Bed & Breakfast*
**SILVER AWARD**
16 Baronsmead, Henley-on-Thames RG9 2DL
t (01491) 578044
e pamelajstuart@aol.com
w amanchris.co.uk

**Apple Ash** ★★★★
*Bed & Breakfast*
**SILVER AWARD**
Woodlands Road, Harpsden RG9 4AB
t (01491) 574198

**Avalon** ★★★ *Bed & Breakfast*
36 Queen Street, Henley-on-Thames RG9 1AP
t (01491) 577829
e avalon@henleybb.co.uk
w henleybb.co.uk

**Azalea House** ★★★★
*Bed & Breakfast*
55 Deanfield Road, Henley-on-Thames RG9 1UU
t (01491) 576407
w azaleahouse.co.uk

**Badgemore Park Golf Club**
★★★★
*Guest Accommodation*
Badgemore, Henley-on-Thames RG9 4NR
t (01491) 637300
e info@badgemorepark.com
w badgemorepark.com

**Bank Farm** ★★ *Farmhouse*
The Old Road, Pishill RG9 6HS
t (01491) 638601
e e.f.lakey@btinternet.com
w stayatbankfarm.co.uk

**The Baskerville** ★★★★ *Inn*
**SILVER AWARD**
Station Road, Lower Shiplake RG9 3NY
t (0118) 940 3332
e enquiries@thebaskerville.com
w thebaskerville.com

**The Beeches** ★★★★
*Bed & Breakfast*
**SILVER AWARD**
3a Coldharbour Close, Henley-on-Thames RG9 1QF
**t** (01491) 579344
**e** henleyduddies@talktalk.net
**w** beechesbandbhenley.co.uk

**Brackenhurst** ★★★
*Bed & Breakfast*
Russells Water RG9 6EU
**t** (01491) 642399
**e** info@foolonthehill.co.uk
**w** foolonthehill.co.uk

**Coldharbour House** ★★★★
*Bed & Breakfast*
3 Coldharbour Close, Henley-on-Thames RG9 1QF
**t** (01491) 575229
**e** coldharbourhouse@aol.com
**w** coldharbourhouse.co.uk

**Denmark House** ★★★★
*Guest Accommodation*
**SILVER AWARD**
Northfield End, Henley-on-Thames RG9 2HN
**t** (01491) 572028
**e** ds.hutchings@virgin.net
**w** denmark-house.net

**Falaise House** ★★★★
*Guest Accommodation*
37 Market Place, Henley-on-Thames RG9 2AA
**t** (01491) 573388

**Garden View**
Rating Applied For
*Bed & Breakfast*
Greys Road, Henley-on-Thames RG9 1TF
**t** (01491) 579010
**e** carolplocka@aol.com
**w** gardenview.org.uk

**Glenroy** ★★★
*Bed & Breakfast*
27 Makins Road, Henley-on-Thames RG9 1PU
**t** (01491) 574403
**e** glenis.welch@virgin.net

**Lenwade** ★★★★★
*Bed & Breakfast*
**SILVER AWARD**
3 Western Road, Henley-on-Thames RG9 1JL
**t** (01491) 573468
**e** jacquie@lenwade.com
**w** lenwade.com

**Little Parmoor Farm** ★★★★
*Farmhouse*
Parmoor RG9 6NL
**t** (01494) 881600
**e** frances@francesemmett.com
**w** parmoor.com

**Old Bell House** ★★★
*Bed & Breakfast*
9 Northfield End, Henley-on-Thames RG9 2JG
**t** (01491) 574350
**e** antony@antonydesign.co.uk

**Old School House** ★★★★
*Bed & Breakfast*
42 Hart Street, Henley-on-Thames RG9 2AU
**t** (01491) 573929
**e** adrian.lake@btinternet.com
**w** oldschoolhousehenley.co.uk/

**The Old Wood** ★★★
*Bed & Breakfast*
197 Greys Road, Henley-on-Thames RG9 1QU
**t** (01491) 573930
**e** janice@janicejones.co.uk

**Orchard Dene Cottage**
★★★★ *Bed & Breakfast*
Lower Assendon, Henley-on-Thames RG9 6AG
**t** (01491) 575490
**e** info@orcharddenecottage.co.uk
**w** orcharddenecottage.co.uk

**Riverside Guest House**
★★★ *Guest Accommodation*
4 River Terrace, Henley-on-Thames RG9 1BG
**t** (01491) 571133
**e** no4riverside@virgin.co.uk
**w** no4riverside.co.uk

**Robhill** ★★★★
*Bed & Breakfast*
267 Greys Road, Henley-on-Thames RG9 1QS
**t** (01491) 577391
**e** jill@robhill.info
**w** robhillbandb.com

**Slaters Farm** ★★★
*Bed & Breakfast*
Church Lane, Rotherfield Peppard RG9 5JL
**t** (01491) 628675
**e** stay@slatersfarm.co.uk

**Stag Hall** ★★★
*Bed & Breakfast*
Stoke Row Road, Kingwood RG9 5NX
**t** (01491) 680338
**e** stag_hall@hotmail.com

**The Walled Garden** ★★★★
*Bed & Breakfast*
Bell Lane, Henley-on-Thames RG9 2HR
**t** (01491) 573142
**e** walledgard@aol.com

## HERNE BAY
Kent

**Bayview** ★★★★
*Bed & Breakfast*
Central Parade, Herne Bay CT6 5JJ
**t** (01227) 741458
**e** info@the-bayview-guesthouse.co.uk
**w** the-bayview-guesthouse.co.uk

**Evening Tide Bed and Breakfast** ★★★★
*Guest House*
97 Central Parade, Herne Bay CT6 5JJ
**t** (01227) 365014
**e** info@eveningtide.co.uk
**w** eveningtide.co.uk

**Priory B&B** ★★★★
*Guest Accommodation*
203 Canterbury Road, Herne Bay CT6 5UG
**t** (01227) 366670
**e** stephen@guy200.demon.co.uk
**w** theprioryband b.co.uk

**Summerhouse** ★★★★
*Bed & Breakfast*
15 Glenbervie Drive, Beltinge, Herne Bay CT6 6QL
**t** (01227) 363192
**e** john.pye1@talktalk.net
**w** beltingesummerhouse.co.uk

**Westgrange House Bed and Breakfast** ★★★★
*Bed & Breakfast*
42 Busheyfield Road, Herne Bay CT6 7LJ
**t** (01227) 740663

## HERNHILL
Kent

**Church Oast** ★★★★
*Bed & Breakfast*
Hernhill, Faversham ME13 9JW
**t** (01227) 750974
**e** jill@geliot.plus.com
**w** churchoast.co.uk

## HERSHAM
Surrey

**Bricklayers Arms** ★★★★ *Inn*
6 Queens Road, Walton-on-Thames KT12 5LS
**t** (01932) 220936
**e** ff@bricklayers-arms.fsworld.co.uk

## HERSTMONCEUX
East Sussex

**Sandhurst** ★★★★
*Guest Accommodation*
Church Road, Herstmonceux, Hailsham BN27 1RG
**t** (01323) 833088
**e** junealanruss@aol.com

**The Stud Farm** ★★★
*Farmhouse*
Bodle Street Green, Hailsham BN27 4RJ
**t** (01323) 832647
**e** timkatemills@aol.com
**w** studfarmsussex.co.uk

**Waldernheath Country House** ★★★★
*Bed & Breakfast*
Hailsham Road, Amberstone, Hailsham BN27 1PJ
**t** (01323) 442259
**e** waldernheath.c.h@btinternet.com
**w** visitsussex.org

## HEVER
Kent

**Becketts** ★★★★
*Bed & Breakfast*
**SILVER AWARD**
Pylegate Farm, Hartfield Road, Cowden, Edenbridge TN8 7HE
**t** (01342) 850514
**e** jacqui@becketts-bandb.co.uk
**w** becketts-bandb.co.uk

## HEYSHOTT
West Sussex

**Little Hoyle** ★★★★
*Bed & Breakfast*
Hoyle Lane, Heyshott, Midhurst GU29 0DX
**t** (01798) 867359
**e** ralphs.littlehoyle@btopenworld.com
**w** smoothhound.co.uk/hotels/littlehoyle

## HIGH HURSTWOOD
East Sussex

**Chillies Granary** ★★★★
*Guest Accommodation*
Chillies Lane, High Hurstwood, Crowborough TN6 3TB
**t** (01892) 655560

**The Orchard** ★★★★
*Bed & Breakfast*
Rocks Lane, High Hurstwood, Uckfield TN22 4BN
**t** (01825) 732946
**e** turtonorchard@aol.com
**w** theorchardbandb.co.uk

## HIGH WYCOMBE
Buckinghamshire

**9 Green Road** ★★★★
*Bed & Breakfast*
**SILVER AWARD**
High Wycombe HP13 5BD
**t** (01494) 437022
**w** lovetostayat9.co.uk

**9 Sandford Gardens** ★★★
*Bed & Breakfast*
Daws Hill, High Wycombe HP11 1QT
**t** (01494) 441723 & 07980 439560

**Amersham Hill Guest House**
★★★ *Guest House*
52 Amersham Hill, High Wycombe HP13 6PQ
**t** (01494) 520635

**The Bell** ★★★ *Inn*
41 Frogmoor, High Wycombe HP13 5DQ
**t** (01494) 525588
**e** info@thebellonline.co.uk
**w** thebellonline.co.uk

**Longforgan** ★★
*Bed & Breakfast*
**SILVER AWARD**
Magpie Lane, Flackwell Heath HP10 9EA
**t** (01628) 525178
**e** bedbreakfasthighwycombe@hotmail.co.uk
**w** bedandbreakfasthighwycombe.co.uk

**The Three Horseshoes Inn**
★★★★ *Inn* **GOLD AWARD**
Horseshoe Road, Bennett End, Radnage, High Wycombe HP14 4EB
**t** (01494) 483273

## HILDENBOROUGH
Kent

**The Barn at Woodview**
★★★★ *Bed & Breakfast*
**SILVER AWARD**
London Road, Watts Cross, Tonbridge TN11 8NQ
**t** (01732) 833167
**e** woodview.barn@ntlworld.com

## HILL BROW
West Sussex

**The Jolly Drover** ★★★★ *Inn*
**SILVER AWARD**
London Road, Hill Brow, Liss GU33 7QL
**t** (01730) 893137
**e** thejollydrover@googlemail.com

**HINTON WALDRIST**
**Oxfordshire**

**The Old Rectory** ★★★★
*Bed & Breakfast*
Hinton Waldrist, Faringdon
SN7 8SA
t (01865) 821228

**HOLMBURY ST MARY**
**Surrey**

**Holmbury Farm** ★★★★
*Guest Accommodation*
Holmbury St Mary, Dorking
RH5 6NB
t (01306) 621443
e virginia@holmsburysheep.co.uk
w smoothhound.co.uk/hotels/holmbury

**Holmbury St Mary YHA** ★★
*Hostel*
Radnor Lane, Dorking
RH5 6NW
t (01306) 730777
e holmbury@yha.org.uk
w yha.org.uk

**HOLYBOURNE**
**Hampshire**

**Upper Neatham Mill Farm Guest House** ★★★★
*Guest House*
Upper Neatham Mill Lane, Holybourne GU34 4EP
t (01420) 542908
e upperneatham@btinternet.com
w upperneatham.co.uk

**HORLEY**
**Surrey**

**Berrens Guest House** ★★★
*Guest House*
62 Massetts Road, Horley
RH6 7DS
t (01293) 430800

**Melville Lodge Guest House**
★★★ *Guest House*
15 Brighton Road, Horley
RH6 7HH
t (01293) 784951
e melvillelodge.guesthouse@tesco.net
w melvillelodgegatwick.co.uk

**Rosemead Guest House**
★★★★ *Guest House*
**SILVER AWARD**
19 Church Road, Horley
RH6 7EY
t (01293) 784965
e info@rosemeadguesthouse.co.uk
w rosemeadguesthouse.co.uk

**The Turret Guest House**
★★★ *Guest Accommodation*
48 Massetts Road, Horley
RH6 7DS
t (01293) 782490 & 07970 066471
e info@theturret.com
w theturret.com

**HORNDEAN**
**Hampshire**

**The Ship & Bell** ★★★ *Inn*
6 London Road, Horndean
PO8 0BZ
t (023) 9259 2107
e shipandbell@fullers.co.uk
w fullersinns.co.uk

**HORSHAM**
**West Sussex**

**The Larches** ★★★
*Bed & Breakfast*
28 Rusper Road, Horsham
RH12 4BD
t (01403) 263392
e ericjanelane@aol.com

**The Wirrals** ★★
*Bed & Breakfast*
1 Downsview Road, Horsham
RH12 4PF
t (01403) 269400
e thewirralsarchibald@btinternet.com
w visitsussex.org

**HULVERSTONE**
**Isle of Wight**

**The Elms** ★★★★
*Bed & Breakfast*
Hulverstone PO30 4EH
t (01983) 741528
e theelmsbnb@aol.com

**HUNGERFORD**
**Berkshire**

**The Garden House** ★★★★
*Bed & Breakfast*
Rear of 34 High Street, Hungerford RG17 0NF
t (01488) 685369
e bevjess@openscreen.co.uk
w openscreen.co.uk/thegardenhouse

**Wilton House** ★★★★
*Bed & Breakfast*
**SILVER AWARD**
33 High Street, Hungerford
RG17 0NF
t (01488) 684228
e welfares@hotmail.com
w wiltonhouse-hungerford.co.uk

**HUNSTON**
**West Sussex**

**Spire Cottage** ★★★★
*Bed & Breakfast*
Church Lane, Hunston, Chichester PO20 1AJ
t (01243) 778937
e jan@spirecottage.co.uk
w spirecottage.co.uk

**HURLEY**
**Berkshire**

**Meadow View** ★★★★★
*Bed & Breakfast*
**SILVER AWARD**
Henley Road, Hurley SL6 5LW
t (01628) 829764
e info@meadowviewbedandbreakfast.co.uk
w meadowviewbedandbreakfast.co.uk

**HURST**
**Hampshire**

**Copper Beeches** ★★★
*Bed & Breakfast*
Torberry Farm, Hurst, Petersfield GU31 5RG
t (01730) 826662
e ianchew@torberry212.fsnet.co.uk
w copperbeeches.homecall.co.uk

**HURSTPIERPOINT**
**West Sussex**

**Wickham Place** ★★★★
*Guest Accommodation*
**SILVER AWARD**
Wickham Drive, Hurstpierpoint, Hassocks
BN6 9AP
t (01273) 832172
e accommodation@wickham-place.co.uk
w smoothhound.co.uk/hotels/wickham

**IBTHORPE**
**Hampshire**

**Staggs Cottage** ★★★★
*Guest Accommodation*
Windmill Hill, Ibthorpe
SP11 0BP
t (01264) 736235
e staggscottage@aol.com
w staggscottage.co.uk

**IVINGHOE**
**Buckinghamshire**

**Bull Lake B&B** ★★★★
*Bed & Breakfast*
Ford End, Ivinghoe LU7 9EA
t (01296) 668834
e enquiries@bull-lake.co.uk
w bull-lake.co.uk

**JORDANS**
**Buckinghamshire**

**Jordans Youth Hostel** ★
*Hostel*
Welders Lane, Beaconsfield
HP9 2SN
t 0870 770 5886
e jordans@yha.org.uk
w yha.org.uk

**KENNINGTON**
**Kent**

**The Conningbrook** ★★★★
*Guest Accommodation*
Canterbury Road, Kennington
TN24 9QR
t (01233) 636863
e conningbrook@shepherdneame.co.uk
w conningbrookashford.co.uk

**Downsview Guest House** ★★★★
*Guest Accommodation*
Willesborough Road, Kennington TN24 9QP
t (01233) 621391
e downsviewguesthouse@msn.com
w ashforddownsview.co.uk

**KIDLINGTON**
**Oxfordshire**

**Warsborough House**
★★★★ *Bed & Breakfast*
52 Mill Street, Kidlington
OX5 2EF
t (01865) 370316

**KILMESTON**
**Hampshire**

**Dean Farm** ★★★★
*Guest Accommodation*
Kilmeston, Alresford SO24 0NL
t (01962) 771286
e warrdeanfarm@btinternet.com
w warrdeanfarm.btinternet.co.uk

**KINGHAM**
**Oxfordshire**

**Tollgate Inn & Restaurant**
★★★★ *Inn*
Church Street, Kingham
OX7 6YA
t (01608) 658389
e info@thetollgate.com
w thetollgate.com

**KINGSDOWN**
**Kent**

**The Gardeners Rest**
★★★★★
*Guest Accommodation*
**GOLD AWARD**
Nemesis, Queensdown Road, Kingsdown, Deal CT14 8EF
t (01304) 371449
e sandra@gardenersrest.me.uk
w gardenersrest.me.uk

**KINGSLEY**
**Hampshire**

**Spring Cottage** ★★★
*Bed & Breakfast*
Main Road, Kingsley
GU35 9NA
t (01420) 472703
e paulineansell@aol.com

**KINGSTON BLOUNT**
**Oxfordshire**

**The Cherry Tree** ★★★
*Guest Accommodation*
High Street, Kingston Blount
OX39 4SJ
t (01844) 352273
e cherrytreepub@btconnect.com
w thecherrytreepub.com

**KINTBURY**
**Berkshire**

**The Dundas Arms** ★★★ *Inn*
Station Road, Kintbury, Hungerford RG17 9UT
t (01488) 658263
e info@dundasarms.co.uk
w dundasarms.co.uk

**LADDINGFORD**
**Kent**

**Chequers Inn** ★★★★ *Inn*
Nr Yalding, Maidstone
ME18 6BP
t (01622) 871266

**LAKE**
**Isle of Wight**

**Ashleigh House** ★★★★
*Guest Accommodation*
81 Sandown Road, Lake
PO36 9LE
t (01983) 402340
e richard@ashleighhousehotel.com
w ashleighhousehotel.com

**Haytor Lodge** ★★★★
*Guest Accommodation*
16 Cliff Path, Lake PO36 8PL
t (01983) 402969
e info@islandbreaks.co.uk

**Osterley Lodge** ★★★★
*Guest Accommodation*
62 Sandown Road, Lake
PO36 9JX
t (01983) 402017
e osterleylodgeiw@aol.com
w netguides.co.uk/wight/basic/osterley.html

**Piers View Guest House** ★★★★
*Guest Accommodation*
20 Cliff Path, Lake PO36 8PL
**t** (01983) 404646
**e** info@islandbreaks.co.uk

## LAMBERHURST Kent

**Woodpecker Barn** ★★★★★
*Bed & Breakfast*
**SILVER AWARD**
Wickhurst Farm, Tunbridge Wells TN3 8BH
**t** (01892) 891958
**e** martinloveday@btinternet.com
**w** woodpeckerbarn.co.uk

## LANE END Buckinghamshire

**Rances** ★★★★
*Bed & Breakfast*
Moor Common HP14 3HR
**t** (01494) 881294
**e** d.is@btopenworld.com

## LANGLEY Kent

**Orchard House** ★★★★
*Bed & Breakfast*
Sutton Road, Maidstone ME17 3LZ
**t** (01622) 862694
**e** orchard_house2004@yahoo.co.uk

## LANGRISH Hampshire

**Upper Parsonage Farm** ★★★★ *Farmhouse*
**SILVER AWARD**
Harvesting Lane, East Meon GU32 1QR
**t** (01730) 823490
**e** sue@atko.demon.co.uk
**w** upperparsonagefarm.co.uk

**Yew Tree Farm House** ★★★
*Bed & Breakfast*
Langrish, Petersfield GU32 1RB
**t** (01730) 264959
**e** jane.sprinks@tesco.net

## LAVANT West Sussex

**Flint Cottage** ★★★★
*Bed & Breakfast*
47 Mid Lavant, Lavant, Chichester PO18 0AA
**t** (01243) 785883
**e** info@flintcottagebedandbreakfast.co.uk
**w** smoothhound.co.uk/hotels/flint

## LECKHAMPSTEAD Buckinghamshire

**Weatherhead Farm** ★★★★
*Farmhouse*
Leckhampstead, Buckingham MK18 5NP
**t** (01280) 860502
**e** weatherheadfarm@aol.com

## LEE COMMON Buckinghamshire

**Lower Bassibones Farm B & B** ★★★★
*Guest Accommodation*
Lower Bassibones Farm, Ballinger Road, Great Missenden HP16 9LA
**t** (01494) 837798
**e** lowerbassibones@yahoo.co.uk
**w** discover-real-england.com

## LEE-ON-THE-SOLENT Hampshire

**Chester Lodge** ★★★★
*Bed & Breakfast*
20 Chester Crescent, Lee-on-the-Solent PO13 9BH
**t** (023) 9255 0894
**e** chesterlodge@btinternet.com

**Leeward House B&B** ★★★★
*Bed & Breakfast*
18 Russell Road, Lee-on-the-Solent PO13 9HP
**t** (023) 9255 6090
**e** enq@leewardhouse.co.uk
**w** leewardhouse.co.uk

**Milvil Corner** ★★★★
*Guest Accommodation*
**SILVER AWARD**
41 Milvil Road, Lee-on-the-Solent PO13 9LU
**t** (023) 9255 3489
**e** enquiries@milvilcorner.co.uk
**w** milvilcorner.co.uk

## LEEDS Kent

**Further Fields** ★★★
*Guest Accommodation*
Caring Lane, Maidstone ME17 1TJ
**t** (01622) 861288
**e** furtherfields@aol.com
**w** furtherfields.co.uk

**West Forge** ★★★
*Guest Accommodation*
Back Street, Maidstone ME17 1TF
**t** (01622) 861428
**w** westforge.co.uk

## LEIGH Kent

**Charcott Farmhouse** ★★★★
*Bed & Breakfast*
Charcott, Tonbridge TN11 8LG
**t** (01892) 870024
**e** charcottfarmhouse@btinternet.com
**w** smoothhound.co.uk/hotels/charcott

## LENHAM Kent

**Bramley Knowle Farm** ★★★★
*Guest Accommodation*
Eastwood Road, Maidstone ME17 1ET
**t** (01622) 858878
**e** diane@bramleyknowlefarm.co.uk
**w** bramleyknowlefarm.co.uk

**The Dog & Bear Hotel** ★★★★ *Inn*
The Square, Lenham, Maidstone ME17 2PG
**t** (01622) 858219
**e** dogbear@shepherd-neame.co.uk
**w** shepherd-neame.co.uk

## LEWES East Sussex

**13 Hill Road** ★★★
*Bed & Breakfast*
Garden Flat, Lewes BN7 1DB
**t** (01273) 477723
**e** kmyles@btclick.com

**Berkeley House** ★★★★
*Guest Accommodation*
2 Albion Street, Lewes BN7 2ND
**t** (01273) 476057
**e** enquiries@berkeleyhouselewes.co.uk
**w** berkeleyhouselewes.co.uk

**The Blacksmiths Arms** ★★★★ *Inn* **SILVER AWARD**
London Road, Offham, Lewes BN7 3QD
**t** (01273) 472971
**e** blacksmithsarms@tiscali.co.uk
**w** theblacksmithsarms-offham.co.uk

**The Crown Inn** ★★
*Guest Accommodation*
191 High Street, Lewes BN7 2NA
**t** (01273) 480670
**e** sales@crowninn-lewes.co.uk
**w** crowninn-lewes.co.uk

**Eckington House** ★★★★
*Guest Accommodation*
**SILVER AWARD**
Ripe, Glyndebourne BN8 6AR
**t** (01323) 811274
**e** suebrianhill@btopenworld.com
**w** eckingtonhouse.co.uk

**Hale Farm House** ★★★★
*Guest Accommodation*
**SILVER AWARD**
Hale Green, Lewes BN8 6HQ
**t** (01825) 872619
**e** s.burrough@virgin.net
**w** halefarmhouse.co.uk

**Langtons House** ★★★★
*Guest Accommodation*
**SILVER AWARD**
143b High Street, Lewes BN7 1XT
**t** (01273) 476644
**e** info@langtonshouse.com
**w** langtonshouse.com

**Lill Stugan** ★★★★
*Guest Accommodation*
33 Houndean Rise, Lewes BN7 1EQ
**t** (01273) 483580
**e** alanagh.raikes@virgin.net

**Millers** ★★★★
*Bed & Breakfast*
**SILVER AWARD**
134 High Street, Lewes BN7 1XS
**t** (01273) 475631
**e** millers134@aol.com
**w** hometown.aol.com/millers134

**Tamberry Hall** ★★★★★
*Guest Accommodation*
**GOLD AWARD**
Eastbourne Road, Halland, Lewes BN8 6PS
**t** (01825) 880090
**e** bedandbreakfast@tamberryhall.fsbusiness.co.uk
**w** tamberryhall.co.uk

## LEYSDOWN ON SEA Kent

**Muswell Manor Holiday Park** ★★★ *Guest Accommodation*
Shellness Road, Leysdown, Sheerness ME12 4RJ
**t** (01795) 510245
**e** mail@muswellmanor.co.uk
**w** muswellmanorholidaypark.com

## LINDFIELD West Sussex

**Little Lywood** ★★★★
*Guest Accommodation*
Ardingly Road, Lindfield, Haywards Heath RH16 2QX
**t** (01444) 892571
**e** nick@littlelywood.freeserve.co.uk

## LITTLEBOURNE Kent

**The Evenhill** ★★★★ *Inn*
62 The Hill, Littlebourne CT3 1TA
**t** (01227) 728073
**w** shepherd-neame.co.uk

**The Pilgrims Rest** ★★★★
*Guest Accommodation*
48-50 High Street, Canterbury CT3 1ST
**t** (01227) 721341
**e** info@thepilgrimsrest.biz
**w** thepilgrimsrest.biz

## LITTLEHAMPTON West Sussex

**Amberley Court** ★★★★
*Guest Accommodation*
**SILVER AWARD**
Crookthorn Lane, Littlehampton BN17 5SN
**t** (01903) 725131
**e** msimmonds06@aol.com
**w** visitsussex.org

**Arun Sands** ★★★
*Guest Accommodation*
84 South Terrace, Littlehampton BN17 5LJ
**t** (01903) 732489
**e** info@arun-sands.co.uk
**w** arun-sands.co.uk

**Arun View Inn** ★★ *Inn*
Wharf Road, Littlehampton BN17 5DD
**t** (01903) 722335
**w** thearunview.co.uk

**Selborne House** ★★★
*Bed & Breakfast*
21 Selborne Road, Littlehampton BN17 5LZ
**t** (01903) 726064
**e** fipickett@hotmail.com
**w** selbornehouse.net

**YHA Littlehampton** ★★★★
*Hostel*
63 Surrey Street, Littlehampton BN17 5AW
**t** (01903) 733177
**e** littlehampton@yha.org.uk
**w** yha.org.uk

## LONG HANBOROUGH Oxfordshire

**The Close Guest House**
★★★ *Guest House*
Witney Road, Long Hanborough OX29 8HF
t (01993) 882485

**Old Farmhouse** ★★★★
*Bed & Breakfast*
Station Hill, Long Hanborough OX29 8JZ
t (01993) 882097
e rvmaundrell@btinternet.com
w countryaccom.co.uk/old-farmhouse

## LONG WITTENHAM Oxfordshire

**The Grange** ★★★
*Bed & Breakfast*
High Street, Long Wittenham OX14 4QH
t (01865) 407808
e graham@grangebb.com
w grangebb.com

**Witta's Ham Cottage**
★★★★ *Bed & Breakfast*
**SILVER AWARD**
High Street, Long Wittenham OX14 4QH
t (01865) 407686
e bandb@wittenham.com

## LONGFIELD Kent

**The Rising Sun Inn** ★★★ *Inn*
Fawkham Green, Fawkham, Longfield DA3 8NL
t (01474) 872291

## LONGPARISH Hampshire

**Yew Cottage Bed & Breakfast** ★★★
*Bed & Breakfast*
Longparish, Andover SP11 6QE
t (01264) 720325
e yewcottage@ukgateway.net

## LOWER BOURNE Surrey

**Kiln Farm Bed and Breakfast**
★★★★ *Bed & Breakfast*
8 Kiln Lane, Lower Bourne GU10 3LR
t (01252) 726083
e raphe_palmer@tiscali.co.uk
w kilnfarm.plus.com

## LYDD ON SEA Kent

**Plovers** ★★★★
*Bed & Breakfast*
**SILVER AWARD**
Toby Road, Lydd-on-Sea TN29 9PG
t (01797) 366935
e troddy@plovers.co.uk
w plovers.co.uk

## LYMINGE Kent

**Roundwood Hall Bed and Breakfast** ★★★★
*Bed & Breakfast*
Stone Street, Lyminge, Folkestone CT18 8DJ
t (01303) 862260
e bnb@roundwoodhall.co.uk
w roundwoodhall.co.uk

## LYMINGTON Hampshire

**Bluebird Restaurant** ★★★
*Bed & Breakfast*
4-5 Quay Street, Lymington SO41 3AS
t (01590) 676908

**Britannia House** ★★★★★
*Guest Accommodation*
**SILVER AWARD**
Mill Lane, Lymington SO41 9AY
t (01590) 672091
e enquiries@britannia-house.com
w britannia-house.com

**Durlston House** ★★★
*Guest Accommodation*
Gosport Street, Lymington SO41 9EG
t (01590) 677364
e durlstonhouse@aol.com
w durlstonhouse.co.uk

**Gorse Meadow Guest House**
★★★ *Guest House*
Sway Road, Pennington, Lymington SO41 8LR
t (01590) 673354
e gorsemeadow@btconnect.com
w gorsemeadowguesthouse.co.uk

**Moonraker Cottage** ★★★★
*Bed & Breakfast*
62 Milford Road, Lymington SO41 8DU
t (01590) 678677
e moonraker62@tiscali.co.uk

**Pennavon House** ★★★★
*Bed & Breakfast*
**SILVER AWARD**
Lower Pennington Lane, Pennington SO41 8AL
t (01590) 673984
e info@pennavon.co.uk
w pennavon.co.uk

**The Rowans** ★★★
*Bed & Breakfast*
76 Southampton Road, Lymington SO41 9GZ
t (01590) 672276
e the.rowans@totalise.co.uk

## LYNDHURST Hampshire

**Acorns of Lyndhurst** ★★★★
*Bed & Breakfast*
**SILVER AWARD**
31 Romsey Road, Lyndhurst SO43 7AR
t (023) 8028 4559
e enquiries@acornsoflyndhurst.co.uk
w acornsoflyndhurst.co.uk

**Burwood Lodge** ★★★★
*Guest Accommodation*
27 Romsey Road, Lyndhurst SO43 7AA
t (023) 8028 2445
e burwood.1@ukonline.co.uk
w burwoodlodge.co.uk

**Clayhill House** ★★★★
*Bed & Breakfast*
Clay Hill, Lyndhurst SO43 7DE
t (023) 8028 2304
e clayhillhouse@tinyworld.co.uk
w clayhillhouse.co.uk

**Englefield** ★★★★
*Guest Accommodation*
Chapel Lane, Lyndhurst SO43 7FG
t (023) 8028 2685
e christine.salmon@talktalk.net

**Hurst End** ★★★
*Bed & Breakfast*
Clayhill, Lyndhurst SO43 7DE
t (023) 8028 2606
e hurst.end@btinternet.com
w hurstend.co.uk

**Lyndhurst House B&B**
★★★★
*Guest Accommodation*
35 Romsey Road, Lyndhurst SO43 7AR
t (023) 8028 2230
e enquiries@lyndhursthousebb.co.uk
w lyndhursthousebb.co.uk

**The Mailmans Arms** ★★★★
*Inn*
71 High Street, Lyndhurst SO43 7BE
t (023) 8028 4196
e info@mailmans-arms.co.uk
w mailmans-arms.co.uk

**Okeover** ★★★
*Bed & Breakfast*
12 Forest Gardens, Lyndhurst SO43 7AF
t (023) 8028 2406
e okeover12@btinternet.com
w okeoveraccommodation.co.uk

**Rosedale Bed & Breakfast**
★★★ *Bed & Breakfast*
24 Shaggs Meadow, Lyndhurst SO43 7BN
t (023) 8028 3793 & (023) 8013 4253
e rosedalebandb@btinternet.com
w rosedalebedandbreakfast.co.uk

## LYNSTED Kent

**The Black Lion** ★★★★
*Bed & Breakfast*
Sittingbourne ME9 0RJ
t (01795) 521229

## MAIDENHEAD Berkshire

**The Black Boys Inn** ★★★★
*Restaurant with Rooms*
**SILVER AWARD**
Henley Road, Hurley, Maidenhead SL6 5NQ
t (01628) 824212

**Braywick Grange** ★★★★
*Bed & Breakfast*
100 Braywick Road, Maidenhead SL6 1DJ
t (01628) 625915
e reception@braywickgrange.co.uk
w braywickgrange.co.uk

**Cartlands Cottage** ★★
*Bed & Breakfast*
Kings Lane, Cookham Dean, Maidenhead SL6 9AY
t (01628) 482196

**Clifton Guest House** ★★★
*Guest House*
21 Craufurd Rise, Maidenhead SL6 7LR
t (01628) 620086
e reservation@cliftonguesthouse.co.uk
w cliftonguesthouse.co.uk

**Gables End** ★★
*Bed & Breakfast*
4 Gables Close, Maidenhead SL6 8QD
t (01628) 639630
e christablight@onetel.com

**Hillcrest** ★★★ *Guest House*
19 Craufurd Rise, Maidenhead SL6 7LR
t (01628) 620086
e reservation@cliftonguesthouse.co.uk
w cliftonguesthouse.co.uk

**Sheephouse Manor** ★★★
*Bed & Breakfast*
Sheephouse Road, Maidenhead SL6 8HJ
t (01628) 776902
e info@sheephousemanor.co.uk
w sheephousemanor.co.uk

**Sunny Cottage** ★★★★
*Guest House*
Manor Lane, Maidenhead SL6 2QW
t (01628) 770731
e beadvr@aol.com
w sunnycottagebb.co.uk

## MAIDSTONE Kent

**At Home** ★★★★
*Guest Accommodation*
39 Marston Drive, Vinters Park, Maidstone ME14 5NE
t (01622) 202196
e steveandlesley@steleybrown.freeserve.co.uk

**Calgary** ★★★
*Bed & Breakfast*
18 Bower Mount Road, Maidstone ME16 8AU
t (01622) 208963
e jandpt@blueyonder.co.uk

**The Granary** ★★★★
*Guest Accommodation*
Lower Farm Road, Boughton Monchelsea, Maidstone ME17 4DD
t (01622) 743532
e sue@granarybandb.co.uk
w granarybandb.co.uk

**Grove House** ★★★★
*Bed & Breakfast*
**SILVER AWARD**
Grove Green Road, Maidstone ME14 5JT
t (01622) 738441

**The Hazels** ★★★★
*Bed & Breakfast*
Yeoman Way, Bearsted, Maidstone ME15 8PQ
t (01622) 737943
e carolbuse@hotmail.com
w the-hazels.co.uk

**The Limes** ★★★★
*Guest Accommodation*
118 Boxley Road, Maidstone ME14 2BD
t (01622) 750629

**Maidstone Lodge ★★★**
*Guest Accommodation*
22/24 London Road, Maidstone ME16 8QL
t (01622) 758778
e maidstonelodge@btinternet.com
w maidstonelodge.co.uk

**Oakwood House ★★★**
*Guest Accommodation*
Oakwood Park, Maidstone ME16 8AE
t (01622) 626600
e oakwoodhouse@kent.gov.uk
w oakwoodhouse-kcc.com

**Penenden Heath Lodge**
★★★★ *Bed & Breakfast*
2 Penenden Heath Road, Penenden Heath ME14 2DA
t (01622) 672562
e penendenheathlodge@blueyonder.co.uk
w penendenheathlodge.com

**Ringlestone House**
★★★★★
*Guest Accommodation*
Ringlestone Road, Harrietsham, Maidstone ME17 1NX
t (01622) 859911
e bookings@ringlestonehouse.co.uk
w ringlestone.co.uk

**Roslin Villa ★★★★**
*Guest House*
11 St Michaels Road, Maidstone ME16 8BS
t (01622) 758301
e info@roslinvillaguesthouse.com
w roslinvillaguesthouse.com

## MARDEN
Kent

**3 Chainhurst Cottages**
★★★★ *Bed & Breakfast*
**SILVER AWARD**
Dairy Lane, Marden TN12 9SU
t (01622) 820483
e heatherscott@waitrose.com
w chainhurstcottages.co.uk

**Tanner House ★★★★**
*Farmhouse*
Tanner Farm, Goudhurst Road, Tonbridge TN12 9ND
t (01622) 831214
e enquiries@tannerfarmpark.co.uk
w tannerfarmpark.co.uk

## MARGATE
Kent

**The Hussar ★★★★** *Inn*
219 Canterbury Road, Margate CT9 5JP
t (01843) 836296
e rdobbs@ukgateway.net
w hussarhotel.co.uk

**Innsbrook House ★★★**
*Guest Accommodation*
Dalby Square, Cliftonville, Margate CT9 2ER
t (01843) 298946
e info@innsbrookhouse.co.uk
w innsbrookhouse.co.uk

**The Malvern Guest House and Blues Grill ★★★**
*Guest House*
29 Eastern Esplanade, Cliftonville, Margate CT9 2HL
t (01843) 290192
e themalvern@aol.com
w malvern-hotel.co.uk

**YHA Margate The Beachcomber ★★** *Hostel*
3-4 Royal Esplanade, Westbrook Bay, Margate CT9 5DL
t (01843) 221616
e margate@yha.org.uk
w yha.org.uk

## MARK CROSS
East Sussex

**Rose Cottage ★★★★**
*Bed & Breakfast*
Mill Lane, Mark Cross, Crowborough TN6 3PJ
t (01892) 852592
e johnandsoniacooper@hotmail.co.uk

## MARLOW
Buckinghamshire

**18 Rookery Court ★★★★**
*Bed & Breakfast*
Marlow SL7 3HR
t (01628) 486451
e gillbullen@rookerycourt.fsnet.co.uk
w bandb-marlow.co.uk

**31 Institute Road ★★**
*Bed & Breakfast*
Marlow SL7 1BJ
t (01628) 485662

**Acorn Lodge ★★★★**
*Bed & Breakfast*
**SILVER AWARD**
79 Marlow Bottom Road, Marlow SL7 3NA
t (01628) 472197
e acornlodge@thamesinternet.com
w acornlodgemarlow.co.uk

**Granny Anne's ★★★**
*Bed & Breakfast*
54 Seymour Park Road, Marlow SL7 3EP
t (01628) 473086
e roger@grannyannes.com
w marlowbedbreakfast.co.uk

**The Hand and Flowers**
★★★★★ *Inn*
West Street, Marlow SL7 2BP
t (01628) 482277
w thehandandflowers.co.uk

**Hazeldene ★★**
*Bed & Breakfast*
53 Stapleton Close, Marlow SL7 1TZ
t (01628) 482183

**Heathercroft ★★★★**
*Bed & Breakfast*
Marlow SL7 2QR
t (01628) 473641
e ellimarlow@aol.com
w heathercroft-marlow.co.uk

**Malvern House ★★★★**
*Guest Accommodation*
Fernie Fields HP12 4SP
t 07792 815846
e krysmaddocks@hotmail.com
w malvernguesthouse.co.uk

**Oak Tree B&B**
Rating Applied For
*Bed & Breakfast*
76 Oaktree Road, Bucks SL7 3EX
t (01628) 475340
e sheila.budd@btinternet.com

**Red Barn Farm ★★★**
*Farmhouse*
Marlow Road, Marlow SL7 3DQ
t (01494) 882820
e redbarnfarm@btinternet.com

**Riverdale ★★★★**
*Bed & Breakfast*
Marlow Bridge Lane, Marlow SL7 1RH
t (01628) 485206
e chrisrawlings@onetel.com
w bed-breakfast-marlow.co.uk

**Swiss Cottage B & B ★★★★**
*Bed & Breakfast*
New Road, Marlow SL7 3NG
t 07752 032407
e swisscottagebb@hotmail.com
w swisscottagemarlow.co.uk

## MARLOW BOTTOM
Buckinghamshire

**Sue Simmons Bed & Breakfast ★★**
*Bed & Breakfast*
61 Hill Farm Road, Marlow Bottom SL7 3LX
t (01628) 475145
e suesimmons@accommodationmarlow.com
w accommodationmarlow.com

**T J O'Reilly's ★★★** *Inn*
61 Marlow Bottom Road, Marlow SL7 3NA
t (01628) 484926

## MARSHBOROUGH
Kent

**Honey Pot Cottage ★★★★**
*Guest Accommodation*
Marshborough Road, Marshborough, Sandwich CT13 0PQ
t (01304) 813374
e honeypotcottage@lycos.com
w honeypotcottage.co.uk

**Southside Bed & Breakfast**
★★★★ *Bed & Breakfast*
Southside, Marshborough Road, Sandwich CT13 0PQ
t (01304) 812802
e reservations.southsidebandb@yahoo.co.uk
w southsidebandb.co.uk

## MERSHAM
Kent

**Garden Cottage at Munday Manor ★★★★★**
*Bed & Breakfast*
**SILVER AWARD**
Munday Manor, Cheesemans Green, Ashford TN25 7HU
t (01233) 720353
e johnrais@aol.com
w mundaymanor.co.uk

**Glebe Place ★★★★**
*Bed & Breakfast*
The Street, Ashford TN25 6ND
t (01233) 500174
e valerieseldon@glebeplaceinkent.co.uk
w glebeplaceinkent.co.uk

## MICHELDEVER
Hampshire

**Willow Cottage ★★★**
*Bed & Breakfast*
Duke Street, Micheldever, Winchester SO21 3DF
t (01962) 774520
e willcott@globalnet.co.uk
w winchesterbedandbreakfast.co.uk

## MIDGHAM
Berkshire

**Eastfield ★★★**
*Bed & Breakfast*
Birds Lane, Midgham RG7 5UL
t (0118) 971 3160

## MIDHURST
West Sussex

**18 Pretoria Avenue ★★★**
*Bed & Breakfast*
Pretoria Avenue, Midhurst GU29 9PP
t (01730) 814868
e ericstratford@uwclub.net

**20 Guillards Oak ★★★★**
*Bed & Breakfast*
Midhurst GU29 9JZ
t (01730) 812550
e coljenmidhurst@tiscali.co.uk

**Carrondune ★★★**
*Bed & Breakfast*
Carron Lane, Midhurst GU29 9LD
t (01730) 813558

**Oakhurst Cottage ★★**
*Bed & Breakfast*
Carron Lane, Midhurst GU29 9LF
t (01730) 813523

**Ye Olde Tea Shoppe ★★★**
*Guest Accommodation*
North Street, Midhurst GU29 9DY
t (01730) 817081
e yeoldeteashoppe@btconnect.com

**Pear Tree Cottage ★★★**
*Bed & Breakfast*
Lamberts Lane, Midhurst GU29 9EF
t (01730) 817216

**Sunnyside ★★★**
*Bed & Breakfast*
Cocking Causeway, Midhurst GU29 9QH
t (01730) 814370

## MILFORD ON SEA
Hampshire

**Alma Mater ★★★★**
*Bed & Breakfast*
4 Knowland Drive, Milford on Sea, Lymington SO41 0RH
t (01590) 642811
e bandbalmamater@aol.com
w almamater.org.uk

**The Bay Trees Bed & Breakfast** ★★★★
*Bed & Breakfast*
**GOLD AWARD**
8 High Street, Milford-on-Sea SO41 0QD
**t** (01590) 642186
**e** rp.fry@virgin.net
**w** baytreebedandbreakfast.co.uk

**Ha'penny House** ★★★★★
*Guest Accommodation*
**SILVER AWARD**
Whitby Road, Milford-on-Sea SO41 0ND
**t** (01590) 641210
**e** info@hapennyhouse.co.uk
**w** hapennyhouse.co.uk/

## MILTON COMMON
Oxfordshire

**Byways** ★★★★
*Bed & Breakfast*
**SILVER AWARD**
Old London Road, Milton Common OX9 2JR
**t** (01844) 279386
**e** byways.mott@tiscali.co.uk
**w** bywaysbedandbreakfast.co.uk

## MILTON KEYNES
Buckinghamshire

**Chantry Farm** ★★★
*Farmhouse*
Pindon End, Hanslope, Milton Keynes MK19 7HL
**t** (01908) 510269
**e** chuff.wake@tiscali.co.uk
**w** chantryfarmbandb.com

**Furtho Manor Farm** ★★★
*Farmhouse*
Northampton Road, Old Stratford, Milton Keynes MK19 6NR
**t** (01908) 542139
**e** furtho@farming.co.uk
**w** furthomanorfarm.co.uk

**Kingfishers** ★ *Guest House*
9 Rylstone Close, Heelands, Milton Keynes MK13 7QT
**t** 07866 424417
**e** enquiry@kingfishersmk.co.uk
**w** kingfishersmk.co.uk

**Spinney Lodge Farm** ★★★
*Farmhouse*
Forest Road, Hanslope MK19 7DE
**t** (01908) 510267

**The White Hart** ★★★★ *Inn*
1 Gun Lane, Sherington MK16 9PE
**t** (01908) 611953
**e** whitehartresort@aol.com
**w** whitehartsherington.com

## MILTON-UNDER-WYCHWOOD
Oxfordshire

**Hillborough House** ★★★★
*Bed & Breakfast*
The Green, Shipton Road, Burford OX7 6JH
**t** (01993) 832352
**e** hillboroughhouse@btinternet.com

## MINSTER
Kent

**Hoo Farmhouse** ★★★★★
*Bed & Breakfast*
**GOLD AWARD**
147 Monkton Road, Minster, Ramsgate CT12 4JB
**t** (01843) 821322
**e** stay@hoofarmhouse.com
**w** hoofarmhouse.com

## MINSTER-IN-SHEPPEY
Kent

**Glen Haven** ★★
*Bed & Breakfast*
Lower Road, Minster-on-Sea, Sheerness ME12 3ST
**t** (01795) 877064
**e** johnstanford@btinternet.com

## MINSTER LOVELL
Oxfordshire

**Hill Grove Farm** ★★★★
*Farmhouse*
Crawley Dry Lane, Minster Lovell OX29 0NA
**t** (01993) 703120
**e** katharinemcbrown@btinternet.com
**w** countryaccom.co.uk/hill-grove-farm/

## MORETON
Oxfordshire

**Elm Tree Farmhouse** ★★★★
*Farmhouse*
Moreton, Thame OX9 2HR
**t** (01844) 213692
**e** wendyvonbergen@btinternet.com
**w** elmtreefarmhouse.co.uk

## MOTTISTONE
Isle of Wight

**Mottistone Manor Farmhouse** ★★★★
*Guest Accommodation*
Mottistone PO30 4ED
**t** (01983) 740207
**e** bookings@bolthols.co.uk
**w** bolthols.co.uk

## MOULSOE
Buckinghamshire

**The Old Stables** ★★★★
*Guest House*
Newport Road, Moulsoe MK16 0HR
**t** (01908) 217766
**e** hermitage.moulsoe@tiscali.co.uk

## NETTLEBED
Oxfordshire

**Parkcorner Farm House** ★★★ *Bed & Breakfast*
Park Corner, Nettlebed RG9 6DX
**t** (01491) 641450
**e** parkcorner_farmhouse@hotmail.com

## NETTLESTEAD
Kent

**Rock Farm House** ★★★★
*Guest Accommodation*
Rock Farm, Gibbs Hill, Maidstone ME18 5HT
**t** (01622) 812244
**w** rockfarmhousebandb.co.uk

## NEW MILTON
Hampshire

**Bashley House** ★★★
*Bed & Breakfast*
Bashley Common Road, New Milton BH25 5SQ
**t** (01425) 610278
**e** burleyv@globalnet.co.uk
**w** bashleyhouse.co.uk

**Beech Lodge** ★★★★
*Guest House*
16 Mount Avenue, New Milton BH25 6NT
**t** (01425) 622130
**e** johnevans856@aol.com
**w** beechlodge.org.uk

**Jobz-A-Gudn** ★★★★
*Bed & Breakfast*
169 Stem Lane, New Milton BH25 5ND
**t** (01425) 615435
**e** info@jobzagudn.com
**w** jobzagudn.com/

**Nyewood Cottage Bed & Breakfast** ★★★★
*Bed & Breakfast*
37 Barton Court Road, New Milton BH25 6NW
**t** (01425) 615321
**e** enquiry@nyewoodcottage.co.uk
**w** nyewoodcottage.co.uk/

**St Ursula** ★★★
*Bed & Breakfast*
30 Hobart Road, New Milton BH25 6EG
**t** (01425) 613515

**Taverners Cottage** ★★★★
*Bed & Breakfast*
**SILVER AWARD**
Bashley Cross Road, Bashley, New Milton BH25 5SZ
**t** (01425) 615403
**e** judith@tavernerscottage.co.uk
**w** tavernerscottage.co.uk

**Willy's Well** ★★★★
*Bed & Breakfast*
Bashley Common Road, Bashley, New Milton BH25 5SF
**t** (01425) 616834
**e** moyramac2@hotmail.com

**Woodlands** ★★★★
*Bed & Breakfast*
Ashley Lane, New Milton BH25 5AQ
**t** (01425) 616425
**e** bealwoodlands@yahoo.co.uk
**w** newforest-bed-and-breakfast.co.uk/2default.asp

## NEWBURY
Berkshire

**160 Craven Road** ★★
*Bed & Breakfast*
Newbury RG14 5NR
**t** (01635) 40522

**19 Kimbers Drive** ★★
*Bed & Breakfast*
Speen RG14 1RQ
**t** (01635) 521571
**w** the-process.com/sandra

**93 Gloucester Road** ★★★★
*Bed & Breakfast*
Newbury RG14 5JJ
**t** (01635) 32376
**e** maggie@newbury2.demon.co.uk

**The Bell at Boxford** ★★★
*Inn*
Boxford, Newbury RG20 8DD
**t** (01488) 608721
**e** paul@bellatboxford.com
**w** bellatboxford.com

**The Carnarvon Arms** ★★★★ *Inn*
Winchester Road, Whitway, Burghclere, Newbury RG20 9LE
**t** (01635) 278222
**e** info@carnarvonarms.com
**w** carnarvonarms.com

**East End Farm** ★★★★
*Guest Accommodation*
East End, Newbury RG20 0AB
**t** (01635) 254895
**e** mp@eastendfarm.co.uk
**w** eastendfarm.co.uk

**Highclere Farm** ★★★★
*Bed & Breakfast*
Highclere Street, Highclere RG20 9PY
**t** (01635) 255013
**e** walshhighclere@newburyweb.net
**w** highclerefarmnewbury.co.uk

**Ingledene Bed and Breakfast** ★★★★
*Guest Accommodation*
225 Andover Road, Newbury RG14 6NG
**t** (01635) 43622
**e** info@ingledenebnb.co.uk
**w** ingledenebnb.co.uk

**Manor Farm House** ★★★★
*Farmhouse* **SILVER AWARD**
Church Street, Hampstead Norreys, Newbury RG18 0TD
**t** (01635) 201276
**e** bettsbedandbreakfast@hotmail.com
**w** bettsbedandbreakfast.co.uk

**The Old Farmhouse** ★★★★
*Bed & Breakfast*
Downend Lane, Chieveley, Newbury RG20 8TN
**t** (01635) 248361
**e** palletts@aol.com
**w** smoothhound.co.uk/hotels/oldfarmhouse

**The Paddock** ★★★
*Bed & Breakfast*
Midgham Green, Midgham RG7 5TT
**t** (0118) 971 3098
**e** midghamgreen@yahoo.co.uk
**w** midghamgreen.co.uk

## NEWFOUND
Hampshire

**Rose Cottage** ★★★★
*Bed & Breakfast*
Newfound RG23 7HF
**t** (01256) 780949
**e** rosecottagebedandbreakfast@btinternet.com
**w** http://uk.geocities.com/rosecottagebedandbreakfast@btinternet.com/

**NEWHAVEN**
**East Sussex**

**Newhaven Lodge Guest House** ★★★ *Guest House*
12 Brighton Road, Newhaven
BN9 9NB
**t** (01273) 513736
**e** newhavenlodge@aol.com
**w** newhavenlodge.co.uk

**NEWICK**
**East Sussex**

**Holly Lodge** ★★★★
*Bed & Breakfast*
**SILVER AWARD**
Oxbottom Lane, Newick,
Lewes BN8 4RA
**t** (01825) 722738
**e** lallie@waitrose.com

**NEWINGTON**
**Oxfordshire**

**Hill Farm** ★★★ *Farmhouse*
Newington, Wallingford
OX10 7AL
**t** (01865) 891173

**NEWPORT**
**Isle of Wight**

**Forest View B&B** ★★★★
*Bed & Breakfast*
1 Forest View, Marks Corner,
Newport PO30 5UD
**t** (01983) 295578
**e** janet@forestviewbb.co.uk
**w** forestviewbb.co.uk/

---

**Litten Park Guest House**
★★★★
*Guest Accommodation*
48 Medina Avenue, Newport
PO30 1EL
**t** (01983) 526836
**e** info@islandbreaks.co.uk

---

**Newport Quay** ★★★★
*Guest Accommodation*
**SILVER AWARD**
41 Quay Street, Newport
PO30 5BA
**t** (01983) 528544
**e** enquiries@newportquayhotel.co.uk
**w** newportquayhotel.co.uk

---

**The Wheatsheaf Inn** ★★★
*Inn*
St Thomas Square, Newport
PO30 1SG
**t** (01983) 523865
**e** information@wheatsheaf-iow.co.uk
**w** wheatsheaf-iow.co.uk

**NEWPORT PAGNELL**
**Buckinghamshire**

**The Clitheroes** ★★
*Bed & Breakfast*
5 Walnut Close, Newport
Pagnell MK16 8JH
**t** (01908) 611643
**e** shirleyderek.clitheroe@btinternet.com

---

**Rosemary House** ★★★
*Guest Accommodation*
**SILVER AWARD**
7 Hill View, Newport Pagnell
MK16 8BE
**t** (01908) 612198
**e** rosemaryhouse@btinternet.com

**NONINGTON**
**Kent**

**Farthingales B&B**
Rating Applied For
*Bed & Breakfast*
Old Court Hill, Dover
CT15 4LQ
**t** (01304) 840174
**e** farthingalesb&b@yahoo.co.uk
**w** farthingales.co.uk

**NORTH BERSTED**
**West Sussex**

**Willow Rise** ★★★★
*Bed & Breakfast*
131 North Bersted Street,
Bognor Regis PO22 9AG
**t** (01243) 829544
**e** gillboon@aol.com
**w** visitsussex.org

**NORTH LEIGH**
**Oxfordshire**

**Elbie House** ★★★★
*Bed & Breakfast*
**SILVER AWARD**
East End, Woodstock
OX29 6PX
**t** (01993) 880166
**e** mandy@cotswoldbreak.co.uk
**w** cotswoldbreak.co.uk

**NORTH MUNDHAM**
**West Sussex**

**The Cottage** ★★★★
*Bed & Breakfast*
**SILVER AWARD**
Church Road, North
Mundham, Chichester
PO20 1JU
**t** (01243) 784586
**e** lambrinudi-bandb@supanet.com
**w** the-thatched-cottage.co.uk

**NORTH NEWINGTON**
**Oxfordshire**

**The Blinking Owl Country Inn** ★★★ *Inn*
Main Street, North Newington
OX15 6AE
**t** (01295) 730650

---

**The Mill House** ★★★★
*Guest Accommodation*
**SILVER AWARD**
North Newington, Banbury
OX15 6AA
**t** (01295) 730212
**e** lamadonett@aol.com
**w** themillhousebanbury.com

**NORTON**
**West Sussex**

**Norton Cottage** ★★★★
*Bed & Breakfast*
**GOLD AWARD**
Norton Lane, Norton
PO20 3NH
**t** (01243) 544805
**e** nortoncottagebb@btinternet.com
**w** nortoncottage.co.uk

**NUTLEY**
**East Sussex**

**West Meadows** ★★★★
*Bed & Breakfast*
**SILVER AWARD**
Bell Lane, Nutley, Forest Row
TN22 3PD
**t** (01825) 712434
**e** west.meadows@virgin.net
**w** westmeadows.co.uk

**OAKLEY**
**Buckinghamshire**

**New Farm** ★★ *Farmhouse*
Oxford Road, Oakley,
Aylesbury HP18 9UR
**t** (01844) 237360

**OAKLEY GREEN**
**Berkshire**

**Rainworth House** ★★★★
*Guest House*
Oakley Green Road, Oakley
Green SL4 5UL
**t** (01753) 856749
**e** info@rainworthhouse.com
**w** rainworthguesthouse.com

**OARE**
**Kent**

**Uplees Lodge** ★★★★
*Guest Accommodation*
Uplees Road, Faversham
ME13 0QR
**t** (01795) 535014
**e** upleeslodge@aol.com

**OCKLEY**
**Surrey**

**The Kings Arms Inn** ★★★★
*Inn*
Stane Street, Ockley RH5 5TS
**t** (01306) 711224
**e** enquiries@thekingsarmsockley.co.uk
**w** thekingsarmsockley.co.uk

**OFFHAM**
**East Sussex**

**The Old Wash House**
★★★★
*Guest Accommodation*
Mill Laine Farm, Offham, Lewes
BN7 3QB
**t** (01273) 475473
**e** harmer@farming.co.uk
**w** milllainebarns.co.uk

**OFFHAM**
**Kent**

**Little Quintain**
Rating Applied For
*Bed & Breakfast*
Teston Road, Offham
ME19 5NR
**t** (01732) 871616
**e** m.lomard@oefs.co.uk
**w** littlequintain.co.uk

**OLD WIVES LEES**
**Kent**

**Pond Cottage** ★★★★★
*Bed & Breakfast*
Selling Road, Canterbury
CT4 8BD
**t** (01227) 751828
**e** jude@judartdesigns.co.uk
**w** judartdesigns.com

**OLNEY**
**Buckinghamshire**

**Colchester House** ★★★★
*Guest Accommodation*
**SILVER AWARD**
26 High Street, Olney
MK46 4BB
**t** (01234) 712602
**e** peter.blenkinsop@btopenworld.com
**w** olneybucks.co.uk

---

**The Lindens** ★★★★
*Guest Accommodation*
30a High Street, Olney
MK46 4BB
**t** (01234) 712891
**e** accommodation@thelindens.com
**w** thelindens.com

**OTFORD**
**Kent**

**Darenth Dene** ★★★
*Bed & Breakfast*
Shoreham Road, Sevenoaks
TN14 5RP
**t** (01959) 522293

**OVERTON**
**Hampshire**

**Mallards**
Rating Applied For
*Bed & Breakfast*
3 Trims Court, Basingstoke
RG25 3JZ
**t** (01256) 770039
**e** mallards@test-the-water.com
**w** test-the-water.co.uk

**OXFORD**
**Oxfordshire**

**Adams Guest House** ★★
*Guest Accommodation*
302 Banbury Road, Oxford
OX2 7ED
**t** (01865) 556118
**e** oxfordadamsguesthouse@hotmail.com

---

**Arden Lodge** ★★★
*Guest Accommodation*
34 Sunderland Avenue, Oxford
OX2 8DX
**t** (01865) 552076

---

**Beaumont Guest House**
★★★ *Guest Accommodation*
234 Abingdon Road, Oxford
OX1 4SP
**t** (01865) 241767
**e** beaumontgh@btinternet.com
**w** oxfordcity.co.uk

---

**Becket House** ★★
*Guest Accommodation*
5 Becket Street, Oxford
OX1 1PP
**t** (01865) 724675
**e** becketguesthouse@yahoo.co.uk

---

**Brenal Guest House** ★★★
*Guest House*
307 Iffley Road, Oxford
OX4 4AG
**t** (01865) 721561

---

**Broomhill** ★★★★
*Bed & Breakfast*
Lincombe Lane, Boars Hill,
Oxford OX1 5DZ
**t** (01865) 735339
**e** sara@broomhill-oxford.co.uk
**w** broomhill-oxford.co.uk

---

**Brown's Guest House** ★★★
*Guest Accommodation*
281 Iffley Road, Oxford
OX4 4AQ
**t** (01865) 246822
**e** brownsgh@hotmail.com
**w** brownsguesthouse.co.uk

**The Bungalow** ★★★
*Guest Accommodation*
Mill Lane, Marston OX3 0QF
t (01865) 557171
e ros.bungalowbb@btinternet.com
w cherwellfarm-oxford-accom.com

**The Buttery** ★★★★
*Guest House*
11-12 Broad Street, Oxford OX1 3AP
t (01865) 811950
e enquiries@thebutteryhotel.co.uk
w thebutteryhotel.co.uk

**Central Backpackers Oxford**
★★ *Backpackers*
13 Park End Street, Oxford OX1 1HH
t (01865) 242288
e oxford@centralbackpackers.co.uk
w centralbackpackers.co.uk

**Chestnuts** ★★
*Bed & Breakfast*
72 Cumnor Hill, Oxford OX2 9HU
t (01865) 863602
e fmjones@phonecoop.coop

**Cornerways** ★★★★
*Bed & Breakfast*
282 Abingdon Road, Oxford OX1 4TA
t (01865) 240135
e jeakings@btopenworld.com

**Cotswold House** ★★★★
*Guest Accommodation*
363 Banbury Road, Oxford OX2 7PL
t (01865) 310558
e d.r.walker@talk21.com
w cotswoldhouse.co.uk

**Department for Continuing Education** ★★★ *Campus*
Rewley House, 1 Wellington Square, Oxford OX1 2JA
t (01865) 280166
e res-ctr@conted.ox.ac.uk
w conted.ox.ac.uk

**Dial House** ★★★★
*Guest House*
25 London Road, Headington, Oxford OX3 7RE
t (01865) 425100
e dialhouse@ntlworld.com
w dialhouseoxford.co.uk

**Falcon Guest House** ★★★
*Guest Accommodation*
88-90 Abingdon Road, Oxford OX1 4PX
t (01865) 511122
e stay@falconoxford.co.uk
w oxfordcity.co.uk

**Five Mile View Guest House**
★★★ *Guest Accommodation*
528 Banbury Road, Oxford OX2 8EG
t (01865) 558747
e 5mileview@cityav.co.uk
w oxfordcity.co.uk

**Gables** ★★★★★
*Guest Accommodation*
6 Cumnor Hill, Oxford OX2 9HA
t (01865) 862153
e stay@gables-oxford.co.uk
w gables-guesthouse.co.uk

**Gorselands Hall** ★★★★
*Guest Accommodation*
**SILVER AWARD**
Boddington Lane, Woodstock OX29 6PU
t (01993) 882292
e hamilton@gorselandshall.com
w gorselandshall.com

**Head of the River** ★★★★
*Inn*
Folly Bridge, St Aldates, Oxford OX1 4LB
t (01865) 721600
e headoftheriver@fullers.co.uk

**Home Farm House** ★★★★
*Bed & Breakfast*
**SILVER AWARD**
Holton, Oxford OX33 1QA
t (01865) 872334
e sonja.barter@tiscali.co.uk
w homefarmholton.co.uk

**Homelea Guest House**
★★★★
*Guest Accommodation*
356 Abingdon Road, Oxford OX1 4TQ
t (01865) 245150
e enquiries@oxford-guesthouse.co.uk
w oxford-guesthouse.co.uk

**Isis Guest House** ★★
*Guest House*
45-53 Iffley Road, Oxford OX4 1ED
t (01865) 248894
e isis@herald.ox.ac.uk
w isisguesthouse.co.uk

**Lakeside Guest House**
★★★★
*Guest Accommodation*
118 Abingdon Road, Oxford OX1 4PZ
t (01865) 244725
e daniella.s@ntlworld.com
w oxfordcity.co.uk

**Lonsdale Guest House** ★★★
*Guest House*
312 Banbury Road, Summertown, Oxford OX2 7ED
t (01865) 554872
e lons.dale.bb@talktalk.net

**Milka's Guest House** ★★★
*Guest Accommodation*
379 Iffley Road, Oxford OX4 4DP
t (01865) 778458
e reservations@milkas.co.uk
w milkas.co.uk

**Mulberry Guest House**
★★★ *Guest Accommodation*
265 London Road, Headington, Oxford OX3 9EH
t (01865) 767114
e stay@mulberryguesthouse.co.uk
w mulberryguesthouse.co.uk

**Newton House** ★★★
*Guest Accommodation*
82/84 Abingdon Road, Oxford OX1 4PL
t (01865) 240561
e newton.house@btinternet.com
w oxfordcity.co.uk

**The Old Black Horse** ★★★★
*Inn*
102 St Clements, Oxford OX4 1AR
t (01865) 244691
e oldblackhorse@googlemail.com
w theoldblackhorsehotel oxford.co.uk/

**Park House** ★★★
*Bed & Breakfast*
7 St Bernard's Road, Oxford OX2 6EH
t (01865) 310824
e krynpark@hotmail.com

**Parklands** ★★★★
*Guest Accommodation*
100 Banbury Road, Oxford OX2 6JU
t (01865) 554374
e stay@parklandsoxford.co.uk
w oxfordcity.co.uk

**Pickwick's Guest House**
★★★★ *Guest House*
15-17 London Road, Headington, Oxford OX3 7SP
t (01865) 750487
e pickwicks@tiscali.co.uk
w pickwicksguesthouse.co.uk

**Remont** ★★★★
*Guest Accommodation*
367 Banbury Road, Summertown, Oxford OX2 7PL
t (01865) 311020
e info@remont-oxford.co.uk
w remont-oxford.co.uk

**The Ridings** ★★★
*Guest Accommodation*
280 Abingdon Road, Oxford OX1 4TA
t (01865) 248364
e pat.mansell@ntlworld.com
w theridingsguesthouse.co.uk

**Sportsview Guest House**
★★★ *Guest Accommodation*
106-110 Abingdon Road, Oxford OX1 4PX
t (01865) 244268
e stay@sportsviewguesthouse.co.uk
w sportsviewguesthouse.co.uk

**Tilbury Lodge** ★★★★
*Guest Accommodation*
**SILVER AWARD**
5 Tilbury Lane, Oxford OX2 9NB
t (01865) 862138

**The Westgate** ★★
*Guest Accommodation*
1 Botley Road, Oxford OX2 0AA
t (01865) 726721

**Whitehouse View Guest House** ★★ *Guest House*
9 Whitehouse Road, Grandpont, Oxford OX1 4PA
t (01865) 721626 & 07831 201259
e sramdoo@aol.com

## PADDOCK WOOD
Kent

**The Annexe, Pinto** ★★★★
*Bed & Breakfast*
Chantlers Hill, Brenchley TN12 6LX
t (01892) 836254
e janemoor@supanet.com

## PARTRIDGE GREEN
West Sussex

**Pound Cottage** ★★★
*Bed & Breakfast*
Mill Lane, Littleworth, Horsham RH13 8JU
t (01403) 710218
e thegeo@poundcott.freeserve.co.uk

## PEMBURY
Kent

**Camden Arms Hotel** ★★★★
*Inn*
High Street, Tunbridge Wells TN2 4PH
t (01892) 822012
e food@camdenarms.co.uk
w camdenarms.co.uk

## PETERSFIELD
Hampshire

**1 The Spain** ★★★★
*Bed & Breakfast*
Sheep Street, Petersfield GU32 3JZ
t (01730) 263261
e allantarver@ntlworld.com
w 1thespain.com

**80 Rushes Road** ★★★
*Bed & Breakfast*
Petersfield GU32 3BP
t (01730) 261638
e collinstudor@waitrose.com
w rushes-road.co.uk

**Border Cottage** ★★★★
*Bed & Breakfast*
4 Heath Road, Petersfield GU31 4DU
t (01730) 263179
e lawrence@bordercottage.co.uk
w bordercottage.co.uk

**Downsview (Petersfield)**
★★★★ *Bed & Breakfast*
58 Heath Road, Petersfield GU31 4EJ
t (01730) 264171
e info@downsview58.co.uk
w downsview58.co.uk

**Heath Farmhouse** ★★★★
*Bed & Breakfast*
Sussex Road, Petersfield GU31 4HU
t (01730) 264709
e info@heathfarmhouse.co.uk
w heathfarmhouse.co.uk

**The Holt** ★★★★
*Bed & Breakfast*
60 Heath Road, Petersfield GU31 4EJ
t (01730) 262836

**JSW** ★★★★
*Restaurant with Rooms*
20 Dragon Street, Petersfield GU31 4JJ
t (01730) 262030
e jsw.restaurant@btconnect.com

**Pipers** ★★★ *Bed & Breakfast*
1 Oaklands Road, Petersfield GU32 2EY
t (01730) 262131

**Quinhay Farmhouse ★★★★**
*Bed & Breakfast*
Alton Road, Froxfield, Petersfield GU32 1BZ
**t** (01730) 827183
**e** janerothery@quinhaybandb.co.uk
**w** quinhaybandb.co.uk

**South Gardens Cottage**
*★★★ Bed & Breakfast*
South Harting, Petersfield GU31 5QJ
**t** (01730) 825040
**e** randjholmes@beeb.net

## PETHAM
Kent

**South Wootton House ★★★**
*Farmhouse*
Capel Lane, Petham CT4 5RG
**t** (01227) 700643
**e** mountfrances@farming.co.uk

## PETWORTH
West Sussex

**Burton Park Farm ★★★**
*Farmhouse*
Burton Park Road, Petworth GU28 0JT
**t** (01798) 342431

**Eedes Cottage ★★★★**
*Bed & Breakfast*
Bignor Park Road, Bury Gate, Pulborough RH20 1EZ
**t** (01798) 831438
**e** eedes.bandb@btinternet.com
**w** visitsussex.org/eedescottage

**Garden Cottage ★★★★**
*Bed & Breakfast*
Park Road, Petworth GU28 0DS
**t** (01798) 342414
**e** a.wolseley@ukonline.co.uk

**Halfway Bridge Inn**
*★★★★★ Inn*
**GOLD AWARD**
Halfway Bridge, Lodsworth, Petworth GU28 9BP
**t** (01798) 861281
**e** enquiries@halfwaybridge.co.uk
**w** halfwaybridge.co.uk

**Old Railway Station ★★★★**
*Guest Accommodation*
Station Road, Petworth GU28 0JF
**t** (01798) 342346
**e** info@old-station.co.uk
**w** old-station.co.uk

**Rectory Cottage ★★★**
*Bed & Breakfast*
Rectory Lane, Petworth GU28 0DB
**t** (01798) 342380
**e** dcradd@aol.com
**w** visitsussex.org

## PEVENSEY BAY
East Sussex

**The Bay ★★★** *Inn*
Eastbourne Road, Pevensey Bay, Pevensey BN24 6EJ
**t** (01323) 768645
**w** thechapmangroup.co.uk

## PISHILL
Oxfordshire

**Orchard House ★★★★**
*Guest Accommodation*
Pishill, Henley-on-Thames RG9 6HJ
**t** (01491) 638351

## PITT
Hampshire

**Enmill Barn ★★★★★**
*Bed & Breakfast*
**SILVER AWARD**
Enmill Barn, Enmill Lane, Winchester SO22 5QR
**t** (01962) 856740
**e** jennywas21@hotmail.com
**w** enmill-barn.co.uk

## PLAITFORD
Hampshire

**The Shoe Inn ★★★★** *Inn*
Salisbury Road, Romsey SO51 6EE
**t** (01794) 322397
**e** theshoeinn@btinteenet.com
**w** shoeinn.co.uk

## PLAY HATCH
Oxfordshire

**The Crown at Playhatch**
*★★★★ Inn*
The Crown, Playhatch RG4 9QN
**t** (0118) 947 2872
**e** info@thecrown.co.uk
**w** thecrown.co.uk

## PLAYDEN
East Sussex

**The Corner House ★★★★**
*Guest Accommodation*
Rye Road, Rye TN31 7UL
**t** (01797) 280439
**e** yvonne@the-corner-house.com
**w** the-corner-house.com

**Playden Oasts Inn ★★★** *Inn*
Rye Road, Playden TN31 7UL
**t** (01797) 223502

## PLUCKLEY
Kent

**Elvey Farm ★★★★**
*Guest Accommodation*
Elvey Lane, Ashford TN27 0SU
**t** (01233) 840442
**e** bookings@elveyfarm.co.uk
**w** elveyfarm.co.uk

## PORCHFIELD
Isle of Wight

**Youngwoods Farm ★★★**
*Farmhouse*
Whitehouse Road, Porchfield PO30 4LJ
**t** (01983) 522170
**e** judith@youngwoods.com
**w** youngwoods.com

## PORTSMOUTH
Hampshire

**Abbey Lodge ★★★**
*Guest House*
30 Waverley Road, Southsea PO5 2PW
**t** (023) 9282 8285
**e** linda@abbeylodge.co.uk
**w** abbeylodge.co.uk

**Albatross Guest House**
*★★★ Guest Accommodation*
51 Waverley Road, Portsmouth PO5 2PJ
**t** (023) 9282 8325
**w** albatrossguesthouse.co.uk

**Arden Guest House ♦♦♦**
*Guest Accommodation*
14 Herbert Road, Portsmouth PO4 0QA
**t** (023) 9282 6409
**e** crichard240@aol.com

**Bembell Court ★★★**
*Guest House*
69 Festing Road, Portsmouth PO4 0NQ
**t** (023) 9273 5915
**e** keith@bembell.co.uk
**w** bembell.co.uk

**Esk Vale Guest House ★★★**
*Guest Accommodation*
39 Granada Road, Portsmouth PO4 0RD
**t** (023) 9286 2639
**e** enquiries@eskvaleguesthouse.co.uk
**w** eskvaleguesthouse.co.uk

**Everley Guest House ★★★**
*Guest House*
33 Festing Road, Portsmouth PO4 0NG
**t** (023) 9273 1001
**e** everleyguesthouse@ntlworld.com
**w** smoothhound.co.uk/hotels/everleyguesthouse

**Fortitude Cottage ★★★★**
*Guest Accommodation*
51 Broad Street, Portsmouth PO1 2JD
**t** (023) 9282 3748
**e** info@fortitudecottage.co.uk
**w** fortitudecottage.co.uk

**Gainsborough House ★★★**
*Guest Accommodation*
9 Malvern Road, Portsmouth PO5 2LZ
**t** (023) 9282 2604
**e** jill.filer@yahoo.co.uk
**w** gainsboroughhouse.co.uk

**Hamilton House Bed & Breakfast ★★★★**
*Guest Accommodation*
95 Victoria Road North, Portsmouth PO5 1PS
**t** (023) 9282 3502
**e** sandra@hamiltonhouse.co.uk
**w** hamiltonhouse.co.uk

**Homestead Guest House**
*★★★ Guest Accommodation*
11 Bembridge Crescent, Portsmouth PO4 0QT
**t** (023) 9273 2362
**e** b.currie1@ntlworld.com
**w** homesteadguesthouse-southsea.co.uk

**Lamorna Guest House ★★**
*Bed & Breakfast*
23 Victoria Road South, Portsmouth PO5 2BX
**t** (023) 9281 1157
**e** merry_kerry2003@yahoo.co.uk
**w** lamornaguesthouse.co.uk

**Waverley Park Lodge Guest House ★★★**
*Guest Accommodation*
99 Waverley Road, Portsmouth PO5 2PL
**t** (023) 9273 0402
**e** waverleyparklodge@yahoo.co.uk
**w** waverleyparklodge.co.uk

**The Woodville ★★★**
*Guest Accommodation*
6 Florence Road, Portsmouth PO5 2NE
**t** (023) 9282 3409
**e** woodvillehotel@boltblue.com

## PRINCES RISBOROUGH
Buckinghamshire

**Coppins B&B ★★**
*Bed & Breakfast*
**SILVER AWARD**
Coppins, New Road, Princes Risborough HP27 0LA
**t** (01844) 344508
**e** jillthomas@thecoppins.co.uk
**w** thecoppins.co.uk

**Drifters Lodge ★★★★**
*Bed & Breakfast*
60 Picts Lane, Princes Risborough HP27 9DX
**t** (01844) 274773
**e** info@drifterslodge.co.uk
**w** drifterslodge.co.uk

**The Old Station ★★★★★**
*Bed & Breakfast*
**SILVER AWARD**
Sandpit Lane, Princes Risborough HP27 9QQ
**t** (01844) 345086
**e** ianmackinson@hotmail.com
**w** theoldstation-bledlow.co.uk

**Solis Ortu ★★★**
*Bed & Breakfast*
Aylesbury Road, Askett HP27 9LY
**t** (01844) 347777
**e** p.and.pr@btinternet.com

## PRIVETT
Hampshire

**The Threshing Barn**
*★★★★★ Bed & Breakfast*
Stocks Lane, Privett GU34 3NZ
**t** (01730) 828383
**e** emma@thethreshingbarn.co.uk
**w** thethreshingbarn.co.uk

## PULBOROUGH
West Sussex

**Barn House Lodge ★★★★**
*Bed & Breakfast*
Barn House Lane, Pulborough RH20 2BS
**t** (01798) 872682
**e** suehj@aol.com

**The Labouring Man ★★★★**
*Inn*
Old London Road, Pulborough RH20 1LF
**t** (01798) 872215
**e** philip.beckett@btconnect.com
**w** thelabouringman.co.uk

**Lyon Cottage ★★**
*Bed & Breakfast*
Bury Gate, Pulborough RH20 1EY
**t** (01798) 865295

**St Cleather** ★★★★
*Bed & Breakfast*
**SILVER AWARD**
Rectory Lane, Pulborough RH20 2AD
**t** (01798) 873038
**e** enquiries@stcleather.me.uk
**w** stcleather.me.uk

## RADNAGE
Buckinghamshire

**Rosling House** ★★★★
*Bed & Breakfast*
**SILVER AWARD**
Radnage Common Road, High Wycombe HP14 4DD
**t** (01494) 482724
**e** c.wheeler1@btinternet.com
**w** roslinghouse.co.uk

## RAINHAM
Kent

**Abigails** ★★
*Guest Accommodation*
17 The Maltings, Rainham, Gillingham ME8 8JL
**t** (01634) 365427
**e** davidjpenfold@btopenworld.com

## RAMSGATE
Kent

**Abbeygail Guest House**
★★★★ *Guest House*
17 Penshurst Road, Ramsgate CT11 8EG
**t** (01843) 594154
**e** abbeygail2004@aol.com
**w** abbeygail.co.uk

**Belvidere Guest House**
★★★ *Guest House*
26 Augusta Road, Ramsgate CT11 8JS
**t** (01843) 588809

**Fairholme Bed and Breakfast**
★★ *Bed & Breakfast*
9 Albion Road, Ramsgate CT11 8DJ
**t** (01843) 583483
**e** gandmwarr@btinternet.com

**Glendevon Guest House**
★★★★ *Guest House*
8 Truro Road, Ramsgate CT11 8DB
**t** (01843) 570909
**e** rebekah.smith1@btinternet.com
**w** glendevonguesthouse.co.uk

**Glenholme Guest House**
★★★ *Guest Accommodation*
6 Crescent Road, Ramsgate CT11 9QU
**t** (01843) 595149

**The Royale Guest House**
★★★ *Guest Accommodation*
7 Royal Road, Ramsgate CT11 9LE
**t** (01843) 594712
**e** sylvbarry@aol.com
**w** theroyaleguesthouse.co.uk

**Spencer Court** ★★★
*Guest Accommodation*
37 Spencer Square, Ramsgate CT11 9LD
**t** (01843) 594582
**e** glendaanken@hotmail.com
**w** smoothhound.co.uk/hotels/spencer

## READING
Berkshire

**Belle Vue House** ★★★★
*Guest Accommodation*
2 Tilehurst Road, Reading RG1 7TN
**t** (0118) 959 4445
**e** bellevuehotel@btconnect.com
**w** bellevuehousehotel.co.uk

**Caversham Lodge** ★★
*Guest House*
133a Caversham Road, Reading RG1 8AS
**t** (0118) 961 2110
**e** raj.roy@hotmail.co.uk

**Dittisham Guest House**
★★★ *Guest Accommodation*
63 Tilehurst Road, Reading RG30 2JL
**t** (0118) 956 9483
**e** dittishamgh@aol.com

**Great Expectations** ★★★
*Inn*
33 London Street, Reading RG1 4PS
**t** (0118) 950 3925
**e** greatexpectations@thechapmansgroup.co.uk

## RINGMER
East Sussex

**Bethany** ★★ *Bed & Breakfast*
25 Ballard Drive, Ringmer, Lewes BN8 5NU
**t** (01273) 812025
**e** dimeadows@rockuk.net

**Bryn-Clai** ★★★★
*Guest Accommodation*
Uckfield Road, Ringmer, Lewes BN8 5RU
**t** (01273) 814042
**w** brynclai.co.uk

## RINGWOOD
Hampshire

**The Auld Kennels** ★★★
*Bed & Breakfast*
215 Christchurch Road, Ringwood BH24 3AN
**t** (01425) 475170
**e** auldkennels@aol.com
**w** auldkennels.co.uk

**Avonmead House** ★★★★
*Bed & Breakfast*
16 Salisbury Road, Ringwood BH24 1AS
**t** (01425) 475531
**e** chrissie.peckham@talktalk.net
**w** avonmeadhouse.co.uk

**Fraser House** ★★★★
*Guest House*
Salisbury Road, Blashford BH24 3PB
**t** (01425) 473958
**e** mail@fraserhouse.net
**w** fraserhouse.net

**High Corner Inn** ★★★ *Inn*
Linwood, Ringwood BH24 3QY
**t** (01425) 473973

**Moortown Lodge** ★★★★
*Guest Accommodation*
244 Christchurch Road, Ringwood BH24 3AS
**t** (01425) 471404
**e** enquiries@moortownlodge.co.uk
**w** moortownlodge.co.uk

**The Star Inn** ★★★★ *Inn*
**SILVER AWARD**
Market Place, Ringwood BH24 1AW
**t** (01425) 473105
**w** thestarringwood.co.uk

**Torre Avon** ★★★★
*Bed & Breakfast*
21 Salisbury Road, Ringwood BH24 1AS
**t** (01425) 472769
**e** b&b@torreavon.freeserve.co.uk
**w** torreavon.freeserve.co.uk

## RINGWOULD
Kent

**Rippledown Environmental Education Centre** ★★★
*Group Hostel*
Ripple Down House, Dover Road, Deal CT14 8HE
**t** (01304) 364854
**e** office@rippledown.com
**w** rippledown.com

## RIPE
East Sussex

**Hall Court Farm** ★★★★★
*Bed & Breakfast*
**SILVER AWARD**
Ripe, Lewes BN8 6AY
**t** (01323) 811496
**e** johnhecks@btconnect.com
**w** hallcourtfarm.co.uk

## RIPLEY
Surrey

**Four Oaks Cottage** ★★★
*Bed & Breakfast*
Polesden Lane, Ripley GU23 6DX
**t** (01483) 225251
**e** fouroaksbb@aol.com
**w** fouroaksbb.co.uk

**The Talbot Inn** ★★★ *Inn*
High Street, Ripley GU23 6BB
**t** (01483) 225188
**e** info@thetalbotinn.com
**w** thetalbotinn.com

## RIVER
Kent

**Heather's Woodlands** ★★★
*Guest Accommodation*
29 London Road, River, Dover CT17 0SF
**t** (01304) 823635

## ROBERTSBRIDGE
East Sussex

**Glenferness** ★★★★
*Bed & Breakfast*
Brightling Road, Robertsbridge TN32 5DP
**t** (01580) 881841
**e** info@glenferness.co.uk
**w** glenferness.co.uk

**Slides Farm B&B** ★★★★★
*Bed & Breakfast*
**SILVER AWARD**
Silverhill, Robertsbridge TN32 5PA
**t** (01580) 880106
**e** slides.farm@btinternet.com
**w** slidesfarm.com

## ROCHESTER
Kent

**Churchfields B&B** ★★
*Bed & Breakfast*
**SILVER AWARD**
6 Churchfields Terrace, St Margarets Street, Rochester ME1 1TQ
**t** (01634) 400 679
**e** info@churchfieldsbandb.co.uk
**w** churchfieldsbandb.co.uk

**The Cottage** ★★★★
*Bed & Breakfast*
66 Borstal Road, Rochester ME1 3BD
**t** (01634) 403888

**Greystones** ★★★★
*Guest Accommodation*
25 Watts Avenue, Rochester ME1 1RX
**t** (01634) 409565

**Guinea Lodge** ★★★
*Guest Accommodation*
435 Maidstone Road, Rochester ME1 3PQ
**t** (01634) 306716

**North Downs Barn** ★★★★
*Bed & Breakfast*
Bush Road, Cuxton, Rochester ME2 1HF
**t** (01634) 296829
**e** alison@northdownsbarn.wanadoo.co.uk
**w** northdownsbarn.co.uk

**Riverview Lodge** ★★
*Guest House*
88 Borstal Road, Rochester ME1 3BD
**t** (01634) 842241

**Salisbury House** ★★★★
*Guest Accommodation*
29 Watts Avenue, Rochester ME1 1RX
**t** (01634) 400182

## RODMELL
East Sussex

**Garden Studio** ★★★★
*Guest Accommodation*
Robin Hill, Mill Lane, Rodmell, Lewes BN7 3HS
**t** (01273) 476715 & 07775 624235

## ROLVENDEN
Kent

**Duck & Drake Cottage** ★★★
*Guest Accommodation*
Sandhurst Lane, Rolvenden, Cranbrook TN17 4PQ
**t** (01580) 241533
**e** duckanddrake@supanet.com

**Green Cottage B&B** ★★
*Bed & Breakfast*
5 Sparkes Wood Avenue, Rolvenden, Tenterden TN17 4LU
**t** (01580) 241765
**e** stevree@onetel.com

## ROMNEY MARSH
Kent

**Coxell House** ★★★★
*Guest Accommodation*
**SILVER AWARD**
9 Manor Road, Lydd, Romney Marsh TN29 9HR
**t** (01797) 322037
**e** coxellhouse@btinternet.com
**w** coxellhouse.co.uk

**Stable Cottage** ★★★★
*Bed & Breakfast*
The Sheiling, Donkey Street, Burmarsh, Romney Marsh TN29 0JN
**t** (01303) 872335 & 07870 918387
**e** eric777@tiscali.co.uk
**w** stablecottageburmarsh.co.uk

## ROMSEY
Hampshire

**The Chalet Guest House** ★★
*Bed & Breakfast*
105 Botley Road, Whitenap SO51 5RQ
**t** (01794) 517299
**e** thechalet@ntlworld.com

**The Dairy at Packridge Farm** ★★★★
*Guest Accommodation*
Packridge Lane, Romsey SO51 9LL
**t** (023) 8073 3073
**e** thedairy@packridgeestate.com
**w** packridgeestate.com

**Nursery Cottage** ★★
*Bed & Breakfast*
The Avenue, East Tytherley SP5 1LF
**t** (01794) 341060
**w** nursery-cottage.com

**Pauncefoot House** ★★★★
*Bed & Breakfast*
Pauncefoot Hill, Romsey SO51 6AA
**t** (01794) 513139
**e** lendupont@aol.com

**Pyesmead Farm** ★★★★
*Farmhouse*
Plaitford, Romsey SO51 6EE
**t** (01794) 323386
**e** pyesmead@talk21.com
**w** pyesmeadfarm.co.uk

**Ranvilles Farm House**
★★★★★ *Bed & Breakfast*
Pauncefoot Hill, Romsey SO51 6AA
**t** (023) 8081 4481
**e** info@ranvilles.com
**w** ranvilles.com

**St Brelades House** ★★★★
*Bed & Breakfast*
Mill Lane, Sherfield English, Romsey SO51 6FN
**t** (01794) 324766
**e** b&b@st-brelades.freeserve.co.uk

**Stoneymarsh Bed & Breakfast** ★★★
*Bed & Breakfast*
Stoneymarsh Cottage, Stoneymarsh, Michelmersh SO51 0LB
**t** (01794) 368867
**e** m.m.moran@btinternet.com

## ROOKLEY
Isle of Wight

**Kennerley House – B&B**
★★★★ *Bed & Breakfast*
Main Road, Rookley PO38 3NB
**t** (01983) 842001
**e** carolfoote@btinternet.com
**w** kennerleyhouse.com

## ROUND GREEN
Kent

**Cordons** ★★★
*Bed & Breakfast*
Round Green Lane, Colliers Green TN17 2NB
**t** (01580) 211633
**w** cordonsbandb.co.uk

## ROWLEDGE
Surrey

**Rosebarton** ★★★★
*Bed & Breakfast*
Cherry Tree Walk, Rowledge GU10 4AD
**t** (01252) 793580
**e** rosebarton@btinternet.com

## ROYAL TUNBRIDGE WELLS
Kent

**191 Upper Grosvenor Road**
★★★ *Bed & Breakfast*
Royal Tunbridge Wells TN1 2EF
**t** (01892) 537305

**40 York Road** ★★★★
*Bed & Breakfast*
Royal Tunbridge Wells TN1 1JY
**t** (01892) 531342
**e** yorkroad@tiscali.co.uk
**w** yorkroad.co.uk

**A & A Studley Cottage** ★★★★
*Guest Accommodation*
**GOLD AWARD**
Bishop's Down Park Road, Royal Tunbridge Wells TN4 8XX
**t** (01892) 539854
**e** cook@studleycottage.co.uk
**w** studleycottage.co.uk

**Alconbury Guest House**
★★★★★ *Bed & Breakfast*
**SILVER AWARD**
41 Molyneux Park Road, Royal Tunbridge Wells TN4 8DX
**t** (01892) 511279
**e** wisepig@telecomplus.org.uk
**w** palace4u.co.uk

**Ash Tree Cottage** ★★★★
*Bed & Breakfast*
**SILVER AWARD**
7 Eden Road, Royal Tunbridge Wells TN1 1TS
**t** (01892) 541317
**e** rogersashtree@excite.com
**w** ashtreekent.co.uk

**Badgers End** ★★
*Bed & Breakfast*
47 Thirlmere Road, Royal Tunbridge Wells TN4 9SS
**t** (01892) 533176

**Bankside** ★★★★
*Bed & Breakfast*
6 Scotts Way, Royal Tunbridge Wells TN2 5RG
**t** (01892) 531776
**e** amkib1@yahoo.co.uk
**w** banksidebedandbreakfast-tunbridgewells.co.uk

**The Beacon** ★★★★
*Guest Accommodation*
Tea Garden Lane, Tunbridge Wells TN3 9JH
**t** (01892) 524252
**e** beaconhotel@btopenworld.com
**w** the-beacon.co.uk

**Bethany House** ★★★★★
*Guest Accommodation*
**GOLD AWARD**
170 St Johns Road, Royal Tunbridge Wells TN4 9UY
**t** (01892) 684363
**e** info@bethanyhousetwells.co.uk
**w** bethanyhousetwells.co.uk

**Blundeston** ★★★★
*Guest Accommodation*
Eden Road, Royal Tunbridge Wells TN1 1TS
**t** (01892) 513030
**e** daysblundeston@excite.com

**The Brick House** ★★★★
*Bed & Breakfast*
**SILVER AWARD**
21 Mount Ephraim Road, Royal Tunbridge Wells TN1 1EN
**t** (01892) 516517
**e** info@thebrickhousebandb.co.uk
**w** thebrickhousebandb.co.uk

**Broadwater** ★★★★
*Bed & Breakfast*
24 Clarendon Way, Royal Tunbridge Wells TN2 5LD
**t** (01892) 528161
**e** david.thompson4@which.net

**Clarken Guest House** ★★
*Guest House*
61 Frant Road, Royal Tunbridge Wells TN2 5LH
**t** (01892) 533397
**e** suekench@hotmail.com

**Danehurst House** ★★★★★
*Bed & Breakfast*
**SILVER AWARD**
41 Lower Green Road, Royal Tunbridge Wells TN4 8TW
**t** (01892) 527739
**e** info@danehurst.net
**w** danehurst.net

**Ford Cottage** ★★★★
*Guest Accommodation*
Linden Park Road, Tunbridge Wells TN2 5QL
**t** (01892) 531419
**e** fordcottage@tinyworld.co.uk

**Great Oaks** ★★
*Bed & Breakfast*
163 St Johns Road, Tunbridge Wells TN4 9UP
**t** (01892) 529992
**e** greatoaks163@tiscali.co.uk

**Hawkenbury Farm** ★★★★
*Bed & Breakfast*
Hawkenbury Road, Royal Tunbridge Wells TN3 9AD
**t** (01892) 536977
**e** rhwright1@aol.com

**Hazelwood House** ★★
*Bed & Breakfast*
**SILVER AWARD**
Bishop's Down Park Road, Royal Tunbridge Wells TN4 8XS
**t** (01892) 545924
**e** judith@hurcomb3.wanadoo.co.uk

**The Lancers**
Rating Applied For
*Bed & Breakfast*
34 Church Road, Royal Tunbridge Wells TN1 1JP
**t** 07964 400147
**e** gilly@thelancers.co.uk
**w** thelancers.co.uk

**Manor Court Farm** ★★★
*Farmhouse*
Ashurst Road, Ashurst, Tunbridge Wells TN3 9TB
**t** (01892) 740279
**e** jsoyke@jsoyke.freeserve.co.uk
**w** manorcourtfarm.co.uk

**The Nightingales** ★★★★
*Bed & Breakfast*
London Road, Southborough TN4 0UJ
**t** (01892) 522384
**e** milliken61@oal.com

**Rosnaree** ★★★
*Bed & Breakfast*
189 Upper Grosvenor Road, Royal Tunbridge Wells TN1 2EF
**t** (01892) 524017
**e** davidann.rosnaree@yahoo.co.uk

**Swan Cottage** ★★★★
*Bed & Breakfast*
17 Warwick Road, Royal Tunbridge Wells TN1 1YL
**t** (01892) 525910
**e** swancot@btinternet.com
**w** swancottage.co.uk

## RUDGWICK
West Sussex

**Alliblaster House** ★★★★★
*Bed & Breakfast*
**GOLD AWARD**
Hillhouse Lane, Rudgwick, Horsham RH12 3BD
**t** (01403) 822860
**e** info@alliblasterhouse.com
**w** alliblasterhouse.com

**Mucky Duck Inn** ★★★★ *Inn*
Tismans Common, Loxwood Road, Horsham RH12 3BW
**t** (01403) 822300
**e** mucky_duck_pub@msn.com
**w** mucky-duck-inn.co.uk

## RUSTINGTON
West Sussex

**Kenmore** ★★★★
*Guest Accommodation*
**SILVER AWARD**
Claigmar Road, Rustington, Littlehampton BN16 2NL
**t** (01903) 784634
**e** thekenmore@hotmail.co.uk
**w** kenmoreguesthouse.co.uk

**Mallon Dene ★★★★**
*Bed & Breakfast*
**SILVER AWARD**
47 Mallon Dene, Littlehampton BN16 2JP
**t** (01903) 775383
**e** jenny@mallondene.co.uk
**w** mallondene.co.uk

## RYDE
Isle of Wight

**Claverton House Bed and Breakfast ★★★★**
*Bed & Breakfast*
Claverton House, 12 The Strand, Ryde PO33 1JE
**t** (01983) 613015
**e** clavertonhouse@aol.com
**w** clavertonhouse.co.uk

Dorset House ★★★
*Guest Accommodation*
31 Dover Street, Ryde PO33 2BW
**t** (01983) 564327
**e** hoteldorset@aol.com
**w** thedorsethotel.co.uk

**Fern Cottage ★★★★**
*Bed & Breakfast*
8 West Street, Ryde PO33 2NW
**t** (01983) 565856
**e** sandra@psdferguson.freeserve.co.uk

Pencombe House ★★★★
*Bed & Breakfast*
Newnham Road, Ryde PO33 3TH
**t** (01983) 567910

Sea View B&B ★★★★
*Bed & Breakfast*
8 Dover Street, Ryde PO33 2AQ
**t** (01983) 810976
**e** seaviewbandbinryde@hotmail.com

Seahaven House ★★★
*Guest Accommodation*
36 St Thomas Street, Ryde PO33 2DL
**t** (01983) 563069
**e** seahaven@netguides.co.uk

**Seaward Guest House ★**
*Guest House*
14-16 George Street, Ryde PO33 2EW
**t** (01983) 563168
**e** bookings@seawardguesthouse.co.uk

Sillwood Acre ★★★★
*Bed & Breakfast*
**SILVER AWARD**
Church Road, Binstead PO33 3TB
**t** (01983) 563553
**e** debbie@sillwood-acre.co.uk
**w** sillwood-acre.co.uk

Trentham Guest House
★★★ *Guest House*
38 The Strand, Ryde PO33 1JF
**t** (01983) 563418
**e** info@trentham-guesthouse.co.uk
**w** trentham-guesthouse.co.uk

## RYE
East Sussex

At Wisteria Corner ★★★★
*Bed & Breakfast*
47 Ferry Road, Rye TN31 7DJ
**t** (01797) 225011
**e** mmpartridge@lineone.net
**w** wisteriacorner.co.uk

**Aviemore Guest House**
★★★ *Guest House*
28-30 Fishmarket Road, Rye TN31 7LP
**t** (01797) 223052
**e** info@aviemorerye.co.uk
**w** aviemorerye.co.uk

Durrant House ★★★★★
*Guest Accommodation*
**GOLD AWARD**
2 Market Street, Rye TN31 7LA
**t** (01797) 223182
**e** info@durranthouse.com
**w** durranthouse.com

Fairacres ★★★★★
*Bed & Breakfast*
**GOLD AWARD**
Udimore Road, Broad Oak TN31 6DG
**t** (01424) 883236
**e** shelagh-john@fairacres.fsworld.co.uk
**w** smoothhound.co.uk/hotels/fairacres

Four Seasons ★★★★
*Guest Accommodation*
**SILVER AWARD**
96 Udimore Road, Rye TN31 7DY
**t** (01797) 224305

**Hayden's ★★★★★**
*Bed & Breakfast*
108 High Street, Rye TN31 7JE
**t** (01797) 224501
**e** richard.hayden@mac.com
**w** cheynehouse.co.uk

**Jeake's House ★★★★★**
*Guest Accommodation*
**GOLD AWARD**
Mermaid Street, Rye TN31 7ET
**t** (01797) 222828
**e** stay@jeakeshouse.com
**w** jeakeshouse.com

Kimbley Cottage ★★★★
*Bed & Breakfast*
Main Street, Peasmarsh TN31 6UL
**t** (01797) 230514
**e** kimbleycot@aol.com
**w** kimbleycottage.co.uk

Leswinton B&B ★★★★
*Bed & Breakfast*
Leswinton, West Undercliff, Rye TN31 7DX
**t** (01797) 224710
**e** leswintonbandb@yahoo.co.uk

Oaklands ★★★★★
*Guest Accommodation*
**SILVER AWARD**
Udimore Road, Rye TN31 6AB
**t** (01797) 229734
**e** info@oaklands-rye.co.uk
**w** oaklands-rye.co.uk

The Place Camber Sands ★★★★
*Guest Accommodation*
New Lydd Road, Rye TN31 7RB
**t** (01797) 225057
**e** enquiries@theplacecambersands.co.uk
**w** theplacecambersands.co.uk

The Rise ★★★★
*Bed & Breakfast*
**GOLD AWARD**
82 Udimore Road, Rye TN31 7DY
**t** (01797) 222285
**e** theriserye@aol.com
**w** therise-rye.co.uk

Ship Inn ★★★ *Inn*
The Strand, Rye TN31 7DB
**t** (01797) 222233
**e** info@shipinnrye.co.uk
**w** shipinnrye.co.uk

**Strand House ★★★★**
*Guest Accommodation*
**SILVER AWARD**
Strand House, Tanyards Lane, The Strand, Winchelsea TN36 4JT
**t** (01797) 226276
**e** info@thestrandhouse.co.uk
**w** thestrandhouse.co.uk

Top o'The Hill at Rye ★★★
*Inn*
Rye Hill, Rye TN31 7NH
**t** (01797) 223284

Vine-Cottage ★★★
*Bed & Breakfast*
Vine Cottage, 25a Udimore Road, Rye TN31 7DS
**t** (01797) 222822

Willow Tree House ★★★★★
*Guest Accommodation*
**SILVER AWARD**
Winchelsea Road, Rye TN31 7EL
**t** (01797) 227820
**e** info@willow-tree-house.com
**w** willow-tree-house.com

## RYE FOREIGN
East Sussex

The Hare & Hounds ★★★★
*Inn*
Rye Road, Rye TN31 7ST
**t** (01797) 230483

## ST LAWRENCE
Isle of Wight

Lisle Combe ★★★
*Guest Accommodation*
Bank End Farm, Undercliff Drive, St Lawrence PO38 1UW
**t** (01983) 852582
**e** lislecombe@yahoo.com
**w** lislecombe.co.uk

Little Orchard ★★★★
*Guest Accommodation*
Undercliff Drive, St Lawrence PO38 1YA
**t** (01983) 731106

## ST LEONARDS
East Sussex

Hastings House ★★★
*Guest Accommodation*
9 Warrior Square, St Leonards-on-Sea, Hastings TN37 6BA
**t** (01424) 422709
**e** sengloy@btconnect.com
**w** hastingshouse.co.uk

Hollington Croft ★★★
*Bed & Breakfast*
272 Battle Road, St Leonards-on-Sea TN37 7BA
**t** (01424) 851795

Marina Lodge ★★★
*Guest House*
123 Marina, St Leonards-on-Sea TN38 0BN
**t** (01424) 715067
**e** marinalodgeguesthse@tiscali.co.uk
**w** marinalodge.co.uk

Melrose Guest House
★★★★ *Guest House*
18 de Cham Road, St Leonards-on-Sea TN37 6JP
**t** (01424) 715163
**e** melrose18@hotmail.com

Rutland ★★★ *Guest House*
17 Grosvenor Crescent, St Leonards-on-Sea TN38 0AA
**t** (01424) 714720
**e** carol@rutlandguesthouse.co.uk
**w** rutlandguesthouse.co.uk

The Sea Spirit Hotel ★★★
*Guest House*
Tower Road West, St Leonards-on-Sea TN38 0RJ
**t** (01424) 729518
**e** lorraineedwards@btinternet.com

Sherwood Guest House
★★★★ *Guest House*
15 Grosvenor Crescent, St Leonards-on-Sea TN38 0AA
**t** (01424) 433331
**e** wendy@sherwoodhastings.co.uk
**w** sherwoodhastings.co.uk

Tower House 1066 ★★★★
*Guest Accommodation*
**SILVER AWARD**
28 Tower Road West, Hastings TN38 0RG
**t** (01424) 427217
**e** reservations@towerhousehotel.com
**w** towerhousehotel.com

## ST-MARGARETS-AT-CLIFFE
Kent

Holm Oaks ★★★★
*Guest Accommodation*
**SILVER AWARD**
Dover Road, St Margarets-at-Cliffe, Dover CT15 6EP
**t** (01304) 852990
**e** holmoaks@invictawiz.co.uk

## ST MARGARET'S BAY
Kent

**Small Acre ★★★★**
*Guest Accommodation*
**SILVER AWARD**
Sea View Road, St Margarets Bay, Dover CT15 6EE
**t** (01304) 851840
**e** marion@smallacre.co.uk
**w** smallacre.co.uk

## SANDFORD
Isle of Wight

The Barn ★★★★ *Farmhouse*
Pound Farm, Shanklin Road, Sandford PO38 3AW
**t** (01983) 840047
**e** barnpoundfarm@barnpoundfarm.free-online.co.uk

## SANDHURST Berkshire

**The Wellington Arms ★★★**
*Inn*
203 Yorktown Road, Sandhurst GU47 9BN
**t** (01252) 872408
**w** thewellingtonarms.co.uk

## SANDHURST Kent

**Lamberden Cottage ★★★★**
*Bed & Breakfast*
Rye Road, Cranbrook TN18 5PH
**t** (01580) 850743
**e** thewalledgarden@hotmail.co.uk
**w** lamberdencottage.co.uk

## SANDOWN Isle of Wight

**The Alendel ★★★**
*Guest House*
1 Leed Street, Sandown PO36 9DA
**t** (01983) 402967
**e** info@alendelhotel.co.uk
**w** alendelhotel.co.uk

**Beaufort House ★★★★**
*Guest House*
30 Broadway, Sandown PO36 9BY
**t** (01983) 403672
**e** web@thebeaufortsandown.co.uk
**w** thebeaufortsandown.co.uk

**The Belgrave ★★**
*Guest Accommodation*
14-16 Beachfield Road, Sandown PO36 8NA
**t** (01983) 404550

**The Bernay ★★★★**
*Guest Accommodation*
24 Victoria Road, Sandown PO36 8AL
**t** (01983) 402205
**e** info@thebernayhotel.co.uk
**w** thebernayhotel.co.uk

**Bertram Lodge ★★★★**
*Guest Accommodation*
3 Leed Street, Sandown PO36 9DA
**t** (01983) 402551
**e** gazz@blodge.fslife.co.uk
**w** bertramlodgehotel.com

**The Caprera – A ★★★**
*Guest House*
Melville Street, Sandown PO36 8LE
**t** (01983) 402482
**e** thecaprera@btconnect.com
**w** thecaprera.com

**Cliff Lodge Guest House**
★★★★ *Guest House*
13 Cliff Path, Lake PO36 8PL
**t** (01983) 402963
**e** clifflodge@uwclub.net
**w** cliff-lodge-isle-of-wight.co.uk

**Copperfield Lodge ★★★★**
*Bed & Breakfast*
**SILVER AWARD**
Newport Road, Apse Heath PO36 9PJ
**t** 07733 262889
**e** copperfieldlodge@aol.com

**The Denewood ★★★★**
*Guest Accommodation*
7-9 Victoria Road, Sandown PO36 8AL
**t** (01983) 402980
**e** holidays@denewoodhotel.co.uk
**w** denewood-hotel.co.uk

**The Fernside ★★★★**
*Guest House*
30 Station Avenue, Sandown PO36 9BW
**t** (01983) 402356
**e** enquiries@thefernside.co.uk
**w** fernsidehotel.co.uk

**Heathfield House ★★★★**
*Guest Accommodation*
52 Melville Street, Sandown PO36 8LF
**t** (01983) 400002
**e** mail@heathfieldhousehotel.com
**w** heathfieldhousehotel.com

**Inglewood Guest House**
★★★ *Guest House*
15 Avenue Road, Sandown PO36 8BN
**t** (01983) 403485
**e** inglewooduk@yahoo.co.uk

**The Montpelier ★★★**
*Guest Accommodation*
Pier Street, Sandown PO36 8JR
**t** (01983) 403964
**e** enquiries@themontpelier.co.uk
**w** themontpelier.co.uk

**Mount Brocas Guest House**
★★★ *Guest House*
15 Beachfield Road, Sandown PO36 8LT
**t** (01983) 406276
**e** mountbrocas1@btconnect.com
**w** wightstay.co.uk/brocas.html

**The Philomel Guest House**
★★★ *Guest House*
21 Carter Street, Sandown PO36 8BL
**t** (01983) 406413
**e** enquiries@philomel-hotel.co.uk
**w** philomel-hotel.co.uk

**Rooftree ★★★★**
*Guest House*
26 The Broadway, Sandown PO36 9BY
**t** (01983) 403175
**e** rooftree@btconnect.com
**w** rooftree-hotel.co.uk

**The Sandhill ★★★**
*Guest Accommodation*
6 Hill Street, Sandown PO36 9DB
**t** (01983) 403635
**e** sandhillsandown@aol.com
**w** sandhill-hotel.co.uk

**Sandown Manor**
Rating Applied For
*Guest House*
Yaverland Road, Sandown PO36 8QP
**t** (01983) 402266
**e** sandownmanor@yahoo.co.uk
**w** sandownmanor.co.uk

**Southwood House ★★★**
*Guest Accommodation*
26 Albert Road, Sandown PO36 8AW
**t** (01983) 407297
**e** southwoodhouse@aol.com
**w** southwoodhouse.co.uk

**Treval Guest House ★★★★**
*Bed & Breakfast*
46 Culver Way, Yaverland PO36 8QJ
**t** (01983) 407910
**e** val-newton@tiscali.co.uk
**w** treval-sandown.co.uk

## SANDWICH Kent

**Molland House B+B ★★★★★**
*Guest Accommodation*
**GOLD AWARD**
Molland Lane, Ash, Sandwich CT3 2JB
**t** (01304) 814210
**e** tracy@mollandhouse.co.uk
**w** mollandhouse.co.uk

## SARRE Kent

**The Crown Inn – The Cherry Brandy House ★★★★** *Inn*
Ramsgate Road, Sarre, Birchington CT7 0LF
**t** (01843) 847808
**e** crown@shepherdneame.co.uk
**w** crownbirchington.co.uk

## SEAFORD East Sussex

**Cornerways ★★★**
*Guest Accommodation*
10 The Covers, Seaford BN25 1DF
**t** (01323) 492400

**Malvern House ★★★**
*Bed & Breakfast*
Alfriston Road, Seaford BN25 3QG
**t** (01323) 492058
**e** malvernbandb@aol.com
**w** malvernhouse.gb.com

**The Silverdale ★★★★**
*Guest House*
21 Sutton Park Road, Seaford BN25 1RH
**t** (01323) 491849
**e** silverdale@mistral.co.uk
**w** silverdaleseaford.co.uk

## SEAVIEW Isle of Wight

**1 Cluniac Cottages ★★★**
*Bed & Breakfast*
Priory Road, Seaview PO34 5BU
**t** (01983) 812119
**e** bill.elfenjay@virgin.net
**w** cluniaccottages.co.uk

**Clover Ridge ★★★★**
*Bed & Breakfast*
**SILVER AWARD**
18 Horestone Rise, Seaview PO34 5DB
**t** (01983) 617377
**e** cloverridge.seaviewiow@virgin.net
**w** cloverridge.co.uk

**Maple Villa B&B ★★**
*Bed & Breakfast*
Oakhill Road, Seaview PO34 5AP
**t** (01983) 614826
**e** mail@maplevilla.co.uk
**w** maplevilla.co.uk

## SEDLESCOMBE East Sussex

**Forge House ★★★★**
*Bed & Breakfast*
The Green, Sedlescombe TN33 0QA
**t** (01424) 870054
**e** jean@bridgetvaughan.wannado.co.uk

## SELBORNE Hampshire

**Ivanhoe ★★★★**
*Bed & Breakfast*
Oakhanger, Selborne GU35 9JG
**t** (01420) 473464
**w** ivanhoe-bnb.co.uk

## SELSEY West Sussex

**Greenacre Bed & Breakfast ★★★★**
*Guest Accommodation*
Manor Farm Court, Selsey PO20 0LY
**t** (01243) 602912
**e** greenacre@zoom.co.uk
**w** visitsussex.org

**Keston House ★★★★**
*Bed & Breakfast*
16 Beacon Drive, Chichester PO20 0TW
**t** (01243) 604513
**e** mrt@mercedes553.wanadoo.co.uk
**w** kestonhouseselsey.co.uk

**Norton Lea Guest House**
★★★ *Bed & Breakfast*
Chichester Road, Selsey, Chichester PO20 9EA
**t** (01243) 605454
**e** nortonlea@aol.com
**w** nortonlea.com

**St Andrews Lodge ★★★★**
*Guest Accommodation*
Chichester Road, Selsey PO20 0LX
**t** (01243) 606899
**e** info@standrewslodge.co.uk
**w** standrewslodge.co.uk

**Vincent Lodge ★★★★**
*Bed & Breakfast*
**SILVER AWARD**
Vincent Road, Selsey PO20 9DJ
**t** (01243) 602985
**e** info@vincentlodge.co.uk
**w** vincentlodge.co.uk

## SEND Surrey

**Sommerhay Barn ★★★★**
*Bed & Breakfast*
Church Lane, Send GU23 7JL
**t** (01483) 210107
**e** angey_watson@hotmail.com

## SEVENOAKS Kent

**40 Robyns Way ★★**
*Bed & Breakfast*
Sevenoaks TN13 3EB
**t** (01732) 452401
**e** ingram7oaks@onetel.com
**w** web.onetel.com/~ingram7oaks/

**56 The Drive ★★★**
*Bed & Breakfast*
Sevenoaks TN13 3AF
t (01732) 453236
e shirley.lloyd@7oaks.net

**Bramber ★★** *Bed & Breakfast*
45 Shoreham Lane, Sevenoaks TN13 3DX
t (01732) 457466

**Crofters ★★★★**
*Bed & Breakfast*
67 Oakhill Road, Sevenoaks TN13 1NU
t (01732) 460189
e ritamarfry@talk21.com

**The Heathers ★★★★★**
*Guest Accommodation*
**SILVER AWARD**
29 White Hart Wood, Sevenoaks TN13 1RS
t (01732) 454061
e ken@beaumontk.fslife.co.uk
w http://the-heathers.mysite.wanadoo-members.co.uk

**Hornshaw House ★★★★**
*Bed & Breakfast*
47 Mount Harry Road, Sevenoaks TN13 3JN
t (01732) 465262
e elizabeth.bates4@btinternet.com
w hornshaw-house.co.uk

**Old Timbertop Cottage**
**★★★★** *Bed & Breakfast*
**SILVER AWARD**
4 Old Timbertop Cottages, Bethel Road, Sevenoaks TN13 3UE
t (01732) 460506
e timbertopcottage@tiscali.co.uk
w timbertopcottage.co.uk

**The Pightle ★★★★**
*Guest Accommodation*
21 White Hart Wood, Sevenoaks TN13 1RS
t (01732) 451678
e emtess@tiscali.co.uk
w thepightle.co.uk

**Robann ★★★**
*Bed & Breakfast*
5 Vestry Cottages, Old Otford Road, Sevenoaks TN14 5EH
t (01732) 456272
e info@robannbandb.co.uk
w robannbandb.co.uk

**The Studio at Double Dance**
**★★★★** *Bed & Breakfast*
**SILVER AWARD**
Penny Cracknell, Double Dance, Bates Hill TN15 9AT
t (01732) 884198
e pennycracknell@doubledance.co.uk
w doubledance.co.uk

## SHALFORD Surrey

**2 Northfield ★★★**
*Bed & Breakfast*
Off Summersbury Drive, Shalford GU4 8JN
t (01483) 570431
e themordens@tiscali.co.uk
w northfieldbnb.net

## SHANKLIN Isle of Wight

**The Appley ★★★★**
*Guest House*
13 Queens Road, Shanklin PO37 6AW
t (01983) 862666
e rod.folds@virgin.net
w appleyhotel.com

**Atholl Court ★★★**
*Guest House*
1 Atherley Road, Shanklin PO37 7AT
t (01983) 862414
e info@atholl-court.co.uk
w atholl-court.co.uk

**The Birkdale ★★★★**
*Guest House* **SILVER AWARD**
5 Grange Road, Shanklin PO37 6NN
t (01983) 862949
e birkdale-iow@hotmail.co.uk
w birkdalehotel.com

**Brooke House ★★★**
*Guest House*
2 St Pauls Avenue, Shanklin PO37 7AL
t (01983) 863162
e brookehousehotel@btconnect.com
w brookehousehotel.co.uk

**The Burlington ★★★**
*Guest House*
6 Chine Avenue, Shanklin PO37 6AG
t (01983) 862090
e burlingtonshanklin@isleofwight.com
w isleofwighthotels.org.uk

**The Chestnuts ★★★★**
*Guest House*
4 Hope Road, Shanklin PO37 6EA
t (01983) 862162
e info@thechestnutsshanklin.co.uk
w thechestnutsshanklin.co.uk

**Claremont Guest House**
**★★★★** *Guest House*
4 Eastmount Road, Shanklin PO37 6DN
t (01983) 862083
e claremont@dsl.pipex.com
w southernuk.com/claremont.htm

**Cliftonville Guest House**
**★★★** *Guest House*
6 Hope Road, Shanklin PO37 6EA
t (01983) 862197
e info@cliftonvillehotel.wanadoo.co.uk
w cliftonvillehotel.com

**The Edgecliffe ★★★★**
*Guest Accommodation*
7 Clarence Gardens, Shanklin PO37 6HA
t (01983) 866199
e edgecliffehtl@aol.com
w wightonline.co.uk/edgecliffehotel

**Foxhills ★★★★★**
*Guest Accommodation*
**GOLD AWARD**
30 Victoria Avenue, Shanklin PO37 6LS
t (01983) 862329
e info@foxhillshotel.co.uk
w foxhillshotel.co.uk

**Grange Bank House ★★★★**
*Guest Accommodation*
**SILVER AWARD**
Grange Road, Shanklin PO37 6NN
t (01983) 862337
e grangebank@btinternet.com
w grangebank.co.uk

**Hambledon ★★★★**
*Guest Accommodation*
11 Queens Road, Shanklin PO37 6AW
t (01983) 862403
e enquiries@hambledon-hotel.co.uk
w hambledon-hotel.co.uk

**The Havelock ★★★★**
*Guest Accommodation*
**SILVER AWARD**
2 Queens Road, Shanklin PO37 6AN
t (01983) 862747
e enquiries@havelockhotel.co.uk
w havelockhotel.co.uk

**The Hazelwood ★★★**
*Guest House*
14 Clarence Road, Shanklin PO37 7BH
t (01983) 862824
e hazelwoodiow@aol.com
w hazelwoodiow.co.uk

**The Heatherleigh ★★★★**
*Guest House* **SILVER AWARD**
17 Queens Road, Shanklin PO37 6AW
t (01983) 862503
e enquiries@heatherleigh.co.uk
w heatherleigh.co.uk

**Ingress Bed & Breakfast**
**★★★** *Guest Accommodation*
St Pauls Crescent, Shanklin PO37 7AN
t (01983) 862623
e info@ingressbandb.co.uk
w ingressbandb.co.uk

**The Kenbury ★★★★**
*Guest Accommodation*
Clarence Road, Shanklin PO37 7BH
t (01983) 862085
e kenbury@isleofwighthotel.co.uk
w isleofwighthotel.co.uk

**The Lincoln ★★★★**
*Guest House*
30 Littlestairs Road, Shanklin PO37 6HS
t (01983) 861171
e enquiries@thelincoln.org.uk
w thelincoln.org.uk

**The Miclaran ★★★**
*Guest House*
37 Littlestairs Road, Shanklin PO37 6HS
t (01983) 862726
e miclaran@btinternet.com
w miclaran.co.uk

**Mount House ★★★**
*Guest House*
20 Arthurs Hill, Shanklin PO37 6EE
t (01983) 862556
e graham.mounthouse@btopenworld.com
w wightstay.co.uk/mount.html

**Overstrand ★★★★**
*Guest Accommodation*
5 Howard Road, Shanklin PO37 6HD
t (01983) 862100
e enquiries@overstrand-hotel.co.uk
w overstrand-hotel.co.uk

**The Palmerston ★★★**
*Guest Accommodation*
16 Palmerston Road, Shanklin PO37 6AS
t (01983) 865547
e info@palmerston-hotel.co.uk
w palmerston-hotel.co.uk

**The Pink Beach Guest House**
**★★★** *Guest House*
20 The Esplanade, Shanklin PO37 6BN
t (01983) 862501
e pinkbeach@btopenworld.com
w pink-beach-hotel.co.uk

**Roseberry ★★★★**
*Guest Accommodation*
3 Alexandra Road, Shanklin PO37 6AF
t (01983) 862805
e herm-beach@tinyworld.co.uk
w roseberryhotel-isleofwight.co.uk

**The Royson ★★★★**
*Guest House*
26 Littlestairs Road, Shanklin PO37 6HS
t (01983) 862163
e info@theroyson.co.uk
w theroyson.co.uk

**The Ryedale ★★★**
*Guest Accommodation*
3 Atherley Road, Shanklin PO37 7AT
t (01983) 862375
e hayley@ryedale-hotel.co.uk
w ryedale-hotel.co.uk

**The St Leonards ★★★★**
*Guest Accommodation*
**SILVER AWARD**
22 Queens Road, Shanklin PO37 6AW
t (01983) 862121
e info@thestleonards.co.uk
w thestleonards.co.uk

**Snowdon House ★★★★**
*Guest Accommodation*
**SILVER AWARD**
19 Queens Road, Shanklin PO37 6AW
t (01983) 862853
e info@snowdonhotel.fsnet.co.uk
w thesnowdonhotel.co.uk

**Somerville ★★★**
*Guest Accommodation*
14 St Georges Road, Shanklin PO37 6BA
t (01983) 862821
e somerville@fsmail.net

**Swiss Cottage** ★★★★
*Guest Accommodation*
10 St Georges Road, Shanklin PO37 6BA
**t** (01983) 862333
**e** info@swiss-cottage.co.uk
**w** swiss-cottage.co.uk

**The Triton**
Rating Applied For
*Guest Accommodation*
23 Atherley Road, Shanklin PO37 7AU
**t** (01983) 862494
**e** jackie@iow-accommodation.com
**w** iow-accommodation.com

**Westbury Lodge** ★★★★
*Guest Accommodation*
**SILVER AWARD**
25 Queens Road, Shanklin PO37 6AW
**t** (01983) 864926
**e** enquiries@westburylodge.co.uk
**w** westburylodge.co.uk

**YMCA Winchester House**
★★★ *Group Hostel*
Sandown Road, Shanklin PO37 6HU
**t** (01489) 772215
**e** winchesterhouse@ymca-fg.org
**w** ymca-fg.org/iow

## SHARPTHORNE
West Sussex

**Courtlands Nurseries**
★★★★ *Bed & Breakfast*
Chilling Street, Sharpthorne, East Grinstead RH19 4JF
**t** (01342) 810780
**e** lindsay.shurvell@virgin.net
**w** courtlandsnurseries.co.uk

## SHEERNESS
Kent

**The Croft Guesthouse** ★★★
*Guest House*
89 Queenborough Road, Sheerness ME12 3DB
**t** (01795) 662003
**e** thecroftguesthouse@hotmail.com
**w** thecroftguesthouse.co.uk

**The Ferry House Inn** ★★★★
*Guest Accommodation*
Harty Ferry Road, Leysdown-on-Sea, Sheerness ME12 4BQ
**t** (01795) 510214
**e** info@theferryhouseinn.co.uk
**w** theferryhouseinn.co.uk

**Invicta Guest House** ★★★
*Guest House*
6 Marine Parade, Sheerness ME12 2AL
**t** (01795) 661731
**w** invictaguesthouse.co.uk

## SHERBORNE ST JOHN
Hampshire

**Manor Farm Stables** ★★★★
*Bed & Breakfast*
**SILVER AWARD**
Vyne Road, Sherborne St John RG24 9HX
**t** (01256) 851324

## SHERE
Surrey

**Burrows Lea Country House**
★★★★
*Guest Accommodation*
Burrows Lea, Hook Lane, Shere GU5 9QG
**t** (01483) 205620
**e** accommodation@burrowslea.org.uk
**w** sanctuary-burrowslea.org.uk

**Lockhurst Hatch Farm**
★★★★ *Farmhouse*
Lockhurst Hatch Lane, Shere GU5 9JN
**t** (01483) 202689
**e** gill@lockhurst-hatch-farm.co.uk
**w** users.waitrose.com/~gmgellatly

**Rookery Nook Bed and Breakfast** ★★★
*Bed & Breakfast*
**SILVER AWARD**
The Square, Shere GU5 9HG
**t** (01483) 209399
**e** info@rookerynook.info
**w** rookerynook.info

## SHILLINGFORD
Oxfordshire

**Alouette Bed & Breakfast**
★★★★ *Bed & Breakfast*
2 Caldicot Close, Shillingford OX10 7HF
**t** (01865) 858600
**e** wendy@alouettebandb.co.uk
**w** alouettebandb.co.uk

**The Kingfisher Inn** ★★★★
*Inn*
27 Henley Road, Shillingford OX10 7EL
**t** (01865) 858595
**e** enquiries@kingfisher-inn.co.uk
**w** kingfisher-inn.co.uk

## SHIPLEY
West Sussex

**Goffsland Farm (B & B)**
★★★★ *Farmhouse*
**SILVER AWARD**
Shipley, Horsham RH13 9BQ
**t** (01403) 730434

## SHIPPON
Oxfordshire

**The White House** ★★
*Bed & Breakfast*
Faringdon Road, Shippon, Abingdon OX13 6LW
**t** (01235) 521998
**e** judymccairns@freeuk.com

## SHIPTON-UNDER-WYCHWOOD
Oxfordshire

**Court Farm** ★★★★
*Bed & Breakfast*
Mawles Lane, Shipton-under-Wychwood OX7 6DA
**t** (01993) 831515
**e** enquiries@courtfarmbb.com
**w** courtfarmbb.com

**Garden Cottage** ★★★
*Bed & Breakfast*
Fiddlers Hill, Shipton-under-Wychwood OX7 6DR
**t** 07803 399697
**e** charmian@gardencottage.wanadoo.co.uk

**Lodge Cottage** ★★★
*Bed & Breakfast*
High Street, Shipton-under-Wychwood OX7 6DG
**t** (01993) 830811
**e** h.a.savill@btopenworld.com

## SHOREHAM
Kent

**Preston Farmhouse** ★★★★
*Farmhouse*
Shoreham Road, Shoreham, Sevenoaks TN14 7UD
**t** (01959) 522029

## SHOREHAM-BY-SEA
West Sussex

**Truleigh Hill Youth Hostel**
★★ *Hostel*
Truleigh Hill, Shoreham-by-Sea BN43 5FB
**t** (01903) 813419

## SHORWELL
Isle of Wight

**Northcourt** ★★★★
*Guest Accommodation*
**SILVER AWARD**
Main Road, Shorwell PO30 3JG
**t** (01983) 740415
**e** enquiries@northcourt.info
**w** northcourt.info

**Westcourt Farm** ★★★★
*Farmhouse* **SILVER AWARD**
Limerstone Road, Shorwell PO30 3LA
**t** (01983) 740233
**e** julie@westcourt-farm.co.uk
**w** westcourt-farm.co.uk

## SIBFORD GOWER
Oxfordshire

**The Horse and Groom Inn**
★★★★ *Inn*
Milcombe, Banbury OX15 4RS
**t** (01295) 722142
**e** argyles@swalcliffe.net
**w** horseandgroom.biz

## SIDLESHAM
West Sussex

**Landseer House** ★★★★
*Bed & Breakfast*
**GOLD AWARD**
Cow Lane, Sidlesham, Chichester PO20 7LN
**t** (01243) 641525
**e** enq@landseerhouse.co.uk
**w** landseerhouse.co.uk

## SIDLESHAM COMMON
West Sussex

**Brimfast House** ★★★
*Bed & Breakfast*
Brimfast Lane, Sidlesham Common, Chichester PO20 7PZ
**t** (01243) 641841
**e** bookings@brimfastbandb.co.uk
**w** brimfastbandb.co.uk

## SINGLETON
West Sussex

**1 Rose Cottage** ★★★★
*Guest Accommodation*
**SILVER AWARD**
Singleton, Chichester PO18 0HP
**t** (01243) 811607
**e** rosecottagesingleton@yahoo.co.uk
**w** 1rosecottage.com

## SITTINGBOURNE
Kent

**Scuttington Manor Guest House** ★★★★ *Guest House*
Dully Road, Tonge, Sittingbourne ME9 9PA
**t** (01795) 521316

**Woodstock Guest House**
★★★★ *Bed & Breakfast*
**SILVER AWARD**
25 Woodstock Road, Sittingbourne ME10 4HJ
**t** (01795) 421516
**e** woodstockbnb@blueyonder.co.uk
**w** woodstockguesthouse.com

## SKIRMETT
Buckinghamshire

**The Old Bakery** ★★★★
*Guest Accommodation*
Henley-on-Thames RG9 6TD
**t** (01491) 638309
**e** lizzroach@aol.com

## SLINFOLD
West Sussex

**Oakwood House Guest House**
Rating Applied For
*Bed & Breakfast*
Five Oaks Road, Horsham RH13 0QW
**t** (01403) 790402

## SLOUGH
Berkshire

**Furnival Lodge** ★★★★
*Guest House*
53-55 Furnival Avenue, Slough SL2 1DH
**t** (01753) 570333
**e** info@furnival-lodge.co.uk
**w** furnival-lodge.co.uk

## SMARDEN
Kent

**Hereford Oast** ★★★★
*Bed & Breakfast*
**SILVER AWARD**
Smarden Bell Road, Smarden, Ashford TN27 8PA
**t** (01233) 770541
**e** suzy@herefordoast.fsnet.co.uk
**w** herefordoast.co.uk

**Snap Mill** ★★★★
*Guest Accommodation*
**SILVER AWARD**
Romden Road, Smarden TN27 8RB
**t** (01233) 770333
**e** snapmill@aol.com
**w** snapmill.co.uk

## SONNING
Berkshire

**The Bull Inn** ★★★★ *Inn*
**SILVER AWARD**
High Street, Sonning RG4 6UP
**t** (0118) 969 3901
**e** bullinn@fullers.co.uk
**w** fullersinns.co.uk

## SOULDERN
Oxfordshire

**Tower Fields** ★★★
*Farmhouse*
Souldern, Bicester OX27 7HY
**t** (01869) 346554
**e** toddyclive@towerfields.com
**w** towerfields.com

## SOUTHAMPTON
Hampshire

**Alcantara Guest House**
★★★★
*Guest Accommodation*
20 Howard Road, Shirley
SO15 5BN
t (023) 8033 2966
e alcantaraguesthouse@sky.com
w alcantaraguesthouse.co.uk

**Amberley Lodge Guest House** ★★★
*Guest Accommodation*
1 Howard Road, Shirley
SO15 5BB
t (023) 8022 3789
e contact@amberleyguesthouse.co.uk
w amberleyguesthouse.co.uk

**Angela House B&B** ★★★
*Bed & Breakfast*
37 Whitehouse Gardens,
Regents Park SO15 0SB
t (023) 8070 3969
e angela.davies37@btinternet.com

**Argyle Lodge Guest House**
★★★★
*Guest Accommodation*
13 Landguard Road, Shirley
SO15 5DL
t (023) 8022 4063
e judith@higgs1236.freeserve.co.uk
w argylelodge.com

**The Avenue Bed and Breakfast**
Rating Applied For
*Bed & Breakfast*
19 The Avenue, Southampton
SO17 1XF
t (023) 8022 1450
e theavenuebandb@aol.com
w southamptonbandb.co.uk/

**Banister Guest House** ★★★
*Guest Accommodation*
11 Brighton Road,
Southampton SO15 2JJ
t (023) 8022 1279
e info@banisterhotel.co.uk
w banisterhotel.co.uk

**Brunswick Lodge** ★★★★
*Guest Accommodation*
100 Anglesea Road, Shirley
SO15 5QS
t (023) 8077 4777
w brunswicklodge.co.uk

**Dormy House** ★★★★
*Guest Accommodation*
21 Barnes Lane, Sarisbury
Green SO31 7DA
t (01489) 572626
e dormyhousehotel@warsash.globalnet.co.uk
w dormyhousehotel.net

**Eaton Court** ★★★
*Guest Accommodation*
32 Hill Lane, Southampton
SO15 5AY
t (023) 8022 3081
e ecourthot@aol.com
w eatoncourtsouthampton.co.uk

**Ellenborough House** ★★★
*Guest Accommodation*
172 Hill Lane, Southampton
SO15 5DB
t (023) 8022 1716
e ellenboroughhse@aol.com
w ellenboroughhouse.co.uk

**Fenland Guest House** ★★★
*Guest Accommodation*
79 Hill Lane, Southampton
SO15 5AD
t (023) 8022 0360
e fenland@btconnect.com
w fenlandguesthouse.co.uk

**Lakeside** ★★★★
*Bed & Breakfast*
West Common, Blackfield
SO45 1XJ
t (023) 8089 8926
e tonycavell@aol.com
w lakesidebandb.net

**Landguard House Guest House** ★★★ *Guest House*
44 Landguard Road,
Southampton SO15 5DP
t (023) 8022 9708
e enquiries@landguardhouse.co.uk
w landguardhouse.co.uk

**Linden Guest House** ★★★
*Guest Accommodation*
51-53 The Polygon,
Southampton SO15 2BP
t (023) 8022 5653
e trisha@lindenguesthouse.net
w lindenguesthouse.net

**Madison House** ★★★
*Guest Accommodation*
137 Hill Lane, Southampton
SO15 5AF
t (023) 8033 3374
e foley@madisonhouse.co.uk
w madisonhouse.co.uk

**Mayfair Guest House**
★★★★
*Guest Accommodation*
11 Landguard Road,
Southampton SO15 5DL
t (023) 8022 9861
e info@themayfairguesthouse.co.uk
w themayfairguesthouse.co.uk

**Mayview Guest House** ★★★
*Guest Accommodation*
30 The Polygon, Southampton
SO15 2BN
t (023) 8022 0907
e info@mayview.co.uk
w mayview.co.uk

**Rivendell Guest House**
★★★★
*Guest Accommodation*
19 Landguard Road, Hill Lane,
Southampton SO15 5DL
t (023) 8022 3240
e rivendelllalley@talktalkbusiness.net

**The Spinnaker** ★★★★ *Inn*
286 Bridge Road, Lower
Swanwick SO31 7EB
t (01489) 572123
e mail@thespinnakerinn.co.uk
w thespinnakerinn.co.uk/

## SOUTHERHAM
East Sussex

**Bramble Barn** ★★★★
*Bed & Breakfast*
Southerham, Lewes BN8 6JN
t (01273) 474924

## SOUTHSEA
Hampshire

**Birchwood Guest House**
★★★★
*Guest Accommodation*
44 Waverley Road, Portsmouth
PO5 2PP
t (023) 9281 1337
e enquiries@birchwood.uk.com
w birchwood.uk.com

**Ferryman Guest House**
★★★ *Guest Accommodation*
16 Victoria Road South,
Portsmouth PO5 2BZ
t (023) 9287 5824
e theferrymanhotel@hotmail.com
w ferryman-hotel.co.uk

**Portsmouth & Southsea Backpackers Lodge** ★★
*Backpackers*
4 Florence Road, Southsea
PO5 2NE
t (023) 9283 2495
e portsmouthbackpackers@hotmail.com
w portsmouthbackpackers.co.uk

**The Retreat** ★★★★
*Guest House* **GOLD AWARD**
35 Grove Road South,
Portsmouth PO5 3QS
t (023) 9235 3701
e theretreatguesthouse@yahoo.co.uk
w theretreatguesthouse.co.uk

**University of Portsmouth**
★★ *Guest Accommodation*
Queen Elizabeth The Queen
Mother Hall, Furze Lane,
Southsea PO4 8LW
t (023) 9284 4884

## STAINES
Surrey

**The Swan** ★★★ *Inn*
The Hythe, Staines TW18 3JB
t (01784) 452494
e swan.hotel@fullers.co.uk
w fullersinns.co.uk

## STANFORD IN THE VALE
Oxfordshire

**Cox's Hall** ★★★★
*Bed & Breakfast*
High Street, Stanford-in-the-Vale, Faringdon SN7 8NQ
t (01367) 710248

## STANSTED
Kent

**The Black Horse** ★★★ *Inn*
Tumblefield Road, Stansted
TN15 7PR
t (01732) 822355
e blackhorsekent@tiscali.co.uk

## STAPLEHURST
Kent

**White Cottage** ★★★★
*Bed & Breakfast*
**SILVER AWARD**
Headcorn Road, Hawkenbury,
Tonbridge TN12 0DU
t (01580) 891480
e john.batten@mac.com
w the-whitecottage.co.uk

## STEEPLE ASTON
Oxfordshire

**Old Toms** ★★★
*Bed & Breakfast*
North Side, Steeple Aston
OX25 4SE
t (01869) 340212
e marymlloyd@aol.com

## STELLING MINNIS
Kent

**Great Field Farm** ★★★★
*Farmhouse* **SILVER AWARD**
Misling Lane, Stelling Minnis,
Canterbury CT4 6DE
t (01227) 709223
e Greatfieldfarm@aol.com
w great-field-farm.co.uk

## STEVENTON
Oxfordshire

**Tethers End** ★★★
*Bed & Breakfast*
Abingdon Road, Steventon,
Abingdon OX13 6RW
t (01235) 834015

## STEYNING
West Sussex

**Nash Manor** ★★★★
*Guest Accommodation*
**SILVER AWARD**
Horsham Road, Steyning
BN44 3AA
t (01903) 814988
e info@nashmanor.co.uk
w nashmanor.co.uk

**The Penfold Gallery Guest House** ★★★★★
*Guest House* **SILVER AWARD**
High Street, Steyning
BN44 3GG
t (01903) 815595
e johnturner57@aol.com
w artyguesthouse.co.uk

## STOCKBRIDGE
Hampshire

**The White Hart Inn** ★★★★
*Inn*
High Street, Stockbridge
SO20 6HF
t (01264) 810663
e whitehart.stockbridge@fullers.co.uk
w accommodating-inns.co.uk

## STOKE ROW
Oxfordshire

**The Cherry Tree Inn** ★★★★
*Inn*
Stoke Row, Henley-on-Thames
RG9 5QA
t (01491) 680430
e info@thecherrytreeinn.com
w thecherrytreeinn.com

## STONE-IN-OXNEY
Kent

**Tighe Farmhouse** ★★★★
*Farmhouse*
Stone-in-Oxney, Tenterden
TN30 7JU
t (01233) 758251
e robin.kingsley@ndierct.co.uk
w accommodationrye.co.uk

## STREATLEY
Berkshire

**Streatley On Thames YHA**
★★★ *Hostel*
Hill House, Reading Road, Streatley RG8 9JJ
t (01491) 872278
e streatley@yha.org.uk
w yhastreatley.org.uk

## STROOD
Kent

**The Sundial** ★★
*Bed & Breakfast*
18 Ranscombe Close, Strood
ME2 2PB
t (01634) 721831
e sean@company8234.freeserve.co.uk

**The White Cottage** ★★★★
*Guest Accommodation*
41 Rede Court Road, Rochester
ME2 3SP
t (01634) 719988

## SUNNINGDALE
Berkshire

**Beaufort House** ★★★★
*Bed & Breakfast*
Broomfield Park, Ascot SL5 0JT
t (01344) 622991
e jenny@beaufort-house.com
w beaufort-house.com

## SWALCLIFFE
Oxfordshire

**Grange Farm Bed and Breakfast** ★★★ *Farmhouse*
Swalcliffe Grange, Swalcliffe
OX15 5EX
t (01295) 780206
e taylor@swalcliffe-grange.freeserve.co.uk
w swalcliffegrange.com

## SWANLEY
Kent

**Greenacres** ★★★★
*Bed & Breakfast*
15 Greenacre Close, Swanley
BR8 8HT
t (01322) 613656
e pauline.snow1@btinternet.com
w greenacrebandb.co.uk

## SWAY
Hampshire

**The Arches** ★★★★
*Bed & Breakfast*
Station Road, Sway, Lymington
SO41 6AA
t (01590) 681339
e lynn@thenewforest.wanadoo.co.uk
w the-arches.co.uk

**Manor Farm** ★★★
*Bed & Breakfast*
Coombe Lane, Sway SO41 6BP
t (01590) 683542

**The Nurse's Cottage** ★★★★
*Guest Accommodation*
Station Road, Sway, Lymington
SO41 6BA
t (01590) 683402

**Tiverton** ★★★★
*Bed & Breakfast*
9 Cruse Close, Sway, Lymington SO41 6AY
t (01590) 683092
e ronrowe@talk21.com
w tivertonnewforest.co.uk

## TAPLOW
Buckinghamshire

**Bridge Cottage Guest House**
★★★ *Guest Accommodation*
Bath Road, Maidenhead
SL6 0AR
t (01628) 626805
e bridgecottagebb@btconnect.com
w bridgecottagebb.co.uk

## TELSCOMBE
East Sussex

**Stud Farm House** ★★★★
*Farmhouse*
Telscombe Village, Newhaven
BN7 3HZ
t (01273) 302486
e ninaamour5@yahoo.co.uk

**TelscombeYouth Hostel** ★★
*Hostel*
Bank Cottages, Telscombe Village, Newhaven BN7 3HZ
t (01273) 301357
e reservations@yha.org.uk
w yha.org.uk

## TENTERDEN
Kent

**Collina House Hotel** ★★★★
*Guest Accommodation*
5 East Hill, Tenterden
TN30 6RL
t (01580) 764852
e enquiries@collinahousehotel.co.uk
w collinahousehotel.co.uk

**Kench Hill Centre**
Rating Applied For
*Hostel*
Appledore Road, Tenterden
TN30 7DG
t (01580) 762073
e admin@kenchhill.co.uk
w kenchhill.co.uk

**Signal Cottage Bed & Breakfast** ★★★★
*Bed & Breakfast*
3 Rogersmead, Tenterden
TN30 6LF
t (01580) 761806

**The White Cottage** ★★★
*Bed & Breakfast*
London Beach, Ashford Road, Tenterden TN30 6SR
t (01233) 850583
e ruth@thewhitecottagebedandbreakfast.co.uk
w thewhitecottagebedandbreakfast.co.uk

## THAKEHAM
West Sussex

**Abingworth Hall**
Rating Applied For
*Guest Accommodation*
Storrington Road, Pulborough
RH20 3EF
t (020) 8511 1534

## THAME
Oxfordshire

**Field Farm** ★★★★
*Farmhouse*
Rycote Lane, North Weston
OX9 2HQ
t (01844) 215428
e suzanne@fieldfarmbandb.co.uk
w fieldfarmbandb.co.uk

## THATCHAM
Berkshire

**One Church Lane** ★★★★
*Bed & Breakfast*
Thatcham RG19 3JL
t (01635) 869098
e johnhousemaster@aol.com

## THURNHAM
Kent

**Black Horse Inn** ★★★★ *Inn*
Pilgrims Way, Thurnham, Maidstone ME14 3LD
t (01622) 737185
e info@welliboot.net
w welliboot.net

**Cold Blow 3** *Bunkhouse*
Cold Blow Farm, Cold Blow Lane, Maidstone ME14 3LR
t (01622) 735038

**Coldblow Farm Bunkbarns**
*Bunkhouse*
Cold Blow Lane, Thurnham, Maidstone ME14 3LR
t (01622) 735038
e campingbarns@yha.org.uk
w coldblow-camping.co.uk

**Coldblow Farm Camping Barn** *Camping Barn*
Cold Blow Lane, Thurnham, Maidstone ME14 3LR
t (01622) 735038
e campingbarns@yha.org.uk
w coldblow-camping.co.uk

## THURSLEY
Surrey

**Hindhead YHA** ★ *Hostel*
Devil's Punchbowl, Off Portmouth Road, Godalming
GU8 6NS
t (01428) 604285
w yha.org.uk

## TONBRIDGE
Kent

**86 Hadlow Road** ★★
*Bed & Breakfast*
Tonbridge TN9 1PA
t (01732) 357332
e aurelia.gemini@talktalk.net

**Fieldswood** ★★★★
*Bed & Breakfast*
**SILVER AWARD**
Hadlow Park, Hadlow, Tonbridge TN11 0HZ
t (01732) 851433
e info@fieldswood.co.uk
w fieldswood.co.uk

## TOTLAND BAY
Isle of Wight

**Chart House** ★★★★
*Guest Accommodation*
**SILVER AWARD**
Madeira Road, Totland Bay
PO39 0BJ
t (01983) 755091
e info@islandbreaks.co.uk

**Clifton House** ★★★
*Guest Accommodation*
Colwell Common Road, Totland Bay PO39 0DD
t (01983) 753237
e clifton.house@btinternet.com

**The Granville** ★★★★
*Bed & Breakfast*
**SILVER AWARD**
Granville Road, Totland Bay
PO39 0AZ
t (01983) 756030
e granvilleiow@googlemail.com
w the-granville.co.uk

**Littledene Lodge** ★★★
*Guest House*
Granville Road, Totland Bay
PO39 0AX
t (01983) 752411
e littledenehotel@aol.com

**Sandy Lane Bed and Breakfast** ★★★★
*Guest Accommodation*
Sandy Lane, Colwell Common Road, Totland Bay PO39 0DD
t (01983) 752240
e louise@sandylane-iow.co.uk
w sandylane-iow.co.uk

**Totland Bay YHA** ★★★
*Hostel*
Hurst Hill, Totland Bay
PO39 0HD
t (01983) 752165
e totland@yha.org.uk
w yha.org.uk

## TROTTON
West Sussex

**Orchard House** ★★★★
*Bed & Breakfast*
**SILVER AWARD**
Mill Lane, Trotton, Midhurst
GU31 5JT
t (01730) 812530
e orchardhouse.trotton@btinternet.com
w orchardhouse.cabanova.com

## TWYFORD
Hampshire

**Highfield Cottage** ★★★★
*Bed & Breakfast*
Old Rectory Lane, Twyford
SO21 1NR
t (01962) 712921
e highfieldcottage@gmail.com
w smoothhound.co.uk/hotels/highfieldcott

**Orchard House** ★★★
*Bed & Breakfast*
Manor Road, Twyford
SO21 1RJ
t (01962) 712087
e susan@smflemons.fsnet.co.uk
w orchardhousetwyford.co.uk

**Twyford House** ★★★★
*Bed & Breakfast*
High Street, Twyford
SO21 1NU
t (01962) 713114
e crchtwyho@aol.com
w twyfordhousebnb.co.uk

### UCKFIELD
East Sussex

**South Paddock** ★★★★★
*Bed & Breakfast*
**SILVER AWARD**
Maresfield Park, Uckfield
TN22 2HA
t (01825) 762335

### UFFINGTON
Oxfordshire

**Norton House** ★★★★
*Guest Accommodation*
**SILVER AWARD**
Broad Street, Uffington,
Faringdon SN7 7RA
t (01367) 820230
e carloberman@aol.com

### UPNOR
Kent

**Arethusa Venture Centre**
★★★ *Activity Accommodation*
Rochester ME2 4XB
t (01634) 719933
e lwright@shaftesbury.org.uk
w arethusa.org.uk

### UPPER FARRINGDON
Hampshire

**Old Timbers** ★★★★
*Bed & Breakfast*
1 Crows Lane, Farringdon
GU34 3ED
t (01420) 588449
e info@oldtimberscottage.co.uk
w oldtimberscottage.co.uk

### UPPER LAMBOURN
Berkshire

**Saxon Cottage** ★★★★
*Guest Accommodation*
Upper Lambourn, Hungerford
RG17 8QN
t (01488) 71503
e judy.gaselee@virgin.net

### VENTNOR
Isle of Wight

**Bonchurch Manor** ★★★★
*Guest Accommodation*
Bonchurch Shute, Bonchurch
PO38 1NU
t (01983) 852868
e reception@bonchurchmanor.com
w bonchurchmanor.com

**Brunswick House** ★★★★
*Guest House*
Victoria Street, Ventnor
PO38 1ET
t (01983) 852656
e brunswick@unicombox.co.uk
w brunswickhouse-web.co.uk

**The Enchanted Manor**
★★★★★
*Guest Accommodation*
**GOLD AWARD**
St Catherine's Point, Sandrock
Road, Niton PO38 2NG
t (01983) 730215
e info@enchantedmanor.co.uk
w enchantedmanor.co.uk

**The Hermitage Country House** ★★★★★
*Guest Accommodation*
**GOLD AWARD**
St Catherines Down, Ventnor
PO38 2PD
t (01983) 730010
e enquiries@hermitage-iow.co.uk
w hermitage-iow.co.uk

**The Leconfield** ★★★★★
*Guest Accommodation*
**GOLD AWARD**
85 Leeson Road, Upper
Bonchurch, Ventnor PO38 1PU
t (01983) 852196
e enquiries@leconfieldhotel.com
w leconfieldhotel.com

**Westfield House** ★★★★
*Bed & Breakfast*
Shore Road, Bonchurch
PO38 1RF
t (01983) 853232
e garethhughesiow@hotmail.co.uk

**Windsor Carlton**
Rating Applied For
*Guest House*
4-5 Alexandra Gardens,
Ventnor PO38 1EE
t (01983) 852543
e windsorcarlton@btinternet.com
w windsorcarltonhotel.co.uk

### VERNHAM DEAN
Hampshire

**Upton Cottage** ★★★
*Bed & Breakfast*
Vernham Dean, Andover
SP11 0JY
t (01264) 737640
e info@uptoncottageb-and-b.co.uk

### WADDESDON
Buckinghamshire

**The Lion** ★★★★ *Inn*
70a High Street, Waddesdon
HP18 0JD
t (01296) 651227
e info@thelionwaddesdon.co.uk
w thelionwaddesdon.co.uk

**The Old Dairy** ★★★
*Bed & Breakfast*
4 High Street, Waddesdon
HP18 0JA
t (01296) 658627
e hconyard@tesco.net
w theolddairywaddesdon.co.uk

### WADHURST
East Sussex

**The Greyhound** ★★★ *Inn*
St James Square, Wadhurst
TN5 7EN
t (01892) 783224
e jharrold@lineone.net

**Spring Cottage** ★★★
*Bed & Breakfast*
90 Felpham Road, Felpham,
Bognor Regis PO22 7PD
t (01243) 868500
e springcottage.bb@virgin.net
w springcottagebb.co.uk

### WALBERTON
West Sussex

**Longacre** ★★★★
*Bed & Breakfast*
The Street, Walberton
BN18 0PY
t (01243) 543542
e longacrebandb@tinyworld.co.uk
w visitsussex.org

### WALLINGFORD
Oxfordshire

**Fords Farm** ★★★★
*Farmhouse* **SILVER AWARD**
Ewelme, Wallingford
OX10 6HU
t (01491) 839272

**Huntington House** ★★★
*Bed & Breakfast*
18 Wood Street, Wallingford
OX10 0AX
t (01491) 839201
e hunting311@aol.com

**Little Gables** ★★★★
*Bed & Breakfast*
166 Crowmarsh Hill,
Crowmarsh Gifford,
Wallingford OX10 8BG
t (01491) 837834 &
07860 148882
e marketing@littlegables.co.uk
w stayingaway.com

**Marsh House** ★★★★
*Bed & Breakfast*
7 Court Drive, Shillingford
OX10 7ER
t (01865) 858496
e marsh.house@talk21.com
w marshhousebandb.co.uk

**North Moreton House**
★★★★★
*Guest Accommodation*
**SILVER AWARD**
High Street, North Moreton
OX11 9AT
t (01235) 813283
e katie@northmoretonhouse.co.uk
w northmoretonhouse.co.uk

### WALMER
Kent

**Hardicot Guest House**
★★★★ *Bed & Breakfast*
Kingsdown Road, Walmer,
Deal CT14 8AW
t (01304) 373867
e guestboss@btopenworld.com
w hardicot-guest-house.co.uk

### WANTAGE
Oxfordshire

**B&B in Wantage** ★★★★
*Bed & Breakfast*
50 Foliat Drive, Wantage
OX12 7AL
t (01235) 760495
e eleanor@eaturner.freeserve.co.uk
w geocities.com/bandbinwantage

**Old Yeomanry House**
★★★★
*Guest Accommodation*
27 Wallingford Street,
Wantage OX12 8AU
t (01235) 772778
e jenny@yeomanryhouse.co.uk
w yeomanryhouse.co.uk

**Regis Guest House** ★★★★
*Guest House* **SILVER AWARD**
12 Charlton Road, Wantage
OX12 8ER
t (01235) 762860
e millie_rastall@hotmail.com
w regisguesthouse.com

### WARNHAM
West Sussex

**Nowhere House** ★★★
*Bed & Breakfast*
Dorking Road, Durfold Hill,
Horsham RH12 3RZ
t (01306) 627272

### WARNINGCAMP
West Sussex

**Furzetor** ★★★★
*Bed & Breakfast*
Clay Lane, Warningcamp,
Arundel BN18 9QN
t (01903) 882974
e furzetor@hotmail.com

**YHA Arundel** ★★★ *Hostel*
Warningcamp, Arundel
BN18 9QY
t (01903) 882204
e arundel@yha.org.uk
w yha.org.uk

### WASH WATER
Berkshire

**The Chase Guest House**
★★★★ *Bed & Breakfast*
**SILVER AWARD**
Waterbourne, Andover Drove
RG20 0LZ
t (01635) 231441
e chaseguesthouse@btconnect.com
w thechaseguesthouse.com

### WATER STRATFORD
Buckinghamshire

**The Rolling Acres** ★★★★
*Bed & Breakfast*
Water Stratford, Buckingham
MK18 5DX
t (01280) 847302
e info@rolling-acres.co.uk

### WATERLOOVILLE
Hampshire

**Fairways**
Rating Applied For
*Guest Accommodation*
The Brow, Waterlooville
PO7 5DA
t (023) 9271 1711
e davidkeeping@ntlworld.com

**Holly Dale** ★★
*Bed & Breakfast*
11 Lovedean Lane,
Waterlooville PO8 8HH
t (023) 9259 2047
e pwengland@uku.co.uk

**New Haven Bed & Breakfast**
★★★ *Bed & Breakfast*
193 London Road,
Waterlooville PO7 7RN
t (023) 9226 8559
e newhaven@toucansurf.com

### WATERSFIELD
West Sussex

**The Willows** ★★★★
*Bed & Breakfast*
London Road, Watersfield,
Pulborough RH20 1NB
t (01798) 831576
e mount@ukonline.co.uk
w mountbandb.co.uk

## WEALD
Oxfordshire

**The Coach House** ★★★★
*Bed & Breakfast*
College Farm, Bridge Street, Bampton OX18 2HG
t (01993) 851041
e info@thecoachhousebampton.co.uk
w thecoachhousebampton.co.uk

## WENDOVER
Buckinghamshire

**17 Icknield Close** ★★★
*Guest Accommodation*
Wendover, Aylesbury HP22 6HG
t (01296) 583285
e grbr.samuels@ntlworld.com

---

**Dunsmore Edge** ★★★
*Bed & Breakfast*
Dunsmore Lane, London Road, Wendover HP22 6PN
t (01296) 623080
e drackford@btinternet.com

## WEST BRABOURNE
Kent

**Bulltown Farmhouse Bed & Breakfast** ★★★★
*Guest Accommodation*
Bulltown Lane, West Brabourne, Ashford TN25 5NB
t (01233) 813505
e wiltons@bulltown.fsnet.co.uk

## WEST CHILTINGTON
West Sussex

**The Old School House B & B** ★★★★★ *Bed & Breakfast*
**SILVER AWARD**
Church Street, Pulborough RH20 2JW
t (01798) 812585
e enquiries@theoldschoolhousebandb.com
w theoldschoolhousebandb.com

## WEST CLANDON
Surrey

**The Oaks** ★★
*Bed & Breakfast*
Highcotts Lane, West Clandon GU4 7XA
t (01483) 222531
e kate_broad@yahoo.co.uk

## WEST HARTING
West Sussex

**Three Quebec** ★★★★
*Bed & Breakfast*
West Harting, Petersfield, Midhurst GU31 5PG
t (01730) 825386
e patriciastevens@threequebec.co.uk
w threequebec.co.uk

## WEST HORSLEY
Surrey

**Silkmore** ★★★★
*Bed & Breakfast*
Silkmore Lane, West Horsley KT24 6JQ
t (01483) 282042
e carolyn@leporello.co.uk

## WEST MALLING
Kent

**Appledene** ★★★★
*Guest Accommodation*
**SILVER AWARD**
164 Norman Road, West Malling ME19 6RW
t (01732) 842071
e appledene@westmalling.freeserve.co.uk
w smoothhound.co.uk/hotelsappledene

## WEST STOKE
West Sussex

**West Stoke House** ★★★★★
*Restaurant with Rooms*
**GOLD AWARD**
Downs Road, West Stoke, Chichester PO18 9BN
t (01243) 575226
e info@weststokehouse.co.uk
w weststokehouse.co.uk

## WEST WITTERING
West Sussex

**The Beach House** ★★★
*Guest House*
Rookwood Road, West Wittering, Witterings PO20 8LT
t (01243) 514800
e info@beachhse.co.uk
w beachhse.co.uk

## WESTCOTT
Surrey

**Corner House Bed & Breakfast** ★★
*Guest Accommodation*
Guildford Road, Westcott RH4 3QE
t (01306) 888798
e ktnyman@tiscali.co.uk

## WESTGATE ON SEA
Kent

**White Lodge Guest House** ★★★★ *Guest House*
12 Domneva Road, Westgate-on-Sea CT8 8PE
t (01843) 831828
e margaret@whitelodge.co.uk
w whitelodge.co.uk

## WESTON-ON-THE-GREEN
Oxfordshire

**Westfield Court House B&B** ★★★★ *Bed & Breakfast*
North Lane, Weston-on-the-Green OX25 3RG
t (01869) 350777
e jbrownwest@aol.com
w westfieldcourthouse.co.uk

---

**Weston Grounds Farm** ★★★
*Farmhouse*
Northampton Road, Weston-on-the-Green, Bicester OX25 3QX
t (01869) 351168

## WESTON TURVILLE
Buckinghamshire

**Loosley House B&B** ★★★
*Guest House*
87 New Road, Weston Turville HP22 5QT
t (01296) 484157
w loosleyhouse.co.uk

## WEYBRIDGE
Surrey

**Riverdene Gardens** ★★★★★
*Guest Accommodation*
**SILVER AWARD**
1 Oatlands Drive, Weybridge KT13 9NA
t (01932) 223574
w riverdenegardens.co.uk

## WHITCHURCH
Hampshire

**Peak House Farm** ★★★
*Farmhouse*
Cole Henley, Whitchurch RG28 7QJ
t (01256) 892052
e peakhouse.farm@btinternet.com
w peakhousefarm.co.uk

## WHITSTABLE
Kent

**Alliston House** ★★★★
*Bed & Breakfast*
**SILVER AWARD**
1 Joy Lane, Whitstable CT5 4LS
t (01227) 779066
e bobgough57@aol.com
w stayinwhitstable.co.uk

---

**The Captain's House** ★★★
*Bed & Breakfast*
56 Harbour Street, Whitstable CT5 1AQ
t (01227) 275156

---

**Copeland House** ★★★★
*Guest House*
4 Island Wall, Whitstable CT5 1EP
t (01227) 266207
e mail@copelandhouse.co.uk
w copelandhouse.co.uk

---

**The Duke of Cumberland** ★★★ *Inn*
High Street, Whitstable CT5 1AP
t (01227) 280617
e enquiries@thedukeinwhitstable.co.uk
w thedukeinwhitstable.co.uk

---

**The Pearl Fisher** ★★★★
*Guest Accommodation*
**SILVER AWARD**
103 Cromwell Road, Whitstable CT5 1NL
t (01227) 771000
e stay@thepearlfisher.co.uk
w thepearlfisher.com

---

**Victoria Villa** ★★★★
*Guest Accommodation*
**GOLD AWARD**
Victoria Street, Whitstable CT5 1JB
t (01227) 779191
e victoria.villa@virgin.net
w victoria-villa.i12.com

---

**Windy Ridge** ★★★★
*Guest Accommodation*
Wraik Hill, Whitstable CT5 3BY
t (01227) 263506
e scott@windyridgewhitstable.co.uk
w windyridgewhitstable.co.uk

## WIGGINTON
Oxfordshire

**Pretty Bush Barn** ★★★★
*Bed & Breakfast*
Wigginton, Banbury OX15 4LD
t (01608) 738262
e trev@prettybushbarn.fsnet.co.uk

## WINCHELSEA
East Sussex

**Winchelsea Lodge Motel** ★★★★
*Guest Accommodation*
Hastings Road, Winchelsea TN36 4AD
t (01797) 226211
e julie.hannah@1066motels.co.uk
w thelodgeatwinchelsea.co.uk

## WINCHESTER
Hampshire

**12 Christchurch Road** ★★★
*Bed & Breakfast*
Winchester SO23 9SR
t (01962) 854272
e pjspatton@yahoo.co.uk

---

**152 Teg Down Meads** ★★★
*Bed & Breakfast*
Winchester SO22 5NS
t (01962) 862628
e l.chalk4@ntlworld.com

---

**29 Christchurch Road** ★★★★★ *Bed & Breakfast*
**SILVER AWARD**
Christchurch Road, Winchester SO23 9SU
t (01962) 868661
e dilke@waitrose.com
w fetherstondilke.com

---

**5 Clifton Terrace** ★★★★
*Bed & Breakfast*
**SILVER AWARD**
Winchester SO22 5BJ
t (01962) 890053
e chrissiejohnston@hotmail.com

---

**53a Parchment Street** ★★★
*Bed & Breakfast*
Winchester SO23 8BA
t (01962) 849962

---

**58 Hyde Street** ★★★
*Bed & Breakfast*
Hyde Street, Winchester SO23 7DY
t (01962) 854646
e gj.harvey@ntlworld.com
w 58hydestreet.co.uk

---

**Acacia** ★★★★
*Bed & Breakfast*
**SILVER AWARD**
44 Kilham Lane, Winchester SO22 5PT
t (01962) 852259
e amelia.shirley@btinternet.com
w btinternet.com/~eric.buchanan

---

**Cheriton House** ★★★
*Bed & Breakfast*
61 Cheriton Road, Winchester SO22 5AY
t (01962) 620374
e cheritonhouse@hotmail.com

**Dawn Cottage** ★★★★★
*Bed & Breakfast*
**SILVER AWARD**
99 Romsey Road, Winchester
SO22 5PQ
t (01962) 869956
e dawncottage@hotmail.com

**Giffard House** ★★★★★
*Guest Accommodation*
**GOLD AWARD**
**50 Christchurch Road,**
**Winchester SO23 9SU**
**t (01962) 852628**
**e giffardhotel@aol.com**
**w giffardhotel.co.uk**

**The King Alfred Pub** ★★★★
*Inn*
Saxon Road, Winchester
SO23 7DJ
t (01962) 854370
e thekingalfredpub@yahoo.co.uk

**Lainston** ★★★
*Bed & Breakfast*
Lainston Close, Winchester
SO22 5LJ
t (01962) 866072
e julian@lainston.co.uk
w lainston.co.uk

**The Lilacs** ★★
*Bed & Breakfast*
1 Harestock Close, Winchester
SO22 6NP
t (01962) 884122
e susanm.pell@ntlworld.com
w smoothhound.co.uk/hotels/lilacs

**R J and V J Weller** ★★★
*Bed & Breakfast*
63 Upper Brook Street,
Winchester SO23 8DG
t (01962) 620367
e robert.weller@ntlworld.com

**Rowanhurst** ★★★★
*Bed & Breakfast*
Northbrook Avenue,
Winchester SO23 0JW
t (01962) 862433
e joanne.kingswell@talk21.com

**St Johns Croft** ★★★
*Bed & Breakfast*
St Johns Street, Winchester
SO23 0HF
t (01962) 859976
e dottyfraser@gmail.com

**St Margaret's** ★★★
*Bed & Breakfast*
3 St Michael's Road,
Winchester SO23 9JE
t (01962) 861450
e brigid@bbrett.f2s.com
w winchesterbandb.com

**Staddle Stones** ★★★★
*Bed & Breakfast*
15b Bereweeke Avenue,
Winchester SO22 6BH
t (01962) 877883
e sheila@staddle-stones.freeserve.co.uk
w staddle-stones.co.uk

**Sycamores** ★★★
*Bed & Breakfast*
4 Bereweeke Close,
Winchester SO22 6AR
t (01962) 867242
e sycamores.b-and-b@virgin.net

**The University of Winchester** ★★★ *Campus*
West Hill, Winchester
SO22 4NR
t (01962) 827322
e conferences@winchester.ac.uk

**Windy Ridge** ★★★
*Bed & Breakfast*
99 Andover Road, Winchester
SO22 6AX
t (01962) 882527
e angela.westall@virgin.net

**The Wykeham Arms** ★★★
*Inn*
75 Kingsgate Street,
Winchester SO23 9PE
t (01962) 853834
e wykeham.arms@fullers.co.uk
w fullersinns.co.uk

## WINDSOR
Berkshire

**3 York Road** ★★★
*Bed & Breakfast*
Windsor SL4 3NX
t (01753) 861741
e kerrin@tiscali.co.uk

**76 Duke Street** ★★★★
*Bed & Breakfast*
Windsor SL4 1SQ
t (01753) 620636
e admin@76dukestreet.co.uk
w 76dukestreet.co.uk

**Alma Lodge Guest House**
★★★ *Guest House*
58 Alma Road, Windsor
SL4 3HA
t (01753) 855620
e info@almalodge.co.uk
w almalodge.co.uk

**Barbara's Bed & Breakfast**
★★★ *Bed & Breakfast*
16 Maidenhead Road, Windsor
SL4 5EQ
t (01753) 840273
e bbandb@btinternet.com

**Bluebell House** ★★★★
*Guest Accommodation*
**Lovel Lane, Woodside,**
**Winkfield, Windsor SL4 2DG**
**t (01344) 886828**
**e registrations@bluebellhousehotel.co.uk**
**w bluebellhousehotel.co.uk**

**The Clarence** ★★★
*Guest House*
**9 Clarence Road, Windsor**
**SL4 5AE**
**t (01753) 864436**
**e clarence.hotel@btconnect.com**
**w clarence-hotel.co.uk**

**The Cottage Inn** ★★★★ *Inn*
Winkfield Street, Winkfield
SL4 4SW
t (01344) 882242
e cottage@btconnect.com
w cottage-inn.co.uk

**Langton House** ★★★★
*Guest Accommodation*
46 Alma Road, Windsor
SL4 3HA
t (01753) 858299
e paul@langtonhouse.co.uk
w langtonhouse.co.uk

**The Oast Barn** ★★★★
*Bed & Breakfast*
Staines Road, Wraysbury
TW19 5BS
t (01784) 481598
e bandb@oastbarn.com
w oastbarn.com

**The Old Farmhouse** ★★★★
*Bed & Breakfast*
**SILVER AWARD**
Dedworth Road, Oakley Green
SL4 4LH
t (01753) 850411
e debbie@theoldfarmhouse.fslife.co.uk
w theoldfarmhousewindsor.com

**Oscar Lodge** ★★
*Guest House*
65 Vansittart Road, Windsor
SL4 5DB
t (01753) 830613
e oscarhotel@btconnect.com
w oscarhotel.co.uk

**The Prince Albert** ★★★ *Inn*
2 Clewer Hill Road, Windsor
SL4 4BS
t (01753) 864788
e theprincealbert@tiscali.co.uk
w theprincealbertpub.com

**Rutlands** ★★★★
*Bed & Breakfast*
St Leonards Road, Windsor
SL4 3DA
t (01753) 859533

**The Trooper** ★★★ *Inn*
97 St Leonard's Road, Windsor
SL4 3BZ
t (01753) 670123
e trooper@fullers.co.uk
w fullersinns.co.uk

**Windsor Edwardian** ★★★★
*Bed & Breakfast*
21 Osborne Road, Windsor
SL4 3EG
t (01753) 858995
e info@windsoredwardian.co.uk
w windsoredwardian.co.uk

## WINSLOW
Buckinghamshire

**Witsend** ★★★
*Bed & Breakfast*
9 Buckingham Road, Winslow
MK18 3DT
t (01296) 712503
e sheila.spatcher@tesco.net

## WITNEY
Oxfordshire

**Crofters Guest House**
★★★★
*Guest Accommodation*
29 Oxford Hill, Witney
OX28 3JU
t (01993) 778165
e crofters.ghouse@virgin.net

**The Laurels (Witney)** ★★★
*Guest House*
53 Burford Road, Witney
OX28 6DR
t (01993) 702193
e thelaurelsbandb@fsmail.net
w thelaurelsguesthouse.co.uk

**Pinkhill Cottage** ★★★★
*Bed & Breakfast*
45 Rack End, Witney
OX29 7SA
t (01865) 300544
e jane@pinkhill.plus.com
w smoothhound.co.uk/hotels/pinkhill

**Quarrydene** ★★★
*Guest Accommodation*
17 Dene Rise, Witney
OX28 6LU
t (01993) 772152
e jeanniemarshall@quarrydene.fsworld.co.uk

**Springhill Farm Bed & Breakfast** ★★★ *Farmhouse*
Cogges, Witney OX29 6UL
t (01993) 704919
e jan@strainge.fsnet.co.uk

**The Witney** ★★★
*Guest Accommodation*
7 Church Green, Witney
OX28 4AZ
t (01993) 702137
e enquiries@thewitneyhotel.co.uk
w thewitneyhotel.co.uk

## WIVELROD
Hampshire

**Halketts** ★★★★
*Bed & Breakfast*
72 Kings Hill, Beech GU34 4AN
t (01420) 562258

## WOBURN SANDS
Buckinghamshire

**The Old Stables** ★★★★
*Guest House*
Bow Brickhill Road, Woburn
Sands MK17 8DE
t (01908) 281340
e info@oldstables.co.uk
w oldstables.co.uk

**Woodley's Cottage**
Rating Applied For
*Guest Accommodation*
2 The Granary, Bow Brickhill
Road, Milton Keynes
MK17 8DE
t (01908) 281460
e info@woodleyscottage.co.uk
w woodleyscottage.co.uk

## WOKING
Surrey

**Grantchester** ★★
*Bed & Breakfast*
Boughton Hall Avenue, Send
GU23 7DF
t (01483) 225383
e gary@hotpotmail.com

**St Columba's House** ★★
*Guest Accommodation*
**Maybury Hill, Woking**
**GU22 8AB**
**t (01483) 766498**
**e retreats@stcolumbas.org.uk**
**w stcolumbashouse.org.uk**

## WOKINGHAM
Berkshire

**The Dukes Head** ★★★ *Inn*
56 Denmark Street,
Wokingham RG40 2BQ
t (0118) 978 0316

**WONERSH**
**Surrey**

**Woodyers Farm ★★★★**
*Bed & Breakfast*
Barnett Lane, Wonersh
GU5 0RX
**t** (01483) 892862
**e** woodyersfarm@hotmail.co.uk

**WOODFALLS**
**Hampshire**

**Woodfalls Inn ★★** *Inn*
The Ridge, Redlynch SP5 2LN
**t** (01725) 513222
**e** enquiries@woodfallsinnhotel.co.uk
**w** woodfallsinn.co.uk

**WOODGREEN**
**Hampshire**

**Cottage Crest ★★★★★**
*Bed & Breakfast*
**SILVER AWARD**
Castle Hill, Woodgreen
SP6 2AX
**t** (01725) 512009
**e** lupita_cadman@yahoo.co.uk
**w** cottage-crest.co.uk

**WOODSTOCK**
**Oxfordshire**

**Blenheim Guest House & Tearooms ★★★★**
*Guest House*
17 Park Street, Woodstock
OX20 1SJ
**t** (01993) 813814
**e** theblenheim@aol.com
**w** theblenheim.com

**The Laurels ★★★★**
*Bed & Breakfast*
**SILVER AWARD**
40 Hensington Road,
Woodstock OX20 1JL
**t** (01993) 812583
**e** stay@laurelsguesthouse.co.uk
**w** laurelsguesthouse.co.uk

**Shepherds Hall ★★★**
*Guest House*
Witney Road, Freeland, Oxford
OX29 8HQ
**t** (01993) 881256
**w** shepherdshall.co.uk

**WOOTTON BRIDGE**
**Isle of Wight**

**Grange Farm B&B ★★★★**
*Farmhouse*
Grange Farm, Staplers Road,
Wootton PO33 4RW
**t** (01983) 882147
**e** info@grange-farm-holidays.co.uk
**w** grange-farm-holidays.co.uk

**WORMINGHALL**
**Buckinghamshire**

**Crabtree Barn ★★★★**
*Farmhouse*
Menmarsh Road, Worminghall
HP18 9JY
**t** (01844) 339719
**e** issy@crabtreebarn.co.uk
**w** crabtreebarn.co.uk

**WORTH**
**Kent**

**The Blue Pigeons Inn ★★★**
*Inn*
The Street, Deal CT14 0DE
**t** (01304) 613245

**Solley Farm House ★★★★★**
*Bed & Breakfast*
**GOLD AWARD**
The Street, Worth, Sandwich
CT14 0DG
**t** (01304) 613701
**e** solleyfarmhouse@tiscali.co.uk
**w** solleyfarmhouse.co.uk

**WORTHING**
**West Sussex**

**Benson's ★★★★**
*Guest Accommodation*
**GOLD AWARD**
Brighton Road, Worthing
BN11 2EU
**t** (01903) 206623
**e** 15bgh4vw@f2s.com
**w** bensonstheguesthouse.co.uk

**Blair House Hotel ★★★★**
*Guest House*
11 St Georges Road, Worthing
BN11 2DS
**t** (01903) 234071
**e** stay@blairhousehotel.co.uk
**w** blairhousehotel.co.uk

**Camelot House ★★★★**
*Guest Accommodation*
20 Gannon Road, Worthing
BN11 2DT
**t** (01903) 204334
**e** stay@camelothouse.co.uk
**w** camelothouse.co.uk

**Edwardian Dreams ★★★★**
*Guest Accommodation*
**SILVER AWARD**
77 Manor Road, Worthing
BN11 4SL
**t** (01903) 218565
**e** info@edwardiandreams.co.uk
**w** edwardiandreams.co.uk

**Glenhill Guest House ★★★**
*Guest Accommodation*
21 Alexandra Road, Worthing
BN11 2DX
**t** (01903) 202756
**e** linda@filmersankey.wanadoo.co.uk
**w** glenhillguesthouse.co.uk

**The Grand Victorian ★★★**
*Guest Accommodation*
27 Railway Approach,
Worthing BN11 1UR
**t** (01903) 230690
**e** grandvictorian@thechapmansgroup.co.uk
**w** chapmansgroup.co.uk

**Haytor Guest House ★★**
*Bed & Breakfast*
5 Salisbury Road, Worthing
BN11 1RB
**t** (01903) 235287
**e** linda.shipley@homecall.co.uk

**Heenefields Guest House ★★★★**
*Guest Accommodation*
98 Heene Road, Worthing
BN11 3RE
**t** (01903) 538780
**e** info@heenefields.com
**w** heenefields.com

**High Beach Guest House ★★★★**
*Guest Accommodation*
201 Brighton Road, Worthing
BN11 2EX
**t** (01903) 236389
**e** infot@highbeachworthing.com
**w** highbeachworthing.com

**High Trees Guest House ★★★** *Guest Accommodation*
2 Warwick Gardens, Worthing
BN11 1PE
**t** (01903) 236668
**e** bill@hightreesguesthouse.co.uk
**w** hightreesguesthouse.co.uk

**Highdown ★★★** *Inn*
Littlehampton Road, Worthing
BN12 6PF
**t** (01903) 700152
**e** highdownhotel@thechapmansgroup.co.uk
**w** highdownhotel.co.uk

**Marine View Inn ★★★**
*Guest Accommodation*
111 Marine Parade, Worthing
BN11 3QG
**t** (01903) 238413
**e** reservations@marineviewhotel.co.uk
**w** marineviewhotel.co.uk

**Merton House ★★★★**
*Guest House*
96 Broadwater Road, Worthing
BN14 8AW
**t** (01903) 238222
**e** stay@mertonhouse.co.uk
**w** mertonhouse.co.uk

**Moorings ★★★★**
*Guest Accommodation*
4 Selden Road, Worthing
BN11 2LL
**t** (01903) 208882
**e** themooringsworthing@hotmail.co.uk
**w** mooringsworthing.co.uk

**The Old Guard House ★★★★** *Bed & Breakfast*
55 Poulters Lane, Worthing
BN14 7ST
**t** (01903) 527470
**e** eddie442002@tiscali.co.uk

**Pebble Beach ★★★**
*Guest Accommodation*
281 Brighton Road, Worthing
BN11 2HG
**t** (01903) 210766
**e** pebblebeach281@aol.com
**w** pebblebeach-worthing.co.uk

**South Dene Guest House ★★★** *Guest Accommodation*
41 Warwick Gardens,
Worthing BN11 1PF
**t** (01903) 232909
**w** south-dene.co.uk

**Tamara Guest House ★★★**
*Bed & Breakfast*
19 Alexandra Road, Worthing
BN11 2DX
**t** (01903) 520332
**w** tamara-worthing.co.uk

**WROXALL**
**Isle of Wight**

**Little Span Farm B&B ★★★**
*Farmhouse*
Rew Lane, Ventnor PO38 3AU
**t** (01983) 852419
**e** info@spanfarm.co.uk
**w** spanfarm.co.uk

**WYE**
**Kent**

**Mistral ★★★★**
*Bed & Breakfast*
3 Oxenturn Road, Wye,
Ashford TN25 5BH
**t** (01233) 813011
**e** geoff@chapman.invictanet.co.uk
**w** chapman.invictanet.co.uk

**The Wife of Bath Restaurant with Rooms ★★★★**
*Restaurant with Rooms*
**SILVER AWARD**
4 Upper Bridge Street, Ashford
TN25 5AF
**t** (01233) 812232
**e** relax@thewifeofbath.com
**w** thewifeofbath.com

**YARMOUTH**
**Isle of Wight**

**Medlars ★★★**
*Bed & Breakfast*
Halletts Shute, Norton,
Yarmouth PO41 0RH
**t** (01983) 761541
**e** e.grey855@btinternet.com
**w** milford.co.uk

# LONDON

## INNER LONDON

### E15

**The Railway Tavern**
Rating Applied For
*Guest Accommodation*
131 Angel Lane, London
E15 1DB
t (020) 8534 3123
e therailwaytavern@btconnect.com
w railwaytavernhotel.co.uk

### EC4

**City of London YHA ★★★**
*Hostel*
36 Carter Lane, London
EC4V 5AB
t (020) 7236 4965
e city@yha.org.uk
w yha.org.uk

### N1

**Kandara Guest House ★★★**
*Guest Accommodation*
68 Ockendon Road, Islington, London N1 3NW
t (020) 7226 5721
e admin@kandara.co.uk
w kandara.co.uk

**University of Westminster-Alexander Fleming Halls of Residence ★★** *Campus*
3 Hoxton Market, Off Pitfield Street, London N1 6HG
t (020) 7911 5181
e comserv@wmin.ac.uk
w wmin.ac.uk/comserv

**Walter Sickert Hall City University ★★★** *Campus*
Graham Street, London N1 8LA
t (020) 7040 8822
e wsh@city.ac.uk
w city.ac.uk/ems

### N4

**Costello Palace ★★**
*Guest Accommodation*
374 Seven Sisters Road, London N4 2PG
t (020) 8802 6551
e costellopalace@ukonline.co.uk
w infotel.co.uk/16419

### N6

**University of Westminster-Furnival House ★★** *Campus*
Chomeley Park, Highgate, London N6 5EU
t (020) 7911 5181
e comserv@wmin.ac.uk
w wmin.ac.uk/comserv

### N7

**Europa ★★★**
*Guest Accommodation*
62 Anson Road, London
N7 0AA
t (020) 7607 5935
e info@europahotellondon.co.uk
w europahotellondon.co.uk

### N8

**White Lodge ★★★**
*Guest Accommodation*
1 Church Lane, London
N8 7BU
t (020) 8348 9765
e info@whitelodgehornsey.co.uk
w whitelodgehornsey.co.uk

### N10

**The Muswell Hill ★★★**
*Guest House*
73 Muswell Hill Road, London
N10 3HT
t (020) 8883 6447
e reception@muswellhillhotel.co.uk
w muswellhillhotel.co.uk

### N22

**Pane Residence ★★**
*Bed & Breakfast*
154 Boundary Road, London
N22 6AE
t (020) 8889 3735

### NW1

**MIC Conferences and Accommodation ★★★★**
*Guest Accommodation*
81-103 Euston Street, London
NW1 2EZ
t (020) 7380 0001
e sales@micentre.com
w micentre.com

**St Pancras YHA ★★★★**
*Hostel*
79-81 Euston Road, London
NW1 2QS
t (020) 7388 9998
e stpancras@yha.org.uk
w yha.org.uk

### NW3

**Dillons ★★★**
*Guest Accommodation*
21 Belsize Park, London
NW3 4DU
t (020) 7794 3360
e desk@dillonshotel.com
w dillonshotel.com

### NW8

**The New Inn ★★★** *Inn*
2 Allitsen Road, St John's Wood, London NW8 6LA
t (020) 7722 0726
e thenewinnlondon@aol.com
w newinnlondon.co.uk

### NW11

**Anchor House ★★★**
*Guest Accommodation*
10 West Heath Drive, London
NW11 7QH
t (020) 8458 8764
e enquir@anchor-hotel.co.uk
w anchor-hotel.co.uk

### SE1

**Great Dover Street Apartments**
Rating Applied For
*Campus*
165 Great Dover Street, London SE1 4XA
t (020) 7407 0069
e vacations.at.kings@kcl.ac.uk
w kcl.ac.uk/kcvb

**St Christopher's Village**
Rating Applied For
*Hostel*
161-165 Borough High Street, London SE1 1HR
t (020) 7407 1856
e bookings@st-christophers.co.uk
w st-christophers.co.uk

**Stamford Street Apartments**
Rating Applied For
*Campus*
127 Stamford Street, Waterloo, London SE1 9NQ
t (020) 7633 9506
e vacations.at.kings@kcl.ac.uk
w kcl.ac.uk/kcvb

**University of Westminster-International House ★★**
*Campus*
1-5 Lambeth Road, London
SE1 6HU
t (020) 7911 5181
e comserv@wmin.ac.uk
w wmin.ac.uk/comserv

### SE3

**59a Lee Road, Blackheath**
★★ *Bed & Breakfast*
London SE3 9EN
t (020) 8318 7244
e ac@blackheath318.freeserve.co.uk

**Greenland Villa ★★★★**
*Guest Accommodation*
9 Charlton Road, London
SE3 7EU
t (020) 8858 4175
e bookings@greenlandvilla.com
w greenlandvilla.com

### SE6

**The Heathers ★★★**
*Bed & Breakfast*
71 Verdant Lane, London
SE6 1JD
t (020) 8698 8340
e berylheath@yahoo.co.uk
w theheathersbb.com

**Tulip Tree House ★★**
*Bed & Breakfast*
41 Minard Road, London
SE6 1NP
t (020) 8697 2596

### SE8

**M B Guest House ★★**
*Guest Accommodation*
7 Bolden Street, London
SE8 4JF
t (020) 8692 7030
e mbguesthouse@yahoo.co.uk

### SE9

**Boru House ★★**
*Bed & Breakfast*
70 Dunvegan Road, London
SE9 1SB
t (020) 8850 0584

### SE10

**16 St Alfeges ★★★★**
*Bed & Breakfast*
16 St Alfege Passage, London
SE10 9JS
t (020) 8853 4337
e nicmesure@yahoo.co.uk
w st-alfeges.co.uk

**The Corner House ★★**
*Guest Accommodation*
28 Royal Hill, London SE10 8RT
t (020) 8692 3023
e joannacourtney@aol.com

### SE13

**Eden Homes ★★★★**
*Guest Accommodation*
Edwin Hall Place, London
SE13 6RN
t 0845 116 1325
e eden.homes@hotmail.co.uk

**Manna House ★★★**
*Bed & Breakfast*
320 Hither Green Lane, London
SE13 6TS
t (020) 8461 5984
e mannahouse@aol.com
w members.aol.com/mannahouse

### SE14

**Annemarten Pepys Road ★★★★**
*Guest Accommodation*
**SILVER AWARD**
Pepys Road, London SE14 5SE
t (020) 7639 1060
e annemarten@pepysroad.com

### SE16

**YHA London Thameside ★★**
*Hostel*
20 Salter Road, London
SE16 5PR
t 0870 770 6010
e thameside@yha.org.uk
w yha.org.uk

### SE18

**Ebenezer Lodge ★★**
*Bed & Breakfast*
St Mary Street, London
SE18 5AN
t (020) 8855 3051
e ebenezerlodge@btconnect.com
w ebenezerlodge.co.uk

**Moordown Garden**
Rating Applied For
*Bed & Breakfast*
227 Moordown, London
SE18 3ND
t 05602 861713
e newtoncampbell316@btinternet.com

### SE20

**Melrose House ★★★★**
*Guest Accommodation*
89 Lennard Road, London
SE20 7LY
t (020) 8776 8884
e melrosehouse@supanet.com
w uk-bedandbreakfast.com

### SW1

**30 Pavilion Road ★★★**
*Guest Accommodation*
London SW1X 0HJ
t (020) 7584 4921
e rgr@searcys.co.uk
w searcys.co.uk

**Carlton ★★**
*Guest Accommodation*
90 Belgrave Road, London
SW1V 2BJ
t (020) 7976 6634
e info@cityhotelcarlton.co.uk
w cityhotelcarlton.co.uk

**Caswell ★★**
*Guest Accommodation*
25 Gloucester Street, London
SW1V 2DB
t (020) 7834 6345
e manager@hotellondon.co.uk
w hotellondon.co.uk

**Central House ★★★**
*Guest Accommodation*
37-41 Belgrave Road, London
SW1V 2BB
t (020) 7834 8036
e info@centralhousehotel.co.uk

**Comfort Inn Buckingham Palace Road ★★★**
*Guest Accommodation*
10 St Georges Drive, Victoria, London SW1V 4BJ
t (020) 7834 2988
e info@comfortinnbuckinghampalacerd.co.uk
w comfortinnbuckinghampalacerd.co.uk

**The Dover ★★**
*Guest Accommodation*
44 Belgrave Road, London
SW1V 1RG
**t** (020) 7821 9085
**e** reception@dover-hotel.co.uk
**w** dover-hotel.co.uk

**Elizabeth ★★★**
*Guest Accommodation*
37 Eccleston Square, London
SW1V 1PB
t (020) 7828 6812
e info@elizabethhotel.com
w elizabethhotel.com

**Georgian House ★★★**
*Guest Accommodation*
35 St Georges Drive, London
SW1V 4DG
t (020) 7834 1438
e reception@georgianhousehotel.co.uk
w georgianhousehotel.co.uk

**Huttons ★★★**
*Guest Accommodation*
55 Belgrave Road, London
SW1V 2BB
t (020) 7834 3726

**The Lord Milner ★★★★★**
*Guest Accommodation*
**SILVER AWARD**
111 Ebury Street, London
SW1W 9QU
t (020) 7881 9880
e info@lordmilner.com
w lordmilner.com

**Luna Simone Guest House**
★★★★ *Guest House*
47 Belgrave Road, London
SW1V 2BB
t (020) 7834 5897

**Melita House ★★★**
*Guest Accommodation*
35 Charlwood Street, London
SW1V 2DU
**t** (020) 7828 0471
**e** reserve@melitahotel.com
**w** melitahotel.com

**Stanley House ★★**
*Guest Accommodation*
19-21 Belgrave Road, London
SW1V 1RB
t (020) 7834 5042 &
(020) 7834 7292
e cmahotel@aol.com
w londonbudgethotels.co.uk

**University of Westminster-Wigram House ★★** *Campus*
84-99 Ashley Gardens, Thirleby Road, London SW1P 1HG
t (020) 7911 5181
e comserv@wmin.ac.uk
w wmin.ac.uk/comserv

**Vandon House ★★★**
*Guest Accommodation*
1 Vandon Street, London
SW1H 0AH
**t** (020) 7799 6780
**e** info@vandonhouse.com
**w** vandonhouse.com

**Victor ★★★**
*Guest Accommodation*
51 Belgrave Road, London
SW1V 2BB
t (020) 7592 9853
w victorhotel.co.uk

**The Victoria Inn London**
★★★ *Guest House*
65-67 Belgrave Road, London
SW1V 2BG
t (020) 7834 6721
e welcome@victoriainn.co.uk
w victoriainn.co.uk

**The Windermere ★★★★**
*Guest Accommodation*
**SILVER AWARD**
142-144 Warwick Way, London SW1V 4JE
t (020) 7834 5163
e reservations@windermere-hotel.co.uk
w windermere-hotel.co.uk

## SW5

**Beaver ★★**
*Guest Accommodation*
57-59 Philbeach Gardens, London SW5 9ED
t (020) 7373 4553
e hotelbeaver@hotmail.com
w beaverhotel.co.uk

**Comfort Inn Earl's Court**
★★★ *Guest Accommodation*
11-13 Penywern Road, London
SW5 9TT
t (020) 7373 6514
e info@comfortinnearlscourt.co.uk
w comfortinnearlscourt.co.uk

**Earls Court ★** *Guest House*
28 Warwick Road, London
SW5 9UD
t (020) 7373 7079
e info@hotelearlscourt.com
w hotelearlscourt.com

**Lord Jim ★★** *Guest House*
25 Penywern Road, London
SW5 9TT
t (020) 7370 6071
e ljh@lgh-hotels.com
w lgh-hotels.com

**Mowbray Court ★★**
*Guest Accommodation*
28-32 Penywern Road, London
SW5 9SU
**t** (020) 7370 2316
**e** mowbraycrthot@hotmail.com
**w** mowbraycourthotel.co.uk

**Rasool Court ★★**
*Guest Accommodation*
19-21 Penywern Road, London
SW5 9TT
t (020) 7373 8900
e rasool@rasool.demon.co.uk
w rasoolcourthotel.com

**YHA Earl's Court ★★★★**
*Hostel*
38 Bolton Gardens, London
SW5 0AQ
t (020) 7373 7083
e earlscourt@yha.org.uk
w yha.org.uk

## SW7

**Imperial College London**
★★★ *Campus*
South Kensington Campus, London SW7 2AZ
t (020) 7594 9507
e reservations@imperial.ac.uk
w imperial-accommodationlink.com

**Meininger City Hostel & Hotel London ★★★★** *Hostel*
65-67 Queen's Gate, London
SW7 5JS
t (020) 3051 8173
e welcome@meininger-hostels.com
w meininger-hostels.com

## SW8

**Comfort Inn London Vauxhall ★★★★**
*Guest Accommodation*
87 South Lambeth Road, London SW8 1RN
t (020) 7735 9494
e stay@comfortinnvx.co.uk
w comfortinnvx.co.uk

## SW9

**Belgrave Oval ★★★★**
*Guest Accommodation*
9-13 Clapham Road, London
SW9 0JD
t (020) 7793 0142
e enquiries@belgravehotel.net

## SW11

**Lavender Guest House**
★★★ *Guest House*
18 Lavender Sweep, London
SW11 1HA
t (020) 7585 2767
w thelavenderguesthouse.com

## SW16

**The Konyots ★**
*Guest Accommodation*
95 Pollards Hill South, London
SW16 4LS
t (020) 8764 0075

## W1

**The Hallam ★★★**
*Guest Accommodation*
12 Hallam Street, London
W1W 6JF
t (020) 7580 1166
e hallam-hotel@hotmail.com
w hallamhotel.com

**International Students House ★★** *Campus*
229 Great Portland Street, Regent's Park, London
W1N 5HD
t (020) 7631 8300
e accom@ish.org.uk
w ish.org.uk

**Lincoln House – Central London ★★**
*Guest Accommodation*
33 Gloucester Place, London
W1U 8HY
**t** (020) 7486 7630
**e** reservations@lincoln-house-hotel.co.uk
**w** lincoln-house-hotel.co.uk

**Marble Arch Inn ★★**
*Guest Accommodation*
49-50 Upper Berkeley Street, London W1H 5QR
**t** (020) 7723 7888
**e** sales@marblearch-inn.co.uk
**w** marblearch-inn.co.uk

**Oxford Street YHA ★★**
*Hostel*
14 Noel Street, London
W1F 8GJ
t (020) 7734 1618
e oxfordst@yha.org.uk
w yha.org.uk

**Piccadilly Backpackers Hostel ★** *Backpackers*
12 Sherwood Street, Piccadilly Circus, London W1F 7BR
t (020) 7434 9009
e bookings@piccadillybackpackers.com
w piccadillybackpackers.com

**YHA London Central**
Rating Applied For
*Hostel*
104-108 Bolsover Street, London W1W 6AB
t (01629) 592633

## W2

**The Abbey Court ★★★★**
*Guest Accommodation*
20 Pembridge Gardens, London W2 4DU
t (020) 7221 7518
e info@abbeycourthotel.co.uk
w abbeycourthotel.co.uk

**Abbey Court & Westpoint**
★★★ *Guest Accommodation*
174 Sussex Gardens, London
W2 1TP
t (020) 7402 0281
e info@abbeycourt.com
w abbeycourthotel.com

**Alexandra ★★★**
*Guest Accommodation*
159-161 Sussex Gardens, London W2 2RY
t (020) 7402 6471
e hotels.leventis-group@virgin.net
w hotels-leventisgroup.co.uk

**Barry House** ★★★
*Guest Accommodation*
12 Sussex Place, London
W2 2TP
**t** (020) 7723 7340
**e** hotel@barryhouse.co.uk
**w** barryhouse.co.uk

**The Cardiff** ★★★
*Guest Accommodation*
5-9 Norfolk Square, London
W2 1RU
**t** (020) 7723 9068
**e** stay@cardiff-hotel.com
**w** cardiff-hotel.com

**Elysee** ★★★
*Guest Accommodation*
25/26 Craven Terrace, London
W2 3EL
t (020) 7402 7633
e info@hotelelysee.co.uk
w hotelelysee.co.uk

**Hyde Park Radnor** ★★★★
*Guest Accommodation*
7-9 Sussex Place, London
W2 2SX
t (020) 7723 5969
e hydeparkradnor@btconnect.com
w hydeparkradnor.com

**Hyde Park Rooms** ★★
*Guest Accommodation*
137 Sussex Gardens, London
W2 2RX
t (020) 7723 0225
e reception@hydeparkrooms.com
w hydeparkrooms.com

**Kingsway Park Hotel Hyde Park** ★★★
*Guest Accommodation*
139 Sussex Gardens, London
W2 2RX
**t** (020) 7723 5677
**e** info@kingswaypark-hotel.com
**w** kingswaypark-hotel.com

**Nayland** ★★★★
*Guest Accommodation*
132-134 Sussex Gardens,
London W2 1UB
t (020) 7723 4615
e info@naylandhotel.com
w naylandhotel.com

**The Oxford** ★★★
*Guest Accommodation*
13-14 Craven Terrace, London
W2 3QD
**t** (020) 7402 6860
**e** oxfordhotel@btconnect.com
**w** oxfordhotellondon.co.uk

**Park Lodge** ★★★
*Guest Accommodation*
73 Queensborough Terrace,
London W2 3SU
t (020) 7229 6424

**Rhodes House** ★★★
*Guest Accommodation*
195 Sussex Gardens, London
W2 2RJ
**t** (020) 7262 5617 &
(020) 7262 0537
**e** chris@rhodeshotel.com
**w** rhodeshotel.com

**St David's and Norfolk Court**
★★ *Guest Accommodation*
16 Norfolk Square, London
W2 1RS
t (020) 7723 3856
e info@stdavidshotels.com
w stdavidshotels.com

## W3

**Park Lodge** ★★★★
*Guest House*
335 Uxbridge Road, London
W3 9RA
t (020) 8992 7874
w parklodge.com

## W4

**Chiswick Guest House** ★★
*Bed & Breakfast*
40 Spencer Road, Chiswick,
London W4 3SP
t (020) 8994 0876
e rooms@chiswickguesthouse.co.uk
w chiswickguesthouse.co.uk

## W5

**Grange Lodge** ★★
*Guest House*
48-50 Grange Road, London
W5 5BX
t (020) 8567 1049
e enquiries@londonlodgehotels.com
w londonlodgehotels.com

## W6

**At Home in London Bayswater (Ref 211)** ★★★★
*Bed & Breakfast*
70 Black Lion Lane, London
W6 9BE
t (020) 8748 1943
e info@athomeinlondon.co.uk
w athomeinlondon.co.uk

**At Home in London Bayswater (Ref 172)**
Rating Applied For
*Guest Accommodation*
70 Black Lion Lane, London
W6 9BE
t (020) 8748 1943
e info@athomeinlondon.co.uk
w athomeinlondon.co.uk

**At Home in London Belgravia (Ref 235)** ★★★★
*Bed & Breakfast*
70 Black Lion Lane, London
W6 9BE
t (020) 8748 1943
e info@athomeinlondon.co.uk
w athomeinlondon.co.uk

**At Home in London Carlisle Place (Ref 275)** ★★★★
*Bed & Breakfast*
70 Black Lion Lane, London
W6 9BE
t (020) 8748 1943
e info@athomeinlondon.co.uk
w athomeinlondon.co.uk

**At Home in London Chelsea (Ref 227)**
Rating Applied For
*Guest Accommodation*
70 Black Lion Lane, London
W6 9BE
t (020) 8748 1943
e info@athomeinlondon.co.uk
w athomeinlondon.co.uk

**At Home in London Chelsea (Ref 193)** ★★
*Bed & Breakfast*
70 Black Lion Lane, London
W6 9BE
t (020) 8748 1943
e info@athomeinlondon.co.uk
w athomeinlondon.co.uk

**At Home in London Chiswick (Ref 267)** ★★★★
*Bed & Breakfast*
**SILVER AWARD**
70 Black Lion Lane, London
W6 9BE
t (020) 8748 1943
e info@athomeinlondon.co.uk
w athomeinlondon.co.uk

**At Home in London Chiswick (Ref 11)** ★★★★
*Bed & Breakfast*
**SILVER AWARD**
70 Black Lion Lane, London
W6 9BE
t (020) 8748 1943
e info@athomeinlondon.co.uk
w athomeinlondon.co.uk

**At Home in London Chiswick (Ref 258)**
Rating Applied For
*Guest Accommodation*
70 Black Lion Lane, London
W6 9BE
t (020) 8748 1943
e info@athomeinlondon.co.uk
w athomeinlondon.co.uk

**At Home in London Hammersmith (Ref 62)**
★★★★ *Bed & Breakfast*
70 Black Lion Lane, London
W6 9BE
t (020) 8748 1943
e info@athomeinlondon.co.uk
w athomeinlondon.co.uk

**At Home in London Holland Park (Ref 248)**
Rating Applied For
*Guest Accommodation*
70 Black Lion Lane, London
W6 9BE
t (020) 8748 1943
e info@athomeinlondon.co.uk
w athomeinlondon.co.uk

**At Home in London Holland Park (Ref 114)**
Rating Applied For
*Guest Accommodation*
70 Black Lion Lane, London
W6 9BE
t (020) 8748 1943
e info@athomeinlondon.co.uk
w athomeinlondon.co.uk

**At Home in London Kensington (Ref 71)**
Rating Applied For
*Guest Accommodation*
70 Black Lion Lane, London
W6 9BE
t (020) 8748 1943
e info@athomeinlondon.co.uk
w athomeinlondon.co.uk

**At Home in London Mayfair (Ref 229)**
Rating Applied For
*Guest Accommodation*
70 Black Lion Lane, London
W6 9BE
t (020) 8748 1943
e info@athomeinlondon.co.uk
w athomeinlondon.co.uk

**At Home in London Notting Hill (Ref 76)**
Rating Applied For
*Guest Accommodation*
70 Black Lion Lane, London
W6 9BE
t (020) 8748 1943
e info@athomeinlondon.co.uk
w athomeinlondon.co.uk

**At Home in London Parsons Green (Ref 36)**
Rating Applied For
*Guest Accommodation*
70 Black Lion Lane, London
W6 9BE
t (020) 8748 1943
e info@athomeinlondon.co.uk
w athomeinlondon.co.uk

**At Home in London South Kensington (Ref 234)**
Rating Applied For
*Guest Accommodation*
70 Black Lion Lane, London
W6 9BE
t (020) 8748 1943
e info@athomeinlondon.co.uk
w athomeinlondon.co.uk

**At Home in London South Kensington (Ref 30)** ★★
*Bed & Breakfast*
70 Black Lion Lane, London
W6 9BE
t (020) 8748 1943
e info@athomeinlondon.co.uk
w athomeinlondon.co.uk

**At Home in London Vauxhall (Ref 134)** ★★★★
*Bed & Breakfast*
70 Black Lion Lane, London
W6 9BE
t (020) 8748 1943
e info@athomeinlondon.co.uk
w athomeinlondon.co.uk

**At Home in London Victoria (Ref 14)**
Rating Applied For
*Guest Accommodation*
70 Black Lion Lane, London
W6 9BE
t (020) 8748 1943
e info@athomeinlondon.co.uk
w athomeinlondon.co.uk

**At Home in London Victoria (Ref 246)**
Rating Applied For
*Guest Accommodation*
70 Black Lion Lane, London
W6 9BE
t (020) 8748 1943
e info@athomeinlondon.co.uk
w athomeinlondon.co.uk

**At Home in London West Kensington (Ref 77)** ★★★
*Bed & Breakfast*
70 Black Lion Lane, London
W6 9BE
t (020) 8748 1943
e info@athomeinlondon.co.uk
w athomeinlondon.co.uk

**At Home in London West Kensington (Ref 69)** ★★★
*Guest Accommodation*
70 Black Lion Lane, London
W6 9BE
t (020) 8748 1943
e info@athomeinlondon.co.uk
w athomeinlondon.co.uk

**At Home in London Westminster (Ref 5)** ★★
*Guest Accommodation*
**GOLD AWARD**
70 Black Lion Lane, London W6 9BE
**t** (020) 8748 1943
**e** info@athomeinlondon.co.uk
**w** athomeinlondon.co.uk

**The Globetrotter Inn London** ★★★★ *Hostel*
Ashlar Court, Ravenscourt Gardens, Stamford Brook, London W6 0TU
**t** (020) 8746 3112
**e** london@globetrotterinns.com
**w** globetrotterinns.com

**Orlando Bed and Breakfast** ★★ *Guest Accommodation*
83 Shepherds Bush Road, London W6 7LR
**t** (020) 7603 4890
**e** hotelorlando@btconnect.com
**w** hotelorlando.co.uk

**St Peters** ★★★
*Guest Accommodation*
407 Goldhawk Road, London W6 0SA
**t** (020) 8741 4239
**e** info@stpetershotel.co.uk
**w** stpetershotel.co.uk

## W8

**Holland House YHA** ★★
*Hostel*
Holland Walk, Kensington, London W8 7QN
**t** (020) 7937 0748
**e** hollandhouse@yha.org.uk
**w** yha.org.uk

## W11

**Nottinghill Guesthouse Ltd** ★★ *Guest Accommodation*
72 Holland Park Avenue, London W11 3QZ
**t** (020) 7229 9233
**e** hotelondon@aol.com
**w** thiswaytolondon.com

## W14

**Ace Hotel** ★★★ *Hostel*
16-22 Gunterstone Road, London W14 9BX
**t** (020) 7602 6600
**e** reception@ace-hotel.co.uk
**w** acehotel.co.uk

## WC1

**Comfort Inn Kings Cross** ★★★★
*Guest Accommodation*
2-5 St Chad's Street, London WC1H 8BD
**t** (020) 7837 1940
**e** info@comfortinnkingscross.co.uk
**w** comfortinnkingscross.co.uk

**Generator Hostel London** ★★★ *Hostel*
37 Tavistock Place, Russell Square, London WC1H 9SE
**t** (020) 7388 7666
**e** london@generatorhostels.com
**w** generatorhostels.com

**Guilford House** ★★
*Guest House*
6 Guilford Street, London WC1N 1DR
**t** (020) 7430 2504
**e** guilford-hotel@lineone.net
**w** guilfordhotel.co.uk

**The Lancaster**
Rating Applied For
*Guest Accommodation*
4-6 Bedford Place, London WC1B 5JD
**t** (020) 7637 3400
**e** info@thelancaster.co.uk
**w** thelancaster.co.uk

## OUTER LONDON

## BEXLEY

**66 Arcadian Avenue** ★★★
*Guest Accommodation*
Bexley DA5 1JW
**t** (020) 8303 5732

**Blendon Lodge** ★★★★
*Bed & Breakfast*
30 Blendon Road, Bexley DA5 1BW
**t** (020) 8303 2571

**Buxted Lodge Bed and Breakfast** ★★★
*Guest Accommodation*
40 Parkhurst Road, Bexley DA5 1AS
**t** (01322) 554010
**e** info@buxtedlodge.co.uk
**w** buxtedlodge.co.uk

## BRENTFORD

**Kings Arms** ★★★ *Inn*
19 Boston Manor Road, Brentford TW8 8EA
**t** (020) 8560 5860
**w** kingsarmsbrentjord.co.uk

## BROMLEY

**Glendevon House** ★★★
*Guest House*
80 Southborough Road, Bromley BR1 2EN
**t** (020) 8467 2183
**w** avishotels.com

## CHISLEHURST

**The Crown Inn** ★★★ *Inn*
School Road, Chislehurst BR7 5PQ
**t** (020) 8467 7326
**e** crownchislehurst@shepherdneame.co.uk
**w** crownchislehurst.co.uk

## CROYDON

**Bramley** ★★★
*Bed & Breakfast*
7 Greencourt Avenue, Croydon CR0 7LD
**t** (020) 8654 6776

**Croydon Court** ★★★
*Guest Accommodation*
597-603 London Road, Thornton Heath CR7 6AY
**t** (020) 8684 3947
**e** bookings@croydencourthotel.co.uk

**Foxley Mount** ★★★
*Bed & Breakfast*
44 Foxley Lane, Purley CR8 3EE
**t** (020) 8660 9751
**e** enquiries@foxleymount.co.uk
**w** foxleymount.co.uk

**Owlets** ★★★ *Bed & Breakfast*
112 Arundel Avenue, South Croydon CR2 8BH
**t** (020) 8657 5213

**The Park** ★★ *Bed & Breakfast*
63 Addington Road, South Croydon CR2 8RD
**t** (020) 8657 8776

**The Woodstock Guest House** ★★★ *Guest House*
30 Woodstock Road, Croydon CR0 1JR
**t** (020) 8680 1489
**e** woodstockhotel@tiscali.co.uk
**w** woodstockhotel.co.uk

## HAMPTON

**The Chestnuts** ★★★★
*Bed & Breakfast*
16 Chestnut Avenue, Hampton TW12 2NU
**t** (020) 8979 8314
**e** thechestnuts_16@fsmail.net

**Houseboat Riverine** ★★★
*Guest Accommodation*
Riverine, Taggs Island, Hampton TW12 2HA
**t** (020) 8979 2266
**e** malcolm@feedtheducks.com
**w** feedtheducks.com

## HARROW

**London B&B**
Rating Applied For
*Bed & Breakfast*
8 Argyle Road, North Harrow HA2 7AJ
**t** (020) 8248 4039
**e** muidoon@dircon.co.uk
**w** serenade.ndirect.co.uk

**Rhondda House** ★★★
*Guest House*
16 Harrow View, Harrow HA1 1RG
**t** (020) 8427 5009
**w** rhonddahouse.com

**University of Westminster-Harrow Hall of Residence** ★★★ *Campus*
Watford Road, Harrow HA1 3TP
**t** (020) 7911 5181
**e** comserv@wmin.ac.uk
**w** wmin.ac.uk/comserv

**West London B&B**
Rating Applied For
*Bed & Breakfast*
15 Beaumont Avenue, Harrow HA2 7AT
**t** (020) 8723 3890
**e** westlondonbandb@msn.com
**w** gt.ision.co.uk

## HAYES

**Shepiston Lodge** ★★★
*Guest House*
31 Shepiston Lane, Hayes UB3 1LJ
**t** (020) 8573 0266
**e** shepistonlodge@aol.com
**w** shepistonlodge.co.uk

## ILFORD

**The Cranbrook** ★★
*Guest Accommodation*
22-24 Coventry Road, Ilford IG1 4QR
**t** (020) 8554 6544

**The Park** ★★
*Guest Accommodation*
327 Cranbrook Road, Ilford IG1 4UE
**t** (020) 8554 9616
**e** parkhotelilford@netscapeonline.co.uk
**w** expresslodging.co.uk

## KEW

**Melbury** ★★★
*Bed & Breakfast*
33 Marksbury Avenue, Richmond TW9 4JE
**t** (020) 8876 3930
**e** jennieallen@mac.com
**w** accommodation-kew-richmond.co.uk

**West Lodge** ★★★
*Bed & Breakfast*
179 Mortlake Road, Richmond TW9 4AW
**t** (020) 8876 0584
**e** westlodge@thakria.demon.co.uk

## KINGSTON UPON THAMES

**40 The Bittoms** ★★
*Bed & Breakfast*
Kingston-upon-Thames KT1 2AP
**t** (020) 8541 3171

**8 St Albans Road** ★★
*Bed & Breakfast*
Kingston-upon-Thames KT2 5HQ
**t** (020) 8549 5910

**Ditton Lodge** ★★★★
*Guest House*
47 Lovelace Road, Long Ditton, Kingston-upon-Thames KT6 6NA
**t** (020) 8399 7482
**w** dittonlodge.co.uk

## PINNER

**Delcon** ★★★ *Bed & Breakfast*
468 Pinner Road, Pinner HA5 5RR
**t** (020) 8863 1054
**e** delcon@homecall.co.uk

## PURLEY

**Ardra Guest House** ★★★★
*Guest Accommodation*
108 Foxley Lane, Purley CR8 3NB
**t** (020) 8668 4483
**e** jillsturgess@yahoo.com

**The Maple House** ★★★★
*Bed & Breakfast*
174 Foxley Lane, Purley CR8 3NF
**t** (020) 8407 5123
**e** trevbrgg@aol.com

**Purley Cross Guest House** ★★★ *Guest House*
50 Brighton Road, Purley CR8 2LG
**t** (020) 8668 4964
**e** bookings@purleycross.com

## RICHMOND

**Chalon House** ★★★★★
*Guest Accommodation*
**GOLD AWARD**
8 Spring Terrace, Richmond TW9 1LW
**t** (020) 8332 1121
**e** chalonhouse@hotmail.com

**Hobart Hall Guest House**
★★ *Guest House*
43-47 Petersham Road, Richmond TW10 6UL
**t** (020) 8940 0435
**e** hobarthall@aol.com
**w** hobarthall.net

**Ivy Cottage** ★★★
*Bed & Breakfast*
Upper Ham Road, Ham Common, Richmond TW10 5LA
**t** (020) 8940 8601 & 07742 278247
**e** taylor@dbta.freeserve.co.uk
**w** dbta.freeserve.co.uk

Larkfield Apartments ★★★
*Guest Accommodation*
19 Larkfield Road, Richmond TW9 2PG
t (020) 8948 6620
e shipplets@ukgateway.net
w shipplets.com

Pro Kew Gardens B & B ★★
*Bed & Breakfast*
15 Pensford Avenue, Richmond TW9 4HR
t (020) 8876 3354
e info@prokewbandb.demon.co.uk
w prokewbandb.demon.co.uk

**The Red Cow** ★★★ *Inn*
59 Sheen Road, Richmond TW9 1YJ
**t** (020) 8940 2511
**e** tom@redcowpub.com
**w** redcowpub.com

Richmond Inn ★★★★
*Guest Accommodation*
50-56 Sheen Road, Richmond TW9 1UG
t (020) 8940 0171
w richmondinnhotel.com

Riverside ★★★
*Guest Accommodation*
23 Petersham Road, Richmond TW10 6UH
t (020) 8940 1339
e riversidehotel@yahoo.com
w riversiderichmond.co.uk

West Park Gardens ★★★
*Bed & Breakfast*
105 Mortlake Road, Richmond TW9 4AA
t (020) 8876 6842
e nj.edwards@ukonline.co.uk

## SIDCUP

Hilbert House ★★★
*Guest Accommodation*
Halfway Street, Sidcup DA15 8DE
t (020) 8300 0549
e annandeddie@talktalk.net

## SURBITON

**The Broadway Lodge** ★★
*Guest House*
41 The Broadway, Tolworth, Surbiton KT6 7DJ
**t** (020) 8399 6555
**e** broadway.lodge@tiscali.co.uk
**w** broadway-stgeorgeslodge.com

## SUTTON

**St Margarets Guest House**
★★ *Guest Accommodation*
31 Devon Road, Sutton SM2 7PE
**t** (020) 8643 0164
**e** margarettrotman@hotmail.com
**w** stmargaretsbandb.co.uk

## TEDDINGTON

**Hazeldene** ★★★★
*Guest Accommodation*
58 Hampton Road, Teddington TW11 0JX
t (020) 8286 8500
e glasslisa58@hotmail.com

King Edwards Grove ★★★
*Bed & Breakfast*
Teddington TW11 9LY
t (020) 8977 7251
e peter.midgley@blueyonder.co.uk

Ladywood ★★★
*Bed & Breakfast*
Teddington TW11 8AP
t (020) 8977 6066
e lyndano@hotmail.com

## TWICKENHAM

11 Spencer Road ★★★
*Bed & Breakfast*
Twickenham TW2 5TH
t (020) 8894 5271
e bruceduff@hotmail.com

136 London Road ★★★
*Bed & Breakfast*
Twickenham TW1 1HD
t (020) 8892 3158
e jenniferjfinnerty@hotmail.com
w accommodation-in-twickenham.co.uk/

39 Grange Avenue ★★★★
*Bed & Breakfast*
Twickenham TW2 5TW
t (020) 8894 1055
e carole@fanfoliage.fsbusiness.co.uk
w thewrightresidence.co.uk

Avalon Cottage ★★
*Bed & Breakfast*
50 Moor Mead Road, Twickenham TW1 1JS
t (020) 8744 2178
e avaloncottage@anftel.com
w avalon-cottage.com

The Old Stables ★★★
*Bed & Breakfast*
1 Bridle Lane, Twickenham TW1 3EG
t (020) 8892 4507
e jennitoolsadams@hotmail.com

Peter and Marilyn Wilkins
★★★★ *Bed & Breakfast*
**SILVER AWARD**
37 Grange Avenue, Strawberry Hill, Twickenham TW2 5TW
t (020) 8898 0412
e wilkins_family@blueyonder.co.uk
w twickenham-accommodation.co.uk

## UPMINSTER

**Corner Farm** ★★
*Guest Accommodation*
Fen Lane, North Ockendon, Upminster RM14 3RB
**t** (01708) 851310
**w** corner-farm.co.uk

## UXBRIDGE

**Brunel University Conference Centre**
★★–★★★ *Campus*
Conference Office, Brunel University, Uxbridge UB8 3PH
t (01895) 238353
e conference@brunel.ac.uk
w brunel.ac.uk/campus/conference

## WELLING

Danson Bed & Breakfast ★★
*Guest Accommodation*
73 Danson Crescent, Welling DA16 2AR
t (020) 8304 1239
e delfreda@ntlworld.com

# SOUTH WEST ENGLAND

## ABBOTSBURY Dorset

Corfe Gate House ★★★★
*Bed & Breakfast*
**SILVER AWARD**
Coryates, Portesham DT3 4HW
t (01305) 871483
e corfegatehouse@aol.com
w corfegatehouse.co.uk

**Swan Lodge** ★★★
*Guest Accommodation*
Rodden Row, Abbotsbury, Weymouth DT3 4JL
**t** (01305) 871249

## ABBOTSKERSWELL Devon

The Coachman's Cottage ★★★★
*Guest Accommodation*
Whiddon, Abbotskerswell TQ12 5LG
t (01803) 872451
e mca@fsb.org.uk
w thecoachmanscottage.co.uk

## ADVENT Cornwall

Higher Trezion ★★★★
*Farmhouse*
Tresinney, Advent, Camelford PL32 9QW
t (01840) 213761
e higher.trezion@btinternet.com
w highertrezion.co.uk

## ALDERHOLT Dorset

Desford Cottage ★★★★
*Bed & Breakfast*
3 Park Lane, Alderholt SP6 3AJ
t (01425) 652434
e shirleyhooley@aol.com

## ALDERTON Gloucestershire

Moors Farm House
★★★★★ *Bed & Breakfast*
**GOLD AWARD**
32 Beckford Road, Alderton GL20 8NL
t (01242) 620523
e moorsfarmhouse@ukworld.net
w moorsfarmhouse.co.uk

## ALMONDSBURY Gloucestershire

Royland Cottage ★★★★
*Farmhouse*
Lower Woodhouse Farm, Fernhill BS32 4LU
t (01454) 610123

## ALTON PANCRAS Dorset

Whiteways Farmhouse Accommodation ★★★★
*Bed & Breakfast*
**SILVER AWARD**
Bookham, Dorchester DT2 7RP
t (01300) 345511
e andy.foot1@btinternet.com
w bookhamcourt.co.uk

## ALVERTON Cornwall

Penzance Youth Hostel ★★
*Hostel*
Castle Horneck, Alverton, Penzance TR18 4LP
t (01736) 362666
e penzance@yha.co.uk

## AMBERLEY Gloucestershire

High Tumps
Rating Applied For
*Bed & Breakfast*
St Chloe Green, Amberley GL5 5AR
t (01453) 873584
e dakavic@btinternet.com

## AMESBURY Wiltshire

Fairlawn ★★★ *Guest House*
42 High Street, Salisbury SP4 7DL
t (01980) 622103
e fairlawnhotel@hotmail.com
w fairlawnhotel.co.uk

The George Hotel ★★★ *Inn*
High Street, Amesbury SP4 7ET
t (01980) 622108
w chapmansgroup.com

### APPLEDORE
Devon

**West Farm** ★★★★★
*Bed & Breakfast*
**SILVER AWARD**
Irsha Street, Appledore
EX39 1RY
**t** (01237) 425269
**e** gail@appledore-devon.co.uk
**w** appledore-devon.co.uk

### ARLINGHAM
Gloucestershire

**Putchers** ★★★★ *Farmhouse*
Overton Lane, Arlingham
GL2 7JJ
**t** (01452) 740400
**e** putchers@btinternet.com
**w** putchers.co.uk

### ASHBURTON
Devon

**Golden Lion House** ★★★★
*Guest House*
58 East Street, East Street,
Newton Abbot TQ13 7AX
**t** 05602 812965
**e** info@goldenlionhouse.com
**w** goldenlionhouse.com

### ASHTON KEYNES
Wiltshire

**Wheatleys Farm** ★★★★
*Farmhouse* **SILVER AWARD**
High Road, Ashton Keynes
SN6 6NX
**t** (01285) 861310
**e** gill@wheatleysfarm.co.uk
**w** wheatleysfarm.co.uk

### ATHELHAMPTON
Dorset

**White Cottage** ★★★★
*Bed & Breakfast*
**SILVER AWARD**
Dorchester DT2 7LG
**t** (01305) 848622
**e** markjamespiper@aol.com
**w** freewebs.com/whitecottagebandb

### ATWORTH
Wiltshire

**Church Farm Atworth**
★★★★ *Farmhouse*
Church Street, Atworth
SN12 8JA
**t** (01225) 702215
**e** churchfarm@tinyonline.co.uk
**w** churchfarm-atworth.freeserve.co.uk/

### AVEBURY
Wiltshire

**Manor Farm** ★★★★
*Bed & Breakfast*
High Street, Avebury SN8 1RF
**t** (01672) 539294

**The New Inn** ★★★
*Guest Accommodation*
Winterbourne Monkton,
Swindon SN4 9NW
**t** (01672) 539240
**e** enquiries@thenewinn.net
**w** thenewinn.net

### AVETON GIFFORD
Devon

**Helliers Farm** ★★★★
*Farmhouse*
Ashford TQ7 4NB
**t** (01548) 550689
**e** helliersfarm@ukonline.co.uk
**w** helliersfarm.co.uk

### AXBRIDGE
Somerset

**The Perchery**
Rating Applied For
*Guest Accommodation*
Jubilee Road, Axbridge
BS26 2DA
**t** (01934) 733783
**e** judith.strange@googlemail.com

### AXMINSTER
Devon

**Hedgehog Corner** ★★★★
*Guest Accommodation*
**SILVER AWARD**
Lyme Road, Axminster
EX13 5SU
**t** (01297) 32036
**e** info@hedgehogcorner.co.uk
**w** hedgehogcorner.co.uk

**Kerrington House** ★★★★★
*Guest Accommodation*
**GOLD AWARD**
Musbury Road, Axminster
EX13 5JR
**t** (01297) 35333
**e** ja.reaney@kerringtonhouse.com
**w** kerringtonhouse.com

**Prestoller House** ★★★★
*Guest Accommodation*
Beavor Lane, Axminster
EX13 5EQ
**t** (01297) 33659
**e** prestollerhouse@btinternet.com
**w** prestollerbedandbreakfast.co.uk

### AYLBURTON
Gloucestershire

**Trimwood House Bed & Breakfast** ★★
*Guest Accommodation*
39 High Street, Aylburton,
Lydney GL15 6DE
**t** (01594) 842163
**e** jackicollie@aol.com

### BABBACOMBE
Devon

**Seabury** ★★★★
*Guest Accommodation*
Manor Road, Babbacombe
TQ1 3JX
**t** (01803) 327255

### BAMPTON
Devon

**The Bark House** ★★★★
*Guest Accommodation*
Oakford Bridge, Bampton
EX16 9HZ
**t** (01398) 351236
**e** barkhousehotel@btconnect.com
**w** thebarkhouse.co.uk

**Lodfin Farm Bed & Breakfast**
★★★★ *Bed & Breakfast*
**SILVER AWARD**
Morebath, Bampton, Tiverton
EX16 9DD
**t** (01398) 331400
**e** info@lodfinfarm.com
**w** lodfinfarm.com

### BARBROOK
Devon

**Culdoon** ★★★★
*Bed & Breakfast*
Cherrybridge, Barbrook
EX35 6PE
**t** (01598) 752335
**e** info@culdoon.co.uk
**w** culdoon.co.uk

### BARNSTAPLE
Devon

**Acland Barton** ★★★
*Farmhouse*
Acland Road, Barnstaple
EX32 0LD
**t** (01271) 830253

**Broomhill Farm** ★★★★
*Farmhouse*
Muddiford, Barnstaple
EX31 4EX
**t** (01271) 850676

**Field House** ★★★★
*Bed & Breakfast*
Muddiford, Barnstaple
EX31 4ET
**t** (01271) 376205
**e** fieldhouse@adslexpress.co.uk

**Little Orchard** ★★★
*Guest Accommodation*
Braunton Road, Barnstaple
EX31 1GA
**t** (01271) 371714
**e** terrychaplin@accanet.com

**Lower Yelland Farm B&B**
★★★★
*Guest Accommodation*
Fremington, Barnstaple
EX31 3EN
**t** (01271) 860101
**e** peterday@loweryellandfarm.co.uk
**w** loweryellandfarm.co.uk

**The Spinney** ★★★★
*Guest House* **SILVER AWARD**
Shirwell, Barnstaple EX31 4JR
**t** (01271) 850282
**e** thespinney@shirwell.fsnet.co.uk
**w** thespinneyshirwell.co.uk

**Westcott Barton** ★★★★
*Guest Accommodation*
Middle Marwood, Barnstaple
EX31 4EF
**t** (01271) 812842
**e** westcott_barton@yahoo.co.uk
**w** westcottbarton.co.uk

### BARWICK
Somerset

**Barwick Farm House** ★★★
*Farmhouse*
Rexs Lane, Yeovil BA22 9TD
**t** (01935) 410779
**e** info@barwickfarmhouse.co.uk
**w** barwickfarmhouse.co.uk

### BATCOMBE
Somerset

**Valley View Farm** ★★★★
*Guest Accommodation*
Hincombe Hill, Shepton Mallet
BA4 6AJ
**t** (01749) 850302
**e** valleyviewfarm@lineone.co.uk
**w** http://mysite.wanadoo-members.co.uk/valleyviewfarm

### BATH
Somerset

**14 Raby Place** ★★★★
*Guest Accommodation*
Bath BA2 4EH
**t** (01225) 465120

**Abbey Rise** ★★★★
*Guest Accommodation*
97 Wells Road, Bath BA2 3AN
**t** (01225) 316177
**e** b&b@abbeyrise.co.uk
**w** abbeyrise.co.uk

**Anabelle's Guest House**
★★★ *Guest House*
6 Manvers Street, Bath
BA1 1JQ
**t** (01225) 330133
**e** dmlotfibath@yahoo.co.uk
**w** anabellesguesthouse.co.uk

**Apple Tree Guest House**
★★★★ *Guest House*
7 Pulteney Gardens, Bath
BA2 4HG
**t** (01225) 337642
**e** enquiries@appletreeguesthouse.co.uk
**w** appletreeguesthouse.co.uk

**Aquae Sulis** ★★★★
*Guest Accommodation*
174/176 Newbridge Road,
Bath BA1 3LE
**t** (01225) 420061
**e** enquiries@aquaesulishotel.co.uk
**w** aquaesulishotel.co.uk

**Ashley House** ★★★
*Guest Accommodation*
8 Pulteney Gardens, Bath
BA2 4HG
**t** (01225) 425027
**e** ashleybath@waitrose.com

**Ashley Villa** ★★★★
*Guest Accommodation*
26 Newbridge Road, Bath
BA1 3JZ
**t** (01225) 421683
**e** reservations@ashleyvilla.co.uk
**w** ashleyvilla.co.uk

**Astor House** ★★★★
*Guest House*
14 Oldfield Road, Bath
BA2 3ND
**t** (01225) 429134
**e** astorhouse.visitus@virgin.net
**w** visitus.co.uk

**Athole Guest House**
★★★★★ *Guest House*
**GOLD AWARD**
33 Upper Oldfield Park, Bath
BA2 3JX
**t** (01225) 320000
**e** info@atholehouse.co.uk
**w** atholehouse.co.uk

**Avon Guest House** ★★★
*Guest House*
1 Pulteney Gardens, Bath
BA2 4HG
t (01225) 313009
e julie@avonguesthousebath.co.uk
w avonguesthousebath.co.uk

**The Ayrlington** ★★★★★
*Guest Accommodation*
**GOLD AWARD**
24-25 Pulteney Road, Bath
BA2 4EZ
t (01225) 425495
e mail@ayrlington.com
w ayrlington.com

**Badminton Villa** ★★★★
*Guest House* **SILVER AWARD**
10 Upper Oldfield Park, Bath
BA2 3JZ
t (01225) 426347
e badmintonvilla@blueyonder.co.uk
w s-h-systems.co.uk

**Bath YHA** ★★★ *Hostel*
Bathwick Hill, Bath BA2 6JZ
t (01225) 465674
e bath@yha.org.uk
w yha.org.uk

**Beckford House B&B**
★★★★ *Bed & Breakfast*
58 Upper Oldfield Park, Bath
BA2 3LB
t (01225) 334959
e info@beckford-house.com
w beckford-house.com

**Belgrave Crescent B&B** ★★
*Bed & Breakfast*
4 Belgrave Crescent, Bath
BA1 5JU
t (01225) 429259
e info@belgravecrescent.co.uk
w belgravecrescent.co.uk

**The Belmont** ★★★
*Guest Accommodation*
7 Belmont, Lansdown Road,
Bath BA1 5DZ
t (01225) 423082
e archie_watson@hotmail.com
w belmontbath.co.uk

**Belvedere Bed & Breakfast**
★★★ *Guest Accommodation*
25 Belvedere, Lansdown Road,
Bath BA1 5ED
t (01225) 330264
e info@belvederewinevaults.co.uk
w belvederewinevaults.co.uk

**Bloomfield House** ★★★★
*Guest House*
146 Bloomfield Road, Bath
BA2 2AS
t (01225) 420105
e info@ecobloomfield.com
w ecobloomfield.com

**Braemar Guest House**
★★★★ *Bed & Breakfast*
43 Wellsway, Bath BA2 4RS
t (01225) 422743
e info@bathbraemar.co.uk
w bathbraemar.co.uk

**Bridgnorth House** ★★★
*Bed & Breakfast*
2 Crescent Gardens, Bath
BA1 2NA
t (01225) 331186
e bridgnorth@live.co.uk
w bridgnorthhouse.co.uk

**The Carfax** ★★★★★
*Guest Accommodation*
13-15 Great Pulteney Street,
Bath BA2 4BS
t (01225) 462089
e reservations@carfaxhotel.co.uk
w carfaxhotel.co.uk

**Chestnuts House** ★★★★
*Guest Accommodation*
**SILVER AWARD**
16 Henrietta Road, Bath
BA2 6LY
t (01225) 334279
e reservations@chestnutshouse.co.uk
w chestnutshouse.co.uk

**Church Farm** ★★★
*Farmhouse*
Monkton Farleigh, Bradford-on-Avon BA15 2QJ
t (01225) 858583 & 07803 966798
e reservations@churchfarmmonktonfarleigh.co.uk
w churchfarmmonktonfarleigh.co.uk

**Corston Fields Farm** ★★★★
*Farmhouse* **SILVER AWARD**
Corston, Bath BA2 9EZ
t (01225) 873305
e corston.fields@btinternet.com
w corstonfields.com

**Crescent Guest House**
★★★★ *Guest House*
21 Crescent Gardens, Bath
BA1 2NA
t (01225) 425945
e info@crescentbath.co.uk
w crescentbath.co.uk

**The Edgar Townhouse** ★★★
*Guest Accommodation*
64 Great Pulteney Street, Bath
BA2 4DN
t (01225) 420619
e edgar-hotel@btconnect.com
w edgar-hotel.co.uk

**The Firs** ★★★★
*Bed & Breakfast*
2 Newbridge Hill, Bath
BA1 3PU
t (01225) 334575
e dawnsandora@gmail.com

**Forres House** ★★★
*Guest House*
172 Newbridge Road, Bath
BA1 3LE
t (01225) 427698
e jj.forres@btinternet.co.uk
w forreshouse.co.uk

**The Garden House** ★★★★
*Bed & Breakfast*
Adelaide Place, Bath BA2 6BU
t 07769 658453
e caroline@gardenhousebath.co.uk

**The Grove Lyncombe Vale Road** ★★★★★
*Bed & Breakfast*
Lyncombe Vale Road, Bath
BA2 4LR
t (01225) 484282
e robertstrickland44@yahoo.co.uk
w bathbandb.com

**Hatt Farm** ★★★★
*Farmhouse*
Old Jockey, Box SN13 8DJ
t (01225) 742989
e b&b@hattfarm.co.uk
w hattfarm.co.uk

**Hermitage** ★★★
*Guest Accommodation*
Bath Road, Box, Corsham
SN13 8DT
t (01225) 744187
e hermitagebb@btconnect.com

**High Beeches** ★★★★
*Guest Accommodation*
156 Midford Road, Combe
Down BA2 5SE
t (01225) 830518
e info@high-beeches.com
w high-beeches.com

**The Hollies** ★★★★
*Guest Accommodation*
**SILVER AWARD**
Hatfield Road, Bath BA2 2BD
t (01225) 313366
e davcartwright@lineone.net
w theholliesbath.co.uk

**Lamp Post Villa** ★★★
*Guest Accommodation*
3 Crescent Gardens, Bath
BA1 2NA
t (01225) 331221
e lamppostvilla@aol.com

**Lavender House** ★★★★
*Guest Accommodation*
17 Bloomfield Park, Bath
BA2 2BY
t (01225) 314500
e post@lavenderhouse-bath.com
w lavenderhouse-bath.com

**Lindisfarne Guest House**
★★★★ *Bed & Breakfast*
41a Warminster Road, Bath
BA2 6XJ
t (01225) 466342
e lindisfarne-bath@talk21.com
w bath.org/hotel/lindisfarne.htm

**Marisha's Guest House**
★★★ *Guest House*
68 Newbridge Hill, Bath
BA1 3QA
t (01225) 446881
e marishasguesthouse@tiscali.co.uk
w marishasinbath.co.uk

**Marlborough House** ★★★★
*Guest Accommodation*
1 Marlborough Lane, Bath
BA1 2NQ
t (01225) 318175
e mars@manque.dircon.co.uk
w marlborough-house.net

**Milton House** ★★★★
*Guest House*
75 Wellsway, Bear Flat, Bath
BA2 4RU
t (01225) 335632
e info@milton-house.co.uk
w milton-house.co.uk

**Parkside** ★★★★
*Guest Accommodation*
11 Marlborough Lane, Bath
BA1 2NQ
t (01225) 429444
e post@parksidebandb.co.uk
w parksidebandb.co.uk

**Pulteney House** ★★★
*Guest Accommodation*
14 Pulteney Road, Bath
BA2 4HA
t (01225) 460991
e pulteney@tinyworld.co.uk
w pulteneyhotel.co.uk

**Radnor Guest House** ★★★★
*Guest House*
9 Pulteney Terrace, Pulteney
Road, Bath BA2 4HJ
t (01225) 316159
e info@radnorguesthouse.co.uk
w radnorguesthouse.co.uk

**Ravenscroft (Sydney Road)**
★★★★ *Bed & Breakfast*
**SILVER AWARD**
Sydney Road, Bath BA2 6NT
t (01225) 469267
e rav.bath@ukonline.co.uk

**The Residence** ★★★★★
*Guest Accommodation*
**GOLD AWARD**
Weston Road, Bath BA1 2XZ
t (01225) 750180
e info@theresidencebath.com
w theresidencebath.com

**Roban House** ★★★★★
*Hostel*
26 Lower Oldfield Park, Bath
BA2 3HP
t (01225) 445390
e info@robanhouse.co.uk
w robanhouse.co.uk

**St Leonards** ★★★★
*Guest Accommodation*
**SILVER AWARD**
Warminster Road, Bath
BA2 6SQ
t (01225) 465838
e stay@stleonardsbath.co.uk
w stleonardsbath.co.uk

**Tasburgh House** ★★★★★
*Guest Accommodation*
Warminster Road, Bath
BA2 6SH
t (01225) 425096
e hotel@bathtasburgh.co.uk
w bathtasburgh.co.uk

**Three Abbey Green** ★★★★
*Guest House* **SILVER AWARD**
3 Abbey Green, Bath
BA1 1NW
t (01225) 428558
e stay@threeabbeygreen.com
w threeabbeygreen.com

**Toghill House Farm** ★★★★
*Farmhouse*
Freezing Hill, Wick BS30 5RT
t (01225) 891261
e accommodation@toghillhousefarm.co.uk
w toghillhousefarm.co.uk

**The Villa Magdala** ★★★★★
*Guest Accommodation*
Henrietta Road, Bath BA2 6LX
t (01225) 466329
e office@villamagdala.co.uk
w villamagdala.co.uk

**Walton Villa** ★★★★
*Guest Accommodation*
3 Newbridge Hill, Bath
BA1 3PW
t (01225) 482792
e walton.villa@virgin.net
w walton.izest.com

**Wellsway Guest House ★★**
*Guest Accommodation*
51 Wellsway, Bath BA2 4RS
**t** (01225) 423434

**Weston Lawn ★★★★**
*Guest Accommodation*
Lucklands Road, Weston
BA1 4AY
**t** (01225) 421362
**e** reservations@westonlawn.co.uk
**w** westonlawn.co.uk

**Wheelwrights Arms ★★★★**
*Inn*
Monkton Combe, Bath
BA2 7HB
**t** (01225) 722287
**e** bookings@wheelwrightsarms.co.uk
**w** wheelwrightsarms.co.uk

## BATHEALTON
Somerset

**Hagley Bridge Farm ★★★★**
*Farmhouse*
Ridge Highway, Bathealton
TA4 2BQ
**t** (01984) 629026
**e** info@hagleybridgefarm.co.uk
**w** hagleybridgefarm.co.uk

## BATHWICK
Somerset

**Greenways ★★★**
*Guest Accommodation*
1 Forester Road, Bathwick
BA2 6QF
**t** (01225) 310132
**e** greenwaysbnb@btinternet.com
**w** greenwaysbath.co.uk

## BAWDRIP
Somerset

**Kings Farm ★★** *Farmhouse*
10 Eastside Lane, Bawdrip
TA7 8QB
**t** (01278) 683233

## BEAMBRIDGE
Somerset

**Beam Bridge Hotel and Restaurant**
Rating Applied For
*Inn*
Beam Bridge, Wellington
TA21 0HB
**t** (01823) 672223

## BEAMINSTER
Dorset

**Headington Bed & Breakfast**
★★★★ *Bed & Breakfast*
Down Road, Mosterton,
Beaminster DT8 3JF
**t** (01308) 867312
**e** headingtonbandb@hotmail.com
**w** beaminsterbedandbreakfast.co.uk

**Kitwhistle Farm ★★★**
*Farmhouse*
Beaminster Down, Beaminster
DT8 3SG
**t** (01308) 862458

**North Buckham Farm**
★★★★ *Farmhouse*
Beaminster DT8 3SH
**t** (01308) 863054
**e** trish@northbuckham.fsnet.co.uk
**w** northbuckhamfarm.co.uk

**The Walnuts ★★★★**
*Guest Accommodation*
**SILVER AWARD**
2 Prout Bridge, Beaminster
DT8 3AY
**t** (01308) 862211
**e** caroline@pielesz.freeserve.co.uk
**w** thewalnuts.co.uk

**Water Meadow House**
★★★★★ *Farmhouse*
**SILVER AWARD**
Bridge Farm, Hooke DT8 3PD
**t** (01308) 862619
**e** enquiries@watermeadowhouse.co.uk
**w** watermeadowhouse.co.uk

## BECKINGTON
Somerset

**Arundel**
Rating Applied For
*Guest Accommodation*
7 Bath Road, Frome BA11 6SW
**t** (01373) 831856
**e** arundel07@hotmail.com
**w** arundel-house.moonfruit.com

**Eden Vale Farm ★★★**
*Farmhouse*
Mill Lane, Frome BA11 6SN
**t** (01373) 830371
**e** bandb@edenvalefarm.co.uk
**w** edenvalefarm.co.uk

## BEER
Devon

**Belmont House B&B ★★★★**
*Guest Accommodation*
Gordon Terrace, Clapps Lane,
Beer EX12 3EN
**t** (01297) 24415
**e** simongooch12345@aol.com
**w** belmonthousebedandbreakfast.co.uk

**YHA Beer ★★★** *Hostel*
Bovey Combe, Townsend,
Seaton EX12 3LL
**t** 0870 770 5690
**e** beer@yha.org.uk
**w** yha.org.uk

## BERE REGIS
Dorset

**The Dorset Golf Resort**
★★★★
*Guest Accommodation*
The Dorset Golf & Country
Club, Hyde BH20 7NT
**t** (01929) 472244
**e** admin@dorsetgolfresort.com
**w** dorsetgolfresort.com

## BERROW
Somerset

**Berrow Links House ★★★★**
*Bed & Breakfast*
**SILVER AWARD**
Coast Road, Berrow TA8 2QS
**t** (01278) 751422
**e** afnt@towens.co.uk

## BERRY HILL
Gloucestershire

**Berry Hill House ★★★**
*Bed & Breakfast*
Park Road, Berry Hill, Coleford
GL16 7AG
**t** (01594) 832325
**e** glynis@berryhillhouse.co.uk
**w** berryhillhouse.co.uk

## BERRY POMEROY
Devon

**Berry Farm ★★★★**
*Farmhouse*
Berry Pomeroy, Totnes
TQ9 6LG
**t** (01803) 863231

## BERRYNARBOR
Devon

**Langleigh Guest House**
★★★★
*Guest Accommodation*
The Village, Berrynarbor
EX34 9SG
**t** (01271) 883410
**e** relax@langleighguesthouse.co.uk
**w** langleighguesthouse.co.uk

**The Lodge ★★★★**
*Guest Accommodation*
Pitt Hill, Ilfracombe EX34 9SG
**t** (01271) 883246
**e** philbridle@aol.com
**w** lodge-country-house-hotel.co.uk

## BIBURY
Gloucestershire

**Cotteswold House ★★★★**
*Bed & Breakfast*
**GOLD AWARD**
Arlington, Bibury, Cirencester
GL7 5ND
**t** (01285) 740609
**e** enquiries@cotteswoldhouse.org.uk
**w** cotteswoldhouse.org.uk

**The William Morris Bed & Breakfast ★★★★**
*Bed & Breakfast*
**SILVER AWARD**
11 The Street, Bibury GL7 5NP
**t** (01285) 740555
**e** ian@ianhoward8.wanadoo.co.uk
**w** thewilliammorris.com

## BIDEFORD
Devon

**Bulworthy Cottage ★★★★**
*Guest House* **SILVER AWARD**
Stoney Cross, Bideford
EX39 4PY
**t** (01271) 858441
**e** bulworthy@aol.com
**w** bulworthycottage.co.uk

**The Mount ★★★★**
*Guest House* **SILVER AWARD**
Northdown Road, Bideford
EX39 3LP
**t** (01237) 473748
**e** andrew@themountbideford.fsnet.co.uk
**w** themountbideford.co.uk

## BILBROOK
Somerset

**Steps Farmhouse ★★★★**
*Guest Accommodation*
Bilbrook, Minehead TA24 6HE
**t** (01984) 640974
**e** info@stepsfarmhouse.co.uk
**w** stepsfarmhouse.co.uk

**The Wayside B & B ★★★★**
*Guest Accommodation*
**SILVER AWARD**
Bilbrook, Minehead TA24 6HE
**t** (01984) 641669
**e** thewayside@tiscali.co.uk
**w** thewayside.co.uk

## BINEGAR
Somerset

**Mansefield House ★★★★**
*Guest Accommodation*
Radstock BA3 4UG
**t** (01749) 840568
**e** mansefieldhouse@aol.com
**w** mansefield-house.co.uk

## BISHOP SUTTON
Somerset

**Centaur ★★★**
*Bed & Breakfast*
Ham Lane, Bristol BS39 5TZ
**t** (01275) 332321

## BISHOP'S CLEEVE
Gloucestershire

**Manor Cottage ★★★**
*Guest Accommodation*
41 Station Road, Bishops
Cleeve GL52 8HH
**t** (01242) 673537
**w** manorcottagecheltenham.co.uk/

## BISHOPS HULL
Somerset

**The Old Mill ★★★★★**
*Bed & Breakfast*
**SILVER AWARD**
Netherclay, Bishops Hull
TA1 5AB
**t** (01823) 289732
**w** theoldmillbandb.co.uk

## BISHOP'S LYDEARD
Somerset

**Four Seasons B&B ★★★★**
*Bed & Breakfast*
Seven Ash, Bishops Lydeard
TA4 3EX
**t** (01823) 430337
**e** info@fourseasonsbedbreakfast.co.uk
**w** fourseasonsbedbreakfast.co.uk

**Pound Farm ★★★★**
*Bed & Breakfast*
Pound Lane, Bishops Lydeard
TA4 3DN
**t** (01823) 433443
**e** david@triscombe.fsworld.co.uk

**West View ★★★★**
*Guest Accommodation*
Minehead Road, Bishops
Lydeard TA4 3BS
**t** (01823) 432223
**e** info@westviewbandb.co.uk
**w** westviewbandb.co.uk

### BISHOPSTON
City of Bristol

**Basca House**
Rating Applied For
*Bed & Breakfast*
19 Broadway Road, Bishopston
BS7 8ES
t (0117) 942 2182

### BISHOPSTONE
Wiltshire

**Cheney Thatch'** ★★★
*Bed & Breakfast*
Oxon Place, Bishopstone
SN6 8PS
t (01793) 790508

### BLACKAWTON
Devon

**Middle Wadstray Farm**
★★★ *Farmhouse*
Middle Wadstray, Totnes
TQ9 7DD
t (01803) 712346
e stella.buckpitt1@btopenworld.com
w middle-wadstray-farm.com

**Washwalk Mill** ★★★★
*Bed & Breakfast*
Blackawton, Totnes TQ9 7AE
t (01803) 712217
e enquiries@washwalkmill.co.uk
w washwalkmill.co.uk

### BLAKENEY
Gloucestershire

**The Old Tump House** ★★★
*Bed & Breakfast*
New Road, Blakeney
GL15 4DG
t (01594) 517333
e georginadangelo@btinternet.com
w oldtumphouse.co.uk

### BLANDFORD FORUM
Dorset

**Anvil Inn** ★★★★ *Inn*
Salisbury Road, Pimperne,
Blandford Forum DT11 8UQ
t (01258) 453431
e theanvil.inn@btconnect.com
w anvilinn.co.uk

**Farnham Farm House**
★★★★★
*Guest Accommodation*
**GOLD AWARD**
Blandford Forum DT11 8DG
t (01725) 516254
e info@farnhamfarmhouse.co.uk
w farnhamfarmhouse.co.uk

**Lower Bryanston Farm B&B**
★★★★ *Farmhouse*
Lower Bryanston, Blandford
Forum DT11 0LS
t (01258) 452009
e andrea@bryanstonfarm.co.uk
w brylow.co.uk

**St Leonards Farmhouse**
★★★★ *Bed & Breakfast*
Wimborne Road, Blandford
Forum DT11 7SB
t (01258) 456635
e info.stleonardsfarmhouse@fsmail.net
w stleonardsfarmhouse.com

### BLATCHBRIDGE
Somerset

**Windwistle Cottage**
Rating Applied For
*Bed & Breakfast*
42 Blatchbridge, Frome
BA11 5EL
t (01373) 463643
e ajchant42@btinternet.com
w windwistle.co.uk

### BLEDINGTON
Gloucestershire

**Kings Head Inn and Restaurant** ★★★★ *Inn*
The Green, Bledington
OX7 6XQ
t (01608) 658365
e kingshead@orr-ewing.com
w kingsheadinn.net

### BLOCKLEY
Gloucestershire

**Arreton House** ★★★★
*Guest Accommodation*
Station Road, Blockley
GL56 9DT
t (01386) 701077
e bandb@arreton.demon.co.uk
w arreton.demon.co.uk

### BLUE ANCHOR
Somerset

**The Langbury** ★★★★
*Guest Accommodation*
Carhampton Road, Blue
Anchor TA24 6LB
t (01643) 821375
e post@langbury.co.uk
w langbury.co.uk

### BODMIN
Cornwall

**Bedknobs B&B** ★★★★
*Bed & Breakfast*
**SILVER AWARD**
Polgwyn, Castle Street, Bodmin
PL31 2DX
t (01208) 77553
e gilly@bedknobs.co.uk
w bedknobs.co.uk

**Bokiddick Farm** ★★★★★
*Farmhouse* **SILVER AWARD**
Bokiddick, Lanivet, Bodmin
PL30 5HP
t (01208) 831481
e gillhugo@bokiddickfarm.co.uk
w bokiddickfarm.co.uk

**Hotel Casi Casa** ★★★
*Guest Accommodation*
11 Higher Bore Street, Bodmin
PL31 1JS
t (01208) 77592
e bookings@hotelcasicasa.co.uk
w hotelcasicasa.co.uk

**Colliford Tavern** ★★★ *Inn*
St Neot, Bodmin PL14 6PZ
t (01208) 821335
e info@colliford.com
w colliford.com

**Elm Grove** ★★★
*Bed & Breakfast*
2 Elm Grove, Cardell Road,
Bodmin PL31 2NJ
t (01208) 74044

**Kemsing** ★★★★
*Guest Accommodation*
44 Crabtree Lane, Bodmin
PL31 1BL
t (01208) 73343
e dianagoom@tiscali.co.uk

**Many Views House** ★★★
*Bed & Breakfast*
Launceston Road, Cooksland,
Bodmin PL31 2AR
t (01208) 269991
e chris@manyviewshouse.co.uk
w manyviewshouse.co.uk

**The Old School House**
★★★★ *Bed & Breakfast*
Averys Green, Cardinham,
Bodmin PL30 4EA
t (01208) 821303
e libby@cardinhambb.co.uk
w cardinhambb.co.uk

**Priory Cottage** ★★★
*Bed & Breakfast*
34 Rhind Street, Bodmin
PL31 2EL
t (01208) 73064
e jackiedingle@yahoo.com
w bodminlive.com

**Rocquaine** ★★★★
*Bed & Breakfast*
13 Westheath Road, Bodmin
PL31 1QQ
t (01208) 72368
e pam@robilliard.freeserve.co.uk

**Scrumptious** ★★
*Bed & Breakfast*
26 Berrycombe Hill, Bodmin
PL31 2PW
t (01208) 75939
e rosmcnary@scrumptious.fsnet.co.uk
w cornwall-online.co.uk

**Suncroft** ★★★★
*Bed & Breakfast*
12 Boxwell Park, Bodmin
PL31 2BG
t (01208) 73408
e tbugdale2000@yahoo.co.uk

**Trewint Farm** ★★★★★
*Bed & Breakfast*
**SILVER AWARD**
Blisland, Bodmin PL30 4HX
t (01208) 851190
e johntipler@btinternet.com

### BOLVENTOR
Cornwall

**Jamaica Inn** ★★★ *Inn*
Bolventor, Launceston
PL15 7TS
t (01566) 86250
e enquiry@jamaicainn.co.uk
w jamaicainn.co.uk

### BOSCASTLE
Cornwall

**Boscastle Harbour Youth Hostel** ★★★★ *Hostel*
Palace Stables, Boscastle
PL35 0HD
t (01840) 250287
e customerservices@yha.org.uk

**Boscastle House**
Rating Applied For
*Guest Accommodation*
Tintagel Road, Boscastle
PL35 0AS
t (01840) 250654
e relax@boscastlehouse.com
w boscastlehouse.com

**Bridge House** ★★★
*Guest Accommodation*
The Bridge, Boscastle
PL35 0HE
t (01840) 250011
e bridgehousebnb@talktalk.net
w cornwall-online.co.uk

**Home Farm Bed and Breakfast** ★★★★ *Farmhouse*
**SILVER AWARD**
Boscastle PL35 0BN
t (01840) 250195
e homefarm.boscastle@tiscali.co.uk
w homefarm-boscastle.co.uk

**Lower Meadows** ★★★★
*Guest Accommodation*
Penally Hill, Boscastle
PL35 0HF
t (01840) 250570
e stay@lowermeadows.co.uk
w lowermeadows.co.uk

**The Old Coach House**
★★★★
*Guest Accommodation*
Tintagel Road, Boscastle
PL35 0AS
t (01840) 250398
e jackiefarm@btinternet.com
w old-coach.co.uk

**Orchard Lodge** ★★★★★
*Guest Accommodation*
**SILVER AWARD**
Gunpool Lane, Boscastle
PL35 0AT
t (01840) 250418
e orchardlodge@fsmail.net
w orchardlodgeboscastle.co.uk

**Reddivallen Farm** ★★★★★
*Guest Accommodation*
**SILVER AWARD**
Trevalga, Boscastle PL35 0EE
t (01840) 250854
e liz@redboscastle.com
w redboscastle.com

**The Riverside** ★★★★★
*Guest Accommodation*
The Bridge, Boscastle
PL35 0HE
t (01840) 250216
e reception@hotelriverside.co.uk
w hotelriverside.co.uk

**Trefoil Farm** ★★★
*Farmhouse*
Camelford Road, Boscastle
PL35 0AD
t (01840) 250606
e trefoilfarm@tiscali.co.uk

**Valency Bed and Breakfast**
★★★★
*Guest Accommodation*
**SILVER AWARD**
Penally Hill, Boscastle
PL35 0HF
t (01840) 250397
e tillinghast@btinternet.com
w valencybandb.com

## BOSSINEY
Cornwall

**King Arthur's Arms** ★★★
*Inn*
Fore Street, Tintagel PL34 0DA
**t** (01840) 770831
**e** kingarthurs.pub@btconnect.com
**w** kingarthursarms.co.uk

**Westcote House** ★★★★
*Bed & Breakfast*
Bossiney Road, Tintagel PL34 0AX
**t** (01840) 779194
**e** stay@westcotehouse.co.uk
**w** westcote-house.co.uk

## BOSSINGTON
Somerset

**Buckley Lodge** ★★★★
*Bed & Breakfast*
Bossington, Minehead TA24 8HQ
**t** (01643) 862521
**e** bucklodgeuk@yahoo.co.uk

**Tudor Cottage** ★★★★
*Bed & Breakfast*
**SILVER AWARD**
Porlock TA24 8HQ
**t** (01643) 862255
**e** bookings@tudorcottage.net
**w** tudorcottage.net

## BOSWINGER
Cornwall

**Boswinger YHA** ★★★ *Hostel*
Boswinger, St Austell PL26 6LL
**t** (01726) 844527

## BOURNEMOUTH
Dorset

**Alexander Lodge** ★★★★
*Guest House*
21 Southern Road, Southbourne BH6 3SR
**t** (01202) 421662
**e** alexanderlodge@yahoo.com
**w** alexanderlodgehotel.co.uk

**The Balincourt** ★★★★★
*Guest Accommodation*
**SILVER AWARD**
58 Christchurch Road, Bournemouth BH1 3PF
**t** (01202) 552962
**e** reservations@balincourt.co.uk
**w** balincourt.co.uk

**Beach Lodge** ★★★★
*Guest Accommodation*
61 Grand Avenue, Southbourne BH6 3TA
**t** (01202) 423396
**e** stay@beach-lodge.co.uk
**w** beach-lodge.co.uk

**The Blue Palms** ★★★★
*Guest Accommodation*
26 Tregonwell Road, Bournemouth BH2 5NS
**t** (01202) 554968
**e** bluepalmshotel@btopenworld.com
**w** bluepalmshotel.com

**Cavendish** ★★★★
*Guest Accommodation*
20 Durley Chine Road, West Cliff BH2 5LF
**t** (01202) 290489
**e** info@cavendishhotel.uk.net
**w** cavendishhotel.uk.net

**The Charlesworth** ★★★
*Guest Accommodation*
35 Tregonwell Road, Bournemouth BH2 5NT
**t** (01202) 779177
**e** enquiries@charlesworthhotel.net
**w** charlesworthhotel.net

**Charlton Lodge** ★★★
*Bed & Breakfast*
826 Ringwood Road, Bournemouth BH11 8NF
**t** (01202) 249977
**e** friggs@cwctv.net

**The Claremont** ★★★★
*Guest Accommodation*
89 St Michaels Road, Bournemouth BH2 5DR
**t** (01202) 290875
**e** info@claremonthotelbournemouth.co.uk
**w** claremonthotelbournemouth.co.uk

**Cransley** ★★★★
*Guest Accommodation*
11 Knyveton Road, East Cliff, Bournemouth BH1 3QG
**t** (01202) 290067
**e** info@cransley.com
**w** cransley.com

**Cremona** ★★★
*Guest Accommodation*
St Michaels Road, West Cliff, Bournemouth BH2 5DP
**t** (01202) 290035
**e** enquiries@cremona.co.uk
**w** cremona.co.uk

**Denewood** ★★★
*Guest Accommodation*
1 Percy Road, Bournemouth BH5 1JE
**t** (01202) 394493
**e** info@denewood.co.uk
**w** denewood.co.uk

**Earlham Lodge** ★★★★
*Guest House*
91 Alumhurst Road, Alum Chine, Bournemouth BH4 8HR
**t** (01202) 761943
**e** earlhamlodge@hotmail.com
**w** earlhamlodge.com

**Fielden Court** ★★★★
*Guest House*
20 Southern Road, Bournemouth BH6 3SR
**t** (01202) 427459
**e** enquiries@fieldencourthotel.co.uk
**w** fieldencourthotel.co.uk

**The Fircliff** ★★★★
*Guest House*
Studland Road, Bournemouth BH4 8HZ
**t** (01202) 765307
**e** coastl@tiscali.co.uk

**Ingledene Guest House** ★★
*Guest House*
20 Gardens View, Bournemouth BH1 3QA
**t** (01202) 291914
**e** ingledenehouse@yahoo.com
**w** ingledenehouse.co.uk

**The Kings Langley** ★★★
*Guest House*
1 West Cliff Road, Bournemouth BH2 5ES
**t** (01202) 557349
**e** john@kingslangleyhotel.com
**w** kingslangleyhotel.com

**Marlins** ★★★★
*Guest Accommodation*
2 West Cliff Road, West Cliff BH2 5EY
**t** (01202) 299645
**e** reservations@marlinshotel.com
**w** marlinshotel.com

**Mount Lodge Guest Accommodation** ★★
*Guest House*
19 Beaulieu Road, Alum Chine BH4 8HY
**t** (01202) 761173
**e** mountlodgehotel@yahoo.co.uk

**The Silver How** ★★★
*Guest Accommodation*
5 West Cliff Gardens, Bournemouth BH2 5HN
**t** (01202) 551537
**e** reservations@silverhowhotel.co.uk
**w** silverhowhotel.co.uk

**Southernhay Guest House** ★★★ *Guest Accommodation*
42 Alum Chine Road, Westbourne, Bournemouth BH4 8DX
**t** (01202) 761251
**e** enquiries@southernhayhotel.co.uk
**w** southernhayhotel.co.uk

**Wenrose** ★★★★
*Guest Accommodation*
23 Drummond Road, Boscombe BH1 4DP
**t** (01202) 396451 & 07778 800804
**e** wenrose@bigfoot.com
**w** bournemouthbedandbreakfast.com

**Winter Dene Guest House** ★★★★
*Guest Accommodation*
11 Durley Road South, West Cliff BH2 5JH
**t** (01202) 554150
**e** info@winterdenehotel.com
**w** winterdenehotel.com

**Wood Lodge** ★★★★
*Guest House*
10 Manor Road, Bournemouth BH1 3EY
**t** (01202) 290891
**e** enquiries@woodlodgehotel.co.uk
**w** woodlodgehotel.co.uk

**The Woodlands** ★★★
*Guest House*
28 Percy Road, Bournemouth BH5 1JG
**t** (01202) 396499
**e** stay@the-woodlands-hotel.co.uk
**w** the-woodlands-hotel.co.uk

## BOURTON-ON-THE-WATER
Gloucestershire

**Alderley Guest House** ★★★★
*Guest Accommodation*
**SILVER AWARD**
Rissington Road, Bourton-on-the-Water GL54 2DX
**t** (01451) 822788
**e** alderleyguesthouse@hotmail.com
**w** alderleyguesthouse.com

**Bella Dorma** ★★★
*Bed & Breakfast*
Station Road, Bourton-on-the-Water GL54 2EN
**t** (01451) 810489
**e** email@belladorma.co.uk
**w** belladorma.co.uk

**Broadlands Guest House** ★★★★
*Guest Accommodation*
Clapton Row, Bourton-on-the-Water GL54 2DN
**t** (01451) 822002
**e** marco@broadlands-guest-house.co.uk
**w** broadlands-guest-house.co.uk

**Coombe House** ★★★★
*Guest Accommodation*
**GOLD AWARD**
Rissington Road, Bourton-on-the-Water GL54 2DT
**t** (01451) 821966
**e** info@coombehouse.net
**w** coombehouse.net

**Elvington Bed and Breakfast** ★★★★ *Bed & Breakfast*
Rissington Road, Bourtin-on-the-Water GL54 2DX
**t** (01451) 822026
**e** the@tuckwells.freeserve.co.uk
**w** bandb.fsnet.co.uk

**Farncombe** ★★★★
*Bed & Breakfast*
Clapton-on-the-Hill, Bourton-on-the-Water GL54 2LG
**t** (01451) 820120
**e** julia@farncombecotswolds.com
**w** farncombecotswolds.com

**Holly House** ★★★★
*Guest Accommodation*
Station Road, Bourton-on-the-Water GL54 2ER
**t** (01451) 821302
**e** paula@hollyhousebourton.co.uk
**w** hollyhousebourton.co.uk

**The Lamb Inn** ★★★★ *Inn*
Great Rissington GL54 2LP
**t** (01451) 820388
**e** enquiry@thelambinn.com
**w** thelambinn.com

**Lansdowne Villa Guest House** ★★★★ *Guest House*
Lansdowne, Bourton-on-the-Water GL54 2AR
**t** (01451) 820673
**e** enquiries@lansdownevilla.co.uk
**w** lansdownevilla.co.uk

**Manor Close** ★★★★
*Bed & Breakfast*
High Street, Bourton-on-the-Water GL54 2AP
**t** (01451) 820339
**e** sheenamanorclose@aol.com

**Meadow Rise** ★★★★
*Bed & Breakfast*
**GOLD AWARD**
Pock Hill Lane, Bourton-on-the-Water GL54 2DD
**t** (01451) 821860
**e** info@meadow-rise.co.uk
**w** meadow-rise.co.uk

**Mousetrap Inn** ★★★ *Inn*
Lansdown, Bourton-on-the-Water GL54 2AR
**t** (01451) 820579
**e** thebatesies@gmail.com
**w** mousetrap-inn.co.uk

**Old New Inn** ★★ *Inn*
The Old New Inn, Bourtin-on-the-Water GL54 2AF
**t** (01451) 820467
**e** reception@theoldnewinn.co.uk
**w** theoldnewinn.co.uk

**The Ridge Guesthouse** ★★★★
*Guest Accommodation*
**SILVER AWARD**
Whiteshoots Hill, Bourton-on-the-Water GL54 2LE
**t** (01451) 820660
**e** info@theridge-guesthouse.co.uk
**w** theridge-guesthouse.co.uk

**Southlands** ★★★★
*Guest Accommodation*
Rissington Road, Bourton-on-the-Water GL54 2DT
**t** (01451) 821987
**e** info@southlands-bb.co.uk
**w** southlands-bb.co.uk

**Touchstone** ★★★★
*Bed & Breakfast*
Little Rissington, Bourton-on-the-Water GL54 2ND
**t** (01451) 822481
**e** touchstone.bb@lineone.net
**w** http://website.lineone.net/~touchstone.bb

**Trevone Bed & Breakfast**
★★★ *Bed & Breakfast*
Moore Road, Bourton-on-the-Water GL54 2AZ
**t** 07740 805250
**e** admin@the-mad-hatter-tearoom.co.uk
**w** the-mad-hatter-tearoom.co.uk

**Webby's Windrush Walk**
★★★ *Bed & Breakfast*
37 Rissington Road, Bourton-on-the-Water GL54 2AY
**t** (01451) 810382
**e** p-webb@hotmail.com
**w** webbys-windrushwalk.co.uk

## BOVEY TRACEY
Devon

**Brookfield House** ★★★★★
*Bed & Breakfast*
**GOLD AWARD**
Challabrook Lane, Bovey Tracey TQ13 9DF
**t** (01626) 836181
**e** enquiries@brookfield-house.com
**w** brookfield-house.com

**Oaklands** ★★★★
*Bed & Breakfast*
Challabrook Lane, Bovey Tracey TQ13 9DF
**t** (01626) 832602
**e** oaklandsbedandbreakfast@sky.com
**w** oaklandsholidaysdevon.co.uk

## BOX
Wiltshire

**Lorne House**
Rating Applied For
*Guest House*
London Road, Box, Corsham SN13 8NA
**t** (01225) 742597
**e** info@lornehouse.box.co.uk
**w** lornehousebox.co.uk

**Norbin Farm** ★★★★
*Farmhouse*
Norbin, Box SN13 8JJ
**t** (01225) 866907
**e** gillhillier@yahoo.co.uk
**w** norbin-farm.co.uk

## BRADFORD-ON-AVON
Wiltshire

**The Beeches Farmhouse**
★★★★ *Farmhouse*
Holt Road, Bradford-on-Avon BA15 1TS
**t** (01225) 865170
**e** beeches-farmhouse@netgates.co.uk
**w** beeches-farmhouse.co.uk

**The Georgian Lodge** ★★
*Guest Accommodation*
25 Bridge Street, Bradford-on-Avon BA15 1BY
**t** (01225) 862268
**e** georgianlodge@btconnect.com
**w** georgianlodgehotel.com

**Great Ashley Farm** ★★★★
*Bed & Breakfast*
**SILVER AWARD**
Great Ashley, Bradford-on-Avon BA15 2PP
**t** (01225) 864563
**e** info@greatashley.co.uk
**w** greatashley.co.uk

**Honeysuckle Cottage**
★★★★ *Bed & Breakfast*
**SILVER AWARD**
95 The Common, Broughton Gifford SN12 8ND
**t** (01225) 782463
**e** info@honeysuckle-cottage.org.uk
**w** honeysuckle-cottage.org.uk

**Springfields** ★★★★
*Guest Accommodation*
Great Ashley, Bradford-on-Avon BA15 2PP
**t** (01225) 866125
**e** springfieldsbnb@talktalk.net
**w** springfields.talktalk.net

## BRADPOLE
Dorset

**Orchard Barn** ★★★★★
*Guest Accommodation*
**SILVER AWARD**
Off Lee Lane, Bradpole DT6 4AR
**t** (01308) 455655
**e** reservations@lodgeatorchardbarn.co.uk
**w** wlodgeatorchardbarn.co.uk

**Spray Copse Farm** ★★★★
*Bed & Breakfast*
Lee Lane, Bridport DT6 4AP
**t** (01308) 458510

## BRADWORTHY
Devon

**Lew Barn** ★★★
*Guest Accommodation*
Bradworthy, Holsworthy EX22 7SQ
**t** (01409) 241964
**e** lewmillington@btinternet.com
**w** lewbarn.co.uk

## BRANKSOME PARK
Dorset

**Grovefield Manor** ★★★★
*Guest House*
18 Pinewood Road, Branksome Park BH13 6JS
**t** (01202) 766798
**e** grovefieldmanor@aol.com
**w** grovefieldmanor.com/

## BRATTON CLOVELLY
Devon

**Eversfield Lodge** ★★★★
*Guest Accommodation*
Ellacott Barton, Bratton Clovelly EX20 4LB
**t** (01837) 871480
**e** bookings@eversfieldlodge.co.uk
**w** eversfieldlodge.co.uk/

## BRATTON FLEMING
Devon

**Haxton Down Farm** ★★★★
*Farmhouse*
Bratton Fleming, Barnstaple EX32 7JL
**t** (01598) 710275
**e** haxtondownfarm@btconnect.com
**w** haxton-down-farm-holidays.co.uk

**Sheltercombe Cottage**
★★★★ *Bed & Breakfast*
Bratton Fleming, Barnstaple EX32 7JL
**t** (01598) 710513
**e** enquiries@sheltercombecottage.co.uk
**w** sheltercombecottage.co.uk

## BRAUNTON
Devon

**The George** ★★★ *Inn*
Exeter Road, Braunton EX33 2JJ
**t** (01271) 812029
**e** enquiries@georgehotel-braunton.co.uk
**w** georgehotel-braunton.co.uk

## BRAYFORD
Devon

**Kimbland Farm** ★★★
*Farmhouse*
Brayford, Barnstaple EX32 7PS
**t** (01598) 710352
**e** info@kimblandfarmholidays.co.uk
**w** kimblandfarmholidays.co.uk

## BREAM
Gloucestershire

**Lindum House** ★★★
*Bed & Breakfast*
Oakwood Road, Bream, Lydney GL15 6HS
**t** (01594) 560378
**e** lynne@lindumhouse.fsworld.co.uk
**w** lindum-house.co.uk

**Rising Sun** ★★★ *Inn*
High Street, Bream, Lydney GL15 6JF
**t** (01594) 564555
**e** jonjo_risingsun@msn.com
**w** therisingsunbream.co.uk

## BREAN
Somerset

**Yew Tree House** ★★★★
*Guest Accommodation*
Hurn Lane, Berrow, Nr Brean, Burnham-on-Sea TA8 2QT
**t** (01278) 751382
**e** yewtree@yewtree-house.co.uk
**w** yewtree-house.co.uk

## BRENDON HILL
Somerset

**Raleghs Cross Inn** ★★★★
*Inn*
Raleghs Cross, Watchet TA23 0LN
**t** (01984) 640343
**e** stay@raleghscross.co.uk
**w** raleghscross.co.uk

## BRENTOR
Devon

**Burnville House** ★★★★★
*Farmhouse* **SILVER AWARD**
Burnville Farm, Brentor PL19 0NE
**t** (01822) 820443
**e** burnvillef@aol.com
**w** burnville.co.uk

## BRIDESTOWE
Devon

**Fox & Hounds** *Camping Barn*
Fox & Hounds Hotel, Bridestowe EX20 4HF
**t** (01822) 820206
**e** info@foxandhoundshotel.com
**w** foxandhoundshotel.com

## BRIDGWATER
Somerset

**The Boat & Anchor Inn**
★★★ *Inn*
Meads Crossing, Huntworth, Bridgwater TA7 0AQ
**t** (01278) 662473
**e** andrea@theboatandanchor.co.uk
**w** theboatandanchor.co.uk

**Chestnut Houseclaveys**
★★★★★
*Guest Accommodation*
**SILVER AWARD**
Hectors Stones, Lower Road, Woolavington TA7 8EF
**t** (01278) 683658
**e** paul@chestnuthousehotel.com
**w** chestnuthousehotel.com

**Hill View** ★★★★
*Bed & Breakfast*
**SILVER AWARD**
55 Liney Road, Westonzoyland, Nr Bridgwater TA7 0EU
**t** (01278) 699027
**e** hillview@westonzoyland.fsbusiness.co.uk
**w** visit-hillview.co.uk

**Manor Farm** ★★★
*Farmhouse*
Waterpits, Broomfield TA5 1AT
**t** (01823) 451266
**e** sue@manorfarmbreaks.co.uk
**w** manorfarmbreaks.co.uk

**The Olive Mill** ★★★★
*Restaurant with Rooms*
Chilton Polden Hill, Bridgwater TA7 9AH
**t** (01278) 722202
**e** enquiries@theolivemill.co.uk
**w** theolivemill.co.uk

## BRIDPORT
Dorset

**The Bookend**
Rating Applied For
*Bed & Breakfast*
Melville Square, Bridport DT6 3LS
**t** (0118) 930 2504

**Britmead House** ★★★★
*Guest Accommodation*
West Bay Road, Bridport DT6 4EG
**t** (01308) 422941
**e** britmead@talk21.com
**w** britmeadhouse.co.uk

**Durbeyfield Guest House**
★★★ *Guest Accommodation*
10 West Bay, Bridport DT6 4EL
**t** (01308) 423307
**e** manager@durbeyfield.co.uk
**w** durbeyfield.co.uk

**Eypeleaze** ★★★★
*Bed & Breakfast*
117 West Bay Road, Bridport DT6 4EQ
**t** (01308) 423363
**e** enquiries@eypeleaze.co.uk
**w** eypeleaze.co.uk

**The Gables** ★★★★
*Bed & Breakfast*
West Allington, Bridport DT6 5BH
**t** (01308) 459963
**e** donaldbroadley@hotmail.com
**w** thegablesbridport.co.uk

**Highway Farm** ★★★★
*Guest Accommodation*
**SILVER AWARD**
West Road, Bridport DT6 6AE
**t** (01308) 424321
**e** bale@highwayfarm.co.uk
**w** highwayfarm.co.uk

**New House Farm** ★★★
*Farmhouse*
Mangerton Lane, Bridport DT6 3SF
**t** (01308) 422884
**e** jane@mangertonlake.freeserve.co.uk
**w** mangertonlake.co.uk

**Patchwork House** ★★★★
*Guest Accommodation*
47 Burton Road, Bridport DT6 4JE
**t** (01308) 456515
**w** patchworkhouse.co.uk

**The Roundham House** ★★★★★
*Guest Accommodation*
**SILVER AWARD**
Roundham Gardens, West Bay Road, Bridport DT6 4BD
**t** (01308) 422753
**e** cyprencom@compuserve.com
**w** roundhamhouse.co.uk

**Southfield** ★★★★
*Bed & Breakfast*
Marsh Gate, Burton Road, Bridport DT6 4JB
**t** (01308) 458910
**e** angela@southfield-westbay.co.uk
**w** southfield-westbay.co.uk

**The Tiger Inn** ★★★ *Inn*
14-16 Barrack Street, Bridport DT6 3LY
**t** (01308) 427543
**e** jacquie@tigerinnbridport.co.uk
**w** tigerinnbridport.co.uk

**The Well** ★★★
*Bed & Breakfast*
St Andrews Well, Bridport DT6 3DL
**t** (01308) 424156
**e** thewellbandb@yahoo.co.uk
**w** thewellbedandbreakfast.co.uk

**The White House**
Rating Applied For
*Bed & Breakfast*
90 West Bay Road, Bridport DT6 4AY
**t** (01308) 458708
**e** enquiries@thewhitehouse.co.uk
**w** thewhitehousebb.co.uk

## BRISLINGTON
City of Bristol

**Woodstock Guest House**
★★★★ *Guest House*
534 Bath Road, Brislington BS4 3JZ
**t** (0117) 987 1613
**e** woodstock@blueyonder.co.uk
**w** woodstockguesthouse.org

## BRISTOL
City of Bristol

**Arches House** ★★★
*Guest Accommodation*
132 Cotham Brow, Bristol BS6 6AE
**t** (0117) 924 7398
**e** ml@arches-hotel.co.uk
**w** arches-hotel.co.uk

**The Bowl Inn and Lilies Restaurant** ★★★ *Inn*
16 Church Road, Almondsbury, Bristol BS32 4DT
**t** (01454) 612757
**e** reception@thebowlinn.co.uk
**w** thebowlinn.co.uk

**Bristol YHA** ★★★ *Hostel*
14 Narrow Quay, Bristol BS1 4QA
**t** (0117) 922 1659
**e** bristol@yha.org.uk
**w** yha.org.uk

**Downs View Guest House**
★★★ *Guest House*
38 Upper Belgrave Road, Bristol BS8 2XN
**t** (0117) 973 7046
**e** bookings@downsviewguesthouse.co.uk
**w** downsviewguesthouse.co.uk

**Norfolk House** ★★★
*Guest Accommodation*
577 Gloucester Road, Bristol BS7 0BW
**t** (0117) 951 3191
**e** 577norfolk@blueyonder.co.uk

**The Paddock** ★★★
*Guest Accommodation*
Hung Road, Shirehampton BS11 9XJ
**t** (0117) 923 5140

**Treborough** ★★
*Bed & Breakfast*
3 Grove Road, Coombe Dingle BS9 2RQ
**t** (0117) 968 2712

**Tyndall's Park** ★★
*Guest Accommodation*
4 Tyndall's Park Road, Clifton BS8 1PG
**t** (0117) 973 5407
**e** contactus@tyndallsparkhotel.co.uk
**w** tyndallsparkhotel.co.uk

**Wesley College** ★★ *Campus*
College Park Drive, Henbury Road, Bristol BS10 7QD
**t** (0117) 959 1200
**e** rogers@wesley-college-bristol.ac.uk
**w** wesley-college-bristol.ac.uk

**Westfield House** ★★★★
*Bed & Breakfast*
37 Stoke Hill, Sneyd Park, Bristol BS9 1LQ
**t** (0117) 962 6119
**e** guest@westfieldhouse.net
**w** westfieldhouse.net

## BRIXHAM
Devon

**The Brioc** ★★★★
*Guest Accommodation*
11 Prospect Road, Brixham TQ5 8HS
**t** (01803) 853540
**e** bill@brioc-hotel.fsnet.co.uk
**w** brioc-hotel.fsnet.co.uk

**Brookside Guest House** ★★★★
*Guest Accommodation*
**GOLD AWARD**
160 New Road, Brixham TQ5 8DA
**t** (01803) 858858
**e** holidays@brooksidebrixham.co.uk
**w** brooksidebrixham.co.uk

**Churston Way Lodge** ★★★
*Guest Accommodation*
2 Churston Way, Brixham TQ5 8DD
**t** (01803) 853315
**e** info@churchstonwaylodge.co.uk
**w** churstonwaylodge.co.uk

**Fair Winds**
Rating Applied For
*Guest House*
166 New Road, Brixham TQ5 8DA
**t** (01803) 857537
**e** paulandgillbrixham@btinternet.com
**w** fairwindsbrixham.co.uk

**Lamorna Guest House**
★★★★ *Guest House*
130 New Road, Brixham TQ5 8DA
**t** (01803) 853954
**e** caroline@lamorna.orangehome.co.uk
**w** lamornabedandbreakfast.co.uk

**Melville Guest House** ★★★
*Guest House*
45 New Road, Brixham TQ5 8NL
**t** (01803) 852033
**e** melvillehotel@brixham45.fsnet.co.uk
**w** smoothhound.co.uk/hotels/melville2

**Midhurst Bed & Breakfast** ★★★★
*Guest Accommodation*
132 New Road, Brixham TQ5 8DA
**t** (01803) 857331
**w** midhurstbnb.co.uk

**Raddicombe Lodge** ★★★★
*Guest Accommodation*
Kingswear Road, Brixham TQ5 0EX
**t** (01803) 882125
**e** stay@raddicombelodge.co.uk
**w** raddicombelodge.co.uk

**Ranscombe House** ★★★★
*Guest Accommodation*
Ranscombe Road, Brixham TQ5 9UP
**t** (01803) 882337
**e** ranscombe@lineone.net
**w** ranscombehousehotel.co.uk

**Redlands** ★★★★
*Guest House*
136 New Road, Brixham TQ5 8DA
**t** (01803) 853813
**e** redlandsbrixham@aol.com
**w** redlandsbrixham.co.uk

**Sampford House** ★★★
*Guest Accommodation*
57-59 King Street, Brixham TQ5 9TH
**t** (01803) 857761
**e** sampfordhouse@yahoo.co.uk
**w** sampfordhouse.co.uk

**Sea Tang Guest House**
★★★★ *Guest House*
67 Berry Head Road, Brixham
TQ5 9AA
t (01803) 854651
e seatangguesthouse@yahoo.co.uk
w smoothhound.co.uk/hotels/seatang

**The Shoalstone** ★★★
*Guest Accommodation*
105 Berry Head Road, Brixham
TQ5 9AG
t (01803) 857919

**Sunnybrook Guest House**
★★★ *Guest House*
156 New Road, Brixham
TQ5 8DA
t (01803) 854386
e info@sunnybrook.co.uk
w sunnybrook.co.uk

**Trefoil Guest House** ★★★★
*Guest House*
134 New Road, Brixham
TQ5 8DA
t (01803) 855266
e david.harmer@virgin.net
w trefoilguesthouse.co.uk

**Westbury Guest House**
★★★★ *Guest House*
51 New Road, Brixham
TQ5 8NL
t (01803) 851684
e info@westburyguesthouse.co.uk
w westburyguesthouse.co.uk

**White Horse Guesthouse**
★★★★ *Guest House*
Dartmouth Road, Churston
Ferrers TQ5 0LL
t (01803) 842381
e bookings@thewhitehorsehotel.co.uk
w thewhitehorsehotel.co.uk

**Woodlands Guest House**
★★★★ *Guest House*
Parkham Road, Brixham
TQ5 9BU
t (01803) 852040
e woodlandsbrixham@btinternet.com
w woodlandsdevon.co.uk

## BRIXTON Devon

**Venn Farm** ★★★★
*Guest Accommodation*
Brixton, Plymouth PL8 2AX
t (01752) 880378
e info@vennfarm.co.uk
w vennfarm.co.uk

## BROAD CHALKE Wiltshire

**Lodge Farmhouse Bed & Breakfast** ★★★★
*Bed & Breakfast*
Lodge Farmhouse, Broad
Chalke, Salisbury SP5 5LU
t (01725) 519242
e mj.roe@virgin.net
w lodge-farmhouse.co.uk

**Old Stoke**
Rating Applied For
*Bed & Breakfast*
Stoke Farthing, Salisbury
SP5 5ED
t (01722) 780513
e stay@oldstoke.co.uk
w oldstoke.co.uk

## BROADCLYST Devon

**Heath Gardens** ★★★★
*Bed & Breakfast*
Broadclyst, Exeter EX5 3HL
t (01392) 462311
e info@heathgardens.co.uk
w heathgardens.co.uk

## BROADHEMBURY Devon

**Stafford Barton Farm**
★★★★ *Farmhouse*
Broadhembury, Honiton
EX14 3LU
t (01404) 841403
e jeanwalters1@tesco.net

## BROADOAK Dorset

**Dunster Farm** ★★★★
*Farmhouse*
Broadoak, Bridport DT6 5NR
t (01308) 424626
e dunsterfarm@ukonline.co.uk
w dunsterfarm.co.uk

## BROADSTONE Dorset

**Ashdell** ★★ *Bed & Breakfast*
85 Dunyeats Road, Broadstone
BH18 8AF
t (01202) 692032
e ian@ashdell.fsnet.co.uk
w ashdell.co.uk

**Honey Lodge** ★★★★
*Bed & Breakfast*
**SILVER AWARD**
41 Dunyeats Road, Broadstone
BH18 8AB
t (01202) 694247
e honey_lodge41@hotmail.com
w honeylodge.co.uk

**Tarven** ★★ *Bed & Breakfast*
Corfe Lodge Road, Broadstone
BH18 9NF
t (01202) 694338
e browning@tarvencorfe.fsnet.co.uk
w tarven.co.uk

**Weston Cottage** ★★★★
*Bed & Breakfast*
6 Macaulay Road, Broadstone
BH18 8AR
t (01202) 699638
e westoncot@aol.com
w westoncottage.org.uk

## BROADWELL Gloucestershire

**The White House** ★★★
*Bed & Breakfast*
2 South Road, Broadwell,
Coleford GL16 7BH
t (01594) 837069
e whitehousebroadwell@yahoo.co.uk
w whitehousebroadwell.co.uk

## BROADWINDSOR Dorset

**Cross Keys House** ★★★★★
*Bed & Breakfast*
**SILVER AWARD**
High Street, Broadwindsor
DT8 3QP
t (01308) 868063
e robin.adeney@care4free.net
w crosskeyshouse.com

## BROMHAM Wiltshire

**Wayside** ★★★★
*Bed & Breakfast*
Chittoe Heath, Bromham
SN15 2EH
t (01380) 850695
e mail@jandlseed.co.uk
w waysideofwiltshire.co.uk

## BROMPTON REGIS Somerset

**The George Inn** ★★★ *Inn*
Dulverton TA22 9NL
t (01398) 371273
e thegeorgeexmoor@btconnect.com
w thegeorgeexmoor.co.uk

## BRUTON Somerset

**Gants Mill & Garden** ★★★★
*Farmhouse*
Gants Mill Lane, Bruton
BA10 0DB
t (01749) 812393
e shingler@gantsmill.co.uk
w gantsmill.co.uk

## BRYHER Isles of Scilly

**Bank Cottage Guest House**
★★★★ *Guest House*
Bryher TR23 0PR
t (01720) 422612
e mac.mace@homecall.co.uk
w bryher-ios.co.uk/bc/bank_cottage/bank_cottage.html

**Soleil D'or** ★★★★
*Bed & Breakfast*
Bryher TR23 0PR
t (01720) 422003

## BUCKERELL Devon

**Broadlands** ★★★★
*Bed & Breakfast*
Buckerell, Honiton EX14 3EP
t (01404) 850894

## BUCKHORN WESTON Dorset

**The Stapleton Arms** ★★★★
*Inn*
Stapleton Arms, Church Hill,
Gillingham SP8 5HS
t (01963) 370396
e relax@thestapletonarms.com
w thestapletonarms.com

## BUCKLAND NEWTON Dorset

**Holyleas House** ★★★★★
*Guest Accommodation*
Buckland Newton, Dorchester
DT2 7DP
t (01300) 345214
e tiabunkall@holyleas.fsnet.co.uk
w holyleashouse.co.uk

**Rew Cottage** ★★★★
*Bed & Breakfast*
Buckland Newton, Dorchester
DT2 7DN
t (01300) 345467

## BUDE Cornwall

**Beach House** ★★★
*Guest Accommodation*
Marine Drive, Widemouth Bay,
Bude EX23 0AW
t (01288) 361256
e beachhousebookings@tiscali.co.uk
w beachhousewidemouth.co.uk

**Bentley House** ★★★★
*Bed & Breakfast*
Killerton Road, Bude
EX23 8EW
t (01288) 353698
e amanda@bentleyhousebude.com
w bentleyhousebude.com

**Bossiney House** ★★★★
*Bed & Breakfast*
1 Flexbury Park Road, Bude
EX23 8HP
t (01288) 353356
w bossineyhousebandb.co.uk

**Brendon Arms** ★★★ *Inn*
Vicarage Road, Bude EX23 8SD
t (01288) 354542
e enquiries@brendonarms.co.uk
w brendonarms.co.uk

**Creathorne Farm Bed & Breakfast** ★★★★★
*Farmhouse* **SILVER AWARD**
The Granary, Creathorne Farm,
Bude EX23 0NE
t (01288) 361077
e alisonnicklen@tiscali.co.uk
w creathornefarm.co.uk

**East Woolley Farm** ★★★★
*Guest Accommodation*
**SILVER AWARD**
Woolley, Bude EX23 9PP
t (01288) 331525
e julia@eastwoolleyfarm.plus.com
w eastwoolleyfarm.co.uk

**The Edgcumbe** ★★★★
*Guest Accommodation*
Summerleaze Crescent, Bude
EX23 8HJ
t (01288) 353846
e info@edgcumbe-hotel.co.uk
w edgcumbe-hotel.co.uk

**The Elms** ★★★
*Bed & Breakfast*
37 Lynstone Road, Bude
EX23 8LR
t (01288) 353429

**The Grosvenor** ★★★
*Guest House*
10 Summerleaze Crescent,
Bude EX23 8HH
t (01288) 352062
e enquiries@thegrosvenor-bude.co.uk
w thegrosvenor-bude.co.uk

**Harefield Cottage** ★★★★
*Guest House* **SILVER AWARD**
Upton, Bude EX23 0LY
t (01288) 352350
e sales@coast-countryside.co.uk
w coast-countryside.co.uk

**Highbre Crest ★★★★**
*Guest Accommodation*
**SILVER AWARD**
Whitstone, Holsworthy
EX22 6UF
**t** (01288) 341002
**e** lindacole285@btinternet.com
**w** highbrecrest.co.uk

**Hillbrook ★★★**
*Guest Accommodation*
37 Killerton Road, Bude
EX23 8EL
**t** (01288) 353156
**e** cathyrushbrook@tiscali.co.uk
**w** http://myweb.tiscali.co.uk/hillbrookinfo

**Langaton Farm ★★★★**
*Farmhouse*
Whitstone, Bude EX22 6TS
**t** (01288) 341215
**e** langatonfarm@hotmail.com
**w** langaton-farm-holidays.co.uk

**Links Side ★★★★**
*Guest House*
7 Burn View, Bude EX23 8BY
**t** (01288) 352410
**e** linksidebude@hotmail.com
**w** linkssidebude.co.uk

**Little Haven ★★★★**
*Bed & Breakfast*
**SILVER AWARD**
Silverton Road, Bude EX23 8EY
**t** (01288) 354719

**Meadow View ★★★★**
*Bed & Breakfast*
6 Kings Hill Close, Bude
EX23 8RR
**t** (01288) 355095

**Oketon B & B**
Rating Applied For
*Guest Accommodation*
11 Flexbury Park Road, Bude
EX23 8HR
**t** (01288) 350614
**e** orrwilcox@aol.com
**w** oketon.co.uk

**The Palms Guest House**
★★★★ *Guest House*
17 Burn View, Bude EX23 8BZ
**t** (01288) 353962
**e** palmsguesthouse@tiscali.co.uk
**w** palms-bude.co.uk

**Riverview ★★★**
*Bed & Breakfast*
Granville Terrace, Bude
EX23 8JZ
**t** (01288) 359399
**e** vennings@beeb.net

**Scadghill Farm ★★★★**
*Guest Accommodation*
**SILVER AWARD**
Stibb, Bude EX23 9HN
**t** (01288) 352373
**e** scadghillfarm@btconnect.com
**w** scadghillfarm.co.uk

**Strands ★★★**
*Guest Accommodation*
Stibb, Bude EX23 9HW
**t** (01288) 353514
**e** brendadunstanbude@yahoo.co.uk

**Stratton Gardens House ★★★★**
*Guest Accommodation*
Cot Hill, Stratton, Bude
EX23 9DN
**t** (01288) 352500
**e** moira@stratton-gardens.co.uk
**w** stratton-gardens.co.uk

**Sunrise Guest House**
★★★★ *Guest House*
**SILVER AWARD**
6 Burn View, Bude EX23 8BY
**t** (01288) 353214
**e** sunriseguest@btconnect.com
**w** sunrise-bude.co.uk

**Surf Haven ★★★★**
*Guest House*
31 Downs View, Bude
EX23 8RG
**t** (01288) 353923
**e** info@surfhaven.co.uk
**w** surfhaven.co.uk

**Tee-Side ★★★★**
*Guest House*
2 Burn View, Bude EX23 8BY
**t** (01288) 352351
**e** rayandjune@tee-side.co.uk
**w** tee-side.co.uk

**Tresillian ★★★★**
*Guest Accommodation*
10 Killerton Road, Bude
EX23 8EL
**t** (01288) 356199
**e** linda.shevlin@btinternet.com
**w** tresillian-bude.co.uk

**Wyvern Guest House**
★★★★ *Guest House*
7 Downs View, Bude EX23 8RF
**t** (01288) 352205
**e** eileen@wyvernhouse.co.uk
**w** wyvernhouse.co.uk

## BUDLEIGH SALTERTON
### Devon

**Downderry House ★★★★★**
*Guest Accommodation*
**GOLD AWARD**
10 Exmouth Road, Budleigh
Salterton EX9 6AQ
**t** (01395) 442663
**e** info@downderryhouse.co.uk
**w** downderryhouse.co.uk

**Hansard House ★★★★**
*Guest Accommodation*
**SILVER AWARD**
3 Northview Road, Budleigh
Salterton EX9 6BY
**t** (01395) 442773
**e** enquiries@hansardhotel.co.uk
**w** hansardhousehotel.co.uk

## BUDOCK WATER
### Cornwall

**Home Country House ★★★**
*Guest Accommodation*
Penjerrick, Falmouth TR11 5EE
**t** (01326) 250427

## BUGLE
### Cornwall

**The Bugle Inn ★★★** *Inn*
57 Fore Street, Bugle, St
Austell PL26 8PB
**t** (01726) 850307
**e** bugleinn@aol.com
**w** bugleinn.co.uk

## BULFORD
### Wiltshire

**The Dovecot ★★★★**
*Bed & Breakfast*
**SILVER AWARD**
Watergate Lane, Bulford
SP4 9DY
**t** (01980) 632625
**e** bandb@thedovecot.com
**w** thedovecot.com

## BULLO PILL
### Gloucestershire

**Grove Farm ★★★★**
*Farmhouse*
Bullo Pill, Newnham GL14 1DZ
**t** (01594) 516304
**e** davidandpennyhill@btopenworld.com
**w** grovefarm-uk.com

## BURLAWN
### Cornwall

**Burlawn Farm ★★★★**
*Farmhouse*
Higher Pengelly Cross,
Wadebridge PL27 7LA
**t** (01208) 815548
**e** burlawnfarm@tiscali.co.uk

**Pengelly Farmhouse, Burlawn ★★★★**
*Bed & Breakfast*
**SILVER AWARD**
Burlawn, Wadebridge
PL27 7LA
**t** (01208) 814217
**e** hodgepete@hotmail.com
**w** pengellyfarm.co.uk

## BURNHAM-ON-SEA
### Somerset

**Ashbourne House ★★★★**
*Guest House*
17 Berrow Road, Burnham-on-Sea TA8 2EY
**t** (01278) 783217
**e** ashbourne.house@btinternet.com
**w** ashbournehouse.biz

**Cloisters ★★★**
*Guest Accommodation*
94 Berrow Road, Burnham-on-Sea TA8 2HN
**t** (01278) 789280

**Knights Rest ★★★**
*Bed & Breakfast*
9 Dunstan Road, Burnham-on-Sea TA8 1ER
**t** (01278) 782318
**e** enquiries@knightsrest.net
**w** knightsrest.net/

**Magnolia House ★★★★**
*Guest House*
26 Manor Road, Burnham-on-Sea TA8 2AS
**t** (01278) 792460
**e** enquiries@magnoliahouse.gb.com
**w** magnoliahouse.gb.com

**The Pink House Bed & Breakfast ★★★**
*Guest Accommodation*
214 Berrow Road, Burnham-on-Sea TA8 2JF
**t** (01278) 765925
**e** lorraine.hansard@hotmail.co.uk
**w** thepinkhousebandb.com

**St Aubyns ★★★★**
*Guest House*
11 Berrow Road, Burnham-on-Sea TA8 2ET
**t** (01278) 773769
**e** mark&steve@staubyns-guesthouse.co.uk
**w** staubyns-guesthouse.co.uk

**Sandhills Guest House ★★★**
*Guest House*
3 Poplar Road, Burnham-on-Sea TA8 2HD
**t** (01278) 781208

**Shalimar Guest House ★★★**
*Guest House*
174 Berrow Road, Burnham-on-Sea TA8 2JE
**t** (01278) 785898

**Walton House ★★★★**
*Guest Accommodation*
148 Berrow Road, Burnham-on-Sea TA8 2PN
**t** (01278) 780034
**e** waltonhousebnb@aol.com
**w** waltonhousebnb.co.uk

**The Warren Guest House**
★★★★ *Guest House*
29 Berrow Road, Burnham-on-Sea TA8 2EZ
**t** (01278) 786726
**e** info@thewarrenguesthouse.co.uk
**w** thewarrenguesthouse.co.uk

## BURTON BRADSTOCK
### Dorset

**Chesil Beach Lodge ★★★★**
*Guest Accommodation*
Coast Road, Burton Bradstock
DT6 4RJ
**t** (01308) 897428
**e** enquiries@chesilbeachlodge.co.uk
**w** chesilbeachlodge.co.uk

**Norburton Hall ★★★★★**
*Guest Accommodation*
**GOLD AWARD**
Shipton Lane, Burton Bradstock
DT6 4NQ
**t** (01308) 897007
**e** info@norburtonhall.com
**w** norburtonhall.com

## BURYAS BRIDGE
### Cornwall

**Meadowside Cottage ★★★**
*Bed & Breakfast*
Catchall, Buryas Bridge
TR19 6AQ
**t** (01736) 811168
**e** bryancuddy1@tiscali.co.uk

## BUTCOMBE
### Somerset

**Butcombe Farm Bed and Breakfast ★★★★**
*Guest Accommodation*
Aldwick Lane, Bristol
BS40 7UW
**t** (01761) 462380
**e** info@butcombe-farm.demon.co.uk
**w** butcombe-farm.demon.co.uk

## CALLINGTON
Cornwall

**Cadson Manor** ★★★★★
*Farmhouse* **SILVER AWARD**
Cadson Farm, Callington
PL17 7HW
**t** (01579) 383969
**e** brenda.crago@btclick.com
**w** cadsonmanor.co.uk

**Hampton Manor** ★★★★
*Guest House*
Alston, Callington PL17 8LX
**t** (01579) 370494
**e** hamptonmanor@supanet.com
**w** hamptonmanor.co.uk

**Higher Manaton** ★★★★
*Farmhouse*
Callington PL17 8PX
**t** (01579) 370460
**e** dtrewin@manaton.fsnet.co.uk
**w** cornwall-devon-bandb.co.uk

**Lower House Guest House**
★★★★ *Guest House*
9 Church Street, Callington
PL17 7AN
**t** (01579) 383491
**e** info@lower-house.com
**w** lower-house.com

## CALNE
Wiltshire

**Chilvester Hill House**
★★★★★
*Guest Accommodation*
**SILVER AWARD**
Chilvester Hill, Calne SN11 0LP
**t** (01249) 813981
**e** gill.dilley@talk21.com
**w** chilvesterhillhouse.co.uk

**High Penn House** ★★★★
*Bed & Breakfast*
High Penn, Calne SN11 8RU
**t** 07740 872065 &
07740 872065
**e** mandyha@btinternet.com
**w** highpenn.com

**Queenwood Lodge**
★★★★★
*Guest Accommodation*
**GOLD AWARD**
Bowood Golf & Country Club,
Derry Hill, Calne SN11 9PQ
**t** (01249) 822228
**e** queenwood@bowood.org
**w** bowood.org

## CAMELFORD
Cornwall

**Countryman Hotel** ★★★
*Guest Accommodation*
7 Victoria Road, Camelford
PL32 9XA
**t** (01840) 212250
**e** countrymanhotel@btopenworld.com
**w** cornwall-online.co.uk

**Culloden Farmhouse**
★★★★ *Bed & Breakfast*
Victoria Road, Camelford
PL32 9XA
**t** (01840) 211128
**e** debbie_balaam@msn.com
**w** cullodenfarmhouse.co.uk

**Kings Acre** ★★★★★
*Guest Accommodation*
**GOLD AWARD**
Camelford PL32 9UR
**t** (01840) 213561
**e** info@kings-acre.com
**w** kings-acre.com

**Melorne Farmhouse**
Rating Applied For
*Bed & Breakfast*
Camelford Station PL32 9TZ
**t** (01840) 211301
**e** jane@melornefarmhouse.com
**w** melornefarmhouse.com

**Penlea House** ★★★
*Bed & Breakfast*
Station Road, Camelford
PL32 9UR
**t** (01840) 212194
**e** jandrews04@supanet.com

**Warmington House** ★★★★
*Bed & Breakfast*
Market Place, Camelford
PL32 9PD
**t** (01840) 214961
**e** enquiries@warmingtonhouse.co.uk
**w** warmingtonhouse.co.uk

## CANNINGTON
Somerset

**Blackmore Farm** ★★★★
*Farmhouse*
Blackmore Lane, Bridgwater
TA5 2NE
**t** (01278) 653442
**e** dyerfarm@aol.com
**w** dyerfarm.co.uk

**Gurney Manor Mill** ★★★★
*Bed & Breakfast*
**SILVER AWARD**
Gurney Street, Cannington
TA5 2HW
**t** (01278) 653582
**e** gurneymill@yahoo.co.uk
**w** gurneymill.freeserve.co.uk

## CARBIS BAY
Cornwall

**Amie** ★★★ *Bed & Breakfast*
Sprenen Close, Carbis Bay
TR26 2QT
**t** (01736) 797643
**e** amie@stives.fsworld.co.uk
**w** accommodationstives.com

**Beechwood House** ★★★★
*Guest Accommodation*
St Ives Road, Carbis Bay, St
Ives TR26 2SX
**t** (01736) 795170
**e** beechwood@carbisbay.wanadoo.co.uk

**Endsleigh Guest House**
★★★★
*Guest Accommodation*
St Ives Road, Carbis Bay
TR26 2SF
**t** (01736) 795777
**e** endsleighguesthouse@tiscali.co.uk
**w** endsleighguesthouse.co.uk

**The Lighthouse B & B**
★★★★★ *Bed & Breakfast*
**SILVER AWARD**
Pannier Lane, Carbis Bay
TR26 2RF
**t** (01736) 793830
**e** info@thelighthousebedandbreakfast.co.uk
**w** thelighthousebedandbreakfast.co.uk

**Tradewinds** ★★★★★
*Guest Accommodation*
**SILVER AWARD**
Pannier Lane, Carbis Bay
TR26 2RF
**t** (01736) 799114
**e** enquiries@tradewinds.co.uk
**w** tradewindsstives.co.uk

## CARNON DOWNS
Cornwall

**Chycara** ★★★★
*Bed & Breakfast*
Chyreen Lane, Carnon Downs,
Truro TR3 6LG
**t** (01872) 865447
**e** info@chycara.co.uk
**w** chycara.co.uk

**Woodsedge** ★★★★
*Bed & Breakfast*
Gig Lane, Carnon Downs,
Truro TR3 6JS
**t** (01872) 870269
**e** linda@woodsedgebb.co.uk
**w** woodsedgebb.co.uk

## CASHMOOR
Dorset

**Cashmoor House** ★★★★
*Farmhouse*
Cashmoor, Blandford Forum
DT11 8DN
**t** (01725) 552339
**e** mary@cashmoorhouse.co.uk
**w** cashmoorhouse.co.uk

## CASTLE CARY
Somerset

**Clanville Manor B & B**
★★★★ *Farmhouse*
**SILVER AWARD**
B3153, Castle Cary BA7 7PJ
**t** (01963) 350124
**e** info@clanvillemanor.co.uk
**w** clanvillemanor.co.uk

**The Coach House** ★★★★
*Farmhouse* **SILVER AWARD**
Main Road, Castle Cary
BA7 7PN
**t** (01963) 240315
**e** liz@alfordcoachhouse.co.uk
**w** alfordcoachhouse.co.uk

**The Pilgrims** ★★★★ *Inn*
**SILVER AWARD**
Lovington, Castle Cary
BA7 7PT
**t** (01963) 240597
**e** jools@thepilgrimsatlovington.co.uk
**w** thepilgrimsatlovington.co.uk

## CASTLE COMBE
Wiltshire

**Fosse Farmhouse** ★★★★
*Bed & Breakfast*
**SILVER AWARD**
Nettleton Shrub, Nettleton
SN14 7NJ
**t** (01249) 782286
**e** caroncooper@compuserve.com
**w** fossefarmhouse.com

**Thorngrove Cottage** ★★★★
*Bed & Breakfast*
Summer Lane, Castle Combe
SN14 7NG
**t** (01249) 782607
**e** chrisdalene@sn147ng.fsnet.co.uk

## CERNE ABBAS
Dorset

**Badger Hill** ★★★★
*Bed & Breakfast*
11 Springfield, Cerne Abbas,
Dorchester DT2 7JZ
**t** (01300) 341698

**The New Inn** ★★★ *Inn*
14 Long Street, Dorchester
DT2 7JF
**t** (01300) 341274
**e** newinn.cerneabbas@virgin.net
**w** newinncarneabbas.co.uk

## CHALFORD
Gloucestershire

**The Ragged Cot Inn** ★★★
*Inn*
Hyde GL6 8PE
**t** (01453) 884643
**e** raggedcotinn.hyde@pathfinder.co.uk

**Sollom Voe** ★★★★
*Bed & Breakfast*
Old Neighbouring, Chalford
GL6 8AA
**t** (01453) 882757
**e** anne.fletcher2324@tiscali.co.uk
**w** sollomvoe.co.uk

## CHALLACOMBE
Devon

**Twitchen Farm** ★★★★
*Farmhouse*
Challacombe, Barnstaple
EX31 4TT
**t** (01598) 763568
**e** holidays@twitchen.co.uk
**w** twitchen.co.uk

## CHARD
Somerset

**Ammonite Lodge** ★★★★
*Guest Accommodation*
43 High Street, Chard
TA20 1QL
**t** (01460) 63839
**e** info@ammonitelodge.co.uk
**w** ammonitelodge.co.uk

**Home Farm** ★★★
*Guest Accommodation*
Hornsbury Hill, Chard
TA20 3DB
**t** (01460) 63731

**Hornsbury Mill** ★★★★
*Guest Accommodation*
**SILVER AWARD**
Eleighwater, Chard TA20 3AQ
**t** (01460) 63317
**e** info@hornsburymill.co.uk
**w** hornsburymill.co.uk

**Lindens House** ★★★
*Bed & Breakfast*
Snowden Cottage Lane, High
Street, Chard TA20 1QS
**t** (01460) 61137
**e** joan@lindenshouse.fsnet.co.uk
**w** lindenshouse.co.uk

**Wambrook Farm** ★★★★
*Farmhouse*
Wambrook, Chard TA20 3DF
**t** (01460) 62371
**e** wambrookfarm@aol.com
**w** wambrookfarm.co.uk

### CHARLTON
Wiltshire

**Horse & Groom Inn** ★★★★
*Inn*
The Street, Charlton, Malmesbury SN16 9DL
**t** (01666) 823904
**e** info@horseandgroominn.com
**w** horseandgroominn.com

### CHARLTON HORETHORNE
Somerset

**Longbar** ★★★
*Bed & Breakfast*
Level Lane, Sherborne DT9 4NN
**t** (01963) 220266
**e** longbar@tinyworld.co.uk
**w** longbarfarm.co.uk

### CHARLTON KINGS
Gloucestershire

**Cotswold Studio** ★★★
*Bed & Breakfast*
Ledmore Road, Charlton Kings GL53 8RA
**t** (01242) 526957
**e** geraldine.white@btinternet.com
**w** cotswoldstudio.co.uk

**Detmore House** ★★
*Bed & Breakfast*
London Road, Charlton Kings GL52 6UT
**t** (01242) 582868
**e** gillkilminster@breathemail.net

**Hilden Lodge** ★★★★
*Guest Accommodation*
London Road, Charlton Kings GL52 6YG
**t** (01242) 583242

### CHARMINSTER
Dorset

**The Inn for All Seasons**
Rating Applied For
*Guest Accommodation*
North Street, Charminster DT2 9QZ
**t** (01305) 264694
**e** informationseasons@aol.com

**Slades Farm** ★★★★
*Bed & Breakfast*
North Street, Charminster DT2 9QZ
**t** (01305) 264032
**e** info@bandbdorset.org.uk
**w** bandbdorset.org.uk

**Three Compasses Inn** ★★★
*Inn*
The Square, Charminster, Dorchester DT2 9QT
**t** (01305) 263618

### CHARMOUTH
Dorset

**The Abbots House** ★★★★★
*Restaurant with Rooms*
The Street, Charmouth DT6 6QF
**t** (01297) 560339
**e** info@abbotshouse.co.uk
**w** theabbotshouse.co.uk

**Befferlands Farm** ★★★★
*Bed & Breakfast*
Charmouth, Bridport DT6 6RD
**t** (01297) 560203
**e** bob@befferlands.freeserve.co.uk
**w** befferlands.co.uk

**Cardsmill Farm** ★★★
*Farmhouse*
Whitchurch Canonicorum, Bridport DT6 6RP
**t** (01297) 489375
**e** cardsmill@aol.com
**w** farmhousedorset.com

**Cliffend** ★★★★
*Guest Accommodation*
Higher Sea Lane, Charmouth, Bridport DT6 6BD
**t** (01297) 561047
**w** cliffend.org.uk

### CHEDDAR
Somerset

**Arundel House** ★★★
*Guest Accommodation*
Church Street, Cheddar BS27 3RA
**t** (01934) 742264
**e** enquiries@arundelhousecheddar.co.uk
**w** arundelhousecheddar.co.uk

**Cheddar YHA** ★★★ *Hostel*
Hillfield, Cheddar BS27 3HN
**t** (01934) 742494
**e** cheddar@yha.org.uk
**w** yha.org.uk

**Chedwell Cottage** ★★★★
*Guest Accommodation*
59 Redcliffe Street, Cheddar BS27 3PF
**t** (01934) 743268

**Constantine** ★★★
*Guest Accommodation*
Lower New Road, Cheddar BS27 3DY
**t** (01934) 741339

**Gordon's** ★★★
*Guest Accommodation*
Cliff Street, Cheddar BS27 3PT
**t** (01934) 742497
**e** info@gordonshotel.co.uk
**w** gordonshotel.co.uk

**Neuholme** ★★
*Guest Accommodation*
The Barrows, Cheddar BS27 3BG
**t** (01934) 742841
**w** neuholme.co.uk

**Wassells House** ★★★★
*Bed & Breakfast*
Upper New Road, Cheddar BS27 3DW
**t** (01934) 744317
**e** enquiries@wassellshouse.co.uk
**w** wassellshouse.co.uk

**Waterside** ★★
*Bed & Breakfast*
Cheddar Road, Axbridge BS26 2DP
**t** (01934) 743182
**e** gillianaldridge@hotmail.com
**w** watersidecheddar.co.uk

**Yew Tree Farm** ★★
*Bed & Breakfast*
Theale, Wedmore BS28 4SN
**t** (01934) 712475
**e** enquiries@yewtreefarmbandb.co.uk
**w** yewtreefarmbandb.co.uk

### CHEDZOY
Somerset

**Apple View** ★★★★
*Farmhouse* **SILVER AWARD**
Temple Farm, Chedzoy TA7 8QR
**t** (01278) 423201
**e** temple_farm@hotmail.com
**w** apple-view.co.uk

### CHELSTON
Devon

**The Elmdene** ★★★★
*Guest Accommodation*
Rathmore Road, Torquay TQ2 6NZ
**t** (01803) 294940
**e** enquiries@elmdenehotel.co.uk
**w** elmdenehotel.co.uk

**Millbrook House** ★★★★
*Guest Accommodation*
Old Mill Road, Torquay TQ2 6AP
**t** (01803) 297394
**e** marksj@sky.com
**w** millbrook-house-hotel.co.uk

**The Parks Hotel**
Rating Applied For
*Guest Accommodation*
Rathmore Road, Torquay TQ2 6NZ
**t** (01803) 292420
**e** enquiries@parks-hotel.co.uk
**w** parks-hotel.co.uk

### CHELTENHAM
Gloucestershire

**33 Montpellier** ★★★★
*Guest Accommodation*
33 Montpellier Terrace, Cheltenham GL50 1UX
**t** (01242) 526009
**e** montpellierhotel@btopenworld.com
**w** montpellier-hotel.co.uk

**Beaumont House** ★★★★★
*Guest Accommodation*
**SILVER AWARD**
56 Shurdington Road, Cheltenham GL53 0JE
**t** (01242) 223311
**e** reservations@bhhotel.co.uk
**w** bhhotel.co.uk

**Bentons** ★★★
*Guest Accommodation*
71 Bath Road, Cheltenham GL53 7LH
**t** (01242) 517417

**Brennan Guest House** ★★★
*Guest Accommodation*
21 St Lukes Road, Cheltenham GL53 7JF
**t** (01242) 525904
**e** colintaylor@blueyonder.co.uk

**Bridge House** ★★★★
*Guest Accommodation*
88 Lansdown Road, Cheltenham GL51 6QR
**t** (01242) 583559
**e** bridgehouse@freeuk.com
**w** bridgehouse88.co.uk

**Burlington House** ★★★★
*Guest Accommodation*
Gloucester Road, Cheltenham GL51 7TB
**t** (01242) 526665
**e** info@burlingtonhouse.net
**w** burlingtonhouse.net

**Butlers** ★★★★
*Guest Accommodation*
**SILVER AWARD**
Western Road, Cheltenham GL50 3RN
**t** (01242) 570771
**e** info@butlers-hotel.co.uk
**w** butlers-hotel.co.uk

**Cheltenham Lawn & Pitville Gallery** ★★★★
*Guest Accommodation*
5 Pittville Lawn, Cheltenham GL52 2BE
**t** (01242) 526638
**e** anthea.millier@cheltenhamlawn.com
**w** cheltenhamlawn.com

**Cheltenham Townhouse** ★★★★
*Guest Accommodation*
12-14 Pittville Lawn, Cheltenham GL52 2BD
**t** (01242) 221922
**e** info@cheltenhamtownhouse.co.uk
**w** cheltenhamtownhouse.co.uk

**Colesbourne Inn** ★★★★ *Inn*
Colesbourne GL53 9NP
**t** (01242) 870376
**e** info@thecolesbourneinn.co.uk
**w** thecolesbourneinn.co.uk

**Crossways Guest House** ★★★★
*Guest Accommodation*
Oriel Place, 57 Bath Road, Cheltenham GL53 7LH
**t** (01242) 527683
**e** cross.ways@btinternet.com
**w** crosswaysguesthouse.com

**Garden House** ★★★★
*Guest Accommodation*
24 Christ Church Road, Cheltenham GL50 2PL
**t** (01242) 522525
**e** miggilorraine@hotmail.com

**Hannafords** ★★★★
*Guest Accommodation*
20 Evesham Road, Cheltenham GL52 2AB
**t** (01242) 524190
**e** sue@hannafords.icom43.net
**w** hannafords.icom43.net

**Hanover House** ★★★★★
*Bed & Breakfast*
**SILVER AWARD**
65 St Georges Road, Cheltenham GL50 3DU
**t** (01242) 541297
**e** hanoverhouse@tiscali.co.uk
**w** hanoverhouse.org

**Leeswood** ★★
*Guest Accommodation*
14 Montpellier Drive, Cheltenham GL50 1TX
**t** (01242) 524813
**e** leeswood@hotmail.com
**w** leeswood.org.uk

**Lypiatt House** ★★★★★
*Guest Accommodation*
Lypiatt Road, Cheltenham
GL50 2QW
**t** (01242) 224994
**e** stay@lypiatt.co.uk
**w** lypiatt.co.uk

**Moorend Park Guest Accommodation** ★★★★
*Guest Accommodation*
Moorend Park Road,
Cheltenham GL53 0LA
**t** (01242) 224441
**e** moorendpark@freeuk.com
**w** moorendpark.freeuk.com

**Oak Tree House** ★★★
*Bed & Breakfast*
26 Swindon Lane, Cheltenham
GL50 4NY
**t** (01242) 248831
**e** oaktreehouse1@activemail.co.uk
**w** cotswolds.info/webpage/oaktreehouse-cheltenham.htm

**The Old Station** ★★★★
*Bed & Breakfast*
Westfield, Notgrove GL54 3BU
**t** (01451) 850305

**Prestbury House** ★★★★
*Guest Accommodation*
The Burgage, Prestbury,
Cheltenham GL52 3DN
**t** (01242) 529533
**e** enquiries@prestburyhouse.co.uk
**w** prestburyhouse.co.uk

**Thirty Two** ★★★★★
*Guest Accommodation*
**GOLD AWARD**
Imperial Square, Cheltenham
GL50 1QZ
**t** (01242) 771110
**e** stay@thirtytwoltd.com
**w** thirtytwoltd.com

**Whittington Lodge Farm**
★★★★ *Farmhouse*
**SILVER AWARD**
Whittington, Cheltenham
GL54 4HB
**t** (01242) 820603
**e** cathy@whittlodgefarm.fslife.co.uk
**w** whittlodgefarm.fslife.co.uk

**The Wynyards** ★★★★
*Bed & Breakfast*
Butts Lane, Woodmancote,
Cheltenham GL52 9QH
**t** (01242) 673876
**w** smoothhound.co.uk/hotels/wynyards

## CHELYNCH
### Somerset

**The Old Stables** ★★★★
*Bed & Breakfast*
Chelynch Road, Shepton
Mallet BA4 4PY
**t** (01749) 880098
**e** maureen.keevil@amserve.net
**w** the-oldstables.co.uk

## CHENSON
### Devon

**Chenson Farm** *Camping Barn*
Chenson EX18 7LF
**t** (01363) 83236

## CHERITON FITZPAINE
### Devon

**The Devon Wine School**
★★★★★ *Bed & Breakfast*
**SILVER AWARD**
Redyeates Farm, Crediton
EX17 4HG
**t** (01363) 866742
**e** alastair@devonwineschool.co.uk
**w** devonwineschool.co.uk

## CHETNOLE
### Dorset

**Chetnole Inn** ★★★★ *Inn*
**SILVER AWARD**
Chetnole, Sherborne DT9 6NY
**t** (01935) 872337
**e** enquiries@thechetnoleinn.co.uk
**w** thechetnoleinn.co.uk

## CHEW MAGNA
### Somerset

**Valley Farm** ★★★★
*Bed & Breakfast*
Sandy Lane, Stanton Drew
BS39 4EL
**t** (01275) 332723
**e** valleyfarm2000@tiscali.co.uk
**w** smoothhound.co.uk

**Woodbarn Farm** ★★★★
*Farmhouse*
Denny Lane, Chew Magna,
Bristol BS40 8SZ
**t** (01275) 332599
**e** woodbarnfarm@hotmail.com
**w** smoothhound.co.uk/hotels/woodbarn

## CHEW STOKE
### Somerset

**Orchard House** ★★★
*Guest Accommodation*
Bristol Road, Chew Stoke
BS40 8UB
**t** (01275) 333143
**e** orchardhse@ukgateway.net
**w** orchardhouse-chewstoke.co.uk

## CHEWTON MENDIP
### Somerset

**Copper Beeches** ★★★★
*Guest Accommodation*
Lower Street, Chewton Mendip
BA3 4GP
**t** (01761) 241496
**e** copperbeechesbandb@tiscali.co.uk
**w** copperbeechesbandb.co.uk

## CHIDEOCK
### Dorset

**Bay Tree House** ★★★★
*Bed & Breakfast*
**SILVER AWARD**
Duck Street, Chideock,
Bridport DT6 6JW
**t** (01297) 489336
**e** jane@baytreechideock.co.uk
**w** baytreechideock.co.uk

## CHILD OKEFORD
### Dorset

**Manor Barn Bed & Breakfast**
★★★★★ *Bed & Breakfast*
**SILVER AWARD**
Upper Street, Child Okeford
DT11 8EF
**t** (01258) 860638
**e** carisorby@btinternet.com
**w** manorbarnbedandbreakfast.co.uk

## CHILSWORTHY
### Devon

**Thorne Park** ★★★★
*Farmhouse*
Holsworthy EX22 7BL
**t** (01409) 253339
**e** thornepark@farming.co.uk
**w** thornepark-devon.co.uk

## CHILTON CANTELO
### Somerset

**Higher Farm** ★★★★
*Bed & Breakfast*
C Cantelo, Yeovil BA22 8BE
**t** (01935) 850213
**e** susankerton@tinyonline.co.uk

## CHIPPENHAM
### Wiltshire

**Church Farm** ★★★★
*Farmhouse*
Hartham, Corsham SN13 0PU
**t** (01249) 715180
**e** churchfarmbandb@hotmail.com
**w** churchfarm.cjb.net

**Glebe House** ★★★★
*Bed & Breakfast*
**SILVER AWARD**
Chittoe, Chippenham
SN15 2EL
**t** (01380) 850864
**e** gscrope@aol.com
**w** glebehouse-chittoe.co.uk

**New Road Guest House**
★★★ *Guest House*
31 New Road, Chippenham
SN15 1HP
**t** (01249) 657259
**e** mail@newroadguesthouse.co.uk
**w** newroadguesthouse.co.uk

**Springlewood House** ★★★
*Guest Accommodation*
Malmesbury Road,
Chippenham SN15 5LR
**t** (01249) 652821
**w** springlewood.co.uk

## CHIPPING CAMPDEN
### Gloucestershire

**Bran Mill Cottage** ★★★
*Bed & Breakfast*
Aston Magna, Moreton-in-Marsh GL56 9QW
**t** (01386) 593517
**e** enquiries@branmillcottage.co.uk
**w** branmillcottage.co.uk

**Brymbo B&B** ★★★★
*Guest Accommodation*
Honeybourne Lane, Mickleton
GL55 6PU
**t** (01386) 438890
**e** enquiries@brymbo.com
**w** brymbo.com

**Dragon House** ★★★★
*Bed & Breakfast*
High Street, Chipping
Campden GL55 6AG
**t** (01386) 840734
**e** valatdragonhouse@btinternet.com
**w** dragonhouse-chipping-campden.com

**The Eight Bells** ★★★★ *Inn*
Church Street, Chipping
Campden GL55 6JG
**t** (01386) 840371
**e** neilhargreaves@bellinn.fsnet.co.uk
**w** eightbellsinn.co.uk

**Gainsborough Cottage**
★★★★ *Bed & Breakfast*
Pear Tree Close, Chipping
Campden GL55 6DB
**t** (01386) 849148
**e** janeayton@btinternet.com
**w** gainsboroughcottage.co.uk

**Home Farm House** ★★★★
*Farmhouse* **SILVER AWARD**
Ebrington, Chipping Campden
GL55 6NL
**t** (01386) 593309
**e** willstanley@farmersweekly.net
**w** homefarminthecotswolds.co.uk

**The Malins** ★★★★
*Bed & Breakfast*
21 Station Road, Blockley
GL56 9ED
**t** (01386) 700402
**e** malinsblockley@btinternet.com
**w** chippingcampden.co.uk/themalins.htm

**Manor Farm** ★★★★
*Farmhouse*
Weston-Subedge, Chipping
Campden GL55 6QH
**t** (01386) 840390
**e** lucy@manorfarmbnb.demon.co.uk
**w** manorfarmbnb.demon.co.uk

**Nineveh Farm** ★★★★★
*Guest Accommodation*
**GOLD AWARD**
Mickleton, Chipping Campden
GL55 6PS
**t** (01386) 438923
**e** stay@nineveh.co.uk
**w** ninevehfarm.co.uk

**Sandalwood House** ★★★★
*Bed & Breakfast*
**SILVER AWARD**
Back Ends, Chipping Campden
GL55 6AU
**t** (01386) 840091
**e** sandalwoodhouse@hotmail.com

**Taplins** ★★★★
*Bed & Breakfast*
5 Aston Road, Chipping
Campden GL55 6HR
**t** (01386) 840927
**e** info@cotswoldstay.co.uk

**Weston Park Farm** ★★★
*Bed & Breakfast*
Dovers Hill, Chipping
Campden GL55 6UW
**t** (01386) 840835
**e** jane_whitehouse@hotmail.com
**w** cotswoldcottages.uk.com

## CHITTLEHAMPTON
### Devon

**Higher Biddacott Farm**
★★★ *Farmhouse*
Chittlehampton, Umberleigh
EX37 9PY
**t** (01769) 540222
**e** waterers.@sosi.net
**w** heavyhorses.net

## CHOLDERTON
### Wiltshire

**Cholderton Bunkhouse**
Rating Applied For
*Hostel*
Cholderton Rare Breeds Farm,
Amesbury Road, Salisbury
SP4 0EW
t (01980) 629438
w choldertoncharliesfarm.com

**Parkhouse Motel ★★★★**
*Guest Accommodation*
Cholderton, Salisbury SP4 0EG
t (01980) 629256

## CHRISTCHURCH
### Dorset

**Druid House ★★★★★**
*Guest Accommodation*
SILVER AWARD
26 Sopers Lane, Christchurch
BH23 1JE
t (01202) 485615
e reservations@druid-house.co.uk
w druid-house.co.uk

**Fisherman's Haunt ★★★** *Inn*
Salisbury Road, Winkton
BH23 7AS
t (01202) 477283
e fishermanshaunt@fullers.co.uk
w fullersinns.co.uk

**Four Seasons B&B ★★★★**
*Bed & Breakfast*
2 Nea Road, Christchurch
BH23 4NA
t (01425) 273408
e melbar1940@aol.com
w 4seasonshighcliffe.co.uk

**Laburnum Lodge ★★★★**
*Bed & Breakfast*
33 Albion Road, Christchurch
BH23 2JQ
t (01202) 471664
e mail@laburnumlodge.info
w laburnumlodge.info

**Salmon's Reach Guest House ★★★**
*Guest Accommodation*
28 Stanpit, Christchurch
BH23 3LZ
t (01202) 477315
e info@salmonsreach.com
w salmonsreach.com

**Seawards ★★★★★**
*Bed & Breakfast*
GOLD AWARD
13 Avon Run Close, Friar's Cliff
BH23 4DT
t (01425) 273188
e seawards13@hotmail.com
w seawards13.plus.com

**Stour Lodge Guest House ★★★★** *Guest House*
54 Stour Road, Christchurch
BH23 1LW
t (01202) 486902
e enquiries@stourlodge.co.uk
w stourlodge.co.uk

## CHRISTIAN MALFORD
### Wiltshire

**Beanhill Farm ★★★★**
*Farmhouse*
Main Road, Christian Malford
SN15 4BS
t (01249) 720672
e bb@beanhillfarm.fsbusiness.co.uk
w beanhillfarmwiltshire.co.uk

## CHUDLEIGH
### Devon

**Higher Rixdale Farm ★★★★**
*Farmhouse*
Luton, Chudleigh TQ13 0BW
t (01626) 867980
e info@higher-rixdale-farm.com
w higher-rixdale-farm.com

## CIRENCESTER
### Gloucestershire

**Abbeymead Guest House ★★★★** *Guest House*
Victoria Road, Cirencester
GL7 1ES
t (01285) 653740
e land0603@aol.com
w abbeymeadguesthouse.com

**Apsley Villa ★★★**
*Guest House*
Victoria Road, Cirencester
GL7 1ES
t (01285) 653489

**Brooklands Farm ★★**
*Farmhouse*
Ewen, Cirencester GL7 6BU
t (01285) 770487 &
07790 948931
w glosfarmhols.co.uk

**The Bungalow ★★★★**
*Guest Accommodation*
SILVER AWARD
93 Victoria Road, Cirencester
GL7 1ES
t (01285) 654179
e info@bandbcirencester.co.uk
w bandbcirencester.co.uk

**Columbrae ★★★★**
*Bed & Breakfast*
3 School Hill, Stratton GL7 2LS
t (01285) 653114
e margaret@columbraebandb.co.uk
w columbraebandb.co.uk

**Dixs Barn ★★★★**
*Bed & Breakfast*
Duntisbourne Abbots,
Cirencester GL7 7JN
t (01285) 821249
e wilcox@dixsbarn.freeserve.co.uk

**The Ivy House ★★★★**
*Guest House*
2 Victoria Road, Cirencester
GL7 1EN
t (01285) 656626
e info@ivyhousecotswolds.com
w ivyhousecotswolds.com

**The Leauses ★★★★**
*Guest Accommodation*
SILVER AWARD
101 Victoria Road, Cirencester
GL7 1EU
t (01285) 653643
e info@theleauses.co.uk
w theleauses.co.uk

**Manor Farm ★★★**
*Farmhouse*
Middle Duntisbourne,
Cirencester GL7 7AR
t (01285) 658145
e enquiries@duntisbourne.com
w duntisbourne.com

**The Old Brewhouse ★★★★**
*Guest Accommodation*
7 London Road, Cirencester
GL7 2PU
t (01285) 656099
e info@theoldbrewhouse.com
w theoldbrewhouse.com

**Raydon House ★★★**
*Guest House*
The Avenue, Cirencester
GL7 1EH
t (01285) 653485
e raydon@gl71eh.freeserve.co.uk
w raydonhousehotel.co.uk

**Riverside House ★★★★**
*Guest Accommodation*
Watermoor Road, Cirencester
GL7 1LF
t (01285) 647642
e riversidehouse@mitsubishi-cars.co.uk
w riversidehouse.org.uk

**The Royal Agricultural College ★★★** *Campus*
Stroud Road, Cirencester
GL7 6JS
t (01285) 652531
e commercial.services@rac.ac.uk
w rac.ac.uk

**Le Spa ★★★★**
*Guest Accommodation*
Gloucester Road, Cirencester
GL7 2LA
t (01285) 653840
e mail@lespa.com
w lespa.com

**The Talbot Inn ★★★★** *Inn*
14 Victoria Road, Cirencester
GL7 1EN
t (01285) 653760
e info@talbotinncotswolds.co.uk
w talbotinncotswolds.co.uk

**The White Lion Inn ★★★**
*Inn*
8 Gloucester Street,
Cirencester GL7 2DG
t (01285) 654053
e mutlow@ashtonkeynes.fsnet.co.uk
w whitelioncirencester.co.uk

## CLAPHAM
### Devon

**Hyperion Stud ★★★★**
*Farmhouse*
Clapham Stud, Clapham
EX6 7YQ
t (01392) 833794
e hyperwell@aol.com
w hyperion-stud.co.uk

**Yeo's Farm ★★★★**
*Farmhouse*
Dunchideock, Exeter EX2 9UJ
t (01392) 883927
e killinger.legg@tiscali.co.uk
w yeos-farm-exeter.co.uk

## CLAVERTON DOWN
### Somerset

**University of Bath ★★–★★★** *Campus*
The Avenue, Claverton Down
BA2 7AY
t (01225) 383926
e beds@bath.ac.uk
w bath.ac.uk/salesandevents

## CLOVELLY
### Devon

**Fuchsia Cottage ★★★★**
*Bed & Breakfast*
Higher Clovelly, Clovelly,
Bideford EX39 5RR
t (01237) 431398
e tom@clovelly-holidays.co.uk
w clovelly-holidays.co.uk

## CLYFFE PYPARD
### Wiltshire

**The Goddard Arms**
*Bunkhouse*
Clyffe Pypard SN4 7PY
t (01793) 731386
e clyffepypard@yha.org.uk

## COALEY
### Gloucestershire

**Waterend Farm ★★★★**
*Farmhouse*
Coaley, Dursley GL11 5DR
t (01453) 899141
e enquiries@waterendfarm.co.uk
w waterendfarm.co.uk

## COBERLEY VILLAGE
### Gloucestershire

**The Old Post Office ★★★★**
*Bed & Breakfast*
Coberley Village, Cheltenham
GL53 9QZ
t (01242) 870694
e pjcarlton@btinternet.com

## CODFORD ST MARY
### Wiltshire

**Glebe Cottage ★★★★**
*Bed & Breakfast*
Church Lane, Codford
BA12 0PJ
t (01985) 850565
e bob.ra@woolrych.net
w glebecottagecodford.co.uk

## COLD ASTON
### Gloucestershire

**Field Ways ★★★★**
*Bed & Breakfast*
Cheltenham GL54 3BJ
t (01451) 810659
e cascadegroup@aol.com

## COLEFORD
### Gloucestershire

**Braceland Adventure Centre**
*Bunkhouse*
Christchurch, Coleford
GL16 7NP
t (01594) 833820
e alison839@btinternet.com
w bracelandadventurecentre.co.uk

**Forest House ★★★★**
*Guest Accommodation*
Cinderhill, Coleford GL16 8HQ
t (01594) 832424
e suesparkes@tumphouse.fsnet.co.uk
w forest-house-hotel.co.uk

## COLLINGBOURNE KINGSTON
### Wiltshire

**Manor Farm B&B ★★★★**
*Farmhouse*
Collingbourne Kingston,
Marlborough SN8 3SD
t (01264) 850859
e stay@manorfm.com
w manorfm.com

**COLN ST ALDWYNS**
**Gloucestershire**

**Deer Park Cottage ★★★★**
*Bed & Breakfast*
Hatherop Road, Coln St Aldwyns GL7 5AR
**t** (01285) 750692
**w** deerparkbandb.co.uk

**COLYFORD**
**Devon**

**Swan Hill House ★★★★**
*Guest House*
Colyford EX24 6QQ
**t** (01297) 553387

**COLYTON**
**Devon**

**The Old Bakehouse ★★★★**
*Bed & Breakfast*
**SILVER AWARD**
Lower Church Street, Colyton EX24 6ND
**t** (01297) 552518
**e** france.bakehouse@hotmail.co.uk
**w** theoldbakehousebandb.co.uk

**Smallicombe Farm ★★★★**
*Guest Accommodation*
**SILVER AWARD**
Northleigh, Colyton EX24 6BU
**t** (01404) 831310
**e** maggie_todd@yahoo.com
**w** smallicombe.com

**COMBE DOWN**
**Somerset**

**Beech Wood ★★★★**
*Bed & Breakfast*
Shaft Road, Combe Down BA2 7HP
**t** (01225) 832242
**e** beechwoodbath@talktalk.net
**w** beechwoodbath.ihoststudio.com/

**Grey Lodge ★★★★**
*Bed & Breakfast*
**SILVER AWARD**
Summer Lane, Combe Down BA2 7EU
**t** (01225) 832069
**e** greylodge@surfree.co.uk
**w** greylodge.co.uk

**COMBE MARTIN**
**Devon**

**Acorns Guest House ★★★★**
*Guest Accommodation*
2 Woodlands, Combe Martin EX34 0AT
**t** (01271) 882769
**e** info@acorns-guesthouse.co.uk
**w** acorns-guesthouse.co.uk

**Blair Lodge Guest House ★★★★** *Guest House*
Moory Meadow, Seaview EX34 0DG
**t** (01271) 882294
**e** info@blairlodge.co.uk
**w** blairlodge.co.uk

**Mellstock House ★★★★**
*Guest Accommodation*
Woodlands, Combe Martin EX34 0AR
**t** (01271) 882592
**e** enquiries@mellstockhouse.co.uk
**w** mellstockhouse.co.uk

**Saffron House ★★★**
*Guest Accommodation*
King Street, Combe Martin EX34 0BX
**t** (01271) 883521
**e** stay@saffronhousehotel.co.uk
**w** saffronhousehotel.co.uk

**COMPTON BASSETT**
**Wiltshire**

**The White Horse Inn ★★★**
*Inn*
Compton Bassett, Calne SN11 8RG
**t** (01249) 813118
**w** comptonbassett.com/thewhitehorse

**COMPTON DUNDON**
**Somerset**

**Rickham House ★★★★**
*Farmhouse*
Street TA11 6QA
**t** (01458) 445056
**e** rickham.house@btconnect.com
**w** rickhamhouse.co.uk

**The Yew Tree @ Church Farm ★★★** *Bed & Breakfast*
School Lane, Somerton TA11 6TE
**t** (01458) 274891
**e** info@yewtreebnb.co.uk
**w** yewtreebnb.co.uk

**CONNOR DOWNS**
**Cornwall**

**Nanterrow Farm B & B ★★★**
*Farmhouse*
Gwithian, Hayle TR27 5BP
**t** (01209) 712282
**e** nanterrow@hotmail.com
**w** nanterrowfarm.co.uk

**CONSTANTINE**
**Cornwall**

**The Old Chapel ★★★★**
*Bed & Breakfast*
Seworgan, Constantine TR11 5QN
**t** (01326) 341418
**e** info@theoldchapelcornwall.co.uk
**w** theoldchapelcornwall.co.uk

**COOMBE BISSETT**
**Wiltshire**

**Evening Hill ★★**
*Bed & Breakfast*
Blandford Road, Coombe Bissett SP5 4LH
**t** (01722) 718561
**e** henrys@eveninghill.com
**w** eveninghill.com

**COOMBE KEYNES**
**Dorset**

**Highfield ★★★**
*Guest Accommodation*
Coombe Keynes, Lulworth Cove BH20 5PS
**t** (01929) 463208
**e** jmitchell@coombekeynes.freeserve.co.uk
**w** highfield-bb.co.uk

**COPPLESTONE**
**Devon**

**Harebell ★★★★**
*Guest Accommodation*
**SILVER AWARD**
Copplestone EX17 5LA
**t** (01363) 84771
**e** kenjwarren@aol.com
**w** harebellbandb.co.uk

**CORFE CASTLE**
**Dorset**

**Bradle Farmhouse ★★★★**
*Farmhouse* **GOLD AWARD**
Bradle Farm, Church Knowle, Wareham BH20 5NU
**t** (01929) 480712
**e** info@bradlefarmhouse.co.uk
**w** bradlefarmhouse.co.uk

**Kingston Country Courtyard ★★★★**
*Guest Accommodation*
Langton Road, Kingston BH20 5LR
**t** (01929) 481066
**e** annfry@kingstoncountrycourtyard.co.uk
**w** kingstoncountrycourtyard.co.uk

**Norden House ★★★**
*Guest Accommodation*
Corfe Castle, Wareham BH20 5DS
**t** (01929) 480177
**e** nordenhouse@fsmail.net
**w** nordenhouse.com

**Westaway ★★★★**
*Bed & Breakfast*
88 West Street, Corfe Castle BH20 5HE
**t** (01929) 480188
**e** ray_hendes@btinternet.com
**w** westaway-corfecastle.co.uk

**CORFE MULLEN**
**Dorset**

**Elms Lodge ★★★★**
*Bed & Breakfast*
**GOLD AWARD**
7 Cogdean Way, Corfe Mullen BH21 3XD
**t** (01202) 699669
**e** elmslodge@hotmail.com
**w** elmslodge.co.uk

**The Goat House ★★**
*Bed & Breakfast*
Pine Road, Wimborne BH21 3DW
**t** (01202) 886783
**e** info@goathouse.co.uk
**w** goathouse.co.uk

**CORSHAM**
**Wiltshire**

**Ashley Wood Farm ★★★★**
*Farmhouse* **SILVER AWARD**
Lower Kingsdown Road, Kingsdown SN13 8BG
**t** (01225) 742288
**e** ashleywoodfarm@hotmail.com
**w** ashleywoodfarm.co.uk

**Pickwick Lodge Farm ★★★★** *Farmhouse*
**SILVER AWARD**
Guyers Lane, Pickwick SN13 0PS
**t** (01249) 712207
**e** bandb@pickwickfarm.co.uk
**w** pickwickfarm.co.uk

**Saltbox Farm ★★★★**
*Farmhouse*
Box, Corsham SN13 8PT
**t** (01225) 742608
**e** bbsaltboxfarm@yahoo.co.uk
**w** saltboxfarm.verypretty.co.uk

**CORTON DENHAM**
**Somerset**

**The Queens Arms ★★★★**
*Inn*
Sherborne DT9 4LR
**t** (01963) 220317
**e** relax@thequeensarms.com
**w** thequeensarms.com

**COSSINGTON**
**Somerset**

**Brookhayes Farm ★★★★**
*Farmhouse*
Bell Lane, Cossington TA7 8LR
**t** (01278) 722559
**e** brookhayesfm@tiscali.co.uk
**w** brookhayes-farm.co.uk

**COVERACK**
**Cornwall**

**Coverack Youth Hostel ★★★** *Hostel*
Parc Behan, School Hill, Helston TR12 6SA
**t** (01326) 280687
**e** coverack@yha.org.uk

**CRANBORNE**
**Dorset**

**Chaseborough Farm ★★**
*Bed & Breakfast*
Gotham, Cranborne, Wimborne BH21 5QY
**t** (01202) 813166
**e** jim.ghinn@tiscali.co.uk
**w** chaseboroughfarm.co.uk

**CRANTOCK**
**Cornwall**

**Tregenna House ★★★★**
*Guest House*
West Pentire Road, Crantock, Newquay TR8 5RZ
**t** (01637) 830222
**e** pete@tregennahouse.co.uk
**w** tregennahouse.co.uk

**CREWKERNE**
**Somerset**

**Honeydown Farm ★★★★**
*Farmhouse*
Seaborough Hill, Crewkerne TA18 8PL
**t** (01460) 72665
**e** c.bacon@honeydown.co.uk
**w** honeydown.co.uk

**CRICKLADE**
**Wiltshire**

**Waterhay Farm ★★★★**
*Farmhouse*
Waterhay, Leigh SN6 6QY
**t** (01285) 861253

**CROWCOMBE**
**Somerset**

**Home Leigh House ★★★★**
*Bed & Breakfast*
Crowcombe TA4 4BL
**t** (01984) 618439
**w** quantockonline.co.uk/adverts/homeleigh/homeleigh_hughesaa.html

## CROYDE
Devon

**Combas Farm** ★★★★
*Farmhouse*
Croyde, Braunton EX33 1PH
t (01271) 890398
w combasfarm.co.uk

**Denham House & Cottages**
★★★★ *Guest House*
North Buckland, Braunton
EX33 1HY
t (01271) 890297
e info@denhamhouse.co.uk
w denhamhouse.co.uk

**Moorsands** ★★★
*Guest Accommodation*
34 Moor Lane, Croyde Bay
EX33 1NP
t (01271) 890781
e paul@moorsands.co.uk
w croyde-bay.com/moorsands.htm

## CULLOMPTON
Devon

**Langford Court North**
★★★★ *Farmhouse*
Langford, Cullompton
EX15 1SQ
t (01884) 277234
e tchattey@yahoo.co.uk

**Newcourt Barton** ★★★★
*Farmhouse* **SILVER AWARD**
Langford, Cullompton
EX15 1SE
t (01884) 277326
e newcourtbarton@btinternet.com
w newcourtbarton-devon.co.uk

## CURRY RIVEL
Somerset

**Orchard Cottage** ★★★★★
*Bed & Breakfast*
Townsend, Curry Rivel
TA10 0HT
t (01458) 251511

## DALWOOD
Devon

**Burrow Way** ★★★★
*Farmhouse*
Dalwood, Axminster EX13 7ES
t (01404) 831802
e burrow.way@tiscali.co.uk

## DARTMOUTH
Devon

**Browns** ★★★★★
*Guest Accommodation*
**SILVER AWARD**
27-29 Victoria Road,
Dartmouth TQ6 9RT
t (01803) 832572
e enquiries@brownshoteldartmouth.co.uk
w brownshoteldartmouth.co.uk

**Capritia Guest House** ★★★
*Bed & Breakfast*
69 Victoria Road, Dartmouth
TQ6 9RX
t (01803) 833419
e kenjohnston@btinternet.com
w capritia.com

**Cladda** ★★★★
*Guest Accommodation*
**SILVER AWARD**
88-90 Victoria Road,
Dartmouth TQ6 9EF
t (01803) 835957
e jordan@cladda-guesthouse.co.uk
w cladda-guesthouse.co.uk

**Hill View House** ★★★★
*Guest Accommodation*
**GOLD AWARD**
76 Victoria Road, Dartmouth
TQ6 9DZ
t (01803) 839372
e enquiries@hillviewdartmouth.co.uk
w hillviewdartmouth.co.uk

**Lower Collaton Farm**
★★★★ *Bed & Breakfast*
Blackawton, Dartmouth
TQ9 7DW
t (01803) 712260
e mussen@lower-collaton-farm.co.uk
w lower-collaton-farm.co.uk

**Mounthaven** ★★★★★
*Guest Accommodation*
**SILVER AWARD**
Mount Boone, Dartmouth
TQ6 9PB
t (01803) 839061
e enquiries@mounthavendartmouth.co.uk
w mounthavendartmouth.co.uk

**Skerries Bed & Breakfast**
★★★★ *Bed & Breakfast*
**SILVER AWARD**
Strete, Dartmouth TQ6 0RH
t (01803) 770775
e jam.skerries@rya-online.net
w skerriesbandb.co.uk

**Valley House** ★★★★
*Bed & Breakfast*
46 Victoria Road, Dartmouth
TQ6 9DZ
t (01803) 834045
e enquiries@valleyhousedartmouth.com
w valleyhousedartmouth.com

**The Victorian House** ★★★★
*Bed & Breakfast*
**SILVER AWARD**
1 Vicarage Hill, Dartmouth
TQ6 9EW
t (01803) 832766
e sue@victorianhouse.org.uk
w victorianhouse.org.uk

## DAWLISH
Devon

**The Beeches Bed & Breakfast**
Rating Applied For
*Guest Accommodation*
15a Old Teignmouth Road,
Dawlish EX7 0NJ
t (01626) 866345
e enquiries@thebeechesbandb.co.uk
w thebeechesbandb.co.uk

**Channel View Guest House**
★★★★ *Guest House*
14 Teignmouth Hill, Westcliff
EX7 9DN
t (01626) 866973
e channelviewguesthouse@fsmail.net
w channelviewguesthouse.co.uk

**Hadleigh House**
Rating Applied For
*Bed & Breakfast*
Exeter Road, Dawlish EX7 0BT
t (01626) 864580
w attheseaside.freeuk.com

**Lammas Park House**
★★★★★
*Guest Accommodation*
**GOLD AWARD**
3 Priory Road, Dawlish EX7 9JF
t (01626) 888064
e lammaspark@hotmail.com
w lammasparkhouse.co.uk

**Lyme Bay House**
Rating Applied For
*Guest Accommodation*
34 West Cliff, Dawlish
EX7 9DN
t (01626) 864211
e enquiries@lymebaydawlish.co.uk
w lymebaydawlish.co.uk

## DAWLISH WARREN
Devon

**Sandays B&B** ★★★★
*Bed & Breakfast*
Warren Road, Dawlish
EX7 0PQ
t (01626) 888973

## DEERHURST
Gloucestershire

**Deerhurst Bed & Breakfast**
★★★★ *Farmhouse*
Deerhurst Priory, Deerhurst
GL19 4BX
t (01684) 293358
e timandcate@aol.com
w deerhurstbandb.co.uk

## DEVIZES
Wiltshire

**Asta B&B** ★★
*Bed & Breakfast*
66 Downlands Road, Devizes
SN10 5EF
t (01380) 722546
e astabedandbreakfast@tiscali.co.uk

**Bramley House** ★★★★
*Bed & Breakfast*
**SILVER AWARD**
5 The Breach, Devizes
SN10 5BJ
t (01380) 729444

**Byde a Whyle** ★★★
*Bed & Breakfast*
29 Roundway Park, Devizes
SN10 2ED
t (01380) 723288
e robert@arbyde.wanadoo.co.uk
w byde-a-whyle.co.uk

**Eastleigh House** ★★★★
*Bed & Breakfast*
3 Eastleigh Road, Devizes
SN10 3EE
t (01380) 726918
e barbara@eastleighhouse.co.uk
w eastleighhouse.co.uk

**The Gables** ★★★★
*Bed & Breakfast*
Bath Road, Devizes SN10 1PH
t (01380) 723086
e enquiries@thegablesdevizes.co.uk
w thegablesdevizes.co.uk

**The Gatehouse** ★★★
*Bed & Breakfast*
Wick Lane, Devizes SN10 5DW
t (01380) 725283
e info@visitdevizes.co.uk
w visitdevizes.co.uk

**Longwater** ★★★
*Bed & Breakfast*
Lower Road, Erlestoke
SN10 5UE
t (01380) 830095

**The Old Manor** ★★★★
*Bed & Breakfast*
The Street, Chirton SN10 3QS
t (01380) 840777
e bandb@theoldmanor.biz
w theoldmanor.biz

**Rosemundy Cottage** ★★★★
*Guest Accommodation*
London Road, Devizes
SN10 2DS
t (01380) 727122
e info@rosemundycottage.co.uk
w rosemundycottage.co.uk

## DIDMARTON
Gloucestershire

**The Kings Arms at Didmarton**
Rating Applied For
*Inn*
The Street, Didmarton,
Badminton GL9 1DT
t (01454) 238245
e bookings@kingsarmsdidmarton.co.uk
w kingsarmsdidmarton.co.uk

## DILTON MARSH
Wiltshire

**Angel Cottage** ★★★★
*Bed & Breakfast*
High Street, Westbury
BA13 4DR
t (01373) 825480
e enquiries@angle-cottage.co.uk
w angel-cottage.co.uk

## DINTON
Wiltshire

**Honeysuckle Homestead**
★★★ *Guest Accommodation*
Dinton, Salisbury SP3 5HA
t (01722) 717887
e honeysuckle@dinton21.freeserve.co.uk
w honeysucklehomestead.co.uk

**Marshwood Farm B&B**
★★★★ *Bed & Breakfast*
Dinton, Salisbury SP3 5ET
**t** (01722) 716334
**e** marshwood1@btconnect.com
**w** marshwoodfarm.co.uk

## DIPTFORD
Devon

**Old Rectory Bed and Breakfast** ★★★★★
*Bed & Breakfast*
**SILVER AWARD**
Diptford, Totnes TQ9 7NY
**t** (01548) 821575
**e** hitchins@oldrectorydiptford.co.uk
**w** oldrectorydiptford.co.uk

## DITTISHAM
Devon

**Downton Lodge** ★★★★
*Guest Accommodation*
Dartmouth TQ6 0JD
**t** (01803) 722252
**e** welcome@downtonlodge.co.uk
**w** downtonlodge.co.uk

## DOLTON
Devon

**Rams Head Inn** ★★★ *Inn*
South Street, Dolton EX19 8QS
**t** (01805) 804255
**e** ramsheadinn@btinternet.com
**w** ramsheadinn.co.uk

## DONHEAD ST ANDREW
Wiltshire

**Oakdale House** ★★★
*Bed & Breakfast*
New Road, Donhead St Andrew SP7 9EG
**t** (01747) 828767
**e** ella@oakdalehouse.co.uk
**w** oakdalehouse.co.uk

## DONHEAD ST MARY
Wiltshire

**Cedar Lodge** ★★★
*Bed & Breakfast*
5 Deweys Place, Donhead St Mary SP7 9LW
**t** (01747) 829240
**e** cedarlodge@onetel.com
**w** cedarlodge.org.uk

## DORCHESTER
Dorset

**Aquila Heights** ★★★★
*Guest Accommodation*
44 Maiden Castle Road, Dorchester DT1 2ES
**t** (01305) 267145
**e** aquila.heights@tiscali.co.uk
**w** aquilaheights.co.uk

**Baytree House** ★★★★
*Bed & Breakfast*
**SILVER AWARD**
4 Athelstan Road, Dorchester DT1 1NR
**t** (01305) 263696
**e** info@baytreedorchester.com
**w** bandbdorchester.co.uk

**Churchview Guest House**
★★★★ *Guest House*
Winterbourne Abbas, Dorchester DT2 9LS
**t** (01305) 889296
**e** stay@churchview.co.uk
**w** churchview.co.uk

**Higher Came Farmhouse**
★★★★
*Guest Accommodation*
**SILVER AWARD**
Higher Came, Dorchester DT2 8NR
**t** (01305) 268908
**e** enquiries@highercame.co.uk
**w** highercame.co.uk

**Sunrise Guest House** ★★★
*Guest House*
34 London Road, Dorchester DT1 1NE
**t** (01305) 262425
**w** sunriseguesthouse dorchester.com

**Tarkaville** ★★★
*Bed & Breakfast*
30 Shaston Crescent, Dorchester DT1 2EB
**t** (01305) 266253
**e** tarkaville@lineone.net

**Westwood House** ★★★★
*Guest House*
29 High West Street, Dorchester DT1 1UP
**t** (01305) 268018
**e** reservations@westwoodhouse.co.uk
**w** westwoodhouse.co.uk

**The White House** ★★★
*Bed & Breakfast*
9 Queens Avenue, Dorchester DT1 2EW
**t** (01305) 266714
**e** sandratwh@yahoo.co.uk
**w** rynhorn.tripod.com/whitehouse/index.htm

**Yalbury Park** ★★★★
*Farmhouse*
Frome Whitfield Farm, Dorchester DT2 7SE
**t** (01305) 250336
**e** yalburypark@tesco.net

**Yellowham Farm** ★★★★
*Guest Accommodation*
**SILVER AWARD**
Yellowham Wood, Dorchester DT2 8RW
**t** (01305) 262892
**e** mail@yellowham.freeserve.co.uk
**w** yellowham.co.uk

## DOWNTON
Wiltshire

**Casterbridge House Bed & Breakfast** ★★★★
*Bed & Breakfast*
140 The Borough, Downton SP5 3LT
**t** (01725) 513270
**e** info@casterbridgehouse.co.uk
**w** casterbridgehouse.co.uk

**Witherington Farm Bed & Breakfast** ★★★★★
*Bed & Breakfast*
**GOLD AWARD**
Witherington, Downton SP5 3QT
**t** (01722) 710222
**e** bandb@witheringtonfarm.co.uk
**w** witheringtonfarm.co.uk

## DRAKEWALLS
Cornwall

**Drakewalls House** ★★★
*Guest House*
Gunnislake PL18 9EG
**t** (01822) 833617
**e** patsmyth_53@hotmail.com
**w** drakewallsbedandbreakfast.co.uk

## DULOE
Cornwall

**Carglonnon Farm** ★★★★
*Farmhouse*
Duloe, Liskeard PL14 4QA
**t** (01579) 320210

**Tremadart House** ★★★★
*Bed & Breakfast*
Tremadart Lane, Duloe, Looe PL14 4PE
**t** (01503) 262766
**e** philipparead@hotmail.co.uk
**w** tremadart.co.uk

## DULVERTON
Somerset

**Ashwick Manor Farm**
★★★★ *Farmhouse*
Dulverton TA22 9QE
**t** (01398) 323371
**e** ashwickmanorfarm@tiscali.co.uk
**w** ashwickmanorfarm.co.uk

**Hawkwell Farm House**
★★★★★ *Bed & Breakfast*
Hawkwell Lane, Dulverton TA22 9RU
**t** (01398) 341708
**e** jan@hawkwellhouse.com
**w** hawkwellfarmhouse.co.uk

**Northcombe** *Bunkhouse*
Northcombe Farm, Dulverton TA22 9JH
**t** (01398) 323602
**e** sally@northcombecampingbarns.fsnet.co.uk

**Springfield Farm** ★★★★
*Farmhouse*
Ashwick, Dulverton TA22 9QD
**t** (01398) 323722
**e** stay@springfieldfarms.co.uk
**w** springfieldfarms.co.uk

**Three Acres Country House**
★★★★★
*Guest Accommodation*
**GOLD AWARD**
Brushford, Dulverton TA22 9AR
**t** (01398) 323730
**e** enquiries@threeacrescountryhouse.co.uk
**w** threeacrescountryhouse.co.uk

**Town Mills** ★★★★
*Guest Accommodation*
**SILVER AWARD**
High Street, Dulverton TA22 9HB
**t** (01398) 323124
**e** townmillsdulverton@btinternet.com
**w** townmillsdulverton.co.uk

**Winsbere House** ★★★★
*Bed & Breakfast*
64 Battleton, Dulverton TA22 9HU
**t** (01398) 323278
**e** info@winsbere.co.uk
**w** winsbere.co.uk

## DUNKESWELL
Devon

**The Old Kennels** ★★★★
*Guest Accommodation*
Stentwood, Dunkeswell EX14 4RW
**t** (01823) 681138
**e** info@theoldkennels.co.uk
**w** theoldkennels.co.uk

## DUNSTER
Somerset

**Exmoor House Dunster**
★★★★
*Guest Accommodation*
**SILVER AWARD**
12 West Street, Dunster TA24 6SN
**t** (01643) 821268
**e** stay@exmoorhousedunster.co.uk
**w** exmoorhousedunster.co.uk

**Millstream Cottages** ★★★★
*Bed & Breakfast*
2 Mill Lane, Minehead TA24 6SW
**t** (01643) 821966
**w** millstreamcottagedunster.co.uk

**Spears Cross** ★★★★★
*Guest Accommodation*
**SILVER AWARD**
1 West Street, Dunster TA24 6SN
**t** (01643) 821439
**e** visit@spearscross.demon.co.uk
**w** spearscross.co.uk

## DURSLEY
Gloucestershire

**Foresters** ★★★★
*Bed & Breakfast*
Chapel Street, Cam GL11 5NX
**t** (01453) 549996
**e** foresters@freeuk.com

## EAST CHARLETON
Devon

**The Barley House** ★★★★
*Bed & Breakfast*
Home Farm Barns, East Charleton TQ7 2AR
**t** (01548) 531882
**e** stay@thebarleyhouse.co.uk
**w** thebarleyhouse.co.uk

## EAST CHINNOCK
Somerset

**Barrows Farmhouse** ★★★★
*Bed & Breakfast*
Weston Street, Yeovil BA22 9EJ
**t** (01935) 864576
**e** barrowsfarmhouse@aol.com
**w** barrowsfarmhouse.com

**Gables Guest House** ★★★
*Guest House*
Yeovil BA22 9DR
**t** (01935) 862237
**e** tony@whitehead7877.freeserve.co.uk

## EAST COKER
### Somerset

**Granary House** ★★★★
*Bed & Breakfast*
**SILVER AWARD**
East Coker, Yeovil BA22 9LY
**t** (01935) 862738
**e** stay@granaryhouse.co.uk
**w** granaryhouse.co.uk

## EAST HARPTREE
### Somerset

**Harptree Court** ★★★★★
*Guest Accommodation*
**SILVER AWARD**
East Harptree, Bristol BS40 6AA
**t** (01761) 221729
**e** location.harptree@tiscali.co.uk
**w** harptreecourt.co.uk

## EAST KENNETT
### Wiltshire

**The Old Forge** ★★★★
*Bed & Breakfast*
**SILVER AWARD**
East Kennett, Marlborough SN8 4EY
**t** (01672) 861686
**e** laura@feeleyfamily.fsnet.co.uk
**w** theoldforge-avebury.co.uk

## EAST LOOE
### Cornwall

**Bridgeside Guest House**
★★★ *Guest House*
Fore Street, East Looe, Looe PL13 1HH
**t** (01503) 263113

**Pine Lodge B&B** ★★★★
*Bed & Breakfast*
Widegates, Looe PL13 1QB
**t** (01503) 240857
**e** bandb@pinelodgelooe.fsnet.co.uk
**w** pinelodgelooe.co.uk

**Sea Breeze Guest House**
★★★ *Guest House*
Lower Chapel Street, East Looe, Looe PL13 1AT
**t** (01503) 263131
**e** annette@seabreeze.wanadoo.co.uk
**w** cornwallexplore.co.uk/seabreeze

## EAST STOKE
### Dorset

**Woodlands Lodge** ★★★★
*Guest Accommodation*
Bindon Lane, East Stoke BH20 6AS
**t** (01929) 462327
**e** atwoodlands@talktalk.net
**w** woodlandscampingpark.co.uk

## EAST STOUR
### Dorset

**Aysgarth** ★★★★
*Bed & Breakfast*
**SILVER AWARD**
Back Street, East Stour, Gillingham SP8 5JY
**t** (01747) 838351
**e** aysgarth@lineone.net

## EAST TYTHERTON
### Wiltshire

**Barnbridge** ★★
*Bed & Breakfast*
East Tytherton, Chippenham SN15 4LT
**t** (01249) 740280
**e** bgiffard@aol.com
**w** barnbridge.co.uk

## EASTON ROYAL
### Wiltshire

**Follets B & B** ★★★★
*Bed & Breakfast*
**SILVER AWARD**
Easton Royal, Pewsey SN9 5LZ
**t** (01672) 810619
**e** margaret@folletsbb.com
**w** folletsbb.com

## EBRINGTON
### Gloucestershire

**Little Gidding** ★★★★
*Bed & Breakfast*
**SILVER AWARD**
Ebrington, Chipping Campden GL55 6NL
**t** (01386) 593302
**e** bookings@ebrington.com
**w** ebrington.com

## EDGE
### Gloucestershire

**The Withyholt** ★★★★
*Bed & Breakfast*
Paul Mead, Edge GL6 6PG
**t** (01452) 813618

## EVERCREECH
### Somerset

**Crossdale Cottage** ★★★
*Bed & Breakfast*
Pecking Mill, Shepton Mallet BA4 6PQ
**t** (01749) 830293
**e** info@crossdalecottage.co.uk
**w** crossdalecottage.co.uk

**The Old Dairy Rooms**
★★★★ *Farmhouse*
Rodmoor Farm, Shepton Mallet BA4 6DW
**t** (01749) 830531
**w** olddairyrooms.co.uk

## EXETER
### Devon

**The Bendene** ★★★★
*Guest Accommodation*
15-16 Richmond Road, Exeter EX4 4JA
**t** (01392) 213526
**e** reservations@bendene.co.uk
**w** bendene.co.uk

**Braeside Guest House**
★★★★ *Guest House*
21 New North Road, Exeter EX4 4HF
**t** (01392) 256875
**e** reception@braeside.biz
**w** braeside.biz

**Clock Tower Guest House**
★★★★
*Guest Accommodation*
16/17 New North Road, Exeter EX4 4HF
**t** (01392) 424545
**e** reservations@clocktowerhotel.co.uk
**w** clocktowerhotel.co.uk

**Culm Vale Country House**
★★★ *Bed & Breakfast*
Culm Vale, Stoke Canon, Exeter EX5 4EG
**t** (01392) 841615
**e** culmvale@hotmail.com
**w** culmvaleaccommodation.co.uk

**Exeter YHA** ★★★ *Hostel*
47 Countess Wear Road, Exeter EX2 6LR
**t** (01392) 873329
**e** exeter@yha.org.uk
**w** yha.org.uk

**The Garden House** ★★★★
*Bed & Breakfast*
**SILVER AWARD**
4 Hoopern Avenue, Pennsylvania EX4 6DN
**t** (01392) 256255
**e** stay@exeterbedandbeakfst.co.uk
**w** exeterbedandbreakfast.co.uk

**The Georgian Lodge** ★★★★
*Guest Accommodation*
5 Bystock Terrace, Exeter EX4 4HY
**t** (01392) 213079
**e** reservations@georgianlodge.com
**w** georgianlodge.com

**The Grange** ★★★★
*Guest Accommodation*
Stoke Hill, Exeter EX4 7JH
**t** (01392) 259723
**e** dudleythegrange@aol.com

**Hayne Barton Milverton Country Holidays** ★★
*Bed & Breakfast*
Whitestone, Exeter EX4 2JN
**t** (01392) 811268
**e** g_milverton@hotmail.com
**w** milvertoncountryholidays.com

**Home Farm** ★★★★
*Farmhouse*
Farringdon, Exeter EX5 2HY
**t** (01395) 232293
**e** rupert_thompson@hotmail.com

**Jades Guest House** ★★★
*Guest House*
65 St Davids Hill, Exeter EX4 4DW
**t** (01392) 435610
**e** jllbkrb@aol.com

**Lower Thornton Farm**
★★★★ *Farmhouse*
**SILVER AWARD**
Kenn, Exeter EX6 7XH
**t** (01392) 833434
**e** alison@lowerthorntonfarm.co.uk
**w** lowerthorntonfarm.co.uk

**Oakcliffe** ★★★ *Guest House*
73 St Davids Hill, Exeter EX4 4DW
**t** (01392) 258288
**e** oakcliffe@excite.com
**w** smoothhound.co.uk/hotels/oakcliffe

**Park View** ★★★
*Guest Accommodation*
8 Howell Road, Exeter EX4 4LG
**t** (01392) 271772
**e** enquiries@parkviewexeter.co.uk
**w** parkviewexeter.co.uk

**Radnor Hotel** ★★★
*Guest Accommodation*
79 St Davids Hill, Exeter EX4 4DW
**t** (01392) 272004
**e** ddweeks@radnorhotel.eclipse.co.uk

**Raffles** ★★★★
*Guest Accommodation*
11 Blackall Road, Exeter EX4 4HD
**t** (01392) 270200
**e** raffleshtl@btinternet.com
**w** raffles-exeter.co.uk

**Rydon Farm** ★★★★
*Farmhouse*
Woodbury, Exeter EX5 1LB
**t** (01395) 232341
**e** sallyglanvill@aol.com
**w** rydonfarmwoodbury.co.uk

**Silversprings** ★★★★
*Guest Accommodation*
**GOLD AWARD**
12 Richmond Road, St David's EX4 4JA
**t** (01392) 494040
**e** juliet@silversprings.co.uk
**w** silversprings.co.uk

**Strete Ralegh Farm** ★★★★
*Bed & Breakfast*
Whimple, Exeter EX5 2PP
**t** (01404) 822464
**e** info@streteraleghfarm.co.uk
**w** streteraleghfarm.co.uk

**Telstar Guest House** ★★★★
*Guest House*
75-77 St Davids Hill, Exeter EX4 4DW
**t** (01392) 272466
**e** reception@telstar-hotel.co.uk
**w** telstar-hotel.co.uk

**Thorverton Arms** ★★★ *Inn*
Thorverton, Exeter EX5 5NS
**t** (01392) 860205
**e** info@thethorvertonarms.co.uk
**w** thethorvertonarms.co.uk

**University of Exeter** ★★★
*Campus*
Sales Office, Lafrowda House, Exeter EX4 6TL
**t** (01392) 215566
**e** conferences@exeter.ac.uk
**w** exeter.ac.uk/hospitality

**White Hart** ★★★
*Guest Accommodation*
66 South Street, Exeter EX1 1EE
**t** (01392) 279897
**e** booking.wh.exeter@eldridge-pope.co.uk
**w** roomattheinn.info

**Woodbine Guesthouse**
★★★★ *Guest House*
1 Woodbine Terrace, Exeter EX4 4LJ
**t** (01392) 203302
**e** info@woodbineguesthouse.co.uk
**w** woodbineguesthouse.co.uk


Look out for establishments participating in the National Accessible Scheme

## EXFORD
Somerset

**Exford YHA** ★★★ *Hostel*
Exe Mead, Exford TA24 7PU
t (01643) 831288
e exford@yha.org.uk
w yha.org.uk

**Exmoor Lodge Guest House**
★★★ *Guest House*
Chapel Street, Exford
TA24 7PY
t (01643) 831694
e exmoor-lodge@talktalk.net
w exmoor-lodge.co.uk

**Stockleigh Lodge** ★★★★
*Guest Accommodation*
B3224, Exford TA24 7PZ
t (01643) 831500
e myra@stockleighexford.freeserve.co.uk
w stockleighexford.freeserve.co.uk

## EXMOUTH
Devon

**The Devoncourt** ★★★★
*Guest Accommodation*
Douglas Avenue, Exmouth
EX8 2EX
t (01395) 272277
e enquiries@devoncourt.com
w devoncourt.com

**New Moorings** ★★★★
*Guest Accommodation*
1 Morton Road, Exmouth
EX8 1AZ
t (01395) 223073
e anneanddave@newmoorings.wanadoo.co.uk
w newmoorings.co.uk

**The Swallows** ★★★★
*Guest Accommodation*
11 Carlton Hill, Exmouth
EX8 2AJ
t (01395) 263937
e p.russo@btclick.com
w exmouth-guide.co.uk/swallows.htm

**Victoria Guest House**
★★★★
*Guest Accommodation*
**SILVER AWARD**
131 Victoria Road, Exmouth
EX8 1DR
t (01395) 222882
e alfred@exmouth.net
w exmouth.net

## FAIRFORD
Gloucestershire

**Hathaway** ★★★★
*Bed & Breakfast*
**SILVER AWARD**
London Road, Fairford
GL7 4AR
t (01285) 712715
e lizian.spurway@btinternet.com

## FALMOUTH
Cornwall

**The Beach House ★★★★**
*Guest Accommodation*
**SILVER AWARD**
**1 Boscawen Road, Falmouth**
**TR11 4EL**
**t (01326) 210407**
**e beachhousefalmouth@hotmail.com**
**w beachhousefalmouth.co.uk**

**Camelot** ★★★★
*Guest Accommodation*
5 Avenue Road, Falmouth
TR11 4AZ
t (01326) 312480
e camelotfalmouth@aol.com
w camelot-guest-house.co.uk

**Castleton Guest House**
★★★ *Guest House*
68 Killigrew Street, Falmouth
TR11 3PR
t (01326) 372644
e dawnemmerson@aol.com

**Chellowdene** ★★★★
*Guest House*
Gyllyngvase Hill, Falmouth
TR11 4DN
t (01326) 314950
e info@chellowdene.co.uk
w chellowdene.co.uk

**Chelsea House ★★★★**
*Guest Accommodation*
**2 Emslie Road, Falmouth**
**TR11 4BG**
**t (01326) 212230**
**e info@chelseahousehotel.com**
**w chelseahousehotel.com**

**Dolvean House** ★★★★★
*Guest House* **SILVER AWARD**
50 Melvill Road, Falmouth
TR11 4DQ
t (01326) 313658
e reservations@dolvean.co.uk
w dolvean.co.uk

**Engleton House Guest House** ★★★
*Guest Accommodation*
67 Killigrew Street, Falmouth
TR11 3PR
t (01326) 372644 & 07736 684666
e dawnemmerson@aol.com
w falmouth-bandb.co.uk

**Grove Hotel** ★★★
*Guest Accommodation*
Grove Place, Falmouth
TR11 4AU
t (01326) 319577
e grovehotel@btconnect.com
w thegrovehotel.net

**Gyllyngvase House** ★★★★
*Guest Accommodation*
Gyllyngvase Road, Falmouth
TR11 4GH
t (01326) 312956
e info@gyllyngvase.co.uk
w gyllyngvase.co.uk

**Hawthorne Dene** ★★★★
*Guest Accommodation*
**SILVER AWARD**
12 Pennance Road, Falmouth
TR11 4EA
t (01326) 311427
e enquiries@hawthornedenehotel.co.uk
w hawthornedenehotel.com

**Headlands** ★★★★
*Guest Accommodation*
4 Avenue Road, Falmouth
TR11 4AZ
t (01326) 311141
e headlandsfalmouth@hotmail.co.uk
w headlandsfalmouth.co.uk

**Highcliffe, Falmouth** ★★★★
*Guest Accommodation*
22 Melvill Road, Falmouth
TR11 4AR
t (01326) 314466
e info@highcliffe-falmouth.co.uk
w stayinfalmouth.co.uk

**Lugo Rock** ★★★★
*Guest Accommodation*
59 Melvill Road, Falmouth
TR11 4DF
t (01326) 311344
e info@lugorockhotel.co.uk
w lugorockhotel.co.uk

**Lyonesse Guest House, Falmouth** ★★★
*Guest Accommodation*
17 Western Terrace, Falmouth
TR11 4QN
t (01326) 313017
e info@lyonessefalmouth.co.uk
w lyonessefalmouth.co.uk

**The Palms Guest House**
★★★★
*Guest Accommodation*
11 Castle Drive, Falmouth
TR11 4NF
t (01326) 314007
e j_miller99@hotmail.com
w thepalmsguesthouse.co.uk

**Poltair** ★★★★ *Guest House*
**SILVER AWARD**
Emslie Road, Falmouth
TR11 4BG
t (01326) 313158
e info@poltair.co.uk
w poltair.co.uk

**The Red House** ★★★★
*Guest Accommodation*
24 Melvill Road, Falmouth
TR11 4AR
t (01326) 311172
e info@theredhousefalmouth.co.uk
w theredhousebandb.co.uk

**Seaward Guest House**
Rating Applied For
*Guest Accommodation*
44 Melvill Road, Falmouth
TR11 4DQ
t (01326) 318100
e phil@seawardguesthousefalmouth.co.uk
w seawardguesthousefalmouth.co.uk

**Telford Guest House**
★★★★ *Guest House*
47 Melvill Road, Falmouth
TR11 4DG
t (01326) 314581
e connolly.sue@btconnect.com
w thetelford-falmouth.co.uk

**Tregedna Lodge** ★★★★
*Hostel*
Maenporth, Falmouth
TR11 5HL
t (01326) 250529
e tregednafarm@btinternet.com
w tregednafarmholidays.co.uk

**Tregenna Guest House**
★★★ *Guest Accommodation*
28 Melvill Road, Falmouth
TR11 4AR
t (01326) 313881
e jayne@corston.wanadoo.co.uk
w tregennafalmouth.co.uk

**Trelawney Guest House**
★★★★
*Guest Accommodation*
6 Melvill Road, Falmouth
TR11 4AS
t (01326) 316607
e trelawney@hotmail.co.uk
w trelawney-guesthouse.co.uk

**Trevaylor** ★★★★
*Guest Accommodation*
8 Pennance Road, Falmouth
TR11 4EA
t (01326) 313041
e info@trevaylorhotel.co.uk
w trevaylorhotel.com

**Wellington House** ★★★★
*Guest Accommodation*
26 Melvill Road, Falmouth
TR11 4AR
t (01326) 319947
e wellingtonhouse@msn.com
w wellingtonhousefalmouth.co.uk

**The Westcott** ★★★★
*Guest Accommodation*
Gyllyngvase Hill, Falmouth
TR11 4DN
t (01326) 311309
e info@westcotthotel.co.uk
w westcotthotel.co.uk

**Wickham Guest House**
★★★ *Guest Accommodation*
Gyllyngvase Terrace, Falmouth
TR11 4DL
t (01326) 311140
e enquiries@wickhamhotel.freeserve.co.uk
w wickham-hotel.co.uk

## FARMBOROUGH
Somerset

**Barrow Vale Farm** ★★★★
*Farmhouse*
Farmborough, Bath BA2 0BL
t (01761) 470300
e cherilynlangley@hotmail.com

## FARRINGTON GURNEY
Somerset

**The Croft Bed & Breakfast**
★★★★ *Bed & Breakfast*
The Croft, Bristol Road, Bristol
BS39 6TJ
t (01761) 453479
w thecroftbandb.com

## FAULKLAND
Somerset

**Lime Kiln Farm** ★★★★
*Bed & Breakfast*
A366, Radstock BA3 5XE
t (01373) 834305
e info@limekilnfarm.co.uk
w limekilnfarm.co.uk

**Old Farm Cottages** ★★★★
*Bed & Breakfast*
The Green, Radstock BA3 5UZ
t (01373) 834597
e maryclark1@hotmail.co.uk

**FEOCK**
**Cornwall**

**Come-To-Good Farm**
★★★★ *Farmhouse*
Feock, Truro TR3 6QS
t (01872) 863828
e info@cometogoodfarm.co.uk
w cometogoodfarm.co.uk

**FIDDINGTON**
**Gloucestershire**

**Hillview B and B** ★★★★
*Guest Accommodation*
**SILVER AWARD**
Fiddington, Ashchurch
GL20 7BJ
t (01684) 293231
e info@tewkesburybandb.co.uk
w tewkesburybandb.co.uk

**FLUSHING**
**Cornwall**

**An Chy Coth** ★★★★
*Bed & Breakfast*
37 Kersey Road, Flushing,
Falmouth TR11 5TR
t (01326) 377028
e anchycoth@hotmail.com

**FORD**
**Gloucestershire**

**The Plough** ★★★★ *Inn*
Ford, Temple Guiting,
Cheltenham GL54 5RU
t (01386) 584215
e info@theploughinnatford.co.uk
w theploughinnatford.co.uk

**FORRABURY**
**Cornwall**

**The Old Parsonage**
★★★★★
*Guest Accommodation*
Green Lane, Boscastle
PL35 0DJ
t (01840) 250339
e enquiries@old-parsonage.com
w old-parsonage.com

**FORTHAMPTON**
**Gloucestershire**

**Lower Lode Inn** ★★ *Inn*
Forthampton GL19 4RE
t (01684) 293224
e lowerlode@tiscali.co.uk

**FOSSEBRIDGE**
**Gloucestershire**

**The Inn at Fossebridge**
★★★★ *Inn*
Cheltenham GL54 3JS
t (01285) 720721
e info@fossebridgeinn.co.uk
w fossebridgeinn.co.uk

**FOWEY**
**Cornwall**

**Coombe Farm B&B** ★★★
*Farmhouse*
Fowey PL23 1HW
t (01726) 833123
e tessapaull@hotmail.com

**Fowey Marine Guest House**
★★★★ *Guest House*
21/27 Station Road, Fowey
PL23 1DF
t (01726) 833920
e enquiries@foweymarine.com
w foweymarine.com

**Old Ferry Inn** ★★★★ *Inn*
Bodinnick-by-Fowey, Fowey
PL23 1LX
t (01726) 870237
e oldferryinn@bodinnick.fsnet.co.uk
w oldferryinn.com

**FRAMPTON-ON-SEVERN**
**Gloucestershire**

**The Bell** ★★★★ *Inn*
The Green, Frampton-on-Severn, Gloucester GL2 7EP
t (01452) 740346
e stay@thebellatframpton.co.uk
w thebellatframpton.co.uk

**FRANCE LYNCH**
**Gloucestershire**

**The Coach House B & B**
★★★★ *Bed & Breakfast*
Highfield Way, Stroud GL6 8LZ
t (01453) 887529
e info@coachhousebnb.co.uk
w coachhousebnb.co.uk

**FRIAR WADDON**
**Dorset**

**Corton Farm** ★★★★
*Bed & Breakfast*
**SILVER AWARD**
Friar Waddon, Weymouth
DT3 4EP
t (01305) 815784
e hollylasseter@corton.org

**Pump Cottage** ★★★
*Bed & Breakfast*
Friar Waddon Road, Upwey
DT3 4EW
t (01305) 816002
e ronjamsden@hotmail.com
w pumpcottagebedandbreakfast.com

**FROME**
**Somerset**

**The Crown** ★★★ *Inn*
Market Place, Frome BA11 1AF
t (01373) 454618
e tomcheeseman@mac.com
w thecrownhotelfrome.co.uk

**The Full Moon** ★★★ *Inn*
Rudge Lane, Frome BA11 2QF
t (01373) 830936
e info@thefullmoon.co.uk
w thefullmoon.co.uk

**Granados** ★★★
*Bed & Breakfast*
East Woodland Road, Frome
BA11 5EL
t (01373) 465317
e granadosbandb@aol.com

**The Lodge** ★★★★
*Bed & Breakfast*
Monkley Lane, Rode Common
BA11 6QQ
t (01373) 830071
e juliemcdougal@btinternet.com

**Lower Grange Farm** ★★★★
*Farmhouse*
Feltham Lane, Frome BA11 5LL
t (01373) 452938
e bandb@thelowergrangefarm.fsnet.co.uk

**Mount Grange** ★★★★
*Guest Accommodation*
25 Bath Road, Frome BA11 2HJ
t (01373) 300159
e mountgrange@blueyonder.co.uk
w mount-grange.co.uk

**Seymours Court** ★★★★
*Farmhouse*
Green Park Lane, Frome
BA11 6TT
t (01373) 830466
e seymourscourt@btinternet.com
w seymourscourt.co.uk

**FROXFIELD**
**Wiltshire**

**The Pelican Inn**
Rating Applied For
*Inn*
Bath Road, Marlborough
SN8 3JY
t (020) 8777 3636
e tu@bcinns.co.uk

**The White House** ★★★★
*Bed & Breakfast*
**SILVER AWARD**
Little Bedwyn, Marlborough
SN8 3JP
t (01672) 870321
e whitehousebandb@btinternet.com
w the-white-house-b-and-b.co.uk

**GILLINGHAM**
**Dorset**

**Lyde Hill Farmhouse** ★★
*Bed & Breakfast*
Woodville, Stour Provost
SP8 5LX
t (01747) 838483

**GITTISHAM**
**Devon**

**Catshayes Farm** ★★★
*Farmhouse*
Gittisham, Honiton EX14 3AE
t (01404) 850302
e catshayesfarm@aol.com
w catshayes-farm-honiton.co.uk

**GLASTONBURY**
**Somerset**

**Apple**
Rating Applied For
*Guest Accommodation*
25 Norbins Road, Glastonbury
BA6 9JF
t (01458) 834547
e applebnb@ukonline.co.uk
w glastonbury.co.uk/accommodation/apple

**Appletree House** ★★★★
*Bed & Breakfast*
27 Bere Lane, Glastonbury
BA6 8BD
t (01458) 830803
e sue@appletreehouse.org.uk
w appletreehouse.org.uk

**The Barn** ★★★
*Bed & Breakfast*
84b Bove Town, Glastonbury
BA6 8JG
t (01458) 832991
e adriangoolden@yahoo.co.uk

**Belle-Vue** ★★★
*Bed & Breakfast*
2 Bere Lane, Glastonbury
BA6 8BA
t (01458) 830385
e belle_vueglastonbury@tiscali.co.uk
w bellevueglastonbury.co.uk

**Chalice Hill House** ★★★★
*Bed & Breakfast*
Dod Lane, Glastonbury
BA6 8BZ
t (01458) 830828
e mail@chalicehill.co.uk
w chalicehill.co.uk

**Cherrywood** ★★★★
*Bed & Breakfast*
11 Rowley Road, Glastonbury
BA6 8HU
t (01458) 833115

**Chestnuts Boutique Bed and Breakfast** ★★★★
*Bed & Breakfast*
**SILVER AWARD**
Bove Town, Glastonbury
BA6 8JG
t (01458) 830562
e jane@glastonburyaccommodation.com
w glastonburyaccommodation.com

**Chindit House**
Rating Applied For
*Guest Accommodation*
23 Wells Road, Glastonbury
BA6 9DN
t (01458) 830404
e peter@chindit-house.co.uk
w chindit-house.co.uk

**Coxwithy House B & B**
★★★★ *Bed & Breakfast*
Coxwithy Lane, Edgarley
BA6 8LA
t (01458) 833021
e jo@coxwithyhouse.co.uk
w coxwithyhouse.co.uk

**Divine Light Bed and Breakfast** ★★★
*Bed & Breakfast*
16a Magdalene Street,
Glastonbury BA6 9EH
t (01458) 835909
e glastonburyrose@lineone.net
w divinelightcentre.co.uk

**Havyatt Cottage** ★★★
*Guest Accommodation*
2 Havyatt, Glastonbury
BA6 8LF
t (01458) 832520
e christinahavyatt@hotmail.co.uk
w havyattcottage.co.uk

**Kylemore House** ★★★
*Guest Accommodation*
16 Lambrook Street,
Glastonbury BA6 8BX
t (01458) 831612
e enquiries@kylemorehouse.co.uk
w kylemorehouse.co.uk

**Little Orchard** ★★★
*Guest Accommodation*
Ashwell Lane, Glastonbury
BA6 8BG
t (01458) 831620
e the.littleorchard@lineone.net
w littleorchardglastonbury.co.uk

**Lower Farm** ★★★★
*Farmhouse* **SILVER AWARD**
High Street, Somerton
TA11 6BA
t (01458) 223237
e lowerfarm@btconnect.com
w lowerfarm.net

**Mapleleaf Middlewick**
★★★★ *Bed & Breakfast*
Wick Lane, Nr Glastonbury
BA6 8JW
t (01458) 832351
e middlewick@btconnect.com
w middlewickholidaycottages.co.uk

**Meare Manor** ★★★★
*Guest Accommodation*
60 St Marys Road, Glastonbury
BA6 9SR
t (01458) 860449
e reception@mearemanor.com
w mearemanor.com

**Melrose House** ★★★★
*Bed & Breakfast*
Coursing Batch, Glastonbury
BA6 8BH
t (01458) 834706
e info@melrose-bandb.co.uk
w melrose-bandb.co.uk

**Pippin** ★★★ *Bed & Breakfast*
4 Ridgeway Gardens,
Glastonbury BA6 8ER
t (01458) 834262
e daphne.slater@talktalk.net
w smoothhound.co.uk/hotels/pippin

**Shambhala Retreat**
Rating Applied For
*Bed & Breakfast*
Coursing Batch, Glastonbury
BA6 8BH
t (01458) 831797
e elisis@shambhalaheartcentre.com
w shambhala.co.uk

**Three Magdalene Street**
★★★★★
*Guest Accommodation*
3 Magdalene Street,
Glastonbury BA6 9EW
t (01458) 832129
e info@numberthree.co.uk
w numberthree.co.uk

**Tordown B & B and Healing Centre** ★★★★
*Guest Accommodation*
5 Ashwell Lane, Glastonbury
BA6 8BG
t (01458) 832287
e info@tordown.com
w tordown.com

**Who'd A Thought It Inn**
★★★ *Inn*
17 Northload Street,
Glastonbury BA6 9JJ
t (01458) 834460
e enquiries@whodathoughtit.co.uk
w whodathoughtit.co.uk

## GLOUCESTER
Gloucestershire

**Albert House** ★★★
*Guest Accommodation*
56-58 Worcester Street,
Gloucester GL1 3AG
t (01452) 502081
e enquiries@alberthotel.com
w alberthotel.com

**Brookthorpe Lodge** ★★★
*Guest House*
Stroud Road, Gloucester
GL4 0UQ
t (01452) 812645
e enquiries@brookthorpelodge.demon.co.uk
w brookthorpelodge.demon.co.uk

**Kilmorie Small Holding**
★★★★
*Guest Accommodation*
Gloucester Road, Corse,
Gloucester GL19 3RQ
t (01452) 840224
e sheila-barnfield@supanet.com
w smoothhound.co.uk/hotels/kilmorie

**Lulworth** ★★★
*Guest Accommodation*
12 Midland Road, Gloucester
GL1 4UF
t (01452) 521881
e lulworth-guest@tiscali.co.uk
w http://myweb.tiscali.co.uk/lulworth

**The Mulberry House** ★★★
*Bed & Breakfast*
2a Heathville Road, Gloucester
GL1 3DP
t (01452) 720079
e themulberryhouse@hotmail.com
w the-mulberry-house.co.uk/

**The New Inn** ★★★ *Inn*
16 Northgate Street,
Gloucester GL1 1SF
t (01452) 522177
e new_inn_hotel@hotmail.com
w newinnglos.com

**Nicki's Guesthouse & Taverna** ★★ *Guest House*
105-107 Westgate Street,
Gloucester GL1 2PG
t (01452) 301359

**The Spalite** ★★★
*Guest House*
121 Southgate Street,
Gloucester GL1 1XQ
t (01452) 380828
e marsh@spalitehotel.fsnet.co.uk
w spalitehotel.co.uk

**Springfields Farm** ★★
*Farmhouse*
Little Witcombe, Gloucester
GL3 4TU
t (01452) 863532

**Town Street Farm** ★★★
*Farmhouse*
Town Street, Tirley, Gloucester
GL19 4HG
t (01452) 780442
e townstreetfarm@hotmail.com
w townstreetfarm.co.uk

## GODNEY
Somerset

**Double-Gate Farm** ★★★★
*Guest Accommodation*
**GOLD AWARD**
Wells BA5 1RX
t (01458) 832217
e doublegatefarm@aol.com
w doublegatefarm.com

## GOLANT
Cornwall

**Golant YHA** ★★★ *Hostel*
Penquite House, Fowey
PL23 1LA
t (01726) 833507

## GONVENA
Cornwall

**Pencarn** ★★★★
*Bed & Breakfast*
Gonvena, Wadebridge
PL27 6DL
t (01208) 814631
e trevor.wiltshire@pencarn.co.uk
w pencarn.co.uk

**St Giles Cottage** ★★★★
*Bed & Breakfast*
Gonvena Hill, Wadebridge
PL27 6DP
t (01208) 813695
e info@stgilescottage.co.uk
w stgilescottage.co.uk

## GOONHILLY DOWNS
Cornwall

**County Cottage** ★★★★
*Bed & Breakfast*
Goonhilly Downs, Helston
TR12 6LQ
t (01326) 221810
e chris@countycottage.co.uk
w countycottage.co.uk

## GORRAN
Cornwall

**Mount Pleasant B&B** ★★★
*Farmhouse*
Mount Pleasant Farm, Gorran,
St Austell PL26 6LR
t (01726) 843918

## GORRAN HAVEN
Cornwall

**Bumblebees** ★★★★
*Bed & Breakfast*
Foxhole Lane, Gorran Haven
PL26 6JP
t (01726) 842219
e bamford@foxhole.vispa.com
w bumblebees.biz

## GRAMPOUND
Cornwall

**Perran House** ★★★
*Guest Accommodation*
Fore Street, Grampound
TR2 4RS
t (01726) 882066

## GREAT RISSINGTON
Gloucestershire

**The Granary Guesthouse**
★★★★ *Bed & Breakfast*
7 Cotswold Meadows, Great
Rissington GL54 2LN
t (01451) 821898
e info@cotswolds-bed-and-breakfasts.co.uk
w cotswolds-bed-and-breakfasts.co.uk

## GREENHAM
Somerset

**Greenham Hall** ★★★★
*Bed & Breakfast*
Wellington TA21 0JJ
t (01823) 672603
e greenhamhall@btopenworld.com
w greenhamhall.co.uk

## GRITTENHAM
Wiltshire

**Orchard View** ★★★★
*Bed & Breakfast*
Chesseley Hill, Grittenham
SN15 4JX
t 07773 480841
e susan.cary@btinternet.com

## GRITTLETON
Wiltshire

**The Neeld Arms Inn** ★★★
*Inn*
The Street, Grittleton
SN14 6AP
t (01249) 782470
e info@neeldarms.co.uk
w neeldarms.co.uk

## GUITING POWER
Gloucestershire

**The Guiting Guest House**
★★★★ *Guest House*
**SILVER AWARD**
Post Office Lane, Guiting
Power, Cheltenham GL54 5TZ
t (01451) 850470
e info@guitingguesthouse.com
w guitingguesthouse.com

**The Hollow Bottom** ★★★★
*Inn*
Winchcombe Road, Guiting
Power GL54 5UX
t (01451) 850392
e hello@hollowbottom.com
w hollowbottom.com

## GULWORTHY
Devon

**Colcharton Farm** ★★★★
*Farmhouse* **SILVER AWARD**
Gulworthy, Tavistock
PL19 8HU
t (01822) 616435
e colchartonfarm@agriplus.net
w visit-dartmoor.co.uk

**Hele Farm** ★★★★
*Farmhouse*
Gulworthy, Tavistock PL19 8PA
t (01822) 833084

## GUNWALLOE
Cornwall

**Glendower** ★★★★
*Guest Accommodation*
**SILVER AWARD**
Gunwalloe, Helston TR12 7QG
t (01326) 561282
e ian.mandy.turner@virgin.net
w glendower-gunwalloe.co.uk

## GWEEK
Cornwall

**Little Australia** ★★★★
*Guest Accommodation*
Nr Gweek, Helston TR12 6BG
t (01326) 221245
e wright.littleoz@hotmail.com
w littleaustraliafarm.co.uk

## HALBERTON
Devon

**The Priory**
Rating Applied For
*Guest Accommodation*
11 High Street, Halberton
EX16 7AF
**t** (01884) 821234
**e** dawn@theprioryhalberton.co.uk
**w** theprioryhalberton.co.uk

## HALSE
Somerset

**Rock House ★★★★**
*Bed & Breakfast*
**SILVER AWARD**
Main Road, Halse TA4 3AF
**t** (01823) 432956
**e** dwolverson@rockhousesomerset.co.uk
**w** rockhousesomerset.co.uk

## HALSTOCK
Dorset

**Quiet Woman House**
★★★★ *Bed & Breakfast*
Halstock, Yeovil BA22 9RX
**t** (01935) 891218
**e** enquiry@qwhdorset.co.uk
**w** qwhdorset.co.uk

## HALWELL
Devon

**Orchard House ★★★★★**
*Bed & Breakfast*
**SILVER AWARD**
Horner, Halwell, Totnes
TQ9 7LB
**t** (01548) 821448
**e** helen@orchard-house-halwell.co.uk
**w** orchard-house-halwell.co.uk

## HAMBROOK
Gloucestershire

**The Coach House ★★★**
*Guest Accommodation*
Bristol Road, Hambrook
BS16 1RY
**t** (0117) 956 6901
**e** info@bristolcoachhouse.co.uk
**w** bristolcoachhouse.co.uk

## HAMWORTHY
Dorset

**Holes Bay B & B ★★**
*Bed & Breakfast*
365 Blandford Road, Poole
BH15 4JL
**t** (01202) 672069
**e** maggie.dixon1@ntlworld.com

---

**Jessimine B&B ★★★**
*Bed & Breakfast*
77 Lake Road, Hamworthy
BH15 4LF
**t** (01202) 257726
**e** anita.saville@ntlworld.com

---

**Sarnia Cherie ★★★★**
*Bed & Breakfast*
375 Blandford Road,
Hamworthy, Poole BH15 4JL
**t** (01202) 679470
**e** criscollier@aol.com
**w** sarniacherie.co.uk

---

**Seashells ★★★**
*Bed & Breakfast*
4 Lake Road, Hamworthy
BH15 4LH
**t** (01202) 671921
**e** chris.tony@ntlworld.com
**w** 4seashells.co.uk

## HARBERTONFORD
Devon

**Pound Court Cottage**
★★★★
*Guest Accommodation*
Old Road, Harbertonford
TQ9 7TA
**t** (01803) 732441
**e** poundcourtcottage@tiscali.co.uk
**w** poundcourtcottage.co.uk

## HARLYN BAY
Cornwall

**The Harlyn Inn ★★★★** *Inn*
Harlyn Bay, Padstow PL28 8SB
**t** (01841) 520207
**e** mail@harlyn-inn.com
**w** harlyn-inn.com

## HARTLAND
Devon

**Elmscott Farm ★★★★**
*Farmhouse*
Hartland, Bideford EX39 6ES
**t** (01237) 441276

---

**Elmscott YHA ★★** *Hostel*
Elmscott, Hartland, Bideford
EX39 6ES
**t** (01237) 441367
**e** reservation@yha.org.uk
**w** yha.org.uk

---

**Gawlish Farm ★★★★**
*Farmhouse*
Hartland, Bideford EX39 6AT
**t** (01237) 441320

---

**Golden Park ★★★★★**
*Bed & Breakfast*
**GOLD AWARD**
Hartland, Bideford EX39 6EP
**t** (01237) 441254
**e** lynda@goldenpark.co.uk
**w** goldenpark.co.uk

---

**Trutrese ★★★**
*Guest Accommodation*
Harton Cross, Hartland
EX39 6AE
**t** (01237) 441274
**e** info@trutrese.com

## HAWKCHURCH
Devon

**The Old Inn ★★★** *Inn*
Axminster EX13 5XD
**t** (01297) 678309
**w** hawkchurch.com

## HAYLE
Cornwall

**Chy Coth ★★★★**
*Bed & Breakfast*
20 Prospect Place, Hayle
TR27 4LT
**t** (01736) 759529
**e** jwellington920@btinternet.com

---

**The Penellen ★★★★**
*Guest Accommodation*
64 Riviere Towans, Hayle
TR27 4AF
**t** (01736) 753777
**e** enquiries@golds-hire.co.uk
**w** golds-hire.co.uk

## HAYTOR
Devon

**Moorlands House**
Rating Applied For
*Guest Accommodation*
Newton Abbot TQ13 9XT
**t** (020) 8511 1534

## HELFORD
Cornwall

**Number 7even ★★★★**
*Bed & Breakfast*
**SILVER AWARD**
7 Minster Fields, Manaccan
TR12 6JG
**t** (01326) 231997
**e** number7even@btinternet.com
**w** number7even.co.uk

## HELSTON
Cornwall

**Hollow Tree House ★★★★**
*Bed & Breakfast*
Church Hill, Helston
TR13 8NW
**t** (01326) 572410
**w** hollowtreehouse.co.uk

---

**Jentone Bed and Breakfast**
★★★★
*Guest Accommodation*
Carnkie, Wendron TR13 0DZ
**t** (01209) 860883
**e** johns@jentone.net
**w** jentone.net

---

**Little Pengwedna Farm**
★★★★ *Farmhouse*
Nancegollan, Helston
TR13 0AY
**t** (01736) 850649
**e** ray@good-holidays.co.uk
**w** good-holidays.co.uk

---

**Lyndale Cottage Guest House ★★★★** *Guest House*
4 Greenbank, Meneage Road,
Helston TR13 8JA
**t** (01326) 561082
**e** enquiries@lyndalecottage.co.uk
**w** lyndalecottage.co.uk

---

**Mandeley Guesthouse ★★★**
*Guest House*
Clodgey Lane, Helston
TR13 8PJ
**t** (01326) 572550
**e** mandeley@btconnect.com
**w** mandeley.co.uk

---

**Strathallan Guest House**
★★★★
*Guest Accommodation*
6 Monument Road, Helston
TR13 8HF
**t** (01326) 573683
**e** strathallangh@aol.com
**w** connexions.co.uk/strathallan

---

**Tregathenan House ★★★★**
*Bed & Breakfast*
The Old Farmhouse,
Tregathenan TR13 0RZ
**t** (01326) 569840
**e** tregathenan@hotmail.com
**w** tregathenan.co.uk

## HEMYOCK
Devon

**Pounds Farm ★★★★**
*Farmhouse*
Hemyock EX15 3QS
**t** (01823) 680802
**e** shillingscottage@yahoo.co.uk
**w** poundsfarm.co.uk

## HENLADE
Somerset

**Barn Close Nurseries ★★★**
*Guest Accommodation*
Stoke Road, Henlade TA3 5DH
**t** (01823) 443507
**e** jujuat66@hotmail.co.uk

## HEXWORTHY
Devon

**The Forest Inn ★★★** *Inn*
Hexworthy, Dartmoor
PL20 6SD
**t** (01364) 631211
**e** info@theforestinn.co.uk
**w** theforestinn.co.uk

## HEYTESBURY
Wiltshire

**The Red Lion ★★★★**
*Guest Accommodation*
42a High Street, Heytesbury
BA12 0EA
**t** (01985) 840315
**e** donna.pease@btinternet.com

---

**The Resting Post ★★★★**
*Bed & Breakfast*
High Street, Heytesbury,
Warminster BA12 0ED
**t** (01985) 840204
**e** enquiries@therestingpost.co.uk
**w** therestingpost.co.uk

## HEYWOOD
Wiltshire

**Redwood Lodge ★★★★**
*Guest Accommodation*
Capps Lane, Westbury
BA13 4NE
**t** (01373) 823949
**w** redwoodlodgeuk.com

## HIGHBRIDGE
Somerset

**46 Church Street ★★★**
*Bed & Breakfast*
Highbridge TA9 3AQ
**t** (01278) 788365

## HIGHCLIFFE
Dorset

**10 Brook Way ★★**
*Bed & Breakfast*
Fiars Cliff BH23 4HA
**t** (01425) 276738
**e** midgefinn@hotmail.com

---

**The Beech Tree ★★★★**
*Guest House*
2 Stuart Road, Highcliffe
BH23 5JS
**t** (01425) 272038
**e** hkowalski@beechtree.info
**w** beechtree.info

---

**Beechcroft Place ★★★★**
*Bed & Breakfast*
**SILVER AWARD**
106 Lymington Road, Highcliffe
BH23 4JX
**t** (01425) 277171
**e** info@beachmeetsforest.co.uk
**w** beachmeetsforest.co.uk

---

**Castle Lodge ★★★★**
*Guest House*
173 Lymington Road, Highcliffe
BH23 4JS
**t** (01425) 275170
**e** sharon@castlelodge-highcliffe.co.uk
**w** castlelodge-highcliffe.co.uk



Look out for establishments participating in the National Accessible Scheme

**Sea Corner** ★★★
*Guest House*
397 Waterford Road, Highcliffe BH23 5JN
**t** (01425) 272731
**e** kevin.seacorner@hotmail.co.uk
**w** seacorner-guesthouse.co.uk

## HILLERSLAND
Gloucestershire

**The Rock** ★★★★
*Guest Accommodation*
Hillersland, Coleford GL16 7NY
**t** (01594) 837893
**e** chris@stayattherock.com
**w** stayattherock.com

## HILMARTON
Wiltshire

**Burfoots** ★★★★
*Bed & Breakfast*
1 The Close, Hilmarton SN11 8TH
**t** (01249) 760492
**e** info@burfoots.co.uk
**w** burfoots.co.uk

## HOLBETON
Devon

**Bugle Rocks** ★★★★
*Bed & Breakfast*
Battisborough Cross, Plymouth PL8 1JX
**t** (01752) 830422
**e** stay@buglerocks.co.uk
**w** buglerocks.co.uk

## HOLCOMBE
Devon

**Ashlawn Cottage**
Rating Applied For
*Guest Accommodation*
Holcombe Road, Holcombe EX7 0JB
**t** (01626) 863622

**Manor Farm** ★★★★
*Farmhouse*
Holcombe Village, Holcombe EX7 0JT
**t** (01626) 863020
**e** humphreyclem@aol.com
**w** farmaccom.com

## HOLMEBRIDGE
Dorset

**Holmebridge House** ★★★
*Bed & Breakfast*
Holmebridge, Wareham BH20 6AF
**t** (01929) 550599
**e** holmebridge@googlemail.com
**w** holmebridgehouse.co.uk

## HOLSWORTHY
Devon

**Bason Farm** ★★★★
*Farmhouse*
Bradford, Holsworthy EX22 7AW
**t** (01409) 281277
**e** info@basonfarmholidays.co.uk
**w** basonfarmholidays.co.uk

**Oak Tree Farm** ★★★★
*Farmhouse*
Burnards House, Holsworthy EX22 7JA
**t** (01409) 254870
**e** colinvalerie.stevens@oaktreelleyns.co.uk
**w** oaktreelleyns.co.uk

## HONITON
Devon

**The Cottage** ★★★★
*Guest Accommodation*
Marsh, Honiton EX14 9AJ
**t** (01460) 234240
**e** buttonstephens@btopenworld.com
**w** cattagemarsh.co.uk

**Lower Luxton Farm** ★★★
*Farmhouse*
Honiton EX14 9PB
**t** (01823) 601269
**e** lwrluxtonfm@hotmail.com
**w** lowerluxtonfarm.co.uk

**Wessington Farm** ★★★★
*Guest Accommodation*
**SILVER AWARD**
Awliscombe, Honiton EX14 3NU
**t** (01404) 42280
**e** bandb@lre9.com
**w** eastdevon.com/bedandbreakfast

## HOPE COVE
Devon

**The Cottage** ★★★
*Guest Accommodation*
Hope Cove, Salcombe TQ7 3HJ
**t** (01548) 561555
**e** info@hopecove.com
**w** hopecove.com

**Sand Pebbles** ★★★★
*Guest Accommodation*
Hope Cove, Kingsbridge TQ7 3HF
**t** (01548) 561673
**e** andrew@sandpebbles.fsnet.co.uk
**w** sandpebbleshotel.co.uk

## HORSINGTON
Somerset

**Half Moon Inn** ★★★ *Inn*
Off Higher Road, Templecombe BA8 0EF
**t** (01963) 370140
**e** halfmoon@horsington.co.uk
**w** horsington.co.uk

## HORTON
Wiltshire

**Partacre** ★★ *Bed & Breakfast*
Horton, Devizes SN10 3NB
**t** (01380) 860261

## HUCCLECOTE
Gloucestershire

**Notley House and The Coach House** ★★★
*Guest Accommodation*
93 Hucclecote Road, Gloucester GL3 3TR
**t** (01452) 611584
**e** notleyhouse@blueyonder.co.uk
**w** notleyhouse.co.uk

## HULLAVINGTON
Wiltshire

**Serendipity Bed and Breakfast** ★★★★
*Bed & Breakfast*
15 The Street, Hullavington SN14 6EF
**t** (01666) 837661
**e** alison.reed@serendipitybedandbreakfast.co.uk

## HUNTLEY
Gloucestershire

**Birdwood Villa Farm** ★★★
*Farmhouse*
Main Road, Birdwood, Gloucester GL19 3EQ
**t** (01452) 750451
**e** birdwood.villafarm@virgin.net
**w** birdwoodvillafarm.co.uk

**Kings Head Inn** ★★★ *Inn*
Birdwood, Gloucester GL19 3EF
**t** (01452) 750348
**e** enquiries@kingsheadbirdwood.co.uk
**w** kingsheadbirdwood.co.uk

## IDDESLEIGH
Devon

**Parsonage Farm** ★★★★
*Farmhouse* **SILVER AWARD**
Iddesleigh, Winkleigh EX19 8SN
**t** (01837) 810318
**e** roseward01@yahoo.co.uk

## IDE
Devon

**Drakes Farm House** ★★★★
*Bed & Breakfast*
Drakes Farm, Exeter EX2 9RL
**t** (01392) 256814
**e** drakesfarm@hotmail.com
**w** drakesfarm-devon.co.uk

## ILFRACOMBE
Devon

**Burnside** ★★★★
*Bed & Breakfast*
34 St Brannocks Road, Ilfracombe EX34 8EQ
**t** (01271) 863097
**e** san-dave@meekb.freeserve.co.uk
**w** burnside-ilfracombe.com

**Cairn House** ★★★
*Guest Accommodation*
43 St Brannocks Road, Ilfracombe EX34 8EH
**t** (01271) 863911
**e** info@cairnhousehotel.co.uk
**w** cairnhousehotel.co.uk

**Combe Lodge** ★★★
*Guest House*
Chambercombe Park Road, Ilfracombe EX34 9QW
**t** (01271) 864518
**e** combelodgehotel@tinyworld.co.uk
**w** combe-lodge.co.uk

**Dorchester Guest House**
★★★★ *Guest House*
59 St Brannocks Road, Ilfracombe EX34 8EQ
**t** (01271) 865472
**e** edwardsna@btinternet.com
**w** the-dorchester.co.uk

**The Elmfield** ★★★
*Guest Accommodation*
Torrs Park, Ilfracombe EX34 8AZ
**t** (01271) 863377
**e** info@theelmfield.com
**w** elmfieldhotelilfracombe.co.uk

**The Graystoke** ★★★★
*Guest House*
58 St Brannocks Road, Ilfracombe EX34 8EQ
**t** (01271) 862328
**e** graystokehotel@aol.com
**w** graystokehotel.com

**Lyncott House** ★★★★
*Guest Accommodation*
56 St Brannocks Road, Ilfracombe EX34 8EQ
**t** (01271) 862425
**w** lyncotthouse.co.uk

**Mullacott** *Camping Barn*
Mullacott Farm, Mullacott Cross EX34 8NA
**t** (01271) 866877
**e** relax@mullacottfarm.co.uk
**w** mullacottfarm.co.uk

**St Brannocks House** ★★★★
*Guest Accommodation*
61 St Brannocks Road, Ilfracombe EX34 8EQ
**t** (01271) 863873
**e** info@stbrannockshouse.co.uk
**w** stbrannockshouse.co.uk

**Sherborne Lodge Hotel** ★★
*Guest Accommodation*
Torrs Park, Ilfracombe EX34 8AY
**t** (01271) 862297
**e** visit@sherborne-lodge.co.uk
**w** sherborne-lodge.co.uk

**Varley House** ★★★★
*Guest Accommodation*
Chambercombe Park, Ilfracombe EX34 9QW
**t** (01271) 863927
**e** info@varleyhouse.co.uk
**w** varleyhouse.co.uk

**Westaway** ★★★★★
*Guest Accommodation*
**SILVER AWARD**
Torrs Park, Ilfracombe EX34 8AY
**t** (01271) 864459
**e** mail@westawayhotel.co.uk
**w** westawayhotel.co.uk

**The Woodlands** ★★★
*Guest Accommodation*
Torrs Park, Ilfracombe EX34 8AZ
**t** (01271) 863098
**e** info@woodlandsdevon.com
**w** woodlandsdevon.com

## ILLOGAN
Cornwall

**Portreath Camping Barn**
*Bunkhouse*
Nance Farm, Illogan TR16 4QX
**t** (01209) 842244
**e** mary.alway@btinternet.com

## ILLOGAN HIGHWAY
Cornwall

**Lyndhurst Guest House**
★★★ *Guest House*
80 Agar Road, Redruth TR15 3NB
**t** (01209) 215146
**e** sales@lyndhurst-guesthouse.net
**w** lyndhurst-guesthouse.net

## ILMINSTER
Somerset

**Dillington House ★★★★★**
*Campus*
Off Bay Hill, Ilminster
TA19 9DT
**t** (01460) 52427
**e** ccrocker@somerset.gov.uk
**w** dillington.com

**Graden ★★★**
*Bed & Breakfast*
Ilminster TA19 0SG
**t** (01460) 52371

## ISLES OF SCILLY

**Browarth ★★★**
*Bed & Breakfast*
Rams Valley, St Mary's
TR21 0JX
**t** (01720) 422353

**Covean Cottage ★★★**
*Guest House*
St Agnes TR22 0PL
**t** (01720) 422620
**e** coveancottage@fsmail.net

**Demelza Bed & Breakfast**
**★★★★** *Bed & Breakfast*
Demelza, Jackson's Hill, St
Marys TR21 0JZ
**t** (01720) 422803
**e** sibleysonscilly@tiscali.co.uk

**The Harbourside ★★★**
*Guest House*
The Quay, St Mary's, Isles of
Scilly TR21 0HU
**t** (01720) 422352
**e** theharbourside@hotmail.co.uk
**w** harbourside-scilly.co.uk

**Nornour ★★★**
*Bed & Breakfast*
Mount Flagon, St Mary's
TR21 0NE
**t** (01720) 423901
**e** mjsenior26@hotmail.com
**w** nornourbandb.co.uk

**Nundeeps ★★★**
*Bed & Breakfast*
Rams Valley, St Mary's
TR21 0JX
**t** (01720) 422517
**e** cook@nundeeps.freeserve.co.uk

**The Old Town Inn ★★★** *Inn*
Old Town, St Martin's
TR21 0NN
**t** (01720) 422301

**Pelistry Cottage ★★★★**
*Bed & Breakfast*
The Parade, St Mary's
TR21 0LP
**t** (01720) 422506
**e** scillyhols@hotmail.com
**w** scillyholidays.com

**Polreath Guest House**
**★★★★** *Bed & Breakfast*
Higher Town, St Martin's
TR25 0QL
**t** (01720) 422046
**e** s.poat@ntlworld.com
**w** polreath.com

## IVYBRIDGE
Devon

**Higher Coarsewell Farm**
**★★★★** *Bed & Breakfast*
Ugborough, Ivybridge
PL21 0HP
**t** (01548) 821560
**e** sue@highercoarsewellfarm.co.uk
**w** highercoarsewellfarm.co.uk

**Hillhead Farm ★★★★**
*Farmhouse* **SILVER AWARD**
Ugborough, Ivybridge
PL21 0HQ
**t** (01752) 892674
**e** info@hillhead-farm.co.uk
**w** hillhead-farm.co.uk

**Venn Farm ★★★** *Farmhouse*
Ugborough, Ivybridge
PL21 0PE
**t** (01364) 73240
**w** smoothhound.co.uk/hotels/vennfarm

## JACOBSTOW
Cornwall

**Broad Langdon B&B ★★★★**
*Guest Accommodation*
**SILVER AWARD**
Broad Langdon, Jacobstow,
Bude EX23 0BZ
**t** (01566) 781656
**e** johnnjo@btinternet.com
**w** broadlangdon.co.uk

## KEYBRIDGE
Cornwall

**Robin's Nest ★★★★**
*Bed & Breakfast*
Riverdale, Keybridge, Bodmin
PL30 4QL
**t** (01208) 851390
**e** jjohn.gerring@telco4u.net
**w** riverdale.me.uk

## KILCOT
Gloucestershire

**Withyland Heights ★★★★**
*Farmhouse*
Beavans Hill, Kilcot GL18 1PG
**t** (01989) 720582
**e** withyland@farming.co.uk

## KILKHAMPTON
Cornwall

**Heatham Farmhouse**
**★★★★** *Farmhouse*
**SILVER AWARD**
Kilkhampton, Bude EX23 9RH
**t** (01288) 321325
**e** heathamfarm@btconnect.com
**w** heathamfarm.co.uk

## KILVE
Somerset

**The Old Mill ★★★★**
*Bed & Breakfast*
A39, Kilve TA5 1EB
**t** (01278) 741571

## KILWORTHY
Devon

**Kilworthy Farm B & B ★★★**
*Farmhouse*
Kilworthy, Tavistock PL19 0JN
**t** (01822) 614477
**e** sandra@kilworthy.co.uk

## KIMMERIDGE
Dorset

**Chaldecotts ★★** *Farmhouse*
Swalland Farm, Kimmeridge
BH20 5PD
**t** (01929) 480936
**e** info@chaldecotts.co.uk
**w** chaldecotts.co.uk

**Kimmeridge Farmhouse**
**★★★★** *Farmhouse*
**GOLD AWARD**
Kimmeridge, Wareham
BH20 5PE
**t** (01929) 480990
**e** kimmeridgefarmhouse@hotmail.com
**w** kimmeridgefarmhouse.co.uk

## KINGSBRIDGE
Devon

**Ashleigh House ★★★**
*Guest Accommodation*
Ashleigh Road, Kingsbridge
TQ7 1HB
**t** (01548) 852893
**e** reception@ashleigh-house.co.uk
**w** ashleigh-house.co.uk

**Globe Inn ★★★★** *Inn*
Frogmore, Kingsbridge
TQ7 2NR
**t** (01548) 531351
**e** enquiries@theglobeinn.co.uk
**w** theglobeinn.co.uk

**Mountain Water Experience**
**★★** *Activity Accommodation*
Courtlands, Kingsbridge
TQ7 4BN
**t** (01548) 550675
**e** mwe@mountainwaterexp.demon.co.uk
**w** mountainwaterexperience.com

**South Allington House**
Rating Applied For
*Farmhouse*
Chivelstone, Kingsbridge
TQ7 2NB
**t** (01548) 511272
**e** barbara@southallingtonhouse.co.uk
**w** southallingtonhouse.co.uk

## KINGSKERSWELL
Devon

**Harewood Guesthouse**
**★★★** *Guest House*
17 Torquay Road,
Kingskerswell TQ12 5HH
**t** (01803) 872228
**e** correneandbill1@blueyonder.co.uk
**w** harewoodguesthouse.pwp.blueyonder.co.uk

## KINGSTON ST MARY
Somerset

**Fulford Grange ★★★★★**
*Bed & Breakfast*
**GOLD AWARD**
Taunton TA2 8AJ
**t** (01823) 451206
**e** enquiries@fulfordgrange.co.uk
**w** fulfordgrange.co.uk

## KINGTON LANGLEY
Wiltshire

**The Moors ★★★**
*Bed & Breakfast*
Malmesbury Road, Kington
Langley SN14 6HT
**t** (01249) 750288
**e** carolinetayler@hotmail.com

## KINGTON ST MICHAEL
Wiltshire

**Arch House ★★★★**
*Bed & Breakfast*
Manor Court, Kington St
Michael SN14 6JA
**t** (01249) 758377
**e** christinejago@btinternet.com
**w** archhousebandb.co.uk

## KNOWSTONE
Devon

**West Bowden Farm ★★★★**
*Farmhouse*
Knowstone, South Molton
EX36 4RP
**t** (01398) 341224
**e** west.bowden@ukf.net
**w** westbowden.ukf.net

## LACOCK
Wiltshire

**King John's Hunting Lodge**
**★★★★** *Bed & Breakfast*
**SILVER AWARD**
21 Church Street, Lacock,
Chippenham SN15 2LB
**t** (01249) 730313
**e** kingjohns@amserve.com

**Lacock Pottery Bed & Breakfast ★★★★**
*Bed & Breakfast*
1 The Tanyard, Church Street,
Chippenham SN15 2LB
**t** (01249) 730266
**e** simonemcdowell@lacockbedandbreakfast.com
**w** lacockbedandbreakfast.com

**Lower Lodge ★★★★**
*Bed & Breakfast*
35 Bowden Hill, Chippenham
SN15 2PP
**t** (01249) 730711
**e** duboulaylowerlodge@hotmail.co.uk

**The Old Rectory ★★★★**
*Guest Accommodation*
Cantax Hill, Lacock SN15 2JZ
**t** (01249) 730335
**e** sexton@oldrectorylacock.co.uk
**w** oldrectorylacock.co.uk

## LADOCK
Cornwall

**Woodland Valley ★★★★**
*Group Hostel*
Ladock, Truro TR2 4PT
**t** (01726) 882268
**e** jones.farm@virgin.net
**w** woodlandvalley.co.uk

## LANDRAKE
Cornwall

**Lantallack Farm ★★★★★**
*Bed & Breakfast*
**GOLD AWARD**
Landrake, Saltash PL12 5AE
**t** (01752) 851281
**e** nickywalker44@tiscali.co.uk
**w** lantallack.co.uk

**LANEAST**
**Cornwall**

**Stitch Park** ★★★★
*Bed & Breakfast*
**SILVER AWARD**
Laneast, Launceston PL15 8PN
**t** (01566) 86687
**e** stitchpark@hotmail.com

**LANESCOT**
**Cornwall**

**Great Pelean Farm** ★★★★
*Farmhouse* **SILVER AWARD**
Tywardreath, Par PL24 2RX
**t** (01726) 812106
**e** andyjones74@hotmail.com
**w** greatpeleanfarm.com

**LANGPORT**
**Somerset**

**Amberley** ★★★★
*Guest Accommodation*
Martock Road, Long Load
TA10 9LD
**t** (01458) 241542
**e** jean.atamberley@talk21.com
**w** amberleybandb.co.uk

**Muchelney Ham Farm**
★★★★ *Farmhouse*
**SILVER AWARD**
Muchelney Ham, Langport
TA10 0DJ
**t** (01458) 250737
**w** muchelneyhamfarm.co.uk

**Orchard Barn** ★★★★
*Bed & Breakfast*
Law Lane, Langport TA10 0LS
**t** (01458) 252310
**e** orchardbarn@zoom.co.uk
**w** orchard-barn.com

**LANIVET**
**Cornwall**

**St Benets Abbey** ★★★★
*Guest Accommodation*
Truro Road, Lanivet, Bodmin
PL30 5HF
**t** (01208) 831352
**e** st.benetsabbey@btconnect.com
**w** stbenetsabbey.com

**Willowbrook** ★★★★
*Guest Accommodation*
Lamorick, Lanivet, Bodmin
PL30 5HB
**t** (01208) 831670
**e** willowbrookbandb@aol.com
**w** welcomingyou.co.uk/willowbrook

**LANREATH-BY-LOOE**
**Cornwall**

**Bocaddon Farm** ★★★★
*Bed & Breakfast*
Looe PL13 2PG
**t** (01503) 220192
**e** holidays@bocaddon.com
**w** bocaddon.com

**LANSALLOS**
**Cornwall**

**Lesquite Farm** ★★★★
*Farmhouse* **SILVER AWARD**
Peakswater, Lansallos, Looe
PL13 2QE
**t** (01503) 220315
**e** tolputt@lesquitepolperro.fsnet.co.uk
**w** lesquite-polperro.fsnet.co.uk

**West Kellow Farm** ★★★★
*Farmhouse* **SILVER AWARD**
Lansallos, Polperro PL13 2QL
**t** (01503) 272089
**e** westkellow@aol.com
**w** westkellow.co.uk

**LANSDOWN**
**Somerset**

**The Blathwayt** ★★★★ *Inn*
Lansdown, Bath BA1 9BT
**t** (01225) 421995
**e** info@theblathwayt-bath.co.uk
**w** theblathwayt-bath.co.uk

**LANTEGLOS**
**Cornwall**

**Trehaida** ★★★★ *Farmhouse*
Whitecross, Fowey PL23 1NF
**t** (01726) 870880
**e** trehaida@btopenworld.com
**w** trehaida.co.uk

**LAUNCESTON**
**Cornwall**

**Berrio Bridge House** ★★★★
*Bed & Breakfast*
**SILVER AWARD**
North Hill, Launceston
PL15 7NL
**t** (01566) 782714
**e** helen@berriobridge.freeserve.co.uk
**w** berriobridgehouse.co.uk

**Glencoe Villa** ★★★
*Guest Accommodation*
13 Race Hill, Launceston
PL15 9BB
**t** (01566) 775819

**Lynher Farmhouse** ★★★★
*Bed & Breakfast*
Lynher Farm, North Hill,
Launceston PL15 7NR
**t** (01566) 782273
**e** pam@lynherfarm.fsnet.co.uk
**w** lynherfarm.co.uk

**Middle Tremollett** ★★★★
*Farmhouse*
Coads Green, Launceston
PL15 7NA
**t** (01566) 782416
**e** btrewin@btinternet.com
**w** tremollett.com

**Oakside** ★★★★
*Bed & Breakfast*
South Petherwin, Launceston
PL15 7JL
**t** (01566) 86733
**e** janet.crossman@tesco.net

**Primrose Cottage** ★★★★★
*Bed & Breakfast*
**SILVER AWARD**
Lawhitton, Launceston
PL15 9PE
**t** (01566) 773645
**e** enquiry@primrosecottagesuites.co.uk
**w** primrosecottagesuites.co.uk

**St Leonards House** ★★★★
*Bed & Breakfast*
Polson, Launceston PL15 9QR
**t** (01566) 779195
**e** enquiries@stleonardshouse.co.uk
**w** stleonardshouse.co.uk

**Thornbank Bed and Breakfast** ★★★
*Bed & Breakfast*
6 Highfield Park Road,
Launceston PL15 7DY
**t** (01566) 776136
**e** bkressinger513@btinternet.com
**w** launcestonbedandbreakfast.co.uk

**Tregood Farm** ★★★
*Bed & Breakfast*
Congdon's Shop, Launceston
PL15 7PN
**t** (01566) 782263 & 07976 239893

**Trevadlock Farm** ★★★★★
*Farmhouse* **SILVER AWARD**
Congdon Shop, Launceston
PL15 7PW
**t** (01566) 782239
**e** trevadlock@farming.co.uk
**w** trevadlock.co.uk

**Wheatley Farm** ★★★★★
*Farmhouse* **GOLD AWARD**
Maxworthy, Launceston
PL15 8LY
**t** (01566) 781232
**e** valerie@wheatley-farm.co.uk
**w** wheatley-farm.co.uk

**LAVERSTOCK**
**Wiltshire**

**20 Potters Way** ★★★
*Bed & Breakfast*
Laverstock, Salisbury SP1 1PY
**t** (01722) 335031

**LECHLADE-ON-THAMES**
**Gloucestershire**

**Cambrai Lodge** ★★★★
*Guest Accommodation*
Oak Street, Lechlade,
Lechlade-on-Thames GL7 3AY
**t** (01367) 253173
**e** cambrailodge@btconnect.com
**w** cambrailodgeguesthouse.co.uk

**New Inn Hotel** ★★★ *Inn*
Market Square, Lechlade-on-Thames GL7 3AB
**t** (01367) 252296
**e** info@newinnhotel.co.uk
**w** newinnhotel.co.uk

**LEEDSTOWN**
**Cornwall**

**Little Pengelly – Farmhouse B&B** ★★★★
*Guest Accommodation*
**SILVER AWARD**
Trenwheal, Leedstown
TR27 6BP
**t** (01736) 850452
**e** maxine@littlepengelly.co.uk
**w** littlepengelly.co.uk

**LEIGHTON**
**Somerset**

**Broadgrove House** ★★★★
*Bed & Breakfast*
Leighton, Frome BA11 4PP
**t** (01373) 836296
**e** broadgrove836@tiscali.co.uk
**w** broadgrovehouse.co.uk

**LELANT**
**Cornwall**

**Hindon Hall** ★★★★★
*Guest Accommodation*
**SILVER AWARD**
Lelant, St Ives TR26 3EN
**t** (01736) 753046
**e** enquiries@hindonhall.co.uk

**LISKEARD**
**Cornwall**

**Hyvue House** ★★★
*Bed & Breakfast*
Endsleigh Terrace, Liskeard
PL14 6BN
**t** (01579) 348175

**Lampen Farm** ★★★★
*Farmhouse*
St Neot, Liskeard PL14 6PB
**t** (01579) 320284
**e** joan@lampenfarm.fsnet.co.uk
**w** lampen-farm.co.uk

**Trecorme Barton** ★★★★
*Farmhouse*
Quethiock, Liskeard PL14 3SH
**t** (01579) 342646
**e** david_renfree@btinternet.com
**w** trecormebarton.co.uk

**Tregondale Farm** ★★★★
*Farmhouse* **GOLD AWARD**
Menheniot, Liskeard PL14 3RG
**t** (01579) 342407
**e** tregondalefarm@btconnect.com
**w** tregondalefarm.co.uk

**Trewint Farm** ★★★★
*Farmhouse* **SILVER AWARD**
Menheniot, Liskeard PL14 3RG
**t** (01579) 347155
**e** holidays@trewintfarn.co.uk
**w** trewintfarm.co.uk

**LITTLE LANGFORD**
**Wiltshire**

**Little Langford Farmhouse**
★★★★★ *Farmhouse*
**GOLD AWARD**
Little Langford, Salisbury
SP3 4NP
**t** (01722) 790205
**e** bandb@littlelangford.co.uk
**w** littlelangford.co.uk

**LITTLE PETHERICK**
**Cornwall**

**Little Tregonna B&B** ★★★★
*Bed & Breakfast*
Wadebridge PL27 7QT
**t** (01841) 540446
**e** jayneclinton@hotmail.co.uk

**LITTLETON PANELL**
**Wiltshire**

**Summerhayes** ★★★★★
*Bed & Breakfast*
**SILVER AWARD**
143 High Street, Littleton Panell
SN10 4EU
**t** (01380) 813521
**e** summerhayesbandb@ukonline.co.uk
**w** summerhayesbandb.co.uk

**LITTON CHENEY**
**Dorset**

**Litton Cheney YHA** ★★★
*Hostel*
Litton Cheney, Dorchester
DT2 9AT
t (01308) 482340

**LIZARD**
**Cornwall**

**Atlantic House** ★★★★★
*Guest Accommodation*
**SILVER AWARD**
Pentreath Lane, The Lizard
TR12 7NY
t (01326) 290399
e atlantichse@aol.com
w atlantichouselizard.co.uk

**Lizard Point Youth Hostel**
★★★ *Hostel*
Yha Lizard, Helston TR12 7NT
t 0870 770 6120

**The Top House Inn** ★★★★
*Inn*
The Top House, Helston
TR12 7NQ
t (01326) 290974
w thetophouselizard.co.uk

**Trethvas Farmhouse** ★★★★
*Farmhouse*
The Lizard, Helston TR12 7AR
t (01326) 290720
e gwen@trethvas.plus.com
w trethvasfarm.com

**LONGBOROUGH**
**Gloucestershire**

**Luckley Farm** ★★★
*Guest Accommodation*
Longborough, Stow-on-the-Wold GL56 0RD
t (01451) 870885
e info@luckley-holidays.co.uk
w luckley-holidays.co.uk

**LONGHOPE**
**Gloucestershire**

**The Farmers Boy Inn** ★★★
*Inn*
Ross Road, Longhope
GL17 0LP
t (01452) 831300
e info@thefarmersboyinn.co.uk
w thefarmersboyinn.co.uk

**LOOE**
**Cornwall**

**Bucklawren Farm** ★★★★
*Farmhouse* **SILVER AWARD**
St Martin, Looe PL13 1NZ
t (01503) 240738
e bucklawren@btopenworld.com
w bucklawren.co.uk

**Coombe Farm** ★★★★
*Guest Accommodation*
Widegates, Looe PL13 1QN
t (01503) 240223
e coombe_farm@hotmail.com
w coombefarmhotel.co.uk

**The Deganwy** ★★★★
*Guest House*
Station Road, East Looe, Looe
PL13 1HL
t (01503) 262984
e enquiries@deganwyhotel.co.uk
w deganwyhotel.co.uk

**Dolphin Guest House**
★★★★ *Guest House*
Station Road, East Looe, Looe
PL13 1HL
t (01503) 262578
e dolphinhouse@btconnect.com
w dolphin-house.co.uk

**Dovers House** ★★★★
*Guest House* **SILVER AWARD**
St Martins Road, St Martin,
Looe PL13 1PB
t (01503) 265468
e twhyte@btconnect.com
w dovershouse.co.uk

**Driftwood** ★★★★
*Guest Accommodation*
Portuan Rd, Hannafore, Looe
PL13 2ND
t (01503) 262990
e picko@westlooe.fsnet.co.uk

**The Gulls** ★★★★
*Guest Accommodation*
Hannafore Road, Looe
PL13 2DE
t (01503) 262531
e enquiries@gullshotel.co.uk
w gullshotel-looe.co.uk

**Hillingdon** ★★★
*Guest House*
Portuan Road, West Looe,
Looe PL13 2DW
t (01503) 262906
e info@hillingdonguesthouse.co.uk
w hillingdonguesthouse.co.uk

**Little Larnick Farm** ★★★★
*Farmhouse* **SILVER AWARD**
Pelynt, Looe PL13 2NB
t (01503) 262837
e littlelarnick@btclick.com
w littlelarnick.co.uk/

**Schooner Point Bed & Breakfast** ★★★★
*Guest Accommodation*
1 Trelawney Terrace, West
Looe, Looe PL13 2AG
t (01503) 262670
e enquiries@schoonerpoint.co.uk
w schoonerpoint.co.uk

**Seaview** ★★★
*Bed & Breakfast*
Portuan Road, Looe PL13 2DW
t (01503) 265837
e sharon@seaviewlooe.fsworld.co.uk
w seaview-looe.co.uk

**Trelren** ★★★ *Bed & Breakfast*
Polperro Road, Looe PL13 2JS
t (01503) 263918
e enquiries@trelren.co.uk
w trelren.co.uk

**The Watermark** ★★★★
*Guest House* **SILVER AWARD**
Hannafore Road, Looe
PL13 2DE
t (01503) 262123
e ash@looe.co.uk
w looe.co.uk

**LOPCOMBE**
**Wiltshire**

**Downs View Bed and Breakfast** ★★★
*Bed & Breakfast*
Stockbridge Road, Lopcombe
Corner SP5 1BW
t 07808 572671
e reservations@downs-view.co.uk

**LOSTWITHIEL**
**Cornwall**

**The Kings Arms**
Rating Applied For
*Guest Accommodation*
Fore Street, Lostwithiel
PL22 0BL
t (01208) 872383

**Tremont House** ★★★★
*Bed & Breakfast*
2 The Terrace, Lostwithiel
PL22 0DT
t (01208) 873055

**LOWER WRAXALL**
**Dorset**

**Lower Wraxhall Farmhouse**
★★★★ *Bed & Breakfast*
Lower Wraxall, Dorchester
DT2 0HL
t (01935) 83218
e judy-thompson@beeb.net

**LULWORTH COVE**
**Dorset**

**Applegrove** ★★★
*Bed & Breakfast*
West Road, West Lulworth,
Lulworth Cove, Wareham
BH20 5RY
t (01929) 400592
e jennyandjohn@applegrove-lulworth.co.uk
w applegrove-lulworth.co.uk

**LYDBROOK**
**Gloucestershire**

**Belvedere House B&B**
★★★★ *Bed & Breakfast*
**SILVER AWARD**
Belvedere House, Lower
Lydbrook, Lydbrook GL17 9NU
t (01594) 860513
e info@belvederehouse.co.uk
w belvederehouse.co.uk

**LYDEARD ST LAWRENCE**
**Somerset**

**Fitzhead Court** ★★★
*Bed & Breakfast*
Taunton TA4 3JP
t (01823) 400923
e kilpatrick@eclipse.co.uk
w fitzheadcourt.eclipse.co.uk

**LYDFORD**
**Devon**

**Lydford Country House**
★★★★ *Guest House*
Lydford, Okehampton
EX20 4AU
t (01822) 820347
e info@lydfordhouse.com
w lydfordhouse.com

**LYDIARD TREGOZE**
**Wiltshire**

**Park Farm** ★★★ *Farmhouse*
Hook Street, Lydiard Tregoze
SN5 3NY
t (01793) 853608

**LYDNEY**
**Gloucestershire**

**Millingbrook Lodge** ★★★★
*Inn*
George Inn, High Street,
Aylburton, Lydney GL15 6DE
t (01594) 845522 &
(01594) 842163
e jackicollie@aol.com
w millingbrooklodge.com

**LYME REGIS**
**Dorset**

**Charnwood Guest House**
★★★★
*Guest Accommodation*
21 Woodmead Road, Lyme
Regis DT7 3AD
t (01297) 445281
e enquiries@lymeregisaccommodation.com
w lymeregisaccommodation.com

**Clappentail House** ★★★★★
*Bed & Breakfast*
**GOLD AWARD**
Uplyme Road, Lyme Regis
DT7 3LP
t (01297) 445739
e pountain@clappentail.freeserve.co.uk

**Clovelly Guest House**
★★★★
*Guest Accommodation*
**SILVER AWARD**
View Road, Lyme Regis
DT7 3AA
t (01297) 444052
e clovelly@lymeregisbnb.com
w lymeregisbnb.com

**Coombe House** ★★★
*Bed & Breakfast*
41 Coombe Street, Lyme Regis
DT7 3PY
t (01297) 443849
e dymps@coombe-house.co.uk
w coombe-house.co.uk

**Devonia Guest House**
★★★★ *Guest House*
2 Woodmead Road, Lyme
Regis DT7 3AB
t (01297) 442869
e bookings@devoniaguest.co.uk
w devoniaguest.co.uk

**Kersbrook Guest Accomodation** ★★★
*Guest Accommodation*
Pound Road, Lyme Regis
DT7 3HX
t (01297) 442596
e alex@kersbrook.co.uk
w kersbrook.co.uk

**The London Guesthouse**
★★★★
*Guest Accommodation*
40 Church Street, Lyme Regis
DT7 3DA
t (01297) 442083
e info@londonlymeregis.co.uk
w londonlymeregis.co.uk

**Lucerne** ★★★★
*Guest Accommodation*
View Road, Lyme Regis
DT7 3AA
t (01297) 443752
e lucerne@lineone.net
w lymeregis.com/lucerne

**Manaton** ★★★★
*Guest Accommodation*
Hill Road, Lyme Regis DT7 3PE
**t** (01297) 445138
**e** enquiries@manaton.net
**w** manaton.net

**Ocean View** ★★★★
*Guest Accommodation*
2 Hadleigh Villas, Silver Street, Lyme Regis DT7 3HR
**t** (01297) 442567
**e** jaybabe@supanet.com
**w** lymeregis.com/ocean/view

**Old Lyme Guest House**
★★★★ *Guest House*
**GOLD AWARD**
29 Coombe Street, Lyme Regis DT7 3PP
**t** (01297) 442929
**e** oldlyme.guesthouse@virgin.net
**w** oldlymeguesthouse.co.uk

**Rotherfield** ★★★★
*Guest Accommodation*
View Road, Lyme Regis DT7 3AA
**t** (01297) 445585
**e** rotherfield@lymeregis.com
**w** rotherfieldguesthouse.com

**St Andrews House** ★★★★
*Guest Accommodation*
Uplyme Road, Lyme Regis DT7 3LP
**t** (01297) 445495
**w** lymeregis.com/standrewshouse

**Southernhaye** ★★★
*Bed & Breakfast*
Pound Road, Lyme Regis DT7 3HX
**t** (01297) 443077
**e** info@southernhaye.co.uk
**w** southernhaye.co.uk

**Springfield** ★★★★
*Guest Accommodation*
Woodmead Road, Lyme Regis DT7 3LJ
**t** (01297) 443409
**e** warren@springfield.vu
**w** springfield.vu

**Thatch** ★★★★
*Bed & Breakfast*
Uplyme Road, Lyme Regis DT7 3LP
**t** (01297) 442212
**e** thatchbb@btinternet.com

## LYNMOUTH
Devon

**Brendon House** ★★★★
*Guest House*
Brendon, Exmoor, Lynton EX35 6PS
**t** (01598) 741206
**e** brendonhouse4u@aol.com
**w** brendonhouse4u.com

**Coombe Farm** ★★★
*Farmhouse*
Countisbury, Lynton EX35 6NF
**t** (01598) 741236
**e** coombefarm@freeuk.com
**w** brendonvalley.co.uk/coombe_farm.htm

**The Heatherville** ★★★★★
*Guest Accommodation*
**SILVER AWARD**
3 Tors Park, Lynmouth EX35 6NB
**t** (01598) 752327
**e** lorraine@theheatherville.co.uk
**w** heatherville.co.uk

**Lorna Doone House** ★★★★
*Guest House*
4 Tors Road, Lynmouth EX35 6ET
**t** (01598) 753354
**e** info@lornadoonehouse.co.uk
**w** lornadoonehouse.co.uk

## LYNTON
Devon

**Castle Hill Guest House**
★★★★ *Guest House*
Castle Hill, Lynton EX35 6JA
**t** (01598) 752291
**e** info@castlehillhotel.co.uk
**w** castlehillhotel.co.uk

**Croft House** ★★★★
*Guest Accommodation*
Lydiate Lane, Lynton EX35 6HE
**t** (01598) 752391
**e** stay@lyntonbandb.co.uk
**w** lyntonbandb.co.uk

**The Denes Guest House**
★★★★ *Guest House*
**SILVER AWARD**
15 Longmead, Lynton EX35 6DQ
**t** (01598) 753573
**e** j.e.mcgowan@btinternet.com
**w** thedenes.com

**Fernleigh Guest House**
★★★★ *Guest House*
Park Street, Lynton EX35 6BY
**t** (01598) 753575
**e** bookings@fernleigh.net
**w** fernleigh.net

**Gable Lodge Guest House**
★★★★ *Guest House*
35 Lee Road, Lynton EX35 6BS
**t** (01598) 752367
**e** gablelodge@btconnect.com
**w** gablelodgelynton.co.uk

**Highcliffe House** ★★★★★
*Guest Accommodation*
**SILVER AWARD**
Sinai Hill, Lynton EX35 6AR
**t** (01598) 752235
**e** info@highcliffehouse.co.uk
**w** highcliffehouse.co.uk

**Higher Bodley Farm** ★★★★
*Farmhouse*
Parracombe EX31 4QN
**t** (01598) 763798
**e** higherbodley@hotmail.co.uk
**w** higherbodleyfarm.co.uk

**Ingleside** ★★★★
*Guest Accommodation*
**SILVER AWARD**
Lee Road, Lynton EX35 6HW
**t** (01598) 752223
**e** keithdiana@supanet.com
**w** ingleside-hotel.co.uk

**Kingford House** ★★★★
*Guest Accommodation*
**SILVER AWARD**
Longmead, Lynton EX35 6DQ
**t** (01598) 752361
**e** tricia@kingfordhouse.co.uk
**w** kingfordhouse.co.uk

**Lee House** ★★★★
*Guest Accommodation*
27-28 Lee Road, Lynton EX35 6BP
**t** (01598) 752364
**e** info@leehouselynton.co.uk
**w** leehouselynton.co.uk

**Longmead House** ★★★★
*Guest Accommodation*
**SILVER AWARD**
9 Longmead, Lynton EX35 6DQ
**t** (01598) 752523
**e** info@longmeadhouse.co.uk
**w** longmeadhouse.co.uk

**Rockvale Hotel** ★★★
*Guest Accommodation*
Lee Road, Lynton EX35 6HW
**t** (01598) 752279
**e** judithwoodland@rockvale.fsbusiness.co.uk
**w** rockvalehotel.co.uk

**South View Guest House**
★★★★
*Guest Accommodation*
23 Lee Road, Lynton EX35 6BP
**t** (01598) 752289
**e** maureenroper@hotmail.com
**w** southview-lynton.co.uk

**Southcliffe** ★★★★
*Guest Accommodation*
**SILVER AWARD**
34 Lee Road, Lynton EX35 6BS
**t** (01598) 753328
**e** info@southcliffe.co.uk
**w** southcliffe.co.uk

**Waterloo House** ★★★★
*Guest House*
Lydiate Lane, Lynton EX35 6AJ
**t** (01598) 753391
**e** relax@waterloohousehotel.com
**w** waterloohousehotel.com

## MAENPORTH
Cornwall

**Avalon Guest House**
Rating Applied For
*Guest Accommodation*
Maenporth, Falmouth TR11 5HN
**t** (01326) 250704
**e** avalon@avalonguesthouse.com
**w** avalonguesthouse.com

## MALMESBURY
Wiltshire

**Kinfield Annexe** ★★★
*Guest Accommodation*
Bremilham Road, Malmesbury SN16 0DQ
**t** (01666) 825041
**e** jennifer.warner1@tesco.net

**Lovett Farm** ★★★★
*Farmhouse*
Little Somerford, Chippenham SN15 5BP
**t** (01666) 823268
**e** sue@lovettfarm.co.uk
**w** lovettfarm.co.uk

**Manor Farm** ★★★★
*Farmhouse*
Corston, Malmesbury SN16 0HF
**t** (01666) 822148
**e** ross@johneavis.wanadoo.co.uk
**w** manorfarmbandb.co.uk

**Marsh Farmhouse** ★★★
*Guest House*
Crudwell Road, Malmesbury SN16 9JL
**t** (01666) 822208

**Oakwood Farm** ★★★
*Farmhouse*
Upper Minety, Malmesbury SN16 9PY
**t** (01666) 860286

## MALPAS
Cornwall

**Woodbury** ★★★★
*Bed & Breakfast*
Malpas, Truro TR1 1SQ
**t** (01872) 271466

## MANATON
Devon

**Great Houndtor**
*Camping Barn*
Manaton, Newton Abbot TQ13 9UW
**t** (01647) 221202

## MANGOTSFIELD
Gloucestershire

**Fern Cottage Bed & Breakfast** ★★★★ *Farmhouse*
**SILVER AWARD**
188 Shortwood Hill, Pucklechurch BS16 9PG
**t** (0117) 937 4966
**e** sueandpete@ferncottagebedandbreakfast.co.uk
**w** ferncottagebedandbreakfast.co.uk

## MANNINGFORD ABBOTS
Wiltshire

**Huntlys Farm** ★★★★
*Farmhouse*
Manningford Abbots, Pewsey SN9 6HZ
**t** (01672) 563663
**e** meg@gimspike.fsnet.co.uk

## MANSTON
Dorset

**Northwood Cottages B&B**
★★★★
*Guest Accommodation*
**SILVER AWARD**
2 Northwood Cottages, Manston DT10 1HD
**t** (01258) 472666
**e** info@northwoodcottages.co.uk
**w** northwoodcottages.co.uk/affiliate/?id=visitbritainbnb

## MANTON
Wiltshire

**Teal Cottage** ★★★★
*Bed & Breakfast*
**SILVER AWARD**
High Street, Manton SN8 4HH
**t** (01672) 513904
**e** tealcottagebandb@yahoo.co.uk
**w** tealcottage.co.uk

**MARAZION**
**Cornwall**

**Chymorvah House ★★★**
*Guest Accommodation*
Marazion TR17 0DQ
t (01736) 710497
e info@chymorvah.co.uk
w chymorvah.co.uk

**Rosario ★★★★**
*Guest Accommodation*
The Square, Marazion
TR17 0BH
t (01736) 711998
w marazion.net

**Rosevidney Manor**
★★★★★
*Guest Accommodation*
**SILVER AWARD**
Tredrea Lane, Rosevidney
TR20 9BX
t (01736) 740811
e gary@rosevidneymanor.co.uk
w rosevidneymanor.co.uk

**MARK**
**Somerset**

**Burnt House Farm ★★★**
*Guest Accommodation*
Yarrow Road, Highbridge
TA9 4LR
t (01278) 641280
e carmenburnthouse@yahoo.co.uk

**MARKET LAVINGTON**
**Wiltshire**

**The Green Dragon ★★★** *Inn*
26-28 High Street, Market Lavington, Devizes SN10 4AG
t (01380) 813235
e greendragonlavington@tiscali.co.uk
w greendragonlavington.co.uk

**MARLBOROUGH**
**Wiltshire**

**Crofton Lodge ★★★★**
*Bed & Breakfast*
**SILVER AWARD**
Crofton, Marlborough
SN8 3DW
t (01672) 870328
e ali@croftonlodge.co.uk
w croftonlodge.co.uk

**The Inn with the Well ★★★**
*Inn*
Marlborough Road, Ogbourne St George SN8 1SQ
t (01672) 841445
e info@theinnwiththewell.co.uk
w theinnwiththewell.co.uk

**Merlin ★★★**
*Guest Accommodation*
36-39 High Street, Marlborough SN8 1LW
t (01672) 512151
e info@merlinhotel.co.uk
w merlinhotel.co.uk

**Upper Westcourt ★★★★**
*Bed & Breakfast*
Westcourt, Burbage SN8 3BW
t (01672) 810307
e prhill@onetel.com
w upperwestcourt.co.uk

**Wernham Farm ★★★**
*Farmhouse*
Clench Common, Marlborough
SN8 4DR
t (01672) 512236
e margglvsf@aol.com
w wernhamfarmhouse.co.uk

**MARTOCK**
**Somerset**

**Bartletts Farm ★★★★**
*Farmhouse*
Isle Brewers, Taunton
TA3 6QN
t (01460) 281423
e sandjpeach@tesco.net
w bartlettsfarm.net

**The White Hart Hotel**
★★★★ *Inn*
East Street, Martock TA12 6JQ
t (01935) 822005
e enquiries@whiteharthotelmartock.co.uk
w whiteharthotelmartock.co.uk

**Wychwood ★★★**
*Bed & Breakfast*
7 Bearley Road, Martock
TA12 6PG
t (01935) 825601
e wychwoodmartock@yahoo.co.uk

**MATCHAMS**
**Dorset**

**Little Paddock B&B ★★★★**
*Bed & Breakfast*
Hurn Road, Matchams
BH24 2BT
t (01425) 470889
e enquiries@little-paddock.com
w little-paddock.com

**MAWGAN PORTH**
**Cornwall**

**Bre-Pen Farm ★★★★**
*Farmhouse*
Mawgan Porth TR8 4AL
t (01637) 860420
e jill.brake@virgin.net
w bre-penfarm.co.uk

**Trevarrian Lodge ★★★**
*Guest House*
Trevarrian, Mawgan Porth
TR8 4AQ
t (01637) 860156
e trevarrian@aol.com
w trevarrianlodge.co.uk

**MAYPOOL**
**Devon**

**Maypool YHA ★★**
*Group Hostel*
Maypool, Brixham TQ5 0ET
t (01803) 842444
e maypool@yha.org.uk
w yha.org.uk

**MEAVY**
**Devon**

**Callisham Farm**
Rating Applied For
*Farmhouse*
Meavy, Yelverton PL20 6PS
t (01822) 853901
e esme@callisham.co.uk
w callisham.co.uk

**MELKSHAM**
**Wiltshire**

**Conigre Farm Hotel and Restaurant**
Rating Applied For
*Restaurant with Rooms*
Semington Road, Melksham
SN12 6BZ
t (01225) 702229
e enquiries@theconigrehotel.co.uk
w theconigrehotel.co.uk

**MERE**
**Wiltshire**

**Castleton House ★★★★**
*Bed & Breakfast*
Castle Street, Warminster
BA12 6JE
t (01747) 860446
e info@castletonhouse.com
w castletonhouse.com

**The Old Police House ★★★**
*Bed & Breakfast*
North Street, Mere BA12 6HH
t (01747) 861768
e gilly.gristwood@btopenworld.com
w westcountrynow.com

**MERRYMEET**
**Cornwall**

**Higher Trevartha Farm**
★★★★ *Farmhouse*
**SILVER AWARD**
Pengover, Liskeard PL14 3NJ
t (01579) 343382

**MEVAGISSEY**
**Cornwall**

**Bacchus B&B ★★★**
*Bed & Breakfast*
Trevarth, Mevagissey
PL26 6RX
t (01726) 843473
e susiecannone@yahoo.co.uk
w bacchus-cornwall.co.uk

**Buckingham House ★★★**
*Guest House*
17 Tregoney Hill, Mevagissey, St Austell PL26 6RD
t (01726) 843375
e housead07@aol.com
w buckinghamhousemevagissey.co.uk

**Corran Farm B&B ★★★★**
*Farmhouse* **SILVER AWARD**
St Ewe, Mevagissey, St Austell
PL26 6ER
t (01726) 842159
e info@corranfarm.co.uk
w corranfarm.co.uk

**Eden B&B ★★★★**
*Guest Accommodation*
**SILVER AWARD**
Omega, Bodrugan Hill
PL26 6PS
t (01726) 842836
e magie@tiscali.co.uk
w visitportmellon.co.uk

**Honeycombe House ★★★★**
*Guest House*
61 Polkirt Hill, Mevagissey
PL26 6UR
t (01726) 843750
e enquiries@honeycombehouse.co.uk
w honeycombehouse.co.uk

**Portmellon Cove Guest House ★★★★★**
*Guest House* **SILVER AWARD**
121 Portmellon Park, Portmellon PL26 6XD
t (01726) 843410
e stay@portmellon-cove.com
w portmellon-cove.com

**Tregilgas Farm ★★★★**
*Farmhouse*
Gorran, St Austell PL26 6ND
t (01726) 842342
e Dclemes88@aol.com
w tregilgasfarmbedandbreaksfast.co.uk

**Tregoney House ★★★**
*Bed & Breakfast*
Tregoney Hill, Mevagissey
PL26 6RD
t (01726) 842760
e dianne.young@hotmail.co.uk
w tregoneyhouse.co.uk

**Tregorran Guest House**
★★★★ *Guest House*
Cliff Street, Mevagissey, St Austell PL26 6QW
t (01726) 842319
e helen@tregorran.co.uk
w tregorran.co.uk

**Wild Air Guest House**
★★★★ *Bed & Breakfast*
**SILVER AWARD**
Polkirt Hill, Mevagissey
PL26 6UX
t (01726) 843302
e clareavent@aol.com
w wildair.co.uk

**MILLBROOK**
**Cornwall**

**Stone Farm ★★★★**
*Farmhouse* **SILVER AWARD**
Whitsand Bay, Millbrook, Torpoint PL10 1JJ
t (01752) 822267
e blake@stone-farm.fsnet.co.uk
w stone-farm.co.uk

**MILTON ABBAS**
**Dorset**

**The Old Bank ★★★**
*Bed & Breakfast*
56-57 The Street, Milton Abbas, Blandford Forum
DT11 0BP
t (01258) 880520
e annieaskew@yahoo.co.uk
w theoldbankmiltonabbas.co.uk

**MILTON DAMEREL**
**Devon**

**Buttermoor Farm ★★★★**
*Farmhouse*
Milton Damerel, Holsworthy
EX22 7PB
t (01409) 261314
e info@buttermoorfarm.co.uk
w buttermoorfarm.co.uk

**MINEHEAD**
**Somerset**

**Bactonleigh ★★★**
*Guest Accommodation*
20 Tregonwell Road, Minehead
TA24 5DU
t (01643) 702147
e info@bactonleigh.co.uk
w bactonleigh.co.uk

**Beverleigh** ★★★★
*Bed & Breakfast*
Beacon Road, Minehead
TA24 5SE
**t** (01643) 708450

**Dunkery Lodge** ★★★★
*Guest Accommodation*
Townsend Road, Minehead
TA24 5RQ
**t** (01643) 706170
**e** stay@dunkery-lodge.co.uk
**w** dunkery-lodge.co.uk

**Glendower House** ★★★★
*Guest House*
30-32 Tregonwell Road,
Minehead TA24 5DU
**t** (01643) 707144
**e** info@glendower-house.co.uk
**w** glendower-house.co.uk

**The Kingsway** ★★★★
*Guest Accommodation*
36 Ponsford Road, Minehead
TA24 5DY
**t** (01643) 702313
**e** kingswayhotel@msn.com
**w** kingswayhotelminehead.co.uk

**Marston Lodge** ★★★
*Guest Accommodation*
St Michaels Road, Minehead
TA24 5JP
**t** (01643) 702510
**e** marstonlodge@aol.com
**w** marstonlodgehotel.co.uk

**Montrose Guest House**
★★★★ *Guest House*
14 Tregonwell Road, Minehead
TA24 5DU
**t** (01643) 706473
**e** montroseminehead@btinternet.com
**w** montroseminehead.co.uk

**Oakfield Guest House**
★★★★★
*Guest Accommodation*
**SILVER AWARD**
Northfield Road, Minehead
TA24 5QH
**t** (01643) 704911
**e** oakfieldminehead@yahoo.com
**w** oakfieldminehead.co.uk

**The Parks** ★★★★
*Guest House* **SILVER AWARD**
26 The Parks, Minehead
TA24 8BT
**t** (01643) 703547
**e** info@parksguesthouse.co.uk
**w** parksguesthouse.co.uk

**Promenade** ★★★
*Guest Accommodation*
The Esplanade, Minehead
TA24 5QS
**t** (01643) 702572
**e** jgph@globalnet.co.uk
**w** johngroons.org.uk

**The Quay Inn** ★★★★ *Inn*
Quay Street, Minehead
TA24 5UJ
**t** (01643) 707323
**e** info@quay-inn.co.uk
**w** quay-inn.co.uk

**Sunfield** ★★★
*Guest Accommodation*
83 Summerland Avenue,
Minehead TA24 5BW
**t** (01643) 703565
**e** stay@sunfieldminehead.co.uk
**w** sunfieldminehead.co.uk

**Tranmere House** ★★★★
*Guest Accommodation*
24 Tregonwell Road, Minehead
TA24 5DU
**t** (01643) 702647
**e** info@tranmereguesthouse.orangehome.co.uk
**w** tranmereguesthouse.co.uk

**Tregonwell House** ★★★
*Guest House*
1 Tregonwell Road, Minehead
TA24 5DT
**t** (01643) 709287
**e** info@tregonwellhouse.co.uk
**w** tregonwellhouse.co.uk

**YHA Minehead** ★★★ *Hostel*
Manor Road, Minehead
TA24 6EW
**t** (01643) 702595
**e** minehead@yha.org.uk
**w** yha.org.uk

## MODBURY
Devon

**Weeke Farm** ★★★
*Farmhouse*
Modbury, Ivybridge PL21 0TT
**t** (01548) 830219

## MOLLAND
Devon

**West Lee Farm** ★★★★
*Farmhouse*
Molland, South Molton
EX36 3NJ
**t** (01398) 341751
**e** maggi.woodward@ukonline.co.uk
**w** westleefarm.co.uk

## MONTACUTE
Somerset

**Carents House** ★★★★
*Bed & Breakfast*
7a Middle Street, Montacute
TA15 6UZ
**t** (01935) 824914
**e** dianasloan@talktalk.net
**w** carentshouse.co.uk

**Montacute Country Tearooms** ★★★
*Bed & Breakfast*
1 South Street, Montacute
TA15 6XD
**t** (01935) 823024
**e** info@montacutemuseum.co.uk
**w** montacutemuseum.co.uk

## MORCOMBELAKE
Dorset

**Wisteria Cottage** ★★★★
*Guest Accommodation*
Taylors Lane, Morcombelake
DT6 6ED
**t** (01297) 489019
**e** dave@dorsetcottage.org.uk
**w** dorsetcottage.org.uk

## MORETON-IN-MARSH
Gloucestershire

**Acacia** ★★
*Guest Accommodation*
New Road, Moreton-in-Marsh
GL56 0AS
**t** (01608) 650130
**e** acaciaguesthouse@tiscali.co.uk

**Fosseway Farm B&B** ★★★★
*Farmhouse*
Stow Road, Moreton-in-Marsh
GL56 0DS
**t** (01608) 650503

**Jasmine Cottage** ★★★
*Bed & Breakfast*
Stretton-on-Fosse, Moreton-in-Marsh GL56 9SA
**t** (01608) 661972
**e** ann@jasminecottage.wanadoo.co.uk
**w** http://jasmine-cottage.mysite.wanadoo-members.co.uk/

**New Farm** ★★★ *Farmhouse*
Dorn, Moreton-in-Marsh
GL56 9NS
**t** (01608) 650782 & 07811 646320
**e** catherinerighton@btinternet.com
**w** newfarmbandb.co.uk

**Old Farm** ★★★ *Farmhouse*
Dorn, Moreton-in-Marsh
GL56 9NS
**t** (01608) 650394
**e** info@oldfarmdorn.co.uk
**w** oldfarmdorn.co.uk

**Treetops** ★★★★
*Guest House*
London Road, Moreton-in-Marsh GL56 0HE
**t** (01608) 651036
**e** treetops1@talk21.com
**w** treetopscotswolds.co.uk

**Windy Ridge House**
★★★★★ *Bed & Breakfast*
**SILVER AWARD**
The Crook, Longborough
GL56 0QY
**t** (01451) 830465
**e** nick@windy-ridge.co.uk
**w** windy-ridge.co.uk

## MORETONHAMPSTEAD
Devon

**Great Sloncombe Farm**
★★★★ *Farmhouse*
Moretonhampstead, Newton
Abbot TQ13 8QF
**t** (01647) 440595
**e** hmerchant@sloncombe.freeserve.co.uk
**w** greatsloncombefarm.co.uk

**Great Wooston Farm**
★★★★
*Guest Accommodation*
Moretonhampstead, Newton
Abbot TQ13 8QA
**t** (01647) 440367 & 07798 670590
**e** info@greatwoostonfarm.com
**w** greatwoostonfarm.com

**Little Wooston Farm** ★★★
*Guest Accommodation*
Moretonhampstead, Newton
Abbot TQ13 8QA
**t** (01647) 440551
**e** jeannecuming@btinternet.com

## MORWENSTOW
Cornwall

**The Bush Inn** ★★★ *Inn*
The Bush Inn Crosstown,
Morwenstow, Bude EX23 9SR
**t** (01288) 331242
**w** bushinn-morwenstow.co.uk

**Willow Tree Cottage** ★★★★
*Bed & Breakfast*
**SILVER AWARD**
Morwenstow, Bude EX23 9SJ
**t** (01288) 331100
**e** rfsphillips@tiscali.co.uk
**w** willowtreecottage.co.uk

## MOTCOMBE
Dorset

**The Coppleridge Inn** ★★★
*Inn*
Motcombe, Shaftesbury
SP7 9HW
**t** (01747) 851980
**e** thecoppleridgeinn@btinternet.com
**w** coppleridge.com

**Pear Tree House** ★★★
*Bed & Breakfast*
Bittles Green, Motcombe
SP7 9NX
**t** (01747) 852647
**e** pocock@motcombe.eclipse.co.uk

## MOUSEHOLE
Cornwall

**Kerris Farm** ★★★★
*Farmhouse*
Kerris, Paul TR19 6UY
**t** (01736) 731309
**e** kerrisfarm@btconnect.com
**w** kerrisfarm.co.uk

**Mousehole B&B** ★★★
*Bed & Breakfast*
Two Foxes Lane, Mousehole
TR19 6QQ
**t** (01736) 731882
**e** twofoxes.m@btopenworld.com

**Tremayne** ★★★
*Guest Accommodation*
Tremayne Restaurant
Accommodation, The Parade,
Penzance TR19 6PS
**t** (01736) 731214
**e** tremayne@mouseholecornwall.fsnet.co.uk

## MUCHELNEY
Somerset

**The Parsonage** ★★★★★
*Guest Accommodation*
**GOLD AWARD**
Silver Street, Muchelney
TA10 0DL
**t** (01458) 259058
**e** valerie@breathe.co.uk
**w** parsonagesomerset.co.uk

**MUDFORD**
Somerset

**Half Moon Inn and Country Lodge ★★★★**
*Guest Accommodation*
Main Street, Yeovil BA21 5TF
**t** (01935) 850289
**e** enquiries@thehalfmooninn.co.uk
**w** thehalfmooninn.co.uk

**MULLION**
Cornwall

**The Mounts Bay Guest House ★★★**
*Guest Accommodation*
Churchtown, Mullion
TR12 7HN
**t** (01326) 241761
**e** jan@mountsbayguesthouse.wanadoo.co.uk
**w** mountsbayguesthouse.co.uk

**Trenance Farmhouse ★★★★**
*Guest Accommodation*
Mullion, Helston TR12 7HB
**t** (01326) 240639
**e** info@trenancefarmholidays.co.uk
**w** trenancefarmholidays.co.uk

**NAUNTON**
Gloucestershire

**Aylworth Manor ★★★★**
*Bed & Breakfast*
Naunton, Cheltenham
GL54 3AH
**t** (01451) 850850
**e** jeaireland@aol.com
**w** aylworthmanor.co.uk

**Fox Hill ★★★★**
*Guest Accommodation*
**SILVER AWARD**
Stow Road, Naunton GL54 5RL
**t** (01451) 850496
**w** smoothhound.co.uk/hotels/foxhillnaunton

**NETHER STOWEY**
Somerset

**Castle of Comfort Country House ★★★★★**
*Guest Accommodation*
**SILVER AWARD**
Dodington, Nether Stowey, Bridgwater TA5 1LE
**t** (01278) 741264
**e** reception@castle-of-comfort.co.uk
**w** castle-of-comfort.co.uk

**The Old Cider House ★★★★**
*Guest Accommodation*
25 Castle Street, Nether Stowey TA5 1LN
**t** (01278) 732228
**e** info@theoldciderhouse.co.uk
**w** theoldciderhouse.co.uk

**The Old House ★★★★**
*Bed & Breakfast*
**SILVER AWARD**
St Mary Street, Nether Stowey TA5 1LJ
**t** (01278) 732392
**e** scourfieldfam@yahoo.co.uk
**w** theoldhouse-quantocks.co.uk

**Stowey Brooke House ★★★★★**
*Guest Accommodation*
**SILVER AWARD**
18 Castle Street, Nether Stowey TA5 1LN
**t** (01278) 733356
**e** markandjackie@stoweybrookehouse.co.uk
**w** stoweybrookehouse.co.uk

**NETHERBURY**
Dorset

**Parnham Farm ★★★★**
*Guest Accommodation*
Crook Hill, Netherbury
DT6 5LY
**t** (01308) 488214
**e** rbbowditch@btconnect.com
**w** parnhamfarm.co.uk

**NEWENT**
Gloucestershire

**The George ★★★** *Inn*
Church Street, Newent
GL18 1PU
**t** (01531) 820203
**e** enquiries@georgehotel.uk.com
**w** georgehotel.uk.com

**Newent Golf Club and Lodges ★★★**
*Guest Accommodation*
Cold Harbour Lane, Newent
GL18 1DJ
**t** (01531) 820478
**e** newentgolf@btconnect.com
**w** newentgolf.co.uk

**Sandyway Nurseries Countryside B & B ★★★**
*Bed & Breakfast*
Redmarley Road, Newent
GL18 1DR
**t** (01531) 820693
**e** jean@sandy.f9.co.uk
**w** visitheartofengland.com/wheretostay/index.htm

**Three Ashes House ★★★★**
*Bed & Breakfast*
**SILVER AWARD**
Ledbury Road, Newent
GL18 1DE
**t** (01531) 820226
**e** judith@threeasheshouse.co.uk

**NEWLAND**
Gloucestershire

**Tan House Farm ★★★**
*Bed & Breakfast*
Laundry Lane, Newland, Coleford GL16 8NQ
**t** (01594) 832222
**e** christiearno@talktalk.net
**w** tanhousefarm.org.uk

**NEWLYN**
Cornwall

**The Smugglers Restaurant**
Rating Applied For
*Guest Accommodation*
Fore Street, Penzance
TR18 5JN
**t** (01736) 331501
**e** smugglersnewlyn@btconnect.com
**w** smugglersnewlyn.co.uk

**NEWMILL**
Cornwall

**Bosulval Old Barn ★★★★**
*Guest Accommodation*
**SILVER AWARD**
Newmill, Penzance TR20 8XA
**t** (01736) 367742
**e** info@laidback-trails.co.uk
**w** laidback-trails.co.uk

**Chy Bowjy ★★★★★**
*Bed & Breakfast*
**SILVER AWARD**
Chysauster, Penzance
TR20 8XA
**t** (01736) 368815
**e** jj@jjassociates.me.uk
**w** chy-bowjy.co.uk

**NEWNHAM**
Gloucestershire

**The Old House Bed & Breakfast ★★★**
*Bed & Breakfast*
High Street, Newnham
GL14 1BW
**t** (01594) 510944
**e** griffiths6@btinternet.com
**w** theoldhousenewnham.co.uk

**NEWQUAY**
Cornwall

**The Alex Guest House ★★★**
*Guest House*
19 Alexandra Road, Newquay
TR7 3ND
**t** (01637) 875311
**e** enquiries@alexguesthouse.co.uk
**w** alexguesthouse.co.uk

**Alicia ★★★★** *Guest House*
136 Henver Road, Newquay
TR7 3EQ
**t** (01637) 874328
**e** alicianewqauy@googlemail.com
**w** alicia-guesthouse.co.uk

**Breaks ★★★★** *Guest House*
80 Crantock Street, Newquay
TR7 1JW
**t** (01637) 874641
**e** info@newquaybreakshotel.co.uk
**w** newquaybreakshotel.co.uk

**The Carlton ★★★★**
*Guest Accommodation*
6 Dane Road, Newquay
TR7 1HL
**t** (01637) 872658
**e** enquiries@carltonhotelnewquay.co.uk
**w** carltonhotelnewquay.co.uk

**Chichester Interest Holidays ★★** *Guest Accommodation*
14 Bay View Terrace, Newquay
TR7 2LR
**t** (01637) 874216
**e** sheila.harper@virgin.net
**w** http://freespace.virgin.net/sheila.harper

**Chynoweth Lodge ★★★★**
*Guest Accommodation*
1 Eliot Gardens, Newquay
TR7 2QE
**t** (01637) 876684
**e** chynowethlodge@btconnect.com
**w** chynowethlodge.co.uk

**The Glendeveor ★★★**
*Guest Accommodation*
25 Mount Wise, Newquay
TR7 2BQ
**t** (01637) 872726
**e** enquiries@glendeveorhotel.co.uk
**w** glendeveorhotel.co.uk

**Godolphin Arms ★★★**
*Guest Accommodation*
86-88 Henver Road, Newquay
TR7 3BL
**t** (01637) 872572
**e** godolphin.arms@btconnect.com
**w** godolphinarmshotel.co.uk

**Goofys ★★★** *Hostel*
5 Headland Road, Newquay
TR7 1HW
**t** (01637) 872684
**e** info@goofys.co.uk
**w** goofys.co.uk

**Gratton Lodge ★★★**
*Guest House*
119 Mount Wise, Newquay
TR7 1QR
**t** (01637) 877011
**e** grattonlodge@fsmail.net
**w** grattonlodge.co.uk

**The Harbour ★★★★**
*Guest Accommodation*
**SILVER AWARD**
North Quay Hill, Newquay
TR7 1HF
**t** (01637) 873040
**e** alanburnett@harbourhotel.co.uk
**w** harbourhotel.co.uk

**Harrington Guest House ★★★** *Guest House*
25 Tolcarne Road, Newquay
TR7 2NQ
**t** (01637) 873581
**e** harringtonguesthouse@yahoo.co.uk
**w** harringtonguesthouse.com

**Hepworth ★★★★**
*Guest Accommodation*
27 Edgecumbe Avenue, Newquay TR7 2NJ
**t** (01637) 873686
**e** hepworthnewquay@aol.com
**w** hepworthhotel.co.uk

**Lynton House ★★★**
*Guest House*
4 The Crescent, Newquay
TR7 1DT
**t** (01637) 873048
**e** info@lyntonhotel.wanadoo.co.uk
**w** lynton-hotel-newquay.co.uk

**The Metro ★★★★**
*Guest Accommodation*
142 Henver Road, Newquay
TR7 3EQ
**t** (01637) 871638
**e** info@metronewquay.co.uk
**w** metronewquay.co.uk

**Pengilley Guest House ★★★**
*Guest House*
12 Trebarwith Crescent, Newquay TR7 1DX
**t** (01637) 872039
**e** jan@pengilley-guesthouse.co.uk
**w** pengilley-guesthouse.co.uk

**Penny Farthing Guest House** ★★★★
*Guest Accommodation*
Headland Road, Newquay
TR7 1HW
t (01304) 205563
e pennyfarthing.dover@btinternet.com
w pennyfarthing.com

**Pensalda Guest House** ★★★
*Guest House*
98 Henver Road, Newquay
TR7 3BL
t (01637) 874601
e karen_pensalda@yahoo.co.uk
w pensalda-guesthouse.co.uk

**Pine Lodge** ★★★★
*Guest Accommodation*
91 Henver Road, Newquay
TR7 3DJ
t (01637) 850897
e enquiries@pinelodgehotel.co.uk
w pinelodgehotel.co.uk

**Reef Surf Lodge** ★★★★
*Hostel*
10-12 Berry Road, Newquay
TR7 1AR
t (01637) 879058
e enquiries@reefsurflodge.com
w reefsurflodge.com

**Roma Guest House** ★★★★
*Guest Accommodation*
1 Atlantic Road, Newquay
TR7 1QJ
t (01637) 875085
e romaghnewquay@aol.com
w romaguesthouse.co.uk

**Surfside B&B** ★★★
*Bed & Breakfast*
35 Mount Wise, Newquay
TR7 2BH
**t (01637) 872707 & 07813 330609**
**e surfsidehotel@btconnect.com**
**w surfsidenewquay.co.uk**

**The Sutherland** ★
*Guest Accommodation*
29 Mount Wise, Newquay
TR7 2BH
t (01637) 879027
e info@sutherlandhotel.co.uk
w sutherlandhotel.co.uk

**Three Beaches** ★★★
*Guest Accommodation*
17 Godophin Way, Newquay
TR7 3BU
t (01637) 873931
e graham@threebeacheshotel.fsnet.co.uk
w threebeacheshotel.co.uk

**Tir Chonaill** ★★★
*Guest Accommodation*
106 Mount Wise, Newquay
TR7 1QP
t (01637) 876492
e tirchonaillhotel@talk21.com
w tirchonaill.co.uk

**Westward B&B** ★★★★
*Guest Accommodation*
25 Edgcumbe Avenue,
Newquay TR7 2NJ
t (01637) 871627
e westwardnewquay@aol.com
w westwardnewquay.co.uk

### NEWTON ABBOT
Devon

**Rock House Bed & Breakfast**
★★★★★ *Bed & Breakfast*
**SILVER AWARD**
Maddacombe Road,
Kingskerswell TQ12 5LF
t (01803) 404990
e alison.rockhouse@blueyonder.co.uk
w rockhouse-cottage.co.uk

### NEWTON POPPLEFORD
Devon

**Milestone Cottage** ★★★
*Bed & Breakfast*
High Street, Newton
Poppleford EX10 0DU
t (01395) 568267
e stay@a1-guesthouse.co.uk
w a1-guesthouse.co.uk

### NEWTON ST LOE
Somerset

**Bath Spa University**
Rating Applied For
*Campus*
Newton Park, Bath BA2 9BN
t (01225) 875669
e conference@bathspa.ac.uk
w bathspa.ac.uk

**Pennsylvania Farm B&B**
★★★★ *Farmhouse*
Newton St Loe, Bath BA2 9JD
t (01225) 314912
e info@pennsylvaniafarm.co.uk
w pennsylvaniafarm.co.uk

### NORTH BRADLEY
Wiltshire

**49a Church Lane** ★★★★
*Bed & Breakfast*
**SILVER AWARD**
North Bradley BA14 0TA
t (01225) 762558
e m-wise@amserve.com

### NORTH CADBURY
Somerset

**Ashlea House** ★★★★
*Guest Accommodation*
**SILVER AWARD**
High Street, Yeovil BA22 7DP
t (01963) 440891
e ashlea@btinternet.com
w ashleahouse.co.uk

### NORTH CERNEY
Gloucestershire

**The Bathurst Arms** ★★★★
*Inn*
Cirencester GL7 7BZ
t (01285) 831281
e james@bathurstarms.com
w bathurstarms.com

### NORTHLEACH
Gloucestershire

**Cotteswold House & Cottage** ★★★★
*Bed & Breakfast*
**SILVER AWARD**
Market Place, Northleach
GL54 3EG
t (01451) 860493
e cotteswoldhouse@aol.com
w cotteswoldhouse.com

**Northfield Bed and Breakfast** ★★★★
*Guest Accommodation*
**SILVER AWARD**
Cirencester Road, Northleach
GL54 3JL
t (01451) 860427
e northfield@loving.orangehome.co.uk
w northfieldbandb.co.uk

### NORTON FITZWARREN
Somerset

**Old Rectory** ★★★★
*Bed & Breakfast*
Rectory Road, Norton
Fitzwarren TA2 6SE
t (01823) 330081
e jw@oldrectorynorton.net
w oldrectorynorton.net

### NORTON ST PHILIP
Somerset

**The Plaine** ★★★★
*Guest Accommodation*
Bell Hill, Bath BA2 7LT
t (01373) 834723
e enquiries@theplaine.co.uk
w theplaine.co.uk

### NORTON SUB HAMDON
Somerset

**Bagnell Cottage** ★★★★
*Bed & Breakfast*
Norton-sub-Hamden TA14 6TF
t (01935) 862802
e eileenbagnellcottage@btinternet.com
w bagnellcottage.com

### OAKDALE
Dorset

**Heathwood Guest House**
★★★ *Guest House*
266 Wimborne Road, Oakdale
BH15 3EF
t (01202) 679176
e heathwoodhotel@tiscali.co.uk
w heathwoodhotel.co.uk

### OAKFORD
Devon

**Harton Farm** ★★★
*Farmhouse*
Oakford, Tiverton EX16 9HH
t (01398) 351209
e lindy@hartonfarm.co.uk
w hartonfarm.co.uk

### OGBOURNE ST GEORGE
Wiltshire

**Blue Barn** ★★★★
*Bed & Breakfast*
Ogbourne St George,
Marlborough SN8 2NT
t (01672) 841082
e jaxs@capalmer.co.uk

**The Sanctuary** ★★★★
*Bed & Breakfast*
Ogbourne St George,
Marlborough SN8 1SQ
t (01672) 841473
e rebecca.macdonald@core-support.co.uk
w the-sanctuary.biz

### OKEFORD FITZPAINE
Dorset

**Okeapple House** ★★★★
*Bed & Breakfast*
Okeford Fitzpaine, Blandford
Forum DT11 0RS
t (01258) 861126
e 51fairmount@tiscali.co.uk

### OKEHAMPTON
Devon

**Charlecott Lodge** ★★★★
*Bed & Breakfast*
38 Station Road, Okehampton
EX20 1EA
t (01837) 53998
e susaneckles@btinternet.com
w charlecott.co.uk

**Knole Farm** ★★★★★
*Farmhouse* **SILVER AWARD**
Bridestowe, Okehampton
EX20 4HA
t (01837) 861241
e mavis.bickle@btconnect.com
w knolefarm-dartmoor-holidays.co.uk

**Lower Trecott Farm** ★★★★
*Bed & Breakfast*
**SILVER AWARD**
Wellsprings Lane, Sampford
Courtenay EX20 2TD
t (01837) 880118
e craig@trecott.fsnet.co.uk
w lowertrecottfarm.co.uk

**Week Farm** ★★★★
*Farmhouse*
Bridestowe, Okehampton
EX20 4HZ
t (01837) 861221
e accom@weekfarmonline.com
w weekfarmonline.com

**YHA Okehampton** ★★★
*Activity Accommodation*
Klondyke Road, Okehampton
EX20 1EW
t (01837) 53916
e okehampton@yha.org.uk
w okehampton-yha.co.uk

### OLD TOWN
Isles of Scilly

**Carn Ithen** ★★★★
*Bed & Breakfast*
**SILVER AWARD**
Trench Lane, Old Town, St
Mary's TR21 0PA
t (01720) 422917
e roz-alfred@carn-ithen.fsnet.co.uk
w scilly-oldtown.com

**The Greenlaws** ★★★★
*Bed & Breakfast*
Old Town, St Mary's
TR21 0NH
t (01720) 422045

### OTTERY ST MARY
Devon

**Pitt Farm** ★★★★ *Farmhouse*
Coombelake, Ottery St Mary
EX11 1NL
t (01404) 812439
e pittfarm@tiscali.co.uk
w pitt-farm-devon.co.uk

### PADSTOW
Cornwall

**1 Caswarth Terrace** ★★
*Bed & Breakfast*
Padstow PL28 8EE
t (01841) 532025

**50 Church Street** ★★★★
*Bed & Breakfast*
**SILVER AWARD**
Padstow PL28 8BG
**t** (01841) 532121
**e** churchstreet50@hotmail.com
**w** 50churchstreet.co.uk

**Althea House** ★★★★★
*Bed & Breakfast*
**SILVER AWARD**
64 Church Street, Padstow
PL28 8BG
**t** (01841) 532579
**e** zooat14@aol.com
**w** altheahouse.co.uk

**Althea Library** ★★★★★
*Guest Accommodation*
**SILVER AWARD**
27 High Street, Padstow
PL28 8BB
**t** (01841) 532717
**e** enquiries@althealibrary.co.uk
**w** althealibrary.co.uk

**Cally Croft** ★★★★
*Bed & Breakfast*
**SILVER AWARD**
26 Raleigh Close, Padstow
PL28 8BQ
**t** (01841) 533726
**e** callycroft@btinternet.com
**w** padstow-callycroft.co.uk

**Chy Veor** ★★★★
*Bed & Breakfast*
24 Hawkins Road, Padstow
PL28 8EU
**t** (01841) 533545
**e** jim@jwhull.fsnet.co.uk

**Chyloweth** ★★★★
*Bed & Breakfast*
Constantine Bay, Padstow
PL28 8JQ
**t** (01841) 521012
**e** roger.vivian@tiscali.co.uk
**w** padstowlive.com

**Coswarth House** ★★★★★
*Bed & Breakfast*
**SILVER AWARD**
12 Dennis Road, Padstow
PL28 8DD
**t** (01841) 534755
**e** coswarthhouse@btinternet.com
**w** coswarthhouse.com

**Cyntwell B&B** ★★★★
*Bed & Breakfast*
4 Cross Street, Padstow
PL28 8AT
**t** (01841) 533447
**e** wendy@wgidlow.fsnet.co.uk
**w** cyntwell.co.uk

**Damara House** ★★★
*Guest Accommodation*
1 Grenville Road, Padstow
PL28 8EX
**t** (01841) 532653
**e** info@sianhowells.com
**w** sianhowells.com

**Garslade Guest House**
★★★★ *Bed & Breakfast*
52 Church Street, Padstow
PL28 8BG
**t** (01841) 533804
**e** garsladeguest@btconnect.com
**w** garslade.com

**Lamorva House** ★★★★
*Guest Accommodation*
3 Sarahs Meadow, Padstow
PL28 8LX
**t** (01841) 533841
**e** lamorva@aol.com
**w** padstowlive.com

**Lellizzick Farm** ★★★★
*Farmhouse* **SILVER AWARD**
Lellizzick, Padstow PL28 8HR
**t** (01841) 532838
**e** lellizzick1@aol.com
**w** lellizzick.co.uk

**Molesworth Manor** ★★★★
*Guest Accommodation*
Little Petherick, Wadebridge
PL27 7QT
**t** (01841) 540292
**e** molesworthmanor@aol.com
**w** molesworthmanor.co.uk

**No 8** ★★★★ *Bed & Breakfast*
8 Drake Road, Padstow
PL28 8ES
**t** (01841) 532541

**Pendeen House** ★★★★
*Bed & Breakfast*
28 Dennis Road, Padstow
PL28 8DE
**t** (01841) 533855
**e** emmacaddis@yahoo.co.uk

**Petrocstowe** ★★★★
*Guest Accommodation*
**SILVER AWARD**
30 Treverbyn Road, Padstow
PL28 8DW
**t** (01841) 532429
**e** andrearichards@btinternet.com
**w** stayinpadstow.co.uk

**Rosmarinus** ★★★★
*Guest Accommodation*
8 Raleigh Close, Padstow
PL28 8BQ
**t** (01841) 533712
**e** richardellis8@aol.com
**w** padstowbb.co.uk

**Symply Padstow** ★★★★
*Bed & Breakfast*
**SILVER AWARD**
32 Dennis Road, Padstow
PL28 8DE
**t** (01841) 532814
**e** info@symply-padstow.co.uk
**w** symply-padstow.co.uk

**Tamarisk** ★★★★
*Bed & Breakfast*
13 Grenville Road, Padstow
PL28 8EX
**t** (01841) 532272

**Trealaw Bed & Breakfast**
★★★★ *Bed & Breakfast*
22 Duke Street, Padstow
PL28 8AB
**t** (01841) 533161
**w** trealaw.com

**Treann** ★★★★
*Guest Accommodation*
Dennis Road, Padstow
PL28 8DE
**t** (01841) 533855
**e** emmacaddis@yahoo.co.uk
**w** treverbynhouse.com/treann.html

**Trethillick Farmhouse**
★★★★ *Farmhouse*
Padstow PL28 8HJ
**t** (01841) 532352
**e** mwatsonsmyth@aol.com

**Treverbyn House** ★★★★
*Guest Accommodation*
**SILVER AWARD**
Station Road, Padstow
PL28 8DA
**t** (01841) 532855
**w** treverbynhouse.com

**Trevorrick Farm – B & B**
★★★★ *Farmhouse*
St Issey, Padstow PL27 7QH
**t** (01841) 540574
**e** info@trevorrick.co.uk
**w** trevorrick.co.uk

**West House** ★★★★
*Bed & Breakfast*
Grenville Rd, Padstow
PL28 8EX
**t** (01841) 533479
**e** willis@bun.com
**w** westhouse-padstow.co.uk

**The White Hart Apartment**
★★★★ *Bed & Breakfast*
**SILVER AWARD**
1 New Street, Padstow
PL28 8EA
**t** (01841) 532350
**e** whthartpad@aol.com
**w** whitehartpadstow.co.uk

**Woodlands Country House**
★★★★★
*Guest Accommodation*
**GOLD AWARD**
Treator, Padstow PL28 8RU
**t** (01841) 532426
**e** enquiries@woodlands-padstow.co.uk
**w** woodlands-padstow.co.uk

## PAIGNTON
## Devon

**Amber House** ★★★★
*Guest Accommodation*
**SILVER AWARD**
6 Roundham Road, Paignton
TQ4 6EZ
**t** (01803) 558372
**e** enquiries@amberhousehotel.co.uk
**w** amberhousehotel.co.uk

**Arden House** ★★★
*Guest House*
10 Youngs Park Road, Paignton
TQ4 6BU
**t** (01803) 558443
**e** info@ardenhousehotel.com
**w** ardenhousehotel.com

**The Ashleigh** ★★★
*Guest Accommodation*
15 Queens Road, Paignton
TQ4 6AT
**t** (01803) 558923
**e** ashleighhotel4@aol.com
**w** ashleigh-hotel.co.uk

**The Bay Sands** ★★★★
*Guest Accommodation*
14 Colin Road, Paignton
TQ3 2NR
**t** (01803) 524877
**e** enquiries@baysands.co.uk
**w** baysands.co.uk

**Beach House** ★★★★
*Guest Accommodation*
39 Garfield Road, Paignton
TQ4 6AX
**t** (01803) 525742
**e** beachhouse@l2222.fsbusiness.co.uk

**Beecroft Lodge** ★★★
*Guest Accommodation*
10 St Andrews Road, Paignton
TQ4 6HA
**t** (01803) 558702
**e** info@beecrofthotel.co.uk
**w** beecrofthotel.co.uk

**Bella Vista Guest House**
★★★ *Guest Accommodation*
Berry Square, Paignton
TQ4 6AZ
**t** (01803) 558122
**e** bellavista@berrysquare.fsbusiness.co.uk
**w** english-riviera.co.uk/accommodation/guest-houses/bella-vista/index.htm

**Benbows Guest House** ★★★
*Guest House*
1 Alta Vista Road, Roundham
TQ4 6DB
**t** (01803) 558128
**e** benbowshotel@btinternet.com
**w** benbowshotel.co.uk

**The Beresford** ★★★★
*Guest Accommodation*
5 Adelphi Road, Paignton
TQ4 6AW
**t** (01803) 551560
**e** info@beresfordhotel.co.uk
**w** beresfordhotel.co.uk

**Birchwood House** ★★★★
*Guest House*
33 St Andrews Road, Paignton
TQ4 6HA
**t** (01803) 551323
**e** dawnbowbeer@hotmail.co.uk
**w** birchwoodhouse.net

**Birklands Guest House**
★★★★ *Guest House*
33 Garfield Road, Paignton
TQ4 6AX
**t** (01803) 556970
**e** trevor@trevor27.freeserve.co.uk
**w** birklands.co.uk

**Blue Waters Lodge** ★★★★
*Guest Accommodation*
4 Leighon Road, Paignton
TQ3 2BQ
**t** (01803) 557749
**e** bluewaters.lodge@virgin.net
**w** bluewaterslodge.co.uk

**Braedene Lodge** ★★★
*Guest House*
22 Manor Road, Paignton
TQ3 2HR
**t** (01803) 551079
**e** stay@braedenehotel.fsnet.co.uk
**w** braedenehotel.co.uk

**Briars** ★★★★
*Guest Accommodation*
26 Sands Road, Paignton
TQ4 6EJ
**t** (01803) 557729
**e** malcolmmandy@hotmail.co.uk
**w** briarshotel.com

**Bristol House** ★★
*Guest House*
Garfield Road, Paignton
TQ4 6AU
t (01803) 558282
e info@bristolhousehotel.com
w bristolhousehotel.com

**Carrington Guest House**
★★★ *Guest House*
10 Beach Road, Paignton
TQ4 6AY
t (01803) 558785
e info@carringtonguesthouse.co.uk
w carringtonguesthouse.co.uk

**Charnwood House** ★★★★
*Guest Accommodation*
Queens Road, Paignton
TQ4 6AT
t (01803) 558889

**The Cherra** ★★★
*Guest Accommodation*
15 Roundham Road, Paignton
TQ4 6DN
t (01803) 550723
e info@cherrahotel.co.uk
w cherrahotel.co.uk

**The Cherwood** ★★★★
*Guest Accommodation*
26 Garfield Road, Paignton
TQ4 6AX
t (01803) 556515
e pauline@cherwood-hotel.co.uk
w cherwood-hotel.co.uk

**Cliveden** ★★★★
*Guest Accommodation*
**27 Garfield Road, Paignton**
**TQ4 6AX**
**t (01803) 557461**
**e ros.mager@btconnect.com**
**w clivedenguesthouse.co.uk**

**Colin House** ★★★★
*Guest Accommodation*
2 Colin Road, Paignton
TQ3 2NR
t (01803) 550609
e karen@colinhouse.co.uk
w colinhouse.co.uk

**The Cosmopolitan** ★★★★
*Guest Accommodation*
2 Kernou Road, Paignton
TQ4 6BA
t (01803) 523118
e mail@paignton-cosmopolitan.com
w paignton-cosmopolitan.com

**Craigmore Guest House**
★★★ *Guest House*
54 Dartmouth Road, Paignton
TQ4 5AN
t (01803) 557373
e cgh@excite.co.uk

**Culverden Guest House**
★★★ *Guest Accommodation*
4 Colin Road, Preston TQ3 2NR
t (01803) 559786
e info@culverdenhotel.co.uk
w culverdenhotel.co.uk

**Easton Court** ★★★★
*Guest House*
5 St Andrews Road, Paignton
TQ4 6HA
t (01803) 555810
e info@eastoncourt.co.uk
w eastoncourt.co.uk

**The Florida** ★★★★
*Guest Accommodation*
9 Colin Road, Paignton
TQ3 2NR
t (01803) 551447
e stay@floridahotelpaignton.co.uk
w floridahotelpaignton.co.uk

**Harbour Lodge** ★★★
*Guest Accommodation*
4 Cleveland Road, Paignton
TQ4 6EN
t (01803) 556932
e enquiries@harbourlodge.co.uk
w harbourlodge.co.uk

**The Mayfield** ★★★★
*Guest Accommodation*
8 Queens Road, Paignton
TQ4 6AT
t (01803) 556802
e mayhot@tiscali.co.uk

**Norbreck** ★★★ *Guest House*
New Street, Paignton TQ3 3HL
t (01803) 558033
e norbreckguesthouse@hotmail.com
w norbreck.com

**Park Lodge Hotel** ★★★
*Guest House*
16-18 Adelphi Road, Paignton
TQ4 6AW
t (01803) 551232

**Richmond Guest House**
Rating Applied For
*Guest House*
19 Norman Road, Paignton
TQ3 2BE
t (01803) 550978
e info@richmondgh.co.uk
w richmondgh.co.uk

**Rockview Guest House**
★★★ *Guest House*
**13 Queens Road, Paignton**
**TQ4 6AT**
**t (01803) 556702**
**e rockview@blueyonder.co.uk**
**w rockview.co.uk**

**Rosemead Guest House**
★★★ *Guest Accommodation*
22 Garfield Road, Paignton
TQ4 6AX
t (01803) 557944
e rosemeadhotel@aol.com
w rosemeadpaignton.co.uk

**Roundham Lodge** ★★★★★
*Guest Accommodation*
**SILVER AWARD**
16 Roundham Road, Paignton
TQ4 6DN
t (01803) 558485
e enquiries@roundham-lodge.co.uk
w roundham-lodge.co.uk

**St Edmunds House** ★★★
*Guest Accommodation*
25 Sands Road, Paignton
TQ4 6EG
t (01803) 558756
e stedmunds@lycos.co.uk
w stedmundshotel.com

**San Brelade** ★★★
*Guest House*
3 Alta Vista Road, Paignton
TQ4 6DB
t (01803) 553725
e info@sanbrelade.co.uk
w hotelsanbrelade.co.uk

**The Sands** ★★★★
*Guest Accommodation*
32 Sands Road, Paignton
TQ4 6EJ
t (01803) 551282
e hotel.sands@virgin.net
w hotelsands.co.uk

**Sea Spray House** ★★★
*Guest Accommodation*
1 Beach Road, Paignton
TQ4 6AY
t (01803) 553141
e mail@seasprayhotel.co.uk
w seasprayhotel.co.uk

**Seacroft Guest House**
★★★★
*Guest Accommodation*
41 Sands Road, Paignton
TQ4 6EG
t (01803) 523791
e enquiries@seacroftguesthouse.co.uk
w seacroftguesthouse.co.uk

**Seaford Sands** ★★★
*Guest Accommodation*
Roundham Road, Paignton
TQ4 6DN
t (01803) 557722
w seafordsandshotel.co.uk

**Seahaven** ★★★
*Guest Accommodation*
2 Beach Road, Paignton
TQ4 6AY
t (01803) 525549
e hotelbookings@seahavenhotel.org.uk
w seahavenhotel.org.uk/

**Seaways** ★★★
*Guest Accommodation*
30 Sands Road, Paignton
TQ4 6EJ
t (01803) 551093
e seawayshotel@aol.com
w seawayshotel.com

**Sonachan House** ★★★★
*Guest Accommodation*
35 St Andrews Road, Paignton
TQ4 6HA
t (01803) 558021
e info@sonachan.co.uk
w sonachan.co.uk

**The Sundale** ★★
*Guest Accommodation*
10 Queens Road, Paignton
TQ4 6AT
t (01803) 557431
e sundalehotel@tiscali.co.uk
w sundalehotelpaignton.co.uk

**Three Palms**
Rating Applied For
*Guest Accommodation*
21 Sands Road, Paignton
TQ4 6EG
t (01803) 551340

**Two Beaches** ★★★★
*Guest Accommodation*
27 St Andrews Road, Paignton
TQ4 6HA
t (01803) 522164
e 2beaches@tiscali.co.uk
w twobeaches.co.uk

**The Wynncroft** ★★★
*Guest Accommodation*
Elmsleigh Park, Paignton
TQ4 5AT
t (01803) 525728
e wynncroft@fsbdial.co.uk
w wynncroft.co.uk

## PAINSWICK
Gloucestershire

**Cardynham House** ★★★★
*Guest Accommodation*
The Cross, Painswick GL6 6XX
t (01452) 814006
e info@cardynham.co.uk
w cardynham.co.uk

**Hambutts Mynd** ★★★
*Guest Accommodation*
Edge Road, Painswick GL6 6UP
t (01452) 812352
e ewarland@aol.com
w accommodation.uk.net/hambutts.htm

**Meadowcote** ★★★★
*Bed & Breakfast*
Stroud Road, Painswick
GL6 6UT
t (01452) 813565
e lockmeadowcote@talktalk.net

**St Annes** ★★★★
*Bed & Breakfast*
Gloucester Street, Painswick
GL6 6QN
t (01452) 812879
e greg-iris@supanet.com
w st-annes-painswick.co.uk

**St Michaels Restaurant**
★★★★
*Restaurant with Rooms*
Victoria Street, Painswick
GL6 6QA
t (01452) 814555
e info@stmickshouse.co.uk
w stmickshouse.co.uk

**Skyrack** ★★★
*Bed & Breakfast*
The Highlands, Painswick
GL6 6SL
t (01452) 812029
e wendyskyrack@hotmail.com

**Thorne** ★★★ *Bed & Breakfast*
Friday Street, Painswick
GL6 6QJ
t (01452) 812476

**Tibbiwell Lodge** ★★★★
*Bed & Breakfast*
Tibbiwell Lane, Stroud
GL6 6YA
t (01452) 812748
e lovell_richard@hotmail.com
w tibbiwelllodgepainswick.webs.com

**Troy House** ★★★
*Bed & Breakfast*
Gloucester Street, Painswick
GL6 6QN
t (01452) 812339
e simonnefrissen@microdia.co.uk
w troy-house.co.uk

**Upper Doreys Mill** ★★★
*Bed & Breakfast*
Edge, Painswick GL6 6NF
t (01452) 812459
e sylvia@doreys.co.uk
w doreys.co.uk

## PAMINGTON
Gloucestershire

**Pamington Court Farm**
★★★★ *Farmhouse*
Pamington, Ashchurch
GL20 8LY
**t** (01684) 772301
**e** mhill@uwclub.net
**w** pamingtoncourtfarm.com

## PANBOROUGH
Somerset

**Garden End Farm** ★★★
*Farmhouse*
Wells Road, Wells BA5 1PN
**t** (01934) 712414
**e** sheila@gardenendfarm.freeserve.co.uk
**w** gardenendfarm.freeserve.co.uk

## PAR
Cornwall

**An Skyber** ★★★★
*Bed & Breakfast*
The Mount, Par PL24 2DA
**t** (01726) 815013
**e** valeriejobes@tiscali.co.uk
**w** an-skyber.co.uk

**Reynards Rest** ★★★★
*Bed & Breakfast*
The Mount, Par PL24 2BZ
**t** (01726) 815770
**e** doug@reynardsrest.co.uk
**w** reynardsrest.co.uk

**The Royal Inn** ★★★★ *Inn*
66 Eastcliffe Road, Par
PL24 2AJ
**t** (01726) 815601
**e** info@royal-inn.co.uk
**w** royal-inn.co.uk

## PARKEND
Gloucestershire

**Deanfield** ★★★★
*Guest Accommodation*
Folly Road, Parkend, Lydney
GL15 4JF
**t** (01594) 562256
**e** deanfieldbb@aol.com
**w** deanfield.org.uk

**Edale House** ★★★★
*Guest House*
Folly Road, Parkend, Lydney
GL15 4JP
**t** (01594) 562835
**e** enquiry@edalehouse.co.uk
**w** edalehouse.co.uk

**The Fountain Inn** ★★★ *Inn*
Parkend, Lydney GL15 4JD
**t** (01594) 562189
**e** thefountaininn@aol.com

## PARKSTONE
Dorset

**Viewpoint Guest House**
★★★★ *Guest House*
11 Constitution Hill Road,
Parkstone BH14 0QB
**t** (01202) 733586
**e** enquiry@viewpoint-gh.co.uk
**w** viewpoint-gh.co.uk

## PAYHEMBURY
Devon

**Yellingham Farm** ★★★★
*Farmhouse* **SILVER AWARD**
Payhembury, Honiton
EX14 3HE
**t** (01404) 850272
**e** janeteast@yellinghamfarm.co.uk
**w** yellinghamfarm.co.uk

## PEDWELL
Somerset

**Polden Vale** ★★★★
*Bed & Breakfast*
Taunton Road, Pedwell
TA7 9BG
**t** (01458) 211114
**e** paul.malabar@onetel.net

**Sunnyside** ★★★★
*Bed & Breakfast*
**SILVER AWARD**
34 Taunton Road, Street
TA7 9BG
**t** (01458) 210097
**e** sunnyside@pedwell.freeuk.com
**w** pedwell.freeuk.com

## PELYNT
Cornwall

**Bake Farm** ★★★★
*Farmhouse*
Pelynt, Looe PL13 2QQ
**t** (01503) 220244
**e** bakefarm@btopenworld.com

**Cardwen Farm** ★★★★
*Farmhouse*
Pelynt, Looe PL13 2LU
**t** (01503) 220213
**e** cardwenfarm@freenet.co.uk
**w** cardwenfarm.com

**Trenderway Farm** ★★★★★
*Farmhouse* **SILVER AWARD**
Pelynt, Looe PL13 2LY
**t** (01503) 272214
**e** trenderwayfarm@hotmail.com
**w** trenderwayfarm.co.uk

## PENHALLOW
Cornwall

**Lambriggan Court** ★★★★
*Guest Accommodation*
Penhallow, Truro TR4 9LU
**t** (01872) 571636
**e** lynn_c_churchill@hotmail.com
**w** lambriggancourt.com

## PENRYN
Cornwall

**Bay View** ★★★
*Bed & Breakfast*
Busvannah, Penryn TR10 9LQ
**t** (01326) 372644
**e** dawnemmerson@aol.com
**w** falmouth-bandb.co.uk

**Sunnyside Bed and Breakfast** ★★★★
*Bed & Breakfast*
Treluswell, Penryn TR10 9AN
**t** (01326) 379254
**e** enquiries.sunnyside@btinternet.com
**w** sunnysidebedandbreakfast.co.uk

## PENSFORD
Somerset

**Green Acres** ★★
*Guest Accommodation*
Stanton Wick, Pensford, Bristol
BS39 4BX
**t** (01761) 490397

**Leigh Farm** ★★ *Farmhouse*
Old Road, Pensford BS39 4BA
**t** (01761) 490281

## PENSILVA
Cornwall

**Penharget Farm** ★★★★
*Farmhouse*
Pensilva, Liskeard PL14 5RJ
**t** (01579) 362221
**e** penhargetfarm@ukonline.co.uk
**w** penharget-farm-cornwall.co.uk

## PENTEWAN
Cornwall

**Ancient Shipbrokers**
★★★★ *Bed & Breakfast*
1 Higher West End, Pentewan
PL26 6BY
**t** (01726) 843370
**e** wendy@shipbrokers.orangehome.co.uk
**w** pentewanbedandbreakfast.com

## PENZANCE
Cornwall

**Carnson House** ★★★
*Guest Accommodation*
2 East Terrace, Penzance
TR18 2TD
**t** (01736) 365589
**e** reception@carnson-house.co.uk
**w** carnson-house.co.uk

**Castallack Farm** ★★★★
*Farmhouse* **SILVER AWARD**
Castallack, Lamorna TR19 6NL
**t** (01736) 731969
**e** info@castallackfarm.co.uk
**w** castallackfarm.co.uk

**Chiverton House** ★★★★
*Guest Accommodation*
**SILVER AWARD**
9 Mennaye Road, Penzance
TR18 4NG
**t** (01736) 332733
**e** alan.waller@sky.com
**w** chivertonhousebedandbreakfast.co.uk

**Con Amore** ★★★★
*Guest Accommodation*
38 Morrab Road, Penzance
TR18 4EX
**t** (01736) 363423
**e** krich30327@aol.com
**w** con-amore.co.uk

**The Corner House** ★★★★
*Guest Accommodation*
20 Marine Terrace, Penzance
TR18 4DL
**t** (01736) 351324
**e** info@thecornerhousepenzance.co.uk
**w** thecornerhousepenzance.co.uk

**Cornerways Guest House**
★★★ *Guest Accommodation*
5 Leskinnick Street, Penzance
TR18 2HA
**t** (01736) 364645
**e** enquiries@cornerways-penzance.co.uk
**w** penzance.co.uk/cornerways

**Glencree House** ★★★★
*Guest Accommodation*
2 Mennaye Road, Penzance
TR18 4NG
**t** (01736) 362026
**e** stay@glencreehouse.co.uk
**w** glencreehouse.co.uk

**Halcyon Guest House**
★★★★ *Guest House*
6 Chyandour Square, Penzance
TR18 3LW
**t** (01736) 366302
**e** pat+bob@halcyon1.co.uk
**w** halcyon1.co.uk

**Harbour Heights Bed and Breakfast** ★★★
*Bed & Breakfast*
Boase Street, Newlyn TR18 5JE
**t** (01736) 350976
**e** anneofnewlyn@aol.com
**w** harbour-heights.co.uk

**Lombard House** ★★★★★
*Guest Accommodation*
16 Regent Terrace, Penzance
TR18 4DW
**t** (01736) 364897
**e** lombardhouse@btconnect.com
**w** lombardhousehotel.com

**Lowenna** ★★★★★
*Guest Accommodation*
**GOLD AWARD**
Raginnis Hill, Mousehole
TR19 6SL
**t** (01736) 731077
**e** mm4lowenna@aol.com

**Lynwood Guest House**
★★★★ *Guest House*
41 Morrab Road, Penzance
TR18 4EX
**t** (01736) 365871
**e** lynwoodpz@aol.com
**w** lynwood-guesthouse.co.uk

**Menwidden Farm** ★★★
*Farmhouse*
Ludgvan, Penzance TR20 8BN
**t** (01736) 740415
**e** coramenwidden@tiscali.co.uk

**The Pendennis** ★★★★
*Guest Accommodation*
Alexandra Road, Penzance
TR18 4LZ
**t** (01736) 363823
**e** thependennis@googlemail.com
**w** thependennis.co.uk

**Penrose Guest House** ★★★
*Guest House*
8 Penrose Terrace, Penzance
TR18 2HQ
**t** (01736) 362782
**e** enquiries@penrosegsthse.co.uk
**w** penrosegsthse.co.uk

**Rose Farm** ★★★★
*Farmhouse*
Chyanhal, Buryas Bridge
TR19 6AN
t (01736) 731808
e penny@rosefarmcornwall.co.uk
w rosefarmcornwall.co.uk

**Shoreline Guest House** ★★★★
*Guest Accommodation*
17 Marine Terrace, The Promenade, Penzance
TR18 4DL
t (01736) 366821
e enquiries@shoreline-penzance.com
w shoreline-penzance.com

**The Summer House** ★★★★★
*Guest Accommodation*
**GOLD AWARD**
Cornwall Terrace, Penzance
TR18 4HL
t (01736) 363744
e reception@summerhouse.cornwall.com
w summerhouse-cornwall.com

**Torwood House** ★★★
*Guest House*
Alexandra Road, Penzance
TR18 4LZ
t (01736) 360063
e lyndasowerby@aol.com
w torwoodhousehotel.co.uk

**Tremont** ★★★★
*Guest Accommodation*
Alexandra Road, Penzance
TR18 4LZ
t (01736) 362614
e info@tremonthotel.co.uk
w tremonthotel.co.uk

**Treventon** ★★★
*Guest House*
Alexandra Place, Penzance
TR18 4NE
t (01736) 363521

**Warwick House** ★★★★
*Guest House*
17 Regent Terrace, Penzance
TR18 4DW
t (01736) 363881
e enquiry@warwickhousepenzance.co.uk
w warwickhousepenzance.co.uk

**Woodstock Guest House**
★★★★ *Guest House*
29 Morrab Road, Penzance
TR18 4EZ
t (01736) 369049
e info@woodstockguesthouse.co.uk
w woodstockguesthouse.co.uk

**Wymering** ★★★
*Guest Accommodation*
Regent Square, Penzance
TR18 4BG
t (01736) 362126
e pam@wymering.com
w wymering.com

## PERRANPORTH
Cornwall

**The Perranporth Inn** ★★★★
*Inn*
St Pirans Road, Perranporth
TR6 0BJ
t (01872) 573234
e perranporthinn@btconnect.com
w perranporthinn.co.uk

**Perranporth Youth Hostel**
★★ *Hostel*
Droskyn Point, Perranporth
TR6 0GS
t (01872) 573812
e perranporth@yha.org.uk

**Tides Reach** ★★★★
*Guest House*
Ponsmere Road, Perranporth
TR6 0BW
t (01872) 572188
e jandf.boyle@virgin.net
w tidesreachhotel.com

**The Whitehouse Inn & Luxury Lodge** ★★★★ *Inn*
Penhallow, Nr Truro, St Agnes
TR4 9LQ
t (01872) 573306
e whitehouseinn@btconnect.com
w whitehousecornwall.co.uk

## PIDDLETRENTHIDE
Dorset

**The European Inn** ★★★★
*Inn* **SILVER AWARD**
Piddletrenthide, Dorchester
DT2 7QT
t (01300) 348308
e info@european-inn.co.uk
w european-inn.co.uk

**The Poachers Inn** ★★★★
*Inn*
Piddletrenthide, Dorchester
DT2 7QX
t (01300) 348358
e thepoachersinn@piddletrenthide.fsbusiness.co.uk
w thepoachersinn.co.uk

## PILSDON
Dorset

**Gerrards Farm** ★★★★
*Farmhouse* **SILVER AWARD**
Pilsdon, Bridport DT6 5PA
t (01308) 867474
e chrisrabbetts@btinternet.com
w gerrardsfarm.co.uk

## PILTON
Somerset

**Bowermead House**
★★★★★ *Bed & Breakfast*
**SILVER AWARD**
Whitstone Hill, Shepton Mallet
BA4 4DT
t (01749) 890744
e w.southcombe@btopenworld.com
w bowermeadhouse.co.uk

## PITCHCOMBE
Gloucestershire

**Gable End** ★★★
*Bed & Breakfast*
Pitchcombe, Stroud GL6 6LN
t (01452) 812166

## PLUSH
Dorset

**Kingsmead** ★★★★
*Bed & Breakfast*
Piddletrenthide, Dorchester
DT2 7QX
t (01300) 348234
e mikehtkingsmead@aol.com

## PLYMOUTH
Devon

**Athenaeum Lodge** ★★★★
*Guest Accommodation*
4 Athenaeum Street, The Hoe, Plymouth PL1 2RQ
t (01752) 665005 & (01752) 670090
e us@athenaeumlodge.com
w athenaeumlodge.com

**Berkeleys of St James**
★★★★
*Guest Accommodation*
4 St James Place East, Plymouth
PL1 3AS
t (01752) 221654
e enquiry@onthehoe.co.uk
w onthehoe.co.uk

**The Bowling Green** ★★★★
*Guest Accommodation*
**SILVER AWARD**
9-10 Osborne Place, Plymouth
PL1 2PU
t (01752) 209090
e info@bowlingreenhotel.com
w bowlingreenhotel.com

**Brittany Guest House**
★★★★ *Guest House*
28 Athenaeum Street, The Hoe, Plymouth PL1 2RQ
t (01752) 262247
e enquiries@brittanyguesthouse.com
w brittanyguesthouse.co.uk

**Caledonia Guest House**
★★★★ *Guest House*
27 Athenaeum Street, Plymouth PL1 2RQ
t (01752) 229052
e info@thecaledonia.co.uk
w thecaledonia.co.uk

**Casa Mia Guest House** ★★★
*Guest House*
201 Citadel Road East, The Hoe PL1 2JF
t (01752) 265742
e janecasamia@googlemail.com
w casa-mia-onthehoe.com

**Citadel House** ★★
*Guest House*
55 Citadel Rd, The Hoe
PL1 3AU
t (01752) 661712
w citadelhouse.co.uk

**Crescent House** ★★★
*Guest House*
18 Garden Crescent, West Hoe, Plymouth PL1 3DA
t (01752) 266424
e crescenthouse18@aol.com

**Four Seasons** ★★★★
*Guest House*
207 Citadel Road East, Plymouth PL1 2JF
t (01752) 223591
e f.seasons@btconnect.com
w fourseasonsguesthouse.co.uk

**Gabber Farm** ★★★
*Farmhouse*
Gabber Lane, Down Thomas, Plymouth PL9 0AW
t (01752) 862269
e gabberfarm@tiscali.co.uk

**The George Guest House**
★★★ *Guest House*
161 Citadel Road, Plymouth
PL1 2HU
t (01752) 661517
e georgeguesthouse@btconnect.com
w accommodationplymouth.co.uk

**Grosvenor Park**
Rating Applied For
*Hostel*
114-116 North Road East, Plymouth PL4 6AH
t (01752) 229312
e gphotel@grosvenorparkhotel.co.uk
w grosvenorparkhotel.co.uk

**Homeleigh Bed & Breakfast**
★★ *Bed & Breakfast*
5 George Lane, Plympton, Plymouth PL7 1LJ
t (01752) 330478
e homeleighbandb@blueyonder.co.uk
w homeleighbandb.co.uk

**Hotspur Guest House**
★★★★ *Guest House*
108 North Road East, Plymouth
PL4 6AW
t (01752) 663928
e info@hotspurguesthouse.co.uk
w hotspurguesthouse.co.uk

**The Imperial** ★★★★★
*Guest Accommodation*
Lockyer Street, The Hoe
PL1 2QD
t (01752) 227311
e info@imperialplymouth.co.uk
w imperialplymouth.co.uk

**Kynance House** ★★
*Guest Accommodation*
113 Citadel Road West, The Hoe PL1 2RN
t (01752) 266821
e info@kynancehotel.co.uk
w kynancehotel.co.uk

**Mariners Guest House** ★★★
*Guest House*
11 Pier Street, West Hoe, Plymouth PL1 3BS
t (01752) 261778
e marinersguesthouse@blueyonder.co.uk
w marinersguesthouse.co.uk

**The Moorings Guest House**
★★★ *Guest Accommodation*
4 Garden Crescent, West Hoe, Plymouth PL1 3DA
t (01752) 250128
e enquiries@themooringsguesthouseplymouth.com
w themooringsguesthouseplymouth.com

**Mount Batten Centre**
★★★★ *Group Hostel*
Lawrence Road, Plymouth
PL9 9SJ
t (01752) 404567

**Number Seven** ★★★★
*Bed & Breakfast*
7 Haddington Road, Stoke
PL2 1RW
t (01752) 564848
e suetorrance@yahoo.co.uk
w numbersevenplymouth.co.uk

**Poppy's Guest House** ★★★
*Guest House*
4 Alfred Street, The Hoe
PL1 2RP
t (01752) 670452
e bookings@poppysguesthouse.co.uk
w smoothhound.co.uk/hotels

**Seymour Guest House** ★★★
*Guest House*
211 Citadel Road East, The Hoe PL1 2JF
t (01752) 667002
e peter@seymourguesthouse.co.uk
w seymourguesthouse.co.uk

**Squires Guest House**
★★★★ *Guest House*
7 St James Place East, Plymouth
PL1 3AS
t (01752) 261459
e info@squiresguesthouse.com
w squiresguesthouse.com

**Sydney Guest House** ★★
*Guest House*
181 North Road West,
Plymouth PL1 5DE
t (01752) 266541

**University of Plymouth**
★★★ *Campus*
Drake Circus, Plymouth
PL4 8AA
t (01752) 232027
e summer-accommodation@plymouth.ac.uk
w plymouth.ac.uk/holidayaccommodation

## POLBATHIC
Cornwall

**Buttervilla Farm** ★★★★
*Farmhouse* **SILVER AWARD**
Polbathic, St Germans, Looe
PL11 3EY
t (01503) 230315
e info@buttervilla.com
w buttervilla.com

## POLGOOTH
Cornwall

**Hunters Moon** ★★★★
*Guest House* **SILVER AWARD**
Chapel Hill, Polgooth PL26 7BU
t (01726) 66445
e enquiries@huntersmooncornwall.co.uk
w huntersmooncornwall.co.uk

## POLKERRIS
Cornwall

**Tregaminion Farm** ★★★★
*Farmhouse*
Polkerris, Par PL24 2TL
t (01726) 812442

## POLPERRO
Cornwall

**Chyavallon** ★★★★
*Bed & Breakfast*
**SILVER AWARD**
Landaviddy Lane, Polperro,
Looe PL13 2RT
t (01503) 272788
w polperro.org/chyavallon/index.html

**Cottage Restaurant (The)**
★★★★
*Restaurant with Rooms*
**SILVER AWARD**
The Coombes, Polperro
PL13 2RQ
t (01503) 272217
w cottagerestaurantpolperro.co.uk

**The Cottles – Polperro**
★★★★ *Guest House*
Longcoombe Lane, Looe
PL13 2PL
t (01503) 272578
e enquiries@cottles-polperro.co.uk
w cottles-polperro.co.uk

**Crumplehorn Inn and Mill**
★★★ *Inn*
Crumplehorn, Polperro, Looe
PL13 2RJ
t (01503) 272348
e host@crumplehorn-inn.co.uk
w crumplehorn-inn.co.uk

**Millie's** ★★★ *Bed & Breakfast*
Crumplehorn, Polperro, Looe
PL13 2RJ
t (01503) 272492

**The Old Mill House Inn**
Rating Applied For
*Inn*
Mill Hill, Polperro PL13 2RP
t (01503) 272362
e enquiries@oldmillhouseinn.co.uk
w oldmillhouseinn.co.uk

## POLZEATH
Cornwall

**White Heron** ★★★★
*Guest House*
Polzeath, Wadebridge
PL27 6TJ
t (01208) 863623
e info@whiteheronhotel.co.uk
w whiteheronhotel.co.uk

## POOLE
Dorset

**Alice Sea Guest House B&B**
★★★ *Bed & Breakfast*
17 Burngate Road, Hamworthy
BH15 4HS
t (01202) 679840
e reginald.coker@ntlworld.com

**Cherry Tree B & B** ★★★
*Bed & Breakfast*
84 Parkstone Heights, Poole
BH14 0RZ
t (01202) 723494
e cherrytree_poole@btinternet.com

**Corkers Restaurant & Cafe Bar with Guest Rooms**
★★★★
*Guest Accommodation*
**SILVER AWARD**
1 High Street, Poole BH15 1AB
t (01202) 681393
e corkers@corkers.co.uk
w corkers.co.uk

**Cranborne House** ★★★★
*Guest Accommodation*
**SILVER AWARD**
45 Shaftesbury Road, Poole
BH15 2LU
t (01202) 685200
w cranborne-house.co.uk

**Danecourt Lodge** ★★★★
*Bed & Breakfast*
**GOLD AWARD**
58 Danecourt Road, Poole
BH14 0PQ
t (01202) 730957
e pat@danecourtlodge.co.uk
w danecourtlodge.co.uk

**Fleetwater Guest House**
★★★★
*Guest Accommodation*
161 Longfleet Road, Poole
BH15 2HS
t (01202) 682509
e fleetwater161@yahoo.co.uk
w fleetwaterguesthouse.co.uk

**Foxes B&B** ★★
*Bed & Breakfast*
**SILVER AWARD**
13 Sandbanks Road, Poole
BH14 8AG
t (01202) 269633
e sue.fox@foxesbandb.co.uk
w foxesbandb.co.uk

**Harbourside Guest House**
★★ *Bed & Breakfast*
195 Blandford Road, Poole
BH15 4AX
t (01202) 673053
e harboursideguesthouse@gmail.com

**Highways** ★★★
*Bed & Breakfast*
29 Fernside Road, Poole
BH15 2QU
t (01202) 677060

**Hove to B&B** ★★★★
*Bed & Breakfast*
7 Salterns Road, Lower
Parkstone BH14 8BJ
t (01202) 241430
e hoveto3@hotmail.com
w hovetobedandbreakfast.com

**Mariners Guest House** ★★★
*Guest House*
26 Sandbanks Road, Poole
BH14 8AQ
t (01202) 247218
e admin@themarinersguesthouse.co.uk
w themarinersguesthouse.co.uk

**Oakborne** ★★★★
*Bed & Breakfast*
116 Ringwood Road, Poole
BH14 0RW
t (01202) 678211
e absmurrey@aol.com
w oakborne.co.uk

**Quayside B&B** ★★
*Guest Accommodation*
9 High Street, Poole BH15 1AB
t (01202) 683733
w poolequayside.co.uk

**The Saltings** ★★★★
*Bed & Breakfast*
**GOLD AWARD**
5 Salterns Way, Poole
BH14 8JR
t (01202) 707349
e saltings_poole@yahoo.co.uk
w the-saltings.com

**Tideway** ★★★★
*Bed & Breakfast*
Beach Road, Upton BH16 5NA
t (01202) 621293
e tideway@tiscali.co.uk
w tidewaybb.co.uk

**Vernon** ★★ *Bed & Breakfast*
96 Blandford Road North,
Beacon Hill, Poole BH16 6AD
t (01202) 625185
e frederick@frendell.wanadoo.co.uk
w vernonbnb.co.uk

## PORLOCK
Somerset

**Exmoor House** ★★★★★
*Guest Accommodation*
**SILVER AWARD**
Minehead Road, Porlock
TA24 8EY
t (01643) 863599
e ann@exmoor-house.co.uk
w exmoor-house.co.uk

**Glen Lodge** ★★★★
*Guest Accommodation*
Hawkcombe, Minehead
TA24 8LN
t (01643) 863371
e glenlodge@gmail.com
w glenlodge.net

**Myrtle Cottage** ★★★
*Bed & Breakfast*
High Street, Porlock TA24 8PU
t (01643) 862978
e bob.steer@virgin.net
w myrtleporlock.co.uk

**Rose Bank Guest House**
★★★★ *Guest House*
**SILVER AWARD**
High Street, Porlock TA24 8PY
t (01643) 862728
e info@rosebankguesthouse.co.uk
w rosebankguesthouse.co.uk

**Sea View** ★★★★
*Bed & Breakfast*
High Bank, Porlock TA24 8NP
t (01643) 863456
e seaview.porlock@btconnect.com
w seaviewporlock.co.uk

## PORT ISAAC
Cornwall

**Anchorage** ★★★★
*Guest Accommodation*
12 The Terrace, Port Isaac
PL29 3SG
t (01208) 880629

**Cornish Arms** ★★★★ *Inn*
Pendoggett, Port Isaac
PL30 3HH
t (01208) 880263
e info@cornisharms.com
w cornisharms.com

**Hathaway Bed and Breakfast** ★★★★
*Guest Accommodation*
Roscarrock Hill, Port Isaac
PL29 3RG
t (01208) 880416
e marion.andrews1@btopenworld.com
w cornwall-online.co.uk

**The Slipway** ★★★★ *Inn*
Harbour Front, Port Isaac
PL29 3RH
t (01208) 880264
e slipway@portisaachotel.com
w portisaachotel.com

**Westaway nr Port Isaac** ★★★★★
*Guest Accommodation*
**SILVER AWARD**
Trelights, Port Isaac PL29 3TF
t (01208) 881156
e info@westawaycornwall.com
w westawaycornwall.com

## PORTHCRESSA
Isles of Scilly

**The Lookout** ★★★★
*Bed & Breakfast*
Porthcressa, St Mary's, Isles of Scilly TR21 0JQ
t (01720) 422132

## PORTHLEVEN
Cornwall

**The Copper Kettle** ★★★★
*Guest Accommodation*
33 Fore Street, Porthleven
TR13 9HQ
t (01326) 565660
e tsue.copperkettle@btinternet.com
w cornishcopperkettle.com

## PORTLAND
Dorset

**Alessandria House** ★★
*Guest Accommodation*
71 Wakeham Easton, Portland
DT5 1HW
t (01305) 822270

**Brackenbury House** ★★★
*Bed & Breakfast*
Fortuneswell, Portland DT5 1LP
t (01305) 826509
e enquiries@brackenburyhouse.co.uk
w brackenburyhouse.co.uk

**Sea View** ★★★
*Bed & Breakfast*
151 Weston Street, Portland
DT5 2DG
t (01305) 821573
e stay@seaviewbandb.co.uk

**YHA Portland** ★★★ *Hostel*
Hardy House, Portland
DT5 1AU
t 0870 770 6000
e portland@yha.org.uk
w yha.org.uk

## PORTON
Wiltshire

**The Porton** ★★★ *Inn*
Station Approach, Porton
SP4 0LA
t (01980) 610203
e info@portonhotel.com
w portonhotel.com

## PORTSCATHO
Cornwall

**Hillside House** ★★★★
*Guest Accommodation*
8 The Square, Portscatho, St Mawes TR2 5HW
t (01872) 580526
e info@hillsidehouse-portscatho.co.uk
w hillsidehouse-portscatho.co.uk

**Rosevine Hotel** ★★★★★
*Guest Accommodation*
**GOLD AWARD**
Porthcurnick Beach, Portscatho, St Mawes
TR2 5EW
t (01872) 580206
w rosevine.co.uk

**Trewithian Farm** ★★★★
*Guest Accommodation*
Portscatho, Truro TR2 5EJ
t (01872) 580293
e enquiries@trewithian-farm.co.uk
w trewithian-farm.co.uk

## POSTBRIDGE
Devon

**Bellever YHA** ★★ *Hostel*
Bellever, Postbridge PL20 6TU
t (01822) 880227
e bellever@yha.org.uk
w yha.org.uk

**Runnage** *Camping Barn*
Runnage Farm, Postbridge
PL20 6TN
t (01822) 880222
e christine@runnagecampingbarns.fsnet.co.uk
w runnagecampingbarns.co.uk

## POTTERNE
Wiltshire

**Four Winds** ★★★
*Bed & Breakfast*
11 Silver Street, Potterne
SN10 5NQ
t (01380) 730334
e angelahousehold@hotmail.com

**Frogsleap** ★★★★
*Bed & Breakfast*
10 Blounts Court, Potterne
SN10 5QA
t (01380) 727761
e crisp@frogsleap.freeserve.co.uk

## POULSHOT
Wiltshire

**Poulshot Lodge** ★★
*Farmhouse*
Poulshot Road, Poulshot
SN10 1RQ
t (01380) 828255

## POUNDSTOCK
Cornwall

**Outdoor Adventure Ltd**
★★★ *Activity Accommodation*
Atlantic Court, Widemouth Bay, Bude EX23 0DF
t (01288) 361312

## PRAA SANDS
Cornwall

**Mzima** ★★★
*Guest Accommodation*
Penlee Close, Praa Sands
TR20 9SR
t (01736) 763856
e marianfoy@prussia-cove-holiday.com

## PRIDDY
Somerset

**Ebborways Farm** ★★
*Guest Accommodation*
Pelting Road, Wells BA5 3BA
t (01749) 676339
e info@ebborwayfarm-bandb.co.uk
w ebborwaysfarm.co.uk

## PURTINGTON
Somerset

**Purtington Barn** ★★★★
*Guest Accommodation*
Chard TA20 4DH
t (01460) 432078
e mail@purtingtonbarn.com
w purtingtonbarn.com

## QUEEN CAMEL
Somerset

**Dairy Court** ★★★★
*Guest Accommodation*
Wales, Queen Camel, Nr Yeovil
BA22 7PA
t (01935) 850003
e enquiries@dairycourt.com
w dairycourt.com

## RADSTOCK
Somerset

**The Radstock** ★★★ *Inn*
Market Place, Radstock
BA3 3AD
t (01761) 420776
e radstockhotel@thechapmansgroup.co.uk
w radstockhotel.co.uk/

## RAMSBURY
Wiltshire

**Marridge Hill Cottage** ★★★
*Bed & Breakfast*
Marridge Hill, Ramsbury
SN8 2HG
t (01672) 520486

## REDHILL
Somerset

**Hailstones Farm** ★★★★
*Farmhouse*
Bristol BS40 5TG
t (01934) 861178
e info@hailstonesfarmbandb.co.uk

## REDLYNCH
Wiltshire

**Forest Edge B&B** ★★★★
*Bed & Breakfast*
Lower Windyeats Cottage, Forest Road, Redlynch
SP5 2PU
t (01725) 511516
e forestedge@hotmail.co.uk
w newforestedge.co.uk

## REDRUTH
Cornwall

**Goonearl Cottage** ★★★★
*Guest House*
Wheal Rose, Scorrier, Redruth
TR16 5DF
t (01209) 891571
e goonearl@onetel.com
w goonearlcottage.com

**Tumblydown Farm** ★★★
*Guest Accommodation*
Tolgus Mount, Redruth
TR15 3TA
t (01209) 211191
w tumblydownfarm.co.uk

## REZARE
Cornwall

**Rezare Farmhouse** ★★★★
*Guest Accommodation*
**SILVER AWARD**
Rezare, Launceston PL15 9NX
t (01579) 371214
e anthony@rezarefarmhouse.co.uk
w rezarefarmhouse.co.uk

## ROCK
Cornwall

**Tzitzikama Lodge Guest House** ★★★★
*Guest Accommodation*
Rock Road, Rock, Wadebridge
PL27 6NP
t (01208) 862839
e tzitzikama.lodge@btinternet.com
w cornwall-online.co.uk

## ROSCROGGAN
Cornwall

**Roscroggan Chapel Guest House** ★★★ *Guest House*
Roscroggan Hill, Roscroggan
TR14 0JA
t (01209) 714696
e enquiries@accommodation-in-cornwall.com
w accommodation-in-cornwall.com

## RUAN HIGH LANES
Cornwall

**New Gonitor Farm** ★★★★
*Farmhouse*
Ruan High Lanes, Truro
TR2 5LE
t (01872) 501345
e rosemary@newgonitorfarm.wanadoo.co.uk

**Trenona Farm Holidays**
★★★ *Farmhouse*
Ruan High Lanes, Truro
TR2 5JS
t (01872) 501339
e info@trenonafarmholidays.co.uk
w trenonafarmholidays.co.uk

## RUAN MINOR
Cornwall

**Chyheira**
Rating Applied For
*Guest Accommodation*
Gun Hill, Ruan Minor
TR12 7LQ
t (01326) 290343
e chrissy@chyheira.co.uk
w chyheira.co.uk

**Skyber** ★★★★
*Bed & Breakfast*
Treal, Ruan Minor TR12 7LS
t (01326) 290684

## RUDFORD
Gloucestershire

**The Dark Barn Lodge**
★★★★
*Guest Accommodation*
Barbers Bridge, Rudford, Gloucester GL2 8DX
t (01452) 790412
e info@barbersbridge.co.uk
w barbersbridge.co.uk

## RUSHALL
Wiltshire

**Chestnuts Cottage** ★★★★
*Bed & Breakfast*
Church Lane, Rushall SN9 6EH
t (01980) 630976
e richard@chestnuts-cot.co.uk

**Little Thatch** ★★★
*Bed & Breakfast*
Rushall, Pewsey SN9 6EN
t (01980) 635282
e enewton@talktalk.net

## ST AGNES
Cornwall

**Little Trevellas Farm** ★★★
*Farmhouse*
Trevellas, St Agnes TR5 0XX
t (01872) 552945
e velvetcrystal@xln.co.uk

**Penkerris** ★★ *Guest House*
Penwinnick Road, St Agnes
TR5 0PA
t (01872) 552262
e info@penkerris.co.uk
w penkerris.co.uk

## ST AGNES
Isles of Scilly

**Hellweathers Guest House**
★★★ *Bed & Breakfast*
St Agnes TR22 0PL
t (01720) 422430

## ST AUSTELL
Cornwall

**Anchorage House** ★★★★★
*Guest Accommodation*
**GOLD AWARD**
Nettles Corner, Boscundle, St Austell PL25 3RH
t (01726) 814071
e info@anchoragehouse.co.uk
w anchoragehouse.co.uk

**The Beech Tree Guest House**
★★★★
*Guest Accommodation*
**SILVER AWARD**
23 Beech Road, St Austell
PL25 4TS
t (01726) 77461
e info@thebeechtreeguesthouse.co.uk
w thebeechtreeguesthouse.co.uk

**Cornerways Guest House**
★★★ *Guest House*
Penwinnick Road, St Austell
PL25 5DS
t (01726) 61579
e nwsurveys@aol.com

**Crossways** ★★★
*Guest Accommodation*
6 Cromwell Road, St Austell
PL25 4PS
t (01726) 77436
e enquiries@crosswaysbandb.co.uk
w crosswaysbandb.co.uk

**Greenbank** ★★★★
*Bed & Breakfast*
39 Southbourne Road, St Austell PL25 4RT
t (01726) 73326
e greenbank@cornish-riviera.co.uk
w cornish-riviera.co.uk/greenbank.htm

**Gwyndra House** ★★★
*Bed & Breakfast*
7 Kings Avenue, St Austell
PL25 4TT
t (01726) 73870
e gwyndrahouse@btconnect.com
w gwyndrahouse.co.uk

**Highland Court Lodge**
★★★★★
*Guest Accommodation*
**GOLD AWARD**
Biscovey Road, Biscovey
PL24 2HW
t (01726) 813320
e enquiries@highlandcourt.co.uk
w highlandcourt.co.uk

**Holly House** ★★★★
*Bed & Breakfast*
84 Truro Road, St Austell
PL25 5JS
t (01726) 70022
e penny@hollyhousecornwall.co.uk
w hollyhousecornwall.co.uk

**Little Grey Cottage** ★★★★
*Bed & Breakfast*
Trethurgy, St Austell PL26 8YD
t (01726) 850486
e info@littlegreycottagebb.co.uk
w littlegreycottagebb.co.uk

**Lowarn** ★★★★
*Bed & Breakfast*
16 Poltair Road, St Austell
PL25 4LT
t (01726) 61669
e lowarne@aol.com

**Lowarth Gwyth** ★★★
*Guest Accommodation*
80 Truro Road, St Austell
PL25 5JS
t (01726) 70513
e ann@lowarthgwyth.co.uk
w lowarthgwyth.co.uk

**Lower Barn Boutique B&B**
★★★★★ *Guest House*
**SILVER AWARD**
Bosue, St Ewe PL26 6EU
t (01726) 844881
e janie@bosue.co.uk
w bosue.co.uk

**Mandalay** ★★★ *Guest House*
School Hill, Mevagissey
PL26 6TQ
t (01726) 842435
e jillconneely@yahoo.com
w mandalayhotel.freeserve.co.uk

**Pen Star House** ★★★★
*Bed & Breakfast*
20 Cromwell Road, St Austell
PL25 4PS
t (01726) 61367
e pen.star@btinternet.com
w penstarguesthouse.co.uk

**Spindrift – St Austell** ★★★
*Bed & Breakfast*
London Apprentice, St Austell
PL26 7AR
t (01726) 69316
e mcguffspindrift@hotmail.com
w spindrift-guesthouse.co.uk

**Tall Ships** ★★★★★
*Bed & Breakfast*
2 Eleven Doors, Charlestown
PL25 3NZ
t (01726) 871095
e tallshipscharlestown@tiscali.co.uk
w tallshipscharlestown.com

**Trevu** ★★★★
*Bed & Breakfast*
10 Courtney Road, St Austell
PL25 4JF
t (01726) 64480
e trevu@tiscali.co.uk
w trevu.co.uk

## ST BRIAVELS
Gloucestershire

**St Briavels Castle YHA** ★★
*Hostel*
Church Street, St Briavels, Lydney GL15 6RG
t 0870 770 6040
e stbriavels@yha.org.uk
w yha.org.uk

## ST BURYAN
Cornwall

**Boskenna Home Farm**
★★★★
*Guest Accommodation*
**SILVER AWARD**
St Buryan, Penzance
TR19 6DQ
t (01736) 810705
e julia@boskenna.co.uk
w boskenna.co.uk

**Downs Barn Farm** ★★★★★
*Farmhouse* **SILVER AWARD**
St Buryan TR19 6DG
t (01736) 810295
e stay@downsbarnfarm.co.uk

**Tredinney Farm B&B**
★★★★
*Guest Accommodation*
Crows-An-Wra, St Buryan
TR19 6HX
t (01736) 810352
e rosemary.warren@btopenworld.com
w tredinneyfarm.co.uk

**Tregiffian Farm** ★★★★
*Farmhouse* **SILVER AWARD**
St Buryan, Penzance TR19 6BG
t (01736) 810243
e vicki@tregiffianfarm.co.uk
w tregiffianfarm.co.uk

**Tregurnow Farm** ★★★★
*Guest Accommodation*
St Buryan, Penzance TR19 6BL
t (01736) 810255
e tregurnow@lamorna.biz
w lamorna.biz

**Trelew Farm** ★★★★
*Guest Accommodation*
St Buryan, Penzance TR19 6ED
t (01736) 810308
e info@trelew.co.uk
w trelew.co.uk

## ST COLUMB MAJOR
Cornwall

**Pennatillie Farm** ★★★★★
*Farmhouse* **SILVER AWARD**
Talskiddy, St Columb Major
TR9 6EF
t (01637) 880280
e angelacolgrove@btconnect.com
w cornish-riviera.co.uk/pennatilliefarm.htm

## ST ERTH PRAZE
Cornwall

**Bostrase Country Guest House** ★★★★
*Guest Accommodation*
Tolroy Farm, Off Tolroy Road, Hayle TR27 6HG
t (01736) 754644
e bostrasecottage@tolroy.wanadoo.co.uk
w bostraseholidays.co.uk

## ST EWE
Cornwall

**The Barns at Polsue**
★★★★★ *Guest House*
**SILVER AWARD**
St Ewe, St Austell PL26 6EW
t (01726) 843686
e polsue@aol.com
w polsue.co.uk

## ST ISSEY
Cornwall

**Cannalidgey Villa Farm**
★★★★ *Farmhouse*
Trenance, Wadebridge
PL27 7RB
t (01208) 812276
e cannalidgey@btinternet.com

**Olde Tredore House** ★★★★
*Bed & Breakfast*
St Issey, Wadebridge
PL27 7QS
t (01841) 540291

**Rose Park** ★★★
*Bed & Breakfast*
Penrose Farm, St Issey, Wadebridge PL27 7RJ
t (01208) 812595

## ST IVES
Cornwall

**Anchorage Guest House**
★★★★
*Guest Accommodation*
5 Bunkers Hill, St Ives TR26 1LJ
t (01736) 797135
e info@theanchoragebandb.co.uk
w theanchoragebandb.co.uk

**Blue Hayes** ★★★★★
*Guest Accommodation*
**GOLD AWARD**
Trelyon Avenue, St Ives
TR26 2AD
t (01736) 797129
e info@bluehayes.co.uk
w bluehayes.co.uk

**Blue Mist** ★★★★
*Guest Accommodation*
6 The Warren, St Ives
TR26 2EA
t (01736) 793386
e stay@blue-mist.co.uk
w blue-mist.co.uk

**Byways** ★★★
*Bed & Breakfast*
22 Steamers Hill, Angarrack
TR27 5JB
t (01736) 753463
e bywaysbb@lineone.net
w bywaysbb.co.uk

**Carlill** ★★★★ *Guest House*
9 Porthminster Terrace, St Ives
TR26 2DQ
t (01736) 796738
e carlill@vodafoneemail.co.uk
w visitcornwall.co.uk

**Carlyon Guest House** ★★★
*Guest House*
18 The Terrace, St Ives
TR26 2BP
t (01736) 795317
e andrea.papworth@btinternet.com
w carlyon-stives.co.uk

**Chy An Gwedhen** ★★★★
*Guest Accommodation*
St Ives Road, Carbis Bay, St Ives TR26 2JN
**t (01736) 798684**
**e info@chyangwedhen.com**
**w chyangwedhen.com**

**Dean Court** ★★★★★
*Guest Accommodation*
**SILVER AWARD**
Trelyon Avenue, St Ives
TR26 2AD
t (01736) 796023
e info@deancourt.vispa.com
w deancourthotel.com

**The Grey Mullet Guest House** ★★★★
*Guest Accommodation*
2 Bunkers Hill, St Ives TR26 1LJ
**t (01736) 796635**
**e greymulletguesthouse@lineone.net**
**w touristnetuk.com/sw/greymullet**

**Longships** ★★★★
*Guest Accommodation*
Talland Road, St Ives TR26 2DF
t (01736) 798180
e longshipshotel@hotmail.co.uk
w longships-hotel.co.uk

**Monterey** ★★★★
*Guest Accommodation*
7 Clodgy View, St Ives
TR26 1JG
t (01736) 794248
e info@monterey-stives.fsnet.co.uk
w monterey-stives.co.uk

**The Olive Branch Guest House**
Rating Applied For
*Bed & Breakfast*
6 Porthminster Terrace, St Ives
TR26 2DQ
t (01736) 795363
e info@theolivebranchstives.co.uk
w theolivebranchstives.co.uk

**Organic Panda Bed & Breakfast** ★★★★
*Guest Accommodation*
1 Pednolver Terrace, St Ives
TR26 2EL
t (01736) 793890
e info@organicpanda.co.uk
w organicpanda.co.uk

**Sea Breeze** ★★★★
*Guest Accommodation*
**SILVER AWARD**
5 Higher Trewidden Road, The Belyars, St Ives TR26 2DP
t (01736) 797549
e jill.yelling@tiscali.co.uk
w seabreeze-stives.co.uk

**Shun Lee House** ★★★★★
*Bed & Breakfast*
**GOLD AWARD**
Trelyon Avenue, St Ives
TR26 2AD
t 07756 012406
e terry@shunleehotel.co.uk
w shunleehotel.co.uk

**Tregony Guest House** ★★★★
*Guest Accommodation*
1 Clodgy View, St Ives
TR26 1JG
t (01736) 795884
e info@tregony.com
w tregony.com

**Treloyhan Manor** ★★★
*Guest Accommodation*
St Ives TR26 2AL
t (01736) 796240
e treloyhan@christianguild.co.uk
w cgholidays.co.uk

### ST JULIOT
Cornwall

**Higher PennyCrocker Farm** ★★★ *Farmhouse*
St Juliot, Boscastle PL35 0BY
t (01840) 250488
e pennycrocker@hotmail.co.uk
w pennycrocker-boscastle.co.uk

**The Old Rectory** ★★★★★
*Guest Accommodation*
**GOLD AWARD**
St Juliot, Boscastle PL35 0BT
t (01840) 250225
e sally@stjuliot.com
w stjuliot.com

### ST JUST
Cornwall

**Land's End YHA** ★★ *Hostel*
Letcha Vean, Cot Valley, St Just-in-Penwith TR19 7NT
t (01736) 788437

### ST JUST-IN-PENWITH
Cornwall

**Bosavern House** ★★★★
*Guest House*
Bosavern, St Just TR19 7RD
t (01736) 788301
e info@bosavern.com
w bosavern.com

**Boswedden House** ★★★
*Guest Accommodation*
Cape Cornwall, St Just
TR19 7NJ
t (01736) 788733
e thelmagriffiths2002@yahoo.co.uk
w boswedden.org.uk

**The Commercial** ★★★★
*Guest Accommodation*
13 Market Square, St Just
TR19 7HE
t (01736) 788455
e enquiries@commercial-hotel.co.uk
w commercial-hotel.co.uk

### ST JUST IN ROSELAND
Cornwall

**Roundhouse Barns** ★★★★
*Bed & Breakfast*
Truro TR2 5JJ
**t (01872) 580038**
**e info@roundhousebarnholidays.co.uk**
**w roundhousebarnholidays.co.uk**

### ST KEVERNE
Cornwall

**Old Temperance House** ★★★★
*Guest Accommodation*
**SILVER AWARD**
The Square, St Keverne
TR12 6NA
t (01326) 280986
e info@oldtemperancehouse.co.uk
w oldtemperancehouse.co.uk

### ST KEW
Cornwall

**Lane End Farm B&B** ★★★★
*Bed & Breakfast*
Pendoggett, Port Isaac
PL30 3HH
t (01208) 880013
e nabmonk@tiscali.co.uk
w visitwadebridge.com

**Tregellist Farm** ★★★★
*Guest Accommodation*
**SILVER AWARD**
Tregellist, St Kew PL30 3HG
t (01208) 880537
e jillcleave@tregellist.fsbusiness.co.uk
w tregellistfarm.co.uk

### ST LEVAN
Cornwall

**Sea View House** ★★★★
*Guest Accommodation*
The Valley, Porthcurno
TR19 6JX
t (01736) 810638
e svhouse@btinternet.com
w seaviewhouseporthcurno.com

### ST MABYN
Cornwall

**Treglown House** ★★★★
*Guest Accommodation*
Haywood Farm, St Mabyn, Wadebridge PL30 3BU
t (01208) 841896
e enquiries@treglownhouse.co.uk
w treglownhouse.co.uk

### ST MARTIN
Cornwall

**Windermere House** ★★★
*Bed & Breakfast*
St Martin's, Looe PL13 1NX
t (01503) 262035
e windermerehouse@btconnect.com
w windermerehouse.co.uk

### ST MARY'S
Isles of Scilly

**Anjeric Guest House** ★★★
*Guest House*
Lower Strand, St Mary's
TR21 0PS
t (01720) 422700
e judyarcher@yahoo.co.uk
w scillyonline.co.uk/accomm/anjeric.html

**Annet** ★★★★
*Bed & Breakfast*
**SILVER AWARD**
St Mary's TR21 0NF
t (01720) 422441
e holidays@annet-cottage.co.uk
w annet-cottage.co.uk

**April Cottage** ★★★★
*Bed & Breakfast*
**SILVER AWARD**
Church Road, St Mary's, Isles of Scilly TR21 0NA
t (01720) 422279
e louisehicks@btinternet.com

**Armeria** ★★ *Bed & Breakfast*
1 Porthloo Terrace, St Mary's
TR21 0NF
t (01720) 422961
e dolphindesigns@btinternet.com

**Auriga Guest House** ★★★★
*Bed & Breakfast*
Porthcressa Road, St Mary's
TR21 0JL
t (01720) 422637
e aurigascilly@aol.com
w scillyonline.co.uk/accomm/auriga.html

**Beachfield House** ★★★★
*Guest House*
Porthloo TR21 0NE
t (01720) 422463
e whomersley@supanet.com

**Belmont** ★★★ *Guest House*
Church Road, St Mary's
TR21 0NA
t (01720) 423154
e enquiries@the-belmont.freeserve.co.uk
w the-belmont.freeserve.co.uk

**Blue Carn Cottage** ★★★★
*Farmhouse*
Old Town, St Mary's
TR21 0NH
t (01720) 422309
e philjroberts@tiscali.co.uk

**Broomfields** ★★★★
*Bed & Breakfast*
Church Road, St Mary's
TR21 0NA
t (01720) 422309

**Buckingham House** ★★★
*Guest House*
The Bank, St Mary's TR21 0HY
t (01720) 422543

**Bylet** ★★★ *Guest House*
Church Road, St Mary's
TR21 0NA
t (01720) 422479
e thebylet@bushinternet.com
w byletholidays.com

**Carntop Guest House**
★★★★ *Guest House*
**SILVER AWARD**
Church Road, St Mary's
TR21 0NA
**t** (01720) 423763
**w** carntop.co.uk

**Colossus** ★★★
*Bed & Breakfast*
Pilot's Retreat, Church Road, St Mary's TR21 0NA
**t** (01720) 423631
**e** enquiries@colossus-scilly.co.uk
**w** colossus-scilly.co.uk

**Crebinick House** ★★★★
*Guest House* **SILVER AWARD**
Church Street, St Mary's, Isles of Scilly TR21 0JT
**t** (01720) 422968
**e** enquiries@crebinick.co.uk
**w** crebinick.co.uk

**Eastbank** ★★★★
*Bed & Breakfast*
Porthloo, St Mary's, Isles of Scilly TR21 0NE
**t** (01720) 423695
**e** enquiries@scilly-holidays.co.uk
**w** scilly-holidays.co.uk

**Evergreen Cottage Guest House** ★★★★ *Guest House*
The Parade, Hugh Town
TR21 0LP
**t** (01720) 422711

**Freesia Guesthouse** ★★★★
*Guest House*
The Parade, St Mary's
TR21 0LP
**t** (01720) 423676
**e** freesiaguesthouse@hotmail.com

**Garrison House** ★★★★
*Bed & Breakfast*
**SILVER AWARD**
Garrison Hill, St Mary's
TR21 0LS
**t** (01720) 422972
**e** garrisonhouse@aol.com
**w** isles-of-scilly.co.uk/guesthouses

**Gunner Rock** ★★★★
*Bed & Breakfast*
Jacksons Hill, Isles of Scilly
TR21 0JZ
**t** (01720) 422595

**Isles of Scilly Country Guest House** ★★★ *Guest House*
Sage House, High Lanes
TR21 0NW
**t** (01720) 422440
**e** scillyguesthouse@hotmail.co.uk
**w** scillyguesthouse.co.uk

**Kistvaen** ★★★★
*Bed & Breakfast*
Sally Port, St Mary's, Isles of Scilly TR21 0JE
**t** (01720) 422002
**e** chivy002@aol.com
**w** kistvaen.co.uk

**Lynwood** ★★★★
*Bed & Breakfast*
Church Street, St Mary's, Isles of Scilly TR21 0JT
**t** (01720) 423313

**Lyonnesse Guest House**
★★★ *Guest House*
Lower Strand, St Mary's, Isles of Scilly TR21 0PS
**t** (01720) 422458

**Mincarlo** ★★★ *Guest House*
Strand, St Mary's, Isles of Scilly
TR21 0PT
**t** (01720) 422513
**e** manager@mincarlo-ios.co.uk
**w** mincarlo-ios.co.uk

**Rose Cottage** ★★★★
*Bed & Breakfast*
**SILVER AWARD**
Strand, St Mary's TR21 0PT
**t** (01720) 422078
**e** rosecottage@infinnet.co.uk

**St Hellena** ★★★
*Bed & Breakfast*
13 Garrison Lane, St Mary's
TR21 0JD
**t** (01720) 423231
**e** mcguiness@st-hellena.fsnet.co.uk
**w** http://sthellena.mysite.freeserve.com

**Santa Maria** ★★★★
*Guest House*
Sallyport, St Mary's TR21 0JE
**t** (01720) 422687

**Shamrock** ★★★★
*Bed & Breakfast*
High Lanes, St Mary's, Isles of Scilly TR21 0NW
**t** (01720) 423269

**Shearwater Guest House**
★★★ *Guest House*
The Parade, St Mary's
TR21 0LP
**t** (01720) 422402
**e** griswalds00@hotmail.com
**w** shearwater-guest-house.co.uk

**Sylina Guesthouse** ★★★★
*Guest House*
Mcfarlands Downs, St Mary's
TR21 0NS
**t** (01720) 422129
**e** relax@sylina.co.uk
**w** sylina.co.uk

**Tolman House** ★★★★
*Guest Accommodation*
**SILVER AWARD**
Old Town, St Mary's, Isles of Scilly TR21 0NH
**t** (01720) 422967
**e** tolmanhouse@hotmail.co.uk
**w** scilly-oldtown.com

**Trelawney** ★★★★
*Guest House*
Church Street, St Mary's
TR21 0JT
**t** (01720) 422377
**e** jharlin@hotmail.com
**w** trelawney-ios.co.uk

**Veronica Lodge** ★★★
*Bed & Breakfast*
The Garrison, St Mary's
TR21 0LS
**t** (01720) 422585
**e** veronicalodge@freenetname.co.uk

**Westford House** ★★★★
*Guest House*
Church Street, St Mary's
TR21 0JT
**t** (01720) 422510

**The Wheelhouse** ★★★★
*Guest House*
Little Porth, St Mary's, Isles of Scilly TR21 0JG
**t** (01720) 422719

**Wingletang Guest House**
★★★ *Guest House*
The Parade, St Mary's
TR21 0LP
**t** (01720) 422381

## ST MAWES
Cornwall

**Gwelesmor** ★★★
*Bed & Breakfast*
Gwelesmor House, 18 Polvarth Estate, St Mawes TR2 5AT
**t** (01326) 270731
**e** phyllismichell@supanet.com

**Trenestral Farm** ★★★
*Farmhouse*
Ruan High Lanes, Truro
TR2 5LX
**t** (01872) 501259

## ST MAWGAN
Cornwall

**Dalswinton House** ★★★★
*Guest Accommodation*
St Mawgan-in-Pydar, Nr Padstow TR8 4EZ
**t** (01637) 860385
**e** dalswintonhouse@tiscali.co.uk
**w** dalswinton.com

## ST MERRYN
Cornwall

**Greenacres** ★★★★
*Bed & Breakfast*
Padstow PL28 8JZ
**t** (01841) 520478
**e** kelly@kellylynden.orangehome.co.uk

**Tregavone Farm** ★★★
*Farmhouse*
St Merryn, Padstow PL28 8JZ
**t** (01841) 520148

**Trewithen Farmhouse**
★★★★
*Guest Accommodation*
**SILVER AWARD**
Trewithen Farm, St Merryn, Padstow PL28 8JZ
**t** (01841) 520420
**e** maystrewithen@aol.com
**w** trewithenfarmhouse.co.uk

## ST MINVER
Cornwall

**Tredower Barton** ★★★
*Bed & Breakfast*
St Minver, Wadebridge
PL27 6RG
**t** (01208) 813501

**Tregwormond Grange**
Rating Applied For
*Farmhouse*
St Minver, Wadebridge
PL27 6RE
**t** (01208) 869660
**e** janetsluggett@hotmail.co.uk

## ST NEOT
Cornwall

**Higher Hobbs** ★★★★
*Bed & Breakfast*
Park Farm, St Neot, Liskeard
PL14 6PU
**t** (01579) 321700
**e** malcmandy@aol.com

**Higher Searles Down**
★★★★ *Bed & Breakfast*
**SILVER AWARD**
St Neot, Bodmin PL14 6QA
**t** (01208) 821412
**e** glen@hsdown.go-plus.net
**w** hsdown.go-plus.net

**Serena House** ★★★★
*Bed & Breakfast*
St Neot, Liskeard PL14 6NG
**t** (01579) 326079

## ST NEWLYN EAST
Cornwall

**Trewerry Mill Guest House**
★★★ *Guest Accommodation*
Trewerry Mill, Trerice, Truro
TR8 5GS
**t** (01872) 510345
**e** trewerry.mill@talktalk.net
**w** trewerrymill.co.uk

## ST TEATH
Cornwall

**Paths End** ★★★★
*Bed & Breakfast*
Trewennen Road, Bodmin
PL30 3JZ
**t** (01208) 850441
**e** btg65@hotmail.com
**w** palmcottage.co.uk

## ST WENN
Cornwall

**Trewithian Farm** ★★★★
*Farmhouse*
St Wenn, Bodmin PL30 5PH
**t** (01208) 895181
**e** ttewithian@hotmail.com

## SALCOMBE
Devon

**Burton Farmhouse and Garden Room Restaurant**
★★★★ *Farmhouse*
Burton Farm, Galmpton
TQ7 3EY
**t** (01548) 561210
**e** anne@burtonfarm.co.uk
**w** burtonfarm.co.uk

**Salcombe YHA** ★★★ *Hostel*
Overbecks, Sharpitor, Salcombe TQ8 8LW
**t** (01548) 842856
**e** salcombe@yha.org.uk
**w** yha.org.uk

## SALISBURY
Wiltshire

**2 Park Lane** ★★★★
*Guest Accommodation*
Castle Road, Salisbury SP1 3NP
**t** (01722) 321001
**e** helen076@btconnect.com
**w** 2parklane.co.uk

**4 Roman Road B&B** ★★★
*Bed & Breakfast*
4 Roman Road, Salisbury
SP2 9BH
**t** (01722) 325808
**e** davidstepkirkman@aol.com

**50 Trinity Street**
Rating Applied For
*Bed & Breakfast*
Trinity Street, Salisbury
SP1 2BD
**t** (01722) 410253
**e** steviesteph@hotmail.co.uk

**78 Belle Vue Road** ★★
*Bed & Breakfast*
Salisbury SP1 3YD
t (01722) 329477

**Alabare House** ★★
*Guest House*
15 Tollgate Road, Salisbury
SP1 2JA
t (01722) 340206
e bookings@alabare.org
w alabare.org

**Ballantynes** ★★
*Bed & Breakfast*
114 Netherhampton Road,
Salisbury SP2 8LZ
t (01722) 325743
e info@ballantynesbandb.com
w ballantynesbandb.com

**Bridge Farm** ★★★★
*Farmhouse* **SILVER AWARD**
Lower Road, Britford SP5 4DY
t (01722) 332376
e mail@bridgefarmbb.co.uk
w bridgefarmbb.co.uk

**Burcombe Manor** ★★
*Bed & Breakfast*
Burcombe Lane, Burcombe,
Salisbury SP2 0EJ
t (01722) 744288
e nickatburcombemanor@btinternet.com
w burcombemanor.co.uk

**Byways House** ★★★
*Guest House*
31 Fowlers Road, Salisbury
SP1 2QP
t (01722) 328364
e info@bywayshouse.co.uk
w bywayshouse.co.uk

**Cawden Cottage** ★★★
*Bed & Breakfast*
Stratford Toney, Salisbury
SP5 4AT
t (01722) 718463
e cawdencottage@yahoo.co.uk
w cawdencottage.co.uk

**Cherrypickers**
Rating Applied For
*Guest Accommodation*
6 Harlington Road, Salisbury
SP2 7LG
t (01722) 335613
e geoffanddi@cherrypickersbandb.co.uk

**Edwardian Lodge** ★★★★
*Guest House*
59 Castle Road, Salisbury
SP1 3RH
t (01722) 413329
e enquiries@edwardianlodge.co.uk
w edwardianlodge.co.uk

**Farthings** ★★★
*Bed & Breakfast*
9 Swaynes Close, Salisbury
SP1 3AE
t (01722) 330749
e gill.rodwell@tiscali.co.uk
w farthingsbandb.co.uk

**Highveld** ★★★
*Bed & Breakfast*
44 Hulse Road, Salisbury
SP1 3LY
t (01722) 338172
e y.sfakianos@btopenworld.com
w salisburybedandbreakfast.com

**Holly Tree House** ★★
*Bed & Breakfast*
53 Wyndham Road, Salisbury
SP1 3AH
t (01722) 322955

**Kinvara House** ★★★
*Bed & Breakfast*
28 Castle Road, Salisbury
SP1 3RJ
t (01722) 325233
e kinvarahouse@aol.com
w kinvarahouse.co.uk

**Leena's Guest House** ★★★
*Guest House*
50 Castle Road, Salisbury
SP1 3RL
t (01722) 335419

**Manor Farm** ★★★★
*Farmhouse*
Burcombe Lane, Burcombe,
Salisbury SP2 0EJ
t (01722) 742177
e suecombes@manorfarmburcombe.fsnet.co.uk
w manorfarmburcombebandb.com

**The Old Rectory Bed & Breakfast** ★★★★
*Bed & Breakfast*
75 Belle Vue Road, Salisbury
SP1 3YE
t (01722) 502702
e stay@theoldrectory-bb.co.uk
w theoldrectory-bb.co.uk

**Rokeby Guest House**
★★★★ *Guest House*
**SILVER AWARD**
3 Wain-A-Long Road, Salisbury
SP1 1LJ
t (01722) 329800
e karenrogers@rokebyguesthouse.co.uk
w rokebyguesthouse.co.uk

**St Anns House**
Rating Applied For
*Guest House*
32 St Ann Street, Salisbury
SP1 2DP
t (01722) 335657
e info@stannshouse.co.uk
w stannshouse.co.uk

**Salisbury Youth Hostel Association** ★★★ *Hostel*
Milford Hill House, Milford Hill
SP1 2QW
t (01722) 327572
e salisbury@yha.org.uk
w yha.org.uk

**Sarum College** ★★
*Guest Accommodation*
19 The Close, Salisbury
SP1 2EE
t (01722) 424800
e lc@sarum.ac.uk
w sarum.ac.uk

**Spire House** ★★★★
*Guest Accommodation*
**SILVER AWARD**
84 Exeter Street, Salisbury
SP1 2SE
t (01722) 339213
e spire.enquiries@btinternet.com
w salisbury-bedandbreakfast.com

**Stratford Lodge** ★★
*Guest Accommodation*
4 Park Lane, Salisbury SP1 3NP
t (01722) 325177
e enquiries@stratfordlodge.co.uk
w stratfordlodge.co.uk

**Swaynes Firs Farm** ★★★
*Farmhouse*
Grimsdyke, Coombe Bissett
SP5 5RF
t (01725) 519240
e swaynes.firs@virgin.net
w swaynesfirs.co.uk

**Victoria Lodge Guest House**
★★★ *Guest House*
61 Castle Road, Salisbury
SP1 3RH
t (01722) 320586
e mail@viclodge.co.uk
w viclodge.co.uk

**Walsworth House** ★★★★★
*Bed & Breakfast*
31 Albany Road, Salisbury
SP1 3YQ
t (01722) 504074
e tkenny@thetalentmanager.co.uk
w walsworthhouse.webeden.co.uk

**Wyndham Park Lodge**
★★★★
*Guest Accommodation*
51 Wyndham Road, Salisbury
SP1 3AB
t (01722) 416517
e enquiries@wyndhamparklodge.co.uk
w wyndhamparklodge.co.uk

### SALTASH Cornwall

**Kilna House** ★★★
*Guest Accommodation*
Tideford, Saltash PL12 5AD
t (01752) 851236
e kilnahouse01@aol.com
w kilnaguesthouse.co.uk

**Riverview B&B** ★★★
*Bed & Breakfast*
82 North Road, Saltash
PL12 6BE
t (01752) 840141
e dvpeterson@btinternet.com
w riverview-saltash.com

### SAMPFORD ARUNDEL Somerset

**Selby House** ★★★★
*Bed & Breakfast*
**SILVER AWARD**
Sampford Arundel, Wellington
TA21 9QE
t (01823) 667384
e enquiries@selbyhouse.co.uk
w selbyhouse.co.uk

### SAMPFORD PEVERELL Devon

**Leonard Moor House**
★★★★ *Farmhouse*
Leonard Moor, Nr Sampford
Peverell, Tiverton EX16 7EL
t (01884) 820881 & 07813 618607
e sue.quick1@btinternet.com
w leonardhousebbaccommodation.com

### SANDFORD Devon

**Ashridge Farm** ★★★★
*Bed & Breakfast*
Sandford EX17 4EN
t (01363) 774292
e info@ashdridgefarm.co.uk
w ashridgefarm.co.uk/

### SANDHURST Gloucestershire

**Brawn Farm** ★★★★
*Farmhouse*
Sandhurst Lane, Sandhurst
GL2 9NR
t (01452) 731010
e brawnfarm@yahoo.co.uk

### SEATON Devon

**Beach End** ★★★★
*Bed & Breakfast*
**SILVER AWARD**
8 Trevelyan Road, Seaton
EX12 2NL
t (01297) 23388

**Beaumont** ★★★★
*Guest House*
Castle Hill, Seaton EX12 2QW
t (01297) 20832
e jane@lymebay.demon.co.uk
w smoothhound.co.uk/hotels/beaumon1.html

**Gatcombe Farm** ★★★★
*Farmhouse*
Seaton EX12 3AA
t (01297) 21235
e bedandbreakfast@gatcombefarm.co.uk
w gatcombe-farm-devon.co.uk

**Holmleigh House Bed & Breakfast** ★★★★
*Guest Accommodation*
Homeleigh, Sea Hill, Seaton
EX12 2QT
t (01297) 625671
e gaynorjones_8@hotmail.com
w holmleighhouse.co.uk

**Pebbles** ★★★★
*Guest Accommodation*
**SILVER AWARD**
Sea Hill, Seaton EX12 2QU
t (01297) 22678
e enquiries@pebbleshouse.co.uk
w pebbleshouse.co.uk

### SEEND Wiltshire

**Rew Farm** ★★★★
*Farmhouse*
Seend Cleeve, Melksham
SN12 6PS
t (01380) 828289

### SELSLEY Gloucestershire

**Little Owl Cottage** ★★★★
*Bed & Breakfast*
**SILVER AWARD**
Selsey Hill, Selsley GL5 5LN
t (01453) 757050
e littleowlcottage@sky.com
w littleowlcottagebedandbreakfast.co.uk

**SEMINGTON**
**Wiltshire**

**Newhouse Farm** ★★★★
*Bed & Breakfast*
Littleton, Semington BA14 6LF
**t** (01380) 870349
**e** stay@newhousefarmwilts.co.uk
**w** newhousefarmwilts.co.uk

**SENNEN**
**Cornwall**

**Treeve Moor House** ★★★★
*Guest Accommodation*
Sennen TR19 7AE
**t** (01736) 871284
**e** info@firstandlastcottages.co.uk
**w** firstandlastcottages.co.uk

**SHAFTESBURY**
**Dorset**

**Glebe Farm** ★★★★★
*Bed & Breakfast*
**SILVER AWARD**
High Street, Ashmore SP5 5AE
**t** (01747) 811974
**e** stay@glebefarmbandb.co.uk
**w** glebefarmbandb.co.uk

**The Old Forge** ★★★
*Bed & Breakfast*
Compton Abbas, Shaftesbury SP7 0NQ
**t** (01747) 811881
**e** theoldforge@hotmail.com
**w** theoldforgedorset.co.uk

**The Retreat** ★★★★
*Guest House* **SILVER AWARD**
47 Bell Street, Shaftesbury SP7 8AE
**t** (01747) 850372
**e** info@the-retreat.org.uk
**w** the-retreat.org.uk

**SHAVE CROSS**
**Dorset**

**Shave Cross Inn** ★★★★ *Inn*
**GOLD AWARD**
Bridport DT6 6HW
**t** (01308) 868358
**e** roy.warburton@virgin.net
**w** theshavecrossinn.co.uk

**SHEPTON MALLET**
**Somerset**

**Belfield House** ★★★
*Guest Accommodation*
34 Charlton Road, Shepton Mallet BA4 5PA
**t** (01749) 344353
**e** info@belfieldhouse.com
**w** belfieldhouse.com

**Bowlish House** ★★★★
*Restaurant with Rooms*
Coombe Lane, Shepton Mallet BA4 5JD
**t** (01749) 342022
**e** info@bowlishhouse.com
**w** bowlishhouse.com

**Littleridge** ★★
*Bed & Breakfast*
46 Compton Road, Shepton Mallet BA4 5QT
**t** (01749) 342983

**Maplestone** ★★★★
*Guest Accommodation*
Quarr, Shepton Mallet BA4 5NP
**t** (01749) 347979
**e** info@maplestonehall.co.uk
**w** maplestonehall.co.uk

**Middleton House** ★★★★
*Guest Accommodation*
68 Compton Road, Shepton Mallet BA4 5QT
**t** (01749) 343720
**e** lynandbob@shepton.freeserve.co.uk

**Temple House Farm** ★★★★
*Farmhouse*
Chelynch Road, Shepton Mallet BA4 4RQ
**t** (01749) 880294
**e** reakesbedbugs@aol.com
**w** templehousefarm.co.uk

**SHERBORNE**
**Dorset**

**The Alders** ★★★★
*Bed & Breakfast*
Sandford Orcas, Sherborne DT9 4SB
**t** (01963) 220666
**e** jonsue@thealdersbb.com
**w** thealdersbb.com

**Bridleways** ★★★
*Bed & Breakfast*
Oborne Road, Sherborne DT9 3RX
**t** (01935) 814716
**e** bridleways@tiscali.co.uk

**Cumberland House** ★★★★
*Bed & Breakfast*
**SILVER AWARD**
Green Hill, Sherborne DT9 4EP
**t** (01935) 817554
**e** sandie@bandbdorset.co.uk
**w** bandbdorset.co.uk

**Honeycombe View** ★★★
*Bed & Breakfast*
Lower Clatcombe, Sherborne DT9 4RH
**t** (01935) 814644
**e** honeycombower@talktalk.net

**The Pheasants B&B** ★★★★
*Bed & Breakfast*
24 Greenhill, Sherborne DT9 4EW
**t** (01935) 815252
**e** info@thepheasants.com
**w** thepheasants.com

**SHILLINGFORD**
**Devon**

**Barleycorn House B&B** ★★★★
*Guest Accommodation*
Shillingford, Tiverton EX16 9AZ
**t** (01398) 332026
**w** barleycornhouse.co.uk

**SHIPHAM**
**Somerset**

**Penscot Inn** ★★★ *Inn*
The Square, Winscombe BS25 1TW
**t** (01934) 842659
**w** penscot.co.uk

**SHUTTA**
**Cornwall**

**Glenfeaden**
Rating Applied For
*Bed & Breakfast*
1 Glenfeaden, Shutta, Looe PL13 1LY
**t** (01503) 264320

**Meneglaze Bed & Breakfast**
★★★★ *Guest House*
Shutta, Looe PL13 1LU
**t** (01503) 269227
**e** meneglaze@tiscali.co.uk

**SIDBURY**
**Devon**

**Rose Cottage Guest House** ★★★★
*Guest Accommodation*
**SILVER AWARD**
Greenhead, Sidbury EX10 0RH
**t** (01395) 597357 & 07891 197218
**e** roz.kendall@btinternet.com
**w** rosecottagesidbury.co.uk

**SIDMOUTH**
**Devon**

**The Barn And Pinn Cottage Guest House** ★★★★
*Guest House* **SILVER AWARD**
Bowd Cross, Sidmouth EX10 0ND
**t** (01395) 513613
**e** jean-whittaker@tiscali.co.uk
**w** barnandpinncottage.co.uk/

**Berwick House** ★★★★
*Guest Accommodation*
Salcombe Road, Sidmouth EX10 8PX
**t** (01395) 513621
**e** reservations@berwick-house.co.uk
**w** berwick-house.co.uk

**Burscombe Farm** ★★★
*Farmhouse*
Burscombe, Sidbury EX10 0QB
**t** (01395) 597648
**e** burscombefarm@fwi.co.uk
**w** burscombefarm-devon.co.uk

**Canterbury Guest House** ★★★★
*Guest Accommodation*
Salcombe Road, Sidmouth EX10 8PR
**t** (01395) 513373
**e** anny@agarton8.wanadoo.co.uk

**Cheriton Guest House**
★★★★ *Guest House*
Vicarage Road, Sidmouth EX10 8UQ
**t** (01395) 513810
**e** sara.land1@virgin.net
**w** smoothhound.co.uk/hotels/cheritong

**Coombe Bank Guest House**
★★★★ *Guest House*
86 Alexandria Road, Sidmouth EX10 9HG
**t** (01395) 514843
**e** info@coombebank.co.uk
**w** coombebank.co.uk

**Dukes** ★★★ *Inn*
The Esplanade, Sidmouth EX10 8AR
**t** (01395) 513320
**e** dukes@hotels-sidmouth.co.uk
**w** hotels-sidmouth.co.uk

**Farmhouse Cottage** ★★★★
*Guest Accommodation*
Church Street, Sidford EX10 9RE
**t** (01395) 577682
**e** farmhousecott@aol.com
**w** farmhousecottagesidmouth.co.uk

**Higher Coombe Farm** ★★★
*Farmhouse*
Tipton St John, Sidmouth EX10 0AX
**t** (01404) 813385
**e** kerstinfarmer@farming.co.uk
**w** smoothhound.co.uk/hotels/higherco

**Hollies Guest House** ★★★★
*Guest House* **SILVER AWARD**
Salcombe Road, Sidmouth EX10 8PU
**t** (01395) 514580
**e** enquiries@holliesguesthouse.co.uk
**w** holliesguesthouse.co.uk

**Kyneton Lodge** ★★★★
*Bed & Breakfast*
87 Alexandria Road, Sidmouth EX10 9HG
**t** (01395) 513213
**e** info@kyneton.co.uk
**w** kyneton.co.uk

**Larkstone House** ★★
*Bed & Breakfast*
22 Connaught Road, Sidmouth EX10 8TT
**t** (01395) 514345

**Lavenders Blue** ★★★★
*Guest House* **SILVER AWARD**
33 Sidford High Street, Sidford, Sidmouth EX10 9SN
**t** (01395) 576656
**e** lavendersbluesidmouth@fsmail.net

**The Long House** ★★★★★
*Bed & Breakfast*
**SILVER AWARD**
Salcombe Hill Road, Sidmouth EX10 0NY
**t** (01395) 577973
**e** pvcia@aol.com
**w** holidaysinsidmouth.co.uk

**Lower Pinn Farm** ★★★★
*Farmhouse*
Peak Hill, Sidmouth EX10 0NN
**t** (01395) 513733
**e** liz@lowerpinnfarm.co.uk
**w** lowerpinnfarm.co.uk

**Lynstead** ★★★★
*Guest House*
Vicarage Road, Sidmouth EX10 8UQ
**t** (01395) 514635
**e** info@lynsteadguesthouse.co.uk
**w** lynsteadguesthouse.co.uk

**Pinn Barton Farm** ★★★★
*Farmhouse* **SILVER AWARD**
Peak Hill, Pinn EX10 0NN
**t** (01395) 514004
**e** betty@pinnbartonfarm.co.uk
**w** pinnbartonfarm.co.uk

**Rose Cottage** ★★★★
*Guest Accommodation*
Coburg Road, Sidmouth EX10 8NF
**t** (01395) 577179
**e** neilsurf@tesco.net

**Ryton Guest House** ★★★
*Guest House*
52-54 Winslade Road, Sidmouth EX10 9EX
**t** (01395) 513981
**e** info@ryton-guest-house.co.uk
**w** ryton-guest-house.co.uk

**The Salty Monk ★★★★★**
*Restaurant with Rooms*
**GOLD AWARD**
**Enjoy England Awards for Excellence Winner**
Church Street, Sidford, Sidmouth EX10 9QP
**t** (01395) 513174
**e** saltymonk@btconnect.com
**w** saltymonk.co.uk

**Sidling Field ★★**
*Bed & Breakfast*
105 Peaslands Road, Sidmouth EX10 8XE
t (01395) 513859
e shenfield@sidlingfield.co.uk
w sidlingfield.co.uk

**Southcombe Guesthouse**
★★★★ *Guest House*
Vicarage Road, Sidmouth EX10 8UQ
t (01395) 513861
e mervyn.james@virgin.net

**Southcroft ★★★★**
*Guest Accommodation*
Arcot Road, Sidmouth EX10 9ES
t (01395) 516903
e southcroft_sidmouth@yahoo.com
w southcroftsidmouth.co.uk

**Southern Cross Guest House**
★★★ *Guest House*
High Street, Newton Poppleford, Sidmouth EX10 0DU
**t** (01395) 568439
**e** timothy.flaher@btconnect.com
**w** southerncrossdevon.co.uk

**Tyrone ★★★★**
*Bed & Breakfast*
Sid Road, Sidmouth EX10 9AL
t (01395) 516753
e tyronehouse@msn.com

**The Willow Bridge ★★★★**
*Guest House*
Millford Road, Sidmouth EX10 8DR
t (01395) 513599

## SILVERTON
Devon

**Three Tuns Inn ★★★** *Inn*
14 Exeter Road, Silverton EX5 4HX
t (01392) 860352
e threetunsinn@btinternet.com
w threetuninn.co.uk

## SIMONSBATH
Somerset

**Emmett's Grange ★★★★**
*Guest Accommodation*
Simonsbath TA24 7LD
t (01643) 831138
e mail@emmettsgrange.co.uk
w emmettsgrange.co.uk

**The Pinkery Centre**
Rating Applied For
*Hostel*
Minehead TA24 7LL
t (01643) 831437

## SIXPENNY HANDLEY
Dorset

**Chase House ★★★**
*Bed & Breakfast*
Deanland, Sixpenny Handley SP5 5PD
t (01725) 552829
e chasehouse1@gmail.com

## SLAUGHTERFORD
Wiltshire

**Manor Farm ★★★**
*Farmhouse*
Slaughterford, Chippenham SN14 8RE
t (01249) 782243
e janmanorfm@hotmail.co.uk

## SLIMBRIDGE
Gloucestershire

**Tudor Arms ★★★** *Inn*
Shepherds Patch, Slimbridge GL2 7BP
t (01453) 890306
e ritatudorarms@aol.com

## SNOWSHILL HILL
Gloucestershire

**Snowshill Hill Estate**
★★★★★ *Farmhouse*
**SILVER AWARD**
Snowshill Hill, Broadway GL56 9TH
t (01386) 853959
e snowshillhill@aol.com
w broadway-cotswolds.co.uk

## SOMERTON
Somerset

**The Brue at Lydford ★★★★**
*Restaurant with Rooms*
West Street, Somerton TA11 7PR
t (01963) 240217
w thebrue.co.uk

**Fosse House Farm ★★★**
*Guest Accommodation*
A37, Lydford-on-Fosse TA11 7DW
t (01963) 240268
e stay@fossehousefarm.co.uk
w fossehousefarm.co.uk

**Littleton House ★★★**
*Bed & Breakfast*
New Street, Somerton TA11 7NU
t (01458) 273072

**Mill House ★★★★★**
*Bed & Breakfast*
**SILVER AWARD**
Mill Road, Somerton TA11 6DF
t (01458) 851215
e b&b@millhousebarton.co.uk
w millhousebarton.co.uk

**The White Hart Inn ★★★**
*Guest Accommodation*
Market Place, Somerton TA11 7LX
**t** (01458) 272314
**e** white.hart@virgin.net
**w** whitehartsomerton.co.uk

## SOUDLEY
Gloucestershire

**White Horse Inn ★★★** *Inn*
Church Road, Soudley, Cinderford GL14 2UA
t (01594) 825968

## SOUTH MOLTON
Devon

**Huxtable Farm ★★★★**
*Farmhouse* **SILVER AWARD**
West Buckland, Barnstaple EX32 0SR
t (01598) 760254
e jackie@huxtablefarm.co.uk
w huxtablefarm.co.uk

**Kerscott Farm ★★★★★**
*Farmhouse* **GOLD AWARD**
Ash Mill, South Molton EX36 4QG
t (01769) 550262
e kerscott.farm@virgin.net
w devon-bandb.co.uk

**Townhouse Barton ★★★**
*Farmhouse*
Nadder Lane, South Molton EX36 4HR
t (01769) 572467
e info@townhousebarton.co.uk
w townhousebarton.co.uk

## SOUTH NEWTON
Wiltshire

**Salisbury Old Mill House**
★★★★ *Bed & Breakfast*
**SILVER AWARD**
Warminster Road, South Newton SP2 0QD
t (01722) 742458
e salisburymill@yahoo.com
w salisburymill.co.uk

## SOUTH PETHERTON
Somerset

**Rock House ★★★★★**
*Guest Accommodation*
**SILVER AWARD**
5 Palmer Street, South Petherton TA13 5DB
t (01460) 241538
e info@stayatrockhouse.co.uk
w stayatrockhouse.co.uk

## SOUTH TEHIDY
Cornwall

**Collingwood ★★★**
*Guest Accommodation*
Mount Whistle Road, South Tehidy TR14 0HU
t (01209) 714696
e enquiries@accommodation-in-cornwall.com
w accommodation-in-cornwall.com

## SOUTH ZEAL
Devon

**The Moors House ★★★★**
*Guest Accommodation*
South Zeal, Okehampton EX20 2PD
t (01837) 840209
e stay@themoorshouse.co.uk
w themoorshouse.co.uk

## SOUTHBOURNE
Dorset

**Mory House ★★★★**
*Guest Accommodation*
**SILVER AWARD**
31 Grand Avenue, Southbourne, Bournemouth BH6 3SY
t (01202) 433553
e stay@moryhouse.co.uk
w moryhouse.co.uk

## SOUTHVILLE
City of Bristol

**The Greenhouse ★★★★**
*Bed & Breakfast*
61 Greenbank Road, Southville BS3 1RJ
t (0117) 902 9166
e kathy@thegreenhousebristol.co.uk
w thegreenhousebristol.co.uk

**The White House Guest Rooms ★★★**
*Guest Accommodation*
28 Dean Lane, Bristol BS3 1DB
t (0117) 953 7725
e info@thewhitehouseguestrooms.co.uk
w thewhitehouseguestrooms.co.uk

## SOUTHWELL
Dorset

**Lobster Farmhouse ★★★**
*Guest Accommodation*
Portland Bill, Portland DT5 2JT
t (01305) 861253

## SPAXTON
Somerset

**Cobb Cottage Bed & Breakfast ★★★**
*Bed & Breakfast*
Four Forks, Spaxton TA5 1BW
t (01278) 671161
w cobbcottage.com

## SPREYTON
Devon

**The Tom Cobley Tavern**
★★★ *Inn*
Spreyton, Crediton EX17 5AL
t (01647) 231314

## STANTON DREW
Somerset

**Greenlands ★★★★**
*Farmhouse*
Stanton Drew, Bristol BS39 4ES
t (01275) 333487

**The Tithe Barn ★★★★**
*Bed & Breakfast*
Sandy Lane, Bristol BS39 4EL
t (01275) 331887
e stephen.jcroucher@btinternet.com
w thetithebarnsomerset.co.uk

## STANTON WICK
Somerset

**The Carpenters Arms**
★★★★ *Inn*
Stanton Wick, Pensford BS39 4BX
t (01761) 490202
e carpenters@buccaneer.co.uk
w the-carpenters-arms.co.uk

## STAUNTON
Gloucestershire

**Steep Meadow ★★★★**
*Bed & Breakfast*
Staunton, Coleford GL16 8PD
t (01594) 832316
e helen@steepmeadow.co.uk
w steepmeadow.co.uk

## STAVERTON
Devon

**Kingston House** ★★★★★
*Guest Accommodation*
**GOLD AWARD**
Staverton, Totnes TQ9 6AR
t (01803) 762235
e info@kingston-estate.co.uk
w kingston-estate.co.uk

## STAVERTON
Gloucestershire

**Staverton House** ★★★★
*Bed & Breakfast*
Church Lane, Staverton
GL51 0TW
t (01242) 680886

## STEEPLE ASHTON
Wiltshire

**Church Farm Steeple Ashton**
★★ *Farmhouse*
5 High Street, Steeple Ashton
BA14 6EL
t (01380) 870518
e susan.churchfarm@tesco.net

**Longs Arms Inn** ★★ *Inn*
High Street, Steeple Ashton
BA14 6EU
t (01380) 870245
e carolinequartley@hotmail.com
w thelongsarms.co.uk/

## STOGUMBER
Somerset

**Hall Farm** ★★★ *Farmhouse*
Station Road, Stogumber
TA4 3TQ
t (01984) 656321

**Knoll Cottage** ★★★★
*Bed & Breakfast*
Vellow Road, Stogumber
TA4 3TN
t (01984) 656689
e mail@knoll-cottage.co.uk
w knoll-cottage.co.uk

**The White Horse Inn** ★★★
*Inn*
High Street, Stogumber
TA4 3TA
t (01984) 656277
e info@whitehorsestogumber.co.uk
w whitehorsestogumber.co.uk

**Wick House** ★★★★
*Guest House*
2 Brook Street, Stogumber,
Taunton TA4 3SZ
t (01984) 656422
e sheila@wickhouse.co.uk
w wickhouse.co.uk

## STOKE ST GREGORY
Somerset

**Meare Green Farm** ★★★★
*Farmhouse*
Meare Green, Stoke St
Gregory TA3 6HT
t (01823) 490759
e info@mearegreenfarm.com
w mearegreenfarm.com

## STOKE SUB HAMDON
Somerset

**Castle Farm** ★★★★
*Farmhouse*
North Street, Stoke-sub-Hamdon TA14 6QS
t (01935) 822231
e karen@castlefarmaccomodation.com
w castlefarmaccomodation.com

## STONEHOUSE
Gloucestershire

**Merton Lodge** ★★
*Bed & Breakfast*
8 Ebley Road, Stonehouse
GL10 2LQ
t (01453) 822018

## STONEY STRATTON
Somerset

**Stratton Farm** ★★★★
*Farmhouse*
High Street, Shepton Mallet
BA4 6DY
t (01749) 830830
w strattonfarm.co.uk

## STOUR ROW
Dorset

**Woodville Farm** ★★★★
*Bed & Breakfast*
Green Lane, Stour Row
SP7 0QD
t (01747) 838241
e woodvillefarm@btconnect.com
w stonebank-chickerell.com

## STOW-ON-THE-WOLD
Gloucestershire

**Aston House** ★★★★
*Bed & Breakfast*
**SILVER AWARD**
Broadwell, Stow-on-the-Wold
GL56 0TJ
t (01451) 830475
e fja@netcomuk.co.uk
w astonhouse.net

**Corsham Field Farmhouse**
★★★ *Farmhouse*
Bledington Road, Stow-on-the-Wold, Cheltenham GL54 1JH
t (01451) 831750
e farmhouse@corshamfield.co.uk
w corshamfield.co.uk

**Cross Keys Cottage** ★★★
*Bed & Breakfast*
Park Street, Stow-on-the-Wold
GL54 1AQ
t (01451) 831128
e rogxmag@hotmail.com

**Little Broom** ★★★★
*Guest Accommodation*
Maugersbury, Stow-on-the-Wold GL54 1HP
t (01451) 830510
w completely-cotswold.com/maugers/accom/broom/broom.htm

**Number Nine** ★★★★
*Bed & Breakfast*
**SILVER AWARD**
Park Street, Stow-on-the-Wold
GL54 1AQ
t (01451) 870333
e enquiries@number-nine.info
w number-nine.info

**South Hill Farmhouse**
★★★★
*Guest Accommodation*
Station Road, Stow-on-the-Wold GL54 1JU
t (01451) 831888
e info@southhill.co.uk
w southhill.co.uk

**Westcote Inn** ★★★★ *Inn*
Nether Westcote, Chipping
Norton OX7 6SD
t (01993) 830888
e info@westcoteinn.co.uk
w westcoteinn.co.uk

**YHA Stow-on-the-Wold**
★★★★ *Hostel*
The Square, Cheltenham
GL54 1AF
t (01451) 830497
e stow@yha.org.uk
w yha.org.uk

## STRATFORD SUB CASTLE
Wiltshire

**Carp Cottage** ★★★
*Guest Accommodation*
Stratford Road, Stratford-sub-Castle SP1 3LH
t (01722) 327219
e carp-cottage@dsl.pipex.com

## STRATTON-ON-THE-FOSSE
Somerset

**Oval House** ★★
*Bed & Breakfast*
Fosse Road, Radstock BA3 4RB
t (01761) 232183
e mellotte@metronet.co.uk
w mellotte.clara.co.uk

## STREET
Somerset

**The Dairy Cottage** ★★★
*Bed & Breakfast*
18 Cranhill Road, Street
BA16 0BY
t (01458) 448484
e gillseddon@hotmail.co.uk
w thedairycottage.co.uk

**Dorm House** ★★★
*Bed & Breakfast*
4 Glaston Road, Street
BA16 0AN
t (01458) 840830
e dormhouse@waitrose.com
w the-dorm.co.uk

**Marshalls Elm Farm** ★★★
*Farmhouse*
B3151, Street BA16 0TZ
t (01458) 442878

**Old Orchard House** ★★★★
*Bed & Breakfast*
Middle Brooks, Street
BA16 0TU
t (01458) 442212
e old.orchard.house@amserve.com
w oldorchardhouse.co.uk

**Street YHA** ★ *Hostel*
The Chalet, Ivythorn Hill, Street
BA16 0TZ
t 0870 770 6056
e street@yha.org.uk
w yha.org.uk

## STROUD
Gloucestershire

**1 Woodchester Lodge**
★★★★ *Bed & Breakfast*
Southfield Road, North
Woodchester, Stroud GL5 5PA
t (01453) 872586
e anne@woodchesterlodge.co.uk
w woodchesterlodge.co.uk

**12 Valley Views** ★★★★
*Bed & Breakfast*
Orchard Close, Middleyard
GL10 3QA
t (01453) 827458
e enquiries@valley-views.com
w valley-views.com

**The Clothiers Arms** ★★★
*Inn*
1 Bath Road, Stroud GL5 3JJ
t (01453) 763801
e harry.counsell@btconnect.com
w clothiersarms.co.uk

**Pretoria Villa** ★★★★
*Bed & Breakfast*
**SILVER AWARD**
Wells Road, Eastcombe, Stroud
GL6 7EE
t (01452) 770435
e pretoriavilla@btinternet.com
w bedandbreakfast-cotswold.co.uk

**Tiled House Farm** ★★★★
*Farmhouse*
Oxlynch, Stonehouse
GL10 3DF
t (01453) 822363
e tiledhousebb@aol.com
w tiledhousebandb.com

**The Yew Tree Bed and Breakfast** ★★★★
*Bed & Breakfast*
Walls Quarry, Brimscombe
GL5 2PA
t (01453) 887980
e info@theyewtreestroud.co.uk
w theyewtreestroud.co.uk

## STUDLAND
Dorset

**Shell Bay Cottage** ★★★★
*Guest Accommodation*
**SILVER AWARD**
Glebe Estate, Swanage
BH19 3AS
t (01929) 450249
e shellbayrose@btinternet.com
w shellbaycottage.com

## STURMINSTER NEWTON
Dorset

**Blackmore Farm Cottage**
★★★★
*Guest Accommodation*
Lydlinch, Sturminster Newton
DT10 2HZ
t (01258) 471624
e blackmorefarmcottagebnb@yahoo.co.uk
w bfcbednbreakfast.co.uk

**Hazeldean Bed & Breakfast**
★★★★ *Bed & Breakfast*
Bath Road, Sturminster Newton
DT10 1DS
**t** (01258) 472224
**e** sarah_grounds@hotmail.com
**w** hazeldeanbnb.co.uk

**Lower Fifehead Farm**
★★★★ *Farmhouse*
Fifehead St Quintin,
Sturminster Newton DT10 2AP
**t** (01258) 817335

## SWANAGE
Dorset

**Amberlea** ★★★ *Guest House*
36 Victoria Avenue, Swanage
BH19 1AP
**t** (01929) 426213
**e** stay@amberleahotel-swanage.co.uk
**w** amberleahotel-swanage.co.uk

**Amberlodge** ★★★
*Guest House*
34 Victoria Avenue, Swanage
BH19 1AP
**t** (01929) 426446
**e** stay@amberlodge-swanage.co.uk
**w** amberlodge-swanage.co.uk

**Arbour House** ★★★
*Guest House*
19 Walrond Road, Swanage
BH19 1PB
**t** (01929) 426237
**e** info@arbourhouseswanage.co.uk
**w** arbourhouseswanage.co.uk

**Bella Vista** ★★★★
*Guest House*
14 Burlington Road, Swanage
BH19 1LS
**t** (01929) 422873
**e** mail@bellavista-swanage.co.uk
**w** bellavista-swanage.co.uk

**The Castleton** ★★★★
*Guest Accommodation*
1 Highcliffe Road, Swanage
BH19 1LW
**t** (01929) 423972
**e** stay@thecastleton.co.uk
**w** thecastleton.co.uk

**Caythorpe House** ★★★
*Guest House*
7 Rempstone Road, Swanage
BH19 1DN
**t** (01929) 422892
**e** enquiries@caythorpehouse.co.uk
**w** caythorpehouse.co.uk

**Clare House** ★★★★
*Guest House* **SILVER AWARD**
1 Park Road, Swanage
BH19 2AA
**t** (01929) 422855
**e** info@clare-house.com
**w** clare-house.com

**Corner Meadow** ★★★
*Bed & Breakfast*
24 Victoria Avenue, Swanage
BH19 1AP
**t** (01929) 423493
**e** geogios@hotmail.co.uk

**Danesfort** ★★★ *Guest House*
Highcliffe Road, Swanage
BH19 1LW
**t** (01929) 424224
**e** reception@danesforthotel.co.uk
**w** danesforthotel.co.uk

**Easter Cottage** ★★★★
*Bed & Breakfast*
**SILVER AWARD**
9 Eldon Terrace, Swanage
BH19 1HA
**t** (01929) 427782
**e** info@eastercottage.co.uk
**w** eastercottage.co.uk

**The Fairway** ★★
*Bed & Breakfast*
De Moulham Road, Swanage
BH19 1NR
**t** (01929) 423367
**e** rita@ritawaller.plus.com
**w** swanagefairway.co.uk

**Glenlee** ★★★★ *Guest House*
6 Cauldon Avenue, Swanage
BH19 1PQ
**t** (01929) 425794
**e** info@glenleehotel.co.uk
**w** glenleehotel.co.uk

**Goodwyns** ★★★★
*Bed & Breakfast*
2 Walrond Road, Swanage
BH19 1PB
**t** (01929) 421088 &
07952 991129
**e** knapman104@btinternet.com

**Grace Gardens Guest House**
★★★★ *Guest House*
28 Victoria Avenue, Swanage
BH19 1AP
**t** (01929) 422502
**e** enquiries@gracegardens.co.uk
**w** gracegardens.co.uk

**The Limes** ★★★
*Guest House*
48 Park Road, Swanage
BH19 2AE
**t** (01929) 422664
**e** info@limeshotel.net
**w** limeshotel.net

**Little Gem** ★ *Guest House*
Cecil Road, Swanage BH19 1JJ
**t** (01929) 427904
**e** info@littlegemguesthouse.co.uk
**w** littlegemguesthouse.co.uk

**Millbrook Guest House**
★★★ *Guest Accommodation*
56 Kings Road West, Swanage
BH19 1HR
**t** (01929) 423443
**e** bob@millbrookswanage.com
**w** millbrookswanage.com

**The Oxford House** ★★★
*Guest House*
5 Park Road, Swanage
BH19 2AA
**t** (01929) 422247
**e** enquiries@oxfordhotelswanage.co.uk
**w** theoxfordswanage.co.uk

**The Oxford Lodge** ★★★
*Guest House*
3 Park Road, Swanage
BH19 2AA
**t** (01929) 422805
**e** info@oxfordlodgeswanage.co.uk
**w** oxfordlodgeswanage.co.uk

**Rivendell Guest House**
★★★★ *Guest House*
58 Kings Road West, Swanage
BH19 1HR
**t** (01929) 421383
**e** kevin@rivendell-guesthouse.co.uk
**w** rivendell-guesthouse.co.uk

**St Michael** ★★★★
*Guest House*
31 Kings Road West, Swanage
BH19 1HF
**t** (01929) 422064

**Sandhaven Guest House**
★★★ *Guest Accommodation*
5 Ulwell Road, Swanage
BH19 1LE
**t** (01929) 422322
**e** mail@sandhaven-guest-house.co.uk
**w** sandhaven-guest-house.co.uk

**Swanage Haven Boutique Guest House** ★★★★
*Guest House*
3 Victoria Road, Swanage
BH19 1LY
**t** (01929) 423088
**e** info@swanagehaven.com
**w** swanagehaven.com

**YHA Swanage** ★★★ *Hostel*
Cluny Crescent, Swanage
BH19 2BS
**t** (01929) 422113
**e** swanage@yha.org.uk
**w** yha.org.uk

## SWEETSHOUSE
Cornwall

**Rew Farm Bed and Breakfast**
★★★★ *Farmhouse*
Sweetshouse, Lanhydrock
PL30 5AW
**t** (01208) 873798
**e** sue.hopper@btopenworld.com
**w** rewfarm.co.uk

## SWIMBRIDGE
Devon

**Barn Cottage** ★★★
*Bed & Breakfast*
Middle Hearson, Swimbridge
EX32 0QH
**t** (01271) 830931
**e** bed@bedandbreakfastdevon.eu
**w** bedandbreakfastdevon.eu

## SWINDON
Wiltshire

**Appletree House** ★★★
*Guest Accommodation*
29 Kingsdown Road, Upper
Stratton SN2 7PE
**t** (01793) 829218
**e** tweed_appletree@hotmail.co.uk

**The Lodge** ★★★★
*Guest Accommodation*
1 Hunt Street, Swindon
SN1 3HW
**t** (01793) 526952 &
(01793) 526904
**e** info@thelodgeswindon.co.uk
**w** thelodgeswindon.co.uk

**The Swandown** ★★★
*Guest Accommodation*
36/37 Victoria Road, Swindon
SN1 3AS
**t** (01793) 536695
**e** swandownhotel@gmail.com
**w** s-h-systems.co.uk/hotels/swandown

## SYDLING ST NICHOLAS
Dorset

**Hazel Cottage** ★★★★
*Bed & Breakfast*
**SILVER AWARD**
1 Waterside Walk, Sydling St
Nicholas DT2 9PJ
**t** (01300) 341618
**e** charlescordy@hazelcottage.ndo.co.uk
**w** hazelcottagedorset.co.uk

**Magiston Farm** ★★
*Farmhouse*
Sydling St Nicholas, Dorchester
DT2 9NR
**t** (01300) 320295

## TALATON
Devon

**Larkbeare Grange** ★★★★★
*Bed & Breakfast*
**GOLD AWARD**
Larkbeare, Talaton EX5 2RY
**t** (01404) 822069
**e** stay@larkbeare.net
**w** larkbeare.net

## TARRANT KEYNESTON
Dorset

**The True Lovers Knot** ★★★
*Inn*
Tarrant Keyneston, Blandford
Forum DT11 9JG
**t** (01258) 452209
**e** info@trueloversknot.co.uk
**w** trueloversknot.co.uk

## TARRANT LAUNCESTON
Dorset

**Ramblers Cottage** ★★★★
*Bed & Breakfast*
Tarrant Launceston, Blandford
Forum DT11 8BY
**t** (01258) 830528
**e** sworrall@ramblerscottage.co.uk
**w** ramblerscottage.co.uk

## TAUNTON
Somerset

**Acorn Lodge** ★★★
*Guest Accommodation*
22 Wellington Road, Taunton
TA1 4EQ
**t** (01823) 337613

**Causeway Cottage** ★★★★
*Bed & Breakfast*
Barbers Lane, West Buckland,
Nr Taunton TA21 9JZ
**t** (01823) 663458
**e** causewaybb@aol.com
**w** causewaycottage.co.uk

**Heathercroft**
Rating Applied For
*Guest Accommodation*
118 Wellington Road, Taunton TA1 5LA
t (01823) 275516

**Lyngford House** ★★★★
*Guest Accommodation*
Selworthy Road, Taunton TA2 8HD
t (01823) 284649
e keldridge@lyngford-house.nhs.uk
w lyngford-house.co.uk

**Pyrland Farm** ★★★★
*Farmhouse*
Cheddon Road, Taunton TA2 7QX
t (01823) 334148
e mary@pyrlandfarm.com
w pyrlandfarm.com

**Staplegrove Lodge** ★★★★
*Bed & Breakfast*
**SILVER AWARD**
Staple Grove, Taunton TA2 6PX
t (01823) 331153
e staplegrovelodge@onetel.com
w staplegrovelodge.co.uk

**Thatched Country Cottage and Garden B&B** ★★★
*Bed & Breakfast*
Pear Tree Cottage, Taunton TA3 7QA
t (01823) 601224
e colvin.parry@virgin.net
w smoothhound.co.uk/hotels/thatch

**Yallands Farmhouse** ★★★★
*Guest Accommodation*
**SILVER AWARD**
Staplegrove, Taunton TA2 6PZ
t (01823) 278979
e mail@yallands.co.uk
w yallands.co.uk

## TAVISTOCK
Devon

**Beera Farmhouse** ★★★★
*Bed & Breakfast*
**GOLD AWARD**
Milton Abbot, Tavistock PL19 8PL
t (01822) 870216
e hilary.tucker@farming.co.uk
w beera-farm.co.uk

**Harrabeer Country House** ★★★★
*Guest Accommodation*
Harrowbeer Lane, Yelverton PL20 6EA
t (01822) 853302
e reception@harrabeer.co.uk
w harrabeer.co.uk

**Higher Woodley Farm**
★★★★ *Farmhouse*
**SILVER AWARD**
Lamerton, Tavistock PL19 8QU
t (01822) 832374
e info@woodleybandb.co.uk
w woodleybandb.co.uk

**Mallards** ★★★★
*Guest House*
48 Plymouth Road, Tavistock PL19 8BU
t (01822) 615171
e mallards-guest-house@tiscali.co.uk
w mallardsoftavistock.co.uk

**Rubbytown Farm** ★★★★
*Farmhouse* **SILVER AWARD**
Gulworthy, Tavistock PL19 8PA
t (01822) 832493
e mary@dartmoor-bb.co.uk
w dartmoor-bb.co.uk

**Tor Cottage** ★★★★★
*Guest Accommodation*
**GOLD AWARD**
Chillaton, Lifton PL16 0JE
t (01822) 860248
e info@torcottage.co.uk
w torcottage.co.uk

## TEDBURN ST MARY
Devon

**Fingle Glen Farm** ★★★
*Farmhouse*
Tedburn St Mary EX6 6AF
t (01647) 61227

**Great Cummins Farm**
★★★★ *Farmhouse*
Tedburn St Mary, Exeter EX6 6BJ
t (01647) 61278
e greatcumminsfarm@yahoo.co.uk

## TEDDINGTON
Gloucestershire

**Bengrove Farm** ★★★
*Farmhouse*
Bengrove, Teddington GL20 8JB
t (01242) 620332
e libby.hopkins@connectfree.co.uk

## TEIGNMOUTH
Devon

**Coombe Bank**
Rating Applied For
*Guest Accommodation*
Landscore Road, Teignmouth TQ14 9JL
t (01626) 772369
e dianne.loach@btopenworld.com
w coombebankhotel.net

**The Craigs** ★★★★
*Bed & Breakfast*
Landscore Road, Teignmouth TQ14 9JL
t (01626) 778003
e thecraigsbandb@btinternet.com

**Dresdon House** ★★★★
*Guest House*
26 Orchard Gardens, Teignmouth TQ14 8DJ
t (01626) 773465
e info@dresdenhouse.com

**Higher Holcombe** ★★★
*Bed & Breakfast*
Holcombe Down Road, Teignmouth TQ14 9NU
t (01626) 777144

**Meran House**
Rating Applied For
*Bed & Breakfast*
Third Drive, Landscore Road, Teignmouth TQ14 9JT
t (01626) 778828

**The Moorings B&B**
★★★★★
*Guest Accommodation*
**SILVER AWARD**
33 Teignmouth Road, Teignmouth TQ14 8UR
t (01626) 770400
e mickywaters@aol.com
w themooringsteignmouth.co.uk

**Old Salty House** ★★★★
*Bed & Breakfast*
21 Northumberland Place, Teignmouth TQ14 8BZ
t (01626) 879574
e oldsaltyhouse@hotmail.co.uk
w oldsaltyhouse.co.uk

**Seaway Guest House**
Rating Applied For
*Guest Accommodation*
27 Northumberland Place, Teignmouth TQ14 8BU
t (01626) 879024
e seawayteignmouth@btinternet.com
w seawayteignmouth.co.uk

**Thomas Luny House**
★★★★★
*Guest Accommodation*
**GOLD AWARD**
Teign Street, Teignmouth TQ14 8EG
t (01626) 772976
e alisonandjohn@thomas-luny-house.co.uk
w thomas-luny-house.co.uk

**The Thornhill** ★★★★
*Guest Accommodation*
Mere Lane, Seafront TQ14 8TA
t (01626) 773460
e thornhillhotel@aol.com
w thornhillhotelteignmouth.co.uk

**Woodside Guesthouse**
Rating Applied For
*Guest House*
17 Hermosa Road, Teignmouth TQ14 9JZ
t (01626) 770681
e sally@falcao.eclipse.co.uk
w woodsideguesthouse.com

## TETBURY
Gloucestershire

**One Market Place** ★★★★
*Bed & Breakfast*
1 Market Place, Tetbury GL8 8DA
t (01666) 504334
e onemarketplace@tiscali.co.uk

## TEWKESBURY
Gloucestershire

**Abbots Court Farm** ★★★
*Farmhouse*
Churchend, Twyning, Tewkesbury GL20 6DA
t (01684) 292515
e abbotscourt@aol.com

**Corner Cottages** ★★★★
*Bed & Breakfast*
Stow Road, Alderton GL20 8NH
t (01242) 620630
e cornercottagebb@talk21.com
w cornercottagebb.co.uk

**Gantier** ★★★★
*Bed & Breakfast*
**SILVER AWARD**
Church Road, Alderton GL20 8NR
t (01242) 620343 & 07787 504872
e johnandsueparry@yahoo.co.uk
w gantier.co.uk

**Green Orchard**
Rating Applied For
*Bed & Breakfast*
Deerhurst Walton, Tewkesbury GL19 4BS
t (01242) 680362
e wendy@green-orchard.co.uk
w green-orchard.co.uk

**Jessop House** ★★★★
*Guest Accommodation*
65 Church Street, Tewkesbury GL20 5RZ
t (01684) 292017
e bookings@jessophousehotel.com
w jessophousehotel.com

**Malvern View Guest House**
★★★ *Guest Accommodation*
1 St Marys Road, Tewkesbury GL20 5SE
t (01684) 292776

## THORNDON CROSS
Devon

**Fairway Lodge** ★★★★
*Guest House*
Thorndon Cross, Okehampton EX20 4NE
t (01837) 55122
e info@fairway-lodge.co.uk
w fairway-lodge.co.uk

## THREE LEGGED CROSS
Dorset

**Southview Guest House**
★★★ *Bed & Breakfast*
Ringwood Road, Three Legged Cross, Wimborne BH21 6QY
t (01202) 813746
e southveiw.guesthouse@btinternet.com
w southview-guest-house.co.uk

**Thatch Cottage** ★★★★
*Guest House*
Ringwood Road, Three Legged Cross, Wimborne BH21 6QY
t (01202) 822042
e dthatchcottage@aol.com
w thatch-cottage.co.uk

## TIBBERTON
Gloucestershire

**The Laurels** ★★
*Guest Accommodation*
Bovone Lane, Tibberton, Gloucester GL2 8EA
t (01452) 790300
e henryandchris.rivers@btinternet.com
w newentbedandbreakfast.co.uk

## TIMSBURY
Somerset

**Pitfour House** ★★★★★
*Guest Accommodation*
**SILVER AWARD**
High Street, Bath BA2 0HT
t (01761) 479554

## TINTAGEL
Cornwall

**The Avalon ★★★★★**
*Guest House*
Atlantic Road, Tintagel
PL34 0DD
**t** (01840) 770116
**e** avalontintagel@googlemail.com
**w** avalon-tintagel.co.uk

Bosayne Guest House ★★★
*Guest Accommodation*
Atlantic Road, Tintagel
PL34 0DE
t (01840) 770514
e kdjewalker@bosayne.wanadoo.co.uk
w bosayne.co.uk

Brooklets Cottage ★★★★
*Bed & Breakfast*
Bossiney Road, Tintagel
PL34 0AE
t (01840) 770395
e brookletscottage@tiscali.co.uk
w brookletscottage.co.uk

The Cottage Teashop
★★★★ *Bed & Breakfast*
Bossiney Road, Tintagel
PL34 0AH
t (01840) 770639
e cotteashop@talk21.com

Four Winds ★★★★
*Bed & Breakfast*
Knight's Close, Atlantic Road,
Tintagel PL34 0DR
t (01840) 770300
e kay4windsaccom@aol.com

Lan-y-mor ★★★
*Bed & Breakfast*
3 Knights Close, Tintagel
PL34 0DR
t (01840) 770933
e dave@dowen20.eclipse.co.uk

**The Mill House ★★★** *Inn*
Trebarwith Strand, Tintagel
PL34 0HD
**t** (01840) 770200
**e** management@themillhouseinn.co.uk
**w** themillhouseinn.co.uk

Tintagel YHA ★★ *Hostel*
Dunderhole Point, Tintagel
PL34 0DW
t (01840) 770334

Trevenna Lodge
Rating Applied For
*Guest House*
Castle Heights, Atlantic Road,
Tintagel PL34 0DE
t (01840) 770264
w trevennalodge.com

## TINTINHULL
Somerset

**The Crown and Victoria Inn**
★★★★ *Inn*
14 Farm Street, Nr Yeovil
BA22 8PZ
**t** (01935) 823341
**e** info@thecrownandvictoria.co.uk
**w** thecrownandvictoria.co.uk

## TISBURY
Wiltshire

Beckford Arms
Rating Applied For
*Inn*
Fonthill Gifford, Tisbury,
Salisbury SP3 6PX
t (01747) 870385

Little Hazels ★★★★
*Bed & Breakfast*
Monmouth Road, Tuckingmill
SP3 6NR
t (01747) 870906
e keeblings@yahoo.com
w littlehazels.co.uk

## TIVERTON
Devon

**Bridge Guest House ★★★**
*Guest House*
23 Angel Hill, Tiverton
EX16 6PE
**t** (01884) 252804
**w** smoothhound.co.uk/hotels/bridgegh.html

Courtyard Bed and Breakfast ★★★★
*Restaurant with Rooms*
19 Fore Street, Bampton
EX16 9ND
t (01398) 331842
e doreen@stonehengeinn.freeserve.co.uk
w bampton.org.uk/

**Exe-Tor ★★★★**
*Bed & Breakfast*
Ashley, Tiverton EX16 5PA
**t** (01884) 253197
**e** jean.wynniatt@tesco.net

Great Bradley Farmhouse
★★★★ *Farmhouse*
SILVER AWARD
Great Bradley Farm, Withleigh
EX16 8JL
t (01884) 256946
e hann@agriplus.net
w greatbradleyfarm-devon.co.uk

## TOLLER PORCORUM
Dorset

Colesmoor Farm ★★★★
*Farmhouse*
Toller Porcorum, Dorchester
DT2 0DU
t (01300) 320812
e rachael@colesmoorfarm.co.uk
w colesmoorfarm.co.uk

Higher Kingcombe Lodge
★★★ *Guest Accommodation*
Higher Kingcombe, Toller
Porcorum DT2 0EH
t (01300) 320537
e info@higherkingcombelodge.co.uk
w higherkingcombelodge.co.uk

The Kingcombe Centre
★★★ *Guest Accommodation*
Lower Kingcombe, Toller
Porcorum DT2 0EQ
t (01300) 320684
e office@kingcombecentre.org.uk
w kingcombecentre.org.uk

## TORPOINT
Cornwall

Bulland House ★★★★
*Bed & Breakfast*
Antony Road, Torpoint
PL11 2PE
t (01752) 813823
e info@averywarmwelcome.co.uk
w averywarmwelcome.co.uk

## TORQUAY
Devon

**Abingdon House ★★★★**
*Guest Accommodation*
104 Avenue Road, Torquay
TQ2 5LF
**t** (01803) 201832
**e** abingdon-house@zen.co.uk
**w** abingdon-house.co.uk

Ashurst Lodge ★★★
*Guest Accommodation*
2-4 St Efrides Road, Torquay
TQ2 5SG
t (01803) 292132
e n.hutch@btopenworld.com
w ashurstlodgehotel.co.uk

Ashwood Grange ★★★★
*Guest Accommodation*
18 Newton Road, Torquay
TQ2 5BZ
t (01803) 212619
e stay@ashwoodgrangehotel.co.uk
w ashwoodgrangehotel.co.uk

Avron House ★★★★
*Guest Accommodation*
70 Windsor Road,
Babbacombe TQ1 1SZ
t (01803) 294182
e avronhouse@blueyonder.co.uk
w avronhouse.co.uk

Babbacombe Guest House
★★★★ *Guest House*
53 Babbacombe Road, Torquay
TQ1 3SN
t (01803) 328071
e babbacombeguest@btinternet.com
w babbacombeguesthouse.com

Babbacombe Palms ★★★★
*Guest Accommodation*
2 York Road, Babbacombe
TQ1 3SG
t (01803) 327087
e reception@babbacombepalms.com
w babbacombepalms.com

Banksea ★★★
*Guest Accommodation*
51 Avenue Road, Torquay
TQ2 5LG
t (01803) 211501

Barangay Richville ★★★★
*Guest House*
Avenue Road, Torquay
TQ2 5LF
t (01803) 296933
e admin@barangayrichville.co.uk
w barangayrichville.co.uk

The Baytree ★★★★
*Guest Accommodation*
14 Bridge Road, Torquay
TQ2 5BA
t (01803) 293718
e enquiries@thebaytreehotel.com
w thebaytreehotel.com

The Belmont ★★★★
*Guest Accommodation*
66 Belgrave Road, Torquay
TQ2 5HY
t (01803) 295028
e enquiries@belmonthoteltorquay.co.uk
w belmonthoteltorquay.co.uk

Bentley Lodge ★★★★
*Guest Accommodation*
SILVER AWARD
Tor Park Road, Torquay
TQ2 5BQ
t (01803) 290698
e cj@bentleylodge.co.uk
w bentleylodge.co.uk

The Berburry ★★★★★
*Guest Accommodation*
GOLD AWARD
64 Bampfylde Road, Torquay
TQ2 5AY
t (01803) 297494
e stay@berburry.co.uk
w berburry.co.uk

Brampton Court ★★★
*Guest Accommodation*
St Lukes Road South, Torquay
TQ2 5NZ
t (01803) 294237
e stay@bramptoncourt.co.uk
w bramptoncourt.co.uk

The Brandize ★★★★
*Guest Accommodation*
19 Avenue Road, Torquay
TQ2 5LB
t (01803) 297798
e stay@brandize.co.uk
w brandize.co.uk

Brocklehurst Guest House
★★★ *Guest House*
Rathmore Road, Chelston
TQ2 6NZ
t (01803) 390883
e enquiries@brocklehursthotel.co.uk
w brocklehursthotel.co.uk

Buckingham Lodge ★★★★
*Guest Accommodation*
Falkland Road, Torquay
TQ2 5JP
t (01803) 293538
e stay@buckinghamlodge.co.uk
w buckinghamlodge.co.uk

The Capri ★★★★
*Guest Accommodation*
12 Torbay Road, Livermead
TQ2 6RG
t (01803) 293158
e stay@caprihoteltorquay.co.uk
w caprihoteltorquay.co.uk

Carlton Court ★★★★★
*Guest Accommodation*
18 Cleveland Road, Torquay
TQ2 5BE
t (01803) 297318
e stay@carlton-court.co.uk
w carlton-court.co.uk

**Cary Court** ★★★★
*Guest House*
Hunsdon Road, Torquay
TQ1 1QB
**t** (01803) 209205
**e** stay@carycourthotel.co.uk
**w** carycourthotel.co.uk

**The Charterhouse** ★★★
*Guest Accommodation*
Cockington Lane, Torquay
TQ2 6QT
**t** (01803) 605804
**e** charterhousehtl@btconnect.com
**w** charterhouse-hotel.co.uk

**Chesterfield** ★★★★
*Guest Accommodation*
62 Belgrave Road, Torquay
TQ2 5HY
**t** (01803) 292318
**e** enquiries@chesterfieldhoteltorquay.co.uk
**w** chesterfieldhoteltorquay.co.uk

**The Cimon** ★★★★
*Guest Accommodation*
82 Abbey Road, Torquay
TQ2 5NP
**t** (01803) 294454
**e** enquiries@hotelcimon.co.uk
**w** hotelcimon.co.uk

**The Cleveland** ★★★★
*Guest Accommodation*
Cleveland Road, Torquay
TQ2 5BD
**t** (01803) 297522
**e** wjennings@hotmail.co.uk
**w** theclevelandtorquay.co.uk

**Cloudlands** ★★★★
*Guest Accommodation*
St Agnes Lane, Torquay
TQ2 6QD
**t** (01803) 606550
**e** info@cloudlands.co.uk
**w** cloudlands.co.uk

**Coombe Court** ★★★★
*Guest Accommodation*
67 Babbacombe Downs Road, Torquay TQ1 3LP
**t** (01803) 327097
**e** enquiries@coombecourthotel.co.uk
**w** coombecourthotel.co.uk

**Cranmore** ★★★★
*Guest House*
89 Avenue Road, Torquay
TQ2 5LH
**t** (01803) 298488
**e** stay@thecranmore.co.uk
**w** thecranmore.co.uk

**Crimdon Dene** ★★★★
*Guest House*
Falkland Road, Torquay
TQ2 5JP
**t** (01803) 294651
**e** marjohn@crimdondenehotel.co.uk
**w** crimdondenehotel.co.uk

**Crown Lodge** ★★★★
*Guest Accommodation*
83 Avenue Road, Torquay
TQ2 5LH
**t** (01803) 298772
**e** stay@crownlodgehotel.co.uk
**w** crownlodgehotel.co.uk

**The Crowndale** ★★★★
*Guest Accommodation*
18 Bridge Road, Torquay
TQ2 5BA
**t** (01803) 293068
**e** info@crowndalehotel.co.uk
**w** crowndalehotel.co.uk

**The Downs** ★★★★
*Guest Accommodation*
41-43 Babbacombe Downs Road, Babbacombe TQ1 3LN
**t** (01803) 328543
**e** enquiries@downshotel.co.uk
**w** downshotel.co.uk

**The Exton** ★★★★
*Guest Accommodation*
12 Bridge Road, Torquay
TQ2 5BA
**t** (01803) 293561
**e** enquiries@extonhotel.co.uk
**w** extonhotel.co.uk

**Fleurie House** ★★★★
*Guest Accommodation*
50 Bampfylde Road, Torquay
TQ2 5AY
**t** (01803) 294869
**e** fleuriehousemandc@btinternet.com
**w** fleuriehouse.co.uk

**The Garlieston Guest House**
★★★ *Guest Accommodation*
Bridge Road, Torquay
TQ2 5BA
**t** (01803) 294050
**e** enquiries@thegarlieston.com
**w** thegarlieston.com

**Garway Lodge Guest House**
★★★ *Guest House*
79 Avenue Road, Torquay
TQ2 5LL
**t** (01803) 293126
**e** garwaylodge@hotmail.com
**w** garwaylodgetorquay.co.uk

**Glendower Hotel** ★★★★
*Guest Accommodation*
Falkland Road, Torquay
TQ2 5JP
**t** (01803) 299988
**e** peter@hoteltorquay.co.uk
**w** hoteltorquay.co.uk

**The Glenross** ★★★★
*Guest Accommodation*
**SILVER AWARD**
25 Avenue Road, Torquay
TQ2 5LB
**t** (01803) 297517
**e** jan@glenross-hotel.co.uk
**w** glenross-hotel.co.uk

**The Glenwood** ★★★★
*Guest Accommodation*
Rowdens Road, Torquay
TQ2 5AZ
**t** (01803) 296318
**e** enquiries@glenwood-hotel.co.uk
**w** glenwood-hotel.co.uk

**Grosvenor House** ★★★★
*Guest Accommodation*
Falkland Road, Torquay
TQ2 5JP
**t** (01803) 294110
**e** etc@grosvenorhousehotel.co.uk
**w** grosvenorhousehotel.co.uk

**Haldon Priors** ★★★★★
*Guest Accommodation*
**SILVER AWARD**
Meadfoot Sea Road, Torquay
TQ1 2LQ
**t** (01803) 213365
**e** travelstyle.ltd@talk21.com
**w** haldonpriors.co.uk

**Haute Epine Guest House**
★★★ *Guest House*
36 Bampfylde Road, Torquay
TQ2 5AR
**t** (01803) 296359
**e** gerald@hauteepineguesthouse.wanadoo.co.uk
**w** haute-epineguesthouse.co.uk

**Haven House** ★★★★
*Guest House*
11 Scarborough Road, Torquay
TQ2 5UJ
**t** (01803) 293390
**e** enquiries@havenhotel.biz
**w** havenhotel.biz

**Heathcliff House** ★★★★
*Guest Accommodation*
16 Newton Road, Torquay
TQ2 5BZ
**t** (01803) 211580
**e** heathcliffhouse@btconnect.com
**w** heathcliffhousehotel.co.uk

**The Hillcroft** ★★★★
*Guest Accommodation*
**SILVER AWARD**
Matlock Terrace, 9 St Lukes Road, Torquay TQ2 5NY
**t** (01803) 297247
**e** info@thehillcroft.co.uk
**w** thehillcroft.co.uk

**Jesmond Dene** ★★
*Guest Accommodation*
85 Abbey Road, Torquay
TQ2 5NN
**t** (01803) 293062

**Kelvin House** ★★★★
*Guest Accommodation*
46 Bampfylde Road, Torquay
TQ2 5AY
**t** (01803) 209093
**e** kelvinhousehotel@amserve.com
**w** kelvinhousehotel.co.uk

**Kethla House** ★★★★
*Guest Accommodation*
33 Belgrave Road, Torquay
TQ2 5HX
**t** (01803) 294995
**e** stay@kethlahouse.co.uk
**w** kethlahouse.co.uk

**Kings Lodge** ★★★★
*Guest Accommodation*
44 Bampfylde Road, Torquay
TQ2 5AY
**t** (01803) 293108
**e** enquiries@kingshotel-torquay.co.uk
**w** kingshoteltorquay.co.uk

**Kingston House** ★★★★★
*Guest Accommodation*
75 Avenue Road, Torquay
TQ2 5LL
**t** (01803) 212760
**e** stay@kingstonhousehotel.co.uk
**w** kingstonhousehotel.co.uk

**Kingsway Lodge Guest House** ★★★★ *Guest House*
95 Avenue Road, Torquay
TQ2 5LH
**t** (01803) 295288
**e** kingswaylodge@hotmail.co.uk
**w** kingswaylodgeguesthouse.co.uk

**Lanscombe House** ★★★★
*Guest Accommodation*
**SILVER AWARD**
Cockington Village, Torquay
TQ2 6XA
**t** (01803) 606938
**e** stay@lanscombehouse.co.uk
**w** lanscombehouse.co.uk

**Lawnswood Guest House**
★★★★
*Guest Accommodation*
6 Scarborough Road, Torquay
TQ2 5UJ
**t** (01803) 292595
**e** welcome@lawnswood.net
**w** lawnswood.net

**Lee House** ★★★
*Guest House*
Torbay Road, Torquay
TQ2 6RG
**t** (01803) 293946
**e** info@leehotel.co.uk
**w** leehotel.co.uk

**Lindum Lodge** ★★★★
*Guest Accommodation*
105 Abbey Road, Torquay
TQ2 5NP
**t** (01803) 292795
**e** enquiries@lindum-hotel.co.uk
**w** lindum-hotel.co.uk

**Melba House** ★★★★
*Guest House*
62 Bampfylde Road, Torquay
TQ2 5AY
**t** (01803) 213167
**e** stay@melbahouse.co.uk
**w** melbahouse.co.uk

**Moonraker Guest House**
★★★★ *Guest House*
St Lukes Road, Torquay
TQ2 5NX
**t** (01803) 297088
**e** enquiries@moonrakerhotel.co.uk

**Mount Edgcombe** ★★★★
*Guest Accommodation*
23 Avenue Road, Torquay
TQ2 5LB
**t** (01803) 292310
**e** info@mountedgcombe.co.uk
**w** mountedgcombe.co.uk

**Mount Nessing** ★★★★
*Guest Accommodation*
St Lukes Road North, Torquay
TQ2 5PD
**t** (01803) 294259
**e** stay@mountnessinghotel.co.uk
**w** mountnessinghotel.co.uk

**The Netley** ★★★
*Guest Accommodation*
52 Bampfylde Road, Torquay
TQ2 5AY
**t** (01803) 295109
**e** thenetley@btconnect.com
**w** thenetleyhotel.co.uk


Look out for establishments participating in the Walkers, Cyclists, Families and Welcome Pets! schemes

**The Norwood** ★★★★
Guest Accommodation
60 Belgrave Road, Torquay
TQ2 5HY
t (01803) 294236
e enquiries@
norwoodhoteltorquay.co.uk
w norwoodhoteltorquay.co.uk

**The Patricia** ★★★★
Guest Accommodation
64 Belgrave Road, Torquay
TQ2 5HY
t (01803) 293339
e info@hotel-patricia.co.uk
w hotel-patricia.co.uk

**The Pines** ★★★
Bed & Breakfast
19 Newton Road, Torre
TQ2 5DB
t (01803) 292882

**Robin Hill International** ★★★★
Guest Accommodation
74 Braddons Hill Road East,
Torquay TQ1 1HF
t (01803) 214518
e jo@robinhillhotel.co.uk
w robinhillhotel.co.uk

**Rutland Lodge**
Rating Applied For
Guest Accommodation
448 Babbacombe Road,
Torquay TQ1 1HW
t (01803) 213972
e rutlandlodge@mac.com

**St Michael's Guest Accommodation** ★★★★
Guest Accommodation
36 Ash Hill Road, Torquay
TQ1 3JD
t (01803) 297391
e st-michaels@fastnet.co.uk
w st-michaelshotel.co.uk

**The Sandpiper** ★★★★
Guest Accommodation
Rowdens Road, Torquay
TQ2 5AZ
t (01803) 292779
e sandpiper57@home13859.
fsnet.co.uk
w sandpiper-hotel.co.uk

**The Sandpiper Lodge** ★★★
Guest Accommodation
96 Avenue Road, Torquay
TQ2 5LF
t (01803) 293293
e johnatsandpiper@aol.com
w sandpiperlodgehotel.co.uk

**Sandway House** ★★★★
Guest Accommodation
72 Belgrave Road, Torquay
TQ2 5HY
t (01803) 298499
e sandwayhotel@
btopenworld.co.uk

**Sea Point** ★★★
Guest Accommodation
Clifton Grove, Old Torwood
Road, Torquay TQ1 1PR
t (01803) 211808
e seapointhotel@hotmail.com
w seapointhotel.co.uk

**The Shirley** ★★★
Guest Accommodation
Braddons Hill Road East,
Torquay TQ1 1HF
t (01803) 293016
e enquiries@shirley-hotel.co.uk
w shirley-hotel.co.uk

**The Somerville** ★★★★
Guest Accommodation
515 Babbacombe Road,
Torquay TQ1 1HJ
t (01803) 294755
e stay@somervillehotel.co.uk
w somervillehotel.co.uk

**South View** ★★★★
Guest Accommodation
12 Scarborough Road, Torquay
TQ2 5UJ
t (01803) 296029
e info@thesouthview.com
w thesouthview.com

**The Southbank** ★★★★
Guest Accommodation
15-17 Belgrave Road, Torquay
TQ2 5HU
t (01803) 296701
e stay@southbankhotel.co.uk
w southbankhotel.co.uk

**Tor Dean** ★★★★
Guest Accommodation
27 Bampfylde Road, Torquay
TQ2 5AY
t (01803) 294669
e stay@tordeanhotel.com
w tordeanhotel.com

**Torbay Star Guest House** ★★★★ Guest House
73 Avenue Road, Torquay
TQ2 5LL
t (01803) 293998
e torbaystar@btinternet.com
w torbaystarguesthouse.co.uk

**Tower Hall** ★★★★
Guest Accommodation
Solsbro Road, Torquay
TQ2 6PF
t (01803) 605292
e john@towerhallhotel.co.uk
w towerhallhotel.co.uk

**Trafalgar House** ★★★★
Guest Accommodation
30 Bridge Road, Torquay
TQ2 5BA
t (01803) 292486
e trafalgar@hotelstorquayuk.com
w hotelstorquayuk.com

**Trouville** ★★★ Guest House
70 Belgrave Road, Torquay
TQ2 5HY
t (01803) 294979
e info@trouvillehoteltorquay.co.uk
w trouvillehoteltorquay.co.uk

**Villa Marina** ★★★★
Guest Accommodation
Tor Park Road, Torquay
TQ2 5BQ
t (01803) 292187
e enquiries@villamarina-torquay.co.uk
w villamarina-torquay.co.uk

**Walnut Lodge** ★★★★
Guest Accommodation
48 Bampfylde Road, Torquay
TQ2 5AY
t (01803) 200471
e stay@walnutlodgetorquay.co.uk
w walnutlodgetorquay.co.uk

**The Waters Edge** ★★★
Guest Accommodation
Torbay Road, Torquay
TQ2 6QH
t (01803) 293876
e enquiries@waters-edge-hotel.co.uk
w waters-edge-hotel.co.uk

**The Wellsway** ★★★★
Guest Accommodation
56 Bampfylde Road, Torquay
TQ2 5AY
t (01803) 215588
e info@wellsway-hotel.co.uk
w wellsway-hotel.co.uk

**The Westbank** ★★★★
Guest Accommodation
SILVER AWARD
54 Bampfylde Road, Torquay
TQ2 5AY
t (01803) 295271
e westbankhotel@onetel.com
w thewestbank.co.uk

**The Westbourne** ★★★★
Guest Accommodation
106 Avenue Road, Torquay
TQ2 5LQ
t (01803) 292927
e enquiries@westbournehoteltorquay.co.uk
w westbournehoteltorquay.co.uk

**The Westbrook** ★★★
Guest House
15 Scarborough Road, Torquay
TQ2 5UJ
t (01803) 292559
e westbrookhotel@tesco.net
w westbrookhotel.net

**The Westgate** ★★★★
Guest Accommodation
SILVER AWARD
Falkland Road, Torquay
TQ2 5JP
t (01803) 295350
e stay@westgatehotel.co.uk
w westgatehotel.co.uk

**Whitburn Guest House** ★★★ Guest House
St Lukes Road North, Torquay
TQ2 5PD
t (01803) 296719
e lazenby1210@btinternet.com
w whitburnguesthouse.co.uk

**Wilsbrook Guest House** ★★★ Guest House
77 Avenue Road, Torquay
TQ2 5LL
t (01803) 298413
e thewilsbrook@hotmail.com
w wilsbrook.co.uk

## TOTNES
### Devon

**The Elbow Room** ★★★★★★
Guest Accommodation
SILVER AWARD
North Street, Totnes TQ9 5NZ
t (01803) 863480
e r.savin@btinternet.com

**Foales Leigh** ★★★★★
Guest Accommodation
SILVER AWARD
Harberton, Totnes TQ9 7SS
t (01803) 862365

**Four Seasons Guest House**
Rating Applied For
Guest House
13 Bridgetown, Totnes
TQ9 5AB
t (01803) 862146
e info@fourseasonstotnes.co.uk
w fourseasonstotnes.co.uk

**Great Court Farm** ★★★★
Farmhouse SILVER AWARD
Weston Lane, Totnes TQ9 6LB
t (01803) 862326
e janet.hooper3@btinternet.com
w greatcourt-totnes.co.uk

**The Great Grubb B&B**
★★★★ Guest House
Fallowfields, Plymouth Road,
Totnes TQ9 5LX
t (01803) 849071
e accommodation@thegreatgrubb.co.uk
w thegreatgrubb.co.uk

**No 12 B&B**
Rating Applied For
Guest Accommodation
12 Cistern Street, Totnes
TQ9 5SP
t (01803) 840359
e jennie-jennie@hotmail.com
w bedandbreakfasttotnes.com

**The Old Forge at Totnes**
★★★★ Guest House
Seymour Place, Totnes
TQ9 5AY
t (01803) 862174
e enq@oldforgetotnes.com
w oldforgetotnes.com

**Steam Packet Inn** ★★★★
Inn
4 St Peters Quay, Totnes
TQ9 5EW
t (01803) 863880
e esther@thesteampacketinn.co.uk
w thesteampacketinn-totnes.co.uk

## TREGONY
### Cornwall

**Penhesken Farm** ★★
Farmhouse
Tregony, Truro TR2 5TG
t (01872) 530629

**Tregonan** ★★★★
Guest Accommodation
SILVER AWARD
Tregony, Truro TR2 5SN
t (01872) 530249
e sandra@tregonan.co.uk
w tregonan.co.uk

## TREHUNIST
### Cornwall

**North Trewint**
Rating Applied For
Bed & Breakfast
Trewint Road, Menheniot
PL14 3RE
t (01579) 344313
e info@northtrewint.co.uk

---

Establishments in bold have a detailed entry in this guide – use the property index to find the page numbers 651

## TREKNOW
Cornwall

**The Bluff Centre**
Rating Applied For
*Guest House*
Tintagel PL34 0EP
**t** (01840) 770033
**e** marianne@bluff.eclipse.co.uk
**w** bluffcentre.co.uk

## TRELILL
Cornwall

**Trelulla, Trelill** ★★★
*Bed & Breakfast*
Trelill, St Kew Highway, Wadebridge PL30 3HT
**t** (01208) 850938
**e** eileenroberts@trelulla.freeserve.co.uk
**w** wadebridgelive

## TRELOWTH
Cornwall

**Polgreen Guesthouse**
Rating Applied For
*Bed & Breakfast*
Trelowth, St Austell PL26 7DZ
**t** (01726) 64546
**e** office@polgreenguesthouse.co.uk
**w** polgreenguesthouse.co.uk

## TREMOUGH
Cornwall

**Glasney Parc (Tremough)**
★★★ *Campus*
Tremough Campus, Treliever Road, Penryn TR10 9EZ
**t** (01326) 370473
**e** holidaylets@tremoughservices.com

## TRENANCE
Cornwall

**Merrymoor Inn** ★★★★
*Guest Accommodation*
Mawgan Porth, Newquay TR8 4BA
**t** (01637) 860258
**e** info@merrymoorinn.com
**w** merrymoorinn.com

## TRESMEER
Cornwall

**Sycamore Farm** ★★★
*Farmhouse*
Tresmeer, Launceston PL15 8QT
**t** (01566) 781339
**e** juliewalters@uwclub.net

## TRESPARRETT
Cornwall

**Oaklands** ★★★★
*Bed & Breakfast*
Tresparrett, Camelford PL32 9SX
**t** (01840) 261302

## TRETHEVY
Cornwall

**Reevescott**
Rating Applied For
*Bed & Breakfast*
Trethevy, Tintagel PL34 0BG
**t** (01840) 770533
**e** john.pen@talktalk.net

## TREVALGA
Cornwall

**Trehane Farm** ★★★★
*Farmhouse*
Trevalga, Boscastle PL35 0EB
**t** (01840) 250510
**e** trehanefarmhouse@virgin.net
**w** cornish-farms.co.uk

## TREVONE
Cornwall

**Trevone Beach House** ★★★★
*Guest Accommodation*
Trevone, Padstow PL28 8QX
**t** (01841) 520469
**e** trevonebeach@aol.com
**w** trevonebeach.co.uk

## TREWARMETT
Cornwall

**Melrosa** ★★★★
*Bed & Breakfast*
Trewarmett, Tintagel PL34 0ES
**t** (01840) 770360
**e** valerie.stephens@btinternet.com

## TREWOON
Cornwall

**Cooperage** ★★★★
*Guest House*
37 Cooperage Road, Trewoon PL25 5SJ
**t** (01726) 70497
**e** lcooperage@tiscali.co.uk
**w** cooperagebb.co.uk

## TREYARNON BAY
Cornwall

**Treyarnon Bay Youth Hostel**
★★★ *Hostel*
Tregonnan, Treyarnon, Padstow PL28 8JR
**t** 0870 770 6076
**e** treyarnon@yha.org.uk

## TROWBRIDGE
Wiltshire

**62b Paxcroft Cottages** ★★★
*Bed & Breakfast*
Paxcroft, Hilperton BA14 6JB
**t** (01225) 765838
**e** paxcroftcottages@hotmail.com
**w** paxcroftcottages.pwp.blueyonder.co.uk

---

**Ring O' Bells** ★★★
*Guest House*
321 Marsh Road, Hilperton Marsh, Trowbridge BA14 7PL
**t** (01225) 754404
**e** ringobells@blueyonder.co.uk
**w** ringobells.biz

## TRUDOXHILL
Somerset

**Trudox Mead Country B & B**
★★★ *Bed & Breakfast*
Foghamshire Lane, Frome BA11 5DR
**t** (01373) 836387
**e** carewprices@greenbee.net
**w** trudoxmead.co.uk

## TRULL
Somerset

**Canonsgrove Farm** ★★★
*Farmhouse*
Trull, Taunton TA3 7PD
**t** (01823) 279720
**e** c.ralph57@btinternet.com
**w** canonsgrovefarm.co.uk

## TRURO
Cornwall

**Bay Tree** ★★ *Guest House*
28 Ferris Town, Truro TR1 3JH
**t** (01872) 240274
**w** baytree-guesthouse.co.uk

---

**Bissick Old Mill** ★★★★
*Guest House*
Ladock, Truro TR2 4PG
**t** (01726) 882557
**e** enquiries@bissickoldmill.plus.com
**w** bissickoldmill.co.uk

---

**Briars** ★★ *Bed & Breakfast*
14 Blackberry Way, Beechwood Parc, Truro TR1 1QX
**t** (01872) 223814
**e** bethinbriars@hotmail.com

---

**Chy-Vista** ★★★★
*Bed & Breakfast*
Higher Penair, St Clement, Truro TR1 1TD
**t** (01872) 270592

---

**Hazelnut Cottage** ★★★★
*Bed & Breakfast*
Perranwell Station, Truro TR3 7PU
**t** (01872) 865082

---

**Palm Tree House** ★★★★
*Bed & Breakfast*
8 Parkins Terrace, Off St Clement Street, Truro TR1 1EJ
**t** (01872) 270100
**e** bodybusiness@btconnect.com

---

**The Rowan Tree** ★★★
*Bed & Breakfast*
3 Parkvedras Terrace, Truro TR1 3DF
**t** (01872) 277928
**e** christinecartlidge@freenet.co.uk

---

**Stanton House** ★★
*Bed & Breakfast*
11 Ferris Town, Truro TR1 3JG
**t** (01872) 223666
**e** chris@stantonjohnson.fsnet.co.uk

---

**The Townhouse Rooms** ★★★★
*Guest Accommodation*
20 Falmouth Road, Truro TR1 2HX
**t** (01872) 277374
**e** info@trurotownhouse.com
**w** trurotownhouse.com

---

**Tregoninny Farm** ★★★★
*Guest Accommodation*
Tresillian, Truro TR2 4AR
**t** (01872) 520529
**e** tregoninny.farm@btopenworld.com
**w** tregoninny.com

---

**Treswithian Barn** ★★★★
*Bed & Breakfast*
Ruan High Lanes, Truro TR2 5JT
**t** (01872) 501274

## TURKDEAN
Gloucestershire

**Yew Tree Cottage** ★★★★★
*Bed & Breakfast*
**SILVER AWARD**
Turkdean GL54 3NT
**t** (01451) 860222
**e** vivien@bestcotswold.com
**w** bestcotswold.com

## TWO WATERS FOOT
Cornwall

**Gillwood Bed and Breakfast**
★★★★ *Bed & Breakfast*
Twowatersfoot, Liskeard, Bodmin PL14 6HR
**t** (01208) 821648
**e** cliffnshelia@tiscali.co.uk
**w** gillwoodbedandbreakfast.com

---

**Tithe Hall Farm** ★★★★
*Farmhouse*
Two Waters Foot, Liskeard PL14 6HL
**t** (01208) 872491
**e** tithehall@tesco.net
**w** tithehallfarm.co.uk

---

**Treverbyn Vean Manor** ★★★★★
*Guest Accommodation*
**GOLD AWARD**
West Wing, Treverbyn Vean, Liskeard PL14 6HN
**t** (01579) 326105
**e** ahindley@mac.com
**w** treverbynvean.co.uk

## TYWARDREATH
Cornwall

**Morbihan Bed and Breakfast**
★★★★ *Bed & Breakfast*
28 Southpark Road, Tywardreath PL24 2PT
**t** (01726) 817247
**e** morbihanbandb@yahoo.co.uk
**w** morbihanguesthouse.co.uk

## UCKINGTON
Gloucestershire

**Linthwaite** ★★
*Bed & Breakfast*
3 Homecroft Drive, Uckington, Cheltenham GL51 9SN
**t** (01242) 680146
**e** a.r.marchand@talk21.com

## ULEY
Gloucestershire

**The Old Crown Inn** ★★★ *Inn*
The Green, Dursley GL11 5SN
**t** (01453) 860502
**e** info@theoldcrownuley.co.uk
**w** theoldcrownuley.co.uk

## UPLODERS
Dorset

**Uploders Farm** ★★★
*Guest Accommodation*
Dorchester Road, Bridport DT6 4NZ
**t** (01308) 423380

### UPLYME
Devon

**Beech Grove House**
★★★★★ *Guest House*
Rhode Lane, Uplyme DT7 3TX
t (01297) 442723
e beechgroveuplyme@aol.com
w beechgrovehouse.co.uk

### UPPER ODDINGTON
Gloucestershire

**Blenheim Cottage** ★★★★★
*Guest Accommodation*
**GOLD AWARD**
Upper Oddington, Stow-on-the-Wold GL56 0XG
t (01451) 831066
e cotswoldsoddington@btinternet.com
w cotswoldsoddington.co.uk

**Uphome** ★★★★
*Guest Accommodation*
Upper Oddington, Stow-on-the-Wold GL56 0XH
t (01451) 831284
e salgodman@hotmail.com
w cotswoldbreaks.co.uk

### UPTON NOBLE
Somerset

**Crosselm** ★★★★ *Farmhouse*
Shepton Mallet BA4 6AX
t (01749) 850201

### VERYAN
Cornwall

**Treverbyn House** ★★★★
*Bed & Breakfast*
Pendower Road, Veryan, Truro TR2 5QL
t (01872) 501201
e holiday@treverbyn.fsbusiness.co.uk
w cornwall-online.co.uk/treverbyn/ctb.htm

### WADEBRIDGE
Cornwall

**Brookdale B & B** ★★★★
*Bed & Breakfast*
Trevanion Road, Wadebridge PL27 7PA
t (01208) 815425
e deegrant@freeuk.com
w brookdalebandb.co.uk

**Brookfields B&B** ★★★★
*Bed & Breakfast*
**SILVER AWARD**
Hendra Lane, St Kew Highway, Wadebridge PL30 3EQ
t (01208) 841698
e robbie@brookfields.info
w brookfields.info

**Homebound B&B** ★★★★
*Bed & Breakfast*
Gonvena Hill, Wadebridge PL27 6DH
t (01208) 812759
e nigelhackling@aol.com
w homebound.me.uk

**Monte Gordo** ★★★
*Bed & Breakfast*
Tregonce Farm, St Issey, Wadebridge PL27 7QJ
t (01208) 812082

**Spring Gardens** ★★★
*Bed & Breakfast*
Bradfords Quay, Wadebridge PL27 6DB
t (01208) 813771
e springjen1@aol.com
w spring-garden.co.uk

**Tregolls Farm** ★★★★
*Guest Accommodation*
St Wenn, Bodmin PL30 5PG
t (01208) 812154
w tregollsfarm.co.uk

### WADEFORD
Somerset

**The Haymaker Inn** ★★★★
*Inn*
Main Road, Chard TA20 3AP
t (01460) 64161
e stevetingle11@hotmail.co.uk

### WAMBROOK
Somerset

**Woodview** ★★★
*Guest Accommodation*
Wambrook Road, Chard TA20 3EH
t (01460) 65368
e enquiries@woodview.org.uk
w woodview.org.uk

### WAREHAM
Dorset

**Anglebury House** ★★★
*Guest Accommodation*
15-17 North Street, Wareham BH20 4AB
t (01929) 552988
e info@angleburyhouse.co.uk
w angleburyhouse.co.uk

**Ashcroft** ★★★
*Bed & Breakfast*
64 Furzebrook Road, Wareham BH20 5AX
t (01929) 552392
e cake@ashcroft-bb.co.uk
w ashcroft-bb.co.uk

**Beryl's B&B** ★★★
*Bed & Breakfast*
2 Heath Cottages, Wareham Road, Wareham BH20 7DF
t (01929) 550138
e beryle@homecall.co.uk
w britainsbestbreaks.co.uk

**Blackmanston Farm** ★★★
*Farmhouse*
Blackmanston, Steeple, Wareham BH20 5NZ
t (01929) 480743
e bobbraisby@yahoo.co.uk
w members.lycos.co.uk/blackmanstonfarm/

**Spurwing Guest House**
★★★★ *Guest House*
10 Sandford Road, Wareham BH20 4DH
t (01929) 553869
e spencers@spurwing.info
w spurwing.info

**Trinity** ★★★★
*Bed & Breakfast*
32 South Street, Wareham BH20 4LU
t (01929) 556689
e enquiries@trinitybnb.co.uk
w trinitybnb.co.uk

### WARMINSTER
Wiltshire

**Corner House** ★★★★★
*Guest Accommodation*
The Square, High Street, Maiden Bradley BA12 7JG
t (01985) 844629
e wildlifeinwilts@tiscali.co.uk
w cornerhousebb.com

**The George Inn** ★★★★ *Inn*
Longbridge Deverill, Warminster BA12 7DG
t (01985) 840396
w thegeorgeinnlongbridgedeverill.co.uk

**Home Farm** ★★★★
*Farmhouse*
221 Boreham Road, Warminster BA12 9HF
t (01985) 213266
e enquiries@homefarmboreham.co.uk
w homefarmboreham.co.uk

### WARMLEY
Gloucestershire

**Ferndale Guest House** ★★★
*Guest House*
Deanery Road, Warmley BS15 9JB
t (0117) 985 8247
e alexandmikewake@yahoo.co.uk
w ferndaleguesthouse.co.uk

### WASHAWAY
Cornwall

**South Tregleath Farm B & B**
★★★★ *Bed & Breakfast*
**SILVER AWARD**
South Tregleath Farm, Bodmin PL30 3AA
t (01208) 72692

### WASHFORD
Somerset

**Langtry Country House**
★★★★★ *Bed & Breakfast*
A39, Washford TA23 0NT
t (01984) 641688
e helga@langtrycountryhouse.co.uk
w langtrycountryhouse.co.uk

**Monkscider House** ★★★★
*Guest Accommodation*
**SILVER AWARD**
Main Road, Washford TA23 0NS
t (01984) 641055
e david@netgates.co.uk
w monksciderhouse.com

### WATCHET
Somerset

**Esplanade House** ★★★★
*Bed & Breakfast*
Esplanade, Watchet TA23 0AJ
t (01984) 633444
w esplanade-house.co.uk

**Trinity Cottage** ★★★★
*Bed & Breakfast*
Mount Lane, Washford TA23 0QY
t (01984) 641676
e abigailtrin@aol.com
w trinitycottage.co.uk

### WATERROW
Somerset

**Handley Farm Accommodation** ★★★★★
*Farmhouse* **GOLD AWARD**
Waterrow, Taunton TA4 2BE
t (01398) 361516
e info@handleyfarm.co.uk
w handleyfarm.co.uk

### WELLINGTON
Somerset

**Backways Farmhouse**
★★★★ *Bed & Breakfast*
Wellington TA21 9RN
t (01823) 660712
e info@backways.co.uk
w users.tinyworld.co.uk/vanessa.archer/home.index.html

**Mantle Cottage** ★★★
*Bed & Breakfast*
34 Mantle Street, Wellington TA21 8AR
t (01823) 668514
e dalsod@aol.com
w mantlecottage.com

### WELLS
Somerset

**30 Mary Road** ★★★
*Guest Accommodation*
Mary Road, Wells BA5 2NF
t (01749) 674031
e triciabailey30@hotmail.com

**55 St Thomas Street** ★★★
*Bed & Breakfast*
46 Church Street, Wells BA5 2UY
t (01749) 676522
e 55sttst@fsbdial.co.uk
w 55stthomas.co.uk

**Baytree House** ★★★★
*Guest Accommodation*
85 Portway, Wells BA5 2BJ
t (01749) 677933
e stay@baytree-house.co.uk
w baytree-house.co.uk

**Beryl** ★★★★★
*Guest Accommodation*
**SILVER AWARD**
Off Hawkers Lane, Wells BA5 3JP
t (01749) 678738
e stay@beryl-wells.co.uk
w beryl-wells.co.uk

**Burcott Mill Historic Watermill and Guesthouse**
★★★★ *Guest House*
Wells BA5 1NJ
t (01749) 673118
e theburts@burcottmill.com
w burcottmill.com

**Burnt House Farm** ★★★★
*Farmhouse*
Burnthouse Drove, Windsor Hill BA4 4JQ
t (01749) 840185
e ehparry@btinternet.com
w burnthousedrove.co.uk

**Cadgwith House** ★★★★
*Bed & Breakfast*
Hawkers Lane, Wells BA5 3JH
t (01749) 677799
e cadgwith.house@yahoo.co.uk
w cadgwithhouse.co.uk

**Canon Grange** ★★★★
*Guest Accommodation*
Cathedral Green, Wells
BA5 2UB
t (01749) 671800
e canongrange@email.com
w canongrange.co.uk

**Dapa House** ★★★★
*Bed & Breakfast*
62 Bath Road, Wells BA5 3LQ
t (01749) 689248
e enquiries@dapahouse.co.uk
w dapahouse.co.uk

**Islington Farm** ★★★★
*Bed & Breakfast*
**Wells BA5 1US**
**t (01749) 673445**
**e islingtonfarm2004@yahoo.co.uk**
**w islingtonfarmatwells.co.uk**

**Mendip House** ★★★
*Guest Accommodation*
46 Portway, Wells BA5 2BN
t (01749) 679719
e info@mendiphousewells.co.uk
w mendiphousewells.co.uk

**Winston House** ★★★★
*Guest Accommodation*
109 Portway, Wells BA5 2BR
t (01749) 673087
e info@winstonhousewells.co.uk
w winstonhousewells.co.uk

**Worth House** ★★★
*Guest Accommodation*
**Worth, Wookey, Wells**
**BA5 1LW**
**t (01749) 672041**
**e margaret@wookey.eclipse.co.uk**

## WELSH BICKNOR
Gloucestershire

**Welsh Bicknor Youth Hostel**
★★ *Hostel*
Welsh Bicknor, Ross-on-Wye
HR9 6JJ
t 0870 770 6086
e welshbicknor@yha.org.uk
w yha.org.uk

## WEMBWORTHY
Devon

**Lymington Arms** ★★★★
*Guest Accommodation*
Lama Cross, Wembworthy,
Chulmleigh EX18 7SA
t (01837) 83572
e tony@lymingtonarms.co.uk

## WEST ASHTON
Wiltshire

**Watergardens**
Rating Applied For
*Bed & Breakfast*
131 Yarnbrook Road, West
Ashton BA14 6AF
t (01225) 766539
e watergardens@btinternet.com
w watergardens-stay.co.uk

## WEST BAY
Dorset

**Beachcroft** ★★★★
*Bed & Breakfast*
23 Forty Foot Way, West Bay,
Bridport DT6 4HD
t (01308) 423604
w beachcroft-westbay.co.uk

**Briarwood House** ★★★★
*Bed & Breakfast*
Old Church Road,
Bothenhampton DT6 4BP
t (01308) 422567
e katharineandpaul@hotmail.co.uk
w briarwoodhouse.co.uk

**Bridport Arms** ★★★★ *Inn*
West Bay DT6 4EN
t (01308) 422994
e reservations@bridportarms.com
w bridportarms.com

**Heatherbell Cottage** ★★★★
*Guest Accommodation*
Hill Close, West Bay, Bridport
DT6 4HW
t (01308) 422998
e heatherbell4bnb@onetel.net.uk
w cu4bnb.com

**Seacroft** ★★★★
*Bed & Breakfast*
**24 Forty Foot Way, West Bay,**
**Bridport DT6 4HD**
**t (01308) 423407**
**e seacroft24@btinternet.com**
**w seacroftbandb.co.uk**

**The West Bay** ★★★ *Inn*
Station Road, West Bay
DT6 4EW
t (01308) 422157
e info@thewestbay.co.uk
w thewestbay.co.uk

## WEST BEXINGTON
Dorset

**Shearwater** ★★★★
*Bed & Breakfast*
Beach Road, West Bexington
DT2 9DG
t (01308) 897863
w shearwater-cottage.com

## WEST COMPTON
Somerset

**Primrose Hill B & B** ★★★★
*Guest Accommodation*
Knowle Farm Bungalow,
Shepton Mallet BA4 4PD
t (01749) 899279
e mail@primrosehillbb.co.uk
w primrosehillbb.co.uk

## WEST HATCH
Somerset

**The Farmers Inn** ★★★★★
*Inn* **SILVER AWARD**
Slough Hill, West Hatch
TA3 5RS
t (01823) 480480
e letsgostay@farmersinnwesthatch.co.uk
w farmersinnwesthatch.co.uk

## WEST HUNTSPILL
Somerset

**Ilex House** ★★★★
*Bed & Breakfast*
**SILVER AWARD**
102 Main Road, West Huntspill
TA9 3QZ
t (01278) 783801
e enquiries@ilexhouse.co.uk
w ilexhouse.co.uk

## WEST LOOE
Cornwall

**The Old Bridge House**
**★★★★** ***Guest House***
**The Quay, West Looe, Looe**
**PL13 2BU**
**t (01503) 263159**
**e mail@theoldbridgehousehotel.co.uk**
**w theoldbridgehousehotel.co.uk**

**Tidal Court** ★★ *Guest House*
Church Street, West Looe,
Looe PL13 2EX
t (01503) 263695

## WEST LULWORTH
Dorset

**Gatton House** ★★★★
*Guest House*
Main Road, West Lulworth,
Wareham BH20 5RL
t (01929) 400252
e avril@gattonhouse.co.uk
w gattonhouse.co.uk

**Lulworth Cove YHA** ★★
*Hostel*
School Lane, Wareham
BH20 5SA
t (01929) 400564
e lulworth@yha.org.uk
w yha.org.uk

**The Old Barn** ★★★
*Guest Accommodation*
Main Road, West Lulworth
BH20 5RL
t (01929) 400305

## WEST MONKTON
Somerset

**Springfield House** ★★★★
*Guest Accommodation*
Walford Cross, Taunton
TA2 8QW
t (01823) 412116
e tina.ridout@btopenworld.com
w springfieldhse.co.uk

## WEST MOORS
Dorset

**Carey** ★★★★
*Bed & Breakfast*
11 Southern Avenue, West
Moors BH22 0BJ
t (01202) 861159
e russell@lesmor.fsnet.co.uk

## WEST OVERTON
Wiltshire

**Cairncot** ★★★
*Bed & Breakfast*
West Overton, Marlborough
SN8 4ER
t (01672) 861617 &
07798 603455
e dm.leigh@virgin.net
w cairncot.co.uk

## WEST PORLOCK
Somerset

**West Porlock House** ★★★★
*Guest Accommodation*
New Road, Porlock TA24 8NX
t (01643) 862880
e westporlockhouse@amserve.com

## WEST PUTFORD
Devon

**South Worden** ★★★★
*Bed & Breakfast*
West Putford EX22 7LG
t (01409) 261448
e southworden@aol.com
w southworden-holsworthy.co.uk

## WEST QUANTOXHEAD
Somerset

**Stilegate Bed and Breakfast**
★★★★★
*Guest Accommodation*
Staple Close, Williton TA4 4DN
t (01984) 639119
e stilegate@aol.com
w stilegate.co.uk

## WEST TAPHOUSE
Cornwall

**Cross Close House B&B**
★★★★ *Bed & Breakfast*
Cross Close, West Taphouse,
Lostwithiel PL22 0RP
t (01579) 320255
e alex.lister1@tesco.net
w cornwall-online.co.uk

## WEST TOLGUS
Cornwall

**Solcett** ★★★★
*Bed & Breakfast*
**SILVER AWARD**
West Tolgus, Redruth
TR15 3TN
t (01209) 218424
e malst@tiscali.co.uk
w visitcornwall.co.uk

## WESTBURY
Wiltshire

**Black Dog Farm** ★★★★
*Farmhouse*
Chapmanslade, Westbury
BA13 4AE
t (01373) 832858
e lynmmills@aol.com

## WESTHAY
Somerset

**New House Farm** ★★★★
*Farmhouse* **SILVER AWARD**
Shapwick Road, Glastonbury
BA6 9TT
t (01458) 860238
e bell-bell@btconnect.com
w newhousefarmbandb.co.uk

## WESTON-SUPER-MARE
Somerset

**The Albany Lodge** ★★★
*Guest House*
9 Clevedon Road, Weston-super-Mare BS23 1DA
t (01934) 629936
e albany@lodgeguesthouse.co.uk
w albanylodgeguesthouse.co.uk

**Cornerways** ★★★
*Bed & Breakfast*
14 Whitecross Road, Weston-super-Mare BS23 1EW
t (01934) 623708
e cornerwaysgh@aol.com
w cornerwaysweston.com

**Flora Glen Guest House**
Rating Applied For
*Guest House*
130 Locking Road, Weston-super-Mare BS23 3HF
**t** (01934) 620592
**w** floraglenguesthouse.com

**Florence Guest House** ★★★
*Guest House*
32 Upper Church Road, Weston-super-Mare BS23 2DX
**t** (01934) 626993
**e** info@florenceguesthouse.co.uk
**w** florenceguesthouse.co.uk

**Grove Lodge** ★★★
*Guest House*
1 Bristol Road Lower, Weston-super-Mare BS23 2PL
**t** (01934) 620494
**e** thegrovelodge@aol.com
**w** grovelodge.info

**Harmony Poynt** ★★★★
*Guest Accommodation*
Park Place, Weston-super-Mare BS23 2BA
**t** (01934) 620258
**e** enquiries@harmonypoynthotel.co.uk
**w** harmonypoynthotel.co.uk

**Kensington Hotel** ★
*Guest Accommodation*
36 Knightstone Road, Weston-super-Mare BS23 2BD
**t** (01934) 621781
**e** helen@kensington50.freeserve.co.uk
**w** kensingtonhotel-weston.co.uk

**Lewinsdale Lodge** ★★★
*Guest Accommodation*
5-7 Clevedon Road, Weston-super-Mare BS23 1DA
**t** (01934) 632501
**e** lewinsdale.lodge@googlemail.com
**w** lewinsdale-hotel.co.uk

**The Lugano** ★★★
*Guest Accommodation*
26 Upper Church Road, Weston-super-Mare BS23 2DX
**t** (01934) 628207
**e** info@luganohotel.co.uk
**w** luganohotel.co.uk

**Milton Lodge Guest House** ★★★ *Guest House*
15 Milton Road, Weston-super-Mare BS23 2SH
**t** (01934) 623161
**e** info@milton-lodge.co.uk
**w** milton-lodge.co.uk

**Moorlands Country House** ★★★ *Guest House*
30 Main Road, Hutton BS24 9QH
**t** (01934) 812283
**e** margaret-holt@hotmail.co.uk
**w** questaccom.co.uk/35

**Orchard House** ★★★★
*Bed & Breakfast*
**SILVER AWARD**
West Wick, Weston-super-Mare BS24 7TF
**t** (01934) 520948
**e** orchardhousewsm@yahoo.co.uk

**Rosita** ★★★
*Guest Accommodation*
30 Upper Church Road, Weston-super-Mare BS23 2DX
**t** (01934) 620823

**Saxonia Guest House** ★★★
*Guest House*
95 Locking Road, Weston-super-Mare BS23 3EW
**t** (01934) 424850
**e** stay@saxoniaguesthouse.com
**w** saxoniaguesthouse.co.uk

**Soraya** ★★ *Guest House*
34 Upper Church Road, Weston-super-Mare BS23 2DX
**t** (01934) 629043
**e** enquiries@hotelsoraya.co.uk

**Spreyton Guest House** ★★★
*Guest House*
72 Locking Road, Weston-super-Mare BS23 3EN
**t** (01934) 416887
**e** info@spreytonguesthouse.com
**w** spreytonguesthouse.com

**Welbeck** ★★
*Guest Accommodation*
Knightstone Road, Marine Parade, Weston-super-Mare BS23 2BB
**t** (01934) 621258
**e** welbeckhotel@aol.com
**w** weston-welbeck.com

## WESTROP
Wiltshire

**Park Farm Barn** ★★★★
*Bed & Breakfast*
Westrop, Corsham SN13 9QF
**t** (01249) 715911
**e** parkfarmbarn@btinternet.com
**w** parkfarmbarn.co.uk

## WESTWARD HO!
Devon

**Brockenhurst** ★★★★
*Bed & Breakfast*
11 Atlantic Way, Westward Ho!, Bideford EX39 1HX
**t** (01237) 423346
**e** info@brockenhurstindevon.co.uk
**w** brockenhurstindevon.co.uk

**Mayfield** ★★★★
*Bed & Breakfast*
Avon Lane, Westward Ho! EX39 1LR
**t** (01237) 477128
**e** mayfieldbandb@hotmail.co.uk
**w** mayfieldbandb.co.uk

## WEYMOUTH
Dorset

**A Knight's Rest Guest House** ★★★ *Guest Accommodation*
93 Dorchester Road, Weymouth DT4 7JY
**t** (01305) 839005
**e** enquiries@aknightsrest.co.uk
**w** aknightsrest.co.uk

**Aaran House** ★★★
*Guest House*
2 The Esplanade, Weymouth DT4 8EA
**t** (01305) 766669
**e** denise.groves@sky.com
**w** aaranhouse.co.uk

**Albern House** ★★★
*Guest House*
13 Holland Road, Weymouth DT4 0AL
**t** (01305) 783951

**The Anchorage** ★★★
*Guest House*
7 The Esplanade, Weymouth DT4 8EB
**t** (01305) 782542
**e** info@anchoragehotelweymouth.co.uk
**w** anchoragehotelweymouth.co.uk

**Arcadia Guest House** ★★★
*Guest House*
7 Waterloo Place, Weymouth DT4 7PA
**t** (01305) 782458
**e** roywilcocks@hotmail.com
**w** arcadiaguesthouse.com

**Ashmira** ★★★★
*Guest Accommodation*
3 Westerhall Road, Weymouth DT4 7SZ
**t** (01305) 786584
**e** ashmirahotel@btconnect.com
**w** ashmirahotel.uk.com

**The Bay Guest House** ★★★★ *Guest House*
10 Waterloo Place, Weymouth DT4 7PE
**t** (01305) 786289
**e** harrisbay@aol.com
**w** thebayguesthouse.co.uk

**Beach Guest House** ★★★
*Guest House*
34 Lennox Street, Weymouth DT4 7HD
**t** (01305) 779212
**e** beachguesthouse@btinternet.com

**The Beach House** ★★★
*Guest Accommodation*
2 Brunswick Terrace, Weymouth DT4 7RR
**t** (01305) 789353
**e** stay@thebeachhouse.co.uk
**w** thebeachhouseweymouth.co.uk

**Beach View Guest House** ★★★ *Guest House*
3 The Esplanade, Weymouth DT4 8EA
**t** (01305) 786528
**e** beachviewweymouth@hotmail.com
**w** beachviewguesthouse.com

**Beaufort Guest House** ★★★
*Guest Accommodation*
24 The Esplanade, Weymouth DT4 8DN
**t** (01305) 782088
**e** info@beaufortguesthouse.co.uk
**w** beaufortguesthouse.co.uk

**The Bourneville** ★★★
*Guest House*
31-32 The Esplanade, Weymouth DT4 8DJ
**t** (01305) 784784
**e** enquiries@bournevillehotel.co.uk
**w** bournevillehotel.co.uk

**Bridge House** ★★★★
*Bed & Breakfast*
13 Frys Close, Portesham DT3 4LQ
**t** (01305) 871685
**e** thea@theaalexander.co.uk
**w** bridgehousebandb.co.uk

**Brierley Guest House** ★★★
*Guest House*
6 Lennox Street, Weymouth DT4 7HD
**t** (01305) 782050

**Brunswick Guest House** ★★★ *Guest Accommodation*
9 Brunswick Terrace, Weymouth DT4 7RW
**t** (01305) 785408
**e** info@brunswickweymouth.co.uk
**w** brunswickweymouth.co.uk

**The Cavendale** ★★★
*Guest Accommodation*
10 The Esplanade, Weymouth DT4 8EB
**t** (01305) 786960
**e** laraine.holder@virgin.net

**Chandlers** ★★★★★
*Guest Accommodation*
**GOLD AWARD**
4 Westerhall Road, Weymouth DT4 7SZ
**t** (01305) 771341
**e** info@chandlershotel.com
**w** chandlershotel.com

**The Channel** ★★★
*Guest Accommodation*
93 The Esplanade, Weymouth DT4 7AY
**t** (01305) 785405
**e** stay@channelhotel.co.uk
**w** channelhotel.co.uk

**The Chatsworth** ★★★★
*Guest Accommodation*
**SILVER AWARD**
14 The Esplanade, Weymouth DT4 8EB
**t** (01305) 785012
**e** david@thechatsworth.co.uk
**w** thechatsworth.co.uk

**The Clarence** ★★★★
*Guest Accommodation*
20 The Esplanade, Weymouth DT4 8DN
**t** (01305) 787573
**e** clarence.hotel1@btconnect.com

**The Concorde** ★★★
*Guest Accommodation*
131 The Esplanade, Weymouth DT4 7EY
**t** (01305) 776900
**e** sunbeam1@gotadsl.co.uk
**w** theconcordehotel.co.uk

**Crofton Guest House** ★★★
*Guest Accommodation*
Lennox Street, Weymouth DT4 7HD
**t** (01305) 785903
**e** webber_36-2003@tiscali.co.uk

**The Cumberland ★★★★**
*Guest Accommodation*
95 The Esplanade, Weymouth DT4 7AT
**t** (01305) 785644
**e** simon_reid@yahoo.co.uk
**w** cumberlandhotelweymouth.co.uk

**The Cunard Guest House ★★★★**
*Guest Accommodation*
45-46 Lennox Street, Weymouth DT4 7HB
**t** (01305) 771546
**e** harrisweymouth@aol.com
**w** cunardguesthouse.co.uk

**Eastney ★★★★** *Guest House*
15 Longfield Road, Weymouth DT4 8RQ
**t** (01305) 771682
**e** eastneyhotel@aol.com
**w** eastneyhotel.co.uk

**Flintstones Guest House ★★★** *Guest House*
10 Carlton Road South, Weymouth DT4 7PJ
**t** (01305) 784153

**Florian Guest House ★★★★**
*Guest Accommodation*
59 Abbotsbury Road, Weymouth DT4 0AQ
**t** (01305) 773836
**e** susiepitman@aol.com
**w** florianguesthouse.co.uk

**Fosters Guest House ★★★**
*Guest Accommodation*
3 Lennox Street, Weymouth DT4 7HB
**t** (01305) 771685

**Gloucester House ★★★**
*Guest Accommodation*
96 The Esplanade, Weymouth DT4 7AT
**t** (01305) 785191
**e** gloucesterwey@aol.com
**w** gloucesterhouseweymouth.co.uk

**Green Gables ★★★★**
*Guest Accommodation*
14 Carlton Road South, Weymouth DT4 7PJ
**t** (01305) 774808
**e** paula@greengablesweymouth.co.uk
**w** greengablesweymouth.co.uk

**The Gresham ★★**
*Guest Accommodation*
120 The Esplanade, Weymouth DT4 7EW
**t** (01305) 785897
**e** stuart.june@btconnect.com
**w** greshamhotel-weymouth.co.uk

**Harbour Lights ★★★★**
*Guest Accommodation*
20 Buxton Road, Weymouth DT4 9PJ
**t** (01305) 783273
**e** harbourlights@btconnect.com
**w** harbourlights-weymouth.co.uk

**Harlequin House ★★★**
*Guest House*
9 Carlton Road South, Weymouth DT4 7PL
**t** (01305) 785598
**e** mike_evans9999@yahoo.com
**w** harlequin-guest-house.co.uk

**Horizon Guest House ★★★**
*Guest Accommodation*
Brunswick Terrace, Weymouth DT4 7RW
**t** (01305) 784916
**e** info@horizonguesthouse.co.uk
**w** horizonguesthouse.co.uk

**Kelston Guesthouse ★★★**
*Guest Accommodation*
1 Lennox Street, Weymouth DT4 7HB
**t** (01305) 780692
**e** stay@kelstonguesthouse.co.uk
**w** kelstonguesthouse.co.uk

**The Kinley ★★★**
*Guest House*
98 The Esplanade, Weymouth DT4 7AT
**t** (01305) 782264
**e** hotelkinley@hotmail.com
**w** hotelkinley.co.uk

**The Langham ★★★**
*Guest Accommodation*
130 The Esplanade, Weymouth DT4 7EX
**t** (01305) 782530
**e** enquiries@langham-hotel.com
**w** langham-hotel.com

**Lichfield House ★★★**
*Guest House*
8 Brunswick Terrace, Weymouth DT4 7RW
**t** (01305) 784112
**e** lich.house@virgin.net
**w** lichfieldhouse.co.uk

**Lilac Villa Guest House ★★★★** *Guest House*
124 Dorchester Road, Weymouth DT4 7LG
**t** (01305) 782670
**e** lilacvilla@ukonline.co.uk

**Lyndale Guest House ★★★**
*Guest Accommodation*
17 Brunswick Terrace, Weymouth DT4 7SD
**t** (01305) 786275
**e** info@lyndaleguesthouseweymouth.co.uk
**w** lyndaleguesthouseweymouth.co.uk

**Mar June Guest House ★★★**
*Guest House*
32 Lennox Street, Weymouth DT4 7HD
**t** (01305) 761320

**Marina Court ★★★**
*Guest Accommodation*
142 The Esplanade, Weymouth DT4 7PB
**t** (01305) 782146
**e** marion@vassie.fsnet.co.uk
**w** marinacourt.co.uk

**The Mayfair ★★★**
*Guest Accommodation*
99 The Esplanade, Weymouth DT4 7BE
**t** (01305) 782094
**e** themayfair.weymouth@hotmail.com
**w** mayfairhotelweymouth.co.uk

**Morven House ★★★★**
*Guest Accommodation*
2 Westerhall Road, Weymouth DT4 7SZ
**t** (01305) 785075
**e** enquiries@morvenweymouth.co.uk
**w** morvenweymouth.co.uk

**Oaklands Edwardian Guesthouse ★★★★**
*Guest Accommodation*
1 Glendinning Avenue, Weymouth DT4 7QF
**t** (01305) 767081
**e** stay@oaklands-guesthouse.co.uk
**w** oaklands-guesthouse.co.uk

**Old Harbour View ★★★★**
*Bed & Breakfast*
12 Trinity Road, Weymouth DT4 8TJ
**t** (01305) 774633 & 07974 422241
**e** pv_1st_ind@yahoo.co.uk

**The Pebbles ★★★★**
*Guest House*
18 Kirtleton Avenue, Weymouth DT4 7PT
**t** (01305) 784331
**e** info@thepebbles.co.uk
**w** thepebbles.co.uk

**The Redcliff ★★★**
*Guest House*
18/19 Brunswick Terrace, Weymouth DT4 7RW
**t** (01305) 784682
**e** contact@redcliffweymouth.co.uk
**w** redcliffweymouth.co.uk

**The Seaham ★★★★**
*Guest House* **SILVER AWARD**
3 Waterloo Place, Weymouth DT4 7NU
**t** (01305) 782010
**e** stay@theseahamweymouth.co.uk
**w** theseahamweymouth.co.uk

**Sou West Lodge ★★★**
*Guest Accommodation*
Rodwell Road, Weymouth DT4 8QT
**t** (01305) 783749
**e** enquiry@souwestlodge.co.uk
**w** souwestlodge.co.uk

**Spindrift Guest House ★★★**
*Guest Accommodation*
11 Brunswick Terrace, Weymouth DT4 7RW
**t** (01305) 773625
**e** stay@spindriftguesthouse.co.uk
**w** spindriftguesthouse.co.uk

**Sunbay Guest House ★★★**
*Guest House*
12 Brunswick Terrace, Weymouth DT4 7RW
**t** (01305) 785992
**e** info@sunbayguesthouse.co.uk
**w** sunbayguesthouse.co.uk

**Timrick Lodge Guest House**
Rating Applied For
*Guest House*
7 Lennox Street, Weymouth DT4 7HD
**t** (01305) 783194
**e** timricklodge@talktalk.net
**w** timricklodge.co.uk

**Trevann Guest House ★★★**
*Guest House*
28 Lennox Street, Weymouth DT4 7HE
**t** (01305) 782604
**e** trevann28@aol.com

**Turks Head ★★★★**
*Guest Accommodation*
8 East Street, Chickerell DT3 4DS
**t** (01305) 783093

**Warwick Court ★★★**
*Guest House*
20 Abbotsbury Road, Weymouth DT4 0AE
**t** (01305) 783261
**e** sharon@warwickcourt.co.uk

**Weymouth Sands ★★★**
*Guest Accommodation*
5 The Esplanade, Weymouth DT4 8EA
**t** (01305) 839022
**e** enquiries@weymouthsands.co.uk
**w** weymouthsands.co.uk

**Wilton Guest House ★★★**
*Guest Accommodation*
5 Gloucester Street, Weymouth DT4 7AP
**t** (01305) 782820
**e** enq@wiltonguesthouse.co.uk
**w** thewiltonguesthouse.co.uk

## WHEDDON CROSS
Somerset

**Exmoor House ★★★★**
*Guest Accommodation*
Wheddon Cross TA24 7DU
**t** (01643) 841432
**e** info@exmoorhouse.com
**w** exmoorhouse.com

**Little Brendon Hill Farm ★★★★★**
*Guest Accommodation*
Summerway, Wheddon Cross TA24 7BG
**t** (01643) 841556
**e** info@exmoorheaven.co.uk
**w** exmoorheaven.co.uk

**Sundial Guest House ★★★★**
*Guest Accommodation*
**SILVER AWARD**
Wheddon Cross TA24 7DP
**t** (01643) 841188
**e** admin@sundialguesthouse.co.uk
**w** sundialguesthouse.co.uk

## WHILBOROUGH
Devon

**Walmer Towers ★★★★**
*Bed & Breakfast*
**SILVER AWARD**
Moles Lane, Whilborough TQ12 5LS
**t** (01803) 872105
**e** walmertowers@btinternet.com
**w** walmertowers.co.uk

### WHITMINSTER
Gloucestershire

**Whitminster Inn** ★★★★ *Inn*
Bristol Road, Gloucester
GL2 7NY
**t** (01452) 740234
**w** whitminsterinn.co.uk

### WHITSTONE
Cornwall

**Whiteleigh Cottage** ★★★★
*Bed & Breakfast*
Whitstone, Holsworthy
EX22 6LB
**t** (01288) 341082
**e** whiteleighcottage@hotmail.com
**w** whiteleighcottage.co.uk

### WHITTINGTON
Gloucestershire

**Ham Hill Farm** ★★★★
*Guest Accommodation*
**SILVER AWARD**
Whittington, Cheltenham
GL54 4EZ
**t** (01242) 584415
**e** hamhillfarm@johndhughes.plus.com

**Whalley Farm House**
★★★★ *Farmhouse*
**SILVER AWARD**
Whittington, Cheltenham
GL54 4HA
**t** (01242) 820213
**e** rowefarms@farmline.com
**w** whalleyfarm.co.uk

### WIDEMOUTH BAY
Cornwall

**Bay View Inn** ★★★★ *Inn*
Marine Drive, Widemouth Bay,
Bude EX23 0AW
**t** (01288) 361273
**e** thebayviewinn@aol.com
**w** bayviewinn.co.uk

### WILLITON
Somerset

**Hartnells B&B** ★★★★
*Bed & Breakfast*
28 Long Street, Williton
TA4 4QU
**t** (01984) 634777
**e** sueton.perrett@btinternet.com
**w** hartnellsbandb.co.uk

### WILTON
Wiltshire

**The Wheatsheaf** ★★★ *Inn*
1 King Street, Wilton SP2 0AX
**t** (01722) 742267
**e** mail@thewheatsheafwilton.co.uk
**w** thewheatsheafwilton.co.uk

### WIMBORNE MINSTER
Dorset

**The Albion** ★★
*Guest Accommodation*
High Street, Wimborne Minster
BH21 1HR
**t** (01202) 882492
**e** albioninn-wimborne@tiscali.co.uk
**w** albioninn-wimborne.co.uk

**Homestay** ★★★
*Bed & Breakfast*
22 West Borough, Wimborne
BH21 1NF
**t** (01202) 849015

**The Kings Head Hotel**
Rating Applied For
*Guest Accommodation*
The Square, Wimborne
BH21 1JG
**t** (01202) 880101
**e** 6474@greeneking.co.uk
**w** oldenglishinns.co.uk

**Lantern Lodge** ★★★★
*Bed & Breakfast*
**SILVER AWARD**
47 Gravel Hill, Merley
BH21 1RW
**t** (01202) 884183
**e** pam@lanternlodge.net
**w** lanternlodge.net

**Long Lane Farmhouse**
★★★★ *Bed & Breakfast*
**SILVER AWARD**
Long Lane, Colehill BH21 7AQ
**t** (01202) 887829
**e** patricksmyth@btinternet.com

**The Old George** ★★★★
*Bed & Breakfast*
**SILVER AWARD**
2 Corn Market, Wimborne
BH21 1JL
**t** (01202) 888510
**e** chrissie_oldgeorge@yahoo.co.uk
**w** theoldgeorge.net

**West Borough** ★★
*Bed & Breakfast*
96 West Borough, Wimborne
BH21 1NH
**t** (01202) 884039

### WINCHCOMBE
Gloucestershire

**Cleevely** ★★★★
*Bed & Breakfast*
Wadfield Farm, Winchcombe
GL54 5AL
**t** (01242) 602059
**e** cleevelybxb@hotmail.com
**w** smoothhound.co.uk/cleevely

**Gower House** ★★★★
*Guest Accommodation*
16 North Street, Winchcombe,
Cheltenham GL54 5LH
**t** (01242) 602616
**e** gowerhouse16@aol.com.uk

**Manor Farm** ★★★★
*Farmhouse*
Greet, Winchcombe,
Cheltenham GL54 5BJ
**t** (01242) 602423
**e** janet@dickandjanet.fsnet.co.uk

**North Farmcote Bed and Breakfast** ★★★★ *Farmhouse*
North Farmcote, Winchcombe
GL54 5AU
**t** (01242) 602304
**e** davideayrs@yahoo.co.uk
**w** glosfarmhols.co.uk/north-farmcote

**One Silk Mill Lane** ★★★★
*Bed & Breakfast*
Silk Mill Lane, Winchcombe
GL54 5HZ
**t** (01242) 603952
**e** jenny.cheshire@virgin.net

**Parks Farm** ★★★★
*Farmhouse*
Sudeley, Winchcombe
GL54 5JB
**t** (01242) 603874
**e** rosemaryawilson@hotmail.com
**w** parksfarm.co.uk

**Postlip Hall Farm** ★★★★
*Farmhouse* **GOLD AWARD**
Winchcombe, Cheltenham
GL54 5AQ
**t** (01242) 603351
**e** postliphallfarm@tiscali.co.uk
**w** smoothhound.co.uk/hotels/postlip

**The White Hart Inn and Restaurant** ★★★ *Inn*
High Street, Winchcombe
GL54 5LJ
**t** (01242) 602359
**e** enquiries@the-white-hart-inn.com
**w** the-white-hart-inn.co.uk

### WINFRITH NEWBURGH
Dorset

**Wynards Farm** ★★★★
*Bed & Breakfast*
Winfrith Newburgh,
Dorchester DT2 8DQ
**t** (01305) 852660
**e** enquiries@wynardsfarm.co.uk
**w** wynardsfarm.co.uk

### WINKLEIGH
Devon

**The Old Parsonage** ★★★★
*Guest Accommodation*
Court Walk, Winkleigh
EX19 8JA
**t** (01837) 83772
**e** tony@lymingtonarms.co.uk
**w** lymingtonarms.co.uk

### WINSFORD
Somerset

**Kemps Farm** ★★★★
*Farmhouse*
Kemps Lane, Winsford
TA24 7HT
**t** (01643) 851312

### WINSHAM
Somerset

**Fulwood House** ★★★★
*Bed & Breakfast*
Ebben Lane, Chard TA20 4EE
**t** (01460) 30163
**e** liz.earl@virgin.net
**w** fulwoodhouse.co.uk

### WINSLEY
Wiltshire

**Conifers** ★★ *Bed & Breakfast*
4 King Alfred Way, Winsley,
Bradford-on-Avon BA15 2NG
**t** (01225) 722482

**Stillmeadow** ★★★★★
*Bed & Breakfast*
18 Bradford Road, Bradford-on-Avon BA15 2HW
**t** (01225) 722119
**e** sue.gilby@btinternet.com
**w** stillmeadow.co.uk

### WINTERBORNE ZELSTON
Dorset

**Brook Farm** ★★★ *Farmhouse*
Winterborne Zelston,
Blandford Forum DT11 9EU
**t** (01929) 459267
**e** kerleybrookfarmzelston@yahoo.co.uk

### WINTERBOURNE STOKE
Wiltshire

**Scotland Lodge Farm**
★★★★ *Bed & Breakfast*
Winterbourne Stoke, Salisbury
SP3 4TF
**t** (01980) 621199
**e** william.lockwood@bigwig.net
**w** smoothhound.co.uk/hotels/scotlandl.html

### WITCOMBE
Gloucestershire

**Crickley Court** ★★★★
*Guest Accommodation*
**SILVER AWARD**
Dog Lane, Witcombe GL3 4UF
**t** (01452) 863634
**e** lispilgrimmorris@yahoo.co.uk
**w** crickleycourt.co.uk

### WITHAM FRIARY
Somerset

**Higher West Barn Farm**
★★★★ *Farmhouse*
**SILVER AWARD**
Bindon Lane, Frome BA11 5HH
**t** (01749) 850819
**e** enquiry@higherwestbarnfarm.co.uk
**w** higherwestbarnfarm.co.uk

### WITHERIDGE
Devon

**Thelbridge Cross Inn**
★★★★ *Inn*
Thelbridge, Crediton EX17 4SQ
**t** (01884) 860316
**e** admin@thelbridgexinn.co.uk
**w** thelbridgexinn.co.uk

### WITHYPOOL
Somerset

**Newland House** ★★★★★
*Guest Accommodation*
**SILVER AWARD**
Minehead TA24 7NF
**t** (01643) 831199
**e** info@newlandhouse-exmoor.co.uk
**w** newlandhouse-exmoor.co.uk

### WIVELISCOMBE
Somerset

**Mill Barn** ★★★★
*Bed & Breakfast*
Jews Farm, Wivelscombe
TA4 2HL
**t** (01984) 624739
**e** tony&marilyn@mill-barn.freeserve.co.uk
**w** mill-barn.freeserve.co.uk

**North Down Farm** ★★★★
*Farmhouse* **SILVER AWARD**
Wiveliscombe TA4 2BL
**t** (01984) 623730
**e** jennycope@btinternet.com
**w** north-down-farm.co.uk

## WOODBOROUGH
Wiltshire

**Well Cottage** ★★★★
*Bed & Breakfast*
Honeystreet, Woodborough
SN9 5PS
**t** (01672) 851577
**e** booking@well-cottage.org.uk
**w** well-cottage.org.uk

## WOODLEIGH
Devon

**Higher Hendham House**
★★★★ *Farmhouse*
Woodleigh, Kingsbridge
TQ7 4DP
**t** (01548) 550015
**e** higherhendhamhouse@fsmail.net
**w** higherhendhamhouse.com

## WOODY BAY
Devon

**Moorlands** ★★★★
*Guest Accommodation*
Woody Bay, Parracombe
EX31 4RA
**t** (01598) 763224
**e** info@moorlandshotel.co.uk
**w** moorlandshotel.co.uk

## WOOKEY HOLE
Somerset

**Whitegate Cottage** ★★
*Bed & Breakfast*
Milton Lane, Wells BA5 1DE
**t** (01749) 675326
**e** sueandnic@whitegate.freeserve.co.uk
**w** synergynet.co.uk/somerset/whitegate.htm

## WOOL
Dorset

**East Burton House** ★★
*Bed & Breakfast*
East Burton Road, Wareham
BH20 6HE
**t** (01929) 462083
**e** info@eastburtonhouse.com
**w** eastburtonhouse.com

**The Withies** ★★★
*Bed & Breakfast*
16 Colliers Lane, Wool
BH20 6DL
**t** (01929) 405339
**e** pazwold@btinternet.com
**w** atthewithies.co.uk

## WOOLACOMBE
Devon

**Castle** ★★★★
*Guest Accommodation*
The Esplanade, Woolacombe
EX34 7DJ
**t** (01271) 870788

**Ossaborough House** ★★★★
*Guest Accommodation*
**SILVER AWARD**
Ossaborough Lane,
Woolacombe EX34 7HJ
**t** (01271) 870297
**e** info@ossaboroughhouse.co.uk
**w** ossaboroughhouse.co.uk

**Sandunes** ★★★★
*Guest House*
Beach Road, Woolacombe
EX34 7BT
**t** (01271) 870661
**e** beaconhts@u.genie.co.uk
**w** sandwool.fsnet.co.uk

**Sunny Nook** ★★★★
*Guest Accommodation*
**SILVER AWARD**
Beach Road, Woolacombe
EX34 7AA
**t** (01271) 870964
**e** kate@sunnynook.co.uk
**w** sunnynook.co.uk

## WOOLMINSTONE
Somerset

**Barn Cottage Bed and Breakfast** ★★★★
*Bed & Breakfast*
**SILVER AWARD**
Lyminster Farm, Woolminstone
TA18 8QP
**t** (01460) 75313
**e** bandbbarncottage@aol.com
**w** smoothhound.co.uk/hotels/barncottage

## WOOTTON COURTENAY
Somerset

**Dunkery Beacon Country House Accommodation**
★★★★ *Guest House*
Dunkery Beacon, Wootton
Courtenay TA24 8RH
**t** (01643) 841241
**e** info@dunkerybeaconaccommodation.co.uk
**w** dunkerybeaconaccommodation.co.uk

## WOOTTON RIVERS
Wiltshire

**The Royal Oak** ★★★ *Inn*
Wootton Rivers, Marlborough
SN8 4NQ
**t** (01672) 810322
**e** royaloak35@hotmail.com
**w** wiltshire-pubs.com

## WORTH MATRAVERS
Dorset

**Chiltern Lodge** ★★
*Bed & Breakfast*
8 Newfoundland Close, Worth
Matravers BH19 3LX
**t** (01929) 439337
**e** densor@btopenworld.com
**w** chilternlodge.co.uk

## WRAXALL
Somerset

**Rose's Farm** ★★★★
*Farmhouse*
Wraxall, Shepton Mallet
BA4 6RQ
**t** (01749) 860261
**e** info@rosesfarm.com
**w** rosesfarm.com

## YATTON KEYNELL
Wiltshire

**Combehead Barn** ★★★★
*Bed & Breakfast*
Giddeahall, Yatton Keynell
SN14 7ES
**t** (01249) 783487
**e** combe2005@aol.com
**w** thebarncombehead.co.uk

## YELVERTON
Devon

**Overcombe House** ★★★★
*Guest Accommodation*
Old Station Road, Yelverton
PL20 7RA
**t** (01822) 853501
**e** enquiries@overcombehotel.co.uk
**w** overcombehotel.co.uk

**The Rosemont** ★★★★
*Guest Accommodation*
Greenbank Terrace, Yelverton
PL20 6DR
**t** (01822) 852175
**e** office@therosemont.co.uk
**w** therosemont.co.uk

## YEOVIL
Somerset

**Greystones Court** ★★★★
*Guest Accommodation*
152 Hendford Hill, Yeovil
BA20 2RG
**t** (01935) 426124
**e** peterandsimone.adlam@btopenworld.com
**w** greystonescourt.com

**Pendomer House** ★★★
*Bed & Breakfast*
Nr Yeovil BA22 9PB
**t** (01935) 862785
**e** enquiries@pendomerhouse.co.uk
**w** pendomerhouse.co.uk

## YEOVILTON
Somerset

**Courtry Farm** ★★★
*Farmhouse*
Bridgehampton, Yeovil
BA22 8HF
**t** (01935) 840327
**e** courtryfarm@hotmail.com

## YORKLEY
Gloucestershire

**Silverdeane** ★★★★
*Bed & Breakfast*
Lower Road, Yorkley, Lydney
GL15 4TQ
**t** (01594) 560262
**e** enquiries@silverdeane.co.uk
**w** silverdeane.co.uk

# Further information



Clockwise: Botany Bay, Kent; Whinstone Lee Tor, Peak District, Derbyshire; Sherwood Pines Forest Park, Nottinghamshire

# Quality assessment schemes

When you're looking for a place to stay, you need a rating system you can trust. Quality ratings are your clear guide to what to expect, in an easy-to-understand form.

National tourist board professional assessors pay unannounced visits to establishments that are new to the rating scheme and stay overnight. Once in the scheme establishments receive an annual pre-arranged day visit, with an overnight stay generally every other year, when the assessors book in anonymously and test all the facilities and services.

Based on internationally recognised star ratings, the system puts great emphasis on quality, and reflects exactly what consumers are looking for. Ratings are awarded from one to five stars – the more stars, the higher the quality and the greater the range of facilities and services provided.

Look out, too, for Enjoy England Gold and Silver Awards, which are awarded to properties achieving the highest levels of quality within their star rating. While the overall rating is based on a combination of facilities and quality, the Gold and Silver Awards are based solely on quality.

## Star ratings

Star ratings are your sign of quality assurance, giving you the confidence to book the accommodation that meets your expectations. All bed and breakfast accommodation that is awarded a star rating will meet the minimum standards – so you can be confident that you will find the basic services that you would expect, such as:

- A clear explanation of booking charges, services offered and cancellation terms
- A full cooked breakfast or substantial continental breakfast
- At least one bathroom or shower room for every six guests
- For a stay of more than one night, rooms cleaned and beds made daily
- Printed advice on how to summon emergency assistance at night
- All statutory obligations will be met.

Proprietors of bed and breakfast accommodation have to provide certain additional facilities and services at the higher star levels, some of which may be important to you:

**THREE-STAR accommodation must provide:**

- Private bathroom/shower room (cannot be shared with the owners)
- Bedrooms must have a washbasin if not en suite.

**FOUR-STAR accommodation must provide:**

- 50% of bedrooms en suite or with private bathroom.

**FIVE-STAR accommodation must provide:**

- All bedrooms with en suite or private bathroom.

Sometimes a bed and breakfast establishment has exceptional bedrooms and bathrooms and offers guests a very special welcome, but cannot achieve a higher star rating because, for example, there are no en suite bedrooms, or it is difficult to put washbasins in the bedrooms (three star). This is sometimes the case with period properties.

## Quality

The availability of additional facilities alone is not enough for an establishment to achieve a higher star rating. Bed and breakfast accommodation has to meet exacting standards for quality in critical areas. Consumer research has shown the critical areas to be: cleanliness, bedrooms, bathrooms, hospitality and food.

# Advice and information

## Making a reservation

When enquiring about accommodation, make sure you check prices, the quality rating and other important details. You will also need to state your requirements clearly and precisely, for example:

- Arrival and departure dates, with acceptable alternatives if appropriate
- The type of accommodation you need – for example, room with twin beds, en suite bathroom
- The terms you want – for example, bed and breakfast only; dinner and breakfast (where provided)
- The age of any children with you, whether you want them to share your room or be next door, and any other special requirements, such as a cot
- Any particular requirements you may have, such as a special diet, ground-floor room.

### Confirmation

Misunderstandings can easily happen over the telephone, so do request a written confirmation, together with details of any terms and conditions.

### Deposits

If you make your reservation weeks or months in advance, you will probably be asked for a deposit, which will then be deducted from the final bill when you leave. The amount will vary from establishment to establishment and could be payment in full at peak times.

### Payment on arrival

Some establishments ask you to pay for your room on arrival if you have not booked it in advance. This is especially likely to happen if you arrive late and have little or no luggage.

If you are asked to pay on arrival, it is a good idea to see your room first, to make sure it meets your requirements.

## Cancellations

### Legal contract

When you accept accommodation that is offered to you, by telephone or in writing, you enter a legally binding contract with the proprietor. This means that if you cancel your booking, fail to take up the accommodation or leave early, the proprietor may be entitled to compensation if he or she cannot re-let for all or a good part of the booked period. You will probably forfeit any deposit you have paid, and may well be asked for an additional payment.

At the time of booking you should be advised of what charges would be made in the event of cancelling the accommodation or leaving early. If this is not mentioned you should ask so that future disputes can be avoided. The proprietor cannot make a claim until after the booked period, and during that time he or she should make every effort to re-let the accommodation. If there is a dispute it is sensible for both sides to seek legal advice on the matter. If you do have to change your travel plans, it is in your own interests to let the proprietor know in writing as soon as possible, to give them a chance to re-let your accommodation.

And remember, if you book by telephone and are asked for your credit card number, you should check whether the proprietor intends charging your credit card account should you later cancel your reservation. A proprietor should not be able to charge your credit card account with a cancellation fee unless he or she has made this clear at the time of your booking and you have agreed. However, to avoid later disputes, we suggest you check whether this is the intention.

## Insurance

A travel or holiday insurance policy will safeguard you if you have to cancel or change your holiday plans. You can arrange a policy quite cheaply through your insurance company or travel agent.

## Arriving late

If you know you will be arriving late in the evening, it is a good idea to say so when you book. If you are delayed on your way, a telephone call to say that you will be late would be appreciated.

## Service charges and tipping

These days many places levy service charges automatically. If they do, they must clearly say so in their offer of accommodation, at the time of booking. The service charge then becomes part of the legal contract when you accept the offer of accommodation.

If a service charge is levied automatically, there is no need to tip the staff, unless they provide some exceptional service. The usual tip for meals is 10% of the total bill.

## Telephone charges

Establishments can set their own charges for telephone calls made through their switchboard or from direct-dial telephones in bedrooms. These charges are often much higher than telephone companies' standard charges (to defray the cost of providing the service).

### Comparing costs

It is a condition of the quality assessment schemes that an establishment's unit charges are on display by the telephones or with the room information. It is not always easy to compare these charges with standard rates, so before using a hotel telephone for long-distance calls, you may decide to ask how the charges compare.

## Security of valuables

You can deposit your valuables with the proprietor or manager during your stay, and we recommend you do this as a sensible precaution. Make sure you obtain a receipt for them. Some places do not accept articles for safe custody, and in that case it is wisest to keep your valuables with you.

## Disclaimer

Some proprietors put up a notice that disclaims liability for property brought on to their premises by a guest. In fact, they can only restrict their liability. By law, a proprietor is liable for the value of the loss or damage to any property (except a car or its contents) of a guest who has engaged overnight accommodation, but if the proprietor has the notice on display, liability is limited to £50 for one article and a total of £100 for any one guest. The notice must be prominently displayed in the reception area or main entrance. These limits do not apply to valuables you have deposited with the proprietor for safekeeping, or to property lost through the default, neglect or wilful act of the proprietor or his staff.

## Travelling with pets

Dogs, cats, ferrets and some other pet mammals can be brought into the UK from certain countries without having to undertake six months' quarantine on arrival provided they meet all the rules of the Pet Travel Scheme (PETS).

For full details, visit the PETS website at
**w** defra.gov.uk/animalh/quarantine/index.htm or contact the PETS Helpline
**t** +44 (0)870 241 1710
**e** quarantine@animalhealth.gsi.gov.uk
Ask for fact sheets which cover dogs and cats, ferrets or domestic rabbits and rodents.

There are no requirements for pets travelling directly between the UK and the Channel Islands. Pets entering Jersey or Guernsey from other countries need to be Pet Travel Scheme compliant and have a valid EU Pet Passport. For more information see jersey.com or visitguernsey.com.

## What to expect

The proprietor/management is required to undertake the following:

- To maintain standards of guest care, cleanliness and service appropriate to the type of establishment;
- To describe accurately in any advertisement, brochure or other printed or electronic media, the facilities and services provided;
- To make clear to visitors exactly what is included in all prices quoted for accommodation, including taxes, and any other surcharges. Details of charges for additional services/facilities should also be made clear;
- To give a clear statement of the policy on cancellations to guests at the time of booking ie by telephone, fax, email, as well as information given in a printed format;
- To adhere to and not to exceed prices quoted at the time of booking for accommodation and other services;
- To advise visitors at the time of booking, and subsequently if any change, if the accommodation offered is in an unconnected annexe or similar and to indicate the location of such accommodation and any difference in comfort and/or amenities from accommodation in the establishment;
- To register all guests on arrival;
- To give each visitor on request details of payments due and a receipt, if required;
- To deal promptly and courteously with all enquiries, requests, bookings and correspondence from visitors;
- To ensure complaint handling procedures are

in place and that complaints received are investigated promptly and courteously and that the outcome is communicated to the visitor;

- To give due consideration to the requirements of visitors with disabilities and visitors with special needs, and to make suitable provision where applicable;
- To provide public liability insurance or comparable arrangements and to comply with all applicable planning, safety and other statutory requirements;
- To allow a quality ratings assessor reasonable access to the establishment on request, to confirm the Code of Conduct is being observed.

## Comments and complaints

### Bed and breakfast accommodation and the law

Places that offer accommodation have legal and statutory responsibilities to their customers, such as providing information about prices, providing adequate fire precautions and safeguarding valuables. They must also describe their accommodation and facilities accurately. All the places featured in this guide have declared that they do fulfil all applicable statutory obligations.

### Information

The proprietors themselves supply the descriptions of their establishments and other information for the entries, (except quality ratings and awards). The publishers cannot guarantee the accuracy of information in this guide, and accept no responsibility for any error or misrepresentation. All liability for loss, disappointment, negligence or other damage caused by reliance on the information contained in this guide, or in the event of bankruptcy or liquidation or cessation of trade of any company, individual or firm mentioned, is hereby excluded. We strongly recommend that you carefully check prices and other details when you book your accommodation.

### Quality signage

All establishments displaying a quality sign have to hold current membership of a quality assessment scheme.

When an establishment is sold, the new owner has to reapply and be reassessed. In some areas the rating may be carried forward in the interim.

### Problems

Of course, we hope you will not have cause for complaint, but problems do occur from time to time. If you are dissatisfied with anything, make your complaint to the management immediately. Then the management can take action at once to investigate the matter and put things right. The longer you leave a complaint, the harder it is to deal with it effectively.

In certain circumstances, the national tourist boards may look into complaints. However, they have no statutory control over establishments or their methods of operating and cannot become involved in legal or contractual matters, nor can they get involved in seeking financial recompense.

If you do have problems that have not been resolved by the proprietor and which you would like to bring to their attention, please write to:

### England

Quality in Tourism, Farncombe House,
Broadway, Worcestershire WR12 7LJ

### Guernsey

Quality Development Manager,
Commerce and Employment Department,
PO Box 459, St Martin, Guernsey GY1 6AF

### Jersey

Tourism Office, Liberation Place,
St Helier, Jersey JE1 1BB

# About the accommodation entries

## Entries

All the accommodation featured in this guide has been assessed or has applied for assessment under a quality assessment scheme.

Assessment under the EnjoyEngland Quality Rose scheme automatically entitles establishments to a listing in this guide. Start your search for a place to stay by looking in the regional sections of this guide where proprietors have paid to have their establishment featured in either a standard entry (includes description, facilities and prices) or an enhanced entry (photograph and extended details). If you can't find what you're looking for, turn to the listing section on the yellow pages for an even wider choice of accommodation.

## Locations

Places to stay are generally listed under the town, city or village where they are located. If a place is in a small village, you may find it listed under a nearby town (providing it is within a seven-mile radius).

Place names are listed alphabetically within each regional section of the guide, along with the name of the ceremonial county they are in and their map reference.

### Map references

These refer to the colour location maps at the front of the guide. The first figure shown is the map number, the following letter and figure indicate the grid reference on the map. Only place names under which standard or enhanced entries (see above) feature appear on the maps. Some entries were included just before the guide went to press, so they do not appear on the maps.

### Addresses

County names, which appear in the place headings, are not repeated in the entries. When you are writing, you should of course make sure you use the full address and postcode.

### Telephone numbers

Telephone numbers are listed below the accommodation address for each entry. Area codes are shown in brackets.

## Prices

The prices shown are only a general guide; they were supplied to us by proprietors in summer 2008. Remember, changes may occur after the guide goes to press, so we strongly advise you to check prices when you book your accommodation.

Prices are shown in pounds sterling and include VAT where applicable. Some places also include a service charge in their standard tariff, so check this when you book.

There are many different ways of quoting prices for accommodation. We use a standardised method in the guide to allow you to compare prices. For example, when we show:

**Bed and breakfast**: the prices shown are per room for overnight accommodation with breakfast. The double room price is for two people. (If a double room is occupied by one person there is sometimes a reduction in price.)

**Evening meal**: the prices shown are per person per night.

Some places only provide a continental breakfast in the set price, and you may have to pay extra if you want a full English breakfast.

### Checking prices

According to UK law, establishments with at least four bedrooms or eight beds must display their charges in the reception area or entrance. There is no legal requirement for hotels in the Channel Islands to display their prices but they should make them clear at the time of booking.

In your own interests, do make sure you check prices and what they include.

### Children's rates

You will find that many places charge a reduced rate for children, especially if they share a room with their parents. Some places charge the full rate, however, when a child occupies a room which might otherwise have been let to an adult. The upper age limit for reductions for children varies from one accommodation to another, so check this when you book.

### Seasonal packages and special promotions

Prices often vary through the year and may be significantly lower outside peak holiday weeks. Many places offer special package rates – fully inclusive weekend breaks, for example – in the autumn, winter and spring. A number of establishments taking an enhanced entry have included any special offers, themed breaks etc that are available.

You can get details of other bargain packages that may be available from the establishments themselves, regional tourism organisations or your local Tourist Information Centre (TIC). Your local travel agent may also have information and can help you make reservations.

## Bathrooms

Each accommodation entry shows you the number of en suite and private bathrooms available. En suite bathroom means the bath or shower and wc are contained behind the main door of the bedroom. Private bathroom means a bath or shower and wc solely for the occupants of one bedroom, on the same floor, reasonably close and with a key provided. If the availability of a bath, rather than a shower, is important to you, remember to check when you book.

## Meals

It is advisable to check availability of meals and set times when making your reservation. Some smaller places may ask you at breakfast whether you want an evening meal. The prices shown in each entry are for bed and breakfast or half board, but many places also offer lunch.

## Opening period

If an entry does not indicate an opening period, please check directly with the hotel.

## Symbols

The at-a-glance symbols included at the end of each entry show many of the services and facilities available at each establishment. You will find the key to these symbols on page 7.

## Smoking

In the UK and the Channel Islands, it is illegal to smoke in enclosed public spaces and places of work. Some establishments may choose to provide designated smoking bedrooms, and may allow smoking in private areas that are not used by any staff. If you wish to smoke, it is advisable to check whether it is allowed when you book.

## Alcoholic drinks

Many places listed in the guide are licensed to serve alcohol. The licence may be restricted – to diners only, for example – so you may want to check this when you book. If they have a bar this is shown by the 🍷 symbol.

## Pets

Many places accept guests with dogs, but we do advise that you check this when you book, and ask if there are any extra charges or rules about exactly where your pet is allowed. The acceptance of dogs is not always extended to cats and it is strongly advised that cat owners contact the establishment well in advance. Some establishments do not accept pets at all. Pets are welcome by arrangement where you see this symbol 🐕.

The quarantine laws have changed, and dogs, cats and ferrets are able to come into Britain and the Channel Islands from over 50 countries. For details of the Pet Travel Scheme (PETS) please turn to page 662.

## Payment accepted

The types of payment accepted by an establishment are listed in the payment accepted section. If you plan to pay by card, check that the establishment will take your particular card before you book. Some proprietors will charge you a higher rate if you pay by credit card rather than cash or cheque. The difference is to cover the percentage paid by the proprietor to the credit card company. When you book by telephone, you may be asked for your credit card number as confirmation. But remember, the proprietor may then charge your credit card account if you cancel your booking. See under Cancellations on page 661.

## Awaiting confirmation of rating

At the time of going to press some establishments featured in this guide had not yet been assessed for their rating for the year 2009 and so their new rating could not be included. Rating Applied For indicates this.

## Property names

Under the Common Standards for assessment, guest accommodation may not include the word 'hotel' in its name. The majority of accommodation in this guide complies with this rule and the national assessing bodies, including VisitBritain, are working towards bringing all guest accommodation in line with this.

# Getting around

## Travelling in London

### London transport

London Underground has 12 lines, each with its own unique colour, so you can easily follow them on the Underground map. Most lines run through central London, and many serve parts of Greater London.

Buses are a quick, convenient way to travel around London, providing plenty of sightseeing opportunities on the way. There are over 6,500 buses in London operating 700 routes every day. You will need to buy a ticket before you board the bus – available from machines at the bus stop – or have a valid Oyster card (see below).

London's National Rail system stretches all over London. Many lines start at the main London railway stations (Paddington, Victoria, Waterloo, Kings Cross) with links to the tube. Trains mainly serve areas outside central London, and travel over ground.

Children usually travel free, or at reduced fare, on all public transport in London.

### Oyster cards

Oyster cards can be used to pay fares on all London Underground, buses, Docklands Light Railway and trams; they are generally not valid for National Rail services in London.

Oyster cards are very easy to use – you just touch the card on sensors at stations or on buses and it always charges you the lowest fare available for your journey. You buy credit for your journey and when it runs out you simply top up with more.

Oyster is available to adults only. Children below the age of 11 can accompany adults free of charge. Children between the ages of 11 and 15 should use the standard child travel card. You can get an Oyster card at any underground station, at one of 3,000 Oyster points around London displaying the London Underground sign (usually shops), or from visitbritaindirect.com.

### London congestion charge

The congestion charge is an £8 daily charge to drive in central London at certain times. Check whether the congestion charge is included in the cost of your car when you book. If your car's pick up point is in the congestion-charging zone, the company may pay the charge for the first day of your hire.

### Low Emission Zone

The Low Emission Zone is an area covering most of Greater London, within which the most polluting diesel-engine vehicles are required to meet specific emissions standards. If your vehicle does not, you will need to pay a daily charge.

Vehicles affected by the Low Emission Zone are older diesel-engine lorries, buses, coaches, large vans, minibuses and other heavy vehicles such as motor caravans and motorised horse boxes. This includes vehicles registered outside of Great Britain. Cars and motorcycles are not affected by the scheme.

For more information visit tfl.gov.uk/roadusers/lez.

## Rail and train travel

Britain's rail network covers all main cities and smaller regional towns. Trains on the network are operated by a few large companies running routes from London to stations all over Britain, and smaller companies running routes in regional areas. You can find up-to-the-minute information about routes, fares and train times on National Rail Enquiries (nationalrail.co.uk). For detailed information about routes and services, refer to the train operators' websites (see page 672).

### Railway passes

BritRail offers a wide selection of passes and tickets giving you freedom to travel on all National Rail services. Passes can also include sleeper services, city and attraction passes and boat tours. Passes can normally be bought from travel agents outside Britain or by visiting the Britrail website (britrail.com).

## Bus and coach travel

### Public buses

Every city and town in Britain has a local bus service. These services are privatised and run by separate companies. The largest bus companies in Britain are First (firstgroup.com/bustravel.php), Stagecoach (stagecoachbus.com), and Arriva (arrivabus.co.uk), which run buses in most UK towns. Outside London, buses usually travel to and from the town centre or busiest part of town. Most towns have a bus station, where you'll be able to find maps and information about routes. Bus route information may also be posted at bus stops.

### Tickets and fares

The cost of a bus ticket normally depends on how far you're travelling. Return fares may be available on some buses, but you usually need to buy a 'single' ticket for each individual journey.

You can buy your ticket when you board a bus, by telling the driver where you are going. One-day and weekly travel cards are available in some towns, and these can be bought from the driver or from an information centre at the bus station. Tickets are valid for each separate journey rather than for a period of time, so if you get off the bus you'll need to buy a new ticket when getting on another bus.

## Domestic flights

Flying is a time-saving alternative to road or rail when it comes to travelling around Britain. Domestic flights are fast and frequent and there are 33 airports across Britain operating domestic routes. You will find airports marked on the maps at the front of this guide.

### Domestic flight advice

Photo ID is required to travel on domestic flights. It is advisable to bring your passport, as not all airlines will accept other forms of photo identification.

There are very high security measures at all airports in Britain. These include restrictions on items that may be carried in hand luggage. It is important that you check with your airline prior to travel, as these restrictions may vary over time. Make sure you allow adequate time for check-in and boarding.

## Cycling

Cycling is a good way to see some of Britain's best scenery and there are many networks of cycling routes. The National Cycle Network offers over 10,000 miles of walking and cycling routes connecting towns and villages, countryside and coast across the UK. For more information and routes see page 674 or visit Sustrans at sustrans.co.uk.

## Think green

If you'd rather leave your car behind and travel by 'green transport' when visiting some of the attractions highlighted in this guide you'll be helping to reduce congestion and pollution as well as supporting conservation charities in their commitment to green travel.

The National Trust encourages visits made by non-car travellers. It offers admission discounts or a voucher for the tea room at a selection of its properties if you arrive on foot, cycle or public transport. (You'll need to produce a valid bus or train ticket if travelling by public transport.)

More information about The National Trust's work to encourage car-free days out can be found at nationaltrust.org.uk. Refer to the section entitled Information for Visitors.

## The Channel Islands

For information about travelling to, and within, the Channel Islands go to jersey.com or visitguernsey.com.

**To help you on your way you'll find a list of useful contacts at the end of this section.**

# England at a glance

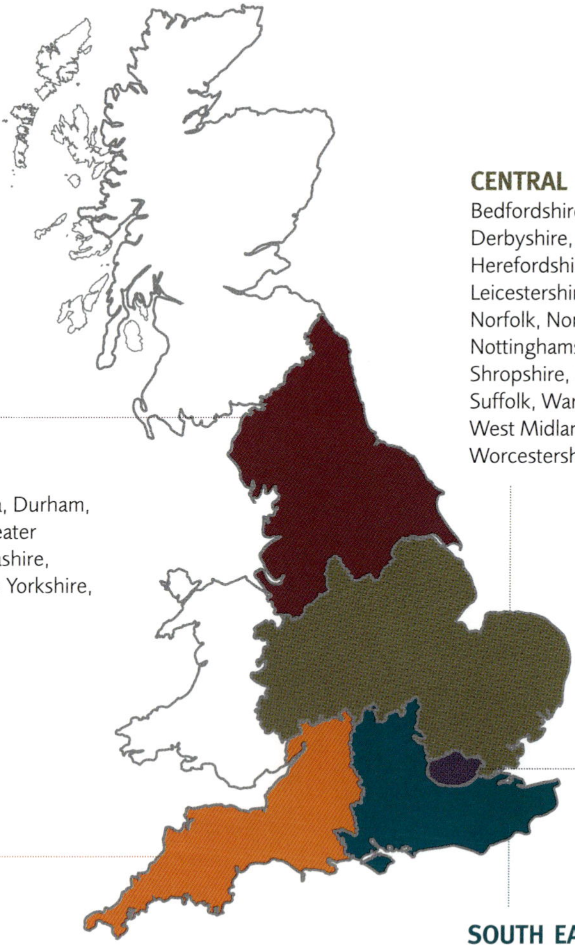

**CENTRAL ENGLAND**
Bedfordshire, Cambridgeshire, Derbyshire, Essex, Herefordshire, Hertfordshire, Leicestershire, Lincolnshire, Norfolk, Northamptonshire, Nottinghamshire, Rutland, Shropshire, Staffordshire, Suffolk, Warwickshire, West Midlands, Worcestershire

**NORTHERN ENGLAND**
Cheshire, Cumbria, Durham, East Yorkshire, Greater Manchester, Lancashire, Merseyside, North Yorkshire, Northumberland, South Yorkshire, Tees Valley, Tyne and Wear, West Yorkshire

**LONDON**

**SOUTH WEST ENGLAND**
Bristol, Cornwall, Devon, Dorset, Gloucestershire, Isles of Scilly, Somerset, Wiltshire

**SOUTH EAST ENGLAND**
Berkshire, Buckinghamshire, East Sussex, Hampshire, Isle of Wight, Kent, London, Oxfordshire, Surrey, West Sussex

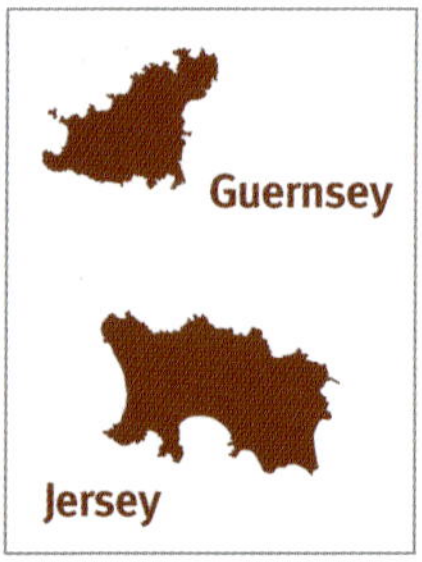


**THE CHANNEL ISLANDS**
Guernsey and Jersey are not drawn to scale

# Counties and regions at a glance

If you know what county you wish to visit you'll find it in the regional section shown below.

| County | Region |
|---|---|
| Bedfordshire | Central England |
| Berkshire | South East England |
| Bristol | South West England |
| Buckinghamshire | South East England |
| Cambridgeshire | Central England |
| Cheshire | Northern England |
| Cornwall | South West England |
| Cumbria | Northern England |
| Derbyshire | Central England |
| Devon | South West England |
| Dorset | South West England |
| Durham | Northern England |
| East Yorkshire | Northern England |
| East Sussex | South East England |
| Essex | Central England |
| Gloucestershire | South West England |
| Greater Manchester | Northern England |
| Hampshire | South East England |
| Herefordshire | Central England |
| Hertfordshire | Central England |
| Isle of Wight | South East England |
| Isles of Scilly | South West England |
| Kent | South East England |
| Lancashire | Northern England |

| County | Region |
|---|---|
| Leicestershire | Central England |
| Lincolnshire | Central England |
| Merseyside | Northern England |
| Norfolk | Central England |
| North Yorkshire | Northern England |
| Northamptonshire | Central England |
| Northumberland | Northern England |
| Nottinghamshire | Central England |
| Oxfordshire | South East England |
| Rutland | Central England |
| Shropshire | Central England |
| Somerset | South West England |
| South Yorkshire | Northern England |
| Staffordshire | Central England |
| Suffolk | Central England |
| Surrey | South East England |
| Tees Valley | Northern England |
| Tyne and Wear | Northern England |
| Warwickshire | Central England |
| West Midlands | Central England |
| West Sussex | South East England |
| West Yorkshire | Northern England |
| Wiltshire | South West England |
| Worcestershire | Central England |

To help readers we do not refer to unitary authorities in this guide.

# By car and by train

## Distance chart

The distances between towns on the chart below are given to the nearest mile, and are measured along routes based on the quickest travelling time, making maximum use of motorways or dual-carriageway roads. The chart is based upon information supplied by the Automobile Association.

**To calculate the distance in kilometres multiply the mileage by 1.6**

**For example:** Brighton to Dover 82 miles x 1.6 =131.2 kilometres

| | Aberdeen | Aberystwyth | Barnstaple | Birmingham | Brighton | Bristol | Cambridge | Cardiff | Carlisle | Carmarthen | Dorchester | Dover | Edinburgh | Exeter | Fort William | Glasgow | Gloucester | Guildford | Hereford | Holyhead | Hull | Inverness | Kendal | Leeds | Lincoln | Liverpool | Maidstone | Manchester | Middlesbrough | Newcastle | Northampton | Norwich | Nottingham | Oxford | Penzance | Perth | Peterborough | Plymouth | Portsmouth | Preston | Salisbury | Sheffield | Shrewsbury | Southampton | Stoke-on-Trent | Stranraer | Taunton | Wick | York |
|---|---|---|---|---|---|---|---|---|---|---|---|---|---|---|---|---|---|---|---|---|---|---|---|---|---|---|---|---|---|---|---|---|---|---|---|---|---|---|---|---|---|---|---|---|---|---|---|---|---|
| Aberystwyth | 472 | | | | | | | | | | | | | | | | | | | | | | | | | | | | | | | | | | | | | | | | | | | | | | | | |
| Barnstaple | 608 | 214 | | | | | | | | | | | | | | | | | | | | | | | | | | | | | | | | | | | | | | | | | | | | | | | |
| Birmingham | 436 | 124 | 180 | | | | | | | | | | | | | | | | | | | | | | | | | | | | | | | | | | | | | | | | | | | | | | |
| Brighton | 613 | 288 | 210 | 171 | | | | | | | | | | | | | | | | | | | | | | | | | | | | | | | | | | | | | | | | | | | | | |
| Bristol | 518 | 130 | 100 | 90 | 169 | | | | | | | | | | | | | | | | | | | | | | | | | | | | | | | | | | | | | | | | | | | | |
| Cambridge | 463 | 215 | 267 | 97 | 120 | 170 | | | | | | | | | | | | | | | | | | | | | | | | | | | | | | | | | | | | | | | | | | | |
| Cardiff | 537 | 111 | 128 | 109 | 202 | 44 | 203 | | | | | | | | | | | | | | | | | | | | | | | | | | | | | | | | | | | | | | | | | | |
| Carlisle | 236 | 236 | 371 | 199 | 376 | 281 | 256 | 300 | | | | | | | | | | | | | | | | | | | | | | | | | | | | | | | | | | | | | | | | | |
| Carmarthen | 520 | 48 | 190 | 172 | 264 | 107 | 266 | 68 | 284 | | | | | | | | | | | | | | | | | | | | | | | | | | | | | | | | | | | | | | | | |
| Dorchester | 600 | 206 | 94 | 172 | 119 | 62 | 184 | 120 | 364 | 182 | | | | | | | | | | | | | | | | | | | | | | | | | | | | | | | | | | | | | | | |
| Dover | 587 | 326 | 272 | 208 | 82 | 205 | 124 | 239 | 381 | 301 | 200 | | | | | | | | | | | | | | | | | | | | | | | | | | | | | | | | | | | | | | |
| Edinburgh | 126 | 336 | 471 | 299 | 476 | 381 | 333 | 400 | 100 | 386 | 463 | 458 | | | | | | | | | | | | | | | | | | | | | | | | | | | | | | | | | | | | | |
| Exeter | 593 | 198 | 44 | 165 | 178 | 84 | 259 | 113 | 356 | 175 | 57 | 248 | 455 | | | | | | | | | | | | | | | | | | | | | | | | | | | | | | | | | | | | |
| Fort William | 156 | 435 | 570 | 398 | 576 | 480 | 456 | 499 | 199 | 485 | 562 | 580 | 137 | 554 | | | | | | | | | | | | | | | | | | | | | | | | | | | | | | | | | | | |
| Glasgow | 150 | 332 | 467 | 295 | 472 | 377 | 353 | 396 | 96 | 382 | 459 | 477 | 47 | 451 | 102 | | | | | | | | | | | | | | | | | | | | | | | | | | | | | | | | | | |
| Gloucester | 484 | 113 | 126 | 56 | 155 | 36 | 150 | 63 | 248 | 125 | 118 | 192 | 346 | 110 | 445 | 343 | | | | | | | | | | | | | | | | | | | | | | | | | | | | | | | | | |
| Guildford | 571 | 224 | 175 | 128 | 44 | 106 | 96 | 139 | 335 | 201 | 97 | 97 | 433 | 150 | 532 | 430 | 99 | | | | | | | | | | | | | | | | | | | | | | | | | | | | | | | | |
| Hereford | 487 | 79 | 144 | 59 | 189 | 54 | 153 | 59 | 250 | 85 | 136 | 225 | 349 | 129 | 448 | 346 | 34 | 133 | | | | | | | | | | | | | | | | | | | | | | | | | | | | | | | |
| Holyhead | 464 | 102 | 339 | 167 | 345 | 249 | 259 | 202 | 228 | 150 | 331 | 369 | 326 | 323 | 425 | 323 | 215 | 302 | 156 | | | | | | | | | | | | | | | | | | | | | | | | | | | | | | |
| Hull | 376 | 227 | 320 | 139 | 258 | 230 | 138 | 250 | 170 | 311 | 312 | 262 | 247 | 304 | 367 | 266 | 196 | 239 | 198 | 218 | | | | | | | | | | | | | | | | | | | | | | | | | | | | | |
| Inverness | 106 | 496 | 631 | 459 | 637 | 541 | 517 | 561 | 260 | 546 | 623 | 641 | 157 | 616 | 66 | 176 | 507 | 595 | 510 | 488 | 430 | | | | | | | | | | | | | | | | | | | | | | | | | | | | |
| Kendal | 283 | 189 | 324 | 153 | 330 | 234 | 251 | 254 | 47 | 240 | 316 | 354 | 145 | 309 | 245 | 143 | 200 | 288 | 203 | 181 | 164 | 307 | | | | | | | | | | | | | | | | | | | | | | | | | | | |
| Leeds | 329 | 173 | 301 | 120 | 262 | 211 | 146 | 230 | 123 | 224 | 293 | 271 | 200 | 265 | 321 | 219 | 177 | 220 | 179 | 165 | 59 | 383 | 110 | | | | | | | | | | | | | | | | | | | | | | | | | | |
| Lincoln | 388 | 199 | 275 | 98 | 216 | 185 | 95 | 205 | 182 | 267 | 246 | 220 | 258 | 260 | 379 | 277 | 151 | 173 | 154 | 204 | 44 | 441 | 176 | 74 | | | | | | | | | | | | | | | | | | | | | | | | | |
| Liverpool | 362 | 110 | 272 | 101 | 278 | 182 | 193 | 202 | 126 | 158 | 264 | 302 | 224 | 257 | 324 | 222 | 148 | 236 | 151 | 102 | 128 | 386 | 79 | 74 | 139 | | | | | | | | | | | | | | | | | | | | | | | | |
| Maidstone | 545 | 284 | 234 | 166 | 50 | 167 | 82 | 200 | 339 | 262 | 161 | 41 | 416 | 209 | 537 | 435 | 153 | 58 | 186 | 327 | 220 | 599 | 313 | 231 | 178 | 261 | | | | | | | | | | | | | | | | | | | | | | | |
| Manchester | 357 | 134 | 261 | 89 | 266 | 171 | 160 | 190 | 120 | 184 | 253 | 290 | 219 | 245 | 318 | 216 | 136 | 224 | 139 | 125 | 97 | 380 | 74 | 44 | 85 | 34 | 248 | | | | | | | | | | | | | | | | | | | | | | |
| Middlesbrough | 276 | 244 | 357 | 176 | 318 | 267 | 197 | 286 | 95 | 294 | 349 | 322 | 146 | 341 | 283 | 190 | 232 | 276 | 235 | 235 | 89 | 308 | 84 | 64 | 122 | 145 | 280 | 114 | | | | | | | | | | | | | | | | | | | | | |
| Newcastle | 235 | 275 | 388 | 207 | 349 | 298 | 229 | 317 | 60 | 325 | 380 | 353 | 106 | 372 | 242 | 153 | 264 | 307 | 266 | 266 | 142 | 267 | 102 | 95 | 154 | 176 | 311 | 145 | 39 | | | | | | | | | | | | | | | | | | | | |
| Northampton | 486 | 174 | 212 | 56 | 133 | 115 | 56 | 162 | 249 | 224 | 159 | 155 | 348 | 196 | 447 | 345 | 79 | 90 | 111 | 217 | 152 | 509 | 203 | 136 | 94 | 151 | 113 | 139 | 189 | 220 | | | | | | | | | | | | | | | | | | | |
| Norwich | 488 | 278 | 329 | 160 | 168 | 233 | 63 | 266 | 282 | 328 | 241 | 172 | 359 | 313 | 480 | 378 | 212 | 160 | 215 | 321 | 147 | 542 | 276 | 174 | 103 | 240 | 130 | 185 | 223 | 254 | 118 | | | | | | | | | | | | | | | | | | |
| Nottingham | 395 | 162 | 232 | 51 | 193 | 142 | 86 | 161 | 189 | 223 | 224 | 210 | 266 | 216 | 387 | 285 | 107 | 151 | 110 | 178 | 93 | 449 | 164 | 77 | 39 | 112 | 168 | 71 | 130 | 161 | 64 | 119 | | | | | | | | | | | | | | | | | |
| Oxford | 510 | 160 | 170 | 68 | 109 | 73 | 82 | 107 | 274 | 169 | 115 | 146 | 373 | 154 | 472 | 370 | 48 | 67 | 81 | 242 | 190 | 534 | 228 | 174 | 132 | 176 | 107 | 164 | 227 | 258 | 44 | 146 | 102 | | | | | | | | | | | | | | | | |
| Penzance | 702 | 308 | 108 | 274 | 287 | 193 | 368 | 222 | 466 | 284 | 167 | 357 | 564 | 109 | 663 | 562 | 220 | 259 | 238 | 434 | 415 | 726 | 419 | 403 | 370 | 367 | 318 | 356 | 451 | 482 | 326 | 433 | 326 | 265 | | | | | | | | | | | | | | | |
| Perth | 86 | 388 | 523 | 351 | 529 | 433 | 378 | 453 | 152 | 438 | 515 | 503 | 42 | 507 | 102 | 64 | 399 | 486 | 401 | 379 | 291 | 114 | 199 | 245 | 303 | 278 | 461 | 275 | 192 | 150 | 400 | 404 | 310 | 426 | 617 | | | | | | | | | | | | | | |
| Peterborough | 435 | 204 | 263 | 86 | 158 | 173 | 37 | 193 | 229 | 255 | 204 | 162 | 306 | 248 | 427 | 325 | 139 | 115 | 142 | 225 | 110 | 489 | 223 | 121 | 51 | 159 | 120 | 132 | 170 | 201 | 45 | 78 | 58 | 86 | 357 | 351 | | | | | | | | | | | | | |
| Plymouth | 633 | 239 | 62 | 205 | 218 | 124 | 299 | 153 | 397 | 215 | 98 | 288 | 495 | 44 | 594 | 493 | 151 | 190 | 169 | 365 | 346 | 657 | 350 | 334 | 301 | 298 | 249 | 287 | 382 | 413 | 257 | 364 | 257 | 196 | 78 | 544 | 288 | | | | | | | | | | | | |
| Portsmouth | 596 | 244 | 162 | 154 | 53 | 125 | 137 | 158 | 360 | 220 | 73 | 141 | 458 | 132 | 558 | 456 | 118 | 45 | 152 | 328 | 276 | 620 | 314 | 260 | 215 | 262 | 102 | 250 | 313 | 344 | 130 | 204 | 188 | 85 | 241 | 508 | 157 | 172 | | | | | | | | | | | |
| Preston | 326 | 146 | 281 | 110 | 287 | 191 | 209 | 211 | 89 | 197 | 273 | 311 | 188 | 266 | 287 | 185 | 157 | 245 | 160 | 138 | 122 | 349 | 43 | 69 | 134 | 36 | 269 | 35 | 103 | 139 | 159 | 235 | 121 | 184 | 375 | 237 | 180 | 306 | 270 | | | | | | | | | | |
| Salisbury | 549 | 184 | 118 | 121 | 90 | 52 | 145 | 98 | 313 | 160 | 39 | 160 | 411 | 93 | 511 | 409 | 72 | 62 | 105 | 281 | 261 | 573 | 267 | 244 | 202 | 215 | 121 | 203 | 298 | 329 | 115 | 212 | 173 | 70 | 203 | 461 | 165 | 134 | 44 | 223 | | | | | | | | | |
| Sheffield | 397 | 166 | 272 | 91 | 233 | 182 | 122 | 201 | 161 | 263 | 264 | 247 | 236 | 256 | 359 | 257 | 148 | 191 | 150 | 157 | 66 | 421 | 115 | 38 | 47 | 79 | 205 | 39 | 100 | 131 | 104 | 148 | 45 | 142 | 366 | 309 | 93 | 297 | 228 | 73 | 212 | | | | | | | | |
| Shrewsbury | 417 | 75 | 220 | 48 | 226 | 130 | 140 | 111 | 181 | 110 | 212 | 250 | 279 | 205 | 379 | 277 | 96 | 184 | 52 | 105 | 162 | 441 | 135 | 119 | 124 | 65 | 208 | 71 | 190 | 221 | 98 | 203 | 87 | 123 | 314 | 329 | 129 | 245 | 209 | 92 | 161 | 88 | | | | | | | |
| Southampton | 578 | 225 | 142 | 135 | 66 | 106 | 136 | 140 | 342 | 201 | 53 | 152 | 440 | 111 | 539 | 437 | 100 | 49 | 133 | 309 | 258 | 601 | 295 | 241 | 199 | 243 | 113 | 232 | 294 | 325 | 111 | 204 | 169 | 67 | 221 | 489 | 157 | 152 | 20 | 252 | 23 | 209 | 191 | | | | | | |
| Stoke-on-Trent | 392 | 112 | 220 | 48 | 226 | 130 | 140 | 150 | 156 | 211 | 212 | 250 | 254 | 205 | 353 | 251 | 96 | 184 | 99 | 123 | 129 | 415 | 109 | 93 | 91 | 57 | 208 | 46 | 164 | 195 | 98 | 172 | 54 | 123 | 314 | 303 | 99 | 245 | 209 | 66 | 161 | 50 | 38 | 191 | | | | | |
| Stranraer | 235 | 342 | 477 | 305 | 482 | 387 | 363 | 406 | 106 | 392 | 469 | 487 | 132 | 461 | 181 | 86 | 352 | 440 | 355 | 333 | 276 | 261 | 153 | 229 | 288 | 232 | 445 | 229 | 201 | 163 | 354 | 388 | 295 | 380 | 571 | 149 | 333 | 502 | 466 | 195 | 418 | 267 | 287 | 447 | 261 | | | | |
| Taunton | 560 | 165 | 50 | 132 | 160 | 51 | 226 | 80 | 323 | 142 | 45 | 224 | 422 | 34 | 521 | 419 | 77 | 126 | 96 | 291 | 272 | 583 | 277 | 261 | 228 | 225 | 185 | 213 | 309 | 340 | 183 | 291 | 184 | 123 | 144 | 471 | 215 | 75 | 114 | 234 | 70 | 224 | 172 | 94 | 172 | 429 | | | |
| Wick | 207 | 597 | 732 | 560 | 738 | 642 | 618 | 662 | 361 | 647 | 724 | 742 | 258 | 716 | 166 | 277 | 606 | 695 | 610 | 588 | 531 | 104 | 408 | 484 | 543 | 487 | 700 | 484 | 409 | 367 | 609 | 644 | 550 | 635 | 826 | 215 | 589 | 757 | 721 | 451 | 673 | 523 | 542 | 702 | 516 | 362 | 684 | | |
| York | 323 | 201 | 314 | 133 | 275 | 224 | 154 | 243 | 116 | 251 | 306 | 279 | 193 | 298 | 314 | 212 | 189 | 233 | 192 | 192 | 38 | 376 | 91 | 24 | 79 | 102 | 237 | 71 | 51 | 89 | 146 | 180 | 87 | 184 | 408 | 239 | 125 | 339 | 269 | 96 | 254 | 57 | 146 | 251 | 120 | 223 | 265 | 477 | |
| LONDON | 550 | 239 | 216 | 121 | 54 | 120 | 59 | 153 | 314 | 215 | 125 | 78 | 413 | 200 | 512 | 410 | 102 | 31 | 136 | 282 | 186 | 574 | 268 | 201 | 143 | 216 | 39 | 204 | 254 | 285 | 68 | 118 | 129 | 56 | 310 | 462 | 86 | 241 | 75 | 225 | 85 | 169 | 163 | 77 | 161 | 420 | 167 | 675 | 211 |

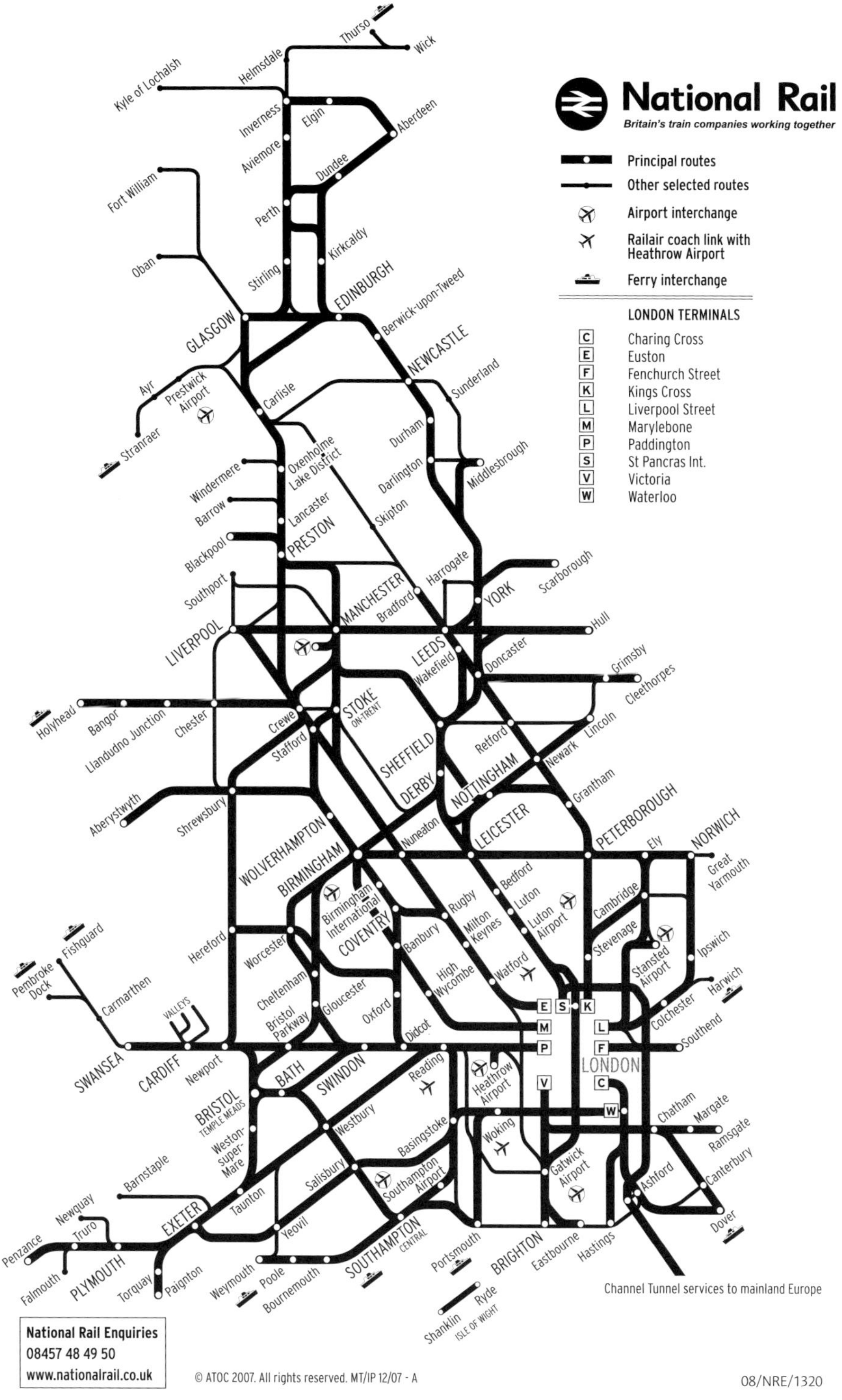
National Rail
Britain's train companies working together
Principal routes
Other selected routes
Airport interchange
Railair coach link with Heathrow Airport
Ferry interchange
LONDON TERMINALS
C Charing Cross
E Euston
F Fenchurch Street
K Kings Cross
L Liverpool Street
M Marylebone
P Paddington
S St Pancras Int.
V Victoria
W Waterloo
Thurso
Wick
Helmsdale
Kyle of Lochalsh
Inverness
Elgin
Aberdeen
Aviemore
Dundee
Fort William
Perth
Kirkcaldy
Oban
Stirling
EDINBURGH
Berwick-upon-Tweed
GLASGOW
NEWCASTLE
Ayr
Prestwick Airport
Carlisle
Sunderland
Stranraer
Oxenholme Lake District
Durham
Windermere
Darlington
Middlesbrough
Barrow
Lancaster
Skipton
PRESTON
Blackpool
Harrogate
Scarborough
Southport
MANCHESTER
Bradford
YORK
LIVERPOOL
Hull
LEEDS
Wakefield
Doncaster
Grimsby
Cleethorpes
Holyhead
Bangor
Llandudno Junction
Chester
Crewe
Stafford
STOKE ON-TRENT
SHEFFIELD
Retford
Lincoln
DERBY
NOTTINGHAM
Newark
Grantham
Aberystwyth
Shrewsbury
WOLVERHAMPTON
Nuneaton
LEICESTER
PETERBOROUGH
BIRMINGHAM
Ely
NORWICH
Great Yarmouth
Birmingham International
COVENTRY
Rugby
Bedford
Luton
Luton Airport
Cambridge
Fishguard
Pembroke Dock
Hereford
Worcester
Banbury
Milton Keynes
Stevenage
Stansted Airport
Ipswich
Cheltenham
Gloucester
High Wycombe
Watford
Harwich
Carmarthen
VALLEYS
Bristol Parkway
Oxford
Colchester
Didcot
Southend
SWANSEA
CARDIFF
Newport
BATH
SWINDON
Reading
Heathrow Airport
LONDON
BRISTOL TEMPLE MEADS
Westbury
Chatham
Margate
Weston-super-Mare
Basingstoke
Woking
Ramsgate
Barnstaple
Salisbury
Southampton Airport
Gatwick Airport
Ashford
Canterbury
Newquay
Taunton
Truro
EXETER
Yeovil
SOUTHAMPTON CENTRAL
Dover
Penzance
Portsmouth
BRIGHTON
Eastbourne
Hastings
Falmouth
PLYMOUTH
Torquay
Paignton
Weymouth
Poole
Bournemouth
Ryde
Shanklin
ISLE OF WIGHT
Channel Tunnel services to mainland Europe
National Rail Enquiries
08457 48 49 50
www.nationalrail.co.uk
© ATOC 2007. All rights reserved. MT/IP 12/07 - A
08/NRE/1320

# Travel information

## General travel information

| | | |
|---|---|---|
| **Streetmap** | streetmap.co.uk | |
| **Transport Direct** (a journey planner) | transportdirect.info | |
| **Transport for London** | tfl.gov.uk | (020) 7222 1234 |
| **Travel Services** | departures-arrivals.com | |
| **Traveline** (public transport information) | traveline.org.uk | 0870 200 2233 |

## Bus & coach

| | | |
|---|---|---|
| **Megabus** | megabus.com | 0901 331 0031 |
| **National Express** | nationalexpress.com | 0870 580 8080 |
| **WA Shearings** | washearings.com | (01942) 823371 |

## Car & car hire

| | | |
|---|---|---|
| **AA** | theaa.com | 0870 600 0371 |
| **Green Flag** | greenflag.co.uk | 0845 246 1557 |
| **RAC** | rac.co.uk | 0870 572 2722 |
| **Alamo** | alamo.co.uk | 0870 400 4562* |
| **Avis** | avis.co.uk | 0844 581 0147 |
| **Budget** | budget.co.uk | 0844 581 2231 |
| **Easycar** | easycar.com | 0906 333 3333 |
| **Enterprise** | enterprise.com | 0870 350 3000* |
| **Hertz** | hertz.co.uk | 0870 844 8844* |
| **Holiday Autos** | holidayautos.co.uk | 0870 400 4461 |
| **National** | nationalcar.co.uk | 0870 400 4581 |
| **Thrifty** | thrifty.co.uk | (01494) 751500 |

## Air

| | | |
|---|---|---|
| **Air Southwest** | airsouthwest.com | 0870 043 4553 |
| **Blue Islands** (Channel Islands) | blueislands.com | 0845 620 2122 |
| **BMI** | flybmi.com | 0870 607 0555 |
| **BMI Baby** | bmibaby.com | 0871 224 0224 |
| **British Airways** | ba.com | 0844 493 0787 |
| **British International** (Isles of Scilly to Penzance) | islesofscillyhelicopter.com | (01736) 363871* |
| **Eastern Airways** | easternairways.com | 0870 366 9989 |
| **Easyjet** | easyjet.com | 0871 244 2366 |
| **Flybe** | flybe.com | 0871 700 2000* |
| **Flyglobespan** | flyglobespan.com | 0871 271 0415* |
| **Jet2.com** | jet2.com | 0871 226 1737* |
| **Manx2** | manx2.com | 0871 200 0440* |
| **Ryanair** | ryanair.com | 0871 246 0000 |
| **Skybus** (Isles of Scilly) | islesofscilly-travel.co.uk | 0845 710 5555 |
| **Thomsonfly** | tomsonfly.com | 0871 231 4869 |
| **VLM** | flyvlm.com | 0871 666 5050 |

## Train

| | | |
|---|---|---|
| **National Rail Enquiries** | nationalrail.co.uk | 0845 748 4950 |
| Consult National Rail Enquiries for up-to-the-minute advice on journey planning, train times and service updates. | | |
| **The Trainline** (online booking) | trainline.co.uk | |
| **UK train operating companies** | rail.co.uk | |
| **Arriva Trains** | arriva.co.uk | 0845 748 4950 |
| **c2c** | c2c-online.co.uk | 0845 601 4873 |
| **Chiltern Railways** | chilternrailways.co.uk | 0845 600 5165 |
| **CrossCountry** | crosscountrytrains.co.uk | 0870 010 0084 |
| **East Midlands Trains** | eastmidlandstrains.co.uk | 0845 712 5678 |
| **Eurostar** | eurostar.com | 0870 518 6186* |
| **First Capital Connect** | firstcapitalconnect.co.uk | 0845 026 4700 |
| **First Great Western** | firstgreatwestern.co.uk | 0845 700 0125 |
| **Gatwick Express** | gatwickexpress.com | 0845 850 1530 |
| **Heathrow Connect** | heathrowconnect.com | 0845 678 6975 |
| **Heathrow Express** | heathrowexpress.com | 0845 600 1515 |
| **Hull Trains** | hulltrains.co.uk | 0845 071 0222 |
| **Island Line** | island-line.co.uk | 0845 748 4950 |
| **London Midland** | londonmidland.com | 0844 811 0133 |
| **Merseyrail** | merseyrail.org | (0151) 702 2071 |
| **National Express East Anglia** | nationalexpresseastanglia.com | 0845 600 7245 |
| **National Express East Coast** | nationalexpresseastcoast.com | 0845 722 5333 |
| **Northern Rail** | northernrail.org | 0845 000 0125 |
| **ScotRail** | firstgroup.com/scotrail | 0845 601 5929 |
| **South Eastern Trains** | southeasternrailway.co.uk | 0845 000 2222 |
| **South West Trains** | southwesttrains.co.uk | 0845 600 0650 |
| **Southern** | southernrailway.com | 0845 127 2920 |
| **Stansted Express** | stanstedexpress.com | 0845 600 7245 |
| **Translink** | nirailways.co.uk | (028) 9066 6630 |
| **Transpennine Express** | tpexpress.co.uk | 0845 600 1671 |
| **Virgin Trains** | virgintrains.co.uk | 0845 722 2333* |

## Ferry

| | | |
|---|---|---|
| **Ferry information** | sailanddrive.com | |
| **Condor Ferries** (Channel Islands) | condorferries.co.uk | 0845 609 1024* |
| **Steam Packet Company** (Isle of Man) | steam-packet.com | 0871 222 1333 |
| **Isles of Scilly Travel** | islesofscilly-travel.co.uk | 0845 710 5555 |
| **Red Funnel** (Isle of Wight) | redfunnel.co.uk | 0870 444 8898 |
| **Wight Link** (Isle of Wight) | wightlink.co.uk | 0871 376 4342 |

Phone numbers listed are for general enquiries unless otherwise stated.

* Booking line only

# National cycle network

Sections of the National Cycle Network are shown on the maps in this guide. The numbers on the maps will appear on the signs along your route 3.
Here are some tips about finding and using a route.

- **Research and plan your route online**
  Log on to **sustrans.org.uk** and click on 'Get cycling' to find information about routes in this guide or other routes you want to use.

- **Order a route map**
  Useful, easy-to-use maps of many of the most popular routes of the National Cycle Network are available from Sustrans, the charity behind the Network. These can be purchased online or by mail order – visit **sustransshop.co.uk** or call **0845 113 0065.**

- **Order Cycling in the UK**
  The official guide to the National Cycle Network gives details of rides all over the UK, detailing 148 routes and profiles of 43 days rides on traffic-free paths and quiet roads.

| ROUTE NUMBER | ROUTE/MAP NAME | START/END OF ROUTE |
|---|---|---|
| **South West** | | |
| 3 | The West Country Way | Padstow – Bristol/Bath |
| 3 & 32 | The Cornish Way | Land's End – Bude |
| 27 | The Devon Coast to Coast | Ilfracombe – Plymouth |
| **South East** | | |
| 4 & 5 | Thames Valley | London – Oxford via Reading |
| 4 | Kennet & Avon | Reading – Bristol |
| 2, 20 & 21 | Downs & Weald | London – Brighton – Hastings |
| **Central England** | | |
| 5 & 54 | West Midlands | Oxford – Derby via Stratford-upon-Avon |
| **Northern England** | | |
| 1 | Coast & Castles South | Newcastle – Berwick-upon-Tweed – Edinburgh |
| 7, 14 & 71 | Sea to Sea (C2C) | Whitehaven/Workington – Sunderland/Newcastle upon Tyne |
| 14 | Three Rivers | Middlesbrough – Durham – South Shields |
| 65 & Regional 52 (W2W) | Yorkshire Moors & Coast | Middlesbrough – Easingwold & Barnard Castle – Whitby |
| 65 & 66 | Yorkshire Wolds, York & Hull | Easingwold – York – Hull |
| 68 | Pennine Cycleway (South Pennines & the Dales) | Holmfirth – Appleby-in-Westmorland/Kendal |
| 68 | Pennine Cycleway North | Appleby-in-Westmorland/Penrith – Berwick-upon-Tweed |
| 72 | Hadrian's Cycleway | Ravenglass – South Shields |
| 62 & 65 | Trans Pennine Trail East | Yorkshire – North Sea |
| 62 | Trans Pennine Trail West | Irish Sea – Yorkshire |
| 67 | Trans Pennine Trail Central | Leeds – Chesterfield |

# National Accessible Scheme index

Establishments participating in the National Accessible Scheme are listed below – those in colour have a detailed entry in this guide. At the front of the guide you can find information about the scheme. Establishments are listed alphabetically by place name within each region.

## Mobility level 1


| | | |
|---|---|---|
| *Beverley* Northern England | **Rudstone Walk Country B&B** ★★★★ | 445 |
| *Blackpool* Northern England | **Holmsdale** ★★★ | 447 |
| *Blackpool* Northern England | **The Lawton** ★★★ | 448 |
| *Bowness-on-Solway* Northern England | **The Old Chapel** ★★★ | 450 |
| *Congleton* Northern England | **Sandhole Farm** ★★★★ | 455 |
| *Denshaw* Northern England | **Cherry Clough Farm House Accommodation** ★★★★ | 457 |
| *Harbottle* Northern England | **The Byre Vegetarian B&B** ★★★★ SILVER | 463 |
| *Haydon Bridge* Northern England | **Shaftoe's** ★★★★ | 466 |
| *Ingleton* Northern England | **Riverside Lodge** ★★★★ | 468 |
| *Kirkbymoorside* Northern England | **The Cornmill** ★★★★ SILVER | 106 |
| *Liverpool* Northern England | **YHA Liverpool** ★★★★ | 109 |
| *Manchester* Northern England | **Manchester YHA** ★★★★ | 476 |
| *Manchester* Northern England | **Luther King House** ★★★ | 111 |
| *Northallerton* Northern England | **Lovesome Hill Farm** ★★★★ SILVER | 479 |
| *Preston* Northern England | **Little Weghill Farm** ★★★★ SILVER | 481 |
| *Scarborough* Northern England | **The Scarborough Travel and Holiday Lodge** ★★★ | 486 |
| *Southport* Northern England | **Sandy Brook Farm** ★★★ | 126 |
| *Threlkeld* Northern England | **Scales Farm Country Guest House** ★★★★ SILVER | 492 |
| *Warrington* Northern England | **Tall Trees Lodge** ★★★ | 132 |
| *Winsford* Northern England | **The Winsford Lodge** ★★★ | 499 |
| *York* Northern England | **The Groves** ★★★ | 502 |
| *Ashbourne* Central England | **Mona Villas Bed and Breakfast** ★★★★ | 505 |
| *Cleethorpes* Central England | **Tudor Terrace Guest House** ★★★★ | 516 |
| *Cressbrook* Central England | **Cressbrook Hall** ★★★★ | 518 |
| *Donington* Central England | **Browntoft House** ★★★★ SILVER | 520 |
| *Ely* Central England | **Casa Nostra Guesthouse** ★★★ | 522 |
| *Gainsborough* Central England | **Blyton (Sunnyside) Ponds** ★★★ | 193 |
| *Halstead* Central England | **The White Hart** ★★★ | 526 |
| *Holbeck* Central England | **Browns** ★★★★★ GOLD | 528 |
| *Leominster* Central England | **YHA Leominster** ★★★★ | 533 |
| *Lighthorne* Central England | **Church Hill Farm B & B** ★★★★ | 534 |
| *Mundesley* Central England | **Overcliff Lodge** ★★★★ | 540 |


Establishments in colour have a detailed entry in this guide.

## Mobility level 1 continued


| | | |
|---|---|---|
| *Shrewsbury* Central England | **Lyth Hill House** ★★★★ GOLD | 547 |
| *Skegness* Central England | **Chatsworth** ★★★ | 226 |
| *West Rudham* Central England | **Oyster House** ★★★★ SILVER | 557 |
| *Wirksworth* Central England | **The Old Lock-Up** ★★★★★ GOLD | 559 |
| *Abingdon* South East England | **Abbey Guest House** ★★★★ | 561 |
| *Biddenden* South East England | **Heron Cottage** ★★★★ | 263 |
| *Folkestone* South East England | **Garden Lodge** ★★★★ | 574 |
| *Headington* South East England | **YHA Oxford** ★★★★ | 577 |
| *Hill Brow* South East England | **The Jolly Drover** ★★★★ SILVER | 578 |
| *Leckhampstead* South East England | **Weatherhead Farm** ★★★★ | 580 |
| *Pulborough* South East England | **The Labouring Man** ★★★★ | 301 |
| *Streatley* South East England | **Streatley On Thames YHA** ★★★ | 594 |
| *Sway* South East England | **The Nurse's Cottage** ★★★★ | 594 |
| *Witney* South East England | **Springhill Farm Bed & Breakfast** ★★★ | 597 |
| *London SW7* | **Meininger City Hostel & Hotel London** ★★★★ | 600 |
| *Boscastle* South West England | **Reddivallen Farm** ★★★★★ SILVER | 607 |
| *Boscastle* South West England | **The Old Coach House** ★★★★ | 361 |
| *Cannington* South West England | **Blackmore Farm** ★★★★ | 613 |
| *Cheltenham* South West England | **Prestbury House** ★★★★ | 372 |
| *Godney* South West England | **Double-Gate Farm** ★★★★ GOLD | 623 |
| *St Mary's* South West England | **Isles of Scilly Country Guest House** ★★★ | 642 |
| *Stow-on-the-Wold* South West England | **YHA Stow-on-the-Wold** ★★★★ | 646 |
| *West Quantoxhead* South West England | **Stilegate Bed and Breakfast** ★★★★★ | 654 |
| *Weston-super-Mare* South West England | **Milton Lodge Guest House** ★★★ | 655 |
| *Weston-super-Mare* South West England | **Saxonia Guest House** ★★★ | 655 |
| *Weston-super-Mare* South West England | **Spreyton Guest House** ★★★ | 655 |
| *Yelverton* South West England | **Overcombe House** ★★★★ | 423 |


## Mobility level 2


| | | |
|---|---|---|
| *Bailiff Bridge* Northern England | **The Lodge at Birkby Hall** ★★★★ SILVER | 442 |
| *Berwick-upon-Tweed* Northern England | **Meadow Hill Guest House** ★★★★ | 444 |
| *Bridlington* Northern England | **Providence Place** ★★★★ | 78 |
| *Haydon Bridge* Northern England | **Grindon Cartshed** ★★★★ | 97 |
| *Helmsley* Northern England | **Helmsley YHA** ★★★ | 466 |
| *Hesleden* Northern England | **The Ship Inn** ★★★★ SILVER | 466 |
| *Lockton* Northern England | **YHA Lockton** ★★★★ | 474 |
| *Manchester* Northern England | **Manchester YHA** ★★★★ | 476 |
| *Newbrough* Northern England | **Carr Edge Farm** ★★★★ | 478 |
| *Ribchester* Northern England | **Riverside Barn** ★★★★★ SILVER | 482 |
| *Runswick Bay* Northern England | **Ellerby** ★★★★ SILVER | 484 |
| *Whitby* Northern England | **Whitby YHA** ★★★★ | 496 |
| *Blaxhall* Central England | **Blaxhall YHA** ★★★ | 508 |
| *Cromer* Central England | **Incleborough House Luxury Bed and Breakfast** ★★★★★ GOLD | 189 |
| *Dereham* Central England | **Greenbanks** ★★★★ | 519 |
| *Manningtree* Central England | **Curlews** ★★★★ SILVER | 213 |
| *Oakamoor* Central England | **Dimmingsdale YHA** ★★ | 542 |
| *Redditch* Central England | **White Hart Inn** ★★★ | 222 |
| *Sheringham* Central England | **Sheringham YHA** ★★ | 547 |
| *Walton-on-the-Naze* Central England | **Bufo Villae Guest House** ★★★★ | 237 |
| *Wangford* Central England | **The Plough Inn** ★★★★ | 556 |
| *Headington* South East England | **YHA Oxford** ★★★★ | 577 |

## Mobility level 2 continued


| | | |
|---|---|---|
| *London NW1* | **St Pancras YHA** ★★★★ | 599 |
| *London SE16* | **YHA London Thameside** ★★ | 599 |
| *Bath* South West England | **The Carfax** ★★★★★ | 605 |
| *Cannington* South West England | **Blackmore Farm** ★★★★ | 613 |
| *Colyton* South West England | **Smallicombe Farm** ★★★★ SILVER | 374 |
| *Godney* South West England | **Double-Gate Farm** ★★★★ GOLD | 623 |
| *Padstow* South West England | **Woodlands Country House** ★★★★★ GOLD | 634 |
| *Parkend* South West England | **The Fountain Inn** ★★★ | 636 |
| *Sandford* South West England | **Ashridge Farm** ★★★★ | 643 |
| *Yelverton* South West England | **Overcombe House** ★★★★ | 423 |


## Mobility level 3 Independent


| | | |
|---|---|---|
| *Harwood Dale* Northern England | **The Grainary** ★★★★ | 464 |
| *Longthwaite* Northern England | **Borrowdale YHA** ★★★★ | 475 |
| *Manchester* Northern England | **Manchester YHA** ★★★★ | 476 |
| *Oakamoor* Central England | **Dimmingsdale YHA** ★★ | 542 |
| *Skegness* Central England | **The Fountaindale** ★★★★ | 548 |
| *Southwold* Central England | **Newlands Country House** ★★★★ | 549 |
| *Tugford* Central England | **Tugford Farm B&B** ★★★★ | 555 |
| *Headington* South East England | **YHA Oxford** ★★★★ | 577 |
| *Warningcamp* South East England | **YHA Arundel** ★★★ | 595 |
| *Alverton* South West England | **Penzance Youth Hostel** ★★ | 603 |
| *Cannington* South West England | **Blackmore Farm** ★★★★ | 613 |
| *Cheddar* South West England | **Cheddar YHA** ★★★ | 614 |
| *Godney* South West England | **Double-Gate Farm** ★★★★ GOLD | 623 |
| *Horsington* South West England | **Half Moon Inn** ★★★ | 625 |
| *Torquay* South West England | **Crown Lodge** ★★★★ | 650 |
| *Truro* South West England | **Tregoninny Farm** ★★★★ | 652 |


## Mobility level 3 Assisted


| | | |
|---|---|---|
| *Manchester* Northern England | **Manchester YHA** ★★★★ | 476 |
| *Oakamoor* Central England | **Dimmingsdale YHA** ★★ | 542 |
| *Tugford* Central England | **Tugford Farm B&B** ★★★★ | 555 |
| *Headington* South East England | **YHA Oxford** ★★★★ | 577 |
| *Alverton* South West England | **Penzance Youth Hostel** ★★ | 603 |
| *Cannington* South West England | **Blackmore Farm** ★★★★ | 613 |
| *Cheddar* South West England | **Cheddar YHA** ★★★ | 614 |
| *Godney* South West England | **Double-Gate Farm** ★★★★ GOLD | 623 |
| *Truro* South West England | **Tregoninny Farm** ★★★★ | 652 |


## Hearing impairment level 1


| | | |
|---|---|---|
| *Whitby* Northern England | **Whitby YHA** ★★★★ | 496 |
| *Sway* South East England | **The Nurse's Cottage** ★★★★ | 594 |
| *Horsington* South West England | **Half Moon Inn** ★★★ | 625 |


## Visual impairment level 1


| | | |
|---|---|---|
| *Helmsley* Northern England | **Helmsley YHA** ★★★ | 466 |
| *Whitby* Northern England | **Whitby YHA** ★★★★ | 496 |
| *Sway* South East England | **The Nurse's Cottage** ★★★★ | 594 |
| *Horsington* South West England | **Half Moon Inn** ★★★ | 625 |


Establishments in colour have a detailed entry in this guide.

# Gold and Silver Award winners

Establishments that have achieved a Gold or Silver Award in recognition of exceptional quality are listed below – those in colour have a detailed entry in this guide. Establishments are listed alphabetically by place name within each region.

## Northern England

### GOLD

*Aldbrough* **West Carlton Country Guest House** ★★★★ 439
*Aldfield* **Bay Tree Farm** ★★★★ 439
*Alnwick* **West Acre House** ★★★★★ 66
*Ambleside* **Barnes Fell Guest House** ★★★★ 440
*Ambleside* **Easedale Lodge Guest House** ★★★★ 440
*Ambleside* **Far Nook** ★★★★ 441
*Ambleside* **Kingswood 'Bee & Bee'** ★★★★ 441
*Ampleforth* **Daleside** ★★★★★ 442
*Ampleforth* **Shallowdale House** ★★★★★ 442
*Askrigg* **Helm** ★★★★★ 442
*Bardon Mill* **Montcoffer** ★★★★★ 443
*Barnard Castle* **Greta House** ★★★★★ 443
*Barnard Castle* **The Homelands** ★★★★ 443
*Bedale* **Mill Close Farm** ★★★★★ 444
*Berwick-upon-Tweed* **No 1 Sallyport** ★★★★★ 445
*Berwick-upon-Tweed* **West Coates** ★★★★★ 445
*Beverley* **Burton Mount Country House** ★★★★★ 445
*Blackpool* **Number One** ★★★★★ 448
*Blackpool* **Number One South Beach** ★★★★★ 448
*Blackpool* **The Waterford** ★★★★ 449
*Boltongate* **Boltongate Old Rectory** ★★★★★ 450
*Borrowdale* **Hazel Bank Country House** ★★★★★ 76
*Brisco* **Crossroads House** ★★★★ 452
*Bruera* **Churton Heath Farm Bed & Breakfast** ★★★★ 452
*Burythorpe* **Low Penhowe** ★★★★★ 452
*Carlisle* **Number Thirty One** ★★★★★ 453
*Cartmel* **Hill Farm B&B For Country Lovers** ★★★★★ 79
*Cockermouth* **Graysonside** ★★★★★ 455
*Coniston* **Coniston Lodge** ★★★★★ 456
*Corbridge* **Riggsacre** ★★★★★ 456
*Crosby Ravensworth* **Crake Trees Manor** ★★★★★ 83
*Darlington* **Clow Beck House** ★★★★★ 457
*Dinnington* **Throapham House Bed & Breakfast** ★★★★★ 458
*Grasmere* **Heron Beck Guest House** ★★★★ 462
*Grasmere* **Lake View Country House** ★★★★ 462
*Grasmere* **Riversdale** ★★★★ 462
*Grassington* **Grassington Lodge** ★★★★★ 92
*Grassington* **Yew Tree House** ★★★★ 462
*Haltwhistle* **Ashcroft Guest House** ★★★★ 463
*Harrogate* **Cold Cotes** ★★★★★ 95
*Harrogate* **Acacia** ★★★★ 463
*Harrogate* **Applewood House** ★★★★ 463
*Harrogate* **Knabbs Ash** ★★★★ 464
*Hawes* **Rookhurst Country House** ★★★★★ 95
*Hawes* **Thorney Mire Barn B&B** ★★★★★ 465
*Hawkshead* **The Drunken Duck Inn** ★★★★★ 465
*Hawkshead Hill* **Summer Hill Country House** ★★★★ 465
*Hebden Bridge* **Holme House** ★★★★★ 97
*Helmsley* **Oldstead Grange** ★★★★★ 466
*Helmsley* **West View Cottage** ★★★★ 466
*Holmfirth* **Sunnybank Guesthouse** ★★★★★ 98
*Huddersfield* **Castle View Guest House** ★★★★★ 467
*Keswick* **Howe Keld** ★★★★ 470
*Kettlesing* **Green Acres** ★★★★ 471
*Kirkby Stephen* **Augill Castle** ★★★★★ 472
*Levisham* **The Moorlands Country House** ★★★★★ 473
*Leyburn* **Waterford House** ★★★★★ 473
*Longframlington* **Lee Farm** ★★★★★ 474

## Northern England continued

### GOLD continued

*Longhorsley* **Thistleyhaugh Farm** ★★★★★ 474
*Middleton-in-Teesdale* **Grove Lodge** ★★★★ 476
*Newbrough* **Allerwash Farmhouse** ★★★★★ 478
*Newton-on-the-Moor* **The Old School** ★★★★★ 479
*Otley* **Scaife Hall Farm** ★★★★ 479
*Pickering* **17 Burgate** ★★★★★ 115
*Pickering* **The Old Vicarage** ★★★★★ 116
*Rastrick* **Elder Lea House** ★★★★★ 482
*Ravenstonedale* **Coldbeck House** ★★★★★ 482
*Ravenstonedale* **A Corner of Eden** ★★★★ 482
*Ripon* **Sharow Cross House** ★★★★★ 483
*Rothbury* **Farm Cottage Guest House** ★★★★★ 483
*Rothbury* **Tosson Tower Farm B&B** ★★★★★ 484
*Sawrey* **West Vale Country House & Restaurant** ★★★★★ 485
*Scotby* **Willowbeck Lodge** ★★★★★ 487
*Sledmere* **Life Hill Farm B&B** ★★★★ 489
*Sleights* **The Lawns** ★★★★★ 489
*Stainburn* **Falconwood** ★★★★★ 490
*Staithes* **Grinkle Lodge** ★★★★★ 490
*Stonyhurst* **Alden Cottage – B&B** ★★★★ 491
*Swarland* **Swarland Old Hall** ★★★★★ 491
*Warkworth* **Roxbro House** ★★★★ 494
*Whitehaven* **Moresby Hall** ★★★★★ 136
*Whitewell* **The Inn at Whitewell** ★★★★★ 136
*Windermere* **Beechwood** ★★★★ 497
*Windermere* **Oakfold House** ★★★★ 499
*Wold Newton* **The Wold Cottage** ★★★★★ 500
*Wooler* **Firwood** ★★★★★ 500
*Wooler* **The Old Manse** ★★★★★ 500
*York* **Alexander House** ★★★★★ 500
*York* **Arnot House** ★★★★★ 500

### SILVER

*Accrington* **Norwood Guest House** ★★★★ 439
*Addingham* **Beck House Farm** ★★★★ 439
*Addingham* **Lumb Beck Farmhouse Bed and Breakfast** ★★★★ 439
*Allendale* **Keenley Thorn Farmhouse** ★★★★ 439
*Alnmouth* **Beech Lodge** ★★★★ 65
*Alnmouth* **Bilton Barns Farmhouse** ★★★★ 439
*Alnmouth* **Westlea** ★★★★ 439
*Alnwick* **Aln House** ★★★★ 439
*Alnwick* **Alndyke Bed and Breakfast** ★★★★ 439
*Alnwick* **Courtyard Garden** ★★★★ 439
*Alnwick* **Norfolk** ★★★★ 440
*Alnwick* **Prudhoe Croft** ★★★★ 440
*Alnwick* **Redfoot Lea Bed & Breakfast** ★★★★ 440
*Alnwick* **Rooftops** ★★★★ 440
*Alston* **Rosemount Cottage** ★★★★ 440
*Ambleside* **Red Bank** ★★★★★ 68
*Ambleside* **Amboseli Lodge** ★★★★ 440
*Ambleside* **Crow How Country House** ★★★★ 440
*Ambleside* **Elder Grove** ★★★★ 441
*Ambleside* **Fern Cottage** ★★★★ 441
*Ambleside* **Fisherbeck** ★★★★ 441
*Ambleside* **Freshfields Guest House** ★★★★ 441
*Ambleside* **High Wray Farm B&B** ★★★★ 441
*Ambleside* **Norwood House** ★★★★ 441
*Ambleside* **Riverside** ★★★★ 441
*Ambleside* **Waterwheel Guesthouse** ★★★★ 441
*Appleby-in-Westmorland* **Broom House** ★★★★ 442
*Arnside* **Number 43** ★★★★★ 442
*Askrigg* **Stoney End** ★★★★★ 442
*Askrigg* **Apothecary's House** ★★★★ 442
*Austwick* **Austwick Hall** ★★★★★ 442
*Aysgarth* **Thornton Lodge** ★★★★★ 69
*Aysgarth* **Heather Cottage Guesthouse** ★★★★ 442
*Aysgarth* **Stow House Country House** ★★★★ 442
*Baildon* **Ford House Farm Bed and Breakfast** ★★★★ 442
*Bailiff Bridge* **The Lodge at Birkby Hall** ★★★★ 442
*Bainton* **Wolds Village Luxury Guest Accommodation** ★★★★ 442
*Bamburgh* **Glenander Bed & Breakfast** ★★★★ 70
*Barlow* **Berewick House** ★★★★ 443
*Barnard Castle* **Crich House Bed & Breakfast** ★★★★ 70
*Barrow-in-Furness* **November House B&B** ★★★★ 70
*Barrowford* **Merok Bed & Breakfast** ★★★★ 443
*Barton* **Higher Farm Bed & Breakfast** ★★★★ 443
*Bassenthwaite* **Herdwick Croft Guest House** ★★★★ 443
*Bassenthwaite* **Highside Farm** ★★★★ 443
*Beadnell* **Beach Court** ★★★★★ 443
*Beadnell* **Low Dover Beadnell Bay** ★★★★★ 444
*Bedale* **Elmfield House** ★★★★ 72
*Belford* **Easington Farm** ★★★★ 444
*Belford* **The Farmhouse Guest House** ★★★★ 444
*Ben Rhydding* **Farmhouse at Wharfedale Grange** ★★★★ 444
*Berwick-upon-Tweed* **Granary Guest House** ★★★★★ 444
*Berwick-upon-Tweed* **Alannah House** ★★★★ 72
*Berwick-upon-Tweed* **Clovelly House** ★★★★ 444
*Berwick-upon-Tweed* **Four North Road** ★★★★ 444
*Berwick-upon-Tweed* **The Old Vicarage Guest House Farm** ★★★★ 445
*Berwick-upon-Tweed* **Whyteside House** ★★★★ 445
*Blaxton* **Beech Grove Lodge** ★★★★ 449
*Blundellsands* **Blundellsands Guesthouse** ★★★★ 449
*Boston Spa* **Four Gables** ★★★★★ 450
*Brampton* **Vallum Barn** ★★★★ 450
*Bridlington* **The Bay Court** ★★★★ 450
*Bridlington* **The Seacourt** ★★★★ 451
*Caldbeck* **Swaledale Watch** ★★★★ 79
*Carleton* **Birklands House** ★★★★ 453

Establishments in colour have a detailed entry in this guide.

## Northern England continued

### SILVER continued


*Carleton* **River Forge Bed & Breakfast** ★★★★ 453
*Carlisle* **Cartref Guest House** ★★★★ 453
*Carlisle* **Courtfield Guest House** ★★★★ 453
*Carlisle* **Fernlee Guest House** ★★★★ 453
*Carnforth* **Capernwray House** ★★★★ 453
*Castle Carrock* **The Weary at Castle Carrock** ★★★★ 453
*Chatton* **South Hazelrigg Farmhouse** ★★★★ 80
*Chester* **Mitchell's of Chester Guest House** ★★★★★ 454
*Chester* **Willow Run Bed & Breakfast** ★★★★ 454
*Chester-le-Street* **Low Urpeth Farm** ★★★★ 455
*Colne* **Blakey Hall Farm** ★★★★ 455
*Coniston* **Yew Tree Farm** ★★★★★ 82
*Coniston* **The Old Rectory** ★★★★ 456
*Corbridge* **Priorfield** ★★★★ 456
*Corbridge* **Town Barns** ★★★★ 456
*Cornhill-on-Tweed* **The Old School House B&B** ★★★★★ 456
*Cornhill-on-Tweed* **The Coach House at Crookham** ★★★★ 456
*Craster* **Stonecroft** ★★★★ 457
*Crayke* **Hazelwood Farm Bed and Breakfast** ★★★★ 457
*Cropton* **High Farm Bed & Breakfast** ★★★★ 457
*Culgaith* **Laurel House** ★★★★ 457
*Cundall* **Cundall Lodge Farm** ★★★★★ 457
*Downholme* **Walburn Hall** ★★★★ 458
*Dufton* **Brow Farm Bed & Breakfast** ★★★★ 85
*Durham* **60 Albert Street** ★★★★ 458
*Durham* **Cathedral View Town House** ★★★★ 86
*Durham* **The Victorian Town House** ★★★★ 88
*Easington* **Townend Farm B & B** ★★★★ 459
*Eastgate-in-Weardale* **Rose Hill Farm** ★★★★ 459
*Ebberston* **Studley House Farm** ★★★★ 459
*Egton Bridge* **Broom House** ★★★★ 88
*Eshott* **Eshott Hall** ★★★★★ 460
*Far Sawrey* **Fair Rigg at Far Sawrey** ★★★★★ 460
*Fence* **Grains Barn Farm** ★★★★★ 460
*Ford* **Hay Farm House** ★★★★ 460
*Gateshead* **The Riding Farm House** ★★★★ 461
*Gilsland* **The Hill on the Wall** ★★★★★ 461
*Gilsland* **Bush Nook Guest House** ★★★★ 461
*Goathland* **Heatherdene** ★★★★ 461
*Goodshaw* **The Old White Horse** ★★★★ 461
*Grasmere* **Beck Allans Guest House** ★★★★ 461
*Great Ayton* **The Kings Head at Newton under Roseberry** ★★★★ 93
*Guilden Sutton* **Roseville** ★★★★★ 462
*Halifax* **Rose Cottage** ★★★★★ 463
*Hamsterley* **Dale End** ★★★★ 463
*Hamsterley* **Hamsterley B&B** ★★★★ 463
*Harbottle* **The Byre Vegetarian B&B** ★★★★ 463
*Harrogate* **18 Park Parade** ★★★★★ 463
*Harrogate* **The Bijou** ★★★★★ 464
*Harrogate* **Bowes Green Farm** ★★★★ 464
*Harrogate* **Brookfield House** ★★★★ 464
*Harrogate* **Central House Farm** ★★★★ 464
*Harrogate* **Franklin View** ★★★★ 464
*Harrogate* **Lavender House** ★★★★ 464
*Hartoft* **Robin's Nest** ★★★★ 464
*Hawes* **The Old Dairy Farm** ★★★★★ 465
*Hawkshead* **Walker Ground Manor** ★★★★★ 465
*Hawkshead* **Yewfield Vegetarian Guest House** ★★★★★ 465
*Haworth* **Ashmount Guest House** ★★★★★ 465
*Haworth* **The Manor Guest House** ★★★★★ 465
*Haworth* **The Old Registry** ★★★★ 465
*Heads Nook* **Croft House** ★★★★ 466
*Heddon-on-the-Wall* **Heddon Lodge** ★★★★ 466
*Hellifield* **Chapel Farm B&B** ★★★★ 466
*Helmsley* **Carlton Lodge** ★★★★ 466
*Helmsley* **Stilworth House** ★★★★ 466
*Hesleden* **The Ship Inn** ★★★★ 466
*Hexham* **Fairshaw Rigg** ★★★★ 466
*Hexham* **Kitty Frisk House** ★★★★ 467
*High Lorton* **Swinside End Farm** ★★★★ 467
*Holmes Chapel* **Padgate Guest House** ★★★★ 467
*Holmfirth* **Uppergate Farm B&B** ★★★★ 467
*Hornsea* **Earlham House Guest House** ★★★★ 467
*Huddersfield* **The Old Co-Op** ★★★★★ 468
*Huddersfield* **Elm Crest** ★★★★ 468
*Huddersfield* **Huddersfield Central Lodge** ★★★★ 99
*Hull* **The Hornbeams** ★★★★★ 468
*Humshaugh* **Carraw Bed and Breakfast** ★★★★ 468
*Hutton-le-Hole* **Burnley House** ★★★★ 468
*Huxley* **Higher Huxley Hall** ★★★★★ 468
*Ings* **The Hill** ★★★★ 469
*Kellah* **Kellah Farm B & B** ★★★★ 469
*Kendal* **Beech House** ★★★★★ 469
*Keswick* **The Grange Country House** ★★★★★ 103
*Keswick* **Abacourt House** ★★★★ 469
*Keswick* **Acorn House** ★★★★ 101
*Keswick* **Allerdale House** ★★★★ 469
*Keswick* **Amble House Guest House** ★★★★ 469
*Keswick* **Badgers Wood** ★★★★ 102
*Keswick* **Braemar Guest House** ★★★★ 469
*Keswick* **Burnside B&B** ★★★★ 469
*Keswick* **Dunsford Guest House** ★★★★ 470
*Keswick* **The Edwardene** ★★★★ 470
*Keswick* **Ellas Crag** ★★★★ 470
*Keswick* **Glendale Guest House** ★★★★ 470
*Keswick* **Keswick Park** ★★★★ 470
*Keswick* **Parkfield Guest House** ★★★★ 471
*Keswick* **Ravensworth House** ★★★★ 471
*Keswick* **Tarn Hows** ★★★★ 471
*Keswick* **Whitehouse** ★★★★ 471

## Northern England continued

### SILVER continued


*Kielder Water* **The Pheasant Inn (by Kielder Water) ★★★★** 105
*Kirkbymoorside* **Brickfields Farm ★★★★★** 472
*Kirkbymoorside* **Ely Cottage ★★★★★** 472
*Kirkbymoorside* **The Cornmill ★★★★** 106
*Kirkwhelpington* **Cornhills Farmhouse ★★★★** 472
*Knaresborough* **The Mitre ★★★★★** 472
*Lakeside* **The Knoll Country House ★★★★★** 472
*Lancaster* **Penny Street Bridge, Lancaster ★★★★** 473
*Leeming Bar* **Little Holtby ★★★★** 473
*Leyburn* **Clyde House ★★★★** 108
*Leyburn* **West Close Farmhouse ★★★★** 473
*Littleborough* **Hollingworth Lake B&B ★★★★★** 474
*Longframlington* **Coquet Bed & Breakfast ★★★★** 474
*Longhoughton* **Swallows' Rest ★★★★** 474
*Longton* **Willow Cottage ★★★★** 475
*Low Row* **Rowleth End Guest House ★★★★** 475
*Lowick* **Burn House Bed & Breakfast ★★★★** 475
*Loxley* **Barnfield House ★★★★** 475
*Lytham St Annes* **Cornubia ★★★★** 475
*Macclesfield* **Red Oaks Farm B&B ★★★★** 475
*Malton* **Red House ★★★★** 476
*Masham* **Park House ★★★★★** 476
*Middleton-in-Teesdale* **Brunswick House ★★★★** 476
*Nantwich* **Coole Hall Farm Bed and Breakfast ★★★★** 478
*New Hutton* **1 Ashes Barn ★★★★** 478
*Northallerton* **Elmscott ★★★★** 479
*Northallerton* **Lovesome Hill Farm ★★★★** 479
*Pateley Bridge* **High Green Farm ★★★★** 480
*Penrith* **The Old School ★★★★★** 480
*Penrith* **Roundthorn Country House ★★★★★** 480
*Pickering* **Apricot Lodge ★★★★★** 480
*Pickering* **Bramwood Guest House ★★★★** 480
*Pickering* **Bridge House ★★★★** 480
*Pickering* **Cawthorne House ★★★★** 115
*Pickering* **Costa House ★★★★** 480
*Pickering* **Eleven Westgate ★★★★** 115
*Pickering* **No 9 B&B ★★★★** 481
*Pickering* **Rains Farm Bed & Breakfast ★★★★** 481
*Pickering* **Wildsmith House ★★★★** 481
*Pontefract* **Tower House Executive Guest House ★★★★★** 481
*Port Carlisle* **Brockelrigg ★★★★★** 116
*Portinscale* **Lakeview ★★★★** 481
*Portinscale* **Powe House ★★★★** 481
*Powburn* **Low Hedgeley Farm ★★★★★** 116
*Preston* **Little Weghill Farm ★★★★** 481
*Rainow* **Harrop Fold Farm Bed & Breakfast ★★★★★** 481
*Rathmell* **Littlebank Guest House ★★★★★** 482
*Reeth* **Cambridge House ★★★★** 482
*Ribchester* **Riverside Barn ★★★★★** 482
*Richmond* **New Skeeby Grange ★★★★★** 118
*Richmond* **Mount Pleasant Farm ★★★★** 482
*Richmond* **Whashton Springs Farm ★★★★** 483
*Ripon* **Mallard Grange ★★★★★** 483
*Ripponden* **Over The Bridge ★★★★** 483
*Robin Hood's Bay* **Lee-Side ★★★★** 483
*Rochdale* **Moss Lodge ★★★★★** 483
*Romaldkirk* **Hollin Croft ★★★★** 483
*Rosedale Abbey* **Sevenford House ★★★★** 483
*Rosedale East* **Ann's Cottage ★★★★** 483
*Rossendale* **Middle Carr Farm ★★★★** 483
*Rothbury* **Katerina's Guest House ★★★★** 484
*Rothbury* **Silverton House ★★★★** 484
*Runswick Bay* **Ellerby ★★★★** 484
*Sandbach* **Bagmere Bank Farm Luxury Bed and Breakfast ★★★★** 484
*Sawrey* **Beechmount Country House ★★★★★** 484
*Scalby* **Scalby Hayes B&B ★★★★** 485
*Scarborough* **The Alexander ★★★★** 485
*Scarborough* **The Helaina ★★★★** 485
*Scarborough* **Killerby Cottage Farm ★★★★** 123
*Scarborough* **Riviera Town House ★★★★** 486
*Scarborough* **Sawdon Heights ★★★★** 123
*Scarborough* **Tall Storeys ★★★★** 487
*Seahouses* **Railston House ★★★★** 487
*Seahouses* **Springwood ★★★★** 487
*Settle* **Halsteads Barn ★★★★★** 487
*Settle* **Mainsfield ★★★★** 487
*Shotley Bridge* **The Manor House Inn ★★★★** 488
*Silsden* **Pickersgill Manor Farm ★★★★** 488
*Skipsea* **Village Farm ★★★★** 488
*Skipton* **Chinthurst ★★★★★** 488
*Skipton* **Cononley Hall Bed & Breakfast ★★★★★** 125
*Slaithwaite* **The Mistal Bed and Breakfast ★★★★★** 489
*Slaley* **The Travellers Rest ★★★★** 489
*Southport* **Ambassador Town House ★★★★** 489
*Southport* **The Waterford ★★★★** 490
*Sprotbrough* **The Old Rectory ★★★★** 490
*Stamford Bridge* **High Catton Grange ★★★★** 490
*Stanhope* **Horsley Hall ★★★★★** 490
*Stannington* **Cheviot View Farmhouse Bed & Breakfast ★★★★** 491
*Stannington* **Robin Hood Inn ★★★★** 491
*Stape* **High Muffles ★★★★** 127
*Stape* **Rawcliffe House Farm ★★★★** 491
*Stape* **Seavy Slack ★★★★** 491
*Startforth* **Startforth House Bed & Breakfast ★★★★** 491
*Staveley* **Staveley Grange ★★★★★** 491
*Stocksfield* **Locksley, Bed & Breakfast ★★★★** 491
*Stokesley* **Willow Cottage ★★★★** 491


Establishments in colour have a detailed entry in this guide.

## Northern England continued

### SILVER continued


*Tarporley* Hill House Farm Bed & Breakfast ★★★★ 492
*Thirsk* **Borrowby Mill, Bed and Breakfast ★★★★** 129
*Thirsk* Laburnum House ★★★★ 492
*Thirsk* The Poplars ★★★★ 492
*Thoralby* The Old Barn ★★★★ 492
*Thornthwaite* Jenkin Hill Cottage ★★★★ 492
*Thornton Dale* **Cherry Garth ★★★★** 130
*Threlkeld* Scales Farm Country Guest House ★★★★ 492
*Thurstonland* Ackroyd House ★★★★★ 493
*Todmorden* Kilnhurst Old Hall ★★★★★ 493
*Tweedmouth* West Sunnyside House ★★★★ 493
*Tynemouth* Martineau Guest House ★★★★ 493
*Ullswater* Elm House ★★★★ 493
*Ullswater* Whitbarrow Farm ★★★★ 493
*Wall* Tantallon House ★★★★ 494
*Wark* **Battlesteads Country Inn & Restaurant ★★★★** 132
*Warkworth* Fairfield House ★★★★★ 494
*Weaverthorpe* Blue Bell Inn ★★★★ 494
*Welburn* Welburn Lodge ★★★★ 494
*West Kirby* **At Peel Hey ★★★★** 133
*Westgate-in-Weardale* Lands Farm ★★★★ 495
*Wetherby* Linton Close ★★★★ 495
*Whickham* East Byermoor Guest House ★★★★ 495
*Whitby* The Langley ★★★★★ 496
*Whitby* Cross Butts Stable Restaurant with Rooms ★★★★ 495
*Whitby* **Gramarye Suites B&B ★★★★** 135
*Whitby* Haven Crest ★★★★ 496
*Whitby* Netherby House ★★★★ 496
*Whitby* The Olde Ford ★★★★ 496
*Whitby* Storrbeck Guest House ★★★★ 496
*Whitestake* Whitestake Farm ★★★★★ 496
*Whitworth* Hindle Pastures ★★★★ 497
*Wigglesworth* Cowper Cottage ★★★★ 497
*Windermere* High View ★★★★★ 498
*Windermere* Storrs Gate House ★★★★★ 499
*Windermere* Braemount House ★★★★ 497
*Windermere* Denehurst Guest House ★★★★ 498
*Windermere* **Fair Rigg ★★★★** 138
*Windermere* **Fairfield House and Gardens ★★★★** 139
*Windermere* Ivy Bank ★★★★ 498
*Windermere* Lingwood Lodge ★★★★ 498
*Windermere* Lonsdale House ★★★★ 499
*Windermere* Mylne Bridge House ★★★★ 499
*Windermere* Oldfield House ★★★★ 499
*Windermere* Ravenscroft ★★★★ 499
*Windermere* **Southview House & Indoor Pool ★★★★** 141
*Windermere* The Westbourne ★★★★ 499
*Wirral* Pendragon House ★★★★ 499
*Wombleton* Rockery Cottage ★★★★ 500
*Wooler* Tilldale House ★★★★ 500
*Wooler* Tillside B&B ★★★★ 500
*York* **Bishops ★★★★★** 144
*York* **23 St Marys ★★★★** 142
*York* **Ascot House ★★★★** 143
*York* **Barbican House ★★★★** 144
*York* Beech House ★★★★ 501
*York* The Bloomsbury ★★★★ 501
*York* Bowmans Guest House ★★★★ 501
*York* Crook Lodge ★★★★ 501
*York* Feversham Lodge ★★★★ 502
*York* Gregory's ★★★★ 502
*York* **The Hazelwood ★★★★** 146
*York* Limes ★★★★ 502


## Central England

### GOLD


*Arley* Tudor Barn ★★★★ 504
*Ashbourne* Omnia Somnia ★★★★★ 505
*Aylsham* **Old Pump House ★★★★★** 170
*Bewdley* Kateshill House ★★★★★ 507
*Biggin-by-Hartington* The Kings at Ivy House ★★★★★ 508
*Billericay* Badgers Rest ★★★★ 508
*Bishop's Castle* Magnolia ★★★★ 508
*Broadway* **Sheepscombe House ★★★★** 177
*Broadway* Windrush House ★★★★ 510
*Brockdish* Grove Thorpe ★★★★★ 510
*Bungay* Earsham Park Farm ★★★★ 511
*Burton Dassett* Caudle Hill Farm ★★★★ 511
*Bury St Edmunds* Manorhouse ★★★★★ 511
*Buxton* **Grendon Guest House ★★★★★** 179
*Chelmsford* Chatton Park House Bed & Breakfast ★★★★★ 515
*Church Stretton* Jinlye Guest House ★★★★★ 515
*Clacton-on-Sea* Pond House Farmhouse Bed and Breakfast ★★★★ 516
*Cleobury Mortimer* Woodview B&B ★★★★ 516
*Clun* New House Farm ★★★★★ 517
*Colchester* Park Hall Country House ★★★★★ 517
*Coventry* Barnacle Hall ★★★★★ 518
*Cromer* Captains House ★★★★★ 518
*Cromer* **Incleborough House Luxury Bed and Breakfast ★★★★★** 189
*Cropston* Horseshoe Cottage Farm ★★★★★ 518
*Cropthorne* Oaklands Farmhouse ★★★★★ 518
*Cropthorne* Cropvale Farm Bed and Breakfast ★★★★ 518
*Crowle* Sunbrae Bed and Breakfast ★★★★ 519

## Central England continued

### GOLD continued


*Diss* **Dickleburgh Hall** ★★★★★ 520
*Diss* **The Old Rectory Hopton** ★★★★★ 520
*East Carleton* **Majority Cottage** ★★★★ 521
*Edale* **Stonecroft Country Guest House** ★★★★ 521
*Ely* **Hill House Farm** ★★★★ 522
*Fakenham* **Holly Lodge** ★★★★★ 523
*Great Oakley* **Zig Zag Cottage** ★★★★ 524
*Hathersage* **Cannon Croft** ★★★★ 527
*Hickling* **The Dairy Barns** ★★★★ 197
*Hindringham* **Field House** ★★★★★ 528
*Holbeck* **Browns** ★★★★★ 528
*Holt* **Byfords** ★★★★★ 528
*Hope* **Underleigh House** ★★★★★ 198
*Hopton Heath* **Hopton House** ★★★★ 529
*Hunstanton* **Gate Lodge** ★★★★ 529
*Ironbridge* **The Library House** ★★★★★ 530
*Kenilworth* **Loweridge Guest House** ★★★★★ 531
*Kidderminster* **Garden Cottages** ★★★★ 531
*Lavenham* **Lavenham Priory** ★★★★★ 532
*Leominster* **Ryelands** ★★★★★ 533
*Lichfield* **Old Rectory** ★★★★ 534
*Little Waltham* **Channels Lodge** ★★★★ 535
*Littleport* **Killiney House** ★★★★★ 535
*Ludlow* **Mr Underhill's** ★★★★★ 536
*Ludlow* **Ravenscourt Manor** ★★★★★ 536
*Matlock* **Robertswood Country House** ★★★★★ 538
*Matlock* **Sheriff Lodge** ★★★★ 538
*Nayland* **White Hart Inn** ★★★★★ 216
*Newmarket* **Birdcage Walk** ★★★★ 540
*North Lopham* **Church Farm House** ★★★★★ 541
*Norwich* **By Appointment** ★★★★ 541
*Nottingham* **Greenwood Lodge City Guesthouse** ★★★★★ 542
*Pembridge* **Lowe Farm B & B** ★★★★ 543
*Pulham Market* **Old Bakery** ★★★★★ 222
*Ross-on-Wye* **Norton House** ★★★★ 544
*Saxmundham* **Moat House Farm** ★★★★ 546
*Shrewsbury* **Lyth Hill House** ★★★★ 547
*Snelston* **Oldfield House** ★★★★★ 549
*Snetterton* **Holly House Guest House** ★★★★★ 549
*Southam* **Wormleighton Hall** ★★★★ 549
*Stalham* **Bramble House** ★★★★ 550
*Stamford* **Rock Lodge** ★★★★★ 550
*Stanton in Peak* **Congreave Farm** ★★★★ 550
*Stowmarket* **Bays Farm** ★★★★★ 231
*Stratford-upon-Avon* **Shakespeare's View** ★★★★★ 552
*Stratford-upon-Avon* **White-Sails** ★★★★★ 552
*Stratford-upon-Avon* **Folly Farm Cottage** ★★★★ 232
*Uppingham* **Spanhoe Lodge** ★★★★★ 236
*Vowchurch* **Yew Tree House** ★★★★ 237
*Wellington Heath* **Hope End House** ★★★★★ 557
*Wells-next-the-Sea* **Normans** ★★★★★ 557
*Wells-next-the-Sea* **Machrimore** ★★★★ 557
*Wells-next-the-Sea* **Meadow View Guest House** ★★★★ 557
*Wigmore* **Pear Tree Farm** ★★★★ 558
*Wirksworth* **The Old Lock-Up** ★★★★★ 559


### SILVER


*Albrighton* **Parkside Farm** ★★★★ 503
*Alton* **The Warren** ★★★★ 504
*Ardleigh* **Park Cottage** ★★★★ 504
*Ashbourne* **Holly Meadow Farm** ★★★★ 505
*Ashbourne* **Shirley Hall** ★★★★ 505
*Ashford in the Water* **River Cottage** ★★★★★ 505
*Ashford in the Water* **Chy-an-Dour** ★★★★ 505
*Assington* **The Case Restaurant with Rooms** ★★★★ 505
*Aston Munslow* **Chadstone** ★★★★★ 170
*Aylmerton* **Driftway Guest House** ★★★★ 505
*Badingham* **Colston Hall** ★★★★ 506
*Bakewell* **Bolehill Farm** ★★★★ 506
*Bakewell* **Castle Hill Farm House** ★★★★ 506
*Bakewell* **The Garden Room** ★★★★ 506
*Balderton* **Newark Lodge Guest House** ★★★★★ 506
*Bamford* **Pioneer House** ★★★★ 171
*Bamford* **Yorkshire Bridge Inn** ★★★★ 171
*Barford* **Westham House B&B** ★★★★ 506
*Barons Cross* **Lavender House** ★★★★ 507
*Barrow-on-Trent* **5 Nook Cottages** ★★★★ 507
*Bartlow* **Westoe Farm** ★★★★★ 507
*Bayston Hill* **Chatford House** ★★★★ 507
*Beccles* **Eveleigh House** ★★★★ 507
*Bedford* **Church Farm** ★★★★ 507
*Bedford* **Cornfields** ★★★★ 172
*Beeston Regis* **Sheringham View Cottage** ★★★★ 507
*Benniworth* **Glebe Farm** ★★★★ 507
*Bildeston* **Silwood Barns** ★★★★ 508
*Bolnhurst* **Old School House** ★★★★ 509
*Bottesford* **The Thatch Restaurant** ★★★★ 509
*Bourne* **Maycroft Cottage Bed and Breakfast** ★★★★ 174
*Brackley* **The Old Surgery** ★★★★ 509
*Bradley* **Yeldersley Old Hall Farm** ★★★★ 509
*Braunston* **Braunston Manor Hotel** ★★★★ 509
*Bridgnorth* **Churchdown House** ★★★★★ 510
*Brightlingsea* **Paxton Dene** ★★★★ 510
*Broadway* **Burhill Farm** ★★★★★ 510
*Broadway* **Dove Cottage** ★★★★ 510
*Broadway* **The Old Stationhouse** ★★★★ 510
*Broadway* **The Olive Branch Guest House** ★★★★ 510
*Broadway* **Whiteacres** ★★★★ 510
*Bromsgrove* **The Durrance** ★★★★ 510


Establishments in colour have a detailed entry in this guide.

## Central England continued

### SILVER continued


*Brooke* **Old Vicarage** ★★★★ 510
*Broseley* **Broseley House** ★★★★ 511
*Broseley* **Rock Dell** ★★★★ 511
*Burnham-on-Crouch* **Mangapp Manor** ★★★★ 511
*Burnham-on-Crouch* **The Railway Hotel** ★★★★ 177
*Burnham Thorpe* **Whitehall Farm** ★★★★ 177
*Bury St Edmunds* **Ounce House** ★★★★★ 511
*Bury St Edmunds* **Brambles Lodge** ★★★★ 178
*Butterton* **Coxon Green Farm** ★★★★ 511
*Buxton* **Westlands** ★★★★★ 512
*Buxton* **9 Green Lane B&B** ★★★★ 511
*Buxton* **Devonshire Lodge Guest House** ★★★★ 512
*Buxton* **Fernydale Farm** ★★★★ 179
*Buxton* **Grosvenor House** ★★★★ 179
*Buxton* **Kingscroft Guest House** ★★★★ 180
*Buxton* **Roseleigh** ★★★★ 512
*Buxton* **Stoneridge Guest House** ★★★★ 512
*Caenby Corner* **Ermine Lodge Bed and Breakfast** ★★★★ 180
*Calver* **Valley View Guest House** ★★★★ 512
*Cambridge* **The Conifers** ★★★★ 513
*Cambridge* **Finches Bed and Breakfast** ★★★★ 513
*Cambridge* **Upton House** ★★★★ 513
*Cambridge* **Worth House** ★★★★ 183
*Cavendish* **Embleton House** ★★★★ 514
*Chapel-en-le-Frith* **High Croft** ★★★★★ 183
*Cheadle* **Ley Fields Farm** ★★★★ 514
*Chesterfield* **Batemans Mill Country Inn & Restaurant** ★★★★ 515
*Cheveley* **1eleven Bed & Breakfast** ★★★★ 515
*Chorleywood* **Ashburton Country House** ★★★★★ 515
*Church Stretton* **Brookfields Guest House** ★★★★★ 515
*Church Stretton* **Juniper Cottage** ★★★★ 515
*Church Stretton* **Mynd House** ★★★★ 516
*Cockfield* **The Old Manse Barn** ★★★★ 517
*Colchester* **Charlie Brown's** ★★★★ 517
*Colchester* **Fridaywood Farm** ★★★★ 517
*Colchester* **Rutland House Bed and Breakfast** ★★★★ 517
*Coltishall* **Seven Acres House** ★★★★★ 186
*Colton* **Colton House** ★★★★★ 186
*Conisholme* **Wickham House** ★★★★★ 518
*Cranwell* **Byards Leap Lodge** ★★★★ 518
*Cross Houses* **Upper Brompton Farm** ★★★★ 518
*Deeping St Nicholas* **St Nicholas House** ★★★★ 519
*Denstone* **Manor House Farm** ★★★★ 519
*Derby* **Thornhill Lodge Guest House** ★★★★ 519
*Dersingham* **Ashdene House** ★★★★ 519
*Dersingham* **The Corner House** ★★★★ 519
*Digby* **Digby Manor Bed & Breakfast** ★★★★ 520
*Diseworth* **Lady Gate Guest House** ★★★★ 520
*Diss* **Strenneth** ★★★★ 520
*Donington* **Browntoft House** ★★★★ 520
*Dorstone* **Highfield** ★★★★ 520
*Droitwich* **The Old Farmhouse** ★★★★★ 520
*Droitwich* **Middleton Grange** ★★★★ 520
*Eardisland* **Lawton Bury Farm B & B** ★★★★ 520
*Earl Soham* **Bridge House** ★★★★ 521
*Earls Colne* **Greenlands Farm** ★★★★ 521
*East Barkwith* **The Grange** ★★★★ 521
*Eckington* **Harrowfields Bed and Breakfast** ★★★★ 521
*Edingthorpe* **Church Farm Barn** ★★★★★ 521
*Elmesthorpe* **Badgers Mount** ★★★★ 521
*Elmstead* **Pheasant Lodge** ★★★★ 521
*Elmswell* **Elmswell Hall B&B** ★★★★ 521
*Elmswell* **Mulberry Farm** ★★★★ 521
*Elton* **Hawthorn Cottage** ★★★★★ 521
*Ely* **96 Lynn Road** ★★★★ 522
*Ely* **Bowmount House** ★★★★ 522
*Ely* **The Grove** ★★★★ 522
*Ely* **Walnut House** ★★★★ 522
*Epping* **The Coach House** ★★★★ 522
*Erpingham* **Saracens Head Inn** ★★★★ 522
*Ewyas Harold* **The Old Rectory – Ewyas Harold** ★★★★ 522
*Eyam* **Bretton Cottage** ★★★★★ 522
*Eye* **Bull Auberge** ★★★★★ 522
*Eye* **Camomile Cottage** ★★★★ 522
*Fairfield* **Barms Farm** ★★★★★ 522
*Fakenham* **Highfield Farm** ★★★★ 523
*Feckenham* **Orchard House** ★★★★ 523
*Feering* **Old Wills Farm** ★★★★ 193
*Felixstowe* **Castle Lodge** ★★★★ 523
*Fernhill Heath* **Dilmore House** ★★★★ 523
*Fillongley* **Grooms Cottage** ★★★★ 523
*Friston* **Old School** ★★★★ 524
*Great Easton* **The Swan Inn** ★★★★ 524
*Great Hormead* **Brick House Farm Bed And Breakfast** ★★★★ 524
*Great Wolford* **The Old Coach House** ★★★★★ 194
*Great Yarmouth* **Barnard House** ★★★★ 525
*Great Yarmouth* **Beaumont House** ★★★★ 525
*Great Yeldham* **The White Hart** ★★★★ 525
*Habrough* **Church Farm** ★★★★ 526
*Halesworth* **Valley Farm Vineyards** ★★★★ 526
*Hanley Castle* **The Chestnuts** ★★★★ 526
*Hanley Swan* **Meadowbank** ★★★★ 526
*Harwich* **Woodview Cottage** ★★★★ 526
*Hatfield Heath* **Friars Farm** ★★★★ 527
*Hathersage* **The Plough Inn** ★★★★ 527
*Haughley* **Haughley House** ★★★★★ 527
*Helhoughton* **Woodfarm House** ★★★★★ 527
*Hereford* **Brandon Lodge** ★★★★ 527

## Central England continued

### SILVER continued


*Hereford* **Old Rectory** ★★★★ 527
*Hintlesham* **College Farm** ★★★★ 197
*Holbeach* **Cackle Hill House** ★★★★ 528
*Holt* **Kadina** ★★★★ 528
*Hope* **Poachers Arms** ★★★★ 528
*Hope Valley* **The Chequers Inn** ★★★★ 198
*Hope Valley* **The Rising Sun** ★★★★ 529
*Horsley* **Horsley Lodge** ★★★★ 199
*Hunstanton* **The Bays Guesthouse** ★★★★★ 529
*Hunstanton* **Burlington House** ★★★★ 529
*Hunstanton* **Deepdene House** ★★★★ 529
*Hunstanton* **Glenberis Bed And Breakfast** ★★★★ 529
*Hunstanton* **The King William IV Country Inn & Restaurant** ★★★★ 199
*Hunstanton* **Linksway Country House** ★★★★ 529
*Hunstanton* **Peacock House** ★★★★ 530
*Hunstanton* **Rose Fitt House** ★★★★ 530
*Ilam* **Beechenhill Farm B&B** ★★★★ 530
*Ingoldisthorpe* **Pencob House** ★★★★ 530
*Ipswich* **Lattice Lodge Guest House** ★★★★ 530
*Ipswich* **Melverley Heights Guest House** ★★★★ 530
*Ipswich* **Sidegate Guesthouse** ★★★★ 530
*Ironbridge* **Bridge House** ★★★★★ 200
*Ironbridge* **The Old Rectory at Broseley** ★★★★★ 200
*Ironbridge* **Severn Lodge** ★★★★★ 530
*Ironbridge* **Coalbrookdale Villa Guest House** ★★★★ 530
*Kenilworth* **Victoria Lodge** ★★★★ 201
*Kettlebaston* **Box Tree Farm** ★★★★ 531
*Kidderminster* **The Brook House** ★★★★ 531
*Kinnerley* **Meadowbank Lodge** ★★★★ 532
*Lavenham* **Guinea House Bed & Breakfast** ★★★★ 203
*Lavenham* **Old Convent** ★★★★ 532
*Leamington Spa* **The Coach House** ★★★★ 204
*Leamington Spa* **No 8 Clarendon Crescent** ★★★★ 533
*Leintwardine* **Lower Buckton Country House** ★★★★ 533
*Leiston* **Field End** ★★★★ 533
*Lincoln* **Creston Villa Guest House** ★★★★★ 206
*Lincoln* **The Old Bakery Restaurant with Rooms** ★★★★ 207
*Lincoln* **The Old Vicarage** ★★★★ 207
*Linton* **The Manor** ★★★★ 534
*Little Compton* **The Old School** ★★★★★ 534
*Little Easton* **Roslyns** ★★★★ 535
*Little Sampford* **Bush Farm** ★★★★ 535
*Littleport* **Glebe House** ★★★★ 535
*Litton* **Hall Farm House** ★★★★ 535
*Long Melford* **High Street Farmhouse** ★★★★ 209
*Loughborough* **Lane End Cottage** ★★★★ 535
*Lowestoft* **The Sandcastle** ★★★★ 536
*Ludlow* **The Clive Bar and Restaurant With Rooms** ★★★★★ 211
*Ludlow* **DeGreys** ★★★★★ 211
*Maltby le Marsh* **Old Mill House B&B** ★★★★ 537
*Malvern* **The Brambles** ★★★★ 537
*Malvern* **Cannara Guest House** ★★★★ 212
*Malvern* **Hidelow House** ★★★★ 537
*Malvern* **The Old Croque** ★★★★ 537
*Malvern* **Orchid House** ★★★★ 537
*Malvern* **Treherne House** ★★★★ 537
*Malvern* **Clevelands** ★★★ 537
*Malvern* **Guarlford Grange** ★★★ 537
*Manningtree* **Curlews** ★★★★ 213
*Manton* **Broccoli Bottom** ★★★★ 537
*Mathon* **Weobley Cross Cottage** ★★★★ 214
*Matlock* **Cascades Gardens** ★★★★★ 538
*Matlock* **B&B Yew Tree Cottage** ★★★★ 538
*Matlock* **Riverbank House** ★★★★ 538
*Matlock* **Town Head Farmhouse** ★★★★ 538
*Matlock Bath* **Sunnybank Guest House** ★★★★ 538
*Medbourne* **Homestead House** ★★★★ 538
*Meole Brace* **Meole Brace Hall** ★★★★★ 539
*Much Wenlock* **Old Quarry Cottage** ★★★★ 539
*Nayland* **The Steam Mill House** ★★★★ 540
*Neatishead* **Regency Guesthouse** ★★★★ 540
*New Balderton* **Bridge House** ★★★★ 540
*Newark* **Crosshill House Bed and Breakfast** ★★★★ 540
*Newport* **Red Gables Country B&B** ★★★★ 217
*North Kilworth* **Old Rectory** ★★★★ 541
*Northampton* **The Poplars** ★★★★ 218
*Northampton* **Roade House Restaurant and Hotel** ★★★★ 541
*Northrepps* **The Stables Church Farm** ★★★★ 541
*Norton Disney* **Brills Farm** ★★★★ 541
*Norwich* **Gilman Lodge Guest House** ★★★★★ 542
*Norwich* **Beaufort Lodge** ★★★★ 541
*Norwich* **Old Lodge** ★★★★ 542
*Old* **Wold Farm** ★★★★ 542
*Old Catton* **Catton Old Hall** ★★★★★ 542
*Orleton* **Rosecroft** ★★★★★ 542
*Osbournby* **Barn Gallery** ★★★★ 542
*Oulton Broad* **The Mill House Bed and Breakfast** ★★★★ 543
*Pentney* **Little Abbey Farm** ★★★★ 543
*Pershore* **Arbour House** ★★★★ 221
*Pleshey* **Bury Farm** ★★★★ 543
*Retford* **Bolham Manor** ★★★★ 544
*Ross-on-Wye* **Lumleys B & B** ★★★★ 544
*Ross-on-Wye* **Walnut Tree Cottage** ★★★★ 544
*Rougham Green* **Oak Farm Barn** ★★★★ 544
*Rugby* **Lawford Hill Farm** ★★★★ 545
*Saffron Walden* **The Cricketers** ★★★★ 545


Establishments in colour have a detailed entry in this guide.

## Central England continued

### SILVER continued


*Saffron Walden* **Rowley Hill Lodge** ★★★★ 545
*St Albans* **Riverside** ★★★★ 545
*St Ives* **Cheriton House** ★★★★★ 223
*Sandy* **Highfield Farm** ★★★★★ 545
*Saxmundham* **Georgian Guest House** ★★★★★ 546
*Scamblesby* **The Paddock at Scamblesby** ★★★★ 546
*Sculthorpe* **Manor Farm Bed & Breakfast** ★★★★ 546
*Shalford* **Lynton House** ★★★ 546
*Shepshed* **Grange Courtyard** ★★★★★ 546
*Sheringham* **Bench Mark House** ★★★★★ 546
*Sheringham* **Cleat House** ★★★★★ 546
*Sheringham* **Fairlawns** ★★★★★ 546
*Sheringham* **Olivedale** ★★★★ 547
*Sheringham* **Sunrays B&B** ★★★★ 547
*Sheringham* **Viburnham House B&B** ★★★★ 224
*Shoby* **Shoby Lodge Farmhouse** ★★★★ 547
*Shotley* **Hill House Farm Bed & Breakfast** ★★★★ 547
*Shrewsbury* **Castlegates House** ★★★★★ 547
*Sibton* **Park Farm** ★★★★ 547
*Skegness* **Stoneleigh** ★★★★ 548
*Snettisham* **Twitchers Retreat** ★★★★ 549
*Solihull* **Chelsea Lodge** ★★★★ 549
*Solihull* **Acorn Guest House** ★★★ 227
*South Cockerington* **West View Bed & Breakfast** ★★★★ 227
*South Scarle* **Greystones** ★★★★ 549
*Spilsby* **Spye House** ★★★★ 228
*Sporle* **Corfield House** ★★★★ 550
*Stafford* **Cedarwood** ★★★★ 550
*Stamford* **Park Farm** ★★★★ 550
*Stansted* **The Cottage** ★★★★ 230
*Stansted Mountfitchet* **Chimneys** ★★★★ 550
*Stanton-by-Bridge* **Ivy House Farm** ★★★★ 230
*Stoke-on-Trent* **Cedar Tree Cottage** ★★★★ 230
*Stottesdon* **Hardwicke Farm Bed & Breakfast** ★★★★ 551
*Stowmarket* **Step House** ★★★★ 551
*Stratford-upon-Avon* **The Howard Arms** ★★★★★ 232
*Stratford-upon-Avon* **Broadlands Guest House** ★★★★ 551
*Stratford-upon-Avon* **Penryn Guest House** ★★★★ 552
*Stratford-upon-Avon* **Victoria Spa Lodge** ★★★★ 552
*Stretton on Dunsmore* **Home Farm (A45)** ★★★★ 552
*Sudbury* **St David's Hall** ★★★★ 552
*Swaffham Bulbeck* **B&B at Martin House** ★★★★ 553
*Swanton Morley* **Carricks at Castle Farm** ★★★★★ 233
*Swanton Morley* **Frogs Hall Farm** ★★★★★ 553
*Symonds Yat East* **Garth Cottage** ★★★★ 553
*Takeley* **Oak Lodge Bed And Breakfast** ★★★★ 553
*Takeley* **Pussy Willow** ★★★★ 553
*Tamworth* **Chestnuts Country Guest House** ★★★★ 553
*Tamworth* **Middleton House Farm** ★★★★ 553
*Tanworth-in-Arden* **Grange Farm** ★★★★ 553
*Tanworth-in-Arden* **Mows Hill Farm** ★★★★ 553
*Telford* **The Old Orleton** ★★★★★ 234
*Telford* **The Mount** ★★★★ 554
*Telford* **West Ridge B&B** ★★★★ 554
*Terrington St John* **The White House** ★★★★ 554
*Thaxted* **Crossways Guesthouse** ★★★★ 554
*Thetford* **Glebe Country House Bed & Breakfast** ★★★★ 554
*Thorndon* **Moat Farm** ★★★★ 554
*Thornham Magna* **Thornham Hall** ★★★★★ 235
*Thornham Magna* **Red House** ★★★★ 554
*Thurlby* **6 The Pingles** ★★★★ 554
*Towcester* **Potcote** ★★★★★ 555
*Towcester* **Slapton Manor Accommodation** ★★★★ 236
*Tunstall* **Manor House** ★★★★ 555
*Uckinghall* **Ivydene House Bed and Breakfast** ★★★★★ 555
*Upton upon Severn* **Tiltridge Farm & Vineyard** ★★★★ 556
*Vowchurch* **The Old Vicarage** ★★★★ 556
*Vowchurch* **Upper Gilvach Farm** ★★★★ 556
*Wadshelf* **Temperance House Farm** ★★★★ 556
*Warwick* **Park Cottage** ★★★★ 557
*Warwick* **The Seven Stars Guest Accommodation** ★★★★ 557
*Warwick* **Shrewley Pools Farm** ★★★★ 557
*Waterhouses* **Leehouse Farm** ★★★★ 238
*Wells-next-the-Sea* **Admiral House** ★★★★ 557
*Wells-next-the-Sea* **Boxwood Guest House** ★★★★ 557
*West Rudham* **Oyster House** ★★★★ 557
*West Runton* **The Old Barn** ★★★★ 558
*Westborough* **The Old Tavern** ★★★★ 558
*Weston-on-Trent* **The Willows** ★★★★ 558
*Wethersfield* **Church Hill House** ★★★★ 558
*Wetton* **The Old Chapel** ★★★★ 558
*Whaley Bridge* **Springbank Guest House (Whaley Bridge)** ★★★★ 558
*Wilton* **Benhall Farmhouse** ★★★★ 558
*Wimbish* **Beeholme House** ★★★★★ 558
*Wimbish* **Newdegate House** ★★★★ 558
*Wingfield* **Gables Farm** ★★★★ 239
*Winster* **Brae Cottage** ★★★★ 559
*Wirksworth* **Avondale Farm** ★★★★ 559
*Wirksworth* **Manor Barn** ★★★★ 559
*Wix* **Periwinkle Cottage** ★★★★ 239
*Woodbridge* **Fir Tree Lodge** ★★★★ 559

# Central England continued

## SILVER continued


*Woodbridge* **St Anne's School House** ★★★★ 559
*Woodhall Spa* **Chaplin House** ★★★★ 240
*Woodhall Spa* **Kirkstead Old Mill Cottage** ★★★★ 240
*Woofferton* **Orchard House** ★★★★ 560
*Woonton* **Rose Cottage – Woonton** ★★★★ 560
*Worcester* **Hill Farm House** ★★★★ 242
*Worcester* **Oldbury Farm** ★★★★ 560
*Worstead* **Hall Farm Guesthouse** ★★★★ 560
*Wortham* **Rookery Farm** ★★★★ 242
*Wroxham* **Coach House** ★★★★ 560
*Wymondham* **Witch Hazel** ★★★★ 560
*Yoxford* **Chapel Cottage** ★★★★ 560


# South East England

## GOLD


*Alton* **The Granary** ★★★★ 561
*Arreton* **Arreton Manor** ★★★★★ 561
*Arundel* **Arundel House Restaurant & Rooms** ★★★★★ 261
*Aylesford* **Wickham Lodge** ★★★★★ 562
*Benson* **Fyfield Manor** ★★★★ 563
*Bexhill-on-Sea* **The Old Vicarage** ★★★★ 564
*Biddenden* **Barclay Farmhouse** ★★★★★ 564
*Biddenden* **Birchley 5 Star Bed & Breakfast** ★★★★★ 564
*Bordon* **Groomes** ★★★★★ 565
*Brenchley* **Hononton Cottage** ★★★★ 565
*Brighton & Hove* **Brightonwave** ★★★★ 566
*Burford* **Westview House** ★★★★ 567
*Burley* **Holmans** ★★★★ 269
*Burmarsh* **Haguelands Farmhouse** ★★★★★ 567
*Bury* **The Barn at Penfolds** ★★★★ 567
*Canterbury* **Magnolia House** ★★★★★ 271
*Canterbury* **The Old Kent Barn** ★★★★★ 568
*Chatham* **Officers Hill** ★★★★★ 569
*Deal* **Number One B and B** ★★★★ 571
*Dover* **Alkham Court Farmhouse B&B** ★★★★★ 571
*Earnley* **Millstone** ★★★★ 572
*Eastbourne* **Ocklynge Manor** ★★★★★ 573
*Eastbourne* **Brayscroft House** ★★★★ 279
*Eastbourne* **Loriston Guest House** ★★★★ 572
*Edenbridge* **Starborough Manor** ★★★★ 573
*Godshill* **Koala Cottage Retreat** ★★★★★ 575
*Hastings* **The Lookout** ★★★★ 577
*Haywards Heath* **Copyhold Hollow Bed & Breakfast** ★★★★ 577
*Heathfield* **Iwood Bed & Breakfast** ★★★★ 286
*High Wycombe* **The Three Horseshoes Inn** ★★★★ 578
*Kingsdown* **The Gardeners Rest** ★★★★★ 579
*Lewes* **Tamberry Hall** ★★★★★ 580
*Milford on Sea* **The Bay Trees Bed & Breakfast** ★★★★ 583
*Minster* **Hoo Farmhouse** ★★★★★ 583
*Norton* **Norton Cottage** ★★★★ 584
*Petworth* **Halfway Bridge Inn** ★★★★★ 586
*Royal Tunbridge Wells* **Bethany House** ★★★★★ 588
*Royal Tunbridge Wells* **A & A Studley Cottage** ★★★★ 588
*Rudgwick* **Alliblaster House** ★★★★★ 588
*Rye* **Durrant House** ★★★★★ 589
*Rye* **Fairacres** ★★★★★ 589
*Rye* **Jeake's House** ★★★★★ 305
*Rye* **The Rise** ★★★★ 589
*Sandwich* **Molland House B+B** ★★★★★ 590
*Shanklin* **Foxhills** ★★★★★ 591
*Sidlesham* **Landseer House** ★★★★ 592
*Southsea* **The Retreat** ★★★★ 593
*Ventnor* **The Enchanted Manor** ★★★★★ 595
*Ventnor* **The Hermitage Country House** ★★★★★ 595
*Ventnor* **The Leconfield** ★★★★★ 595
*West Stoke* **West Stoke House** ★★★★★ 596
*Whitstable* **Victoria Villa** ★★★★ 596
*Winchester* **Giffard House** ★★★★★ 311
*Worth* **Solley Farm House** ★★★★★ 598
*Worthing* **Benson's** ★★★★ 598


## SILVER


*Abinger Common* **Leylands Farm** ★★★★ 561
*Aldington* **Fostums** ★★★★ 561
*Alton* **Boundary House** ★★★★ 561
*Alton* **Shepherds Court** ★★★★ 561
*Alverstone Garden Village* **Bluebell Wood Bed & Breakfast** ★★★★ 561
*Andover* **May Cottage** ★★★★ 261
*Arundel* **Pindars** ★★★★ 562
*Arundel* **The Townhouse** ★★★★ 562
*Ashurst* **Kingswood Cottage** ★★★★ 562
*Awbridge* **Crofton Country Bed and Breakfast** ★★★★★ 562
*Awbridge* **Woodpeckers B&B** ★★★★ 562
*Aylesbury* **Tanamera** ★★★★ 262
*Banbury* **Banbury Cross B&B** ★★★★ 562
*Barton on Sea* **Grandco Lodge** ★★★★ 563
*Basingstoke* **Millfield House** ★★★★ 563
*Battle* **A White Lodge** ★★★★ 563
*Battle* **Tollgate Farm House** ★★★★ 563
*Benenden* **The Holt** ★★★★ 563
*Bethersden* **The Old Stables** ★★★★ 563
*Bexhill-on-Sea* **The Old Manse** ★★★★★ 564
*Bexhill-on-Sea* **Arden House** ★★★★ 563
*Bexhill-on-Sea* **Dunselma** ★★★★ 564
*Biddenden* **Whitfield Farm** ★★★★ 564
*Binstead* **Newnham Farm** ★★★★★ 564


Establishments in colour have a detailed entry in this guide.

## South East England continued

### SILVER continued


*Bognor Regis* **Alderwasley Cottage** ★★★★ 564
*Bonchurch* **Winterbourne Country House** ★★★★★ 265
*Borden* **Holly House Bed & Breakfast** ★★★★ 565
*Bosham* **Good Hope** ★★★★ 565
*Brede* **The Mill House** ★★★★ 565
*Brighton & Hove* **The Cavalaire** ★★★★ 566
*Brighton & Hove* **Leona House** ★★★★ 566
*Brighton & Hove* **Sea Breeze** ★★★★ 566
*Broad Oak* **Hazelhurst B&B** ★★★★ 566
*Broadstairs* **Anchor Lodge** ★★★★ 566
*Broadstairs* **Copperfields Guest House** ★★★★ 566
*Broadstairs* **The Devonhurst** ★★★★ 566
*Broadstairs* **Number 68** ★★★★ 566
*Broadstairs* **South Lodge Guest House** ★★★★ 566
*Broadstairs* **Viking** ★★★★ 567
*Burford* **Barley Park** ★★★★ 567
*Burgess Hill* **Wellhouse** ★★★★ 567
*Cadnam* **Twin Oaks Guest House** ★★★★ 270
*Canterbury* **Thanington** ★★★★★ 568
*Canterbury* **Bower Farm House** ★★★★ 270
*Canterbury* **Castle House** ★★★★ 567
*Canterbury* **Harriet House** ★★★★ 568
*Canterbury* **Oak Cottage** ★★★★ 272
*Catherington* **Lone Barn** ★★★★ 568
*Chart Sutton* **White House Farm** ★★★★ 569
*Checkendon* **Larchdown Farm** ★★★★ 569
*Chichester* **Friary Close** ★★★★ 569
*Chichester* **West Faldie** ★★★★ 569
*Chichester* **Woodstock House** ★★★★ 273
*Chieveley* **Thatched House B&B** ★★★★ 569
*Chipping Norton* **Rectory Farm** ★★★★★ 570
*Chipping Norton* **The Forge** ★★★★ 570
*Cliffe Woods* **Orchard Cottage** ★★★★ 570
*Colworth* **Glencroft** ★★★★ 570
*Cranbrook* **Hallwood Farm Oast** ★★★★★ 570
*Cranbrook* **Bull Farm Oast** ★★★★ 570
*Cross-in-Hand* **High Brow** ★★★★ 570
*Crossbush* **April Cottage** ★★★★ 570
*Crowborough* **Braemore** ★★★★ 570
*Crowborough* **Yew House Bed & Breakfast** ★★★★ 275
*Cuckfield* **Highbridge Mill** ★★★★ 275
*Dorking* **Denbies Farmhouse** ★★★★ 277
*Dorking* **Stylehurst Farm** ★★★★ 571
*Dover* **Colret House** ★★★★ 277
*Dover* **East Lee Guest House** ★★★★ 571
*Dover* **Loddington House** ★★★★ 571
*East Ashling* **The Dairy Farm** ★★★★ 572
*East Cowes* **Crossways House** ★★★★ 572
*Eastbourne* **Guest House Pavilion** ★★★★ 572
*Eastbourne* **The Guesthouse East** ★★★★ 572
*Eastbourne* **Southcroft** ★★★★ 573
*Eastergate* **Mount Pleasant House** ★★★★ 573
*Edenbridge* **Mowshurst Farm House** ★★★★ 573
*Ewhurst Green* **Clouds Bed and Breakfast** ★★★★★ 573
*Faversham* **Gladstone House** ★★ 574
*Forton* **The Barn House B&B** ★★★★★ 281
*Framfield* **Beggars Barn** ★★★★ 574
*Fulbrook* **Star Cottage** ★★★★ 575
*Gatcombe* **Freewaters** ★★★★ 575
*Gatcombe* **Little Gatcombe Farm** ★★★★ 575
*Gatwick* **The Lawn Guest House** ★★★★ 281
*Godalming* **Heath House** ★★★★ 575
*Godalming* **Highview** ★★ 575
*Goodwood* **The Coach House** ★★★★ 575
*Graffham* **Withy** ★★★★★ 575
*Graffham* **Brook Barn** ★★★★ 575
*Grafty Green* **Foxes Earth Bed & Breakfast** ★★★★ 575
*Gravesend* **Eastcourt Oast** ★★ 575
*Greatstone* **White Horses Cottage** ★★★★ 575
*Guildford* **Plaegan House** ★★★★ 284
*Hailsham* **Hailsham Grange** ★★★★★ 284
*Hastings* **Swan House** ★★★★★ 286
*Hastings* **Seaspray** ★★★★ 285
*Hawkley* **Scotland Farm Countryside Bed and Breakfast** ★★★★ 577
*Hayling Island* **The Coach House** ★★★★ 577
*Henley-on-Thames* **Lenwade** ★★★★★ 287
*Henley-on-Thames* **Alushta** ★★★★ 577
*Henley-on-Thames* **Amanchris** ★★★★ 577
*Henley-on-Thames* **Apple Ash** ★★★★ 577
*Henley-on-Thames* **The Baskerville** ★★★★ 287
*Henley-on-Thames* **The Beeches** ★★★★ 578
*Henley-on-Thames* **Denmark House** ★★★★ 578
*Hever* **Becketts** ★★★★ 288
*High Wycombe* **9 Green Road** ★★★★ 289
*High Wycombe* **Longforgan** ★★ 578
*Hildenborough* **The Barn at Woodview** ★★★★ 578
*Hill Brow* **The Jolly Drover** ★★★★ 578
*Horley* **Rosemead Guest House** ★★★★ 579
*Hungerford* **Wilton House** ★★★★ 579
*Hurley* **Meadow View** ★★★★★ 579
*Hurstpierpoint* **Wickham Place** ★★★★ 579
*Lamberhurst* **Woodpecker Barn** ★★★★★ 290
*Langrish* **Upper Parsonage Farm** ★★★★ 580
*Lee-on-the-Solent* **Milvil Corner** ★★★★ 580
*Lewes* **The Blacksmiths Arms** ★★★★ 290
*Lewes* **Eckington House** ★★★★ 580
*Lewes* **Hale Farm House** ★★★★ 580
*Lewes* **Langtons House** ★★★★ 580
*Lewes* **Millers** ★★★★ 580
*Littlehampton* **Amberley Court** ★★★★ 580
*Long Wittenham* **Witta's Ham Cottage** ★★★★ 581
*Lydd on Sea* **Plovers** ★★★★ 581

## South East England continued

### SILVER continued


*Lymington* **Britannia House** ★★★★★ 291
*Lymington* **Pennavon House** ★★★★ 581
*Lyndhurst* **Acorns of Lyndhurst** ★★★★ 581
*Maidenhead* **The Black Boys Inn** ★★★★ 292
*Maidstone* **Grove House** ★★★★ 292
*Marden* **3 Chainhurst Cottages** ★★★★ 582
*Marlow* **Acorn Lodge** ★★★★ 582
*Mersham* **Garden Cottage at Munday Manor** ★★★★★ 582
*Milford on Sea* **Ha'penny House** ★★★★★ 583
*Milton Common* **Byways** ★★★★ 583
*New Milton* **Taverners Cottage** ★★★★ 295
*Newbury* **Manor Farm House** ★★★★ 296
*Newick* **Holly Lodge** ★★★★ 584
*Newport* **Newport Quay** ★★★★ 584
*Newport Pagnell* **Rosemary House** ★★★ 297
*North Leigh* **Elbie House** ★★★★ 584
*North Mundham* **The Cottage** ★★★★ 584
*North Newington* **The Mill House** ★★★★ 584
*Nutley* **West Meadows** ★★★★ 584
*Olney* **Colchester House** ★★★★ 584
*Oxford* **Gorselands Hall** ★★★★ 585
*Oxford* **Home Farm House** ★★★★ 585
*Oxford* **Tilbury Lodge** ★★★★ 585
*Pitt* **Enmill Barn** ★★★★★ 586
*Princes Risborough* **The Old Station** ★★★★★ 586
*Princes Risborough* **Coppins B&B** ★★ 586
*Pulborough* **St Cleather** ★★★★ 587
*Radnage* **Rosling House** ★★★★ 587
*Ringwood* **The Star Inn** ★★★★ 587
*Ripe* **Hall Court Farm** ★★★★★ 587
*Robertsbridge* **Slides Farm B&B** ★★★★★ 587
*Rochester* **Churchfields B&B** ★★ 302
*Romney Marsh* **Coxell House** ★★★★ 588
*Royal Tunbridge Wells* **Alconbury Guest House** ★★★★★ 588
*Royal Tunbridge Wells* **Danehurst House** ★★★★★ 588
*Royal Tunbridge Wells* **Ash Tree Cottage** ★★★★ 588
*Royal Tunbridge Wells* **The Brick House** ★★★★ 588
*Royal Tunbridge Wells* **Hazelwood House** ★★ 588
*Rustington* **Kenmore** ★★★★ 304
*Rustington* **Mallon Dene** ★★★★ 589
*Ryde* **Sillwood Acre** ★★★★ 589
*Rye* **Oaklands** ★★★★★ 589
*Rye* **Willow Tree House** ★★★★★ 589
*Rye* **Four Seasons** ★★★★ 589
*Rye* **Strand House** ★★★★ 305
*St Leonards* **Tower House 1066** ★★★★ 589
*St-Margarets-at-Cliffe* **Holm Oaks** ★★★★ 589
*St Margaret's Bay* **Small Acre** ★★★★ 306
*Sandown* **Copperfield Lodge** ★★★★ 590
*Seaview* **Clover Ridge** ★★★★ 590
*Selsey* **Vincent Lodge** ★★★★ 590
*Sevenoaks* **The Heathers** ★★★★★ 591
*Sevenoaks* **Old Timbertop Cottage** ★★★★ 591
*Sevenoaks* **The Studio at Double Dance** ★★★★ 591
*Shanklin* **The Birkdale** ★★★★ 591
*Shanklin* **Grange Bank House** ★★★★ 591
*Shanklin* **The Havelock** ★★★★ 591
*Shanklin* **The Heatherleigh** ★★★★ 307
*Shanklin* **The St Leonards** ★★★★ 591
*Shanklin* **Snowdon House** ★★★★ 591
*Shanklin* **Westbury Lodge** ★★★★ 592
*Sherborne St John* **Manor Farm Stables** ★★★★ 592
*Shere* **Rookery Nook Bed and Breakfast** ★★★ 592
*Shipley* **Goffsland Farm (B & B)** ★★★★ 592
*Shorwell* **Northcourt** ★★★★ 592
*Shorwell* **Westcourt Farm** ★★★★ 592
*Singleton* **1 Rose Cottage** ★★★★ 592
*Sittingbourne* **Woodstock Guest House** ★★★★ 592
*Smarden* **Hereford Oast** ★★★★ 592
*Smarden* **Snap Mill** ★★★★ 592
*Sonning* **The Bull Inn** ★★★★ 592
*Staplehurst* **White Cottage** ★★★★ 593
*Stelling Minnis* **Great Field Farm** ★★★★ 308
*Steyning* **The Penfold Gallery Guest House** ★★★★★ 593
*Steyning* **Nash Manor** ★★★★ 593
*Tonbridge* **Fieldswood** ★★★★ 594
*Totland Bay* **Chart House** ★★★★ 594
*Totland Bay* **The Granville** ★★★★ 594
*Trotton* **Orchard House** ★★★★ 594
*Uckfield* **South Paddock** ★★★★★ 595
*Uffington* **Norton House** ★★★★ 309
*Wallingford* **North Moreton House** ★★★★★ 595
*Wallingford* **Fords Farm** ★★★★ 595
*Wantage* **Regis Guest House** ★★★★ 595
*Wash Water* **The Chase Guest House** ★★★★ 595
*West Chiltington* **The Old School House B & B** ★★★★★ 596
*West Malling* **Appledene** ★★★★ 596
*Weybridge* **Riverdene Gardens** ★★★★★ 596
*Whitstable* **Alliston House** ★★★★ 596
*Whitstable* **The Pearl Fisher** ★★★★ 596
*Winchester* **29 Christchurch Road** ★★★★★ 596
*Winchester* **Dawn Cottage** ★★★★★ 597
*Winchester* **5 Clifton Terrace** ★★★★ 596
*Winchester* **Acacia** ★★★★ 596
*Windsor* **The Old Farmhouse** ★★★★ 597
*Woodgreen* **Cottage Crest** ★★★★★ 598
*Woodstock* **The Laurels** ★★★★ 314
*Worthing* **Edwardian Dreams** ★★★★ 598
*Wye* **The Wife of Bath Restaurant with Rooms** ★★★★ 598


Establishments in colour have a detailed entry in this guide.

## London

### GOLD


*London W6* **At Home in London Westminster (Ref 5)** ★★ 602
*Richmond* **Chalon House** ★★★★★ 602


### SILVER


*London SE14* **Annemarten Pepys Road** ★★★★ 599
*London SW1* **The Lord Milner** ★★★★★ 600
*London SW1* **The Windermere** ★★★★ 600
*London W6* **At Home in London Chiswick (Ref 267)** ★★★★ 601
*London W6* **At Home in London Chiswick (Ref 11)** ★★★★ 601
*Twickenham* **Peter and Marilyn Wilkins** ★★★★ 603


## South West England

### GOLD


*Alderton* **Moors Farm House** ★★★★★ 603
*Axminster* **Kerrington House** ★★★★★ 604
*Bath* **Athole Guest House** ★★★★★ 356
*Bath* **The Ayrlington** ★★★★★ 356
*Bath* **The Residence** ★★★★★ 358
*Bibury* **Cotteswold House** ★★★★ 359
*Blandford Forum* **Farnham Farm House** ★★★★★ 360
*Bourton-on-the-Water* **Coombe House** ★★★★ 608
*Bourton-on-the-Water* **Meadow Rise** ★★★★ 609
*Bovey Tracey* **Brookfield House** ★★★★★ 363
*Brixham* **Brookside Guest House** ★★★★ 610
*Budleigh Salterton* **Downderry House** ★★★★★ 612
*Burton Bradstock* **Norburton Hall** ★★★★★ 612
*Calne* **Queenwood Lodge** ★★★★★ 613
*Camelford* **Kings Acre** ★★★★★ 613
*Cheltenham* **Thirty Two** ★★★★★ 615
*Chipping Campden* **Nineveh Farm** ★★★★★ 615
*Christchurch* **Seawards** ★★★★★ 616
*Corfe Castle* **Bradle Farmhouse** ★★★★ 617
*Corfe Mullen* **Elms Lodge** ★★★★ 617
*Dartmouth* **Hill View House** ★★★★ 618
*Dawlish* **Lammas Park House** ★★★★★ 618
*Downton* **Witherington Farm Bed & Breakfast** ★★★★★ 619
*Dulverton* **Three Acres Country House** ★★★★★ 619
*Exeter* **Silversprings** ★★★★ 620
*Godney* **Double-Gate Farm** ★★★★ 623
*Hartland* **Golden Park** ★★★★★ 624
*Kimmeridge* **Kimmeridge Farmhouse** ★★★★ 626
*Kingston St Mary* **Fulford Grange** ★★★★★ 626
*Landrake* **Lantallack Farm** ★★★★★ 626
*Launceston* **Wheatley Farm** ★★★★★ 627
*Liskeard* **Tregondale Farm** ★★★★ 627
*Little Langford* **Little Langford Farmhouse** ★★★★★ 627
*Lyme Regis* **Clappentail House** ★★★★★ 628
*Lyme Regis* **Old Lyme Guest House** ★★★★ 629
*Muchelney* **The Parsonage** ★★★★★ 631
*Padstow* **Woodlands Country House** ★★★★★ 634
*Penzance* **Lowenna** ★★★★★ 636
*Penzance* **The Summer House** ★★★★★ 395
*Poole* **Danecourt Lodge** ★★★★ 638
*Poole* **The Saltings** ★★★★ 638
*Portscatho* **Rosevine Hotel** ★★★★★ 639
*St Austell* **Anchorage House** ★★★★★ 401
*St Austell* **Highland Court Lodge** ★★★★★ 401
*St Ives* **Blue Hayes** ★★★★★ 640
*St Ives* **Shun Lee House** ★★★★★ 641
*St Juliot* **The Old Rectory** ★★★★★ 641
*Shave Cross* **Shave Cross Inn** ★★★★ 407
*Sidmouth* **The Salty Monk** ★★★★★ 408
*South Molton* **Kerscott Farm** ★★★★★ 645
*Staverton* **Kingston House** ★★★★★ 646
*Talaton* **Larkbeare Grange** ★★★★★ 647
*Tavistock* **Tor Cottage** ★★★★★ 413
*Tavistock* **Beera Farmhouse** ★★★★ 648
*Teignmouth* **Thomas Luny House** ★★★★★ 648
*Torquay* **The Berburry** ★★★★★ 649
*Two Waters Foot* **Treverbyn Vean Manor** ★★★★★ 652
*Upper Oddington* **Blenheim Cottage** ★★★★★ 653
*Waterrow* **Handley Farm Accommodation** ★★★★★ 653
*Weymouth* **Chandlers** ★★★★★ 655
*Winchcombe* **Postlip Hall Farm** ★★★★ 657


### SILVER


*Abbotsbury* **Corfe Gate House** ★★★★ 603
*Alton Pancras* **Whiteways Farmhouse Accommodation** ★★★★ 603
*Appledore* **West Farm** ★★★★★ 604
*Ashton Keynes* **Wheatleys Farm** ★★★★ 604
*Athelhampton* **White Cottage** ★★★★ 354
*Axminster* **Hedgehog Corner** ★★★★ 604
*Bampton* **Lodfin Farm Bed & Breakfast** ★★★★ 604
*Barnstaple* **The Spinney** ★★★★ 355
*Bath* **Badminton Villa** ★★★★ 605
*Bath* **Chestnuts House** ★★★★ 357
*Bath* **Corston Fields Farm** ★★★★ 605
*Bath* **The Hollies** ★★★★ 605
*Bath* **Ravenscroft (Sydney Road)** ★★★★ 605
*Bath* **St Leonards** ★★★★ 605
*Bath* **Three Abbey Green** ★★★★ 605
*Beaminster* **Water Meadow House** ★★★★★ 606
*Beaminster* **The Walnuts** ★★★★ 606
*Berrow* **Berrow Links House** ★★★★ 606
*Bibury* **The William Morris Bed & Breakfast** ★★★★ 606
*Bideford* **Bulworthy Cottage** ★★★★ 606
*Bideford* **The Mount** ★★★★ 606

## South West England continued

### SILVER continued


*Bilbrook* The Wayside B & B ★★★★ 606
*Bishops Hull* The Old Mill ★★★★★ 606
*Bodmin* Bokiddick Farm ★★★★★ 607
*Bodmin* Trewint Farm ★★★★★ 607
*Bodmin* Bedknobs B&B ★★★★ 607
*Boscastle* Orchard Lodge ★★★★★ 607
*Boscastle* Reddivallen Farm ★★★★★ 607
*Boscastle* Home Farm Bed and Breakfast ★★★★ 607
*Boscastle* Valency Bed and Breakfast ★★★★ 607
*Bossington* Tudor Cottage ★★★★ 608
*Bournemouth* The Balincourt ★★★★★ 608
*Bourton-on-the-Water* Alderley Guest House ★★★★ 608
*Bourton-on-the-Water* The Ridge Guesthouse ★★★★ 609
*Bradford-on-Avon* Great Ashley Farm ★★★★ 609
*Bradford-on-Avon* Honeysuckle Cottage ★★★★ 609
*Bradpole* Orchard Barn ★★★★★ 609
*Brentor* Burnville House ★★★★★ 609
*Bridgwater* Chestnut Houseclaveys ★★★★★ 609
*Bridgwater* **Hill View** ★★★★ 365
*Bridport* The Roundham House ★★★★★ 610
*Bridport* Highway Farm ★★★★ 610
*Broadstone* Honey Lodge ★★★★ 611
*Broadwindsor* Cross Keys House ★★★★★ 611
*Bude* Creathorne Farm Bed & Breakfast ★★★★★ 611
*Bude* East Woolley Farm ★★★★ 611
*Bude* **Harefield Cottage** ★★★★ 368
*Bude* Highbre Crest ★★★★ 612
*Bude* Little Haven ★★★★ 612
*Bude* **Scadghill Farm** ★★★★ 368
*Bude* Sunrise Guest House ★★★★ 612
*Budleigh Salterton* **Hansard House** ★★★★ 369
*Bulford* The Dovecot ★★★★ 612
*Burlawn* Pengelly Farmhouse, Burlawn ★★★★ 612
*Callington* Cadson Manor ★★★★★ 613
*Calne* Chilvester Hill House ★★★★★ 613
*Cannington* Gurney Manor Mill ★★★★ 613
*Carbis Bay* The Lighthouse B & B ★★★★★ 613
*Carbis Bay* Tradewinds ★★★★★ 613
*Castle Cary* Clanville Manor B & B ★★★★ 613
*Castle Cary* The Coach House ★★★★ 613
*Castle Cary* The Pilgrims ★★★★ 613
*Castle Combe* Fosse Farmhouse ★★★★ 613
*Chard* Hornsbury Mill ★★★★ 613
*Chedzoy* Apple View ★★★★ 614
*Cheltenham* Beaumont House ★★★★★ 614
*Cheltenham* Hanover House ★★★★★ 614
*Cheltenham* **Butlers** ★★★★ 371
*Cheltenham* Whittington Lodge Farm ★★★★ 615
*Cheriton Fitzpaine* The Devon Wine School ★★★★★ 615
*Chetnole* Chetnole Inn ★★★★ 615
*Chideock* Bay Tree House ★★★★ 615
*Child Okeford* **Manor Barn Bed & Breakfast** ★★★★★ 372
*Chippenham* Glebe House ★★★★ 615
*Chipping Campden* Home Farm House ★★★★ 615
*Chipping Campden* Sandalwood House ★★★★ 615
*Christchurch* Druid House ★★★★★ 616
*Cirencester* The Bungalow ★★★★ 616
*Cirencester* The Leauses ★★★★ 616
*Colyton* **The Old Bakehouse** ★★★★ 374
*Colyton* **Smallicombe Farm** ★★★★ 374
*Combe Down* Grey Lodge ★★★★ 617
*Copplestone* Harebell ★★★★ 617
*Corsham* Ashley Wood Farm ★★★★ 617
*Corsham* Pickwick Lodge Farm ★★★★ 617
*Cullompton* Newcourt Barton ★★★★ 618
*Dartmouth* Browns ★★★★★ 618
*Dartmouth* Mounthaven ★★★★★ 618
*Dartmouth* Cladda ★★★★ 618
*Dartmouth* Skerries Bed & Breakfast ★★★★ 618
*Dartmouth* The Victorian House ★★★★ 618
*Devizes* Bramley House ★★★★ 618
*Diptford* Old Rectory Bed and Breakfast ★★★★★ 619
*Dorchester* Baytree House ★★★★ 619
*Dorchester* Higher Came Farmhouse ★★★★ 619
*Dorchester* **Yellowham Farm** ★★★★ 377
*Dulverton* Town Mills ★★★★ 619
*Dunster* Spears Cross ★★★★★ 619
*Dunster* Exmoor House Dunster ★★★★ 619
*East Coker* Granary House ★★★★ 620
*East Harptree* **Harptree Court** ★★★★★ 377
*East Kennett* The Old Forge ★★★★ 620
*East Stour* Aysgarth ★★★★ 620
*Easton Royal* Follets B & B ★★★★ 620
*Ebrington* Little Gidding ★★★★ 620
*Exeter* The Garden House ★★★★ 620
*Exeter* Lower Thornton Farm ★★★★ 620
*Exmouth* Victoria Guest House ★★★★ 621
*Fairford* Hathaway ★★★★ 621
*Falmouth* Dolvean House ★★★★★ 621
*Falmouth* **The Beach House** ★★★★ 379
*Falmouth* Hawthorne Dene ★★★★ 621
*Falmouth* Poltair ★★★★ 621
*Fiddington* Hillview B and B ★★★★ 622
*Friar Waddon* Corton Farm ★★★★ 622
*Froxfield* The White House ★★★★ 622
*Glastonbury* Chestnuts Boutique Bed and Breakfast ★★★★ 622
*Glastonbury* Lower Farm ★★★★ 623
*Guiting Power* **The Guiting Guest House** ★★★★ 382


Establishments in colour have a detailed entry in this guide.

## South West England continued

### SILVER continued


*Gulworthy* **Colcharton Farm** ★★★★ 623
*Gunwalloe* **Glendower** ★★★★ 623
*Halse* **Rock House** ★★★★ 624
*Halwell* **Orchard House** ★★★★★ 382
*Helford* **Number 7even** ★★★★ 624
*Highcliffe* **Beechcroft Place** ★★★★ 624
*Honiton* **Wessington Farm** ★★★★ 625
*Iddesleigh* **Parsonage Farm** ★★★★ 625
*Ilfracombe* **Westaway** ★★★★★ 625
*Ivybridge* **Hillhead Farm** ★★★★ 626
*Jacobstow* **Broad Langdon B&B** ★★★★ 626
*Kilkhampton* **Heatham Farmhouse** ★★★★ 626
*Lacock* **King John's Hunting Lodge** ★★★★ 384
*Laneast* **Stitch Park** ★★★★ 627
*Lanescot* **Great Pelean Farm** ★★★★ 627
*Langport* **Muchelney Ham Farm** ★★★★ 627
*Lansallos* **Lesquite Farm** ★★★★ 627
*Lansallos* **West Kellow Farm** ★★★★ 627
*Launceston* **Primrose Cottage** ★★★★★ 385
*Launceston* **Trevadlock Farm** ★★★★★ 385
*Launceston* **Berrio Bridge House** ★★★★ 627
*Leedstown* **Little Pengelly – Farmhouse B&B** ★★★★ 627
*Lelant* **Hindon Hall** ★★★★★ 627
*Liskeard* **Trewint Farm** ★★★★ 627
*Littleton Panell* **Summerhayes** ★★★★★ 627
*Lizard* **Atlantic House** ★★★★★ 628
*Looe* **Bucklawren Farm** ★★★★ 386
*Looe* **Dovers House** ★★★★ 387
*Looe* **Little Larnick Farm** ★★★★ 628
*Looe* **The Watermark** ★★★★ 628
*Lydbrook* **Belvedere House B&B** ★★★★ 628
*Lyme Regis* **Clovelly Guest House** ★★★★ 628
*Lynmouth* **The Heatherville** ★★★★★ 629
*Lynton* **Highcliffe House** ★★★★★ 629
*Lynton* **The Denes Guest House** ★★★★ 387
*Lynton* **Ingleside** ★★★★ 629
*Lynton* **Kingford House** ★★★★ 388
*Lynton* **Longmead House** ★★★★ 388
*Lynton* **Southcliffe** ★★★★ 629
*Mangotsfield* **Fern Cottage Bed & Breakfast** ★★★★ 629
*Manston* **Northwood Cottages B&B** ★★★★ 629
*Manton* **Teal Cottage** ★★★★ 629
*Marazion* **Rosevidney Manor** ★★★★★ 630
*Marlborough* **Crofton Lodge** ★★★★ 389
*Merrymeet* **Higher Trevartha Farm** ★★★★ 630
*Mevagissey* **Portmellon Cove Guest House** ★★★★★ 630
*Mevagissey* **Corran Farm B&B** ★★★★ 390
*Mevagissey* **Eden B&B** ★★★★ 630
*Mevagissey* **Wild Air Guest House** ★★★★ 630
*Millbrook* **Stone Farm** ★★★★ 630
*Minehead* **Oakfield Guest House** ★★★★★ 631
*Minehead* **The Parks** ★★★★ 631
*Moreton-in-Marsh* **Windy Ridge House** ★★★★★ 631
*Morwenstow* **Willow Tree Cottage** ★★★★ 631
*Naunton* **Fox Hill** ★★★★ 632
*Nether Stowey* **Castle of Comfort Country House** ★★★★★ 393
*Nether Stowey* **Stowey Brooke House** ★★★★★ 632
*Nether Stowey* **The Old House** ★★★★ 632
*Newent* **Three Ashes House** ★★★★ 632
*Newmill* **Chy Bowjy** ★★★★★ 632
*Newmill* **Bosulval Old Barn** ★★★★ 632
*Newquay* **The Harbour** ★★★★ 632
*Newton Abbot* **Rock House Bed & Breakfast** ★★★★★ 633
*North Bradley* **49a Church Lane** ★★★★ 633
*North Cadbury* **Ashlea House** ★★★★ 633
*Northleach* **Cotteswold House & Cottage** ★★★★ 633
*Northleach* **Northfield Bed and Breakfast** ★★★★ 633
*Okehampton* **Knole Farm** ★★★★★ 633
*Okehampton* **Lower Trecott Farm** ★★★★ 633
*Old Town* **Carn Ithen** ★★★★ 633
*Padstow* **Althea House** ★★★★★ 634
*Padstow* **Althea Library** ★★★★★ 634
*Padstow* **Coswarth House** ★★★★★ 634
*Padstow* **50 Church Street** ★★★★ 634
*Padstow* **Cally Croft** ★★★★ 634
*Padstow* **Lellizzick Farm** ★★★★ 634
*Padstow* **Petrocstowe** ★★★★ 634
*Padstow* **Symply Padstow** ★★★★ 634
*Padstow* **Treverbyn House** ★★★★ 634
*Padstow* **The White Hart Apartment** ★★★★ 634
*Paignton* **Roundham Lodge** ★★★★★ 635
*Paignton* **Amber House** ★★★★ 634
*Payhembury* **Yellingham Farm** ★★★★ 636
*Pedwell* **Sunnyside** ★★★★ 636
*Pelynt* **Trenderway Farm** ★★★★★ 636
*Penzance* **Castallack Farm** ★★★★ 636
*Penzance* **Chiverton House** ★★★★ 636
*Piddletrenthide* **The European Inn** ★★★★ 637
*Pilsdon* **Gerrards Farm** ★★★★ 637
*Pilton* **Bowermead House** ★★★★★ 637
*Plymouth* **The Bowling Green** ★★★★ 397
*Polbathic* **Buttervilla Farm** ★★★★ 638
*Polgooth* **Hunters Moon** ★★★★ 638
*Polperro* **Chyavallon** ★★★★ 638
*Polperro* **Cottage Restaurant (The)** ★★★★ 638
*Poole* **Corkers Restaurant & Cafe Bar with Guest Rooms** ★★★★ 638
*Poole* **Cranborne House** ★★★★ 638
*Poole* **Foxes B&B** ★★ 638

## South West England continued

### SILVER continued


*Porlock* **Exmoor House** ★★★★★ 638
*Porlock* **Rose Bank Guest House** ★★★★ 638
*Port Isaac* **Westaway nr Port Isaac** ★★★★★ 639
*Rezare* **Rezare Farmhouse** ★★★★ 639
*St Austell* **Lower Barn Boutique B&B** ★★★★★ 640
*St Austell* **The Beech Tree Guest House** ★★★★ 640
*St Buryan* **Downs Barn Farm** ★★★★★ 640
*St Buryan* **Boskenna Home Farm** ★★★★ 640
*St Buryan* **Tregiffian Farm** ★★★★ 640
*St Columb Major* **Pennatillie Farm** ★★★★★ 402
*St Ewe* **The Barns at Polsue** ★★★★★ 640
*St Ives* **Dean Court** ★★★★★ 641
*St Ives* **Sea Breeze** ★★★★ 641
*St Keverne* **Old Temperance House** ★★★★ 641
*St Kew* **Tregellist Farm** ★★★★ 641
*St Mary's* **Annet** ★★★★ 641
*St Mary's* **April Cottage** ★★★★ 641
*St Mary's* **Carntop Guest House** ★★★★ 642
*St Mary's* **Crebinick House** ★★★★ 642
*St Mary's* **Garrison House** ★★★★ 642
*St Mary's* **Rose Cottage** ★★★★ 642
*St Mary's* **Tolman House** ★★★★ 642
*St Merryn* **Trewithen Farmhouse** ★★★★ 642
*St Neot* **Higher Searles Down** ★★★★ 642
*Salisbury* **Bridge Farm** ★★★★ 643
*Salisbury* **Rokeby Guest House** ★★★★ 643
*Salisbury* **Spire House** ★★★★ 643
*Sampford Arundel* **Selby House** ★★★★ 643
*Seaton* **Beach End** ★★★★ 643
*Seaton* **Pebbles** ★★★★ 643
*Selsley* **Little Owl Cottage** ★★★★ 643
*Shaftesbury* **Glebe Farm** ★★★★★ 644
*Shaftesbury* **The Retreat** ★★★★ 407
*Sherborne* **Cumberland House** ★★★★ 644
*Sidbury* **Rose Cottage Guest House** ★★★★ 644
*Sidmouth* **The Long House** ★★★★★ 644
*Sidmouth* **The Barn And Pinn Cottage Guest House** ★★★★ 644
*Sidmouth* **Hollies Guest House** ★★★★ 644
*Sidmouth* **Lavenders Blue** ★★★★ 408
*Sidmouth* **Pinn Barton Farm** ★★★★ 644
*Snowshill Hill* **Snowshill Hill Estate** ★★★★★ 645
*Somerton* **Mill House** ★★★★★ 645
*South Molton* **Huxtable Farm** ★★★★ 645
*South Newton* **Salisbury Old Mill House** ★★★★ 645
*South Petherton* **Rock House** ★★★★★ 645
*Southbourne* **Mory House** ★★★★ 645
*Stow-on-the-Wold* **Aston House** ★★★★ 646
*Stow-on-the-Wold* **Number Nine** ★★★★ 646
*Stroud* **Pretoria Villa** ★★★★ 411
*Studland* **Shell Bay Cottage** ★★★★ 646
*Swanage* **Clare House** ★★★★ 647
*Swanage* **Easter Cottage** ★★★★ 647
*Sydling St Nicholas* **Hazel Cottage** ★★★★ 647
*Taunton* **Staplegrove Lodge** ★★★★ 648
*Taunton* **Yallands Farmhouse** ★★★★ 648
*Tavistock* **Higher Woodley Farm** ★★★★ 648
*Tavistock* **Rubbytown Farm** ★★★★ 648
*Teignmouth* **The Moorings B&B** ★★★★★ 648
*Tewkesbury* **Gantier** ★★★★ 648
*Timsbury* **Pitfour House** ★★★★★ 648
*Tiverton* **Great Bradley Farmhouse** ★★★★ 649
*Torquay* **Haldon Priors** ★★★★★ 416
*Torquay* **Bentley Lodge** ★★★★ 649
*Torquay* **The Glenross** ★★★★ 650
*Torquay* **The Hillcroft** ★★★★ 650
*Torquay* **Lanscombe House** ★★★★ 650
*Torquay* **The Westbank** ★★★★ 651
*Torquay* **The Westgate** ★★★★ 651
*Totnes* **The Elbow Room** ★★★★★ 651
*Totnes* **Foales Leigh** ★★★★★ 651
*Totnes* **Great Court Farm** ★★★★ 651
*Tregony* **Tregonan** ★★★★ 651
*Turkdean* **Yew Tree Cottage** ★★★★★ 652
*Wadebridge* **Brookfields B&B** ★★★★ 653
*Washaway* **South Tregleath Farm B & B** ★★★★ 653
*Washford* **Monkscider House** ★★★★ 653
*Wells* **Beryl** ★★★★★ 653
*West Hatch* **The Farmers Inn** ★★★★★ 654
*West Huntspill* **Ilex House** ★★★★ 654
*West Tolgus* **Solcett** ★★★★ 654
*Westhay* **New House Farm** ★★★★ 654
*Weston-super-Mare* **Orchard House** ★★★★ 655
*Weymouth* **The Chatsworth** ★★★★ 655
*Weymouth* **The Seaham** ★★★★ 656
*Wheddon Cross* **Sundial Guest House** ★★★★ 656
*Whilborough* **Walmer Towers** ★★★★ 656
*Whittington* **Ham Hill Farm** ★★★★ 657
*Whittington* **Whalley Farm House** ★★★★ 657
*Wimborne Minster* **Lantern Lodge** ★★★★ 657
*Wimborne Minster* **Long Lane Farmhouse** ★★★★ 657
*Wimborne Minster* **The Old George** ★★★★ 657
*Witcombe* **Crickley Court** ★★★★ 657
*Witham Friary* **Higher West Barn Farm** ★★★★ 657
*Withypool* **Newland House** ★★★★★ 657
*Wiveliscombe* **North Down Farm** ★★★★ 657
*Woolacombe* **Ossaborough House** ★★★★ 658
*Woolacombe* **Sunny Nook** ★★★★ 423
*Woolminstone* **Barn Cottage Bed and Breakfast** ★★★★ 658

# Walkers and cyclists welcome

Establishments participating in the Walkers Welcome and Cyclists Welcome schemes provide special facilities and actively encourage these recreations. Accommodation with a detailed entry in this guide is listed below. Place names are listed alphabetically within each region.

## Walkers Welcome and Cyclists Welcome

| | | |
|---|---|---|
| *Ambleside* Northern England | **Wordsworths Guest House** ★★★★ | 68 |
| *Beal* Northern England | **Brock Mill Farmhouse** ★★★ | 71 |
| *Berwick-upon-Tweed* Northern England | **Alannah House** ★★★★ SILVER | 72 |
| *Burnley* Northern England | **Ormerod** ★★★ | 79 |
| *Castleside* Northern England | **Bee Cottage Guesthouse** ★★★★ | 80 |
| *Dalby* Northern England | **South Moor Farm** ★★★★ | 84 |
| *Egton Bridge* Northern England | **Broom House** ★★★★ SILVER | 88 |
| *Foulridge* Northern England | **Hare & Hounds Foulridge** ★★★ | 89 |
| *Giggleswick* Northern England | **The Harts Head Inn** ★★★★ | 90 |
| *Grantley* Northern England | **St Georges Court** ★★★★ | 92 |
| *Haworth* Northern England | **Rosebud Cottage** ★★★★ | 96 |
| *Haydon Bridge* Northern England | **Grindon Cartshed** ★★★★ | 97 |
| *Hexham* Northern England | **HallBarns B&B** ★★★★ | 98 |
| *Ingleton* Northern England | **Springfield Country Guest House** ★★★★ | 100 |
| *Keswick* Northern England | **Sandon Guesthouse** ★★★★ | 104 |
| *Keswick* Northern England | **Newlands Fell Guesthouse** ★★★ | 104 |
| *Kirkbymoorside* Northern England | **The Cornmill** ★★★★ SILVER | 106 |
| *Macclesfield* Northern England | **Moorhayes House** ★★★ | 110 |
| *Pickering* Northern England | **The Old Vicarage** ★★★★★ GOLD | 116 |
| *Pickering* Northern England | **Eleven Westgate** ★★★★ SILVER | 115 |
| *Richmond* Northern England | **Frenchgate Guest House** ★★★★ | 118 |
| *Saltburn-by-the-Sea* Northern England | **The Arches** ★★★★ | 121 |
| *Stape* Northern England | **High Muffles** ★★★★ SILVER | 127 |
| *Thornton Dale* Northern England | **Cherry Garth** ★★★★ SILVER | 130 |
| *Beccles* Central England | **Pinetrees** ★★★★ | 172 |
| *Bishop's Castle* Central England | **Inn on the Green** ★★★★ | 174 |
| *Bourne* Central England | **Maycroft Cottage Bed and Breakfast** ★★★★ SILVER | 174 |
| *Brampton Abbotts* Central England | **Brampton Cottage** ★★★ | 175 |
| *Broadway* Central England | **Lowerfield Farm** ★★★★ | 176 |
| *Buxton* Central England | **Fernydale Farm** ★★★★ SILVER | 179 |
| *Chapel-en-le-Frith* Central England | **High Croft** ★★★★★ SILVER | 183 |
| *Clun* Central England | **The White Horse Inn** ★★★ | 185 |
| *Hickling* Central England | **The Dairy Barns** ★★★★ GOLD | 197 |
| *Hunstanton* Central England | **The King William IV Country Inn & Restaurant** ★★★★ SILVER | 199 |
| *Hunstanton* Central England | **The Lodge** ★★★★ | 200 |
| *Ironbridge* Central England | **The Old Rectory at Broseley** ★★★★★ SILVER | 200 |

## Walkers Welcome and Cyclists Welcome continued


| | | |
|---|---|---|
| *Leicester* Central England | **Wondai B&B** ★★★ | 205 |
| *Lincoln* Central England | **Welbeck Cottage B&B** ★★★★ | 208 |
| *Lincoln* Central England | **Goodlane B&B** ★★★ | 206 |
| *Long Compton* Central England | **Butlers Road Farm** ★★★ | 208 |
| *Ludlow* Central England | **Elm Lodge B&B** ★★★★ | 211 |
| *Market Drayton* Central England | **The Hermitage** ★★★ | 214 |
| *Mumby* Central England | **Brambles** ★★★★ | 215 |
| *Newport* Central England | **Red Gables Country B&B** ★★★★ SILVER | 217 |
| *Norwich* Central England | **Cavell House** ★★★★ | 219 |
| *Pershore* Central England | **Arbour House** ★★★★ SILVER | 221 |
| *South Walsham* Central England | **Old Hall Farm** ★★★★ | 227 |
| *Wainfleet* Central England | **Willow Farm** ★★★ | 237 |
| *Woodnewton* Central England | **Bridge Cottage** ★★★★ | 241 |
| *Bognor Regis* South East England | **White Horses Felpham** ★★★★ | 264 |
| *Burford* South East England | **Cotland House B&B** ★★★★ | 269 |
| *Burley* South East England | **Wayside Cottage** ★★★★ | 270 |
| *Canterbury* South East England | **Clare Ellen Guest House** ★★★★ | 271 |
| *Chichester* South East England | **Woodstock House** ★★★★ SILVER | 273 |
| *Chinnor* South East England | **The Croft** ★★★★ | 274 |
| *Colwell Bay* South East England | **Rockstone Cottage** ★★★★ | 274 |
| *Henley-on-Thames* South East England | **Bank Farm** ★★ | 287 |
| *Pluckley* South East England | **Elvey Farm** ★★★★ | 300 |
| *Pulborough* South East England | **The Labouring Man** ★★★★ | 301 |
| *Ramsgate* South East England | **Glendevon Guest House** ★★★★ | 301 |
| *Sandown* South East England | **Mount Brocas Guest House** ★★★ | 307 |
| *Athelhampton* South West England | **White Cottage** ★★★★ SILVER | 354 |
| *Bath* South West England | **Wheelwrights Arms** ★★★★ | 359 |
| *Bridport* South West England | **The Well** ★★★ | 365 |
| *Colyton* South West England | **The Old Bakehouse** ★★★★ SILVER | 374 |
| *Dinton* South West England | **Marshwood Farm B&B** ★★★★ | 376 |
| *Kingsbridge* South West England | **Ashleigh House** ★★★ | 384 |
| *Lynton* South West England | **Higher Bodley Farm** ★★★★ | 387 |
| *Market Lavington* South West England | **The Green Dragon** ★★★ | 389 |
| *Martock* South West England | **The White Hart Hotel** ★★★★ | 389 |
| *Nether Stowey* South West England | **Castle of Comfort Country House** ★★★★★ SILVER | 393 |
| *Pensford* South West England | **Green Acres** ★★ | 394 |
| *Porlock* South West England | **Glen Lodge** ★★★★ | 398 |
| *St Just in Roseland* South West England | **Roundhouse Barns** ★★★★ | 403 |
| *Sidmouth* South West England | **The Salty Monk** ★★★★★ GOLD | 408 |
| *Tintagel* South West England | **The Avalon** ★★★★★ | 414 |
| *Wells* South West England | **Burnt House Farm** ★★★★ | 419 |
| *Yelverton* South West England | **Overcombe House** ★★★★ | 423 |


## Walkers Welcome


| | | |
|---|---|---|
| *Keswick* Northern England | **The Grange Country House** ★★★★★ SILVER | 103 |
| *Keswick* Northern England | **Appletrees** ★★★★ | 101 |
| *Pickering* Northern England | **17 Burgate** ★★★★★ GOLD | 115 |
| *York* Northern England | **Alcuin Lodge Guest House** ★★★★ | 142 |
| *Hope* Central England | **Underleigh House** ★★★★★ GOLD | 198 |
| *Tenbury Wells* Central England | **Millbrook** ★★★★ | 234 |
| *Rochester* South East England | **Churchfields B&B** ★★ SILVER | 302 |
| *Rye* South East England | **Hayden's** ★★★★★ | 305 |
| *Callington* South West England | **Hampton Manor** ★★★★ | 369 |
| *Mullion* South West England | **Trenance Farmhouse** ★★★★ | 393 |


## Cyclists Welcome


| | | |
|---|---|---|
| *Meppershall* Central England | **Old Joe's** ★★ | 215 |

# Families and pets welcome

Establishments participating in the Families Welcome or Welcome Pets! schemes are listed below. They provide special facilities and actively encourage families or guests with pets. Establishments in bold have a detailed entry in this guide. Place names are listed alphabetically within each region.

| | | |
|---|---|---|
| **Families and Pets Welcome** | | |
| *Dalby* Northern England | **South Moor Farm** ★★★★ | 84 |
| *Macclesfield* Northern England | **Astle Farm East** ★★ | 110 |
| *Hunstanton* Central England | **The Lodge** ★★★★ | 200 |
| **Families Welcome** | | |
| *Barrow-in-Furness* Northern England | **November House B&B** ★★★★ SILVER | 70 |
| *Keswick* Northern England | **Littletown Farm** ★★★ | 104 |
| *Keswick* Northern England | **Newlands Fell Guesthouse** ★★★ | 104 |
| *Kielder Water* Northern England | **The Pheasant Inn (by Kielder Water)** ★★★★ SILVER | 105 |
| *Canterbury* South East England | **Clare Ellen Guest House** ★★★★ | 271 |
| *Athelhampton* South West England | **White Cottage** ★★★★ SILVER | 354 |
| **Pets Welcome** | | |
| *Ambleside* Northern England | **The Old Vicarage** ★★★★ | 67 |
| *Cockermouth* Northern England | **Rose Cottage** ★★★★ | 81 |
| *Grinton* Northern England | **The Bridge Inn** ★★★ | 93 |
| *Kendal* Northern England | **The Glen** ★★★★ | 101 |
| *Kirkby Lonsdale* Northern England | **Copper Kettle Restaurant & Guest House** ★★ | 105 |
| *Windermere* Northern England | **Fairfield House and Gardens** ★★★★ SILVER | 139 |
| *Ely* Central England | **The Old School B & B** ★★★★ | 191 |
| *Frinton-on-Sea* Central England | **Russell Lodge** ★★★ | 193 |
| *Knipton* Central England | **Manners Arms** ★★★★ | 202 |
| *Malvern* Central England | **Cannara Guest House** ★★★★ SILVER | 212 |
| *Mumby* Central England | **Brambles** ★★★★ | 215 |
| *Stoke-on-Trent* Central England | **Verdon Guest House** ★★ | 231 |
| *Wainfleet* Central England | **Willow Farm** ★★★ | 237 |
| *Adderbury* South East England | **The Bell Inn** ★★★ | 259 |
| *Eastbourne* South East England | **The Gladwyn** ★★★★ | 279 |
| *Marlow* South East England | **The Hand and Flowers** ★★★★★ | 293 |
| *Pluckley* South East England | **Elvey Farm** ★★★★ | 300 |
| *Richmond* London | **Ivy Cottage** ★★★ | 336 |
| *Marlborough* South West England | **Crofton Lodge** ★★★★ SILVER | 389 |
| *St Agnes* South West England | **Little Trevellas Farm** ★★★ | 400 |
| *St Mawgan* South West England | **Dalswinton House** ★★★★ | 403 |

# Quick reference index

If you're looking for a specific facility use this index to see at-a-glance detailed accommodation entries that match your requirement. Establishments are listed alphabetically by place name within each region.

## Indoor pool


| | | |
|---|---|---|
| *Ambleside* Northern England | **The Old Vicarage ★★★★** | 67 |
| *Ambleside* Northern England | **Wateredge Inn ★★★★** | 68 |
| *Windermere* Northern England | **Southview House & Indoor Pool ★★★★** SILVER | 141 |
| *Windermere* Northern England | **The Cranleigh ★★★** | 138 |
| *Cambridge* Central England | **Harry's Bed and Breakfast ★★★★** | 182 |
| *Creaton* Central England | **Highgate House – A Sundial Group Venue ★★★★** | 188 |
| *Lincoln* Central England | **Damon's Motel ★★★★** | 206 |
| *Nayland* Central England | **Gladwins Farm ★★★★** | 216 |
| *Sudbury* Central England | **Hillview Studio ★★★** | 233 |
| *Abingdon* South East England | **Kingfisher Barn ★★★★** | 259 |
| *Freshwater* South East England | **The Orchards ★★★★** | 281 |
| *Glastonbury* South West England | **Mapleleaf Middlewick ★★★★** | 382 |
| *Lanreath-by-Looe* South West England | **Bocaddon Farm ★★★★** | 384 |
| *Rudford* South West England | **The Dark Barn Lodge ★★★★** | 400 |
| *St Austell* South West England | **Anchorage House ★★★★★** GOLD | 401 |


## Outdoor pool


| | | |
|---|---|---|
| *Alvechurch* Central England | **Woodlands Bed and Breakfast ★★★★** | 169 |
| *Cambridge* Central England | **Harry's Bed and Breakfast ★★★★** | 182 |
| *Castleton* Central England | **Ye Olde Cheshire Cheese Inn ★★★** | 183 |
| *Empingham* Central England | **Shacklewell Lodge ★★★★** | 191 |
| *Toppesfield* Central England | **Harrow Hill Cottage ★★★** | 235 |
| *Bonchurch* South East England | **Winterbourne Country House ★★★★★** SILVER | 265 |
| *Canterbury* South East England | **Clare Ellen Guest House ★★★★** | 271 |
| *Detling* South East England | **Wealden Hall ★★★★** | 276 |
| *Milton Keynes* South East England | **Chantry Farm ★★★** | 294 |
| *Newbury* South East England | **East End Farm ★★★★** | 296 |
| *Bath* South West England | **Church Farm ★★★** | 357 |
| *Bath* South West England | **Hermitage ★★★** | 357 |
| *Blandford Forum* South West England | **Farnham Farm House ★★★★★** GOLD | 360 |
| *Devizes* South West England | **Rosemundy Cottage ★★★★** | 376 |
| *Dorchester* South West England | **Sunrise Guest House ★★★** | 376 |
| *Hemyock* South West England | **Pounds Farm ★★★★** | 383 |
| *Marlborough* South West England | **Crofton Lodge ★★★★** SILVER | 389 |
| *Matchams* South West England | **Little Paddock B&B ★★★★** | 389 |
| *Mullion* South West England | **Trenance Farmhouse ★★★★** | 393 |
| *Nether Stowey* South West England | **Castle of Comfort Country House ★★★★★** SILVER | 393 |
| *St Mawgan* South West England | **Dalswinton House ★★★★** | 403 |


Establishments listed here have a detailed entry in this guide.

## Outdoor pool continued


| | | |
|---|---|---|
| *Tavistock* South West England | **Tor Cottage ★★★★★** GOLD | 413 |
| *Torquay* South West England | **Haldon Priors ★★★★★** SILVER | 416 |


## Evening meal by arrangement


| | | |
|---|---|---|
| *Alderley Edge* Northern England | **Mayfield Bed & Breakfast @ Sheila's ★★★** | 64 |
| *Allendale* Northern England | **High Keenley Fell Farm ★★★★** | 64 |
| *Alnmouth* Northern England | **Alnmouth Golf Club ★★★** | 64 |
| *Alnwick* Northern England | **The Masons Arms Country Inn ★★★★** | 65 |
| *Alnwick* Northern England | **The Queens Head Hotel ★★★★** | 66 |
| *Alnwick* Northern England | **Alnwick Lodge ★★★** | 65 |
| *Ambleside* Northern England | **Dower House ★★★★** | 66 |
| *Ambleside* Northern England | **Wateredge Inn ★★★★** | 68 |
| *Aysgarth* Northern England | **Thornton Lodge ★★★★★** SILVER | 69 |
| *Aysgarth* Northern England | **Wheatsheaf Inn ★★★** | 69 |
| *Bardon Mill* Northern England | **Twice Brewed Inn ★★★** | 70 |
| *Barrow-in-Furness* Northern England | **November House B&B ★★★★** SILVER | 70 |
| *Bassenthwaite* Northern England | **Ouse Bridge House ★★★★** | 71 |
| *Bedale* Northern England | **The Castle Arms Inn ★★★★** | 71 |
| *Bedale* Northern England | **Elmfield House ★★★★** SILVER | 72 |
| *Berwick-upon-Tweed* Northern England | **The Cat Inn ★★★** | 72 |
| *Bishop Wilton* Northern England | **High Belthorpe ★★★** | 73 |
| *Blackpool* Northern England | **The Berwick ★★★★** | 74 |
| *Blackpool* Northern England | **Edenfield Guest House ★★★★** | 74 |
| *Blackpool* Northern England | **The Raffles Guest Accommodation ★★★★** | 75 |
| *Blackpool* Northern England | **Ash Lodge ★★★** | 73 |
| *Blackpool* Northern England | **Cardoh Lodge ★★★** | 74 |
| *Blackpool* Northern England | **Hadley ★★★** | 74 |
| *Blackpool* Northern England | **Norville House ★★★** | 75 |
| *Blackpool* Northern England | **The Valentine ★★★** | 76 |
| *Bolton-by-Bowland* Northern England | **Middle Flass Lodge ★★★★** | 76 |
| *Borrowdale* Northern England | **Hazel Bank Country House ★★★★★** GOLD | 76 |
| *Braithwaite* Northern England | **Coledale Inn ★★★** | 77 |
| *Brampton* Northern England | **Blacksmiths Arms ★★★★** | 77 |
| *Brampton* Northern England | **Scarrowhill House ★★★★** | 77 |
| *Bridlington* Northern England | **Providence Place ★★★★** | 78 |
| *Buckden* Northern England | **The White Lion Inn ★★★** | 79 |
| *Castleside* Northern England | **Bee Cottage Guesthouse ★★★★** | 80 |
| *Chester* Northern England | **Golborne Manor ★★★★** | 80 |
| *Clitheroe* Northern England | **Bayley Arms ★★★★** | 81 |
| *Cockermouth* Northern England | **Rose Cottage ★★★★** | 81 |
| *Coniston* Northern England | **Yew Tree Farm ★★★★★** SILVER | 82 |
| *Corbridge* Northern England | **Fellcroft ★★★★** | 83 |
| *Crosby Ravensworth* Northern England | **Crake Trees Manor ★★★★★** GOLD | 83 |
| *Dalby* Northern England | **South Moor Farm ★★★★** | 84 |
| *Danby* Northern England | **The Fox & Hounds Inn ★★★★** | 84 |
| *Doncaster* Northern England | **The Balmoral ★★★** | 85 |
| *Doncaster* Northern England | **Park Inn ★★★** | 85 |
| *Durham* Northern England | **Garden House ★★★** | 87 |
| *Durham* Northern England | **The Avenue Inn ★★** | 86 |
| *Durham* Northern England | **St Chad's College ★★** | 87 |
| *Durham* Northern England | **St Johns College ★★** | 87 |
| *Egton Bridge* Northern England | **Broom House ★★★★** SILVER | 88 |
| *Ellingham* Northern England | **The Pack Horse Inn ★★★** | 88 |
| *Foulridge* Northern England | **Hare & Hounds Foulridge ★★★** | 89 |
| *Garstang* Northern England | **Guys Thatched Hamlet ★★★★** | 90 |
| *Giggleswick* Northern England | **The Harts Head Inn ★★★★** | 90 |
| *Gilsland* Northern England | **Gilsland Spa ★★★★** | 90 |
| *Grange-over-Sands* Northern England | **Greenacres Country Guesthouse ★★★★** | 91 |

## Evening meal by arrangement continued


| | | |
|---|---|---|
| *Grange-over-Sands* Northern England | **The Lymehurst ★★★★** | 91 |
| *Great Ayton* Northern England | **The Kings Head at Newton under Roseberry ★★★★** SILVER | 93 |
| *Great Eccleston* Northern England | **The Cartford Inn ★★★★** | 93 |
| *Grinton* Northern England | **The Bridge Inn ★★★** | 93 |
| *Guisborough* Northern England | **Fox Inn ★★★** | 94 |
| *Guisborough* Northern England | **Three Fiddles ★★** | 94 |
| *Harrogate* Northern England | **Cold Cotes ★★★★★** GOLD | 95 |
| *Hawes* Northern England | **Rookhurst Country House ★★★★★** GOLD | 95 |
| *Hawkshead* Northern England | **Crosslands Farm ★★★★** | 95 |
| *Hawkshead* Northern England | **Ivy House & Restaurant ★★★★** | 96 |
| *Haworth* Northern England | **Rosebud Cottage ★★★★** | 96 |
| *Haworth* Northern England | **The Bronte ★★★** | 96 |
| *Haydon Bridge* Northern England | **Grindon Cartshed ★★★★** | 97 |
| *Hexham* Northern England | **HallBarns B&B ★★★★** | 98 |
| *Huddersfield* Northern England | **Cambridge Lodge ★★★** | 99 |
| *Irthington* Northern England | **Newtown Farm ★★★** | 100 |
| *Kermincham* Northern England | **The Fields Farm ★★★★** | 101 |
| *Keswick* Northern England | **Lindisfarne House ★★★★** | 103 |
| *Keswick* Northern England | **Newlands Fell Guesthouse ★★★** | 104 |
| *Kielder* Northern England | **Twenty Seven ★★** | 105 |
| *Kielder Water* Northern England | **The Pheasant Inn (by Kielder Water) ★★★★** SILVER | 105 |
| *Kirkby Lonsdale* Northern England | **Copper Kettle Restaurant & Guest House ★★** | 105 |
| *Kirkbymoorside* Northern England | **The Cornmill ★★★★** SILVER | 106 |
| *Knaresborough* Northern England | **Gallon House ★★★★★** | 106 |
| *Leeds* Northern England | **The Glengarth ★★★** | 107 |
| *Leeds* Northern England | **St Michael's Guest House ★★★** | 108 |
| *Leeds* Northern England | **The Moorlea ★★** | 108 |
| *Liverpool* Northern England | **Aachen ★★★** | 109 |
| *Liversedge* Northern England | **Heirloom Carriage Driving B&B ★★** | 110 |
| *Manchester* Northern England | **Stay Inn – Manchester ★★★** | 111 |
| *Morecambe* Northern England | **The Clifton ★★★** | 112 |
| *Morecambe* Northern England | **Silverwell ★★★** | 112 |
| *Newbiggin-on-Lune* Northern England | **Tranna Hill ★★★★** | 113 |
| *Newcastle upon Tyne* Northern England | **The Keelman's Lodge ★★★★** | 113 |
| *Newcastle upon Tyne* Northern England | **Clifton House ★★★** | 113 |
| *Oldham* Northern England | **Grains Bar Farm ★★★** | 114 |
| *Ovington* Northern England | **The Four Alls ★★★** | 114 |
| *Pickering* Northern England | **The Hawthornes ★★★★** | 116 |
| *Port Carlisle* Northern England | **Brockelrigg ★★★★★** SILVER | 116 |
| *Ripon* Northern England | **The Royal Oak ★★★★** | 119 |
| *Runswick Bay* Northern England | **The Firs ★★★★** | 120 |
| *St Bees* Northern England | **Fleatham House ★★★★★** | 121 |
| *Sale* Northern England | **The Belforte House ★★★** | 121 |
| *Saltburn-by-the-Sea* Northern England | **The Arches ★★★★** | 121 |
| *Scarborough* Northern England | **Killerby Cottage Farm ★★★★** SILVER | 123 |
| *Scarborough* Northern England | **Brontes Guest House ★★★** | 122 |
| *Scarborough* Northern England | **Robyn's Guest House ★★★** | 123 |
| *Scarborough* Northern England | **The Thoresby ★★★** | 124 |
| *Settle* Northern England | **Maypole Inn ★★★** | 125 |
| *Sheffield* Northern England | **Parson House Farm ★★★** | 125 |
| *Shelley* Northern England | **Three Acres Inn and Restaurant ★★★★** | 125 |
| *Skipton* Northern England | **Napier's Restaurant & Accommodation ★★★★** | 126 |
| *Skipton* Northern England | **The Woolly Sheep ★★★** | 126 |
| *Stanley* Northern England | **Oak Tree Inn ★★** | 127 |
| *Stockton-on-Tees* Northern England | **The Parkwood ★★★** | 128 |
| *Tarporley* Northern England | **Foresters Arms ★★★** | 129 |
| *Thirsk* Northern England | **Borrowby Mill, Bed and Breakfast ★★★★** SILVER | 129 |

## Evening meal by arrangement continued


| | | |
|---|---|---|
| *Thirsk* Northern England | **Manor House Cottage** ★★★★ | 129 |
| *Thixendale* Northern England | **The Cross Keys** ★★★ | 130 |
| *Thornton Dale* Northern England | **Bridgefoot Guest House** ★★★★ | 130 |
| *Thornton Dale* Northern England | **Cherry Garth** ★★★★ SILVER | 130 |
| *Threlkeld* Northern England | **Horse and Farrier Inn** ★★★★ | 131 |
| *Wall* Northern England | **The Hadrian Wall Inn** ★★★ | 131 |
| *Wark* Northern England | **Battlesteads Country Inn & Restaurant** ★★★★ SILVER | 132 |
| *Warrington* Northern England | **New House Farm Cottages** ★★ | 132 |
| *West Kirby* Northern England | **At Peel Hey** ★★★★ SILVER | 133 |
| *West Woodburn* Northern England | **Bay Horse Inn** ★★★ | 134 |
| *Whalley* Northern England | **Whalley Abbey** ★★★★ | 134 |
| *Whitby* Northern England | **Sneaton Castle Centre** ★★★★ | 135 |
| *Whitby* Northern England | **Wentworth House** ★★★ | 135 |
| *Whitehaven* Northern England | **Moresby Hall** ★★★★★ GOLD | 136 |
| *Whitewell* Northern England | **The Inn at Whitewell** ★★★★★ GOLD | 136 |
| *Whitley Bay* Northern England | **Lindsay Guest House** ★★★★ | 136 |
| *Windermere* Northern England | **Fairfield House and Gardens** ★★★★ SILVER | 139 |
| *Windermere* Northern England | **Bowfell Cottage** ★★★ | 137 |
| *Workington* Northern England | **Old Ginn House** ★★★★ | 141 |
| *York* Northern England | **The Lighthorseman** ★★★★ | 147 |
| *York* Northern England | **Manor Guest House** ★★★★ | 148 |
| *York* Northern England | **The Windmill** ★★★★ | 149 |
| *Aldborough* Central England | **Butterfly Cottage** ★★★★ | 166 |
| *Alton* Central England | **Fields Farm** ★★★★ | 167 |
| *Alton* Central England | **Bulls Head Inn** ★★★ | 167 |
| *Alvechurch* Central England | **Woodlands Bed and Breakfast** ★★★★ | 169 |
| *Aston Munslow* Central England | **Chadstone** ★★★★★ SILVER | 170 |
| *Aylsham* Central England | **Old Pump House** ★★★★★ GOLD | 170 |
| *Barrow upon Soar* Central England | **Hunting Lodge** ★★★★ | 171 |
| *Bedford* Central England | **Cornfields** ★★★★ SILVER | 172 |
| *Beeston* Central England | **Hylands** ★★★ | 173 |
| *Birmingham* Central England | **Rollason Wood** ★★ | 173 |
| *Bishop's Castle* Central England | **Inn on the Green** ★★★★ | 174 |
| *Bradwell* Central England | **Travellers Rest** ★★★ | 175 |
| *Brigg* Central England | **Holcombe Guest House** ★★★★ | 175 |
| *Broadway* Central England | **The Bell at Willersey** ★★★★ | 176 |
| *Broadway* Central England | **Farncombe Estate Centre** ★★★★ | 176 |
| *Broadway* Central England | **Lowerfield Farm** ★★★★ | 176 |
| *Burnham-on-Crouch* Central England | **The Railway Hotel** ★★★★ SILVER | 177 |
| *Buxton* Central England | **Grendon Guest House** ★★★★★ GOLD | 179 |
| *Buxton* Central England | **Fernydale Farm** ★★★★ SILVER | 179 |
| *Buxton* Central England | **Kingscroft Guest House** ★★★★ SILVER | 180 |
| *Buxton* Central England | **Devonshire Arms** ★★★ | 178 |
| *Castleton* Central England | **Ye Olde Cheshire Cheese Inn** ★★★ | 183 |
| *Cheadle* Central England | **Rakeway House Farm B&B** ★★★★ | 184 |
| *Chesterfield* Central England | **Clarendon Guest House** ★★★ | 184 |
| *Cheveley* Central England | **Old Farmhouse** ★★★★ | 184 |
| *Clun* Central England | **The White Horse Inn** ★★★ | 185 |
| *Colton* Central England | **Colton House** ★★★★★ SILVER | 186 |
| *Corby* Central England | **Manor Farm Guest House** ★★★★ | 187 |
| *Coventry* Central England | **Ashleigh House** ★★★ | 188 |
| *Coventry* Central England | **Highcroft Guest House** ★★★ | 188 |
| *Creaton* Central England | **Highgate House – A Sundial Group Venue** ★★★★ | 188 |
| *Cromer* Central England | **Incleborough House Luxury Bed and Breakfast** ★★★★★ GOLD | 189 |
| *Dereham* Central England | **Hunters Hall** ★★★★ | 189 |
| *Elmswell* Central England | **Kiln Farm** ★★★★ | 190 |
| *Ely* Central England | **Anchor Inn** ★★★★ | 191 |

## Evening meal by arrangement continued


| | | |
|---|---|---|
| *Empingham* Central England | **Shacklewell Lodge** ★★★★ | 191 |
| *Fakenham* Central England | **Abbott Farm** ★★★ | 192 |
| *Gainsborough* Central England | **Blyton (Sunnyside) Ponds** ★★★ | 193 |
| *Grantham* Central England | **The Cedars** ★★★★ | 194 |
| *Great Yarmouth* Central England | **Cavendish House** ★★★ | 195 |
| *Hereford* Central England | **Hedley Lodge** ★★★★ | 196 |
| *Hevingham* Central England | **Marsham Arms Inn** ★★★★ | 197 |
| *Hickling* Central England | **The Dairy Barns** ★★★★ GOLD | 197 |
| *Hilton* Central England | **Tudor Rose** ★★★★ | 197 |
| *Hope Valley* Central England | **The Chequers Inn** ★★★★ SILVER | 198 |
| *Horsley* Central England | **Horsley Lodge** ★★★★ SILVER | 199 |
| *Hundon* Central England | **The Plough Inn** Applied | 199 |
| *Hunstanton* Central England | **The King William IV Country Inn & Restaurant** ★★★★ SILVER | 199 |
| *Hunstanton* Central England | **The Lodge** ★★★★ | 200 |
| *Kettering* Central England | **Dairy Farm** ★★★ | 201 |
| *Kettleburgh* Central England | **Church Farm** ★★★ | 202 |
| *Knipton* Central England | **Manners Arms** ★★★★ | 202 |
| *Latchingdon* Central England | **Crouch Valley Lodge** ★★★ | 203 |
| *Leadenham* Central England | **George Hotel** ★★★ | 203 |
| *Lincoln* Central England | **Damon's Motel** ★★★★ | 206 |
| *Lincoln* Central England | **The Old Bakery Restaurant with Rooms** ★★★★ SILVER | 207 |
| *Lincoln* Central England | **Welbeck Cottage B&B** ★★★★ | 208 |
| *Lincoln* Central England | **Duke William Inn** ★★★ | 206 |
| *Little Cawthorpe* Central England | **The Royal Oak Inn – The Splash** ★★★★ | 208 |
| *Loughborough* Central England | **Charnwood Lodge** ★★★★ | 209 |
| *Loughborough* Central England | **Highbury Guest House** ★★★★ | 210 |
| *Ludlow* Central England | **The Clive Bar and Restaurant With Rooms** ★★★★★ SILVER | 211 |
| *Ludlow* Central England | **Cecil Guest House** ★★★ | 211 |
| *Mablethorpe* Central England | **The Cannon Guest House** ★★★ | 212 |
| *Market Drayton* Central England | **The Hermitage** ★★★ | 214 |
| *Mumby* Central England | **Brambles** ★★★★ | 215 |
| *Mundford* Central England | **Colveston Manor** ★★★★ | 215 |
| *Nayland* Central England | **White Hart Inn** ★★★★★ GOLD | 216 |
| *Newton St Margarets* Central England | **Marises Barn** ★★★★ | 217 |
| *Northampton* Central England | **The Poplars** ★★★★ SILVER | 218 |
| *Norwich* Central England | **Cavell House** ★★★★ | 219 |
| *Pershore* Central England | **Anchor Inn & Restaurant** ★★★ | 221 |
| *Ross-on-Wye* Central England | **Broome Farm** ★★★★ | 222 |
| *Sheringham* Central England | **Viburnham House B&B** ★★★★ SILVER | 224 |
| *Shifnal* Central England | **Odfellows – The Wine Bar** ★★★ | 225 |
| *Shingle Street* Central England | **Lark Cottage** ★★★★ | 225 |
| *Sibton* Central England | **Sibton White Horse Inn** ★★★★ | 226 |
| *Skegness* Central England | **Chatsworth** ★★★ | 226 |
| *Skegness* Central England | **Roosevelt Lodge** ★★★ | 226 |
| *Stafford* Central England | **Wyndale Guest House** ★★★ | 229 |
| *Stamford* Central England | **Candlesticks** ★★★ | 229 |
| *Stansted* Central England | **The White House** ★★★★ | 230 |
| *Stoke-on-Trent* Central England | **Reynolds Hey** ★★★★ | 231 |
| *Stratford-upon-Avon* Central England | **The Howard Arms** ★★★★★ SILVER | 232 |
| *Stratford-upon-Avon* Central England | **Folly Farm Cottage** ★★★★ GOLD | 232 |
| *Telford* Central England | **The Old Orleton** ★★★★★ SILVER | 234 |
| *Thompson* Central England | **Chequers Inn** ★★★★ | 234 |
| *Thornham Magna* Central England | **Thornham Hall** ★★★★★ SILVER | 235 |
| *Thornton Curtis* Central England | **Thornton Hunt Inn** ★★★★ | 235 |
| *Toppesfield* Central England | **Harrow Hill Cottage** ★★★ | 235 |
| *Uppingham* Central England | **Spanhoe Lodge** ★★★★★ GOLD | 236 |

## Evening meal by arrangement continued


| | | |
|---|---|---|
| *Vowchurch* Central England | **Yew Tree House** ★★★★ GOLD | 237 |
| *Wainfleet* Central England | **Willow Farm** ★★★ | 237 |
| *Whitney-on-Wye* Central England | **Rhydspence Inn** ★★★★ | 238 |
| *Woodhall Spa* Central England | **Chaplin House** ★★★★ SILVER | 240 |
| *Woodhall Spa* Central England | **Village Limits Motel** ★★★★ | 241 |
| *Woodhurst* Central England | **The Raptor Foundation** ★★★ | 241 |
| *Woolpit* Central England | **Bull Inn and Restaurant** ★★★ | 241 |
| *Worcester* Central England | **Holland House** ★★★ | 242 |
| *Wrentham* Central England | **Five Bells** ★★★ | 243 |
| *Adderbury* South East England | **The Bell Inn** ★★★ | 259 |
| *Arundel* South East England | **Arundel House Restaurant & Rooms** ★★★★★ GOLD | 261 |
| *Ashford* South East England | **Dean Court Farm** ★★★ | 262 |
| *Banbury* South East England | **St Martins House** ★★★★ | 262 |
| *Barham* South East England | **The Duke of Cumberland** ★★★★ | 263 |
| *Biddenden* South East England | **Heron Cottage** ★★★★ | 263 |
| *Bladbean* South East England | **Molehills** ★★★★ | 264 |
| *Brede* South East England | **2 Stonelink Cottages** ★★ | 265 |
| *Brighton & Hove* South East England | **The Townhouse Brighton** ★★★★ | 267 |
| *Brize Norton* South East England | **The Priory** ★★★ | 268 |
| *Broadstairs* South East England | **Bay Tree Broadstairs** ★★★★ | 268 |
| *Brookland* South East England | **The Royal Oak** ★★★★ | 268 |
| *Burley* South East England | **Wayside Cottage** ★★★★ | 270 |
| *Canterbury* South East England | **Magnolia House** ★★★★★ GOLD | 271 |
| *Canterbury* South East England | **Clare Ellen Guest House** ★★★★ | 271 |
| *Canterbury* South East England | **Hornbeams** ★★★★ | 271 |
| *Crowborough* South East England | **Yew House Bed & Breakfast** ★★★★ SILVER | 275 |
| *Cuckfield* South East England | **Highbridge Mill** ★★★★ SILVER | 275 |
| *Dymchurch* South East England | **Waterside Guest House** ★★★★ | 278 |
| *East Ashling* South East England | **Horse & Groom** ★★★★ | 278 |
| *Eastbourne* South East England | **Brayscroft House** ★★★★ GOLD | 279 |
| *Eastbourne* South East England | **The Birling Gap** ★★★ | 278 |
| *Fordingbridge* South East England | **The Three Lions** ★★★★ | 280 |
| *Freshwater* South East England | **The Orchards** ★★★★ | 281 |
| *Guildford* South East England | **Littlefield Manor** ★★★ | 283 |
| *Haslemere* South East England | **Sheps Hollow** ★★★ | 285 |
| *Haslemere* South East England | **The Wheatsheaf Inn** ★★★ | 285 |
| *Hastings* South East England | **Swan House** ★★★★★ SILVER | 286 |
| *Henley-on-Thames* South East England | **The Baskerville** ★★★★ SILVER | 287 |
| *Kingham* South East England | **Tollgate Inn & Restaurant** ★★★★ | 290 |
| *Lamberhurst* South East England | **Woodpecker Barn** ★★★★★ SILVER | 290 |
| *Lewes* South East England | **The Blacksmiths Arms** ★★★★ SILVER | 290 |
| *Littlehampton* South East England | **Arun View Inn** ★★ | 290 |
| *Longfield* South East England | **The Rising Sun Inn** ★★★ | 291 |
| *Lymington* South East England | **Britannia House** ★★★★★ SILVER | 291 |
| *Lymington* South East England | **Gorse Meadow Guest House** ★★★ | 291 |
| *Lyndhurst* South East England | **Rosedale Bed & Breakfast** ★★★ | 292 |
| *Marlow* South East England | **The Hand and Flowers** ★★★★★ | 293 |
| *Newbury* South East England | **The Carnarvon Arms** ★★★★ | 296 |
| *Newbury* South East England | **East End Farm** ★★★★ | 296 |
| *Newbury* South East England | **The Bell at Boxford** ★★★ | 295 |
| *Newport Pagnell* South East England | **Rosemary House** ★★★ SILVER | 297 |
| *Pluckley* South East England | **Elvey Farm** ★★★★ | 300 |
| *Pulborough* South East England | **The Labouring Man** ★★★★ | 301 |
| *Royal Tunbridge Wells* South East England | **The Beacon** ★★★★ | 303 |
| *Rye* South East England | **Strand House** ★★★★ SILVER | 305 |
| *Sandhurst* South East England | **Lamberden Cottage** ★★★★ | 306 |
| *Sandhurst* South East England | **The Wellington Arms** ★★★ | 306 |
| *Shanklin* South East England | **The Palmerston** ★★★ | 307 |

## ✕ Evening meal by arrangement continued


| | | |
|---|---|---|
| *Sheerness* South East England | **The Ferry House Inn** ★★★★ SILVER | 308 |
| *Thurnham* South East England | **Black Horse Inn** ★★★★ | 309 |
| *Winchester* South East England | **The Wykeham Arms** ★★★ | 312 |
| *Windsor* South East England | **Bluebell House** ★★★★ | 313 |
| *Woking* South East England | **St Columba's House** ★★ | 313 |
| *Woodstock* South East England | **Shepherds Hall** ★★★ | 314 |
| *London NW1* | **MIC Conferences and Accommodation** ★★★★ | 330 |
| *London W2* | **Kingsway Park Hotel Hyde Park** ★★★ | 334 |
| *Richmond* London | **Ivy Cottage** ★★★ | 336 |
| *Richmond* London | **The Red Cow** ★★★ | 336 |
| *Surbiton* London | **The Broadway Lodge** ★★ | 336 |
| *Abbotsbury* South West England | **Swan Lodge** ★★★ | 354 |
| *Athelhampton* South West England | **White Cottage** ★★★★ SILVER | 354 |
| *Avebury* South West England | **The New Inn** ★★★ | 355 |
| *Barnstaple* South West England | **The Spinney** ★★★★ SILVER | 355 |
| *Barnstaple* South West England | **Westcott Barton** ★★★★ | 356 |
| *Bath* South West England | **The Residence** ★★★★★ GOLD | 358 |
| *Bath* South West England | **Wheelwrights Arms** ★★★★ | 359 |
| *Blandford Forum* South West England | **Anvil Inn** ★★★★ | 359 |
| *Bolventor* South West England | **Jamaica Inn** ★★★ | 360 |
| *Bournemouth* South West England | **Wood Lodge** ★★★★ | 362 |
| *Bournemouth* South West England | **The Kings Langley** ★★★ | 362 |
| *Bourton-on-the-Water* South West England | **Mousetrap Inn** ★★★ | 363 |
| *Bridgwater* South West England | **The Olive Mill** ★★★★ | 365 |
| *Bridport* South West England | **The Tiger Inn** ★★★ | 365 |
| *Bristol* South West England | **The Bowl Inn and Lilies Restaurant** ★★★ | 366 |
| *Bude* South West England | **Harefield Cottage** ★★★★ SILVER | 368 |
| *Bude* South West England | **Scadghill Farm** ★★★★ SILVER | 368 |
| *Bude* South West England | **Surf Haven** ★★★★ | 368 |
| *Bude* South West England | **Beach House** ★★★ | 367 |
| *Budleigh Salterton* South West England | **Hansard House** ★★★★ SILVER | 369 |
| *Callington* South West England | **Hampton Manor** ★★★★ | 369 |
| *Charlton* South West England | **Horse & Groom Inn** ★★★★ | 370 |
| *Charminster* South West England | **Three Compasses Inn** ★★★ | 370 |
| *Cheddar* South West England | **Yew Tree Farm** ★★ | 371 |
| *Child Okeford* South West England | **Manor Barn Bed & Breakfast** ★★★★★ SILVER | 372 |
| *Chipping Campden* South West England | **The Eight Bells** ★★★★ | 373 |
| *Cholderton* South West England | **Parkhouse Motel** ★★★★ | 373 |
| *Cirencester* South West England | **Riverside House** ★★★★ | 373 |
| *Colyton* South West England | **The Old Bakehouse** ★★★★ SILVER | 374 |
| *Corfe Castle* South West England | **Norden House** ★★★ | 375 |
| *East Harptree* South West England | **Harptree Court** ★★★★★ SILVER | 377 |
| *Exeter* South West England | **Thorverton Arms** ★★★ | 379 |
| *Ford* South West England | **The Plough** ★★★★ | 380 |
| *Fossebridge* South West England | **The Inn at Fossebridge** ★★★★ | 380 |
| *Frampton-on-Severn* South West England | **The Bell** ★★★★ | 381 |
| *Guiting Power* South West England | **The Guiting Guest House** ★★★★ SILVER | 382 |
| *Honiton* South West England | **Lower Luxton Farm** ★★★ | 383 |
| *Launceston* South West England | **Primrose Cottage** ★★★★★ SILVER | 385 |
| *Lizard* South West England | **The Top House Inn** ★★★★ | 386 |
| *Lynton* South West England | **The Denes Guest House** ★★★★ SILVER | 387 |
| *Lynton* South West England | **Higher Bodley Farm** ★★★★ | 387 |
| *Lynton* South West England | **Kingford House** ★★★★ SILVER | 388 |
| *Market Lavington* South West England | **The Green Dragon** ★★★ | 389 |
| *Marlborough* South West England | **Crofton Lodge** ★★★★ SILVER | 389 |
| *Martock* South West England | **The White Hart Hotel** ★★★★ | 389 |
| *Mevagissey* South West England | **Tregilgas Farm** ★★★★ | 390 |
| *Milton Damerel* South West England | **Buttermoor Farm** ★★★★ | 390 |

## Evening meal by arrangement continued


| | | |
|---|---|---|
| *Moretonhampstead* South West England | **Little Wooston Farm** ★★★ | 392 |
| *Morwenstow* South West England | **The Bush Inn** ★★★ | 392 |
| *Nether Stowey* South West England | **Castle of Comfort Country House** ★★★★★ SILVER | 393 |
| *Paignton* South West England | **Cliveden** ★★★★ | 394 |
| *Paignton* South West England | **Rockview Guest House** ★★★ | 394 |
| *Par* South West England | **The Royal Inn** ★★★★ | 394 |
| *Penzance* South West England | **The Summer House** ★★★★★ GOLD | 395 |
| *Penzance* South West England | **Cornerways Guest House** ★★★ | 395 |
| *Penzance* South West England | **Menwidden Farm** ★★★ | 395 |
| *Perranporth* South West England | **Tides Reach** ★★★★ | 396 |
| *Perranporth* South West England | **The Whitehouse Inn & Luxury Lodge** ★★★★ | 396 |
| *Plymouth* South West England | **Gabber Farm** ★★★ | 397 |
| *Polzeath* South West England | **White Heron** ★★★★ | 398 |
| *Porlock* South West England | **Glen Lodge** ★★★★ | 398 |
| *Port Isaac* South West England | **Cornish Arms** ★★★★ | 398 |
| *Port Isaac* South West England | **The Slipway** ★★★★ | 398 |
| *Redruth* South West England | **Goonearl Cottage** ★★★★ | 399 |
| *Rudford* South West England | **The Dark Barn Lodge** ★★★★ | 400 |
| *St Agnes* South West England | **Penkerris** ★★ | 401 |
| *St Austell* South West England | **Anchorage House** ★★★★★ GOLD | 401 |
| *St Austell* South West England | **Highland Court Lodge** ★★★★★ GOLD | 401 |
| *St Columb Major* South West England | **Pennatillie Farm** ★★★★★ SILVER | 402 |
| *St Mawgan* South West England | **Dalswinton House** ★★★★ | 403 |
| *Shave Cross* South West England | **Shave Cross Inn** ★★★★ GOLD | 407 |
| *Sidmouth* South West England | **The Salty Monk** ★★★★★ GOLD | 408 |
| *Somerton* South West England | **The White Hart Inn** ★★★ | 409 |
| *Stogumber* South West England | **Wick House** ★★★★ | 409 |
| *Stow-on-the-Wold* South West England | **Westcote Inn** ★★★★ | 410 |
| *Street* South West England | **Old Orchard House** ★★★★ | 410 |
| *Stroud* South West England | **1 Woodchester Lodge** ★★★★ | 410 |
| *Taunton* South West England | **Causeway Cottage** ★★★★ | 412 |
| *Tavistock* South West England | **Harrabeer Country House** ★★★★ | 412 |
| *Tewkesbury* South West England | **Green Orchard** Applied | 413 |
| *Tintagel* South West England | **The Mill House** ★★★ | 414 |
| *Tintinhull* South West England | **The Crown and Victoria Inn** ★★★★ | 414 |
| *Tiverton* South West England | **Bridge Guest House** ★★★ | 414 |
| *Torquay* South West England | **Abingdon House** ★★★★ | 415 |
| *Torquay* South West England | **Coombe Court** ★★★★ | 415 |
| *Torquay* South West England | **The Norwood** ★★★★ | 416 |
| *Torquay* South West England | **The Sandpiper Lodge** ★★★ | 416 |
| *Uley* South West England | **The Old Crown Inn** ★★★ | 418 |
| *Wadebridge* South West England | **Tregolls Farm** ★★★★ | 418 |
| *West Looe* South West England | **The Old Bridge House** ★★★★ | 420 |
| *Weymouth* South West England | **Oaklands Edwardian Guesthouse** ★★★★ | 421 |
| *Weymouth* South West England | **The Kinley** ★★★ | 421 |
| *Wimborne Minster* South West England | **The Albion** ★★ | 422 |
| *Guernsey* The Channel Islands | **Auberge du Val** ★★★★ | 436 |
| *Jersey* The Channel Islands | **Fairholme** ★★★ | 437 |

# Budget accommodation

If you're travelling on a budget, the following establishments offer accommodation from £25 per person per night or less. This may be for a single room or based on two people sharing a room. These prices are only an indication – please check carefully before confirming a reservation. Establishments are listed alphabetically by place name within each region. See also the index of hostel and campus accommodation on page 709.

## Northern England


*Alnwick* **The Masons Arms Country Inn** ★★★★ 65
*Ambleside* **Wordsworths Guest House** ★★★★ 68
*Ambleside* **Ferndale Lodge** ★★★ 66
*Bacup* **Rossbrook House** ★★★★ 69
*Bardon Mill* **Twice Brewed Inn** ★★★ 70
*Barrow-in-Furness* **November House B&B** ★★★★ SILVER 70
*Beverley* **Eastgate Guest House** ★★★★ 73
*Bishop Wilton* **High Belthorpe** ★★★ 73
*Blackpool* **The Berwick** ★★★★ 74
*Blackpool* **Edenfield Guest House** ★★★★ 74
*Blackpool* **Ash Lodge** ★★★ 73
*Blackpool* **Cardoh Lodge** ★★★ 74
*Blackpool* **Hadley** ★★★ 74
*Blackpool* **Norville House** ★★★ 75
*Blackpool* **The South Beach** ★★★ 75
*Blackpool* **The Valentine** ★★★ 76
*Blackpool* **The Manor Grove** ★★ 75
*Bradford* **Ivy Guest House** ★★ 76
*Bridlington* **Lincoln House** ★★★★ 78
*Bridlington* **Providence Place** ★★★★ 78
*Bridlington* **The Waverley** ★★★ 78
*Buckden* **The White Lion Inn** ★★★ 79
*Burnley* **Ormerod** ★★★ 79
*Corbridge* **Broxdale** ★★★★ 82
*Craster* **Howick Scar Farmhouse** ★★★ 83
*Darlington* **Boot & Shoe** ★★★ 84
*Dent* **Stone Close Tea Room & Guest House** ★★★ 84
*Doncaster* **The Balmoral** ★★★ 85
*Doncaster* **Park Inn** ★★★ 85
*Doncaster* **Rock Farm** ★★★ 85
*Durham* **The Avenue Inn** ★★ 86
*Durham* **St Chad's College** ★★ 87
*Durham* **St Johns College** ★★ 87
*Foulridge* **Hare & Hounds Foulridge** ★★★ 89
*Garstang* **Ashdene** ★★★ 89
*Grange-over-Sands* **The Lymehurst** ★★★★ 91
*Guisborough* **Fox Inn** ★★★ 94
*Guisborough* **Three Fiddles** ★★ 94
*Harbottle* **Parsonside Bed & Breakfast** ★★★★ 94
*Hawkshead* **Crosslands Farm** ★★★★ 95
*Haworth* **The Bronte** ★★★ 96
*Haworth* **The Apothecary Guest House** ★★ 96
*Hebden* **Court Croft** ★★★ 97
*Huddersfield* **Cambridge Lodge** ★★★ 99
*Ingleton* **Springfield Country Guest House** ★★★★ 100
*Keswick* **Sandon Guesthouse** ★★★★ 104
*Kirkby Lonsdale* **Ullathorns Farm** ★★★★ 106
*Kirkby Lonsdale* **Copper Kettle Restaurant & Guest House** ★★ 105
*Knutsford* **Moat Hall Motel** ★★★ 107
*Leeds* **Avalon Guest House** ★★★★ 107
*Leeds* **The Glengarth** ★★★ 107
*Leeds* **St Michael's Guest House** ★★★ 108
*Leeds* **The Moorlea** ★★ 108
*Little Bollington* **Bollington Hall Farm** ★★ 108
*Liverpool* **Holme-Leigh Guest House** ★★★ 109
*Liversedge* **Heirloom Carriage Driving B&B** ★★ 110
*Macclesfield* **Astle Farm East** ★★ 110
*Manchester* **Luther King House** ★★★ 111
*Morecambe* **Silverwell** ★★★ 112
*Newcastle upon Tyne* **Stonehaven Lodge** ★★★ 114


Establishments listed here have a detailed entry in this guide.

## Northern England continued


*Preesall* **Grassendale** ★★★ 117
*Redcar* **Armada Guest House** ★★★ 117
*Ripon* **The White Horse** ★★★ 120
*Ryton* **A1 Hedgefield House** ★★★ 120
*Sale* **The Belforte House** ★★★ 121
*Scarborough* **Howdale** ★★★★ 123
*Scarborough* **Smugglers Rock Country House** ★★★★ 124
*Scarborough* **The Whiteley** ★★★★ 124
*Scarborough* **Brontes Guest House** ★★★ 122
*Scarborough* **Dolphin Guest House** ★★★ 122
*Scarborough* **The Thoresby** ★★★ 124
*Sheffield* **Parson House Farm** ★★★ 125
*Sunderland* **Felicitations** ★★★ 128
*Thirsk* **Manor House Cottage** ★★★★ 129
*Thirsk* **Town Pasture Farm** ★★★★ 129
*Thornton-Cleveleys* **Four Seasons Guest House** ★★ 130
*Warrington* **Tall Trees Lodge** ★★★ 132
*West Witton* **The Old Star** ★★★ 134
*Whitby* **Wentworth House** ★★★ 135
*Windermere* **College House** ★★★★ 137
*Windermere* **Lindisfarne Guest House** ★★★★ 140
*Windermere* **Southview House & Indoor Pool** ★★★★ SILVER 141
*Windermere* **Bowfell Cottage** ★★★ 137
*Windermere* **Elim Lodge** ★★★ 138
*York* **The Lighthorseman** ★★★★ 147
*York* **Fourposter Lodge** ★★★ 146
*York* **Greenside** ★★★ 146


## Central England


*Acton* **Barbies** ★★ 166
*Alton* **Fields Farm** ★★★★ 167
*Alton* **Windy Arbour** ★★★★ 168
*Alton* **Hillside Farm** ★★★ 168
*Bakewell* **Housley Cottage** ★★★★ 170
*Beccles* **Pinetrees** ★★★★ 172
*Birmingham* **Elmdon Guest House** ★★★ 173
*Birmingham* **Rollason Wood** ★★ 173
*Bourne* **Maycroft Cottage Bed and Breakfast** ★★★★ SILVER 174
*Brackley* **Astwell Mill** ★★★★ 174
*Brampton Abbotts* **Brampton Cottage** ★★★ 175
*Brigg* **Holcombe Guest House** ★★★★ 175
*Cambridge* **The Poplars** ★★★★ 182
*Cambridge* **Tudor Cottage** ★★★★ 182
*Cambridge* **Avondale** ★★★ 181
*Cambridge* **Southampton Guest House** ★★★ 182
*Cheadle* **Rakeway House Farm B&B** ★★★★ 184
*Cherry Hinton* **Old Rosemary Branch** ★★ 184
*Chesterfield* **Abigails Guest House** ★★★ 184
*Chesterfield* **Clarendon Guest House** ★★★ 184
*Colchester* **Scheregate Guesthouse** ★★ 185
*Coventry* **Ashdowns Guest House** ★★★ 187
*Coventry* **Ashleigh House** ★★★ 188
*Coventry* **Bede Guest House** ★★★ 188
*Coventry* **Highcroft Guest House** ★★★ 188
*Derby* **Bonehill Farm** ★★★ 189
*Docking* **Jubilee Lodge** ★★★★ 190
*Endon* **Hollinhurst Farm** ★★★ 192
*Eye Kettleby* **Old Guadaloupe B&B** ★★★★ 192
*Framlingham* **High House Farm** ★★★ 193
*Frinton-on-Sea* **Russell Lodge** ★★★ 193
*Great Baddow* **Homecroft** ★★★ 194
*Great Yarmouth* **Cavendish House** ★★★ 195
*Halesworth* **Fen-Way Guest House** ★★★★ 195
*Hatfield Broad Oak* **Bury House** ★★★ 195
*Honington* **North View Guesthouse** ★★★ 198
*Kettering* **Dairy Farm** ★★★ 201
*Kexby* **The Grange** ★★★ 202
*Leadenham* **George Hotel** ★★★ 203
*Leamington Spa* **Braeside Bed & Breakfast** ★★★★ 204
*Leamington Spa* **The Coach House** ★★★★ SILVER 204
*Leamington Spa* **Charnwood Guest House** ★★★ 204
*Leicester* **Abinger Guest House** ★★★ 205
*Leicester* **Wondai B&B** ★★★ 205
*Lincoln* **Savill Guest House** ★★★★ 207
*Lincoln* **Welbeck Cottage B&B** ★★★★ 208
*Long Compton* **Butlers Road Farm** ★★★ 208
*Long Melford* **High Street Farmhouse** ★★★★ SILVER 209
*Loughborough* **Charnwood Lodge** ★★★★ 209
*Loughborough* **Highbury Guest House** ★★★★ 210
*Loughborough* **Peachnook Guest House** ★★ 210
*Ludlow* **Cecil Guest House** ★★★ 211
*Mablethorpe* **The Cannon Guest House** ★★★ 212
*Market Drayton* **The Hermitage** ★★★ 214
*Meppershall* **Old Joe's** ★★ 215
*Meriden* **Bonnifinglas Guest House** ★★★ 215
*Mumby* **Brambles** ★★★★ 215
*Mundford* **Colveston Manor** ★★★★ 215
*Newark* **Ivy Farm B&B** ★★★ 217
*Norwich* **Edmar Lodge** ★★★ 219
*Orsett* **Jays Lodge** ★★★★ 220
*Overstrand* **Cliff Cottage Bed and Breakfast** ★★★ 221
*Pershore* **Anchor Inn & Restaurant** ★★★ 221
*Redditch* **White Hart Inn** ★★★ 222
*Ross-on-Wye* **Broome Farm** ★★★★ 222
*Ruskington* **Sunnyside Farm** ★★★ 223
*St Albans* **Tresco** ★★★ 223
*Sandy* **The Tythe Barn** ★★★★ 224
*Skegness* **The Grafton Guest House** ★★★ 226
*Skegness* **Roosevelt Lodge** ★★★ 226
*Solihull* **Acorn Guest House** ★★★ SILVER 227

## Central England continued


*South Walsham* **Old Hall Farm** ★★★★ 227
*Stoke-on-Trent* **Reynolds Hey** ★★★★ 231
*Stoke-on-Trent* **Verdon Guest House** ★★ 231
*Sudbury* **Hillview Studio** ★★★ 233
*Telford* **The Mill House** ★★★★ 233
*Toppesfield* **Harrow Hill Cottage** ★★★ 235
*Towcester* **Slapton Manor Accommodation** ★★★★ SILVER 236
*Tunstall* **The Victoria** ★★★ 236
*Wainfleet* **Willow Farm** ★★★ 237
*Walton-on-the-Naze* **Bufo Villae Guest House** ★★★★ 237
*Waterhouses* **Leehouse Farm** ★★★★ SILVER 238
*West Bridgford* **Firs Guesthouse** ★★★ 238
*Wishaw* **Ash House** ★★★★ 239
*Woodhurst* **The Raptor Foundation** ★★★ 241
*Worcester* **Hill Farm House** ★★★★ SILVER 242
*Wortham* **Rookery Farm** ★★★★ SILVER 242


## South East England


*Bladbean* **Molehills** ★★★★ 264
*Bognor Regis* **Jubilee Guest House** ★★★ 264
*Brede* **2 Stonelink Cottages** ★★ 265
*Brighton & Hove* **Andorra Guest Accommodation** ★★★ 266
*Brighton & Hove* **Atlantic Seafront** ★★★ 266
*Brockenhurst* **Goldenhayes** ★★ 268
*Brookland* **The Royal Oak** ★★★★ 268
*Chalgrove* **Cornerstones** ★★ 272
*Danehill* **New Glenmore** ★★★★ 276
*Dummer* **Oakdown Farm Bungalow** ★★★ 278
*Faversham* **Barnsfield** ★★★ 280
*Faversham* **Tenterden House** ★★★ 280
*Folkestone* **The Rob Roy Guest House** ★★★ 280
*Freshwater* **The Orchards** ★★★★ 281
*Hastings* **The Old Town Guest House** Applied 285
*Henfield* **1 The Laurels** ★★★★ 286
*Henley-on-Thames* **Orchard Dene Cottage** ★★★★ 288
*Littlehampton* **Arun View Inn** ★★ 290
*Midhurst* **Oakhurst Cottage** ★★ 293
*Milton Keynes* **Kingfishers** ★ 294
*Oxford* **Becket House** ★★ 297
*Oxford* **Whitehouse View Guest House** ★★ 299
*Reading* **Dittisham Guest House** ★★★ 301
*Royal Tunbridge Wells* **Hawkenbury Farm** ★★★★ 303
*Ryde* **Claverton House Bed and Breakfast** ★★★★ 304
*Ryde* **Fern Cottage** ★★★★ 304
*Ryde* **Seaward Guest House** ★ 304
*St Margaret's Bay* **Small Acre** ★★★★ SILVER 306
*Sandown* **The Montpelier** ★★★ 306
*Sandown* **Mount Brocas Guest House** ★★★ 307
*Shanklin* **Ingress Bed & Breakfast** ★★★ 307
*Shanklin* **The Palmerston** ★★★ 307
*Stelling Minnis* **Great Field Farm** ★★★★ SILVER 308
*Wantage* **B&B in Wantage** ★★★★ 310
*Winchester* **12 Christchurch Road** ★★★ 311
*Wroxall* **Little Span Farm B&B** ★★★ 314


## London


*London N7* **Europa** ★★★ 329
*London N22* **Pane Residence** ★★ 330
*London SE6* **The Heathers** ★★★ 331
*London SW1* **The Dover** ★★ 331
*London W1* **Marble Arch Inn** ★★ 333
*London W2* **The Oxford** ★★★ 334
*Sutton* **St Margarets Guest House** ★★ 337
*Upminster* **Corner Farm** ★★ 337


## South West England


*Boscastle* **The Old Coach House** ★★★★ 361
*Bournemouth* **Cremona** ★★★ 361
*Bournemouth* **The Kings Langley** ★★★ 362
*Bournemouth* **Southernhay Guest House** ★★★ 362
*Bourton-on-the-Water* **Mousetrap Inn** ★★★ 363
*Broad Chalke* **Lodge Farmhouse Bed & Breakfast** ★★★★ 367
*Broadclyst* **Heath Gardens** ★★★★ 367
*Bude* **Surf Haven** ★★★★ 368
*Cheddar* **Waterside** ★★ 371
*Clovelly* **Fuchsia Cottage** ★★★★ 374
*Dorchester* **Sunrise Guest House** ★★★ 376
*Drakewalls* **Drakewalls House** ★★★ 377
*Exeter* **Culm Vale Country House** ★★★ 378
*Gillingham* **Lyde Hill Farmhouse** ★★ 381
*Honiton* **Lower Luxton Farm** ★★★ 383
*Launceston* **Trevadlock Farm** ★★★★★ SILVER 385
*Launceston* **Oakside** ★★★★ 385
*Lechlade-on-Thames* **New Inn Hotel** ★★★ 386
*Lynton* **The Denes Guest House** ★★★★ SILVER 387
*Lynton* **Higher Bodley Farm** ★★★★ 387
*Mevagissey* **Tregilgas Farm** ★★★★ 390
*Milton Damerel* **Buttermoor Farm** ★★★★ 390
*Moretonhampstead* **Little Wooston Farm** ★★★ 392
*Newquay* **Surfside B&B** ★★★ 393
*Newquay* **Chichester Interest Holidays** ★★ 393
*Paignton* **Cliveden** ★★★★ 394
*Paignton* **Rockview Guest House** ★★★ 394
*Penzance* **Wymering** ★★★ 395
*Plymouth* **Athenaeum Lodge** ★★★★ 396
*Plymouth* **Brittany Guest House** ★★★★ 397

## South West England continued


*Plymouth* **Four Seasons** ★★★★ 397
*Plymouth* **Gabber Farm** ★★★ 397
*Portland* **Alessandria House** ★★ 399
*Ruan High Lanes* **New Gonitor Farm** ★★★★ 400
*St Agnes* **Penkerris** ★★ 401
*St Minver* **Tredower Barton** ★★★ 404
*Salisbury* **Highveld** ★★★ 405
*Sherborne* **Honeycombe View** ★★★ 407
*Sidmouth* **Southern Cross Guest House** ★★★ 408
*Somerton* **The White Hart Inn** ★★★ 409
*Stow-on-the-Wold* **Corsham Field Farmhouse** ★★★ 409
*Street* **Old Orchard House** ★★★★ 410
*Tewkesbury* **Abbots Court Farm** ★★★ 413
*Tiverton* **Exe-Tor** ★★★★ 415
*Torquay* **Abingdon House** ★★★★ 415
*Torquay* **The Norwood** ★★★★ 416
*Torquay* **The Sandpiper Lodge** ★★★ 416
*Torquay* **Wilsbrook Guest House** ★★★ 416
*Truro* **Palm Tree House** ★★★★ 417
*Wells* **30 Mary Road** ★★★ 419
*West Looe* **Tidal Court** ★★ 420
*Weymouth* **Oaklands Edwardian Guesthouse** ★★★★ 421
*Weymouth* **Sou West Lodge** ★★★ 422
*Wimborne Minster* **The Albion** ★★ 422
*Winsley* **Conifers** ★★ 422
*Winterborne Zelston* **Brook Farm** ★★★ 422


## The Channel Islands


*Guernsey* **Auberge du Val** ★★★★ 436
*Jersey* **Fairholme** ★★★ 437
*Jersey* **St Magloire Guest House** ★★★ 437
*Jersey* **Villa d'Oro Guest House** ★★★ 437

Country ways
The Countryside Rights of Way Act gives people new rights to walk on areas of open countryside and registered common land.
To find out where you can go and what you can do, as well as information about taking your dog to the countryside, go online at countrysideaccess.gov.uk.
And when you're out and about...

# Hostel and campus accommodation

The following establishments all have a detailed entry in this guide.

## Hostels

| | | |
|---|---|---|
| *Berwick-upon-Tweed* Northern England | **Berwick Backpackers** ★★★★ BACKPACKER | 72 |
| *Heddon-on-the-Wall* Northern England | **Houghton North Farm** ★★★★ HOSTEL | 97 |
| *Keswick* Northern England | **Fisher-Gill Camping Barn** CAMPING BARN | 103 |
| *Liverpool* Northern England | **YHA Liverpool** ★★★★ HOSTEL | 109 |
| *Whitby* Northern England | **Sneaton Castle Centre** ★★★ HOSTEL | 135 |
| *London WC1* | **Generator Hostel London** ★★★ HOSTEL | 335 |

## Campus accommodation

| | | |
|---|---|---|
| *Huddersfield* Northern England | **Storthes Hall Park** ★★★ CAMPUS | 99 |
| *Norwich* Central England | **Broadview Lodge** ★★★★ CAMPUS | 219 |
| *Winchester* South East England | **The University of Winchester** ★★★ CAMPUS | 312 |

# Bank holiday dates for your diary

| holiday | 2009 | 2010 |
|---|---|---|
| **New Year's Day** | 1 January | 1 January |
| **Good Friday** | 10 April | 2 April |
| **Easter Monday** | 13 April | 5 April |
| **Early May Bank Holiday** | 4 May | 3 May |
| **Liberation Day** (Channel Islands) | 9 May | 9 May |
| **Spring Bank Holiday** | 25 May | 31 May |
| **Summer Bank Holiday** | 31 August | 30 August |
| **Christmas Day Holiday** | 25 December | 27 December |
| **Boxing Day Holiday** | 28 December | 28 December |

# Index by property name

Accommodation with a detailed entry in this guide is listed below.

## b continued page



## c page



## d page

## d continued



## e



## f



## g



## h

## h continued page



## i page



## j page



## k page



## l page



## m page



## n page

## n continued page



## o page



## p page



## q page



## r page



## s page

## s continued page



## t page



## u page



## v page



## w page



## y page

# Index by place name

The following places all have detailed accommodation entries in this guide. If the place where you wish to stay is not shown, the location maps (starting on page 32) will help you to find somewhere to stay in the area.

## c continued

## k continued page



## l page



## m page



## n page



## o page



## p page



## q page



## r page



## s page

**Published by:** Heritage House Group (Ketteringham Hall, Wymondham, Norfolk NR18 9RS; t (01603) 819420; f (01603) 814325; hhgroup.co.uk) on behalf of VisitBritain, Thames Road, Blacks Road, London W6 9EL
Publishing Manager: Tess Lugos
Production Manager: Iris Buckley
Compilation, design, copywriting, production and advertisement sales: Jackson Lowe Marketing, 3 St Andrews Place, Southover Road, Lewes, East Sussex BN7 1UP
t (01273) 487487 jacksonlowe.com
Cover design: Jamieson Eley, Nick McCann
Typesetting: Marlinzo Services, Somerset and Jackson Lowe Marketing
Accommodation maps: Based on digital map data © ESR Cartography, 2008
Touring maps: © VisitBritain 2005. National Parks, Areas of Outstanding Natural Beauty, National Trails and Heritage Coast based on information supplied by Natural England. Cycle Networks provided by Sustrans
Printing and binding: 1010 Printing International Ltd, China

**Front cover:** The Salty Monk Restaurant with Rooms, Sidmouth, Devon
**Back cover:** britainonview/Rod Edwards

**Photography credits:** britainonview/David Angel/ANPA/Daniel Bosworth/Martin Brent/brightononview/Alan Chandler/East Midlands Tourism/East of England Tourism/Eden Project/Rod Edwards/Damir Fabijanic/FCO/Klaus Hagmeier/Joanna Henderson/Adrian Houston/Kent Tourism Alliance/Simon Kreitem/Lee Valley Regional Park/Pawel Libera/James McCormick/McCormick-McAdam/Doug McKinlay/Eric Nathan/David Noton/NWDA/Tony Pleavin/Grant Pritchard/Ingrid Rasmussen/Olivier Roques-Ro/David Sellman/Andy Sewell/Jon Spaull/Thanet District Council/Troika/Visit Chester & Cheshire/Michael Walter/Juliet White/Worcestershire County Council; Iris Buckley; cumbriaphoto.co.uk/Ben Barden/Cumbria Tourism; The Deep; Imperial War Museum North; Michael Jackson; Jersey Tourism; Allan McPhail; NTPL/Rob Judges; One NorthEast Tourism; Mark Passmore; South West News Service; Thermae Bath Spa/ Matt Cardy; Visit Bristol; VisitGuernsey; visitlondonimages/britainonview


ISBN 978-0-7095-8447-6

**A VisitBritain Publishing guide**